The original theatre of the City of New York
from the mid-sixties to the mid-seventies.
Book 3.

Peter Schumann's
Bread and Puppet Theatre

VOLUME 1

Peter Schumann's Bread and Puppet Theatre was originally conceived as the fourth book in the series, *The Original Theatre of the City of New York*, on the culturally revolutionary florescence of the American Theatre, circa 1963–73, considered as a facet of that decade's libertarian spirit, and as part of The New American Art (c.1947–73). The first two books were *Queer Theatre* and *The Theatre of Visions of Robert Wilson*. On being reissued, *Schumann's Bread and Puppet Theatre: Volume 1* is now the third book in the series and *Volume 2* becomes the fourth. A fifth book, *Richard Foreman*: *The Ontological-Hysteric Theatre, 1968–86* is projected for 2009. The author of the series is a German-born doctor of philosophy and writer of poetry, and lives in New York City.

Peter Schumann, 31 years old. *Photograph by R. Joyce.*

Stefan Brecht

The original theatre of the
City of New York from the
mid-sixties to the mid-seventies.
Book 3.

Peter Schumann's
Bread and Puppet Theatre

Volume 1

Methuen Drama

To my sister Barbara, affectionately,
with gratitude, with admiration.

First published in two volumes as a Methuen Drama Paperback original in 1988 by Methuen Drama.

Methuen Drama
A & C Black Publishers Limited
36 Soho Square
London W1D 3QY

Copyright © Stefan Brecht 1988

Copyright in all the quoted material, whether from Peter Schumann or anyone else, is the property of the individual authors.
The copyright in the photos by B. Brown and H. Widner is held by Stefan Brecht.
The copyright in all other photos, except where noted otherwise, is owned by the individual photographers.

ISBN: 978 0 413 59890 5

ISBN for Volume 2: 978 0 413 60510 8

A CIP catalogue record for this book is available from the British Library.
All rights reserved. No part of this publication may be reproduced in any form or by any means – graphic, electronic or mechanical, including photocopying, recording, taping or information storage and retrieval systems – without the written permission of A & C Black Publishers Limited.

This book is produced using paper that is made from wood grown in managed, sustainable forests. It is natural, renewable and recyclable. The logging and manufacturing processes conform to the environmental regulations of the country of origin.

Contents

Volume 1

I	1934 Summer 1963. Lehr und Wanderjahre. Germany and the encounter of America.	1
II	How it worked. The relations of production of an independent theatre.	155
III	The product. Expansion of the medium of puppetry through masked performance. The tempting problem of sound. The irritating problem of words.	271
IV	Fall 1963–69. The sixties, or the New York period.	337
IV(1)	The four periods of Schumann's work, 1963–83. Puppet making, religious observances and children's theatre during the first period, fall 1963–69.	339
IV(2)	The Vietnam War. Street agitation during the sixties.	461
IV(3)	Indoors theatre during the sixties. Creation of the medium and attainment of mastery. Restrictive inspiration by peace agitation.	599

Volume 2 (*also available from Methuen Drama*)

V	1970–74. The Goddard period. Reconstitution of the medium on a personal basis: without the Peace Movement frame. Attempts to reach real America.	1
VI	1975–78. The initial Dopp Farm period. Morality plays, and circus as communal celebration of nature.	271
VII	1979–83. The later Dopp Farm period. Prophetic theatre of doom condemning civilization. The atom bomb, famine, terror.	455

Bibliography	649
Appendices	657

Preface

Schumann is one of the great artists of the twentieth century. This is substantially my excuse for the length of this book. The excellence of much of his work apart, some points of interest (not alien to his stature) are the following. He has invented a magnificent new medium, the 'live puppet' show or 'puppet masque'. He has been one of the few directors to develop and consistently use 'alienation'. He has dealt with the issues of the age. His work – moral theatre – is a major statement from the Left and presents the interest of an effort to carry on a large enterprise outside of the money economy. The changes of his communicational mode over a quarter century have reflected those of the alienated but expressive and socially oriented among the young. His masks alone – but they are for use in performance – would suffice to make him a major artist. Representing his feelings more purely than do his shows, they make a distinct statement of note.

Stefan Brecht

Part I.
1934 – summer 1963.

Training, the German vacuum, the unacceptability of Art (sculpture, dance), reversion to puppetry: a new performance medium, combining sculpture and dance, in the guise of a folk art.

Contents: Part I

1. Childhood. Kultur, war, puppeteering. — 5
2. *Hyperion*. Evangel of the faith that, adapted to his personality and changing times, has guided Schumann as artist. Nobility (Schumann: simplicity) vs. meanness, baseness. The spiritual regeneration of mankind as aim of art. — 14
3. German Lehr- and Wanderjahre, 1954-1961. Dance the vocation, project of a German renewal through dance, the ambition to become an artistic Genghis Khan. Germany a spiritual vacuum. Failure. — 24
4. Seven years of abortive sculpturing, apprenticeship for his later puppeteering. — 44
5. Amerika. The suburban cocktail party of executives, the working city in movement. Summer '61. — 51
6. First stay in the Big City. Autumn '61-spring '62. The Rev. Tyler and his Uranian Alchemy Players. — 61
7. *Totentanz*. May-November '62. Terminates his dance ambitions. The dialectic of death. Sculpture comes to the aid of dance: use of masks to liberate amateurs for performance. — 83
8. Manifesto. — 97
9. Vermont interlude, summer '62-spring '63. Putney School. Schumann after an 18-year pause takes up puppetry again. The shows. — 102
10. Puppets, summer '62-spring '63. — 116
11. Summer of '63, semblance of an itinerant puppeteer. Schumann as Johnny the Abductor and Rinaldini the Girl-Killer. Beer and scatology. Puppeteering as fun. — 125
12. Manteos: celastic and big puppets. — 136
13. How Bob saw him. — 142
14. Four periods of Schumann's creative activity 1963-1983. — 146

1. Childhood. Kultur, war, puppeteering.

Peter Schumann was born, second youngest of five children, on the 11th of June, 1934, in Lueben, Silesia, not far from what was then Breslau, almost a suburb of it in fact, into the family of a gentle Lutheran schoolmaster, and at least until the Great War of '39-'45, apparently had somewhat of an idyllic childhood[1] — learning from his mother the recipe of the

---

1. Some of the quality of Schumann's childhood home may perhaps be inferred from the impression his parents made on a '60s associate of Schumann's, visiting them with him in the summer of '69, a man of good nature and yet also good sense, Bob Ernstthal:
'Peter's father and mother were extremely nice. I met them a couple of times in Germany. I just loved them. They're wonderful. Nice, nice people. Really nice. And his brother, who I met a couple of times, once in America — I think he came — and once in Germany. Older brother. His parents — his father was a schoolmaster in Germany. Secondary school, I think, or Gymnasium. Something like that. A very sweet guy. And his mother, also. Really very nice. God, I have wonderful memories of them. They live on the edge of a forest in Germany and they have this little house. They retired, I believe. It was all just — we went there at one time — we'll go into that later — on one of the European tours. We took time off and visited them for a while. My impression was a very sunny, summery visit with them. Almost Chekhov. Something very idyllic. Very nice. (I: Christian?) Yes. (I: Believing Christians?) Yes. Protestants. (I: But I mean, was that part of the picture?) Yes, of them. In a way — it's almost like the old Germany that got smashed in the war. The fineness, the philosophy. The elegance of living. The whole gestalt of a Germany that is great. You know what I mean. That got smashed and run down and discredited, etcetera. But after the war, with peacetime, they got it together again. There was that very elegant quality of European life that they really were an example of. They were very nice, extremely. And he always liked them.' — (Ernstthal, interview.)
'But his mother has — and in her letters — there is something so spiritual or good about her. I think she finished — or maybe she was just tutored, because she came from this — a better off family. But she worked as a nurse in the — during the First World War, not on the front but in hospitals and all, and then I think most of her education came through her husband who was a teacher, and she would read the books and they would discuss them and they would have friends in and discuss these ideas, and not just books but the ideas, and — but her tie or her bond — she was very close to nature and in a very beautiful way — just sort of the way she would describe how beautiful it is. When I came there with our babies, our first baby — and she would just say, "Let the sun shine on the baby because there's something just very good about it." It's not just healthy or it's getting vitamin D, but the sun is just a beautiful source of everything; of love and light and all and so to be in the path of the ray of sun is more than just getting vitamins or whatever (Laughs). And so much, or the same attitude toward water. Peter would tell me how their tradition at Easter was that you go to a spring, you know, pure water, and that you wash your face before you say anything and that is — I don't know how often they did it really — but just the whole idea of doing — of having this very direct and — I'm sure I'm missing the vocabulary for it. I don't think I'd know it in German but when I say spiritual, then it sounds sort of, I don't know, too intellectual. And her letters are very beautiful this way. Also, the way she would speak. She's always been very interested in contemporary, you know, in politics and reading the newspaper and seeing — and then she kind of sees or senses forces, you know, an evil force, something terrible that's coming, or a promising force like the anti-nuclear movement in Germany. She just sees that if they are mixed up or confused, they're long-haired

heavy black Eastern bread, the father reading to his children from among the stories recorded by the brothers Grimm;[2] and from the Bible? We may presume the child's ear open to the Book's loud, harsh, Jewish voice, unsilenced even in the IIIrd Reich. (Later, Schumann had his father for a teacher in his German literature classes and hated it, admitting his father was a good teacher.) To his interviewer Kourilsky[3] he mentions, some 30 years later, the Kasperl Theater and the circus[4] – the midsummer night arts of the country people in these northern countries. But the war went badly, and with many others the family fled (he remembers the crowded train, the vomit in the corridor) before the Russians (1944): first to a farm in Schleswig-Holstein (1944-45),[5] but eventually to Hanover, a city like so many German cities – and perhaps Germany – in its essence destroyed by the bombers from the West. The Western bomber rather than the Eastern tank would be the focus of the boy's later dominant theme as an artist, that of war: the irruption of fire in a peaceful village.[6] These were

---

or unwashed or whatever, it's something that's a hopeful – you know, they're for this goodness, an innate goodness in things. So it's a very moral way of looking at the world, but it's not religious at all. It's not a Christian – she doesn't talk about Christian.' — (Elka, interview.) (Elka: Ms. Elka Leigh Scott Schumann.)

2. 'He loved his mother and loves his mother and respects her very much, and he knew that his parents wanted the best for him and so much of his – of his appreciation of literature – of Hölderlin, for example, came through his parents and his father who love German literature but read and recited Pushkin and the *Arabian Nights* and *Grimm's Fairy Tales* all their childhood long so – and he was a very, really appreciative of that ... and Peter's relationship with his parents was really very strong and warm.' — (Elka, interview.)

3. Françoise Kourilsky, *Le Bread and Puppet Theatre*, Lausanne, 1971. Kourilsky interviewed Schumann in 1968 and 1969. I shall quote this source as 'Kourilsky, '71.'

4. '... ce monde itinérant totalement différent du monde civilisé, avec ses acrobates étonnants, ses animaux étranges, toutes les choses les plus extraordinaires: cela ressemblait à la vie des désirs imaginaires que la bourgeoisie ne voulait pas réaliser, c'était extérieur à notre societé et cela venait *vers* nous. Le cirque tenait dans ses bras les rêves impossibles de notre monde.' — (Schumann, in Kourilsky, '71.)

5. 'Until he was ten, the Schumann family lived in the Silesian village of Brokau, near the industrial city of Breslau, which was renamed Wroclaw after the end of World War II, when this portion of what had been eastern Germany was incorporated into Poland. Late in 1944 his family fled from their home barely ahead of the Soviet army, with the whole horizon ablaze behind them and other frantic refugees clinging to the roof and windows of the last train. He remembers the town on fire, the black smoke and explosions from the inferno of Breslau as it burned.

His mother had baked the rye grain she had saved into hard, long-lasting sourdough loaves, just like the hundreds that he shares out to visitors at his festival now, and they survived on these till they reached Schleswig-Holstein and could live on what grain they were able to glean from the harvested fields – while she knitted sweaters for the winter from the wool that Peter, his two brothers and his sister picked off the pasture fences where sheep had grazed. At the community oven in the new town, she cut miniature suns onto the tops of loaves to mark them off from other people's. It was a sign of familyhood and survival that he still uses when baking bread, except that his suns look like puppet animals, the rays being "legs" sticking off a round body.' — (Hoagland, *Let 'em Have*, '83.)

6. Thus Bob Ernstthal, an associate of Schumann's from the summer of '63 onward, à propos of one of Schumann's earliest shows, the '62 *Fire*:

'I believe there was a show in the *Putney Puppet Tales* having to do with fire and there was a village and there was a fire — as you know, Peter is reluctant, he doesn't describe his past, but I remember that he was the Fireman. The Red Man was used as the Fireman and it was something about a fire in the town. And I think it relates to that automobile crash we did in that first version when I'm reading the Apocalypse (in the *Apocalypse* show of the summer of '63 (SSB)) — it had to do with that kind of thing. It was always like — it was always a scene — you remember the later woodcuts of wolves rushing through the town and things like that — a really recurrent theme was fire in the village. Earthquake in the village — fire — burning and running away and a peaceful village and wolves descend on it — beasts coming in out of the hills — that kind of feeling — apocalyptic, horrific feeling erupting onto a peaceful scene. A terrifying fire out of the sky. Undoubtedly from his feeling in Silesia when they left. It must be from that. I mean, it's like you just can't shake it. And he had brothers and sisters and he saw — I believe he was young enough — it was just at that time, I think, when it wasn't like his whole life was fleeing. I think he saw his world broken when he was old enough to really understand it. I think he probably was a young boy when he saw this war erupt into his life. And his father — like I was saying — his father, like Mr. Good Man — these very early things — I found that one there, *The Good Life of Mr. Miller*, (show of the winter of '62-'63) and all that. His father is really the image of the "good man." He really, really is. He was a school headmaster, I think, of this little school, and he has that feeling of being the "good burgher" — without the bad parts. He's a very kindly — civilization, I mean. Germany was highly civilized, as you know, and I think he saw — that was the image of the "good life" of Mr. Miller being suddenly bombed and fire coming out of the sky and burning up the village — and wolves. They didn't have a lot to eat, I think, also, in those years when they were fleeing and stuff. He mentioned it once in a while, but I think he had to go steal eggs from farmers and steal things from the farms and a little bit of wheat, you know, a little bit of stuff, and it really — it recurred — it was like a nightmare for him. It never stopped. (I: How did the Red Man puppet look? Redheaded?) He was red-headed and he had kind of an elongated or rounded face. It was a pointer. It was the pointing figure — it was a — it was a gesture of panic. In a certain way, it was like panic. (I: Even in the mask itself?) Ah — the mask was more serene but the hand was a very — a pointer — pointing like: "Get out!" It was the fire imagery. It was the imagery of alarm. "Alarm! Sound the cry!" That's how I remember it being described, like I said, as the Fireman. He used to refer to it as the Fireman.' — (Ernstthal, interview.)

Air raids on the railroad yards and industrial suburbs of Breslau extended to Lueben, and Schumann remembers (conversation, '82) that there were many of them, though as he remembers it children were afraid only because the grownups were. Speaking of this, the only vivid memories he brings up are not of these air raids, but of waking up early one morning in the peaceful Schleswig-Holstein countryside to which the family had fled and seeing small, scattered fires in the nearby woods and waking up his parents to tell them. There were no air raids in this rural area: probably a bomber had simply discharged its cargo to lighten its return flight. They had planted a garden and one day, working in the garden, the family witnessed (like Brueghel's plowman, the fall of Icarus) the offshore bombing of a ship. Schumann remembers the water spurting up where the bombs hit it. The ship was a German ship transporting Polish and Russian prisoners of war. The bloated bodies washed up on the beach for several days afterwards. The local farmers would gather them by the truckload for mass burial. We remember what we are afraid of in the guise of other images — images from situations in which we were safe and not afraid: spectators. When the world scares us it shakes us: our bee's work of graphic storing becomes disorganized. The memory of what happened as distinct from the memory that something happened like Freud's dreamwork functions substitutively: what we retain denotes other events. Might some of the power of art reside in its providing us with such safe substitutes, substitutes we can recall without fear that the pain that attended what they substitute for

the hard post-war years still, but apparently the young Schumann, in a somewhat normal manner, made his way through a Hanover Gymnasium, the Lutherschule, to the office of principal of which his father had been appointed. He received his Abitur in 1953.

His home was formally Christian, and Christian at heart, but not fervently so, but unemphatically.[7] German Kultur, whether Protestant,

---

will come back also? But he has occasionally spoken of the bombings also:

'I also think he's very deeply affected by the war he lived through in Germany, which has sparked his feelings, and his sympathies, and his empathizing with the whole rest of the world. (I: Does he ever talk about that war and his childhood experiences?) A little bit. He remembers as a child hearing bombs and hearing the noise and being very afraid and it seems like he and his brothers and sister were with his mother much of the time and she seemed to be the one that would soothe them or take care of them during the times when he – I guess he was very scared. And he talks about times where she would make the bread that he makes now and that would be what they ate. That's what they survived on for days.... I remember him always talking about the noise and hearing the bombs and being very scared.' — (Fernandez, interview.)

'Extremely magnetic and driven. Driven, and probably driven by psychological forces, of what he had seen as a youngster himself. And expressive always, almost like reiterating that same point over and over again, expressing in that one way or partially – reiterating the death over and over again.' — (Palmer, interview.)

I asked Dr. Irving Oyle, quondam standup comedian, what Schumann was like when he met him in Provincetown in the summer of '63:

'Just an interesting person, you know. Theatrical person. Well, he was heavy, Germanic. I got the sense he'd been severely wounded by the war. I think he – I get the impression that he experienced the Dresden fire storm or something like that – he was down on war.' — (Oyle, interview.)

7. 'They would go to church Christmas and Easter, I think, pretty much and that would be it.' — (Elka interview.)

His boyhood friend, Dieter Starosky (cf. infra), in '83 commenting on his engagement in Leftist causes during the '60s, thought he was probably as uncommitted to them as, despite his work's Christian trappings, to Christianity, and remembered him as during the later '50s hardly committed to Christ and the Bible even just as guides in life:

'Na, ich denke da hat, ich würde gar nicht sagen unbedingt links, vielmehr gegen dieses organisierte Grausame hat er wahrscheinlich ankämpfen wollen. Er wollte irgendwie den Menschen zeigen, wie das menschliche, sagen wir mal eine Mutter oder so, wie die leidet. Ich denke, er hat auch da die politischen Dinge, er hat sich dafür gebrauchen lassen, hat seine Sachen dafür zur Verfügung gestellt. Sowohl jetzt, ich will nicht sagen, dass er sich da verkauft, aber er, wenn er einigermassen damit übereinstimmt, dann nimmt er eben die Themen, wie er auch so Themen aus der Bibel nimmt. Die nimmt er, wie er sie gebrauchen kann. I hab ihn da oftmals angesprochen, weil mich die Bibel sehr interessiert und ich bin also eher darauf das auch zu verstehen, dass man das in seinem Leben anwendet. Aber ich glaub, das ist ihm gar nicht so wichtig, ihm reicht die Geschichte, der ganze Rahmen, das reicht ihm, nicht dass man den Kern der Aussage begreift.

Naja, das Christentum ist nach meiner Meinung also, wenn man ihn auf den Kern der Sache anspricht, auf den Kern der Bibel, da weicht er auch gerne aus, denn ich halte Weihnachten feiern und Ostern feiern halte ich nicht gerade für den Ausdruck des Christlichen. Das ist das traditionelle Christliche.... Wie ich den Peter verstehe. Wenn ich ihn immer daraufhin angesprochen hab, das war ihm zu, zu moralisch, zu sehr wie eine Sektierergruppe oder so, ja oder wie eben so Frauen die so eine Kirchenorganisation vertraten und das mochte er nicht.... Wie gesagt, da kann man mit'm Peter also, liess er auch gar nicht

Catholic or Jewish is not areligious, but is quietly religious. And his home was not Nazi, but neither was it in opposition: its windows were closed to the stench, those years, of German politics at home and abroad. The vulgarities and horrors of the regime were not spoken of in the children's presence.[8] This also was not untypical of the teachers, officials, businessmen carrying German Kultur. Schumann thus became insidiously Christian, and, until in America political engagement offered him an opportunity for meaningful art, quite apolitical.

While still at the Gymnasium, Schumann made masks for an arts class project, and did stone carving on his own (Schumann, interview, '79).[9] During his last year at the Gymnasium he staged a performance of a mime or dance sort, based on or derived from a play called *The Magic Lantern*, by Heinrich v. Heisler, a member of the Georgekreis:

'(Elka: Say a few words about that play you directed, because you talked a lot about that when I first met you, by —) By Heinrich von Heisler. That wasn't so important, that *play*, but I got a group of people together with whom I tried to do plays without props, without words, without music; the people represented architecture, or plants, or animals or various age groups — that was something that I very much tried, and it ended up as *dance*, at the end of that. That was still in high school, and right after high school. (Elka: You talked about that a lot. Even though I never saw it, I only saw some snap-shots at your mother's, but that's very vivid in *my* memory of what was very strong in *you*, and I don't think you *ever* mentioned puppetry in those years.) You might call it *mime* or something similar to that. I wasn't aware of any specific tradition for that. That was only — just a bunch of people who *tried* out things with me, theatrical movements that were not meant for an *audience*, but just were meant to be performed for other people who participated.' (Schumann, interview, '79.)

He formed[10] one of those intimate, one-on-one friendship associations

---

mit sich argumentieren. Ihm war die geschichtliche, also diese Geschichte als Hintergrund, das war ihm genug und das, da hat er genommen, was er kriegte, was ihm passte.' — (Starosky, interview.)

Though Starosky is a fundamentalist, so that what he in others judges lack of commitment to Christianity, others, Christian or non-Christian, might still consider commitment, I suspect that Schumann's break with 'bourgeois' values in the mid-'50s comprised some degree of rejection of the Christian values of his parents.

8. '(His father) did continue teaching and he did — felt, I think, that things were bad and wrong but his parents were not outspoken dissidents.... (His father) had fought in the First World War and was crippled. He had a bad leg so he wasn't in the Second World War.' — (Elka, interview.)

9. 'Au lycée, Peter Schumann fait des spectacles expérimentaux utilisant essentiellement les mouvements du corps. Les arts plastiques l'attirent. Il aime beaucoup les Expressionistes, Kirchner, Heckel, Nolde, tous les artistes du groupe *Die Brücke*..., dont il reprend de cette époque une des techniques préférées: la gravure sur bois.' — (Kourilsky, '71.)

10. 'Das hat er gamacht, das hat er gemacht. Wir haben von Sokrates, also Plato die, die Apologie des Sokrates gemacht. Und ich hatte da eine Musik dazu geschrieben und auch selber mitgespielt und irgendwie ist er dadurch aufmerksam geworden und da hat er mich

peculiar to adolescence with a fellow student, Dieter Starosky, like himself an idealist youth from a genteel background, a soul-brothership of the sort celebrated in what according to Elka, his wife, was their Bible, Hölderlin's *Hyperion*. Dieter, in the American vernacular his buddy, became his first associate in the arts, the only (nearly)[11] equally associated associate he was ever to have.[12]

Among the friends of the Schumann family were the Max Jacobs. During Peter Schumann's childhood in Silesia, the children of the two families played and went to school together. When, after the war, the Jacobs stayed on in Saxony – part, first of the Russian zone of occupation, then of the German Democratic Republic – which they did until some time in the '50s (they moved to Hamburg then), they would still periodically come to visit the Schumanns 'in the West.' Max Jacob was a puppeteer, by his Hohnsteiner Puppenspiele, the Obraszow of Germany, or the Bill Baird,[13] the man who rediscovered 'fist puppetry; sort of the folksy arts of puppetry of which only some little bits of remainders still existed' (Schumann, interviewed on my behalf by his son Ephraim Schumann in October 1979, mostly in the presence of his wife Elka, quoted in the sequel as 'Schumann, interview, '79.'). The Schumann children went to the Jacobs' puppet shows, Peter Schumann 'watched a lot of their shows' (ibid.), liked the old standbys, especially the *Puppenfaust* ('liked it – the "idea of it" – better than Goethe's *Faust*'), finding out only later, during his teens, when he did a great deal of reading, what it was he had seen, and liked puppet shows 'much, much' better than the theatre, and the Jacobs gave them puppets as presents. All the Schumann children played these puppets, and Peter did puppet shows with his brothers and sisters, with one brother and sister in particular, and with the children of

---

angesprochen. Und da kam eigentlich der erste Kontakt zustande. Da zeigte er mir dann seine Skulpturen und es war für mich faszinierend, also was von ihm als Person ausging. — (Starowsky, interview.)

11. 'Wir haben also genauso gelitten, wie auch Erfüllung zusammen gefunden, in dem, was wir für Vorstellungen hatten und ich hab ihm praktisch geholfen dabei dieses (...) zu erfüllen, denn die Ideen kamen immer vom Peter, das stimmt. Wir haben uns dann bereichert gegenseitig, aber die Vorstellungen, diese ganzen Impulse, die Initiativen, die kamen von ihm.' — (Starosky, interview.)

12. 'Another German that I met only once, who came on a visit, who was a cellist – that was an original puppeteer in Europe. And I remember seeing Peter and this young man together and the respect that was between them. It was like somebody at last, was on the beam.' — (Palmer, interview.)

13. 'Well, that is not true of Bill Baird, it's true of Obraszow and Max Jacob . . . . (Jacob) had a friend who was a good woodcarver and carved him the heads for his puppets. I don't remember his name. And he collected a little company around himself and made puppet shows and eventually had a repertoire that included *Faust* and *Freischütz* and old standard plays like that, that puppeteers had done before him.' — (Schumann, interview, '79.)

Jacob's puppet carver was Theo Eggnik Riga, 'master pupil' of Prof. Winde of the Dresden Academy of Arts. — (Marie Jacob, letter, '82.)

friends of the family: 'I was a dedicated puppeteer when I was a kid. I did a *lot* of puppet shows.' — (ibid.)

When he got out of high school, he 'and a friend' attended an 'all-round' puppetry workshop — a 'long weekend or something like that' — given by the Jacobs, where 'everyone built his own head and made up his own costume and then in some fashion several people together would produce a little play.' (ibid.) From Schumann's turns of phrase, I get the impression that he did not, after his early childhood, altogether dig the specifics — stereotypes of folksiness — of the Hohnsteiner Handpuppenspiele.[14] Soon after he left high school, he abandoned puppetry:[15]

'When I grew up, and I was an art student and a young artist, I always had the longing to eventually do puppetry. I always liked that the *best* of all the things that I'd seen. I always — I thought this kind of relationship to an *audience*, that a puppeteer has, is the most desirable. (Elka: But certainly when I met you and those years that I knew you, your early twenties, I don't remember your mentioning puppetry at all as an ideal or goal. I think during that time you would have scorned something so little and cute and like geraniums growing in a pot or something, and you talked of mass choreography and some huge events that were like Oberammergau, sort of, or like the circus. Something in which there was no audience or relation to audience: where things were done for their own sake, and *that* was very much dominant in your mind and the thought of puppetry didn't come until Putney.) It's true. I forgot about it for years. I thought about puppetry and then forgot about it. Many years.'   (Schumann, interview, '79.)

Jacob contributed to Schumann's lasting conception of himself as really a wandering folk artist, and of his puppetry as a popular art. Schumann was to realize this ideal of puppetry twice: on Coney Island in the spring and summer of '70, and from the mid-'70s onward by his once-a-year Circus

---

14. 'Yes, they are no good (Obraszow's puppets). He doesn't have any good puppets. He has no taste — he's a real — in contrast to Max Jacob, who does have — not that he has very good taste, but he had good carvers and they were all from wood — Max Jacob's puppets — and that made a big difference. He had real old fashioned craftsmen working puppets for him and those were beautiful. Simple, folk-kind carving like one would find in the Bavarian forest or in the Black Forest, but they were good — they were good. I have seen much better puppets than Obraszow does in the Russian Petrushka puppets that perform in — supposedly they still do — in supermarkets and so on and in Russian stores. — (Schumann, interview, '82.)

15. When one reads Max Jacob's delightful *Mein Kasper und ich* (originally published around 1962, 2nd edition 1981), it occurs to one that Jacob may in fact have above all transmitted to the young Schumann an image of the puppeteering profession as still not only in principle but as regards feasible exercise of it an itinerant 'volksverbunden' trade. When Jacob was barely starting, in the early 1920s, he has just received his first puppet — Kasper — as a present. There were still

'in Sachsen und auch in Thüringen Puppenspielerfamilien, die auf eine grosse Tradition zurückblicken konnten. Sie hatten Marionetten und spielten wochenlang in den Dörfen. Die ländliche Bevölkerung hing sehr an diesen Puppenspielern, die mit ihren Wohnwagen von einem Ort zum anderen zogen, und liebte die von ihnen dargebotenen Volksstücke.

in Glover, Vermont. He abandoned puppetry when he left high school, but the medium remained in his mind, and after an interval of some nine years, his early interest in it provided him the key by which to resolve his hesitation between sculpture and dance, and his reservations concerning them, in our century essentially elitist and egoist arts.

Einmal hörten wir, dass in einem Nachbardorf "Die Genoveva" gespielt werden sollte. Als besondere Attraktion stand auf dem Theaterzettel, ich besitze ihn noch heute: "Zum Schluss Genoveva auf dem Paradebette mit bengalischer Beleuchtung." Wir besuchten die Vorstellung und erlebten die Ergriffenheit der dörflichen Zuschauer über das Schicksal der Genoveva. Uns selbst amüsierte das stelzbeinige Pathos und die unfreiwillige Komik, mit der das Spiel durchsetzt war.' — (loc. cit.)

But Jacob's puppetry developed neither from this popular tradition, nor from the one he refers to immediately following this citation, the art tradition — he mentions a performance of a Mozart 'Singspiel,' probably 'Bastien and Bastienne' by the 'Brannsche Marionetten-Theater Münchner Künstler.' — but from the 'Wandervögelbewegung,' the Teutonizing, highly organized and highly ideological, non-smoking, non-drinking, vegetarian, nature loving, hiking movement; a way of life for many young people of the lower and middle classes, as for the young Jacob, devoted — during free time — not only to wandering (a way of 'coming into possession' of the German landscape), but to intense camaraderie and a somewhat communal life at the movement's homes and out of doors, involving not only cooking together but also mutual and communal entertainment, especially music: Jacob became a puppeteer as an autodidact: gradually developing his art playing for his fellow Wandervögel good-naturedly satirical Kasper-skits about the movement, and then branching out, still in the context of the movement, playing for village and small town audiences on the occasions of Wandervögel encounters and for village schools to which the teachers, themselves Wandervögel (there were many lower school teachers in the movement), would invite him; and his first fellow performers were Wandervögel also, his one and only play for these audiences a 'Kaspers Heldentat' concocted by him, and which he could vary at liberty, since a heroic deed of some sort was what Kasper was supposed to perform anyhow. The Wandervögelbewegung was a Volksbewegung, making allowance for its contrived character: by developing within it, and by its initial address to juvenile and rural audiences Jacob's puppetry developed as a popular art, and was like the traditional rural popular puppetry also in being itinerant. Ultimately he became known for having developed hand puppetry beyond those traditional popular origins and forms:

'Als Max Jacob mit seinem Spiel begann, war Handpuppenspiel auf dem Jahrmarkt zu Hause. Max Jacob, und mit ihm einige andere Puppenspieler, wandten sich von den Derbheiten des Jahrmarktkaspers ab und bewirkten eine Reform, durch die Kasperspiel nicht nur für Kinder, sondern auch und gerade für Erwachsene einen neuen Wert in künstlerischer Hinsicht bekam. Diese Reform hatte weitreichende Folgen, hat bedeutende Änderungen hervorgerufen und wirkt immer noch weiter. Die Spielweise ist als Hohnsteiner Stil ein Begriff geworden. Unter ihm ist in technischer Hinsicht die Loslösung der Handpuppe von der Spielleiste und damit die Eroberung des Bühnenraums zu verstehen (something Schumann was in his own way also to accomplish (SSB)); inhaltlich wird darunter der Weg von einfacher, vordergründiger, oft sehr grober Kost zu sensibleren Spielen verstanden (id.) die auch das Aufgreifen literarischer Stoffer für die Erwachsenen möglich machte (Schumann's work is not analogous to Jacob's in this respect (SSB)). Max Jacob's Kasper beherrschte seine Spiele als eine Gestalt, die sich allem Positiven im Leben zur Seite stellte, und zugleich sich nicht scheute, zu allen aktuellen Problemen Stellung zu beziehen. Dieser Kasper war weder autoritär noch antiautoritär, er war einfach *un*autoritär und verkörperte ein Stück gesunden Menschenverstands.' — (Fr. Arndt, introduction to '81 edition of Jacob, *Mein Kasper*.)

As regards specifics, Jacob's puppet theatre seems to have differed toto coelo from what Schumann came up with, notably in five regards: the center of Jacob's theatre (when he didn't do literature) seems to have been Kasper, a non-malevolent but decidedly satiric clown, to Jacob representing himself; though he decidedly wanted an improving effect on his audiences, Jacob had a horror of the 'raised index finger'; the primary effect his puppet theatre seems to have aimed at was laughter – amusement: puppet theatre to him was in essence comedy; there seems to have been nothing morbid about Jacob or his theatre, he had a positive view of life and accentuated the positive; his puppets were pretty awful, except for a few that Till de Kock made for him, conventional and insinuatingly good-natured caricatures, with the scantiest and most superficial psychological and social references, and no other, nowhere as original or powerful as those of the popular German tradition surviving into the early 20th century, though lacking the smart-alecky slickness of post-World-War-II puppets East and West. And of course: his was strictly a hand puppet theatre.

I retain, then, as the formative experiences of Schumann's childhood the sudden descent of the gigantic fiery tidal wave of war onto the warm and happy innocent life of a peaceful village; the appealing figure of the simple man of the people, wandering across the land, entertainer of children, free of the cares of respectable people, but welcomed by them, as artist, as entertainer and as man, nevertheless; and that high fine culture, literature-and-music-bound, of the Old Germany – assaulted, shattered by that tidal wave, and, significantly, quite distinct from, and in some ways even the opposite, of that itinerant folk artist's art, stance and existential mode, combining aspects of refinement and discipline identifying to the boy his parents, but most particularly, seeing as how the man was also his teacher at the Gymnasium, his father.

2. *Hyperion*. Evangel of the faith that, adapted to his personality and changed times, has guided Schumann as artist. Nobility (Schumann: simplicity) vs. meanness, baseness. The spiritual regeneration of mankind as aim of art.

'Ich kann sagen, wir haben, wir haben des öfteren mal Bücher verbrannt, weil, da sammeln sich dann immer wieder Bücher und wenn wir dann wieder mal aufbrachen, dann haben wir fast, fast alles verbrannt: alle Abiturzeugnisse und das alles wurde verbrannt und manchmal blieb nur der *Hyperion* übrig und eventuell die Bibel oder mal die Bagavad Gita oder so, ja. Und wenn wir uns was besorgt haben, dann haben wir uns halt das immer wieder als erstes besorgt. Und wir haben also auch manche, also ziemlich viel laut vorgelesen, einander vorgelesen.'
(Starosky, interview.)

'I did not like Rilke. I felt that in German literature (*Hyperion*) was about the purest and greatest that I had learned to know. That was so – maybe just that, so pure and straight out of the mind. It wasn't ashamed to be feeling. It wasn't ashamed of itself. It didn't have any of these complications that literature has a lot. It was like fairy tale straight-forward literature. *Hyperion* was quite different from the hymns and the late poetry. I didn't read *Hyperion* any more and I started liking that poetry much more than that prose. It's a great love story. It is also a great friendship that's portrayed in it. It is also about a dream of a young modern man about some anarchic revolution, not in Germany but in Greece, because that was his whole inner alignment. It's something where a modern man protests his modern civilization, rejects it and finds some – and creates some ideal time. That is his solution. Now – meantime I couldn't read that book any more. I tried to. I tried a couple of times. And now that's gone. I don't know. It was very particular to that time. Whereas with the poetry, I still am tremendously attracted.)
(Schumann, interview, '83.)

Young Schumann's Bible, *Hyperion*, the great poet Hölderlin's epistolary novel for ladies, as insufferable in diction as in spirit, written 1796/98, but begun some four or five years earlier, was conceived and executed during the decade of idealist disappointment by the realization of the ideals of the French Revolution. It advances an ideal of nobility.

The noble man or woman that Hölderlin proposes to us as ideal is a person preemptively dominated in mind and conduct by a fervent love of the Good; a positive, not a censorious love; a love of a spiritually defined good; a love supported by a generous faith in the meaningfulness of the world in terms of an organization of it according to a benign design, a faith taking the form of a loving communion with nature. The Good spiritually conceived is neither a chicken in every pot nor producers' ownership of the means of production but the existence of spirit according to its true nature. Hölderlin indicates the nature of this nature by the terms 'living spirit', but the biting edge of the conception is that spirit, not in its form of the spirituality of nature (the which = the mutual support of its parts = all-pervasive love) but in its form of human spirit is capable of existing otherwise than according to its true nature: number one, as the lowness of selfish materialism, shading off into the brutality of a pursuit of sensuous satisfactions, number two, as mechanicity of the soul, the ossification of the spirit into present forms (concretely: the preset forms of custom, morality and religion furnished the individual by society for appropriate enactment of one of the social roles). Man is capable of lowness by a confinement within his/her animal nature, capable of psychic mechanization by confinement within a social role – the bad alternatives of bourgeois calculation or peasant crudity and of petty-bourgeois self-satisfied and righteous Philistinism. Either way he/she detracts from the sum total of true spirituality in the world by a perversion of the spirit within him/her. Nobility is attained by elevation above that lowness not fixing the soul into preset and prescribed patterns. It is not only an elevation of the spirit to ideal objectives, but an idealist and generously emotional magnanimity. The Good to the pursuit of which somebody noble devotes his/her life is thus specifically the ennoblement of humanity, the reign of the living spirit within all men. Not, note, their moral and/or intellectual improvement, for this would be a goal acknowleged and if it fit into social role even pursued by mechanical souls; nor improvement of the material conditions of life: a goal that the base might well in their collectively materialist and selfish interest pursue.

As the *Hyperion* makes clear in its Platonizing description of its hero's development getting to be noble ain't that easy. It requires first of all educative personal contacts – Hölderlin in real life was a tutor and he wrote the book as Platonist educator. We are all subject to the despiritualizing forces of our animal nature and of society: to overcome them requires the help of and intimacy with (noble) others: specifically (in the case of a male individual which is what this book is about) an Older Man ('Adamas' in the book) whom we can adore and who – adoration leading to emulation – sets our soul on its upward path, Young Male Friends to whom we can attach ourselves in an erotically tinged and competitive mutual soul-brotherhood ('Alabanda'), the friends mutually goading one another on to the risks of active pursuit of the ideal, each by his different strength making up for the other's weaknesses, and a Noble Woman ('Diotima') to fall into requited love with, this (chaste) relationship fostering an inner stability of noble motive and a desire by a noble life to be worthy of and admired by her. These three kinds of ennobling love are all natural to a young man growing up, but evidently some luck is required for finding the right persons and hitting it off with them; and in some milieux chances might be especially slim. There are two further near-

requirements or requirements for individual ennoblement: also not necessarily apt to be fulfilled. The one is a frequentation of nature inspiring and affirming faith in the universal immanent lovingness of the world beyond man, the presence of the living spirit within it: Hölderlin's particular point, important to him, being that mankind's near-universal perversion of spirit makes such solacing inspiration 'well-nigh' indispensible for keeping up the courage indispensible to nobility. This presents problems not only to the urbanite and any busy person, but to youths caught up in a practical relationship to nature, e.g. the agriculturalist's. The other is inspiration by noble art, a point less stressed but crucial to Hölderlin (since it assigns a noble role to artistic endeavour), and in *Hyperion* made both by a lecture Hyperion gives on the Athenians of the Periclean age, and by advice given him by Diotima: at a time when Alabanda urges him on to (noble) political action (intervention in the Greek insurrectionary movement against Turkish despotism), she urges him rather to develop his artistic talents so that he can nobly deploy them for his ideals. Ideal images produced by art are the only adequate images of the ideal, and − soul food − are indispensible guides and enthusiasmers for individual ennoblement. In an age or country lacking them it is hard or impossible to become noble.

Hyperion effectively presents a vicious circle. For the difficulties of ennoblement are largely due to the deficiency of nobility in the world, which thus tends to perpetuate itself. For if the majority of people are either base- or low-minded if not in the grip of their animal passions and downright brutal, or else escape this condition only by falling into the soul-stunting mechanisms of custom and of conventional religion and morality or of particular role-performances, not only are chances for the ennobling personal encounters small, but the obstacles posed by these predominant categories of people to soul-saving communion with nature and to the production of soul-stirring noble art − ignored by the base, derided by the mechanical-souled, its potential producers despised by both types − are correspondingly great. But the harder it is made for any generation of individuals to become or remain noble, the harder it will be for the next.

The image of mankind *Hyperion* presents is thus one of a few fortunate noble individuals isolated in a sea of spiritual perversion, the ignoble or narrow-minded many. This situation of course precisely presents to the noble the challenge by response to which to prove their nobility and make it real: the challenge of the ennoblement of this miserable humanity. In addition to offering its spiritualist ideal of 'what it means to be human', the doctrine of the living spirit and the ideal of nobility, and a pedagogic theory on how nobility is fostered in people, it raises the problem of how to behave nobly (how to pursue the ennoblement of mankind, its spiritual regeneration), a problem of how the good society, one of noble individuals and one fostering nobility, might historically yet be attained.

It discusses two alternative modes of noble action (and two corresponding paths of humanity towards true spirituality): political action, artistic action, the former the choice of the idealist ideologues and politicians of the French Revolution, the historical event that above all stirred the young Hölderlin (and his friend Hegel), the latter e.g. Hölderlin's choice. The political action in principle available to the noble individual, the spiritualist idealist, and one commended to noble German youth in some of Hölderlin's poetry written before *Hyperion*, is quite specific: it is insurrectionary or revolutionary (not propagandistic, or not primarily propagandistic or educative, but essentially military), and its goals are political, viz. the liberal goals of national independence and individual liberty, i.e. a constitutional form guaranteeing individual liberty and minimizing the state's regulatory interference. This was Hyperion's choice. Artistic action, on the other hand, though it might (a point not raised in the novel) support such political action propagandistically, might also be quite apolitical (merely presenting the ideals of the living spirit), and it might even oppose direct political action: which is what in fact *Hyperion* does: both by its story — its hero's insurrectionary tentative is defeated by the baseness of his followers (simple mountain folk) who commence to plunder and pillage and are routed by the Turks in this state of base indiscipline — besides which the book brings up the basic embarrassing fact about the Greek independence movement from the mid-18th century onward, namely that it was largely engineered by Russian despotism for the sake of an extension of Russian imperial power: not only is Hyperion's insurrection aided by the Russians, but Hyperion, having been defeated as guerilla, enlists in the Imperial Russian navy — and by its hero's discourse: his friend Alabanda is a member of a sinister conspiratorial movement (the book in a splendid passage describes his originally or 'basically' idealist co-conspirators' corruption by their political action), and Hyperion argues with him about his more proximate political objective which, more in line with the *Republic* than with the *Symposium*, and more in line with the ideals of 1793 than with those of 1789, is a strong state, regulating virtue: Hyperion does not believe that government regulation can promote their spiritual ideals. *Hyperion* thus is a justification of Hölderlin's defection from the politics inspiring him at the beginning of the '90s, and an argument in favor of the artistic or even the exclusively artistic promotion of the advent of the good society, the realization of the Good. It expresses the disaffection from politics of many of the original idealistic supporters of the French Revolution.

The basic thrust of its argument against the political pursuit of its ideals is not against either political action or political objectives per se, but against the authoritarianism of the politics it envisages: insurrectionary action, government regulation, essentially: imposition of a way of life by force: it opposes them as inappropriate to its ideals: destroying the spiritual nobility of the conspirators, insurrectionaries, power-holders no less than of the populations they seek to reform. But it is no accident or historical limitation that it considers only the imposition of reform by force: there is no other way to reform a humanity both the rulers and the ruled of which are largely either basely materialist and egoist or at best petty-minded performers of their assigned social roles. Given the state of humanity, the political-minded noble individual is faced with the choice of debasing authoritarianism and ineffectuality: politics is inadvisable for him or her.

This leaves art. Abdication from the challenge of reform of humanity would be base. *Hyperion* suggests a third alternative: the private activity of pedagogy in personal relationships of the sort it describes as factors of individual ennoblement, the preceptorial inspiration of younger people, mutual spiritual vivification among young people of the same sex, allied in friendship, spiritual sustainment between man and woman. This would be noble action of a more restricted scope than art or politics, but though its possible contribution to mankind's spiritual regeneration would be lesser, it would be more certain. I don't from the book's standpoint see any objection to this choice and in fact it clearly is a way of life and line of endeavor from its standpoint incumbent on the high-minded. But limitation to it is excluded for artistically gifted individuals: I would go so far as to say that for an artistically gifted individual to pursue idealist goals in his private life only but not as artist would from Hyperion's standpoint be ignoble.

Hyperion does not deal with the problems of an artistic pursuit of its ideals. But they are clearly implicit in the diatribe of Hyperion against the Philistinism of the Germans – their 'mechanical-souledness' – concluding the novel. They are analogous to the problems of a political pursuit of mankind's spiritual regeneration. On the one hand, mankind may be presumed largely impervious to a noble art.[1] On the other hand adaptation of the art to the receptivities of the base-minded or the narrow-spirited would expose the artist to the danger of becoming base or narrow-minded him- or herself, and though, presuming artistic talent, it would be effective, it would be more apt to strengthen the baseness or the narrow tastes and prejudices of its consumers than to detach them from their materialism, egoism or brutal sensuousness or to make them transcend the limitations of their social roles.

Hyperion lastingly influenced Schumann, I would say. Presenting views, feelings, attitudes to him that were already his, it strengthened and clari-

---

1. Hölderlin, late in life, expressed his sense of failure: 'Öfters hab ich Gesang versucht aber sie hörten dich nicht./ Denn so wollte die heil'ge Natur du sangest du für sie in/ deiner Jugend nicht singend/ Du sprachest zur Gottheit, aber dies habt ihr all vergessen,/ dass immer die Erstlinge Sterblichen nicht, dass sie den/ Göttern gehören. Gemeiner muss, alltäglicher muss die/ Frucht erst werden, dann wird sie den Sterblichen eigen.' — (F. Hölderlin, *Aber die Sprache.*)

fied them and raised them to the level of principle. It defined for him his own alienated position in the Germany of the 1950s. It gave form to his own idealism: equally opposed to soul-destroying base materialism and selfishness – to consumerism and the striving for higher income – and to soul-stultifying conventionalities of morality and religion and acceptance of role; and equally vast in its ambitions: the spiritual regeneration of the Germans and ultimately of all mankind. It confirmed his own distaste for politics and his own artistic inclinations. Its stress on a purifying relationship with nature was highly congenial to him; and its negative judgment of humanity met with his own. Its conception of art – not to be pursued for its own sake nor for self-expression, but in the service of high ideals and for the good of humanity – was his own, but provided encouragement. And the problems it implied for an idealistic and spiritually oriented pursuit of art in a base or at best Philistine environment were his own.

The coincidence of Schumann's views and feelings with those of Hölderlin in the *Hyperion*, Schumann's adherence to the gospel of the living spirit, makes the book a key to his work. I have gone to some trouble to indicate the nature of the agreement because Schumann's attempts at solutions to those problems of the idealist artist with spiritual and humanitarian ideals both then and subsequently diverged totally from Hölderlin's. These divergences are less indicative of disagreement than of disparities of personality and of a difference of historical situation: the same problems, attaching to the same general position and tentative are in a different situation attacked differently by a man of different temperament.

Whereas Hölderlin (as he emerges in his letters and poems) was of an open, loving and outgoing nature, but also soft and pliant, and naturally ascetic and chaste, of weak sexual temperament, virtually free of personal feelings of sinfulness or guilt, and far more given (though his personal life was miserable) to enthusiastic appreciation of the beautiful and good – of the evidences of spirit in nature and in man – than to complaint or castigation of evil, Schumann (as he appears from his work and from second hand reports) is an intensely private man, reserved and emotionally cautious, energetic rather than enthusiastic, forceful and dominant rather than loving, tender rather than loving, and, robustly sensual by nature, ascetic by discipline, and above all – given, precisely, the two traits distinguishing him from Hölderlin, namely his erotic and other appetitiveness and his need to dominate, an inward lust for power, and the conflict between these needs and the ideals and the spirituality he shares with Hölderlin – beset and preoccupied by a sense of personal sinfulness, of guilt (of which there is no trace in Hölderlin's poems) and apt to project them outward in a focus on evil rather than on good, and in an ideal of unconflicted innocence and simplicity contrary to his own nature.

These differences pertain primarily to the differences in content in the two men's work, which, besides the two I have indicated – Schumann's focus on evil (the evils of power and greed) rather than on good, and his reduction of Hölderlin's ideal of actively enterprising, daring nobility to one of passively accepting, suffering or content simplicity of mind and innocence of heart – primarily relate to the primordial role of death in his work. In Hölderlin's poems as in *Hyperion* (Diotima's strangely content and incidental dying), death appears as quite incidental aspect of life, and even positively: as affirmation of the reign of the spirit and of its unity in all its material manifestations, in the life of an individual, the life of the earth into which he or she decomposes, others' remembering awareness of him or her. In Schumann's work death is the main figure, primarily in its eschatological association with Judgment, Heaven and Hell (the Dance of Death theme), secondarily – and, though this is not what Schumann intends, no less negatively and threateningly – as integral aspect of life, its cost. His is a world of demons, Hölderlin's one of Apollonian harmony. But this vast difference arises from shared ideals: nobly presented by Hölderlin, grimly or humorously contrasted with reality by Schumann: promoted by both.

Their historical situations present a gross similarity: as the libertarian ideals of 18th century humanism had been fatally fractured by the post-revolutionary development of France – terror, directoire, Napoleon – so the communitarian ideals of 19th century socialism have been fatally fractured by the post-revolutionary development of the Soviet Union. Each man worked in an age of snatched-away goals, for the reasonably specific goals that to a preceding generation of idealists had seemed an attainable Utopia substituted a generic (and correspondingly vague) goal of spiritual regeneration: for Hölderlin positively defined by love or even as love, for Schumann negatively as escape from the pettiness and meanness of people around him.

But the big pertinent difference in their historical situations is the passing of an addressable elite. It is pertinent because artistic form is addressive gesture, and addressive gesture depends on whom the artist imagines he/she is addressing. After all, doing art *is* part of a person's social life. But what kind of a phantom public shadowily occupies an artist's (or intellectual's) interior gallery – other both than the artists, intellectuals, bohemians, etc. he/she hangs around with and other also, at least quite possibly, than the people for whom he/she actually works and that are paying him/her – is not up to the free work of the imagination, but depends on what the artist can plausibly imagine. I.e. he/she has to construe his/her addresses out of the confusing indices furnished him/her by actual society. Thus my father fantastically imagined as his audience a non-existing proletarian elite. Hölderlin in the accents of classic Greece addressed himself to an elite he desperately constructed out of a few encounters of his student days: a humanistically educated, cultured

German Youth: certainly not the enlightened bourgeoisie addressed by Diderot or that Marx and Engels imagined they perceived in the Manchester of the 1850s getting ready to 'assume state power', but still a stratum by their families and prospects relating to as similar a class as the difference in national histories allowed. The disaffected artist or intellectual (the one we are here concerned with), though dependent also on scattered personal encounters, construe their image of an addressable audience that it makes sense for them to address out of indices furnished by the reformist and oppositional movements of their time.

Since Hölderlin's time, the development of the corporate economy and of its correlate, the pseudo-democratic, economy-regulating, services state and the integration into them of what up to maybe the mid-19th century appeared as a bourgeois as well as of what up to maybe the 1920s appeared as a working class elite have done away with addressable oppositional elites – socially possibly effective class-carriers of reformist or revolutionary ideals. These publics have become unimaginable. This was certainly Schumann's situation both in Germany and later in America – my father had constructed his imaginary audience out of perceptions and movements of the time of the Great Depression. We can still to some extent construe the political life of the West in terms of a class struggle: but a historicist interpretation of this class struggle as tending toward a utopian future has for the greater part of the century seemed merely an ideological ploy. When Hölderlin, appropriate to this, addressed himself to a culturally defined elite, this was no doubt to a considerable extent against his better judgment, but the political activities of such an elite in the Germany of 1810-20 and again at the end of the '40s show that it was not purely arbitrary fancy. In Schumann's case, not only his experience of his parents' quietism during the Third Reich, but the record of the 'gebildeten Stände' during the '30s and, with isolated negligible exceptions, during the war simply precluded such address: 'Bildung' had been proven irrelevant to a regeneration of the spirit and as form of the spirit was definitely not on the 'live' but on the 'mechanical' side. (And in fact with few exceptions neither art nor thought have in the West since World War I addressed themselves either formally or even just pro forma to the cultured.) Hölderlin's work addressed itself to individuals in whom he could suppose the 'living spirit' active: unselfish young idealists preoccupied by the welfare of their fellow men; and who, though not in the aggregate amounting to what since the 1820s has been considered a 'social class', were not just a scattering of isolated and powerless – historically irrelevant – individuals either, but could be seen as a social stratum (elite of a 'class' or not) potentially exercising an important, directed influence on the future.

The gospel of the *Hyperion* constrains the artist to the objective of redeeming the virtually unredeemable – the base- and/or mean-spirited majority. Hölderlin's solution for himself was address to an elite that might by leadership effect this. Schumann no longer had this option. He tried two different approaches, one in Germany in the 1950s, another one in America subsequently.

His first approach was based on the view that art could not – not substantially – affect, i.e. alter the mind-set of, addressees, its consumers: an audience. The audience could be assumed to a decisive extent to be base- and/or mean-spirited and in this state virtually impervious to idealist address. The exceptions would not be (socially, historically) significant. He thus devised the idea that an art could be devised that would – in the desired direction – affect not its audience but its practitioners and that would be of a sort not restricting its practice to the talented and skilled. If the practice of such an art, open to all and spiritually regenerating its practitioners could be established, he seems to have felt, it might (somehow) spread: though it is hard to see why he should have thought indirectly salutary proselytizing of practitioners by such an art more feasible than directly salutary effects on audiences. The art he thought might in this way – just possibly – effect the ennoblement of mankind was dance. The effort or perhaps more basically the desperate fantasy encouraging it collapsed '59-'60.

In America, he has tried a communicative art, addressed to an audience: predicated on the assumption that though people by and large were in the senses outlined base- and/or mean-spirited, that was not all they were, that there was in the population though little or no nobility a residue of simplicity of spirit and innocence of heart that could be appealed to, opening them to address of corresponding form, and potential for spiritual regeneration through such address. This art was puppetry, a people's and children's art, in a variety of ways drawing not on classical but on medieval antecedents.

Simplicity and innocence characterize the noble (and Hölderlin himself), but in the sense in which they came to characterize Schumann's work and at least in a residual way the audience he imagined himself addressing they have different and in some ways opposite associations. The kind of spirit Schumann came to strive to express, to appeal to and to foster is characterized not by idealism, but by naive attachment to the simple things of life, to the values and pleasures of family, work and community, not by an urge to reform or improve humanity, but by fellowship, helpfulness, respect for the person, not by love, but by gentleness and good will, and by acceptance and contentment, not by ambition or striving for perfection. This ideal is not anything that Hölderlin would have objected to, but he is not particularly concerned with it either in *Hyperion* or in his poetry. The art form that Schumann developed under the aegis of this ideal was utterly different from Hölderlin's. That the gospel of *Hyperion* or a way of thinking very close to it motivates it is suggested, however, above all by a coincidence of objectives (spiritual regeneration) and of oppositions (to baseness, meanness in the senses adumbrated), by a kinship of the forms of spirit idealized (they differ only as the self-conscious differs from the unselfconscious), and by indications that Schumann adopted this art form not as direct and appropriate expression of his most intimate personal concerns, but under the obligation of an allegiance to the *Hyperion*'s gospel: for his masks, his most direct expression, neither express nor address nor seem designed to foster the simplicity and innocence the spectacles he uses them in express, address and are designed to foster, but are on the subject of guilt: of death, eschatologically.

Schumann's responsiveness to Hölderlin's noble spiritualism suggests that the patently different set of values he in America substituted for it in his work — pacifism, asceticism, simplicity of life, thought and action, utility to fellow men — are to a relevant extent given meaning by that noble spiritualism, are to be interpreted as particular sub-form of it, and not viewed as simply other, let alone opposite. It also suggests a certain degree of consciousness and deliberateness on Schumann's part in giving it this form, a process of self-censorship, self-denial and self-restriction, even: some insincerity in the service of his ideals, a degree of artificiality: a strategy. These are considerations to keep in mind in considering his work. But they should be balanced by consideration of the influence of his personality on his work; by his relation to power, guilt and death: *Naturally* inclining him to *deviate* from Hölderlin's views and place accents differently; and perhaps independently, say in reaction against his own nature, inclining him to make the particular applications of it he did make. There is more to his work than its simplicities, and some of it related to ideals of nobility and spirituality, but some of it also to his struggles with himself.

3. German Lehr- and Wanderjahre, 1954-1961. Dance the vocation. Project of a German renewal through dance, the ambition to become an artistic Genghis Khan. Germany a spiritual vacuum[1]. Failure.

Upon leaving the Gymnasium, he studied for a year (1953-4) at a Hannover academy of arts heavily named the Werkkunstschule, studied sculpture under Professor Scheuernstuhl (Chairscrubber), learned to do plaster casting, in the spirit of Byron, Dr. Winkelman and Hölderlin, took off for Greece ('54), returned, briefly signed up at the Hochschule für Bildende Künste in Berlin (1955), found himself unable/unwilling to attend classes, quit. This concluded his formal education. Probably this is when he gave up the idea of becoming a professional sculptor. He was now a drop-out. He had rebelled. There was apparently no break with his parents, but he had rebelled against them and against Kultur. He went to Munich, a city that at least since Mad Ludwig has in Germany counted as congenial to artistic searching free spirits.

On her way to her native Russia, her first visit since her childhood, Elka Leigh Scott,[2] his future wife, encountered his friend Dieter there in

---

1. 'Germany was a – well, very difficult place. But not difficult enough. It was – well, I worked in different areas.... What we looked for (Schumann is speaking of his dance projects during the second half of the '50s (SSB)) – I don't know, in Germany it didn't seem to make *sense* – we couldn't – we didn't know what *for*, when we did it. (I: That's what I meant. How about politics?) Yeah. There was no such thing as politics. In Germany there were no *politics* – no visible politics. There was nothing – no – it was just going on – what was going on. There were complaints about what Mr. Adenauer did when Schumann went out of the – came out of the limelight, but it wasn't big. There was nothing – no great wrongs or rights or anything. It was an awful – yeah, really a vacuum – empty scene – empty-headed and unintelligent and I had no interest in that at all. I just found everything was wrong, that's all – I think, so did many of my friends. But what one tries to do is to – oh, I don't know.' — (Schumann, interview, '82.)

2. Russian-born daughter, American, of the engineer John Scott who during the '20s and or '30s had worked in the Soviet Union and later became a conservative editor of *Time* magazine. Also granddaughter of the grow-it-yourself ecologist Scott Nearing. She is shy, genteel, opinionated and intolerant, ferociously protective of her husband, harbors deep resentments against him, is amazingly prudish, withal 'somehow very innocent' (still in the '80s), with a pleasing, clear girlish voice. A graduate of Putney School and Bryn Mawr, profoundly imbued with a sense of her own incompetence and insignificance, a New England-type Christian, i.e. not really at all religious, but beset by conscience, she has from almost the time of their first meeting in '56 been totally devoted to her husband. The rigors of the roles of wife of an artist, wife of a Great Man, wife of Peter Schumann notwithstanding, she is a beautiful person.

He met Elka in 1956 in Munich, where she was studying on her junior year abroad from Bryn Mawr College. Though Bryn Mawr is a conventional first-class college, at that

Elka Schumann, Glover, VT., 1982. *Photograph by B. Brown.*

the early summer of '56. Dieter and he had by then been working together, apparently with a primary orientation toward free-form music, for over a year.³ They were trying to get together a dance group, asked her to join — apparently Dieter was wont to approach people striking him as suitable on the street.⁴ A motorcyclist a few days later gave Schumann, who was bicycling to a Martin Buber lecture, a fractured skull.

---

point she had had a singularly unconventional history. She had been born in Russia but deported with her family across Siberia and through Japan to the United States in 1941 when she was five years old — scarcely two weeks ahead of the German invasion of Russia, indeed — which gave her a complex and scary baptism in world affairs rather like Peter's. Her father was an American Communist who had dropped out of the University of Wisconsin a decade earlier to learn arc welding and help the Revolution at its source. He had married an educated peasant woman in the remote city of Magnitogorsk, but had lately taken up the more controversial activity of journalism.

Elka did speak German in Munich, nevertheless, because her father had made a 120-degree political turn, becoming a war correspondent, based in Stockholm, for *Time* magazine and then the magazine's bureau chief in Berlin after the war. Eventually, he was a special assistant to Henry Luce and dedicated a book called *China: The Hungry Dragon* to him in 1967. He had a reputation as a loner and a mystery man about the *Time* offices in New York, an individual who seemed to have arrived from the Soviet Union with his ideas fully formed, unlike other apostates from Communism like Whittaker Chambers, and who travelled abroad so frequently on closemouthed missions for Luce or for James A. Linen, then the company's president, as to arouse the joking rumor that he might be an intelligence agent, using *Time* as a cover.

He called himself John Scott to distinguish himself from his father, Scott Nearing, an economics professor from Pennsylvania who had been expelled from a brief stint in the Communist Party for contradicting a Leninist theory about ten years before John Scott was in his turn kicked out of Russia. Nearing, instead of turning conservative afterwards, took to the woods of southern Vermont — his 'cyclone cellar', as he called it — in 1932, to pioneer the back-to-the-land movement a little later with his books like *Living the Good Life: How to Live Sanely and Simply in a Troubled World* and *The Maple Sugar Book*. Though Nearing remained an angry, vocal radical, he tends to be treated respectfully in the memoirs of antiradical intellectuals like Whittaker Chambers and Sidney Hook. Chambers, in his book *Witness*, for instance, describes him as really a 'species of Christian socialist.' (After John Scott died in 1976, Elka's mother became an evangelizing born-again Christian.)' — (Hoagland, Let 'em Have, '83.)

3. 'Wir haben halt über alles gesprochen. Aber nach dem Abitur sind wir dann zusammen weggezogen und haben versucht eine Verbindung zu finden zwischen Musik, Darstellung und Text und Sprache, wobei die Sprache hauptsächlich von ihm kam, also die Grundideen kamen von Peter immer und wir haben also sehr viel improvisiert in 'ner Musik — unkonventionell improvisiert, also nicht nach Harmonien.... Ich hab erst später dann zur Musik getunden. Also ich hab zwar Musik gespielt und gemacht und eben weit weg von der Harmonie und dem sauber spielen, rein spielen, wie man's auf der Hochschule lernt.... Er spielte drauf zu und er konnte also unaufhörlich, das, das hatte für mich zu wenig Schema, das hatte für mich zu wenig Struktur. Ich wollte einen ganzen Block in diesem Charakter machen und dann plötzlich abbrechen und dann eine neues Thema oder etwas wirklich entwickeln, was dann sichtbar wirklich ein neues Thema hervorbrachte oder ein anderes, einen anderen Impuls, eine andere Geschwindigkeit, ein anderes Tempo und soetwas.' — (Starosky, interview.)

4. '... Und da hat ich ihm auch ziemlich viel geholfen, also ich bin viel durch die Strassen gegangen undwer mir schien, der würde dazu passen, den hab ich angesprochen und hab

Schumann, though at all times, in various hovels, keeping busy sculpting, painting and printing, with Dieter pursued this project of a dance group for the next five years.[5] By and large unsuccessfully. He couldn't find the kind of people he wanted, people that moved 'right',[6] people that were willing to commit themselves totally to the work, people that were willing to do the kind of thing he wanted: under his direction. He had trouble communicating his ideas and no doubt put people off by his effective insistence on absolute leadership. There was more talk than dancing.[7]

---

ihn eingeladen, die haben wir also miteinbezogen, wenn sie sich dazu gebrauchen liessen.' — (Starosky, interview.)

5. He and Dieter apparently also fooled around with minimalist happenings of a dadaist type, e.g. during their '57 Balkan trip:

'... a dada skit in which he stood on the tail of his wagon holding a stone, then maybe dropped it after half an hour.' — (Hoagland, Let 'em Have, '83.)

Mostly he remembers more what leads up to his later puppetry. But such a memory is selective and collective: in actual fact, he and Dieter probably were into nihilist art quite a bit.

'Years ago I travelled with horse and waggon through Austria and Bavaria doing fiddling and maskdancing by the side of the road. But the shows were solitary performances for trees rather than humans and the horse went lame and the waggon broke.' — (Schumann, *Bread and Rosebuds*, April 1970.)

6. '... this idea of something being right, a movement, a note, a way a tune will be produced.... Yeah. I think of the word 'richtig' as being – which is much more sort of vague, but the way it was used was a very specific thing. It was like something coming into focus and either it came into focus or it dissipated...' — (Elka, interview.)

'Wir haben schon immer Leute miteinbezogen, aber nicht jeder war dann geeignet dazu, das dann richtig umzusetzen, wie wir's uns vorstellten.... Da wurde auch auf derbe einfache, was wir auch sehr viel geübt haben und mit Neuhinzugekommenden und das ist interessant, schlicht zu gehen, also eine Strecke zu gehen. Da merkte man auch, dass ein, ein normaler Mensch nicht mal mehr gehen kann. Das hab ich an mir selber auch bemerkt. Und zwar so gehen, dass es wirklich Freude macht, dass das Gehen wirklich alle Fasern erfasst. Die meisten waren dann entweder zu verkrampft oder sie wollten eine, eine, schon wieder etwas künstlerisches draus machen und da sieht man auch zum Beispiel der Gedanke, wenn man, wenn man mit Menschen zusammen ist, die sich natürlich ausdrücken können, die also sich nichts vormachen, mit den kann man auch wie in einem Volk gut auskommen. Aber wenn man mit einer Menge von Heuchlern oder Verklemmten zusammen ist, das wird dann schwierig, das Zusammenleben... und die Gesamtidee war eben doch auch schon andere miteinzubeziehen und je mehr damit verbunden waren, wie gesagt, hier in Deutschland hat's ja keiner so lang ausgehalten wie ich in dieser Zeit, so er dann selbstschöpferisch tätig war. Weil entweder die Einzelnen nicht reinpassten oder es hatte für sie keinen Sinn und ein oder zwei, die wollten halt studieren, die wollten irgendwie an der Akademie sowas machen. Aber das hat uns eigentlich nicht verletzt, in Gegenteil, das haben wir irgendwie abgetan, das war für uns indiskutabel, uns da an der Schule sich da noch ausbilden zu lassen und sich treten zu lassen.' — (Starosky, interview.)

7. '(Elka referring to the '53/'54 *Magic Lantern* and the work it developed into:) And is that what you continued to try to do in those early years that we were together, because you planned very, very *hard* to get a group of people together to work on something, and....) Well, there were always people, it seemed to me, to work on these *dances* – what did we call them? *Dance 1, Dance 2, Dance 3*. If you recall, there was a bunch of people who came to Munich. What disappointed me was their lack of commitment, discipline,

The modesty of 'starting a dance group' is deceptive. The actual project was the renewal of the world, or at least Germany. The group was by its work to regenerate itself spiritually: itself. Not the audience. But it was to grow (and grow and grow and grow): by a proselytizing effect on spectators. (The only analogues I can think of: the wandering flagellants of the 14th century; the Revivalist movements of the early 19th century in the U.S. and the United Kingdom.) Starosky in retrospect (interview, '83) goes so far as to characterize as the essence of Schumann's project at that time simply the gathering of a vast followership of which he would be 'king.'[8] This idealist megalomania was the context of his central project

---

and working ability, and commitment to an experiment that didn't tell you beforehand what the outcome would be. One that didn't make it sweet and nice. (Elka: And you were probably a very confusing and harsh director, too, because I don't think you helped people to try to find out what it was that you wanted to do.) Right. But my interest wasn't just to organize people into something that would be neat for a performance, but it was more of an extension of my own wish to be a dancer, so I danced most of the parts myself, and the rest of what was organized around that dancing was an experiment with fabrics and ropes and chains and objects of sorts, and sounds, an organization for chorus movements.' — (Schumann, interview, '79.)

'But Peter was looking for these people who could move this way and periodically we'd make a big effort to get together in order to produce something and there was never much of a response. But also he didn't understand what he wanted and he was unclear, or curt or – or whatever, so I wasn't the only one who maybe felt (Laugh) . . . . No. He seemed very isolated, yeah, and maybe that was partly the romance of it but, you know, a feeling of some unique person, and unique event, completely misunderstood or unappreciated by the surrounding world and also after a while it got to feel very, sort of, not what he was doing felt sterile, but the atmosphere felt so dead and because no matter how he tried and he would you know, every now and then get some people who were a little bit interested, it just seemed never to find any kind of a revelation in a bigger group of people, which Peter felt very strongly . . . . But the dances were really done – I mean were done not that often. It was a lot of preparation and a lot of talking and theorizing about it, but it was always hard to get the people together, the group and – gosh, my memory's really bad about that. I mean I remember the Occamstrasse, the sort of cellar theatre and a lot of candles lit and some of the music being made there, but of the actual, the dance is sort of like – it was strange – it was very hard to get close to. It was very rarely – and I think there was probably a contradiction there. I mean, talk about, you know, large groups of people and he wanted to bring it up but then the performances would often be – the posters would be illegible so that people couldn't know where to go if they wanted to come, or the mood wasn't right, some things wouldn't be gotten, the poster wasn't right and my clearest earliest memory of the dances was the *Totentanz*. (I: In New York?) In New York . . . . Well I remember very frustrating rehearsals where I discovered more and more that I was not capable of doing these things that were –' — (Elka, interview.)

'Mein Beitrag war, wenn ich das jetzt von mir aus beurteile, aus dem Detail heraus, ja, da konnt ich vielleicht etwas dazu beitragen, aus der Mentalität heraus, während die Gesamtidee, die hat, die war so irgendwie in seinem Kopf festgesetzt. Oftmals wusste er's nicht, aber war fast stur, er ging auf etwas hinzu ohne es vielleicht – auch oftmals Missverständnisse, direkt Missverständnisse intellektueller Art, aber auch geschmacklicher Art.' — (Starosky, interview.)

8. 'Und am liebsten wär's uns gewesen, wenn das das Publikum hätte, nicht, dass diese Trennung so scharf wär zwischen Publikum, das dann einfach mal applaudiert und sich

during the years ending with *Totentanz* in '61, a project in the words of Elka that I have quoted before involving:

'mass choreography and some huge events that were like Oberammergau, sort of, or like the circus.' (Elka in Schumann, interview, '79.)

The essence of the regeneration, as far as I can make out from Elka's recollections was to be a turning away from the dehumanization, the materialism of modern civilization, the hunger for goods, gadgets, comforts,

---

bedankt und dann geht's wieder. Sollte ja mehr Kontakt (...) (I: Sie sprachen von Problemen. Was meinten sie?) Ja, doch schon, vor allen Dingen, um auch mal, um auch zu zeigen, weshalb das nicht die Erfüllung seines künstlerischen Strebens war, auf der Bühne zu stehen und ein Publikum vor sich zu haben. Diese Schranke, also diese Barriere da, diese abgrundtiefe Schlucht dazwischen, zwischen dem Darstellenden und dem Zuhörenden. Der eine ist der Aktive und der andere ist der total Passive und das geht irgendwie am Leben vorbei. Das macht den einen zum sich Produzierenden, das kann ihn auch zum Heuchler machen und den anderen macht es total frustriert und steril. Das wollten wir eigentlich auch vermeiden.... Erstmal dadurch, dass man, dass wir möglichst versucht haben innerhalb von Aktionen oder so, nicht das auf einer Bühne zu machen, gut, wenn es sich nicht anders ergab, haben wir eben auf einer Bühne getanzt. Das war aber nur hin und wieder, das war nicht das, was wir anstrebten. In einer Aufführung macht, aber das war nicht das Ziel, der Sinn und Zweck für die ganze Arbeit. Und einmal dadurch, sondern dass wir öfter so auf gleicher Ebene mit den Zuschauern uns dargestellt haben und möglichst immer wieder aus den Zuschauern Leute gesucht haben, die sich dann nachher zum Gespräch eingefunden haben (...) Ja, also nicht sie in ihrer Reserve zu lassen und selber die Gruppe, ja hier wir sind die Darstellenden und isoliert, sondern, dass ein Funke überspringt und dass soetwas wie, was sagen wir denn da, das also ein literarisches Vorbild ist, also von Genghis Khan als eine Horde oder so, in dieser Richtung halt, dass eben ein Volk zustande kommt, das sich meinetwegen selber sein Brot bäckt, dass selber 'n Stück Land hat, dass selber Vieh hat, dass selber Pferde hat und selber auch vielleicht woanders hinzieht – (I: Das war die Auffassung?) Ja, das war, ja das war zumindest etwas, was, was mitspielte, vielleicht sogar sehr wesentlich mitspielte. Und nicht Kunst um der Kunst Willen, also dass man jetzt irgendwo arriviert wird oder anerkannt wird in den Hallen der Kunst oder der Künstlernamen. (I: Und als Samenkorn einer neuen Lebensweise, ja?) Ja. Einer Lebensweise, die sich wirklich ausleben kann in all den Fähigkeiten, die wir bekommen haben und so. Praktisch, dass die Phantasie wieder aufleben kann, dass die Kreativität wieder lebendig werden kann. Deswegen sagte ich vorhin, wir leben. (I: Sie haben mehrmals Genghis Khan erwähnt. War das für sie damals ein Begriff?) Ja, dem Peter war das 'n bisschen 'ne Idealvorstellung, dass er wirklich ein Volk hinter sich hatte und das ihm wahrscheinlich sogar auch auf jedes Wort gehorchte und eben mitmachte und er eben wirklich, dass er ganze Landstriche überziehen konnte. (I: Erschrecklich.) Ja, sicher, da gab es kein Tabu, nicht, auch wie gesagt, den Nietzsche was der Nietzsche im *Zarathustra* geschrieben hat und ich meine, für mich sind die Dinge jetzt schon so lange her, das ist ja fast 30 Jahre her, das sind irgendwie schon verblasste Erinnerungen. Aber dieser, dieser, diese Vorstellung, ein Volk zu regieren, also ich seh da immer noch mehr in ihm den Wunsch, dass er wie ein König sei als in'ner, als Künstler, nicht, dass man in'ner Zeitung als Künstler von ihm spricht, über ihn als Künstler spricht, möchte vielmehr in Aktion getreten sein mit einem Volk, das von einem König geleitet wird. Aber nicht so, so, als irgendwie als Sektenführer, als religiöser Dämon oder so (...). Es war eben eine gewisse Einseitigkeit, eine gewisse Einspurigkeit, die man da eben lernte und er wollte was Gesamtes kreieren, was Gesamtes machen, (und) das eben auch ins Leben umsetzen, möglichst mit einem Volk.' — (Starosky, interview.)

29

possessions, and for an economic security assuring continued access to them, a turn toward a 'simple life.'⁹ Schumann held onto these ideals: a sub-text of his work during the '60s, they were prominently promoted by his work of the '70s. At the time, they were surely to some extent a reaction against the '50s consumerism, exceedingly strong in the Bundesrepublik.

We note that Schumann's artistic ambitions, whatever their motivation, were ethically oriented. Good was to be achieved, and a good not only for him. The art was to be not just indulgence, nor just entertainment, but means of salvation: for the artist and for his fellow men. That the ethics in

---

Starosky figures that Schumann realized this project with his Vermont circuses:
'So wie ich das beurteilen kann, ich hab es noch nicht miterlebt, aber da hat er eigentlich ein Grossteil von dem erreicht, was er sich in seinen Traüumen erahnt hat, dass er eben eine grosse Menge von Menschen zusammenbringen kann, die sich da auch leiten lassen, die sich dirigieren lassen und freiwillig, also nicht so unter dem Taktstock eines Choreographen, sondern die, die wirklich Freude daran haben und die das freiwillig gern mitmachen. Die selber sich auch nicht als Statisten gebrauchen lassen, sondern selber erfüllt sind davon.' — (Starosky, interview.)

9. 'Wir wollten unbedingt hier diese Zivilisation verlassen, wir wollten in ein Land gehen, wo man gern leben kann . . . . Er war in Griechenland mal und hat also davon erzählt, aber wir wollten weiter, wir wollten nach Afghanistan, mit einem Pferd. Wir haben uns ein Pferd und einen Wagen besorgt und sind dann über die Alpen mit dem Pferdewagen. Wir sind gescheitert, weil uns die Mittel ausgingen, wir kamen dann nicht mehr über die Grenze nach Jugoslawien – die haben dann (...) verlangt.... Wir haben erstmal die Pässe überquert mit allen Eskapaden und allen Schwierigkeiten mit so einem Wagen, der dem Pferd praktisch in die Hufe schiebt, wenn es bergab ging und manches mal haben wir 'n Radbruch erlebt, dass die Speichen rausgebrochen waren, wenn wir den Wagen bremsen wollten. Es war eben auch der Drang, raus aus dieser, aus dieser abgestaubten Zivilisation. Aber wir sahen eben, dann sind wir also zurück und haben uns dann ein Auto besorgt, ein altes Auto, und haben den gleichen Versuch mit dem Auto gemacht und mitten in der Türkei sind uns die Mucken ausgegangen und letzlich hatten wir beide so den Drang wieder zu arbeiten und nicht nur zu vagabundieren, da sind wir wieder zurück. Also das Arbeiten war dann eine stärkere Kraft, als frei zu sein. Und dann merkt man ja auch, wenn man in 'n Orient kommt, da ist man aus 'm (...), das ist ganz anders, da kann man unter Umständen als Mitteleuropäer in eine Festung geraten und in eine Sackgasse geraten. Wir sind auch manchmal von der Polizei verfolgt worden, einfach, weil wir so andersaussahen, anders als – deswegen konnte man auf der Strasse gehen und man wurde köstlich behandelt, wie halt so Terroristen, obwohl dergleichen überhaupt nicht dahinter stand. (I: Was haben sie da abgelehnt? Was erschien ihnen als das eigentlich Schlimme?) Ich fang mal bei mir an diesem Fall. Für mich waren also dieses Schulsystem, Prüfungen und Beruf und dass man was machen und leisten müsse, was also in zahlbarer Münze herauskommt oder in einem Zeugnisbrief oder soetwas, das war so am Leben vorbei, das wir, dass ich bereit was dafür alles zu opfern, um mir das Leben zu geben, also sagen wir, dem Leben näher zu kommen. Und bei'm Peter, er sprach immer sehr respektvoll von seinen Lehrern, also, nicht, dass er da die verachtet hätte, die Lehrer an der Akademie und so, obgleich er natürlich den Raum hatte sich von dem akademischen Stil zu befreien. Das war ganz ohne Frage, aber er sprach immer respektvoll und hat sich wahrscheinlich in allen Dingen auch darauf bezogen. Nur es war eben eine gewisse Einseitigkeit, eine gewisse Einspurigkeit, die man da eben lernte und er wollte was Gesamtes kreiern, was Gesamtes machen, das eben auch ins Leben umsetzen, möglichst eben mit einem Volk.' — (Starosky, interview.)

question at this time apparently were amoral, an ethics 'beyond Good and Evil' in the sense of Nietzche's Zarathustra,[10] qualifies but does not abrogate this.

Elka (interview, '83) hints at another component of this ideology: Deutschtümlerei, a prideful faith in a German cultural mission and in an innate capacity of the German nation or people to fulfill it — an essential and distinguishing power and simplicity or purity of a German spirit. This Germanicism in Schumann's case was political only in a very large sense. The means he had in mind were spiritual, and in particular artistic. There is no hint at it in any work or writing of Schumann's known to me, nor have I ever heard him say anything in any way suggesting it. It's an ideology going back to the 1820s, or even to the years after 1806. Elka thinks that it faded out of Schumann's thinking during the late '50s, in some small part perhaps due to her influence, more under the impact on him of newspaper writing and documentaries dealing with the concentration camps; his reflections on Germany's Nazi past then also preparing him for the political positions he took in the U.S., '63 and following.[11]

---

10. 'Wenn ich also vielmehr, mich bemüh', den Kern der biblischen Aussage zu verstehen. Und da, da weicht er aus, also wenn man ihn daraufhin anspricht, das ist ihm zu moralisch, er hat nicht gerne die Unterscheidung zwischen gut und böse. Ich kan mich erinnern, er machte lieber die Unterscheidung zwischen schön und hässlich oder so. Ja, gut und böse, das mochte er gar nicht, obgleich er unter dem Bösem leidet, aber diese Unterscheidung gut und böse war ihm nie sehr sympatisch. Natürlich, das soll nicht heissen, dass er jetzt das Hinschlachten in Vietnam oder so, dass er das für gut heisst, das heisst er bestimmt für schlecht, nicht, also alles Töten usw., aber ich kann mir denken, dass er für seinen Zweck also unter Umständen Genghis Khan oder solche oder Zarathustra oder solche Dinge, dass er die auch einsetzen würde.' — (Starosky, interview.)

11. 'Peter was pretty ignorant, I think of many of the things when I met him. I think I really told him, or maybe he would have found these things out anyway at that time because in the mid-fifties I know in the Süddeutsche Zeitung, at that time a big series came out on documentation of the Nazi atrocities of the concentration camps. I kept some in the old Bible we have. The women who rebound the Bible said it was bad for the old paper to have this acid paper in there. But it was something like that we followed and there were many movies, including movies that the Nazis had taken of the Polish or the Warsaw Ghetto. I think there was one that was a whole movie that was just — well, it was put together later but it was in the context of that whole piece of history. (I: What about politics? Was there — at this time he was not interested in politics?) No. (I: Did that happen suddenly when he came to America or was there —) I think that having his eyes opened in Germany to the Nazi past was important. I think for many — I mean I was aware being there as also because of my Russian background how — oh and I hated this German sort of self pity and most Germans I thought felt so sorry for themselves and they just didn't.... And Peter didn't have any of this self pity or anything but he just wasn't aware of the extent, I think, of what Germany had done. So I think that was part — I would say that was important, I think, for him.... I think Peter's awareness of maybe Germany's — the recent history of Europe was happening during these years so — (I: Fifty-six to fifty-eight.) The late fifties.... (I: Did you talk about this then, the Nazi — how did he integrate that with his other conceptions, or not at all, or — was it important in his mind or —) I think maybe I sensed in his, in some of the philosophizing or whatever of — when we first met a sort of

Schumann himself describes the effect on him of this realization that there was this chamber of horrors there, that had recently seen quite a bit of activity, as distrust of the bourgeoisie and of bourgeois culture, i.e. as reinforcement of what I think of as his rebellion against his family's 'Kultur.'[12]

---

latent — I don't know. I read these things later in art history books and I can't remember these sort of turn of the century, 1920s, '30s art historians who saw Gothic art as the expression of this Germanness that was something very special in the whole history of mankind; there was nothing quite as strong; Italian, southern things were somehow soft and decadent and this German thing had something really — this edge and this power that no other art had and I think there was something maybe like that in Peter's talk. Also, I've seen, not a Deutschland Über Alles but a sort of a — I mean even now he certainly appreciates certain German artists very, very much but I wonder if this exposure to Germany's recent history plus when he came to America seeing more things, you know, and simply meeting more people and all just took away that (laughing) possibility of — I don't — some things that I wouldn't — but when you talk about politics, it wasn't — in a way, I think, Peter's — at that point his search or what he was looking for really turned its back to all these — to everything mundane and practical and everyday, including the daily newspaper, including elections, or who was mayor, whatever. All these things seemed very like shadows, very secondary compared to the search for these very big truths and very big concepts.' — (Elka, interview.)

12. '(I: Elka was saying that when she first met you you were not particularly aware of the more recent Nazi history of Germany but that in the mid-fifties, '56, '58, whatever, you became aware of the Nazi thing, of the concentration camps, and that sort of thing, and that it made a difference to you, somehow changed important realities of yours at that point.) That is true. I must say I don't know for what reason. I guess because of all the whispering that your parents did during the war. We were really excluded from talks or from information. We were kept out of the room. I didn't have a picture of what happened there at all until the time when I saw concentration camp films. That was an area that made a big difference, not in words because when it was related in words it always sounded as if, okay, there was another poor — numbers didn't mean so much because they — but to be confronted with that you have to see that. It dawned on me really slowly what that was and it was not with the help of my parents. It was something that I — with Elka — (I: What did it mean to you then?) Well, the incredible revelation of it is that when I did see that these normal bourgeois people that one was surrounded by had — I would say these *educated*, these *cultured*, these fine arts educated people had this, that means *us*, had this fantastic ability to cruelty, to — the most devilish acts — that were committed there by the normal vulgar bourgeoisie. I once saw a documentary where — I think it was Himmler, either Himmler or Heidrich — who expressed at some portion of his speech — said something like, in an address to his men, that all it *needed* was the understanding of what these things are *good* for, to be able to do them, that this was a new morale of being above this little bit of cruelty, of destruction and being a higher kind of person because of it. So these — it was as easy as that. They created a sort of artificial idealism that all one had to do is believe these philosophers, what they said there, and then one could do pretty much anything. That was one side of it. But the more — I don't think that the Nazi regime was so much so full of this — of that kind of a person — of those big romanticizers. I think it was probably more — what was more frightening was to think that these very down-to-earth, one would think, good natured family people were able to do these things, without even an idealistic commitment. So that was a gruesome experience to think that, and that it must have been the people all around, 'cause it wasn't done by a few, it was done by thousands and thousands. There is the other — the thing that school teachers and that Germans

The ideals were high, the ambition strong, the projects vast. Dance was the medium chosen. The projects proved, by and large, unrealizable. Returned to Munich, after various peregrinations,[13] in the spring of '59, there are more or less public weekly performances of a somewhat undefined sort announced by beautiful illegible posters, though mostly just

---

generally after the war tried to do is definitely to wash it off themselves, to always say, "Well, it was those SS people, that's what did it. The army was wonderful. The army was this old Prussian educated, very –." I would think my parents had that idea also.' — (Schumann, interview, '83.) It may also have gotten away from his Nietzchean rejection of morality.

13. Returning from Russia, Elka in the early fall of '56, before going on to Paris to tell her parents she is not going back to finish college that year — her father suspects the Russians have brainwashed her — finds him back at his parents' in Hannover. She is told word will be left for her at the youth hostel in Freiburg in the Black Forest where to find him and Dieter: she joins them near there, in Denslingen in the Altmühltal in October, rents a room near them. They all live there till February ('57). The two friends are still wanting to start a dance group, but he is also trying to make a living selling sculptures, prints, printed fabrics (which Elka, unsuccessfully, tries to hawk), and this sidetracks the dance project. Toward the end of the winter things sort of 'fall apart,' so Elka in the spring leaves to finish college back home while Dieter and Peter go on a trip to Turkey together. She had not been invited. As she later put it: 'He wanted to kind of withdraw from this sordid world and kind of go – the idea was to go off into the East, into the wilderness, which he finally did do with his friend, and they did go to Turkey, but it was like a holy quest or a mission, not to accomplish something.' — (Elka, interview.) Sometime during this year ('57) Schumann makes a trip to Sweden. Then, apparently, he lives for a year in a 'basement gallery' in Frankfurt, 'filled with pictures and drawings and stuff' which he leaves behind. Both in Sweden and Frankfurt he – unsuccessfully, on the whole – offers his services as dance instructor – instructor in his own kind of dancing. Returning from the U.S. in the summer of '58, Elka – on spec – looks him up in an abandoned medieval village near Sisteron in southern France. There are a few other Germans there – Dieter is apparently not around – and the idea is they will start an artistic commune. There is no water on the hill. He and Elka are now living together. The project is not working out, she and Schumann go together to Sweden, Schumann having been invited by a gallery owner in Linköping to come and do portrait sculptures of town notables. They stay a dark and cold winter ('58/'59), Schumann doing 'lots of paintings' on the side, and then, by way of Hannover, where for a couple of months they stay at his parents' – the situation becomes untenable, Schumann, sculpting in the basement, is trecking plaster dust upstairs into his mother's neat apartment – they go back to Munich, leaving behind his concrete castings, arriving there in the spring ('59) with the money Schumann had earned in Sweden. It seems a lot but goes quick, Elka is pregnant with Tamara, their oldest child, they are not married, the decent burghers won't rent to them, they move from one horrible dump to another, sometimes have to stay outside of town. Tamara is born in August 1959 in Salzburg, their second oldest, Ephraim – they got married just before Tamara was born – in Moosach, a small place near Munich, where they move in 1960. These two years in and around Munich were hard: 'I wasn't – I looked – I don't know if I went out of my way to look strange or whatever, but I certainly didn't try to look proper, so I would get a lot of stares and I had long hair and I would not go barefoot but I'd wear sandals and long flowery skirts and so I think in Germany I must have looked gypsy-like with all the bad connotations of it or something – strange and alien and dirty (Laugh). And Peter had a beard which made him really stand out in Germany at that time . . . . It was very hard to find a place to live. Nobody wanted to rent to us. We had no steady income or job and we

didn't look respectable.... And it got very depressing. Somehow Peter made quite a lot of money in Sweden. We thought, well, this will last us. We didn't think that far ahead but it seemed like we'd have enough to live for months, and months, and months, and we would find a place to live and work and the whole problem of a place to live got terrible because we would answer ads and we would put up notices and nobody would rent to us. I stayed for a while with my old former landlady, the one I lived with during my junior year, a very sweet, very sweet German hausfrau in Schwabingen in Munich and she sort of took me in for a while. She had to rent rooms for money and couldn't rent to a couple, and we weren't married, which made looking for an apartment even harder and as I became more pregnant that became really a little harder. And we put a notice in the paper – oh no, we saw a notice in the paper of a place outside of Munich, the one in Riedenburg, and we answered it and we were very hopeless. We did find a place with an old lady in a part of Munich which I'm sure has been torn down, which was really a medieval – it was somewhere near the Messegelände, the Octoberfest place, but it was a hovel, a real medieval hovel and to get to the room that she was renting you had to walk through the apartment. And there was this little room in the back with, you know, grimy and black and a tiny little window. It was something like Dickens. She was a horrible old – (Laughing) really mean and greedy for money and it was – I think we stayed there – we took it because it was the only thing that had come up. We really couldn't stay there at all. So then when we answered this ad for the place in Riedenburg we had very little hope. I think we even told them then – and the whole thing of finding a place to stay was getting really bad because we wanted – I think I wanted to get married and Peter didn't object, but we couldn't get married until we had our residence and our pass and we couldn't find that until we were married. I mean it was sort of a really a bind. And this man, when we went to the interview at this place, I mean, then he was a well-to-do – I don't know if he was nobility – a well-off man who owned this whole little castle complex and he was renting rooms in the carriage house, and we explained our problem to him and he, I think, was really – a favor that he did to us because we were so disreputable looking. But he did rent to us and then after that we were able to – we got married.... We spent a whole lot of time just looking for this place to live and Peter had found that Occamstrasse is a place where he could work, but that whole time we were just staying with friends, or with my old landlady, or sort of camping out in this impossible little room. And it's sort of like – I can see New York now. You just realized you can't afford renting an apartment and having a studio, plus at that time everything was so much more strict and, you know, respectable. The demands for respectability were so strong that would eliminate us just constantly from consideration for living in the city. And then after we were in Riedenburg, which was very beautiful but there – Peter had no workroom there at all. We had a tiny little – two little rooms on two different levels on the third floor of this carriage house and he couldn't work there. But at least it gave us a place to be in where Tamara was born. I mean she wasn't born there but we lived there, but then we really felt we had to move closer to the city but not into the city because that just seemed impossible, so that's when we found the place in Moosach.... We were living off the money that Peter had made in Sweden and my parents have always been very helpful and generous to me so when they came, the first time they met Peter – oh I remember one of the first places we got in Munich, and I think that was before my pregnancy showed, was a sort of a Kellerwohnung two rooms in a suburb of Munich, and I think the rooms were really bad. They had very little light and the people who owned the house – it wasn't an apartment house. It was just a one-family house and they wanted to make more money by renting out these two rooms and they kind of made them possible by painting them new and all that, but I think the only reason they rented to us was because they were so bad that nobody else would take them. And we took them and my parents came to visit that early summer and were very, very dismayed at finding us living in this cellar. It wasn't a dirty cellar. It was a neatly painted cellar but it still wasn't anything that they wanted for their daughter to have. We have these funny photographs of our families meeting in the – Peter's mother and father came and my

music – Schumann on the violin, Dieter on the cello – perhaps with some text,[14] their first public performance, just he and Starosky, without music, perhaps one at a Communist youth festival in Vienna (Starosky, interview) – a group – with a rather unstable membership – 'friends and enemies,' Schumann says – is forming[15] – the Schumanns sometimes remember it as the Gruppe für Neuen Tanz, it also, at least on occasion, called itself Elilant, a meaningless, arbitrary name, Schumann says – the name of a monk in Benediktbeuren – there were rehearsals, some halfway definite dance compositions – *Tanz 1, Tanz 2,* – began to emerge, in May '60, the group got a prize, and sometime between then and the early summer of '61 it went on a tour of some major German cities. They had no kind of success, hardly any or no press notices, the group was chronically on the verge of extinction. The final product and apparently the relatively most substantial achievement, and the one closest to satisfying him, of this ambition of Schumann's was not produced with this group, nor even with Starosky – who in '60/'61 made up his mind he was going to be a pro-

---

parents were there. They were all very cordial, (Laughing) hoping everything would turn out all right.' — (Elka, interview.)

14. 'Ja, so wie ich mich erinnere, waren das also keine Geschichten. Wir haben zwar auch mal textlichen Hintergrund gemacht, aber das mehr Gedichte, statt Geschichten, also die Gedichte hatten so Charakter vielleicht wie Rimbaud oder wie Hölderlin oder noch andere. Und da kann man also keine Handlungen davon ableiten, nicht. So war etwa auch die Darstellung in der Zeit, so dass man nicht sagen kann, hier entwickelt sich eine Geschichte, ein Drama, mit einem Aufstieg und einem Abstieg, mit einer Lösung oder so einer Problemstellung bis zu einer Lösung. Das hatte es an sich nicht. Diese Geschichten waren mehr – ich nenn mal nur ein Beispiel; da hatten wir eine Gruppe von Menschen, die gegen einen Einzelnen ausströmte und entweder ging der Einzelne zugrunde oder die Gruppe wurde weggedrängt und ich sagte das glaub ich eben schon, statt einer Thematik wurde da eben mehr eine Dynamik zum Ausdruck gebracht.... Wir haben zum Beispiel auch, Gedichte, die er geschrieben hat, die hab' ich rezitiert und er hat mit der Geige dazu gespielt, ja. Oder wir haben sie eben auf Tonband aufgenommen und dazu getanzt eben, zum Teil haben wir das Tonband auch dazu verwendet.'

15. 'I tried this dance – dance rehearsals in the village near Munich where we lived – in Moosach. People came out there and we worked together on dances. Now the dances were always meant to include what we did in music, and to include what I did in sculpture or in painting or drawing. But, naturally, they were also a big problem in: What did *people* do? Who participated? What kind of a group that was – it was a bunch of very good friends and a bunch of enemies. It was a great difficulty to keep people together. (I: The same people – being the friends and the enemies?) Sometimes, but it was a group of outsiders to the Munich "culture." People who were against what was going on in – at that time with the established art gallery scene or performance scene in Munich, which was pretty traditionalistic and boring. (I: Was it traditionalistic – not outré modern?) No – right, it was that kind of ultra modern stuff that had already become tradition by that time. So it was a pretty boring scene – so, I think a lot of what we did was done with people who were opposing that. Who felt like revolting or – no, that's a big word for that kind of thing. But it was a hard thing to keep these people together – *that* I remember – *really* hard, and to get performances going.' — (Schumann, interview, '82.)

fessional musician and refused to follow Schumann to America[16] – and not in Germany, but in America: the *Totentanz* Schumann did with the Alchemy Players in New York City in 1961.

Just what that dancing was to be like and how it fit into the friends' underlying project of a German renaissance or world renewal is hard to make out.

'Und wie gesagt, wir sind dann aus Hannover weggegangen. Er hatte da auch einige Freunde, die Bildhauerei gemacht haben. Wir sind dann nach München gegangen und da haben versucht, dann soetwas zusammenzustellen mit'm Theater, Tanz und Musik. Das war ein Suchen. Da war ein Unfall von ihm, da hatte er sowas wie'n Schädelbruch. Da ist er wieder zurückgekommen, da lernte er auch seine Frau kennen. Und dann haben wir so einige Aufführungen gemacht. Meine sogar, eine der ersten wäre gewesen, dass wir mal in Wien bei so einem kommunistischen Jugendfest (...) zu zweit ohne Musik muss das gewesen sein. (I: Was war das (...)?) Das ist, man kann, es war keine Pantomime, dazu fehlte das Thema. Es war auch nicht nur der expressive Tanz, es war – Ja wissen sie, es war, wie, wenn man von einem Maler hört, ja, wie findest du die Farben – sagt er, er geht den Farben nach, er geht den Formen nach und findet. So sind wir den Bewegungen nachgegangen, waren also viel mehr wie in 'ner Musik, wenn man ein Thema setzt, nicht ein literarisches Thema, sondern ein Thema, was zu der Materie passt. Also sagen wir Stakkato oder Legato oder statisch oder geschmeidig und so in diesem Sinne. So hab ich das jedenfalls damals verstanden. Vielleicht hatte er noch andere Begriffe. Wir haben uns auch manches mal missverstanden und trotzdem haben wir zusammengearbeitet. (I: Ja nun, aber zum Beispiel, dann also, hat man sich dann festgelegt auf die Bewegungen und die dann in der Vorstellung wiederholt oder war das mehr improvisatorisch (...)?) Ja, prinzipiell haben wir uns festgelegt auf den Charakter dieses Stückes, aber wir haben nie, wie im Ballett die Schritte markiert, wieviel Schritte und was kommt

---

16. 'Peter hatte 'ne Familie und hatte so, hatte 'ne ganz andere Atmosphäre bekommen als vorher.... Da gingen die Wege langsam auseinander.... die Tätigkeit was nicht mehr so homogen, wie sie vorher war. Und da öffnete sich mir der Weg zur Musik und den bin ich dann gegangen.... Ich hab dann Musik gelernt, direkt, also Tonleiter spielen und dieses alles, Konzerte üben und Sonaten spielen. Das setzte ganz andere Massstäbe voraus, dass man sich in ein Schema hineinfügt wissen sie? Dass man bereit ist, also sich selber aufzugeben, was man selber vor hat erst mal abzulegen ein Handwerk zu lernen. Und beim Peter war es weniger Handwerk, es war mehr leben, (...) wie Freunde zusammen die Dinge sahen... hat mir das nie gesagt, also, ob ihn das verletzt hat, sehr verletzt hat, dass wir dann auseinandergegangen sind, dass ich dann nicht mit nach Amerika gegangen bin.... Er hat mich auch später immer noch mal eingeladen, aber wie gesagt, ich wollte mich da nicht mehr abhängig machen. (I: Handelte sich's aber darum, um die Abhängigkeit?) Ne, also abhängig ist vielleicht gar nicht das Richtige. Aber ich dachte, es ist besser, er geht, er macht die Sache alleine. Das hat ihm wahrscheinlich auch mehr geholfen. Ich weiss nicht, ob, ich möchte mich da auch nicht zu wichtig nehmen in dieser ganzen Sache, aber es war für ihn schon sehr gut, dass er nach America gegangen ist, da musste er völlig umdenken, sowohl in seiner Sprache, da konnte er kein Hölderlin gebrauchen, da musste er eine einfache Sprache, da hatte er auch diese Bücher, diese, wir soll ich sagen, die Zeichnungen mit paar Worten und musste er so klar sprechen, dass es eben jeder verstehen kann.'
— (Starosky, interview.)

dann. Sondern da war sehr viel von der Improvisation abhängig. Deswegen haben wir, wir sahen das eben nicht nur als, als eine Kunst an, die man lernt und immer wieder reproduzieren kann, wie wenn man etwas nach Noten oder Choreografie macht, sondern das sollte eigentlich viel mehr Leben sein. Auch wie wir in München dann in einem Keller den wir gemietet hatten, getanzt hatten, hinter einem, hinter einem (...) Vorhang (...). Also dann haben wir manchmal unter einem grossem Sack Formen gemacht, also praktisch um lebendige Formen statt der Skulptur, lebendige Formen zu gestalten. Das war, sollte mehr Leben sein.' (Starosky, interview.)

'But there was something more than that, there was some kind of a magic rightness about – that you were searching for in the way people moved. They either moved right or they moved wrong and there was nothing – in a way, it was completely fatalistic, it wasn't something you could rehearse and get better at, it was an essence in the movement that you were looking for and you constantly discarded people, and I know, because I was trying so hard to be in that, too, and I was completely incapable of it and actually the only person you found who *did* have the rightness and with whom you could work was Dieter, your friend.'
(Elka Schumann in Schumann, interview, '70.)

'It was a new dance and it was a dance that did not have anything to do with classical ballet or folk dance and a completely radical idea but not just a dance but a whole way of living in a very, sort of in a rarefied atmosphere or sort of – I don't want to make fun of it, but it's hard to repeat it without it sounding ridiculous or funny or very extreme or – I never thought then that there was anything silly or – about it but it was a real kind of a turning one's back on all established art forms, scorning galleries, theater-going public and all that and trying to get back to a very basic kind of dance that depended on moving and the term, I remember, was always "the right way." (Little laugh) And it had nothing to do with training or with grace or whatever. It was sort of being in a certain state of mind where whatever you did you knew was right and that knowing that it was right gave it its rightness and there was quite a lot of – the vocabulary around it was all very holy and very ecstatic, I guess, and his ideas were very – they were very strong and that was very attractive about him I guess it was so – compared to so many of my contemporaries who were all kind of wishy-washy, getting their liberal education and kind of bogged down in very small mundane and personal problems. Peter had a real world – a vision of something very, very big and beautiful and –' (Elka, interview.)

Elka goes on to describe this 'way' as the 'way of looking at life' of Hyperion in Schumann's and Dieter's 'holy book.'

'And that was like a manifesto for me, and I read it and it was – my German was – I could understand it but I didn't have the whole background. I guess it's a very – where you go behind it, words and understandings behind it, but it all impressed me as being very – it was turning, going away from materialism and practical considerations and pettiness and looking for something pure, very pure and very beautiful, and it was a way of being with nature, you know, one with nature and with people when things were right in a very special way. I don't know if I – because when you're in that atmosphere it all sounds right and then when you're out of it, or older, (Laugh) and grown beyond it then it's very hard to describe it without, without having it sound — I think he had visions of hundreds of people, roomfuls of people all doing one thing, a walking across the room, the right way of picking an object up or raising an arm, something like that, but I was never able to do (Laughing) — the first years where I tried and never — and always felt that I couldn't do it.... Maybe it was my self-consciousness. Yes, I think so. And I've always been (Laughing) — so this is sort of, I felt like an outcast or somebody who is sort of damned (Laughing).' (Elka, interview.)

'Because in Germany I simply tried an idea of dance in which I said: finish this — this aestheticism of dance, where a selection of movements — an arbitrary choice, usually from the rococo period really, is taken and is made into "King of All Movements" and the vocabulary of dance relies on that aestheticism; and we said, well, movement — anything — any movement, any arbitrary movement, any itching, any normal movements, from walking to the up-and-down-getting of the body — is a dance. So let's make dances that consists of these movements. And I went around to dance studios, teaching that kind of dance in Germany, actually. I went to a dance studio in Frankfurt, I remember, I went in Sweden, when I was in Sweden — to dance studios, and presented myself as a teacher of that method — which was not a method — which was just to walk with people and make choreography out of walking, sitting down, getting up, moving objects, and such things. And it was easier, at any time, to work with non-dancers. I always got stuck with working with dancers in that thing.' (Schumann, interview '82.)

'What we tried was very pure and strong, but what we did was probably ridiculous. It was aggressive and often almost silly. We did dance concerts where we just didn't do anything. Where we invited people to come and yet prepared nothing. And you walked around holding a stone in your hand — or playing a fiddle and a cello for the longest time and then changing the positions of the chairs, or something. It was — we just said: we want to give what at that moment we want to do, and that's it.' (Schumann, interview, '82.)

'For this pure dance you would not be dressed in sneakers and jeans and tee shirts but you would be wearing these beautiful home made and, if possible, you know, hand spun and hand woven, but that wasn't that important. But the things that you would make yourself, and I don't know if you saw these old photos of the *Totentanz*, but Peter just took old rotting burlap and a big needle and thread and just sort of, you know just kind of put the stuff around somebody and sewed them up so these very, very crude and quickly made costumes — you know it was part of the dance, the visual.... I think at that time, too, it was just make it, you know. It doesn't matter if the seams are neat or nice, and if you find the stuff in the garbage that's just as good as going and buying it somewhere, but that it be, in a way, as basic or as sort of starting from scratch as this kind of dance was, without ideas of costumes and fitted things and, you know, but the beauty of a big piece of cloth that just falls in a certain way.... He played the violin and that also was part of this idea was to not use Bach or, you know, compose music for it, but to create your own music and with that, creation of the music was — was also very important but in my memory the big thing that included all these arts was the dance.

'A cette époque, je n'avais pas le moindre intérêt à rendre ces compositions intelligibles, à faire qu'elles aient un sens pour quelqu'un. Je les voulais simplement comme des créations qui fonctionnent en elles-mêmes.'

(Schumann, in Kourilsky, '71.)

Schumann's thinking at the time seems to run along the lines: man's potentials are the individual's; their actualization is inhibited by conceptualized principles, and by the 'outer-directed' crowd-life and materialistic orientation of modern times; the individual should live simply, intuitively, originatively (non-imitatively); art should be of the same sort, and guidance to such a life. These ideals would work against doing art in any established form, e.g. dance according to the patterns or canons of classical ballet, and also against imitating even artists one admired and that inspired one, dancers like Kreutzberg, Wigman or Cunningham.[17] The dance he aimed at was to be a realization of such a life, and also a promotion of it.

We note that these ideals preclude art for its own sake or for the sake of the artist. Pursued either way, it destroys, self-contained addition to it, the simplicity of life. Pursued for its own sake it is an alienation, pursued for the artist's, a corruption of the artist. Art needs an ethical motivation: a promotion of human life realizing its potentials.

---

17. Schumann briefly liked Kreutzberg's dancing, presumably in Kurt Joss' *Der grüne Tisch*. In this work, inspired by a Dance-of-Death mural in the Lübeck Marienkirche, Death is Mars and at the end, as he does in Schumann's *King Story* the Great Warrior subdues the Profiteer. I see no formal resemblance between Joss' and Schumann's work. The resemblance of certain masks made by Sigrud Leeder for a projected *Dance of Death* of Joss in '27 to Schumann's Vietnamese Woman mask seems merely the generic resemblance between face-cast masks, death masks or not. Schumann saw Cunningham in Germany, probably at the 'balletabend' at the Cologne Friedrich Wilhelm Gymnasium, organized by the 'Atelier Mary Bauermeister' of Cologne, at which, on May 10th, 1960, Carolyn Brown, Merce Cunningham, John Cage and David Tudor were the performers. Kourilsky, '71, thinks that this exposure to John Cage – with whom, she says he shared 'free use of sound, acrobatics, jokes' – may have contributed to his decision a few months later to visit the U.S. I doubt it. Nor was there any influence, except possibly, on Schumann's later music, by Cage. The elegance, sophistication and formality of Cunningham are quite alien to Schumann.

'I liked people who I didn't see. I like Mary Wigman whose performances I never saw, Laban ... I liked the idea of that upsetting period in dance but – at that time in Germany there wasn't much of that left. There were some students of those people who performed and even those I didn't have much of a chance to see, so it was more a liking for something that I had an idea about what it was like – more from photos and from writing about them.' — (Schumann, interview, '83.)

Starosky remembers that Schumann altogether rejected Kreutzberg's style:

'Solche Leute unter den Tänzern, denn Mary Wigman war ja auch schon etwas länger her, gut, dann den, diesen Marcel Marceau, der reine Pantomime, naja gut, das hat man gesehen bei dem Jean Louis Barrault da war also diese Romantik, das hat ihm auch irgendwie was gegeben. Aber wenn das Thema dann auf Harald Kreutzberg kam, das war also total aus. Der Harald Kreutzberg, der hat, war für ihn einer, der praktisch nur von Pose zu Pose sprang, der dazwischen kein Leben hatte, der also praktisch sich selber wie im Spiegel sah oder die Zwischenbewegungen zwischen den Posen, diese Zeit, die war nicht ausgefüllt, die war nicht belebt.' — (Starosky, interview.)

Schumann's ideology provided him with an ethical justification for wanting to be an artist. But there were two difficulties: his faith in dance as the medium was weakened not just by his lack of success with audiences, but, because of his difficulties in getting others to work with him, by doubts as to its intrinsic suitability; and these doubts were further strengthened both by his growing awareness of his nation's Nazi past, a time of brutality acquiesced in, and by the absence, during the '50s, of what he could regard as significant or valid political movements and even issues. Dance might not be a suitable means, and the end might be unattainable even by other means.

Elilant — five male dancers — at a competitive dance festival, May 8th, 1960 — 14 groups, 90 choreographers — jointly organized by the Munich Amerikahaus and the Society of Friends of the Ballet, in the category 'modern' (there was also 'jazz' and 'classical') were awarded second prize for amateurs (no first prize was awarded), the statue of a ballerina, for a piece they had in a spirit of mockery called *Das Ballett*.[18]

'Endlich öffnet sich der Vorhang. Aus dem düsteren Grau der Kulissen schälen sich langsam weisse Hände, konturenlose Körper mit schwarzen Gesichtern und wirren Haaren. Zu der Musik von hell und dumpf stampfenden Hölzern beginnen die Körper zu zucken, sich schmerzverzerrt zu winden. Fabrikhallengeräusche werden zur Musik, es klirrt, dröhnt und rasselt. Die fünf jungen Tänzer der Studentengruppe Elilant arbeiten nun vermutlich an imaginären Maschinen oder trainieren Sportarten. Ein erster zaghafter Pfiff aus dem Publikum geht sofort in Beifall unter. Dann pfeift, lacht, zischt, murrt, klatscht und ruft es 'Bravo' aus der Menge, bis der Vorhang über dem experimentellen Stück "Das Ballett" niedergeht. Damit hatte sich die Agressivität des Publikums für diesen Abend erschöpft, es wurde nur noch geklatscht.'

(Monika Schlecht, *Süddeutsche Zeitung*, 5/9/60.)

Kourilsky, '71, quotes Elka on this dance:

'C'était un spectacle tout à fait brut. Il est difficile de le raconter. Il comportait de

---

18. 'It was done with a small group of friends who came out to this village to rehearse it with me and then we involved a larger group of people later on, certainly before the performances. We performed it in a few odd places like, I remember, a youth center somewhere in Munich and then for a ballet contest. I believe that was in the year '59. The Amerika Haus in Munich announced a contest of modern ballet to — with the condition that all the ballets would be created with American music. So what we did was, we pretended that the music was by somebody called Leigh Scott, which was Mama's maiden name, and with that we fulfilled the condition for entering it. They never checked back on who the composer was. Actually, I composed the music, so there wasn't any real problem with that part of it. We performed in different workshop situations in and around Munich: in a film studio (Film Studio Occamstrasse), in a youth club, in the Städtisches Museum — the Museum Lehnbachstrasse — at the ballet contest, and then we made a tour. We performed at the Technische Hochschule in Hannover, and we performed at the Paedagogische Hochschule in Hamburg. I recall these instances — there may have been more — probably not many more.' — (Schumann interview, '79.)

nombreux effets contrastés: station debout immobile succédant à un mouvement frénétique; noir puis brusquement lumière. Certains passages, comme celui où un homme empêtré dans ses cordes essayait de s'en défaire, étaient très impressionnants.'

Ernstthal, a subsequent collaborator, in '63 from Schumann got the impression that these dances had been 'very strange dances in bags and with heavy dark make-up. Part of it was like great, big sewn burlap bags with arms sticking out, and different kinds of movement – very heavy, Germanic, dark, existential dances.' — (Ernstthal, interview.)

'Let me describe to you what the show looked like as far as I remember. For the whole stage, for the background and the two sides of the stage, I painted big scrolls of paper with life-size – that is, with people-size hands, and another scroll with people-size faces. Maybe I should say those were scrolls that were about six feet tall each and they represented, each of them, a row of upright hands and a row of frontal faces. They were mounted, if I recall that right, hands on the bottom and faces on the top, all around the stage. The event in the middle of the stage involved people with painted faces and with costumes that we had made for the occasion from rags and dyed fabrics, a lot of burlap, a big burlap bag, a lot of black and white painting on hands and on faces, horizontally separated faces, half-black, half-white, or vertically separated half-black, half-white faces.'

(Schumann, interview, '79.)

As Schumann remembers it in '82, maybe *Ballett* didn't have those backdrops, but had perhaps as many as twenty people in it, lasted 15-20 minutes and Ms. Schlecht's account is 'totally wrong' (Schumann, interview, '82), but Schumann may be confusing it with some other show or shows of theirs:

'I'll bet it was many more people, because part of the dance was a crowd of people in a bag with hands sticking out of the bag. And the other part was a fight between two people – and I remember that either I, or Dieter and I played violins for that, so that already amounts to quite a few people. The fight and the violin playing – so we had live sound in it and there were several dances. One was a fight that was simultaneously with that bag and then there was a chair dance, with tumbling over of chairs.... I think they came in, sitting on chairs and moving on the chairs, and then there was a tumbling over chairs and getting the chairs on top of them – having the hands at the bottom of the chairs – and moving the chairs.'

(Schumann, interview, '82.)

In a manifesto-essay on his May '62 New York City *Totentanz* (Schumann, *Totentanz wie er am 15. Mai . . .*), Schumann speaks of two prior versions of it done in Germany 'two years ago by a group of New Dancers,' i.e. about the time of *Ballet*. In '82 he is no longer sure he did anything called 'Totentanz' in Germany at all. But Starosky remembers it:

'... und zwar nach, erstmal diese Holzschnitte von – (I: Holbein. oder von wem sind die? Es gibt doch Holbeinholzschnitte davon?) Ja, ja, da war auch das

Thema, Totentanz, stimmt, das fällt mir gerade jetzt ein.... Also natürlich waren das keine Illustrationen, nochmalige Illustrationen von dem Totentanz, von den Holzschnitten, aber das waren eben, was ich vorhin schon sagte, Massen gegen Einzelmenschen, einer unterlag oder so oder es war auch eben ein Kampf, auch zwischen den Gebietern ein Kampf und nicht so sehr, dass da der Sensenmann kam oder der Teufel. Aber einfach diese, der Amerikaner sagt das (...), ja, dieses Straucheln, unterliegen oder mit verbissener Art, wie eben sein, so 'n Mongole oder so, ja, dass der dann durch seine Brutalität – wie gesagt, da waren wir beide so unterschiedlich in den Mentalitäten. Er war also richtig, also allein in den Bewegungen, dass er, er liebte das Stampfen und dieses Harte und ich versuchte mehr die, die Bewegungen vom Intellektuellen her, waren die mehr geprägt. Ich hab ja oftmals, also wo auch, körperliches mit durchdacht und mitempfunden, aber auch den Raum, der Raum war mir immer sehr wichtig bei der Bewegung, dass man den ganzen Raum ausmisst und auch, man hat ja oftmals eine Idee, man hatte was im Kopf und dann gehe ich auf das Ziel zu. Das kann man ja auch im Tanz darstellen. Nicht, dass ich meinetwegen, ja, sagen wir wie Rilke da diesen goldenen Käfig oder so darstellt, dieses Rastlose oder Hin und Her oder meinetwegen eine geometrische Form im Raum beschreiben, dass man also nicht nur die Impulse beim Tanz zum Ausdruck bringt sondern dass man da auch eine gewisse Geometrie mitreinbringt. Und das, da hatten wir auch, da sind wir auch einander vorbeigegangen da war er sehr impulsiv und ich war vielleicht, ich weiss nicht, wie ich das sagen soll, genauso war's auch in der Musik.... Ich weiss nicht, ob ich das jetzt mit Worten widergeben kann – da waren wir beide solche Gegensätze, da krachte es auch manchmal auseinander und trotzdem waren wir eben, hat sich das dann doch bereichert.'

(Starosky interview.)

What Starosky remembers from it is the image of the individual's self-affirmation not only against but in subjugation of the crowd, carried by dancing of Schumann's which he remembers as 'brutal' and as characteristic of Schumann's style of dancing. Whether Schumann so danced Death or not, the piece apparently carried the boyish daydream of Genghis Khanian leadership that seems to have obsessed him.

The Dance of Death, in literature and frescoes going back to the early 15th and perhaps the 14th century, probably a French invention, is a double Christian allegory, rooted in the notions that death is God's wages for our sins, and that it exposes us to his judgment: allegory of dying – a harvest of souls that will be followed by winnowing – and of life: the phase of our existence in which we are apt to sin, and in which how much we sin is up to us, i.e. allegory of sinful living and simply of sinning. The dance mostly is allegorical in both ways. Insofar as it represents life, the figure of Death is really that of the Devil, tempter in this life, proximate punisher in the next. That it is this double allegory, i.e. is ambiguous, makes sense: the terror of death and the anxiety to live fully, i.e. rightly, positively and privately, are related. The sins that the dance (together with their future punishment) represents in the images of the various Dances of Death comprise most everything pleasurable, but in the main and focally come down to sex and to the enjoyment of social prerogative. The images of Death as the beautiful woman's lover abound, and the allegory's standard point is that Death spares no one, i.e. does not spare the Rich and Powerful. Insofar as the allegory pointed to the sinfulness of the Rich and Powerful it was social criticism. Insofar as it pointed to the Judgment awaiting them, it was social apology: told the poor and weak to forget their envy and resentment.

Preoccupied by anti-war agitation, Schumann dropped the Dance of Death theme '63-'69: but from '70 onward it again emerged in his work as a major preoccupation. Essentially, it expressed his awareness of his own sinfulness, which came down to just two things, obviously to his lechery, inobviously to his craving to dominate or lust for power.

Both Schlecht's review of *Ballett* and Starosky's memory of Schumann's dancing place it squarely in the German modern expressionist tradition. So do Elka's references to the importance of the theme of the opposition of the individual to 'the many' in Schumann's work of the '50s. For expressionism in painting, acting, playwriting and the movies had this theme, a theme expressing panic. 1919, when the German armies flooded back into the country, was the great tragic moment of modern history, that of the working class revolution that didn't happen: the moment when Oriental Despotism took over the socialist tradition, reducing it to tool of the industrialization of backward economies, a tool of capital formation, a belated 'original accumulation' in the sense of Marx. Expressionism was the German artists' negative reaction to the prospect of a 'disappearance of the individual' under communism. Turning the heroic late 19th century pre-fascist (we still find it in *Mein Kampf* and in the Mussolini's writing, D'Annunzio, etc.) image of the brutally self-affirming individual enterpriser into the negative image of the hysterical individual, schizophrenically sensing his own dissolution, but affirming his own worth and reality even in this disgusting state, the expressionists provided a last-ditch individualism. By the mid-20th century, the development of capitalism had provided the theme with some new meaning: the depersonalization of social relations in people's private lives and pursuits of a living now seemed to threaten individuality almost as much as the socialization of the individual in societies without private ownership of means of production. The problem of how to be somebody had taken on a third dimension. Having apparently preoccupied Schumann in the '50s, he abandoned this expressionist topic/problem when he went from dance to his new medium of puppeteering in '62. But it subsequently resurfaced in his work whenever his otherwise and generally preoccupant concern with the evil of warlike power weakened under an access of pessimism – during his second and fourth periods of creativity (cf. infra).

4. Seven years of abortive sculpturing, apprenticeship for his later puppeteering.

Though, thus, he gave up the pursuit of a technical education in the arts at the age of twenty-one, and for the next seven years put his mind to dreams of dance performance, he in fact continued to spend a good deal of time on sculpting, painting and printing. One gets the feeling that this is what he did in fact — even though his mind was on performing and on performance projects — spend his time on: not a preoccupant concern but what he naturally (obsessively) did: sign of a vocation.[1] Talking about it in retrospect, and after he had become a 'puppeteer', he stresses the sculpting and painting intended for performances, tends to think of figures he sculpted as puppets, and the masks he made stand out to him. But I suspect that at the time there was not that much of a performance nexus, and that though he hated the idea of making objects just so they would be standing or hanging somewhere, divorced from the making of them, from their maker and from his life and intents: to be looked at or to alter a space, and not even, the state of civilization being what it was, like the Christian art of the Middle Ages by convened allegories integrated into the lives of a community of viewers, this did not in fact orient him toward the production of objects for possible performances with them, but simply condemned him to the frustration of making things for discarding.[2]

The truth is, I don't think he has the genius of a painter or sculptor — just as I have never seen him move in a way that would suggest he could have been a great dancer: his sense of color arrangements and of organization of space work, and sometimes magnificently, when deployed ancillarily to an outpouring of emotion in his finally arrived-at medium, via moving, grotesquely deformed human figures; not otherwise. The reason for this, I would say, is that his emotion attaches to the dialectic of individual and society. He is trite when dealing with either term of this dialectic, the pathos of the individual, the terror or the warmth of the group. The wellspring of his art is at the point of his awareness of their intersection and conflict. This he perceives clearly and feels strongly about. Dialectic is not just relation, nor conjunct of opposition and interdependency. Neither dance nor the plastic or graphic arts seem suitable media for its representation, at any rate not in forms of them available to contemporaries.[3]

---

1. 'Wherever he was one of the first things he wanted to do was find clay so he could sculpt and get wood or whatever for woodcuts.' — (Elka, interview.)
2. His exposition in Danbury, Connecticut in October '61 may be taken as the end of this period of art for nothing.
3. 'I did like Barlach, but I also like Maillol. I liked some of Rodin's work. I liked Dadaist stuff. That sounds like a big Sammelsurium (laugh). I think that's what it was. It was very

He did stone carving on his own when he was at the Gymnasium, 'just as something that I wanted to do' – (Schumann, interview, '79) and learned plaster casting after he left it, at the Hannover Werkkunstschule. I don't know that he ever did any metal casting or wood carving except of blocks for printing – or, after high school, stone carving – but he did freeform (chickenwire) reinforced plaster or concrete sculptures, made plaster molds from clay or face masks, and plaster casts from these, made composite plaster casts and paper maché molds and casts. He worked in plaster and paper maché, and experimented with different types of paper maché. I suspect his sculpturing skills did not extend beyond this, but he made a virtue of necessity – or out of his disinclination to learn more – by an ethics or aesthetics of cheapness (though not, in Germany as yet, it seems, of the use of junk – a point of ethics for him later, though never of aesthetics): the expensive or at any rate the manifestly expensive art work would be a signpost away from salvation. And implicitly (as later on explicitly) the art work's impermanence probably was valued by him: less danger of its alienation from life. He did portrait heads, semi-abstract figures of animals,[4] seated figures, dancers, a giant woman with a baby,

---

different styles and things that impressed me. Now I don't like Barlach any more, but at that time I liked his sculpture, what he could do in sculpture. I really liked that a lot. I like him less now. I find the stylizations that he does, I find them a bit arbitrary and sort of unnecessary. They are forced, sort of an adopted style he stuck to instead of something alive where he sort of arrives at the style. It's like an assumed style. There is Lehmbruck. Lehmbruck I like very much. I still like him just as much as I did then. Lehmbruck, I really like that man a lot. That's very tender, beautiful stuff. And I hadn't discovered any of these sort of Arp and those people, Lipschitz and those guys. I still don't care too much for them. Arp, yes, but the other sort of avant garde of that time I didn't care so much for them.' — (Schumann, interview, '83.)
'He admired master painters like Rembrandt and Michelangelo, Matisse and Paul Klee, George Grosz and Vasily Kandinsky – "who was the brain of modern art," he says, "Kandinsky more than Picasso, who was an acrobat, and empty like most acrobats." The expressionist painter Paula Modersohn-Becker and the sculptor Wilhelm Lehmbruck affected him particularly personally, and Ernst Ludwig Kirchner, "who was the most difficult and spiteful of the German expressionists, with mean, wild colors," he adds with some delight, "and Erich Heckel, who was part of him." His own painted landscapes and animals resemble Kirchner's, and his country scenes are a bit like Heckel's. His heads remind one of Emil Nolde's, and, like Edward Munch, he pictures the end of the world. Expressionist sculpture and painting were nonantomical, seeking a free, flat spontaneity; and Peter, with papier-mâché as his usual material and polychrome painting overlaying that, is only minimally three-dimensional. He is a sculptor against form, a sculptor trying not to be sculptural.' — (Hoagland, *Let 'em Have*, '83.)
4. 'Als ich ihn kennengelernt hatte (1953/54 (SSB)), hatte er sehr weiche Formen, er hatte, ich kann mich erinnern, ein Kopf von einem asiatischen oder chinesischen Menschen. Das waren solch weiche Formen, die haben mich damals beeindruckt und fast das Gegenteil von seinem Benehmen waren seine Formen ... oder Tiere, so eine Katze, ganz weich ineinander, also keine harten Konturen, sondern weiche Konturen. Das hatte sehr viel Plastik, das ging, drängte von innen heraus und brachte also keine Härten.' — (Starosky, interview.)

groups, groups relating to individuals. . . .[5]

---

5. 'Elka: You were a very good technician of all those techniques. To my mind. I was very impressed by how masterfully you did the plaster casting, and your mastery of the clay is really – it wouldn't have made a big difference to you if it hadn't been – if you hadn't been so good at it, but I was impressed by that sort of Germanic tradition.) That plaster casting that you shoot for is to cast like the Italians do – recast all their famous sculpture into plaster – so that what you are shooting for is to make light-weight, fine-walled, equal-walled plaster casts. And you get that only when you work with your hands instead of with tools, (Elka: And fast.) so you have to work fast. A quiet hand to throw it on equally, and then check on your – that your wall stays equally thin. There is a risk in that, because the thinner you go, the more likely it is that the cast breaks. (Elka: You made pretty complicated casts too, not just – I'm not talking of the masks, but I remember sculptures of seated cats that sort of went – the forms went into abstract shapes that were quite complicated and the cast had to be made in many pieces and taken out –) I never enjoyed that piece-mount making. I always liked to make very simple casts. In addition to the things that we (the Gruppe Elilant or the Gruppe für Neuen Tanz, 1958 ff. (SSB)) used directly in these shows, I produced a lot of drawings and a lot of sculpture at the same time.' — (Schumann, interview, '79.)

'One was a cat, I remember, a very sort of stylized Egyptian black cat. Oh, people, human figures, varied expressions, I guess, not – I think most of his things were, you know you – recognizable shapes and very – there's one that's here which was used for the backdrop for *Fire* and it was made in Germany . . . . It was chalk, charcoal with some color in it.' — (Elka, interview.)

Kourilsky, '71 describes this backdrop: 'des corps enlacés, figures géométriques,' painted fabric, in *Fire* hung over the arched – black – backdrop.

'. . . and to my mind, the sculpture that *wasn't* used in these dances was part of the same idea for what Mama called "Oberammergau", or something like that, or circus. There were a lot of 2 ft., 2½ ft. seated figures in plaster. I did some work in stone, in granite and sandstone. I did a lot of wire structures that got paper maché applied over them. (Elka: That was a substitute for bronze, wasn't it?) Yes. Yes, I was very proud to have found a way of – (Elka: A cheap art of making very –) cheap sculpture with a paper maché that I made from newspaper and toilet paper and various mixtures of paper and some cheap glue in it and some chicken wire, and a lot of these groupings were quite similar. Many, many people grouped together, contrasted to single people, very often quite similar to what we did in the dances, later on. (Elka: They were like sketches for your choreography – for your dance. And I'm just looking at this photo now with the big figure with the chicken wire mother and child (probably for the Munich *Totentanz* (SSB)), and in the back is a little relief of paper maché on a board, and that's just what you did – it's the same thing that you did about three years later when you came to America. You made a whole lot of these paper maché wire figures that were grouped as dancers in different compositions of group versus single.) I also made these round-shaped worlds that were similar to these lanterns that you were talking about. (Elka: and tables and chairs were very important in these things. There was often a table –) People sitting at a table, or just a table and chair and a group of people in other chairs.' — (Schumann, interview, '79.)

'Like his original stuff was plaster: chairs. He used to be a sculptor – these Giaccometti-like stick figures or chairs. A whole long piece of chairs with wire covered with plaster. Chairs – arrangements – or people – just an arrangement of people. It was kind of – actually a lot like Giaccometti and other people who do like table pieces; that kind of thing.' — (Ernstthal, interview.)

The portrait sculptures he made in Sweden in the winter '58/59:

'He modeled them in clay and then cast them in plaster and made a sort of a packing wad over them so they looked like a gray – you know they weren't just naked plaster.

Besides the sculptures, Schumann was also turning out drawings, and prints and paintings, both of these apparently chiefly on fabrics: scarves, hangings, robes for possible use in performances. I don't know what instruction, if any, he has received in any of these techniques.[6]

He also made (paper maché) masks and stick puppets and at least one figure for use in performances, the aforementioned giant woman with baby, that he in retrospect has considered a puppet, probably improperly if only because it was not for manipulation but only for sitting there.[7] He

---

They had a shading on them. And then over each portrait he did – he sort of took one characteristic – I know one man had this very long neck. The portraits are very recognizable. I was quite impressed by his skill. Up till then I'd known – you know he would make wild expressionistic, often pretty abstract things and here were these very recognizable portraits. Another man who had huge jowls, he made him just whole neck and head came out right out of the base like this, like a sort of a beehive, and he kind of emphasized that. And somebody else maybe he made a huge forehead.' — (Elka, interview.)

6. '(Elka: And . . . in Munich you made beautiful posters that were completely illegible. (These were for week-end performances by Schumann and Starosky. (SSB)) And you made me very big drawings that were all over the wall, those huge faces. But many of your paintings then were abstract – about the costumes. Besides, this work in sculpture that you did, I think you should mention your painting and graphic art work and one of the projects. One of our money-making projects that didn't work at all was for you to do painting and printing on fabric. It's hard to sell pictures, but we thought if the pictures were printed on fabric, then people would be more likely to buy them as tablecloths or wall hangings or scarves. I remember, we had very little money then and we spent some of our last marks on buying silk and rayon and we dyed that and you did printing or painting on those and then I hitchhiked around to art galleries and gift stores and tried to sell these things there, and I never succeeded. I guess I'm not a salesperson. At the same time as you were painting paintings or printing woodcuts, you also had this interest in working with fabric and you talked a lot of using the fabrics as robes for these figures that would be in the dances that you invisioned. Some huge, very striking, and very important in the composition of the dances, would be the robe and the design on the robe and the way it would be held.) We did use some of these things.' — (Schumann, interview, '79.)

7. 'Then there were masks used. At least in one of the performances I recall, in the film studio on Occamstrasse in Munich, we used giant faces that I had made, paper maché faces and one giant figure of a woman who had a little baby mounted on her stomach, out of chicken wire and paper maché. (Ephraim: Was that a puppet or a mask with a structure?) It was a puppet that had no limbs, no joints, so it could only move as a whole, arms and all, and the masks were similar to what we have still in the theatre, they were faces with fabric hanging from them. (Elka: We still have some of them.) No, those are different masks. Those are masks that we used – not in that particular performance. Those were masks that were used on the face of the dancer.' — (Schumann, interview, '79.)

'J'avais déjà fait des marionnettes à Munich, sans réussir vraiment à les utiliser. C'étaient simplement de grosses têtes montées sur tige et prolongées par du tissu, elles ne pouvaient pas très bien bouger. Mais j'avais l'impression que si je me mettais à en refaire, cette fois-ci je les utiliserais.' — (Kourilsky, '71.)

When Ephraim, the interviewer, asks his father whether thus in fact only masks, but no puppets were used, Schumann responds: 'That I find hard to define. I would call those things puppets, those effigies that we used there, whether – to describe the mama with the baby on her belly and also the big masks that had fabric dangling from them. But I remember that we experimented at that time a lot and that we didn't in all performances use these

had made his first masks 'for a project in arts class' (Schumann, interview, '79) while at the Gymnasium. On his trip to the Balkans with his friend Dieter, in '57, a year in which he 'made lots of masks' (ibid.), he and Dieter put on performances with these masks. (ibid.) The first masks Elka actually remembers him making, partly because she helped make them, were made later, when they lived near Munich, in '59 and/or '60, half a dozen or so fine, carefully sculptured, waxed and painted masks made with Japanese rice paper.[8] Three of them, Elka recalls, were half-masks

---

things. I remember also that for these performances I tried hand puppets. I had built hand puppets, or rather, puppets that are the size of hand puppets that were operated on little rods. See, Mom doesn't even remember those and I remember them because they were hanging up, later on they were hanging up, and down the staircase in Moosach. They were little paper maché heads with fabric on them, with little hands and they had sticks inside of them. They were rod puppets and they were meant to be used out of this big burlap bag, it was a big black burlap bag in which people performed, danced, moved; a bag that had in the dance the function of a womb that kept moving and eventually gave birth to something. The puppets were meant to come out of the holes out of which the hands came when we performed the dance with the hands sticking out of several holes in this dance in different positions. Those holes were also meant to be used for those puppets but we never performed it that way. We experimented.' — (Schumann, interview, '79.)

8. '(Ephraim: Did you make the masks and puppets in the same way and were their looks anything similar to the sculpture that you made before 1961 in Germany?) What would you say? (Elka: I think you certainly used many of the same techniques – you did the clay and plaster, and you were – I mean – I think your first masks were made in negative plaster casts. You used that method of making the original model in clay and making the plaster cast over it and pulling the clay out – smearing it with soap and then casting it in plaster – and I helped you a lot. I remember we did a lot of that kind. And that's the way you make most your most *careful* masks, you make them the same way, except you use celastic instead. Did you make face masks in Germany?) Yes. (Elka: Of whom? And why?) Several people. I think some of them for fitting the masks. (Elka: These are all techniques you learned in sculpture school and art school?) Yeah. Well, the masks – the only difference is, in Germany, if you recall, the masks that we made together in (?), and later in Moosach – I was very interested in the beauty of the material – to get with such cheap material a really beautiful *result*, that to my mind seemed more beautiful than bronze casts or anything, and so I tried a *lot* of different ways of making paper maché – I remember we had a method of putting suet – melted suet into the masks, and using, on top of the suet, a cold glue with a rice paper – something like that – as the first layer. And that effect of the soaked rice paper laying on top of the suet which greased the surface, which soaked into that soft paper, made a very strong – first of all, it was a very tight-fitting, exact replica that you had there, because the rice paper would get so *deep* into the crevices of your plaster mold that it would pick up any scratch, not only finger scratches, on the clay, even the brush stroke which you have in your plaster cast would also be showing up in your final mask. So you have an extremely fine kind of – (Elka: And they are very strong, because we have some of those *still*, and they are 20 years old.) And they are very finely rendered and very good replicas. You couldn't get it any better with any casting method. (Ephraim: You stopped using the rice paper?) (Elka: (laughing) It was very expensive.) It wasn't that expensive, it was just a very tedious process that – it took a long time to make one mask.' — (Schumann, interview, '79.)

'I took much more care in Germany on these masks. I had done masks before, but the *Dance of Death* masks in Germany were a real discovery for me, in mask building. What I

intended for use in dance performances. Or for recitals to music? But that they were in fact used in dances seems doubtful. The performers in those German dance concerts had painted faces: masks were used rarely, if ever. But the idea at least was there. When Schumann did *Totentanz* in New York, he sent back for his German-made masks, and used them.

They tend to be either Neanderthal-like grave skeleton masks, skull-like above all in their narrow, separate jaws (the dead as objects of contemplation), or Africanoid and geometricizing, high-expressive, though neither demonic nor animalic,[9] but physiognomic abstracts of living humans, and either with widely open mouth-holes, or, perhaps mostly, mouth-and-jawless half masks.[10] They — and not only the Japanese rice paper ones — were

---

wanted from masks and how to get contrasts from one mask to another and how to make big features in the face and how to work the mouth and the eyes and all those things — to just utilize the whole means of roundness — of roundness in the face. So — and I also had a very nice experience with the type of paper maché I used. I made plaster casts from the original — from the clay thing — and then I used a white glue — a hard glue — and I used a Japanese paper — a rice paper, and laid that on a layer of suet which I had brushed into the — hot suet, which I had brushed into the plaster negative. And the rice paper would take the crevices and the detail like a cast. I mean, as fine as any cast method would do. Plus, it would soak up the grease from the suet that was laid in as a separator for the paper to come off the plaster mold — so the result was something that — sort of a glazed surface. A glazed, shiny, a wax effect that I liked very much. It was real fun. With every detail, even the scratch of a fingernail in the clay would be reproduced this way. So it made fun to work on detail and was fun to work on them — on the masks — on the technical part of them. And then, in America I made a very primitive set of masks that were sort of just purpose-serving masks. I just made rough shapes and made them directly over clay — I didn't bother about the casting — so that the surfaces were not important any more, and the paper — I didn't use rice paper, I used newspaper and all the playful — the nice things about the technical, it was gone. It was just quick, and purposeful. Yes, I see the difference in that. (I: Wasn't much of the detail quite useless in a performance?) Yeah. (I: I mean, the waxiness might not have been but the detail?) Yes, the waxiness also was useless in the performance. Not only that, they turned out to be unpractical, these good German masks, because they hurt people. They were heavier — they were too heavy — they had sharp edges — they were stiff as wood, unflexible — they distorted with time, from hanging or lying, you know, it was hard to support them well. And the new ones I made thinner. They were flexible, they were softer and they were rougher, so they were good enough for theatre performance.' — (Schumann, interview, December '82.)
9. Schumann did not name these masks individually, but tried to variegate them: 'animal creatures and fat and skinny and mean and jolly' — (Schumann, interview, December '82) but I have seen no animalic ones.
10. 'Ja, die Masken waren also nicht in dem Masse die übergrossen und auch nicht die unterkleinen Masken, sondern die waren praktisch so, dass man sie mit in die Lebensform mithineinbezog so, gut der Kopf war grösser und der Ausdruck war extrem farbig, war, die Farbe war immer nur grau, graue Schattierungen. Weiss kaum, also meist so graue Schattierungen, wie man eben so Ton oder eherne Sachen macht in 'ner Bildhauerei, nicht, also gar keine Farbkontraste und auch keine übergrossen Formen, auch nicht dieses kühle Weiss, was er jetzt zum Beispiel hat und ganz andere Welten dann wieder (...). War alles bestimmt auch finsterer — so als Zuschauer, tierisch ernster.... anfänglich waren sie auch weich, dann wurden sie mal hart, auch in der Farbe eben, also dieses Grau und jetzt ('83(?)

made with a care devoted to their sculptural quality, that Schumann never again expended on his masks. (For one thing, of course, he in America stopped making his masks himself.) They were original but of no interest. The sculptor really had nothing to say. Also, they were impractical, heavy and sharp-edged inside and bad fits, and when, lying around, they lost shape, this detracted from their quality, since, their being sculptures, their shape was essential to them.

By the spring of '61, following a break-up of his company engineered or finalized, deliberately or not, by him, a way of starting out on a new approach to his work that was to prove a pattern in his life, Schumann, a drop-out from art school, with limited formal training and limited skills in the two disparate art forms tempting him, a failure, really, in both of them, unsuccessful and unrecognized, his redemptive ideals tattered, and the ambition relating to them surely weakened, penniless, a hippie with two babies and a wife, decided to accept an invitation from his in-laws to come visit them in Ridgefield, Connecticut. I presume they paid for the trip. He was 27 years old.

> '... und ... über des kühnen
> Herkules Säulen hinaus, zu neuen seligen Inseln
> Tragen die Hoffnungen ihn ...'
>
> (F. Hölderlin, *Der Archipelagus*.)

(SSB)) hab ich wieder gesehen zum Beispiel wie ein Engel, eine übergrosse Figur, Engel mit diesen hängenden zerfetzten Gewändern und oben so ein Lächeln, so ein smiling, also fast (...) diese Ausdrücke. Das scheint also wie der Anfang, in dieser Atmosphäre empfunden zu sein.' — (Starosky, interview.)

5. Amerika. The suburban cocktail party of executives, the working city in movement. Summer '61.

'(I: And the idea was simply to render a visit to your in-laws? Present their grandchildren to them?) Yeah. We'd put it off for ages, because I'd always said I'd never go to America. I hated everything that came from America, so I had no interest at all. And then, I think we had a bad fight with our company and something and we were – oh awfully – felt awful in Munich – and we said let's go on a journey. That's all. That's how it was. And then when we got here we just stayed.' (Schumann, interview, '82.)

His brother-in-law picked them up and drove them out to Mr. Scott's house:

'Also, John Scott was wealthy. That's the reason number two. Again, never to be mentioned or anything. But it's true, if you're a poor artist and you marry a girl with a wealthy father, you might tend to go towards that, more, although, again, he was very strict with his relationships with them. Plus, he hated his guts because he worked for *Time* magazine – John Scott, Elka's father. Always at odds. And Peter, of course, would never clean up to go to their house in Ridgefield, which is very – it's real beautiful – also, I believe he built it himself. Or built a lot of it himself. Big, imposing house with a balcony or a patio overlooking the hills of Connecticut. A mansion of a man who is an editor of *Time* magazine. No small potatoes. But he hated his guts. But I *think* there was also money coming from that direction because they had kids, and I think there was some support there. The relationship with the Scotts was quite a different matter (from Schumann's relationship – loving – with his own parents (SSB)), I think it was always strained. Because it was before – he wasn't a beatnik. And that was the only thing that was current at that time. Also, again, that's where I am coming from mentally. And it was all very, very new, and they didn't like it at all. They didn't like his *politics* at all. And he didn't like them one bit.' (Ernstthal, interview.)

Elka wouldn't ever put it like Bob, of course, but she wouldn't even see it that way:

'My parents really had a hard time with Peter. They thought he was a real irresponsible and strange man. I know when my – when I must have gone back, when I returned home, this prodigal daughter returning home and my mother, she wasn't – you know she didn't really try to interrogate me about what was happening but of course she was curious and she wanted to know who this person was and I had been so close mouthed and cryptic about describing obviously this person who's the reason that I didn't come home and I think because of my not confiding or not being open about it I think they just imagined the worst possible things. At one point she asked some – is he some kind of terrible pervert or whatever it was. You know she just couldn't imagine, couldn't – but I think it helped my parents a lot to meet his parents who are so sweet and respectable and intelligent and proper and also I think that gave them some hope. But after we moved to – after we came to America I think my father grudgingly sort of developed an admiration for Peter and he just – because he works hard and even though politically they are really, really far apart, and my father just kept getting more and more conservative from, I don't know when – maybe from the time he left Russia that he sort of began . . . . It wasn't politics too much but as the Vietnam war issue came up more, plus I think, the welfare issue. We weren't on welfare but we did get Medicaid or – we got free medical care. (I: This was later.) This was later. (I: Sixty-three, sixty-four.) Yeah, right, that my father really looked down at that, I think. Oh, I would get surplus food, surplus cheese and I think that embarrassed or shamed him, I think, and here I got the best education they could look to find and here I was – yeah. They also didn't like us living in this really slum part of New York. They thought that a proper husband – (I: But when you first came you had the two children by that time?) Yes. (I: And you were intending to go back to Munich?) Mm-hmm. (I: But you had –) I don't remember fights or anything. I think they were trying to be cordial and my father arranged for Peter to have an exhibit in a Danbury town.'

(Elka, interview.)

Schumann kept working, however:

'He made a lot of sculpture, paper maché on wire, not counting the cement and plastic things that he'd made . . . . In fact, he filled the whole house up within the couple of months of the summer. He took all the – my father saves lumber and doors and Peter had mounted all these sculptures on all of them and every morning – the little figures. My mother got really tired of opening the oven and seeing – (I: The kitchen oven?) The kitchen oven and seeing the little (Laughing) – and I learned photography and our neighbor, a very nice Hungarian artist and doctor, a dermatologist, helped me set up a little darkroom and I took photos of Peter's things and made up sort of a portfolio of these sculptures for him to take around to the galleries, and he did that, I don't know, for weeks but he got really disgusted with it because it was also this sort of you weren't in fashion or else even if someone was interested in your work there would be a waiting list of two years. He went to the Museum of Modern Art and the Guggenheim also and showed his things and was sent out the door and dismissed, and I think after, not a long time after – a few weeks – he just came back and said "because if I'm doing this there's no time to make anything. I'm not going to spend my time trying to sell my stuff. That's just stupid." '

(Elka, interview.)

The show the Scotts had arranged for him got a review which allows us some idea of what he had been doing so far and now stopped doing:

'Who could imagine that any show following Tauno Kauppi at the Hoffman Fuel offices on White Street would provoke even more storm and discussion than that artist's metal assemblages?

Yet such is actually the case with the sculptures, drawings and woodcuts of Peter Schumann now on display at the fuel company's offices.

The young German artist has fashioned sculptures consisting of thin, elongated shapes, some eight to ten inches tall, obviously representing the human figure living or dead, with spindly arms outstretched in groping fashion, arranged in groups large and small. In two instances the sculptures are part of structures which rest on the floor. In the others they are fixed against a background support which hangs against the wall in the manner of a picture or bas relief.

There are only three drawings, each large in size and done in charcoal on paper. Once again groups of featureless figures are to be seen in various movements and postures. Some appear to be land-based, others are floating in space.

Finally, the exhibit consists of a number of woodcuts. Several of these come closer to traditional pictorial concepts and art.

The sculpture, drawings and woodcuts show groups without centralized composition, uniform faceless beings arranged in uninterrupted rows of arbitrarily combined masses. Without symbolic gesture or any kind of anecdotal connotation these figures are rhythmically added together in simple postures: standing, lying, kneeling. Many of these sculptures are made of paper maché, a favorite material with children, covering wire frames. This has proved an effective and inexpensive solution of technical difficulties. There is a trace of Dadaism in this absolute lack of interest in creating aesthetically pleasing forms and in bringing out the beauty of materials. Looking at these works, people are often reminded of a post-atomic war world.

Here is expressionism, but it is obvious that the origins of this expressionism lie more in Mondrian and Kline than the early twentieth century art revolution of Germany. That movement consciously used distortion and every violent effect, whereas this sculpture works with understatement rather than exaggeration. In contrast to distortion, the figures here are embryonic, formless, anonymous. And, in formation, they represent anarchy. The figures must be seen as a new race with a language as yet unrealized – they lie in an open, untouched field of sculptural possibilities.

On the whole, this sculpture is a typical post-abstraction product; Peter Schumann developed this style after several years of concentrating on large abstract drawings, which evolved into such populated sculptural landscapes out of drastically simplified figures. Ideally these works, many times enlarged, should cover walls and facades and stand in squares, because they are meant to be an integral part of an architectural setting.

Schumann's work has a jarring impact. It is not pretty. For anyone immersed in traditional art ideas, or even in modern abstract expressionism, it may not be easy to take, particularly at first view. But, once again it represents the serious, intense efforts of a young man of forceful inner vision, and it demands to be seen. Visitors may see the show at the Hoffman Fuel offices during regular business hours until November 27.' — (Elka Schumann (?), *Art of Peter Schumann Stirs Interest Discussion*, article, 1961, Connecticut newspaper, in Bread and Puppet Theatre files.)

They stayed at the Scott's for the summer, Schumann escaping for frequent visits to New York, going 'a lot to galleries and museums' (Elka, interview), but also checking out the new dance:

'walked around trying to find interesting performances and interesting performance people who did things that I thought I could cope with, I could find joining-in company from. So I walked into the studio of Merce Cunningham (then just off West 14th Street, above the Living Theatre space (SSB)), whom I had seen performing in Europe. And through him I learned to know a group of people who worked with Robert Dunn on a dance and choreographers' workshop – Yvonne Rainer – I am trying to recall the names – Dick Levin – a whole group of people whose names I don't recall too well now. I did not participate but I observed. Remy Charlip was in that workshop also. I observed these workshop sessions and got to be friendly with some of the people in this group, for example, this Dick Levin, a very tall young man who moved very well and was very interesting, intelligent, to do experiments with. I also went to Alwin Nikolais' Henry Street Settlement Dance Studio, and tried to find dancers there. I had the idea of simply continuing dance as I had done in Germany and I found very interesting what I saw other people do in New York. In Germany I felt very isolated and very unsatisfied with what happened with these performances that I did, or even this – finding people to work with. (Ephraim: So the show (*Totentanz* (SSB)) is really different when you did it in New York because of the people?) Well, I didn't – see, the show that we finally did, I couldn't do with these dancers because they were all people of a different kind of thinking, of education, in dance, that I didn't care for and didn't want in my dance. They were all very analytical about what they did in dance and they were all very involved with Cage's work and Cunningham's work, which I wasn't. So I did not find a good way of achieving these things with them.'

(Schumann, interview, '79.)

I.e., he didn't attend classes of Cunningham's, he attended Robert Dunn's classes:[1]

'In his studio where all these choreographers participated. Remy Charlip and Yvonne Rainer and all the kind of people who later on did their own – had their own dance groups and theatre groups.'

(Schumann, interview, '82.)

Rainer (*Work, 1961-73*) has described the kind of stuff 'this group of people' were up to. E.g. Simone Forti did

'an improvisation in our studio that affected me deeply. She scattered bits and pieces of rags and wood around the floor, landscape-like. Then she simply sat in one place for a while, occasionally changed her position or moved to another place. She brought the godlike image of the "dancer" down to human scale.'

---

1. The Judson Dance Theater, according to Sally Banes' *Democracy's Body: Judson Dance Theater 1962-1964* (1984) started from the class in dance composition that Robert Dunn, a student of John Cage's offered in the fall of 1960 in Merce Cunningham's studio. Wendy Perron in a review of this book in the *Village Voice* of January 15, 1985 characterizes the work of the Judson dancers in terms making its proximity to what Schumann had been trying to do in Germany rather clear:
'The dances they made were raw, plain, stripped to the essentials, sometimes didactic, but more often giddy with ideas and messy with innocent physicality. The unwritten imperative was to break down polarities – dance/nondance, director/performer, virtuosity/awkwardness. Judson dancers worked against the conventions of pointed toes, pulled-up torso, exaggerated projection, and the theme-and-variations format that pervaded modern dance. They performed with relaxed, alert bodies, allowing the audience to see the natural effort as opposed to the stylization of a trained dancer.'

Aileen Pasloff:

'a solo ... performed at the Living Theater that really knocked me out, called *Tea at the Palaz of Hoon*. She wore a red dress with a bustle; sat in a throne-like chair; outlined her own features, breasts and nipples with a pencil; kind of "bumped" around the chair ... It was very female, funny, robust and stylish. She also stuck the pencil in her mouth and chattered with her teeth.'

'Elaine Summer's numbered styrofoam blocks, Steve Paxton's diagrammed ball which he spun and stopped with his index finger, Trisha Brown's dice, Steve's preoccupation with eating. The emphasis on aleatory composition reached ridiculous proportions sometimes ... the Cagean idea that chance offered an alternative to the masterpiece was operating very strongly.'

This cultural revolution was essentially the performer's: each performer choreographing an involvement with things (instead of with space — or with people) for him-herself specifically: designed to result in a non-dance subjecting dance to the personal there-being of that particular performer, a person. I.e.: a thing. The insurrection, a decomposition, subsidized by the state and by the great capitalist foundations, eventually, e.g. in the cases of Pasloff and Rainer, paid off in some beautiful tender work and moments. It cleansed Schumann qua dancer of the highfaluting violence of German expressionism, brought home to him, I would say, that the dance was for him a blind alley — discrediting the emotional intensity of expressionism, while convincingly defining as its only alternatives either a to him pointless aesthetic formalism or a to him equally pointlesss trivial concern with the self and the moment of existence. He had — naively — wanted to preserve in a reduction of dance to a demonstration of the human body in its actual if not true world of the everyday — coping with sitting down — both German bourgeois culture's pretensions to a preoccupation by the higher things in life (the spiritual) — his parents' values — and German romanticism's — the 19th century German student movement's, rebellious German bourgeois youth's — equally fake pretensions to a preoccupation by the (universal) transcendental and irrational. This naiveté was provincial. Germany in the '50s was province. Arrived at (what in the '60s still was) the world capital, its dancers immediately showed him this was ludicrous. But purged of those pretensions, a demonstration of the everyday body either was exercise of personal vanity or else, at best, pathetic complaint with pretensions of cool. Cunningham's high road, on the other hand (from which the Judson dancers departed) conflicted with his social conscience:[2]

Schumann: 'Je ne me sens pas lié à eux. Leur travail est un travail d'intensité, et pour moi il y a une grande différence entre une oeuvre d'intensité qui constam-

---

2. 'Das amerikanische Tanz-Festival, das in jährlicher Folge nun zum 14. Male im Connecticut-College, New London, stattfand, zeigte die Eigebnisse einer sechswöchigen Tanzarbeit. Neun repräsentative Ensembles und ein grosser Stab von Tanzerziehern und

ment se renforce en elle-même et pour elle-même, et un travail qui delibérément sacrifie cette puissance interne dans l'intérêt du geste communautaire d'une oeuvre faite *avec* les autres et *pour* les autres. Une oeuvre d'art qui n'est pas prise en charge par une communauté, ça ne m'intéresse pas. J'admire beaucoup Merce Cunningham, mais il ne m'était vraiment pas possible de continuer à travailler avec des gens qui faisaient porter tout leur intérêt sur la danse elle-même. Qui peut dire que ce mouvement musculaire a un sens? Pour qu'il ait un sens, il ne suffit pas de le porter à son plus haut degré d'intensité, il faut user de comparaisons avec le milieu social ou l'on vit, ou bien avec les histoires qu'on a lues le matin dans son journal, où bien encore avec sa propre vie, et ne pas compter sur la technicité de l'expérimentation, sur le corps physique seulement.' (Schumann in Kourilsky, '71.)

'Cunningham is a classical dancer and a fantastic one, too. What he uses is ballet, and he twists it – he distorts it – but it's classical ballet technique with the distortations and the sculpting that he invents for the body. But technically it's as strict, as classical as can be. There's no – but he arrives at new movements – at things that the ballet doesn't know. The positions that he comes to and even the moves that he does – but the body – the style of movement – how shall I say

---

Choreographen gaben einen umfassenden Überblick über den "modern dance" in den USA. Dem europäischen Besucher wurde so das Besondere dieser Tanzform im Gegensatz zu den Überbleibseln der expressionistischen Tanzbewegung in Deutschland vorgeführt.
Zwei Jose Limon Aufführungen brachte das Festival: 'Performance,' mit der Musik von W. Schuman: eine schnelle Folge von zügigen Massenzenen, voller phantastischer Gags, und, viel weniger überzeugend, die Uraufführung von 'The Moirai,' mit der Musik von H. Aitken: ein Tanz mit vier grossen Tänzern – Betty Jones, Lola Huth, Ruth Currier, Chester Wolenski – leider nur übertrieben symbolisch interpretiert.
Merce Cunningham stützte sich in 'Aeon' – Musik: John Cage – auf ein etwas buddhistisch gefärbtes Programm.
Seine choreographische Leistung beeinträchtigte das jedoch nicht. 'Aeon' ist ein sehr ruhiger Tanz, der auch in schnellen Partien aufgelöster Bewegungen seine statische Struktur spüren liess. In imaginären Handhabungen, teilweise unter dadaistischer Anwendung von gegenständlichen Fremdkörpern (Federhosen, Tüchern, Stricken), entsteht eine nicht menschliche und dock sinnvolle Atmosphäre. Die Musik von Cage, die mit heftigen Lautstärkenunterschieden, von schreienden bis zu kaum noch wahrnehmbaren Geräuschen arbeitete, und die auch im wesentlichen statisch strukturiert war, existierte selbständig, illustrierte nicht nur den Tanz. Noch eindrucksvoller war die zweite Cunningham-Choreographie, 'Crises' (Musik: C. Nancarrow), eine auf das knappste reduzierte Komposition, die an keiner Stelle Überfluss verriet.
Bemerkenswert sind auch die Choreographien von Paul Taylor, 'Insects and Heroes' und 'Resonances' von Ruth Currier, beides Uraufführungen, mit ziemlich trivialer Ballett-Musik, aber Beispiele für die fast exzentrich raffinierte Ausnützung moderner choreographischer – nur choreographischer – Möglichkeiten, mit einem Gepräge, das sehr deutlich Verwandtschaft mit surrealistischer Malweise verrät.
Weitere Ensembles des Festivals waren: Doris Humphrey Repertory Group, La Meri Repertory Group mit sogenannter Folklore, Jack Moore and Dance Company und Anna Sokolow Dance Company. Ausserdem sah man Unterricht im Graham-Stil, Limon- oder Cunningham-Stil, und die Ergebnisse der Arbeit der Tanzstudenten. Eine traurige Bilanz. Denn diesem Tanznachwuchs fehlt, was die Generation der Lehrer und Choreographen noch besass: eine Idee, eine bestimmte Überzeugung vom Tanz.' — (Schumann, *Welt*, September 19, '61.)

that? You know, how they pick up their bodies, how they stretch their legs, how they stretch their arms – it's all – it's classical ballet.'
(Schumann, interview, '82.)

The graphic and sculptural arts at this same time in New York were irrupting into performance art, the 'happenings' produced 1959-62 by Allan Kaprow, Red Grooms, Robert Whitman, Jim Dine, Yayoi Kusama, Claes Oldenburg, performance-analogues of the contemporary 'environment' and 'assemblage' sculptures of Rauschenberg, George Segal, et al.[3] Schumann's introduction to this may have been by way of Oldenburg, with whom he became acquainted at about this time. These stagings of the American landscape, of people in a destructive and, hence, destroyed environment of junk, in their anarchic way as artful as Schumann's ('64 ff.) classically controlled ones, were like them in being pictorial compositions, and *crowded* ones, crowded into a three-dimensional space that they filled explosively.

The earlier nativistic liberation movement, the one in painting, might

---

3. Cf. Allan Kaprow's magnificent 1966 *Assemblage, Environments and Happenings*, a work remaindered by Harry N. Abrams, Inc. at $10, a book largely written in 1959, finished in 1961, presenting happenings not as theatre but as extended, totalized environments, and these as 'plastic art.' In fact, Kaprow's beautiful essay is structured (cf. the transition, pg. 187-8, to the dogmatic exposition pg. 188-208) as prescription for preventing happenings from being misunderstood as theatre. Looking at stills of the performance work of Grooms, Dine and Oldenburg during '59-'62, it appears a powerful spontaneous artistic antagonist reaction to the dirt, decadence and anarchy and indeed the POVERTY of The Big City and the American Big City in particular, and in particular a registration of its anthropofag horrible-terribleness: a revolutionary art form, no less, continuing the similar German revolt of 1916-24 in an American vein, its humor specifically American. Such, however, was not the effect on the audiences. What came across was the artist as enfant terrible and as subject matter of his own work, and the boring quality of the happenings, due to a cunning manipulation of their temporal structures, sterilized the art's outcry against the decadent urban-industrial-capitalist system – in an almost apologetic way, as did the humor. This effective submission to the system antedated the rewarded changeover to collectible pop art. But for a moment there, those boys related visibly:

'The Judson Gallery was for artists to show their work. Claes Oldenburg and the then assistant minister, Bud Scott, planned shows for the year 1958-1959 that included a two-months-long super-happening experimental art program called the *Ray Gun Specs*, in which almost all of the people doing happenings and experimental art work in the city took part. Oldenburg's *Snapshots from the City* was the first piece on the happenings program. In the basement gallery were Oldenburg and his wife, Pat, covered in bandages and paint, charging about, dying. It was like a Shinbone Alley aftermath of Hiroshima in Manhattan. There were shreds of buildings – objects made of cardboard with blackened edges – and Claes moved about like a modern mummy waving a bottle and being a cross between a Bowery bum and an accident victim. It was very hard to see because the space was so crammed. The lights blinked on and off (Lucas Samaras had been told simply to turn them on and off 32 times during the piece, at any intervals) ... The roots for this theater field are in Europe. Certainly there is something of the understructure of European cities in a Brechtian way that stands out in his work, but it also spells Chicago and Red Hook and Coney Island and midnight Italian madness of gangsters and death and living on dimes.' — (Hansen, *A Primer of Happenings and Time/Space Art*, '65.)

have held no message for Schumann,[4] but he came on the scene when dance and sculpture, the art forms he had failed to find an outlet in, were going feral, and he

> 'found – not people doing exactly what he was doing – but – just a whole much more open atmosphere – to the happenings, to all the garbage art . . . all around – artists and – you know you felt there were people putting on the happenings of theatre. You know you didn't have to wait, or you rented a store front and did a show or – things felt really open.' (Elka, interview.)

Trying, ever industrious, to peddle his stuff – crude, derivative – and failing, he checked out the dancers turned walkers in their lofts and the humorous salesmen of industrial junk. But walking the hot streets he met The City, the gigantic bone mill, grinding gaily, ferociously (now dark meat rather than pale), the shamelessly naked image of power. It told him 'There is no place for you here, but there is room. You are on your own.' Not that this city talks to one; it is not stylistically turned to address; it refuses us a matrix by an upthrust of its grimy shoulders as it looks coldly past us into the sky. What defines it is not misery, but the power of the brutality of its indifference, an indifference that is equally (and thus more perfectly indifference) a boundless egalitarian tolerance: evident in the filth and the visual anarchy of its slums, unequalled by the cities of Europe where a bourgeoisie (no such animal in the U.S.) has had its representatives decentify the working class districts, and where brutality is adulterated by hypocritical quaintness and masked as order, and intimidates. The complement of this indifference is energy, and unlike the energy of, for instance, the Ruhr Valley, it is the energy of countless individuals, personal drive, evident in the flux of the advertisements and in the ant trails of the streets. Even the energy of its skyscrapers, the workshops of the great corporations, elsewhere manipulatively dominative energy, here flares out from their glittering windows as the energy of many scrambling individuals. The cold fever of the urban performers complements the indifference of the urban sculpture: each presupposes and reinforces the other. And the artist's self-assertive response – competitive imitation and negation of the city's challenge – is to both, to the filthy city's brute majesty and refusal to be a home and to its anarchist violence: as e.g. in New York since I was young, the paint-spattered huge canvases, indolently self-equilibrating integrations of chance, turned out serially by abstract expressionists or the exuberantly leaping saxophone solos of jazz escaping the hypnosis of bebop into free form – or, I would say, the huge Christs, Fatsos and

---

4. 'The starburst of abstract expressionism was around, as well as happenings, junk painting, and a collage art of found objects expressing the glut of a society of excesses. Peter had discovered Franz Kline in Europe, and now was moved by Willem de Kooning. He may have picked up a bit of the prankish quality and the technique of using paint as form (but not the cynicism) of the schools of Robert Rauschenberg and Claes Oldenburg – whose apartment he sublet.' — (Hoagland, *Let 'em Have*, '83.)

Death Riders, crude and august, flowers of protest that Schumann soon would fashion.

'But we did want to move into the city because that whole atmosphere and the scene and the contacts and the possibilities of working with people was so – seemed so rich there, whereas Connecticut in the suburbs it was like Moosach, having – being better off but it was no – even if he could have arranged another exhibit maybe in another town it wouldn't have gone anywhere, whereas in New York it seemed like a real ferment of ideas and interests and people.'

(Elka, interview.)

Four things in particular, with no analogues in the Germany of the '50s, seem to have started Schumann for the first time in his life, in New York City in 1961, on artistic communication: (1) the demonstration to him by avant garde performance art that a live relationship between artist and public was achievable, one in which the art was the artist's direct response to modern life, unconfirmed by canons or traditions of art, and the public took it in and appreciated it without reference to any such canons or traditions (though in the case of this avant garde art still as art, product of an artist and unrelated to life); (2) the demonstration to him by the dancing and music playing of R. O. Tyler and his Uranian Alchemy Players that art that was a part of living (as that avant garde art wasn't) and independent of artistic training or skills (on which that avant garde art very much depended) and that could be appreciated as part of living and without categorization of it as art could be (and was being) produced; (3) something like spontaneous community efforts (notably rent strikes on the Lower East Side) (cf. infra, part IV (2)) to improve conditions of ordinary life in the community, conditions that could be viewed as radically evil, so that those efforts would be aiming at merely adequate or minimal conditions only: offering to art a function (support of the movement and needs) not presupposing any power of its own to change people, and yet justifying it from an idealist view (inasmuch as community as opposed to competitive co-existence and adequate conditions of ordinary life as opposed to any kind of affluence are preconditions for the life of the spirit; (4) an idealist movement (the pacifist Peace Movement, brought to Schumann's attention through his association with the Living Theatre) opposing a major evil: offering to art not only that same function, but an opportunity both to participate directly in the life of the spirit (as form of which that movement could be viewed), and to address the ordinary man as regards it and in terms of his participation in it, namely his moral and religious values, and his opportunity to increase his share of it (by opposing the war). The fact is of course that Schumann could no more help doing art than breathing. Hölderlin's exit into madness, or Rimbaud's into commerce was unavailable to him. But those four encounters energized and guided him, and – in conjunction – in spite of his unalteredly negative view of the spiritual capacities of men generally, and of the generality of modern man in particular, guided him into doing art of a sort he had hitherto not attempted: communicative art; addressed to the common man. Whereas his dance in Germany had addressed itself to no one, had been uncommunicative and had not been intended as communication, and his proselytizing for it had addressed itself to the uncommon man.

6. First stay in the Big City. Autumn '61-spring '62. The Rev. Tyler and his Uranian Alchemy Players.

They settled in on East 4th Street, between Avenues C and D. This is the Lower East Side, a slum, once Yiddish, Polack and Ukranian, in the '60s increasingly Puerto Rican. The super two doors down was Richard O. Tyler, print-maker, maker and vendor of chapbooks,[1] Uranian ambassador, temple minister unacknowledged by the I.R.S., capo and spiritual

---

1. Born April 1st, 1926 in Lansing, Michigan, having during World War II served in the U.S. Army Parachute Infantry in the Pacific area and then, for a year, under pro-consul D. MacArthur in Japan, in the civil service, Tyler had returned to study art at the Chicago Art Institute. In 1958, after an apparently fairly successful career as a commercial artist, deciding to go into the art business for himself, but to adapt commerce to art, rather than vice versa, he had founded the Uranian Press. This is what it says in the introduction to his *The Life and Death of the Chickenman*, an autobiographical report on his schizophrenic dope apotheosis and suicide in 15 woodcuts, in *Exodus*, No. 2 (fall '59), published by the Judson Memorial Church's Judson Studio. He sold his stuff off a cart, printed it in his rent-free basement. A cancer in his face killed Tyler in 1983.

'(Schumann) did a *Totentanz* at Judson Church with a group of people, that we later either worked with or became friends with. And this was a group around Dick Tyler – Richard Tyler, who did this kind of stuff. He was a woodcut artist and a graphic and a printer and he did things like that. The best – I have a collection of some of his stuff. But he was a friend. He was like – when drugs were considered schizophrenic – there were drugs to produce schizophrenia and he was one of the first victims of it in a way. He was totally nuts. But a great artist. He did a death – doomsday scene, a woodcut, that I really wish I had. It's this incredibly big, intricate woodcut of the whole city going mad and – he lived in a basement. He was the superintendent. They lived in this basement, hermetically sealed basement on East 4th Street, surrounded by junkies. Anyway, Richard Tyler, Charlie Adams, who stayed with us for many years, played the trumpet, Don West was another guy. This was like a strange little cabal of these really very strange characters. And he had met them when he had done *Totentanz* at Judson Church.' — (Ernstthal interview.)

'Der Dick bezeichnete sich immer als Anarchisten. Ich hab nie gewusst ob ich 'n Kommunist oder 'n Anarchist bin, dat war im Grunde genommen auch scheissegal. Aber wir hatten politische Meinungen oder so Interessen, die hab'n wir nie geteilt. Für den Dick waren die, die Lower Eastsider nur 'n dummet Pack. Der hat die nicht gern gemocht, der hat sich schon, der hatte 'ne sehr arrogante Haltung.... Ja, ja. Der hat sich auch Auserwählte gegriffen und hat den noch wat beigebracht. Mir hat er zum Beispiel auch gezeigt, wie man die Holzschnitte besser (...) Aber ich meine so die Kinder von der Strasse, da waren immer so'n paar, ich weiss nicht, wie er darauf gekommen ist, er war ja selber immer sehr widersprüchlich. Ich hab da nie durchgeblickt.... er hat ungefähr 2,000 Holzschnitte gemacht.... Die hat er in einem Raum gestapelt. Aber nicht einfach so, wie ich, so Brett auf Brett, sondern die sind mit Leistchen abgedeckt, dann kommt der nächste, also – die zeigt er nur nicht. Die hat er mir gezeigt, der hat, soviel ich weiss hat er das ganze Neue Testament illustriert, mit Figuren, die aber aus der die aus der jetzigen Zeit stammen. Szenen, die aus der jetzigen Zeit stammen könnten, bezogen aber auf die politischen (...). Die hat er niemandem gezeigt, zeigt er nicht, ist 'ne grosse Ehre, wenn man 'n paar zu Gesicht kriegt.' — (Eckhardt, interview.)

𝔊reetings

from

Dorothea Baer
Kenneth Sheppard   Ralph Mucklefoot
Michael Martin, app.   Richard O. Tyler   Conrad Skalba, app.
absentia, Ronald Short, app.   photo by Howard Smi

Uranian Press N.Y.C.

The Rev. R. O. Tyler and family, c.1960. *Photograph by Howard Smith.*

guide of the Uranian Alchemy Players,[2] American jokester. Schumann 'happened to meet him in the street – didn't just meet him, but also a lot of other people, very interesting people.' — (Schumann, interview, '79.)

---

2. The Uranian Alchemy Players:
 '... our musical department. A five-piece group with far-out sounds. We use them, along with slides, and a tape reading. Kind of a presentation you might say.' — (Tyler to interviewer, *Village Voice*, April 6, '60.)

THE
Agt.

𝕿𝖍𝖊 ideal agent must be so psychologically well-balanced as to appear normal.

Hand set & printed at Uranian Press by R.O.T.

Schumann had not given up on dance. He tried to get the Robert Dunn crowd interested — a shift, inasmuch as these were sort of professional dancers — but without much luck:

'I was very happy to meet Dick Tyler because it was at a time when I was very frustrated with the dancers I had met in Cunningham's studio and the Alwin Nikolais in the Henry Street Settlement House, because I simply could not keep these people together — I didn't have a telephone and it was very hard to arrange rehearsals. And it was also — they were involved in so many other people's dances — everybody was in several people's choreographies. And most often in their own, so they were very hard people to deal with. Yvonne Rainer was in it for a while, and Simone Morris and Dick Levine — those are names I recall — and they are difficult people, and then when I met Richard, that was like — he committed himself and his group to this dance, so that was a very solid thing, even though the people were, in themselves, much more messed up people than the dancers. (I: Not dancers at all.) Not dancers at all — yeah.' (Schumann, interview, '82).

'(Elka: Maybe we should discover a little more the quality of what the people you work with are like, what made those people right for the kind of work you were trying to do. 'Cause you didn't find that kind of spirit or attitude or willingness to try these things among the people in Germany and you didn't find it among the sort of professional dancers and yet this group of people somehow were able to realize the thing you were trying to do.) It's not that easy to describe what made Dicky Tyler and his people different. For one thing, what made them different was that they had no ambitions to be dancers, to be in the — in any enterprise of art or anything like that. They were people who were grouped around this strange and intense man that Dick Tyler is, to listen to his speech and to — which I could not understand because my English was too bad — and to smoke pot with him and to make music with him and to learn skills from him. He taught a lot of kids on that block how to print, using printing presses and how to carve into wood and make woodcuts with him, make print books from the woodcuts, he had a whole very, very broad and big enterprise going there, with kids and people from the street. (Ephraim: Did he do anything with theatre or was it something new for him to —?) It was, to use dance or, then, maybe not. I mean his music was very theatrical. (Elka: Some of it was just talking.) The music that he did together with his people was — was done for solstice and for special occasions, for ceremonies that were always special planetarian occasions that were carefully chosen and they were done with candlelight and began with smoking and a lot of caretaking for the distribution of instruments and such things. Those events happened at Judson Church and so there was theatricality there at least and Dorothy made films — that's right. Dorothy, Dick's wife, made quite fantastic films with children in masks and things.' (Schumann, interview, '79.)

'He used to have them in Judson Church — in the loft of Judson Church. And they were sometimes very big. Many people would come and he would — he and Dorothy would take — would read the constellation of the stars first and light many candles and people would smoke dope and a lot of incense was burned and instruments distributed and then the musicking started and so on — it was very fine — I mean, it depended a lot on, as you say, who came there — what people participated. And we got — and one very good instrument got lost the first time we participated. Elka had a beautiful flute — and sort of the best one can have.

And after the event was over it was gone and then we spent the rest of the night walking, following one lead after another, knocking on people's doors who had attended this meeting, trying to find that instrument. That's how I recall these events. But now that they're at his house, I think that problem is eliminated. Hope so.' (Schumann, interview, '82.)

The sessions of the Uranian Alchemy Players, a fairly disreputable bunch, alcoholics, junkies, ex-cons, though in one sense just convivial get-togethers, jam sessions — basically jazz — in which skill at the instrument didn't, but the capacity for collective participation in collective improvisation did count, were religious services, conducted in a matter-of-fact and strictly humorous fashion. Jam sessions when not done for an audience, i.e. not directed at listeners, and when the competitive element is suppressed — Tyler's staging suppressed it — tend to be religious because unlike in audience-less chamber music playing the individual player has to produce — improvise — himself — i.e., be there — and invest this spectral but real self in the community: he is not simply doing without himself as in the case of chamber music. Jazz is a gift from Africa. Religion is communion. By '61 there were tentatives to expand these services beyond the musical, e.g. the Alchemy Players in the spring of '61 at the Judson did the first play that Robert Nichols, a later associate of Schumann's wrote, a play with music by a Black composer:

'Chas. Adams was there. They came very late, were all gassed, it was a bomb or maybe it was tremendous. Around this time I listened to them play (or worship) in the church (Judson) each got in a corner in the darkness and gave out. Was weird and beautiful.' (Nichols, letter, May '82.)

Nichols attended one of the Players' *Totentanz* performances (May 30, '62):

'In the basketball gym at Judson.... All was exciting around Judson those days. It was hot. Audience sitting one end on floor. Performers in grey masks, vigorous muscular movement. Remember I liked seeing men dance in this way (Didn't know whose show it was.)' (Nichols, ibid.)

Tyler is in absolute terms a major figure: a great man, though not a major figure: by his energetic, risk-taking and generous life-style; by his theory; and by his concerts. (He is also probably the greatest XXth century woodcut artist: I know of none other that has had anything to tell.)

He figured that the times, considered sub species aeternitatis, called for a Sacrifice: of consciousness, a heroic deed to nudge the wheel of evolution — of the world-soul's evolution; but that this dive was not only dangerous in more ways than one, but probably only the half of it: needing to be supplemented by alchemical creativity, the serving-out of the abiding essences. His art doesn't go this far. It is concerned with that sacrifice, and with the terror of the times that call for it and indeed, atomic bomb and all, produce it in the form of people's breakdowns and with the terror of these breakdowns: a man at night drowning in a swirling black freezing river, his stiffening hands continually slipping off the white floes as he tries to reach shore. This is how that inward journey actually is: the archetypes are nowhere in sight. Where this mission is undertaken by artistic means, the image produced is that of a groaning man. This mission is reported on, not any achievement of it.

'In this paper Creativity is to be understood in the sense of a Self Documented life work toward a more fully integrated individual, able to bridge consciousness and the unconscious, achieve effective communication between these states, and impart the result in a symbol system seeking to evolve self transcedence to the point of holding in consciousness the knowledge of unity with the universe. The involuntary achievement of this state produces the dissociation of schizophrenia. However, a mild schizophrenia artificially induced in the individual oriented toward a working philosophical balance of the archetypical creative image action of the unconscious, with the reasoning "reality" of the conscious, will produce an increasingly controlable [3]mantram able to express a deepened conception of reality through expression of more fundamental psychical occurrences.

The magnetic empathy of Freud's "oceanic feeling" is more easily aroused and apt to be automatically induced, by the document deepened beyond the confines of the personality. This product of the intuitive, in turn, will possess intrinsic power for transformation, through a direct action upon the unconscious of the beholder, bypassing the conscious with an "archetypal twinge" that may induce a wakening to the dream state of timeless soul longing for "universal interconnection."

A warning!

I cannot too Seriously Stress the Great Danger of dehumanization and derangement, due to careless contact of the unconscious constellations! This seemingly simple system of balance sought through "sacrifice of consciousness," demands that Sacrifice, be seen as such, and Consciousness be most carefully considered as the culmination of an immeasurable span of struggle from the race sleep state, thus never a "nothing-but" condition automatically acquired. The unimaginable vastness of the deep unconsciousness is only dimly comprehensible by comparison to the Planetary Past, and as such, contains a sum total of living energy held in check by only the most thin veneer of hereditary consciousness, hard won. Once unconscious contact is Intentionally Established, an energy channel is opened to the archetypes, that is autonomous and self strengthening to the point of possible unbidden possession of consciousness, and the same circuits established for Creative Action, automatically open to the Yang and Yin balance of Violent, vandalistic, nihilistic, Murderous destruction, for which the only proven protection of consciousness is through a Personal Religious Projection. The sanctioning support of a superior power is the promise of the Super Conscious, which constantly seeks the supply of archetypal energy from the universal unconscious, in order to bring the cycle of "universal interconnection" to flower in the Conscious.'

(Tyler, *Creativity as a Mantic Procedure of the Intuitive Function*, '60.)

---

3. Mantra — Literally, instrument of thought. — (Tyler's footnote.)

Note that in Schumann's case also, if we look at the essence of his subsequent artistic production, his heads (sculptures), in isolation, the larger — in his case also altogether humanitarian — message is not there, but only the PAIN of the schizophrenic, man delivered from the bounds of realist reason, and indeed the repeated image of this man's raw interface with being. This could reasonably be viewed as Schumann's sacrifice of himself as a sculptor; and in any event as a sacrifice of 'consciousness' in his essential art.

Tyler, in the Atomic Year 17 – 1961 – saw the threat of nuclear war as crucial contemporary fact, saw it as symptom of the preponderant form of madness, rational madness, and saw as only salvation a mass transformation of consciousness from the intellectual to the intuitive, recommending LSD as means. Schumann's art is dominated by the same diagnosis, and ideologically differs only on the remedy.

Tyler, when Schumann got associated with him (fall of '61/'62) was on the downgrade. This had nothing to do with his boozing and dope taking. He had, in '59, as part of a 'younger generation' (cf. quote of Oldenburg infra) – Tyler, Oldenburg, Dine, Grooms, Tyler's wife Dorothea Baer – the 'older generation' apparently comprising such people as Cage, Kaprow, George Brecht, perhaps R. Whitman – been on the verge of making it, promoted by an alliance between the recently founded *Village*

Voice and the Judson Memorial Church on Washington Square, then developing its role as promoter of the arts. An article in the *Voice* by Meyer and Eli Levin, 'Churchyard Sanctuary for Pushcart Artist', had drawn attention to his prints and chapbooks:

'While walking south of Washington Square in New York we came across something unusual — a black and red pushcart with an awning over it had been forced in behind the railing that stands about three feet out from the Judson Church on Thompson Street. Over the cart hung a sign, "Fine Art Editions ... Chapbooks ... Broadsides."'

In October, he, Dine, Oldenburg and others as 'Judson Group' had an exposition at the Judson Gallery.

Exodus, a Judson publication, the later *Judson Review*, in the fall of '59 published his *Life and Death of Chickenman*. In December, Red Grooms did *The Burning Building* at what he called his 'museum' at 148 Delancey Street, and January to March '60, Oldenburg had his *Ray Gun* exhibition at the Judson Gallery. Red Grooms' *The Magic Train Ride* at the new uptown Reuben Gallery in Jan. '60, pointed the way to the art collectors' market — a salvation found by Grooms much later only, in the '70s, but attained by Oldenburg that spring, with his *Ray Gun* show at the Reuben.[4] In March (March 7th) '60, when Oldenburg did his first theatre piece, *Snapshots from the City*, *Life* had a two-page spread on Tyler's 'apprentice', nine-year-old Ronald Short, author, illustrator and printer of *The Adventures of Tom Gray* ('The candor and innocence of the penny history may best be achieved today by the child, whose world is still populated with hero and monster, and whose access to the "deeper stratum and purer source" enables us to participate most closely in the birth of art' — from Tyler's introduction to this work — a remark heralding some aspects of Schumann's later work and evoking Tyler's and Schumann's shared inclination toward the popular arts of older days.) On April 1st, '60, Tyler and his Uranian Alchemical Players were to give a One Night Only grand Psychasthenic Spectacle at the church, apparently in connection with an exhibition there (at the Gallery) by Uranus (Tyler), March 25th through April 14th.

The show got Tyler a second article in the *Voice* (April 6) and was immediately followed, April 15 — May 5 by a One Man (sic) show of 'constructions and paintings' by Dorothea Baer.

The article, 'Tyler the Chapman. Art — From Pushcart into Judson Gallery,' by J. R. Goddard, mentions as exhibit a poster announcing a performance by the Uranian Alchemy Players of something called *Frog's*

---

4. By May '63 (issue of May 26), the *Washington Post* was quoting 'Robert Scull, the noted collector' (New York City taxi tycoon) on happenings (on two happenings earlier in May at the Washington Gallery of Modern Art): 'This is an occasion! One of the best happenings Claes Oldenburg has done and how good to have an "uptown audience!"'

𝔄ttention   ⋒   𝔄ttention

has
Recently Returned
safely & successfully

From a privateering pioneering exploration expedition into Archaic Layers of the Mind, laden with Booty & Spoils, secured at the greatest personal Risk & Danger, & now offered for your in(tro)spection.

Apotrophic Objects, Archaeological Aberrations, & Oracular Observations - daringly dipped & fearsomely filched from the Deep Unconscious, & patinæd by the Personal with rich ritual 'irrelevancies' religiously rendered & rightly represented.

𝔖ee

The treasure trophies taken by the Powerful Penticle of the Nihilistic Necromancer, used to Yoke the Catalyst to the Cornucopia. - 'queer bizarrisms & scatological obscenities of the symbolical relationship to reality' - All Alive & Loaded with Power to break down boundaries with Neophyte Neolithic Neologisms, & Exotic Exorcisms Extraordinary.

𝔓ear

atavistic   animistic

SOUNDS

anarchistic   archaistic

𝔉eel

The Phyletic Fascination of the Evolutionary Disease as you are drawn into the Envisioned Vortex of the Horror Vacui, into the spaceless timeless Mythological Matrix of 're-birth, divine intervention & salvation through sacrifice.'

Now to be Seen

at 𝔍udson 𝔊allery, 239 Thompson St. N.Y.C. Wash. Sq. So.

Opening (7 to 11 p.m.) March 25 & showing through April 14th
gallery open 7 day week, from 2 until 5 p.m.

Flyer for March 25 – April 14, 1960. *Uranus Exhibition at Judson Gallery.*

Shock Dream, an 'Artaudianpsychodrama' (Tyler, interview) a 'live musical slide reading of psychasthenic selections from '*Projections in a Burning Building*,' a psychodrama rendered in the Artaudian tradition.'

    The Uranian Alchemy Players had been formed to perform *Frog's Shock Dream*, but apparently the Rev. Moody never gave his consent to doing it at Judson; or was it the full *Projections from a Burning Building* Tyler didn't get to do? Whichever it was, the refusal seems to have put the quietus on Tyler's incipient emergence. When, in the summer of '62, Al

Carmines, confectioner of campy musicals and Gertrude Stein operas, replaced Bud Scott as the artistic director at Judson, his disinterest in the neo-surrealist/dadaist happenings movement merely provided supplemental assurance that Tyler was not going to make it in the Village either in that area or as print artist. And his prints did not have the commodity-derived bright commodity appeal that would have gotten him uptown sales. Schumann, on the other hand, with an art that in some respects was not unlike Tyler's — in its populism, its focus on the violence at the heart of the times, its concern with people and with communicating to them an awareness of that violence and its horrors, a certain primitivism, naiveté and good humor — proved able to keep a minimum of support from the Village establishment going, partly by a greater respectability (Christianism instead of dope and schizophrenia), partly by engagement in the Peace Movement.

Though Schumann, like Tyler, never did any happenings, a scene or network of people in which happenings were important, though perhaps not as far as they were concerned quite the defining element, was Schumann's artistic milieu during his first year in America, and both for this reason and because happenings in fact were a synthesis of performing with sculptural and graphic arts which is what Schumann had in Germany perhaps been groping for and which '63 following he in quite another way was to achieve with his puppeteering, a discussion by Oldenburg of this scene '58/'60 and of the influence of Tyler and of Tyler's *Frog's Shock Dream* project on his *Snapshots of the City* may be of interest. Although we can identify elements of continuity, Schumann's first year in America resulted in a complete change of direction in his art to which Oldenburg's identification of an Artaudian expressionist trend at the end of the '50s and the beginning of the '60s among the 'younger generation' of performance artists coming from sculpture and graphics seems relevant:

'KOSTELANETZ — What kind of theatrical awareness did you have when you presented your first theatre piece, *Snapshots from the City*?
OLDENBURG — Since that was as late as March, 1960, I had by then seen everyone give performances, except Jimmy Dine, who gave his first at that time too. That is, I had seen pieces by Robert Whitman, Red Grooms, Allan Kaprow, Dick Higgins, and perhaps George Brecht. I was aware of a tradition called "happenings" and also the experiments lumped with happenings although they had a different sort of inspiration, such as Red Grooms's *The Burning Building*. I had also seen the productions at The Living Theatre. I was influenced of course by all these things, but since my purpose was making all this useful to myself, I wasn't trying to be the first one to do anything. At the time, I made an analysis of what was going on. I felt that there were two possible choices whose differences then looked very clear to me. There were people, both performers and spectators, who would go to one kind of theatre and ignore the other. I remember very well that the late Bob Thompson said he would not see a Kaprow, for example, because he was in the Red Grooms piece. I remember that when a Red Grooms

piece and a Kaprow were put together at the Reuben Gallery, in January of 1960, there was really a lack of communication between the two groups; they divided between an emotional and a rational expression. The latter had come out of Cage's ideas and what Kaprow had done with the *18 Happenings*.

KOSTELANETZ — Was Cage known to be anti-expression — against the conspicuous display of personal emotion or even individual taste?

OLDENBURG — At that time, he appeared to be. I remember how clearly his put-down of (Edgard) Varese stuck in my mind. In *"The History of Experimental Music in the U.S."*, in *Silence*, page 69, Cage wrote, "It is clear that ways must be discovered to allow noises and tones to be just noises and tones, not exponents subservient to Varese's imagination."

KOSTELANETZ — Cage objected to Varese's desire to create something out of himself and of his own, rather than accept the surprises his environment created for him.

OLDENBURG — On the other hand, there existed at that time a strong influence from both Artaud and certain people who just went that way, like Red Grooms and The Living Theatre and Dick Tyler. Tyler, who was and is a printmaker, introduced me to Artaud's text, *The Theatre and Its Double*. He was my "super" at 330 East Fourth Street, between Avenues C and D, where he lived in the basement. He had his print-maker's press there and I saw him almost every day. The assistant minister at Judson (Memorial Church) at that time, Bud Scott, appreciated him very much. Tyler had a cart, which he kept in the Judson backyard and from which he sold his "magic" pamphlets. They were about such things as salvation through schizophrenia — all kinds of mind-breakers, that were then revolutionary but have now become commonplace. He was very interested in theatre and he also had a little group that was among the first to play music at Judson. It was an anti-music that I used to call "no-music." They would use various instruments in all the "wrong" ways and play them for hours. Anyway, the story of Dick Tyler is a long one that has not been written. Now he has taken a lighthouse in Nova Scotia, and he commutes from there.

KOSTELANETZ — How was Tyler Artaudian?

OLDENBURG — I've never absorbed Artaud very thoroughly. His theatre was, as you say, an expressionist theatre, which I tended to lump with all the expressionist theatre I could think of, as well as certain German films like (*The Cabinet of Dr.*) *Caligari* (1919) and *M* (1931) — things with a terrifying mood and horrible experiences. Of the things that were revolutionary at the time, that direction posed one possibility.

KOSTELANETZ — This was opposed to the Cagean stream . . .

OLDENBURG — . . . which was a revolution too. It consisted of silence — in accepting the world . . .

KOSTELANETZ — . . . and in being able to perform anything.

OLDENBURG — At this time, this separation seemed extremely clear. Now, it is different, as the two streams have sort of run together. Cage turned out to be a more complex person than he seemed at that time, and his influence has become so mixed up with other things. For instance, as Kaprow is now much less dependent upon chance procedures, he has become more of an expressionist.

KOSTELANETZ — He expects his pieces to create some emotional involvement, and to fulfill this purpose he generally inserts a degree of physical danger; and this is very much in the Artaud tradition.

OLDENBURG – The fact that these traditions flow together and that people who do happenings can draw upon one or the other is one reason why happenings are confusing to an audience. When I did happenings at The Ray Gun Theatre, I drew upon both streams. I would make a very engaging and emotional sequence which I would suddenly stop and drop, to start something entirely different.

I remember very well a Tyler piece, that was never put on, in which the audience at the Judson was to be gathered into a pit. There was supposed to be a stage at one end; and on it Tyler planned to put a friend of his who had a steel plate in his head from a war injury. He was to sit there, tied up; and I had the part of hitting him in the head with a baseball bat. There were other details I can't remember, but that one stays with me very clearly, because I didn't feel like doing that. At the climax of the piece, bombs would be thrown down at the audience, who would be so terrified and wounded that Tyler expected they would panic. He wanted to do it in the chapel of the Church, which at that time was not used for performances; so this was one among the reasons why it was never performed.

I don't think this piece had much circulation, but it had a great influence on me. I think you can see in the photographs of *Snapshots* that there is a great element of cruelty and suffering which may be theatrical. I wasn't really suffering at that point, but I looked as though I were suffering. Just before the performance, I accidentally cut my finger rather deeply, went over to St. Vincent's Hospital, where I sat around for a long time; and I think that experience directly contributed to the choices of costume and so on that I made for the piece.

KOSTELANETZ – Wasn't there an element of cruelty in keeping the audience in the dark for fifteen minutes?

OLDENBURG – Not only were they in the dark, but they had a great deal of difficulty seeing, because of the small opening to the room in which it was performed. The audience was in another room, and they had to look through a doorway. So, there were many people in a dark room, and only a few of them could see. There was a lot of jostling around. Often, too, the unpredictable and unprofessional surroundings of the performances produced suffering, simply by lack of foresight or sufficient provision for the audience. One must admit, though, that such indifference is a form of cruelty. Here was this mixture of my acting out suffering and forcing the audience to undergo suffering; yet the whole idea of the piece was rather objective – I was going to translate myself analytically from an inanimate object to an animate one.

I suspect that *Snapshots* had more of an expressionist effect than later pieces; it was partly because of the tremendous involvement which anything at the Judson at that time inspired. There was a great sense of crisis constantly; there was the style of the time and the place. They were starting to reach out into the community, and the community was flowing in there. The place had a lot of action then.

What I'm trying to get at is that I tried to make an analysis at this time of the theatre that could be done, and then I decided what *I* wanted to do; and I was very selective about what I took; I think I came out with a synthesis that was something quite personal.

KOSTELANETZ – Where did you stand at this time, around 1960, in relation to Bob Whitman?

OLDENBURG – Well, the two things about Whitman then that interested me most were his use of material – stuff like clothing; he had a deep feeling for any kind of fabric — and his sense of time, that was the second thing. He has spoken about his pieces being sculpture in time.

KOSTELANETZ – As you were extremely interested in both time and material in *Snapshots*, wasn't his position then very close to yours?

OLDENBURG – Absolutely. His style was also very personal and highly aesthetic. His things were so beautiful and lyrical they were almost precious.

KOSTELANETZ – How did, say, Kaprow's example work upon you?

OLDENBURG – My position, you must understand, has always been on the outside. I didn't live in New Jersey, and I wasn't part of the New Jersey school, of which Kaprow was the leader. I didn't study with Cage. I discovered this whole area when I was looking for a gallery in 1958 and came across Red Grooms, who had started the City Gallery, which was the prototype of the Judson and many other informal artist-run places which also housed performances. Another later stopping-place of Red's perambulating was, for instance, the Delancey Street Museum, a loft which has recently become the home of Peter Schumann's Bread and Puppet Theatre.

At the same time, I found Jim Dine, who had also found Red. The City Gallery was a splinter from the Hansa Gallery, and we formed the younger generation. After having my first one-man show at the Judson, I went away for the summer; and when I came back I saw Kaprow open the Reuben Gallery with his *18 Happenings in 6 Parts*. It wasn't until then that I gradually came to realize the existence of this New Jersey group. It included Whitman and Lucas Samaras, who both had been students of Kaprow's and were very much influenced by him, at the same time that they had their own entirely different ideas. Also through Kaprow, I met George Segal and Roy Lichtenstein. That year, of course, I had started the Judson Gallery with Jim Dine, Dick Tyler and Phyllis Yampolsky. Although I had seen Kaprow at a Hansa picnic at George Segal's farm in 1958, the Reuben performance was my first meaningful point of contact with him. I had earlier read his piece on Jackson Pollock, which impressed me.

KOSTELANETZ – How did you do your first piece?

OLDENBURG – *Snapshots* was done in the beginning of March, 1960. I had created a "street" inside the Judson Gallery; a metaphoric "street" constructed out of paper and street materials; and it had a "floor collage" with all kinds of found objects on it — a "landscape" of the street; and the white walls showing through the construction were to be taken as open space.

KOSTELANETZ – Would you have preferred to have done this on a real street?

OLDENBURG – The original performance was supposed to take place in front of the Judson on Thompson Street. It was called *Post No Bills*. We had planned to block the street at the moment of performance by stalling a car, but the more I thought about the piece, the more I felt it was very closely connected with the construction I had made. I decided that I wanted to show my construction at the same time that I presented a performance. When people eventually came into the Judson Gallery, they saw me on the street as an object. So, from my first performance, my theatre work was linked to my sculpture or my construction. I was literally *in* my construction. Otherwise, I was trying to work from the inanimate situation to an animate one, from no-motion into motion.

KOSTELANETZ – To what does the title refer?

OLDENBURG – They were snapshots in the sense that flashes of light froze the action. I was obsessed at the time with something that lay between action and stillness; freezing the motion was a painterly and a theatrical idea. Originally, I had wanted to bring things from a very still state to a very slow state to a very fast state; but I settled for the snapshot device, which made the effect of the thing really painterly. You can see that in the photographs of it. As the people came in, for fifteen minutes Pat and I were on the stage not moving — bodies that were not exactly buried but part of the landscape; it was a three-dimensional panorama like the things you see in museums. There were thirty-two flickers; and as Lucas is rather perverse, he once or twice waited a long time before he put the light on. Otherwise, you couldn't see a damn thing, and we were doing all these things in total darkness.

My piece was the beginning of the night's performances. The audience left that little place, which was also the gallery, and went into the anteroom of the gymnasium, where Al Hansen had his piece for W.C. Fields. They went from there into the main gym where Kaprow did his piece with the boot (*Coca Cola, Shirley Cannonball?*) and from there back to the anteroom where Whitman did his piece. The evening closed with Higgins' piece, which is in fact interminable — counting in German until everybody left. The idea was to give a spectrum of what was going on. I organized the show.

KOSTELANETZ — How large was the audience?

OLDENBURG — About two hundred; and we gave it for three nights. Most of the faces were familiar.

KOSTELANETZ — Did any newspapers cover it?

OLDENBURG — In those days, the Voice was very excited about off-Broadway. They were creating off-Broadway, and they had just invented the Obie Award. But they were only interested in theatre as they understood it. Jerry Tallmer did a put-down review of happenings at the Reuben Gallery in the early sixties, and that was supposed to seal the fate of happenings. Things have changed a lot. Now almost anything you care to do they will cover and celebrate. Happenings are news.

KOSTELANETZ — Did you create a tradition as a result of your own performance?

OLDENBURG — The understanding of what we all have done is still not cleared up. Everything that everyone has done seems to have flowed together, as far as historical criticism is concerned. The necessary distinctions have not been made. Perhaps it's a word for artists, non-artists, fashion, revolution, politics, pop, and who knows what else. I have poured a lot of innovations into the tradition, but the critic is yet to come who will bother to sort out individual contributions. Michael Kirby was fanatically devoted to letting things speak for themselves.

KOSTELANETZ — Would you say, then, that the notion of "painter's theatre" is not very useful, because even among the painters exist not only different styles but different artistic traditions and different artistic ancestors?

OLDENBURG — Yet something you could say about my performances to individualize them is that as they are very much connected with my work as a painter and sculptor, they correspond to certain periods of my work. For example, the first three pieces — *Snapshots, Blackouts* (December 1960), and *Fotodeath/ Ironworks* (February, 1961) — are limited in color to black and white, and they have a great deal to do with darkness. This would also describe my work at that time, when I worked entirely with materials from the street and paper, as well as

used no color. These three pieces also have a quality of desperation and misery about them; they deal with events of the street and its inhabitants, beggars and cripples. The sculptural pieces from *The Store* (December, 1961) and *Ray Gun Theatre* (1962), by contrast, are very colorful and warmly lighted – intimate.'
(Kostelanetz, *The Theatre of Mixed Means*, 1968.)

The terrified struggle of individuals to establish a space identifiably their own in an environment at the same time extremely simplified and utterly chaotic (the sum of these struggles: New York City) was in avant garde performance art at the time Schumann walked into the scene according to his friend Oldenburg's dichotomy represented by the 'rationalist' 'withdrawers into silence'; that environment by the 'emotional' 'expressionists.' These, however, as his account shows, managed as much as did those others by their elegant works to arrange these representations of reality into precisely such spaces for themselves (and got into them): an egocentrism on which the rigidly idealist German could not pick up on since it could strike him only as perversion of Art. What these rowdy free enterprises – as they were at that moment in historical time only – demonstrated to him, however, was that performances could be put on that were unrespectable in form, did not, by their form, either cater or endorse a revelation. German dadaism around the time of the first world war and German expressionism just after it had been of this sort, but the repeats of them that *faute de mieux* he had a world war later attempted no longer were: a tradition hallowed them; and there was nothing else of the sort around in Germany for him to latch onto either. Secondly, what he learned was that he could as painter/sculptor do performance art. He still had to get his dance off his chest (and it might gain him an entree), and he proceeded to do so: but, significantly, he was not himself going to dance. The dance would be his as director, not as extension of his dancing.

'Rbt. Ernsthal. 848 Ashbury St. S/F CA 941

        Uranian Phalanstery
        328 E. 4th St.
        New York, 10009
        May 8th 1979

Dear Bob: Stefan Brecht visited me yesterday upon your recommendation, after interviewing you in San Francisco on early Peter Schumann (U.S.) action (pre B/P theater); bringing me yr S/F address, which I haven't had since sometime in the '70's, when I received the "Annual Co. Calender" mailing return'd from (941)

        (NOT FORWARDABLE ...
        ADDRESSEE UNKNOWN)

This letter to you allows me to write out my rememberances, & to give the subject some reflection; assembling supporting material which I shall present to Mr. Brecht with a copy of this letter (cc

        PETER
        BRUNO
        CHARLIE)

I assume you recvd the book "Bread & Puppet Theater" Les Loges Paris 2e 1978, sent by the Publisher from "Peter & Co. Merry Christmas."

see Hist. du Bread & Puppet Theater: In the Beginning.... NYC. OCT. 1963 In a loft at 148 Delancey St. on the Lower East Side three friends Bruno Eckardt, Bob Ernstthal & Peter Schumann created the Bread & Puppet Theater ... having arrived from Germany two years earlier with his wife & children.

Peter & Elka with three children, moved on the block in 1962. My Kumpania was then in operation as (URANIAN PHALANSTERY) (uranian press) (330 e. 4 st.) (n y 9, n y) ... operating from a cellar, staffed by schoolboys, who print Chapbooks, tracts & broadsides, sold from a pushcart with a "Letter of Protection & Permission" to operate a "bookbarrow" on Church Grounds (V.V. Aug. 19th 1959)

(E. 4th St.
(between Ave.
(C & D # 350
(a tenement
(since demolished
(across from
(RUSSIAN ORTHO-
(DOX UKRANIAN
(CHURCH

(" Apl. 6th 1960)

Our theater Co., "The Uranian Alchemy Players", was formed in 1959 for the production of "Frogs Shock Dream". SEE...
at Judson Mews Church (Wash. Sq. NYC.)   (CLAES OLDENBURG
where we were still operating the barrow   (CONVERSATIONS Tract...
weekends with Band Master &   (supporting material)
Master Chapman Ken Sheppard. A member of our organization, "Wheelman & 1st Horn" Charlie Adams, was Sexton of Judson Church at that time, allowing us access to the main church space

w/CHOIR
ORGAN LOFT
GRAND PIANO ... fantastic acoustics ...

under the all covering "Arts Programme", we were able to hold regular rehearsals on nites we kept the cart open, & to hit on the full moons in the main hall for a couple of seasons. My theater is Bullfinch & Jung out of Artaud & Alice Bailey. We were able to "woodshed" on playing the Planetary Hour

system (4e)   "Letters on Occult Medi-
& "Ray Ruler"   tation" (sound & color
with "Esoteric Astrology",   chap.) AAB. LUCIS TRUST PUB.
AAB SEVEN DAYS Vol. 3, "Treatise on Cosmic Fire"
                         for MOVEMENT & DANCE, with the
goal sought through Theater being "Esoteric Healing"
                         Vol 4. SEVEN RAYS AAB LUCIS PUB.
with a RE.LIGHTING provided through SOUND & COLOR
                         MOVEMENT
                         RITUAL & MYTH
see URANIAN PRESS CHAPBOOKS.SUPPORTING MATERIAL.
    "Creativity as a Mantic Proceedure of the Intuitive Function"

STOLEN PAPER 1959 "CULT APPEAL & PROTEST STATEMENT" REVIEW ED. 1977   URANIAN TRACT SOC. CHAPBOOK.INC.1978 & RELEASE of all Planetary Prisoners ... We had seven regulars, eleven counting apprentices, who had learned to move around and easily achieve amazing overtones w/Charles Ives overlay echos from a man stationed INSIDE the organ pipe chamber (Heavy Vib. Box) LaMont Young, who was just starting his long TURTLETONE Time, was working on his drone piano, would sometimes sit in with Terry Riley & others. The Uranian Phalanstery Workshop, under Dorothea's direction, were in production & shooting an 8MM epic film "The Quest", with preteen children of members & neighbors (CLASSIC, MYTH)   making paper machee masks, stick puppet figures, props, costumes & scenery.

When we had money for film & processing, we would load the troop in Charlies Station wagon for a days shooting in the wilds of Staten Island, & a couple of times all the way up to "Dick's Castle" on the Hudson, up near Bear Mountain Bridge. Great stuff, & gave the Band members a chance to blow out in the woods. Peter, now a neighbor, showed us the wonderful masks he had created for his dance theater production of "TOTENTANZ" in Munich 1961, & as he was temporarily "sans Co.", proposed that my people present the piece in Gotham that spring. I agreed, & he and Elka joined our organization[5] URANIAN PHALANSTERY; were issued Agt. cards, w/are carried to this day on the URANIAN EMBASSY rosters as "active international" in good standing (17 yrs.) Being myself but a "common show" quacksalver, I could see that Schumann was an impresario with Circus eyes, & a true Maestro with a lovely family, who had trooped with him on a one wagon puppet show tour of the Balkans in '60; here truely was "Action in the Role". See STOLEN PAPER REVIEW CHAPBOOK.URANIAN PRESS.NYC. Peter attended a full moon band rehearsal in the darkend three story chamber of the Chapel, with its giant cross, & removable benches in the vault space, this was the perfect place for TOTENTANZ. This was of course true, but the same ban on using the space for performances was in effect, that had prevented "Frogs Shock Dream" from being performed in 1959. "Happenings", & the neodada nihilism was still not considered a proper use of sacred space. Agreeing to act as "Patch" on his request, (we still had a powerful ally in Associate Minister Bud Scott, see OLDENBURG TRACT) who opon meeting Peter & his family, was so impressed he obtained permission for "TOTENTANZ".DEATHDANCE. to be performed as a <u>dance concert</u> in the sanctuary of Judson Church on TUE.MAY 15th.11PM to 1230AM. 1962. (Twelve "Alchemy Player" agts. present w/seven members performing.[6] "... DANCE OF DEATH ... CONCEIVED & DIRECTED BY PETER SCHUMANN, it was performed by the ALCHEMY PLAYERS." see HOWARD SMITH DANCE REVIEW "STRANGE EXCITEMENT" VV.May24th 1962) Smiths dynamite provocative review,

---

5. Leigh Schumann (Elka) joined August 29, 1962; Peter Schumann July 11, 1962.
6. Dick Tyler himself played Death in the whole 4-performance 61/62 series (Tyler, Interview, V/7/79). According to a small notebook of his entitled 'Totentanz History', Barbara and Peter Moore, Joseph Phon and Jonas Mekas were among the participants, and performance took or was to take 1 hr 20 min.

plus word of mouth, made for a popular demand return performance on WED.May 30th, booked this time into the "Hall of Issues" space, a cramped "soapbox" gallery, Peter was furious at this change of space, & a compromise was reached when the "Sports & Rec. Dir." agreed to let us use the gymspace for the one hour dance concert repeat perform. "<u>TOTENTANZ</u>". Alchemy Players ... Sure Enough, the Baptist Congregational Board had spooked on a "Deathdance" being performed in the Sanctuary of Judson Memorial Church ... the strange review, & word of mouth reports of "band of beatnik crazys" carrying on with weird orgeastic midnite rituals ... strange sounds & people prevailed. (After this performance, (11 Agts. present, 7 performing, May.30th 1962) Peter refused to have anything more to do with Judson Memorial Church, Bud Scott, ASSOC. MINISTER, resigned shortly thereafter, & with his wife & family joined a religious commune in New Jersey. The new Assoc. Min. of Culture[7] made a clean sweep, & we shortly lost our pushcart parking space "in the churchyard", & also pulled out of Judson never to return ... Claes Oldenburg had now done well enough with his Store & Ray Gun Theater on third st. off 1st Ave., that he was able to vacate #10 rear 330 E. 4th St., & move to a loft on 14th st. off 1st Ave. where he then started manufacturing Softwear Artifacts. The Peter Schumann Family then moved into #10 rear 330 east 4th st. (between Aves C & D) I rented the three rooms basement front for a print shop, (while living at #332, apt. 32, next door rear) from Max Bossman in 1957. An old operator, this was his last building & he enjoyed collecting the ten monthly rents in person, a good landlord, he listened to all complaints, & would do repairs when it was called for. The drains were a horror with years of pouring liquid chicken fat down the toilets. Max gave me free rent, elect. & gas (3 rms ft.) plus the whole basement (4 rooms with water) to become Super of #330 (10 family) in 1958, I was Supt. To the Temple #328 rear, the #326 (3 fam.) & #322 (4 fam.) brownstones, standing on "shape ups" for West St. "platform" work; with Dorothea teaching part time at the Grand St. Settlement House. Being Super, gave me the right to "bring in my people" when there was a vacancy in 330 – The Terrible O'Connor Family, who's boys terrorized the building, pulled out of #10, & Bossman was pleased to rent the apt. to Claes; a "Real Gentleman & Educated Man" was the landlord's judgement. Even when the old yentas reported that "he didn't have any furniture to speak of, slept on a mattress on the floor, making big (OIL PAINTING PICTURES) & messing up the rooms with plaster, making sculptures." When Oldenburg started soft sculpture, the giant hamburger in vinal plastic, the same gossips reported that his "nice little wife" ran a <u>sewing machine</u> all night long. (They were all retired garment workers & knew a "pieceworkshop" operation when they heard it.) Bossman now understood that my people were "Artists from Bohemia" who paid their rent & gave little trouble. So Peter, a "Sculptor Artist from Europe" was welcomed as a solid family man with a wife & three children. Bruno Eckhardt with his wife & son had arrived from Germany, & were living in three depressing rear rooms in a 6th St. tenement off Ave. D, with Bruno working as a moving man for Bill Mallory who ran an

---

7. Al Carmines, the party that, I guess, sponsored the 'Judson Dance Theatre' – it is interesting to see that a *choice* was made here: the art of the Lower East Side crazies with their distinct life styles (e.g. dope) was in fact squelched; middle class harmless art was promoted at its expense.

unlicensed outlaw moving co. from an answering service at that address, giving us all temporary employment at times. That summer the Eckardt family moved into apt. #2, (5 rms.rear) at #330 ... In Sept. of 1962 we were to perform the TOTENTANZ in Putney, Vt., at the Putney School where Elka Schumann was to tutor in russian language, & Peter hoped to teach Puppetry. Chas. Adams, Dorothea Bear, Don Bass,[8] Bruno Eckardt, Marty Greenbaum, Bruce and Robin Grund, Sally Morris, Bill Mallory, Elka & Peter Schumann, Kenneth Sheppard, & Relytor Uranian[9] would do a one hour TOTENTANZ on Sat. SEPT. 22nd (7PM) Putney School Sward (?); Vermont weekender. The Band went up in Charlie's station wagon & Bill Mallory's van. Dorothea got enough good footage of the afternoon rehearsal to produce her esoteric 8MM film classic "TOTENTANZ". (The actual dance performance produced a drenching rain that left the grass sward a bog that put dancers in real danger of drowning, if on the bottom of the "body pile" numbers) The final performance of "Totentanz" by the Alchemy Players was to be Sat. Nov.10th 1962. Billed in the Nov.8th V.Voice as "... a medieval masked deathdance around Wash. Sq. Fountain, 4 pm";[10] it was actually performed at Circle in the Sq. theater on 6th Ave in a last minute change — The "Second Call World Wide GENERAL STRIKE For Peace" MON.NOV.5th.SUN.NOV.11th posters also announced a 10PM production of FIRE, by the Alchemy Players at the Living Theater (cor.6th Ave & 14th ST.) (We (A/P) had not rehearsed this piece, & would be a seven piece pit band, while Peter & the "Putney Puppet Theater" people (Jan, Ann & Ion), with Bill Mallory & Bruno Eckhardt, produced this piece.) When asked by the interviewer "how did this production of Fire compare to the famous protest FIRE of 1965," I could only answer that the one affect retained in my mind was this wonderful use of the "Sausage Machine" (whole puppydog in one end, string of sausages out the other) ... & the fact that JUDITH MALINA of Living Theater was very angry at our use of "apprenticeboychapman" coming out of the pit, to buzz the aisles with Tracts & "American Flag Fan Cigars" for sale ... (a common practice in "Uranian Alchemy Player" action). From the beginning of our association for this "season of '67 Totentanztour" Peter had been antagonistic to the use of Astrological methods (We had agreed to omit "URANIAN" & do the TOTENTANZ as "Alchemy Players".) &/or Metaphysics (a six piece Alchemy Player unit consisting of CHAS ADAMS . DON BASS . DOROTHEA BAER . REGGIE DANIALS . KEN SHEPPARD . RENTOR URANIAN . MARCHED FROM Thompson st. to Times sq. SUN.FEB.4th.1962 in Peace parade, on this final day of the 1st World Wide Gen. Strike; with the DEATH mask & DRUM) This Event, marked "The End of the World", as predicted by various Indian Philosophers; or by the unprecedented close grouping of seven planets in the Sign of Aquarius. (I'm sure

---

8. Richard Tyler's brother, I believe.
9. Tyler's *Totentanz History* in addition mentions ' "Black Duke" — Haitian student,' but not Marty Greenbaum.
10. 'The second General Strike for Peace is now well underway ... two performances by the Alchemy Players on Sat., November 30 — a medieval masked dance called "Totentanz" around Washington Square Fountain at 4 p.m. and a dance production with life-sized puppets at 10 p.m. and midnight at the Living Theatre, 14th Street and Sixth Avenue.' — (*Village Voice*, Nov. 3 (?), 1961.)

JULIAN BECK (LIVING THEATER) appreciated this fact...) There had been some "band member" dissention about Pete from the beginning also. Some resented the fact of the troupes name being changed & submitting to Peters (to them) harsh European "Nonsense Maestro" style — My people were "old Bohemians", shell shocked Vets, beatnick dopers, hustlers & street people; artists & musicians. (The Chap.w/Band Master, Ken Sheppard, learned ALTO SAX in Greenhaven, & went on to the ATTICA HOUSE BAND) We lost two members REGGIE DANIALS & RUTH WALDINGER the opening nite of Totentanz (MAR 15th) in a directional dispute — Next this faction would only take direction from Peter, through me (MAY 30th)... The Putney production, because it entailed travel, w/shooting the movie, was highly enjoyed by all; however, they still considered Peter to be a "Greenhorn" & "squarehead", although they all loved Bruno. With the final production of "TOTENTANZ" Sat. Nov. 10th62. the Apprentice Boys & Chapman, under Master Chapman Ken Sheppard, in open revolt stated that they <u>would not</u> work with "Puppets", dance & musicals, but NO PUPPETS for Pete [11]... w/no hard feelings in the Familia, Solveg Schumann is my god daughter, and Ben Ekardt my godson. Peter returned to Putney to form the "Earth Co." puppet theater which produced posters & chapbooks under that title in N.Y. & Vt. '63. In 1964 we showed the 8MM TOTENTANZ film at the B/P Theater 148 Delancey St. loft, & were permitted to sell the "cigar tract", as we had been allowed by the previous "Delancey St. Museum" shows at that address when Red Grooms & Bob Thompson had their theater.

In 1963, we became international with (the) Uranian Phalansterian Workshop Store Mythological Museum Hampton N.S. BOSILOCAN in New Scotland. Peter & Elka w/four children, Victor Kaplan with wife & two children and Charlie Adams came up in 1965 for the opening of the Uranian Phalanstery Film Soc. SUMMER COMEDY SEASON, at the Store. (NOW the "Chas. DEGAULLE Mun. Theater"... back room w/benches for SUN. showings of 8MM COMEDY W/URANIAN footage... Adm. 25c w/free bag popcorn) & although I spoke of the old time ANNUAL FAIR SUMMER EVENT (   ) old time COUNTY FAIRS a natural for Punch & Judy shows — booked as CULTURE — ect. Pete got a place in STRONG MAINE. 04989 (now known as the "Blackbird Theater" farm). Charlie Adams went with him; also taking a rundown farm with a great barn for theater... Pete didn't stay long in Strong.MA. but Charlie loved the place (played with the TOWN BAND) & by hook & crook was able to operate there until 1970 when the big ski Outfit

---

[11]. 'I think I've never seen Peter drunk. Really drunk. A lot of other people — Dick Tyler, for one, and lots of people that we know — who were really serious about — Dick Tyler, for instance, had a real problem. A great, great artist. A great artist. But — that's why I wonder sometimes if he's still alive. I think he's probably — they moved to Nova Scotia, finally, I think — and still has — and he's just a madman. But he had a real bad drinking problem. We had to finally bar — (Question from interviewer about drugs. (SSB)) No, he didn't take drugs. What happened was, he became a wino, actually, in later times, and he was a real — like this real scuzzy, drunken scene, and we had to bar him, finally, from the theatre, after once having to throw him out and he fell down the stairs, and taking a sculpture — this big plaster lady that was on top of the stairs — with him, crashing down two straight flights onto Delancey Street.' — (Ernstthal, interview.)

speculators forced him out...) Charlie took the URANIAN REENLISTMENT in '71, & is now "In Good Standing" working with "Shoestring Theater Co." 41 BRACKETT ST. Portland Ma.04101. Bruno Eckardt is also ok according to his son
MALERSTRAS 8.56 WUPPERTAL 1.
WEST GERMANY
Benny, who visited me from GER. last summer here in NYC & up to Nova Scotia and is composing ballads & working as a gardner in the housing Projects. drop him a Line... I told Mr. Brecht that I hadn't seen you since 1968, when you were living in a Bowery loft over the Bum (   ) (NOW TIN PALACE) cor. 3rd. & (printing publishing) "BLACKMASK" (a shortlived marxist paper) when you went to Europe with the 1968 "Bread & Puppet Theater" tour, when you went on to India to a closed Ashram. I received a P/C Galilie & Jerusalem from you 72, & a mailing from Calif. from "Foundation of Revelation 59 SCOTT ST. SF CA. Brecht said you mentioned an "early burn-out" guru. I hope it wasn't Father, the Indian Beggar from Gorkhara, West Bengal "Lord of the SIVA KALPA" in this the 15th year of same; who's portrait to this day hangs in an honored position in our Temple Entry Hall (right over the sign in book. Dorothea said he had "rogues eyes") "Lost Atlantis" ended I only hope "Shotsy Morning Star in her speedy Porsche car, Lew Gottlieb, Patty & Buzz" get the old man back to "the unknown village of Gorkhara" ... (& you-an X.SMP.TROT)... I hope you enjoy this letter & the bag of supporting material SMALL PACKET Printed Matter EDUCATIONAL MATERIAL etc. and will write & visit when next in Gotham.
Love
Rev. Relytor Dr. Urania
Uranian Phalanstery
328 E. 4 St., N.Y.C.
New York, 10009 U.S.A.'

7. *Totentanz*. May-November '62. Terminates his dance ambitions. The dialectic of death. Sculpture comes to the aid of dance: use of masks to liberate amateurs for performance.

Whether Schumann had ever called anything he did in Germany a 'dance of death' is not clear any more, he is not sure, guesses maybe not. But that what he tried to get Tyler's people to do in the sanctuary of Judson Church on May 15th ('62), in the gym or Hall of Issues of the church on May 30th, and again, outdoors in a meadow at Putney School, Putney, Vt. on September 22nd, and November 10th at a Greenwich Village theatre, the Circle in the Square,[1] and at least sometimes advertised

---

1. 'a medieval masked dance called *Totentanz* around Washington Square Fountain at 4 p.m.' was announced by the November 8th Voice as part of the activities planned by the N.Y. Committee for a General Strike for Peace: to be done by the Alchemy Players – no mention of Schumann. But it wasn't done there. There seems to have been a fifth performance of something like this *Totentanz* that summer. Peter Moore, the photographer who had taken pictures of the springtime New York performance, caught Schumann participating in a Woodstock, N.Y. shindig in August, the 'Ergo Suits Artists' Carnival,' on August 17th, and one of the photographs shows a group of five *Totentanz*-masked sportively dressed youths parading past the K Gallery there, one beating the drum, two between them carrying a Halloweenish sign, 'Deathdance 9 p.m. Tonight.'

bilingually as '*Totentanz/Dance of Death*' comprised elements of what he had done in Munich or even consisted more or less entirely of such elements seems certain – whereas, *par contre*, when he says (interview, '82) that the 'ideas' in it came 'mostly from the dances in Munich, that were redone' this may very well be misleading, namely if we were to take 'ideas' to refer to intellectual content and not just to particular working ideas, which is what (in that interview) he *seems* to have in mind:

'there was a Janus dance with the double-headed big mask into which several people fitted, separating each chapter of the dance. That was a recurring dance that went through the piece, (some of these "chapters" being: (SSB)) this dance in the womb, we called it, that was the big bag dance, and another one, those people then crawling out of the bag, and another one was the chair dance, with tumbling over of chairs ... (we) came in, sitting on chairs and getting the chairs on top of (us), having the hands at the bottom of the chairs, and moving the chairs, and the "crawling dance" ... a fight between two people that was simultaneous with that (womb) bag ...'

Whether the intellectual content was the same is not clear. The New York '62 *Dance of Death* had a very definite over-all structure embodying very definite ideas (cf. infra) and there is no evidence that this was the case for any of his German dance productions, nor that he even entertained those ideas before he crossed the ocean. It is not inconceivable to me that the title and perhaps even the theme came from R.O. Tyler: who had done Dance of Death woodcuts.

'Auch dieses sehr starke, diese sehr starke Beziehung vom Dick zum Peter, weil der Dick in dieser Sache wat gesehen hat, wat er selber nämlich wiedergegeben hat, sein, sein, diese Toten, seine Art von Totentänzen. Ich weiss nicht, ob sie diese Drucke kennen ... das war'n seine eignen Ideen.' (Eckardt, interview.)

The four performances apparently varied a good deal from one another in detail, and especially the outdoors one was quite different from the others, but especially the first one, done in the sanctuary at night, other than that it was a dance probably had as much (and perhaps more) in common with the mystic jam sessions by which Tyler there had celebrated the unity of spirit with the cosmos as with the German dances by which Schumann had celebrated the integrity of simple man.

The last of the New York productions was sponsored by Judith Malina's and Julian Beck's Living Theatre: they got the Circle in the Square for him, and it was presented as part of the second 'World Wide Strike for Peace,' which like the first Strike for Peace in February (in the central event of which, a parade February 4th from the Village mid-town, Tyler, in the Death mask, made by Schumann, he wore as Death in *Totentanz* – he and Schumann on different occasions both did that part – and as in the show beating a drum, marched leading six Alchemy Players), was a set of pacifist demonstrations initiated and sponsored by the Living Theatre, anarchist and phantasmagoric forerunners of the subsequent peace agitation of the '60s. The Living Theatre was going political at this time. They had done my father's *He Who Says Yes/He Who Says No* as long ago as 1951 and his *In the Jungle of Cities* in (December) '60, but in the fall of this year ('62), they did his subversive, brutally comic treatment of soldiering *Man is Man*, and their next play, in May '63, was another anti-war play, Kenneth Brown's *The Brig*. Gelber's *The Apple* ('61) and *Man is Man* framed their sponsorship of Schumann. A remark, quoted by Kourilsky (Kourilsky, '71), of Maurice Blanc's, in the cast of *Man is Man*, late Sensitive Young Hero of the Bread & Puppet Theatre, evokes the work atmosphere of the Living Theatre at this time:

'Au Living Theatre, je sentais comme un démon obsédant tout le monde, comme si chacun souhaitait une explosion de plus en plus grandiose et recherchait l'intensité du désastre. C'était une atmosphère constante de drame – fascinante d'une certaine façon, mais je me sens mieux au Bread and Puppet Theatre, où il n'y a pas du tout cette sorte d'émotivité forcenée, frénétique.' (Kourilsky, '71.)

Both as regards Tyler and the Living Theatre, Schumann was entering the New York theatre scene under the sign of Artaud: as befitted his expressionist proclivities, of which the N. Y. *Totentanz* was the wake. That *Totentanz* was somewhat in this spirit was also suggested by a review of it provided by the Judson-*Village Voice* alliance, a review that must at this point in his life – a failure all around, living on his father-in-law, etc. – have provided important encouragement to Schumann, its superficiality notwithstanding:

'Something weird took place Tuesday night, May 15, in the sanctuary of Judson Memorial Church. It was called "Totentanz" or "Dance of Death." Whether or not this was a happening doesn't matter because something really did happen and it was strangely exciting, full of eerie surprises and odd humor. Conceived and directed by Peter Schumann, it was performed by the Alchemy Players.

In the orthodox sense of the word the dancers are not really dancers and they double as their own musicians who really don't play music. Voices, a drum, violin, trumpet, flute, saxophone, tambourine, harmonica, bells, and someone clapping his hands are used as instruments to produce sounds in alternating currents of funeral dirges, kindergarten bands, primitive rituals, and a diabolic symphony warming up. Throughout the performance the participants (and even some of the audience) all wear ghostly gray-white masks that in themselves create an instant supernatural atmosphere of impending doom. The lighting is stark and effective. The performers, most of whom are barefoot, display a basic sense of drama and a schizophrenic follow-the-leader type of choreography.

At the beginning it all seems a little forced and seriously clever, but soon you are carried away by a driving physical and psychic spontaneity that becomes ever deeper as the performers become more hypnotically involved in their improvised self-possession.

You shouldn't be told beforehand of the actual scenes, movements, and incidents because if you go to see the next (and possibly last) performance, at the Judson Hall of Issues on Wednesday, May 30, you will know too many details and surprise is an important part of the inspiration of "Totentanz."

What is really important in watching it is not so much what is going on in front of your eyes but what it is doing to your mind, and if you go with the tight mood of the careful intellectual, trying to symbolize and categorize, things might become like a tedious nightmare instead of the pagan exorcism that was intended. "Totentanz" is capable of leading you into funny realms, spectral areas, and many strange thoughts.'

(Howard Smith, *(Dance) Strange Excitement, Village Voice*, May 24, '62.)

Arthur Sainer, as mush-headed a critic as he is a playwright, retrospectively esteemed it (he saw the November 10 performance) a 'use of ritual' by which the Bread and Puppet Theatre became 'one of the earliest ensembles to employ ritual':

'*The Totentanz*, a ritual dance of death, performed by young men and women and one or two children, all in black garments. To the accompaniment of a steady percussive beat, they circle about and leap, circle about and leap until one by one they drop, until one by one they are symbolically dead. And then, after death, they rise, to die again. A constant death and resurrection.

But what is so effective, so moving about this troupe is the commitment to the dance, the concentration, the belief in the efficiency of the theatrical statement. All performed wordlessly, anonymously. The action goes past energy to belief, it isn't the will that's engaged but the soul that wills. Something is taking place that goes beyond theatre, that becomes theatre because it goes beyond it: it goes through theatre and, leaving it, striking at an atavistic nerve, it becomes theatre. Becomes what it's almost become indifferent to, gets there by going past it.

And so gets to us, affects us because we become incapable of seeing it as theatre, we move into the essential area of simply seeing and feeling, we lose the power and the need to judge, we can't ask of it because we're caught up in answering it. And what it asks of us is not to see it but to see ourselves. And we do see ourselves by seeing it. We see the death of man and simultaneously see one man, each his own man, from death to resurrection, the resurrection of all to that of each. In some way the death embodies us so that we begin to partake of it, and also of the resurrection. It's not that we include ourselves through a local extension, that we rationally see ourselves in the scheme of death, but rather that, like seeing an auto accident that wrenches us, we are shaken into a comprehension of the terms of the universe, not its intent but its effect. We come to see ourselves dying ourselves. We are died and dying. We comprehend and are comprehended. We are watching and the witnesses are being witnessed.'

(Sainer, *Radical Theatre Notebook*, '75.)

'(I: You did the Putney performance out of doors in a meadow and with a fire. That must have been very different.) Yeah. It was. It was very different because all the people in it were New York City people that had, it seemed, never in their life been to any countryside and they filled themselves with dope and went totally wild. And for them it was a fantastic adventure. They walked through these meadows and hills and they got lost in a very dreamy — totally lost — they didn't know what to do and how to deal with cold or wind or anything. They just filled themselves with dope and were in a trance, really, when they did it. But for them that seemed to be the best thing to do — it was a memorable dance. They wanted to be in *ecstasy* at the time when they did it. Yeah. I preferred that very much to —

they seemed very real to me — they seemed very honest and real and straightforward people compared to the dancers and intellectual people that I had worked with before in Cunningham's studio and Alwin Nikolais' studio where I did these dance tryouts. I was very happy with that situation.' (Schumann, interview, '82.)

He 'liked' the Alchemy Players 'on tour and found it wasn't easy to be with' them, but it 'was the right crew for this dance' — (Schumann, interview, '79.)

'(I: You didn't have any rehearsals?) No. They were — it was very hard to get a rehearsal together. A lot of things were left up to the individuals — of how to do it. There were no such choreography rehearsals other than the real arranging of the whole scene. There was only the structuring of the dance rehearsed; but what — how a person danced — I decided only on how fast he danced and what beat was given, and such things. But on the whole, I had to use what came out of them. (I: Wasn't that completely different from the Moosach-Munich German situation?) It was different, yeah. It was different, and it was not.'

(Schumann, interview, '82.)

Schumann while at Putney School described his New York *Dance of Death* in an unpublished manifesto entitled *The Dance of Death as it was anonymously performed at Judson Church in New York on May 15th 1962 (& repeated in the Hall of Issues, New York, on May 30th 1962):*

'In the foyer of the church hang the emblems of the Dance of Death: drawings and sculptures of rows of empty chairs, boxes painted with figures and filled with groups of figures, big drawings with hundreds of figures, face molds of the dancers and musicians, big posters with descriptive representations of the dance and with explanations:

"All artistic activities are magical operations and music is the mystery of the universe exerting the all uniting power in nature. A most powerful conceiver, it allures the celestial influences. That the planets whirling in their orbs produce sounds, is a discovery of Pythagoras. The spheres produce tones of the nucleus of all that exists, and men who can imitate this celestial harmony have traced their way back to this sublime realm, where moving according to these ideal figures, they then capture the magical meanings of the earliest sacred dances performed in mystical rites, movements that cause the gods to rejoice, and echoes to haunt the planets, creating great curative forces."

Agrippa von Nettesheim
(Henry Cornelius:
De Oculta Philosophia
1531)

and:

Deathdance is one of the oldest forms of dance. Dances of death were performed throughout the middleages in the churches of Europe. Our dance is the new execution of the old rite. You will see the third version tonight. The first and the second version of Totentanz were performed two years ago in Germany by a group of New Dancers. Our Deathdance is a wild feast against death.

We ask you to take a mask and sit in front of the dance on the pedestal. The chorus sitting on the pedestal, shaped and enlarged by the masks, is the chorus of judges, of bourgeois, watching demons, waiting to be killed. We have no interest in art. (We are no pupils of any kind of dance.) Our interest is in purpose, in joy, in ecstasy. Our dance is the exaltation of common life to dance.

This is a serious and self conscious dance.

The nave of the church is empty, the audience sits along the walls beneath the columns. On a podium below the enormous wooden cross stand more than 40 chairs with masks. In the beginning, the dancers, who all throughout the whole dance wear uncolored, very plastic masks, some of them enclosing the head, and everyday clothing, are busy trying to talk members of the audience into sitting on the podium and wearing the masks.

Act 1. The Overture.

The ten masked dancers and musicians, among them a gigantic Negro and his five year old son, briefly stand in the hall without moving while death beats the drum.

Act 2. The Celebration.

The whole group walks in a line, playing music, to below the podium, and there performs an extended concert with violin, flute, drum, bell, horn, mouth harp, hand clapping, tambourine and trumpet, a continuous crescendo growing into driven jazz, an unorganized music that out of independently running voices coalesces into rhythms and delicate regularities. When the music has become very loud and fast, the first of the dancers puts aside his instrument, dances around Death, jumps in all directions, does a spasmic, wildly excessive ("aus allen Fugen platzenden") dance all over the floor until he collapses, exhausted. And thus one dancer after another, leaping, stomping, throwing out his arms and legs, does his dance, ending by throwing himself on top of those already prone. Then Death steps forward and takes his seat on the heap of the demons, and one hears only his muted drumbeats. The lights go off, a projector light hits the heap which suddenly begins to move, throwing Death off it, and continues to move in place, like a nest of worms or snakes, in a crawling motion of seemingly unconnected arms, legs and masks. This continues for quite a while before the crowd separates and the full light goes back on. You see Death and the musicians lying on the floor. A dragging, low music of saxophone, trumpet, flute and drum begins, while the masked performers crawl and push against one another, down on the floor, at first fighting, then gradually moving ever more slowly and finally their movement dying along with the music.

Act 3. The Janus Dance.

A gigantic double-headed mask, screaming loudly, horribly jumps into the projector's cone of light, swinging arms and legs. Death runs in a circle around it, beats out frenetic whirls on the drum, pushes and shoves it off.

Act 4. The Fanfare.

The trumpeter runs diagonally through the hall, stops, makes hectic sounds, the masks come running in, run back out again, individual ones among them reappear, groups, then all together, run throughout the space, again disappear.

Act 5. First repetition of the Janus Dance.

Act 6. The Dance of Birth.

A big, dark, shapeless mass is crouching in the projector light, a globe, a womb. There is movement inside of it and from it sounds a chorus of manifold low voices melting into one another. From behind it, somewhere in the dark, one hears the death drum. The singing develops, becomes clearer, the movements of the mass grow larger, it begins to move from its place, to crawl. A masked figure with an instrument drops from the dark clump and starts to play notes. The mass continues to move and loses more bodies, all starting to make music. The more emaciated the big bag becomes, the more violently it moves, arms reach out of it, it rolls on the floor, leaps, runs, forms sharply defined sculptures. Then it stands, shivering.

Act 7. Second repetition of the Janus Dance.

Act 8. Third repetition of the Janus Dance.

Surrounded by all the other masks, to the accompaniment of deafening yells, the Janus mask is chased in. It is pushed back out.

Act 9. The Chairs.

All masks enter, many of them carrying chairs, sit down, get up on the chairs, some sit for a long time without moving, others throw chairs up into the air, push chairs, balance on chairs, or seated in couples facing one another, stroke one another's hands. The group is close together. At times it is unmoving, sometimes all move, sometimes an individual undertakes a big action: pushes all the seated ones close together, throws them down, carries them off. This lasts a long time. Finally someone starts rolling out the chairs and those seated on them and the others join him in doing this.

Act 10. The Ceremony.

In the cone of light the dancers carry the drumbeating Death seated in a chair high above their shoulders in a wide circle through the hall, deposit him in the center, the musicians (all with drums, horns or wooden beating instruments) pace out the space in a wide circuit, the dancers take one another by the hand and dance around Death. Slow and fast, leaping and standing they throughout a long dance dance around Death, who sits on his chair and beats his drum. Finally, to the hammering of the music, they work themselves into circling the chair on a run. At their highest speed they run out in a chain.

Act 11. Death's Dance.

Death performs a long solo dance, jumps among the audience, falls, drums on the floor crawling over it, with his drum stick draws his signs in the air in the four corners of the hall, carries on, is aggressive, acts dignified.

Act 12. The End.

The lights flare on to a great noise and one sees the masks falling on the ground. This is repeated three times.

Concluding remark. The whole dance lasts almost an hour and a half and there are no intermissions. It should not be performed on a stage, but in a space allowing the audience to participate in the action. (A girl in the audience participated in the singing and, in the Chairs, in the dancing.) In addition to the choir of seated masks on the podium, it had been planned to supply the entire audience with masks, and to distribute it in rows and choruses in the space. But it had not been possible to make enough masks. There were about two months of rehearsal, but details were not worked out. Music and dance were spontaneous throughout. All the dancers were amateurs, nobody had any kind of schooling. Each participant participated both as dancer and as musician.'[2]

(Schumann, *The Dance of Death* . . . . Translated from the German by S. Brecht.)

Death beats the drum for masked men and a masked boy. (1. Opening.) The living – but they are wearing these grey lifeless masks – individually challenge Death and are subdued by the challenge. Death reigns. But Death cannot maintain Himself: He is overthrown. The reborn fight. Their fights exhaust them. They die. Death dies. (2. Celebration.) Death expulses a ferocious two-faced giant. (3. First Janus dance.) Heralded agitation of the living. (4. The fanfare.) (5. Second Janus dance.) The living are born, individuated, generate energy, freeze. (6. The dance of birth.) (7. Third Janus dance.) The living chase the two-faced giant. (8. Fourth Janus dance.) The living install themselves but will not stay put. (9. The chairs.) The living celebrate death. (10. The ceremony.) Aggressive Death gives a show of his life and dignity. (11. The dance of death.) The living repeatedly perform the catastrophe of their deaths. (12. Finale.)

The essential point is that the living dance with death. Dancing is life at its intensest (though it also has the feature of unconscious following – of whatever music the living hear.) In the 14th century, death was the wages of sin – life's lustful dance was led by the devil. Since Adam ate of the apple, and Lucifer's horde was unleashed on his descendants, man naturally danced with death. In the medieval sculptures, this dance is harmonious, courtly. Schumann put the antagonism between the living and their dying in. Whether Schumann had the death of eternal damnation and the dance of sin-committance in mind, we cannot tell. From his

---

2. His original staging plan had been:

'1. Stand. 2. Tune. 3. Big Mask. 4. Trumpet. 5. Big Mask. 6. Sack. 7. Big Mask. 8. Chairs. 9. Big Mask. 10. Ceremony. 11. Big Mask. 12. Death. 13. Fall 3 times.'

He dropped the fifth Janus dance (Act 1. in the staging plan), so that Death's triumphant solo immediately follows his adoration by the living, and he made the fourth one (9. in the staging plan) precede rather than follow the unquiet installation of the living (Chairs), so that in the performance the third and last contention of Death with Time (if that is what Janus represents) was immediately followed by a rivaling contention of the living with Time (that fourth Janus dance).

description, the dance seems to have associated life mostly with agitation, excitation, individuation, ostentation, fighting − turmoil, antagonism, vanity, and to the extent Death set the beat for this nasty and undignified conduct, perhaps the dance conveyed a sense of life as grotesque spasm, the curve of gesture into extinction. Though this would be an image of life as war wedded to peace, Schumann has denied that with Janus he had the Roman god of war and peace in mind, seems to say he had to do with a looking both backward and forward: 'I thought of Janus as the representative of January − being the beginning of the year.' (Schumann, interview, '82.) Might we think of him as human time: history? sequence of generations? and/or maturation cum decay? Or as hurried, harassed, ambitious and frustrated, self-conflicting life − Life? Counter-piece, in the dance, of Death? It's murky (as, however, is to us what we are doing and what we are like), partly because Schumann was not clear headed and/or refused the position-takings by which the dumber ones among us resolve their doubts, partly perhaps simply because while the dance's message was reasonably clear, it was not of a sort conveyable by verbal description.

Clearly, it was by no means as thoughtless or haphazard a piece as he later has sometimes pretended. Rather it was a conceptual dance, an allegory. Clearly, also, it was not a commemoration of the dead, integrating the ancestors into the community[3], nor a stern evocation of mortality; and if it was a celebration of death as integral to life, condition for and recurrent preamble of rebirth (negation subject to its own negation), it was not a happy one − the piece was dark.

Some manner of idealization of life − didactic evocation of what it really is and how it should be lived − seems to have been a central intent of

---

3. Schumann in '82 puts the concept of *Totentanz*: to provide a new-type ceremony of service for the dead for a culture that doesn't have any:

'But I think our *Totentanz* ideas was more to provide in a culture that doesn't − that doesn't have a service for the dead, in a real sense, to create a dance that could be used like that. That could be a ceremony, better than the normal setting up of a gravestone. That was the idea; to make a − to create something for what I felt doesn't exist in our culture. (I: The incorporation of the dead with the living in the on-going community.) Yeah. In a way, it's a definition of culture, I think, what people do with their dead − how they relate to their dead − and we come to New York and see the Brooklyn graveyards or, normally in America you see a graveyard, you realize that that is a vacuum − that's something that doesn't exist. It's a quick discarding of people into a little factory of stones and get rid of them and get away from − there isn't even any "getting". In Europe I saw horrible graveyards, too, but then on Sundays and special days they get decorated and people plant flowers and women still go to their husbands' gravesides and like that. But America, I think, has extremely little of that − or nothing. (I: How did *Totentanz* − this actual piece − relate to that, though. To that idea of a commemoration of the dead or a recognition of the dead?) Yeah, that's a good question. I guess it didn't. In any detail. But that was − that was only its overall − it wanted to provoke that thought but it didn't in detail describe any of what might be a ceremony for the dead − that we would propose. It only said: Here it is. This is a ceremony for dying and the dead and the ceremony is totally made up and invented and not relating to old ceremonies that exist.' — (Schumann, interview, '82.)

Schumann's dance work in Germany, though if we go by the newspaper review of his 1960 *Ballett*, the work did not realize this intent.

The dialectic of life and death has been the central mystery of Schumann's work. Conceived in the Hegelian manner, it comprises four ideas:

(1) Death, non-trivially conceived is not merely the absence of life – spiritual non-being, physical non-functioning – but, as compendium of life-destroying forces, a destructive force acting on life.

(2) This force arises from life. The processes of living, the acts in which we are alive create and feed it. Living is always also directed against life. Life is lethal.

(3) Whatever is alive is continually exposed to this force, and coping with it is the essence of living, the mechanism of life and the core of the experience of it. Living consists in resisting death.

(4) Conceived as supervened state of inanimation, death is an attribute of individuality. An individual's death is the destruction of their individuality only, however. It does not touch whatever in them transcends their individuality. As destruction of individuality death is a positive event, fountain of the life of other individuals. As separation of individuals' aspects of universality from mere singularity it is also a positive event, a definition of essence. An individual dies in every creative act of theirs.

The implication for living to Schumann seems to be: define your values and objectives in terms of opposition to the forces opposing life: don't ignore them: the purely positive objectives and values are misleading evasions, resignations to death. He in his shows seems to me to have ignored another implication: don't let the lethal entailments of your life-affirmative acts inhibit you.

The dialectic of life and death provides a grim outlook on life: that it is a preoccupation with death. This outlook is expressed by Schumann's masks.

'Ihr wandelt droben im Licht
  Auf weichem Boden, selige Genien!
    Glänzende Götterlüfte
      Rühren euch leicht,
        Wie die Finger der Künstlerin
        Heilige Saiten.
Schicksallos, wie der schlafende
  Säugling, atmen die Himmlischen;
    Keusch bewahrt
      In bescheidener Knospe,
        Blühet ewig
          Ihnen der Geist,
            Und die seligen Augen
              Blicken in stiller
                Ewiger Klarheit.

> Doch uns ist gegeben
>> Auf keiner Stätte zu ruhn,
>>> Es schwinden, es fallen
>>>> Die leidenden Menschen
>>>>> Blindlings von einer
>>>>>> Stunde zur andern,
>>>>>>> Wie Wasser von Klippe
>>>>>>>> Zu Klippe geworfen,
>>>>>>>>> Jahrlang ins Ungewisse hinab.'
>>>>>>>>>> (Hölderlin, *Hyperion's Schicksalslied.*)

Totentanz was his first masked dance — masks were used at most occasionally and incidentally in his German dance work. He sent back to Germany for some masks, about a dozen, and made new ones: the 'Janus' mask intended for two or more performers, a mask, the 'Big Mask', for Ken Sheppard whose head was too big for the masks he had, as well as some for at least some of the performers other than Sheppard, and some for distribution to the spectators he wanted to figure as 'judges or bourgeois' in the performances.[4]

What decided him to use masks is obscure. Conceivably, Dorothea Baer's use of masks in her movies might have had something to do with it.

---

[4] 'I cast all the players' faces, and then made masks that fitted over their faces — made masks over the cast of their faces so they would fit better.' — (Schumann, interview '79.)

Whether he used the German masks at all is thus doubtful.

'. . . one of the masks . . . was made for a very tall black man who couldn't fit on any of the masks that we had from Germany and I made him a new mask. (Elka: He was a friend of Dick Tyler's.) Right, Ken (Ken Sheppard (SSB)), he died some five years ago. (So (SSB)) one Negro mask I made in New York, and I had quite a few sent over from Germany, but I made, I think, just as many for this dance — actually many, many more, because I remember the first performances of *Totentanz* (in New York (SSB)) we may have been only some fifteen people in the performance but we handed out at least thirty or forty masks to the audience for each performance. We put a part of the audience on raised seats in masks — that was part of what we wanted to have in this performance. Maybe a dozen (masks) were sent from Germany and the rest were all made in New York — but it wasn't just puppets and masks that we used, there also was a big bag used; and there were chairs used and there was a whole big room full of drawings through which people had to go before they could see the dance. That was part of the show — black and white drawings. I cast all the players' faces, and then made masks that fitted their faces, and made masks over the cast of their faces so they would fit better.' — (Schumann, interview '79.)

'We wanted a part of the audience to be an immediate part of the performance by putting the masks on them, putting them on chairs, having them sit without moving and act like a jury that sits above the trial. So that's — that was done with, I would think, about 30, maybe 30 masks that were given out to people as they came into the door and they were sitting on . . . that's this front altar area is raised. That's where they were sitting on big chairs there . . . no. No, the *Totentanz* thing was where — that the whole play was put down a bit by having these people sitting above them. The whole play was at all times watched by these masked weirdos.' — (Schumann, interview, '83.)

According to himself[5] the idea was Tyler's, and the masks were to cut down on Tyler's people's inhibition against making fools of themselves cavorting about. Schumann's German experience had been that amateurs could no more move authentically ('richtig') than professional dancers. He may have thought of the masks as aids to such movement. But he was on his way to a use of puppets dispensing with the requirement of authenticity.

Looking at the pictures Moore took of the piece, the masks are clearly ancillary to motion: but, though in their sculptural self-assertiveness a little deplacé-looking, powerful. I suspect that with these utter anarchistic amateurs making trouble for him during rehearsals, on top of not being able to dance to begin with, i.e. with not even any of the seriousness about – respect for – it that his German buddies (who had discontented him by their ultimate lack of devotion to dancing) had had and had surely displayed, Schumann grabbed at masking them to make up for the deficiencies of the motion: the masks giving focus and definition to certain poses or gestures which, it seems from the photos, he may have been able to get them to assume/make.

Moore's photos show just a few men in movement (some guys moving) and compositions of their groupings by asymmetries within wholes. The men are wearing light-colored shirts (short-sleeved, practical, loose, their collars open), dark pants, white socks so that their feet and their lower arms plus hands contrast white to their dark bodies, and by this contrast go with and bring out the highly sculptured face masks covering their faces. The show thus seems to have been rather a dance with masks than really a masked dance, and hardly dance in any strong sense at all, rather just movement with exaggerated, sustained, strained and/or excessive poses. The masks perhaps made dance out of what without them would

---

5 '(I: Now, in New York City, at least, in *Totentanz* you used masks. Did everybody have a mask on among the dancers?) Yes, I think so. Yeah, in New York, yes. In Munich, no. In Munich we used painted faces. (I: And no masks?) I'm sure we used masks sometimes, in some dances. We did quite a few different dances and some were done with masks. (I: Like the Janus mask? Or the Death skull masks – did you use those in Germany?) They came from Germany, so we must have used them there. (I: I was wondering, you see, whether, somehow, you see – Moore made a few pictures of the New York *Totentanz* and I looked at them and they looked very good, but, that is to say – they look, I thought: No rehearsals, no dancers. Then I thought: Well, they're wearing masks. That, alone, gives a lot of focus to the thing. And then I was wondering whether perhaps this particular piece of work and experience may have led you on to greater reliance on masks. You see, this thing compared to the Munich thing.) Right, right. Yeah, I think so. Probably, yes. I think, in Richard Tyler's group, with them, they insisted on masks. I probably tried without masks – some of the things – and they insisted on masks. That was – what the mask does to the dancer – that he is not seen – that he can perform something else – that was very important to them. And I think it was a real collaboration of a typical Richard Tyler idea and of what I wanted to do.' — (Schumann, interview, '82.)

have been just uninteresting movement lacking compositional tension, but in themselves were more on exhibition than integral elements.

'(I: The masks — my impression is — correct me if I'm wrong — that the masks in the New York *Totentanz* were somewhat similar to one another except for the skull mask and the Janus mask — that they were two exceptions and that the other dancers probably had somewhat similar and close-fitting face masks, probably?) No, the masks were not that similar. There were two types of masks that were used, and one were — I should have some sample pieces — but they were quite different — were masks that I made in Germany, and I had written to Dieter to send them to me. And they were very finely wrought masks that I had made into plaster molds with great, great care. They were real results of a long time of work on masks. Whereas, the new ones that I made in New York, then, I didn't have enough for that group, so I made new ones in New York. They were much more shoddy and by far not as good. They were quickly done. (I: Also more close fitting?) Maybe more close fitting; more openings for eyes and noses, and so on, for easier breathing and more practical ideas, but not as good as the old masks. I remember that very clearly — that there was a big difference between these German masks that I had sent over and these newly made masks. (I: You know, they were in the background — different *Totentanz* masks, and they were quite different from one another — the German ones. Anyhow — okay. But, to me there are two kinds of masks in your work. As regards masks worn by performers that fit over the face, etcetera, the one is these more sculptured things where the nose comes out further or whatever, and I don't even quite know how they're supported on the face, because they're quite different from the human face. And then, the others are like, you know, Vietnamese women and so on, which are derived from actual face masks.) But that, I hadn't arrived at yet. To make masks like those: well-fitting masks. All the masks were awkward, and big nose and big eye bulges and mouths, etcetera. (I: What about the mask for Ken Sheppard — the black fellow. You made a special mask?) That is what later we used as a King Herod mask. Yeah, that was also not a well-fitting mask. It was not, you know, it wasn't a half mask that's fitted on — it was a mask that fit over his own head. (I: It fitted over his whole head and it rested on his —) shoulder.'

(Schumann, interview, '82.)

To my eye and mind, these masks for the German and New York *Totentanz* are, for two reasons, merely essays. First of all, they look to me done more from a sculptor's than from a performance person's viewpoint. Secondly, to the extent envisaged for performance, ill-considered. As sculptures, they marginally are in the tradition of the Cubist-time neo-colonialist exploitation of commercially debased African tribal masks by European artists struck by the way those objects of trade break up space: faces unwillingly allowing themselves to be projected out into a three-dimensionality destroying a face's crucial presentation by its owner as picture of him- (or her-) self. Schumann hadn't quite seriously thought of them as yet as to be seen worn by somebody — a performer. He knew they would be seen worn, but wasn't quite operating with this knowledge yet, or he just simply made them without thinking of their use by performers.

Their deployment in space is too vigorous for performance masks. As art objects they break up space, induce a turbulence for the eye appeased, if at all, by themselves only, but not absorbable into the larger to-be-appeased, turbulence of the performer's motion. His later masks don't go in and out so much. (The three-dimensional arrestiveness of individual features — eyes, noses — also made the production of these masks difficult and time-consuming.) They look all right sitting on a shelf. Secondly, they are made without consideration of the body. A mask on a performer is the focus, but has to work as focus as part and top of the body. If it makes the eye jump to it, it destroys the performance. This is, as regards use in performance, the fault of these '59-'62 masks, because Schumann put too much into their expressions. They are too decidedly smiling, shouting or anguished for there to be much left over for the performer to do with his arms or legs, his clad body. The sculptor that made them had no intercourse with, didn't trust the dancer that was to use them.

When considered as sculpture, the New York City-made *Totentanz* masks are clearly inferior to the Munich ones (which they copy). Neither the component shapes nor their relations are as well-defined. They have, however, gained in expressive force.

8. Manifesto.

When Schumann in '62 at Putney wrote his 'description' of the May '62 Judson *Totentanz* performances, he prefaced it, by way of introduction, by a programmatic ecstatic manifesto, calling for art of a genuinely folkloristic sort, i.e. not born of art, but sincere and adequate direct response, unconfined by prevailing canons, to the existing historical and social situation, free of not only distracting technical or other sophistication, but of the vanity of personal expression and identification, informed by the nature of the age and devoted to or at any rate in effect achieving a genuine concrete utility to the living, 'necessary' in these objective senses, not in any personal sense. He announced his readiness for producing such art.

The manifesto proclaimed the necessity of art, i.e. not of taking in other people's art, but of doing art, and proclaimed it as actually everybody's need. It stipulated the kind of art that everybody ought to be creating: a response to life, and thus to the actual historical situation people find themselves in; bypassing or transcending, not expressing individual peculiarity; helpful to others; not borrowing the forms of or reproducing art of another age; not response or attempt to contribute to existing contemporary art, to the given art being done and recognized as such or as good; not application of technique and independent of technical skills. This might be summed up: art should be produced not as art, but as response to life; not as expression of individuality, but of what is shared with others; and not as luxury, but out of felt need; and not so that the products (art works) might be there, but for the sake of doing it. His identification of such art as folk art, as religious, and as helpful to others seem relatively supplementary.

Since this manifesto introduces Schumann's account of the 'anonymous' Judson dance program, and since it so preponderantly exemplifies the art called for by dance and music as virtually to identify it with them, Schumann seems to have felt that the New York *Totentanz* has come pretty close to the manifesto's ideal.[1] Music and dance are more direct

---

1. I can personally attest that the jam session festival celebrations at Tyler's East 4th Street Uranian Temple in '79/'80 were still wonderful events not unlike what Schumann in this manifesto seems to call for.

Eckhardt felt that with both his Munich dances and with *Totentanz* Schumann was on the wrong road, and one he abandoned after *Totentanz*: with perhaps the pre-*King Story* show of the summer of '62 (*Burning Towns?*) the rebeginning – the beginning of an art for others, not for Schumann himself:

'Ja, also ich weiss nicht, welchen Einfluss ich auf Peter ausgeübt habe. Ich hab'n ein Einfluss aus ihn ausgeübt, aber inwieweit, inwieweit das gegangen ist, also ich kann jetzt nicht behaupten, dass ich der, ich irgendwie Steine ins Rollen gebracht hätte, aber vielleicht bin

responses than poetry or drama (made indirect by language) or than painting and sculpture (made indirect by the detachment of the art work). When he wrote the manifesto, Schumann was going into puppetry. Presumably he felt it was going to be an art form allowing art in the spirit of the manifesto.

'Nowadays the term "folklore" is understood to mean singing folk songs, dancing folk dances, etc., i.e. stealing from some period or other its innermost being, its glory. Folklore never called itself "folklore". What nowadays one means by the term in the period in question was as right as nourishment, as necessary as nourishment, and was simply good nourishment ("die schöner Nahrung"). There are still some places where something like that exists. But only he has it for whom it's a necessity, who can't sing anything except just that, who needs no other song and no other place. Those who sing Yiddish songs as well as Spanish ones, and those that have it on phonograph records hereby betray themselves. They are the users and the gourmets ("die Nutzniësser und die Geniesser"): they don't have it.

Only he who has only one soul has a soul, only he who has only one song has a song, and similarly for dance. If, feeling our way back to the origin, we knew more precisely what it means to "have" a dance – to dance in forms that one has not chosen, in forms specifically resulting from everything one does in life and in action, in forms that are ineluctable, bare of artifice, devoid of refinements of detail – if one we could intuit in dancing or in music this little bit of necessity, we would already have a grip on how to begin to dance or to make music. I know how much nonsense is spoken about "necessity". Any just three quarters intelligent painter nowadays justifies his work with concepts of this sort. But by "necessity" I don't mean anything personal. I don't mean this Something to which, irresponsibly, one feels oneself driven. (A Berliner may feel himself driven to dance in Spanish only.) To explain the real and useful necessity that I have in mind I have to evoke the image of an unusual human being, that of the ordinary person, that rarest among human characters, the human being that lives in his age, that reacts spontaneously to what his age teaches him, who makes his life out of what his age does to him, who in no way has recourse to what has already been developed – a naked, whipped, daring human being, one who is ordinary because no queerness, no particular inclination or passion, no genius ear, no genius eye, no

---

ich einer der Steine gewesen, einer der Leute gewesen, die die Sache da beflügelt haben, ja. So, wie ich, ich den Peter kennengelernt habe, da hatte der, der hatte seinen *Totentanz*, der *Totentanz*, die Masken, die der war ja mit seinem *Totentanz* verheiratet. Die Masken, die hingen im Zimmer und die Kinder spielten mit den Masken und die Masken gehörten zum Peter und Peter gehörte zu den Masken. Dat war 'n Stück von ihm und 'n Stück aus, aus seinem Glaubensbekenntnis. Und er hat aus diesem *Totentanz*, er hat selber gesehen, dat diese, ich kann mich jetzt nicht richtig ausdrücken, wie ich den *Totentanz* ihn bezeichnen soll .... Der Peter hatte in München, wir hatten noch das Zelt von seiner experimentallen Tanzgruppe und davon hielt ich gar nichts. Dat war, für mich war dat 'ne snobistische Art 'n Drama zu machen (...). Ich hab diese Fähigkeit nicht gehabt, daeinzusteigen. Und vor allen Dingen hatte ich auch kein Respekt und kein Verständnis für die, so für die ganze Ausdrucksform, nicht, dat war übrigens beim *Totentanz* genau derselbe, der *Totentanz* der hat mir nicht gut gefallen. Dat war für mich, dat war für mich irgendwie wat, dat war wat für Peter, aber nicht für die Leute jemacht, nicht. Und dat war unser, naja gut. So ging dat los irgendwie, nicht (i.e. their disagreements (SSB)). — (Eckhardt, interview.)

genius love, no however beautiful eccentricity, seduces him away into the past, into peculiarity and into selfhood, a human being at the same time sufficiently chaste and sufficiently daredevil to achieve what is necessary, that which in his age is possible. I can make this clear by some verbal images. Somebody that plays Bach may be a great person and may be very useful to his students and listeners. But he can change nothing and he cannot hope to change anything. He cannot hope to do anything real. He is harmless and is, himself, helpless, does nothing by his playing to feed the hungry, to get rid of wrongs – I mean: to create joy beyond personal gain and personal enjoyment. Another, somebody in some Spanish village, a genuine flamenco player, listening to jazz in bars, seeing tourists, having cars in his head, no longer is a flamenco player: regardless of how beautifully he plays. He may still – suffering, pained, sorrowing for flamenco – be a genuine musician. But he is no longer a flamenco player in the grandeur of flamenco. He too can put something very beautiful and very valuable into the world, but he too can no longer help it, cannot live with it according to its demands.

Only the Ordinary Human Being can do that, the individual who is not protected by any particular love or by an age other than his own, who is forced to make a music that is necessary – not only personally necessary, but the unique music resuming the age, possible in the age, the one kind of music that might help.

I intend nothing pompous by this. Nor am I calling for a muse lightening the leisure time of the working class – though I like it better than that self-grafted, self-beautiful muse that has made connection with the modern banking establishment. Every age, every present, has to find its music, its solution, no matter what, but in any event not politics or games, culture mongering or anything like that, but music, spirit, dance, language, image, religion, a norm, a law, a potential: its own structure and order, a salvation that can be achieved only in specific terms, out of *this* age, *this* present, a simple inwardness capable of life so that it can be of help in the external world.

This, I think, is clear. I know what fashion and philosophy have to say concerning it. I know this cherished ideal of a science able to milk everything, to spell out the detail of everything, to piece together anything. I have no answer for students. One can study anything.

I am speaking of a big opportunity and a real one – though it's not something that can be achieved routinely. That's why I prefer to put it this way: it has almost begun to come into being. A big effort might bring it into being. I mean our real "folklore", the practice of a possible spiritual genuine life. Its practive: for an order is never born from mere spirituality, from the circumlocution of something or from any interpretation, no matter how true. Only practice, only music, dance, language, image, only the practice of religion can give birth to religion.

For many this will sound like an attempt to save the honor of art – just an artistic idea. I am not going to try to correct that impression. I don't want by their own body to demonstrate to anybody who does not have the longing for it – and where is such a person, with such a longing, to be found anyway?! – what dance is: this primary, everyday, wasted capacity. And I have no desire to sharpen the eyes and ears of anybody who does not yearn for this so that their eyes and ears might regain their conscience, might acquire power. I am not speaking of art at all. For "art" refers to the same secondary state intended by the concept of folklore. Whatever else it refers to, "art" refers to a product pacified before it has come into existence, to the art work, a thing by tradition enshrouded in love, captured to serve a particular, exclusively personal function, a thing that to historians registers an absurd value, absurd because not projected into reality. I am speaking of the chaos that is rich in mercies, of life in the rough, of the reality-worked-into-life attaching to the old festivities. I am speaking of joy ("die Freude"). All that is spiritual is made of joy. What I am saying is that without such means as dance and music a really chosen and really real life is not possible. The opportunity that I am speaking of makes me shudder perceiving it. It devours all, admits of no superfluity, disallows Bach and Beethoven, Luther and Rilke, permits only one thing, the Whole, the Something in which all the mercies of old might come to life again. (I am not saying to stop reading Rilke, not to listen to Bach anymore.) The art of folklore now achievable by us, the great improvisation, has no need to borrow from the past. But it has a thousand relationships of love, it knows the oldest times. It comes from the place in which at any time a melody has been meaningful.

The manifesto, the imperative, that follows from this goes like this:

Forget the notes. Don't waste your hearing on training. Get together, three or four of you, and make the music, whether with chairs and mugs and spoons or with fiddles and flutes, let the structures come into being, absolve your service to the world made out of sound, make a mess, hear fugues, do nothing, hear the littlest units. There can be no other relationship to music any more than this: to lower it to the status of an ordinary activity. There are no longer any principles of selection, no limits, no scales. Only the moral criterion of utilizability is left us, the challenge to find a music intensifying and sanctifying all that is heard. For we are now making a useful music, a music whose order is the order of music, a music for the new world.

It is as of now possible to create something that will console for centuries of specialist art, centuries in which the highest human power was as though in waste guided into side channels, centuries of proud professional idiocy, centuries of human dilletantism. We can now do for real what has been made in pictures for the pictures only, we can now actually live expressionism: which was only a revolution useful to art dealers and art critics. We are dancers. We are expressionists. We are Christians, pagans, Buddhists, Jews, everything, we live the oldest life. We don't need the categories of history. Creativity is not to be found at the universities nor in the Heideggers, Adornos and Picassos. We all stem from countries and communities that have never yet dared live with their demons. We unleash our spirits.'

(Schumann, *The Dance of Death*... Translation by S. Brecht.)

The manifesto indicates, I would say, what Schumann over the years has aimed at. A modern equivalent of pre-rococo Christian church art. But he didn't make it. The movies and jazz have come as close to such an unselfconscious folk art as anything, but they come under what he refers to as 'eine dem Arbeiterstand die Mussezeit aufhellende Muse', a muse putting some light into the leisure time of the working classes. Schumann would probably deny they were the 'Praxis eines ... geistigen echten Lebens', the practice of an authentic spiritual life ('authentic' being, incidentally, a Heideggerian term criticized by Adorno), as also that they 'satisfy the hunger of the starving' or promote the 'elimination of evils', that they 'help the world.'

Schumann's art has diverged from what the manifesto called for by its reliance on the archaic folk art medium of puppetry and medieval forms of drama, and on Christian iconography: in effect, if not by intention, requiring the spectator to make allowance for these forms as devices, and making his own response to contemporary life indirect and artful because of his reliance on them.

What Schumann is here responding to is the work of Tyler's Alchemy Players and their music in particular (and probably also their dancing in Putney): an art that is 'necessary' in being an 'ordinary' man's unalloyedly genuine response to the life of his age. His own work in dance up to the New York *Totentanz* on the other hand would probably be art of the sort that 'always' 'also' is meant by the word 'art' and that the *Manifesto* rejects: 'the already pacified result: the work of art, thing wrapped by tradition in love and caught for the sake of a particular and exclusively personal function, in which every historian divines a value that is absurd because never radiated into reality.' He was in the sequel, with Charlie Adams' help to try for that ordinary man's genuine response in his music. But though his puppetry turned out consistently a genuine response to his age: whether it can relevantly be viewed as an ordinary man's response, even once we have made allowance for the fact that an ordinary man has to be alienated, talented and has to have an altogether unusual personality to respond to his age genuinely, seems doubtful to me. But the art of Tyler's group (and much of Afro-American music) and Tyler's own art as print-maker can probably be described in these terms.

9. Vermont interlude, summer '62-spring '63. Putney School. Schumann after an 18-year pause takes up puppetry again. The shows.

A former Russian teacher of Elka's having recommended her as her sabbatical replacement, 1962/3, at Putney School, Putney, Vt., Elka's old prep school, and Elka having been hired sometime in the spring of '62, and having signed up for post-graduate work at Wyndham College, Putney for part of the summer of '62, her father giving her the money for the tuition and probably more besides, the Schumanns moved up to Putney, 'into a nice little country house, a farm house on the side of the road' (Elka, interview) provided by the school — the first decent housing of their own — sometime in the late spring or early summer of '62, Schumann going up ahead to fix it up — he painted the curtains (later using them in a show, *The Story of the World*). The idea was that Schumann was to mind the kids, do the cooking. He applied for the job of a dance teacher at the school, but didn't get it, either somebody had seen *Totentanz* in New York, or they didn't decide on his appointment till after they had seen it in Putney in September, and 'they definitely didn't want that kind of dance there' — (Elka, interview).[1]

They already had a sculpture and an art teacher. But he was hired to be in charge of puppetry 'activities,' two or three evenings a week for an hour or an hour and a half. And he got a job as art instructor at a local private grammar school. One doesn't get the impression that he was fleeing New York, or even the horrors of East 4th Street, but rather that he was leaving it reluctantly, under the force of economic necessity, and under the stern gaze of his in-laws, worried about their daughter.

If he was turned down as dance teacher in the fall, that summer's puppeteering (cf. infra) would have prompted him to offer doing puppetry with the kids and his turn to puppeteering would have been independent of this. If, as seems more likely, the matter was decided in the spring, puppeteering would have occurred to him as something to do at the school, his turn to it inspired by his desire to have something official to do

---

1. 'The *Dance of Death* was a bad introduction to Putney School where they wanted a Dance of Life. I was proposing to them, well, while my wife teaches Russian I might as well teach dance and my introduction to that was that I invited all the Alchemy Players up there and we performed the *Dance of Death* and sent them all screaming and it ended up with a big fire in the middle of this, and a lot of smoke and everybody coughing, and everybody — the teachers were all very upset. I guess the students enjoyed it. I didn't get the dance teacher job (they hired a nice girl from Bennington to do that).' — (Schumann, interview, '79.)

up there and earn a little pocket money. This latter is more likely.[2] What made him think of it was probably less the use of masks in *Totentanz* than that it was something appropriate for kids. He may even have thought of it as a marketable profession. Basically, I would say, he had realized that as he had not the gifts of a great dancer or choreographer, he did not have those of a great sculptor either.

He started making puppets — and not hand puppets but rod puppets, which he hadn't used before, nor, it seems even seen — right away when he got to Putney, and then used them in August — August 17 — in Woodstock, New York, at something called the 'Ergo Suits Artists' Carnival', at least two of them: the Red Man or 'The Pointer' and the Blue Man and his Son, a double puppet, above the traditional hand puppet curtain in a play called *Burning Towns*, his first puppetry show, repeated August 31 and September 2 in New York City at the Judson Memorial Church and later that year, November 10, at the Living Theatre, at 14th Street and Sixth Avenue, in a production which the *Village Voice* (November 8, '62) announced as an Alchemy Players' 'dance production with life-size puppets at 10 p.m. and midnight'. As we have seen, Tyler's people refused to be the German martinet's puppets, and just contributed music, so that, as Tyler remembers it (confusing, however, this production with a *Fire* done later that year, in December, also at the Living Theatre), Schumann had some 'Putney Puppet Theatre' people — 'Jan, Ann and Jon' — with one Bill Mallory, and with a new German associate, Bruno Eckhardt,[3] for performers. Schumann now remembers nothing about *Burning Towns* (except that it did not relate to Grooms' *Burning Building*, which he hadn't seen), and Tyler only that (in its November presentation) it had a 'sausage machine' in it, making sausages out of (puppet) people. Schumann (interview, '82) thinks this may have been an independent little skit, *The Sausage Machine*, the machine being a 'cardboard box with a crank on it — some kind of machine parts painted on it — I think little puppets were stuffed into it and coming out as sausages' (ibid.), probably an image for cannon fodder. Bruno Eckhardt, Schumann's first associate in the U.S., remembers (Eckhardt, interview) doing a predecessor of the two later *King Stories* (*The Great King and the Mosquito, The Great King Makes*

---

2. 'I think the puppetry was sort of out of the blue. He thought, rather than be there and just babysit or just do his private art here this was — as far as the salary goes it was very minimal — the teachers who ran the activities in the evening were on very — that was a very low salary so he wasn't doing it because it would really bring in a lot of money, but it was like he was doing something with people, with students who were available and there weren't many there. I think at first there were maybe eight or ten were in his group. Some dropped out.' — (Elka, interview.)

3. During the winter of '61/'62, the Schumanns had occupied #10 rear of 330 E.4th St., and Eckhardt, his wife Eva and their son Benny, #2 rear. The two fathers met (Elka, letter, June '82) taking their offspring to the Houston Street playground. Eckhardt and Eva became members of Schumann's first troupe in the fall of '63.

War) with Schumann in Woodstock.[4] I suspect this was *Burning Towns*. Apparently it was a far cruder and far more violent image of war, beset by reminiscences of the Third Reich, than the later *King Story* versions: the puppets delimiting the playing area are finished off by a shot in the back of the head, kicked into the dirt.

---

4. 'There were three *King Stories*. Some of them had quite a bit of mask play in them – not just puppets.... There was a bunch of masks that were cardboard boxes, painted faces and arms of players were sticking out, and a mask on top of the cardboard box. And then there were sword fights between two such cardboard boxes.' (Schumann, interview, December '82.) But whether there was such a 'carton puppet' *King Story* or not, there was a third and original one – perhaps called '*Burning Towns*' – played in Woodstock that summer and remembered by Bruno Eckhardt:

'Ja, das war 'ne schöne Zeit, da war'n wir noch gut zusammen. Und das war, ich bin da, ich bin da ganz drin aufgegangen. So, so, die, diese Genickschusszene, mit dem, mit dem, wo die Masken gekillt werden, die haben wir in.... Um unseren Spielplatz, hier war der Vorhang mit den Puppen und Peter und ich wir haben den Krieg gespielt. Und um diesen Platz waren Masken in den Boden gesteckt. Die begrenzten also praktisch unsern Spielraum. Und nach dieser sehr gewalttätigen Szene, wir waren beide damals gut trainiert, der Peter war sowieso ziemlich sportlich, da haben wir, da haben wir mit, auch mit unserer körperlichen Leistung ganz schönen Eindruck gemacht. Um, um irgendwann hochzubringen, was den Leuten dort gar nicht bewusst war. Die Leuten wussten nicht, was Krieg ist. Das'n Comic-Strip (...) Und ich bin dann hinterher rumgegangen und hab die, diese Puppet mit Genickschuss erledigt. Das war, das sah grausig aus. So 'ne dicke Wumme, das knallte auch laut und dann, bei jedem Schuss und Tritt, nicht, und dann flog die Maske in 'n Dreck. Und das war so, so, dat hat sich dieser komische Clown da, bin ja nie mit dem klar gekommen, der der ist ja jetzt in diesem Business ist irgendwie ... Muppet – Kollege (I: ja, ja (...) heisst der) Ne, is'n andrer ... Henson, Jim Henson, der hat sich damals furchtbar aufgeregt darüber. Weil, weil der Henson, der ist jüdisch und wir waren Deutsche. Und dann hat er, dann hat er uns gesagt, wir wären Faschisten und er könnte sich mit dem, mit dem Widersacher (?) überhaupt nicht zufrieden geben. Das wär 'ne Schweinerei und Unverschämtheit. Naja und da haben wir uns lang mit dem unterhalten ... Dat war (...) auch die beste *Kingstory*. Also wir hatten mehrere *Kingstories*. Wir haben komischerweise, wir haben diese *Kingstory* hinterher, soviel ich mich erinnern kann, haben wir die in dieser Form nicht mehr gespielt. Die war lustig, wir haben dann hauptsächlich die letzten, die zwei gespielt, *der König und die Fliege* und dann *Kingstory* und *der grosse Krieger*. Das war ungefähr so (...), 'ne Veränderung der ersten *Königsgeschichte*, so, nicht. Die war'n bisschen poetischer, aber mir hat die Anfängliche besser gefallen.... Ich hab das erste Lied, ich hab das erste Lied im Theater gebracht. Und dat war, dat war die Soldaten-Story. Ich weiss jetzt den Zusammenhang nicht mehr, wie dat alles so gelaufen ist. Auf alle Fälle, der Peter, der kam aus Putney und hatte diese wunderschöne dreiköpfige Soldatenpuppe und dann hatten wir 'ne Pappkanone, es gab noch andre Puppen, natürlich, die People war auch immer da, nicht, also der Leute waren natürlich auch immer da. Und dann haben wir und dann haben wir dieses Stück, dieses Soldatenstück ... das war vor der *Kingstory*. Dann haben wir im, in Woodstock zum ersten Mal, da auf diesem, da war so'n Künstlerfestival da haben wir dat aufgeführt und da hab ich dieses saublöde Lied mitreingebracht:

        Heiliger Maria und Joseph
        Wenn wir am Rhein marschiern

Kenn sie dat nicht? Heidi heido heida.... Heidi heido heida, ein Müll, also, dat haben die Truppen immer gegröhlt, wenn die hier durchmarschiert sind. Und dat hat eine ungeheuer penetrant faschistische Aussage, kriegt man wirklich Angst, ja, und wir haben dat so

To judge from Moore's photos, the Woodstock summer *Burning Towns* combined the play of puppets of radically diverse sizes above a curtain, in sophisticated compositions, and with an apparent tendency for the puppets to burst out from their curtain-delimited proper sphere of existence behind the curtain into the space of seeing (not quite, perhaps, as far as one can judge from Moore's photos, the audience's space) between audience and curtain, with music and stylized narrative play by mummers in that space in front of the curtain (or off to one side and around it), and with savantly primitive displays of written titles and naive pictures on the curtain and in the air. The combination is achieved with an ostentatious lack of neatness, but with extreme care, notably as to relative placements. The mode of composition we might metaphorically say is centrifugality limited by central attraction: the contained explosion characteristic of our age: rather than placement within a contained space or area, whether contained materially or within a frame, suggested by a composition; and rather than, also, geometric arrangement (the classic symmetries, diagonals, unitary perspectives). The puppetry in these photos figures as only one of the elements of the theatrical event. The diversity of the puppets and their 'dynamic' relationships echo the diversity of the elements and *their* 'dynamic' relationships. The ostentatious lack of neatness is alienatory (verfremdend) and incites to creative apprehension.

Returned, in early September, from the Judson *Burning Towns*, to Putney, he started working with the kids, and as first product of this work, early on in October, for the Fall Foliage Festival offered the first of his shows to bear the name of *Fire*,[5] and in December, this time in an

---

gemacht und ich hab dem Peter dat auch irgenwie erklärt, wie ich das gesehen hab, in diesem scheppernden stampfenden Gleichschritt, wenn die Kompanien zum Schiessstand bei uns, bei uns war gleich 'n Schiessstand, ich wohnte so am Waldrand, so'n bisschen da, dann kamen die angedonnert und haben dieses Lied einem in die Ohren gestampft, das hab ich ja nie vergessen. Und dat sollte dann der ständige Begleiter werden. Ich hab das manchmal gehasst, ja, mir wurd manchmal kotzübel, aber dat war drin, dat war in der Show drin, dat hat auf die Leute 'ne ungeheure Wirkung gehabt.' — (Erkhardt, interview.)

5. Bob Ernstthal, an associate of Schumann's the following summer, in '79, partly guessing, partly drawing on recollections of impressions Schumann gave him in the summer and fall of '63, surmises that this first *Fire* encapsulated a lasting theme of Schumann's work, the sudden destructive descent of war on a peaceful, even idyllic and rural community and was derived from traumatic childhood memories of this sort, and that a figure in it, the Red Man, represented an unheeded warner like Schumann's later Chicken Little, and represented Schumann himself (in his puppeteering activity): 'The Red Man was used as the Fireman and it was something about fire in the town. In fact, I think he had little fire trucks and bells ringing, going through the village ... "There's a fire! There's a fire!"' — (Ernstthal, interview.)

If Ernstthal were right, the '62 *Fire* would probably have been the first presentation of Schumann's dominant theme: war on civilians by fire from the air. But this was at any rate not the play's ostensible topic:

attempt to get as many kids as possible in the grammar school involved, with them did a nativity show, like his later ones called *The Christmas Story*,[6] the first of his public celebrations of Christmas.

Whether doing a nativity play – a Medieval genre – in the XXth century accorded with his manifesto of earlier that year seems debatable. It

---

'It was simply about fire. About the excuses people have for not extinguishing fire. That was the first part of it, and then powers of fire, and then helping hands that extinguish fire. Sort of these ideas. The Fireman was really fire – was the representative of fire itself. And the warning was done by a pair of hands. There was a puppet that just consisted of hands, or they were a bunch of hands – the show ended with hands. It wasn't a curtain show only, it was a curtain show and then there was a wheelbarrow and somebody was wheeled around in a wheelbarrow in it, so there was a parade part of it somewhere inside the show. Things were carried away and brought back.' — (Schumann, interview, '82.)

'A show about all kinds of different puppets trying to – to extinguish a fire, and then they couldn't, and then a big pair of hands came out, and, I think, showed them, sort of, like that. But (the) wheelbarrow, and various things that I don't recall. There was lots of text in it, talking in it. It was a puppet show played behind a curtain like the *King Story*, because that's the style of puppet that I built for it, but there was at least a narrator outside, with a drum, plus there definitely was a parade away from the stage and back to it. I believe it was the Rattle Dragon that sat on the wheelbarrow. We had a dragon with beer cans or lids or something like that.' — (Schumann, interview, '79.)

'It didn't have a logical plot or – it was outdoors. It was (done) over a curtain, I think, (with) these wire puppets. It was short and lively and had a connection. (I: Was it about war?) It was (about) threat, a threat, so I think it could have been war.' — (Elka, interview.)

6. 'They had hired a new guy to be the director of that grammar school and I was on good terms with him and he actually helped me operate puppets in some of the (Putney School (SSB)) Sunday events and some of the children had worked with me sometimes, so I got the whole school involved. I made the *Christmas Story* with the whole school – all the kids in that school – there may have been some, I don't know, forty kids, something like that. Thirty or forty kids took part in it then and it sort of ended up like the basic first draft to the *Christmas Story* that later on I ended up doing a lot in New York.' — (Schumann, interview, '79.)

'It was not at all a puppet show, it was a big project, with many, many kids. With singing and with a chorus dressed in white, as angels, singing and with kids performing parts. It was not a puppet show. There were some puppets used, probably, but not much at all. There were masks used.' — (Schumann, interview, '82.)

'... was first performed with 40 children, Christmas 1962, at Putney School, Vermont. The play was never written down. It developed out of rehearsals when the old Christmas story was reenacted with the use of everything we could lay our hands on: puppets, costumes, pipes, drums, milk crates, candles...' — (Advertisement for the '65 *Christmas Story, Village Voice*, December 23, '65.)

'There were masks used ... for the shepherds, little hand puppets for the people of Jerusalem ... the "Big Mask" for King Herod. Donkey and cow were already there. I think they were – well, I'm not sure, I think they were wall puppets but not little ones; ... operated above the curtain on sticks ... Mary and Joseph were two kids, they did not wear masks, they were in front of the stage. (Elka: They were played the same as they were later in New York, by the kids?) Yeah. Later on I made masks for them and they performed with masks. I made little hand puppets especially for that – with the kids ... The angel was a hand puppet.' — (Schumann, interview, '79.)

would be consistent, if it sprung on the part of all participants from still alive feelings connected with the images. There is room for doubt here.

Schumann had been in New York in November for *Burning Towns*. During the Christmas recess, he again nipped down to the big city and, continuing his association with the Living Theatre – apparently congenial to him, a flyer of his of January '63 refers to them as the Loving Theatre – he did (Thursday and Friday, December 20 and 21) a *Christmas Story* at their Sixth Avenue loft. It was 'very different' (Schumann, interview, '79) from the one at Putney,[7] and was 'performed with kids of friends of mine, and a few other people, I can't recall who. The only people in the audience were Elka's mother and a friend of hers.' — (Schumann, interview, '79.)

He followed this up at the end of December by another show at the Living Theatre, one which in its reprise immediately afterwards, January 2-7, '63, at the Judson Church, was called *A Festival of Puppets*,[8] and

---

7. Presumably, not as regards the story, but in that while the Putney show was done by several dozen costumed small kids and had a lot of singing and music in it, the Living Theatre one was done as puppet show, with a few puppeteers and two small kids, with at most a little '(pipe blowing' on the 'Peace Organ' (cf. infra) for music – above a curtain, with mostly only Mary and Joseph – done, without masks, by the two kids (Schumann, interview, '79) in front of it, 'walking through the aisles and going to sleep and coming back, etc.' (Schumann, interview, '82), partly with hand puppets, e.g. for the people of Nazareth, and apparently for the annunciatory angel, partly with the new kind of puppets Schumann had been making at Putney, rod puppets, e.g. Herod's three comic red-nosed soldiers on one stick, or by puppets functioning pretty much or wholly as such rod puppets, but having older masks for their heads, e.g. the Herod puppet who came 'bouncing over in front of the curtain, . . . a horror, fast moving and shouting' (ibid.) and whose head was the 'big mask' from *Totentanz*. And there were also 'wall' or cutout puppets, operated above the curtain 'on sticks.' (Schumann, interview, '79.) He says (ibid.) 'masks were used for the shepherds.' I don't think his memory is too reliable about any of this.

'I wanted to do shows that made sense and it seemed that to make a show for the customers that existed would make sense. So when I came to New York to do that *Christmas Story* I remember the biggest part of that *Christmas Story* was that about an hour before the performance I started the advertising for it. So I had a cardboard box that was painted as a Madonna and my arms stuck out on the side, and I had a mask – a Madonna mask in the cutout where my face was, and I walked around and announced the show – up and down 14th Street, around that area, and tried to get people to come into the – that was the nicest part of the performance as I recall, because it was very difficult and very exciting and very – without any results, because we ended up performing with one or two people in the audience, and the performers were never there on time. We often had to replace somebody immediately and had to play the donkey and Joseph together or some ridiculous – some ridiculous way – slipped on one costume and did that for a while and then put on the other one. (I: Were the Innocents massacred at the Living Theatre or were they saved by any –?) I think in the original versions they were massacred and then in the later *Christmas Story* that was stopped.' — (Schumann, interview, '82.)

8. Schumann in '82 calls these shows 'very messy assemblages of drawings and puppets – pretty wild happenings of short little sketches that quickly found a title. The title was put on there and then performed, so they probably changed pretty fast, from one performance to another.' This makes the titles unreliable guides to what he did. Bruno Eckhardt performed with him in the shows.

comprised items entitled *The Ceremony of the Things*, 'done in the Hall of Issues, and then ended up with something like a parade out into the street. It was about objects,' (Schumann, interview, '79), *The Story About the Great Man* (possibly *King Story II* or *III*), *The Battle* (probably a 'crankie'), *Fire* (adapted from the autumn Putney *Fire?*), *The Cow*, and *One Story About Everybody, Starting With Breakfast* (probably a '*Mr. Miller Story*', cf. infra). He remembers also at the Living Theatre doing something called *The Peace Organ*.

'I had found an old organ in Vermont that I had brought to New York – all the pipes of an organ – and I played them like a concert, conducting, seating people like organ pipes, blowing them, and then conducting them – which ones blew. It was probably just part of a show, and I can't tell if it was part of *The Christmas Story* or part of other events.' (Schumann, interview, '79.)

'The Living Theatre was on 14th Street at Sixth Avenue, upstairs in that old department store. A marvelous theatrical setup. And they had Monday nights for free. The first time I saw Peter was during the Christmas season and he had the most incredible and beautiful thing, I don't know if anybody's ever seen it, and may have, but it was a Baroque organ in which he pulled out stops and the stops would be little angels and would be human beings and it was really marvellous. It took up the entire stage of the Living Theatre. He had built it and it was a Dresden-like – quite beautiful, quite elegant. And as I recall, gold and pink and very – (And his troupe) sang the *Hallelujah Chorus* and they sang German Christmas songs. They were angels, and they were organists and they were musicians.'
(Bissinger, interview.)

This 'puppet festival' was billed as 'produced by the People Puppet Theater,' not, like *Burning Towns* had been, by the Putney Puppet Players.

Moore's photos of the Judson 'Puppet Festival' show combat in free space, not by puppets above or even in front of a curtain – between masked performers (the photo in which Schumann's face shows may show him just after the end of the play) in what Schumann later views as puppet costume: torso-enclosing carton boxes with painting on them, in an early version of *King Story, King Story III*. Schumann seems to have advanced considerably toward his subsequent form of theatre: from hand puppets toward, as he at this time called them, 'live puppets.' Decor and costumes are still very 'modern,' but now not in the expressionist but rather in the Dadaist-Surrealist tradition. Schumann's subsequent work can hardly be considered in this tradition – he rather systematically avoids the 'modern.'

At Putney that winter, Schumann would do puppet shows in their living room, their puppets mostly perhaps made by himself, and the shows put on by himself, though often also with the help of the kids in his 'activities' sessions, and of kids in Elka's Russian classes, 'taking pity with such beautiful enterprises and to help out.' (Schumann, interview, '79): mostly hand puppet shows above the curtain, but also using his new rod or wire puppets. Many or most of these *Putney Puppet Tales* were *Mr. Miller Stories*, where Mr. Miller is Everyman, but the stories are lyrical rather

than didactic or moralistic (Elka: 'like Sufi stories, like Hassidic, like Baal-shem Tov stories, that had no point, or, or, – I was furious (laughs) . . . they didn't make sense') (interview, '79),[9] and Mr. Miller is not the only one in them, there is Mrs. Miller, the Blue Murderer, the Peace Angel, the Leprechaun, a 4- or 6-armed witch, puppets he had first used in *Fire*, . . . But he also did small-scale versions of his *King Stories*, *The Great King and the Mosquito*, later called *King Story II*, and *The Great King Makes War*, later called *King Story III*, of *Fire*, of the *Ceremony of the Things*, of something called *Genesis*. To the extent he could get invitations, the students were willing to come along as performers, and the school authorities would allow them to, he performed some of these shows and combinations of them at some of the Ivy League schools, Bennington, Goddard, Harvard, Dartmouth. He was also making 'crankies': series of black drawings on paper scrolls illustrating the accompanying narration of a story when unwound: *The Battle, Rinaldini the Beautiful*; and linoleum-cut *Mr. Miller Story* comic books:

An exhibition, March 13-30 ('63) of drawings and 'textile posters' of his at the Harvard College Adams House on the Charles River gold coast led to a free Adams House presentation, April 13th, by him and 'The Putney School Puppet Theater', of a show he called *The Story of the World*, made up of *Putney Puppet Tales* and, probably some new material:

'This past Saturday the Adams House dining room was the scene of the most unusual and for some of us the most exciting theater experience of the Harvard season. It is hard to find an accurate label for the performance: it broke through customary genres and divisions of character, audience and artist, in a strange melange of myth, symbolism, sermon, dance and music. Its creator, Peter Schumann, calls it The Live Puppet Theater, but to call it a puppet show hardly gives an idea of the drama's sophistication and variety.

. . . Most Adams House members will remember his recent exhibit of graphics and charcoals in the lower common room and the small dining room. The performance and the exhibit have, indeed, elements in common, but of the performance first . . .

A large eyeless gold head and equally large gold hand appeared in the spotlight

---

9. 'Mr. Miller was – that, I thought was his father, looking back – the same as Mr. Good Man. And that's kind of like those – the Everyman theme, the Good Man motif. Mr. Miller; this is his wife, this is his daughter, Mr. Miller goes for a walk, Mr. Miller breaks bread. It was like a proto-version of Everyman type of story. And there were often some of those little books, the linoleum cuts and stuff and the man sits down at the table, the man eats his dinner, the man goes to sleep, the man dreams of sheep, the man wakes up. That kind of thing. The Mr. Miller Stories were – as I remember, there was a crankie, I believe a crankie kind of movie that was Mr. Miller's movie – like that, a story, an instructional – actually it was like a Lehrstück, that kind: "Now you see Mr. Miller driving his car. He goes to his house. Here you see Mr. Miller coming and saying hello to his wife. 'Hello, wife.' 'Hello, Mr. Miller.' It was very, kind of simplistic." ' — (Ernstthal, interview.)

get up   cofee wife   bye-bye   car   office
joke   lunch joke   busy   busy busy busy
3 o'clock 4 o'clock 5 o'clock   6 o'clock   7 o'clock
dinner   feelings soup   cheese   john dessert
mary   twist   ecstasy   12 o'clock

above the low curtain that marked the "stage". It was God, surveying Chaos ... "and God went to look upon all the things that weren't there yet ... and he decided he should make something, and the first thing he made was the darkness." The light went out. "And he saw the darkness was very dark, so he created light..." Adam is created and then Eve, and God asks, "Adam, you like?" (Peter Schumann's thick accent) "She's just peachy!" answers a distinctly American puppet voice. An atmosphere of folk tale, a humor of incongruity, and an occasional gratuitous but delightful touch provided by Mr. Schumann's difficulty with English idioms.

This scene, The Creation, was followed by Production, The Banquet, The King, War, Peace, The Genius, Love, Fire, and Death. Aside from the obvious connection of the first and last scenes there does not seem to have been any logical or aesthetic order, but rather a progression of ideas. In between scenes, Mr. Schumann and his helpers produced weirdly rhythmic and strident music of a flavor between the Japanese and electronic on what after turned out to be an assortment of plastic horns, a drum, a kazoo and a Jew's harp. The puppets, their heads strongly sculptured, were handled simply, but sometimes with wit, as in the love scenes. Once, in the wordless scene of Peace, Mr. Schumann achieved a dance-like beauty with the slow and sweeping movement of his Peace-Angel. The puppeteers did not hesitate to enter the action along with the puppets: a masked actor appeared to roughly administer the royal toothbrush and breakfast to the blustering monarch-puppet, etc.

For the Banquet's surrealistic satire, the puppets were completely laid aside. In this scene the actors, in masks, talked nonsense, were silent, and devoured a plateful of balloons at whistle-blasts by toastmaster Schumann. Again, in War the actors appeared, to do a dance-mime battle in masks and cardboard armor. The triumphant warrior turns to the King, demands his reward. When he is refused, "revolution" ensues with the death of the King and his Nazi-like soldiers and the warrior assuming the King's place complete with royal toothbrush, breakfast, and puppet ministers. The sequence became a bitter allegory of contemporary history. Mr. Schumann (in a new mask) then showed a "movie" – a "documentary" as he called it, of a medieval war. It was a painted scroll worked by two cranks. The battling kings are numbered one through six, suggesting in their anonymous hard faces the cruel follies of governments ... "... Now comes the really funny part. See, the soldiers are dying. They die so gracefully, like dancers ... and the birds fly away ..." Here Mr. Schumann was at his most eloquent, drawing perhaps on the fund of his European experience. The restraint of his simple forms in the surrealistic frame of the "movie" forcefully conveyed his bitter satire of and protest against war.

The drama was not always this exciting. The second love scene was only too familiar and merely amusing. Also there were some disturbing faults in timing and gaps in the action which Mr. Schumann's asides to the audience failed to smooth over.

The Story of the World, with its starkly simple action, interplay of character and actor, and dissonant music, might be placed in the tradition of Brecht. But it is "farther out" and to enjoy it fully one must have a certain taste for an interplay of levels and genres. Some might appreciate its naivete, but not its surrealism; others its satire, but find its music repetitious or disturbing. Dave Lelyveld, certainly an intelligent observer, found the show "clever, but boring:" its best moments standing out as "potential elements of a good thing." He regretted the lack of a full dramatic development; he "started liking it, but then it just slipped away." Certainly this type of half-improvised drama depends heavily on audience unity and rapport; this rapport was sometimes noticeably missing and the unfortunately small audience was a disparate conglomeration of Friends, Tocsin, Adams House, Cambridge and faculty. Mr. Schumann himself told me afterwards that he felt the performance had been off and the audience unresponsive. This reviewer, however, was completely carried away by the strength of conception, wit and variety of the drama. For me it was a delightful and refreshing evening.

The Exhibit – a comment.

For me, Saturday's performance was a key to the art exhibit, which I had previously found puzzling. Where I had before been put off by the surface naivete of his technique, I could now see a deeply sincere primitivism, a sought-for simplicity, reducing the human drama to fundamental evocative elements – man, woman, face, chair, house, tree, sun, etc. His work is a poetry of visual symbols stripped of the picturesque, the descriptive values of the literary and photographic art of the past. Schumann's art work sometimes shows weaknesses analogous to those of his drama – excessive muddiness of tone, confused composition and excess subjectivity: when the visionary fails to move us, it becomes merely puerile; but sometimes he achieves exquisite effects, as in the strongly rhythmic composition of horses, reminiscent of pre-historic wall paintings, or that of the dying armies in the War 'movie'. In some of his longer scrolls he creates depth and spatial structure with mysteriously simple juxtapositions of light and shade, and his faces emerging from darkness sometimes equal the emotional power of the best of Käthe Kollwitz." (John Weber, Harvard's *Adams House Oak Leaf.*)

The Story of the World like much of Schumann's work subsequently is in a birth-life-death sequence borrowed from the schema heaven-world-last judgment frequent in medieval Christian iconography (in this case 'good' death replacing the last judgment), like it presents an essentially ahistorical, non-linear view of the human situation, and makes three points: (1) life is essentially very simple, no need to get pompous or profound about it, it not only can be summed up with 'child-like' simplicity, but that's the best way to present it, (2) it's not a confused mess of diverse incidents and facts, there are only a few important things that can happen to one or that one can do or that one may have to deal with, (3) these essential constituents of life divide into good ones (love, nature, art, family life) and bad ones (war, rulers, law, money, material excess), (4) the good things relate to the bad as does peace to war. To present this kind of outlook, the ordinary one, simplified and purified, requires courage of an artist. Schumann, a complicated, brooding and intelligent man, deliberately chose this outlook as what he wanted his art to present, not vice versa adapted his statement to a medium he happened into; and he chose it, because he thought it was the crucial statement for art or for his art to make, cutting out, in most of his work, both his actual dominant (I would say) view of life: that it is tragic, and even the mystery of life; and any special perspective such as all men have, dumb or clever.

The positive view of death in the concluding scene may correspond to the positive view of it apparently intended by *Totentanz*. The scenes between the opening *Genesis* and this concluding scene can be viewed as arbitrary assemblage, but he probably thought of them as representation of Life: life as relation to nature (2-4), as social/historical reality (5-10), as a personal thing (11-18).

He compounded the show out of stuff he had worked up since the preceding summer, e.g. scenes 5-7 were *The King and the Mosquito, The King Makes War*, and the *Battle* crankie.

Schumann this winter, then had decisively turned to puppet performance as his medium. Only the following winter did he arrive at his definitive form of it, a transition obscured by his insistence that he is doing traditional, albeit eclectically inter-cultural puppet theatre. By and large, that winter his puppetry was still traditional: flat and narrative. The puppeteers — setting aside the cardboard box knights and masked narrators/musicians — had not yet entered the puppets:

'We did many experiments and the experiments usually involved a puppet curtain, a few rod puppets that were operated behind it, a few hand puppets that were operated behind it, objects either held up by hand or mounted on a stick, such as chairs, boots, the towel, a piece of cardboard with something painted on it, like a sausage machine in one case, various things, balloons, plus, a narrator in front, with an instrument to either conduct a dialogue with the puppets or to narrate the show. But the narrator would also often double up as an operator of puppets, and be outside as the musician and quite often I found myself in the position even if the story was rehearsed for several people, that I performed it all by myself, jumping from behind the curtain to the front, in that fashion. All these stories: *Mr. Miller Stories, Genesis, Story of the World*, and there were many other titles, they were all in this fashion. They were done with pretty much the same set of puppets. There was a whole bunch of little hand puppets that were also involved, and then things that were painted on flat things — on cardboard and so on — that were held up and used that way, like the gun for the three soldiers, or this sausage machine I required, or, I remember, shoes, or a wig of hair to represent the ladies. (Ephraim: ... those shows were done with the Putney students?) Every show, yes, and every show was basically only performed one time, because there was so much improvisation and that could not be repeated.' (Schumann, interview, '79.)

The Story of the World.

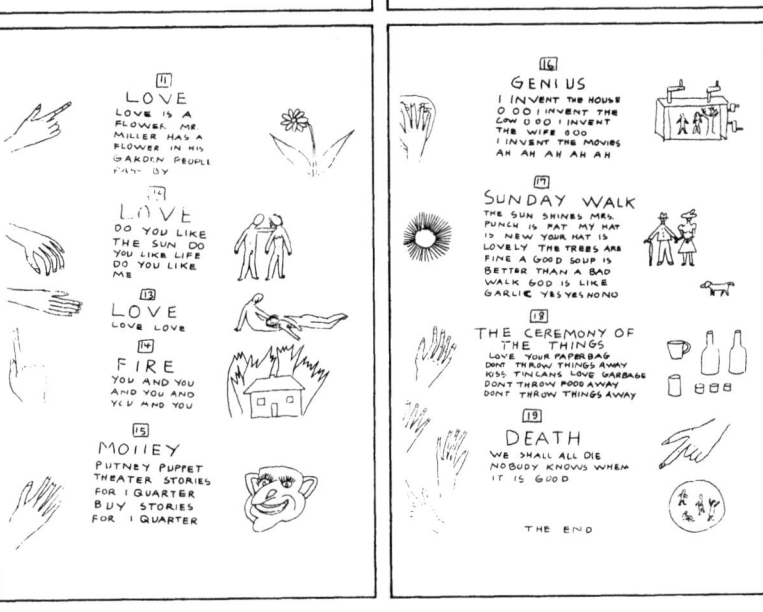

1 CREATION
GOD WAS ALONE GOD
MADE THE WORLD
GOD MADE ADAM
GOD MADE EVE
GOD MADE THE APPLE
GOD THREW ADAM
AND EVE OUT OF
PARADISE

2 PRODUCTION
APPLES APPLES APPLES
APPLES APPLES APPLES
APPLES APPLES APPLES

3 BANQUET
APPLES ARE EATEN
APPLES EXPLODE

4 WIND
SEE WIND
FEEL WIND
LISTEN TO WIND
DRINK WIND

5 KING
ROYAL SUN ROYAL
TOOTHBRUSH ROYAL
BREAKFAST ROYAL
NEWS THE KING
IS BORED
A MOSQUITO

6 WAR
ROYAL SUN ROYAL
TOOTHBRUSH ROYAL
BREAKFAST ROYAL
NEWS THE KING
IS BORED WAR

7 WAR
SWORDS CRIES
BLOOD CRIES BLOOD
SERIOUS WAR

8 LAST WAR
NO SWORDS NO
CRIES NO BLOOD NO
CRIES NO BLOOD
NO SERIOUS WAR

9 PEACE
THE SINGING
ANGEL OF PEACE

10 COURT
JUDGES
ANGEL
HANGMAN

11 LOVE
LOVE IS A
FLOWER. MR.
MILLER HAS A
FLOWER IN HIS
GARDEN PEOPLE
PASS BY

12 LOVE
DO YOU LIKE
THE SUN DO
YOU LIKE LIFE
DO YOU LIKE
ME

13 LOVE
LOVE LOVE

14 FIRE
YOU AND YOU
AND YOU AND
YOU AND YOU

15 MONEY
PUTNEY PUPPET
THEATER STORIES
FOR 1 QUARTER
BUY STORIES
FOR 1 QUARTER

16 GENIUS
I INVENT THE HOUSE
O O O I INVENT THE
COW O O O I INVENT
THE WIFE O O O
I INVENT THE MOVIES
AH AH AH AH AH

17 SUNDAY WALK
THE SUN SHINES MRS.
PUNCH IS FAT MY HAT
IS NEW YOUR HAT IS
LOVELY THE TREES ARE
FINE A GOOD SOUP IS
BETTER THAN A BAD
WALK GOD IS LIKE
GARLIC YES YES NO NO

18 THE CEREMONY OF THE THINGS
LOVE YOUR PAPER BAG
DONT THROW THINGS AWAY
KISS TIN CANS LOVE GARBAGE
DONT THROW FOOD AWAY
DONT THROW THINGS AWAY

19 DEATH
WE SHALL ALL DIE
NOBODY KNOWS WHEN
IT IS GOOD

THE END

10. Puppets, summer '62-spring '63.

Starting in the summer of '62 at Putney, in addition to making small hand puppets in the Kasperl Theater tradition (though he used string manipulation 1970 ff., he never made anything like traditional string-operated marionettes, the other popular Western tradition), he 'built' (his term) the first generation of puppets peculiar to him: paper maché wire rod puppets,[1] puppets with paper maché heads (sometimes hands), operated from the inside by twined wire. He later 'when the wire went too often and too much and kinked and broke' (Schumann, interview '87) substituted wood sticks for the wire in some or all of these puppets. Some of this puppet building may have been done during part of his twice-a-week puppetry classes, but apparently he built these puppets mostly on his own.

Rod puppets are heads on a stick or wire, normally with an additional stick or wire to move the arms or one of the arms, i.e. typically two-rod puppets, held up above the operator's head and operated from behind a curtain hiding the operator, i.e. used in the fashion of hand puppets, but much larger[2] and with larger gestures, and light enough to be held up in one hand. Ernstthal, (interview) thinks of them as Schumann's 'first tentative exploitation of puppets as moving sculpture' − as Schumann's attempt to put mobility into his German sculptures. Their heads were 'almost made from plaster casts, in the lost plaster cast fashion − thin walls which are chiselled off'. (Schumann, interview, '79.) Their typically being two-rod puppets (with separate arm movement) made them different from the 'stock' puppets − heads on sticks − that Schumann also used, e.g. the people in *King Story*. But the essential feature of the Putney rod puppets was that each by its construction was given its peculiar possibilities and restrictions of movement, i.e. characteristic gestures.[3] Though reverting to

---

1. '(Elka: Didn't you think for the longest time that you had invented the rod puppet?) Yes, you're right. I never knew of rod puppets. (Laughs.) But anyway, these were my invention of rod puppets. (Ephraim: For the *King Story?*) Mm. But actually, I've never seen rod puppets that have the rods *inside* in disguise − inside the puppet rather than − you know, a rod puppet is usually built so that the head stick is inside and then the hands are operated from outside the puppet. That's quite different.' — (Schumann, interview, '79.)
2. 'I think we would call kid-size. Which is like the size of a six-year-old child. No. In fact, I have to take that back. I have a feeling these *King Story* puppets were actually people-size. But if you take − like if you just cut yourself off at the waist and held you up, it would seem small. In other words, they were actually life-size I think, but they didn't create a life-size impression. But in style they were about . . . I think heads were about . . . probably head-size. And hands were about hand-size.' — (Ernstthal, interview.)
3. 'He was in many plays. Probably in the *Burning Towns*, also − stuff like that. I bet he was one of the chief actors in all those little shows at that time. I was very proud of that − having discovered that method: to put your hands inside a puppet. You know, to build a puppet with two rods. In the King it's the two arms coming together like this − so the

it with his animal puppets of 1974 onwards, once Schumann got into big puppets he no longer much explored this approach to construction: gesturally individuating construction.

These summer-of-'62-to-spring-of-'63 Putney rod puppets are in Schumann's mind primarily associated with their uses in either the *Mr. Miller Stories* or *King Story* but many or most were used in both at different times then, as well as in the other shows of this period, and weren't built for any particular show at all. *Birdcatcher* ('64/'65) seems the first and one of the few shows of his, all the puppets of which were built for it (Schumann, interview, '79), and not used in other shows.

The disassociation of the masks and puppets from performance — from what they do in a show — and from story, and even from character is an interesting fact about Schumann's approach. We can think of it as a way in which he remained and has remained a sculptor — a puppet or even a mask sculptor. But there are two main aspects to his shows that allow this disassociation: the figures in them are not so much psychological characters (and as such, story elements) or persons, as rather concretizations of aspects of social and of moral existence (as well as replicas of personal visions that he himself might not be able to specify the social and moral correlates of); and the stories are parables the social and moral themes or points of which to a large degree repeat from one story to another, and to the extent they are not parables they are the incidental underpinnings of serially presented personal visions, again to some considerable extent, from one to another, variants of the same few essential visions.

Stylistically, Schumann with these Putney period rod puppets seems to go in two directions away from his German sculptor's approach. Some of the puppets — generally the Mr. Miller ones — advance toward a traditional puppetry puppet style, not too far from the wooden Kasperl hand puppets: ridiculous and inoffensively grotesque personages. This line might eventually have gained him the kind of acceptance American and European puppeteers have procured in this century — even TV appearances. But

---

hands, the wire frame hands, end up in wires that bend to a joint and then are attached to a broomstick. Then the head is separate. So what you get is you get head movements separate from arm movements. You're also getting a certain amount of body movement — you can make a guy fat by contracting. By putting these — so you can make them like this and like this. It's a great variety of movements possible, but, naturally, you can't separate the hands movements and you can't — it's very limited and yet you find a lot of things like that. It was a very nice method to find. So some of these were single hand movements — like the Red Man had just the right arm, and the left arm was attached to the head rod — and some were double hand movements, like the King. (I: Well, the invention, then, was the separate connections?) What you could do with two rods inside. Yes, and how you would connect. Whether you would connect one hand to sort of make the hand still by connecting it to the head, or whether you would put it on a rod with the other hand. Every one had a specialized gesture, that way. Every puppet was specialized for one type of gesture. And I liked that a lot. That was fun.' — (Schumann, interview, December '82.)

he, immediately, as of the fall of '63, abandoned it. Some of the puppets, e.g. the Red Man, the Blue Man and his Son, the Peace Angel — generally, perhaps, the *King Story* puppets, not drawing on any puppeteering stylistic tradition I know of, but to my eye stylistically similar to primitive stone sculpture (I am thinking of Mesolithic fertility figures, of Olmec and Olmecoid, and of Bronze Age Aegean figures in stone), characterized by abstraction, severity and grandeur, point in the direction he then pursued. Along this line, he remained in the tradition of (lithic) sculpture per se.

Ernstthal (ibid.) thinks of these Putney *King Story* puppets as 'rounder' than later ones: 'In a certain way more tentative — the style hadn't solidified too much.' (ibid.) Their heads tend in fact to be elongated — narrow ovals — but they are rounded in the sense that their facial planes tend not to be accentuated. They are less 'sculptural' than either the earlier or the later puppets, and they have less expression than either the later or the earlier puppets. They are in these senses more neutral than their predecessors and followers. I think we can view them as transitional: Schumann had by now realized that sculpting heads for performances was different than sculpting heads or masks for being looked at on their own, so he was careful not to make them too interesting either as sculptured objects or as images of faces. He was going to trust movement to individuate the puppets (and built them so they could differ characteristically by movement), and wanted heads that would (as, say, in Barlach sculptures) by their shapes go nicely with gestures. But on the other hand, he had not yet fully realized, at least not for puppet-making purposes, the cardinal principle that a puppet is identified by its face, and had not yet found the solution worked out in his next generation of puppets, the non-individualizing characterization of faces by their affective moral qualities, nor had yet found a sculpturally strong shaping of the heads completed by the puppet's body and of a piece with it. The puppet bodies were still incidental to him: he thought of heads and upper limbs, which made sense for a puppet show above a curtain.[4]

---

4. Elka thinks there is no break between the styles of Schumann's German and of his American masks, that from his German days on, he has maintained two styles: an abstractive geometric and an amorphous vegetablelike one:

'In the museum there's one of the little booths downstairs has mainly the old puppets. It has Mr. Miller and Mrs. Miller. There are the *King Story* puppets from that time and I think you see a real similarity in all of them and I think it's very connected to the sculpture he did in Germany. I guess Peter has really these two styles and one of them is the very defined sort of strong, very sort of strong features, simplified planes and abstract and sort of simplified forms, and the other one is something that's much more undefined or where the form is very ... some kind of, that are almost vegetable-like. When he made these birds and fish for my parents they're these kind of — they're very big and simple shapes but not this kind of clarity and sharp edge but a kind of cloud-like feeling about them. When I think of the god faces, that golden one is something similar. It's very — and some of the disciples, which are also pretty early, have this kind of amorphous look about them. Also,

Among the wire-operated puppets made summer '62-spring '63 in Putney, Vermont, were notably: the King, the Priest, the Red Man or Fireman (the Pointer), the Blue Man and his Son, the Rattle Demon or Rattle Dragon, the Three Soldiers puppet, the People or White Faces, an Angel or Peace Angel and the Professors,[5] all primarily *King Story* puppets, and Mr. and Mrs. Miller, primarily *Mr. Miller Stories* puppets. The Millers, the Peace Angel, a Leprechaun puppet, a cymbal player with a pot lid in one hand and a metal stick in the other, and a Blue Murderer puppet, originally with a paper maché knife in one hand, later with something metallic so he could hit a gong, all were made in the summer of '62 and used in the fall of '62 *Fire* before being used in *Mr. Miller Stories*. (Schumann, interview, December '82.) A puppet with 'HELP' on its hand was made for *Fire*, but wasn't used. — (Schumann, interview, December, '82.)

---

the *Dead Man Rises* puppets, they're white and they're painted in with features but they have this undefined quality, so I don't think there was any — I wouldn't say there was a definite break or change in his things.' — (Elka, interview.)

5. '... the *King Story* puppets are made with a wire inside. This wire wrapped around maybe two or three times, around itself. Flexible steel wire. The kind that you bend – has no spring in it. Like clothes hangers, only a thicker metal. (Two or three pieces of wire) wrapped together so you could bend it – infinitely flexible – the wire could be bent. So you could move them. I mean, the King – there was always two wires. It was very clever, in fact. The King had one wire in the head and one wire that branched out into the hand. So his movement was like this. And then you could bend it. But it was still essentially this kind of movement. Head – and hands. And that was the principle. If you took (the puppet down), you could set it, and the hands would move, right? They could also move up and down because it was loose under the frame. They could move up and down. The head could move from side to side. That was the essential movement. That was the King – the one stick went to the head. And the other stick went to both hands. It was clever. The King had the two hands on one stick. The Priest had – was like this, so the Priest's movement was like this – forward from the chest and out like this. And the head was on another stick. So he could be praying or things like that. The Red Man was the pointer. He had one hand sewn into the garment like this, that was immovable. He had a head stick and this long pointy finger. So he had one hand, but it could really do stuff. Gesture – two sticks. One was the head and one was this long pointy finger. The Red Man – with the pointy head – it was all very raw. There was no shoulder or anything fancy. Just wire. But it was good because he had this one hand and he could do lots of movement with it because it was on one stick. So the Red Man was a pointer. He was like a *Fire* figure, in fact. Like that's where he started, as a *Fire* figure. A fireman. He was red. He was red faced. The Blue Man and his Son was a big and a small blue head and a blue bag. And they each had a stick, so they didn't have any hands. But they could move together and apart – a technique which was used later in some of the *Crucifixion* puppets – the big ones. (Ernstthal probably means the disciple puppets made in the fall of '63 and used in the spring of '64 *Easter Story* and in other things also (SSB)). There was one puppet that was two people together. It was actually very tender. It was a nice movement, because they would kind of rub heads together and they could gesture and stuff together. It was a man and his son in this one puppet. And the Demon was an arc of wire with a demon head. Demonic head. This was the puppets in the beginning. And he was attached all around with the lids of cans

The Red Man, Ernstthal thinks, was used in the Putney *Fire* as Fireman. He '... was red-headed and he had kind of an elongated or rounded face.' — (ibid.):

'It was a pointer. It was the pointing figure — it was a gesture of panic. In a certain way it was like a panic. The mask was more serene but the hand was a very — a pointer — pointing like: "Get out!" It was like a — it was the *Fire* imagery. It was the imagery of alarm. "Alarm! Sound the cry!" That's how I remember it being described — like I said, as the Fireman. He used to refer to it as the Fireman, and it was a great gesture — do you know the Leonardo painting of St. John the Baptist? It was that same gesture, actually. It's one of my favorite paintings and it had the same quality, because the hand was on this long stick, but it could also be kind of curved and turned like that — the same way — and usually at his death, when the death blow was struck, it would go up like that and point up and then cross. It was a very good puppet — I mean, it was a really expressive puppet. The face was serene. It was (a) life-size (puppet).'

Its left arm was sewn to his head. The Professors, hand puppets with gnarled, lumpy heads and huge black-rimmed eyeglasses, appeared, arguing, in *Burning Towns* as well as, later, in *King Story*. They are reasonably realistic caricatures of Gymnasium teachers: serious, worried, salaried.

The White Faces — 'white masks on sticks' (Ernstthal, interview, '79), may, Ernstthal thinks (ibid.), have been among Schumann's first Putney experiments. He seems (ibid.) to think of them as developments of *Totentanz* death masks. They were the People of *King Story*. They never had any clothes.

The Three Soldiers (Elka, Schumann interview, '79): 'little funny soldiers with red noses' were 'three heads with a burlap body. Three heads like — actually Brechtian style' — (Ernstthal, interview, '79):

'They very much — that was the only thing that was specifically Brechtian I ever

---

— can lids, so you could play him like this. (The can lids were) attached to the wire. It would rattle — it was a rattle demon kind of — and you could play him with two hands. It was just an arc. And they could move and go forward and backward and — rraaaah, like that. It was a loud noise attached to it. There was a big fight and the cannon and they (the soldiers, the cannon, the dragon (SSB)) were chasing from one side to the other, back and forth, and they shoot the dragon and it goes "ahhghghghgh" and it would rattle — death rattle. It was almost like an oriental kind of dragon or rattle demon — that kind of thing. (I: What is the impression he gave?) Noise. And a big stickout tongue and a kind of a jumping around demonic being. Not like a dragon. More like a rattle demon of the Far East or some kind of snake — witch doctor's cure — kind of character. You know what I mean? Noise and a mask and ahhh — like that, and making lots and lots of noise. And the people were all afraid of it because it was so noisy and so wild that it would — the movement was like this, and like this, so the thing really moved and it was very scary. In fact, even then, I mean, kids would back away. That was always like true. Kids were always terrified of these things. It was just scary. It was very noisy and it looked very demonic. (And) three-headed soldiers.' — (Ernstthal, interview, '79.)

remember. It was the hats. They had those kind of funny like Galy Gay World I doughboy hat. They were three-headed and they had these flat World War I hats. Not World War II, but flat.' — (ibid.)

With their frog mouths and button noses, the soldiers were funny — simpletons — rather than gruesome (dumbness remained a characteristic of Schumann's soldier puppets, but it got gruesome). This was a primitive puppet, a stick puppet, operated with one stick. A cardboard gun was used with them.

The head of the Rattle Demon or Rattle Dragon apparently was used as the narrator's mask when Schumann and Ernstthal '63-'65 agitated with the *Rat Movie* on the streets of the Lower East Side. In indoor shows, he was 'mostly' used in front of the curtain. The performer held him and danced with him.' — (Schumann, interview, '82.)

The King (of *King Story*) — 'a *very* peculiar looking king, to tell you the truth, he had bumps and he had these like horn things and funny jangly cloth hanging from the neck. It was a peculiar — totally peculiar king.' — (Ernstthal, interview, '79.)

'He was in many plays. Probably in the *Burning Towns*, also, stuff like that I bet he was one of the chief actors in all those little shows at that time. I was very proud of that — having discovered that method: to put your hands inside a puppet. You know, to build a puppet with two rods. In the King it's the two arms coming together like this — so the hands, the wire frame hands, end up in wires that bend to a joint and then are attached to a broomstick. Then the head is separate. So what you get is you get head movements separate from arm movements. You're also getting a certain amount of body movement. You can make the guy fat by contracting. By putting these — so you can make them like this and like this. It's a great variety of movements possible, but, naturally, you can't separate the hand movements and you can't — it's very limited and yet you find a lot of things in that. It was a very nice method to find. So some of these were single hand movements — like the Red Man had just the right arm, and the left arm was attached to the head rod — and some were double hand movements, like the King. (I: Well, the invention, then, was the separate connections?) What you could do with two rods inside. Yes, and how you would connect. Whether you would connect one hand to sort of make the hand still by connecting it to the head, or whether you would put it on a rod with the other hand. Every one had a specialized gesture, that way. Every puppet was specialized for one type of gesture and I liked that a lot. That was fun.' (Schumann, interview, December '82.)

The *Mr. Miller* puppets apparently were technically along the lines of the *King Story* ones — rod puppets — though stylistically more in the 'funny' Kasperl hand puppet tradition, but not endearing.

Mr. Miller seemed 'stuffed' (Schumann, interview, '79) 'because the arms were on a horizontal rod held up by an upright rod' (ibid.). He was a 'fat, stuffed puppet with big fat working gloves, stuffed working gloves, and long, horizontal wire that was curved around — that made him look very *big* – and had a big nose, big ears, a red face, bald-headed, and he became the hero of many little puppet shows that I did.' – (ibid.):

'... a kind of an Everyman. An all-round, multi-purpose character who could go through any fllimsy story. The idea was to make many stories and to have one character who went through them, and he was the guy. Mr. Miller was an arbitrary choice ... Mr. Miller never had a character. He – yeah, he did, in some stories, but he lost it for another story. So that wasn't very consistent. He was a fatso, you know – fattish. He was played, mostly, without his body. If you can imagine the rod and just the head and then big, fat arms leaning over, and sort of leaning – like somebody leaning in the window sill that's a bit too high. That kind of appearance – that was his major way of –'

(Schumann, interview, December '82.)

Whereas Mr. Miller had those dumb black hands, Mrs. Miller, *extremely* ugly, hardly human, with her coxcomb hair and big protruding eyeballs, had witch- or bird-like four-fingered spindly paper maché hands on sleeves that the operator slipped over his arms (Schumann, interview, '82). She ... 'had yellow hair, big bulgy eyes and a little white collar, a little bit like the collar of a judge, sort of gathered, ruffled fabric around her neck, and very ugly hands.' (Schumann, interview, '79.) Like Mr. Miller, she was a two-rod puppet.

Of hand puppets, Ernstthal remembers the two Johnny and Susan puppets of their *Johnny and Susan* summer '63 show: the former 'looked a little like Peter. Kind of broad in the bottom – it was triangular-shaped, and a big nose' – apparently a one-finger part of this puppet show was a dog that would bark and bother Johnny and be pushed away. There was also a puppet for Susan's father. Ernstthal thinks the hand puppets later used in the Delancey Street Bread and Puppet Museum *Fairy Tales*, e.g. a fisherman, had been made in Putney, seeing as how Schumann later was no longer interested in making hand puppets, 'paper maché, in fact half-masks, made over a little clay form and then hair or cloth put over the back of them.' — (Ernstthal, interview. '79.)

Among the '62 Living Theatre *Christmas Story* puppets, the Schumanns in '79 remembered a black and white cow, either with a three-dimensional paper maché head and a cloth body, or, like the donkey puppet from that show, a cutout raised above the curtain from a stick (a 'wall puppet', Schumann calls it), shepherds' masks (paper maché heads, I take it), little hand puppets for the people of Jerusalem, and for the angel, according to Schumann in '82, the big, wingless rod puppet Peace Angel that 'held a white flag and spindle through her hands) (Schumann, interview, '83) and appears in one of Moore's August '62 Woodstock photos, was probably used: there may have been a small hand puppet angel around also. The mask of the big angel, a black-robed, spindly-handed figure, is one of the more cubist-Africanoid sculptures of Schumann's of that time: a geometric abstract of curves. The King Herod puppet's head was the 'Big

Mask' worn by Ken Sheppard in the New York City '62 *Totentanz*. Joseph wore a face mask, as did the shepherds, whose masks, 'colored masks, with sort of bright red cheeks, slowly got damaged by being used too much' (Schumann, interview, '83), and then were replaced by face masks taken from life masks of Negro kids Schumann worked with in the '66 *Chicken Little*. Mary wore a face mask – the one later used by Schumann as 'White Lady', and then as 'Resurrection Angel', on stilts? There was a Three Kings puppet, its mask one 'that has three faces and is worn by a player who has his face in the center. It's tied on. It has a back head to it.' (Schumann, interview, '83.) The Three Kings stilt puppet in *Washerwoman Nativity* ('79) was a copy of it.

The 'big golden god head' (Elka, interview, '83) made for the *Genesis/Story of the World* show, like the large golden hand that went with it and that Elka thinks was lost when they lost the Courthouse, was flat, with 'claws behind it and two sticks, so it was to be played above a puppet curtain' — (Schumann, interview, '83):

'... Large, oval, way over life-size, maybe three feet tall, with very soft, amorphous features, not sharp-ridged, no eyes, just the nose and the mouth are indicated. And the hand was up in this gesture (palm out, fingers pointing up (SSB)).'
(Elka, interview, '83.)'

It was the first of a series, the next one made for Nichols' *Everyman* ('64), the two after that in '70 or '70 and '71, one first used in a July 4th parade of '70, the other in *Emilia* in February '71.

In '79 (but not in '82) Schumann remembers box puppets built on Suffolk Street, i.e. around October '63, called 'Gloria' puppets – two or three of them that he described as:

'Giant faces painted on cardboard boxes and holes on the side of the cardboard boxes to stick your arms out, and to operate swords. And we did dances to drumbeats, and battles and fights, hopping around with these creatures.'

In '82 he remembers during this period using:

'... a bunch of cardboard puppets – Madonna-type puppets, where the whole figure was painted on a fairly tall cardboard box and an opening was left for the face and usually a mask was inserted there. I believe we had several of those –'

One clear memory he has is walking down 14th Street advertising his '62 *Christmas Story* at the Living Theatre in one of these boxes: with a mask he considered a 'Mary' mask.

In Peter Moore's photos of the January '63 Judson Gallery *Puppet Festival* we see these carton box puppets. In Schumann's terminology, they would be 'puppets with inside operators'. They were apparently of different constructions: the performer's head – masked: the photos show both the 'Janus' and the 'Big Mask' worn – may stick out of the top or a hole might be left for his masked face in front, the box enclosing his head also; his arms or hands might stick out the front or sides. The boxes probably generally went down to just above crotch and buttocks. Chances are, he used these puppets to perform early versions of *King Story* – pieces that became *King Story*. I very much doubt that he made any of these after the spring of '63 at the very latest: they were 'puppets' of '62. Performing in them was an extension of masked performance (such as in *Totentanz*): probably suggested to him by doing puppetry with the wire-moved Putney rod puppets.

In Moore's photos of the January 1963 *'Puppet Festival'* at the Judson we see a third type of puppets that Schumann had been making during this period, 'box puppets': carton boxes with holes in them, for the wearer's ('operator's') neck and arms, variously painted, with pictures on them, for a performer to wear around his or her torso, their (masked) head and their arms and legs sticking out. This kind of puppet was apparently just a sideline. But, qua puppets with an 'inside operator', they can be viewed as the first appearance of the 'live puppet' subsequently central to his work. The 'live puppet' combined the ideas of a puppet shell with the operating mechanisms of the rod puppets. He used them in *Burning Towns* and perhaps in early versions of *King Story*. He advertised his '62 Living Theatre *Christmas Story* walking down 14th Street dressed in one of them – with a mask he considered a 'Mary' mask. When I interviewed him in '79, he remembers building some on Suffolk St. still, i.e. around October '63, two or three of them. He called them 'Gloria puppets' and described them as:

'giant faces painted on cardboard boxes and holes on the side ... to stick your arms out and to operate swords. And we did dances to drumbeats, and battles and fights, hopping around with these creatures.'

He didn't remember building them this late when I interviewed him in '82, just using them, perhaps – 'Madonna-type puppets'. I doubt he made any after the spring of '63 – he took time out during the summer, and in the fall got busy on his new center-pole puppets.

11. Summer of '63, semblance of an itinerant puppeteer. Schumann as Johnny the Abductor and Rinaldini the Girl-Killer. Beer and scatology. Puppeteering as fun.

By the spring of '63, Schumann probably had had it with Putney:

'He had worked at Putney School with all these wealthy kids. Kids of wealthy parents. And he wanted to take – I think he just wanted to shit on the whole trip – to use his phrase – and get out and go by himself. Because I think the pressure of all that, and the creamy – he called these people creamy – I think he was sick of it. And I think he just wanted to take off by himself and get drunk a little – cut loose. Just like this. Plus he had three kids. Solveig was a baby – as I remember, when I first met him, Solveig was a baby, and Tamara. Ephraim was called Brotzek, Little Brother, at that time. So I knew him as Brotzek. He was a real little tyke and Solveig was the baby. And Tamara was maybe three or four. So, anyway, that was my impression, that he wanted to leave Putney and leave the school – leave all that business and take off and get loose. Be poor, and just cut loose. Drink beer – be by himself. Take off. He had had to teach kids and do kind of pageants and things that were a little soft. I think he possibly could have stayed there, because he was very talented with people. He had good connections and people liked him and stuff. But Peter was really too serious an artist to stay there. For one thing, it was all rich kids. And also, he's not a teacher. Never has been. And never probably will be. He's an artist. So it wasn't really critical. It wasn't really the thing to do.' (Ernstthal, interview.)

'We moved out of Putney ... I moved out in June. Mom went in June at the end of the Putney term to Wyndham to finish her degree, and I built myself a tent over a trailer and I used our jeep to pull the trailer around and I built the cranky box into the trailer, and I went around and performed the crankies and little Punch and Judy type shows by the side of the road. (Ephraim: The one that's in Connecticut, that jeep? Elka: Yeah.) Um, hm. (Elka: It was a jeep and a trailer from my parents.) The jeep was – the trailer I bought from – from a maintenance man who lived in the same house with Stefan and Fernando. (Elka: But then it ended up in Ridgefield, right?) Yeah, I left it there. (Elka: And the whole trailer is covered with words and phrases and words painted in white on canvas.)' (Schumann, interview, '79.)

On *his* trailer it says 'HELLO, GOOD-BYE, ENJOY, MORNING, FLOWER...'

So, as the 'Moosach Puppet Theater,' he leaves. Pretty soon – in mid-July – he meets Bob Ernstthal, then nineteen to his twenty-nine:

'I was out of college, Brown University. I went to Provincetown. Really basically dropped out. Kind of at loose ends. Living in Provincetown. Not quite knowing what was going on ... and a friend of mine had a book store in Provincetown. And one evening this strange German guy came in and wanted to do a puppet show. And we were there and we saw it. And it was really unintelligible. He was trying to do this puppet show. I think it was some kind of early version of the *King Story*. I forget what he called it. And it was really unintelligible. (I: In the bookshop?) Right out in front of the bookshop. He set up the curtain right out front and he was giving the show. It *was* unintelligible. He was holding up puppets, yelling, doing the sound effects, and he had a very good German accent. And it was pretty strange. But interesting. Different, you know. He was holding up puppets and making noise and moving around and then dropping them and picking up other ones . . . And he had this jeep and a trailer. This army jeep and this trailer painted with names and a cloth cover like a tent on this little teeny trailer which he kept *everything* in, in which he lived. And he asked if he could park – we had a driveway kind of thing – if he could park up by our driveway. We were living at the house of Prescott Townsend, who was a notorious Boston, Beacon Hill homosexual from way back. We didn't know that at the time because it was more naive in those days. (I: Who's we, by the way?) Oh, it was just college friends. (I: And what names were painted on the truck?) Mr. Goodman, The King, Everyman, The Blue Man. It was all names just painted diagonally across the front of the trailer. It was an open jeep and trailer and all the names across it, painted . . . . And he asked if he could park his trailer and his jeep up there. He was really wild. He was living on the bread and lard and garlic,[1] and beer. And brewer's yeast. That was his diet. Because garlic is a natural stimulant. But, of course, if you eat that much garlic it comes out your hair and your armpits and just everything. Totally he was engulfed in this cloud of garlic. He was pretty wild. He was pretty much of a wild man and very Germanic – he considered beer food, and he was eating *rather* poorly, so he spent a lot of time in the bars, or in the bar there. Dance. Sometimes he would get drunk and he would dance, with the girls or just by himself, and just dance and go nuts in his own way.[2] It was the very end of Provincetown. And he was very gruff and self-determined always – as usual. And then, the next day he came and he used our bathroom or something, because he was parked out in the driveway. And the next day I said, 'Maybe you would want some help. You want some help in putting the show on, or –' I could see he needed somebody else there because he was trying to do the whole show himself, which was impossible. You could imagine doing all those shows totally by himself. It didn't really make any sense. So I asked him if maybe he would want some help. I had done some theatre in high school and college and this and that, and it looked like fun. It looked like fun

---

1. The reader will recall that according to Dioscorides the moly, black-rooted and white-flowering, that Hermes gave Ulysses as antidote to Circe's metamorphosing powers, was *Allium subhirsutum*, (wild) garlic.
2. '(I: Was that art dancing, in any way?) Yes. It was his own world. It was in a way – I wouldn't call it disco dancing, but it was definitely in his own world. He would get – it was kind of like his own version of jitterbug. Like – it was in fact, now that I think of it, like a mockery of the dance that people were doing at that time. It was always mocking. He would take the gestures and the movements of that time that were popular, and extend them. But he would abstract them. And – you know what it was like? From what I've seen, it sound ridiculous, but Twyla Tharp. It was like taking those things and making them a mockery. It was a mockery. This frenzied mockery of the mores and of the society of that time.' — (Ernstthal, interview.)

to me. So he said, "Oh yeah, we try it out, okay." So we drove out to the dunes, to some sand dunes somewhere, and drove out into the sand, and went back in the trailer. The trailer had openings on the side that could button down like flaps. You could play out the side. And all the puppets were hung in there. He slept in it, plus he kept the brewer's yeast in those little compartments and the brewer's yeast spilled, so the whole place smelled like brewer's yeast, which has a – very *fine*, you know – it's a very fine powder. And he said, "Here, hold this. Do this." And we started working out the show. From the truck, out in the sand dunes. From this little trailer. The trailer was about the size of this couch. It was a little eight-foot trailer. Just a flatbed trailer. And he built up the sides and he made this iron structure, over which a tent – it was like a tent. It was like an army tent. It was up when he drove and it was hooked onto the jeep. One little flap in the side, so it was like a puppet theatre. Like a crankie movie, actually. It was about that size. And then behind the opening was a cloth so you couldn't see behind it. So we would play by crouching down and reaching up underneath like that. It was kind of a strange cranked thing. So, he said, "Well, this is the show," and we just kinda made up the show. There was nobody there, and we just rehearsed – the first rehearsal. It was: the king wakes up in the morning and gets his teeth brushed. It was what we would call now *King Story II*. There were two *King Stories* originally when I met Peter. One was *King Story I*, which was serious, but there was also a *King Story II*, which was a comedy, sort of. And then we got this art gallery across the street, backing onto the water. It was Sal's Art Gallery, I guess. And we did a show there right away. (I: Next day?) Two days. And we did a show that was made on a ladder reading from the Book of Revelations. *The Apocalypse*.' (Ernstthal, interview.)

They did *Apocalypse* (cf. infra) for the grown-ups; *King Story II* for kids. And they probably did other things on both shows as well. Bob's mother saw them at Sal's – the gruff, Teutonic Schumann in his garlic-sweat cloud 'terrified' her.

'Peter Schumann, who has brought his Moosach Puppet Theatre to Provincetown to the delight of the children (and even the adults), laughed when asked about the origin of his puppetry: "All chance," he said. The name "Moosach," which Peter has chosen for his puppet theatre, derives from the little Bavarian village of Moosach to which Peter will return next fall when his wife has finished a teaching engagement at the Putney School in Vermont. The puppets themselves belie (sic) Peter's sculptural training for they reveal a solid sence (sic) of form as well as an exciting feeling for the theatre. His engagement this week at the Front Street Gallery ... will be an unusual opportunity for young and old alike to enjoy an ancient but living art which is not often seen at its best in this country. Bob Ernstthal of New York will be Mr. Schumann's able assistant puppeteer.'
(Notice, *Provincetown New Beacon*.)

So they embarked on a tour for the remainder of the summer.

'And then he asked me to go on a tour. He said, "Let's go. Let's go on a tour. We can sleep in the trailer." If we laid down – it was six feet long – there were little boxes on the side and there was a space in the middle. So when we slept in it, we just laid down side by side, and just slept in it. I felt a little bit like *La Strada*

– it was, in fact, a lot like *La Strada*. I remember that was the image I had, because it was this completely strange show, with this very strange guy. Against the pleadings of my mother, we took off. So what we did was put – I don't think I had anything. He had a sleeping bag. That's about it. And we drove off. Against the pleadings of my mother, to whom the scene was nightmarish. And I was so happy being in *La Strada*. Remember in *La Strada*, the motorcycle with this crazy little shed thing on the back where they sleep, and all his stuff was there. It was a little like that. And there we were, going off down the road. And we went to places like a girls' camp. We'd drive into the girls' camp, talk to the director, give a puppet show for the girls. And I don't think we'd get any money or anything like that. Do the show. Peter would be outside and I would be inside playing the puppets. For kids' shows that was our technique, our standard. (I: Outside, doing what?) He would be playing the drum and narrating, kind of: "And now you see –", "And then the King –". And I would do the puppets. (I: Well, that's strange.) Yeah. (I: Him, the puppeteer and you the English-speaking person.) Yeah, but he felt he was being more in control outside, see? The outside guy would control it and the inside guy just had the movement. So he would be in control. Later on, this stuff changed. I mean, as time went on, things like that changed. As I remember, in those days, he would be outside. Maybe he did change. We went to a girls' camp; we went to York Beach, Maine. I remember that place, which was kind of a resort like – like Bar Harbor. York Beach was like a more low class resort. It had a boardwalk. It had rides. And we'd pull up on the beach and beat the drum. We went to a town, and we got the fire house. In another town we rented or got the fire house from the fire chief and we'd drive through the town in this jeep, with masks on, blowing these little horns, these little plastic horns. And be yelling, "Puppet Show! Three o'clock at the fire house!" And that would get these big crowds. People would follow us. Kids would follow us along through the town. And we'd go to the fire house and play these shows and – (I: Did people like the shows?) I don't think so. I think they were pretty baffling. I think people were fairly baffled. Fairly baffled by the shows. I have a feeling we dropped the *Apocalypse*, because it was too abstract. And it wasn't really worked out. And I think we did a version of *King Story I*. And *King Story II*, that's right. "Heigh-dee, heigh do," and then the big gun would shoot the king ... It was very rough. Some people liked it. Like I knew a girl named Carol Miller who later became a singer. I had met her in later years. And she remembered. She saw us at York Beach, Maine. And she remembered it totally. I mean she remembered the experience completely. And she thought it was great. So I think there were those among the people who really liked it. And I think it wasn't that bad. It was very unusual. It was very musical. It was bright colors. And quite unique, although it wasn't – as usual, I mean, Peter would never appeal to the taste of people. That's for sure. (I: Musical?) Well, he had these horns – these little tin whistles. Horns, jew's-harp, little snare drum, a trumpet. I could play the trumpet, but real badly. And it had an energy and a color to it, and a vital quality to it that made it really funny and unique. Plus, the whole mode was very new. In fact, totally new. In other words – he had a beard – always wore a beard. And we were kind of scruffy. And the whole mode of it was very new. This was before anything was known about beards or long hair. It was very new. And it had a certain energy. Like you'd just pull up on the street and string a rope, take out clothes pins, posters, and make a stage. In the summer of '63, we were entertainers and would make twenty dollars a day and spent twenty dollars a day. Or ten might be more like it. And we'd sleep in the car. And you couldn't – it wasn't the Bread & Puppet Theatre or anything like that at that time. You never knew what was gonna come of it, it was just fun and a strange adventure. It wasn't known that this would become something.

Provincetown was a very arty scene, in general. This was before hippies; and beatniks, of course, wouldn't be seen dead in a place like Provincetown. So it was the older bohemians – the wealthy bohemians – the art collectors – the art gallery guys – the painters – Hans Hoffmann's school and, you know, the established, well-known painters, and it was a very old art colony scene. And Peter showed up there with bright – he was like a German Expressionist, more, and he was wild in the sense of he didn't fit in – he jutted out. Although he was never a wild person – except that one time when he got drunk and danced and danced and danced. Just danced his head off that night at the bar – this bar that was the scene. So, I really should say that he was never wild in a personal sense.

Peter came out of the Middle Ages in a certain way. The imagery was more like – he had an internal imagery that was totally out of time. Much more like a medieval vagabond – troubadour – not even that, not even that – let me collect my thoughts on that. Let me go pee.

This question, though is really great, because it's like – like I said, my image was a little bit like *La Strada* – Zampano – he was like that kind of character: "And here you see, I can break, with the simple expansion of my chest muscles, this steel chain. If there are any ladies in the audience who might be offended by the sight of blood – I suggest you look away." I mean, that's about the level we were playing. That was the flavor of it and like I think that was the imagery in a certain way – on one level – okay – one thing: he was totally out of the United States mold and he was totally out of the mold of the time – two things. For one thing, he was – it was like he was an archetype – not of a troubadour, that's really wrong – that's really not what it was, because a troubadour has a romantic image. And he was the antithesis of a romantic – he was just the opposite. That's why I said more like Zampanone than like a troubadour. (I: How about Chagall's little guy with the violin, and how about Chaplin, in –) Yeah. Charlie Chaplin was, if anything, Peter's main influence, frankly. It really was. If there was any major main influence, it would be the Tramp. So, if anything, it was in that style – actually, it's true. Chagall – not. Too soft – too soft and too Jewish and too sweet, loving. Chagall has a very loving, romantic, almost feeling. Peter was much more harsh than that. It was like a wanderer – he was like a wanderer – like a travelling showman, but it was really from another age. It was like the travelling puppet show combined with –." (Ernstthal, interview.)

Their output that July and August was, as Ernstthal saw it, predominantly – whether it came off like that or not – intended as light entertainment, in fact, much of it stuff for kids: ***Mr. Miller Stories***,[3] ***Johnnie and Susie***,[4]

---

3. Dr. Irving Oyle, before becoming a successful New York practitioner in the Medicaid racket, and then a California quack, had been a standup comic. He worked with Schumann for a number of years, having made his acquaintance that summer:

'He was touring with his Mr. Miller theatre. He had a truck or a little trailer, jeep and trailer, and this Mr. Miller puppet, with the long, floppy arms was hanging out and he was touring around the countryside. And we just got to talking and picked up his puppets and started playing with them. (I: What was Mr. Miller like?) He was a puppet, Everyman. One of his Everyman puppets. (I: Did you see his *Mr. Miller* show?) No. He was working it up then. His habit was — you probably know — is to make a new puppet and then play with it for a while. Just demonstrate it before audiences and just see what it would do before he worked it into an actual scene. So he was fooling around with Mr. Miller at that time. That was one of his first puppets.' — (Oyle, interview.)

'And at the same time, Irving Oyle met us. And later on, through the years, he was like the only person that had any respectability; had a house and any money, or anything. So we really — he was our friend for many years. He would be in shows occasionally and different things . . . Plus, Irving Oyle lived near there (near the Spencer Memorial Church where '63-'67 the Bread & Puppet did most of their religious shows (SSB)) – lived about four blocks from there, on State Street and that's where Irving came in — we used to huddle — get together at his house and stuff. He was the only substantial person that we knew for years — Irving, Pearl — and they gave us lots of help. We used to go there, eat and — one time when I got very sick and I was living at the loft, he — I went to their house to be sick in, because it was the only place that had any — it was the only person that we knew that was at all realistic or set up for doing anything. (I: Bathroom.) Bathroom. Clean room, right, hot water — and go there and take showers.' — (Ernstthal, interview.)

'He's nuts, but in the nicest fashion. He's a sweet guy. Really very half-baked and I don't mean that in a bad way. But he ran a clinic on Thompson Square for a while at which he professed to be astonished that he got quite rich at it. And he got quite rich because he was taking poor people in, a very good thing to do what he was doing. He was marvelous, but of course they all had Medicaid and eventually the money started to pour in from Medicaid. And Irving professed to be very surprised at this. And the more I think about it, as a doctor he couldn't have been very surprised, you know. At some level he knew very well. That was good. But that's certainly not to put him down. But there's a sort of innocence about him, too. He had a clinic on Avenue — between B and C on 11th Street, I believe. It was in the 1960s.' — (Bissinger, interview.)

4. '*Johnny and Susie* was our attempt at a kids' show. And that was just yacking it up with puppets. And we used to do these — these kids' shows and we would crack up. The audience probably wouldn't get it, but we would be backstage laughing our heads off. It was just these totally silly — something about — God, I can't remember. "I wanta get married. Won't you marry me?' And it was this little puppet that looked a little like Peter. That was Johnny, and he did this — the first bit was the guy, the puppet coming up and talking and this little worm coming up, tickling him. It was funny — like, and he turned around and he'd chase it back and push it down and he'd go up and he'd talk again and this little worm would come on. And then they'd just do this bit with the finger and that was the long part of it — pushing the finger down with his nose: "Get down." No, it wasn't even a worm. It was barking. He'd go: "Rrrr-ark!" And he'd tell him, "Get back, get back." And he'd push it back. "Get down." (I: What was he talking about?) He was saying about the show and how great it was. We were just improvising. We were just fooling around. And it was something about — (I: And Susie?) Susie was this kind of demure, girlish — as I remember, it was something like this — that kind of a girlish trip. That kind of thing. High voice, girlish and she wanted to get married and the father was grumpy and the father didn't want them to get married and they tricked the father and — it was just a — oh, and they had a car. That was one of the things. Jesus, this is really going back. See, these shows were dropped and never really — nothing ever really happened with them. We had the car — the same one from the car crash. And they went — they drove away, took a trip in the car. It was like a toy car — a little toy car. They'd run it along the theatre — the curtain. They took a trip in the country and met different people. The only thing that

echoed that was in the *Christmas Story*, when Mary and Joseph would come to different houses. That's what I think it was. They would drive. They were running away from their father and they drove in the car — Rrrrrr, driving along, and they'd meet someone, another puppet. And the puppet would want toll for the road and they'd give him money and he'd hold them up for a toll in the road and then they would go on and it was that kind of picaresque story. It was just totally improvised theatre. Really funny and delightful, and that was — it was that kind of a story: "Let's get married" — "oh, you have to ask my father. Yes, yes, ask my father first." And they'd go in to the father and the father would say, "No, no." We were playing like two at a time, you know. Leaning over each other and playing two and one would get down and take another one and put that one up. That kind of thing. And it was so improvised, like I said, that we used to crack up totally. I remember that. We would tell a joke or, again, usually about shit. Finding shit on the street. I remember that. "Lying there like a piece of deposit. Don't get up. You're lying there like a piece of deposit in the street," and that was a big funny. And we would just crack up. We would have a great time. The audience probably, perhaps, didn't get it or whatever. But, you know what I mean. It was like "in" jokes. We would have jokes. We would be laughing our heads off behind the stage. Sometimes to the point of not being able to continue. Not being able to continue the show, but — anyway, it was that kind of just real loose style of show. Humorous. Improvised totally. Different from time to time, but with this basic idea of the girl and the boy and the mean mother, and they run away and they find all these stupid people in the world — and then they wind up singing together.' — (Ernstthal, interview.)

Ernstthal seems to have enjoyed Schumann's humor that summer. On the whole, however, he did not think it suitable for kids' shows, thought it crude, and thought that Schumann in addition was disqualified as entertainer of children by dark obsessions with war that kept invading even his pieces for children:

'It was trying to be like kids' shows, but Peter never was good at kids' shows because his humor is — first of all, it's scatalogical. Like Germans tend to be, I've noticed. It had to do with shit a lot . . . it wasn't exactly something that would appeal to kids. The color and the movement . . . The king would take a morning shit. That was hilarious. Anything to do with shit or farting or asses was just the funniest thing. That was characteristic. And Peter — like his term of derision was always, "Oh, I shit on it." Always. If he would get mad at something, he'd shit on it . . . The shows were not entertaining. And that's what my mother saw and why it was so strange. Because, that was the whole point. The shows, even for kids, even at the beach in Maine or at this church that we played in somewhere in Vermont. In these places the shows were always dark . . . because of Peter's nature. It was very hard for him. But we would do funny kids's shows and stuff, but it always had a bite to it. In a way he was obsessed. It's like this: He was obsessed with soldiers — soldiers marching in and soldiers killing. So that even in a light show, like *King Story II*, the king gets shot with a cannon, because of a mosquito. It wasn't what we call entertaining. So even — except for the Johnny and Susie and all that, it had — not what was known to the people as entertainment. And that is why my mother and the people who knew us — or, say my mother, or normal people, found it totally bizarre. And it had no chance for success, because we would never do anything for the audience. That was the first principle. Never — you'd never — sounds funny, in a way, but it's still the same way — never give the audience anything they wanted . . . And he would never — like, I felt that I was — the softness of it. In other words, Peter by himself was almost at that point — especially caught up in anger and obsession in a certain way. An obsession with soldiers, an obsession with death, obsession with darkness and soldiers and war. And at that time, war was far from the American scene.' — (Ernstthal, interview.)

King Story II,⁵ the crankie *Rinaldini*.⁶ In addition, they had two serious shows for adults, *Apocalypse* and a serious(er) version of *King Story*, apparently an approach to the third and (later) main version of it called *King Story I*, but this summer as yet either from the outset or eventually

---

5. 'The king wakes up in the morning and gets his teeth brushed. A comedy, sort of, about the king who gets up and has an advisor kind of brush his teeth, and then there was a mosquito, which is a little piece of cloth on the end of a coat hanger. And the mosquito was bothering the king and he called the soldiers. The soldiers came in and they were three heads with a burlap body. Three heads like – actually, Brechtian in style. And they marched in: "Heigh-dee, heigh-do, heigh-da," like that, with this painted cannon. And they came in with the cannon and they shot the mosquito with the cannon and killed the king by accident. That was the story. It was supposed to be a comedy. I must say we worked on this comic version of the *King Story* for years. Years. And then, it never really developed into anything. It's funny – I mean, that was one show, you know what I mean, that really never got going – that never became a coherent show. But that was the idea... The king and his royal toothbrush and his royal bath and his royal breakfast that was served, and he ate it, and the mosquito coming in and the soldiers and the cannon shooting the king... And that was the one about the mosquito falling in the face of the king – landing on his nose. The soldiers coming. And the king saying, 'No, no, no, don't shoot!' Wham, they shoot! And he goes tumbling over. And he gets killed, or in different versions – see, the shows were never – only toward the end were they ever in anything considered fixed form.' — (Ernstthal, interview.)

According to a report in the *Frankfurter Rundschau* of May 25, '68, apparently based on accounts by Bruno Eckhardt, Schumann had with Eckhardt performed *King Story II* at a Puppeteers' Festival at the beginning of the summer, before he met Ernstthal, and its success had convinced him that he had found his proper metier in puppetry:

'Die Show beim interamerikanischen Puppenspieler-Festival von 1963 gehörte einem Aussenseiter. Eine kleine, als Beatniks avisierte Schar aus New York, unter Führung des gebürtigen Deutschen Peter Schumann, war ausgezogen, die Nightclub- und Walt-Disney-Puppentheater das Fürchten zu lehren.

Schumann weigerte sich, auf einer "Mickey-maus-Bühne" zu spielen, und verlegte seine Vorstellung auf die sumpfige Theaterwiese. "Das Stück," so wird uns berichtet, "schlug ein ... Es zeigte das Privatleben eines Königs und war – in einer weitgehend improvisierten Handlung –" den Erinnerungen aus dem Land des blauäugigen Kriegsgottes' gewidmet.

Schumann, seit 1960 in America zu Hause und als Puppenspieler blutiger Anfänger, wusste nach diesem Erfolg, dass er zu seinem eigentlichen Metier gefunden hatte; er begann in jenem apostolischen Sendungsbewusstsein das ihm schon in den Jahren zuvor als Bildhauer und Tänzer eigen war, mit den Möglichkeiten des Puppentheaters zu experimentieren.' — (Manfred Rieger, 'Brot und Puppen,' *Frankfurter Rundschau*, May 25, '68.)

6. '*Rinaldini* who also – was based on a song. In a way that's how I think, he saw himself, a little, also ... *Rinaldini*, the great lover, who throws his girlfriend Rosa into the water. Oh, it's terrific – it's a great show. Anyway – but he's like a rogue: "Rinaldini was a great robber. Taa-daa-da-da." And goes with his men across the water: "Row – row – row." And they row out and back and Rosa's there and: "Should he throw his girlfriend into the water?" And the men say yes and Rinaldini says no and then he winds up throwing his girlfriend into the water and the sharks ate her up and the moral is: You should learn to swim ... So, on one hand he was that roguish image that I really think he took seriously ...' — (Ernstthal, interview.)

provided with a happier ending (as in *The Story of the World* the war scenes were followed by a peace scene).[7]

Basically, he probably needed big puppets to do something tragic or otherwise awesome. With the rod puppets killing and brutality still, as with hand puppets, came out as fun.

King Story (I) remained a staple in Schumann's repertory for many years. It can be viewed as warning against bellicose anti-communism and against recourse to war and to violence (or force) generally. But the dragon is a strange beast. Its devastations of the countryside are attested to in many myths: yet one wonders if perhaps not some of its bad reputation has been engineered by the very heroes that win the hand of the King's daughter by killing it, usurpatory founders of dynasties: the violence of The State is always legitimized by the violence of the anarchy allegedly kept in check by it. I.e.: Schumann's twisting of the myth is a piece of anarchist propaganda. And there is more to the matter than this: what is the dragon in the soul (Bettelheim has recently certified this term, 'soul', in good Freudian standing) whose violence Schumann perhaps tells us not to do violence to? Let us feed him the virgins he craves![8]

Apocalypse seems to have been a surrealistically – or whimsically – illustrated, very somber Bible reading, radically compressing the Bible into

---

7. 'Once there was a great king and the king had a priest and the king had a red man, and king had a blue man-and-a-son ... We used the soldiers. Three-headed soldiers. (I: And there was a dragon in there also?) Yeah. The dragon was threatening the village and he called the soldiers and they came in: "Heigh-dee, heigh-do, heigh-dah" and with this painted cannon. They killed the dragon and there was a big fight and the cannon, and they were chasing from one side to the other side, back and forth, and they shoot the dragon and it goes "Ahhhghghgh" and it would rattle – death rattle. And killed everyone. No. The end of the *King Story* is something we worked out later in the years. I know that. And I think it was considered too violent. It was too violent to blast everyone out. In other words, the *King Story* (in the winter of '63/'64 *again* (SSB)) developed into a story where everyone was killed at the end. But I think it was something like a flower came out of the cannon at the end and the soldiers marched off and everybody was happy. I think we tempered that ending. I think that the ending of everybody getting killed was a later invention. So the ending was – it wasn't as stark. The show wasn't as stark. The playing wasn't as stark and the ending was more comic. They didn't even shoot the king and they all got around and danced together at the end because they'd killed the dragon, or something like that.' — (Ernstthal, interview.)

8. Murray Levy, who did the *King Story* King for a while from September '68 onward:

'... I saw the dragon as the revolution – the revolutionary movement. I always saw it as that, or even – I could do the *King Story* today, and in fact I did it, I had a theatre of my own called Bilder Theater in Berlin, and we did the *King Story* all over Germany ... and we did the *King Story* as one of our pieces and it was long after the Vietnam war was finished and people – we talked about, a lot, about what the dragon was, among ourselves as well. We never talked about that in the Puppet Theatre so much – I mean, with Peter. But, like the dragon took on the dimensions of fear, of any kind of fear or change or – so we transferred it to personal fears as well.' — (Levy, interview.)

genesis and end of the world, the final times being the present ones, nuclear war represented by a car crash, the time between beginning and end, as in some of the somber eschatologies of the late Middle Ages (Bosch's *Hay Wagon*) merely the negligible preparation for the bad end: the death-in-life theme of *Totentanz*, but unequivocally negative.[9] Elka came to see them do it, July 30th, as an evening program, following an afternoon children's program (photo on the front page of the Valley News, July 31, '63) – children 50 cents, adults $1 – at St. Barnabas Church in Norwich, N.H.[10] Schumann successfully reworked *King Story*

---

9. '... a show that was made on a ladder, reading from the Book of Revelations. And Peter, behind the stage, holding up objects of different kinds, which had a direct or mostly indirect relation to the reading that was going on. I was reading from the Book of Revelations ... Another show, about the end of the world. It's very poetic – the Beast of 666 and all that. And it was very heavy. And then at the end, I remember it, he came out with little cars, little toy cars in front of the stage, in front of this hanging curtain, which was all our blankets pinned up to a string, he did this automobile crash. And everybody died. And that was the end of the world. It was the end of the story. It was a very heavy, peculiar show.' — (Ernstthal, interview.)

It started with creation:
'God made plants ... And he held up a plant, or a flower ... And God made water, and then I think he squirted water over the curtain. And then I think the Apocalypse part might have been the car crash or something on that order. I forget whether we did one, then the other, or if they melded into one.' — (Ernstthal, interview.)

'It was a very abstract – very strange. And no one really understood it. And it probably wasn't really that good. Peter would be out there playing the jew's-harp, and I was just reading. It wasn't a clear – there wasn't any kind of narrative or clear thing. It was all abstract imagery. Going along with this Apocalypse reading ... I have a feeling we dropped the *Apocalypse* because it was too abstract. And it wasn't really worked out .... (Schumann) wasn't a beatnik.

And that was the only thing that was current at that time. (I: What were his politics?) Hating of authority. And considering the whole world is full of police, basically, and he hated them. (I: Anarchism rather than socialism?) Yes. At that time. Just sheer, in a way like a – if anything, it was Kafkaesque, or a nightmare. Considering society as a nightmare. Considering society as if it was a gigantic tank that is one inch from your head. Just about to let go. Considering the whole world as this monster. That was – well, the first thing he did was the *Apocalypse* – the Beast of Babylon. A vision of the whole society blowing itself to smithereens.

It was infusing the mythology of the day (the Christian history of the world (SSB)) with the real – the reality of it. And that, to me, in a way, the Apocalypse and all – and the Revelation – to me, that's what was happening. That's what happened in the '60s in New York. It happened, but happened on the mental plane. Through drugs, and the whole experience was a crashing through into the post-Christian era, which is now. That was the turmoil of the times.' — (Ernstthal, interview.)

10. The context of the St. Barnabas *Apocalypse* was a (Third) Festival of Art and Worship (July 28-August 4) there. It concluded with two lectures by the Rev. Glenesk of Spencer Memorial Church, Brooklyn – one with dancing by Fred Herko – on *The Church and Creative Dancing* and on *Christianity in the Arts*. Glenesk '63-'67 sponsored most of the Bread & Puppet Christmas and Easter shows at Spencer.

'He was the first one to open his church to us. We made fun of him, in a way, because

with new puppets during the coming fall and winter. Similar attempts with *Apocalypse* failed. *King Story* became the point of departure for his 'regular theater' puppetry.

---

he was the classical liberal priest and stuff, but really he really was a good guy. He was a good guy. He suffered mockery, I think, because he had a career to think of and was, in a certain way, self-serving in the arts and he had also this old-time congregation in Brooklyn. He was really trying to straddle his artistic feeling with this congregation that was mostly old ladies. But he gave us a lot of help and support – in the same way the Peace Movement in the early '60s couldn't have survived without the churches, and the peace people tended to mock them a little because they were in such a straight role. Nevertheless, Glenesk really did us a favor.' — (Ernstthal, interview.)

12. Manteos: celastic and big puppets.

At the beginning of that summer of '63, early in June, before he met Bob, Schumann had attended the 27th annual Puppeteers of America Festival in Hurleyville, N.Y. in the Catskills. Here, at the New Morningside Hotel, he learned about celastic, lighter than paper maché, more durable (tougher), and quicker, and perhaps, discounting the acetone fumes, easier to work with,[1] and to some extent a precondition for the large puppets he

---

1. 'Technique de Fabrication des Marionettes.
Matériel et produits nécessaires
Terre glaise, vaseline, célastic (sorte de toile plastifiée se trouvant aux Etats-Unis ou en Allemagne), acétone, colle plastique, couteau à palette, couteau à lame très courte et élargie ("cutter"), gesso (enduit acrylique), peinture acrylique.
Procédé de fabrication
— Faire avec de la terre glaise une forme qui va devenir le moule de la marionnette ou de l'un de ses éléments.
— Enduire le moule de vaseline.
— Déchirer en morceaux une feuille de célastic. Après avoir plongé un morceau de célastic dans l'acétone, l'appliquer sur le moule; le presser à l'aide du couteau à palette afin de faire sortir l'air. Prendre un autre morceau, l'appliquer en ayant soin qu'il chevauche largement sur le précédent, et ainsi de suite, jusqu'à ce que le moule soit entièrement recouvert.
— Laisser sécher toute une journée ce qui constitue le masque.
— Le lendemain, à l'aide du "cutter", couper le masque de telle façon qu'il se détache aisément du moule. Celui-ci, resté intact, peut resservir.
— Reconstituer le masque en recollant les parties à l'aide de longues bandes de célastic qu'on applique à l'intérieur et à l'extérieur.
— Pour égaliser le masque, mettre de la colle plastique aux endroits où les morceaux de célastic se chevauchent. Polir avec du papier de verre.
— Recouvrir le masque de gesso, laisser sécher. Peindre.
La technique que je viens de décrire est celle qui est employée à l'heure actuelle de façon courante par le Bread and Puppet Theatre. Les marionnettes ainsi construites sont extrêmement solides. Mais Peter Schumann est parti de la simple technique dite du "papiétage," qu'il continue à utiliser pour les petites marionnettes, et qui réclame un matériel plus rudimentaire: du papier journal et de la colle en poudre pour tapissier à délayer dans de l'eau. Le procédé de fabrication est sensiblement le même, si ce n'est que des bandes de papier kraft doivent alterner aver le paper journal sur six couches au moins, pour former un masque de carton suffisament dur.
Pour certains éléments (exemple: les mains des personnages de *King's Story*), on utilise du fil de fer (laiton ou fil électrique d'installation). Ce bâti est recouvert de papier journal trempe dans de la colle. Certains masques sont obtenus à partir du moulage d'un visage. Technique courante: appliquer sur le visage enduit de vaseline une couche de plâtre pour moulage, laisser sécher. Appliquer une seconde couche de plâtre plus épaisse que la première. Laisser sécher, retirer.
Traiter ensuite ce moule de plâtre comme un moule de terre glaise.' — (Kourilsky, '71.)

A 'List of materials needed' for a Bread & Puppet Workshop that Schumann sent ahead of time when he was going to do a show from scratch in '75 at the Davis campus of the University of California gives an idea what the group then worked with:
(1) Clay: don't buy it, but borrow it from a pottery or sculpture studio, it's re-usable. (Or

started making that fall,[2] and he encountered the inspiration for these large puppets, the Manteo family's *Orlando Furioso* marionettes, 'Papa

---

else dig it out from a clay-pit or brickyard.) I need the clay wet and ready, and in a quantity – a bathtub full. For the clay: a sturdy table to build on.
(2) Celastic: this is the main expense, and we need it if we want to work fast (papier-mache over wet clay takes too long to dry.) We need one roll heavy-weight and one roll medium-weight. (Celastic is a chemically impregnated cloth which is stiff like very thick leather. When wet with acetone it becomes very limber like a wet cloth. When it dries it becomes stiff again.)
(3) Acetone we'll need about ten gal. which should be bought from a chemical plant or sculpture studio, and not in one gal. containers from a hardware or drug store (too expensive that way). Hopefully we can work outside with the celastic and acetone; if not, we would have to use organic vapour protection (gas-masks).
(4) Rubber gloves, in any case (10 pair). (For working with the acetone.)
(5) Acrylic paints in quart jar sizes, bright red and burnt umber. Housepaint: 3 gallons white 1 gal. black. Paint brushes, all sizes, including ordinary housepaint brushes.
(6) 50 lbs. moulding plaster. (Later increased to 200 lbs. (Shank))
(7) For flags and banners we need: 4 sheets of standard, untempered masonite (hardboard, utility brown board) 4 ft × 8 ft. 4 lbs. printer' ink: 2 lbs. bright red, 1 lb. black, 1 lb. white. 1 gal. paint thinner. Rollers for printing, a couple very big ones, but don't buy! I can bring them.
(8) White fabric: either collect old bed sheets, or buy cheap muslin (unstarched) by the part of bolt (50-100 yards). It's for printing, dyeing, costumes, backdrops, etc.
(9) For puppet-bodies: sticks, dowels, 2 × 4's, broomsticks, branches, pipes. Hopefully we needn't buy these, but can work with whatever you've got in the shop.
(10) Hardware (again to borrow, use, return): pliers, wirecutters, staple-gun, staple-pliers, drill, sewing-machine, saws, trowel, putty-knives, hammer and nails, wire of different thickness . . . .
(11) Glutoline wallpaper paste and vaseline.
Besides it would be good to advise the workshop participants to start collecting other useful, old materials: old fabric, old clothes, old mop-heads, bottle-caps, etc. (In a later letter he added to the list two bushels of rye grain or wheat for bread and a large mixing bowl. — (Shank (Th.) *The B & P's Anti-Bicentennial*, Theatre Quarterly, V, 19, '75.)
Different thicknesses of celastic are obtainable. The thinner celastic gives better detail, but the mask is weaker. Almost all B & P masks since the fall of '63 have been of celastic, but occasionally, mostly to save money on materials, Schumann has had his mask makers use paper maché. E.g. Hoagland in '82 saw volunteers at the '82 circus
'molding a whole variety of masks from many layers of shopping-bag paper steeped and stiffened in wallpaper glue, and drying and painting these.' — (Hoagland, *Let 'em*, '83)
2. Ernstthal, speaking of their first work with celastic that fall:
'. . . the celastic changed everything. (I: How, for instance?) We could turn out – Peter could make a clay head. All right. And then he taught me how to cast – plaster casting. So I would cast it. We'd use a double wall – I think it is called a double wall or clay wall technique of plaster casting. And then we'd take the plaster cast off and he could be doing another head. And I could be doing the celastic, and stuff, and we could really churn them out. We did a lot of puppets really *fast* because of celastic. In Suffolk Street what we did was we made the Great Warrior – we discovered celastic as a medium. And the discovery of celastic – I think Peter had *heard* of it – we used to get it at a place uptown in the theater district. I went there so many times to get it, to get these big rolls of it, and acetone. I remember once I had a bicycle and driving up Third Avenue or something, with this big roll of celastic strapped to my back. Anyway, before I'd go on the subway or whatever, we

Manteo's Life-Sized Marionettes,' 3/4 human-size puppets,[3] with which a succession of Manteos, in the *dolce idioma* still current in the Catania (Sicily) of the late 19th century, from the First to the Second World War performed Ariosto's heroic legend in New York City's Italian neighborhoods:

'In 1963 I went to a festival celebrating over 300 American and foreign puppeteers. Thanks to this meeting I became acquainted with the Sicilian puppet theater. Everything else was nice or not nice, sweet or not sweet and by all means little, not so much in size as in content and intent. Everything was plush and latex and Walt Disney-y and basically about funny- and bunny-rabbits. Maybe I should call that the modest approach of this profession and not complain about it, and I should be glad that there were no Hamlet and Faust productions by foam-rubber specialists. But the Kasper of my childhood had been such a beautifully tough, down-to-earth, real and manly little man that I could not help looking for his life, whatever the shape of that likeness might be.'

(Schumann, *God Himself*, '67.)

'I moved from small puppets to the huge ones after I visited a Sicilian theatre in which large puppets were used. I saw there a pure and strong line. I only saw a short excerpt from a play that lasts one year — it is performed two hours every night with big, heavy wooden puppets. They play it only for male audiences. When they performed they wore mikes around their necks — so close that I could hear every intake of breath. The puppets were made from solid wood and metal — they made the whole stage shake. There were fighting scenes in which ten puppets would jump in the air and clash together. Every puppet must have weighed eighty or ninety pounds. They were held by heavy iron rods and they would move

---

would go up and get our celastic in these big rolls from this place — theatrical supplies. That made it possible to start the bigger scale. (I: Why?) Because it was *lighter*. It was *one* coat. If we had done those big-scale puppets like these in paper maché, it would have taken us a week to do one head, because paper maché takes many, many layers. Later on in Denmark I discovered what they called in Danish *glopa* which is what they put under linoleum. What it is is a kind of raggy under-flooring that you soak and squeeze out and use glue, you can do paper maché — in maybe four layers. Nevertheless, it's a long, tedious process. But celastic, you can make great, big things in one layer. So that started the bigger stuff. — (Ernstthal, interview.)

They made the 13 or 14 'Crucifixion puppets' ' heads 'in less than a week — maybe we'd cast three at a time. But the celastic made it possible to make the positive in a few hours.' — (Ernstthal, interview.)

3. '. . . made of wood, various metals, and cloth, weigh from forty to a hundred and forty pounds each, and are controlled from above with two iron rods and a thick string. A heavy rod connected to the puppet's head makes it possible for him to walk, fight, nod, swivel when he speaks, and suffer decapitation when a mortal sword blow arrives. In the Manteo scheme of things, a dying marionette almost always loses his head. A thinner rod attaches to the right hand — in the case of a knight or an enemy warrior, this is the sword-bearing hand — and the thick string manipulates the left, or shield-bearing, arm. Ariosto's women squabble often, but rarely with weapons. This leaves them free to talk with their hands, which, thanks to the crew on the bridge, they do fluently.' — (Mark Singer, '*Opera Dei Pupi*,' *The New Yorker*, September 17, '79.)

roughly to the center of the stage. It was the greatest theatre I have ever seen. By the way, those guys live in Coney Island now – working as mechanics. They don't make theatre anymore. They used to perform on Mulberry Street in Little Italy. But no more. (TDR: What was so good about the Sicilian theatre?) It was great because the artists invented a way of telling, a way of translating and creating a reality, that first of all defines reality. Even though I didn't understand a word of the Sicilian dialect I could sense the purity of this theatre. It was necessary. I feel that art in the modern world is generally superfluous. Either we should find a true need for it, or give it up. We named our theatre Bread & Puppet because we felt that the theatre should be as basic as bread.'

(Brown and Seitz, *With the Bread & Puppet Theatre, TDR* 38, '68.)

'In the Sicilian puppet show, when the Pope is sick, the sickness comes flying down from the ceiling in the form of blood and lands on him. When the sickness is taken away by the doctor, these spots are painted a different color and taken away in a bag. The translation of the language is so detailed, so real. We don't have that anymore. We call it symbolism nowadays, when somebody does that, but that isn't symbolism. It's the nature of real language to do that, to make something understandable, to detail something to the point that it is very clear. But we don't dare to use real language. Our language is only a destroyed small portion of language. We are inhibited by all the implications that we have learned in school, by all the sciences. But we are looking for it, for a real communicable language.'

(Schumann interviewed by Kourilsky in '73, in F. Kourilsky, *Dada and Circus, Tulane Drama Review* '61.)

'Even though the Sicilian puppets were not any bigger than my *King Story* puppets, they *looked* much larger in the framework that they were used in, and I was fascinated by the *strength* of that *size* that told the stories that reenacted these battle scenes with these *Orlando Furioso* furious events, and when I came back that fall, after travelling during the summer, and then settled in New York in the fall of '63, my whole idea for puppets was to build *giant* puppets, so I built these yellow people, Jesus and his disciples, and the fool and the soldiers, and the beast.' (Schumann, interview, '79.)

The Manteo puppets, being operated from the outside, were not 'live puppets' – with inside operators – like the big puppets he made that fall:[4] he was inspired by them stylistically rather than technically.

The Manteo show is crude. First of all, it has only two elements: romantic but decent love and fighting, and the fighting seems to provide most of the action, the heroic Christian knights, except when subjected to a sneak attack, defeating though only after three or four rounds, the

---

4. Which is why he has sometimes compared to them not his inside-operated big '63/'64, but his outside-operated giant '65 and '66 puppets:

'Die Stockpuppen, wie wir sie bei den ersten religiösen Spielen im Auftrag einer New Yorker Kirche verwendeten, gab es seit Jahrtausenden in Java oder China, die Riesenpuppen, welche von 3-5 Schauspielern getragen und bewegt werden, in Sizilien, bei den Indianern und in Indien.' — (Schumann, *Das Brot & Puppen-Theater, tendenzen*, Nov. '66-Feb. '67.)

Christian or heathen villains. This gets kind of dull. Secondly — but here I may be wrong, having seen only the current Manteo, a poor puppeteer, operate the puppets — the puppets seem generally — perhaps they all are — two-rod puppets, one for the puppet as a whole, one for its right arm, so that not only is there no leg control during the fast action (the giant-seeming gleaming, armored figures bashing into one another, their legs dangling), but most gesturing (there is some head manipulation, achieved I don't know how) is right arm gesturing, notably the knights hitting their shields or, in a contemptuous gesture preliminary to fighting, their opponent's armor with the swords attached to their fists (the sword's being attached badly limits the gestural opportunities for the romantic scenes. At best the lover puts his sworded right hand behind his back in discoursing with his lady). Still, as you sit and watch, some of the medieval romance and adventure, a kind of high idealism and the spirit of risky action in a world all background, emerges from the rough low class tones of the puppeteers' voices, and holds you. I heard no narration: the story, as in real theatre, comes from dialogue; but in this sense this is story-telling puppetry: the action, dominant in Punch and Judy, is subordinated to the story. Schumann's puppetry is in this story-telling tradition; nuanced, three-dimensionally pictorial groupings replacing the drama/humor of actions, except that, having assumed into puppetry the allegoric universalism of the Morality Play, and a poetic shorthand of abstraction, his stories are not of the fates of characters, but of Man's fate.

Schumann liked the Manteo puppets for their power and roughness:[5] they reassured him as to the possibilities of puppetry. The plastic, the cuteness and commercial good humor of the American puppeteers had disgusted (and probably discouraged) him. The Manteo puppets showed him puppetry could be serious business.

'The very small puppets are best for comedy. The really large ones — the eighteen-foot ones — are also at their best when they are buffoons. The medium-size puppets are very good for drama.'

(Schumann, in Brown and Seitz, *With the Bread & Puppet Theatre, TDR* 38.)

His giant puppets of '65, '66 were buffoonish, but during the '70s he built

---

5. Max Jacob, after the National Socialist regime had put the village fair, family, oldtime, popular (volkstümlich) 'marionettists' into a single trade association with the artistic (school and concert hall oriented) 'puppeteers,' much to the chagrin of the latter, of whom Jacob invited a group of the marionettists to a festive afternoon at which the vulgars were treated to a Hohnsteiner puppet performance:

'Einer der ganz alten Spieler nahm mich zur Seite und meinte: "Herr Jacob, ich begreife doch nicht so recht, weiso Sie einen so grossen Erfolg in aller Welt haben. Ihre Kasperpuppen sind doch so klein, dass man sie kaum sieht. Und wir haben in unserem Theater Marionetten mit echten Haaren, und sie sind ein Meter gross. Da müsste unser Erfolg doch auch grösser sein!" — (Jacob, *Mein Kasperl*, '81.)

ones — a solar deity, a death rider, for instance — that were awesome. But he is right about the big — 'medium sizes' — ones.

At Hurleyville he saw that he might get the values of dance from puppets and the values of sculpture as well, how with big dancing puppets he could do the dance of death in life with the awesomeness befitting it. His seven years' conflict between the big mute dead statements of monumental sculpture and the authentic expression of the individual's felt life in dance was resolved. Now all he had to do was to find a way to make puppets that were live. Here *Totentanz* showed the way: he would make puppets of his performers, make puppets worked from the inside. His timid and awkward dancers had been freed and aggrandized by masks. The puppet would work as mask.

13. How Bob saw him.

Young Ernstthal became Schumann's collaborator, i.e. had the privilege and in fact pleasure of working his arse off for him during much of his heroic period of the '60s:

'But he was very gruff, to say the least, and didn't give a shit about anybody, or what anybody thought. That's why we were so good. But he was also very – he was gruff. Simple. He still is. (I: What was he gruff about?) Well, he was just – he never explained anything. He never was humane. He would just say, "Do it – let's do it like this." And we – the truth is, I really liked Peter and we got along really well. And, in fact, I don't know if it's legitimate to say it, but I feel like for years I was the intermediary between Peter and the other people, because he was so sure of himself and just so direct and abrupt and gruff. But I really liked him and understood after a while what was going on and what we were doing and I got into it and I could – I was the American side. The softer side, of it. I kind of translated it into a more – he was unapproachable. He was very unapproachable. He would never take suggestions. And one of the great things about him also was that he never cared for praise or blame, ever. In other words, we would – the show was theatre. Based on work. And we would do this great show, like *Fire*, and it would be the last night or something. And sometimes it would be so great. I mean, you could tell. It was theatre history. It was fabulous. Newport in 1967. We did a show there. And all he would say was: "We'll start a new show tomorrow. Tomorrow afternoon let's work out our next one." That's all, or what we should do next, or what was wrong. He never cared – he never basked in praise at all. Nor did he give a shit what anyone thought, ever. About blaming. If it was obscure – which it really was – I mean, in early days the things were pretty obscure – tended to be obscure. So that was his virtue. Because he just didn't care. Didn't care what anybody said. So anyway, he was frightening because he was so much that way. He had the barest of civilities in his nature. Of course, it mellowed out, in time – very much so, when things got going. The early days were really different, because it was so new.

Whatever it was, the direction was always forward. And that's why he succeeded. Because it was always forward. No matter how good the show was, he would often say it was shitty. And no matter how poor the show was, he would sometimes really like it. But it didn't matter whether he liked it or disliked it. It had really no relevance. So it was always just go ahead. It was total work. Whatever it was, it was just work. And that's also why during those years it really – probably saved my life, because I was in the mainstream of American things that were going on on the Lower East Side at that time. The anarchists and dope and all this stuff. That was really – that was my milieu.

There were always dark undercurrents ... because of Peter's nature. It was very hard for him. We would do funny kids' shows and stuff – but it always had a bite to it. In a way he was obsessed. It's like this: He was obsessed with soldiers – soldiers marching in and soldiers killing .... Peter by himself was almost, at that point, especially, caught up in anger and obsession in a certain way. An obsession with soldiers, an obsession with death, obsession with darkness and soldiers and war. And at that time, war was far from the American scene. Peter was — it was like a nightmare that he was trying to get out, or exorcise. He has a dark nature. (I: The image of the man. What would it be in the summer of '63?) It was like a dark humor. It was also a totally — he was really, as always, he has a real conflict between a loving side and the dark side. Like, essentially, he's really a loving person. He transmits all that love inside to a very staunch family relation. He was a very staunch family man. And the good life. That was the trip. Mr. Miller and the good life. A lot of these real early linoleum blocks and stuff, talk about the good life. These kinds of things. The celebration of the ordinary. So his love and his happy quality was a very strict celebration of ordinary life qualities. For instance, I don't know if this has anything to do with it, but in the middle of the tour, or during the tour, after we'd been all these different places and just driven around, he decided we were going to go to Putney and we're going to see Elka. I realized at the time that he just — he was horny and he wanted to see his wife. But he would never say that or loosen up enough to make that a reason. Do you know what I mean? There was always another reason. But it was clear. He'd been away from her for a long time, and he was horny.

And — I should really qualify this thing about drinking, because he would drink a lot of beer and stuff, but he was never, ever — in a way I could almost say I have never seen him drunk. I think I've never seen Peter drunk. Really drunk.

But it was my impression of Peter — he was obsessive. He was an obsessive. He was obsessed with his own internal imagery, absolutely. But he had that kind of genius of never giving up. He had the kind of genius of never straying, ever, from his point. He never gave in. Never took, either, what anybody else said as important.

He was very strict — a good life was his ideal. So, like I say, his love was all centered around the family, this family and the kids. But it was a very strict version of the good life. Maybe like her grandfather's, Scott Nearing. It was a very, very strict version: "This is good." Like the bread, you know. Uncompromising. A little bitter, and very hard to chew. But it was good, with a capital G. This is Good. This is Good for you. This is Good policy for you. A Good way to live. Da, da, da. "This is the Good life," in *detail*. In absolute detail. Without humor. Also, it's a very European sensibility. That's the other thing I remember. Distinctly. He was definitely a European.

Another great thing of Peter and why he survived so well is that he never dealt with theory. Even these things you see that he wrote, these little paragraphs and stuff — *Streets and Theater*, you know, the few things — they're all very, very — like woodcuts, almost. They're blocked out. He never dabbled. He never discussed them. And that's why we were so good. That's why he kept going so long, when other people crashed on their ass. Including the Mime Troupe and all those others, because they were constantly dealing with ideology. He never dealt with ideology and no one could care about ideology, because it wasn't the *point*. Just do it. Doesn't matter. Including the Christian stories. We *evoked* the mythology, the reality of the mythology.

So, on one hand he was that roguish image that I really think he took seriously. *Rinaldini* was one of his first Paper Movies and he had it when I met him and it was — we did it on this '63 summer job — *Rinaldini* so he did, definitely have a certain roguish quality to him, but on the other hand he had the "good life" routine which was very deep and ingrained in him. The Good Life. On one hand it was duty — on one hand he got Elka pregnant and married her and he was a wild bohemian — very serious artist. But I think his sense of duty was extremely strong and in a certain way he lost his adolescence. So, it would come out once in a while — like with this dancing in Provincetown — drinking beer — in fact, the whole summer tour — to laugh and loosen up a little bit because he missed it. He was a very serious artist and you had Elka and they had a family and they had to really pull it together real fast. So he, in a way — he didn't have his romance. He lost out on his period of romantic life in a certain way. And I feel like, in fact, years later it came out when he started with women more. But in the beginning it was — he was very, very strict with himself and he was always — in fact, I've heard it said and other people have said it — that when they met Peter — in fact, I've thought it — they always assumed that his wife or his girlfriend would be very beautiful — would be a real beauty — or a dancer more, you know, a real sharp looking, beautiful girl — and Elka didn't fit that image. She was the earth mother like — that lovely, wonderful person who really held it together incredibly under terrific circumstances. When I brought Sarah, my first wife, to New York to 6th Street where we were gonna live, she just cried one day. She couldn't believe it — she'd never even been in New York. So anyway, but what I meant, it was like — in a certain way it was like — it was out of a dream a little — on one end there was the working class ethic, although he was a middle class boy. The work ethic. And the 'poor' ethic, that money is shit and all that — being poor. So he had a Protestant, Lutheran shit and money ethic — that it was evil — that it was bad and that the devil is always at hand. Temptation, filthy money, etcetera and so on and so on. And he — but it's true — what was that image? It's almost hard to — I know — it's interesting because it's — I just loved it because it was so poetic — what I'm saying was he was so out of time — he was so serious, on one hand, and yet his stuff was so fanciful on the other. That he was so serious about doing the right thing and he was so strict in certain ways and yet he didn't dress, talk, act, or do anything like anybody else. Nor did he give a shit what anybody thought of him. And at the same time we'd put on masks and blow these Woolworth tin horns and little kazoos and stuff and ride through town beating on a drum and collecting people for a show. So on one hand he was fanciful and light-weight — on the other, he was totally serious about it, which was even more strange, because he took it all so — so seriously.

He became an institution and all that — afterwards — more — it became a recognized thing and I feel like that squeezed him a bit because when it was nothing — when we were nobody — he was at home on the road and being an outsider. He's a total outsider, possibly, so to run a commune is the last role that he should play and it was absurd for him to think he could do it — you know what I mean, he's a total and perennial outsider. But the image of him was totally European, number one, nothing to do with anything American. For one thing, he had a German accent — he was more at home in German — he had that European — towards life — kind of a wry and sarcastic attitude — a very masculine mistrust of women, I would have to say, at that time. As a — anything that would take away his anxiety he ran away from — really — including women and dope. Again, it didn't fit in — right? It didn't fit in to relax the anxiety, the tension, because he was just driven by the tension and it was the European tradition of anxious theatre, or worried, and that there was no solution to it and that there was never an end to it. There was no end to the anxiety – no end to the pain of the world. That's why our most successful things were always painful. The lightweight things were never that successful. They never really worked.

I think he was always guilty. I don't think he ever threw it off. And he probably tried – but he could never – the thing is, he would never give up his guilt, because he would give up the mainspring of his art. Because our great stuff was all based on guilt: *Fire* was based on guilt, in a certain way. I mean, it was to depress people and to make people feel for the sacrifice of others. And morality – and a finger pointing at everybody, saying: "Look at you, you fat pigs – while other people are starving." I think he could never get over his – the guilt.'

(Ernstthal, interview.)

From all those years of work of Ernstthal's, there remains not one mask or puppet: they were all Schumann's.

14. Four periods of Schumann's creative activity 1963-1983.

Art, though it may present itself otherwise, is communication. Communication normally has formal features communicating something about it itself, features that function as manner or gesture of communication. Its content is apt to contribute further information about it: for a definition of its gesture toward the communicatee; and so are the circumstances under which it is undertaken. Some of the information, notably that from content, may only tell us what gesture the communicator would want to be perceived as making toward the audience, and for him/her to be misrepresenting themselves would not be unusual: it is an everyday occurrence. But the sum of the information would be an important – even crucial – part of the communication – and, answering the question 'what is he/she up to?', a part crucial for an understanding or other e.g. emotional intake of it, so much so that one normally looks for it so as to be able to interpret the communication, and would tend to define the objective gesture, what it in fact was, independent of the communicator's intentions, and normally would tell us also what he/she had meant it to be.

A communicational gesture may indicate that no communication is intended: that the communication is not one. But if it doesn't, it will normally besides indicating that the communication is – meant to be – one, indicate of what sort it is supposed to be, and will normally do so by indicating what the communicator hopes to achieve by it, what its effect is to be or in what area its effect is to be, or else by indicating what prompts the communicator to communicate, what his/her reason or motive is. Such definition of function or purpose will normally at the same time define a relationship between communicator and communicatee, i.e. roles that the communicator conceives him/herself and them to be playing in the event, the emission and receipt of the communication.

Though Schumann's stock of metaphors and the basic ideas he has expressed by them have, as far as I can make out, remained fairly constant over the twenty-year period under consideration (the images carrying the metaphors and the topics the ideas are applied to varying), and though he has striven to maintain his communicational gesture overtly constant – an odd mixture: somewhat courtly and aloof, detached, yet also easy and relaxed, courteous and even friendly, all in all the gentlemanly gesture of a private person making offerings ex professio, his feelings about the world – life, humanity, things – or mood have varied (remaining fairly constant, so far as one can tell from his output, over periods of four to seven years), more, it would seem, as a result of his work, i.e. of the activity of expressing a given kind of feeling or mood – perhaps exhausting their expressive potentials relative to his ideas or putting these ideas in a new light or making him want to convey a different aspect of the ideas and/or cummulatively due to the absence of response he was privately hoping for or that, indifference to response notwithstanding, affected him — and perhaps because one's basic feelings/mood change in some rhythm as one grows older — than because of changes either in his personal circumstances[1] or in the world,[2] though probably to some extent responding to changes in the Climate of Opinion in the social strata and sub-strata furnishing his audiences and associates and even in the Public at large; and with these feelings, his feelings about those he was addressing by his work — his audiences or the audiences he wished for or imagined himself addressing — or humanity — have varied, and thus his effective communicational gesture. The four periods of his creativity are separated by crises both in his personal and work circumstances and in his ability to arrive at conceptualizations serviceable for his work.

The cause of crises in the careers of individuals routinely achieving the impossible may be sought in a weakening of their powers and this in turn in a weakening of their faith in what they're doing, manifest to themselves as difficulty of conceptualization in the work process. 1960-'61: inability to embody his life-death dialectic in a dance work. 1969: inability to accomodate the benign God of the Christians in a biblical representation of history. 1973: inability to identify theatrically serviceable reasons for hope for humanity, given man's predatory and competitive character. 1978: inability in pageants to accommodate the destructive efficiency of civilization to an anthropocentric pantheism.

Very roughly we can say he felt discouraged, disturbed, down during a second and fourth period — c. '70-'74, '79 following — and the opposite — confident and affirmative — during a first and third period: c. '63-'69, '75-'78. When he was up, he felt good about addressing people by his art, addressed them fairly directly and as though sure about his reasons for

---

1. The death of his father in '72 presumably affected him, as it would any man, strongly, but I doubt it affected his 'communicational gesture;' but the passage of his children out of adolescence ('78/'81) probably relevantly affected his mind set. As for the self-caused changes, matrimony and first children ('59/'61), onset of promiscuity ('69/'70(?)): they are as much effects as causes of basic attitude changes. ·

2. To my mind the larger world, the historical situation, has been fairly constant since the pacificatory integration of Western working classes into the power structure of Western societies in the Great Depression, Stalin's institution of a progressive (industrializing) despotism in the Soviet Union, the collapse of European world hegemony and the perfection of nuclear weaponry, expression and means of the total opposition between free enterprise capitalism and state capitalism in the '40s. And probably to Schumann's also. The Vietnam War was no great shakes: Schumann could have maintained his communicational gesture relative to other matters when it ended; and in fact changed his stance before it was over.

doing so and the effects he wanted to have on them; when he was down, his address seemed more indirect, he seemed more concerned with what he was doing and how he was doing it than with those addressed and its effects on or via them. All this time, up or down, he didn't think much of those he meant to address, the ordinary man, the people (and thought worse of those he in fact got to address), held them in low esteem, and thought things were bad and getting worse and were likely to end in a catastrophe for humanity at large. But he was always polite, and mostly careful to leave a little hope.

During the first of these periods, his communicational gesture was in the manner of a challenge: he indicated some manner of guilt on the part of his audiences, and, though in an aloof manner, that, moral realities being what they are, they had better straighten up and fly right. It indicated that the desired effect was proximately on conscience, beyond that on political expression, beyond that on the quantity of brutality in the world. It defined the communicator as concerned director of conscience, the art consumer as responsible fellow man who knew better: adventitiously exposed to the art work.

During his second period, the gesture of his work was monstrative: he pointed to the world's suffering, its causes in man, the islets of reprieve (the family): nary a suggestion that anybody, for instance the spectator do anything about it: the barker's gesture at an amusement park horror show. the indication was not so much of an effect as of a motive: the communicator desired to express a perception. The gesture defined him as expositor of reality, and the art consumer as one made privy to his view of it: privileged co-spectator, rather than recipient of information.

During the third period, the gesture was invitational: that of the officiant at a (thank- and praise- rather than prayerful) celebration of the ultimate powers (those of maternal life in nature): he invited his neighbors to join him in a hosanna. Humanity's suffering was subsumed under the world's overall generically resurrective proclivity; and so was the citizen's duty (now represented as something he owed it to himself to discharge) to interfere with crime. The indication was neither of an effect nor of a motive, but of a function – an institutional function – of the event: a get together (in bad times, admittedly) for selfless rejoicing. The communicator appeared as lavishly provident host at a feast for the simple in spirit, and these, the audience, were defined as presumptively like-minded congregation.

Of late, during the fourth period, the gesture has been ambiguous: it has in fact been prophetic: he is warning us that the end is near (subsidiarily charging that the convenant has been broken); but as a carry-over from the preceding period's formalism there is a transparent overlay of prayer, prayer that the worst may be avoided, a prayer in distress, and the hint of a gesture that we are expected to join in. But the dominant gesture is prophetic: the shuddering divulgation of a vision from which the visionary recoils, and the charge – an accusatory component – that we are guilty and deserve our fate, having brought it on ourselves. The communicator hereby is defining himself as the unfortunate possessor of clear sight at grips with what he is seeing (rather, really, than communicating with anybody) and who, since the situation is virtually beyond remedy, has little if any hope of an effect but is helplessly moved to utterance by the terror of his vision – and the consumers of the art work proximately defined as victims of the artist's obsessive perspicuity, ultimately as sinners in court.

Having originally risen to moral challenge and incitement to remedial action (his art a reminder of duty under the circumstances), he retreated from his protest and adopted a non-confrontational (and non-provocative) expository stance (his art now a representation); which he then after a while gave up in turn, advancing (his art become a festivity) to an affirmation of fellowship; a posture which and the attendant transcendental optimism of which then after a while became untenable and were given up by him for a stance in the main turned away from the audience and focused on doom: his art, subsidiarily warning and accusation, in the main a cry of terror.

The overall major variables of this development of the formal social character of his work on the one hand have been the alternatives of a positive, negative and neutral relation to an audience, in which regard the development has been an advance from negative to neutral to positive, followed by negative again, on the other hand, alternatives with respect to involvement with the audience, in which respect its phases have been: direct relation (moral challenge of the other), indirect relation (presentation of a representation to an other), communion (offer of occasion for a joint action), no relation (the artist at grips with his vision and not communicationally motivated or oriented at all), i.e. a retreat from the direct to the indirect, was followed by an advance to intimacy, a greater involvement than the original one, which was again followed by a retreat, but a more total one, a break (though, as I have indicated, a camouflaged one):

> negative direct relation;
> neutral indirect relation;
> positive intimacy;
> negative non-relation.

We may perhaps view these shifts as the desperate plays of an idealist artist whose idealism comprises both a negative view of humanity among other things attributing to it a near-total imperviousness to attempts to improve it by art and a moral sense precluding the luxury of art not devoted to an improvement of humanity, but whom in any event inner necessity compels to do art, to cope with the dilemma posed by his idealism: his successive gestures of communication his phantom solutions of it,[3] attempts to evade it. I see his addressive modes in phases (1) and (3) as attempts to break through that imperviousness, adopted in spite of a sense of futility, or with that sense suppressed by an access of enthusiasm that after a while runs dry, those of phases (2) and (4) as retreats from commitment to communication, the work being carried on in a spirit of defiance. As a being profoundly moral, Schumann has had to keep on trying to communicate. As an artist, he had to keep on doing art. As an intellectual, he was profoundly sceptical of the efficacy of his moralist artistry; and out of this scepticism kept changing his art and its communicational form. I don't think Schumann's European low view of humanity and pessimism wavered much: but they were periodically overcome by America's incitement to communicate or by some blind enthusiasm arising from the pleasure of using his new medium in a new way.

Communication is the social relation:
communicator ⟶ means of communication ⟶ communicatee;
Schumann's puppeteering the relation:
Schumann ⟶ (puppeteers ⟶ puppets) ⟶ audience.

The variation of Schumann's gesture toward the audience has, though not exclusively, once we make allowances for the veiling effect of his recurrent recourse to previous modes to a considerable extent been defined by variation of the puppeteers' relation, within the spectacle, to the puppets: by changes of performance style.

(1) After some experimentation, '63/'65, but generally during the '60s, '63-'69, the image was in the service of the message and this was made clear by a quite unembarrassed, unashamed use of puppet-handlers visible to the audience, not really part of the show, though Schumann now might enjoy the little operators next to a giant puppet, now a gang of fresh-faced kids rushing about arranging things: certain puppet gestures, the puppets generally specializing in special gestures, though especially so during the '60s, were the focus of his directing, they were not just to show, but to 'dramatize' some moral point, intensively embody what it 'meant in human terms' – often enough, normally: war-making and/or war suffering, and the visible actions of the operators apostrophized the audience even if their demeanor – they – didn't, held up and framed those gesture-conveyed intensities of feeling that were to convey the message, and so made address evident. They made the puppet's simple gestures telling rather than allegorically representative.

The 'mime' that was also done on his stage was, I think, then more

---

3. Thus also my father, à propos of 'socialist realism' and in the perspective of a global spread of the Soviet system, once remarked, without seeing this as in the least a reason for not advancing the advent of socialism by his art, that it was very well possible that art might disappear for some centuries.

important than he liked or likes to allow, and involved people-rather-than-puppets on the stage that were 'really part of the show' (not addressive frame), but it was 'epic' in the sense of my father's use of the term with reference to acting, and of the sort aimed at by Ronny Davis (San Francisco Mime Troupe) during the same period (or that Chaikin, acting B. Brecht for the Becks at the beginning of the '60s, briefly got into before he started developing his own Open Theatre kind of thing):[4]

'Mime as practiced by the Mime Troupe, should not be confused with pantomime. Davis describes the difference as that between the work of Charles Chaplin and Marcel Marceau. In pantomime the artist uses no props, but creates, as Marceau does, the illusion of working with these props. The mime is more concerned with the clash of ideas than with technical gimmicks, and uses any and all props, including his voice, to portray these ideas. Mime differs from ordinary theatre, explains Cohon (Peter Cohon, around '67 in the San Francisco Mime Troupe (SSB)) in that it is "a ballet of ideas. We don't want people to empathize but to judge."'

(R. Hurwitt, *Revolution Stage, East Village Other*, November 15-30, '67.)

When Schumann during the second half of '69 got tired of dependence on performers, he didn't just have in mind the underplayed gestural and mimicral pathos of certain of his un-masked performers, but this epic mime as well.

The mime shows tended not to be of the morally challenging sort typical of the period, but as in the non-mime performances of this period the puppet operators "held up" the puppets and their gesture to the audience, hereby addressing the challenge to them – e.g. in the street demonstrations – so in the mime shows, the performers presented their gestures to the audience.

(2) The essence of his spectacles' style during the second monstrative rather than incitatory phase was the compositional use of puppets and masked shrouded operators, semi-puppets, their gestures components of a picture, inserted into a stage frame: operators and mimes substantially absent, and absent also the narrative and/or addressive element, either by being altogether absent, or by explicitly accompanying the referring to the spectacle: the quasi-narrators relating to it rather than to the audience. The simple, emotionally intensively charged gestures of the puppets or masked and shrouded operators now are no longer the primary and focal elements, but rather are integrated major or key elements of compositions. The effect now is closer to that of dance (e.g. *Simple Light*), though sometimes to a dance disarticulated into a more or less comic mechanical ballet with objects, or into a 'happening.'

(3) During the third communally celebratory phase, the puppet appears as

---

4. Cf. Jotterand, *Le nouveau theatre americain.*

figure in the depth of a landscape, its gesture now less important than its stature and displacement through space, and gesture less important now also than during the two preceding phases in being often subordinate to stance or to pattern of motion. The puppet is located – we locate it – and thus has a sculptural aspect. This is the art, notably, of his circus pageants, but to some extent modifies (in the 'morality plays' of this period) stage styles also. These spectacles have the character of events – rather than of demonstrations or representations. Humans characteristically appear as transporters of the puppets – rather than as operators of them; sometimes as decorative participants in the event with no theatrical function, at least not any in any narrow sense of 'theatrical'. They have no intrinsic relation to the puppets. Rather they relate to them and to the event as does the audience, representing it within the show, linking it to the show as though to say 'it's your show as much as ours, the difference between our active and your passive role in the event is negligible.'

(4) During his so far last phase the focus of his staging shifted again, now to an interaction between puppets, typically but not always dummies, and performers, and/or between masks and puppet shells, the elements of puppets, and performers: the operators of the puppets now staged as performers, not just operators, performers manipulating the puppets or puppet elements, with a focus on this interaction. This puppetry may perhaps be thought of as a variant – an expressionist variant – of the performance mode of Bunraku,[5] like it in that the focus includes the manipulation, quite unlike it in that the manipulators in no way figure as gods or agents of fate, but as embroiled. The company is allowing the audience to see what it is at grips with: the puppeteers as in the prior three phases standing for Schumann and performing his gesture.

As his performance style has varied in terms of variations in the relation puppeteer-puppet, so the style of his masks and puppets has varied in terms of variations in their relation to performance. During his up-phases they are designed as implements of performance, and for communication. During his down-phases they are styled to be focal objects, and become private.

1956-1960. Schumann starts out, in Germany, as an artist in the humble medium of paper maché, bent on proving its adequacy, given artisanly care, ingenuity and improvement, for making beautiful objects: a vindication of spirit over matter. He uses the lost plaster cast technique, special paper, special glue. The objects themselves don't stand for anything much. Their use in performance is incidental.

1961-1962. He next, catching on to the spirit of New York and America, locates value in the doing of something in the public place: the

---

5. Cf. Susan Sontag's *Note on Bunraku*, in the program of the appearances, March 12-19, '83 at New York City of Osaka Bunraku Troupe, reproduced as Appendix XIII.

performance itself is the thing, doing must not be obscured by Things. He makes his masks directly over clay, hastily, not bothering to invent new shapes, just grabbing the ones he had already done, makes quick copies and uses them. For the sake of ease of performance he uses life casts of the performers' faces so the masks will fit better. The performance also is of a sort he has already done, but he now uses Things to enhance its power: masked dance. The masks substitute for skill.

1962-1963. This now leads him on to the idea of exploiting the power of those things more directly and intensively for performance: showing them in postures and movement and shaping them to make these effective rather than for power of thinghood: puppetry. Puppetry over a curtain. The puppets are like masked dancers: their wire-levers are inside them. Each is specialized for one type of gesture. Instead of masks for performers, he makes heads for these puppets. For making them he reverts to his old method – lost plaster casts. It is probably the puppetry, a play with things, that gives him the idea of a people-puppetry, something close to his old medium of dance performance, but making use not only of masks, but also of puppet bodies: painted carton-box bodies.

1963-1964. He discovers a new modern means, celastic, facilitating the production of his things (it does not significantly change their appearance) and allowing a new avenue to power of performance, size. He still makes his things by the old careful lost plaster cast method. They are styled for size now: the heads and the garments are simpler, more approximate. These puppets are essentially just enlarged versions of the wire rod puppets, still intended for play above a curtain, wooden sticks and poles replacing the wire for the added strength needed for the size. But some of them develop the carton-box puppet idea: they have inside operators. Their size allows for it, and their weight invites it since it makes just holding them up an essential and important part of using them. And one of them is made specifically for being seen in front of the curtain: moving on the ground.

1964-1969. During the new few years, further sacrificing static thing-appeal (texture, detail), he radically simplifies his production methods (by making masks and heads directly over clay), aggressively pushes his exploitation of size (giant puppets), incorporates the puppet operators into the performance (outside operators, then: formally dressed in white), develops the gestural potentials of big puppets (short stick head handles, puppet heads mounted on top of operators' heads) to a point where they can be effectively and diversely used in front of the curtain or without one, and enriches performance by combinations of big puppets and face-mask-masked performers, and by mime: performance specifically qua communication the guiding aim in all this.

1970-1974. His next period as regards puppet and mask making is one of experimentation, playfulness, liberation. He develops his staging in two opposite directions, a hand- or marionette puppet stage-like box-theatre and outdoor large-area performance, but his puppet- and mask-making is not focused on enhancing the peculiar powers of these performance modes. (E.g. he did not develop puppets for the string operation he essayed for the box format.) In stark contrast to the preceding period it is not subordinate to performance. One attempt to increase gestural scope and freedom by innovation in puppet construction (back pack puppets) is a failure. Another innovation or semi-innovation (bulbhead puppets) actually reduces gestural scope and freedom. He allows himself luxuries of refinement by new techniques of celastic sculpturing (small piece, large sheet), essays a new material (fiberglass), and, getting away from the idea of head and body representation (by draped abstract non-human non-animal bodies, crowd puppets), gains a new freedom in puppet design.

1974-1978. His new freedom in puppet design is during the following period once again put into the service of performance by the important use of four puppet types designed for movement as part of a picture in a setting, three of them broached during the preceding period (stilt puppets, kite-like puppets, puppets with cutout heads and cutout puppets, animal puppets with wooden frameworks). His puppet heads again become simple, but are now, like the clean-cut puppet bodies of this period, well defined, and color becomes an important concern. Whereas during the preceding period, the spectacles sometimes appeared the upshot of the puppets' appearances and movements, during this period, the puppets, however striking, register as the spectacles' implements. But he now conceives of performance as utterance of feelings that are or should be shared rather than as address from-to, and the puppets and masks are styled accordingly: not for transmission but for embodiment.

1979-1983. During a so far last phase, his work then seemed to move into still another phase, characterized by an exposition of the means of the medium (masks, puppet coverings, puppet handling) and the integration of this exposition into performance by means of graphically elaborated puppet handling, aesthetically and semantically integrated into performance, and by the expository use of masks and puppet shells: use of theatrically handled dummy puppets, and choral movements of hand held masks not or not only used for masking and of puppet half shells. His focus is on the medium itself. In the masks and costuming there is a concommitant but not obviously related tendency toward individuation, the representation of individuals. This part, but quite consistently with this, the puppets are styled as dramatis personae, social figures in interaction.

Part II.
How it worked.

Contents: Part II

1. Modus vivendi. Back to the Lower East Side Life of poverty in a slum. — 159
2. Modus operandi. The start. The elements. Minimalization of costs. The objective: art as non-remunerative non-commodity. Not quite attainable. — 166
3. Modus operandi I. The places. '63 –. — 169
4. Modus operandi II. The costs of labor. Limits to their reduction. — 180
5. Modus operandi II. Finance. Funding rejected. Touring the essential revenue source. — 189
6. Modus operandi III. Labor procurement. Motivations. The variables of its formula. Structural forces. — 201
7. Modus operandi III. The labor force. From group of pals to group of acolytes to horde of hippies to commune to seasonal workforce to salaried employees. 1963 –. — 218
8. Modus operandi IV. The work. Puppet-making. — 254
9. Modus operandi IV. The work. Show-making. Rehearsals as show-making experiments with the puppets. — 262

1. Modus vivendi. Back to the Lower East Side. A Life of poverty in a slum. Later in the country. The lasting modus vivendi: A life of poverty.

'(Ephraim: So, when did we move to New York? When was that?) In the fall of '63 we moved back to New York. (Elka: To Suffolk Street. A beautiful apartment that Peter found for us.) Yeah, it was a wonderful tiny, tiny little storefront on Suffolk Street. (Elka: Storefront. No windows, no walls, no doors.) My tryouts with celastic and acetone in the front and you all lived in the back room. (All laugh.) Then I found the loft – no, then I first found the apartment through Claes Oldenburg. I knew him and he was moving out of his apartment. (Elka: He was successful.) He was getting to be successful – a successful sculptor. He was a happening-maker and he sculpted and he was living on the same block that we had lived on before we knew him. (Elka: He had a better apartment than we had – big and sunny.) Much nicer, so we moved into his apartment. He gave it to us. And we also found this Delancey Street loft then, a beautiful loft that Red Grooms had had before us. (Elka: How did you find it? Did you just – ?) By chance. I didn't know that Red Grooms had had it.' (Schumann, interview, '79.)

'He decided he wanted to move to the East Side, which at that time was a real mixed bag of a slum. So we went to New York and we found two storefronts adjoining. At 148 Suffolk Street and 152 Suffolk Street. And there were gypsies living in these storefronts – actually before – the studio was 148. I think it's the same as the Delancey – no, wait a second – anyway, it was on Suffolk Street between Rivington and Stanton Street. (I: Still a very rough area.) Yeah. At that time it was mostly Puerto Rican, as I remember. And we moved. There were *two* storefronts in two different buildings, but next to each other. And one was a phone company depot of some kind and the other was where gypsies were living, and one was boarded up in front, so it was like a living place – there was no – it was just boarded up. And next door was a glass window. So on the one side he moved in with Elka and the kids, which was really tacky – really rough. They were living like gypsies in the *one* side, and next door I lived. I moved, and there was a studio, a little room. There was a studio and behind it was a *teeny* room, and we hung all the puppets in it, and there was a little bed in there and I slept there. And we moved to Suffolk Street and that was our first Lower East Side place, I think, in about six to eight months and possibly a year – no, I don't think it was a whole year. I think in about eight months, I was walking down to Delancey Street, which was a block away, and I noticed that above Max's there was, I believe, a For Lease sign in the top loft above Max's bar, and there were gypsies living on the *second* floor. And I came back – or I looked at it, and I told Peter, "Hey, there's a loft on the corner. Let's go find out what's going on." So he went up there and it was about $80 a month, or something. And he rented it – I think it was the spring of '64. It might have been right in the middle of the year. I remember it was sunny. So it's possible that we lived there a couple of months and then maybe in November or something we saw this loft. It *had* been Red Grooms' – he had his museum there. Anyway, he called it a museum. So the question was: we thought we knew — that it was a beautiful loft-space. It seemed that way at the time. We filled it up in a year. It was just overstuffed. And I slept in the back. But we had to call it something so it wouldn't attract the attention of the fire department. And we had a feeling we might have people up there, etcetera, etcetera, so we wanted to call it a museum. So that's when the Bread & Puppet Museum came into existence — when we moved to 148 Delancey Street, because we needed a name for it. I mean, before, we didn't have a *name*. We didn't have a *theatre*, we didn't have a *name*. Why did we need it? Probably we moved in in late '63, like in November. Moved our stuff in. (I: He lived there too?) No, I think at that time he still probably lived on Suffolk Street, on the top floor — sixth floor. And they had a real apartment. A flat. It was found by Dick Tyler, who was the superintendent. I don't — I guess it was in his building — Dick Tyler's building — and there was a vacancy, and then they moved into it — East 4th Street — which is now the worst junky place in the whole city. Just about always was, actually, pretty much. And they moved there, and the theatre and I moved up to 148 Delancey Street. (Ernstthal, interview.)

The Schumanns had moved into the Suffolk Street rat hole so Schumann could have a place to work in — 'it was Peter's idea of what a great apartment was because the studio was attached right to it' (Elka, interview) — but Elka couldn't take it — 'And after I moved in I just said I can't take it because it's just not good enough for me' (ibid.) — so 'after a very few weeks' they moved to #10 rear, 330 East 4th Street into the apartment vacated by the upwardly mobile Oldenburg, quickly, to benefit from its being rent controlled. This was still between C and D. Maxie, their third child, was born here — Elka remembers their apartments by what children were born in them or what school they went to while living there. Tyler's had his three antique presses in the basement. Some two years later, in '65, not long before Tamara entered first grade, they moved to East 6th Street, between B and A, I think, the place that made Ernstthal's wife cry when she saw it, though it was a step up from East 4th, three tiny rooms, as I recall it, and a kitchenette, but they had five children by now.[1] Bruno Eckhardt who with his wife was living on the ground floor had told them of the place. Marie, their last child, was born here. They stayed here for the remainder of their time in New York, till the beginning of 1970:

'(Elka: Our children were getting bigger, our apartment with its rent of $23 a month was very nice, we were lucky to have it, but when we got back from that big tour, it really was getting terribly small and —) Plus I found a young boy who

---

1. 'Beer was sort of a great treat (for the Bread & Puppet group in '66 (SSB)) — especially for Peter, who seemed not to get to beer too often — I think the only time he ever got a cigar was when you have it to him. They were very poor. He was still — as I understand it — was still painting walls at that point. They were still living in that railroad apartment where they terrified me by having a Christmas tree with candles, where it was absolutely obvious that it was terribly dangerous — five children sleeping in tiers — and I remember that the first time your name came into the conversation was that you had been mugged in the hallway down below. — (Ashley, interview.)

pulled a knife on Solveig and took a doll from her. (Elka: That wasn't so unusual in that area. And I got held up – I'd gone to the bank. I was sort of the treasurer for the theatre and I picked up people's salaries at the bank once a week, and on one day, someone just followed me and held me up with a gun in our hall. It was just before schools were out. And almost everybody else who was living in our area of the city had been robbed in their apartments at least a dozen – not a dozen but several times. People just found out, they didn't even bother – like Bart Lane, he didn't even bother putting a lock on his door because he'd been broken into so many times, it was easier to just keep his door open. And everything had been taken.)' (Schumann, interview, '79.)

They lived (and have continued to live) a life of poverty, the life of the really poor, and though it wasn't exactly voluntary poverty, in that maybe Schumann really didn't have anything to sell that would have paid for bigger and better apartments, yet it was, inasmuch as the way Schumann went and the way he went about it not only totally excluded remunerativeness, but systematically and by design minimized the take. And Elka was busy with the kids. Her parents helped, and it was their help, I am sure, that enabled them to survive at all, but the Schumanns are proud people and weren't about to live off her old man – and especially so since Scott's gains to Schumann were ill-gotten. They weren't worse off than they had been in Munich. But there was now the family, good-sized, and the feeling of being responsible for the children, and they were in their thirties.[2]

---

2. 'You know I can remember he lived all that time – was it on 5th Street or 4th Street – down by Avenue B or C, in a tiny little apartment, with five children, in two rooms, or something like that. I think Elka used to make a large pot of stew at the beginning of the week. The poverty in which they lived was very hard for anyone to really understand. I mean, most of those other theatre people would certainly not be – I was already sold out to the academic world and all that, and everybody – some of the people who were particularly concerned with the purity of his political message – I don't know anyone who would have been able to live under the vow of poverty, so to speak, that Peter and his family were experiencing. And his refusal to accept money from federal sources during that time. I don't think anybody of that stature, or who did that much work so thoroughly, lived up to his belief and convictions to such a degree with so much of his life. (I: I think there were actually one or two.) I know that he simply would not consider that sort of thing. (I: He would not make applications for grants?) I think that he must certainly have been urged to do so. Probably by people connected – I mean, he must have been allowed to know that if he applied he'd get it. He simply wouldn't do it. I remember feeling at that time what I called the vow of poverty, which he probably wouldn't think of that way at all. It tended, in my mind anyway, to make Peter, in addition to an individual who's a friend of mine, be a kind of – he represents something, which is a terrible thing to say about a friend, but it's a kind of position, a kind of physicalization of an absolute, that there is nobody who could have done what he did to such a degree and lived it so thoroughly. And the idea of somebody – I know of no one in the theatre, in our time anyway, who has done it to that degree. And it therefore becomes a kind of one end of a certain scale in one's way of thinking about this with the kind of Broadway mentality perhaps being the opposite end of the scale. I can think of a lot of people who have certain elements of that, but I know of no one

The Lower East Side, their home during the '60s – and also where most of the people then working with Schumann lived – a rat- and cockroach-infested slum, then and still the New York purchasing area for white junkies, full of junkies and pushers, thus a high burglary- and mugging-risk area (the Schumanns and the people working in the Bread and Puppet Theatre were more or less all mugged and/or robbed repeatedly), has been so much subject to arson (on the part of landlords and junkies) that it has just about as high a proportion of burnt-out (but not necessarily altogether unoccupied) houses as Bedford-Stuyvesant and the South Bronx, Black ghettoes, and, due both to the bad garbage collecting typical of poor areas and to the habits of its densely-packed immigrant population (largely Puerto Rican since the '60s), is filthy. Some of its streets, though, and notably the area around Tompkins Square Park, its center, are high-energy and almost cheery in warm weather. There was in the '60s and still is a good deal of left-wing-of-the-Democratic party organizing, Movement for Puerto Rican Independence and old-timey anarchist and socialist activity (evident in the graffiti and the posters), and there are a few good and relatively cheap fruit and vegetable stands and Ukranian butchers. The large influx during the '60s of hippies (making it the East Coast's grey Haight-Ashbury) – not so much into junk as rather consumers of speed, marijuana and LSD – young adventurers with their own ideas – also (until at the end of the '60s the party got desperate) improved the area, bringing with it a few health food stores and bookshops (poetry, the underground press, mysticism) and a sleazy counterculture organ, *The East Village Other*. These were people supporting the Peace Movement and with personal or snob/status interests in dance, the theatre. It was a tough and mean area, its best features the desperation, energy and alienation of many of its inhabitants. There were and are a few theatres, notably Ellen Stewart's La Mama, also a bar with Black shows in a backroom, off Tompkins Square Park – Papp's Shakespeare Festival Company hums in the no-man's land between the Lower East Side and Greenwich Village: Schumann's Delancey Street Museum was similarly located in the borderland. None of these places were 'of' the Lower East Side.

These people and these streets made an artist of Schumann, and a great one. Not that Schumann, except for cherishing his own poverty, has ever

---

who has it to such a thorough degree. With no hypocrisy or even vanity in relation to it. He just took it as a normal development. Most of those – some of these people, anyway, who were active in the theatre around that time, if they lived for two months that way would be explaining to the society what it had done to them, you know. See what you have done to me. I have to live like this. But it just was not part of Peter's nature to do that. He did not publicize the extremity of his commitment or his – the conditions under which he lived. I must say, you'd have to include Elka along with that. An amazing woman who obviously, you know, lived part and parcel with that kind of a conviction and determination. It was an amazing thing just to watch. That was total theatre in itself.' — (Shapli, interview.)

been interested in poverty – or in its characteristic, misery – but the slum kept his apocalyptic vision honed, and somehow the concentration and intensity of the unfulfilled needs of its inhabitants, and their visibility, translated for him into the need for his work that his ethics made a requirement for doing it: even though his art came to deal not with poverty but with war.[3]

---

3. 'The scene in New York was challenging; I mean, you needed to struggle, to win, to fight, and to get involved politically. And I think that is very healthy. I never had before, but in New York you couldn't help it. The whole scene was so evil it was designed for somebody who needed to get his nose into cold water and be shown what people really live like in some areas of the world. So our productions were from the beginning oriented towards social issues. And almost all of them one way or another had to do with Vietnam.'
— (Schumann, in Rough, *An Interview with Peter Schumann, Dramatics*, December 1973.)

'Germany was a vacuum. My political awareness I owe to America and to the Lower East Side.' – (Schumann in Kunin, *The B & P Theatre, Vermont Life*, Spring '77.)

'New York was a very refreshing, very shocking, refreshing experience there. It was just the idea to go with pieces into the street. I really got that in New York – I really saw it in that scene. It seemed to me that suddenly there were *people* there – on the Lower East Side – really, specifically where we *lived* – for whom it would make sense to produce *art*. In Germany I felt that to produce art is total surplus and nonsense, and with too many books and too many galleries and too many everything – and so, why do it? And on the Lower East Side it felt if one could produce a piece of art in the street there, and people would *take* it, then, at least, one would do that – you know – that first requirement that there's a clientele for what you do.' — (Schumann, interview, '82.)

'For thousands of years, artists have been developing the brain of the arts, sacrificing themselves for the most specialized areas, in order to control art, to know how it works in itself, and how it affects its audience. In the healthiest moments of history it looks as if art is an almost natural by-product of human behavior, an almost useful thing. In the sick periods of history, art* is self sufficient, has loose and superfluous connections to society, is scientific and extremely conscious of its self-imposed limitations. Art is by no means the essentially unchangeable expression of a human alikeness throughout the centuries that it is believed to be today. Art is not an up and down of abstractions, a going and coming of perfection, depending on individual capacities. Art is longing for its self-fulfillment and its salvation as much as humans are longing for it and actually art is the most struggling and dynamic part of the human longing. Its longing for the simple result which puts the countless chaotic streams of feelings and expressions together – and does not leave a single one out – could not be fulfilled if it would not be completely one with the human course toward heaven or hell.

What is the end and salvation of art? Certainly not a mere object of art in any surroundings. And certainly an object or event of mainly social importance, be it a still thing being used for an action, or be it an event of movements, of sounds, or a gathering of words. It makes little sense to talk both about a development in art or an aim of art if this is not admitted. And still we shall understand art as an inner potency, as a most powerful struggle towards our end, whatever this end is: our death, our belief, or the final good life. Art is a way of life, (the way of life), the awareness of the conscience as well as the awareness of the flesh and all the cells of the flesh of the whole world.' — (Schumann, *Bread & Puppet Theater. Pamphlet #2.* (Unpublished draft of Easter '64 program at Spencer Church, *The Puppet Christ*.)

---

*I am using 'art' in the sense of the German word 'Kunst' which means literature and music as well as painting, etc. (Schumann's footnote).

I stress the modus vivendi and the locale because the Village, Greenwich Village, which is where he became visibly involved — his field of operations — is quite other. It had been and then, notably in terms of the 'coffee houses' and the young folksong artists, still was, like the Schwabing, bohemian; there was and still is a solid though somewhat elderly working class population, Italian, with fewer ties to the Mafia than in adjoining Little Italy; and there are the students and faculty of New York University, but essentially it is a tourist center for kids from the outer boroughs and the New Jersey towns across the river, for college students down from the Ivy colleges, and for uptown and real-America couples, and living area for genteel liberals. It was notably these last that Schumann was supported by and that furnished his audiences and that got and kept him involved in the Peace Movement. They, and not any Puerto Ricans, hippies (unless they were working for him), gypsies or dour Slavs were the people he had for acquaintances and visited with. They were sort of like his parents, though not so well educated. But the Village and these people meant nothing to him. He needed them, but they gave him neither energy nor ideas.[4] If he had been forced to do puppetry for poor people, he would have been a real folk artist. His ideas and images were unsuitable for the American (though perhaps not for the Mexican or Brazilian) poor, and the American poor only want dance music to dance and listen to and movies for instruction in style and deportment.

Schumann took his family and theatre out of the city in the spring of '70, became resident artist at Goddard College, near Plainfield, Vermont. This was the country so the air was better. No muggings. For a while there was plenty of living space in the main farm house on Cate Farm. Then resident puppeteers started aggregating, and in '71 or '72 the Schumanns moved into a smaller house, where space was a little cramped again. There was still almost no money to live on, but the available food was fresher and Elka quickly planted a vegetable garden — which soon, however, had to support the puppeteers as well. They had exchanged urban for rural poverty — to the Schumanns a vast improvement. They love nature and it was better for the kids, they thought. The ambience here was college: definitely not an improvement. In '74 they moved to a farm near Glover, Vermont, belonging to Elka's parents, which they then gave to Elka. Here there was plenty of space (except in summer when the circus puppeteers affluxed in great numbers), there was the 'sugar bush,' and the ambience now was modern rural, they had 'neighbors.' The farm and its barn are beautiful. Heating was a problem: they now paid for it them-

---

4. 'Peter and Elka and their five kids live on East 6th Street. It's not affluence. And when he cringes at the over-gracious push of the ladies from SANE it's because he's more at home with a certain under-graciousness on the part of some of the New Left. He himself, never grand nor brutish, has nicely avoided New York "style." ' — (Maurice Blanc, *Clowning With the Life Force*, *Village Voice*, September 5, '68.)

selves. Still no money, but they continued to eat good healthy food, the kids skied. In '80, a house was built for Elka uphill from the farm — the summer crowds had got too much for her, and there was now a small group of resident puppeteers in the farmhouse — a small house — and the Schumanns moved into it. It's a tiny, poor house without much charm, but cozy inside, and with splendid views. They started keeping various animals — chickens, a goat, a pig, etc. As the kids started to leave for college, Elka and Schumann got more space, though they did not necessarily welcome this: the house had, I think they had felt, been adequate for the seven of them. Neighbors or no neighbors, I would say, and the proximity of Goddard and other colleges notwithstanding, they now lived in a void, though this did not necessarily bother either of them, what with the work, nature, books and records. They still live not too far from what the American middle class and organized working class would consider the poverty line.

The man minimized his personal expenses. High principles — repression of materialism/consumerism, distaste for the costly facilities of industrial culture, ideal of the simple life — and the true benefits of conformity to them notwithstanding, this involved costs: to him, to his wife, to his children; and required support: his wife's, his wife's family's. Some of this support, that of his wife's family, involved some compromise with principle. The over-all design: maximalization of independence.

2. Modus operandi. The start. The elements. Minimalization of costs. The objective: art as non-remunerative non-commodity. Not quite attainable.

Schumann, immediately he moved into the Suffolk Street storefronts, started to work making big puppets — bought celastic, acetone, the necessary lumber, started to get hold of fabrics, went to work. He had Bob to help him, probably also Eckhardt (and to a lesser extent Eckhardt's wife), Elka surely did what she could, there was Charlie Adams from the Alchemy Players, some others came around, including kids from the neighborhood. Within a few weeks, probably in October ('63) they rented the skylight-lit little loft at 3-story 148 Delancey Street, the place that before the previous tenant had been Red Grooms' and that now became the Bread & Puppet 'Museum', a work- and storage place (the big puppets presented more of a storage problem than hand or rod puppets), and a place where they might perform: the loft peaked up to the skylight, so there was room for the big puppets, the wooden milk crates then still in use that you could pick up on the street, stacked, I believe, in tiers, served for seats. He hung the masks he had on the walls — that made it a de facto museum. Their first recorded performance — recorded by a free notice in the *Village Voice* of November 14 — of an untitled 'puppet show' was on November 17, a Sunday, in the afternoon — thus probably a children's show. This was the first (so recorded) of a run of Sunday afternoon children's shows, extending to one on Sunday, December 22nd: entrance against a 'contribution.' (Since this was not a licensed theatre, no price of admission could legally be charged.) On Saturday, December 21st, at 5 and 9 P.M., they did the *Christmas Story* there, the third version of it after the Putney and Living Theatre ones of the previous year. Entrance was free. On Sunday, December 29, they did their first *Christmas Story* at a church, at the Rev. Glenesk's Spencer Memorial Church on Remsen Street, in Brooklyn Heights. On February 1st, '64, a Saturday, at 9 P.M., at the Museum, they did their first 'serious' play for adults, announced (in the *Voice*'s 'Off-off B'way' column, not the children's entertainment notice section) as a 'tragedy with puppets,' the reworked *King Story*, now called '*King Story I*,' with some of the new big puppets in it: others of which had been used in the December 21st *Christmas Story* already.

The foregoing brings up some main elements of Schumann's operation: three of the four types of output during the '60s: religious observances, kiddie shows, indoors theatre for adults; and some lasting requirements; and work place, a performance place of his own, performance places elsewhere, revenue from spectators, the labor of others, publicity.

The kind of puppetry he was getting into can't be done as cottage industry: he needed work (and storage) space in addition to living quarters. He couldn't perform in his living room (had he had one): if only because his puppets since his Putney living room hand puppet performances had grown too big. He needed media publicity: hand bills, handed out or pasted on walls, don't suffice. Nor do street puppet parades, though he tried them for his '62 and '63 Christmas shows, and later on made a regular practice of parades similar to circus parades. He needed an income because he had operating expenses: minimally for puppet-making materials, heat and/or rent, transportation (for clay and puppets if for nothing else). And he needed labor power, the labor of others: not only for performance, but for making the puppets and rehearsing them, the rehearsals, the way he worked, being the creation of the show, and the making of them more than he could handle by himself.

The principle of his operation was minimalization of money costs. First as regards materials. He was generally able to locate clay pits where he could with his group dig it up free of charge, though during the New York years he needed a car to haul it in. The center pole dowels for the large puppets had to be bought, but some of the lumber, for instance broom handles, could be found on the streets, as could much of the fabric[1] (it would be harder now after two more decades of decline in the garment industry), and for a while Bob Ernstthal's father, who was in the fabric industry, provided material, e.g. all of the material for the first *Birdcatcher*, free — and from some point on at a discount.[2] Tinting could sometimes be done with tea or coffee grounds. Oils were, from '64 onward, abandoned for acrylics. The big expense item was the celastic[3] (acetone was relatively cheap), but, with some exceptions, its advantages for speedy production were such that Schumann stuck with it — bought it from theatrical supply stores. I shall discuss his work and performance places in the sequel, here note only that he paid no rent for his performance spaces in New York

---

1. '... remember the *Crucifixion* puppets? They had these gold colored clothes clothes on them? We found — I think it was Eva Eckhardt, Bruno's wife, who found this incredible pile — all the stuff came up out of the garbage. And she found this incredible pile of fabric. Unbelievable pile, and that's what all those puppets are made out of. One day, I remember, it was like a gold mine or something. Incredible. She came in with this pile of fabric. It was in the garbage. Someone had thrown them away.' — (Ernstthal, interview.)
2. 'Like I said, my father was in the textile business so we got these tons of fabric — and after a while he stopped giving it to us and he started charging us wholesale price because we used so much of it — you know, it just couldn't go on. I'd go up there and come back with these bolts and bolts of this fabric.' — (Ernstthal, interview.)
3. 'Peter did say to me one time — very early on — that he felt guilty about using celastic at a hundred dollars a roll when he didn't have money to give to his puppeteers. When it would be much cheaper to use paper maché. Except that paper maché was too heavy and it wasn't flexible and it didn't travel as well. So, he felt guilty but he had no other recourse. He had to use celastic.' — (Ashley, interview.)

from mid-'66 to early '70 (but his heating bills toward the end of the '60s were considerable), from the spring of '70 until the summer of '73 had neither rent nor heating expenses, paid a nominal rent (to Elka's parents for Dopp Farm) from the summer of '73 until '76, when Mr. Scott gave the place to Elka, on Dopp Farm from '74 onward cut his own firewood. For transportation he during much of the '60s had Charlie Adams' car: in '70 he bought an old school bus and that's what he used from then on. His publicity medium until '68 was the Village Voice. Only during the '70s did other papers such as the New York Times begin to review him with any regularity (cf. infra). He placed some paid ads in the Voice, but it gave him a good deal of free notice in its 'Off-off-Broadway' listings and 'What's On for Children' column, and from '66 to '68, otherwise also. The big expense item, as it turned out (cf. infra), was labor: not initially: but from '67 onward. To defray its costs, as well as the however much minimized other costs, he needed an income. The theatre had to be revenue producing: he couldn't stay entirely outside the money-economy, the exchange of commodities. Which ideally has been his objective – not to have his art turn into a commodity. To avoid, as art producer, financial dependence.

3. Modus operandi I. The places. '63 –.

Schumann had museums later, elaborately installed relief or puppet installations, but the reason this first place was called a 'museum' were the city fire regulations, or, rather, though the place was in fact a bit of a fire trap, their enforcement. Like the sanitation and building codes, they are enforced only if the operator has not been keeping up his bribe payments to the inspectors and doesn't have any pull higher up making this unnecessary, and even then not very much because there are not enough inspectors. But in '63/'64, the authorities, city and federal, acting as rearguard of the spirit of the '50s, were waging a minor guerilla war on the immorality of the times, and the *Village Voice* was, in a small way, on the other side, e.g. reported extensively and with sympathy for the defendant on the trials of the Living Theatre, indicted in January '64 on a charge of having obstructed the federal agents who the preceding October when *The Brig*, hard on the Marine Corps, was running there had closed it down for non-payment of federal taxes, and found guilty in May or June '64 – the *Voice* gave them three Obies on May 28 – and in March '64, their critic of amateur movies, Jonas Mekas was arrested for showing an indecent, lewd and obscene film, Jack Smith's *Flaming Creatures*. He was convicted in June. The city was harrassing coffee houses, unlicensed for entertainment, featuring avant garde theatre or out-of-line folk singers, and was, the *Voice* claimed, tracking them down in its 'What's On' listing: 'License Bureau Goes Small-Game Hunting,' *Village Voice*, February 6, '64, in 'City Puts Bomb Under Off-Beat Culture Scene,' March 26, and similarly again in an article on April 2nd. The February article noted that 'Peter Schumann of the Bread & Puppet Theatre' had been 'served a summons by the License Bureau for holding a puppet demonstration in his loft and specifying the amount of contribution.' So Schumann's ads at this time were sometimes a little tortuous, e.g. advertising 'demonstrations' of ('over-life-sized') puppets. Sometime in '64, the Rev. Glenesk solved some of these problems for him by listing him as sexton – it seems that as sexton Schumann could legally ask for contributions. (Thus the Reverend was later, Glenesk, *Puppets Tell*, '69, able to say the theatre had been 'based' in his church, in private conversations pointing out a further advantage of the arrangement for Schumann: his ecclesiastic status made him draft-exempt.)

The reason for 'Bread' in the theatre's name was that Schumann soon after they started inviting audiences started after performances distributing pieces of bread to them, the dark bread his mother had served her family during the bad wars years and after, made of home-ground rye, and which he now baked himself, not to supplement the puppetry with something more substantial, but, he later said, on the contrary, as sign that it was substantial – nourishing and healthy – like art ought to be (or at least that this was how he intended his art to be.) Taken in this sense, the gesture comes close to being an apology for the moralistic gravity of his theatre – as though he were explaining: art is not supposed to be cake. Audiences usually take it merely as a friendly gesture, indicating that the group means them well – they are not just customers, aren't being taken. When Schumann is doing the distributing there is a slight suggestion that he is relating to the audience as host to guests – something a little different in that it involves a rank order. Commentators have sensed an allusion to Christian communion. Schumann would not admit this, but there is something to it: he thinks of art as properly a community event, and a religious one, and thinks of his theatre as of this nature; and to think of the bread that is broken and shared together as representing the natural world in which man lives and which he ought to till and share in a brotherly fashion would not be far from his mind either, nor that this natural world might truly be viewed as the body of God.

Schumann kept the Delancey Street Museum from October '63 to about the beginning of June '66 when the rent was raised.[1] By then he had worked out his number and had his first 'hit' (*Fire*), i.e. was attracting the attention of the downtown intelligentsia (he didn't hold it) – so Joseph Papp, who had given up on Lincoln Center and was moving his Shakespeare Festival Company into the Astor Library Memorial Building (on Lafayette Street off Cooper Square, which is the main point of transit between the East Village and Greenwich Village), and who likes to promote art alongside of his own operation (he has been a longtime sponsor both of the Bread and Puppet Theatre and the Mabou Mines) offered him (rent-free) accommodations while renovating. Schumann moved in sometime during the second half of '66. The Bread and Puppet Theatre had its home base, two big rooms, there until renovations were finished. They moved out at the end of October '67.[2]

---

1. His last performance there recorded in the *Village Voice* is one of *Fire*, May 20th, 1966 (*Village Voice*, May 19, '66). Allan Katzman in an article in the *East Village Other* (issue of May 15-June 1, '66) quotes Schumann to the effect that 'recently' his landlord decided to raise his rent from $60 to $90, which would make it too difficult for him to continue his theatre.' Taking this together with a performance on June 19, '66 of a children's show, *The Big City Story* at the Bridge Theatre, we may perhaps assume that they left the Delancey Street loft late in May or early in June '66.
2. 'Then the fall came and Joe Papp said, I bought this building and while I'm renovating it, you can work downstairs in two rooms, if you don't mind plaster falling on your heads all the time. The Public Theater. So that's what we did for a year. There was nobody else working in the building. There was a little old caretaker, Mr. Abraham, who would let us in and out. He and I liked each other very much. And we had one room there where we made puppets and another room where we did shows. And we had children's workshops. And new people came and joined us. Some came and left, others came and stayed, like Amy Trompetter.' — (Margo Sherman, interview.)

Ernstthal remembers the move from Delancey Street to Papp's place as motivated by lack of space on Delancey Street and due to an invitation from Papp to use space there for

Through the intermediary of St. Marks in the Bouwerie, they had had limited and occasional access to a city-owned building, the 'Old Courthouse,' on Second Avenue at 2nd Street, a large, nobly proportioned two-story red brick building since early in '67. Soon after they had to leave Papp's, in November '67, they got exclusive use of the main space there, the large, high-ceilinged former court room on the second floor, and by July '68, they had almost the entire building (someone else was using the former jail cells in the basement) to themselves: at a dollar a year. Though there were apparently restrictions on their using the place for public performances, this was a splendid deal, but under pressure from the radical-artistic community incautiously letting others in on it, they lost the place: the city took it back while they were gone on their Europe tour of '69. They had it from November '67 to March '69.[3]

---

free while he was remodeling, and thinks they moved during the summer (of '66) soon after a performance at the Bridge Theatre — perhaps one June 19. He thinks they started building the Grey Lady puppets (used February 2, '67 in *Bach Cantata #140*) almost immediately after moving in (but it was probably after the August-September parks *Chicken Little*), then not using them for anything for quite a while. So perhaps they moved in June/July '66, started working there in September/November '66, started performing there in January '67. The first performance at the Astor Library Landmark Building recorded in the *Village Voice* is a nativity performed there January 7, '67 (*Village Voice*, January 5, '67.) The last performance there was on October 28, '67: *Chicken Little (Says Goodbye Shakespeare)*. (*Village Voice*, October 26, '67.)

They cleared out by the end of October '67.

'*Fire* was our first step in a certain way into real recognition. And I feel that's why Joe Papp invited us in. I think Bernard Friedman or somebody came to see. So that was our entree, you know, into the more set-up theatrical world . . . I remember moving to the Shakespeare Festival almost as soon as they bought it or as soon as they got it, that's when he let us in. Because it was such a big place that he let us in those lower rooms there. And they were constructing and doing the work on them at the same time. In other words, we were a transitional group. I think when they had cleaned it up we were asked to leave — or they needed it — they made a theatre there. It was a cafeteria and it was a big room — two big rooms downstairs — huge rooms . . . Yeah, on the street level . . . there was a side door — you'd come in, turn to the right and there would be — it used to be the cafeteria, where they'd serve meals, as I remember — two great, big rooms. One room and then another great, big room where we played and that was a real explosion — expansion — that was great . . . And that invitation from Joe Papp and all that. Of course, Joe Papp at that time is not the lion that he is now. Although he's always been — he had the same nature — now everybody knows about it. As far as I can tell, he's a great guy, frankly, as I remember him. He was very generous and very kind and very — he was good. Joe Papp was real good. He had a good heart and he said, here, take it, I don't need it now. Maybe later we'll use it, but here's this huge space, why don't you come in? I mean, he was — I think we paid no rent or anything. And in all our dealings with him — The Bridge Theatre we only played briefly, a couple of times in a couple of things. And I think it was probably right before we moved into Papp's theatre. Because once we moved into the Shakespeare Festival there was clay and we built a whole new bunch of stuff. I believe the grey ladies were built immediately we got there and we must have done a bunch of more puppets. — (Ernstthal, interview.)

3. St. Marks in the Bouwerie, the Second Avenue church that got known for its marathon

They started looking again and finally found a small cast-iron building, formerly a bank, at the Brooklyn end of the Brooklyn Bridge, practically in its shadow, and carried on operations here – at #1 Front Street, Bankside, Brooklyn Heights – from January 4 to March 2, 1970.[4] But there

---

poetry readings had been renting the place from the city Department of Real Estate since July 1966, using it until July 1968 as headquarters for its federally funded arts project, but also letting the Bread & Puppet Theatre work there occasionally from at least January '67 onward, e.g. to rehearse the *Bach Cantata #140* (performed February 2, '67) or their parade in the Spring Mobilization to End the War in Vietnam on April 15th. They were already at Papp's place then, but perhaps didn't want to get him involved in the anti-war activity, or, both of these demonstrations being big, didn't have enough space at his place. In October, when they had to leave Papp's place they still weren't sure of the Courthouse: the *Voice* on October 12 solicited space for them 'large enough to store many large and small puppets, to hold children's workshops in puppetry, and to continue designing and building plays.' But from November '67 onward they had use of the big upstairs courtroom, supported (the heating was a big expense item there – about $100 a week) from November '67 until March '68, by a grant from the New York State Council on the Arts, in return for which they did work with children from 'the community,' on which they reported in the *Bread & Puppet Diary/November '67-March '68*. From July '68 onward, when the St. Marks arts project lost federal funding, they rented the building directly from the city Real Estate Department for a dollar a year, and now, except for some movie makers left over from the arts project, using the 15 cells in the basement for storage and shooting a 'science-fiction story about authoritarian society' – the heroine was currently in the hands of the police, but the police were not villains, Rapoport, animator of the Rainbow Division Film Company, was 'just using the serial as a form of comment,' and was trying to raise the money for a second reel – had full use of the building – they probably were not supposed to put on performances there, but, at least during their last few months there, December '68-March '69, apparently did. When they left for Europe, they subleased the place to the Pageant Players. These let the Motherfuckers, a somewhat wild, drug-using counter-culture gang, whom Schumann had until then with difficulty kept out, use it and the city authorities unfavorably disposed toward the Motherfuckers – they apparently had a wild party there – evicted them and the Pageant Players, and when Schumann returned from Europe in November of '69, would not let him back in, claiming he had no right to sub-lease to the Pageant Players. The police, Schumann thinks, threw out some of the things they had left – 'some of our biggest masks – some giant masks', and others they had stored in the cellar had been ruined. — (Schumann, interview, '79.)

4. 'And I remember, we must have been also looking for studios, but we thought we had so much money after this tour, which had made money, and we looked at rents and at places and the rents were just impossible. The rents were like $2,000 a month – or they were just outrageous. We finally *did* find this building, the bank across the Brooklyn Bridge, at the other end of the Brooklyn Bridge, and we moved in there, and the rent was maybe $400 or $500. Yes, we shared it with somebody ... we couldn't stay there for very long. (Elka: And our hosts had rent-raising parties .... But that's when *The Difficult Life* was created.) — (Schumann, interview, '79.)

'The Bread and Puppet Theater was in The Bank in Brooklyn from January 4 till March 2, 1970, subletting from Ray Levine and sharing the ground floor with a pony and Saturday night rent-raising parties. We paid $200 a month and $50 more for use of floor upstairs, and all the heat expenses. But there was almost no heat (dangerous kerosene stove), no sink, no phone (hot water from a pipe upstairs, cold water in the cellar). Glad to move out. But beautiful, unforgettable walks across the Brooklyn Bridge!' — (Elka Schumann, *The Bank*, '70.)

was no room here for performing, and scarcely for rehearsing, and anyhow, they were 'thrown out,' Schumann says (Schumann, *Bread & Rosebuds*, newsletter, April 25, '70), but then were helped to get an old vaudeville theatre or the like, the 'Old Boston Theater,' belonging to Nathan's Hot Dogs, in Coney Island, On Surf Avenue – #1205 – leased to Schumann at a nominal annual rent.[5] They moved in in mid-March, were performing by May, performed, with Schumann there in May and June. He was, however, by this time, leaving New York City for Vermont – left in June, returning only briefly that summer for a circus parade, didn't go there in '71 except for a single performance (and by this time was making his puppets and doing his rehearsals in Vermont), and worked there, rehearsing and performing, in the summer of '72, and that was the end of New York bases for the Bread and Puppet Theatre.

Not counting his street demonstrations and his religious observances,

---

'Enjoyed those January and February cold spells with mostly no heat under the Brooklyn Bridge, in a bank, built a stage and a lot of little puppets sort of marionettes there until we were thrown out again.' — (Schumann, *Bread & Rosebuds*, April 25 '70.)

'(Elka: The conditions were hard there. There was no heat, no water, a pony in the same room, and parties – rent-raising parties – every weekend, so everything we did had to be cleaned out completely so our sub-landlord . . .) Rent-raising parties for the landlord, so – it was a bit difficult, that time.' — (Schumann, interview, '79.)

'Well, we have those (Vermont) landscapes that were done in the bank – terrible weather – Bart Lane was there, working on them very hard. I never knew how he lived. I mean, I thought he would die, it was so cold in that bank. The horse was over in the corner standing knee-deep in used hay, and infections in its feet and everything, and there was no heat.' — (Ashley, interview.)

5. 'Hurrah! It's the Old Boston Theater on 1205 Surf Avenue which used to be a people place where you had a movie and a beer for 15 cents. We got there through the friendliness of Nathan's Mr. and Mrs. Handworker, Dick Levy and Marketta Kimbrell of the City Street Theater and the New York Shakespeare Festival. It costs only 4 hotdogs a year and we have a one-year lease. And it belongs to Nathan's Famous Superhotdogs Inc. The ceiling is leaking, there is no heat and hardly any light and water yet – but the place is ideal for us and besides Nathan's wants to help us find more light and water. – No more *Village Voice* or other publicity necessary – the world is all there, especially kids, superlarge families and old people' — (Schumann, *Bread & Rosebuds*, April 25, '70.)

'It had been, I think, a spook house and a pinball machine place, I don't know what you call it, an arcade of some sort. It was a large room with a balcony, like a mezzanine. (I: On both sides or in the rear?) Pretty much like a U – no, I think it went all the way around the whole building. I mean there was a room cut out for an office in the upstairs and the costume room was on one part and much of it was just junk in storage from the past games that had been there. The front of the building were two huge garage doors, so when we wanted to play we would open the garage doors and there was an anteroom, I guess like what used to be a lobby or where you bought your tickets or whatever, and we would do our outdoor street shows from that front room that opened right out into the street, and then there was a separate door that entered the inner theatre . . . . I guess if we had had seats to seat people it would have seated 100 . . . . It was quite large. A big building. (I: And there was a regular stage?) No. Just a flat floor and we put up leggings and teasers and made a stage. There was no raised stage. — (Fernandez, interview.)

most of his showings while he had the Museum and then the space at Papp's were at the Museum and then at Papp's: as I noted, he didn't perform for a public much at the Courthouse, though the lines between rehearsals (with various people around), open rehearsals and public performances were, in his case, during the '60s indistinct – people saw shows of his at the Courthouse not mentioned in the *Voice*. There were a few, a very few showings during the '60s neither at those bases nor in churches, e.g. they did a children's show, *The Emperor's New Clothes*, at the Brooklyn Children's Museum sometime in '64, put on the *Christmas Story* at the Pocket Theatre, Third Avenue at 13th Street from December 10, '64 to January 4, '65 (90c admission), another children's show, *The Winter Tale*, at the Bridge Theatre, 4 St. Marks Place, like the Pocket Theatre, where e.g. La Monte Young played October 31 and November 1, '64, an avant-garde film-music-etc. emporium, in February-March '65, subsequently in this same performance space[6] – where again admission was charged – doing another children's show, *The Big City Story* on June 19, '65, and *Leaf Feeling the Moonlight* in November '65, at something called the 'Metro North Community Center,' at 331 East 100th Street, in Harlem, on June 5th, '65 did *Flower Mountain*, and at the Trotzkyite Militant Labor Forum performed *Fire* on June 10, '66, gave the one and only performance of *Bach Cantata #140* at the Village Theatre, an enormous barn at Second Avenue and 6th Street, in the winter of '67/'68 performed *A Man Says Goodbye* for the kids at the Adams School for the Neurologically Disturbed, managed to present *King Story* at a turbulent meeting at the Fillmore Theatre, October 22, '68 and played a fairy tale program, *Blue Raven Beauty* late in March and/or early in April '69 at La Mama Theatre on East 4th Street. This is surely not a complete list, but it is not very far from complete for the '60s.

Now it seems clear, that even after he had his 'hit' *Fire*, in '66, he

---

6. 'Real typical tiny, little – tiny little stages, fixed seating, raised platform out front and raised auditorium, as far as I remember. In the Bridge it was raked like this and in the Pocket Theater it was slanted – the auditorium. And both pretty boring, uninteresting theatres.... We didn't use their curtain. We always played with open curtain and I'm sure the Bridge didn't even have a curtain.... Not much backstage. I think it was done pretty much in the open. We probably had a curtain up for the kids' shows and played above the curtain and used the curtain for entrances, too – to the front of it. And then *Leaf Feeling the Moonlight* had these three black curtains. And in the Pocket Theater we played, I think, only the *Christmas Story* and that would have been done – yeah, with just our curtain, I think, just the puppet curtain – head-height curtain, nothing else – I don't think so.... It was very disagreeable to all of us to be in the Pocket Theater. In the Bridge it was different. That was a nicer atmosphere. (I: You mean the people or you mean the space?) The space, also. The space was a nicer space. I mean, the Pocket Theater was these red seats, plush seats going up – very few seats, it seemed, but more than one thinks. They fit so many into these tiny, little places when they're slanted. And hardly any audience – I only have bad recollections of that one – I don't know – what else it was. I think it was not good. — (Schumann, interview, '82.)

wouldn't have had enough of a paying — or non-paying — audience to sustain a continuous operation — continuous, that is, from one weekend to another, but a continuous output of work, which is pretty much what we have had from him since '63 — in a rented theatre, with him, the company, paying the rent, and probably not enough of a paying audience, even, to get himself invited much to other people's, whether for a fee or for a share of the gate,[7] at least not in New York. Not in New York, (1) because his stuff wasn't avant-garde enough, in fact it wasn't avant-garde in any sense, even in the spurious accepted sense, (2) its moral focus, simplicity of viewpoint and childlike humor were even repulsive to some, (3) at the moment he could otherwise maybe have made it, '68-'70, the downtown or offbeat (Off-off-Broadway) fashions made it seem more irrelevant — nice but unimportant — than ever: sex, violence, the individual's search for identity were riding high, (4) what helped him get bookings in Europe, that it came from America and yet had European resonances; and at colleges outside of New York, that it was what was going on in New York and was elevated without being stuffy, could get him neither audiences nor bookings in New York: people knew that his stuff wasn't 'where it was at.' (The arts thrive on fashion and that's how it should be.)

All this is irrelevant, however, though this has not prevented Schumann from feeling bitter about New York. The essential point is quite another, namely that Schumann's art during the '60s, with one or two exceptions, *Leaf, Dead Man Rises*, was not designed for being framed by a theatre, and, perhaps even more importantly, that Schumann didn't want — then or later — its effects affected by the identification of it as theatre resulting from its being presented in a theatre: he didn't want it taken in as art, and in particular not as theatre art, which he thought of in the European manner, as bourgeois (and petty-bourgeois) art for bourgeois and petty-bourgeois audiences. If he was going to show his things indoors he therefore preferred non-theatre spaces.[8] This attitude relaxed in Europe and at

---

7. His bookings, in '65, at the avantgardizing Bridge were brief, unsuccessful, out of place, and due to the management's lack of character.

'I was living with Arthur Sainer and we had a theatre, the Bridge, and we would invite theatre companies to perform there and underground movies and dance. And a guy who was working for us, John Rottenberg, said, I've worked with them and they are wonderful. And we hadn't yet seen them, we'd seen the ads in the paper . . . so we said, sure. We showed underground movies every weekend, that's what paid the bills. Certainly going to the theatre or poetry or music did not pay the bills, but it was underground movies. So we showed everybody's films. People, all the Judson dancers, would come there to perform. Meredith, Yvonne, probably, probably Carolee. Music, Malcolm Godstein and Philip Corner probably did some concerts there . . . experimental performance works.' — (Margo Sherman, interview.)

8. An interview of 1970 conveys his feelings about playing in theatres, though in a slightly skewed manner, because he was then in a somewhat revolutionary mood, and because what he is mostly talking about is the alternative between playing in theatres ('regular' theatres,

colleges (where moreover the performance space might not be a theatre), partly because it was away from home (not the real thing anyhow, from his viewpoint, a reproduction), partly because he needed the money. Certain art-dispensing and/or politically engaged Protestant churches provided Schumann with a major outlet during the '60s, mainly for his Christmas and Easter spectacles (and in '67 and '68 Thanksgiving ones), but, though especially during the winter '67/'68 when they felt unable to perform at the Courthouse, for other things as well: Spencer Memorial (Presbyterian) in Brooklyn, now a warehouse, Judson Memorial (Baptist)[9]

really) and playing on the street:
'(I: Wie sieht das mit dem Räumen aus, in denen ihr spielt? Eure Puppen, eure Musik und meist auch die Choreographie sind doch eigentlich auf Strassentheater zugeschnitten. In Europa haben die Vorstellungen, die in Theatern stattfanden, viel von den, was das Bread and Puppet ist, verloren.) Das ist richtig, das haben wir auch von der Tournee gelernt. Wir haben oft in Theatern spielen müssen, die uns nicht gefielen und die ein bestimmtes Publikum diktierten, das uns nicht gefiel. Und es prägt einen automatisch Avantgarde, etwas Kostbares. Die Kritiker messen nach denselben Massstäben, wie sie irgendeine Inszenierung messen, und das Publikum auch. Wenn zu uns ein Publikum kommt, wir es zur Oper geht, sind wir fehl am Platze, deshalb gehen wir lieber zu den Leuten. Wir haben unsere besten Vorstellungen in den Strassen gehabt. Manchmal bekommt die Sache einfach dadurch einen Sinn, dass du dich da mit deinem ganzen Zeug auf der Strasse befindest. Die Leute kommen aus ihren gewohnten Bahnen, und plötzlich sehen sie diese grossen Puppen, und sie sehen etwas Theatralisches, aber ausserhalb des Theaters. Sie sind nicht darauf vorbereitet, indem sie Eintrittsgeld bezahlt haben, um etwas zu sehen, sondern sie stehen plötzlich vor einer Sache, mit der sie konfrontiert sind. Wir haben allerdings auch böse Erfahrungen gemacht, die Pageant Players und das Burning City sind schon verprügelt worden, deshalb lassen wir uns jetzt immer einladen von den Gemeindeverwaltungen oder irgendwelchen Organisationen. Als wir in Harlem spielten, waren wir dort nie ohne Einladung hingegangen. Das ist auch gut wegen der Polizei, weil bei solchen Veranstaltungen meistens jemand von den Zeitungen da ist, der über irgendwelche Gewaltaktionen berichten könnte. Für unsere neue Tour in die Südstaaten haben wir die Idee, in einem Zirkuszelt zu spielen, was wir an Stellen aufbauen können, wo alle hinkommen. Wir werden, wenn wir in eine Stadt kommen, an verschiedenen Stellen kleine Stücke spielen und den Leuten sagen, wo unser Zelt steht und dass sie dort hinkommen sollen. Dort spielen, zum Teil auch deshalb, weil wir nicht so sehr am Theater interessiert sind wie andere Gruppen. Die meisten Mitglieder unserer Gruppe sind weder Schauspieler noch Pantomimen. Die meisten kommen, weil sie politisch interessiert sind. Wenn wir Schauspieler bei uns hatten, war es meist sehr schwer, sie in die Arbeit zu integrieren. Was uns zusammenbringt, ist nicht die Sache, Theater zu machen, sondern dass wir über verschiedene Dinge mit Leuten, dem Publikum, reden wollen. Man kann das mit einem Maler vergleichen; der setzt sich auch nicht in eine stille Ecke und malt einfach, weil ihm das gefällt, sondern er malt, weil er das jemandem zu zeigen, und das beinhaltet, dass er wissen muss, wem er es zeigen will und wohin er gehen muss, um ihn zu finden. Wir sind nicht sehr daran interessiert, das Theater zu revolutionieren, möglicherweise entsteht eines Tages das beste Theater aus den konventionellsten Formen. Ein Theater ist gut, wenn es für die Leute einen Sinn ergibt. Ein kleines Theater, das nur darauf zielt, gibt es in Amerika noch nicht.' — (Schumann, in Heilmeyer and Frolich, *now/Theater der Erfahrung*, 1971.)
9. 'And Spencer was the first – he (Glenesk) was bold in a way for all his – he's a very timid-sounding and very gentle-sounding guy – but in a way he did a lot, gutsy things – in his own way. I've got a lot of respect for the guy, actually. Judson had its own damn

and Washington Square Methodist Church off Washington Square, St. Peter's (Lutheran) at 54th Street and Lexington Avenue, since torn down and resurrected as part of a Citicorp edifice, St. Clement's (Episcopal) Church. The exodus to the suburbs of their white middle class congregations gave certain idealistic and/or weirdo ministers a chance to try to keep things going by subverting their temples to off-beat art and politics. They did *Birdcatcher*, December 20, '64 at Spencer Memorial, *Wounds of Vietnam*, February 4, '67 and the second run of *Fire*, November 27, '67 to April 1, '68, at Washington Square Methodist, a series of 'experimental plays' or 'protest demonstrations,' January-February '68 at St. Peter's, *Speech* and *Johnny* at Washington Square Methodist, March 30 and 31, '68, *Cry* at St. Peter's, December 5, 6, 7, '69. This in addition to the Christmas, Easter (and Thanksgiving) plays.

Schumann in the '70 interview expressed a preference for street performances, but during the '60s in fact — as later — if we except political performances at political events, of which however during the '60s there were a great deal, they didn't perform on the streets all that much. They at the insistence of filmmakers performed *Birdcatcher* in a Harlem parking lot in the winter of '64/'65, did *Flower Mountain* in the churchyard of St. Mark's May 29 and 30, '65, and later again in Washington Square Park that summer performed the result of a workshop with children, *The Pied Piper of Harlem*, on the block between First and Second Avenues on East 100th Street in Harlem, August 28 — September 4, '66 put on the product of another workshop with children, *Chicken Little*, in three parks, on the Lower East Side, in Harlem, in the Bronx, and July 31 and August 20, '67 did a version of it of their own on Gottesman Plaza, at the intersection of 91st Street and Amsterdam Avenue and at Columbus Park in Chinatown, got up the annual 'Ragamuffin Parade' in Washington Square Park on October 31, '68 — contributed their dragon to it — and participated with the prologue to *Cry* in a city New Year celebration by the Bethesda Fountain in Central Park on December 31, '68. This again is surely not a complete record for the '60s, but it is fairly complete and makes clear that they were in no way a street theatre.

Touring was not yet an established practice for him during the '60s. He presented his work of the '60s to New York City. There are two major exceptions to this, at the end of this period, the first two of his tours in

---

theatre and it had Al Carmines doing his own stuff. And Rochelle Owens and playwrights ... and the dancers, Yvonne Rainer, Fred Herko and that whole scene. So Judson really wasn't that open to us. I think, essentially because of Al Carmines having his own theatre — which is natural — that's his — that was his turf — it was his trip — and that was what he was doing. He had his own musical theatre and his own musical ideas. Like I said, we were definitely out of the theatrical swing of things, so Al Carmines didn't have much time for us — which is natural — I understand it — he did his own things — he did musicals.' — (Ernstthal, interview.)

Europe, April 10 to the end of May or the beginning of June '68 and April-November '69, both not only to, but essentially to France, to the Nancy Young Theatre of the World Festivals – the tours by which he first won public recognition as a major artist, having never won it in New York – the first chiefly with *Fire*, the second chiefly with *Cry*; two fairly important exceptions: two Newport Folk Festival appearances, the first July 12, '67, chiefly with *Chicken Little*, the second in the summer of '68 with *The Bible*, this last one not nearly as important as the first; and two minor exceptions, again at the end of this period, an attendance July 13-16, '68 at the 10th annual Drama Workshop of the National Council of Churches in Denver, Colorado, and one at a San Francisco State College Second Radical Theatre Festival in September '68 (showing mainly *King Story* and *Reiteration*) – the Denver appearance didn't amount to anything, but the San Francisco one established him with the Radical Youth Movement. Other than this, there are only a few piddling excursions – he did *King Story* at the Ohayo Mountain Hall in Woodstock, New York, July 11, '64, he showed up at Expo '67 in Montreal with *Speech* and *A Man Says Goodbye* on Hiroshima Day, August 6, '67, appeared with the same two radical skits and *Dead Man Rises* at the Long Wharf Theatre in New Haven, Connecticut, July 19 and 20, '67 and at the Epworth Methodist Church in Boston with *Speech* in November '67, did things entitled *The Bible* from a play in progress, the *Cry*, locally in some small places in Maine, in July '68 – and some visits to colleges – too few and scattered to merit the name of 'tours' – of which there is no record and the particulars of which neither he nor his people remember, but which are significant, because college tours were to be a (relatively) major source of income for the theatre.

From June '70 onward Schumann had substantially rent-free (except for briefly '75, '76) and substantially assured (except briefly '73, '74) accommodations, first as artist in residence on Goddard College's Cate Farm, then on his in-laws' farm in Glover township, both in Vermont. On Cate Farm he had a large barn as workspace – he fixed up a performance space in it – there was performance space at Goddard College, summers work could be done out of doors, which was good also because of the acetone fumes, and he had a large meadow going down to the Winooskie River as outdoors performance area. In Glover he again had a large barn to work in (he never set up an indoors performance space here), and a beautiful meadow pit – previously a gravel pit, I believe – for his annual circuses. He had everything! – except an audience. The off-beat Goddard faculty, the pseudo-hippie Goddard student body, the assorted artistic types that had settled in the area didn't add up to one, nor his neighbors in Glover. From '74 onward his annual two-day circuses (the first one on Cate Farm) to which people come from near and afar in a minuscule way solved this problem, but otherwise, for this whole period – though '70-'74 he tended to show his new shows first on Cate Farm, at Goddard, or in various nearby towns with colleges, but mostly only once or twice – he was dependent on touring and on visits to New York City (where he tended to perform at Crystal Field's and George Bartenieff's Theatre for the New City, Second Avenue at 10th Street,[10] occasionally performed at St. John's Cathedral, uptown, once in Central Park).

---

10. 'Off-Off-Broadway has gentrified: The number of productions has shrunk, the degree of risk and innovation has dwindled even more.

Spaces that were run on free-form creative chaos suddenly find themselves with managing directors, corporate fund-raisers, and Broadway producers on their advisory boards. The theaters look for glossy, pretested scripts that can make a commercial transfer. Where they once asked the playwright to shift his own scenery, now they want cable rights and a percentage on the cast album.

That's why George Bartenieff and Crystal Field, at Theater for the New City, are heroes. TNC is a last bastion of the true Off-Off spirit. Other theaters do five productions a year; TNC does 30 to 40, as it has been doing since 1971. It's wandered from its first home in Westbeth to Jane Street to Second Avenue, where it's been since 1977. But the lease is up in February and the landlord wants a 300 per cent rent increase. Second Avenue is very popular these days – a lot of fashionable people came down there to go to the theater and decided to stay. TNC is in negotiation with the city for the use of an old market building on First Avenue, currently underused by the Sanitation Department.

Meantime, they're having one of their best seasons ever, with new works by Maria Irene Fornes, Ronald Tavel, Robert Heide, Joan Schenkar, Amlin Gray, Kenneth Bernard, Rosalyn Drexler, and more. About a third of their season, every.year, is made up of work commissioned from writers like these; one early result of the program was *Buried Child*. Then there are guest companies like Bloolips, Bread & Puppet Theater, and Mabou Mines, which first dazzled the world with its Beckett trilogy on Jane Street. Yes, the productions are often done on a shoestring and a prayer, and there's plenty of trash in the interstices: it wouldn't be creative chaos if it weren't chaos first. But the fact is that TNC, along with La Mama and a very few others, is the most exciting theater in New York at present, and in our pablumized culture, that's heroic.' — (Michael Feingold, *Still Off-Off After All These Years*, Village Voice, January 4, '84.)

4. Modus operandi II: The costs of labor. Limits to their reduction.

Ideally, Schumann would have paid nothing for labor. Not just to reduce expenses and thus dependency, but because he feels that the work he has to offer is and should be its own reward, and is in support of good causes, help in the pursuit of which should not require remuneration, and that, generally, to work for a living is not good. In addition he has wanted neither the dependency of others on him or on the remunerativeness of his theatre for a living, nor the responsibility for seeing to it that his theatre was sufficiently remunerative to enable its producers to survive financially. For a while, until '67, he got his help for free, but there were reasons why this could not continue indefinitely. There were three or four major reasons. For one thing, he needed to make some little money off his theatre (1) for living expenses for himself and his family, (2) to finance the theatre. But if he made any surplus, though in particular of course one that helped him support himself and his family, it was difficult and seemed unfair not to spread the money around a little. Since the theatre was very much his own, this was so even when the surplus was not allocated to his living expenses but just was to go back into the operation.

Secondly, as it turned out, he really needed a core of long-term and pretty much full-time associates. He could take on totally inexperienced people, but he could hardly, for any length of time, carry on with only such. And though he needed more people at some times than at others, he really needed some experienced help pretty much continuously. Though there were again and again financially independent individuals not only able but willing to work for him fairly steadily over extended periods, there were not enough, and people like that tended to have their own interests and a strong desire, however hopeless, to be creative on their own. But people that didn't have a source of income (lovers, parents, trust funds) they didn't have to work for needed at least some minimal pay if they were to devote themselves more or less full time over extended periods to the work he needed done.

Thirdly, his labor needs in the course of just a few years grew pretty big, and, in part, somewhat sophisticated (new types of more flexible big puppets, more use of mime), and in this regard emphatically a need for experienced, i.e. long-term, associates. He had acquired a name for himself, the demand for his appearance at rallies or in parades had grown, as also the opportunity (as also a certain demand) for continuous performing, i.e. for shows every weekend, all weekend. And his shows (and political parades) grew bigger, requiring more puppets, masks, costumes, performers. This actually was the crucial long-term cause of his perennial need for labor: he had from the very beginning, in Germany already, been oriented toward big shows (for big audiences), and has throughout his career again and again, first in his parades, then, from '69 onward, in his other work, given in to this essential ambition of his, not unrelated to a desire for a great effect, i.e. for power. His projects always kept getting bigger.[1] Recurrently he would get hold of himself and plan something small: but invariably within half a year or a year he was back to big productions. His essential vision has always been of a grand spectacle with lots of masks, puppets, picture, and people in it, if possible with music. Even back in Germany he apparently never thought of just solo or duo shows. Another thing, also since his German days, work in a group or of a group has seemed the only right kind of work to him, the work itself the sanctified thing, and the working group redeemed. But the bigger his labor needs, the less could he dispense with a core of laborers in need of at least some minimal financial aid. Even when he only periodically needed a big group or a substantial core group of experienced people, there was a need for having people available for the occasion, and there were difficul-

---

1. '(I: Where did he go wrong in your opinion? What bothered you? A major thing?) Elka: Something I felt that I've sort of given up feeling, maybe because my fears haven't materialized. But it's that the things, the pieces, just kept getting – everything kept growing and I felt it was just out of all bounds and the puppets got bigger and bigger and more and more people were needed to do the shows and – (I: When was this now? Late '70s, early '70s?) Well, I guess I felt it probably starting from the '60s, before we even – I mean, there were the Disciple- and Jesus-size puppets, and then there were the Mother Earth size, you know, the really big puppets. And then there were a few, and then there were many. And now there was one giant Washerwoman. No. Actually, the summer that we made one we made four. I thought that was just not – and people who were working on them really – this last summer I made a shirt for one of the Garbagemen. I think I just sewed for maybe a good ten days sewing the squares together and then sewing the – and the Washerwomen, the whole costume is made out of patches where you first have to take old clothes and rip them apart and cut out the squares and then sew the squares together. So I thought it was like really sort of an indecent demand on people to do – to do one would be all right, but to do four, and under such pressure, because there are so many other projects that needed working on. But the people who worked on them loved it. They though it was very – they really felt that was a wonderful experience and the result was really – everyone was very happy and then last summer when Peter said, "I've got an idea. Let's make a Garbageman." And immediately several people said, "Let's make four so we can have a square dance." (Laughing) So I think I've gotten a bit more, a little bit more, maybe more, you know, more perspective about, or gotten over some of these fears of – I mean, for a while it felt like the theatre – when we were just starting, we could put – we, he and I, if we had to move somewhere, we could put the puppets into boxes or we could pick them up and take them somewhere, or, you know, if we had to get them somewhere we could do it but then after a while it was too much for that and you had to have other people. And that dependency, I think, was sort of frightening to me because I'd think, what if nobody came; what if things would be planned that needed lots of people and lots of times there would be a very slow response, and there you'd be. And I think that was one of my ideas with the little puppet shows (the ones she did '71 following (SSB)), just to get people who are very dependable, and keep things in manageable proportions. But I think I've stopped.' — (Elka, interview.)

181

ties about getting rid of people. His over-all part-solution to his labor problem (cf. infra) was recruitment of temporary inexperienced unpaid volunteers, but to use them he needed a core of people that could quickly whip them into shape. The history of the Bread and Puppet Theatre is to some extent that of the labor problems arising from his orientation toward big shows.

Up until the time of weekend shows Fridays and Saturdays or sometimes just Saturdays for grown-ups, Sunday afternoons for children, at Papp's place, and of college tours in the summer of '67, the theatre was, with two exceptions — Eckhardt and Schumann got paid by the city for working with Harlem kids for a couple of weeks in the summer of '65 and for the following summer's park project there were ten 'paid volunteers' (Schumann), i.e. city stipends to ten of them — strictly a losing proposition, and nobody got paid anything.[2]

'By the summer of '67 we were performing every weekend and there was enough money to pay a core company a survival wage. It was $35 for a single person and $50 for a family, a person with a family. (I: How big a core was there?) Not very big. It was Bob (Ernstthal), Peter, Charlie (Adams), Margo (Sherman). I think we may have been the only ones on salary.' (Sherman, interview.)

The summer or fall of '67 was also when the group started touring, i.e. performing at colleges (Bennington, Goddard, Mount Holyoke, Duke,

---

2. '(I: May I ask you where did *your* money come from during that time?) That's a good question. I don't remember *money*. I know that all my years in New York I never paid more than fifty dollars a month *rent*. (I: The economic question is relevant.) It is relevant and the truth is I can't remember now. I don't know what I lived on. I really don't. It just slips my mind. Like I say, I know that we never paid more than fifty dollars a month. I probably lived on less than a hundred dollars a month. We did moving jobs. We did house painting. Things like that. But still, I don't think we — the money thing is a real unknown. It's a big question. I just don't know. I can't remember. In the back (of the Delancey Street loft) there was this kind of fake plywood wall, and behind it was the storage and the puppets and the trunks. And over the trunks was a mattress I slept on. And a chair. And a milk crate for a table. And I had a hotplate. A double hotplate. And I used to live on — Ratner's was right next door, right? I used to live on bagels, butter, pizza across the street, and Pepsi Cola for a long time. And Hostess cupcakes. Then I changed my diet. That's when I got into health food and macrobiotics, because I could buy a hundred pounds of rice for $17 and live on it for months. And it was healthy.' — (Ernstthal, interview.)

'For example, if you are doing a project like the Bronx project — that was, you know, a paid project. (I: Right, that one, but wasn't that sort of outstanding?) That's about it, yeah. It was outstanding. Every now and then there would be some money exchanged. The time was good and the cooperative baby sitting was good. The soup pot was very communal, so you could all manage. We all had rent control in New York City and lived for $30 a month. Wonderful.' — (Palmer, interview.)

Margo Sherman had been supported by her lover, Arthur Sainer, until she joined the theatre (in March '66), but broke up with him once she did (Sainer: 'Margo, you are married to the Puppet Theatre now.'), so had to go out and get work — in a bookshop, typing for the War Resisters' League WIN after that. — (Sherman, interview.)

University of North Carolina, Wesleyan, ...) outside of New York: another source of these wages.

The arrangement of somewhat fixed, very low weekly supporting allowances paid to core-group members — but probably a growing number of such — seems to have continued, except for the six-week Europe tour of '68 and the nine-month one of '69, until the spring of '70.

Kourilsky (Kourilsky, '71) for the winter '67/'68 reports:

'Un groupe permanent de cinq marionnettistes est désormais régulièrement rémunéré: 35 dollars par semaine; 40 à 45 dollars pour un couple avec un ou deux enfants; 50 dollars pour Schumann qui a cinq enfants.'

(Kourilsky, '71.)

'(I: Let me ask you one quick question also here, were you people generally getting paid up in Maine? (I.e. in the summer of '68. (SSB))) I think the whole — yes, some of us were getting expenses and cigarette money. (I: At Newport? (This would be in the summer of '68 also. (SSB))) No, we always, we always were about $35 a week and expenses. And the food and lodging — that sticks — that stays in my head about what we were getting. And then, at the end of a big tour or something, we would get a bonus. Couple of hundred dollars — four or five hundred dollars.' (Levy, interview.)

'(I: But was it fun for you to do it, or was it spriritually elevating, or both, or ...) I didn't think of it as spiritually elevating. For me, it was like ... it was professional. Suddenly I was being paid to do theatre and that made it ... Yeah, it made a big difference ... you know. (I: How much were you being paid?) Oh God, what ... I don't know. In 1968? Don't laugh, I think it was fifteen dollars a week. (I: That's very good.) I don't know how I paid my rent. Oh yeah, I used to substitute in day care — that's how I paid my rent. How else did I pay my rent? I don't remember. But the rent wasn't high at that time — it couldn't have been more than fifty bucks or something really low. But anyway, I was being paid and I was doing theatre and that was great.' (Leherrissier, interview.)

The '68 tour (but it was just Schumann, Sherman, Blanc, Ernstthal and the Oyles and Eckhardts) yielded room, board, transport and pocket money (the Eckhardts perhaps, the Oyles probably not so benefiting):

'(I: And did you make money, a lot of money? I mean, what for you would be a lot of money?) Yeah. We made some money, I cannot remember how much it was. (I: But — can you remember the idea, not the figure — didn't it suddenly strike you, well, by God!) Of course, it was a very thrilling idea to think that — But we were so terribly naive that we didn't have good contracts. Probably we could have earned a whole lot of money, but we didn't. We earned, let's say, five hundred, we brought back let's say five hundred dollars or a thousand dollars at most. (I: As a group?) As a group. I think something like that, maybe five hundred. It was terribly thrilling. (I: Were you people on salary during that time?) Well, no in Europe, I don't remember that we were .... It was all so very casual. Of course, we got room and board and maybe we got a little pocket money.' (Sherman, interview.)[3]

For the dissent-torn but quite successful '69 tour, both allowances (I have not heard of fixed per diems) and bonuses, i.e. shares in net profits from the tour (after deduction of a theatre-share) were apparently greater; as also complaints that they were not big enough.

'(I: Do you remember how much people were being paid?) I remember that in Belgrade – we went to the Theater Biteff – a festival – and we were being paid something like – oh – maybe it was sixty or a hundred dollars at that time – in dinars. Yugoslavian money. And somehow the rumor got around that we had to spend it in Yugoslavia. And we were leaving the next day and we all raced to the department – I bought a sweater I still have – I got a bag of cashew nuts – three pounds – and stuff like that.' (Ernstthal, interview.)

Ashley, speaking of Bread and Puppet tours, but the '69 one in particular, à propos of Tanith Noble's remarks about it:

'I heard all the stories about the bad times on the tours and the meanness amongst people about – particularly about money. They were always fighting about money – coming back on the bus, people were saying: I want my share of the money. I remember people being very cranky about money – coming back and being very angry with Peter about they needed money and they didn't have any. And Peter saying, fuck off, I'm going to take the money for the circus whether you like it or not – they were very angry and there were hard feelings. Seemed like every tour they came back – even in the States they sometimes had quarrels about money.' (Ashley, interview.)[4]

I.e. the argument was about what share if any, the theatre itself – by then an incorporated entity – was entitled to. When they came back, they had to look for a place to work and perform:

'We thought we had so much money after this tour, which had made money, and we looked at rents and at places and the rents were just impossible. The rents were like $2,000 – a month – or they were just outrageous. We finally did find this building, the bank across the Brooklyn Bridge, at the other end of the Brooklyn Bridge, and we moved in there, and the rent was maybe $400 or $500."
(Elka in Schumann, interview, '79.)

'Our savings from Europe are being eaten up fast with 11 $35 salaries, petty cash, tools, celastic, the tent which we got for the new life, big car failure purchase, Bill's mail-truck and 1 more travelling van. Expected income plus the

---

3. When a booking agency initiated in '67 by Ronald Davis of the San Francisco Mime Troupe – cf. E. Munk's interview with Gottlieb and Jurges, *Booking the Revolution, Tulane Drama Review* #44 (summer '69) – in the fall of '68 brought the Living Theatre over, the weekly charge of each of its 34 members was $150 – but this of course included per diems.
4. Elka thinks Ashley's report is 'very subjective' and comments 'on the whole there was surprisingly little fighting about money.' Schumann, she says, 'finds this report untypical.' — (Elka, letter, September 10, '84.)

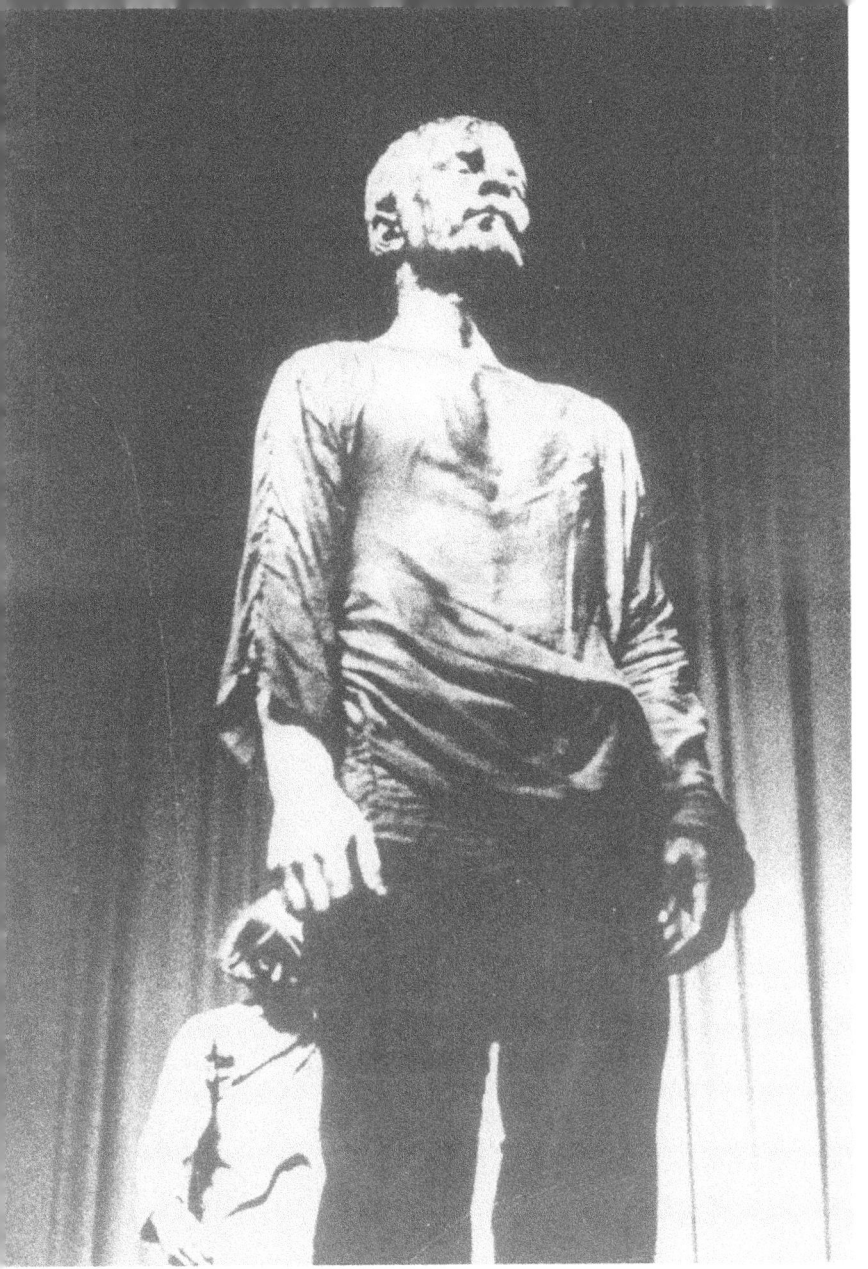

Peter Schumann, dancer.
First version of *Totentanz*, Germany, 1959.

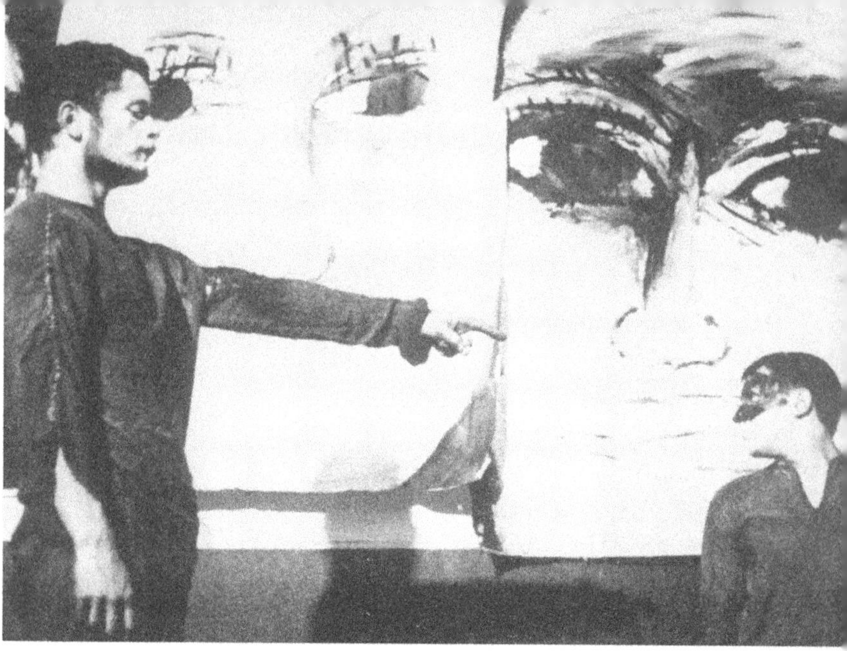

Dancing, Germany, 1959–61. First version of *Totentanz*.

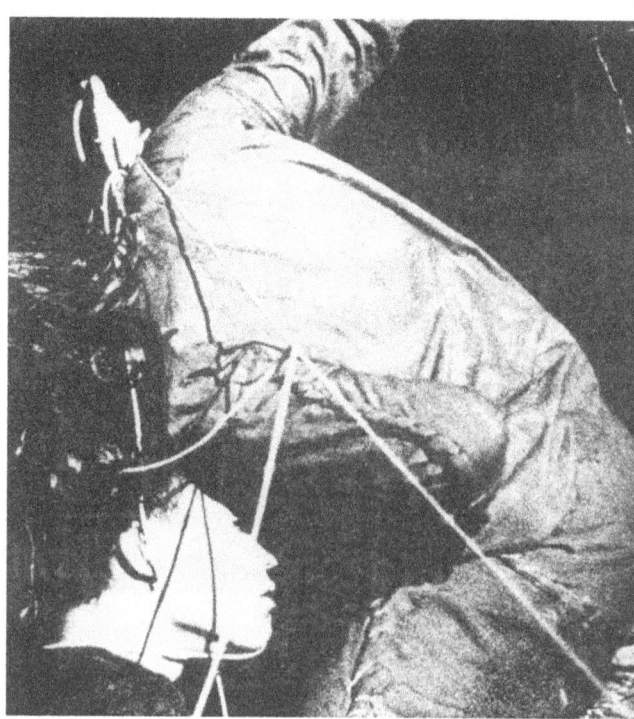

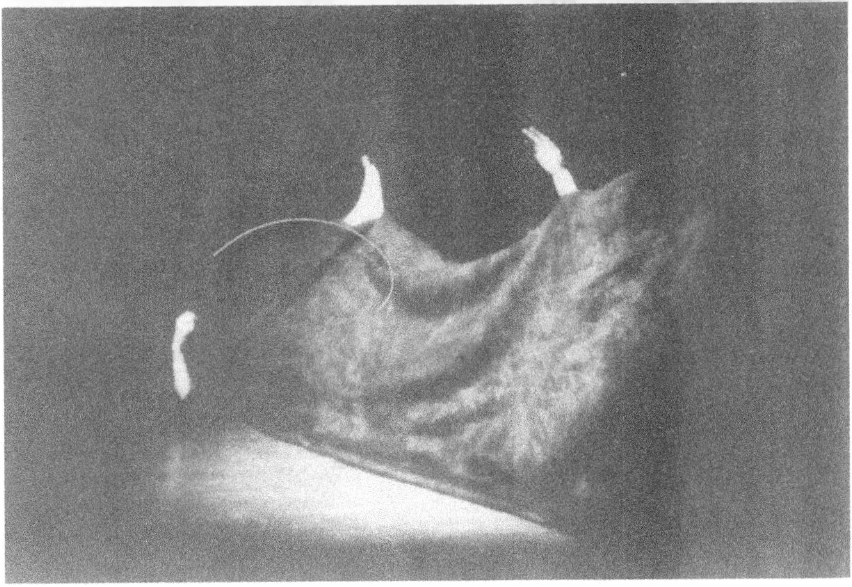

Birth Dance: The Womb

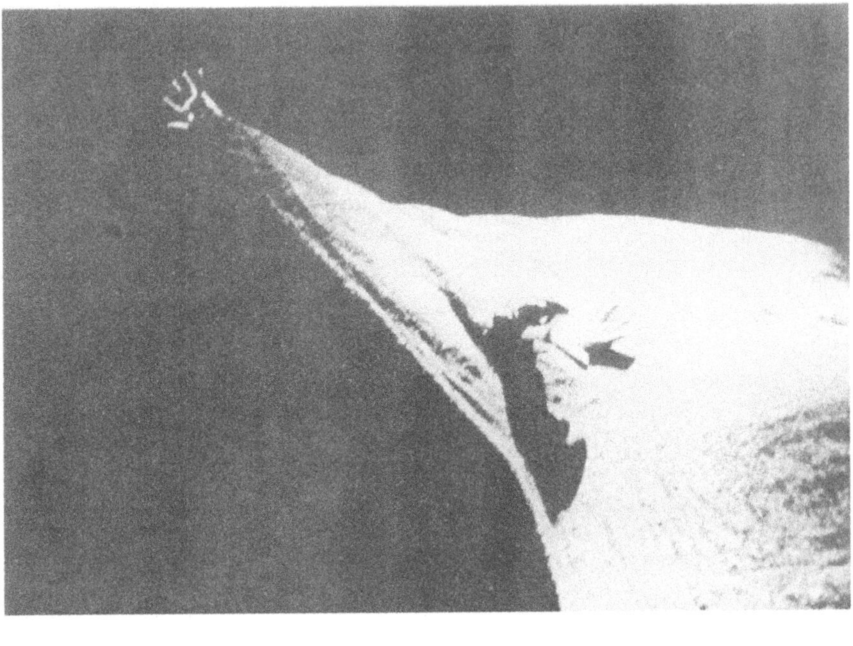

Above: Masks made in Germany, 1959–61, paper mache, made from a cast, used in dance performances.
(Photos: B. Brown)

Right: Janus mask made in New York City 1962, for *Totentanz*, made directly on clay.

Below: The Big Mask made for Ken Shepard, used in *Totentanz*.
(Photos: B. Brown)

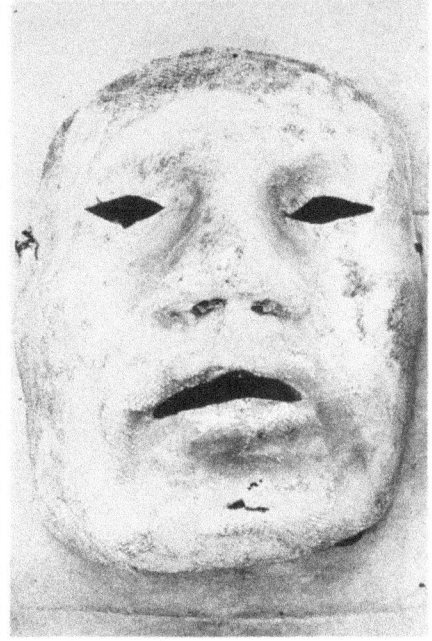
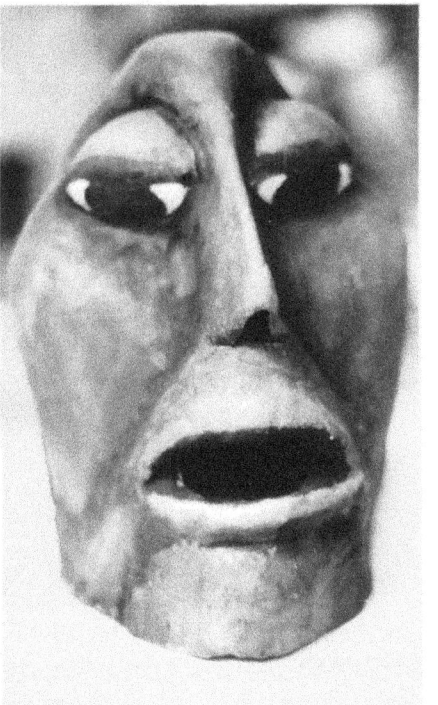

Above left: Mary mask made in New York City, 1963 for *Christmas Story* from a plaster mold.

Above right: Face mask made in the plaster cast of a face, used in *Murder Mystery*, 1964.
(Photos: B. Brown)

Left: Indian mask used in Bob Nichols' *Everyman*, 1964.
(Photo: H. Widmer)

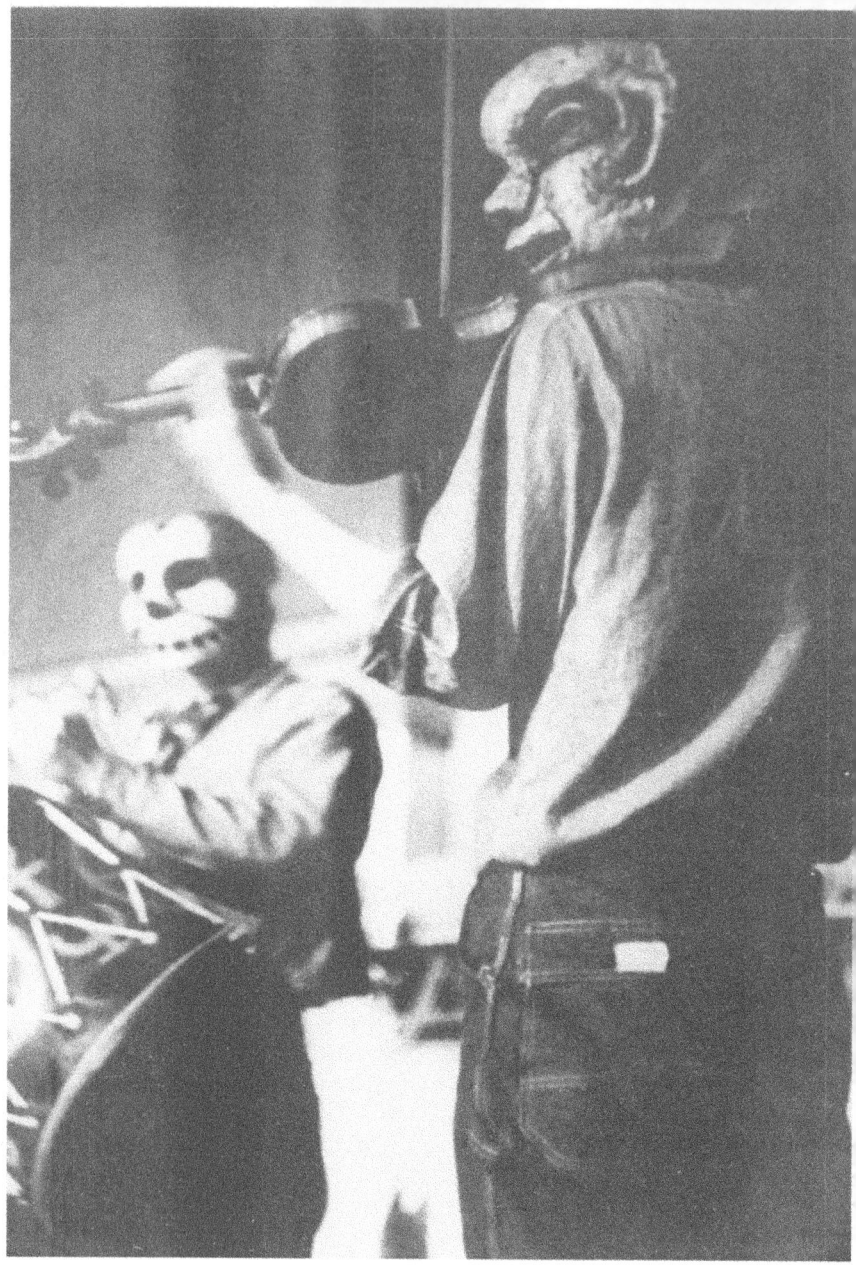

Totentanz performance May 15, 1962, Judson Church, New York City. R. O. Tyler on drum, Peter Schumann playing the violin.

Totentanz, first performance, Alchemy Players.
(Photo: P. Moore)

Burning Towns, Woodstock, N.Y., Ergo Suits Artists Carnival,
August 17, 1962.

Burning Towns, Woodstock, N.Y., Ergo Suits Artists Carnival, August 17, 1962.

Below and opposite: Burning Towns, Judson Church, New York City, August 31, 1962.
(Photos: P. Moore)

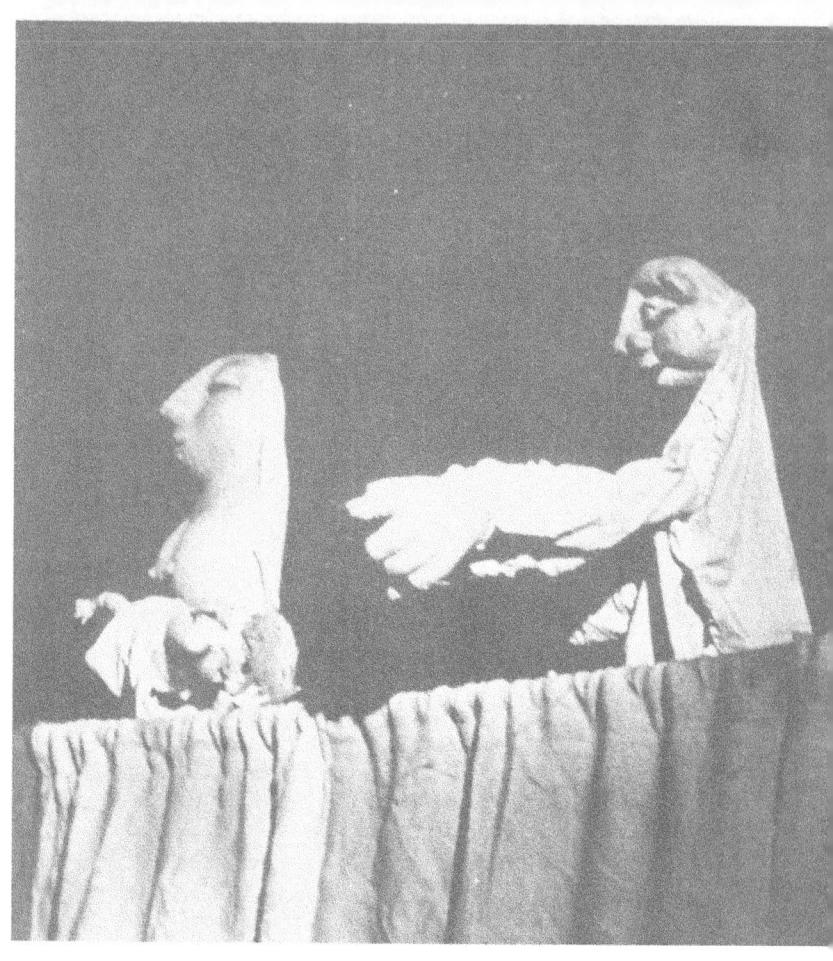

Puppet Festival, Living Theater, New York City, 1962.
(Photo: P. Moore)

Rod puppet made in Putney, Vermont, 1962. First King in *King Story*.

Double rod puppet made in Putney for early versions of *King Story*. The Blue Man and his Son, 1962.

Hand puppets made in Putney, 1962–63, used in *King Story*.
(Photos: B. Brown)

Stick puppets used in *King Story*, 1962.

Rod puppet, The Three Soldiers, *Mr. M* stories and Putney, Vermont, *Fire*.
(Photos: B. Brown)

Carton puppet for Puppet Festival, Jud Gallery, 1963.
(Photo: P. Moore)

 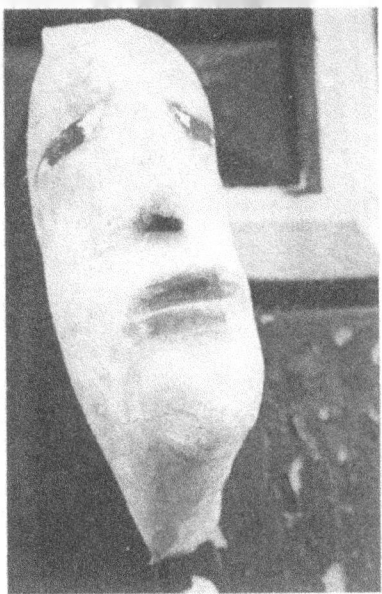

Above left: Giant center pole puppet, Mother Earth, used in *Chicken Little*, 1966. *Above right:* Celastic mask made from cast, used on a short stick over costumed performer's head. River, used in *Leaf Feeling The Moonlight*, 1965. *Below left:* Celastic head, one of the first to be made directly over clay. Uncle Fatso, made by Schumann and child participants in a Harlem workshop in 1965, used in parades. (Photos: H. Widmer) *Below right:* Grey Lady mask operated on a short stick over operator's head, used in *Grey Lady Cantatas*, made in 1967. (Photo: B. Brown)

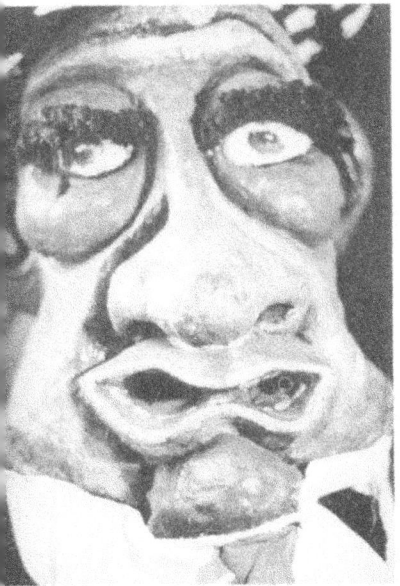 

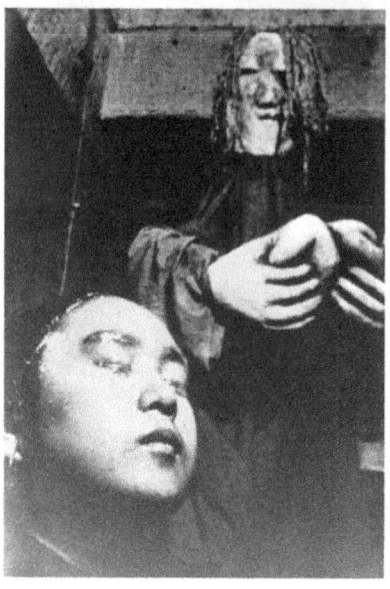 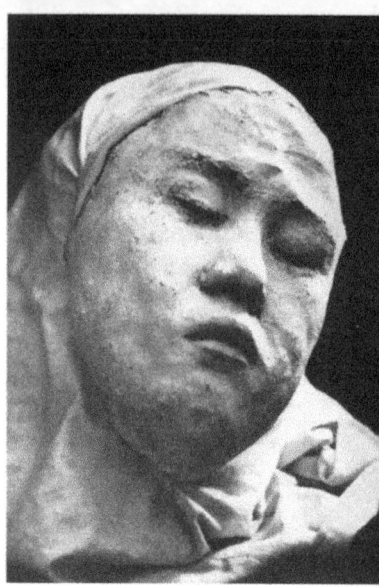

Left: Ms. Li Minh from whose face Schumann got his Vietnamese woman mask made in 1965.

Right: Vietnamese Woman mask made 1967 for second run of *Fire*.
(Photo: R. Bellak)

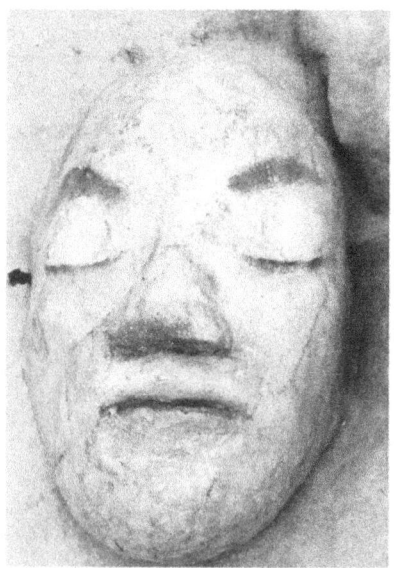 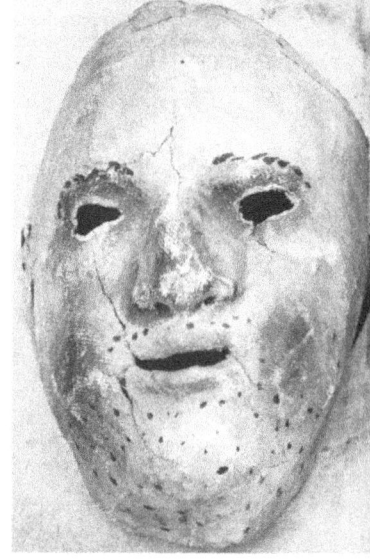

Left: Celastic mask, made into clay mold, blind Vietnamese Woman without eye slits, used in *Fire*, 1966.

Right: Celastic mask, made into clay mold, used in *Murder Mystery* as Drunkard, 1964.
(Photos: B. Brown)

rest of the savings will allow $600 per month (that is what we are spending now per week) from May 15 till October 1st when we want to go on a Westcoast tour.'   Schumann, *Bread and Rosebuds*, April 25, '70.)

So the salaries were discontinued. On Coney Island that summer:

'Then we'd do all these shows and we did them all summer. All the time. Maybe we wouldn't work on Mondays and Tuesdays, days off. All the other time we'd work. And we'd pass the hat and from the hat passing – I got a salary because I was a primary actor. (I: How much did you get?) I don't know – $10 a week. Not very much. But somehow I was able to manage on it with Arthur (Binder). I don't know how I managed but I did and the rest of them just split up the hat. They were just squeaking by really.'   (Leherrissier, interview.)

For the next nine years, until the spring of '79, there were no salaries. During the many U.S. and overseas tours (nine overseas tours during this period) transportation, and normally both room and board and per diem allowances were paid, and if there was a surplus, shares (including a share for the theatre) were paid out. Room and board and some medical expenses were provided to puppeteers living on Cate Farm '70 to '74 (and Elka's parents' farm at Glover was in '73 rented for some), the number of such puppeteers increasing from one or two to around twenty during this time, and room and board was provided for the puppeteers invited to work on the annual summer circuses '74 following during their stay – normally probably around 4-6 weeks.[5] Freeing himself from the burden of

---

5. Bread and Puppet Theater   (An apology for this sounding so clumsy and rigid;
RD 2, Glover   some of this info may not apply to you, some you
Vermont 05839   may know already, but, based on past experience,
June, 1976   such a sheet is needed to avoid unnecessary
     misunderstandings.)

Some Information About the B&P
'76 Circus and Some Guidelines
for People Coming To Work On it

(1) Although all puppeteers will have the opportunity to work on and perform small original sideshows of their own (either using their own puppets & masks or B&P's), the bulk of everyone's time and efforts will go into B&P projects, like: the building and rehearsing of sideshows, pageant and circus proper, preparing facilities, stages and grounds for the event, and of course, there are always the household chores: clean-up and cooking, wood-chopping and shopping, for the big group of people we will be by July, for sure.

(2) Meals will be provided and basic laundry needs taken care of (hopefully no water shortage this summer). Living-sleeping spaces are primitive; besides the few rooms already occupied there's the barn, storage areas, 2 busses, the sugar house. But there is lots of land, so if you have a solid tent, bring it. Please provide your own bedding (sheets, pillows, blankets – the nights can be cold), and when possible, a mattress.

(A contradictory footnote: if you have the money and the wish to contribute to the food-budget, we'll accept it, but we don't expect it.) (Bread and Puppet Theatre circular to circus volunteers, 1976.)

(3) Bread and Puppet Theater cannot be responsible for dentist and doctors bills, and other personal expenses.

salaries early in '70, Schumann until '74 took on the burden of a responsibility for support in kind, a burden shared, however, by the puppeteers themselves and by Elka, inasmuch as, after an initial period, especially, during which Goddard College food chits helped feed the company,[6] a certain proportion of the food was provided from the gradually extensive Cate Farm vegetable gardens[7] – touring providing the money for the remainder.

---

(4) We cannot cover your transportation costs to get here and return home. But if you bring a vehicle and it is used for the Circus or group living needs (shopping trips, touring shows, hauling equipment, etc.) we'll help maintain it.
 Don't feel obliged to share your car; if you want to be the sole driver, or not use it at all, that's ok.
(5) Some useful things to bring along if you have them: whites (shirt, pants/skirts), musical instruments, bowl and cup. If you care for keeping your things, label them.
(6) Bread and Puppet Theater has no grants or public or private foundation support. It is a tax-exempt, non-profit cultural enterprise. It is not an employer and does not pay salaries for work done on its projects (at best there is a sharing of 'profit' at the end of a tour). People who join the work on specific projects are participants/volunteers/apprentices, NOT employees. Therefore you cannot make claims for unemployment compensation on the grounds of the time you spent here.
6. 'The entire core group of puppeteers and Schumanns were welcome (as part of the invitation tendered Schumann to be resident artist at Goddard (SSB)) to dine in the college dining hall or take chits. And the chits could be used to take food out of the commissary. You could turn in three chits and get a 50-pound bag of flour. You could turn in one chit and get twenty-five bananas, or whatever. Yes, they were – it was a very generous arrangement . . . . If they said that they were willing to support the Schumann family and five people – just picking (a number) – then there were food chits for that number of people. Elka used to save them up for the circus rather than spend them so that the workers on the circus could be given chits to go eat. Because it meant that you didn't have to cook, clean, serve and clean up afterwards a whole bunch of people. They could go and eat at the dining hall and then come back. That didn't work out because they didn't come back fast enough. They felt they were workers, they were entitled to an hour off for lunch. Peter always thought they could eat while they were shopping, or something.) — (Ashley, interview.)
 Elka (Letter, September 10, 1984.) comments: 'Ashley's understanding of (the) Goddard situation (is) completely off. Notwithstanding Pres. Witherspoon's generosity, Goddard personnel were sceptical/hostile to us and made getting food assistance so uncomfortable that we soon gave up trying to get cafeteria meals. That was reinstated briefly during (the) 1974 Circus rehearsals, I believe.'
7. 'I'm sure we had a garden the first year (1970, at Cate Farm (SSB)). We came in June . . . The Cate Farm garden became very communal after the first year or two. I guess after the second year because the first year it was mainly our family and the second year it was all sort of new people. But certainly by '74 the garden – there were maybe five or six plots and different people were in charge of different gardens and you were very proud of them and did . . . really beautiful – very intricately planted sections. And some, like Katarina – Paul Zaloom's girlfriend's from Germany – was a very, very interesting garden and with companion planting and sort of esoteric aspects of gardening and –. But when we moved here – I mean, Cate Farm was a communal situation in that way that we were all there as a theatre in residence at Goddard. When we came here, it was my family's farm and the group had disbanded and it was our family that moved here so the garden always felt like

Cash expenses[8] for food by '73 had reached $13,966, in '74 totalled $15,952 (and these '74 expenses presumably the expenses for the first half of the year only), but fell radically in '75, after the company had been disbanded: to $2,983, and in '76 amounted to $9,422 (at Glover: $3,911, on tour $5,511) in '77 to $5,389 (Glover: $4,894, on tour, $495). From the same source, I get annual 'fees' 73-77, apparently monies paid out to members of the company as shares: $18,337 in '73, $22,541 in '74 ('Cate Farm disbanding bonuses'), $3,421 in '75, $9,076 in '76, $23,161 in '77 (of which $18,754 as Glover 'fees,' $4,407 as touring 'fees'). But these figures straddle two radically different situations: from June '70 to July '74, a resident commune of puppeteers was provided (provided itself with) food, Goddard providing the lodging, from '75 through '78, the theatre provided food – and to a core group lodging – for somewhere around six weeks each summer to visiting puppeteers working on the circus.

In '79 salaries were reinstituted:

'People were paid fees according to their participation on tours until about 1977, when I began to get a regular $100 a week salary. Up till then our family had gotten that portion of the tour that everybody else got, except we had gotten more. But starting in late November of '77 I began getting a steady $100 a week and then in April in '79 we instituted a salary for six of us – year round.'

(Elka, in Schumann, interview, '83.)

---

my garden, and I remember I felt very possessive about it and our family did most of it. And now – it got very big and very unwieldy and at this point there are two gardens and the puppeteers grow most of the – (for) the circus . . . which is a big, big production. (I: It still is a relevant item, the garden?) Oh yeah, oh yeah . . . I think that after all the touring they do all year, all of them really look forward to raising the garden and want to do it and want to do it more seriously and I think that's something that probably some of them really regret not being able to do more. (I: So you would say that from '79 to '82, growing your own crops has been a significant item economically and in terms of what people do?) Yeah. (I: I had the impression that it had petered out.) No, no. In fact, we are getting – I mean our family has always kept it and we've added chickens and raising a pig in the summer and things like that. But I'd say from '75 to about '80, the gardening was mainly my – I did most of the gardening and I ordered the plants and I really did most of the planting and the work and so on. (I: More so than at Cate Farm?) In Cate Farm it was much more shared, especially the last summer. I think I only had a – you know, I did a small section of it and other people – (I: This must have taken a lot of work.) Yeah. — (Elka, interview.)

'This has been our third summer of gardenings. We certainly had fresh food every day all summer long, from the first radish in late May until cabbage and corn season, plus a big freezer full of wonders, plus beets, squash, pumpkins, garlic, potatoes stored through late fall, plus tomatoes on the window sills, plus 5 bushels of apples sliced and strung under the ceiling, and more. But we still have a lot to learn to provide for our large lunch and supper tables. Since our cash is from puppet shows only, the schedules of garden and theater experience difficulties with each other. Our system of chores changes frequently. Our organization is as yet uninvented. And besides all that, the validity of our profession is often dubious to ourselves.' — (Schumann, Newsletter, *Bread and Rosebuds*, November '72.)

8. Bread and Puppet accounts. Cf. Appendix XV.

By 1980, salaries apparently were around $52 a week for four puppeteers and Schumann, in '81, $60, in '82, $75, Elka each getting twice the amount.[9] The per diems on tours in '80 amounted to $60 a week, in '81 they were $100, in '82, $115. In 1981 (apparently since 1980) there was a 'Medical Fund': people who had worked in Bread and Puppet for 6-7 months in a year had access to it: it paid half the cost of medical and dental fees. (Minutes of Annual Bread and Puppet Meeting, January 9, '82.) These per diems in '80 came to $8,744, in '81 to $15,558, and food expenses during these two years amounted to $8,899 and $13,562 respectively.

---

9. 'When you cite that Elka gets twice as much money as everyone else, readers should know that that is meant for our whole family. We never got a salary for each child, at most three, usually two or one extra, so three, four or five salaries for a family of seven. Whenever there was a puppeteer with a child or children, the same procedure was followed, the puppeteer receiving either a whole or half a salary per child.' — (Elka, letter of September 10, 1984.)

5. Modus operandi II. Finance. Funding rejected. Touring the essential revenue source.

The problem of costs was acerbated by Schumann's unwillingness to make money. Ideally, he would have preferred not to be paid anything for his shows, but particularly not by the audience: the buyer-seller relationship distorting, even perverting the nature of the event, whether qua the artist's act of art — a concentrated showing of his relation to the world for the sake of his own awareness and mastery of it, or qua relation between artist and people — communion in a community, in which the artist participates as freely giving of himself. Short of getting nothing, if he had to receive money, he preferred getting very little and getting it voluntarily. Getting very little was a minimum requirement, getting it voluntarily close to one: exclusivity of attendance on financial grounds would have made doing art at all meaningless. Possibly there were high admission charges in some of the 'fancy theatres' (Elka) Schumann on some of his European tours played in, but his record is 99% clean: his shows have been either simply free, or admission was against truly not just pretendedly voluntary contributions, or only very low admission was charged — fifty cents, a dollar, two dollars.[1]

There was an alternative or complement to getting money from the audience: get it from a third party — subsidies. Such revenue would not

---

1. Exceptions, '62-'68, as indicated by *Village Voice* ads and notices, from admission against contributions of unspecified amount: *Christmas Story*, Living Theatre, December 20, 21, '62, 50c, same, Museum, December 21, '63, free, same, Museum, January 4, 5, '64, free, *Two King Stories*, Museum, Saturdays and Sundays, February '64, free, *The Puppet Christ*, Judson Poets' Theatre, August 31, September 1, 2, '64, contributions to go for Mississippi Summer Project, *Birdcatcher*, Museum, October '64, $1, *Christmas Story*, Pocket Theatre, December '64, 90c, *The Great Passion*, Spencer Memorial Church, March '65, contribution $1, *King Story* and *Leaf*, Bridge Theatre, November '65, $2, *Christmas Story*, Bridge Theatre, December '65, afternoons: adults, $1, children, 50c, evenings, adults $2, children, $1, *Christmas Story*, Spencer Memorial Church, December '65, contribution $1.50, *Winter Story*, etc. Bridge Theatre, February '66, adults, $1, children 50c, *Fire*, Museum, May 20, '66, benefit for the New York Workshop in Non-Violence, admission $1.50, *Big City Story*, etc. Bridge Theatre, June 19, '66, adults, $1, children, 50c, *Bach Cantata #140*, Village Theatre, February 2, '67, $1, *Wounds*, Washington Square Methodist Church, February 4, '67, free, *Christmas Story*, P.S. 122, December 10, '67, 25c, 50c per family, excerpts from *Cry*, St. Clement's Church, March 17, '68, benefit for David Mitchell, tickets $3, 4, ?, Washington Square Methodist Church, March 30, 31, '68, benefit for Radical Booking Agency, contributions $2, 3, *Christmas Story*, Muse, Brooklyn, December 28, '68, free.

Coney Island, '70:

'We want to play for a dime a nickel or nothing if possible. Rides and shows in Coney Island are now 25 to 75 cents, much higher than local kids can afford.' — (Schumann, *Bread and Rosebuds*, April 25, '70.)

pervert his relation to the audience: the audience would be as much the beneficiary as he. But the problem here was to find a funder dependency on whom would not endanger his art, alliance with whom would not compromise it and him. Even unconditionally accorded funding is dangerous, namely if it can be discontinued. It engenders, especially over a period, a dependency of the work process, if not of the mind, so that in case of discontinuance of the subsidy, it might be impossible to continue the work as it has in the meantime come to be, especially since in the meantime other approaches to making the work possible will not have been made.[2] And if the work is, as Schumann's is, partisan, an alliance subsidizer-subsidizee like any other alliance may be compromising. There is in the case of people like Schumann no reason to bring up adages à la Who Pays the Piper. Nor to speak of 'integrity' – people out to protect their 'integrity' are ipso facto corrupt: vainglorious. Schumann, cf. infra, has not wanted to be subsidized by grants or 'awards' either from the great cultural foundations funded by capitalists that in the U.S. play the role money-disbursing Ministries of Culture play elsewhere and that formerly kings, noblemen and the church played, nor by the State, i.e. the state and federal agencies that since Johnson's regime supplement their activities. On the whole, cf. infra for particulars, he has stuck to this stance, stuck to it even when he was broke and offered money.[3]

---

2. Cf. Appendix XII, Friedman, *When the Curtain Fell on the Workers' Theatre*.
3. Ronnie Davis of the San Francisco Mime Troupe:
'You cannot buy Peter Schumann,' Davis said, 'but that means that Peter Schumann can't make any money either ('he's really embarrassed to make money'). Sure I'm political but I don't believe that means I have to donate my services. I know what our show is worth and I expect to get paid for it. But the situation in New York is that if you make money you have sold out. Guerillas should live off the land, sustained by the people – not feel that fasting is the only means of purity.' — (R. Wetzsteon, *San Francisco Mime Troupe. Theatre of Revolution: Protest or Celebration?*, Village Voice, November 30, '67.)
In March '65, he accepted a grant from the Foundation of Contemporary Performance Arts (Directors: John Cage, Elaine de Kooning, Jill Jakes, Jasper Johns, Billy Klüver), possibly a clean donor. That same year and the following he put his puppetry in the service of the city's youth programs (I have mentioned these '65 and '66 summer parks programs).
'There was a big brouhaha about should we take the money from the city, you know, which was government, to do the Bronx project. And, you know, to me that was perfectly clean, but there were objections even at that level. He was being very pure. You know when you have nothing, you can be very pure. Peter had the idea, and I agreed with it, because I was studying psychology – now, what was I going to do, go into the mental health system? You see, and give IQ tests to black people and do Rorschachs for institutional cases who are never going to get therapy anyway, and, you know, like, could I support that system? So the hippies were the dropouts from those systems. Don't go into business. Don't go into institutionally oppressive situations. Don't serve them. And Peter presented an alternative. Okay, you make a play, you go out on the street, and you get money. And when I came to California, if the plays were good – I worked a long time after I left Peter, doing street theatre. The plays were good, you could support 15 people

Over the years, individuals have probably given him a relatively considerable amount of money, but except for knowing that Mabel Chrystie Dennison (who gave the group a house in Strong, Maine, in '68 that is said to have cost $5,000),[4] gave money from time to time, and a few

---

from them. It was wonderful. And it felt to me totally clean. It was like ice cream, you know. You're not abusing anybody. But remember the times then, the institutional life and everybody kinda going in lockstep with that. And then the army came along. Everybody dropped out. Well, then everybody was evaluating, not only through drugs, but through other introspection. Well, what about these institutions? You know? Don't they just further the cause of, you know, people that have power? Peter was very anti-power. I like that.'
— (Palmer, interview.)

The basic idea of these '60s programs for minority kids — their older brothers raring to rumble, their oldest brothers off in Vietnam with the volunteer army — was to cool it in the streets. Still, the giant Uncle Fatso puppet the first project yielded was immediately paraded in an anti-landlord demonstration in Spanish Harlem and then served in many peace demonstrations, and the next summer's puppet-yield had similar uses, not revolutionary, but 'resistance' — left. For the winter of '67/'68, Schumann accepted a '$4,800 grant from the New York State Council of the Arts administered through Ken Dewey' (Bread and Puppet Diary, November 1967-March 1968): perhaps Schumann was willing to accept money from Dewey that he would have hesitated to accept from that Council. His Coney Island theatre had another grant from the Council '71/'72: 'A member of the company applied' for it, 'and Schumann says he must have signed the application himself but he doesn't remember it. It was surely an aberration.' (B. Goldensohn, *Peter Schumann's Bread & Puppet Theater*, *The Iowa Review*, Spring '77.) Apparently Ashley applied for and accepted it. In January of '71, as part of the fourth set of awards granted by the National Endowment for the Arts to 'aid in the development of new playwrights, new plays and new theater techniques' (*New York Times*, January 19, '71), the Bread & Puppet Theatre was awarded $5,000 (the Open Theatre, the Performance Group and La Mama each got $20,000.). Apparently Schumann refused the money because the NEA 'was the agency of a government embroiled in Southeast Asia conflict' (a New York Associated Press interview of Schumann by William Glover, printed in the *Ann Arbor News* of October 8, '72). In '77, the year Schumann received one-fourth of the Dutch Erasmus prize, the familiar notice stating 'funding in part by' appears in flyers of his for the, to my knowledge, first time: the flyers for his *Ave Maris Stella*, funded in part by 'The Vermont Council on the Arts'. And similarly, at the '78 circus: the Vermont Council had contributed $3,000. The publication of Schumann's *This Is* ('80) was 'assisted by a grant from the Literature Program of the National Endowment for the Arts.' Except for Schumann's mentioning in an interview (M. Thomas, *Pavement Artists*, *Plays and Players*, May 1967) that the Guggenheim Foundation 'had turned him down without even looking at his stuff', this is all I have heard of funding.

4. Ashley (interview), who gives Ken Dewey the credit for getting the theatre incorporated as a non-profit corporation in '68 or '69, says that one reason Dewey did it was because he thought that the way the theatre could survive would be for people to be able to give money — 'the kind of people who might give money because they could get a tax deduction out of it', but adds that this 'proved to be false. There was nobody around giving money who wanted a tax deduction — even Mabel Dennison didn't particularly seem to want one.'

Elka (Letter of September 10, '84) remarks: 'Gifts went to (the) Bread and Puppet, not to Peter, and it's unfair to give (the) impression that Peter pocketed the money.' I am sure Schumann never 'pocketed' any money. I am speaking about donations to the theatre.

figures in Bread and Puppet accounts,' I have no information on this. I don't think these private donations, though at times they may have been a life saver, were a crucial factor.

Schumann foreclosed revenues in yet another way. Not only has he not wanted to play in fancy theatres, he for a long time, into the early '70s, has not wanted to play in theatres – 'regular' theatres – at all. The bias against fancy theatres was a bias against bourgeois or well-heeled audiences. The bias against theatres was due to his belief that these places by inclining audiences to relate to shows as entertainment or in aesthetic terms, qua art, or as 'culture' shielded them against the shows' relevancy to their actual lives.[6]

Nothing but principle was from his success with *Fire* in '66 onward mitigating against subsidization by government and/or foundations. It has been the economic foundation of avant-garde performing art since the early '60s. He would have been supported. As regards his policies of free admission or admission against voluntary contributions, we might say that his unlicensed home-bases – the Delancey St. Museum, etc. – during the '60s made them mandatory anyhow, and that both before and after '66 when his political demonstrations and *Fire* got him a name in New York he couldn't have gotten enough of an audience on a fixed admissions basis to make a change-over advisable or even feasible. Not that his New York reviews from '66 onward weren't favorable enough, but partly because it would have required rent (for a licensed theatre) that would have eaten up the profits, partly because it would have cut down on the impecunious and informal audience his work appealed to, an audience largely limited to people of like political convictions – and partly because very soon after he made it, by '68, the Off-off-Broadway fashion trend, conformity to which determined audience interest, became strong and decidedly excluded his kind of work: sex, nudity, violence, a focus on The Individual and on performers were in: the Living Theatre, the Performance Group, the Open

---

5. Donations in '73, $3,897, in '74, $1,372, in '75, $1,249, in '76, $1,799, in '77, $3,550, gifts in '80, $10,948, in '81, $14,373. But in '80, there was a special fund raising drive (yield: 'over 5,000' by October) to help build a house for Elka Schumann, and Maurice Blanc, who when he died soon after made Schumann his heir, gave $5,083.01.'

In '80, the theatre opened a seedy shop in seedy Hardwick, Vermont, calling it 'Cheap Art': selling posters and such. It made $522.25 the first year. In '83, Schumann had a sign in his driveway advertising bread for sale two days a week.

6. '(TDR: Does the audience react differently in the street than they do indoors?) We've had our best – and sometimes our most stupid – performances in the streets. Sometimes you make your point because your point is simply to be there in the street. It stops people in their tracks – to see those large puppets, to see something theatrical outside of theatre. They can't take the attitude that they've paid money to go into a theatre to "see something". Suddenly there is this thing in front of them, confronting them.' — (Schumann, in: Brown & Seitz, *Interview with Peter Schuman*, TDR, 30 (Winter 1968).)

Theatre, etc. Barely in, he was out. But altogether, he never made it in New York the way he made it in Europe.

His first three tours in Europe ('68, '69, winter '71, '72) got him a name in Europe that the plays he showed on them never got him in New York City (or in America): that of a great original artist and a theatre artist, not just the reputation given him by the New York critics of a man with a fair talent for staging overly simple-minded, even crude political parables, whose flaws as author and director were redeemed by his genius as a mask-maker − or almost, not quite, redeemed. European critics and audiences were better able to appreciate the combination of sophistication and primitivism (simplicity, childlikeness, naiveté), the high moral tenor, and the religiosity and/or mysticism of his work than were American critics and audiences: partly because of native traditions in all three respects, absent in America, partly because of greater European sophistication, and a greater willingness to accept an artist's individuality and/or idiosyncracies, partly because his shows were seen as coming from America and benefited from a credit given things American and from a relaxation of standards and antipathies that might have been operative with respect to native products. Until, in '75/'76, he acquired a local − Vermont, French Canadian − audience for his once-a-year circuses, Schumann's only appeal in America was on the one hand to an audience of liberal sophisticates in New York City, that he didn't particularly want, the appreciation from which was largely politically motivated (a motivation that weakened considerably after the '60s Peace Movement) and the greater part of which from '68 onward preferred the stronger and more trendy fare of other 'avant-garde' Off-off Broadway theatre, and a not too dissimilar audience of college kids across the country to a considerable extent motivated by interest in what was 'happening' in New York, and the effective appeal to which therefore was weakened by his lukewarm reception in New York City. Whether other admission policies would have made his theatre in New York City or later in Vermont lucrative is doubtful, but that they were based on principled choice is certain.

His New York operation basically lost money even while, for the first few years, the labor was unpaid; and continued to lose money thereafter, in spite of his (modest) fame as creator of *Fire* and as peace agitator;[7] his local shows at Goddard, '70-'73, certainly lost money; and his Cate Farm circus of '74 as well as his Glover circuses, '75-'79 and '81 (he did his '80 circus in France, on a contractual basis, and to make money, and made $34,978.56 on it: I have no figures for the '81 ff. circuses) lost money. The Bread and Puppet Theatre spent $4,900 more than it earned on the '74 circus, $2,175 more than it earned on the '75 circus, $3,245 more

---

7. Some old members of the company like to feel that their modest allowances from '67 onward came out of a box office net. I think they are fooling themselves.

than it earned on the '76 circus, lost $6,208 on the '77, $5,574 on the '78, $3,918 on the '79, $7,760 on the '81 circus. His home shows consistently lost money. The basic reason for this was not lack of appreciation by local audiences, but that his home operations, wherever they were, were staged non-commercially and without any consideration for gain or loss, in fact rather with aversion to gain.

When the Schumanns got back to New York in the fall of '63, all they had was the little they had saved from Elka's salary as teacher at Putney School. Schumann then proceeded (it's now been twenty years) to support himself and his wife (Elka has not earned money on her own since then, discounting some minute amounts from her high school performances '71 ff.) and five kids while maintaining a theatrical activity that on its home bases cost him money. Support from Elka's parents probably accounts for how the family could survive given the very small allowances from theatrical earnings he allowed himself and Elka. How the theatre survived is another question.

His first idea was an appeal to what has, especially as regards European hand puppetry, traditionally been a major audience for puppetry, children. They were going to make money with children's shows, Punch and Judy, fairy tales, the comic *King Story*.[8] Although he never, during the '60s, quite gave up on this (cf. infra), and although he in fact got some quite appreciative reviews (cf. infra), this was not particularly successful. If the basic reason here was probably that his humor did not much appeal to American children, brought up on TV rather than on fairy tales, and not too amused by silliness, the reason for the initial lack of success of the Museum's weekend shows for grown-ups was probably not so much their lack of modernity and the reasons cited supra, as rather simply that until '66 he was not in command of the medium, a medium he had created. People could come and admire the puppets, but he had not yet learned how to use them. He had recourse to some expedients, e.g. face-masks people could send home as Christmas gifts,[9] but basically, the putative aid from his in-laws apart, he, Eckhardt and Ernstthal got by by occasional jobs of the sort traditional to impecunious male New York artists (the

---

8. 'That was one of the first shows we did, that was supposed to be fairy tales and we tried this elusive pursuit of doing fairy tales. (I: When was this?) Right in the beginning. Right when we got to Delancey Street. So it was '63. With *King Story*. We were trying to do – work up kids' things, because, for one thing, everyone knew that if we could develop a kids' show we could make money.' — (Ernstthal, interview.)

9. 'Finished mask is $10. – if you come to him at the Delancey St. loft. It's $20 – if he comes to you . . . For an extra $2.50, he will give your mask a more important wood look with dark and light stain. Of course if you really care, you can have it recast in bronze.' — (From a longish article, *Don't Skimp, Send Your Face*, in the *New York Herald Tribune* of December 18, '63.)

'Send your face home for Christmas/exact reproduction/life mask $10/Bread & Puppet Museum . . . / by appointment.' — (Ad, *Village Voice*, November 25, '65.)

female dancers and actresses waitress), viz. apartment painting and light moving.[10] He had given performances at some colleges in the winter of '62/'63, but for some reason, possibly the lack of transport for the big puppets, he didn't take this up again until probably no earlier than the summer of '67, by which time he had some reviews to submit.

Basically, then, over the years, the labor has not, except the first few years, been free; horticulture since '70 cut down on its money costs a little, but surely not very much; there have been other expenses; funding contributed scarcely at all; donations helped, but only to a limited extent; and the home operations of the theatre consistently lost money.

The way Schumann after the first few heroic years kept his theatre going was by touring. He toured college campuses in the U.S. and he toured Europe (and went to Australia, North Africa and South America as well) playing in regular theatres. By far most of his theatrical revenue came from the European tours. Europe has been his economic basis. Ethically, so to speak, the crucial thing was he didn't have to sock the audiences. College audiences may generally have gotten in for free, both they and the European audiences, with, I think, only rare exceptions in fancy European theatres, at worst got in for low admissions, sometimes nominal ones, and in any event, Schumann got paid not by them, either directly at a box office of his own, or indirectly by getting a share of the gate, but by the sponsors. He kept his art a non-commodity by his policy of admission against voluntary contributions in his successive home-bases in New York City, at Goddard, on Dopp Farm, and abroad, as far as the audiences were concerned, he kept it (instructing the people arranging his tours accordingly and fighting them on the issue) a low-priced commodity available to all.

Nevertheless, this dichotomy between home-base theatre in his 'community', effectively subsidized by touring, and the toured theatre involved some compromise with principle: not only the small compromise of small fixed admissions abroad, and perhaps sometimes at colleges, but the larger, though not devastating one, of selling his art to sponsors for a fee. He somehow figured that the foreign and the college sponsorship – the foreign sponsors mostly national, provincial or community cultural agencies of government – Florence, Iran, Aubervilliers, France, Rhein-Hessen – the colleges more often than not pretty classy ones with hefty endowments – either did not have the drawbacks of eventual dependency and compromising associations, e.g. weren't fighting wars in Vietnam, or else had them, but to a lesser extent. To some extent he probably kept up

---

10. '... and all of this wasn't that easy because Bruno and I had our painting companies, and when that didn't work so well, you know, we did furniture moving, so those things, I guess they came first, and so whenever we found a job to paint apartments we shared apartments.' — (Schumann, interview, '79.)

the junkie's illusion that he could stop touring any time he wanted to (and still keep doing theatre). Only now and then, e.g. on the Nov.-Dec. '73 tour or that of the summer of '80 (when he felt he had become integrated into the tourist business), was he oppressed by the feeling that he had to tour to keep going.

From the first one onward — I know of twenty of them[11] — the foreign tours yielded surpluses for the theatre;[12] and so did the U.S. ones.[13]

---

11. (1) April 10-end of May or beginning of June '68, Europe, chiefly France, with *Fire* as the main offering.
(2) April-November '69, Europe, chief offering *Cry of the People*.
(3) December 4, '71-February 15, '72, Europe, chiefly Germany, chief offerings: *Grey Lady Cantatas II & III, Birdcatcher*.
(4) November-December '73, Europe, *Simple Light, Attica*.
(5) March '75, Schumann alone, Paris, 2 weeks, *Grey Lady Cantata VI*.
(6) August '75, Mannheim, Germany, Peter and Tamara Schumann and Murray Levy's group, 10 days, *White Horse Butcher*.
(7) September '75, Martinique, 4 people, *White Horse Butcher*.
(8) January-March '76, North Africa, Eastern and Western Europe, 28-30 people (kids included), *Our Domestic Resurrection*.
(9) September/October '76, Bonn, Brussels, Belgrade, Florence, Rome, 9 people, 8 weeks, *White Horse Butcher*, (small) circus, *Chile*.
(10) November '76, Florence, Schumann only, 2 weeks, *Masaccio* paper-maché workshop.
(11) May-June '77, France, Italy, Switzerland, 8 weeks, *Joan of Arc, White Horse Butcher*.
(12) February/March '78, Australia, (Schumann only).
(13) May/July '78, Europe and South America, *Joan of Arc, White Horse Butcher*.
(14) October-December '78, Italy, *Masaniello*.
(15) March-May '79, Holland, England, Scotland, France, *Washerwoman Cantatas I, II*.
(16) December '79, France, *Washerwoman Cantatas*.
(17) April/September '80, England, France and Italy with *Stations of the Cross*. April-June, 6-week workshop in Lyons, July-August, and 6-week tour in France and Yugoslavia, with *Story of Bread*.
(18) January/February '81, 3 weeks, France, *Washerwoman Nativity*, performed 12 times.
(19) Sometime in '81, Cuba, *The Story of One*, (4 times).
(20) Later in '81 (?), 6 weeks, Germany, Italy, *Goya, Woyzeck*.

12. The pursuit of gain did not sit too well with the more radical puppeteers on the '69 tour:

'There were those who wanted to go to the people ... Bruno thought we should go to the factories — right? We should go to the streets — we should play for free — we should get our message to the people. We should condemn the theatre owners — condemn the theatrical promoters. And essentially condemn and deny the actual people who had put this stuff together for us ... They felt we should bolt from them and condemn them as capitalists — and we should go the factories ... Peter felt he had to honor his commitments ... And he didn't give a shit who the audience was — really ... You see, we were popular ... The pitfalls of popularity. Because people would flock to the theatres to see us — at the same time in France the Black Panthers were being lionized — in French intellectual circles. Eldridge Cleaver was considered — really, you know, a tremendous ideologue and really smart and all that. So the Bread and Puppet Theatre was considered really hot stuff. So the liberals flocked to it and when we'd play a show we were jammed constantly. But then there were those who felt that this was a cop-out. It happened to Bob Dylan — it happened all up and down the line. It was: you are copping out; you're being a capitalist; you're making money; you're doing this or that and the other thing ... Taking thirty-five people and plane loads of equipment to Europe is no small matter. And there was a certain amount of logistics and a certain amount of money that was involved. And some of the places we played were fairly well-paying — obviously — and the crowds flocked to see us and naturally there was — I was not aware of it but there was obviously a money — there was money — thousands of dollars — being passed around.' — (Ernstthal, interview.)

'There were student uprisings all over Europe. People taking over the universities, and asking us to perform, and we having to perform in theatres for money, and sometimes liking it and sometimes hating it. And then going to the schools and performing for free for the students. Once we actually left a place, I think it's the only time we have done that. It was in — must have been the Piccolo Teatro, Milano. Productions d'aujourd'hui Berger were supposedly booking our whole tour ...' — (Sherman, interview.)

The third tour:

'It seemed like it was a good tour and Schumann (after it (SSB)) was hot to get to work and there was some money and we planned shows on Coney Island.' — (Konnoff, interview.)

Schumann has as his proximate reason for disbanding the company in '74 cited how 'horrible' the fourth tour at the end of '73 was, partly because in addition to the 25 or so travelling puppeteers, he needed twenty volunteers wherever he went to put on the show, and his resentment at having to go on such horrible tours to support the company:

'It was sometimes very hard to train people into it because training time was too short to tell people what we were doing. We just told them what to do and we just rehearsed with them and that got — they complained and they hated it and they didn't want to do it ... So at the end of that tour we decided to stop the theatre. (Elka: *You* decided.) Yes ... They (the local volunteers (SSB)) knew that we had a contract, that we got paid and they wanted to be paid too and we just couldn't afford that — the expenses of touring and of having to bring some of that money back to the farm to be able to continue didn't allow for paying twenty other people ... I wanted to disband a company that made its livelihood on doing theatre performances. I wanted to disband *that* company and work again in theatre, and get a group of people together who wanted to *do* what they did — and then *maybe* make some money with that, but not to be running an organization with the obligation of having to feed twenty people.' — (Schumann, interview, '79.)

Elka speaks of the fifth tour as being the first one that made money, but I think she means: for the family. It was a solo tour of Schumann's with a net profit of $616. — (Bread and Puppet accounts.)

'(Elka: Christian (Dupavillon) put it together in something like three weeks, I think, because you just told him you wanted to do it, and he found the theatre, and he found the people to work with you and it was very successful and made some money which you very much needed at that time. That was about the first thing that we — that you did that made money.) Right. — (Schumann, interview, '79.)

13. As Ernstthal (interview) remembers it, they had done 'a lot of touring to the girls' schools — Bryn Mawr and Radcliffe and Bennington ' — before their July '67 performance at Newport, Rhode Island. But of two of the plays he said they toured, *A Man Says Goodbye* and *Dead Man Rises*, one, *Dead Man* was hardly in shape before its New York City opening in May '67, the other hardly before its New York City opening in July '67, so I think he may be mistaken, and that their touring probably started in the summer or fall of '67:

'We had no organization whatsoever essentially. It all went through Peter's home and he just jotted it down and we'd go there. You know, "Can you come to Bennington on September 3rd?" "Oh, let's see. Okay." And Margo (Sherman) was trying to help out. She would call Bryn Mawr or she would call you know another school up there and we would try to go there also. She'd try to set it up .... We went to Harvard and played

The two success stories in American puppetry are Jim Henson's and Peter Schumann's, with Bill Baird a sad third. Henson sold his puppetry to the People by way of the Corporations, and made lots of money. Schumann sold his to the liberal intelligentsia and made no money. That wasn't the audience he wanted: he wanted the People for an audience. But Henson got that audience by giving the People what it wanted and what the Corporations wanted it to want and get: pap.[14] There is no question

---

there in a church and then we went up to Bennington and down through ... Mount Holyoke ...' — (Ernstthal, interview.)

Leherissier (interview) remembers touring *King Story* at colleges toward the end of '68.

Soon after they returned from their 2nd European tour, in the spring of '70, Bill Dalrymple took a group for a tour of colleges in the Southeast, and during the summer Konnoff took another one to Canada, and late in the fall still another one to the West Coast. In July Schumann had taken *Grey Lady Cantata II* to a couple of places in Connecticut. (Schumann, interview, '79.) Some tours of the '70s: March/April '71 *Domestic Resurrection Circus*, New England, August '71 *Birdcatcher*, Canada, September-October '71, New York State campuses, *Birdcatcher* and *Grey Lady Cantata II* and *Whitewashing*, Easter '73, Canada and New England, two months, *Stations of the Cross*, summer '73, abortive 'fun in the parks' tour in New Jersey (set up to finance the fourth European tour (Konnoff, interview)), May '75, solo visit of Schumann's to the University of California's Davis campus for a workshop-show, *Monument to Ishi*, May '75, Quebec, 3 days, Schumann and John Bell, workshop, November-December '75, Vermont and New England, 8-10 people, *Our Domestic Resurrection*, April '76, University of North Dakota, 3 days, workshop, August-September '76, New England and New York City, 3 weeks, *White Horse Butcher*, March '77, Montreal colleges, 10 days, *Joan of Arc*, March '77, University of North Carolina, one week, *Joan of Arc*, August-September '77, New England and New York City, 4 weeks, *Masaniello*, October '77, New England, 3 days, *Joan of Arc*, beginning of '78, to Oregon and back, without Schumann.

Year	Company profits Overseas tours	Canadian tours and U.S. tours other than local
'75	$ 5,499	$ 4,370
'76	12,703	363
'77	21,638	224
'81	37,761	12,681

14. 'Der Henson, der hat das (dependency on the factory system's technology (SSB)) ja bis, bis zur Absurdität gesteigert. Der hat mechanische Puppen entwickelt, die, da läuft jetzt so'n Breitwandfilm, nicht, über, über ... Dat is'n totales Einsteigen in diesen, diesen Konsum, sensationhungrigen Sumpf da, nicht, der, der, so man keine Phantasie mehr hat, da setzt die Technik ein. Ich hab zum Beispiel gesehen, hab selber Puppen gebaut (...), vielen Puppen gebaut. Aber diese Art von Puppenbauen, ich glaub der Henson, der könnte alle arbeitslosen schweizer Uhrenmechaniker bei sich einstellen, der würd eine Herde von diesen mechanischen Puppen bauen, nicht. Der hat ja Geld genug, der kann dat ja investieren, nicht. Und so entwickelt sich durch diese ungeheure Macht das Massenmediums – jeder kennt hier *Sesamstrasse* ... Ja, wissen sie auch wie die entstanden sind und warum? Oder wie man, warum man die so eingeblendet hat? Die *Sesamstrasse* ist entstanden nach den grossen Aufständen in Harlem, wo die 126. Strasse ist, glaub ich, die grosse Querstrasse. Die ist damals in Flammen und Schutt aufgegangen, und in Schutt und Trümmer, nicht. Und da war zum Beispiel, da konnten wir gar nicht nach Harlem rein, ich konnt nicht nach Harlem rein, ich hatt ja da 'n Painting-Job zu tun. Ich hab oft in Harlem gearbeitet. Und ich bin auch mit den Leuten klar gekommen, da hat mir keiner was getan,

of integrity here: Henson's horrible corruption is his essence, and Schumann tried to adapt – not only by his 'silly circus', especially after it got apolitical, but simply by putting service to humanity as he conceived it, and simplicity, ahead of self-expression. He bypassed the corporate control not by rigid purity but by the compromises involved in touring. These compromises were, I think, negligible – not nearly the ethical problem (itself probably not too severe) that his relation to his labor force was.

The Muppets are puppets that made money. Schumann could never have done anything like them. The puppets themselves are neither here nor there.[15] But the shows were often truly funny, I guess: among the few I

---

weil ich hatt da meine Arbeitsklamotten, da ist wie'n Priestergewand, das ist doch, umgibt einen mit Würde, ja, weil die meisten da kleine mahr haben und man ist kein Tourist, den man ein auf den Schädel zischt – ich würd das auch machen, wenn ich's Haus voller Kinder habe oder oder ich weiss nicht, ist so furchtbar da ... Und kurz danach hat der, nach dieser Beruhigung der Sache, da wurde, mir war dat vollkommen verständlich, weil ich diese Situation so gut kannte. Mir war vollkommen verständlich, dat dat Massenmedium da ganz gezielt in die Hütten strahlen muss, nicht wahr, wie idyllisch doch die Low Estside ist. Wer einmal in'ner Low Estside gelebt hat, und kennt den ganzen (...) da, der kann andere Lieder pfeifen. Und dann kam der, der, der Typ in'ner Tonne, nicht, wer die Tonne kennt, überall diese Tonnen, ja diese furchtbaren depremierenden Tonnen, dat ist also sowat von, sowieso so depremierend wird durch allet, nicht, dann überall wo man gaht sieht man diese Mülltonnen, die verfolgen ein dat ganze Leben lang, nicht. Wenn man nachts nach Hause geht und hat Ein im, im Kasten oder wat – bums irgenwo gehts wieder an diese verdammte Tonne ... In der *Sesamstrasse* da kommt die Tonne immer vor und zwar wohnt da jemand drin. Da wohnt so'ne Puppe drin, die wohnt in'ner Tonne. Das ist unheimlich witzig, nicht. Ich hab da sehr empfindliche Gefühle. Und dann sieht man noch diese alten Aufgänge, die so typisch sind für die Estside und diese ganzen Feuerleitern und dat Klimbamborium hier. Dat ist alles mit diesen ganzen Elementen, die so charakteristisch für die Estside sind und auch für Harlem, die sind da mit drin und die werden verarbeitet, vergoldet. Dat ist nichts anderes als psychologisch Kriegsführung. Und dat hat sich so, dat ist so'ne Massenindustrie geworden – die Deutschen die haben jetzt hier ihre deutsche *Sesamstrasse*. Das ist 'ne weltweite Bewegung geworden, 'ne Sesambewegung. Es gibt zum Beispiel keine vernüftigen Kinderprogramme, die, dat einzige, also dat Kinderprogramm, wat immer 100%ig durchgezogen wird, dat ist *Sesamstrasse*. Das'n Ding, ja (...) Ich bin überzeugt dat die Chinesen, die werden jetzt auch – die werden jetzt auch bald ihre chinesische Sesamsendung haben ... Also ich meine, dat wat er uns vorgeworfen hat, in allen Anfängen, da war er nur so'n kleiner TV-Kauz oder hat da seine Werbespots gemacht, da hätte sich jeder von uns geschämt, weil wir sowat in unserm ganzen Leben nicht gemacht haben, genau wie bei einem Herren, weil wir, so'ne Hurerei, dat gibt es nicht. Und dieser Mann, der beschuldigt uns so ungeheurer Sachen. Ich war wirklich sauer, wenn ich nicht wüsste, dat der, dat der uns so furchtbar missverstanden hätte, dann wär ich mit ihm wütend geworden, denn der hat uns wirklich auch, der hat uns beschimpft, als Faschisten – ich als Faschist!' — (Eckhardt, interview.)

15. The violet Yorick of the first Muppet TV program (1954), *Sam and His Friends*, 'a living hunger,' is the only Henson puppet at all like Schumann's. Depending on the angle he's shot at – his yellow-pupilled eyes, deep in their sockets – most other Henson puppets' eyes have no pupils and are on top of the face – look different, depending on the angle – and on whether his jaw is down or up, he can almost attain to the dignity of looking a bit dangerous, and in no way jolly.

The corporations sponsor Henson because his puppets are degraded but harmless human

saw there were some funny ones; the comedy is intelligent; the puppets' acting — movements — and the voices with them are in the great tradition of American comedy, film or stage, their timing is superb. Ideologically, what the Muppet shows I saw come down to is the portrayal of (1) commercial man, buyer or seller, (2) employed/employing man, but especially employed man: as man as such. Their comedy and intelligence depend on these two situations, the sale/purchase (e.g. people selling themselves as entertainers or whatever), work situations in the framework of wage labor, and in particular depend on the degrading and alienatory aspects of commerce and wage employment; and the shows have comic as well as emotional appeal insofar as and only insofar as the viewer accepts the equation of this late- or post-capitalist creature with humanity. This ideology of course is false and foolish. Henson sold because what he sold was the corporate ideology.

---

beings, and because he makes them loveable to the People by their quirks of intransigence, and so makes the People, employees and customers of the Corporations, more docile in their analogous degradation.

6. Modus operandi III. Labor procurement. Motivations. The variables of its formula. Structural forces.

Schumann needed to have some people keeping working with him and he needed from time to time lots of people to help prepare or put on a show. He never made any money to speak of in NYC, nor could he ever have supported even a small theatre just in Vermont out of its revenues. College tours and European tours produced theatrical revenue: but they called for dramatically increased amounts of labor. Schumann has managed over the years to maintain a core group of regulars — of shifting composition — and to attract sizable groups of temporary volunteer helpers when he needed them. The remunerative mode has varied. The chief problem has been keeping down the number of remuneratees — largely, though not exactly or consistently, identical with the core group. Since altogether the normal or supposedly normal rewards, whether in the nature of remuneration or other, have been slight, the operation poses two interesting problems: what has made this labor procurement work? how does the core group work — what keeps it going?

Schumann's attitude toward his labor force has consistently been that he furnished them an opportunity: not so much the opportunity for learning from the work, certainly not the opportunity for expressing themselves by contributing to it, not really the opportunity for associating with him, but the opportunity to do the work: which he regards as in itself — and not because of its possible but doubtful effects on audiences — highly salutary, both in providing an ennobling discipline imposed on and a spiritualization of existence, saving it from the degradations of a materialist civilization, and mystic moments of communion in performance not too unlike those of participation in religious services.[1]

---

1. 'And I came in and started — yeah, started joining in. It sounded like a great deal. I liked the work. I liked what he was doing. I liked the way he worked. I thought he was pulling together images out of the darkness, you know. I don't know. (I: How did you know if you hadn't seen anything?) I guess I — yeah, how did I know? A good question. I'm trying to think. (I: Was it politics, was it religion?) It wasn't politics. No, it was art. It was art. And it was energy and it was the work. It was working hard and it's something concrete and he spieled a lot about that ... There was the whole idea that the work was good and that the making the bread was good and by the sweat of our bodies and, you know, the labor of our — I'm trying to remember. I don't know if he really talked that, but it was a real current that ran through things. (I: But if he said anything, that would be the spiel?) Yeah, yeah, that's what I'm — I have this impression that we were sort of told that the gratification in this thing was the work of it rather than the end product, or something like that. Or, somehow that would be talking about the play, that the play had to be gone through and worked through each time rather than created and finished. But each time it had to be created and the work was the important thing.' — (M. Lippen, interview.)

This totally sincere and though not unrelated to guilt not altogether unrealistic view, governing his own life, has over the years fairly consistently made him feel imposed on and pulled down by his work force, partly by their not always only implicit demands for individual attention, affection or appreciation, their desire for individual status as performers or for work allowing them individual expression or the exercise of talent or artistry and their recurrent attempt to have a voice in shaping the work of the group as a whole, partly by the financial responsibility for the group as a whole, and the efforts – making incursions into his working time and his concentration – of keeping it going when recurrently (due to the grandiosity of his projects) it grows big. He really wants lots of people working with him, but he resents them at the same time. Ideally, as far as he is concerned they would all be spiritually and financially self-supporting. But at the same time he wants them wholeheartedly and full-time devoted to the work; and wants that work to be distinctively the realization of his projects.

Independently of their occasional delusions that their creative process was collective, Schumann can be said to have used (the term 'exploited' would be a little too strong: the use was not detrimental to them) the people working for him. The association has allowed his but not to any significant extent their personal self-expression, artistic development and becoming-known ('fame' would be too strong a term), and their joint enterprise has been directed by him to these ends – although in a sincere and moral spirit: in conscious pursuit not of personal but of social and humanitarian ends.

Although he habitually speaks of the company's decisions, objectives and preferences in the first person plural, they have all been his and influenced only negligibly by his associates. The theatre's advertisements during the '60s frequently and critical notices invariably identified the group as 'Peter Schumann's Bread and Puppet Theatre', something that other American groups, e.g. the Performance Group, the Ridiculous Theatrical Company, the Open Theatre, the Living Theatre have scrupulously avoided or prevented: although the directors' parts in these groups were often equally determinative. On the other hand, up to 1980, anonymity was preserved in almost all performance programs, i.e. the members of the group were not named and nobody knew who did what. His performers' names are unknown to the public. This practice, also, was exceptional.

Two features of the work process have been crucial in making the theatre's creations Schumann's: with almost no exceptions, all mask molds, and, where the masks were made directly over clay, the sculpting of the clay, have been Schumann's work: and the performance modes evolved by him only to a minor extent allow any influence of a performer's interpretation of his/her part on his/her performance, besides which Schumann's play-making procedures preclude such interpretations almost totally anyhow. In his work with performers on a part, he responds to and uses their ways, personality and even ideas on how to do it, so that the resulting performance to some extent depends on these: but he has always retained close control over this use of the performer, and there has been no way for performers to make of this being-used even in part or coincidentally their own creative or self-expressive activity.

Finally, with the exception, perhaps, of skill and boldness in narrating or m.c.ing, his performers don't learn anything by working for him that they can use independently of him, i.e. without using or − badly − imitating his masks and puppets and story-telling modes. Over a period of time they may acquire skills in mask- or puppet-making and in one or more of the performance modes he has developed: but of a sort so integrated in his after all very peculiar performance-mode they are scarcely utilizable independently of it and even just simply: of his ideas, of him. A major reason for this is that he is in his medium an autodidact and one contemptuous of craft as such and of technical perfection, so that the techniques he has developed are all narrowly adapted expedients for his own artistic objectives. You don't become a good mime or dancer by working with him, you become good at doing just precisely the − peculiar − kind of thing he does. So in this sense again, you are not working for yourself, you are working for Schumann: Schumann is using you, you are not using him.

So, if they are being used, why do they do it? Part of the answer is that those that do it have nothing better to do: they can't get it up on their own. The other part is that there *are* satisfactions.

People joining the group or helping with its work were motivated by a variety of factors: admiration of Schumann as a person[2] and/or of his lifestyle, his moral concern, lack of materialism, family life, probity, hard work;[3] a need to belong to a group and attraction to the particular core-

---

2. 'I met Robert Wilson once and I observed him at the rehearsal in Berlin, *Death and Destruction of Detroit*, and I don't like his person. His person seems − doesn't move me. It is not someone I want to come − I am drawn to. Now, Peter, the minute that I *saw* him, I knew, I said, he is somebody that I want to be near.' — (Levy, interview.)

'Well, the tendency is to − he is an overwhelming personality . . . . He has an enormous amount of intensity in his body and his person. For young people, that is a very startling thing to find. He doesn't get sidetracked in great emotional scenes of yelling, right, which demonstrates weakness. And which − so the young people coming to him see a really enormous − he is an enormous figure there. And in any theatre, voluntary or − since then I have had my own groups and roles get − somehow, it is not just the work, the roles begin to form, papa comes there or mama goes there, sister goes there, brother goes there, we transfer. In something so personal, like performing, you are risking making a fool out of yourself, you are taking a big risk, when you go up on the stage. So that you, one is, at least I am, really vulnerable and I really saw him as a great figure there, he was a very, very important significant person for me. Still is, on certain levels. I just came from visiting him. But I preferred working with him when we were small.' — (Levy, interview.)

3. 'I never felt artistic around Peter, but I felt fulfilled. He didn't validate my artistry, but I

group in existence at a given time;[4] political ideas or objectives that they think shared or promoted by the group; notably those of the Peace Movement of the '60s or of the back-to-basics ecology and commune movement of the earlier '70s, a fondness for the work produced and/or admiration for its artistry; ambitions to be in the theatre and develop as a performer,[5]

---

felt very fulfilled in a kind of a unified way. The life and the work and the theatrical style, in a unified way. I've never forgotten that. A tremendous teacher. He embodied it. His life-style and his work were all one thing. That was very rare then. It was extremely rare. (I: How so?) I had never met anybody who could pull that together. I'd met artists who were dissatisfied and scholars who were trying very hard to maintain themselves in school – I was in my twenties then. I met dissidents of all kinds. But everything was disconcerted. Peter had a unified life. And I admired that very much. He had a family and a work and an art and that was all in one place.' — (Palmer, interview.)

4. 'It was also a collective action. There were many people there. Tremendous. For the times? Unheard of. Unheard of for those times. We were in isolated little tenement places in the Lower East Side, everybody doing their own activity. Nothing unified. There wasn't a piece of beauty on the street.... There was nothing. And then, all of a sudden, these gorgeous things would walk down the street. To me, it was magnificent. For what? A voter registration drive. Great. Make Puerto Rican people vote for something. So you bring incredible works of art and you march them around.' — (Palmer, interview.)

5. '(I: You said that here you had always wanted to act and now you were really acting.) Right. (I: And then I brought up the question, to what extent is a person in a mask or manipulated – now do you remember?) Okay. Acting may be different than doing theatre. I was doing theatre. We were performing, we were going out and affecting audiences – people who were paying us money to do what we wanted to do. I was just totally delighted to actually be doing theatre and getting paid for theatre. That made a terrific difference for me in terms of my own – as a theatre maker, okay, better than an actor, you know? I was eighteen then – '68 – no, wait a minute – I was nineteen, so my family was very down on the whole acting trip. I wanted to go to the School of the Arts and they put up with it because they couldn't break my arm and make me go to dental school. So, but then, when I did this, it just confirmed my old suspicion that that was what I would do best. I don't know if I said it on the tape the last time, but probably since I was about three or four, I thought that's what I would do. Maybe four. And I knew that if other things failed, that would be a real possibility for me. So, what does it mean to be performing with Bread and Puppet as an actor? ... It's not acting (I: It's not acting, but it is nevertheless not nothing. It's not a mechanical thing.) Right. For Sure. Also there was singing – we did a lot of singing then, and singing was very important to me. And just basically, the whole thing – okay, someone had contacted us to do a job so we were going to all get in the car and go to this college and bring our props and set up and do the show and afterwards people would be glad we came, which was – it was emotionally satisfying for me, not to be working as a what – a nursery school teacher? It meant that I was already getting experience in my field, and you know, in the Bread and Puppet, as I said to you before, I met people in those years whose connections later on – look, in the times I traveled with Bread & Puppet abroad, more so than in this country, I really got to see what it was to work in theatre, and met all kinds of theatre producers or theatre whatever – contacts that will be valuable for life. You could then say, okay, well, I think I'm going to go to Copenhagen and work with that street theatre I met when we happened to be somewhere. It was really out of the frying pan into the fire for me. When I studied at the New York School of the Arts, it was great to be working toward a professional goal and then suddenly, even though I was getting paid very little, suddenly it wasn't – oh, boy, I'll say it, it wasn't

having fun, whether in getting the show together or in performing;[6] one of the two kinds of enjoyment in working with the big puppets: the loss of self-hood that occurs in a concentrating on moving the puppet right (in giving it life, a transfer to it of one's self-hood),[7] the exercise of a per-

---

Brecht, right? It wasn't an actor's heyday – you just weren't going to be able to fill your deeper parts as an actor. (I: Did you feel that then?) I certainly did. When I was eighteen years old – Stefan, put your chair up so you don't fall over – I played Mother Courage. It was in high school, and it was our senior class play. I had a Ford Foundation scholarship the summer before to study the theatre workshop at Montclair State College in New Jersey, and I went, and it was wonderful. That summer, they produced *The Good Woman of Szechuan*, among others, so I played the boy. I had a part and there were not just high school students, this was a theatre workshop for teachers of theatre and for high school students, so it was a nice program, actually. The teachers of theatre were all actors themselves and so were the kids working with adults, really, and it was nice.... Okay, so, I had these parts in the two shows. Big deal – but what else did we do. Oh, that summer, we worked on *Twelfth Night*. I played Viola, and we worked very hard. Pretty much the same group of people who are still actors today. And then it just dried up. It dried up. There's nobody else coming out of there. (I: He must have been either a good teacher –) He's still the teacher, but it's different now. Maybe the administration is different or the kids are different – I don't know what it is, but something is very different.... Anyway, so when I met Peter, for me it just seemed like the normal thing to do. If they invited me I should do it. So I did, and as far as my saying well, there wasn't really a job for me as an actor – this was the first time I was getting paid. (I: That's a great feeling – the money part.) Well, it's nice when you can actually pay your rent and say, I paid my rent by doing what I do best. Right from the very beginning, there were all kinds of good parts, also – even if you were behind a mask, there was all kinds of room for exploration and to crystallize something from nothing. Peter was very open to suggestions.) — (Leherissier, interview.)
6. 'Well, I just came there for fun, and he and I quarreled. He was like my father – real Germanic. Doesn't matter how much – well, you gotta get a lot of work done, but it's really important that you sweat and grunt and groan while you're doing it. Although, you see, he did have that saving grace. Every once in a while, he'd allow himself – you know, people would have parties. And I was just flat out coming there for the fun of it because I liked to do it. He never fired me, though, because I was good. Threatened to fire me a thousand times. (I: As a performer? Or good at making puppets?) As a performer. So I was good. You know, I would do little hand puppets. I liked the hand puppet. I did all the hand puppetry for a while and I liked the little hand puppets, because I made it funny – fooled around – it was very much – I always maintained the same attitude that we had struck up when we first met in Provincetown when we were both on vacation. You know, that state. Then he would go into his work space. Now, for me, this was his work but I was on vacation, you know. (I: Well, what was his argument about that?) You have to work hard. I mean, you don't just come into a theatre and just do it because it's fun. And I managed to do that. (I: And got away with it. I've had similar problems that way.) And you always got a sense that you weren't doing enough. And I guess that was his attitude toward himself. He really drove himself. No matter how much he did, it wasn't enough – or how much anybody else did, which was never more than 1/50th of what he did. He would work at it day and night for weeks. Constantly. He was always working. And he had – he got impatient with people who had other interests. He got very impatient with the personal things that were going on.' — (Oyle, interview.)
7. 'I felt like I was learning a lot about physical acting. We did *Fire* again. Peter had done *Fire* before I joined the company, and I saw it performed, and then he decided to revive it,

former's power over an audience, without the self-exposure that makes acting feel so perilous, namely: shielded from view by the mask or puppet,

---

and I was given a lot of work to do in that. And I felt like I learned a lot. (I: What did you learn?) About physicality in acting, from doing – the slow was not difficult ever for me – to do slow things. That was hard for other people, but not for me. I learned that – something about the impulse to do something and that any part of the body can lead. You might have an impulse to turn and the elbow might give you the beginning of it and everything else would follow. I discovered one day while I was acting in *Fire* that my face behind the mask was moving a lot. And it was only then that I realized I was acting . . . it was always a very spiritual experience to be inside of one of the *Crucifixion* puppets or the Mary puppet. One felt better than oneself, better than one's own little person filled with anxieties. Suddenly I felt ennobled because one was responsible for something that was larger, that was mythic. Like it changed my breathing process. It was uplifting in a way. It was very, very hard working with Grey Lady puppets . . . . It was slightly different in *Fire*. Deeper, much deeper breathing. Of course, because your arms are lifted, and so the whole chest is opened up. (I: Your arms are lifted, supporting –?) To hold the dowel which is the spine of the puppet – the yellow or the blue Mary. So everything is lifted, and so your breathing is deeper, and the rib cage is open. Doing *Fire* was very interesting in that you physically wouldn't want to do it – at the last minute you wouldn't. A lot of performers have this experience with some plays – that before it's time to do this particular play, you feel tired and depressed and you don't want to do it. And doing it was like going through a tunnel and coming out on the other side – like going to Mass must be for some people who are Catholic. It was a real, real experience. And we used to do it once a week.' — (Sherman, interview.)

'The Easter show and all the other shows were very exciting from the very beginning, and you'd get all revved up to do it. *Christmas Story*, Easter show. But *Fire* – and I've had this experience from time to time with other shows – you would not, you couldn't get revved up to do it. It was almost like you'd have to get revved down. You would find yourself depressed before you do it. (I: But why?) Well, it was a very small stage. I think you couldn't breathe very well in those white Vietnamese masks. It was stifling. Everything was going to be very, very slow. So you had to slow down all of your processes — really get – it wasn't a heightening of, like the way the *Christmas Story* or the Easter show was. It was – of death – a play about death. I'm glad you asked the question, because I never could understand it until just trying to find the words now. So you have to release everyday life and go down, down, down, down. But once it started I was completely into it . . . . It felt like the richest spiritual experience I had ever had, but that it wasn't unfamiliar. It felt like all the people have the knowledge of the possibility of this kind of experience. (I: What kind?) Well, what I call a spiritual experience, of deep concentration, utter deep concentration, and so everything else just falls away. Deep concentration which is sustained for a very long time. It has a form, and a Mass does. I'm trying to describe it. I remember – well, I had to do the last scene which was the self-immolation. With the tape. It was strenuous in a very contained way. And it felt like a selfless gift. See, I was always afraid that acting was show-off, selfish. And this didn't feel that way.' — (Sherman, interview.)

'For a person inside one of these puppets there is no sense of acting: the heads are ill-fitting, the robes are clumsy, sight is limited. The experience is more religious than artistic. I, an average, nondescript person, give my body to this Vietnamese lady mask and robe. I use my energy to move her forward. She, then, becomes a personage worthy of notice. I disappear. It is my disappearance that makes the Vietnamese spirit visible.' — (K. Taylor, *People's Theater*, 1972.)

and absolved of responsibility;[8] or, finally, the masochistic expiatory or ecstatic pleasure of losing yourself in hard work, or of moving as a puppet at the bidding of another.[9]

---

8. 'Fire was tremendous because I was invisible. And so long as I was invisible I could express myself – so *personally* freeing – men and women are very interchangeable in their costuming and behind the mask. The play was built around these five people, and everybody was sort of interchangeable.' — (Palmer, interview.)
'We had a two-man puppet. He was the hands and I was the head. So we were under the skirt of this 15-foot lady, you know, which was in the middle of Madison Square Garden. And it was the most freeing experience, because I could see through the gauze but I couldn't be seen. And in that situation I feel very – very liberated. So Irving and I were the giant puppet, and then there were the masses of people and the skull masks and the various things around. That stands out to me. I could still feel that experience of being hidden and yet expressive.' — (Palmer, interview.
'I could do something in public because I was hidden. Now, that was a personal thing. You know, like an actor doesn't have that problem, but I did. So, it was for me personally liberating because I could be expressive in a protected situation. I can see you. I can move this puppet so that the total direction of the crowd is up there and I'm down here and covered. And for me, personally, it was liberating, however berated that might be.' — (Palmer, interview.)
9. In re her performance as White Lady in *Dead Man*:
'And there was a lot of very difficult movement, like you have to hold a posture for a very long time. You have to be able to have great strength – almost like endurance to be able to handle the thing. And I could project myself into that. I could endure and I could see myself as somehow giving through that.' — (Palmer, interview.)
'The actor then mounts a tall ladder and now, like a tent, there is drawn down over him a giant figure of the Christus with long hands uplifted in benediction. From now until the end of the play the actor will sit there, suffering the heat and discomfort. In the conventional theatre the actor would either shed all those encumbrances or his place be taken by another actor. Here, however, it is as though by accepting all this that the actor enters into an imaginative identification with Christ who had to bear the burden of mankind's sorrows. One is reminded how in the Mass the priest is said to be no longer himself but becomes the representative of Christ. At the end of this play, when the actor is revealed his long hair is lank and wet, his face running with sweat and taut with pain; it is seen to be a kind of Passion and, as in Grotowski's theatre, a total offering of the actor in an act of love.' — (Roose-Evans, *Experimental Theatre*.)
Rehearsal: developing the part:
'Then he would start to just move the images around to see what looked good with what. And that would also be my job – to be under the puppet. To be able to see its capacities, such as they were. Holding the neck and the arms, what it looks like in space and what kind of a walk you need and how you group them and – a lot of it was very boring, you know. It's very much like being under somebody else's will, because you're underneath a big piece of drapery and you can't see yourself. You have to do it by visualizing what it might look like from the outside. And you're being directed by somebody who says: "This way, that way." So it's really being ... like at someone else's will. It's an interesting experience. Being very without personality. (I: You are a puppet.) Yes. Which also, in a way, is liberating, if you accept the constraint. And in a way you can find some extremely rare way of presenting it, in its constrained way. It also can make you feel will-less, which I think is part of the difficulties Peter encountered. (I: Encountered?) Among the people.... But I know that the ones that were most friends of the theatre were ones that were able to go in and out of it. Would come for a project and then leave and lead their own lives and then come back and ... but if you became dependent on it, it was not

George Ashley, one of Schumann's '66 recruits, speaks of the 'power' of *A Man Says Goodbye* and, especially, *Fire*, for a spectator, as consisting in its ability to make the spectator believe what it said:

'What was powerful was that I believed it. I truly believed what they were saying about the devastation of war was true. But the truth of it would convey something very serious about war to people who hadn't thought about it much.'
(Ashley, interview.)

Ashley goes on to discuss the power of these plays over performers in them, his implicit point here being simply that it is the same: bringing out the terrible truth of the matter — the real horror of it all — is as affective as having it brought out by another for one: the mode of performance assuring or promoting the participatory experience, again something that at least during the '60s apparently distinguished Schumann's theatre from most theatre. To the extent this 'devastating' effect of being in Schumann's little plays then was a positive experience — a catharsis? — this would go some way toward explaining why people worked for him: a performance was its own reward, and not even in terms of any relation to the audience, nor of the satisfactions of skill exercised and concentration:

'The power there — the power in *Fire* — you know, the woman, who was ordinarily played by Margo — I suppose was always played by Margo — in *Fire*, Margo sometimes got hurt when she would collapse onto that structure of chicken wire and wood. She would fall on it and she would sometimes get torn — her flesh would be cut. What I learned later is that the power of that piece is also internal. Sometimes, when I performed it in those limited experiences in Iran, I would come out from behind that mask in tears. I mean, it was overwhelming. And it was also — when well done — *A Man Says Goodbye to His Mother* was also overwhelming. And I don't know what word to use — it wasn't poignance, it was devastating. It was more than just a poignant experience. There was another one, later, in which he made me weep on stage as a participant. He did another war play and a man died on the stage and another character came and removed the shoes from this dead person and put them on his own feet and walked away. I saw that during the war. I saw somebody whose shoes had gotten destroyed, for one reason or another, taking shoes off another man to wear. I saw it and it happened on the stage that, although we had rehearsed this piece thoroughly and presented it out in Brooklyn, that I was overwhelmed by it. And I was so overwhelmed that when they took me to the subway to go back into the city, I was standing, waiting for the subway car and somebody grabbed me by the shoulder and shook me and it was a policeman, and he said, what are you doing, and I said, why, I'm waiting for my train, and he said, now look, look what you are doing, and I was smoking a cigarette. I didn't even know where I was — I didn't know I was smoking a cigarette.'
(Ashley, interview.)

---

good.... I had spent four years. But in the end you realize that you have to be something on your own. It's just a question of dependency. At some point you have to break it. Peter never stopped anyone from leaving.' — (Palmer, interview.)

I should add that Ashley went through the war as an infantry man, was captured, as prisoner of war experienced one of its cataclysmic events, the great bombing of Dresden. He was prepared to be affected by a veridic treatment of war. But one way or another, most of the people that worked with Schumann during the '60s were. Before '66 they were, with the exception of Ernstthal, older people with 'problems,' i.e. who had tried to deal with the world, and the kids that then, to the end of the decade influxed similarly, had opened themselves up to the world (and had accordingly gotten hurt). It wasn't till '70 and after that he got the blander, more college young types that he has mostly had since then. So within the mask or puppet, sequestered with themselves (while on stage), they were able to savor the life/death/murder issue presented with emotional immediacy. Shielded from the audience, they lived through their part, and their part was not a make-believe character, but a symbolic concretization of a basic moral problem.

Ideological concurrence mostly, at least up until the mid-'70s provided the initial and general motivation: either a moral and political concurrence, the belief that the Bread and Puppet Theatre's work was politically and/or morally valid and valuable, and participation in it therefore intrinsically worthwhile, or a more spiritual or mystic concurrence (scarcely a specifically religious, let alone dogmatically religious one) – a belief that Schumann was dealing with essential spiritual realities in his work, and that participation in the work would get one in touch with them and was worthwhile also because it would help audiences do so. A decision to join generally presupposed one or another of these beliefs, but was apt to be proximately stimulated in addition by admiration for the work qua art and faith in Schumann's artistic genius. The desire to be near genius and in its field of operation in most cases has probably provided some motivation: but in most cases, I suspect, would not have been sufficient to induce a decision to join, unless the ideological motivations had been there too.

As schema of the group's structure, I see a leader with a powerful personality whose interest, approval and even affection are desired and competed for;[10] the leader's tendency to withhold, but with exceptions, affection, to

---

10. 'I felt myself very dependent on his recognition, in an odd kind of way. Recognition for my labor, recognition for my – for the things that I felt shaky about – to validate me, personally. I think that's very common with actors in a group, that they need the recognition, that they're kind of shaky themselves, so they need recognition from the pater familias. If I didn't get that, I felt very unworthy. And Peter tends not to be a flattering or a reassuring person. So that was difficult, although we all managed, somehow. But the interactions were, to me – like children, which I thought of myself, even though I was close to thirty years old, I still felt like a child there – the reactions of the children striving to please the father. At the same time, the father espouses the idea of a group of equals, but it didn't quite happen that way. Mainly because we were also projecting all of our power

to him: "Tell me what to do", you see, which is very common. We all want freedom and then we don't know what to do with it. We know how to get it, but we — but I never felt Peter would undercut anybody, you know — like, well, "Do your creative work and then I'll judge and condemn you." I never felt that in Peter. But I felt an awful lot of us willing to give up — give up, you know: "Just tell me what to do." So if Peter had a dry space, we all went dry. How silly. This is also why, one by one, I think people left. When they were ready, you see. Now, there are a lot of ways of leaving. You can leave with a fight. You can leave with a "You're holding me down. You're using me." You can leave with "You have lost your political convictions. It's not the right thing –', you know, an argument of some kind. Or you can leave because you know you should leave. It's like that.' — (Palmer, interview.)

'Now there was a big dance, and a day and a half to put it together. And in a puppet that I really didn't have — I didn't know it, but at Newport I didn't have much to do — I mean just — so I couldn't do it and I felt that I disappointed him and everything. That is another thing about Peter; one gets the sense that if you can't do it right, then you're disappointing him, not that he yells at you or curses you out or anything — the way a lot of directors do — but you sense disappointment in yourself and from him and you feel worse, in some ways. And then the narration — but the narration was too complicated for me to do in a short time, because the *King Story* has all to do with drum beats and appearances and coming in and so I did the King, and that is what I stayed with — with Peter for years and years. I was doing the King. I was like his classical King, he said.' —(Levy, interview.)

'Bruno (Eckhardt) had a very, very big problem and he left the tour — no, he stayed until the end. He didn't come back. He felt that he couldn't get warmth and love from Peter, which is what he wanted, which ultimately became my problem. (I: What kind of a man was he?) Bruno? I've seen him since, a couple of years ago in Berlin. He's about my height and weight — a bit heavier, rather round, a guy who in those days was heavy into resistance and also a man who needed love from Peter. He was like a teddy bear, I thought. (I: And he drank, also?) Yes. (I: Then Schumann did not give warmth and love to people?) Not to the men, anyway.... He just seemed to be more accessible to the women than the men.... Some people get it and some people don't.... With Schumann, we're doing such primal things, such images of mother, child, father — these are pictures that move in on one, so that one begins — awakens to these images and needs to have them filled up somehow and he is unable to — he can't give everybody what they want — what they need — he can't. He's a person like anybody else. So it's like an occupational hazard or whatever.... I just went up to visit Peter in Vermont and he's very busy coordinating groups of hundreds of people. Baking the bread, and the contradictions — he's providing, he's presenting the role of the father figure and because of our own, or my own need to get love from that father figure, I ran into problems. So what happened was, I would stay for two years and then I'd leave and do my own group, then he'd invite me back and I'd come back and do another couple of years.... In the '70s. I don't even remember the years. But then, each time I left Peter, I could only think of continuing in this direction. I was really taken completely by it, it just wiped me out, and so all my own group work was puppet shows. I'd do some of his and some of my own and then I'd keep coming back to it.... Around December (1969), the beginning of January — and I was unhappy then, I felt contact with Peter was zero. He didn't seem to be interested to talk about anything. (I: Did you think there was a change in your relationship?) Yes, I felt he was getting interested in other people. (I: Like who?) Nobody in particular, I mean, I just didn't think — I wasn't feeling slighted, I was just feeling that he lost interest. (I: What had you used to talk about?) We were always working — we were always doing a show, and when we weren't doing the show we were building mostly, and I felt frustrated. (I: This communication must have continued with the Brooklyn situation — the communication in terms of working together.) No, we weren't doing so many shows.... It's not just — it's not even how much you say, it's a kind of recognition that somebody is there, which for some — his head was filled up, maybe with his plans to move, with whatever his personal shit is, he

accord preferential interest to newcomers, to get bored with people, and to accord approval only sparsely and selectively, now more to one person, now more to another, and generally according to not too well determinable standards; followers above the average in need of interest, approval, affection; a leader's buddy, #1 man, or lieutenant, given more and greater responsibilities and performance opportunities than others,[11] and perhaps just a little more or greater — these responsibilities and opportunities being also demands put on them — than they can in the long run handle; a majority of followers just as well content not to have the risky position of the leader's #1 man and unlike the candidates for that position, though competing for the leader's interest and so on, forming satisfying liaisons with one another in terms of the group's identity; and a privileged female member of the group, provocative sex object with a quietly hysterical personality, who gets away with things, who is or is not, but is suspected of being the leader's mistress[12] — which increases or even engenders her

---

was getting that together, maybe. It was difficult for me, so I figured it was time to go . . . . — (Levy, interview.)

11. '(I: How does that work, Murray, in a group? Number one and all that — changing one for the other — what is the idea, or what is the mechanism?) It's hard to describe. There are jobs to do. We call them jobs, we don't call them parts. They're jobs, because ego isn't involved, it isn't look at my face, look at my body — that's not what it's about. It's about doing a job, even — from baking bread to carrying a giant puppet. They're all part of the jobs, and for me, being asked to do a job was important at that point, because you just don't do the job, you've got to get asked with Peter. He asks you and you do it. So to that extent — for a long while he was asking me to do all the jobs. I was baking bread and doing all kinds of things and then I wasn't doing it anymore, and I felt — (I: But you did Uncle Fatso, that was a major —) But it — yeah. It wasn't enough or something. Something was missing. Something was making me unhappy.' — (Levy, interview.)

'And it was only then, those of us who wanted to be there, who consciously decided that that was what we were going to do and weren't — and I think because — because of my loyalty at that point, Peter and me got very close. And then, after that, I was doing all the jobs that — that were like extra work — extra jobs, not just being in the chorus — he was asking me to do extra jobs. He picks what he calls favorites. (I: What kind of extra jobs?) Like play a puppet that is alone and not en masse. To do — to play a puppet alone instead of in a mass. (I: Because you were close, that —) Well, he liked me. I think a lot of Peter's decisions come on how he feels about somebody. Because he gets young children to do things, too, because he likes them. (I: Yeah, but also, in particular, people in his eyes are put into what he wants — are better than others, no?) Yeah. (I: You said you were rehearsing this thing all of the time, trying to do it right.) I found it hard to tell when I was doing it right, through him, because he was always critical. He maintains that is part of his tactic — he maintains a certain — sometimes, not always — he, with me, anyway, he was always very critical.' –(Levy, interview.)

12. These suspicions made Schumann appear to many members of his group as a persistent lecher, and therefore, since there was no doubt that he at the same time was an altogether devoted family man, as dual. They saw him as going from Catherine Merrill in '65 to Margo Sherman in '66 to Andrea Woodner in '67, to a young French girl '70-'72, to Carlene Fernandez '74-'76. This may all be mere fantasy, but whether it is or not, it contributed to the leader's image, and this seems important to me as regards the operating

attractiveness, and enhances either the followers' admiration for the leader or their affectionate compassion for his human frailty — and who as the group's feminine principle[13] acerbates the male followers' urge to do their work more than well (according to the leader's criteria endorsed by her) in order to win her approval or admiration.

The binding forces of this structure are psychologically costly, and when the costs exceed the benefits, the follower splits — at least temporarily. The #1 man's position is unstable, he is eventually replaced and splits. Similarly for the carrier of the female principle.

I suspect that some not too distant variant of this group structure is indispensable for enterprises without leaders who are integrated into a society's power structure and/or able to pay their way.

Schumann's labor-procurement formula turned out to comprise five variables: (1) a core-group of regulars, and four main types of irregulars: (2) short-time enthusiasts, (3) old-time associates, (4) workshop attendants, (5) volunteers.

At almost any time '63-'83, Schumann has had the help of a few, typically four to eight people, working for him more or less full time and continuously, and having this work as the main concern in their lives for an extended period, several years, typically perhaps three to six years, though in some cases much longer, with a typical pattern being one or more extended interruptions, typically perhaps half a year to a year and a half, and repeated returns (a pattern weakening the distinction between the regulars and the old-time associate irregulars.) This would be the 'core-group', the Bread and Puppet puppeteers *sensu strictu*, the company. Their most valuable features to Schumann would be first, their familiarity with his creative and operating procedures, second, their development, over a period, of specific skills and interests.

A considerable number of people over the years, typically the girl friends of male regulars, or the female friends of female regulars or

---

principle of the group. If it is not a mere fantasy, Schumann's work fails to express a major part of his personality.

'He liked the girls, Peter. You must have uncovered that part of his career.... He was really scared.... not scared of women. He was scared he was going to get either punished by God or.... He was worried about syphilis. But I got the sense more that he was fearing the wrath of God.' — (Oyle, interview.)

13. 'He (Schumann) let it be easy for me. Even though I knew there were like these undercurrents. Already, I think, at some early point, Margo started to be jealous of the power I was accumulating as a performer in the theatre. I was another woman — I was the first woman to come and work in the theatre who did anything to give Margo the elbow at all. And I certainly didn't succeed in it, but — I really don't know if I really tried — it just sort of worked out that way. I don't know why. I mean, Peter inevitably stayed with Margo. Truly. Probably still does. That's unimportant to me, because enough has happened in my life in the meantime so that I don't have these worries.' — (Leherrissier, interview.)

workshop-attendants, for short periods, a few weeks, a month or two, became intensely involved in the Bread and Puppet work-processes, usually puppet-making rather than performing, usually dropping out for personal reasons and because the attraction for them had in the first place been a superficial social one, subject to lapse, e.g. the group situation rather than art or politics or Schumann's genius.

Friends and admirers of Schumann's, generally his own age, personal acquaintances mostly, with whom he and Elka would sustain some social contact, while probably never becoming regulars, would enjoy performing in one or another of his shows, notably his Easter, Christmas or Thanksgiving shows of the '60s, and, generally liberals and opponents of the Vietnam war, might march, appropriately garbed, in his sections of demonstrations during those years. They might also occasionally lend a hand with the puppet-making, and might provide hospitality to the puppeteers and/or provide some money. Sometimes, for brief periods, they would even become regulars; and some regulars, ceasing to be regulars, would enter this network of old-time associates. Typically, they would be man and wife couples, and more intellectuals or writers than artists.

Schumann's puppetry workshops, starting with his puppetry 'activity' sessions at Putney School in '62/'63 and his art classes at the grammar school there, and by way of the 'community-service' workshops at the Courthouse in '67/'68 continuing to his puppetry workshops and weekly 'puppet news' activities at Goddard College in '72 to the workshops with students at colleges visited on tours by which he '73 ff. (and Bill Dalrymple already in the spring of '70) would get together a performance of a given play at the college in question, have been a major source of labor for him. The idea here is that the attendants will learn something. In fact, mostly all they get is the pleasure of participation. The regulars were indispensable for these 'teaching' activities; and the workshops were a major source of regulars, especially '70/'71: in '70 Schumann had in fact hoped that he might be able indefinitely to defray his labor needs out of workshops with Goddard College students – dispense with a 'core group' altogether, perhaps. But this did not work out (cf. part V). The volunteer recruitment on tours, also on the formal basis of 'workshops' advertised as such, asystematically initiated during the '69 tour of *Cry*, carefully planned as of the '72 tour of *Stations*, often proved difficult and vexatious, and was inherently hazardous. The practice required flexibility – in the construction of shows, in rehearsals – since Schumann could not be sure how many 'students' he would be able to get, sometimes had to start rehearsals not knowing (cf. infra his June '82 New York City pageant and parade) – and diplomacy: a mixture of firmness and permissiveness in dealing with these 'students.' And not having time on any stop of a tour, he could rehearse only the very simplest, rudimentary sort of performances: so the parts had to be or had potentially to be like that.

Finally, he has by word-of-mouth and/or press solicitation, probably starting in '65 (an April 17, Washington, D.C. demonstration or an October 16 New York City peace parade), procured the help of volunteers in the preparation and execution of specific shows calling for a large number of participants and a correspondingly great amount of work on puppets, chiefly, but not only anti-war demonstrations of the '60s, drawing on the pool of opponents of the war in New York City.[14]

The work of the theatre as regards its final output, though perhaps not always as regards its organization – who does what when – has, with perhaps some loosening September '68-December '69, and during '73, been autocratically governed by Schumann, both as regards masks and puppets, and as regards the content and staging of the shows. Masks, puppets, content, staging are – and not just grosso modo, but in their fine detail – as Schumann wants them to be. Only to a negligible extent do they express the ideas or sensibilities of other members of the group. There

---

14. The earliest ad I have found solicits help for a 1966 Memorial Day demonstration:

'Bread and Puppet Theatre needs Women for Memorial Day peace parade. Come to Rehearsal Sunday, May 20, 8 p.m. at 412 Grant Street, near Clinton. Sponsored by the Bread and Puppet Theatre/Veterans and Reservists to End the War in Vietnam.'

The *Bach Cantata #140* was his first 'theatre' piece requiring a large number of performers – perhaps a hundred: a (free) notice in the *Voice* called for them:

'Puppet Helpers. The Bread and Puppet Theatre needs volunteers for a production of Bach's Cantata #140 . . . in conjunction with the Judson Chamber Ensemble. Hands are needed for puppet-making workshops and puppet operation. Call . . .' (Notice, *Village Voice*, January 19, '67.)

A month later, he needed help with the enlarged indoor version of *Chicken Little*, and the *Voice* obliged him by another notice:

'Puppet Workshops. The Bread and Puppet Theatre is holding workshops in experimentation for new productions on Tuesdays and Wednesdays from 6:30 to 8:30 p.m. at the Old Astor Library . . . .' — (Notice, *Village Voice*, February 16, '67.)

A year later, repeated ads solicit help in the preparation of *Johnny Comes Marching Home:*

'*Papier Mache Against the War* ! ! ! ! Volunteers needed ! ! ! ! Saturday 11-6. Weekdays and evenings call Bread and Puppet Theatre . . . Old Court House, Second Avenue at 2nd Street.' (*Village Voice* ad of February 1, '68.) A repeat of the ad the ff. Thursday specifies: 'printing and glueing workshop.' A month after this, Schumann advertises for performers in that year's ('68) Easter show:

An ad of March 28, '68: 'Many people needed for Bread and Puppet's *Crucifixion Against the War* rehearsals, Sunday, March 31, 12 noon, Old Courthouse . . . .'

When, in late '68 he had settled down to working up his next big production, *The Cry of the People for Meat*, he needed a larger number of performers for touring it in Europe, so he had to expand the core group from perhaps half a dozen to about 20 people, and at that, he apparently needed additional volunteers over there. Workshop volunteers were procured through the still helpful *Village Voice*. A notice of November 28, '68 announces 'free theatre workshops at which puppet and mask building and operation will be taught' Monday and Wednesday evenings at the Old Courthouse, ads of December 19 and 26, '68 and of January 2 and 9, '69, announce 'open drama and puppetry workshops' there at the same times. These volunteers probably procured him not only labor for the preparation of the tour, but some additional tourers as well.

has been hardly even the semblance of give-and-take between him and others, of an influence of discussions or suggestions on their final forms. The tradition is that of European theatre: the director as ruler. Omar Shapli sees this as involving a conflict (between oppressiveness and permissiveness) within Schumann's own nature, and as reflected by Schumann's view of human society: as perennially and unalterably in the grip of a conflict between controlling powerful authority and an essential yielding – femine – people. We might add to this that Schumann is not happy about these conflicts (within himself and in the world), does not resolve them intellectually by a view of power as necessary evil, but emotionally and ideologically sides with the people and condemns power.

'But it's very hard to – I mean, when you're looking at what is presenting itself as a social statement, you're also looking at a very strong statement of a single person in a kind of crisis – perpetual crisis between opposites – that has a pessimistic overtone to it. (I: Crisis between opposites?) Well, between oppression and vulnerability. I think that's probably true. That's getting very presumptuous, in a way, because I don't really know that much about Peter's inner life, except what I feel that I see in his work. (I: His vulnerability?) Well, you know, it's a funny thing. We're jumping a bit and maybe we ought to. From what I know of the way he does work, Peter is both very permissive and very autocratic at once with the people he works with. You know, from the few occasions when I've seen him working and from my talks with people who have been with it. There's a very open, almost anarchistic atmosphere to the beginning of work on a piece. But somehow it always follows precisely and exactly where Peter wants it to go, down to the slightest movement, the smallest rhythm, and so on. He retains and projects almost complete control over his work, at least a good part of his work. Now that's a kind of anomaly, I think. Dealing with a social community, the Bread and Puppet Theatre, and that aspect of it is one of the strongest statements. On the other hand, you're dealing with a projection of one man's vision, almost completely. Much more completely than in almost any other theatre that I know of. Both of these things seem to be true and to relate it to the subject, the content of all of that, I think it's possible that that is a reflection of aspects of Peter. I mean, Peter who wants to put it all the way he wants it and Peter who is an extremely vulnerable and open and generous being in the world. And if you put it in social terms wider than that it doesn't seem to me that it ever really comes to any attempts to resolve the social questions it describes. It places them always in terms of there are simple people who are basically good, who are victimized and who have more resilience than Uncle Fatso thinks they have, and they endure. This is one – of course, the oldest themes of anything and it obviously must be valid in a certain way, since it's been there as long as we can recall. But it does have questions that go with it and that are there and – the authority figure. I think that Peter has an Uncle Fatso aspect of himself as a man who wants it his own way and gets it his own way and he probably is aware of that. He must. How couldn't he be? And yet, is perceived as the enemy. There is never an attempt that I know of in his work to do, say what Anouilh tried to do with Creon, you know, something like that. To say, well you needed Uncle Fatso, or qualified you must have an Uncle Fatso, or how else can things go on. Of course, that could be a question

of a position, too. I remember in the Anouilh case it certainly seemed a question to me. But, I mean, there isn't any attempt to view society or life as a set of contradictions for which there is a key, you know. Like a balance between this and a certain amount of that. Uncle Fatso just becomes a little more perceptive and the good people become just a little more ruthless, but maybe things will be all right. That is alien, I think, to the thought of his productions, and alien to his own view of the world.'
(Shapli, interview.)

Schumann's problem with power emerges from statements made by one of my interviewees, herself a willful woman.

'(I: You felt that the Easter and Christmas plays also were political?) Oh yes. I loved them. I thought they were ancient and about humanitarian activities, but also very specific. And I wouldn't limit politics to naming the politician who happens to be there at that moment. But I thought of that definitely as a political human stance. (I: How would you describe that in either of those two?) Well, it was always about power. Peter works a lot with power issues, and shared power vs. kingly power – and life. Everyday life, as a very beautiful and valid situation – without having to have powerful attributes in it. The power is in the simplicity of the thing. And to me that's a political statement. Because we were so – or at least I was so involved in the power of intellectual studies in graduate school and power of all kinds, and we felt so out of power. So to have somebody say that, you know, like a cup of coffee, some bread, is a powerful thing. It makes – it meant something to me.... (I: Could you find a common general theme in all of Peter's work?) The challenge to authority.... The strongest moments that I remember are, you cannot serve two masters. You can either serve God or Mammon. That's like a reiterated thing – two masters. Power. Worldly power, or devotion to life. Life being this very simple idea of life. Food, drink, children, small house. That. But it's always the *simple* life. And threatened, or menaced by the authority. And the interactions of those who challenge. There was also, almost like a mythic quality about Peter, that – when you say it, it sounds incongruous, but it played theatrically very well. But the content was very often the last tribunal. Somehow these evil people, these evildoers, somehow they face a last tribunal under God. There's some spiritual dimension that Schumann never actually spelled out, but it was always alluded to. Death always came, who took away the wrongdoer. The angel came to rescue. Sort of like something beyond real life, that stands as a tribunal for this interaction of power and submission. And very often the protection of the weak. That's so strong. The protection of the weak ... I also felt that Peter required a tremendous amount of personal power in order to be able to direct. He needed people to believe in him completely. And that's not unusual, I would imagine, although I'm not a theatrical person with directors – who need to have a kind of charge built up among the players. And I could not give that, because I felt that I would have to lend myself to this theatre, you know, when he needed me, and essentially would be abandoned, you see, when the theatre moved on.... (referring to her apprehensions, at the time Schumann quit New York for the country, of what working with him in the country would be like:)

Then everything would depend, you see, on Peter's good will or on the charge that could be built up around the creativity. And I felt in the time we are now we're trying to build personal creativity as well as that kind of collective thing. That's very hard to do around somebody who is as stunning as Peter is. To develop a self is hard in that situation.' (Palmer, interview.)

To her mind, what is in question here are not just the intrinsic exigencies of creative activity dependent on the cooperative effort of others, nor intrinsic managerial exigencies of group effort, but psychological frailties of Schumann's:

'Feeling on one hand very dependent on the group interaction – wanting to act as a group and yet needing to be a leader – and projecting, very often, feelings against the group, that we were lesser than, or weak, as a way of asserting his leadership. That one dynamic.' (Palmer, interview.)

'See, I couldn't have been anti-power unless there was a powerful person in front of me. Not at that time. But I could join a cause . . . . Until I got my wings going. But I never really felt – at the time I was very rebellious . . . . I happen to have a personality that, on one hand is extremely rebellious, and the other hand is extremely conservative. That's not everybody. That's just me. So, conservative in the sense that I want to have the right authority in front of me. But I push against that authority. That's how I find my individuality. It's like I can take a teacher and take pot shots at their theory and the stronger the teacher will contend with me, the sharper I get. And Peter was a teacher for me. And the more militant he would get on a point, the more I could push against it, thereby finding my own. Probably very difficult for Peter, but that's what I did. (I: But what would the point be here?) The idea of collective action, which was his statement but not his actuality. Okay, Peter, if this is our theatre and these are our puppets, we manage it – we decide where we're gonna go – you don't take jobs – we take jobs, you see?' (Palmer, interview.)

7. Modus Operandi III. The labor force. From group of pals to group of acolytes to horde of hippies to commune to seasonal workforce to salaried employees. 1963 –.

We owe to the Village's reacquisition during the early '60s of its 1920's reputation as hotbed of the arts, a portrait of the Bread and Puppet crew in those early days, illustrating an article in the *Saturday Evening Post*'s World's Fair issue of May 23, '64 on the 'new American capital of Bohemia' – the Village. It shows the Bread and Puppet artistes posing awkwardly in the Museum with masks from their current offerings: 'Artistes of the Bread & Puppet Theater – where the spectators sit on milk crates – whoop it up in their loft on Delancey Street': Bruno Eckhardt, looking slightly insane, but in a German *Philistine* way, sits out front with a tambourine, Schumann, young, next to him, two milk crates over, with a kiddingly triumphant, impish lift of the nose, his arms raised in the sackcloth of his Fireman/Red Man puppet, a big-nosed, heavy-eyed bugger of a puppet, pointing to something out of the photo frame, mild-looking Arthur Stearns, 'Beanie' Kunis is standing behind Eckhardt, on one hand the passably traditional fairy tale wolf-panther head of the Demon from the old *King Story*, in the crook of his left arm a plaster cast head, Ernstthal behind Schumann, a mere kid, his hair wild, peering at us through his glasses, pretending to blow a trumpet. Squeezed in behind and between him and Kunis, the Dr. Oyle, the group's hand puppet comedian, blandly serious, displaying half of the Janus head, more emphatically African-Picasso than the Red Man, and in the background, gentle and nice, two people that I haven't heard much about, Larry and Margaret Lewis, holding the consternated really terror-struck-looking *King Story* people masks, faces of foolish burghers on short sticks.

Charlie Adams[1] is not there, alcoholic amateur painter, musician extra-

---

1. 'He was the one guy who had a car and he had this beat-up Chevy – '53 Chevy station wagon ... a maniac driver – I've seen him go through places that were too small for the car. I am convinced it was made out of rubber. He was a strange guy. He was the kind of guy who would fix a light fixture in the ceiling – take the socket off without turning off the electricity. And you'd say "How could you do it?" "Well, the trick is only to touch one wire at a time." ' — (Ernstthal, interview.)

'Charlie Adams really impressed me, the intensity of the performance and the commitment – in *Reiteration*.... He just played the drums and played Death.... Well it was *King Story* he played Death and then in *Reiteration* he played the trumpet.... (I: Adams' music contributed a great deal, the trumpet and the drums?) For me yes. (I: And what was it like?) I'd have to say frightening. It wasn't like acting, it was just very on *attack*, especially the *drums*. And strong. And it was just a parade or just trying to be a musical effect, it was a *voice*, in the show ....' — (Konnoff, interview.)

Artistes of the Bread and Puppet Theater, *Saturday Evening Post*, May 23, '64. Photograph by Marvin Lichtner.

ordinary, fabricator of junk instruments — a strong drummer — but he is very much of a regular until April '68, when, perhaps triggered by the Reverend King's assassination, he runs amok, smashing puppets, at the Courthouse[2] — so he and his wife, Mary Kelly, a quiet Catholic girl, an ex-nun, who also worked with the group during the '60s — 'full time' by the summer of '67 — do not go on that spring's tour to Europe. They rejoin the group for its first attempt at communal living in Maine, during the summer of '68, but Mary buys a separate house for them nearby, and they end up settling there. Adams goes with the group to San Francisco in September, and he and Mary are still around the Courthouse that winter, but not much into things any more,[3] and that's it.

'Beanie' and the Lewises are not much heard from after this spring. If we omit them, the first 'core' group or group of regulars would have consisted of Elka, the two Eckhardts, Ernstthal, Charlie Adams, and Dr. Oyle.[4] Much appreciated humorist in the group's Christmas and Easter shows and key performer as lecturing physician in the February 4, '67 *Wounds*, Oyle and his wife Pearl, who also helps out during these years, but definitely an ancillary, as in a way they both are qua benign hosts of the group in their Brooklyn home, get to go on the first European tour in

---

2. 'I don't remember what this fight was about but he went crazy one night and just ran round the Courthouse trying to destroy puppets. Mary (Kelly) was there and he was very violent. It was the same week that people were being assassinated, Martin Luther King or Kennedy.' — (Sherman, interview.)

'... trying to kill Peter ... (I: Why did he want to kill Peter?) I think he was on drugs. I got there after it had started — I walked in on it — and he was ricocheting off the walls — he was completely berserk. Breaking, tearing — I don't know what started it. At that point I was not a member of the inner core group ....' — (Ashley, interview.)

3. By the fall of '68, when Leherissier joined up, 'Murray Levy was there then. When I first met the theatre, Margo was there, Murray Levy was there, Peter, Bob Ernstthal, Charlie Adams and Mary Kelly. But they were sort of not really working that hard back then, because they were emotionally troubled. So they were sort of off on the side, and basically it was Murray, Bob, Peter, Margo and me when I first met them.'—(Leherissier, interview.)

4. 'Elka: Who were you working with at the time (in 1964 (SSB)?) Well, Bob Ernstthal .... He helped, and Bruno helped and I met possibly Irving (Oyle). Maybe not. Maybe Andy Trompetter. Charlie Adams — but he didn't like to work, he liked to perform. But he had workers there. People who came off and on and helped. Then there were these young boys, Bob Walters and Ken O'Leary, and the Puerto Rican, Orlando, who was very nice, who helped quite a bit. (Elka: Did Jules (Rabin) and Helen (Rabin) come?) That must have been a year later. When did we start anti-war things?' — (Schumann, interview, '79.)

'(I: Who was in the first *Crucifixion*? (Easter '64)) Bruno, Eva, probably, Ken O'Leary, and Orlando and Bob Walters and Irving Oyle and ... and Margaret (Lewis) and Larry (Lewis), possibly Charlie Adams, a girl called Catherine (Solomon, probably, rather than Merrill (SSB)). A girl who just came some day — what is her name? Luger is her last name, she lived in Paris for a decade. (Elka: Oh, she's doing pottery and jewelry — Sally Luger.)' – (Schumann, interview, '79.)

the spring of '68, though they don't stay for all of it, and they are pretty much out of the picture from then on, probably moving to California not too much later.

Ernstthal's forte was his vocal delivery, voice and humor as narrator and dialogist, he had a warm vibrant voice and down-to-earth but not fake diction, but he really worked — made masks, did 'everything.'[5] Though Eckhardt — German, Schumann's own age, of a ruder humor — was more Schumann's friend, buddy, than he, he was Schumann's right-hand man.

Outside of the group's work, Bob had an intense Lower East Side life revolving around dope, sex, anarchist politics and poetry.[6] His work at the theatre 'kept him sane,' he has said ('79.) He left for a first time after the June '66 Bridge show, but was back for the *Chicken Little* parks project in August: He had had a brief affair with the new first lady — she replaced Eva as 'feminine principle' — Catherine Merrill, a Safeway heiress and amateur potter, the 'classic liberal girl' (Ernstthal), but then had 'lost out' with her — the motivation was along these lines, but Schumann and he had also been rivals for her affections. He quit again,[7] just when his replacement as Schumann's right-hand man, Murray Levy, joined, after the Europe tour of '68 — 'He said, "I'm leaving the Puppet Theatre" ... in those days when people left, it was very traumatic for Peter ... he would say things like "you're betraying me"' (Sherman, interview) — rejoined, with hopes for an executive position, during the second Europe tour in '69, but left, those hopes having been disappointed,[8] feeling Schumann no longer trusted him, and having had sustained ideological disagreements with Schumann throughout the tour, though, as he recalls it in '79, the precipitating reason was the way Schumann treated people

---

5. 'Peter was the *sculptor*, essentially. And I helped him make — do the physical construction. I felt — I was an *apprentice*. And I made — I did the *handwork*, but Peter did the sculpting, and the painting. But everything — all steps in between that, I would have to do . . . . Yes.' — (Ernstthal, interview.)
6. E.g. Bob in '63-'64 was with Murray Bodkin a.k.a. Lewis Herber (subsequently author of *The Ecology of Freedom*) and Allan Hoffman, a member of the New York Federation of Anarchists (headquarters at 641 East 9th Street), publisher of *The Legacy of Domination, A Draft Introduction to a Statement of Views*, and of the one issue of the magazine *Good Soup* (edited by Bob). After the Metro closed, the three anarchists founded the Bowery Poets Co-op. Ernstthal also was one of the publisher/editors of *Black Mask*.
7. 'Everything really peaked out in that year. When I got back to New York, though, I felt that I couldn't live in New York anymore. It was too de — it was too gross — it was too terrible. And I also wanted to move on personally — with my life and this and that. And we had somebody who wanted me to come and start a theatre in New Mexico so I went to New Mexico and we found this little house with land around it and I started working on — we had a puppet theater and we did shows. Anyway, so I started to remake my life and I was doing crafts and we had this nice place and we had goats —.' — (Ernstthal, interview.)
8. Cf. Part IV(3), section 24.

manipulatively[9] and without concern.[10] He did puppetry with his wife in Denmark, where he had quit, went to California.

Eckhardt, from the much-bombed Ruhr – he attributes the gentleness of Schumann's anti-war plays to his not having experienced the real hardships of the war [11] – 15,000 dead in one bombing attack in the Ruhr town where Eckhardt then lived – a self-taught anarchist like his grandfather, son of a barkeeper – conscious of Schumann's superior social status as son of a teacher – a hobo in his youth – for three years – not just a romantically wandering artist, briefly, like Schumann – who had seen the inside of jails – had come to the U.S. in '61, naively, to make money: he was going to stay for a year, work hard as stone mason (he had six weeks' experience in the trade), make enough money to build himself a house on a plot he owned. The stark reality of the Lower East Side – and the as he thought Mafia stonemason's union — hit him hard, he crawled into a hole, his wife got a job. He was a painter, but found himself unable to use the medium. When after a year or two he pulled himself together, he started house-painting, did reasonably well, bought an old car. With help from Richard Tyler, he got into making and printing woodcuts. He and Schumann worked together apartment-painting. He was an anti-clerical atheist, politically in a non-doctrinal manner a radical radical: unlike Schumann a thorough and basic rebel. Tyler and his people apart, he was Schumann's first American collaborator. He got into *Totentanz* (Eckhardt, interview), worked with Schumann on and in his '62 playlets, with lengthy interruptions – he and his wife returned to Germany in '66 or '67 – and many disputes, increasingly violent – primarily he found Schumann's pacifism and Lutheran quietism and authoritarianism increasingly objectionable, in '68 and '69 thought support of the Vietcong's struggle incum-

---

9. 'Peter essentially mocked Bruno and also used the technique in the group – which was that he would accuse someone of something – of *doing* something – and make him – and *really* condemn him for it – and then forgive him. Thereby gaining an incredible power over everyone.' — (Ernstthal, interview.)

10. 'People were fighting all the time and it was getting – people were not liking each other – it was degenerating. There was no more common purpose – it was getting – poor – it was getting difficult. Finally, Peter was saying "If you don't like it, leave" – which was *another* idle threat. Because how could they leave? Nobody had any money – plus, they would face – like exile and be really stupid – and look stupid, and it would hurt the theatre.... So I think it may have been like September 3rd – something like that. Anyway, so I said: "Well, fuck you. I'm leaving. If that's the way you are going to treat people and that's what it's going to be like – I'm leaving" – which I did.' — (Ernstthal, interview.)

11. 'Ich mein, ich will überhaupt nun nicht immer Recht gehabt haben, aber das war'n bestimmte Sachen die haben mich damals, also, die haben mir so hart zugesetzt, weil ich den Krieg auch in voller Blüte erlebt hab, wirklich dick. Im Krieg bin ich hier gewesen, wo die grossen Bombardements waren. Und ich hatte 'ne ganz andere Vorstellung oder auch das war mir alles nicht kräftig genug auch dieses Strassentheater wie der junge, dieses Vietnam – *A Man Says Goodbye to his Mother*' — — (Eckhardt, interview.)

bent on the group – but he also resented what he felt was the deterioration of the group's initial collaborative work process into a dictatorial work process executing Schumann's projects[12] – he worked with Schumann

---

12. '(I: Hatte sich da '68/'69 was geändert?) Ja, da hatte sich, ja. Ich had zum Beispiel und mich hat das ungeheuer gestört und ich hatte das vorher auch noch nie beobachtet, dass der Peter sich in 'ne Mitte aufbaut und alle sitzen drumheran und hören jetzt genauso mit unheimlicher Konzentration 'nen Vortrag zu, wie man bestimmte Szenen macht und wie man sie nicht macht. Dat war, dat war schon so, ich mein gut, reden kann man immer, wenn einer dat bessere Idee hat, dann hat er auch dat Sagen, is klar, aber dat war schon, dat war schon irgendwie so verteilt, wie ich dat vorher nicht in Erinnerung hatte ... er war seiner Sache schon sicher, ha. Abber ich hatte immer das Gefühl, dass die, dass Leute, dass Leute irgendwie nicht zum Zuge kamen, denn jeder hat Ideen und Gedanken und dat ist night so, dass alle Ideen und Gedanken aus einer Quelle kommen sollen dann bahnt sich, irgenwo bahnt sich wat an, wat man im Grunde genommen an sich nicht haben wollte. Ich glaube, ich hab immer an 'ne Zusammenarbeit geglaubt, und mein Innerstes das bäumt sich dagegen auf, jemanden gegenüberzusitzen, der 'ne bestimmte Autorität für sich ganz normal und selbstverständlich beansprucht ... Dat ist sein Theater, aber er, nun gut. Ich hab dat, ich hab dat bis zu 'ner gewissen Sache hab ich dat, ich hab dat irgendwie akzeptiert. Aber ich bin von den Erfahrungen ausgegangen, die wir miteinander hatten und dat konnte ruhig sein Theater sein, ja, ich bin ihm um den Namen nicht neidisch gewesen oder irgendwie so, ja. Es drehte sich eben einfach um die Art und Weise, wie man eben Dinge produziert, wie dat von statten geht. Und dat war vorher wirklich anders.' — (Eckhardt, interview.)

Dat ging um diesen, dat warn, dat warn, politische, für mich war dat'ne politische Auseinandersetzung. Dat ging los mit dem Streit um die Posters. Wir hatten uns Siebdruckmaterial besorgt und haben dann Posters gemacht über die Show. Und ich hab Posters gemacht über 'Das Salz der Erde.' Dat waren vietnamesische Freiheitskämpfer, die hab ich, dat waren immer so zwei Reihen von Guerilleros, die, die, so in voller Montur und unten drunter hab ich 'n Spruch geschrieben. Ich weiss jetzt nicht mehr, welcher Spruch dat war, aber der Spruch, der stammte nicht von mir. Der war, irgendwie kam der aus der Quelle die dem Peter auch vertraut sein müsste. Und da gab es den ersten Ärger. Und da hab ich 'n zweites Blatt grad gemacht und zwar das kannt ich nich aus'm Kopf, das hab ich, das hab ich abgezeichnet, vom Photo. Ich das nur 'n bisschen verändert. Dat waren drei Guerilla-Kämpfer, die auf'm zerschossenen Hubschrauber stehen. Und war an sich 'n sehr bekanntes Photo (...) Und die Plakate waren sehr schön, dat ist nicht jetzt so, weil ich dat, weil ich sagen will, wie schön ich dat gemacht hab, die waren einfach schön geworden und die wurden auch am schnellsten verkauft. Dat Geld kam in die Theaterkasse, für unsere weitere Existenz und so. Und dat hatte, dat hatte den Peter gewurmt, dat war, und dann hat er so und dann hat er angefangen seine Autorität auszuspielen gegen die ich auch irgendwie so machtlos war und (...) Rollen, die ich früher gemacht habe, anderen zuzuteilen, nicht. Und dat war auch sowat, naja, dar war dat Ding gelaufen, dat wusst ich ganz genau. Wir haben uns dann in Berlin nochmal ernsthaft unterhalten, ich hab gesagt, Peter, ich hau jetzt nicht ab, ich geh erst, wenn du gehst. Aber ich geh jetzt nicht. Vor allen Dingen, wat sollt ich denn machen? Wo soll ich den hingehen, soll ich im Strassengraben schlafen? Ich hatte, ich hatte kein zuhause mehr. Ich war von meiner Familie weg, ich hatte mich vom Peter getrennt und meine Zukunft war ungewiss. Und wie ich dann vom Theater weggegangen bin, da kriegt ich 700 Mark ausgezahlt, dat war mein Anteil. Ich war ziemlich sauer, er hatte 'ne ganze Menge, also für Theater, er wollte sich 'n Zirkuszelt kaufen und so weiter. Under der hat natürlich da wat auf die hohe Kante gelegt. Ich bin dann mit den 700 Mark nach Berlin, ich bin zwischendurch krank geworden, wie die abgefahren sind, dann hab ich wegen der Delly, an der ich sehr gehangen hab (...) aber ich

until the summer of '69, when he was drummed out of the group at a court martial convened by Schumann, on his discharge getting 700DM. The formal charge was an attack on Schumann he had contributed to a group diary, his actual offense, he thought, were certain pro-Vietcong posters he had contributed to the group's poster sales. They were too radical and they sold too well. His humanitarian and anti-authoritarian anarchism was incompatible with Schumann's persistent flirt with a transcendental Jesus – the salvation of man can only be the work of man – and with Schumann's dictatorial directorship: he came to see himself as Thomas Münzer to Schumann's Luther,[13] – Luther, the betrayer of the peasantry.[14]

Eckhardt's major contribution to performances had apparently been his vigorous appearance in the big puppets, notably as Great Warrior in *King*

---

wollte nicht wegen der rüberfahren. Da hab ich, da hab ich in, in, da hab ich in Paris in so'ne Art Nervenzusammenbruch gekriegt mit 'nem sehr starken Asthmaanfall. Und die Leute, bei denen ich da einquartiert war, dat warn, dat warn französische Spiessbürger. Die haben sich nicht viel um mich gekümmert, die kriegten da hinterher Angst, dat mir nicht doch irgendwie wat zustöast und dann haben die doch 'n Artzt geholt. Dat haben die bezahlt auch. Und da hatte ich, ich hatte überhaupt keine Medikamente und dann habe ich Medikamente gehabt und dann hab ich mich eines Morgens, ich hab da acht Tage im Bett gelegen, inso'ner kleinen Kammer, ich hab auch in der ganzen Zeit so gut wie nix gegessen. Dann hab ich mich voll mit Medikamente gestopft und bin morgens um vier oder fünf, praktisch mitten in der Nacht, bin ich zum Gare de Lyon. oder wie dat heisst gefahren und hab mich in 'n Zug gesetzt Richtung Germany. Und da, da hat so mein neues Leben angefangen, von meinen einigen, wieder angefangen, ja.' — (Eckhardt, interview.)
13. 'Ja, also ich, für mich hat er immer so den alten Luther rezipiert, auch so das patriarchalische, das Familienoberhaupt und so, viele Kinder .... Ich habe den, den Jesus, den hab ich als einen Mensch gedacht, das war an sich mein Clown (the Clown in Eckhardt's *Scheisskopf* (SSB)). Das war der Mensch, der, der ja sich aufgibt für eine Sache. Er war nicht, ja ich bin auch Gottes Sohn, nicht, ich hab die Frechheit dat zu behaupten. Und nichts, oder zum Beispiel Peters Interpretation zum Beispiel dort, da hat er ein Stück gemacht (*Simple Light*, '72 (SSB)), da kommt klar heraus, was so in seinem Kpft vorgeht. Dass nach einer langen Evolutionsgeschichte der, der, dieses von Urgöttern, Dämonen, Bestien und menschwerdenden Menschen plötzlich dieses strahlende Licht erscheint, die Geburt Christi .... Ich find das nicht so gut. Ich hab das in Berlin gesehen .... Und mein Hader, mein Hader mit ihm wär, dass ich diese Interpretation oder diese Darstellung nicht akzeptieren, nicht, dat is mir zu, dat war mir zu einfach und vor allen Dingen ich hab da immer, ich hab da immer 'ne Glorifizierung drin, drin gewittert, die ich irgendwie so, so, satt bekannt war und für mich, für mich, wenn wir die, die Kreuzigungsgeschichte in der Brooklyn church da gespielt haben, da fing an sich meine Auseinandersetzung mit dem Peter schon an, weil – Die war damals noch friedlich.' — (Eckhardt, interview.)
14. 'And I think that was part of the conflict that Peter was stronger in character than Bruno, although Bruno was an excellent artist. Although he tried to do things *with* him, Peter was essentially too full of his own things to *possibly* have anybody else doing anything with him. That was part of it, and it was really – and that was very sad, the Peter and Bruno story, because Bruno had a somewhat weaker character although he had a very straight artistic .... Part of it was that pressure, because they were *friends* and yet Peter always had to be boss.' — (Ernstthal, interview.)
'He and Eva, who was very beautiful, had a son, Benjamin. He was a baby. Bruno worked as an orderly in a hospital in the Bronx, carrying dead bodies or something ....

Story.[15] Eckhardt's flamenco guitar playing, his singing — he later became a street singer — as also his woodcuts were much appreciated in the group: but not used in the puppetry much. The exception was a show, *The God Pan, King Scheisskopf and his Clown*, that the Bread and Puppet Theatre did a few times January-February '65. His name did not appear in the *Village Voice* notice. This was a flip-over show of a gigantic book of woodcuts of his, *King Scheisskopf and his Clown*, initially narrated by himself, then — because, he says (interview, '83), he could not keep from attacking the audience — by Schumann.[16] The book is a kind of autobiography. May-June '67, The Bread and Puppet Theatre announced (*Village Voice*, May 18, 25, June 1) an 'exhibition: *King Scheisskopf and his Clown* and new work by the Great German Woodcutter Bruno Eckhardt.' This appears to have been an unnarrated showing. Eckhardt by this time, I believe, was no longer in the U.S.

A composition of some of these beautiful woodcuts — Pan, playing the flute, giving a present to a child, a pair of lovers — the Dionysiac dimension of life absent in Schumann's work — were reproduced in the July '67 issue of WIN, with a notice that they were for sale at the Bread and Puppet Theatre, then on Lafayette Street.

Eckhardt left the book with Schumann. It has been lost.[17]

They were friends. Peter and Bruno and the families were friends. And they spoke German all the time. It was basically a German-speaking trip, actually, in the beginning. I didn't — my family — my father and stuff were German, so I know a very, very loose smattering. I grew up in the generation where German was considered a language to be talked and not let the kids know what you were talking about.... The last time I saw him was in '69, at the European tour. He was having a real bad time. He was really drinking a lot and his political thing was — he was — I don't know what happened. I've heard they split up later.... I either think he's doing real well or he died, one or the other... Bruno was a very, very talented woodcut artist, very talented. And *terrific* guitar player — flamenco, primarily — and also could pick up lots of other kinds of style. And he was really, really good. And I think that was part of the conflict that Peter was stronger in character than Bruno, although Bruno was an excellent artist.' — (Ernstthal, interview.)

15. 'His muscle work was so extraordinary. I was afraid, viscerally afraid.' — (Sherman, interview.)

16. 'Ja, ja, das wurde gezeigt, so nach Art der alten Moritatensänger, mit'm Zeigestock, immer ein Blatt.... Ich hab, ich hab das einmal gemacht, aber ich muss sagen, ich war'n sehr schlechter Vortragskünstler und vor allen Dingen bin ich immer in Versuchung gekommen, das Publikum zu beleidigen. Ich weiss nicht warum, das war, das war Blödsinn, das war abschreckend, ja. Das hat die Leute abgeschreckt, aber die Geschichte ist nicht abschreckend. Und ich hab da so meistens meine Geschichte (...) gequasselt, na ziemlich versaut, nicht. Und dann haben das andere gemacht. Der Peter konnte das gut, ich weiss nicht, wer das noch gemacht hat, ich weiss es nicht mehr.' — (Eckhardt, interview.)

17. 'In fact, he did the biggest book in the world. He did this gigantic book with a huge wooden cover of a story in woodcuts. It was really great. I have no idea where it is. (I: One copy?) Yeah. You couldn't ever throw it out — it's too big ... (I: You don't know the title of it?) No. It was a big book and it was these big woodcuts, about a clown. It was his

Ms. Eckhardt and Ms. Schumann are not in the *Saturday Evening Post* picture. They are probably home, minding the babies:

'Eva was working quite a lot too, but, then, both Mom and Eva had small children, so –' (Schumann, interview, '79.)

The two wives contributed particularly to the Delancey Street children's shows, tried to develop fairy tale plays themselves and performed them, Eva apparently particularly good at performing for children. Eva in Ernstthal's words was the group's 'first feminine principle':

'(I: Eckhardt and his wife, did they perform?) Yeah, they performed. The very first things. Right. And that was one of the interesting things about *language*. They were performed by people who were not really in command of the English language. Bruno – Eva was more – had more of a command of it. Bruno had a *crude* command.... Eva was the feminine side of the whole show, at that time. Elka had three kids, and took Bennie, who was Eva's kid. And Eva was the girl. That sounds funny in a way, but otherwise it was a very rough-hewn masculine theatre and Eva was very feminine. I actually had a crush on her, because she was – I considered her quite beautiful. So she was the feminine side in those very early days of the theatre. She was the girl.... Like I said, Eva, to me, was the feminine aspect of things. She was talented. I can't remember *specifically* what she was. She had a *nice* singing voice, and she was a hearty German girl, I always thought, also quite beautiful. Really. I thought she was very – she had a very – she was the feminine side of things. That's all I can – (I: In the original setup,

---

own story about a clown facing the government because there was a law against making music. It was like a Jesus story, frankly. And the government – they put him on trial and they accuse him of singing in public or something. He was killed, or something. It was this very heavy kind of almost crucifixion, clown story.' — (Ernstthal, interview.)

'Wir haben, die meisten Blöcke die sind mir geklaut worden. Ich hab damals 'ne Geschichte gemacht, 'ne zusammenhängende Geschichte und die, die war ein Buch. Da hatte ich so, das war'ne grauslige Arbeit. Ich hab die Holzschnitte auf Packpapier geklebt, (...) das war'n zich Holzschnitte. Und die Blätter die war'n, die war'n irgendwie so, so schwarz. Und das ganze Buch, da hat mir einer 'n Deckel für gemacht, also 'n Einband. Das wog ungefähr 80, 90 Pfund. (...)
I habe das dem Peter dagelassen. Die Schnitte die warn'n nicht alle gut, die hatten auch, die war'n grob. 'n paar davon, die mocht' ich nicht, ich mochte sie nicht alle. Aber die Geschichte, die Geschichte, das war meine Geschichte. Ob die gut war oder schlecht, das weiss ich nicht. Ich kann mich an die, an den Fortlauf kann ich mich, kann ich mich erinnern genau. Ich weiss nur, dass er ist, wie im Märchen. Der Clown wird, der Clown wird umgebracht und die Leute oder das Volk, die befinden sich ganz zuletzt auf einem riesengrossen Zug, irgendwohin, nach Irgendwo, das ist ein unbestimmtes Ziel. Und die Geschichte endet auch im, im, die hat eigentlich kein Ende, die kann man immer weiter machen. Weil der Clown, der, der ist zwar gestorben, aber er lebt trotzdem, und ich würde jetzt, wenn ich, ich will, ich will, wenn ich jetzt weiter arbeite, ich hab da lange Zeit versäumt, ich habe meine, ich hab, ich hab die Jahre über Lieder gemacht, dann will ich diese Geschichte neu machen. Von Anfang an ....' — (Eckhardt, interview.)

maybe. But also in performances?) Yeah. She was – I don't remember. In these pictures it shows her playing, but I don't remember – she played some of the kids' stuff and tried to give that *light* side of it – (laugh) as I said, that endless pursuit of the kids' show that we could never do – that would never really come off – but she would give that – she had a kindly motherly side. She had a three-year-old son and she had that aspect of understanding how to deal, in *theatre*, with kids, and making fairy tales.' (Ernstthal, interview.)

Elka, then, appears to have been a more marginal member of the original group than Eva. She had more babies to take care of, Schumann was more a believer in 'Kinder, Küche, Kirche' than Eckhardt, Elka's feelings of inadequacy relative to her husband seem to have been strong from their German days onward. Still, she and Eva seem to a large extent to have handled the group's children's theatre activities for the first few years (cf. infra, IV), and when, finally, in '71, she became an active puppeteer – on her own, with all-woman groups, first the Dancing Bear Theater, then the Hardscrabble Mountain Puppeteers – she devoted herself to puppeteering – mostly hand-puppet puppeteering – for children: doing her own versions of *The Christmas Story* at high schools (cf. infra), and fairy tales, e.g. Oscar Wilde's *The Selfish Giant*, a Puerto Rican folktale, *Perez and Martina*, *The Life of Solomon Grundy*, a Chaucer tale, *The Rocks Removed*. Her contributions to Schumann's puppetry – apart from raising the kids and providing a home for him, being the group's chief seamstress (no small matter) more or less throughout the '60s and '70s, and its chief archivist, accountant and correspondent, and doing much of its gardening (a not unimportant part of its economic basis) and a major share of its cooking during the '70s (a job that during the annual circuses of the second half of the '70s reached heroic proportions) – seem limited: though I suspect her of understating them. She promoted Schumann's use of Sacred Harp singing '72 ff., and figure of the Washerwoman ('77 ff.), modeled on her, seems to have been largely her inspiration, and with it the changeover in the theatre's image of woman from the ethereal and passive to the earthy and active. I suspect that over the years her influence on Schumann's work has been in the directions of making it less obscure, more reticent on sexual matters, and more devout – Christian – in tone.

The original core-group pretty much lasted until and was pretty much gone by the fall of '68, though both Eckhardt and Ernstthal tried reentry on the occasion of the turbulent Europe tour of '69, both getting into violent conflicts with Schumann, ostensibly on ideological grounds. Its distinctive characteristic was that it was pretty much made up of strong, independently minded and emotionally turbulent men, crazies, with considerable talent and will of their own. This was the group with whom Schumann worked while he floundered and experimented, during the time he worked out how to use his puppets, created his medium, a time, also, in which he was unknown: becoming known through his peace parades in the course of '65, through *Fire* in '66. He was not the ruler in this group, nor conceived of as such by its members: whose contributions to what he became were, I would say, considerable.[18] As Eckhardt puts it, Schumann had the soup, but they put in the meat.[19]

During the mid-'60s, starting in '65, '66, many of them in the spring and summer of '66, a good dozen more people entered the group, in terms of regularity of attendance, amount of work contributed and visibility in performances and in demonstrations to varying degrees but on the whole perhaps becoming pretty much 'regulars' or 'insiders.' By and large, these people also tended to leave by the end of '68, a few lasting beyond, into the early Vermont years, '70, '71, '72, some 'around' even later. This first generation of recruits, which with the original members makes up the

---

18. '(I: When you came in there (summer of '66 (SSB)) did you have a feeling of a group?) Very strong feeling of a group. There was the inner core – because surrounding them were people who had to be told what to do, when to do it, and they may or may not do it and they may or may not come back again. But there was a recognizable core which was very strong.... They seemed to have a great respect for one another and nobody ever shirked their chores. So the socializing was – we would go in the backyard (of the Oyle's (SSB)) and have lunch there sometimes. Or later on, after rehearsals, go and have a beer or something. They (the Oyles) would frequently make lunches for people who were working very hard.... There was no drugs and no sex as far as I knew – it was clearly a very working relationship and sharing and it was built around an admiration for Peter, I knew of no drugs. They were too poor to have liquor.' — (Ashley, interview.)

'George is wrong about the "drugs" – Bob (Ernstthal) and the others, not Peter, they smoked a lot.' — (Sherman, interview.)

'The (Delancey Street Museum) had a cupola on the roof, where a river breeze blew in the summer and his helpers enjoyed smoking marijuana after rehearsals while watching the police station across the way.' — (E. Hoagland, '83.)

19. 'Ja, wir haben, wir haben damals die ersten Gehversuche mit den Neugeborenen gemacht und da wusste weder der Peter noch ich, wie man dat überhaupt richtig macht, diese Dinger zu bewegen. Dat musste alles dat musste rausgefunden werden. Und wir haben auch über dieses Volkstheater Annoncen gesetzt, da konnte dann jeder gucken kommen. Das war "Open Rehearsals" so nannte sich das. Und aus diesem "Open Rehearsals" da hat sich dann auch wat entwickelt und dat war, dat war nicht immer so, dann war da der Peter der da 'ne Idee im Kopf hatte, gut, er hatte 'ne Idee im Kopf, 'ne Suppe und da fehlte dat Fleisch irgendwie dran. Und dat Fleisch wurde – gut war 'en gute ehrliche Arbeit. Und dat wurde nicht ehrlich und gut, wenn er wirklich so alles im Vorraus so hatte, nicht, er konnte manchmal sehr dominierend sein und dann kam der Puppenspieler da hinterm Vorhang nicht vor und Peter war dauernd davor, nicht. Der war dann, dann so im Laufe der Jahre sagen wir mal hinterher 'ne Puppe. Und dat war die Gefahr, dat man eben im Laufe der Perioden so gedemütigt wird, 'ne Puppe zu sein, dat man die Sache aufgibt und dat ist, dat hatt 'n Nachteil, weil wir 'n, in dieser schwierigen Arbeit, da 'n ständiger Spieler erforderlich war. Dat konnte nicht immer sein, das Leute kommen und gehen, nicht wahr, und wir sagen, nu halt mal die Puppen (...), dat geht ja auch. Wie bei 'ner Band, fliegt einer raus, kommt der nächste und sag pass auf, du machst die Akkorde un wenn du's nicht tust, Scheiss drauf, werden wir den nächsten nehmen. Und 'n Team, 'n gutes eingearbeitetes Team, dat war, dat war manchmal, manchmal war es heikel, da waren zu viele neue, dat war so'n Wechsel dauernd. Und die, die zuerst ständig dabei waren, dat war der Bob Ernstthal und ja und ich.' — (Eckhardt, interview.)

over-all core group of the '60s, essentially is brought in in the context of the group's anti-Vietnam-war work, which is at its most intensive and extensive in '65-'66, and of Schumann's arriving at a definition of and achievement of mastery in his new medium in the winter of '65/'66 (and of his success with *Fire* early in '66): some of them rich liberal college girls, some of them aspiring actors and actresses. They soften the group, clarify and affirm Schumann's superordinate and dominant status, and shift the group's definition and aura from individual rebellion and anarchy (Ernstthal, Adams and Eckhardt were all anarchists) toward a liberal idealism defined by pacifism and ideals of art — artistic purity and integrity.

The more important names: Robert Nichols (spring '64-February '67), Helen and Jules Rabin (end(?) of '65-?), Catherine Merrill (spring '65-spring '66), Helen Hunter Palmer (beginning of '66-September '67), Andy and Amy Trompetter (spring '66-summer '68), Margo Lee Sherman (spring '66-spring '71, and...), George Ashley (Summer '66-fall '70), Arnie Lippen (spring '66-end '68), Mary Benson (? – end '69), Maurice Blanc ('67-end '69), Andrea Woodner (fall '67-fall '68), Irene Leherissier (September '68-beginning '72), Mabel Dennison ('67 (?)-beginning '69). The dates are approximate.

I shall give some particulars about these people, not because what they were like individually mattered much to the shows, but to indicate how Schumann got his work force and how its nature changed. Schumann went his own way and the shows expressed him and his development, not only because *he* made the molds for the masks and masked the performers, but also because their individuality, with the kind of performing he got out of them didn't make much difference. It is probable that the over-all air and character of the shows changed with the over-all character of the labor force, but though this might have to some slight extent fucked him up a bit now and then – as though where a painter just can't get the right kind of pigment for a while for some reason, can't afford it, or there is some scarcity – by and large it probably fitted in with his own artistic development, the nature of the recruits attracted not being fortuitous relative to this. It must be remembered though that though the core group would pretty much do the work on the puppets and on the children's and indoor adult shows (which on the whole until the end of the '60s had small casts), the help of irregular ancillaries – friends, lovers, family, acquaintances – and of recruited volunteers for the bigger street parades (which with the one of November 11, '65 grew very big) was essential. The core-group is not the whole picture.

Bob Nichols[20] was from the spring of '64 until the spring of '68 some-

---

20. Bob Nichols, a Village personality, landscape architect with a particular interest in children's playgrounds, writer and poet, pacifist and anarchist, was the founder in the fall of '61, of the Judson Poets' Theatre, and for about a year its director (then displaced by

thing of a collaborator and promoter of Schumann's. He had seen Schumann's *Totentanz* in '62, went to see his '63 (I think) *Christmas Story* in Brooklyn, loved it, wrote a review of it for the *Voice* that the *Voice* rejected, but that the *Tulane Drama Review* later (in 1970) published, and probably was in his '64 Easter show. I have no record of his having been active with the group much after the spring of '68, but as long as he was in New York (he settled in Vermont with Grace Paley) he saw all of Schumann's shows there, and like George Ashley and George and Mabel Dennison, has been going up to more or less all of Schumann's Glover, Vermont circuses.

---

the vulgarisers Kornfeld and Carmines), at that time was the husband of Mary Perrot Nichols, the editor of the *Village Voice*, and a proponent of street theatre (cf. Appendix VIII.)

When in June '64 he did a street version of *Everyman* (production managers: Grace Paley, his wife later, active in the Village Peace Center, Jules Rabin, a long-time supporter of Schumann's) Schumann provided masks and a chorus of 'creatures':

'New Group Planning Plays in the Streets. A new theatre group has been formed under the auspices of the Judson Poets' Theatre and the Greenwich Village Peace Center to perform plays in the streets of the village from the back of a truck. The group's first production planned for June will be Robert Nichols' modernized version of "Everyman." The story was originally commissioned by Julian Beck and Judith Malina of the Living Theatre. Masks and chorus for the play will be provided by Peter Schumann's Bread and Puppet Museum. Casting try-outs will be held on Saturday, Sunday and Monday evenings at Peace Center, 224 W 4th Street.' — (*Village Voice* notice, May 7, 1964.)

'At 3:45 on a hot Sunday afternoon a tiny, bright procession winds around Washington Square. It consists of four men, naked to the waist, wearing huge masks painted to represent animals and insects. One man beats a drum, another is blowing a horn, a third carries a pair of cymbals. They hold a sign which advertises "Everyman, a Street Play presented by the Peace Center," and by the time they have marched twice around the Square their gay and rackety music has drawn perhaps 50 people away from the folk-singing mob at the fountain. Beating the drum and blowing the horn, the musicians lead their audience to a truck parked on Thompson Street across from Judson Church, where a crowd has already gathered. The audience moves close to the truck, the players step out in their street clothes to be introduced and the play begins.

It opens, of course, with a drum roll. Then God, wearing a big gold mask with an enormous mouth, comes out and tells the audience what they are about to see ... God summons Death, who wears a black cloak with a stylized skull on his head and tells him to fetch Everyman....' — (Kempton, 'Everyman in Scary City,' *Village Voice*, July 2 '64.)

Nichols was associated with the Bread and Puppet Theatre *Digging for the Poverty Program* and *Flower Mountain* of May-July '65 – cf. infra – and worked with them in Harlem in the summer of '65, reviewed (*Village Voice*, February 17, '66) from *Fire*, managed the theatre-poetry part of the January-February '67 Week of the Angry Arts Against the War in Vietnam, introducing the Bread and Puppet *Wounds of Vietnam* into his contribution to it at the Washington Square Methodist Church, and probably helped them get their *Bach Cantata #140* on, and his contribution to the '68 Angry Arts Week, *Peasant Life*, was done together with Schumann's which was that year's version of the *Crucifixion*. He had himself performed in the '66 *Crucifixion*, and in other *Crucifixions* and/or *Christmas Stories* of Schumann's.

'Bob Nichols used to be in the Crucifixion shows. He has a way of using his body that was extraordinary, and also if he had to speak, for example, in the *Christmas Story* he would

I don't know just when the Schumanns got acquainted with the Rabins, but they probably got acquainted — the Oyles were friends of the group, the Rabins friends of the Schumanns — in late '64 or early '65: to judge by Rabin's coverage of Schumann's '65 peace demonstrations in his *Vietnam: Theory and Theater* (*Liberation*, March 1966), and Rabin is still 'Schumann's intellectual friend.' He is an anthropologist of sorts, and an academician — was, then on the Goddard College faculty, one of the people getting Schumann his resident artist position there in early '70. Helen Rabin, then pregnant, did Mary in Schumann's '63 *Christmas Story*, in December '71 she was in Elka's first theatre group. Jules Rabin was among the paid volunteers in the '66 parks project, one of the demonstrators (the Oyles were among them also) in his December '66 demonstrations at St. Patrick's Cathedral. I mention him here because of his close relation with Schumann and reputed influence on his political ideas: he apparently never worked with the group very much, properly is not a 'regular' or core-group member.

Catherine Merrill was among the more important of the new accessions, a central figure, star in *Leaf*, by November '65. She seems to have had a gift for delicate, subdued movement particularly adapted to the poetic mood of *Leaf* and the new kind of big puppet used in it, and a nice singing voice, a high soprano, but she didn't last. She was out before the summer of '66.[21]

Helen Hunter Palmer had taken her two-year-old son to the '64 *Christmas Story*, had loved it, had made friends with Elka, had helped her

---

do the genealogy. He was a beautiful speaker. I would listen a lot to the way he would send his voice and his spirit out. A lot of people, they would get very awkward. They wouldn't even know how to walk across the stage. And Bob had a way of, well, he looked like he had a reason for coming out. But it was a natural reason, it wasn't a contrived reason. And it was like, you could feel in his body, "I'm going to tell you something." Not in a grown-up talking down to a child, but like a story-teller, "there's something I have to say." And it was very natural and beautiful.' — (Sherman, interview.)

21. 'She was, there are some women that are like Circe in a way. They just draw you in by keeping you out.... She was like that. You'd go crazy with passion for her. Like we had an affair briefly. That was before I went to California. So I was a single guy. I was having lots of affairs and knew lots of girls. But Catherine had this magnetic quality and she would just draw you in and make love enough so you couldn't stand to be away from her and then she'd just turn it off. She was dangerous. She wasn't even that pretty. But she had this incredible animal magnetism, sexuality, that like I said, now that I think of it, was reflected in the intensity of some of the shows that were going around at that time. But this pressure that she had. It was really extraordinary. Because she wasn't that special in many ways and when you think back on it.... She was fairly good looking and all that, but it was just something about her that you just had to be in bed with her constantly. She would just let it out enough so it was just like a taste. She'd drive you nuts, essentially. She's one of those women that just drives you completely nuts, just because of the way she is. She couldn't help it. And to tell you the truth, I don't think she meant to. She really didn't mean to. She was a nice girl.' — (Ernstthal, interview.)

sew puppet robes. She was supporting herself and her child as a dress designer and seamstress while taking psychology in graduate school). She started performing when she replaced one Kathy Solomon, briefly a member of the group, in *Fire*, early in '66.[22] She left – in December '67 – because, she felt (Palmer, interview) the group's work was becoming less political, more just theatre, later became a psychic. I suppose she meant not that the theatre pieces were becoming less political, but that the theatre was not demonstrating on the streets as much as earlier. This was true.[23]

Andy – 'who was a suicide, interesting man, a Dutch Jew, who never quite recovered from his early situation' (Palmer, interview), and Amy Trompetter – 'again (like Mary Kelly (SSB)) a very straight, genteel kind of girl, Amy. Very genteel. And Andy had made some films and was a little bit wilder' (Ernstthal, inverview) – were in the group by the time of the '66 Easter show. They hung in there until the end of that Maine summer of '68, had liked the country – 'during that summer finally got the idea to start their own theatre and were invited by the city of Portland to run a children's theatre' (Sherman, interview), started the Blackbird Theater – a puppet theatre, more or less, I believe. They lived until '74 in the house the group had stayed in, but, like so many others, they worked again, repeatedly, with the group during the following years, e.g. were working at Cate Farm (Schumann then was away on his third tour to Europe) in the winter of '71/'72. Amy worked with Schumann on the sculpturing project (*Masaccio*) in Florence, Italy, in '76, performed in his *Washerwoman Nativity* in '82 . . . .[24] There is a memorial for Andy, dead at age 37, in the Glover farm pinewoods, a puppet in his likeness, with a blackbird on its forearm.

Unlike some of these ladies, Margo Lee Sherman who the year before had dropped out of Sarah Lawrence when a theatre instructor, Wilford Leach, whom she much admired, discontent with the students, stopped teaching there and had become diffusively active in the Village art scene,

---

22. 'She was a modern dancer and also trained as psychologist . . . . And so, when she acted, it looked like modern dancing. And that had such a strong style that it didn't quite jibe with a lot of the Bread and Puppet things. But when it did jibe, it was marvellous. When she did the White Lady in *Dead Man Rises*, it was gorgeous. Nobody else could do it so smoothly . . . in that way, which required a great deal of control. So that's where her modern dance training was fabulous.' — (Sherman, interview).

23. 'The people who had stronger personalities had a harder time with Peter . . . someone like Helen, who had a very strong personality. She had an argument at Christmastime, and that's when she left . . . at Washington Methodist Church. She just got angry . . . at Peter and walked out. I think she wanted to play more parts in the show, she wanted to do more acting, and he wasn't giving her more acting because she wasn't really good at it.' — (Sherman, interview.)

24. 'I really don't see myself working with Peter in a regular way. Because most of the puppeteers are just sort of like this – Amy Trompetter being the exception – they are sort of Peter junkies. Anything Peter says goes. I don't want to become – I don't want to give over my soul to anyone, really.' — (Leherrissier, interview.)

tried to stay out of the onerous physical work of the group, making up for it after a while by taking over from Elka much of the clerical work. She was chiefly interested in acting[25] and got her way, becoming[26] one of the company's two bareface actors – Maurice Blanc being the other one – and the only star the company has ever had.

She and Sainer had arranged for the Bread and Puppet '65 Bridge productions and she entered the group at the suggestion of Merrill whom she replaced as the group's focal cunt (cf. II. 6). She was a performer in Schumann's March 26, '66 Fifth Avenue parade demonstration, then working on the puppets for the '66 Easter show and performing in that show.[27] She left at the end of the second European tour, in December '69,[28] for a life as gardening wife in a commune (the New Hamburger

---

25. 'I discovered one day while I was acting in *Fire* (Winter '67/'68(SSB)) that my face behind the mask was moving a lot. And it was only then that I realized I was acting. I never realized I was acting.' — (Sherman, interview.)

26. 'And I was the star, the lead, Chicken Little (in *Chicken Little*, summer of '67 (SSB)). And not only that, I had to take off my mask. I was rehearsing without the mask because it was hot and sweaty in New York, and they said, oh, oh, that's good, you have to leave the mask off. And this was really terrifying, to have my face naked.' — (Sherman, interview.)

When Schumann, '66, '67, got into mime work, she was one of his mainstays.

27. 'And I became friends with Catherine Merrill. And she was talking about Peter all the time. And I respected her and she was working with the Puppet Theatre and she was doing pottery. And I said to myself, maybe I should do one of those two things, I mean work with the Puppet Theatre or do pottery. And she said, Peter needs you, join the Puppet Theatre. So I did. (I: Why did you drop out of college?) Because I was passionately interested in the theatre. I was living in the city with Arthur and I would commute up to school. And school wasn't that interesting to me. My teacher there, whom I worshipped, had stopped directing plays. Wilford Leach. He's directing now, but at that time, he stopped directing at schools because he got so fed up with the students . . . . And I was so involved with Arthur and his life and his work, and I knew that the people up at school didn't like his work, and I directed some of his plays up there, and I wasn't getting support from them. I wanted to be in the city, working, involved in the city . . . . Actually, before I joined, like a week before I joined, there was one of those Fifth Avenue parades against the war. So I participated in that . . . . Okay, so then, I called up . . . to join . . . . "Okay, come down and do celastics." So I went to Delancey street and they were building some new demon masks for the *Crucifixion* show that was coming up in a couple of weeks – maybe a week, I think it was just a week. And I immediately met Andy Trompetter, who must have joined the same day or the same week that I did . . . . I remember very much doing celastic with Andy and other people, but I had immediate contact with him because he was funny. So we sat in this little place on Delancey Street, with the windows open so we'd have a little ventilation – fumes, and for a week we did celastic, demon masks, and then after a week rehearsals began at Spencer church in Brooklyn Heights. And I met the other people. We'd go there, I can't remember how often, every day, and we would rehearse. And I felt like I understood it all, entirely, from even the beginning, instinctively. I just knew exactly what he was talking about. And I felt so in love with it, but not blind in love, just – I know it, I know what it's all about. And I understood how to act in it, how to perform. And he immediately began asking me to do acting things.' — (Sherman, interview.)

28. '(I: And why?) Well, as I say, I don't like touring, so – I didn't have a very good time

Commune near Plainfield, Vermont), but was back in for a tour with a sub-group to Iran by the fall of '70, and with the main group by the spring of '71, and has been in and out since then, one of the ancillaries, but a privileged one, getting to pick what she does. She is not a good actress. Doing male parts in a mask (the first one perhaps as Hungry Young Man in a skit in the summer of '66, a mime part), which Schumann has liked to have her do – she was Christ in the '72 *Stations* – she is not too bad.

George Ashley got caught up in Schumann's puppeteering during their *Chicken Little* parks project in the summer of '66. Of a good Chicago family, he had worked his way up to an executive position chez Hertz, matching numbers – not astonishingly, he soon found himself doing administrative work at the Bread and Puppet too. But he performed with them whenever he could – quitting auto rentals soon after, I believe, to commence a sluggish career as outside administrative assistant to the performance avant-garde. A gentle, well-meaning, very charming man, altogether devoted to the art of others, a maker of postcards, and a very good – beloved – friend of mine. After the company left New York, he was no longer able to work with them, but for a while, until perhaps the summer of '70, he would go up there weekends to work on projects, and

---

on the tour – and I felt that my work wasn't growing because I wanted more and more to do acting (I: As distinct from –?) Puppetry or mime work. Mostly I did mime work in the Puppet Theatre. And I wanted to do acting – plays – words – but I didn't have all of that – although I studied acting – I didn't have all of that armor of protection that would get me to go to a – open audition or shit like that – I felt – so I couldn't – and as I hadn't found a way into it in Europe – and I had also done some writing – poetry – and I had a boyfriend – I thought maybe I can live a very quiet life something I've never had before – a family life – a husband – and stuff like that – and I didn't want to live in New York because I had been raped – (I: What did Schumann say about your leaving?) I don't remember Peter saying – I don't remember what he said. I certainly remember what Elka said (laugh): "And you'll come crawling back!" She just said it like that – was out of control. It was like – the only time that she ever let her – It was the only time that she let her hostility about the fact that several years before I had slept with her husband – that was the only time that she let it out.' (Sherman, interview.) She had been sleeping with him on that tour, fortunately, as she put it, without being in love with him. He at this particular time, wanted to get rid of actors in his company.

'(I: You like Margo's acting – you use her a lot . . . . But how do you like it? What quality is it that –) Well, I like her very, slender, elongated limbs on her body and the movements she was able to do, especially when she was very slow. And I had a very – and I always had an actress in the theatre who could work with masks. And she could do that. She was very able to put on a mask and do that. But, naturally, what an actress does in our theatre isn't *acting* and is so *limited* in the terms of a modern actress and all the ambitions of such people that both these – usually these characters dropped out of the theatre at some point – including Margo, Irene, and whoever. They just – they wanted to do things that I felt they couldn't do, like voice and acting; that's *where our interests part*, and that kind of acting I dislike and can't do anything with so that's – no, for me, these – several of these female big parts that we had from *Fire* on, I think – from the show *Fire* on all the time in the theatre . . . .' — (Schumann, interview, '82.)

he went on a tour to Iran on which Schumann was not along in the fall of '70.

Arnie Lippen entered the group with that same '66 parks project,[29] wasn't invited on the '68 spring tour, didn't join the '68 Maine summer commune, but again showed up at the Courthouse that winter, bringing along Mary Benson Lippen. Mary had been married to him until '65 when they had divorced, and Arnie had joined the '66 parks project with a girl friend, but by '68 they were together again, and she was soon working 'full time.' She started 'working evenings during December' and then 'just started in January. I had another job at that time. So then it started full time. Usually from 9 in the morning till around 10 at night.' (Mary Benson, interview.) They both went on the '69 tour.[30]

Schumann ('we') 'learned to know' Maurice Blanc on the occasion of the February '67 Week of the Angry Arts at Washington Square Methodist Church. He first performed in the Bread and Puppet Theatre in the '67 Thanksgiving show and then in the '69 *Christmas Story*, was one of the five people Schumann invited on his first tour to Europe in the spring of '68 and he was along on the second in '69 as well, but that was it: Schumann loved him well enough, but at that moment wanted no more actors. Or perhaps Maurice – he is dead – did not want to leave New York, or, like Margo then, figured he wasn't 'growing' as an actor with the group. He was an amateur painter and an actor and worked for Schumann as actor. He died in '82 or so and left Schumann some $36.000 in his will.[31] His ashes are kept on the grounds of Dopp Farm in Glover and there is a memorial to him in the pine forest there.

Irene Leherrissier, first introduced in September '67 by a friend of hers,

---

29. 'And the fellow who was so strong who married the very beautiful woman – short and wiry man who now teaches out in Brooklyn and he married the exquisitely beautiful woman with blonde hair – thick blonde hair. Arnie Lippen was a powerhouse. He was everywhere – he had more energy than anybody I'd ever seen. He could climb up on top of anything – it was totally amazing, the amount of energy he had, the physical strength and agility that he had. Climb, crawl, hang, perch.' — (Ashley, interview.)

30. '(I: Winter of 1968, you did these three plays around New England and New York City.) New York State, also, mostly New England. Oh, Arnie Lippen was there also. You should talk with Arnie. He lives in Brooklyn. He's a good guy, and his wife Mary joined us for that tour but then after the tour left the tour. But he hadn't worked with Peter in quite a while. Arnie was in charge of the technical stuff. He's a very good guy. His wife is slightly wacko, but she's trying to get her act together. Yes, Arnie was there then, too. Arnie would always drive a truck or something. Very reliable guy. Peter really needed reliable people. There was a lot, really, to get done.' — (Leherrissier, interview.)

'But I remember there was a lot of costuming stuff. And that's something that I – sort of pulling together costuming stuff and neatening it up. I remember being involved in that. And I still get involved in that when I see him. I'm only beginning to let go of the idea that it has to be neatened up. So I guess there was some feeling like I was taking care of the raggedy edges ...' — (Mary Lippen, interview.)

31. Elka (Letter of September 10, 1984) thinks it worthwhile to specify that 'Maurice's money (was) left to Peter and me, and in case of our deaths, to our children, for 'continuing

Andrea Woodner, who was doing a Bennington work project at the Courthouse (never a core-group member, Woodner turned up again for a summer's communal living with the group in Maine, in '68 – Ernstthal admired her wealthy father's two-story balconied living room), a beautiful person, a '60s flowerchild, a manic-depressive (but not too much so not in the meantime to have gotten an M.A. in anthropology and started her doctoral program), into acting, also wanted to be an actress but neither with the motivation of vanity of the ordinary actor nor with the hard dry ambition of certain actors, an excellent actress, however, the first of the two good ones I have known in the group (the other being, later, Barbara Leber, who, however, may be a better mime than actress). She entered the group effectively only in December '68, when many new people did. Getting involved, on behalf of a lover, in the factional infighting in the group during the '69 tour, she left it, in October '69, before its end, but rejoined soon after, joining its Coney Island contingent in March '70, was in and out, a fairly important performer, carrying on an intense and violent competition with Sherman for choice parts, until the end of the European tour of December '71/February '72. Her father was a conservative gunsmith, an artisan, Margo's a kind of show biz worker – automobile shows for General Motors: unlike the fathers of some of the gentler ladies, not rich either one, so the daughters were, for good or bad, more real.

The first appearance of Mabel Chrystie's – a trust fund heiress during the '60s doing educational work with difficult children on the Lower East Side – her 1st Street School has been described by her later husband, George Dennison – with the Bread and Puppet Theatre that I have heard of was in the '68 Easter show, in which she did 'Mary part' in alternation with Margo Sherman. But I think she was around the group earlier. She has never properly been of it, but has been a steady moral and financial supporter, e.g. bought them the $5000 house in Maine they stayed in in '68, and at least during the winter '68/'69 worked on the puppets fairly steadily.[32] George Dennison's article on *Fire* in the *Voice* was vital in gaining Schumann the degree of recognition he achieved in New York. The Dennisons also have been among the annual pilgrims to the Glover, Vermont circus.

---

the work of the B & P . . . We gave half of it to the B & P, divided (the) remainder into five funds for (our) children's education, which they are using up now. Savings on our salaries (are) impossible.'

32. 'And Mabel Dennison was coming around all the time then. She would like just come over at night and help build puppets or something. I am very fond of Mabel. She's just a real nice person to talk to – she later didn't come so much but she was always very – like she would invite us, if we had worked hard on a rehearsal she would say, please come over for dinner and she'd have all 16 of us over for dinner or something, just this magnanimous kind of generous person. In the fall of '68 Mabel was coming almost every day. There were kids' workshops in the afternoon'. — (Leherrissier, interview.)

Schumann's view of his labor force up to this point, the spring of '68:

'In New York I had a scattered crew who came to rehearsals and then disbanded again. Basically, I worked solo with help.'
(Schumann in an interview with Margarita Barab, Country Journal, Plainfield, Vermont, July 18, '74.)

The third Bread and Puppet core-group generation, the second generation of recruits, essentially the original core-group during the earlier Vermont years, or from the beginning of '70 onward, arrived in three waves: joining the Bread and Puppet commune in Strong, Maine in the summer of '68 (Michael Appleby, Murray Levy, Sara Peattie, Darryl Henriquez), joining the work programs at the Courthouse, November '68-March '69 (Eric Berne, Bill Dalrymple, George Konnoff – less importantly, German Mouré, from Colombia, Uwe Krieger from Berlin, Deborah Knight, Michael Appleby's new girlfriend, Manny Narciza),[33] joining the Europe

---

[33].'And then more and more people dropped in. Eric Berne came from California. (I: This was all in the winter of 1968? Before the tour to Europe?) Okay, so I'd say like in January of 1969, all these people appeared – Sara Peattie came from Boston, Michael Appleby, Debbie Knight came from Boston – she was Michael's girlfriend . . . . (I: Can I ask you one question? Why did all these people appear in 1969?) Well, because we were going on this European thing, and he needed these people to play in <i>The Cry</i> – he had to make up <i>The Cry</i>. (I: The idea being that at all times various people might show up or not but then this was a time for trying to get them to be members of the group.) He didn't want a big group unless he was going on a trip, but he had these jobs lined up, and his agent at the time, Gans – Berger – Ginsberger, really – and Ginsberger had all these jobs and Peter wanted to do the show, so he needed these people to be in it. So he got people that he knew or had met previously. At some point they all started coming and living in the Courthouse. There was this guy, Uwe Krieger, who became my boyfriend – he sort of fell into the theatre. He was invited on the tour, and this guy Manny Narciza came, and Murray was there, of course, and Mabel Dennison was coming around all the time then. So, anyway, all these people finally arrived from all these places here and there – basically, Peter needed a big group to crawl around in beasts and to be the people molding each other, Adam and Eve and all this other stuff. So Margo had a wonderful part and I got a really nice part – I was really pleased with the part I got . . . Eric (Berne) had been acting with the San Francisco Mime Troupe . . . .' — (Leherissier, interview.)

'It was a cross-section. There were some older people, not kids – Appleby, Michael Appleby and the woman who later became his wife and Carol Grosberg, who was very political in those days – it was a young, but mature group, I think. It wasn't kids – it wasn't what I see in Vermont now, very young kids. These were people who knew the streets a little bit more.' — (Levy, interview.)

'(I: So you were planning the tour and working on it?) And rehearsing. It was a very exciting time because it was very organized. The other days were terribly exciting and not organized. And this was just exciting in the sense of every day rehearsing from 10 to 1, a lunch break, and rehearsing again from 2 to 6. That can be thrilling too, that routine. And you know that the whole thing is going towards building a great big show, and taking it on a big tour of Europe. So there was quite a good spirit in the group, and there were a lot of people working. Whereas before there was like an inner core, and other people coming and going, this was a large group that felt, we're all part of this together. Carol Grosberg was there, Sara Peattie, who was only a 16-year-old.' — (Sherman, interview.)

tour of '69, and then the March-June '70 Coney Island contingent and/or Bill Dalrymple's overlapping tour of the Southeast (Axel Gros, a German, Carlene Fernandez, Susan Bettmann, Harvey Spevak (who had, however, previously been in the '68 *Crucifixion*), Bill Whelan – and, less importantly: Pascal Ortega, Brigitte Lane, Claude Roche, Anique Detolle, Tanith Noble, all of them French, Bart Lane, Arthur Bernstein.

This second wave of recruits arrive in the context of the revolutionary atmosphere of '68-'69 and early '70 and of Schumann's attainment of international stature, some of them European students, many of them, and this perhaps defines this recruitment overall, New Left and/or Resistance Movement youngsters. It was by no means a bunch of revolutionaries, but still, rather than liberals they were radicals – although not anarchists or Communists, nor even necessarily politically minded – and arriving in this now very large group – an important factor: it had grown from a small, intimate group of six to nine to a large one of a dozen and a half to two dozen people – and a group that had a commune character – in Maine, on the '69 tour, on Coney Island, on Dalrymple's tour of southeastern campuses, they tended to perceive the work as significant contribution, potentially, to a reform of society. The operative self-definition of the group (its nature as far as the members were concerned, thence its aura) was no longer in terms of participation in a Peace Movement or of the achievement of exquisite theatre: the idea of what it was doing was now: hard practical work in the cause of a rejuvenation of society in terms of radical ideals, by a perception of real influence the work might have, and the theatre was conceived as a living commune, relating to Schumann as pater familias and inspirational guide. The reason for the growth in the group's size June '68 to June '70 was at first that Schumann wanted to do a big spectacle with a big cast on his next tour to Europe, and was able to get it due to his European fame, his name in the Peace Movement, and his artistic achievements in theatres and in peace parades. Then during the '69 tour, additional people joined up in an, during those times, uncontrollable manner, or came over after.

When he came back to New York from that tour, he was fed up with having a big company, with its arguments and demands and communal living style, – and also in particular wanted to get rid of actors – and as means for ridding himself of it utilized a tour, under a lieutenant, Bill Dalrymple, to the south Atlantic states in the spring of '70, the installation, in June, of a separate Bread and Puppet group in Coney Island and a tour under another lieutenant, George Konnoff, in the fall of '70 to California.[34] He himself, with his family went up to the farm, Cate Farm

---

34. 'The whole situation with Coney Island was that Bill (Dalrymple) came back with a ton of people and there was no work for them there, basically, and Peter was leaving, so we had a great mass of sort of socially interested young performers.' — (Konnoff, interview.)

Goddard College in Plainfield, Vt. was putting at his disposal, and invited only two people to join him there: Harvey Spevak, a musician who had been in the '68 *Crucifixion* and on the '69 tour, and Bill Dalrymple, two people he got along with and needed. This strategem in fact for a moment worked pretty well, he got down to a very small group on the farm, that could more or less be provided for on the basis of arrangements with Goddard and of a vegetable garden.

But the number of resident puppeteers soon started growing again. There were some two dozen people there, working on the circus show, during the summer of '71, eight or ten of them living on Cate Farm.[35] By the fall of '71, because of the tour of *Birdcatcher* in New York State, there

---

'No, there was no offer (by Schumann, to the participants in Konnoff's western tour (SSB)) to come back. See, that was a strange time, too, that Peter was really *offering* to run the company the way it was in New York because they'd have to *live* at the farm and that was not explored yet, and he invited a *few* people back, so it did leave a lot of people who ... because the company had grown sort of out of his hands anyhow. Bill's company wound up staying in Coney Island, were never *encouraged* to be a part of the *company* because it never – you know, couldn't offer them any likely *livelihood*, didn't have enough work, so, yes, a few people went back and by that time Peter had gotten some nasty letters about the tour from different people. And that was – I don't know what. We never talked about it a lot. He was *worried*, and – worried about getting his *puppets* back, too. He really didn't – well, not that he didn't know what was going on, but if you know, it definitely – things weren't going on as planned ... so, I decided not to go back or – he offered to let me keep *Fire* and perform it, and I decided not to go back. Maybe I thought I was going to get spanked, I don't know. I had hepatitis by the way. But, Pascal took the puppets back, and I kept the bus.' — (Konnoff, interview.)

35. '(I: About how many people would you say were in Plainfield?) 25. (I: A lot of people.) Yes, and there were already problems with – okay, so Elka had made this garden, and we were eating her garden out of house and home, you know. She didn't have any food left, practically, but okay. And also we really weren't eating that well. We really didn't have that much money then at all, so we were eating a lot of vegetables and practically no protein. When I think about it, it's amazing we really didn't get sick. People did start getting sick after a while. (I: How long did that last?) We might have been there a month or more. Five weeks. July, into early August. People started getting sick because we weren't washing the dishes. Something was wrong. Also people started getting bored. Very bored. For me that was one of Peter's low ebbs. (I: For him too, perhaps, you think?) Probably not. He liked it. He thought it was real funny. He loves all these tongue in cheek things ....' — (Leherissier, interview.)

'(I: Who was in the group?) There were the people who had moved up to Cate Farm. Sue Bettmann. Sara Peattie. There were the few students from Goddard College who joined the puppet theatre, like Pamela MacDonald and Avram Patt, Nick Williams, Mark Dannenhauer. There were people who joined us who were not from Goddard. Very few Goddard people ever ... (I: How many people would you say were living at Cate Farm?) Maybe eight or ten. See, some of the people didn't live on Cate Farm, but they were full-time members, like Pamela, she lived with her mother two miles away. Paul Zaloom had his own little house, and was living with some other people a few miles away. He didn't work with us that summer, but he began working with us in the fall. I don't think it was overcrowded. There was a chicken coop. George Konnoff, Sara Peattie. And then, of course, there were other people, whose names I can't remember, and would just turn up.' — (Sherman, interview.)

were around 20 resident puppeteers, and he took about a dozen and a half puppeteers to Europe with *Birdcatcher* December '71-February '72, almost all of these were Goddard recruits (Sherman, interview), a quite distinct third generation of recruits (cf. infra), with the survivors of the preceding one forming the core group of the early Vermont years, a fourth core group generation. By the end of '72, he was touring *Simple Light* with around 18 people again. This second inflation partly had the same reason as the first one, he was doing pieces with large casts (his '71 circus and *Birdcatcher*, but then especially his '72 *Simple Light*)[36] — and doing huge spectacles had really been his basic intention ever since his German days — but also had another reason: when he went to Goddard in June '70 he had hoped to be able to work largely with volunteer labor recruited from among the Goddard undergraduates by means of workshops and puppetry projects, but this, for several reasons, didn't fully work out (cf. infra V).

Still, by and large the labor picture '70--74 was: an initially small but soon growing and finally sizable resident work force, partly a core-group of New York survivors and Goddard recruits, partly hangers-on, but all of them really working pretty hard most of the time — out there in the sticks there really wasn't much else to do[37] — sustained by a vegetable garden and — rather than by Goddard food chits — by touring income, and a student body labor pool utilized by workshops and puppetry projects. On college tours, sometimes without Schumann, led by a lieutenant, local students were often recruited for prepared performances, rehearsed on the spot. It was desired of Schumann that he be a guru but he had his own problems.

Murray Levy, after a time with the Free Southern Theatre left it when King was killed, the squeeze against whites in that theatre being already strong by then anyhow, went to Berlin where he had heard things were happening on the Left, organized a welcoming committee with a red flag for Schumann, when on his '68 tour Schumann arrived there, hung around, felt welcome, liked *A Man*, followed Schumann back to the U.S., became a member of the group in Maine in June '68,[38] threw himself into

---

36. 'The tour with *Birdcatcher* and the *Grey Lady* (December '71-February '72 (SBB)) was a pretty big tour. There were a lot of Goddard students on that tour and I think it was after that tour also, first of all, that a lot of people left and then that, you know, probably the group built up more members by the time *Simple Light* came along, and that was another big show, and it also had Goddard students. And there were people who left after *Simple Light*.' — (Fernandez, interview.)

37. 'It was a place where we (Ashley came up to work weekends in '70 (SSB)) were working uninterrupted by any need to do anything except work. (I: What was the nature of the group?) They were willing workers at the shrine.' — (Ashley, interview.)

38. 'I was working at the Free Southern Theatre '64 'til the middle of '68 and I heard that there was this street theatre doing great new things but I wasn't interested in that at that point, I was really interested in the civil rights movement and in making a contri-

cleansing orgy of work there that summer,[39] replacing Ernstthal as Schumann's #1 hard-working man. His sympathies on the radical left, and, himself soft, attracted to the tough-acting, he made friends in the winter '68/'69 with the Motherfuckers who cost Schumann the Courthouse, pretty much stayed out of the factional fights during the '69 Europe tour, arrived back in the U.S. felt the boss had lost interest in him,

---

bution to that in fighting that war. So I didn't look him up or anything, but then, when Martin Luther King died, I left and the business was happening in Germany in '68, the – with the students – that excited me and . . . it seemed to be vital, strong and where the change was happening. So I went there alone. That June while I was in Berlin I was having a little bit of problem with the authorities 'cause I was publishing a newspaper for the GIs, I was involved in trying to affect the Viet Nam war through work and so I met Peter, and then I heard while I was in this Berlin group, we were called the US Campaign Against the War in Viet Nam, and we were doing all kinds of things. We were raising money to send to the NLF through publishing a paper for the GIs, we were going to nightclubs with the GIs – would go and in a group in a car – and we would go into the club together and spread out and everybody would be at a different little place trying to talk to the people there. That was – seemed to me – I was finished with theatre then, I was thinking that the only thing that mattered was stopping this war and nothing else but, then I heard that this Peter Schumann was coming to Berlin – it was like June then – and so I — and so I organized a little group of – a little band and met him at the Berlin Bahnhof, at the Bahnhof – and when he came off the plane we were waving a really great red banner and making much music. It was fun and it was also heavy political greeting at the same time. And he received us very, very warmly. He was very touched by this welcome that we gave him and we had very, very wonderful rapport and there was only a few people there. There was Margo Sherman, there was Bruno Eckhardt and Bob Ernstthal and Charlie Adams and Maurice Blanc. There was only a few people there and they were only doing *Fire* and *A Man Says Goodbye to His Mother*. That was all that they were doing, maybe one more street show. And, when he was – they were in Berlin for about a week and we were together all the time and when he was leaving I said I loved what he was doing and I realized I was again hungry to do theatre. Every night I was with him. I helped with the setup, I was just kind of helping out and loving and seeing every show and being moved by it and thinking, My God, this is where I want to go, and I felt like a kid seeing the circus for the first time. Take me with you . . . I was crazy about *A Man Says Goodbye*, it was so tight, it was clear, it was so moving for me. In the midst of the work that I was doing it was really where it was at . . . So, I said I would love very much to work with you, so he says well then, come, we are going to Maine this summer and you can come and work together.' — (Murray Levy, interview.)

39. '. . . we started work on *The Cry of the People for Meat*, which became the great love of mine, I mean we did it then for a year after that . . . Maine was a lot of people, it was a very, very rural farm, it was northern Maine – Strong — near farming people. And it was in the backwoods there, and there was, well, wood burning fire and there were a lot of people. And I had a little tiny closet room where I slept. There was work, the work with Peter starts in the morning and it goes through, and then, when it was too hot we would take a break and go swimming and work at night, with car lights. Set up the cars and light the area so that we could see and I was crazy about him and – and there were people there who were upset that there wasn't more time taken for their personal problems, for their personal needs. They came more for therapy than they did to make theatre and so – but I didn't share their – at that point I didn't, anyway. I was too – too full of curiosity and excitement. I wanted to learn, I wanted to do it . . . There were nights when we were

keenly felt the lack of affection[40] – Bill Dalrymple had become the right-hand-man – did the part of Uncle Fatso in *Difficult Life*, decided to leave the group before it opened on Coney Island, left and started his own 'puppet' theatre, the Stomachache Theatre, did street theatre – which he felt the Bread and Puppet Theatre had pretty much stopped doing – with pieces of Schumann's (*King Story, A Man, Dead Man*) and with crankies of Bertolt Brecht poems. Like so many others, he couldn't stay away, in spite of each time feeling rejected,[41] kept at intervals rejoining, the first

working with these beasts when I wasn't in – when I would see it and I couldn't believe it. This bordered on something really medieval or whatever, you know – it just struck me as being one of the strongest visual experiences I had ever had. I didn't know what it meant, but I didn't care. I mean, like the Bob Dylan song: "Something is happening here and you don't know what it is, do you Mr. Jones" – or "Mrs. Jones?" But I was carried by the intensity and the effort. I thought – I worked myself to a frazzle – really, I just threw myself into it – I, through exhaustion, passed exhaustion to another state – it was a really strong work. It wasn't like in – like any other theatre I have ever done, which after a certain number of times people want a break. This was a blitz kind of working that I felt was cleansing in its – it was cleansing to me, 'cause I needed that at that point.' — (Murray Levy, interview.)

40. 'And I was unhappy then, I felt contact with Peter was zero. He didn't seem to be interested to talk about anything. (I: Did you think there was a change in your relationship?) Yes. I felt he was getting interested in other people. (I: Like who?) Nobody in particular, I mean, I just didn't think – I wasn't feeling slighted, I was just feeling that he lost interest. (What did you used to talk about?) We were always working, we were always doing a show – there's a communication when you're doing a show, and when we weren't doing the show we were building mostly and I felt frustrated. (I: This communication must have continued with the Brooklyn situation, the communication in terms of working together.) No, we weren't doing so many shows ... I was in Brooklyn for a few months and then I left ... It's not just – it's not even how much you say, it's a kind of recognition that somebody is there, which for some – his head was filled up, maybe with his plans to move, whatever his own personal shit is, he was getting that together, maybe. It was difficult for me so I figured it was time to go ... Bill became his number one man. So then – (I: How does that work, Murray, in a group? Number one and all that – changing one for the other – what is the idea, or what is the mechanism?) It's hard to describe. There are jobs to do. We call them jobs, we don't call them parts. They're jobs, because ego isn't involved, it isn't look at my face, look at my body, that's not what it's about, it's about doing a job, even – from baking bread to carrying a giant puppet, they're all part of the jobs, and for me, being asked to do a job was important at that point, because you just don't do the job, you've got to get asked with Peter. He asks you and you do it. So to that extent – for a long while he was asking me not to do all the jobs. I was baking bread and doing all kinds of things and then I wasn't doing it anymore, and I felt – (I: But you did Uncle Fatso – that was a major –) But it – yeah. It wasn't enough or something. Something was missing – something was making me unhappy.' — (Murray Levy, interview.)

41. 'I came back for another circus but I learned something there that was also – that also really upset me. (I: What was that?) This was four years ago, the first Glover circus ... I put *The Red Shoes* there – I started to work on it, rather. And we did it as a side show. It was about a 15 or 20 minute side show. And I asked Peter to come and look at it, and he didn't have time, but on the other hand I felt really lousy. (I: No, but one should have time for a thing like that.) I mean, that is what I mean ... and I was going to dance in the *Red*

time for the July '71 circus, after a violent blow-up during the October '71 New York State tour (Levy felt it was wrong for Schumann to be carrying on a love affair with the young French woman Tanith Noble (with the group from the spring of '70 until then) while leaving Elka at home as weeping 'Grey Lady', actually asks for a group vote on the matter) leaving again, but joining again in December for the third Europe tour, with more terrible arguments between him and Schumann, etc. through the '70s. I saw him doing the lights for a show in '82, grown obscenely fat. He was a hard worker and, as long as Schumann repressed his acting, a strong mime.

George Konnoff some time before September '68, when Schumann's pieces at Ronnie Davis' Radical Theatre Festival in San Francisco, and in particular Charlie Adams' drumming and Death (in *King Story*)[42] impressed him, had left Ronnie Davis' more cautious Mime Troupe for the Diggers and their provocative theatrical street activity, working – or playing – with the Free City Puppets, but in the fall of '68 felt speed and horse were cutting down too much on the work the Diggers were actually doing, the scene was deteriorating, and went to join the Bread and Puppet Theatre in New York.[43] He helped out on the preparation of *Cry*

Shoes, too, but then I got so unhappy with the lack of any kind of – at least look at it and criticize it, for God's sake, you're the master, so to speak. And he didn't, and so I dropped out – I didn't do any dancing and I got – I asked somebody else to dance, but I was going to dance . . . But then, interesting thing, when I went back to Europe – well, I went back with Peter.' — (Murray Levy, interview.)

42. 'Well, I was very impressed. There were – I don't know if I was that impressed with the *shows* at that point as even more with the performers. Charlie Adams really impressed me, the intensity of the performance and the commitment. And in Margo's, you know, and then Peter's performing – he did the Great Warrior in *King Story*. It was, you know, it was a whole weekend of shows and of course there was Teatro Campesino, which I have seen quite a bit and been around, and Mime Troupe was performing, and I just thought this whole new theatrical experience – in the political theatre I had been in before, like the minstrel shows and this and that, they would – they start a lot of verbal jokes and a lot of excessive talk, I mean I analyzed that later, and *Reiteration* had this structure and this movement, and they both to me seemed very *intense*, but it was very uncluttered and restful. You know, I could just get into absorbing those movements. And I think I saw that *Reiteration* probably, because they played it around five or six times. It was relevant to me politically and I thought it made a lot of sense theatrically. There was also that Peter was very friendly. You know, I'd never – for a while I hadn't been around any theatre people and they said, "Come in, sit down"; it wasn't quite the same with working with the most experienced semi- or halfway professionally or, you know, not academically – you know, in the Mime Troupe it was aggressive.' — (Konnoff, interview.)

43. 'George came in a very funny way. I remember one day we were upstairs in the Courthouse, it was a Saturday afternoon and all the puppeteers had left and I was there with Peter, and a ring came on the bell downstairs and we went to that big window to see who it was and there was this kind of blond-haired, long-haired hippie in white clothes and Peter and I looked out and he said "Hi, I've just come from California. I'm here to work with you." And Peter said to me, "Oh, yeah?" But there was George and he's like a

for Europe that winter, but, apparently sort of on probation, did not go to Europe with the group, fooled around the Courthouse while they were gone, went back to California for a couple of months, was back early in March '70 when the next piece, *Difficult Life* had already been worked up, performed in it, went off with a group joining Bill Dalrymple's tour in the southeast with a *Cry of the People* pageant version (dependent on the recruitment of local college students, a mode of labor procural that had informally worked on the '69 *Cry* tour, and later, notably in '72 and '73 when *Simple Light* was taken on tour was systematically and importantly employed) came back and worked with the Coney Island Bread and Puppet group, took it up to Toronto to do some festival shows, and then in the fall of '70 took these people — more or less the bulk of the Coney Island group — on a circus tour to California.[44] Largely because of the circus, a show Konnoff didn't feel on top of, the tour was a disaster,[45]

---

person in long standing now. I think Peter loves George in some very permanent way. I don't know. George is a very good guy. Very good guy. "Hi, I just came from California. I'm here to work with you." And Peter made it hard for him.' — (Leherrissier, interview.)
44. 'Well — we had eighteen plus people and really no place to go so part of the talking was that Peter okayed a tour to California that I had proposed, you know, as something that I would like to do. And through Goddard we had a food allowance (which helped to feed the group during circus rehearsals at Cate Farm in July-August (SSB)) and we made a little bit of money on this Toronto thing and we left to prepare for this tour, which turned out to be a *Resurrection Circus*, which at that point I hadn't thought about what it was going to be. I actually went up a little bit earlier to (Cate Farm) to start working on ideas with Peter while the company was still (on Coney Island.' — (Konnoff, interview.)
So at this point Konnoff was a lieutenant — one of two, the other being Dalrymple.
45. 'Well, one thing, one thing was the show was not under our belt enough, and I didn't feel, or felt *later* that I didn't have enough *handle* on it to be a sort of assistant director to keep it together or make changes or improve things, because I just was . . . I wasn't at ease with it. Plus, we were eighteen people in the school bus and we were ill-prepared for it. We were exhausted *already* from the *summer*, and all the personal problems and things like that became really difficult, when you are driving the long distances that we were driving, our work was spotty, and we had a *huge* amount of shows and the bus was really over-loaded and we had the circus tent — and then we had this.' — (Konnoff, interview.)
'And George managed the tour and Pascal Ortega was there and Hillary Rawlings, George's girlfriend who was this very woman's lib. Somewhere in Indio, California we blew a rod in the bus. We blew the rod in the desert and all this smoke came out and George's little boy was there and we left him in the bus in the hysteria of getting out of the bus and we had to run back and get the kid out of the bus, he was asleep, and then these guys offered to fix the engine if one of us hippie girls would sleep with his nephew. Cause he had never gotten a girl.
Well, Sara Peattie was there and she said very emphatically, "I don't know about this. I know what's right and I know what's wrong and this is wrong." She said no way should we be doing this. So then Hillary decided she would volunteer, and told all of us little bourgeois girls a lesson about we were whores inside of a private relationship anyway so what difference did it make really. Next thing we heard — this was at the time of the Manson murders — right at that time. The next thing we knew, we went to Pomona, the next thing we heard George . . . . They stayed behind so Hillary could turn the trick for was that Peter okayed a tour to California that I had proposed, you know, as something

he decided to discontinue it in California, in Kansas gave half the company notice effective on arrival, the group disbanded in California, and Konnoff, uneasy about the master's displeasure, took off for Spain. He was back (too late for the 'building' of the puppets) for *Birdcatcher* in May '71, the project, he thinks, for which the company (and the number of residents on Cate Farm) grew big again – by the fall of '71 (Konnoff had gone to Europe for the summer, returned for the tour of *Birdcatcher* and *Whitewashing* in New York State in October) about 20 people were living on Cate Farm. He stayed at the Farm – 'Actually got a space' – when Schumann took a group to Europe with *Birdcatcher* (December '71-February '72.), in the spring worked on a student 'puppet newspaper' project and the small shows growing out of it, in the summer was more or less in charge of the Coney Island projects, and stayed right on through until the theatre left Cate Farm in the fall of '74. He seems to have been the group's most used member during the Goddard years. The Western laid-backness that made him a good show narrator might have made him a good tour leader for a communitarian group, except that it was for real.

Carlene Fernandez saw the theatre in the spring of '70 in her native Florida – Dalrymple's tour of the southeast. A musician as much as anything – piano, the flute – she was teaching them at a private school and giving private lessons while going to the University of South Florida – she followed them, she was twenty at the time, up to Coney Island and joined, attracted by the art and the politics – 'what was being said about, you know, the war, and then of course the artistic aspect is what drew me into it, the lighting and sound and the visual thing. Like I was moved into another time and place which was very exciting. And I liked the people that I met and at one time they needed a little bit of extra help with the music so I helped them.' (Fernandez, interview.) She stayed at the theatre at first, then in Bart Lane's and Harvey Spevak's apartment in Manhattan, then 'we got an abandoned house in Coney Island that the city was going to tear down and many of us moved into that house.' (ibid.) 'My main job was music, taking care of instruments, playing . . .' (ibid.) Her first performing job was as Strong Man on a circus parade at the Bronx Zoo. In the fall she was briefly on Cate Farm, Schumann rehearsed her in *Fire*, she went on Konnoff's tour to California, left the disbanding group there, returned to Florida on the first of several returns home (often

---

For what?) They thought they were the Manson people. They had seen two men and a woman leaving the area and thought they were them. Hippies. Then they let them go when they found out they weren't but meantime Hillary didn't do it because George figured he didn't want his girlfriend sleeping with the nephew of the garage guy. (I: Narrow-minded bastard. So was the bus fixed?) Yes, we got the bus fixed, paid the money. And we did shows in Pomona and that was okay, but it wasn't too great. The shows weren't that terrific.' — (Leherrissier, interview.)

for health reasons), was back at Cate Farm in the spring of '71, started working on puppets – not yet on masks:

'I hadn't really broken into that part of the work where I felt comfortable just going in and working with masks. I did a lot of watching and that kind of thing. I did some minimal stuff, building dummies and more that kind of thing, working on and helping with costumes, dyeing fabric (for the many costumes of *Birdcatcher* (SSB)). (Fernandez, interview.)

She went back to Florida after the circus, in August, didn't return until October or November '72, did not go with the group on its tour of New York and New England with *Simple Light*, stayed behind and with Avram Patt, one of the Goddard recruits, took two plays to Washington University in St. Louis, by now herself one of the regulars. She left again – renewed appendix trouble – and returned a year later, in November or December '73, while the group was in Europe with *Simple Light*. At the end of the year she and Sara Peattie (a small round person, one of the best performers that Schumann has had in the area of masked movement between mime and dance, of delicate, simple and gentle grace, who had first shown up, 16 years old, Michael Appleby's then-girlfriend, brought by him, during the summer of '68 Maine retreat) did a small tour with *Christmas Story*. She had now become very good at celastic work, was one of the people doing exceptionally fine work with very small pieces of celastic worked directly on the clay. She stayed with the group till the spring of '76 – was the only puppeteer Schumann asked to accompany him from Cate Farm and Goddard up to his new base in Glover, Vermont, helped install the barn there – left at Elka's suggestion. Stayed in the area, went to study archeology in Burlington, Vermont.

Bill Dalrymple 'came by' (at the Courthouse in the winter of '68/'69, 'he was living at Columbia then, sort of hiding out' (Leherrissier, interview) – he was a draft evader, apparently actively sought by the F.B.I. during his tenure with the Bread and Puppet Theatre (I don't see how he could have managed). Leherrissier says of him that the 'became a director later': he got to run his own little tours, besides the big one to the southeast early in '70, and became someone Schumann was personally attached to, and Schumann's lieutenant. A charming man, he was in the entire history of the Bread and Puppet Theatre the only recruit to it to have genuine leadership ability and talents as stage director. He was killed in a car accident in France in '73.

Bill Whelan, a painter, had made some dragon heads for a Coney Island circus parade in the spring of '70, and during the next four years seems to have worked pretty steadily as mask maker for Schumann – he did not like to get involved in other activities – or with people – too much, but took on specific tasks mask-making and worked hard at them. He introduced two new celastic techniques for achieving fine results even though working directly over clay, small-piece and large-sheet working, and made some of the best masks the group ever came up with. He tried fiberglass:

'Marie Antoinette ... is part of the Bulbhead series ... A double chin, ugly monster lady ... the head must have been made built together with the other Bulbheads. It's the same style of work, and I'll bet I did them all in a row, because I had celastic workers. Very good – people who at that time had made an art out of that – how to use that celastic – and were extremely skillful. And these are made as if in a plaster cast but they're not. They're made directly over clay. (I: That's amazing...) It is. Because they have more detail than a lot of things that were made in plaster casts. So the people who were best at that, I think, were Bill Whelan – He was a puppeteer with us; very good was Carlene Fernandez; and Barbara Leber and then, later on Genevieve Yeuillaz. She did quite a bit of our good celastic work too. But I think the best ones were really Bill Whelan and Carlene. (I: What made them so good? What's the difference?) Their work? Any material – whether it's masonry or whatever it is – it takes more than just the knowledge of how to swing the hammer. You become sensitive to your material – that's what sculpting is all about – to be sensitive to clay – and some sculptors prefer clay to plaster and to wood and what have you – or stone to wood – you can do – you can understand the piece of sculpture that's made in clay as a celastic worker and then really get that piece of sculpture. Or you can muddle it up – make it wishy-washy – make it terrible – lose all of its characteristics in the process – you can misunderstand how the eye is built – you can misunderstand the identations around the nose – you can change the whole character of the mask by misunderstanding what's there in the clay. And these people had it. They looked at the thing – they saw it – and they could do the real thing. And I really – and I worked with them – we worked together on this. They did most of the work, but I came into it and helped them to see it and to get it.... So these people were really lovingly involved in really fine, delicate craftsmanship. The best we ever did with that material.' (Schumann, interview, December '82.)

'He paints and does etchings and drawings, very naturalistic, very nice landscapes and he seemed very unhappy in the bigger participation of the group and I think partly to find a job that he could do that would, although we'd give him something specific and not and kind of take him out of maybe rehearsals and tours and things. He was one of the volunteers when Peter would say, "Let's find another material besides celastic – Maybe fiberglass" and Bill, I remember, said, "I volunteer to research it and experiment with it and try it out", and he did that.' (Elka, interview.)

At the beginning of the '70s, then, the core of his group largely consisted of young rebels who had in their lives (not just in their minds) rejected the values, objectives and activities of middle class America, but had managed to avoid both of the extremes of this rebellion, hippiedom and political commitment, decided, but ultimately judicious risk-takers.

His next generation of recruits, '70/71, was different. Their values were not necessarily radically other than those of the late-'60s generation, but they were not rebels, they had not in fact rebelled, and their awareness had not been politicized. They and their predecessors might be for and against the same things, but whereas those gentle rebels had been importantly and often primarily against, they were importantly and primarily for.[46] To a large extent they were students at Goddard, probably among the more serious and idealistic ones. Some of the names: Pamela MacDonald, 'who had a marvellous voice' (Schuman, interview, August '82), and for a year or two (June '70-November '71) did some operatic singing for Schumann), Avram Patt (June '70-February '72), Chris Hartmann (June '70-September '71) (who had been with the Arissa Theater in California), Mark Dannenhauer, Paul Zaloom (October '71-mid '70s) son of the pistachio king of America (Ashley), a comedian, a mediocre one, who was good as an m.c. for the circus shows, and later struck out on his own, Marc Estrin, a musician, director of the Plainfield Community Chorus,[47] Larry Gordon, also a musician, director of the Word of Mouth

---

46. Ashley, speaking of the decrease of intensity and tightness in Schumann's work after he left New York, is tempted to attribute it to the changed character of the people working for him:
'I mean, the elegance, the form, the intricacy of the work that was done on *The Cry of the People for Meat* ('68-'69 (SSB)) for instance, which was so structured, so elegant, so powerful as a dance piece – just as dance – and pageant – he's never done anything quite like that since and I'm wondering if it's because he has different people to work with . . . none of the people that are with him now are crazy . . . . What he was in that first (period) was partly because through the contributions of Ernstthal and the young Margo and Michael Appleby and other people . . . all of them loonies – except Arnie (Lippen) (who was) very sane – but the rest of them were all pretty bonkers. (I: And you think that fed into the work and into him.) In energy – the fact that they could read a paper at 10 in the morning and have a little book out by 2 in the afternoon – would be drawn, reproduced and ready to be distributed – that kind of manic energy was there. Now they are very effective, they work very well, they use up their time, divide up responsibility, apportion details that have to be done and do them all. Everything is fine. Where is that passion? I don't know.' — (Ashley, interview.)
'I remember there were a lot of Goddard students and that was unusual and from the people who had worked in New York who had overlapped and were at Cate Farm there was a certain amount of tension with Peter now paying so much attention to the Goddard students (Pamela MacDonald, Avram Patt, Mark Dannenhauer were becoming members of the core-group (SSB)) and being so excited working with the students. And I think they felt slightly neglected and I know there was a little bit of tension.' — (Fernandez, interview.)
'That was actually a different group after the *Birdcatcher* crew was gone. Either out of college or done with the theatre for whatever reason, had had enough, and it was, you know, like a new start, and things, I think, had settled down into –. Living arrangements and the whole conflicts. Murray was gone. You know. Things had really made a transition. Sue Bettman was gone. — (Konnoff, interview.)
47. 'There was this guy on the 1972 tour called Marc Estrin. A blond-haired guy I met up at Goddard, he used to teach up there and now works in Burlington, Vermont as a paramedic, I don't know. He did some very nice work for Peter and he was a real help to Peter on that 1971-72 tour, he was like the other responsible grown-up, but Marc was working on – he was preparing a course on Beethoven during that whole tour, so he would go to rehearsals and rehearse with us, but he would never go to bars with us, never

Chorus, Barbara Leber, recruited in August '70, as girl friend of a recent recruit, Avram Patt, to do a Goddess in *Grey Lady Cantata II* (mostly done with Goddard students), and by October '71 when she went along on a New York State tour was counted as a member:[48] a beautiful woman and an excellent mime, she has stuck with the group, in later years taking over accounting functions. Estrin and Gordon were not puppeteers and not 'under' Schumann, but independent musical operators that continued to work with him, off and on, during the '70s.

During the fourth Europe tour, November-December '73 – with *Simple Light* – Schumann decided he would disband the company, and he made a formal announcement of this upon their return: they would do a big circus yet that summer, then there would be no more company.

The labor situation now – from the circus of the summer of '75 onward – changed again. Since the group had been disbanded and the base moved from Goddard to Elka's parents' farm at Glover, its base henceforth, after the '74 circus, Schumann and his family had been almost by themselves: Carlene Fernandez was the only puppeteer asked to come along, Kenny Eisenbraun had briefly been to help install the Glover Puppet Museum, Mark Dannenhauer and his 'little family' were living with them, having moved up there in '73 already, but otherwise there were no puppeteers there until that next or '75 circus. (John Bell was living with George Konnoff nearby in Woodbury: 'So did the other people. They stayed in the area. They worked on their own. They did their own little theatres actually and performances.' (Schumann, interview, '83.)) The regular labor force and core-group developed in '75, would no longer be a self-constituted, resident commune, semi-open to newcomers if they were friends or lovers of members, but a much smaller work-group, and the periodically needed larger irregular work force of puppeteers would no longer be supplied by workshop and 'puppet news' projects from a local student body (though Goddard, not too far away, has in fact continued to provide perhaps even the bulk of the labor force for Schumann's

---

go to restaurants with us, he would buy his food in a grocery store and go back to his room and continue his research, which was basically academic. He was of course going to listening libraries and listening to Beethoven all the time, and he basically entertained himself. Quite apart from this dog-eat-dog thing.' — (Leherissier, interview.)

48. '(Elka:) When the group was disbanded in '74, John (Bell) and Trudi (Cohen) had just begun to get involved in Bread and Puppet projects. They were those sort of newcomers. They just graduated from college and they were barely fringe members tentatively getting involved, whereas Barbara (Leber) was already pretty experienced then ... she'd come very, very early. And she had sort of gone through her apprenticeship and was already an old-timer.) The first tour I remember her was the *Birdcatcher* tour. (Elka: She was in the *Grey Lady Cantata* as a goddess. She –) Yeah, but that was very tentative, I think. (Elka: Yeah. She came in as Avram's girlfriend and for a while it was just that kind of relationship where she was there anyway so she was in the show.)' — (Schumann, interview. '83.)

annual circuses), but, on an informal basis, partly by the now very large circle of former puppeteers,[49] and partly by local people, a few who were residents of Barton, Glover, or Lyndonville, Vermonters generally, notably faculty and students from the state university at Montpelier and from Goddard, many of these Vermonters former New Yorkers who had settled up there,[50] and people from all over the northeast. The two sources overlapped: many former puppeteers had settled in the area. The circus 'sideshows' helped to attract some of these volunteers: they could set up their own shows. The core-group from '75 onward fluctuated around half a dozen people. Some winters, Schumann would work quite by himself, and there were shows away from Glover that he did by himself, e.g. the *Grey Lady Cantata #6* in Paris, in March '75 with local performers, often on a workshop basis, e.g. *A Monument to Ishi* on the Davis campus of the University of California in May '75, the first production of *Joan of Arc*, in February '77, at John Abbot College in Montreal, the first production of *Ave Maris Stella* at Montpelier, Vermont in December '77. But there were a few people who worked with him quite steadily, and are still (in '83) with him: Barbara Leber, whom I have already mentioned, John Bell (an excellent narrator, dialogist and announcer) and Trudi Cohen, John's wife, who became in particular his

---

49. Hoagland (*Let 'em Have*, '83) on the attendants of a friends-and-helpers' party following the '82 Glover circus:

'A jiggling New York inventiveness was in the room – that city-on-strings that had been so important to Peter in greasing his fluency. In New York it was not just an abstract idea that you whip your act together out of junk and afterwards throw it away. But his old buddies from the radical movement of twenty years ago still had faces that looked to be in the throes of integrity. Earth mothers with sensitive, sisterly husbands who, as it turned out, had had trust funds to live on all along and had moved from New York to northern New England were embracing other earth mothers who didn't have trust funds and consequently still had an eight-hour drive back to the city ahead of them.'

50. 'The Bread and Puppet Theater is the only commune in northeastern Vermont that has actually worked out, and one could notice survivors of the communes that failed contentedly wandering around: Lost Nation, New Hamburger, Bean Hollow, Toad Hall, Entropy Acres, Mad Brook, Mullein Hill.

Most of the throng who throw themselves into the festivities are not semiprofessional actors from Manhattan and Boston, acting students from Atlanta and Berkeley, or 1960s radicals and 1970s hippies. Even less are they likely to be native Vermonters from around the neighborhood. Instead, like the audience, they are mostly the so-called New Vermonters – educated, city-bred, middle-class people who have moved to the country within the past ten years to get away from the city and participate in the new or fictional Vermont. One meets doctors who wish that they were carpenters and carpenters who ought to be doctors, ministers who look like car mechanics and car mechanics with a lawyerly manner, painters who say that their work has been stymied badly, and organic farmers going through the mess of a divorce or on the mend from an operation for bowel cancer. They are people who will fly to Amsterdam or Idaho on vacation and yet suppose, when they get back, that the little communities they return to are true 1920s-type small Vermont towns – that, say, Cabot or Brownington is different from Danville or Lowell.'
— (Hoagland, *Let 'em Have*, '83, on volunteers for the '82 circus.)

musical arranger, director and regular musician, but who is also a gifted performer as puppet-mime, both of whom were recruits of '73, and in '74, recent college graduates, 'had just begun to get involved in Bread and Puppet projects' (Elka, interview) and Michael Romanyshyn, who apparently first joined up for the '75 circus, a gifted puppet operator who has occasionally put on shows of his own. These four (and, less regularly, some others: Richard Norcross, Linda Elbow, Howie Cantor, Joanne Schultz, Genevieve Yeuillaz, Nancy Tindall, . . .) were the core group.[51] Except for summers, when, for the circus, many others lived at the farm, they were the only resident puppeteers.

'In '74, after the circus, things were really cut off. These relationships were clearly cut off. We really said no more of this dependency on each other. So John lived with other people — with George Konnoff, I believe — in Woodbury. So did other people. They stayed in the area. They worked on their own. They did their own little theatres actually and performances and the next time I met them was to discuss the possibility of doing a '75 circus here, and then John moved in, I think Barbara, I think Trudi, Michael came later — I think he was part already of the '75 circus. (Elka: But maybe the year before we built the house (a separate house

---

51. 'John Bell, a stalwart from the Cate Farm days, lives in the old farmhouse with his wife Trudi and plays a mean trombone and guitar in performances, as well as pennywhistle, double bass and recorder. He is the troupe's electrician, drives the trip school bus, and can speak Italian, sing in Yiddish, tell long jokes in Quebecois patois, and, ambling on six-foot stilts in gorilla costume, will balance on his shoulders a ten-year-old boy dressed as a baby gorilla, while hailing the audience with gestures from the forests of the Pliocene. Yet out of costume he would appear to be only a tall, nondescript, self-effacing young man with a permanent expression that looks as if he were about to cry.

Barbara Leber, another trouper from Cate Farm, is a sturdy blonde with the face of Petrushka and a Pinocchio bravado whenever she is "on." She does the preparation painting of backdrops and side scenery, has a gym-teacher's manner in ordinary life, but she is wonderfully serviceable in Schumann's productions, able to improvise in dancing style a portrait of a fecund, and then a poisoned, Earth, when ecological poems are read.

Michael Romanyshyn dropped out of high school in Maine a few years ago to adopt the precarious life of a puppeteer. He is Schumann's particular protege, though more like a regular circus performer, now, and is nobody's foil. He does demons, clowns, gunfighters, bumpkins, and fireworks and dragon displays, and tears about the hippodrome balancing a puppet on a twenty-foot pole on the bridge of his nose — claiming, like any good puppeteer, that his purpose is always to focus the gaze of the crowd upon the lofty little rag puppet, though in fact he has developed such presence, agility and speed, such a superstar's physical flair and nose for slapstick humor that it would be impossible for anybody to watch the puppet instead of him.

These three are ubiquitous. And Joanne Schultz, the soul of the On-the-Lam Band in New York City, is a mercurial personality from the Goddard commune, a dashing would-be actress who returns to Vermont every summer to put her spontaneity at the service of puppetry again. Paul Zaloom is a Syrian-American comedian from the old commune who comes back from New York's Tribeca neighborhood to beat a sharp snare drum and play master of ceremonies with splendid panache. Genevieve Yeuillaz, the Parisian actress whose resembles the Mona Lisa — like Godface's flies over for a holiday month to assist with mask sculpture and to dance and run with a flag and project her fine timing and voice.' — (Hoagland, *Let 'em Have*, '83.)

built for the Schumanns on the Glover farm in '80 (SSB)) there was no permanent place for the puppeteers to live. Everyone would live here in the summer, but in the winter and between tours people stayed with friends or for a while a group of them rented a house in Montpelier ... For the summer they were here, but there was a very, a big lack of rootedness, or a feeling of where their home was because the house down there (the old farmhouse (SSB)) was ours and even though people stayed next door, it felt very temporary. And one year the group rented the house over the hills here in Dexter – on the other side of Glover – in '79. But that was already after we had decided on this permanent group.'
(Schumann, interview, '83.)

I.e., there was a working class revolution in the theatre in '79, the puppeteers became corporation employees, wage-laborers, with medical insurance. This was the opposite of the arrangement Schumann in '74/'75 had wanted, his and the puppeteers' mutual independence, but it also formalized the actual situation that had developed since then: a closer and stronger mutual dependence.

Schematically: an original group of temperamentally profoundly alienated, often frustrated independent people with strong unstable personalities and personal problems (or solutions), notably liquor and/or dope, many of them anarchists, was during the mid-sixties adulterated by an influx of liberals and pacifists, some young upper-class women with social concerns, some youngsters with ambitions in theatre. An influx at the end of the '60s of young rebels, European and American, politically active on the left, many of them kids that had paid their dues in the Resistance Movement, utterly changed the group into an idealistic commune. In the course of the early '70s, changing times and an influx of apolitical young non-rebels with more positive ideals (ecology, communal living) modified the group, personal and artistic rather than social or political concerns came to predominate. A disbandment of the group in the mid-'70s changed it into an (ultimately, from 1979 onward, salaried) work unit effectively devoted to the execution of Schumann's projects, and to nothing else, their experience of life, their training, their learning processes pretty much confined to this work, cut off from the world, their isolation between Hardwick and Lyndonville in no way diminished by their over-frequent money-making forays into the European culture market or their excursions to Second Avenue and 10th Street, Manhattan, to exhibit their craft products, living with one another, talking to one another.

8. Modus Operandi IV. The work. Puppet-making.

Among the many kinds of work that needed to be done, the focal ones are puppet-making, show-making and performing. Puppet-making breaks down into mask-making and puppet-building, puppet-building into making the puppet's structure and its dress. Shows were made partly in Schumann's private head and notebooks, partly, thereupon, by 'rehearsals,' especially when, the typical case, no script resulted from those private labors, but to some extent often even when there was a script, a script being the typical result, sooner or later, of the 'rehearsals,' and therefore often or even mostly existing if a show had been done before. Schumann made his shows by trying out different things for the performers to do with given puppets: a show typically was created not as realization of a script, but as upshot of a series of 'rehearsals' in the nature of experiments with puppets, rehearsals only gradually coming down to re-hearsals, 'repetitions,' starting out literally as 'Proben': essays.

And puppet-making very often was not guided by or directed toward the making of any very clearly conceived or written-down show, with its figures or characters in mind, though perhaps typically Schumann had *some* idea of what kind of figure in what kind of show he wanted as he worked on the clay or the mold of a mask – certainly not always. To a degree Schumann has functioned as independent mask-sculptor and puppet-maker, handing over to himself qua show-maker, unsolicited or solicited but not too closely specified masks and puppets. Realistically – an artist needs to be sly because he has to be sly with himself in order not to wreck things in his own head – Schumann probably as puppet-maker mostly knew pretty well whither he was heading, show-wise, his puppet-making was bespoke. But he seems to have tried to keep a certain openness there, a certain freedom for himself as puppet-maker from himself as show-maker. Traditionally, puppet-show-makers East or West don't make their own puppets, but traditionally, also, puppet-making is traditional, i.e. though the show-makers may not draw pictures for the puppet-makers as to what they want, the round of figures has been around for a long time and the puppet-maker is making a mask and puppet of a known type for which he knows or believes there is some demand. But Schumann as puppet-maker even for his Christmas and Easter shows, even for his Punch and Judy shows (least so there, perhaps) has been a traditionless puppet-maker – he pulled the faces from nature, dreams and accident – the accidents of hands in clay – and his 'Vorbilder' were not older puppets but sculpture, notably German Medieval sculpture, and painting, notably, perhaps, I am not erudite enough to say this with certainty, Renaissance Italian painting, i.e. when art-inspired, inspired by arts other than puppet-making.

Puppet-making and show-making, then, have by Schumann and the group been carried on as somewhat independent activities, with show-making more inspired by the results of puppet-making, puppet-making less by envisaged shows than one might expect, and with Schumann oriented toward maintaining a continuous and rapid − intensive − work process closely controlled by himself as regards output in both areas.[1]

---

1. 'The search for a model of a poor theater goes on as success in the previous forms has brought its deprivations. In the case of the Bread & Puppet, the model of the poor theater is one that allows uncompromising control by Schumann of the conditions, in fact the entire ambience, of his art. Although a communal living style might have created the conditions for a profound collaboration, it has in fact created the reverse, the conditions for a solitary artist to shape a company that performed his work for a while with the fewest possible concessions to financial need, that is, to popular success and the tastes of the theater circuit.

Stefan Brecht succeeded in upsetting the members of the company with a program credit on *The Cry of the People for Meat* that he composed for his *TDR* article, not because it was untrue but because it violated the general decorum of modesty and anonymity. The credit reads:

Conceived, produced, directed and narrated by Peter Schumann
performed by his Bread and Puppet Theater.
Masks, costumes, lighting and music by Peter Schumann,
with much help and a little inspiration from the company.

This, in fact, allocates the credits with precision. It is *his* Bread and Puppet Theater. This is worthy of mention because Schumann is a modest man and does not appear for bows at the end of performances. His name rarely appears on program credits, which seldom do more than give the name of the company.

I do not wish to overstate this issue. Schumann controls as most directors do − a puppeteer will perform a gesture a certain way or introduce a variation and Schumann will accept or reject it. It is, of course, within the framework of his scenarios and very detailed instructions.

There are other aspects of this theater that both keep down expenses and allow his control. The decor and music are distinctively homemade, and the masks, of course, are Schumann's sculpture. That he has described theater as an extension of sculpture suggests the degree to which the model of the autonomous and individual artist still motivates him. And this is a basic denial of the form of the theater as given. The Bread and Puppet is without actors and their expensive and demanding personalities. There are instead puppeteers without glamor, virtuosity, or bodies and voices that are trained to impersonate. In their masks they *personify*. Anyone can "play" the King of Hell.' — (B. Goldensohn, *Peter Schumann's Bread & Puppet Theater, Iowa Review*, '77.)

'And that's what − I understood that what made the theatre great was Peter's mind. I worked really well with it, and we developed things together, but it was Peter's − like *Fire*, for instance. I *distinctly* remember we developed it *together*, and stuff, but to even consider doing it as a group effort was senseless. That's one thing that I understood then and understand now. You can't have two people painting a painting − or two people writing a show. It doesn't matter. I mean, we got into such a − we were so much swimming in that sea, of the theatre, that we could work together as one mind, but it was still Peter's trip and if it wasn't − if it ever left that globe, it would fall. In my mind, when the Mime Troupe lost Ronnie Davis and Sandy Archer it wasn't that good any more, see, because it was their insight impulse, that did it. So, understanding that, I worked really happily, and involved with it, and didn't try to *compete* . . . . Either you do it, like if I go into *my* life and what happened in the meantime and all that, different things come up and

Bread and Puppet masks are derived either from clay sculptures or from people's faces. When from a clay sculpture, either directly from the clay or by way of a plaster cast into which the final mask is molded;[2] when from a face, by modeling either into the face cast or into a plaster cast made from it. Masks molded over face casts may be made with deliberate distor-

---

– like when I was in Denmark I had my *own* theatre, that was mine then, and they did what *I* wanted to do, and the people who worked for me essentially helped me, but I did what I wanted to do. I did a show, this terrific show, in '76. This terrific show, with a bunch of flakes, essentially, but by cracking the whip a little, and by doing it my way, the show was one of the best I've ever seen. But they were so flaky that they didn't want to continue. They weren't theatre people. So, anyway, that's what I learned. I understand that you have to have the final say. Somebody has to say, "This is what we do." Even though we *change* it a million times. Even though what we call rehearsals, with this endless going over and over, and changing and changing and, and never ever anything being finished, always things in progress, always things being mutable.' — (Ernstthal, interview.)

2. Instances of Schumann's two from-clay procedures in '75:

'*A Note on Techniques for Making Masks and Banners*

Masks for Deer

A Deer head is sculpted from clay, and then coated with Vaseline. Celastic, a stiff chemically impregnated fabric, is cut into strips, dipped in acetone to soften, and put over the clay model until it is entirely covered. When the Celastic has dried and become stiff again, the mask is cut in half and removed from the clay model. The halves are put together again with acetone-moistened strips of Celastic. Wood putty is used on the rough parts of the mask to smooth it. The masks are painted white and then shaded black. Twigs are put in the holes left for antlers. Two light-weight boards about 3 feet long are attached to the mask. The person inside places one of these on top of his head and holds it on by a strip of cloth tied under his chin. The other board is held in front of the operator with his hands. This armature and the operator are hidden by the Deer's muslin body.

Masks for Hunchback Witches

These masks are made by a method which duplicates more exactly the details of the clay model. After sculpting a clay face, it is coated with Vaseline and then covered with two layers of moulding plaster. The second layer should be smoothed with a trowel for greater strength. When the plaster has dried, it is removed from the clay face, which is softened by letting it stand in water. The inside of the negative plaster mould is dried in the sun. Then strips of light-weight Celastic, dipped in acetone, are pressed into the mould. When the Celastic has dried and is stiff, it is removed from the mould, trimmed, painted white, and shaded with black. Hemp rope is unravelled, dyed black and sewn to the top of the mask as hair.' — (Th. Shank, *The Bread and Puppet's Anti-Bicentennial, Theatre Quarterly*, V, 19, '75.)

'We dig clay out of the ground wherever we find it, keep it moist in old bath tubs and garbage cans and throttle it from time to time with stale home-brewed beer. For big masks we build a foundation from stones, cement blocks and wire. After the clay figure has been modeled, it is either duplicated in plaster (for better detail or to make more than one copy) or it is directly covered with paper maché or with celastic, and when this cover has dried, it is lifted off the clay or cut off it. The finished mask is strengthened from the inside with wood or wire, if it needs it, and is covered on the outside with foundation (Grundierung), and is painted.' — (Schumann, *Puppen & Masken*, '73.)

tions from the cast. The final mask is apt to be painted, and perhaps given a patina.

The masks have almost with no exceptions been of Schumann's design: he molds the clay, and if the mask is derived from a face cast but with deliberate divergencies from it, he is apt to have made it. On the other hand, though he shies away from no part of the work-processes, the bulk of the celastic has been worked up by his helpers, and the bulk of the final masks have been made by them.

By and large, with the major exceptions clustering in the years '71-'74, his primary objective has been expressive rather than formal value, and the primary intent has been not sculptural effect, but effect in performance. He speaks of his masks and puppets as being in and of themselves junk, of value only insofar useable or used. The period mentioned was, apparently due to Bill Whelan's influence, one of experimentation and fine mask making, molding with very small pieces of celastic, giving fine contours, use of large, sometimes single sheets, giving effects independent of the mold — both, in their different ways, perhaps attempts to sculpt in celastic, using the clay sculpture as only point of departure — complex and composite masks, elaborate mask-painting. These techniques tended to involve a certain degree of artistic independence of the mask-makers from Schumann. But this was in these regards an exceptional period. In the main, the masks have been modeled for grand effect, so that departures from the clay mold (or plaster cast) due to haste or to the labor force's lack of skill have not mattered, and so that, also, there was no opportunity for the help to express itself by nuance.

Working with celastic is hard and, because of the acetone, unpleasant work.[3] Hard also because Schumann often wanted a large quantity of masks turned out quickly, whether for the large peace demonstrations of '65 and '66, or for the larger shows.[4] Though Schumann was dependent

---

3. 'Now, by the way, I can't get near acetone. I think my acetone level has disappeared, because I used to be in a big hole, be in there working in this celastic. And I didn't mind it then. I don't know if it's physical. We used to put cigarette butts in the acetone. Only, once it caught fire. But it was just in the pans, so it wasn't so bad. It just made this big flame. There was no safety or health considerations. But now, as I say, I can't — acetone really turns my stomach. And I tend to think it's because I was filled up on it. We didn't use any masks. We kept the door open, unless it was cold. It evaporated and made your hands real cold. So I do remember, actually, that that's true — the theatre was unheated — the loft, Delancey Street — and in the winter I remember working with acetone because it evaporates really fast, and you work with it and your hands would just get ice cold. Evaporate and get very cold. And I think we would occasionally try things like rubber gloves, but as I remember the acetone ate through those gloves, so we used hands. But I remember over that winter it did tend to get real cold, and — but we worked with acetone. That was probably the winter of '63 and '64.' — (Ernstthal, interview.)

4. 'Okay, so then I called up to join. "Okay, come down and do celastics." So I went to Delancey Street and they were building some new demon masks for the *Crucifixion* show that was coming up in a couple of weeks — maybe a week — I think it was just a week. And

on certain performers that did not care for puppet-making and managed pretty well to stay out of it, and was tolerant of this, he tended to esteem true puppeteers only those involving themselves closely in puppet-making and putting out a great deal of work doing it.

I don't think he has made any mask with movable parts.

Schumann's puppet construction has been as untraditionalistic as his mask-making. He seems to have learned very little from existing types of construction, and this apparently intentionally, wanting to be not imitative, but to work with a conscious orientation toward the essence of the matter, the type of movement that could be obtained from a given type of con-

---

I immediately met Andy Trompetter, who must have joined the same day or the same week that I did. I remember very much doing celastic with Andy and other people, but I had immediate contact with him because he was funny. So we sat in this little place on Delancey Street, with the windows open so we'd have a little ventilation – fumes – and for a week we did celastic, demon masks, and then after a week rehearsals began. Well, of course, the other people had already been there, so it seemed like everybody knew the process and I had to understand from watching, because it was all familiar to them, and it wasn't really explained to the newcomers. Well, there were all these puppets that they kept referring to the way you refer to your friend: "the yellow people, they're over there," "the Jesus, his dress is ripped again, would you repair it?", "oh, I know where we can get burlap at discount." The purchasing of materials was a very primary activity. Finding things at wholesale prices, burlap to repair the yellow people, I remember that was going on. And Helen Palmer, who at that time was called Helen Hunter, was one of the chief movers. She's an incredibly energetic person. So she was in charge of all the sewing. She was also in charge of the children – we had children in the show and she was the only person who could hold them together – take care of them. (I: What does that mean, work on the celastic for the demon masks?) Well, Peter had sculpted these masks out of clay and then we had to cover the clay with celastic. Well, I guess Ephraim will go into detail about that. You tear the celastic into pieces and you dip it in acetone and you cover the clay, which you've already put some vaseline over, and it dries. And then you move it and it's plastic, wood, sanding, priming and painting. (I: That process, did that change during the next five years? Do you remember anything?) I don't think it changed by the next five years, but it has changed a little bit in the last – I would say since the *Simple Light* show people have gotten more advanced with celastic techniques. Until then, we always used fairly small pieces of celastic. And then Bill Whelan was doing the celastic on the *Simple Light* puppets, he discovered that if you're really, really good at it you can use a large piece and get it to really take the shape of the clay. And there was a lot less waste and you have a much smoother texture. I haven't done it much and I'm not good at it, but Genevieve is fabulous at it. She's in charge of that now. Genevieve Yeuillaz. She's French and she works with the Bread and Puppet Theatre during a good part of each year. — (Sherman, interview.)

During '66 and '67:

'When we had a big project, like in the early work, the Fifth Avenue parade was, you know, you'd just forget about everything else. We worked continuously. But that was for short bursts of time, you know. Maybe three or four weeks, to get the thing going. And then we would not do that. The process consisted like – it depended on the action. Like a parade action would be: All right, we need a series of something. We need a series of skulls or a series of Vietnam women or a series of something. Then Peter would sculpt the series and he would work very fast and almost continuously. Like once he got started, he would just go. And it was like coming behind somebody, you know. Each piece would

struction.' His '62/'63 rod puppets were produced in ignorance of existing rod puppet types (and differed from them), and when in '63 his seeing the big Sicilian puppets of the Manteos inspired him to make his first generation of big puppets, his construction differed totally from theirs – was not even a variant of theirs. He was not interested in how other American puppeteers constructed their puppets, and when during his visits to Europe on tours during the '70s he went to puppet shows and puppet museums, it was not to learn the craft, but mainly with an interest in how the puppets looked and moved. He has produced a succession of types of differently constructed puppets, and apparently always with a view to type of movement obtainable – not, that is, with a view to modifications that would facilitate operation of the puppet resulting in a type of movement he had already obtained. He has not been interested in ease of operation, perhaps on the contrary welcoming aspects of movement resulting from difficulty of operation.[6] Nor has he been interested in freedom of

---

have to be vaselined and, how do you say – the celastic and the fumes were very bad. It was like being a minor casualty in the Vietnam war, you know. You were working with these huge needles, trying to get through the celastics, and you know – you just put out a notice for workers to come, you know, and God knows where they came from. The Movement, you know. Different places, you put a notice up and you get 35 people there one day and I usually had to kind of organize the cloth crew, the drapery and the other parts of it. So I did lots and lots of cloth on these big industrial sewing machines. And if somebody could sew, then you put them to sew. And if they couldn't, then you had to do it yourself and if they couldn't do that, well, you'd teach them something to do. But you had to keep everybody busy, you know, and participating. And the major thing was the – then when they were put together and glued together, it was like you could start sculpting and then there was all of this work – just labor. He kind of immersed himself in the labor. And then, when it was all sort of half done, you know, and you could get it up on rods so you could get the thing moving.' — (Palmer, interview.)

5. '(TDR: What are you trying to do?) We want to work directly into and out of the interior of people. A demonic thing. (TDR: Why use masks and puppets whose expressions can't change?) Oh, they change greatly. Puppets have tremendous possibilities in their faces and bodies and hands. I build them not as sculpture but as actors. I experiment with movement – with their stiffness or floppiness.' — (Schumann in Brown and Seitz, *With the Bread and Puppet Theatre*, TDR 38, '68.)

6. '(I: In *The Cry of the People* you have these beasts that come forward toward the audience. Many of them. Twelve, twenty – something. Cumbersome masks and they're squeezed together and it's hard to move and they move forward and they move back. It's a very strenuous thing. And my impression was that he anticipated the physical difficulty of it to get the effects.) Oh, absolutely. Well, he would devise a puppet that would be – he would build the difficulty into the puppet. You're absolutely right. To get the effect . . . like Yama, King Hell was a huge, monstrous thing, and it took some holding so that you saw this monster like wobbling and having a little trouble holding himself up, you know, and you actually transmit it, feeling your whole body through the puppet. The way you'd have to make it move. It would have to move the way he wanted it to move. You couldn't move it any other way.' — (Oyle, interview.)

'Schumann's fidelity to his present puppets is such that whoever operates them does not look down on and manipulate them from above or wriggle them on the end of the hand. Rather, he staggers along, gazing up at the looming fringes of the puppet's costume while

movement per se or in the range of movement obtainable from a given construction — nor in life-like movement any more than in life-like appearance, nor in small or complex movements. Rather, he has aimed at types of construction resulting in a narrow range of simple,[7] abstract movements — or in qualities of immobility, as in stationary dummies, puppets that can only be carried and rotated, dolls put in some place, moved to another, removed. His construction materials have generally been wood, string and wire, the wood raw sawed lumber, less frequently branches or saplings — cheapness and simplicity the desiderata as regards the components, simplicity also the desideratum as regards construction and operation. He has avoided construction calling for complex operation, demanding skill. And whereas the masks or puppet heads tend to be sturdy, due to having been made of a heavy grade of celastic or due simply to the overlapping of pieces of celastic — the very work methods that tend to make them rough rather than fine work — the puppets generally have not been built for the rigors of transport or to last: broken or torn components could easily be replaced.

Cheapness and simplicity have also been the desiderata of his puppet dress-making. During the later '70s there was a trend toward gayer, more colorful dress and more varied and brighter colors, and also some more theatrical costumes, but up to then he for fifteen years tended toward black, greys, faded browns and yellows, with occasional blues for poetry and sometimes the demonic, and reds for drama, blood and evil, and away from costumes and even imitation of clothes, especially European clothes. Burlap has been a favorite materials of his. The operative objective has been the pictorial effect in composition and/or the type of movement that could be achieved with a given manner of cutting and draping or fitting, the movement desired being always simple and abstract. A puppet's dress is its body, but Schumann has not been interested in suggestions of flesh or muscle or effects of corporeal ponderosity or even presence. As between pictorial composition and type of movement, his preoccupation has varied, sometimes a painterly orientation has been foremost, sometimes a concern with performance as dance.

Here again, as in the case of the mask-making, the amount of work, given the size and mostly the number of puppets, involved in tinting, cut-

---

supporting a pole that by itself may weigh as much as sixty pounds. And loving the proud traditionalism of the art — Indian effigies thirty feet tall, Indonesian, Turkish, Flemish constructions, Japanese Bunraku and No theater — Peter is actually glad it's so arduous to dance for a mile on stilts or to heft the heavy poles that hold up Yama or the Nature God (called Marvin by the puppet handlers.)' — (Hoagland, *Let 'em Have*, '83.)

7. 'Moi qui ai essayé tant bien que mal de m'initier à une science du mouvement, quand Peter me dit pour bouger une marionnette: "Non, non, tout le corps doit bouger à la même vitesse," c'est vraiment un concept nouveau pour moi.' — (Eric Berne in Kourilsky, '71.)

ting, sewing, fitting has been considerable: real work, often of a fairly mechanical sort, and rarely calling for skill, onerous work.

Schumann prints his own posters, mainly, I believe, from woodcuts, and from '70 onward flags and banners became an important part of certain of his shows, the 'circuses', and these were printed from woodcuts.[8] From '71 onward (*Birdcatcher*, circus of '74, *Monument to Ishi*, '75, . . .) he used costumes with pictures printed from woodcuts on them.

---

8. '*Banners and Flags*
Designs are drawn on pieces of untempered masonite (hardboard or utility brown board) about 3 feet square. The part of the design which is to remain white on the banner is carved into relief using wood-carving tools. Using a large rubber roller, the completed printing block is then inked with printers' ink to which a drying agent has been added. A piece of unstarched muslin or a bed sheet is now cautiously lowered onto the printing surface by two people holding the cloth by the corners. It is pressed on to the inked areas with hands and then rubbed with spoons, doorknobs or other hard smooth objects until the ink has come through in all inked areas. The banner is then removed and hung up to dry.' — (Th. Shank, *The Bread and Puppet's Anti-Bicentennial, Theatre Quarterly*, V, 19, '75.)

9. Modus operandi IV. The work. Show-making. Rehearsals as show-making experiments with the puppets.

The inspiration for Schumann's shows was until '72 or '73 normally provided him by current political events — by the newspapers, the *New York Times* in particular. Thereafter, rather abruptly, no longer, music he happened to hear became a major source of inspiration, sometimes particular figures, e.g. St. Francis, inspired him, or out of his perennial preoccupations some pressing contemporary aspect — the atom bomb, Third World undernourishment, the work of women, ecology, children's idealism — crystallised, certain puppets — the Grey Ladies, the White Lady — provided variable subject matter for different shows, or the terms of an image — e.g. the dompting and killing of horses — come to him, possibly in a dream, inspired him. Just how far his musing and note-making[1] developed the inspirations toward imagery and sequence of images before he started the second phase of show-making, the work with puppets, I don't know. I suspect in most cases some of the way but not all that far — that his shows have tended to be importantly, perhaps preponderantly the result of his work with the puppets. Concerning this work, however, he at different times, for fairly extended periods, had rather specific directive ideas, not the same ones at different times, and these ideas — a notion of the kind of puppetry he was going to attempt — and a notion of the kind of performance space he was going to utilize how — he would also bring to the work with the puppets, and the show would result at least as much from these form-of-performance and problem-to-be-solved ideas as from the work with the puppets, and probably more from them than from preconceived themes or pre-imagined imagery. None of this preliminary work would particularly concern his puppeteers, they would normally be involved in it only to an infinitesimal extent. He wouldn't talk about it — at most perhaps ask a respected confidante or two 'what do you think about doing . . .', and without too much response to their reply. The work with the puppets would then in most cases probably to a greater or lesser extent alter his intentions in particular regards, e.g. a show intended to be largely a marionette show might end up with only a few strings — his attempts at marionettry during the early '70s were in this fashion largely

---

1. '. . . they are sort of my "summer brain," because in summer my brain gets drained and I write things down in order not to forget them. So I keep a notebook with me and I write down ideas for various things. But I write down everything, from materials, from needs of organization, everything; to the ideas and the writing of the plays. That all in there. (I: Arbeitsbücher?) Yeah. (I: Dreams. Of yours — or —) Might also be in there. (I: Are they important? In your work?) Yes, because most shows show up in them. Most shows are in

abortive — or some particular manner of use of particular puppets that might have been central before the work with puppets might prove impracticable with the performers he had, or given how the puppets looked in action. Each puppet tends to have its built-in and quite limited gesticular range and capacities; but Schumann can't know what they are — how far they extend — ahead of exercising the puppet; and the image of its possibilities he gets from a certain set of uses of it over a time period is never necessarily definitive; he has to liberate himself from preconceptions, he may make discoveries, or he may be able to adapt the puppet's style to his technical project, images or content-ideas, or to other puppets used.

Making allowance for the preliminary content-ideas and images, and the formal or technical objectives in re kind of puppetry, space utilization to be attempted, Schumann's shows here resulted from this 'experimentation with the puppets': a kind of work that for him has been not just a means of staging a show for a public, but a process of discovery and of work with its own value and satisfaction.[2]

The work with the puppets — 'rehearsals' — is also work with the performers. First, in that they normally have to be rehearsed in whatever Schumann settles on, have to learn their 'parts', and made to do it 'right.' Some of the parts get fairly complicated and making a given puppet move as Schumann wants it is not all that easy, experience, a sense of rhythm, a combination of discretion and aggressiveness (or perhaps better: assertiveness, decisiveness) enter into it, though not the amount of skill required by most kinds of puppeteering other than Schumann's. Second, in the sense that Schumann also gets ideas from the puppeteers, not so much from what they might have to say,[3] but from the particular way a given

---

there. But I have a very hard time finding things in there because I never organized them and never wrote dates in for them.' — (Schumann, interview, '82.)

2. 'It's a strange ... for all we worked and rehearsed ... we ... rehearsed constantly, there was this quality of improvisation, somehow. It's very peculiar when you think of it, because nothing was set. What the rehearsals were — were not to get things *ready*. But they were just to constantly mutate the shows. constantly change them and rearranging. So there was this process - instead of getting something ready to be finished, it was just, we would just ... we would just work ... would just ... that was part of the whole ethic ... was ... that you work ... and in itself is of value, without anyone there.'
— (Ernstthal, interview.)

3. Not that most people who really worked in the group for some length of time can't remember some particular little effect they contributed, e.g.:

'I was very — I felt like I had a lot — I was very interested in the process of the creation and had a lot of ideas about how things should go and was sort of verbal about what I thought should be or would work or wouldn't work or stuff. People had that, you know, had the opportunity to say what they thought and I was very interested in what I thought. (I: What was the result?) Of people saying what they thought? I felt like some things

individual moves a puppet, their style of movement translating into one of its, from gestures they happen to make that he likes, and particular talents of theirs that before this work, if he hasn't worked with them before, Schumann was not aware of, or else that he hadn't thought of, but that watching or listening occurs to him should be used, e.g. a talent for song, for narration, for mime, for masked movement. Also, if he has already used the puppet with a different performer ('operator' — a term Schumann prefers because it reduces the role of the performer and increases that of the puppet, and because it has the sound of work rather than of art), the work with the new performer may force him to modify his ideas as to how to use it: he will adapt what he does to the new performer's talents, and limitations and to his or her personality as this personality comes across through the puppet's movements.[4] But for the performers, most of this

---

caught on or were tried. (I: Do you remember any?) Yes, I remember my most brilliant idea, which was at the end of the *Dead Man Rises* — there's a part where the man and the woman are dancing together and ripped-up pieces of paper are dropped over the backdrop so that it looks like petals or Danae or some kind of shower — light, fluttery things, you know. That was real nice. (I: You suggested that?) Yeah. (I: What about Danae?) She's the goddess who Jupiter — he had her by shower. She was lying naked by a window and he came in like sunlight or like gold or something and that was his approach. (I: What was your idea, then?) That during this wedding scene — well, that that shower would be like that — would be like the marriage — like the shower, you know, the apple blossoms kind of marriage thing would be like sunlight would be like rice would be suitable. And it was. It looked nice. It was with that White Lady — that beautiful White Lady.' — (M. Lippen, interview.)

In actual fact the confetti looked like snow and had an effect of desolation.

4. 'Peter had a way of being able to work with an individual and make a mood. I don't know if it came from the puppet or the person under the puppet. This has always been a question to me. Since one is working — it's not with a person — it's a piece of sculpture.' — (Palmer, interview.)

'*Leaf Feeling the Moonlight* was a play that Cathy was in. Cathy Merrill. And which she — it was the same puppet that I was in *The Dead Man Rises*. It was the precursor. It's very interesting how Peter works. He had a play like *Leaf Feeling the Moonlight*, which was a presentational play. In other words, the puppet comes out and presents itself in different ways. Then there's an interaction between that and another figure. Very simple. And simple lines. Peter then gets a feeling for that and will try to move that same puppet into different contexts. You can see the line of activity for, like the Easter play. Well, the disciples can move in certain groupings, you see, so he remembers that and then he'll move them in different ways. But the difference was — it was interesting. The same puppet, the same costume, the same face, and the beginning of *The Dead Man Rises*, which was a good play — it was like a reiteration of *Leaf Feeling the Moonlight* — didn't work at all. So a new person under the same puppet has to do it a different way. And once Peter sees something, he can do it. (I: How can you describe this? You saw it?) Yes. It was much stiller. Much less movement. Cathy didn't move it nearly as much as I did. Cathy, I felt was an artist and could — saw the possibilities of this beautiful piece of sculpture being illuminated in different ways... I was not. I moved... It was more the sculptural, visual thing. And my idea was to move it. So I liked the motion part of it.' — (Palmer, interview.)

work consists neither in inventing anything, nor in bullshitting with the director, but in standing there waiting for him to tell them what to do and then doing it — and mostly over and over. It is an extremely passive and submissive kind of work for the performer[5] — though Schumann claims it takes not only passion but also intelligence to do it well.[6] There are different operating modes, however, and Bread and Puppet performance modes in which no puppet is being operated, and some of the modes give more scope to a performer's creativeness than others.

The normal show-making 'rehearsal' procedure then would be for Schumann to tell the group or single individual in concrete — not psychological or story,[7] though occasionally to convey a kinesthetic sense of the

---

5. 'He is sculpting, in one thing he is sculpting and the person is like that — is underneath — is like the stone underneath and the sculptor is on top.' — (Levy, interview.)

6. 'Je dois avouer que cela me passione d'amener les gens à comprendre ce que c'est que de faire bouger une marionnette et la chorégraphie en détail de ses mouvements. Cela n'a rien à voir avec le travail sur les mouvements d'un danseur ou d'un acteur, et il est important de trouver des gens qui aient cette passion, ce talent et cette intelligence de la manipulation des marionnettes. Nous faisons plusieurs répétitions pour essayer de trouver des mouvements qui soient adéquats, qui explorent vraiment ce qu'il est possible de faire avec ce petit bout de tête et ce morceau de tissu qui en part.' — (Schumann in Kourilsky, '71.)

7. '. . . these actors; they have a lot of trouble in our company, because the questions they ask I can't answer. They ask me funny questions. (I: Like: what's his character, or something?) Yeah. And about the feelings they portray or their — (I: George (Bartenieff) doesn't ask you about feelings, does he?) Well, not exactly with that word, but he wants — he definitely would love to get more direction. He would love to get more — I don't know, even, what that is. What they are looking for — but it reminds me of other actors I've worked with. They want to know what they are portraying — what they are — you know, they have that idea that they have to portray something. A character. And I don't know that — it doesn't even interest me — I don't know what that is, the character. I want to see the result of what the character comes out as with the words you put in his mouth and the gestures you give him, and so on. So I can only describe the gesture I want, but I can't describe what's behind it. And he wants what's behind it. When the murderer stands on — comes in on these shoes. Do they mean that these are all the people that he killed? I don't even think that way. It's just empty shoes — a bunch of empty shoes seems to be befitting for the murderer, that's all. But then, to explain it like that to me, kills it. I don't want that . . . and in a show (*Diagonal Man*) like this it's totally confusing to them because they don't have a sense of what they're telling to people. None of them. They get — it's the same with the *Thunder Storm* show. They were totally lost. They relied on people coming to them after the show and telling them something. And then, people didn't do that. People were sort of careful — they didn't know, themselves, how to take it — and so their friends didn't come to them and tell them: "I liked it," or "I didn't like it," or "This was good," and "That wasn't," and so on — they didn't do that, so they didn't — they were confused for a long time until they felt the joy of performing it in detail, I think. And that's where they become like musicians, and they just love doing that. The show warms up to them. It's a good way — it's a dangerous way, because they could take any piece of junk and make it into a good show, also. With no judgment, no — it doesn't say anything about the show — just about their ability to be attached (I: But I have an impression, sort of, that per-

movement, in metaphorical[8] – terms where to move or how to move their arms inside a puppet or without one or where to move it or what gesture to make it make or what type of movement to impart to it, giving his instructions carefully[9] but not too precisely or minutely, but general terms, so that there would be room for them to do it one way rather than another, and then to watch them do it, perhaps repeatedly, either accepting what he saw for the show, or altering his instructions, and again watching until he had something acceptable.[10] The performer would be

---

formances become interesting and good if they're made from a number of somewhat disjunct viewpoints.) It's true – right. It's very important to have it disjunct and not come with an overall philosophy of the show. It's very disturbing to have such a philosophy. But the trick of telling an actor: "Never mind how wrong it is," but giving him a certain direction – it's true that that's needed very much, and I do that also, but I also find that in this show, this was very hard to find an angle for him – how to say these lines. I couldn't say do it as a drunkard. Actually we tried that. Or do it as a wild man. Or be a little petit bourgeois after eating a goose. Or a preacher, you know – I thought of a preacher. Sort of a phony street preacher who stands there preaching abstracta that don't quite make sense to himself, but for some reason he gets paid for that and that's what he does. — (Schumann, interview, December '82.)
8. 'He would describe how you're supposed to move in space, you know. A lot of people would say, well, Bread and Puppet, everything moves slowly. Peter wouldn't describe it moves slowly. He might say, "Don't move so fast," but he would give you a real direction. He would say, "If your hand is moving from this point to this point just think of it moving through space, pushing the space, going through the space." He wouldn't talk about what . . . "Give me this effect," you know, he would just exactly tell you what to do in the moment.' — (Fernandez, interview.)
9. 'He would watch. He would let you go, say, in an improvisation or something, let you go and he would just watch and then stop and you'd talk about it and there was not a lot of this chaos. If you're trying to do something and somebody's yelling to you direction while you're acting it out and, you know . . . . And you felt like you could go so far without sort of being constricted but yet you felt safe that if you started to go out too far he would just stop and say, "Okay, stop." (I: Did you have a feeling that as a result of this sort of thing in some way you had yourself built up your way of doing it?) Sometimes that would happen or sometimes you would feel very comfortable with something you were doing and Peter wouldn't like it. Sometimes you felt very awkward and he would like it and keep it . . . I'll say about his directing: he worked so carefully and slowly through something . . . if you were working close with him, now I'm talking about, like in a real close directing situation, at the end of it you were clear, very sure of yourself, you know, confident of what was going to be right if you did something a certain way. You felt sure of yourself because he had gone so carefully through each step and that is just a good feeling, you know. Other directors, they're often a lot more highstrung. They have a set idea of what they want to see so they're just trying to make you move into this pattern so that they get the effect that they have in their mind. And Peter, his mind is pliable . . . you may perform a show 50 times and every time you perform it it's going to be slightly different because in between time he works on it, he moves it, he alters it, he changes it a little bit. So his directing . . . he was right there with you. I don't know, sort of molding (laugh) molding it as you go along.' — (Fernandez, interview.)
10. 'So I remember coming back and playing them all. And there was all this crawling

apt from what Schumann accepted and rejected to acquire a kinesthetic sense[11] or a feel for or even a conception or interpretation of the part that they could presume and work with in doing other parts of the show with the same puppet or mask or in the same 'part', Schumann then independently judging the resulting visual effect: but not, if he could help it at all — which with actors would not always be possible — giving his instructions in terms of such a 'feel,' conception or interpretation, or discussing them with the performer.[12]

---

around on the floor, like a football team, really. He would have maneuvers and he would blow the whistle and you'd have to go this way and then you would have to turn over and roll on our backs. He had all these little schemes he wanted to work out and we had to do it, no matter what. Peter could never envision anything — he would have to see it enacted, which sometimes — he would have us doing really weird things; things that we would later on have to throw out completely.' — (Leherissier, interview.)

11. '*Fire* had a particular rhythm for the whole show. It had a certain pace and to begin the show we wore white gloves that were real quiet so that if you clapped your hands . . . and we would sit backstage for at least half an hour and we would make music, like tapping a glass with your fingernail, clapping very quietly and . . . . Before the show began. For us it was the beginning of the show. You're all ready. Everything's go. We would meet backstage and it was almost like your heartbeat would start to tick in the right time so that you could go through the whole show in the right tempo. Sometimes we'd even have our masks on already.' — (Sherman, interview.)

12. Helen Palmer as the White Lady in *Dead Man Rises*:
'And at the time we didn't know it was anything but, you know, a story that Peter brought out, and I would move. He would give a line and I would try to move the puppet to express the quality that he had in the line. And then he would arrange lights and scene and move again. It was just a question of saying — of him saying, "All right, now that's right." So then I would assume that quality and try to carry it into the next line.' — (Palmer, interview.)

'Then I had a personal — one Christmas Eve I went up to the big complex in Westchester — White Plains, where they performed. There's a big stage up there. And they were performing on the stage. And they needed people underneath the giant puppets, and I became one. And we were given rhythms to count: and two and three. And I was given perhaps up to twenty to count. I couldn't see where I was going. I simply had to step up steps and over a dam with a great puppet over my head. And, as I stood under there and counted, I began to change too, you know, this physical change was happening, and it became a wonderful experience.

I remember reading, years before, that when Joseph von Sternberg first brought Marlene Dietrich to this country, he had worked with her in Germany. Then he brought her here and he began to work in the Hollywood studios. And he never would explain to her — and subsequently, I found, to almost any of the other actors — what they were to do. He'd simply tell them to count. Count to twelve. Which was an enormous amount of time to not think of anything to do. "Count to twelve", he would say to Marlene, "and lower your eyes and raise them". And he would scream, "You know, you're so stupid you can't count to twelve!" Peter wouldn't explain to you, either, what you were doing. "Count to twelve." — "You're so stupid you can't count", you know. That's all that was expected of you. Nothing else. As a matter of fact, I see this. Once I witnessed it, it became a very interesting thing to watch the few of Peter's stars. Nobody was ever a star in Peter's —

Most parts would retain a margin of indeterminacy, of choice for the performer, and here, if anywhere, some satisfaction of creativeness might accrue,[13] though Schumann would be apt to resist – and eliminate – as disturbing excrescence – any actual shaping of the part or performance giving it distinct individuality or too much nuance.[14]

These 'rehearsals', because the puppets are heavy and, if you are inside them, hot, and the masks hindering, and because of the many repetitions of doing things the same way or in slightly different ways and also because what you are doing is neither a creative nor a learning process for you (though both for Schumann), are like the other work processes hard work.[15]

---

the nearest you'd come to being a star was when you'd get to work without a mask. (I: Margo, Maurice?) Margo and Maurice were the only two I ever knew, and Maurice – it's very clear why he doesn't wear a mask. He is a mask, you know, that wonderful face. And Margo Lee, of course, is the virgin in Western culture, you know. And they're past masters at counting rather than thinking. They'll do anything Peter tells them to do. One, two, three, four, walk off the roof, and they do it.' — (Bissinger, interview.)

'Equally, to peer through the pinholes of a mask breaks down the preconceptions of a lifetime, which is especially important because part of Schumann's method is never to explain to anybody what he "means". He leaves people to grope toward their own understanding in the darkness of his masks and the fragilities of stilt walking, or in conferences with one another, of which there are many. Watching the result, he will speed up a sequence or, with a laugh, try to reduce a sideshow's scale. "We can't advocate world anarchy. That's too big a project for us." ' — (Hoagland, *Let 'em Have*, '83 on rehearsals for '82 circus.)

13. '... les sons et les mouvements sont trouvés par accident, mais ils le sont bien souvent en réponse à une tâche concrète indiquée par le metteur en scène: la spontanéité est rejetée au profit du travail nécessaire à la production d'une action. Schumann dit par exemple: "Faites entrer les amis de Johnny," mais il n'indique jamais comment le faire: c'est à l'acteur de le trouver. Parfois, il dit ce qui ne va pas, ou il ne dit rien du tout. Si une action lui paraît vraiment "trouvée" comme la naissance de Caïn sous les coups du Grand Guerrier, il peut alors donner certaines indications pour préciser les gestes. Mais ceux-ci ne sont jamais définitivement fixés et l'acteur peut les modifier au cours même des représentations. Cela est vrai même de *Fire* où tous les gestes semblent calculés d'avance. De nombreux passages de *The Cry*, les généalogies, par exemple, sont laissés indéterminés. Il ne s'agit pas d'une improvisation totale – la structure de la scène ne change pas, l'image proposée reste la même chaque soir – mais plutôt d'une liberté de choix laissée à l'acteur à l'intérieur de limites fixées à l'avance. Ainsi l'acteur se trouve constamment obligé d'inventer: le spectacle s'élabore avec lui.' — (Kourilsky, '71.)

14. 'Ralph Lee among mask-makers is second only to Schumann in the U.S., and is Lee who runs the Greenwich Village parade. Lee remarked that Schumann's work is "reliably inspiring" (the same words that the theatrical director Joseph Chaikin later used, expressing wonderment that anybody could be nowadays) and doesn't require developed actors – needs amateurs, indeed, who will not infect with foreign stylization the visions he presents.' — (Hoagland, *Let 'em Have*, '83.)

15. 'In so much as in the working on it and the development of it, we weren't concerned with – we were – we would be in those beasts sometimes, crawling on the ground, in the

heat, sweating bullets, for hours on end and there was something about redoing it and the sounds that were coming in on us that had – that had elements of real suffering, and not "as if." And because we really suffered through those things, that when we did do it – And things had a way of taking their time – he uses time in an enormously wonderful way, letting something happen for a long time and then it changes. I mean, sometimes it gets too long and it gets boring, but that is the risk that you take. Most of the time it doesn't – most of the time it is right on. And that is where ritual, for me, comes in. The ritual of eating is one of preparation and coming together and of it happening. Not fast foods. Fast foods is no longer ritual. We have come away from that and the same way I felt, taking the time for things to really develop for me – it took on the dimensions of ritual.' — (Levy, interview.)

Part III.
The product.

Contents: Part III

1. Variety of performance modes: extensions of Puppetry. — 275
2. Acting modes. Approximations of puppet-like acting. — 279
3. Ceremonial movement, the alienation of ceremony, primordiality of moral address. The puppet style. — 285
4. A theatre of mute, grandiose and live puppets, expressive sculptures in a movement of gestures, the puppets define the space. — 295
5. The puppet and the mask. The power of the mask, the dependency of the puppet. Schumann's theatre alienates masked performance by the form of puppetry. — 306
6. Music, speech, pursuit of an integration of man's vocal dimension according to a principle of an organization out of context of means. Ideal of the self-integrating sounds of implements. Ideal of the substitution of non-verbal for verbal utterance. — 322
7. Graphics: to be used as active scenic element. — 329
8. New York City critical response: His marvellous masks apart, his work is soporific, primitive and obscure though (as of *Fire*) he is probably a great artist. — 331

1. Variety of performance modes: extensions of puppetry.

Schumann makes a point of its being puppetry that he and his group are doing, smuggling into the term some insinuation of folk art and some identification with tradition.[1] But he's not scrabbling for a living at this, he has indulged in the luxuries of propaganda and art, not folk at all, his puppets and puppetry are his own inventions, he has draped himself in the false cloak of folkloricity and tradition, and though puppets − animated artifact figures − and the more-than-man-sized ones operated from the inside in particular − define his shows to perception, the crux of his 'puppetry' has been variety and composition of modes of performance, not all puppet-operating, nor even masked.

Performance mode is variegated by the different sizes and kinds (and operating modes) of puppets appearing in given performances. Giant, big, small and tiny puppets are apt to appear in the same performance, as also perhaps cutouts, dummies, dolls, inside-operated puppets, outside-operated ones, handled, flown and pulled ones. This on the one hand is a negative device, making illusion weaker and more difficult and desacralizing performance, but on the other an enrichment of means making up for the intentionally limited movement capacities and effect-modes of individual puppets and types of puppets:

'Puppets and masks ... come in all sizes and shapes that express their nature. "It is like narrative, which gives things the size and brightness and dimension you wish", Mr. Schumann said.'
(Blau, *A Bread & Puppet Visit*, New York Times, September 9, '77.)

Among the Bread and Puppet performance modes, we may distinguish, first puppet-operation in which the puppet is the audience focus from puppet-operation in which the operation or the operator shares this focus −

---

1. On Schumann's romantic conception of folk art, cf. e.g. his *God Himself/Problems Concerning Puppetry & Folkmusic & Folkart in the Light of God & MacNamara*, '67 (cf. Appendix III), an angry and in its detail silly polemic against commercial pseudo-folkart and its integration into the only apparently innocuous entertainment in our society lethargizing the citizenry into acceptance of a morbid pseudo-life and support of the lethal evils of warlike capitalism. Against such pseudo folk art it promotes the myth of a true folk art traditionally at home in the streets, art of poetic circus folk and puppeteers, politically relevant, unswervingly moral, and concerned with the essentials, mindful of God and in touch with the demons. But real folk art has been an apolitical, amoral and irreligious (though superstitious) celebration of life, cf. jazz and the blues − not mentioned by Schumann.

the operation and/or operator itself an element of the theatrical experience, and second both of these — puppet-operation — from performance without a puppet, and within this latter category, third, masked performance simulating that of a puppet from other types of performance, masked or not. Among the crucial distinctions: operation of puppets from behind a curtain, operation in front of or without a curtain; inside operation of a puppet vs. visible operation of it from outside of it; inside operation of a puppet vs. masked performance in a loose garment and in puppet-style; outside visible operation of puppets in a style making it distinctly a part of the theatrical performance as such vs. informal operation; puppet-operating and stagehand-type activities in formal white and/or in a ceremonial or festive manner vs. informal, workmanlike activities ditto in everyday clothes. Because of the multiplicity of relevant theatrical similarities and distinctions any one breakdown of Bread and Puppet performance modes is apt to be somewhat misleading in its groupings.

(1) Puppet-operating.
    (a) the operator invisible.
        (i) operating a rod or stick puppet or a hand puppet above a curtain.
        (ii) operating a life-size or life-size-plus puppet from within.
        (iii) operating a puppet by strings from a curtained second story or from within another puppet.
        (iv) moving small dolls and other toy-size objects by horizontal strings from the wings.
        (v) carrying and moving masonite cutout or half-shell puppets hidden behind them.
        (vi) arranging and rearranging dummies between scenes.

(2) Visible operator.
    (a) carrying and moving a giant pole puppet overhead, e.g. parading it, making it gesture or dance or greet another. The carriers may or may not be covered or fully covered by its dress, arm-movers won't be:
        (i) operators integrated into theatrical picture by ceremonial or festive movement and/or dress.
        (ii) no such integration.
            (1) but integrated by opposition.
            (2) operators incidental.
    (b) operation of a mannequin or dummy strapped to the operator's front:
        (i) interaction between mannequin and operator acted out.
        (ii) without appearance of interaction.

- (c) operation of a dummy or puppet not attached to the operator.
  - (i) interaction as supra.
  - (ii) no interaction.
- (d) holding, carrying and moving large masks or half-shell puppets, so that sometimes the operator is hidden, sometimes not.
- (e) operating a dummy or its head or hands by strings from exposed second story platform (bridge).
- (f) placing or displacing, removing small dolls.

(3) No puppet.
- (a) puppet-like movement by puppet-like performer: masked, in a loose garment hiding his/her outline.
- (b) gesturally abstract movement by masked or veiled performer, in dress delivering up his/her outlines and the movements of his/her limbs:
  - (i) mime.
  - (ii) dance.[2]
  - (iii) intermediate between mime and dance:
    - (1) on stilts.
    - (2) not on stilts.
- (c) unmasked, unveiled performance:
  - (i) ceremonial movement or as though in a rite.
  - (ii) mime.
  - (iii) acting, other than ceremonial movement and mime:
    - (1) presentational acting.
    - (2) simple doing.
    - (3) play-making group activity.
- (d) stagehand-type activities:
  - (i) integrated into theatrical picture by ceremonial or festive movement and/or dress.
  - (ii) no such integration:
    - (1) but integrated by opposition.
    - (2) incidental instrumental activities.
- (e) narration, with flip-book, crankie, or chart, or to action by other performers, and in this case with narrator visible or speaking from wings; quotation-style delivery of other performers' dialogue; barkering, m.c.ing.
- (f) musical performance, vocal or instrumental.

Roughly: over a period of time Schumann brought the puppets out in

---

2. Until Susan Dennison's spectacular demon stilt dance in the '83 circus pageant, dancing had been pretty much Schumann's personal prerogative, e.g. as spirit of Herod in *Washerwoman Nativity*, or as Uncle Sam or White Lady stilt dancer in his circuses.

front of the curtain, brought the operators out from inside the puppet, gave the operators roles, advanced to interactions between them and the puppets, and he added masked performers who were pseudo-puppets, and unmasked performers acting or doing things in the area of mime, dance and ceremony. He did this step-wise and retaining modes whose limits he had transgressed alongside the new modes and did it in a way retaining for the enriched mix the over-all aspect of puppetry.

2. Acting modes. Approximations of puppet-like acting.

Performing in the Bread and Puppet Theatre has not just been puppet-operating. The operating of the puppets — often or mostly being a visible part of the performance — has been stylized in ways involving various kinds of acting, and there has been a great deal of performance not involving operation of a puppet. Bread and Puppet performances have, however, been puppetry in a very general but important sense: the different performance modes have approximated the puppet-like. The movement of the animated artifact figure is not its own but another's, and it is this kind of movement, installed movement, that Schumann has made the characteristic of his theatre, has obtained for performance other than by manipulated puppets from his puppeteers.

There is to this, as to everything involving purpose, a dialectic: in pushing puppetry beyond its limits, Schumann has had to allow performance in which the appearance of movement instituted by another may appear given his or her movements by the *performer*, and though the puppet style of performance is dependent on the suppression of appearance of virtuosity, skill, talent and personality, first, it calls for its own peculiar kinds of skill and personality, and second, having to get performance in this style from substantially unrewarded labor — labor unrewarded e.g. by the ego satisfactions other styles of performance might accord — and dependent on their devotion and energy, Schumann had to accept the appearance in performances of their personalities and of the skills acquired by them during extended periods of loyal service. Moreover, he is seducible and if someone can come up with mime, dance or acting that thrills him, may give them leeway or create occasions for them if it goes against the austerities of style he cherishes. Also, he uses 'interesting parts' as rewards to performers. What one sees, therefore, in Bread and Puppet performance, is puppet movement at its limits.

Schumann has consistently opposed 'acting' in his theatre and has pretty much kept it, though not — though he keeps bitching about the difficulty of working with them — actors, out of his theatre: namely acting in the normal sense of representational, psychologizing acting, involving the pretense of being the character presented, attempting to create the illusion that the performer is that character, i.e. moves and speaks out of or actuated by that fictitious psyche.[1] Such acting is doubly

---

1. In *A Man*, the actor Maurice Blanc did a soldier who at one point is said to feel fear. Schumann prevented him from acting out that fear. My father tells of getting the idea of doing soldiers in white-face from Karl Valentin's, the Swabian comic's 'Furcht ham's. Weiss san's' — 'they are scared — white-faced.' But in Schumann's play how the soldier felt was not to the point, only what he did and whether it was right or wrong.

not puppetish: the performer seems moved by his/her assumed psyche, and this, the illusion aside, is clearly his/her own doing and achievement from minute to minute.

But Schumann has fairly consistently allowed mime, and what we might call 'presentational' acting – acting presenting a character in movement or speech without attempt at psychological indications or at creating an illusion of identification – has cropped up: notably '66-'68 when from simply opposing war Schumann was slipping into presenting both support of and some modes of opposition to it as problems: two kinds of 'presentational' acting closer to the ritual than to the possession by spirits from which normal 'psychologizing' acting is derived. And in addition to these two, he has employed three other kinds of performance that in a wide sense may be thought of as acting – i.e. that involve imitation and even (as mime and presentational acting do not) pretense – namely the 'simple doing' of things as 'anyone' might do them, where the pretense is that it's

---

'But you know I had seen other people do that piece and once again Peter's narration of it is so extraordinary, because it was thrown away, because it is not made into a self-important series of announcements, a man says goodbye to his mother, he does this, he does that. It's riveting. He is a narrative artist in his own right like nobody that I've ever seen. He can pick up and keep you with it without raising an inflection beyond the necessary level, without any kind of overt sweat, he keeps it going. And what struck me at the time was the contrast between that attitude and the hype formal trackings of the event (by the narrator (SSB)) was both jarring and just right.

Whereas most people, when they take material like that, the fact of putting themselves up in all this very formal getup, causes them to assume a very formal delivery, a very formal sense of self, of pompous in fact. You know, the piece involved, the times I've seen it, three musicians. One of them was Peter, one of them did the drum and others did other instruments. They all wore death masks with some shrouds coming with them. The mother who was Margo, who is I think a superb actress in Peter's work and one of the people who flourished in that work, and not many people really learned how to do it to that degree. She was really remarkable at it. She was the mother who later became the Vietnamese woman always wearing masks. And Maurice Blanc who never wore a mask in the piece – of course, Maurice had a face that was almost so mask-like in itself – but at one public session (Shapli is speaking of a '68 Art and Religion workshop (SSB)) a question came up about when Peter says the man is afraid. It's a simple direction and then we hear the march again and Maurice walks by. The question is should Maurice show fear? And a great discussion went into this in which Peter participated without taking sides. The theologians and Christians and so forth were all quite interested. Mostly they wanted him to show fear because otherwise how can you see that the man is undergoing changes, that up to now has been very confident about things and now suddenly he's in a strange country and people don't love him and of course he's going to be afraid.

And I remember saying at the time that I didn't think Maurice should show fear or anything else, that although he wasn't wearing a mask in any way, and that the extraordinary thing was in Peter's saying that line (as narrator saying that the man is afraid (SSB)) he had changed the context in which you see Maurice. So one moment he says the man doesn't show fear and you see him walking along and you see him in the context of that and next the man is afraid. Then you hear the march and you see him as you saw him before and you see a totally different impression of a human being who is changed because the context is changed.' — (Shapli, interview.)

not a theatre situation, group appearances of the performers with some show of spontaneity and personal engagement (real enough, mostly, but still artificial when you have to make a show of it in public view at a precise moment and in another man's play) acting out the making of the play, and, the most important type of acting in his theatre, ceremonious or ritualistic performance in which, as in blessings (transfer of manna), religious ablutions or annointments, or in the distribution of wine and bread with the pretense they are the blood and flesh of a savior, the presence of the sacred and/or the inward transcendentality of the action is indicated.

Mime and presentational acting are puppet-like in that they are ostentatiously imitative, and 'simple doing,' other than in self-made solo shows, by its artistic self-abnegation and task-performance character: the performer is doing what is called for and what he/she has been told to do, and what art is called for (Schumann denies that any is: the performer should not worry about the 'how') must be inevident. Performance as member of the group authorially pretending to be making the play is puppet-like for the same reasons, and also because ego is shown submerged in the group – not as in a Greek chorus bewailing the working of fate, but as in the group of operatic villagers joyously attending the master's wedding. In ceremonious performance sacral powers seem to be ruling the performer's actions. But all these performance modes are at the limits of the puppet-like and easily and often deviate from it. E.g. 'simple doing' the way Schumann does it[2] becomes a bravura show of concentrated energy in the tradition of German Expressionist theatre.

Schumann's use of mime, the reductive presentation of gesture, rendering its Gestalt, and of presentational performance, representation of gesture focusing the audience on its function or significance as action, may be illustrated from the stage version of *Chicken Little* and of *A Man Says Goodbye*, both of '67.

Both in the comedy and in the tragedy, masked and unmasked non-puppeteering performance took the form of something like mime, with the masked performance (Margo Sherman in the Polish photos) something like imitation of a puppet and something like dance mime, the unmasked

---

2. Cf. Schumann as cowboy in *Cry*, infra.
3. 'In "A Man Says Goodbye to His Mother," we see the quintessential facts of military murder. Here, the simplicity is brutally direct. A man is called to war, kisses his mother goodbye, is given weapons, kills his enemy, is decorated, is killed, is mourned, is forgotten. The story is all pictures, and the actors (the word simply does not apply) merely present the images. There is no playing of emotion and no character portrayals, actors are simply the mechanisms which convey the moving sculpture through which the story is unfolded. It is thoroughly un-human, even spectral, but this reinforces the nightmarish quality of what is being depicted.' — (C. Marowitz, *theatre abroad/London: off-off Broadway, Village Voice*, September 5, '68.)

Rehearsals of *A Man Says Goodbye to His Mother* in Poland in 1969. Photos by Piotr Barasz and Eustachy Kossakowski, *Poland* magazine, March 1970.

Chicken Little at the Newport, Rhode Island Folk Festival in July 1967. *Daily News* photo. *Newport Daily News*, July 15, 1967.

performance more in the 'epic' style supposedly promoted by my father as director. Note how Murray Levy holds the airplane: a presentational gesture, not a representational one, and how he mimics the 'mortal blow' struck him; and the stylization of the Chicken Little performer's comedy gesture of — I suppose — frustration. In both masked and unmasked, comic and tragic performance what Schumann apparently got out of at least some of his people was control and restraint in the abstractive presentation of isolated gestural poses: a puppet kind of thing that (1) is not — though it could easily slip into — acting (representation), (2) though a puppet-kind-of-thing is a bona fide non-puppeteering performance mode sui generis.

Both types of performance were important in Schumann's theatre '66-'68, but as far as I can tell the 'representational' type of acting by the time of *Cry* ('69) had pretty much been replaced by ceremonial performance or simply by non-acting.[4]

---

4. Eric Berne, who left the Mime Troupe for the Bread and Puppet Theatre in '69, and who had been a 'regular actor' before he joined the Mime Troupe (quoted in Kourilsky, '71):

' "J'ai appris autant en faisant simplement une entrée et une sortie dans la généalogie du *Cry* qu'en jouant toute une comédie. C'est une façon différente de jouer, absolument non psychologique, qui est totalement négligé aux Etats-Unis. Même à la Mime Troupe, vous devez faire preuve de tempérament sur la scène et cela engage immédiatement votre moi, tandis que dans le théâtre de Peter, vous n'avez pas de nom, il n'y a pas à broder, vous fonctionnez presque comme un machiniste. A la Mime Troupe, j'ai apprix l'excès, au Bread and Puppet l'économie. Ronnie (Davis) parle toujours de bruit, Peter de silence : savoir créer les deux est important pour un acteur.'

Schumann préfère donc travailler avec "des gens qui n'ont pas l'ambition d'être acteurs, que cela intéresse de marcher jusqu'à une table et de prendre un verre et ne faire que cela, plutôt qu'avec des gens qui veulent travailler le *comment* aller à la table et prendre le verre". Il ajoute : "De la part des acteurs, je veux ce que l'on fait dans *The Cry*, qu'ils se conduisent comme tout le monde, qu'ils mettent la table, qu'ils prennent du pain et qu'ils le distribuent, ou bien qu'ils chantent tous sur un ton puissant ou sur un ton doux, ou bien qu'ils s'engagent dans une activité, mais sans simuler une caractéristique de l'esprit humain." ' — (Kourilsky, '71.)

3. Ceremonial movement, the alienation of ceremony, primordiality of moral address. The puppet style.

Slow movement is generally taken as hallmark of the Bread and Puppet style — the slow rise of a disciple's arm, a chunk of paper maché bread in his hand, the slow procession of an army across green hills — and this is correct, by and large puppets and performers move at sub-normal speeds, and the scene-dividing speedy motions of stage clearers or of banner carriers in on a gallop, or the inserts of the jerky, jiggly motion above a curtain of small hand puppets are within the convention the contrasting abnormalcies. The slowness seems appropriate to the large creatures (puppets), gives time for the power of the masks to assert itself, hauls us back from the everyday speeding toward goals the plays put in doubt.[1] Deceleration — relative to everyday life — seems the rule for ceremonies and perhaps for rites — together with sudden speedings up — as though in the manner of a spreading out of time into a small semblance of eternity and a cutting off of purpose. Ceremonial movement is the Bread and Puppet performance style, the alternative mostly chosen by Schumann both to epic — alienatory, narrative — performance and definitely to the variety, modern and old, of mimetically expressive acting performance styles focused on indications of psychology and character. Time is motion, ceremony converts it into a supra-added fifth dimension of space,[2] a canvas on which a Bread and Puppet spectacle is painted in strokes of gesture. Besides slowed-down-ness, ceremoniality requires evenness of gesture: increase of metricality over the normal, even measure, deemphasized accents, simplicity: the confinement of movement, including displacement, to gesture, and the reduction of gesture to essentials, abstraction of gesture; and exaggeration: the enlargement of gesture. Its demands on the performer — when the performer is inside operator of a puppet made on him/her by the puppet[3] — are concentration and restraint, rather than

---

1. 'His extraordinary "rootedness," as (Ralph Lee said), provides him with this simplicity, which at its best is not simplistic but enables him to develop the action with mesmerizing slowness, forcing upon the audience time to remember, imagine or anticipate, until they become his collaborators, a pace which can be overwhelming when the unfolding details are of suffering and death.' — (Hoagland, *Let 'em Have*, '83.)
2. The four dimensions of space: the eye's axis of purposive depth, the chest's axis of confrontation and the body's vertical axis of lostness (or to the superstitious redemption), and the dimension of space, locus of each man's pointal process within the process of the cosmos.
3. Palmer on her performance as White Lady in *Dead Man Rises*:
  'The figure was a white face like the moon. A very simple woman's face. And it was imbedded in the most marvellous costume I've ever seen. It essentially was a net. There was a tremendous amount of net which could be manipulated in very simple and graceful ways, the net. It was like a presentational piece, for presenting this figure over and over

skill or gifts, and a mobilization and continuous investment of energy kept 'behind' the performance, below its surface, strong but not violent gesture. The concentration required is kinesthetic, similar to a dancer's, and conflicts with another requirement on — or at least temptation for — a Bread and Puppet performer, that of awareness of pose, i.e. of pictorial effect.

Because in it the paradigmatic performances are those of puppet operators and masked performers, not those of seeing and kinesthetically self-visualizing, eye-self-monitoring actors or mimes, this awareness is not visual, but it is still a distraction from that sustained concentration on unnaturally slow movement.

Ceremonial or ritual gesture is not just careful, stately, slow, but indicates the sacred (or the intrinsically good) or its presence — perhaps even its presence within the action performed or the performance of it, and indicates — there is no other way of doing it — a spiritual state appropriate to the sacred or intrinsically good or to its presence: awe, respect, spiritual concentration (inwardness). Bread and Puppet performance is ceremonial in this strong sense.[4]

The ceremonial gesture, when performed by masked performers — 'live puppets' — gives the Bread and Puppet Theatre its grandeur. When performed by actors without mask, not puppets, it is disgusting by its pretentiousness. It infracts the modesty incumbent on man in his relation to man (and thus on an actor in relation to an audience). For the sacred or good indicated, it substitutes the feelings of the performer with respect to it — the performer. And being, in the theatre, make-believe, it is sacrilegious, and should it happen to be authentic, embarrassing, because of the stupidity it reveals. But in a masked performer or 'live puppet' it is removed from the performer, and if the artistry of the mask and the intelli-

---

again in different situations. The journey was very slow, long walk, which happened on several levels, around a piece of scenery that Peter had drawn of grey trees. The journey went in and out of this very simple set so the figure would appear and disappear and reappear and disappear. And lights were manipulated to help ... so that the lights were always shining on this face which would appear and disappear like a moon during this journey ... To me it was a character who appeared and disappeared, went outward and went inward ... had a relationship and then a long, long journey all alone. And the idea was to be able to show to the audience or the group the gradual tension that went on in this inner journey and how it built. So you had a very straightforward walk. The only way that this mannequin could really be managed, you see, and that's the constraint of these puppets. At the same time, if you can get a characteristic walk with any of these very constraining puppets, then you have something like a live person who really reads.' — (Palmer, interview.)

4. 'Theatre is a form of religion. It is fun. It preaches sermons and it builds up a self-sufficient ritual where the actors try to raise their lives to the purity and ecstasy of the actions in which they participate.' — (Schumann, statement accompanying *The Puppet Christ*, 1964, Appendix I.)

David Wade reviewing *Fire* (*The Times Saturday Review*, London, May 4, '68) thought: 'These players have a superb sense of ritual and a command of hieratic gesture.'

gence of the operative conceptualizations are adequate to it (as they generally are in the Bread and Puppet Theatre), it is the gesture appropriate to communal rituals (the performer being as much part of this community as the spectator), to celebrations of social union and/or of integration into a cosmos, and is not disgusting, but elevating.

Though the defining style of Bread and Puppet performers and performances is ceremony or ritual, and this not just formally, but with the indication that it's for real, that (1) sanctities and absolute goods attaching to ordinary life are evoked, and (2) that the (theatre's) evocation of them, the performance, partakes of them, Bread and Puppet performance is not just ceremony or ritual, nor stylized only and purely as them, but on the contrary deliberately comprises conflicting stylistic elements, partly designed (only) to prevent the degradation of ceremony/ritual into art, i.e. mere form, aesthetic pattern, and to preclude trance or contemplation that might shield the spectator against message, partly designed to alienate the ceremony/ritual, to put it into perspective by relating it (a) to actual life, (b) to the activity of performance and to its elements and devices, the performers, the masks and puppets.

The slowness, evenness and simplicity (abstraction) of ceremonial gesture continually poses the danger of meaninglessness, and its contained strength may merely generate unspecific tension. The ritual/ceremonial form tends over long periods to drain rituals and ceremonies whose gestural significations and further (symbolic, transcendental) meanings originally (except for esoteric components) were probably perfectly clear to participants and spectators of meaning. Where the rituals and ceremonies are, as in the case of the Bread and Puppet Theatre, contemporary inventions and not even intended for repetition (the one feature incompatible with regarding them as rituals), this is not the case. But care nevertheless has to be exercised to retain meaningfulness by the articulation of gesture and by clear indication of the direction of movements – of where they are headed. It's not enough that it be done (as in the case of many older religious rites), it must be made clear what is being done. Thus in the Bread and Puppet we tend to see simple things done clearly and with some incisiveness. This abrogates ceremoniality. A certain naturalness of movement, not altogether compatible with awesomeness, is retained or interspersed.

It is important to Schumann that like his masks and puppets the performance retain a certain roughness and crudity, a lack of finish, a certain imprecision, both representationally and aesthetically, stopping definitely short of not only smoothness and slickness, perfection of any kind (other than in concentration on to him essential meanings, and inducement of emotion to him appropriate to those meanings), but of sophistication of any kind, subtlety, nuance or embellishment. This applies equally to story and words and to movement. Avoidance of prettiness (he does not always avoid cuteness) is quite compatible with ceremonial awesomeness. But roughness, crudity and imprecision – street shoes visible under the puppet skirt, the covering mask sloppily handled so that the performer's head is partly visible at the edges, gestures a little shaky in the outline, some careless steps – the point being that he does not control performance down to the last detail, and takes care not to, he leaves much execution up to the performers, and often or even normally simply does not rehearse often enough for ballet clockwork precision – mar ceremony. The resulting impression of amateurishness, of childlike playing, of the primitiveness of popular as opposed to the sophistication and high technical level of 'high' art, of the slipshod and made-to-do is an essential part of the Bread and Puppet performance style. The flaws, deficiencies and poverties in question are not deliberately placed or contrived: they are allowed; individual occurrences of them are apt to be unintended, may even be regretted, but in their aggregate the production methods assure they will be there; and the overall effect they have on the style is quite deliberate. This roughness or crudity of Bread and Puppet performances does not assimilate their ceremonial style to that of the so-called 'primitive' cultures, nor does it merely weaken the power of their ceremoniousness – it in the end doesn't, the spectator is carried away in spite of it –: it alienates[5] the ceremony of the performance, makes the point that it is not there for its own sake, but is something gotten up and invented as part of a transaction between the performers and the audience by which the latter is to be put in touch with ultimate realities, with the ultimate realities of their lives outside of the performance. It's almost as though Schumann and his group were telling us: 'Forget the performance. It's not important.'

We might say: Schumann builds a systematic sabotage of art into his art. He does this not only by the higher pretensions (higher than merely artistic ones) of that ceremoniousness, and by formal primitivism, but by certain aesthetic disparatenesses disrupting aesthetic unity – e.g. the different sizes and kinds of puppets in the same performance, the different modes of performance in the same performance, sometimes almost giving

---

5. 'C'est en effet à la "leçon d'écriture" du théâtre de marionnettes japonais plus qu'à la théorie brechtienne de la distanciation qu'il faut penser ici. "Je suppose – dit Peter Schumann – que l'on pourrait interpréter ce que nous faisons comme des effets d'éloignement, mais ce n'est pas là pour moi une question de philosophie, nous n'utilisons pas consciemment cette méthode, et nous n'en avons pas besoin, tout simplement parce que nous employons des marionnettes". Il est dans la nature des marionnettes fe créer une distance et il suffit de les mettre en rapport avec des acteurs pour "éloigner" la représentation. Tout le Bunraku relève en fait l'idée de distanciation: les trois hommes qui actionnent la marionnette sont visibles et il est impossible de les oublier: la marionnette n'est pas là pour nous faire croire quelque chose. Dans le théâtre de marionnettes sicilien – dit-il – lorsqu'on veut dire: "L'homme est malade," on voit la maladie voler à travers les airs et atterrir sur l'homme. C'est une idée fantastique. Ce n'est pas un effet d'éloignement au sens où Brecht l'entend.' — (Kourilsky, '71.)

it the aspect of a variety show – by narrative forms: actual narrations, and framing devices that he, at any rate, regards as pseudo-narratory: presenting the spectacle as illustration of an unspoken text; by incursions of the work process and 'out of character' appearances of the performers as sponsoring individuals into the performance – integrated into the show 'by opposition' or incidental to it; and by actions ostentatiously displaying the puppet character of the puppets or the mask-character of the masks, temporarily dispersing the magic of their illusion. The basic function of these acts of sabotage is the one mentioned: the spectacle is to work as a transaction relating the spectators to their basic realities.

These realities, as far as Schumann and his work are concerned, are those of a moral order, perhaps, but not unambiguously, supranatural, anchored in, perhaps immanent to the world life cycle, possibly a cosmic life cycle. A Bread and Puppet spectacle evokes these essences, its gestures are pared down for clean and clear reference to them, its ceremoniousness is adapted to their awesome absoluteness, its primitivism and alienatory features mitigate its ceremoniousness for the sake of recalling to the audience that they are there to be put in mind of them.

The gestures and images are to denote these essences. They are shaped to be denotative, and shaped and selected – the area of reference is conceptually small, poor – to denote these moral but real essences. The notion that good and evil and their kinds are real, part of a natural, perhaps a cosmic order, implies that pathos is uncalled for: it attaches to these realities themselves, the gestures need not be pathetic. The vocabulary of pathetic gestures, drawing attention to the goodness, suffering, malevolence, tragic flaws of individuals and their conflicts in the psyche does not render the evocation of an objective moral order more effective, but merely debases that order's majesty, and distracts the spectator from the moral by having him fascinated by the vagaries of individual coping with it.

E.g. when Schumann, from the mid-'70s on, started using flocks and herds of puppet animals – stilt-flamingos, kite-gulls, cows, deer or sheep – in his pageants, he for each species of animals rehearsed with their operators a few – two, three or four – simple movements characteristic in an abstract way of the species in question, to be mechanically repeated, a few movement patterns of reaction – hesitation, confusion, fear – to be executed discretionally but sparingly and sensitively at a certain juncture – and perhaps a way to lie down and die. The essences in this case, brought out by simple conformity to instructions, without timidity or bravura, were the natures of different biological species; but conceived in the context of a world view valuing the integration into nature of mammalian species other than man and counterposing animal innocence to human predation.

I have so far not mentioned the most outstanding Bread and Puppet performance element, and, for a Bread and Puppet performer, the crucial element of the performance situation: the presence and power of the mask.

First and foremost, as regards the import for performers, the mask that may be on his or her own face, but then also the face of a puppet he or she is operating whan that face is not over their face, and in fact, masks and puppets' faces worn or controlled by anyone on stage – and not even at that moment, perhaps, but just before or soon after: the movements even of unmasked performers must adjust to that power.

The masks and puppet faces are powerful first in that they gather in the attention of the audience more than – except at certain contrived moments – the face of an actor, because of their abstraction and concentration of expression (I am speaking of Schumann's masks in particular, and other good – abstract but meaningful – masks) and do so even when the puppet as a whole has a powerful functional and/or sculptural finish and wholeness or unity (Schumann's 'Sharkplane' and flying 'Peace Dove' or 'Angel of Peace' puppets being good examples of this); and secondly because of the powerful effect they have on focused attention. I would say that their power is comparable rather to the power in acting of a great voice well and strongly used than to the power of facial expressions or gestures – though in the movies closeups of faces may affect one as strongly as a masked or a puppet face.

Their power has four or five major implications for performance: relatively little needs be done with them to achieve a considerable effect or alteration of effect – slight movements of theirs have considerable impact – too much, too rapid, too irregular, too complicated movement of them blurs the image more than it would if they were less powerful – restraint is crucial; movements of the body and of the limbs must be in accord with their character – their power makes the requirement of this accord strong – movements of the body and of the limbs must have the simplicity of the puppet head or masks, an equal clarity and degree of abstraction – too much fussiness or sophistication of these movements may not impair the impact of puppet face or mask, but is out of place, becomes ridiculous, given the dominance of the simple statement made by the mask or puppet face; and these movements must have the force, the energy or strength and incisiveness of the mask's or puppet face's expression – hesitations ruin any theatrical performance, but in the context of puppets and masks, vagueness, ambiguity, the lack of accent of movement, unclear beginnings and ends or outlines are even more disturbing, I would say, than in other theatre, if only because in other theatre they can be given human values of their own, can be reintegrated into a sequential registry of plausible expression or characterization – something can be made of them in terms of meaning or psychology – but not in a theatre in which the emphasis and focus is on the powerful and set statements of the masks and puppet heads, or at any rate, of Schumann's masks and puppet heads.

His or her masks, to the performer, especially when the performer has had training as an actor, is apt to figure negatively as something hiding his or her face and reducing, in this respect, his or her powers of expression. The performer is apt to tend to try to compensate by bodily gestures, trying to body mime to express some of what his or her face is not available for expressing. In fact, however, a masked performer's mask is more powerfully the focus of spectators' attention than an unmasked performer's naked face – if only by its unequivocality. Powerful effects are achieved by its mere presentation. The performer must therefore be guided to act out of a continued consciousness of his or her artificial face, moving in awareness that this is where he or she carries the audience, and that whatever is writ on the mask is what to the audience he or she is, and that his or her body-whole is that false face's frame. And that even when the musical effects of dance or the expressive effects of mime are intended, his or her movements must be consonant with the mask, must flow out of it.[6]

The abstract movements of the large puppets are similarly powerful and exercise the same restraints on the performers.

Masks and puppets thus not only dominate the performance image, they condition the performance styles of its live components, the puppeteers. This conditioning extends not only to the puppet operators, who because of the size of the puppets appear as their servants rather than as in much other puppet theatre their masters and whose movements appear finalistically controlled by the puppets they operate and the masks they wear, but to the ceremonious quasi-mimes, quasi-dancers and quasi-actors:[7]

---

6. 'But actually there were a lot of technical points. I remember Peter talking about the way to wear a mask, which is quite different from the way most theatrical mask people talk about it. I mean it has – of course, everybody has different points on it. The Commedia people will say this – but Peter used to say that the focus of the energy when you're in mask is the face. Now that sounds logical, except that it's very extraordinary to a lot of people – I mean, who consider that when you wear a mask you eliminate the face and that you have to somehow put the bulk of the expression in other parts of the body, be it the hand, you know, the mid-section or whatever, to show with the body what the face cannot show. Peter is very clear on the point that that is completely wrong. That when the mask is there the face has become more than ever the point of focus for everything, so that an actor who really digests that point in his body will de-emphasize, except for very specific accents and functions, the usages of the rest of his body and put the total emphasis on the face. This means that the slightest movement of the mask is charged with concentrated significance . . . . But a lot of people will take the position that I've just told you. That when you're wearing a mask what it means is you have to put into the arms, into the rest of the body what you cannot show in the face . . . . But an actor who grasps that in what he's doing is really quite an actor.' — (Shapli, interview.)

7. 'When we did *A Man Says Goodbye*, for instance, and I was doing the Bob Ernstthal – the part that he had – that I had seen him do in Berlin, he wanted – I didn't – I reacted to the narration that I was hearing, you know, I let it move in on me, I mean I was – and he felt that that – he felt that that was too much acting. Too much acting. He wanted neutral, not – which may or may not be better or worse. But I began to understand what the nature of demonstration is, cause the piece was really a demonstration. And since then I have – I

learned a lot ... in *Man Says Goodbye* I was without a mask the whole time. And he always – he knew I came from an acting background, so he: "The actor, the actor", things like that. We used to – one time I said, well, Peter if you don't like anything I do I might as well leave, I mean I don't want to hang you up. He said, no, no, I like what you do. So that is what made me say it might have been a tactic. To bring you along to where he wanted me to go. Which is what happens with everybody who works for him.' — (Levy, interview.)

'The following year at NYU I was teaching my second – I guess my second year I was teaching in the theatre program.... And I had a workshop with some of the third year students – a miscellaneous workshop – and I asked him one time to come down and participate. And he came down with Margo Sherman and this other fellow whose name I can never remember.... And this was the time when Peter was playing around with the exercise of the piece that he called *Reiteration*, which used that as the theme for this set of variations – quite fascinating. I never saw where it went to. I only saw him working on it. But I never was convinced that it was going to go anywhere. But the journey was quite fascinating. And he began sort of working that way and he tried to incorporate – asked people to participate, and he brought them up and gave them masks and tried to get them involved in it. The result was a lot of confusion. These students who had been going to acting classes for four years and whatever, and with some sort of intent to go into the theatre as actors, even those who were familiar with his work didn't really know what to make of it when they were placed on stage. Should they act, for instance? Attempts to do that were catastrophic, of course. What should they do? Well, they should just stand there. And here they should raise their hand and here they should say the line. But this isn't acting. This isn't acting at all. You don't need an actor to do this. Peter would of course agree with most of this and try to get on with the work. But it outlined to me very clearly – I mean, there I had a very romantic notion myself that somehow we were going to develop a new kind of actor that incorporated this sort of awareness and other kinds of things and so on, and it's extremely difficult. I mean, in effect, Peter's work has almost nothing to do with acting as we usually consider the term. So it wasn't altogether because the kids were stupid, or had evil intents or had lacked perception, although they may have, some of them I think did. It was really because it wasn't their craft they were being confronted with and they were trying to find a way to relate it. It was painful to me. It was painful because – and angering to me. Angering because I was aware after a while that some of those students were looking at this crazy man up there with the masks who was talking in his little quiet German accent and sort of being a bit of a clown, you know, smiling happily when as far as they could see, nothing was going on. And I got quite angry. I mean, I didn't say – I said it to him later on – that I wanted them to be aware of the fact that they were dealing with one of the quintessentially significant and large artists working in the theatre now. And if they were unable to incorporate or view his presence and work, that's one thing. But that they should not lose sight of the fact that it would be stupid of them not to be able to learn something from him. But it didn't work out too well. And I remember at the end I was with Margo and Peter and Peter said – this was very interesting, he was always very generous with such things – he said, I think it worked rather well, don't you? And Margo said, no, it didn't work very well, and I resented the event. And he said, why? – looking quite surprised. And she said because I think it was calculated to ridicule those students. It was interesting, because she was seeing it exactly the opposite way that I was seeing it. Both of them were quite correct. The students felt – I mean, the stupid ones felt the theatre was being ridiculed. Margo saw that in effect the students were being ridiculed. She was more right than I was, of course.... Well, what I think now is quite different from what I thought then. What I think now is that they could have – you see, I think that our program is fairly effective at training people to function well in the theatre. But I don't think any kind of training situation in itself resolves the kind of lodestone question about artistry. You know, the simple exchange of sparks that has to do with enlarging your capacity to make jumps. Startling jumps that don't seem to

puppet-like not only because like in those in a trance or possessed (dance is traditionally expression of possession), their movement proclaims governance by spiritual realities inspiring them, but because of the primitivism of their arts, by Schumann deliberately kept simple and unskillful and non-individualizing, reduced to the rudimentary so they will complement the simple powerful action of masks and of puppet gestures and so they will to the spectator proclaim the primordial importance of the message. It even extends to the two non-ceremonious performance modes I have mentioned, the cheerfully festive and the matter-of-fact practical or work-a-day: though here chiefly because in these modes the kids and young people working for Schumann seem so empty-headed, their cheer and/or conscientious task-performances quite unrelated to the gravity of the

---

follow from the logic of training in some kind of way. I mean, I think that a fine acting teacher will be able to do that also within certain ways. You know, when I send my students now to see Peter's work, and I do it quite a lot, I tell them not to think of this as something that is an extensioin of their work. This is just simply to experience it. And if they experience it sufficiently it will leave a mark on them which obviously will have some effect on who they are and how they work. In other words, I don't think the effect on an actor is essentially different from the effect on anyone else, except that as an actor it may affect somebody the way — what kind of a broker he is, for all I know. And it certainly should affect an actor in the kind of actor he is.' — (Shapli, interview.)

'Le problème de travailler avec des acteurs, c'est qu'ils ont des émotions aussi bien que des corps. Les marionnettes sont plus mobiles, plus expressives, plus visuelles, elles donnent plus de choix, elles peuvent êtres petites ou immenses. Et en mêlant des gens et des marionnettes dans un spectacle, voux pouvez obtenir un effet de contraste. Des gens entrent en rampant dans un masque, ou en sortent, le contraste peut être qu'ils sont plus petits ou le contraire.... Quand un acteur avec son talent particulier se joint à la troupe, il n'y trouve pas les tâches qui l'aideraient à se développer. Nous avons toujours des problèmes avec les acteurs professionnels qui ont été formés selon la "Méthode" américaine. Les interprétations modernes du système de Stanislavski produisent un blocage mental qui rend le travail impossible. Dès que quelqu'un cherche à devenir acteur, il y a quelque chose qui ne va pas psychologiquement. On le voit suivre un programme à fin strictement personnelle, il apprend tout ce dont justement nous voulons nous débarrasser: le souci de sa personne, l'expression de soi....' — (Kourilsky, '71.)

'Schumann's work is superficially Artaudian, in that it relies almost exclusively on objects and imagery and transcends the naturalistic limitations of actors and characters, but actually much closer to Craig's notions about dehumanized performers and super-marionettes. Artaud's aim was to penetrate beyond psychology into metaphysics; for him, metaphysics lay BEHIND realism. For Schumann, it lies above it. Whereas Artaud idealized the actor and wanted him to become an aesthetic athlete, Schumann finds him a necessary evil, to be tolerated but not encouraged. His theatrical form is more closely allied to effigy and sculpture than to the performing arts. Artaud's ideal theatre is rooted in human extremity, and his quest is always to destroy the familiar in order to rediscover the essential. The essence of Schumann's aesthetic is embodied in his puppets, not his text nor even his action. With him, the mask is the message.' — (C. Marowitz, *theatre abroad. London: Off-off-B'way, Village Voice,* September 5, '68.)

'So far as acting goes, I'm sure a Bread and Puppet actor will never find happiness. There is really no respect for actors in Bread and Puppet.' — (Leherrissier, interview.)

masks' and puppets' and the performance's message, the struggle between good and evil: obviously – they haven't, it would appear, seeing them in these modes, been through the mill – beyond their ken. The performers, in these various ways, appear as puppets.[8]

---

8. 'Helpers who materialize two months beforehand are given short stilts and told to make bigger ones when they have become proficient on those. They are also handed masks, to get the feel of being a Washerwoman or a Garbageman. Stilts will convert anybody into a puppet – stumbling, tripping, relearning how to walk, and then forever swaying slightly in order to keep upright.' — (Hoagland, *Let 'em Have*, '83, on the rehearsals for the '82 circus.)

'When the performers do "act," they are still very much like puppets. Actions are represented without emotions; there is gesture but no attempt at identification with the character. The Brechtian alienation is natural with the puppets, but here it is extended to all of the performers. Both the actors and the puppets demonstrate the story without any attempt at psychology.'

(*Bread and Puppet Theatre. The Stations of the Cross. Tulane Drama Review* #55 — (September 1972.)

4. A theatre of mute, grandiose and live puppets, expressive sculptures in a movement of gestures, the puppets define the space.

Only his hand puppets and, very rarely, his rod puppets when played over the curtain, speak, and these are minor exceptions. His other puppets and his masked performers have no voice. What they might be saying is sometimes said for them, generally in the manner of quotation, by a narrator or from the wings, but this also is infrequent. Dialogue is only a very minor feature of his theatre. Narration, music, sound frame an essentially and almost purely visual theatre.

This visual theatre consists of movement and sculpture (I shall briefly discuss the element of painting infra): the sculpture of the masks or puppet heads, and the sculpture of the whole bodies or masked performers, compounded of these heads and of their bodies, the which appear neither as bodies nor as dress, but as dressed bodies, and whose sculptural quality is due partly (especially in the case of the giant puppets) to the abstract shapes of their parts, partly to their overall abstract shape (in the case of most of his big, life-size or life-size-plus puppets whose dress is apt to be loose, oriental). In some shows similarly abstract large paper maché or celastic hands figure as sculptures.

The large masks or puppet heads are striking, the large puppets imposing, both are often immobile in place, movements are slow: so the spectator often abstracting from their movement and their mobility, is relating to them – especially to the heads – as he or she might to sculpture. But they retain their aspect of sculptures even when moving and seen as mobile or in motion; in fact, only then seem fully to acquire it, not having it e.g. in the Glover puppet museum.

This seems paradoxical. One would normally, I think, think of sculpture and motion as relating antithetically. We may disregard as mistaken the museumgoer's view of sculpture as isolate in space, as appreciable in abstraction from its effect on the viewer's awareness of the space within which it exerts its action. From this viewpoint a sculpture's movement would be merely a distraction, confusing the perception of it. The traditional and true view of sculpture is of it as element of architecture, exerting a projective radiation structuring the space around it, its space and that of the viewer. This it does, together with other fixed, shaped objects in the area, proximately by the configuration of its surfaces and disposition of its mass, but ultimately, even in the case of non-representational sculpture, by gathering up like an equation, some movement into the peace and potency of a posture – in the case of non-representational sculpture: their balance, thereby absorbing movement around them, subduing it by their potent stillness. Good sculpture sculptures its field for restfulness for the viewing occupants of the field, peace of mind and concentration. But if this is the nature of sculpture and of its action, would not movement be as destructive of its peculiar sculptural effect as e.g. speech? The moving sculpture, one might think, not only would disturbingly be restructuring the area in a continuous way — and how could this make for peace of mind, spiritual concentration? — it might never be able to achieve any ordering of it in the first place; and if its very point is an arrest of movement denoted, the representation of movement in stillness, would not its movement necessarily negate the essence of it?

Schumann conceives of his puppets as moving sculptures; as sculptures, but sculptures made to be seen in motion. To the foregoing objection, he opposes that since sculptures in the piazza or park, the courtyard, the cathedral create stillness for the moving field-user, moving sculpture may do so for the still viewer:

'And that was sort of the original idea. That's what one does. You can take a piece of sculpture, put it outside and do things with it — move it — (I: But, you see, in these processions — the ones where the village is blessed and the houses — it's the local figure of Mary or of a saint from the church who extraordinarily moves on that day —) This is true, but on the other hand, if you walk into a cathedral, in contrast to walking into a bank, to my mind, the concentration of thought and of, well, very specific thought — it's hard to express what specific thought — is achieved through these humanized walls and columns more than through *anything*. Architecture — slightly over life-size replicas of human beings in various styles, includes us, the bodies that walk around there, in an incredible way that you will never feel in a bank or in a modern building that prides itself with its neutrality — with its — as if allowing us to think anything quite through, to concentrate on anything. It's not *true*. In that space, our bodies moving and those bodies not moving, get a lot from each other. The idea of having those bodies move and *our* bodies be still offers itself, you know, it's very easily thinkable. Actually, I think, the renaissance *did* that a *lot*. We don't have much *records* of that, but they *did*. They had a deus ex machina — they really *performed* it. They mounted a *lot* of sculpture that moved; created plays with mechanical dolls and life-size figures that would swing through the space in the church and appear from pulpits and various corners . . . . I just feel that movement can hardly be more disturbing or defeating the limits of sculpture — or contradicting that than the fact that the well-dressed citizens of Florence were confronted with gigantic over-life-size nudes. I mean, what an affront to a dressed society, you know. You have these giant, totally undressed, nude beauties standing around them. (I: You think of the very large saints that are carried?) Yeah. One that was described to me was in — somewhere — Barcelona or somewhere, where they not only carried one of these big madonnas and then, when they walk up the steps, they do a job of trembling that figure before they put her down — in different stages. So, they actually do move her, more than just move her around. That's one side of it. The other side is when you look at other forms of mask theater. You look at Tahitian mask theatre, which also I have never seen in performance but in pictures — but I have seen

Japanese forms of theatre – there is certainly a great attempt made at achieving something of the concentration of sculpture with human bodies. You know, that stillness and non-moving composition in a space that they create in a courtyard that gets defined totally by nothing but their bodies that hardly move. And, if they move, then it doesn't amount to more than the contrast of the position of one sculpture to another – must be the desire to achieve concentration such as sculpture has. Well, sculpture isn't *invented* yet. There's more to sculpture than what has been done. Sculpture can move. Calder's sculpture moves a little bit. That's okay. I don't think he's so great, but not so bad.' (Schumann, interview, '82.)

His theatre in fact not infrequently achieves this goal of the spectator's inward concentration. I would think that if it does so by an action involving the type of effect ascribed supra to sculpture qua sculpture, it must do so because of some manner of appropriateness of the movement to the sculpture, and vice versa. E.g., on a general level, non-representational motion for non-representational sculpture, mimetic motion for mimetic, gestural motion for expressionist sculpture.

I would describe Schumann's sculpture as, in the tradition of Gothic medieval and XXth century expressionist sculpture, expressive rather than mimetic, designed to catch what individuals may express rather than their individuations. They are physiognomically quite implausible: their shape is fantasy. They are cracked swollen lumps. They abstract an inner state or motion, but not as feature of the individual or the moment, but rather it itself, a generic spiritual reality – state, action or suffering – perhaps instantiated by individuals, a temperament possessing and acting from within, a fate acting on and through an individual. The masks do not portray expressions as modifications of a face – many of them are hardly face-like – but as essence of it. Similarly for the puppet contours. Many, perhaps most of them show pain, suffering; fewer anger, ferocity; still fewer serenity, benignity; some malice, cunning. They appear as concentrated concretions of these.

Assume now that such sculpture move – as some madonnas are said occasionally to smile or weep. And assume that it moves in the appropriate manner, that is, gesturally, its movement abstract, and the abstraction of it focused on expression; and with the accent of the expression neither on it qua act nor on the individual expressed, but on what is expressed – sorrow, pity, anger, good will. Such movement – gestural movement and this kind of universalizing gestural movement – is the movement characteristic of the Bread and Puppet Theatre, and relates immanently to this sculpture, extending its expression into gesture, not disrupting the sculpture's pacificatory domination of its space, but, on the contrary, achieving it.

I in fact don't buy Schumann's argument that moving sculpture is sculpture. I think that his dance and sculpture were weak and imitative and that he realized this by '61/'62, but at almost the same time, '62/'63, under the impact of New York City avant-garde performance art and of what Tyler's Alchemy Players by their music and movement made of his *Totentanz*, perceived the area in which his true genius could flourish: the gesturally focused performance of masked figures or puppets; his encounter in the summer of '63 with the big puppets of the Manteos then further pointing the way. His masks and puppets are weak when immobile and viewed as sculpture, viz. as shaped matter in space. Their power in his Dopp Farm (Glover) puppet museum, '75 following proves this: it arises from their theatrical arrangement. To make his masks work for performance, he had to abstain from trying to make them powerful as sculpture: qua sculpture, the masks he made in America are even weaker than the ones he had made in Germany: he had to dilute their sculptural effect to achieve their effect in performance. He adapted their expressiveness to gesture.

'Okay – another question – what else would you like to know – how else can we persuade you to participate and find more people to perform in the pageant? It's very important to do this – that's why we brought all this junk here – tons and tons of junk – and now we have to find people to move it; upright it so that it's not junk anymore – comes to life, because these things are very – very, very simple structures and just junk if you take them by what they really are – the materials and the assemblages of very simple materials. And they become creatures and meaningful things only through these rehearsals that we want to do with them. Through what they move like and what they do in context with each other.' (Schumann, address to volunteers for *Fight Against the End of the World* parade and/or pageant, New York City, June 2, '83.)

My definition of Schumann's sculptural style as expressionist needs to be qualified: expressions on Schumann's masks and puppet heads are obscure. They are expressions that an attentive and astonishable regard might reveal *in* expressions, compounded of the shadows of what we sell and buy as expressions. Not actual expressions. The term 'existentialist expressionism' might apply to Schumann's head sculptures, by 'existence' meaning a materiality neither nauseous nor nauseating, but difficult to bear, though essential and ineluctable – nearly unbearable; and essential in that it is not a materiation of spirit, a crutch for souls, but substantial materiality tending toward transcendence, self-destructively, and by this tendency painfully. The extreme crudity of these masks[1] is essential to this expressionism: not only to lead the eye away from or past both face and outer or signifying expression – to true expression – but to signify the tension between spirit and flesh. The movement then, in the main, is to implement this existentialist expressionism. Both sculpture and movement

---

1. 'Though (Ralph) Lee's masks are a good deal more polished and ornate (than Schumann's (SSB)), he generously suggested that Schumann's by their exceptional simplicity and what is deliberately left uncovered or unfinished, demonstrate what is necessary in mask creation and what is not.' — (Hoagland, *Let 'em Have*, '83.)

lack the raw violence by which Gothic and Late Wilhelminian/Weimar expressionism liberated feeling. Instead Schumann has been concerned with an underground of feeling — perhaps just anxiety.

To some extent Schumann's predicament has been that he never found a theatrical equivalent of his sculpture — he came up with political, moralizing, religiously conventional substitutes instead; and with approximative movement devices: great stuff (or I wouldn't be writing this book), but not what we glimpse in the masks. The foregoing simplifies and exaggerates slightly — I am trying to get at what he seems to me to have aimed at. It would be misleading to say that his theatre turned out existentialist expressionism. It didn't. But some such terminology seems to me needed to indicate what he broached.[2]

---

2. 'The puppets create the first and most striking impression of this theater, the miraculous sense of the static mask in motion, where the few words come through with the inwardness of possession by a great force — through the face of the sleeper into the inner movement of the dream. But Schumann's puppets are quite unlike the masks of Attic drama. The voice that rings through them is not individual: only the masks are. One responds to the puppet, not to a person revealed through words, since the words are seldom spoken by the puppets, but by a narrator off to the side.

The puppets move with a dream-like rightness that is adapted to their size. The large ones move slowly, occasionally breaking the pace with startling and often terrifying suddenness. We are not dealing with pompous solemnity, but with a sense of motion that the subconscious recognizes. Visually it is similar to film, which can condense time and action, alternate scenes, and shift focus with the subjective freedom of the dream. (Think of flight and implacable pursuit.) Likewise, the puppets move with a sense not of unreality but of those distortions proper to an inward sense of reality, for their size and motion have the air of dream. Thus this theater can deal utterly unselfconsciously with the fabulous:

> THERE IS A DEAD MAN LYING IN THE RIVER. (Bell)
> WHAT WILL WE DO WITH THE DEAD MAN? (Bell)
> I WILL TIE THE MAN TO THE BACK OF THE RIVER
> AND TAKE HIM TO MY HOUSE. (Bell)
> (From *The Dead Man Rises*)

In this context nothing seems more natural than the resurrection that follows. In *Ordet*, Carl Dreyer tries to force a resurrection out of the fabulous and into the casual world of plots and motives where we explain magic away as a violation of confidence, a sleight of hand, and whatever power it has in *Ordet* depends entirely on our initial acceptance of the moony world where resurrection is normal. The normalcy of the miraculous indicates that we are dealing with a primitive system of conventions similar to those of folk tales, and the preconceptual thought processes of childhood, of our earliest attempts to understand the world.

The basic elements of the medium of allegorical puppet theater correspond closely to Piaget's description of the patterns of thought in childhood. For example, allegorical causation is like the *post hoc* nature of syncretic thought. Psychomachia depends for its persuasiveness on the early sense of imminent justice. Schumann's use of primitive expressive sounds (twittering, moaning, etc.) has the emotive weight of pre-verbal struggles for articulation and, similarly, the dissociation of speaker and figure seems in itself to be an emblem of the separation of the child from the verbal world of adults. The very enterprise of allegorizing with puppets is rooted in animism and concretizing, both of which are basic modes of thought of childhood.

Though he later resisted definitions of his puppetry as synthesis of sculpture and dance,[3] this is how in '63/'64, when he started developing it, he thought of it: as extension of sculpture by dance.[4]

As I have indicated, I find 'gestural movement' more appropriate than 'dance.' Not that there isn't dance focused on expression of feelings and

---

This is not to say that it is a theater for children, but rather that the medium has its roots in the inner lives we carry with us from childhood: the structure of primitive cognitive styles; explosive psychic material composed of fantasies of power and helplessness, of incomprehensible forces, of magical fulfillment of wishes; of human animals and animal humans; of giants and dolls; and above all the sense of disparity between the puppet and its human role. One is seized by one's childhood. This is apparent in the way Schumann alternates simple moral absolutism with perceptual ambiguity, uses satiric ingenues with a child's vision of moral issues, and characterizes stylized and exaggerated gestures, and in general by the freedom with which the mysterious and playful enter this world. The first time I saw the Bread and Puppet in New York in the mid-sixties, I felt that I was in the presence of remarkable artistic power, and it has taken me years to begin to understand this kind of fascination. I found myself resisting an understanding of the use of the materials of childhood for two reasons: first, it seems to minimize the seriousness of the theater, which is vulnerable to any association with childhood merely because the use of puppets suggests that it is entertainment for children; and second, the process of maturity seems to put one acutely out of touch with childhood.' — (B. Goldensohn, *Peter Schumann's Bread & Puppet Theater, Iowa Review,* '77.)

3. '(Elka: This question is almost like asking what art influences — what made a strong impression on you in the field of sculpture, or — you probably didn't see mask exhibits, but certainly *sculpture* played a great role in your high school.) That doesn't make you a puppeteer, if your are influenced by — that you like sculpture. (Elka: But your puppetry is so much a marriage of —) I don't know about that — it's your opinion. I like to sculpt, but — and I went to school, and this is my background, to be a sculptor. I can just as well say my background is to be a baker. (Elka: But the interest in *dance* and choreography on the one hand and your interest and your experience as a sculptor and graphic artist, on the other — that combination is certainly — the puppetry seems like a very logical —)' — (Schumann, interview, '79.)

4. 'Puppet theater is an extension of sculpture. Imagine a cathedral, not as a decorated religious place, but as a theater with Christ and the saints and gargoyles being set in motion by puppeteers, talking to the worshippers, participating in the ritual of music and words. Puppet theater is of action rather than of dialogue. The action is reduced to the simplest dance-like and specialized gestures. Our ten-foot rod puppets were invented as dancers . . . .' — (Schumann, *Bread and Puppets,* program, *The Puppet Christ,* Easter '64.)

Schumann's *Bread & Puppets: A Way of Life* published in *Motive,* in February '65 (Appendix II), a two-part essay (*Puppet Theater as an Extension of Sculpture, Puppet Theater as an Extension of Dance*), an essay which Schumann may have written in '63/'64 (Kourilsky, '71 says it was written in '63) similarly conceptualizes his puppetry as joint extension of sculpture and dance: sculpture extended by dance, dance extended to include 'movement . . . separated from its purpose' of any object, e.g. a chair. The thrust of this essay's discussion of dance is that the Bread and Puppet puppetry develops such movement as theatre medium the way the 'modern theater' develops speech, two primary means of communication, and that 'powerful' communication requires the 'organization' of these means 'out of context', i.e. in independence of one another. Schumann, though he says 'in theater, dance is the most powerful means of communication', does not here call for its substitution for speech. He seems to hint that an analogously independent 'organization' of the verbal medium is what is needed. The '64 program, however, makes this substitution.

operating with stylizations of conventional or pre-conventional body language for it, and gestural in this sense, but it seems to me decent to keep time-wise regularity of movement part of the term's denotation, and Schumann's theatre has nothing to do with this. The term 'dance' has not seemed appropriate to me to the movement of his large puppets individually or in twos or threes. The only time it has come to my mind is à propos of his stage-handling of crowds, of masses (dozens, say) of beasts (*Cry*) or people (*Simple Light*). His elitist Germanic category-couples, leader-mass, crowd-individual jump into operation on these occasions, and he stages the masses-crowds in sub-intellectual biological rhythms and puts in individuals, alternatively dompters or victims of the masses-crowds, in counterpoint movements. Anger and fear may, of course, be gesturally expressed, but when they take over, the patterns of movement and vocal utterance become simplified into curves of rhythmic reiteration in which they are not gesture but hormonally controlled muscular response of an essentially spasmic sort: the leader's angry oratory, the victim's shaking or slinking recoil, the crowd's angry and fearful surges. This is as much material for dance as are the sexual rhythms, but Schumann's theatre deals with it only marginally. His fascist ideology is marginal – a personal atavism.

All puppets (and not just Schumann's), though to different extents, have the power of gesture, i.e. can be operated to abstract from the coordinate fullness of a human's body motions gesturally significant patterns in relative isolation, some a great variety of fairly similar, others only relatively few and/or not too similar gestures, the abstraction enhancing the power of the gesture.[5] But whereas Schumann (except perhaps for his hand puppets) focuses on this power, many other puppeteers and schools of puppetry rather focus on mimetic similitude and lifelikeness, on movement patterns indicative of a working psyche. This has not been Schumann's concern. As he is not interested in giving the impression of a living body's fullness, complexity and/or harmony of organic coordination,

---

5. Cf. Schumann, *Bread and Puppets: A Way of Life*, *Motive*, February '65. Appendix II.

Kourilsky gives some nice examples of this:

'On aura ainsi une marionnette pour chaque fonction, presque pour chaque activité humaine: montrer du doigt (The Pointer), nourrir (The Feeder), prier (le prêtre de *King's Story*), tuer (le Grand Guerrier), frapper (le soldat d'Hérode), etc. Le geste pourra même se détacher du corps: le poing d'Uncle Fatso, qui est à lui seul une marionnette, va frapper celui à qui il parle de paix, explicitant ainsi la parabole: "Méfiez-vous de faux prophètes." Et l'action de pleurer peut être rendue évidente par une seule larme (*Mississippi*).' — (Kourilsky, '71.)

Schumann, in an interview rendered obscure by bad editing, says that puppets have 'terrific intrinsic power' because 'the movements of the human body are so intricate – the harmonious details of a live body make a smooth tonality. But in a puppet there is movement that is simple and uncomplicated – there isn't so much detail, and so there seems to be increased size and power.' — (Schumann in Brown and Seitz, *With the Bread & Puppet Theatre, Tulane Drama Review* #38.)

he is not interested either in creating the impression that his puppets have a psyche, i.e. impressions of psychological process (will, intellect, feeling) giving rise to the movements: basically, for the reason that he is interested rather in the moral aspects of the action, its social meaning, and its cosmic place, and not at all in character or individuation.

Because he values the abstractive power of puppets and has no desire to achieve the psychological reference and verisimilitude of drama and actors,[6] but ultimately also because he does not wish to acknowledge the crucial importance to this theatre of the puppet 'operators' as performers – as animators of the puppets, he has not had much – in fact, anything – to say about the features that I find distinctive of his puppetry: gestural movement, animation, or interplay of masked or unmasked performers and of operators with puppets. I suppose both the ideas that his puppets' movements are expressive and that they are live strike him as pointing in the wrong direction – toward psychology and mimesis. But if gesture (as in theatre) is abstracted from its psychological concomitants – the indications of the psychological processes leading to and attending the gesture – gestural performance is not psychologizing nor mimetic but brings out essential characters – modes of being in a moral universe.[7]

Schumann in the early days thought of his puppets as live, and this in fact is a distinctive feature of them, most particularly of his large puppets with invisible inside operators, the puppets he started making in the fall

---

6. He has flirted with the idea that puppets have a built-in 'Verfremdungseffekt' that actors lack:

'One wouldn't gain anything by making the puppets more real. We want to exploit the feelings you have as much as possible. So, in puppetry, if you want to say something you have that chance of speaking by the contrast of sizes: if you want somebody little, you just make him little; and then he *is* little and unimportant. There really isn't this type of puppetry anywhere else that I know of, but even if it's the little puppets you saw in your growing-up, there is still that sense of strangeness ... of a different size, that you wouldn't have with a real actor. Puppetry is admitting that we do "theatre", and still believing; whereas in theatre, you are constantly persuaded to believe what you see (never mind that the actors aren't real). Actors want you to believe them, but you needn't believe puppets. You see them move and you listen to them. It is a strange relationship. You don't waste time believing they are real.' — (Schumann, in W.H. Rough, *An Interview with Peter Schumann, Dramatics*, December '73.)

I doubt that puppets absolutely lack the illusionistic power that actors have. But Schumann is not interested in using them as simulacra of people, i.e. so that spectators will believe them souled, motivated, possessed of will. He uses them for allegories in which they are embodiments of principles, forces or powers, and in this respect, his puppets are believable, illusionistic: the spectator accepts them as such embodiments, and the humanness of their motions promotes this without promoting acceptance of them as people.

7. Hoagland (*Let 'em Have*, '83), on rehearsals for the '82 circus:

'The tigers didn't twist enough as they paced and slunk. Two persons were inside each painted suit, with a rubber hose for a backbone. "The spins are good, but you must do more turns. Your turns aren't good enough. Never turn in the same directions as your partner turns. Hurry up. Faster," he said.'

'63, but also, to varying extents, of his other puppets not played over a curtain, even, sometimes, of dummies handled by visible operators.

By this I don't mean that they create the illusion of being alive in the sense of their movement seeming individually actuated, motivated or responsive. The anthropomorph ones do not seem to possess will, nor the zoomorph ones instinct. Internal and self-oriented actuation is of course part of what is usually meant by 'life' even as regards plants. What I do mean is only that they give rise to the illusion that they are individuated and corporeal agents or agencies, moving in a purposive or otherwise finalistic (objective-oriented, teleological) manner. The illusion overrides their patent movement by outside agencies, the puppeteers, substituting for it not any kind of working out of its objectives or movements by the individual figure in question, life in the strong sense of organic life, but action due to forces acting within and through it and not in turn emanating from any other individuals, e.g. the puppeteers actually moving it. They are seen – to the extent illusion is operative – as acting[8] embodiments of principle, and as individuated representations of essences. Their movement is live. It tends to have the teleological quality of the movements of the living, and it tends to lack that margin of the mechanical of the externally induced characteristic of most other puppetry.

This smoothness and directedness of his puppets' movements, and their gestural quality – the dynamics of their inception, articulation and termination that make them seem expressive, deliberately significatory – as well as the absence of a qualifying jerkiness and rigidity – is due, I think, to the simplicity of Schumann's puppet mechanisms – their supporting structures and transmission mechanisms – e.g. few jointed limbs, no mobile faces, no string-boards – it seems to allow for a translation of the operators' movements into the puppets' involving a relatively small loss of organicity – to the slowness, controlled energy and incisiveness of their operation, most of all perhaps to the deliberate gestural abstraction, limited gestural vocabulary, and non-psychological significations of their movements. Schumann does not aim at lifelike gesticulation or displacement, but at significant evocative essences of human existence, and within this limited realm

---

8. 'Mich haben Masken und Puppen seit meiner Bildhauerlehre fasziniert, von den kleinsten bis zu den grössten. Ich habe so nach für alle möglichen Zwecke – auch für das normale Puppenspiel – alle in plastischer und technischer Hinsicht denkbaren Puppen gebaut und mire jedesmal eingebildet, ich hätte das erfunden. Die Stockpuppen, wir wir sie bei den ersten religiösen Spielen im Auftrag einer New Yorker Kirche verwendeten, gab es seit Jahrtausenden in Java oder China, die Riesenpuppen, welche von 3-5 Schauspielern – sogenannten Operateuren – getragen und bewegt werden, in Sizilien, bei den Indianern und in Indien. Von der allgemeinen Verbreitung von Masken und Kopfpuppen ganz zu schweigen. Wichtig ist, dass sich unsere Puppen selbst bewegen, den Eindruck erwecken, als handelten sie. Nicht nur pantomimisch oder gestisch.' — (*Peter Schumann/Bread & Puppets/Das Brot und Puppen-Theater, tendenzen*, November '66-February '67, (Schumann, interviewed by tendenzen.))

– on which the sculptural expressiveness of the puppets and their gestures make the spectators focus – can achieve a liveness of movement, that within the wider realm of a lifelike deportment of lifelike individuals with given characters he could not achieve; he constructs his puppets and trains his operators with this limitation in view. Within this chosen area, his operators' lives (though not their personalities) flow into his puppets, and sufficiently so to be convincing to spectators guided not to the psychic causes of the gestures, but to their meaning.

The operators of the puppets are often visible. Even when they are inside the puppet, we know there is a person inside. The illusion that the puppets have independent movement, move on their own, is *weaker* in his theatre than in much other puppet theatre. But his theatre does not ask us to believe this either and thus does not expose itself to the limits of such illusion. Qua allegorical figures representative of the forces of good and evil, his puppets are perfectly believable. We see the liveness of their movements as the life of those forces. Not as the life of the flesh, nor as the effects of the will.

Their action is restricted to representation of what they stand for, gestures embodying the principles or forces they embody.

His puppets are grandiose creatures. This is first and foremost due to their size. But it is also due to their awesome sculpture and to their august, stately gestique; and to the virtual absence of mechanical movement. They are not comic – as hand puppets and marionettes almost invariably are: the giant puppets are sometimes used for humorous effect, and may be – in a small, quiet way – funny, but even then, when what they do is funny, don't turn into comic figures. Quite a few of his masks and puppets have been grotesque, a few – relatively few – caricatures: but up until the end of the '70s at least, they with no exception I can recall have had power, stature and dignity, and so have predisposed his theatre to the presentation of a somber view of human existence, in which humor occurs as touches of humor, not as expression of a comic sense of life, a somber view not viewing human existence as a slight matter, but a truly melancholy view. Which is not quite the same as a tragic view which is what Noh masks seem to predispose Noh for, unless by tragedy we mean the tragedy of the human race as a whole, not any individual tragedy.

The figures in his theatre have been human or animal. Sometimes (*The Difficult Life of Uncle Fatso*) we see a living cloud or mountain. His theatre represents humanity within the continuum of the animal kingdom (this is explicit in *The Cry of the People for Meat*) and as, in principle, integrated into an organic nature. This living world, however, though perhaps entirely natural, is seen from a moral point of view. It comprises a Force or Power of Evil appearing in demonic creatures and contortions (the peasant view of nature). And it appears also, occasionally, perhaps as a solar configuration, but mostly in the faces and figures of women, something like a

Divine Goodness – a passive principle. The shapes, poses and movements of the puppets are perceived by the audience neither on a simply physical plane, nor in psychological terms, but in terms of morality. A morality, however, defined by an immanentist morals: evil and goodness as living constituents of a living world. The puppet sculpture and the puppet dance of this theatre are adapted to this presentation. Speechless, they move as sculpturally self-contained embodiments of vital powers, forces and principles, in the dance rhythms of these forces', powers' and principles' nomic contest.

It is because it is live that this puppet theatre, unlike most puppet theatre remains close to the original form of theatre, the masked dance of magic and/or spirit-banning ceremonials.[9]

---

9. Cf. Schumann's easy transition from an evocation of the grandeur of the traditional forms of puppet theatre to pre-theatre masked dance in his *God Himself: Problems Concerning Puppetry* . . . , 1965: 'Masks are older than actors, faces of wood and stone are older than mimes. Masked dancers and the effigies they carry are certainly at the origin of theater.' — (Appendix III.)

5. The puppet and the mask. The power of the mask, the dependency of the puppet. Schumann's theatre alienates masked performance by the form of puppetry.

The formula 'live puppetry' for what Schumann is doing, almost seems to amount to saying that Schumann, when in the fall of '63 he enlarged his puppets, actually abandoned puppetry, and that his theatre is not puppet theatre at all, but simply live performance using masks, and centrally – setting the tone – head masks and garments that go with these and suggest bodies corresponding to the heads.[1] These garments would be what essentially distinguishes his theatre from most traditions of masked acting theatre, with the absence of speech the second important distinction. The similarity to puppetry would lie in the illusion produced that we were seeing the movement of these suggested bodies other than the performers', and would be strengthened by the sculptural quality of the masks (giving them perceptual independence from the performers' heads) and by the ceremonial and abstractly gestural quality of the movements (enhancing their perceptual independence from the movements of the performers).

That his theatre is not puppetry is supported by the intuitive (though, of course, culturally conditioned) idea of puppetry. This idea seems to preclude the puppet-operators being inside the puppets. It focuses on the use of a transmission mechanism translating movements of the operators into movements of the puppets in such a way as to leave them residually mechanical, with hand puppets and their movements a special case, but not really an exception. Any arrangement involving confusion of puppet and operator or of the movements of the one with those of the other gets us away from this idea of puppetry: the idea that something *clearly* lifeless is being *given* life. That the puppet is in and of itself lifeless is part, not only of the idea, but of the very appreciation and enjoyment of puppetry; that the illusion that the puppet is alive arises in spite not only of the fact that it is not, but in spite of one's awareness that it is not, is intrinsic to a puppet spectacle, as puppetry is ordinarily understood. This particular conflict between knowledge and illusion (absent in Schumann's theatre) seems essential not only for an appreciation of the skill or art of the puppeteer, but for the kind of meaning a puppet spectacle has for the spectator: an imitation of active man by inanimate objects, reflecting back on man, marginally but crucially, doubt as to his freedom of will. This attainder arises from our perception of the puppet as powerless, a perception which has led to the use of the term 'puppet' to designate an apparently independently active agent in reality subject to the will of others. Schumann's

---

1. '... and he has evolved a theater of masks more than of puppets because he likes and choreographs the human body so much.' — (Hoagland, *Let 'em Have*, quoting Ralph Lee.)

puppets, even when operated by visible outside operators, are not so perceived.

Heinrich von Kleist's suggestion that the mechanical movements of a puppet, if engendered — without other action on it — by the application to its center of gravity of a machine force operating according to an appropriate mathematical formula would be more graceful than any human being's, let alone a court dancer's, in fact could be equalled in grace only by God were He to dance, implies that the perceived deficiencies of puppets' movements, viz. their shortfall of the coordination into the unity of grace, is only incidental. But his suggestion is only a metaphor for his true meaning: that (1) consciousness diminishes artistic performance the more it serves as conduit of a self-consciousness afflicted by the desire to please — by vanity — because (2) it would to this extent fail to apply the performer's force to his or her true spiritual center of gravity, the true movement of which alone results in the grace of art, but that (3) man's finite consciousness is prone to this affliction diverting him from his true self for the sake of gratuitous attention to others — which is why puppets rival (deficient) human grace. Kleist is in fact saying the opposite of what he appears to say. Only if an artist's concern with external form is ordinated by his/her concern with producing him- or herself truly can he/she succeed as an artist — an independent concern with form produces the graceless jerkings of a Hampelmann — of court dancers and ordinary artists. This is true, and it also embodies the foregoing perception of puppetry. That the desire to please (not the usual but a correct definition of vanity) is the crucial obstacle to artistry, and that it is at the heart of formalism is also true.

Puppeteering is animated, I would say, by two delights of the puppeteer's: to reproduce humanity in small, giving a close-up view of a view from the distance of it, and to see it jerk on its strings, a humiliation of his fellow men the more acerbic the more lifelike he can get the jerkings to be, with graceful inclinations of the head, shy aversions of the face, proud archings of the chest, but all still dictated, involuntary, and at least just barely visibly so, in which he is not necessarily in play arrogating the powers of God (or of God and Satan preoccupied by their contestive game with one another), getting on top, but may also just be commenting on these fools' blind confidence in being somebodies, in a bitter awareness of his own obsessions (not the least of which, for all of us, is the obsession to stay alive), two alternate stances also explaining the desire to show people as small as they are. If such is shown us in play, we can all delight in seeing our fellow humanity reduced.

The figure of Punch, a foolish trickster, probably misshapen, a hunchback dwarf perhaps, weak, his foolishness quite genuine, though equivalently the sly cunning of the underdog, the villainous peasant serf or the lazy black slave, and the divine inspiration of the epileptic, queer, mentally deranged, possessed augurs of the Paleolithic, on this stage is exceptional. Lowest of the low, he is elevated above the general degradation of man on this stage — it is the puppeteer (an adult playing like a child) himself.[2]

The resonances of Punch (there is no Punch in Schumann's theatre) are manifold, e.g. he evokes the Negro or Irishman who adopts the protective image of the funny, i.e. ridiculous but harmless, hence endearing, Negro or Irishman (any race in a position of inferiority will have exemplars adopting this gambit), as well as the servant or serf surviving by cunning defraudation of his master in small matters (though not the servant in Hegel's dialectic of master and servant moving to reverse their relationship), but there is only one connotation of power: Punch reminds us of Trickster, the God-to-be according to Weston LeBarre, apotheosis of the conjuring shaman, a primitive God still discernible in various pantheons. But in fact, Punch, most insolent of puppets, even talking back to his master, the puppeteer, never in character or action rises above the essential servility of the puppet. (Robert Anton's puppetry centers on such aborted rebellion.)

There is a sinister type of puppet, the automaton, sinister because its mechanism is its own, and we are afraid that the puppet might escape our control and out of resentment dumbly turn against us. The ponderous awkwardness of the robot's movements suggests that we have taken a risk in setting up a machine whose movements are determined blindly by its mechanism rather than being responses to our moment-by-moment manipulation, intimations of the gestures of a murder of which we would be the victim, though ultimately the author also. The subjection characteristic of puppets here strains its limits.

The subordinate status of puppets is expressed also by the appearance and movements of the main type of modern puppet, the figures of the animated cartoon. As Jay Gould has pointed out in his *Biological Homage to Mickey Mouse*, they are subject as regards their proportions and the shape of their parts, to neoteny; and though as far as I can see their animators might easily have made them move like men or animals, they in fact are careful in their movements to preserve a trace of their sequential origin; they move like miraculous toys. The cartoon puppets are not capable of being sinister, and since they are drawings only, moved by a wheel, the sinister aspect of the puppet character as such is at its weakest in them also. But the abandon with which in the best cartoon movies these androids are kicked and thrown about, tortured, flattened and distorted,

---

2. 'The older Punchinello was far less restricted in his actions and circumstances than his modern successor. He fought with allegorical figures representing want and weariness as well as with his wife and with the police, was on intimate terms with the patriarchs and the seven champions of Christendom, sat on the lap of the queen of Sheba, had kings and dukes for his companions, and cheated the Inquisition as well as the common hangman.' — (R. Mortimer Wheeler, *Punch* (art.), *Encyclopedia Britanica*, 11th ed.)

dismembered and exploded, though immensely enjoyable and satisfying, is at its edges also a little frightening.

The mask is quite another. It is, above all, the mystery. Hiding the performer, it bereaves us of the signs by which to beware, and we do not know who it is. It thus gives superiority to the performer, and the effect on the audience is the opposite of that of the puppet.

Note that a simply veiled or shrouded person is mysterious, and that the mystery is produced and persists even if we know who it is and know that person; and that this mystery is totally independent of whether we feel that, shroud or veil apart, they are in any way mysterious.

The way the word is used, mysteriousness may attach to a lack of information merely (our inability to identify the person, or to explain how something happened or came about); or to a seeming paradox or other impossibility. In the case of the hidden or featureless face, oddly, it seems of the latter, stronger sort, something that seems the case and yet, it seems, could not be so. It is not only the feeling 'it could be anybody', it is as though we *saw* anybody.

A puppet, to a greater or lesser extent, takes on its animator's life. It may even, notably if the operator delivers its speech or has designed it and its performance, or when its construction is such that it rather directly and sensitively reproduces the operator's way of moving, take on some of his or her personality. A mask, on the contrary, gives its lack of life and its identity to the wearer of it. He or she becomes it, and all the wearer's vivacity is constrained within the bond of its inanimation. The puppet borrows from its operator; the mask gives to its wearer. Put on, the mask becomes a face; only when played does the puppet become a puppet, an extension of the master, who, if in evidence, if anything, becomes more fully him or herself, active in the use of the puppet, him or herself amplified by its play. In the puppet we see life in death, in the masked performer, death in life.

When we see a puppet come to life we are delighted, but not astounded. We fall into our illusion by a sleight-of-mind. But when a person puts on a mask, the transformation is astounding, in fact, unbelievable. The person becomes another; we are torn into the illusion, but their metamorphosis is frightening rather than delightful; and as the delight in the wearing of a mask relates to a feeling of irresponsibility and power, so the delight in confronting the wearer of a mask relates to the thrill of danger – a masked person is sinister. This intimidation is of course the essence of Halloween, but even a Mardi Gras cortege is scary. Only in theatre, with the stage well separated from the audience, is the fearsomeness of the mask mitigated into strangeness, coldness and awesomeness.

Yet, even so (there is pleasure in danger), the delightfulness of puppetry and the astoundingness of masks and of the masque, though quite different from one another, both belong to a realm of experience distinctly counterposed to that of high culture, but mistakenly identified as frivolous: for the realm of delight and astonishment provided by jugglers, magicians, fireworks, bright lights, waterfalls and fountains, the play of children and the self-destructive excesses of the poor extends without break, continuously to caresses and orgasms, to fornication, to the coming of spring, and to the pleasure parents take in their children, seeing them learn to walk or to talk or hearing their displays of wit. The same spring is touched in all these cases, and the leap of our spirit is the same. We are taken by surprise at a sudden eclosure of capacities increasing our and the world's wealth. Subjectively, although, of course, not in fact, these are experiences of miracles.

We mask ourselves, first of all, from childhood on, by basic expressions of calm, of competence, and of self-containment, reassuring the others we will observe some limits of competition and aggression; secondarily, for social intercourse, with expressions of consideration indicative of cooperativeness, to hide our deficiencies in these regards – lacks and oppositenesses of the inner fact. We allow ourselves to be made puppets by conditioning, i.e. by a deficiency and economy of reason, becoming puppets to the extent our deployments have become responses to signs the advisability of the learned response to which we no longer consider, and have probably not considered sufficiently in the first place. The theatre of unmasked performers, even when by its content designed for the contrary, sustains these degradations by denying them: puppet theatre and masked theatre, by their forms – even when by their content they are designed to sustain them – make us uneasy by revealing them, showing us the premature incursions of death into our lived lives.

Gordon Craig has pointed out that masks by appropriately abstractive sculpturing may better serve as symbols of the mind than the faces of actors obscured by the flux of irrelevant expressions;[3] and Gide that they

---

3. 'Gordon Craig, in his writings on the Theatre, speaks for the Mask over and over again. He sees the gain to the Theatre which is attached to this thing. What he tells us is not new, . . . it is what all artists know, but there lies intrinsic value today in hearing it definitely from the mouth of an artist sprung from one of the most productive families of the English stage. He tells us that human facial expression is for the most part valueless, and that the laws of his Art tell him that "It is better, provided it is not dull, that instead of six hundred expressions, but six expressions shall appear upon the face." Later on he gives an example: "The Judge sits in Judgment upon the Prisoner, and he shall display but two expressions, each of which is in just proportion with the other. He has two masks and on each mask one main *statement*, these statements being tempered by Reflections, . . . the hopes and fears and the rest of not merely the Judge, but of Justice and Injustice." Craig "aims at taking us beyond reality; he replaces the pattern of the thing itself by the pattern which that thing evokes in the mind, the symbol of the thing." In saying this Arthur Symons recognises in Craig a descendent of the family of the ancient artists of the Theatre, for his aim was theirs, and the Mask a part of their strength, – the Mask, the symbol of the Human face. It is this sense of being beyond reality which permeates all great art. We see it in the little clumsily painted pictures of those periods when the true

may be better indicators of contemporary social reality than the faces of actors, because the actor, to be theatrical, is forced to mirror the spectator, who wears the contemporary masks dissimulating contemporary existence.[4] To this we may add that the faces of young actors are apt to be fatuous and empty, and those of older actors so ravaged by their use for the insincerities and muscular exaggerations of their many parts as to be incapable of any expression other than that of weary cynicism; and that the theatrical expressions of actors in any country and decade form an artificial language, formed not for the imitation of life, but for the presentation of a misrepresentative ideology concerning the 'truly' human. Gide does not presume that mask makers are more truthful than other people, only that masks can achieve theatrical effectiveness without aping the contemporary facial misrepresentations of social reality. This leaves the question of how they can do this. Craig, to my mind, correctly emphasizes the abstractive potentials of mask-sculpturing, the symbolic functioning of the masked face, and the interference with signification of expressiveness, but does not indicate how the masked face functions as symbol of 'reality.'

The mask is a false face. The perceptor's conflict is between the illusion that it is a face and the knowledge that it isn't. This conflict makes encounter with a masked person delicious. As in the case of the conflict between the illusion that a puppet has a will and the knowledge that it doesn't, but unlike the case of the conflict between the illusion that an actor has the character acted and the knowledge that they have another one, their own, the conflict in the case of the mask is metaphysical inasmuch as it raises the question of what a face is and whether it is what it is usually considered to be: pictorial outwardness of personality or character, and (by its muscular modifications of the moment, that is, expression)

---

beyond was of more importance than a right perspective, when the perspective of thought and feeling held its true value.... Masks carry conviction when he who creates them is an artist, for the artist limits the statements which he places upon these masks. The face of the actor carries no such conviction: it is over-full of fleeting expression,... frail, restless; disturbed and disturbing, and, as Craig says elsewhere, on this account not *material* with which to make a work of art ... the Mask must return to the Stage to restore expression, ... the visible expression of the mind.' — (John Balance, *A Note on Masks*, *The Mask*, Vol. I, #1, March 1908.)

4. 'When one speaks of the history of drama, it is important, perhaps more important more important than anything else, to ask: *Where is the mask?* In the audience, or on the stage? In the theater, or in life? It is here *or* there, never both at once. The most brilliant periods of drama, those in which the mask is triumphant on the stage, are those in which hypocrisy ceases to mask life. On the contrary, those in which what Condorcet calls "the hypocrisy of manners" is triumphant are the very periods in which the mask is snatched from the face of the actor and he is required to be not beautiful but natural; that is to say, if I rightly understand, that he must take his models from reality, or at least from the semblances of it to be seen in his audience; and that is to say, from a monotonous and already masked humanity. — (Gide, *My Theater* in E.T. Kirby, *The Mask*, *The Drama Review*, #55.)

visual sign of disposition and intent; or whether it is, perhaps, in truth, no guide at all, but merely a brave front, displaying merely a vague scattering of learned dissemblances, sets and grimaces plastered on it by society, displaying nothing of the kaleidoscope of fantasies and desires within. The contradiction between illusion and knowledge within the perception of a mask tinges that perception with the suspicion that faces dissemble not the presence of a person, but the absence of one.

The mask's power is derived from the economy of the face in ordinary life. The face is the body's significatory concentrate and serves in communication – like all signs it doesn't necessarily carry the same meaning for sender and receiver. It has three functions: it is an I.O.U. of humanness; from it its owner's personality or character (or even his or her very personness) is construed, an inference the owner seeks to guide by the momentary modifications of his or her face called 'expression'; and it furnishes probabilities of particular intent and desire.

The look at the face identifies a fellow fleshly mortal, still barely afloat on his/her internal ocean of disorganizing time, that tenuous concatenation of cells, as well as a fellow human being specifically, member of the species, to some extent bound to a code of conduct toward other fellow members such as oneself (e.g. murder is difficult, sex circumscribed), and the look at their face reassures one as to the existence of this precarious margin of safety: the look itself a kind of sign in the nature of an attempted reminder of this contract or reaffirmation of it on one's own part with a request for a confirmation in response, virtually the exhibition of one's own face in a proposed communication between faces. A look at a person's back would do none of this.

A face operates as a sign and as a restraint on action (signal). It is the face of a particular person, and as a sign, the sign of that individual's traits or type (and disposition and intent): a subject's qualities; and as signal, the signal of that individual's demands for our consideration and of eventualities of conduct on their part to prepare for – the lineaments of specific possibilities placed in time and space. Makeup, at most, heightens these effects.

A mask alters the face by reversing the relationship of universals to particular. In the masked face, the false face, perceived as false, but even so as face, the extrojected individual we supply it with is imagined or perceived as individuation of universals. The mask carries its representational character into the face it becomes for us. A masked figure is at the same time a symbolic work of art and the living embodiment of what it symbolizes.

A man's naked face is read as evidence of particulated individuality:[5]

---

[5]. '(I: How do you choose when to use a puppet and when to use a live person?) As soon

the mask perceived as face is read for its indication of essences: qualities that the naked face conveys only as his/her aspects of character or personality, as accidentiae of a particulated individuality.

Since we extend our conventions for the interpretation of faces to animals, the universalizing power of masks extends to animal masks. As Schumann's salesmen with their salesmen masks convey an anxious corruption of the soul, so his cow masks, fearful yearning, his deer masks a delicate dependency on the world. But the illusion of reality engendered by the combination of the mask with the merest adumbration of a corresponding body and with a live performer inside mask and body, moving them in some abstraction of the movement of cows or deer, is that of perceiving not a real salesman, cow or deer, but the corporeal essence of salesman, cow or deer – concretizations of anxious corruption, fearful yearning or of delicate dependency on the world.

Obviously, the first impact of a mask is as withdrawal of the identifying and reassuring signs of the face it hides: the masked face as gesture of refusal and of rejection. (The executioner's mask, mostly thought of as his more or less practical protection against the odium attaching to his profession, carries this message of disruption for the benefit of his clients, as also the torturer's mask.) The 'false face' effect is superimposed on this negative effect of hiding.

The striking feature of masks is their inexpressiveness, due simply to their relative rigidity. They are not subject to the muscular control by which a face is made to carry an expression. What on a real face would pass for one, a smile, or fear, say, or outrage – for any expression can be put on a mask – in a mask is assimilated into the concretion of essences construed from it – seen not as a volitionally projected sign of disposition and intent, or as intended communication at all, but as revelation of an identity. A masked face in this respect is like a mirror that fails to reflect one's face, or like a wall in a place where one expects a mirror. We may speak of a mask's fixed expression, but an unalterably fixed, an atrophied

---

as you put a mask on, to me you're a puppet. Puppets are ideographs, emblems either of character, state of mind, or emotion. One puppet represents anger, another puppet represents power – they become archetypes, ideas. Schumann's Fatso has no personality; he represents all rich businessmen who run the world – he's the archetype. Take *Savages*: I I was supposed to design costumes for Brazilian Indians, and Brazilian Indians don't wear anything. If you use nude people, it's distracting and it becomes extremely personalized. (I: How about using puppets as a distancing device?) That's part of what I've been talking about. They objectify. That's what Brecht was all about, and why his plays work so well in puppetry. Puppets automatically distance you. Some people think that's dehumanizing and anti-emotional, but I find it more moving that way. You don't get caught up in the idiosyncracies of a performer and can focus on the essence of character or emotion.' — (Julie Taymore in *Working with Puppets, Interviews by C. Lee Jenner, Performing Arts Journal* #19, '83.)

expression is, like a rictus, inexpressive; and similarly, in a moveable mask, the abrupt succession of expressions. What renders a fixed expression expressive, when it happens to be expressive, is an indication or the suspicion that its wearer has fixed it and is in some manner maintaining it, an indication lacking in masks.

Obviously, the indication of character or personality by a face is in large measure the sum of residual imprints on it of the more frequent among its past transient expressions, but as such, is not an expression, but an indication of a reason for expressions, viz. of what kind of a person it is. Masks are restricted to this functional dimension of faces; but for this reason are the stronger in it. A smile distracts from the nature of the smiler, and so for all expressions. A person disappears into the relations they are by their expressions seen to be trying to establish to one.

The 'false face' effect, due to the sustained inconsistency in our apperception of worn masks (or of their wearers), transmutes the personal identity inferred from real faces into its converse, a personalisation of universals; the fixity of the mask (and in the case of movable masks their mechanical motion) sustains this leap into transcendentality by cutting the links of the false face to the living will of an individual, thus undercutting perception of this individual as individual essence. At the same time it strengthens the other component of face-perception, the perception of identity: the transcendental personage as which the mask wearer illusively appears has an immutable identity such as possessed, for instance, by gods and demons. They are the appearance of principle. They are supra-natural persons.

There is still a further effect of masks. They project power. They have this effect even when it is most unlikely – a witch or hobgoblin mask on a small kid taunting us for money on Halloween lends meaning – apparent substance – to 'trick or treat', to the threat of a trick played on us. Power is the capacity for doing harm or good. We impute power to – sense the power of – a masked person as we do supranatural identity: in the grip of an illusion we know to be an illusion and yet can't dispel:the inconsistency of which with what we know to be the case does not matter. The reason for this imputation – or part of it – is that on the one hand we impute to the illusively perceived supernatural person will, and awareness (as we would on the strength of their face to any person) and because of their presence some capacity of working their will on us and some awareness, however oblique or general, of ourselves, but on the other hand feel ourselves quite powerless to touch this person, to resist it or affect it in any way. It is there, in our spatio-temporal reality, but it is also not there, being not of our order of being, and we can't operate on it. The relation is one-way. Note that we do not impute power over us to the character portrayed by an actor. It is not supranatural, so that, to the extent the illusion is operative, the relation would be two-way, but in addition there is no relation: we do not feel in the sphere of either that character's will or awareness. But a masked person's personification of greed or goodness is experienced as relevant to us. The mask's projection of power is unsettling or pacifying, depending on its character. If, e.g. transculturally, we can't read that character, the mask is unsettling. And though in some cultures, ritual masks, because of their power when worn, are sacred, a mask not worn is just a thing.

If, as Schleiermacher proposed, the essence of religion is the experience of supranatural power, the foregoing adds up to saying that encounters with mask-wearers provide religious or proto-religious experiences.[6]

If puppetry reveals to us a grotesquely quarrelsome, impotent humanity, the mask, since it is unlike makeup − not simply the face of another − yields us the spectacle of a secret world, arcane but in the face of the mask no longer cryptic − of persons not encountered in life, seeming powerful, of concentrated being, not relating to us, though we relate to them.

I am here speaking simply of anybody that has put on any mask. A child, say, one's own, in daylight, standing there. The only condition is that one take in the mask.

Who these persons are depends on the mask and on our preconceptions. Originally, they might have been incarnations of powers of nature that men were directly exposed to; somewhat later perhaps the ancestors, the surviving dead, potentially helpful, but dangerous, to be satisfied − their generations fused, individuated lineages, the powers of custom and rank. Nowadays, e.g. in the case of Schumann's theatre, they are apt to be per-

---

[6] 'The gods wear masks; the gods are unmasked as men.' — (Weston LaBarre, *Ghostdance*.)

I.e., in initiation − such as puberty − rites:
'If cults make symbolic brothers, the nearly universal use of masks in *initiation ceremonies* suggests that symbolic fathers (shamans or initiators) *impersonate* symbolic fathers (gods) or real fathers (ancestors). The Kàgaba virtually say as much in a Kàgaba text taken down by Preuss (Preuss in Klindt-Jensen, *Grundestrupkedelen*, Copenhagen, '61), in which we learn that the Dema-like primeval priests *took off their faces* at the end of their order-creating activities *so that mortal men might wear them as masks* and thus be able to carry out the ceremonies needed to preserve the order.' — (Weston LaBarre, op. cit.)

'I studied in Japan for a year. Puppetry is a revered art form there. Bunraku has an intensity and release which I think audiences can find liberating. The puppets, dolls, and masked figures of many primitive societies were mediums through which the Gods spoke to men, often to cure. That involves the release of an emotion or exorcism of an illness, seen as a foreign presence. Japan hasn't been a primitive society for centuries, but Bunraku is a sophisticated form that does, however, retain some of that original ritual purpose. The puppet can express large emotions, display feeling publicly, that would be impermissible in daily life and embarrassing in a human actor. You see, puppets have no egos. they can become emblems of heightened or extreme emotional states: passions, rage, sorrow. The kind of release provided is the serious counterpart of the laughter produced by comedy. With puppets you can laugh about things or behavior that real actors could never get away with.' — (Bruce D. Schwartz, interviewed by C. Lee Jenner, *Working With Puppets, Performing Arts Journal* #19, '83.)

sonifications of a moral order. But as Kant showed, a moral order presupposes a religious one, emanation of an absolute ego, and from the mid-'70s onward, the religiosity of Schumann's morals, the red herrings of a religion in most regards not his, the Christian one, disappearing, became evident in his theatre.

Paleolithically, before agriculture, when men lived directly off other living beings (growing and multiplying or not, according to their own natural principles), conscious of the superiority their intelligence conferred on them, but apprehensive also, fearful of the ferocious animals, of poisonous plants, insecure in the face of the growth and decline, the dispersals and migrations of populations, apprehensive of the effects of their own depredations, the mask and the dress that went with it served them to signify (whistling in the dark) their mind's guaranteed adequacy to the dangers posed by those uncertainties; consequence of the rule of the spirit in them over the plant and animal kingdoms, and more particularly, perhaps because the dangers and uncertainties of the hunt were greater, over animals. (I suppose there was a relation between women, dolls representing women, and plant fertility, but know nothing about it.) A man masked as a bird or beast, the mask and his dress mingling the traits of species and genera, dressed in pelts or feathers, wearing horns, antlers, teeth or claws as real exemplar and manifestation, represented a spirit to which the principles of natural life were intrinsic, equivalently – the forces of nature immanently subject to human intelligence – spirit in animal form, life as spirit – the master of animals.[7] The dancing shaman's mask, robe and ornaments were certainly not a disguise – everyone knew him – they showed in external form the true inward unity of a man's cunning with the ferocity of living nature, and showed it in the group's representative, a unity ordinarily not a fact, but attainable by special men through special training and with special means, and with their help by others. I.e. the masked and robed shaman underwent a spiritual transformation, it was felt, in which from being a man, albeit an extraordinary man, he became a being in which the spirit of man the hunter and the generic spirit of the hunted were one, so that his mask and garb did not merely signify this fusion, but themselves partook of this duality: physical objects obtained in the hunt, the actual face and body of the master of animals. Mask and garb, I would say, thus not only were not disguises, they were not just insignia, symbols or representations of an inward reassuring unity of man and nature, nor even just suitable apparel for a spiritual being transcending the antagonism between hungry man and the world; they were themselves part of that spiritual being. Nor did they – another misinterpretation –

---

7. The Magdalenian portrait of a shaman – horse-tailed, bear-pawed, wolf-eared, pop-eyed, antlered, in the Cave of the Three Brothers Bégouën in Ariège, signifies the historical birth of God. — (Cf. S. Geidion, *The Eternal Present: The Beginnings of Art*, London, 1957.)

effect that transformation. The shaman's spirit effected it — they were affected by it.

I evoke the origins of the mask and of the garb that goes with it, from which Schumann drew his theatre, and in which theatre originated, not as a historical aside, but because they presume and indicate powers that the mask still possesses, regardless of how it is used, although not regardless of how it is made.

Traditionally, sculptures represent supernatural beings, and dance indicates possession (e.g. in Voodoo ceremonies, by loas into which the souls of ancestors have been assimilated); the masked performer, and in particular the masked dancer, congruently with this is traditionally perceived as incorporating what, from a 'naturalist' viewpoint, are transcendental beings, by way of a possession by them — that is, a mystery of psychic transubstantiation. In Schumann's theatre we are presented with what seems to me a closely related illusion: the presentation by puppet-like figures of (opposing) principles, powers and forces immanent to nature and natural man that these figures seem to incorporate. Schumann's shows have consistently had political and social reference, but of a clearly and directly moralistic kind, and this in terms of an immanentist morals, not merely subjective and relative evaluation, but obligations that are real by the nature of things. I think it is a power peculiar to masks that has enabled his theatre to do this. It is a power of masks that goes beyond their utility for presenting social and political relationships.[8]

The tradition within which to view Schumann's puppet theatre, then, is really not that of the puppet theatre, a folk and children's entertainment on a small stage, viewed through a framing opening, deploying small hand puppets, small marionettes on strings, or larger rod puppets, a theatre the European exemplars of which once by its relations to the commedia del arte had vitality, but which in its 20th century survivals and revivals is with one or two exceptions totally trivial; but that of masked dance and drama, one of the oldest of all art forms, going back to pre-agricultural shamanistic and totemic ritual, the spirit religions and spirit magic of hunter-gatherers faintly discernible in cave painting, paleolithic stone and

---

[8]. '(I: And you said that masks affected you — could you say a word about that? That, to me has always been a strong thing — a very strong thing, but hard to define.) At that point it was only face masks. The *Dead Man Rises* masks were ghost ones — I mean they were just figures moving around. It was impressive. I hadn't seen that before, either. And, well, the face masks were the first that I had seen used in theatre and they seemed to be very elegant. And in *Fire*, for instance, you could, by the wearing of these masks and these costumes — you transcend the Vietnamese and American — it didn't matter — 'cause the picture was what was happening, and not the person. (I: Right, for instance, race would be irrelevant. The performer, as such, would be, and his race.) Yeah, it would be irrelevant, and I thought that that was also — I also reacted to that.' — (Levy, interview.)

Levy had been an actor in the Free Southern Theatre.

bone (fertility-cult?) figurines, or the 'primitive' masks and sculptures of Africa and Oceania? Within this tradition, the more relevant reference is not to those origins, but to their sequels in the high civilizations of Asia, more particularly (as far as my deplorably narrow ken extends) perhaps those of Japan, Noh opera for the masks, Bunraku theatre for the puppets. Schumann, at least from '63/'64 onward, joins this tradition, not by way of Craig and Jooss, but by way of the ecclesiastic sculpture in wood or stone of the German Middle Ages, and 20th century expressionist German graphics and sculpture.

In this perspective we can say that Schumann implemented his masks with garments flimsily suggestive of bodies going with the masks' faces. The resulting pseudo-puppets had the effect of personalizations of a moral order making the demands of such an order on us (an effect depending not only on their appearance, but also on an enacted action placing or identifying the figures for us in that order, and to allusion to known figures of legend, caricature and the news). They in this sense represented power – power of this sort, and they incorporated or had this power by the efficacy of their representation and the force of the illusion (always, of course, imperfect) that they were real (rather than compounds of performers, masks and garments). The personalizations were concrete in that they appeared as the embodiments of specific social and psychological (ideological, attitudinal) traits and types, e.g. not all goodness, but feminine goodness or not femininity per se but traits of it for us represented in the Virgin Mary, or the femininity of motherhood, etc. They were abstract in that they appeared as representational embodiments of these traits or types, and not as particular individuals (as they would have, if acted by actors). They made demands and had power because the moral significance for us of these traits and types made their evocation exhortatory. E.g. the figure of a warmongering plutocrat, recognizably evil, demanded resistance to war – projected not only the power over us of imperialist capitalism, but – and primarily – of moral imperatives of opposition to it (I leave aside here the question of the nature of such power, presumably engendered by aculturation and childhood socialization). Here again, the portraiture of an individual as such by an actor could not do this, whatever the efficacy of its appeal to conscience or its informational content would be. The acted figure, however exemplary, could not appear as that moral force.

Schumann's theatre can be said to be essentially a theatre of masked performance inasmuch as the magic of the mask, its mystery, its transcendental reference, its evocation of the supernatural, and its power give it its chief impact and are the essential means for its redemptive purpose, while

---

9. 'His masks . . . use the past boldly, and suggest African, pre-Columbian and Asiatic masks, Easter Island heads, Chinese temple sculpture, Lehmbruck, Grosz . . . .' — (Hoagland, *Let 'em Have*, '83.)

the essential features of the puppet, its dependency, its residual mechanicity, and its dialectic of borrowed life play no role in it.

If, nevertheless, Schumann's theatre can properly be called puppetry, this is not particularly because, though he started from masked performance, he arrived at it by way of a return to a traditional form of puppetry, but because he made of the manipulation of his masked figures a major element of it, used to alienate the masked ceremony for the sake of making address to the audience explicit.

Having realized the power of masks, he proceeded to let them work their mystery in a new form of puppet theatre: one that depended on awe, rather than inviting condescension, and essentially tragic (though he would perhaps not admit this) rather than comic (though he tries for humor). The tragic quality of his theatre is conveyed most directly by the appearance of indifference to us of his puppets — no longer, like traditional puppets, playthings — not, like actors, humans posturing before us in the ridiculousness of their pretense — totally unconcerned and yet appearing to us as the lineaments of our fate. This quality is not redeemed by the appearance of visible puppet operators — these appear as the puppets' servants. Only secondarily does his theatre's tragic quality appear as content — the perennial defeat of good by bad.

Schumann's masks make him one of the great plastic artists of our age. They carry a contrapuntal emotion into his stories, the sadness of death. Not infrequently they are skull masks. Often they are masks taken from face casts, but such masks are as though from the faces of the dead — undesiring, mysteriously superior, having lost the sweet vulnerability of the faces of sleepers. The beautiful people in his plays wear these masks, the moonlike faces, gray, white, silver, of oriental peasant ladies, moving through his world slowly and gracefully, figurations of Chinese serenity, wisdom of style, not alleviating this world's Germanic barbarity, but putting its ponderous agitation in perspective, qualifying it as foolish. Then there are the faces of those who sit in the shadow of death, yellowish, pink or purple, the faces of ordinary men and women, with expressions not so much of suffering as of dumbly inward concentration too weak to ennoble, sometimes only the shields of insensitivity borne by dull self-preoccupation — the grotesquely molded faces of worriers, short on time, irritable and arbitrary, narrow-minded, caught up in rules and routines to the point of petrification, ugly by the meanness of misery. These are the faces of the living dead. There are the faces of strange monstrous creatures and of malevolent devils, ogres, and demons — though also of benign fairies, pale, faint, or of unmasculine dreamers. These are the agents of death, often gigantic authorities — outside of time, neither alive nor dead. And there are the tiny, vivacious puppets, ridiculous imps looking on, jumping out of the stomachs or pockets of giants or popping up at the upper edge of a curtain with some crack. They have time but are not using it.

Sitting in the New York subway, I notice how similar the Negro – but not only the Negro – faces of the people opposite me are to Peter Schumann's masks. The reason being, I would say, partly that these people do not relate to one another or myself, partly that I do not relate to them, and no one having or communicating any purposes relative to others, not only do the faces – their expressions 'inward,' really not ex-pressions – in fact, not function significantly, but look otherwise than when so functioning, namely devoid of indications of query or intent or expectation. But I am myself a subway rider, not looking at them with regard to such indication or symbolization – I am not searching for it, am not synthesizing their faces in terms of it, so that their ACTUAL FEATURES are allowed by them to emerge, while I allow myself to see them: small assemblies of eyes, nose and mouth in expanses of cheek, the noses vastly irregular, not simply pyramids, the mouths set in curvatures resulting from lifetimelong overlays of expressive and even more, perhaps, of reactive settings, the eyes not isolated from one another or from their brows nor from their twin caves: this grotesque assembly of forward-probing sensors and assimilators momentarily not functioning as such, but similar to a group of lakes or of lakes and hills on a landscape seen in bird-perspective, a fortuitous wrenching of the expanse of the forward side of the head. The longer one looks at these faces in this subterranean non-repose of theirs, the more the head emerges. 'Face', as usually seen, begins to seem an artifact of the functional imagination, a convenient but arbitrary isolatum of the potential interactor. The sculptural whole – the head – asserts itself in all its bizarre extensions backward and upward: its 'face' the part of its surface on which time's abrasion has planed, area of impact and of formative destruction. And if the ride is long enough, the head recedes into the neck, which – this is winter, still – seems the rim of a container from which emerges the head. The sculptural view of faces follows this same recessive path. The similarity of subway faces to Schumann's masks seems due to a preponderant part of suffering – of responses to the unpleasant, arriving from the outside – in shaping them. This relative formative impotence of joy or pleasure may or may not be due to its relative rarity in the experiences of a lifetime; and perhaps since this subway system is reserved for the poor, whose working day it extends, the faces are similar to those masks, at least in part because of the high incidence of victims that ride on the subway. A striking feature of Schumann's masks is the irregularity, in fact the approximativeness of the faces, especially on the head masks; but inspection of subway faces suggests these masks are in this respect realistic. His face masks are often expressive of serenity, which reminds us that people use their faces more as masks than for expression, a stunning under- and mis-employment of their faces. Similar things to these could be said of the clad bodies of Daumier's figures, especially, in my memory, of their shoulders and backs in coats or overcoats: amazing (but verifiably realistic) distortions of the human body as we imagine it and as the graphically unskilled or graphically skilled but mendacious among us would draw it. Which, in turn, reminds us that Schumann's theatre is primarily a theatre of faces: his hard stare on men's titantic struggle with Time.

6. Music, speech, pursuit of an integration of man's vocal dimension according to a principle of an organization out of context of means. Ideal of the self-integrating sounds of implements. Ideal of the substitution of non-verbal for verbal utterance.

In '82, acknowledging that his theatre's puppetry was of a new kind, he suggested (interview) that the closest thing to it might be opera, and came up with the formula, 'noise-making and music and sculpture and painting, independently of one another developing their powers.'

'63-'65, Schumann seems to have conceived of the theatre he was trying to create as a combination of sculpture and dance, i.e.: of the sculptural abstractions of expressions of his puppets and masks with the gestural abstractions of their movements. He seems to have had in mind a theatre substituting body movement – or rather the combination of sculpturally abstracted facial expression, body presence and of gesture formalized as in dance – for speech.

But he incidentally indicated an approach that probably has been crucial in shaping his theatre: an 'organization out of context' of theatre's several kinds of means: of, for instance, movement and speech. (Schumann, *Bread and Puppets: A Way of Life*, '65.) I.e. the development of body movement into the distinct medium and language of puppets' abstract gestures, of facial expression into the distinct medium and language of mask sculpture, of speech into the quotational parts of narration separated from the supposed speakers and their gestures, and given some manner of formalization or stylization ('organization') of its own, transposed into some aesthetic abstraction transmitting essentials. As his puppets' expressions, the masks, make another statement than their movement, or the same statement independently, their being, to the spectator, no fusion in psychological terms, and Schumann's solitary work with the clay naturally giving rise in him to quite other, more inward, thoughts and feelings, than his work on the movement of the puppets, inevitably social, and as both the masks and the puppet movement abstract, concentrate and elevate dimensions of persons in the flesh, so, given that idea of an 'organization out of context of means', as guidance, one would look for ways of separating speech from faces and movements, for ways of abstracting, concentrating and elevating it. The art work is to explode man into his separate dimensions of appearance and communication, communicating with the audience via each dimension, rendered a separate artistic medium, separately: as concert of independent media. The 'mixed media' idea, but applied not to technical contrivances but to the dimensions of man's natural and phenomenal social existence. E.g. speech given the form of narration, and narration given on the one hand some aesthetically pleasing ('valid') form, on the other some semantically focalizing form, in both regards departing from natural speech. This, rather than the suppression of speech, is what he has attempted over the years.

His puppets – other than his hand puppets – did not turn out mutely incidentally. They weren't meant to talk. Schumann made his masks so that figures with such faces would have no verbal thoughts to express, and so that looking at them we would not expect them to talk. The figures whose faces they are express themselves by their expressions, and what these expressions express is inconsistent with discursive address: too simple and abstract, compatible with abstract gestures but by way of vocal utterance at most with sighs, moans, growls. Speech is the venture of particular individuals, and his puppets represent not such but abstractions. Even the individuals he started making in '80 (*Story of Bread, Diagonal Man*) are – caricatural – abstractions representing the idea of a particular individuality.

When he advanced the formula 'sculpture plus dance' for his theatre – facial expression and gesture – he left out not only speech but also music, i.e. sound. This may have been a simple oversight during a time when an elimination of speech preoccupied him: for he started developing sound accompaniment right away. (*King Story*, '64.) Speaking of his Delancey Street Museum period:

'Getting into puppetry was how to combine – how to make a language out of sculpture and music. It was a very difficult enterprise in that it was so open-ended; there was no tradition one could lean on or there was no tradition one could imitate – there was nothing there. It felt so open that I was enjoying the variety more than the search for results, really . . . what to do with language – that was a very big problem all the time – how to do that – whether one would start, tell a story, or just give a little, words and glimpses . . . there were a dozen shows (between *Murder Mystery* and *Leaf* (SSB)) that had titles and had ideas but nothing was achieved – you know, it didn't work, between the narration and what was done there.' (Schumann, interview, '82.)

I believe that Schumann started out with this in mind: his moving cathedral figures were to move silently and not in silence: but to an analogue of churchly music or of the imaginary music one may hear in the colored light of Gothic cathedrals. And I think that in his hopeful imagination, there were no words at all – maybe not even titles. Or perhaps just a little per piece.

He never or hardly ever achieved this. One hears again and again of his performers requiring explanations – not just of their part, but of the piece – and of Schumann giving in and throwing them scraps of signs, narrative: partly, I would say, so they could function at least until they had started doing their part (then a performer's self-illusioning imagination provides him sustenance), partly because he figured the piece wouldn't work for an audience either if his own dummies got so little satisfaction out of it as it was, wordless.[1]

His ideal, I think, has throughout been a theatre of wordless sculptured de- and configurations of the human form in a world of sounds making sense the way music does, but rather than drawing on the melodic, harmonic and/or rhythmic pattern-references defining a culture's music for that culture's ears as music, relying on the ear's capacity out of the brute sound of things — other than musical instruments, since these are made to produce sounds shaped and abstracted according to the culture's convention[2] — drawn from them, to create by an immersion in the sound produced an inner order: an ideal perhaps not too far from John Cage's: a non-music of sounds functioning as humanly meaningful time-configurtors: throwing against the puppets' man-signs the peculiar torture of man-minds (as every man's tortures the man), death's teasings, together with

---

1. 'The theatrical means that Schumann uses to deal with this material of childhood is pre-dramatic. It is a theater of pageants, tableaux, and processions where sculpture walks, parades, tableaux, and processions where sculpture walks, parades, or dances. The art of drama begins with texts, whereas Schumann "pushes for a place where some language is achieved ... we find from language what we really want." He works with stylized expressive gestures from which language is very remote but which, unlike mime, never seek to substitute themselves for languages. As he works, words are "achieved" with great difficulty, and are usually of great simplicity. As pieces evolve, the company struggles through its bafflement to present the actions that Schumann lays out. After late-night sessions with friends, full of questions, criticism, exhortation, home brew, and strong coffee, a few hand painted signs or words may appear in the next rehearsal as the work takes shape. Language seems to enter to organize and clarify work that is initially conceived visually.' — (B. Goldensohn, *Peter Schumann's Bread & Puppet* Theater, '77.)

2. Kourilsky, reporting Bread and Puppet practice in the '60s:
'Certains des instruments utilisés par le Bread and Puppet Theatre sont traditionnels. Instruments à percussion: grosse caisse, tambour, tambourin, bongo. Instruments à vent, essentiellement des cuivres à la sonorité pleine, au timbre clair et brillant: cornet à piston, cor d'harmonie, cor de chasse, trompette. Pratiquement pas d'instruments à cordes si ce n'est un violon; encore celui-ci est-il le plus souvent "électrique", Peter Schumann y attachant un micro qui prolonge et amplifie la vibration de la corde. D'autres instruments sont des jouets d'enfants: sifflets, petites trompettes ou flûtes en plastique, criquets, piano miniature, crécelle, etc., ou bien des instruments rudimentaires comme le mirliton qui renvoie la voix humaine amplifiée et déformée.

Cependant, la plupart des instruments sont inventés. "Une bonne partie de la musique du théâtre provient d'instruments que nous avons construits nous-mêmes — dit Peter Schumann. Un jour, par exemple, quelqu'un nous a fourni un vieil orgue en bois et nous avons monté toute une symphonie à partir de ces grands et de ces petits tuyaux qui avaient un son étrange qu'on a pu fort bien intégrer dans le théâtre. Une autre fois, j'ai découvert que les agitateurs de machines à laver pour faire tourner le linge étaient de merveilleux cors et nous avons construit tout un orchestre d'agitateurs que nous avons utilisés lors d'une parade à New York." D'autres objets sortis de la vie quotidienne servent à produire des sons à la fois étranges et familiers: couvercles de casseroles utilisés comme des cymbales, vieux bidons d'essence remplis de cailloux ou de morceaux de ferraille, bouts de tuyaux en caoutchouc, certains percés de trous pour servir de flûte, d'autres attachés à un bidon vide dans lequel on souffle comme dans une trompe et qui produit une sorte de son étouffé, lancinant comme le gémissement d'une sirène.' — (Kourilsky, '71.)

what temporary successes man-mind may achieve in rising through time or suspending itself within and against it, a sound-vocabulary of the soul's time of mood, hope, despair, momentary relief.

Whereas adding speech, vehicle of discursive thought, to puppet gesture seems always to have figured for him as a problem that regrettably had to be dealt with, music, vehicle of emotion, to him has felt as the appropriate, not only needed but enriching, completing complement, its addition a challenge he willingly met; and probably a complement he felt in fact — potentially — obviates the need for speech: thought just a poor translation of emotion. But he has had to settle for both.

One reason he did not achieve speechless theatre with autonomously effective but still integrated sound was that it required, really, a universal myth, the Jungian kind of thing, or Frazer's: so the sounded spectacle would be inwardly meaningful and comprehensible to quieted spectators in Timbuktu or Paris or even New York; and his own confused thoughts about the dialectic of Life and Death didn't furnish this Story or Action, wasn't good enough; he found no transverbal universal myth for a key: neither his village woman assailed from the air's ocean (myth form of the '60s), nor his grey mother fleeing into the solitude of the snow (myth of the early '70s), nor his Good Friday's cross-antlered stag's or gently fierce unicorn's slaughter (myth of '75-'78) had that power. So he had recourse (1) to the Church-slicked-over and manipulated stories of a Jewish sect, Christianism, a poor substitute, especially also since this was no longer the Middle Ages in Europe, and this particular religion was dead in men's minds — had died, actually at the time of Francois Rabelais, of Hieronymous von Aaken of Hertogenbosch, of Erasmus of Rotterdam, (2) to morality, which Kant was the last with conviction to say is intuitive, but which in fact is constraining nonsense foisted on survival-anxious egos by social power structures, (3) the politics of war, an epi-phenomenon. But these lack existential truth and so need verbal nudges.

In addition, apparently, he didn't find the music. His search for this music to be furnished by singularly invented instruments through Chance, recommending itself by an intuitively apprehended rightness of the sounds surprisingly furnished was unsuccessful: perhaps his aural intuition was not adequate to the search. The post-medieval music that he mostly during the '70s had recourse to as well as the medieval music that he finally ('77, '78 — *Ave Maris Stella, Wolkenstein*) tried turned out systematically phony[3] —

---

3. 'Safford Cape, the Belgian builder of beautiful, authentic medieval musical instruments plays beautiful, authentic medieval music on the concert stage.... But the life of people and the language and art which their life brings forth has nothing to do with style.... Early medieval music had harsh and pure tone and rhythm, was fierce, not cautious, you can hear rust and cracks in the instruments, and babies crying and men shouting in the background. I don't want to hear such music in Lincoln Center, and any garbage can drum solo by any kid in New York is more medieval music to my ears. — (Schumann, *God Himself,* ... in *Sing Out!* March '67.)

to his own perception – his recourse to it a mere reflex seeing as how he had already had recourse to the poor Christian myth it was allied to.

Bunraku like Western opera couples music with narration not with the visual action, and uses it for dramatic effect and emotional enhancement. Schumann has coupled it and sounds with the visual action, and done this in an attempt – it has been largely unsuccessful – to make this action plus the music/sounds independent of narration (and of all verbal indication or expression). He has used it for emotional effect and dramatization – notably drumming – but in the main either to sustain his pretense that his is a folk art – Dixieland jazz, folk tunes sung or fiddled – or for spiritual elevation and to anchor his tales in Christian convention: Bach and medieval music; or else – and this, I think, has been what he really wanted to do, but rarely if ever (perhaps in *Leaf*, '65, *Fire* '66) got right or worked out to his own satisfaction – using chimes, the raucous noises of instruments homemade from junk, e.g. washing machine agitators, garden hoses, Japanese instruments – as a time marker and attention vivifier, for spiritual enhancement: to make time real and set a delicate or harsh structure of it over against his masks' intimations of mortality.

In '72, he attempted to use folk or quasi-folk choral music (*Hallelujah, Stations*), but thought he retained this solution in an ancillary way, soon (summer of '73, a time when he wasn't doing much and was in a depression) bethought himself that this was the wrong path – one reason being, probably, that the 'shaped note' Sacred Harp singing of *Stations* when appropriately rehearsed turned out sounding quite conventional – that his search of the '60s for sound retrieved by the ear from cacophony had been the right path, and that he should follow it from the point he had reached in '70/'71 in his *Grey Lady Cantatas II and III*: the use of self-organizing sound produced by Things, but (1) including an elementary musical structure, (2) comprising lyrically deployed voice:

'Worker who works, tries to improve himself, they say. Puppeteer who puppeteers, tries to improve himself. How?

Puppetry means the gardening of puppets and music. Music we can not borrow from anywhere. Music has to convey its speech and gossip as clearly as everyday language. There are all kinds of instrumental angels in History, but none of them will help us to find the music that we need.

We have employed a few Sacred Harp hymns and sunshine melodies over the years. But don't let that deceive anybody. The nature of our progression towards a comprehensive unity between the puppets' wiggling and their heartbeat's utterances is something else, and relies on new sounds, not on Sacred Harp hymns. And so, over the years, our washing-machine-agitator horns, our storms (? – Schumann first wrote "tin cans," then crossed it out) and noises and the composition of our washing-machine-agitator horns and (?) and noises into cantatas and sonatas have become self-reliant and unafraid. Often they do what the storyteller used to do in our earlier pieces: hold speeches, moralize on impertinent issues, address themselves boldly to an audience, and cry for reasons of imper-

manence. The musical experience for puppeteers lies not so much in the bottoms of Campbell's soup cans, but rather in the slow hiking and climbing process with light-hearted clicking and sliding sounds which eventually have to be carried to their natural height. To get prepared for this height there exists no plushed or studious guidance, no fiddle lesson, no 12-tone system. (I am not saying that we don't want to parade anymore and trumpet eternal Johnny-comes-marching-homes and beat the holy boom-booms in praise or defiance of muggy old every-day-as-it-is. That's O.K.'
(Schumann, *Vermont Puppet Theater's Desire*, draft of an essay, dated July 18, '73.)

Schumann in the *Grey Lady Cantatas II & III*, used a melodic theme, baroque and Hebrew respectively, as basis for a sequence of interludes that progressively, by partial and distorted renditions, assembled and approached a concluding full and straight rendition of the melody in instrumentally accompanied song, the scenes of the play not in a discernible progressive or non-progressively integrative, assemblive or purificative sequence, but also abutting in a full and pure statement of a sustained theme, i.e. in the end, but only in the end, presenting a like development. These may be instances of using − in a very particular way − music as active and as independent but integrated performance element. *Grey Lady Cantata II* was wordless, *Grey Lady Cantata III* had a dialogue of brief exclamations.

But he did not immediately pursue this path. Instead, he first ('74, *Jephthah* to Carissimi's *Jephthah*, *Grey Lady Cantata V* to Tallis' *Lamentations of Jeremiah* and Bach's *Cantata #40*) reverted to an approach first essayed in his '67 *Bach Cantata #140*, to the use of pre-romantic classical, i.e. primarily contrapuntal and melodic rather than harmonic, choral music, integrally presented as a whole, its formal development and unity intact, cleanly independent half of the performance, equal complement. When he did resume his attempt to work out his own kind of music, he next ('76-'78) reverted to the form of *Hallelujah* and *Stations*, a chorus singing individual verses in alternation with visual scenes. This retained the effective parity of music with the '74 uses of the classics, or even gave the music primacy, but destroyed the music's developmental integrity (one effect of which was that the words, and with them their meaning, came across more powerfully), and with it *some* of that reference to fixed pattern traditionally distinguishing music from other sound. He settled with this form for a number of years, the characteristic form of his 'Initial Dopp Farm period': *Joan of Arc, Ave Maris Stella* of '77, perhaps *Wolkenstein* of '78. But he returned to the path envisaged by him in '73 during his next creative phase, with *Washerwoman Cantata II − Nativity* ('79): attempting, in the alternation pattern, the use of unconventional instruments in the construction of intuitively organizing sound. He pursued this further with an *Insurrection Oratorio* and an 'opera,' *The End Falls Before the Beginning*, both of '83.

All his experiments with music from '72 onward comprised the use of language: he used choral music. Both because this language was integrated with the music, i.e. had the form of song, *was* music (though still vehicle of discursive thought), and because it did not directly relate to the visual action (the sculpture and dance), was not the speech of the figures, nor indication of the action, and in most cases followed and/or preceded the visual action rather than accompanying it, it was a use of language along the line of an 'organization of means out of context': separating, abstracting, elevating and concentrating man's third and 'highest' communicational mode, speech, as his masks and the movement of his puppets did the other two, facial expression and bodily gesture.

But over the years, an intended wordless spectacle of sculptured face masks and moving statuary, the faces moved almost as though almost against will in acquiescent assertions of life to the sound of the voice, of things declaiming feeling, a comedie humaine, has pierced through the spectacle sabotaged and degraded by substitute myths and poor words.

7. Graphics: to be used as active scenic element.

Painting, e.g. acrylics on backdrop and wing panels and curtains, woodcut or linoleum prints on the same or on costumes and banners, paint on masks, has been an element of his theatre since 1966.[1] It has been an independent element in the sense of not just complementing or supporting the effect of other elements – the puppets qua sculpture, the kinetics of the puppetry, a story – inasmuch as he has never allowed its artifact character to be submerged by its representational character as scenery or by its decorative character e.g. as costume ornamentation, and has generally (in the acrylics more than the prints) maintained its distinctive naive style. It has mostly been pretty and sentimental – grey for sadness, desolation and despair, or in primary colors for joy and springtime: with, still in this genre, the pale blue and white Tree of Life backdrop/curtain/sail and Ark-for-All of '70/'71 the only thing good. He is a lousy painter, but he is a good print-artist, and here his medium is black on white and, rarely, grey on white. His '77 *White Horse Butcher* book proves this, though more generally the valid point is probably that his use of colors, like of language, is spoilt by a lack of command of the medium and willful bad taste – the crude effect seduces him, but unlike in the case of his puppet masks, he can't handle it. E.g. the successive black Negro faces painted on masonite he showed in conjunction with his *Revenge of the Law* play in the fall of '72 were powerful.

His overall ideal was the use of pictures as not only independently contributive but as active, i.e. moving elements of performance: used in analogy to moving sculpture or to the modificatory assembly of a piece of music in the course of a performance. He used backdrops this way in some plays of the early '70s: successive panels, turned to view in view of the audience, showing the action independently of and divergently from how the puppets show it in *Whitewashing* ('73); a landscape backdrop panel moved away from the audience in the course of a person's walk in *Grey Lady Cantata II* ('70); the replacement of landscapes by an instigatory figure in the play to illustrate the walk of a person whom we see setting out on this walk, but then no more. (*Grey Lady Cantata III*, '71.) This same play, as part of a living room interior had a portrait that in response to the action changed expression: I don't know how this was handled. He later (*Washerwoman Nativity*, '79) attempted active use of pictures in another way, used like masks: pictures, partly cutouts of landscape elements are danced or walked across. The in-view distribution to performers

---

1. The first use of painting, I believe, was the black and white fabric woodcut print of a landscape – hill, village, trees – hung on the black backdrop of *Fire* ('66). The next, the not too dissimilar landscapes framing *Dead Man* ('67).

for a dance-of-death sequence in a '74 circus of poncho-type robes made of two black-on-white prints in the classic dance-of-death genre, one for the back, one for the front, and these performers' dressing in them, is perhaps also still in this 'active use' area. All of the pictures, black on white or gray on white, paintings or printes, used '70-'74 in this manner were splendid also simply as graphic art. The flowers and cows in '79 were in the sentimental naive genre. But on the whole, as in the case of music, Schumann's use of pictures has not realized his ambitions. The major important of painting to his theatre has been rather the orientation of his staging toward pictorial compositions – tableaux.

8. New York City critical response: His marvellous masks apart, his work is soporific, primitive and obscure though (as of *Fire*) he is probably a great artist.

Critical response to Schumann's work was at least until '67 almost entirely confined to the *Village Voice*, but this was the case also for most other Off-off Broadway theatre, as also the *Voice*'s benign neglect of the work. His American reviews start with Howard Smith's (positive if vacuous) review of *Totentanz*. (*Village Voice*, May 24, '62.) In '63 (December 18), the New York *Herald Tribune*, fleet of foot, chipped in with a friendly article, with photos, à propos of his money-earning face cast selling attempts ('Don't skimp, send your face'), and in '64 the same paper was the first to direct attention to his children's shows (Gail Sheehy, *Giving Them Bread and Puppets*, March 22, '64, quite a positive, chatty article). Then Peter Share (*Theatre for Children*) in the *Voice* of March 26, '64 found these shows 'not quite ready yet', though the masks were 'marvellous', and in May of that year (May 23), the Saturday Evening Post in the big photo I have mentioned found the Bread and Puppet crew among the 'new bohemians' of Greenwich Village, but didn't say what they were doing. Early the following year (January 2) came the first left-wing approbation, a series of photos by Robert Joyce of Schumann's Lower East Side housing agitation, with a paragraph about this work of his and mention of his current theatre production. This was followed by some more tolerably leftish attention, *Some Notes on Peter Schumann* by Margaret Riggs in the monthly *Motive* of February '65, accompanied by an article of Schumann's, *Bread and Puppets: A Way of Life*, and photos. A photo by McDarrah on the front page of the *Village Voice* of March 11 showed Schumann's puppets walking about the Village in a peace parade, Beth Bryant listed the Bread and Puppet in her *New Inside Guide to Greenwich Village* (spring or summer of '65), the *Voice* (November 11, '65) had a photo of Schumann and Merrill working on *King Story*, and then Howard Smith's eye again fell on the Bread and Puppet Theatre (*theatre journal, Village Voice*, November 18, '65): he found their puppets in *King Story* and *Leaf* at the Bridge Theatre – a place to review – 'marvellous' (*Voice* reviewers have a shared critical vocabulary), but complained that Schumann's timing put him to sleep, a complaint subsequently recurring in the *Voice*, indication they were working their reporters too hard.

A most positive but severely restrained accolade directed at *Fire* by Bob Nichols followed (*Village Voice*, February 17, '65): except for Smith's wafflings about *Totentanz* in '62, the first serious approval in the *Voice*, and really, the Riggs article apart, anywhere, and the harbinger of a degree of critical acceptance. Its being followed in turn by an enthusiastic review of Schumann's children's shows at the Bridge Theatre by Victoria Wren (*A Child's New York, Village Voice*, March 3, '66) suggests Schumann was 'in,' halfway through the run of *Fire* at the museum. His friend Jules Rabin that same month drew attention to him on the Left by an ambitiously conceived but confused article on his peace parades in *Liberation* (*Vietnam: Theory and Theatre*), Jean Hersholt beamed the *New York Times'* approval on the family man Schumann by her photo- and recipe-supplemented *Sculptor Finds Art in Baking Too* (*New York Times*, March 7, '66), and Smith having changed his name from Howard to Michael, roused himself, or tried to, from his torpor, in his *theatre journal* (*Village Voice*, March 10, '66) to find *Fire*, one of five pieces reviewed in this review: a nearly perfect poem of images succeeding one another, alas, again, too slowly. McDarrah got a photo of a Fifth Avenue peace parade with Schumann's puppets in it on the front page of the *Voice* (March 31, '66), and in May (May 26) the *Voice* reported it had awarded Schumann one of its Obies, one of five special citations for meritorious work. Allan Katzman, editor of the East Village hippie double of the *Voice*, *The East Village Other*, honored Schumann by reprinting part of Rabin's article in his organ under his own name (Katzman, *The Bread and the Puppet, East Village Other*, May 15—June 1, '66), the *New York Times* published a handsome photo of Schumann's 'Vietnamese woman' on a Memorial Day Parade, and there now followed, in the *Voice*, in June (June 2nd) the only serious—thoughtful—critical consideration Schumann ever got in America, the only one suggesting, as quite a number of European reviews have done, that here was Art! — and here was possibly a great artist, George Dennison's review of *Fire* (*Bread and Puppet Theatre*). Dennison, not being a regular *Voice* reviewer, did not find the play's rhythm sleep-inducing. The *Voice* on August 11 carried another McDarrah photo of Bread and Puppet marching puppets, and on September 1 (Rasa Gustaiti *Bread and Puppets: The Children Build a Children's Theatre*), added its delight at Schumann's work with 'underprivileged' children that summer to that of the *New York Times* six days earlier (*Do-it-yourself Drama is Fostered by City, New York Times*, August 27, '66): Schumann was even getting respectable. Joe Flaherty's mick-wise cop-baiting report on a Bread and Puppet anti-church caper of the end of that year, *The Puppets for Peace: Abduction at Cathedral* (*Village Voice*, January 5, '67) was in no way to make him less so. M. Nadle's *The Unsolved Problem. Angry Arts Aiming Through the Barrier* (*Village Voice*, February 9, '67) picked out Schumann's *Wounds of Vietnam* from among the other Angry Arts Week expressions of disapproval of American intervention in Vietnam for being effective propaganda just by not being a propaganda statement, an approval of Schumann's artistry and good taste echoed in that bastion of knowledgeable good taste, *The New Yorker*. (*Dissent*, February 11, '67.)

On the Left, Albert Bermel (*Doll Houses*) in the *New Leader* (May 8,

'67) couldn't make nothing of the revised *Leaf*, nor could Ben Reade (*The Demonic Protest of the Bread and Puppet Theatre*) make much of Schumann's work, but he hyped it up. Michael Thomas published an interview with Schumann in *Plays and Players* (*Pavement Artists*) (May 1, '67), just as though street theatre were theatre. But now the *Voice* turned sour (from having been bored and then enthusiastic): A.D. Coleman, (*The Christmas Story 1967, Village Voice*, December 21, '67), found Schumann's *Christmas Story* insufficiently revolutionary. That he wasn't far off the beam was immediately confirmed by Dan Sullivan's approval of the same spectacle (*Children's Theatres Bring Some Goodies*) in the *New York Times* (December 23, '67). Sullivan thought the show's irreverence was Christian. Apparently the downtown interest in Schumann had percolated up to 42nd Street, for Sullivan had already been to see *Fire* and reported favorably on it. (*A Stylish Year for Off-off-B'way, New York Times*, January 18, '68.) These were the *Times*' first sign of awareness of his work in the theatre, and for three years more the only ones. A *Voice* article (February 16, '68) on a Bread and Puppet 'garbage parade' shows the Bread and Puppet settling down to sensible liberal concerns, Michael Smith in his *theatre journal* grudgingly commends it for the 'convincing pathos' of its Easter show (*Village Voice*, April 11, '68), though finding the piece obscure and offensively idiosyncratic, and Charles Marowitz (*theatre abroad. London: off-off-Broadway, Village Voice*, May 23, '68) thinks their shows are better suited for the street than for theatres. Lita Eliscu (*theatre? East Village Other*, April 5-11, '68) tears herself away from her preoccupation with more avant garde theater, e.g. Schechner's, for a brief but hectic report on *Johnny*, and Candy Silbersten wholeheartedly and breathlessly endorses the Bread and Puppet's work. (*Theatre: bread and puppets, Escapade*, June '68.)

The Bread and Puppet Theatre had ended the rerun of *Fire* in April and for the remainder of the decade didn't play much in New York City. But Maurice Blanc got a chance sensitively to report on their ongoing work on *Cry* (*Bread and Puppet Theatre. Clowning with the Life Force, Village Voice*, September 5, '68), *Time* magazine (October 18, '68) gave a so severely factual report on *Reiteration* it's downright unilluminating, the *New York Times* published a nice photo of the Bread and Puppet Headquarters at the Old Courthouse (January 8, '69), and Julius Novick (*Theatre: The Christmas Story, Village Voice*, January 9, '69) tore the *Christmas Story* apart: it has no viewpoint, it has no structure and fails even as simple narrative — there are 'magnificently sculptured heads.' The *Voice* was back to its approval of the masks of '64 and '65 (though now finding them magnificent rather than marvellous), but otherwise this is actually the first severely negative review of the Bread and Puppet Theatre in the *Voice*. Arthur Sainer's enthusiastic ('ultimately a work of genius') though niggling and carping *Theater: The Cry of the People for Meat* in the *Voice* at the end of that year (December 25) – Schumann insufficiently appreciates the Judaic tradition in Christianity – does not mitigate Schumann's lasting impression that the *Voice* had hated him,[1] nor his unexpressed but implicit conviction that it had been a major factor in preventing him from establishing himself in New York theatre. 'The *Village Voice* despised us except Arthur Sainer' (Margo Sherman, interview), but Leherrissier (interview) thinks the *Voice* review of *Cry* (*Cry* had been a hit in the garment district – Gottlieb in the *Woman's Wear Daily* of December 12, '69 went positively ape over it) actually decided him to leave the city. Which he did in June '70. Neither the *Voice* nor any other New York paper reported on his work on Coney Island during the spring and summer of '70 – it's too far out there. The *New York Times* (February 11, '70) caught his Uncle Fatso smiting the righteous in Foley Square.

The New York City drama critics of the '70s, men unwillingly seeking refuge in their middle ages, e.g. Gussow at the *Times*, Novick in the *Voice*, had without much either looking at it or thinking about it, in the usual unmonitored fashion, accepted that his work was 'significant,' and that he had stature, was a figure on the scene. He thus was fairly reliably reviewed whenever he brought a show into town (cf. infra, my discussions of the individual plays). Gussow (*New York Times*, January 21, '80) expressed the underlying unexamined judgment by calling him an 'American national living treasure' – à propos of a play that he didn't particularly enjoy or esteem. On the other hand, when Gussow found his next New York offering 'not entirely accessible' and 'lulling' (*New York Times*, March 4, '81), this was also typical of the reviews these critics had been giving him: they were telling 'the public' that he was dull and obscure, and normally added to this an indication that his obscurity did not arise from profundity – they indicated his was simple-minded – but from artistic failure: he was unable

---

1. 'They know nothing, these people. (I: No, but the announcement, you see.) Oh, I see. But even that is unreliable because I remember from then that they were so hostile to us that they very often did not print our announcements. Very often. We had so much trouble with them – they gave us nothing but trouble. They either refused or out of negligence they did not print announcements. (I: Why? Just bitchiness or –) Bitchiness, yes. They disliked us very strongly. I don't know why – I personally disliked the reviewers and I think that was the reason. (I: Yeah, but that was later –) No. Right in the beginning, I remember. You must have read some of those old reviews, or remember them, about *King Story*: the most ridiculous thing they've ever seen and stuff like that. They hated it and we hated them. But we needed them to advertise the shows. (I: Of course. But, also, do you think that the people in the advertising area there would know anything about what anybody else did, or –) Yeah – you're right – maybe not. Maybe I was a bit hyped up about that. Isn't it the editor that decides all these things – of what is worthwhile being – (I: I don't think they would know about it. Of course, in the early days it was a small paper.) Yeah: it was a small paper – it was maybe all the same people did that – (I: You thought it was a conspiracy –) I thought it was a conspiracy.' —— (Schumann, interview, '82.)

to shape his pieces. His reaction was self-sabotage: when he brought a show, he did not provide his self-appointed New York publicity man, George Ashley, with the needed material.[2]

---

2. '(I: Do you remember him talking about New York in a bad way?) Yeah. I've heard him do that before. (I: What did he talk about?) About this being his hometown and not being able to get an audience. Basically he said it was his home town, even though it wasn't his home town. This is where he got started.' (Konnoff, interview. We were talking about Schumann's discontent with the reaction of a Coney Island audience to his play *Birdcatcher in Hell*, July 4, '72. They were "unresponsive," he didn't like either the audience or the response.)

Part IV.
The sixties, or the New York period.

'Der Sänger, der Pfeifer, alle leichten Gaukler, die armen, deren Herz sich an Schein und Schimmer der Erde hing und, eitel, das Eitle pries, weinen hier, weiden mehr Tränen in der Hölle, denn Wasser liegt in dem tiefen Meer.'
(Mechthild v. Magdeburg.)

Service in a political movement: non-egotistical art. The finding of a form. Performance focus on street agitation. The big-city street demonstration: non-verbal instruction to the mass, as paradigm. The moral address to responsible parties obviates the need for addressive or presentational gesture as theatrical form. Thus leaving the artist out of it. Performance as appeal to guilt: concentrated to make it sink in. The theme of guilt.

Part IV (1).
1963-1983. Puppet-making, religious observances and children's theatre, fall '63-'69.

'Es sah aber der achtsame Mann
Das Angesicht des Gottes
Damals, da, beim Geheimnisse des Weinstocks sie
Zusammensassen, zu der Stunde des Gastmahls.
Und in der grossen Seele, wohlauswählend, den Tod
Aussprach der Herr, und die letzte Liebe, denn nie genug
Hatt' er von Güte zu sagen
Der Worte, damals, und zu bejahn Bejahendes. Aber sein Licht war
Tod. Denn karg ist das Zürnen der Welt.
Das aber erkannt er. Alles ist gut. Drauf starb er.
Es sahen aber, gebückt, des ungeachtet, vor Gott die Gestalt
Des Verleugnenden, so wie wenn
Ein Jahrhundert sich biegt, nachdenklich, in der Freude der Wahrheit
Noch zuletzt die Freunde.

Doch trauerten sie, da nun
Es Abend worden. Nämlich rein
Zu sein, ist Geschick, ein Leben das ein Herz hat,
Vor solchem Angesicht, . . .
. . . Zu viel aber
Der Liebe, wo Anbetung ist,
Ist gefahrreich, triffet am meisten. Jene wollten aber
Vom Angesichte des Herrn
Nicht lassen und der Heimat. Eingeboren
wie Feuer war in dem Eisen das, und ihnen
Zur Seite ging, wie eine Seuche, der Schatten des Lieben.
Drum sandt er ihnen
Den Geist . . .'

(F. Hölderlin, *Patmos*, fragment of a late version.)

Contents: Part IV (1)

1. First productive period: its nature. — 343
2. The four types of output during the '60s. — 345
3. Big puppets, first batch, '63/64. The Christian pole puppet: mobilized Gothic statuary. — 347
4. Puppets, masks, '64-'69. — 361
5. Schumann's theatre religious: designed to inspire awe. — 386
6. The Christianism of Schumann's theatre. If mere device a dangerous one. Probably more than a mere device. — 388
7. Christianity teaches submission to power, guilt, fear of death, the rejection of the world and the taming of the flesh. — 395
8. Nature in Schumann's theatre: not the real McCoy. Life worshipped, clipped of its exuberance. — 398
9. Schumann on human nature: better repress it. Repressed human nature the ideal. — 404
10. The beauty of Schumann's position. A eulogy of saintliness in the historical perspective of the restrained poor and weak and the unrestrained rich and powerful. — 416
11. How I feel about it. Saintliness is nice but the release of greedy passion is good. — 419
12. The shows of Jesus. The condition of humanity. The persecuted and the poor. — 422
13. Observances of Christmas. 1963-1969. — 433
14. Observances of Easter. 1964-1969. — 441
15. Puppetry for children. 1963-1967. — 446
16. Puppetry with children. 1965, 1966. — 453

1. First productive period: its nature.

We, in September of '63, find Schumann a puppeteer. He had over a year of performance practice behind him. He had, in *Genesis, Apocalypse,* the *Christmas Story*, the emergent *King Story*, and probably *Fire* and *Burning Towns* too, sketched out puppetry expressions of the major themes preoccupying him. He had turned his sculptor's skills to puppet-making, and, most importantly, had realized that the traditions did not limit him: he could make what kind of puppets he liked. By combining aspects of the big, open-space Sicilian puppets with aspects of the use of masks as in the American versions of *Totentanz*, he had found the idea central to his puppeteering henceforth: live puppets: the puppet show as masque, the masque as puppet show. After a period of experimentation – two years – 1964 and 1965 – it enabled him to make use of his skills and talents as choreographer, and to use puppetry for the only kind of theatre he was interested in: serious and grand theatre. He was ready to go. Or not quite, perhaps. What was yet lacking was a morally and intellectually adequate reason for doing anything: art as such did not, to him, afford such a reason; and a mode of address. But even here, New York City, and the Lower East Side in particular, had begun to give him the answer. He now entered his first period of productivity.

The time from September '63 until December '69, from *King Story I*, ending with the defeat, in front of the curtain, of the Great Warrior by Death, to the *Cry of the People for Meat*, a summation of his work up to then, ending with the crucifixion of Christ by his disciples, is a first period in his productive life. Its determinative element is his participation in New York City street agitation. Its defining feature is his address to the people with a view to change in the great democracy's politics: simple, direct moral instruction, diffusing from his parades into his theatre shows, giving thought to his twice-a-year Christian observances in churches, fucking up his children's shows. The crucial development within this period is that of a critical attitude toward the common man; greedy celebrator of Thanksgiving, callous killer abroad, receptive listener to presidential addresses promising him the Great Society but promoting war, patriotic father of victim soldiers, crier for meat. By '67, the common man turns from solicited audience to subject matter of his theatre. This leads him into his second period, '70 ff. He turns his acquired techniques – a medium – into a tool for describing the more complex reality it recalls to him.

Schumann's overall approach to theatre during this first period can be described as follows: he was going to address people on issues of evident and great concern to them, issues that they could do something about, and with respect to which they had moral responsibilities, he was going to do it with a view to getting them to exercise those responsibilities; and he was going to do it theatrically rather than verbally, but, given the theatrical mode, straightforwardly: as effectively as possible, but not pretending to do anything else, in no way hiding the nature of his enterprise from them, but keeping what they were exposed to from him clear, in the doing of it, in the content and form of his theatre: avoiding all manner and circumstance of presentation that might make other identification of it possible, whether e.g. that he was making a living, was out to entertain them, or was trying to have a good time or to give vent to his feelings or realize himself as an artist, or even was just doing theatre.

2. The four types of output during the '60s.

Schumann's theatre during his New York period in a fairly clean and obvious way divides into religious observances (Christmas, Easter), shows for children, political street agitation, and theatre proper, meaning indoors plays for adults.[1]

The life of the artist in his work. Family, sex, and money, the enjoyment of a city or country are the background and the underground, incidental. You gotta fuck, you gotta eat, you use your eyes, if you can afford it you organize yourself a home and provide for procreation. But you are, grow and decline in your work.

During his Lower East Side Manhattan period, Schumann's work had his street stuff as its backbone and in a simple manner abruptly rayed off into the four directions indicated, quasi dictated by duty, and came together in the end with *Cry*, a periodic statement of position (as *Story of the World* had been). Such a structure of productivity in the case of an artist, a little bundle of essential intentions, indicates and is his character at the time, the nature of his life.

This quadripartite division, though it ignores identity and consistency of ideas, images and techniques, is not arbitrary and to a significant extent distinguishes his first productive period from its sequels. The religious observances tied into the people's pre-existing mythology and basic imagery – presenting the Jesus story – at the appropriate times of year – providing his work with a basic slow beat – designed for and performed at (with relatively few exceptions) the appropriate places, churches. They

---

1. 'Some of our shows are in the streets and some are outside. The inside shows are meant for the Insides, the outside shows are meant to be as big and loud as possible.' (Schumann, *Streets and Puppets*, preamble to Schumann, *God Himself*, '67. The preamble was more particularly addressed to the audience of his *Chicken Little* at the '67 Newport Folk Festival where he did it out-of-doors.

'(Ph. du Vignal: Et à propos des enfants justement . . .) Pour moi, justement, c'est très important qu'il n'y ait pas de coupure; et dans le théâtre professional, justement, il y a cette coupure: on fait des spectacles pour les enfants jusqu'à dix ans, et puis pour les enfants jusqu'à douze ans, et puis pour les grandes personnes. Et pour le public, c'est la même chose, nous espérons jouer pour tout le monde, nous souhaitons que les gens viennent avec leurs enfants quand nous jouons . . . Il nous semble très important qu'il y ait des familles toutes ensemble, pour qu'on puisse leur parler, et pas ce que fait notre civilisation qui sépare les gens en catégories, en particulier en catégories d'éducation: éducation pour les enfants, pour les adolescents, pour les grandes personnes! Mais ce nouveau langage qui reste à trouver pour le théâtre a plus de possibilités: on peut parler à tous.' (Schumann, interviewed by Ph. du Vignal in Paris, November '69, interview apparently published in *L'Art Vivant*, perhaps no. 6 of December '69, then apparently republished in *Theatre*.)

Schumann has made innocuous circus in northern Vermont for families, the number of babies at these August events is amazing; and his pageants up there also appeal to all ages. But during the '60s, in any case, he consistently distinguished afternoon programs for children from evening programs for adults, and tried to provide kid stuff for kids.

were a participation in the community's ritual life. The kid's shows were a relatively continuous week-end afternoons continuation of traditions of European puppetry, using traditional European material, notably fairy tales, and were aimed at a special audience, children, by their humorous tone, content and — less so — form. The political agitation was a participation in the community's political life, generally on occasions set by others, in response, mostly, to requests for the contribution and taking the form of contribution and participation. It was designed for the street and addressed the citizenry. It was an irregular but, at least during the mid-'60s, densely spaced activity. The regular theatre was distinguished by a relative importance of artistic concern: Schumann primarily experimented with form, developed his medium through the work on these performances week-end evenings for adults.

After '69, this way of categorizing his output becomes largely irrelevant. Sub- or side-groups more or less took over the Christmas and children's shows, the Easter show was cast into a surrealist and liturgical form remote from popular modern Christianity, the street agitation petered out. From '74 on, a division into summer circuses and toured theatre shows seems the most adequate; or into circus constituents and morality plays.

3. Big puppets, first batch, '63/'64. The Christian pole puppet: mobilized Gothic statuary.

While still in the Suffolk Street storefronts, without as yet the little skylighted loft on Delancey Street to work or perform[1] in, in September and October of '63, right away, Schumann started building a set of big puppets,[2] seven or eight to 14-15 feet tall from the hems of their garments to the tops of their heads. As the two-rod puppets had added arm gesture to stick puppets and elevated hand puppet gesticulation to the abstract simplicity of gesture, so these pole puppets added a body to the rod puppets and gave them the semblance of aggrandized humanity.

Their heads, a foot-and-a-half to two-and-a-half feet tall, being made of celastic were lightweight, and were held aloft (and thus the whole puppet, its garment being suspended from its neck or head) by an inside operator. A pole or dowel, more or less along the lines of a broom handle, but sometimes longer, was fastened into the head, and was held by the operator. Normally, especially for parading purposes – the alternative was very long poles that could be rested on the ground, but this increased the puppet's stiffness – resting in a holster attached to his belt (these puppets were heavy and were generally operated by men), the operator normally had a free hand to hold and move a second dowel or stick, also inside the puppet's garment attached to a celastic hand at the end of a sleeve – the puppet either having only one arm and hand or, if it had two, the other hand being joined to the moved one in some gestural position, e.g. in

---

1. '... the loft had the fortunate feature of a *big* hole (laughs) in the middle of the ceiling – a skylight. Which was so tall that we could play all these really tall, tall puppets. And all these puppets – these new Jesus and disciple and Fool and Mary puppets were all experimented in the loft, because of that nice feature. I remember one time when we performed, that Jim Henson, the guy who does this Muppet stuff, he came and he performed this little frog, so I remember how ridiculous that was when we did this big puppet show, *Elements of World War II*, or something like that, and this very gentle nice man came with his little frog and performed his frog tricks that he is now so famous for.' — (Schumann, interview, '79.)
2. Ernstthal is not sure of what puppets were made at Suffolk Street September-October '63 and which at the Delancey Street Museum, November '63 ff.:

'... like I said, we got to Suffolk Street and we made these big puppets ... (I: It sounds like it was a whole explosion of things, in the spring of '64.) Because we moved to the loft. And suddenly we got all this space ... when we did the heads of the Crucifixion puppets we completed all the heads within a week, because they were celastic and because of this two-man casting and sculpting team ... disciples, Jesus, the Spiessers, the soldiers, the stovepipe soldiers, and all that – they all – Peter can work very fast ....' — (Ernstthal, interview.)

prayer.[3] If, as in the case of the 'Jesus' puppet, the puppet had two arms, operated by separate sticks, its center pole in a parade, resting in a belt-holster, was in addition strapped to the operator by a belt around the operator's chest, so he had both hands free to hold the arm rods.

The garments were floor-length robes, gave the puppets a monumental quality and moved with the movement of the operator masked by them. Though the theatrical possibilities of these grandiose but awkward puppets were severely restricted, and though Schumann made some other types of puppets at the same time, these pole puppets were the point of departure for all of Schumann's later puppets, his key invention: by their scale and its awesomeness, and the power of stateliness of their movements image-wise defining the range of Schumann's future theatrical tentatives by defining a definite range within it at the outset.

The rod puppets hadn't even had torsos: the very idea of a 'body' was alien to them. Their garments when they were played arranged themselves with the arms into artistic, not realistic, patterns and were gathered for this abstract effect to begin with. But being not just upper bodies but integral beings, these pole puppets could in principle (so to speak) come out from behind the curtain which the rod and stick puppets needed (and – up high

---

3. '(I: But the structure – the skeleton?) It was different because of this one thing. One simple thing. That the *King Story* puppets, the wire ones, could hold up an object of that size and lightness. But the *big* ones could not be held up with *wire* 'cause they were too big and heavy. So they had to be done on dowels because they were heavier. When we went to bigger puppets we'd have to use dowels. Now, the thing about dowels is that you can't bend them. We had to use wood because that was the only thing that could support it. They became more rigid, necessarily. (I: Where did you get the dowels?) Actually, we bought them. Because – we used broomsticks and stuff a lot, for other things, but when we made this bigger style of *Crucifixion* puppets, the Easter ones, we'd use store bought (dowels) (from) a lumber yard. Like these soldiers that we made. (They) were like four puppets, all hung together. So we got extra dowels. They were all like joined. They were *one* puppet with four heads. We called them Spiessers. Three heads, with six hands. And they were played by four people. And they would talk: "Ahhh" – and move around together. So there would be a central pole and either – well, sometimes the hands were like this. Two poles. A head pole and a hand pole. The hands were joined. (The poles) would go inside the fabric. Actually, originally, we'd just kind of do like this. We got kids' holsters for guns, and put them right in the front here, and held them like flagpoles, like (an) honor guard – they have those things, but they are around the waist. And we'd hold them and we'd play them *up*, like that, over our heads. Still with two sticks. So they were either – sometimes the hand would be sewn in and the one hand would move. Sometimes, I think with the Jesus puppet, for instance, we would have *two* hands on rods, but you'd kind of hold the one hand and the head rod *together*, and then move one hand. But then you could put it back, see, and fix it and hold that on, and then get the other. In a way you could imitate a double gesture, but essentially they were all one-man puppets and things like the soldiers and the Spiessers and stuff were played by two of us. The Spiessers, I know, had the hands all sewn in, although there were wires coming from them. So, in other words, you could play the puppet, and let the hands all droop, like play the heads. But then you could grab a hand and make her reach, and make a movement with it, then let it hang again, or then get another hand. . . .' — (Ernstthal, interview.)

– profited by as much as little hand puppets did) and could fill open three-dimensional space quite otherwise powerfully than could on their little stages the marionettes of traditional marionette theatre. In fact, they were to an extent wasted behind a curtain, prevented by it – above the curtain – from exercising their full power. And Schumann did in fact right away try out at least certain ones of them on the floor, in front of the curtain (and relatively soon used them to full effect on the street and – processionally – within the space of churches). But it took him several years of experimentation before he mastered their use (and that of other types of big puppets 'derived' from them) in open stage-type space.[4]

---

4. E.g. in *King Story* originally, only the Great Warrior and Death appeared in front of it, full-bodied on their own legs. In two unadvertised shows in which Schumann in the fall and winter of '63 experimented with his new puppets, *Apocalypse* and *Elements of World War II*, apparently all the puppets were worked in the air from behind a curtain. Similarly, for the '63 *Christmas Story*, probably only Mary and Joseph and their donkey appeared – for their trek – in front of the curtain, though Schumann (interview, '82) thinks that maybe King Herod did, too.

'All the big puppets – the Jesus puppet and all those puppets – were originally played above a curtain. We had this steep, high ceiling, and that's how we played it. (I: When you built the Jesus and the disciples, for instance, did you have in mind using them above a curtain?) Yeah. That was the idea, to build way tall rod puppets that would be operated behind a curtain. (I: You saw these big Manteo puppets doing their fights and so on in an open space, and they inspired you to make these big puppets of yours, but then you still did them above a curtain, in the air? That's surprising. To me, one of the most impressive things about the Manteo puppets, compared to hand puppets and such would be they are out in space.) Right, it's true – out there in space. (I: But that wasn't –?) No. I didn't know how to do that and I thought it could be done better if one would do it above a curtain because of the use of objects. That one could hold up a chair and a shovel and, you know, and operate them from underneath and sticks and –' – (Schumann, interview, '82.)

Granting that puppetry above the curtain is flat, Schumann nonetheless sees certain advantages in it: visibility and a way of creating a theatre, namely, simply by holding up the curtain (which can then alternatively or alternately function as backdrop):

'Right. It has no depth. That way it's not even *similar* to the Sicilian puppets, because what they work with is really *depth*, more than any form of puppetry that I've seen, or any form of theatre. The Sicilian stages that I saw in Paris and in Sicily were always – and then in Belgium – in Belgium they have an adoption of Sicilian stage also. Belgian puppetry is influenced by Sicilian puppetry and they use stages – very deep, with sometimes as many as eight legs, for things to come and – with small rooms where people sit in depth and the stage is as deep as the auditorium, or tiny, little, very little – not very wide and that makes a very strong impression of a courtyard – of a battle – of a meeting of people – how in this *deep* space, how they meet. So you're right – above a curtain everything is flat – but then you have the in-front-of-the-curtain. See, and the invention – when I started working with that *curtain*, I was very happy about that invention of *holding* up the curtain like that because what it meant was that you – with very few people you could create an immediate, you know, stage, where everybody can see. That seemed to me a very practical solution to street shows – to have that curtain. A curtain is sort of like a flag – people look at it – it's red or bright and then on top of it is something that moves, and they – it's high enough up, everybody can see it. That's right, it has no depth. You can hardly do anything with depth – it all disappears. Move backward from the curtain, it cuts off people's view, so it becomes shorter. But I like that curtain with rod puppets above the curtain.'—(Schumann, interview, '82.)

The problem was partly the power of these puppets: the space they — by their aura, by projection — defined was so vast: curtailment of it not only reduced but to some extent sabotaged their effect. Partly, the problem was their gestural limitation, not only by their size and ponderousness, but by their very construction; first, they had no neck movement: their heads and bodies moved as one, and second: the operator did not have too much freedom in moving either the center pole nor the arm rod, and had no free hand to modify the fall of the garment. The first problem was eventually solved by mixing puppet types and sizes and performance modes, essentially perhaps by combining the use of big puppets with the use of masked performers (and of mime): the human scale by a contrast relationship restructured and integrated the big (and even giant) puppets' space-structuring effects. The second problem was solved by developing new types of big puppets capable of head movement and allowing their operators more freedom and control in producing their gestures.[5]

Schumann's productive outburst '63/'64 focused on these pole puppets. His core output consisted of a group that with reference to their use in his Easter plays '64 and following were called the 'Crucifixion' puppets, with reference to the color of their burlap garments and the skin tone of their masks, as well as to their use in Vietnam-related demonstrations, the 'yellow people': Jesus and his Twelve Disciples. Other puppets used in these shows and/or in his Christmas shows made during this Suffolk

---

[5]. 'Mostly, the puppets are rod puppets, so you have very limited things you can do with it, like the Twelve Apostles, the disciples. It's just a single rod with a head, you know. You can just move it around, so it's a sculptural display rather than a movement display. The others (later ones! (SSB)), the ones that were mounted on the head or had independent hands, were much more movable.' — (Palmer, interview.)

Sometime during the '60s, probably for a *Crucifixion* at Judson Church in '67, Schumann made a set of armless disciples: an instance, as in the case of his giant effigy puppets of the '70s, of his working toward the sculptural statuary effect.

'The original (*Crucifixion*) had the right number of disciples and then, later on, we made many more. I just wanted to make it bigger, I think. I had more people available. Instead of just twelve people around that table I wanted to have a mass of people there. And that (no arms, hands) was what was needed for this kind of crowd scene. That you cut out all those little movements and make a more crowd choreography of walking, of kneeling down, of bending over and such things. The first version of that kind of crowd scene, I think, we did in Washington Square Church, where we did performances with them being tied up and pulled through the church. And they didn't need any hands or anything for that. All the little gestures were lost. (I: But in the Last Supper, for instance, you would want the arm gestures?) The Last Supper never had much arm gestures in it because the Feeder (puppet) had the arm gestures. The Feeder just goes around and feeds them the bread and the wine and they bend forward for that. The arm gestures, we never got much from them, really — from those disciple puppets. I think that's probably why the second set didn't get them. Wasn't much needed. Judas had a dance with his arms — I remember that — he had sort of fists — but the others — there are some of these praying big hands that were — yes, we rehearsed that for many times — this one guy, sort of fat looking fellow with hands like this. And some are more delicate — little hands, like this — strange folding positions. It was taken out.' — (Schumann, interview, December '82.)

Street/ early Delancey Street period were the Spiesser(s) puppet, mockers of Jesus, the Pointer, pointing up the lesson of something, the Dancers, celebrating the annunciation to Mary, the Red Devil or Big Fool, tempting Jesus on the mountain, a 'Mary' puppet for the *Crucifixion* shows, also used as Angel of Annunciation in the *Christmas Story*, replacing an earlier one that had been lost, and which Schumann used as Angel of Resurrection '74 ff., a 'Joseph' face mask, and face masks for the shepherds replacing the Putney paper maché ones, these last, 'pink, flesh-colored — red cheeks, red nose, realistic sort of snub-nose masks, sort of drunken looking shepherds — not face-casts.' (Schumann, interview, '79.)[6] His primary output thus was definitely and specifically Christian: a surprising fact in view of his earlier areligiosity. These Christian puppets are the mobilized church statuary as which Schumann identified them in his program for the *Puppet Christ* (Spencer Memorial Church, Easter '64),[7] and surely were inspired by this conception — progressively less applicable to his later puppets. Their very rigidity makes them sculptural even in movement. The Red Devil can be conceived of as mobilized gargoyle. With the exception of the 'Red Devil', they continue the 'sculptural' line of his Putney puppet-making, not its whittling 'Kasperl' line. The Putney 'Peace Angel' stylistically is their predecessor.[8]

Among the other puppets made at this time there were a number of soldier masks and puppets, notably the 'Stovepipe Soldiers' puppet, and a 'Beast' puppet, both stick puppets, on the uses of which some of his earlier staging 'experiments' (*Elements*, November-December '63, *Apocalypse*, winter '63/'64) focused, a large pole puppet, 'The Great Warrior', focus (in front of the curtain) of the new versions (February-April '64) of *King Story*, and some rod puppets for his economically central children's theatre, his Punch and Judy shows: Punch, Judy, 'The Cop', 'The Landlord'.

---

6. Bob Nichols, in an account of a *Christmas Story* performance, probably, though he dates it '62, of '63 mentions a number of other puppets at least some of which were probably made at this time, too: the Bugler (with a 'grotesque mask'), a three-headed wise men puppet, reminding him of Picasso's drawings, the three shepherds ('from Brueghel'), an angel ('rises up from behind the curtain on a pole, stands fifteen feet high'), though this is probably the *Crucifixion* 'Mary' puppet.

7. 'Puppet theater is an extension of sculpture, imagine a cathedral, not as a decorated religious place, but as a theatre with Christ and the saints and gargoyles being set in motion by puppeteers, talking to the worshippers, participating in the ritual of the music and words.' — (Schumann, *Bread and Puppet Theater*, program, of *The Puppet Christ*, May-June '64. Cf. Appendix I.)

8. Schumann thinks of Jesus and the disciples as 'very Renaissancish' in their tones: yellows, umbers, browns — and in their shapes? —: 'They have a bit of this Piero della Francesca sweetness to them'. (Schumann, interview, December '82.) He used oil paints on them, 'the last time I used oil paints. Then I changed to acrylics — it was so much easier. It's too expensive — oil paints. That's — that's the major reason. Slower — more expensive. You get tones that you don't get with acrylics with oil, but I never was for the delicacies — I don't think they matter that much'. — (Schumann, ibid.)

'The Great Warrior' was directly inspired by the Manteo knights, the Punch and Judy puppets continued the Putney 'Kasperl' line.

The typical masks, whether puppet heads or face masks, of this first set were of celastic, made inside plaster molds, not directly over the clay, oil-, not acrylic-painted. The *Crucifixion* puppets' heads were made by the 'lost plaster' method: the molds destroyed to get the celastic heads out of them: which kept the features of these closer to the clay sculptures? Schumann was expending the sculptural care he had expended on his German rice-paper masks, a finesse he dropped once he got going on his shows with some self-assurance ('65-'71) – reverting to it later ('72-'73) only under the special circumstances of having skilled assistants with plenty of time for this available to him.

Christ is now ('82) in the Glover Museum, from the top of his head to the hem of his yellow burlap coat (with its handsome pattern of spreading vertical folds down from the neck) 18 or so feet tall. He has a celastic

---

9. '... the building of Uncle Fatso ('65 (SSB)) was, as I said, direct mounting of celastic over the clay original. You can imagine: the clay is the composition, the original, and then the question is how do you salvage and make this mold into something that is light enough to be used as a puppet? So you either use paper maché or celastic. Sometimes the celastic is put directly over the clay and cut off to be lifted from the clay and remounted and reinforced from the inside, and sometimes, as in the Christ puppets, it's done in plaster. There are two reasons for not working directly from the clay but working into the plaster mold. One is when you want to make more than one copy, you're better off having the first mold. And the second is that you want a certain finesse in sculpture; fineness of line, sharpness of contours, sharpness of crevices, surface exactness, then, for best results, you have to mold it, so what is done is that you cast plaster over the clay; you remove the mold from the clay, or you dig out the clay from the mold. You brush separator in – usually a layer of shellac, and then on top of that, some kind of oil – vaseline, or what I like best is suet, and then it hardens inside the plaster mold. Onto that surface you apply your celastic in little pieces that overlap. You let it dry and then you take it out. If the head is a full-sized head, you have needed two molds that then get pasted together – after they get taken out – separated. But in the case of the Christ and the disciple puppets – the yellow people, we used to call them, because they wore yellow burlap dresses – we made lost molds. We chiselled out the plaster from celastic. The reason for that is we did not put a very thick film of separator inside the mold and we didn't care for making several copies of each face. (I: So first you made the clay. Then you put plaster on top. Why is it more precise?) See, when you work a material over a clay mold, you add the thickness of the material, the precision of your work to the original – you don't just have what you have in the clay, in other words, you make it clumsier by the materials that you apply on top of it – whereas when you work into a mold, you work against the cast of the precise cast of the original. You're working against the inside of it, so your skin surface, the skin of your sculpture, is going to be precisely – if you do the application right – is going to be precisely what the original was. So when you enlarge puppets like the Christ puppets – when you remove such masks out of their molds – you end up with slight distortions from the bend and wiggling that is needed to pull them out of the mold. You often lose some of your best features to that bending and wriggling and swaying that happens when you take them out of the mold. Unless they are molded with the preconceived notion of pulling them out. But with these, for instance, it would have been hard to pull them out, and the chiselling off of the plaster, that really gave us the best results. — (Schumann, interview, '79.)

neck prolonging the head, which emphasizes his overall bottle shape. His head, in Schumann's early style — a little bulgy, cheeks and chin, which are red, curving out — is tiny actually, almost a joke, with a concentrated, grave, commanding expression, looking down along his long nose. His hands are as long as his face, perhaps a foot and a half, with all fingers, thumb included, joined; golden brown hands. Unlike the disciples, he was constructed to have the operator operate his two hands separately. As theirs, his center pole rested in a belt holster dangling in the operator's groin area, but the second support it needed, higher up, was in his case provided, not by the operator's hand or hands, but by a belt around the operator's neck or shoulders, so that both of the operator's hands were free to manipulate his. For some production of the *Crucifixion* during the '60s (and in *Cry* in '69), Jesus was superimposed on one or two operators on a six foot ladder, one sitting on top, one standing half way up; and sometimes the ladder was put on a dolly and wheeled around. (Schumann, interview, '79.)

The disciples are there also, seated at table, heads bigger and higher than His, almost seven feet tall seated, some standing perhaps nine or ten feet tall. They are of many different races, some yellow, two of them Blacks, one a dark, purplish brown, one a greyish purple. They are all very solid or meaty looking — full. They wear many expressions; not foolish, petty or pained throughout, by any means, they are just a wide variety of mature men, a representative sample of humanity, looking at us or looking down. The eyes of most of them are painted on. Their hands are generally joined (thus operable by one hand), but in many ways. Disciples made later in the '60s for a 'more crowd choreography' (Schumann, interview, December '82) were made armless (cf. infra).

The disciple puppets, because of their yellow robes[10] looked like Buddhist monks. This reenforced their use in Vietnam demonstrations, especially when Diem and the Buddhists clashed, in '63.

The Blue Judas[11] was apparently built specifically for the '64 *Cruci-*

---

10. 'The *Crucifixion* puppets had these gold colored clothes on them. We found — I think it was Eva Burckhardt, Bruno's wife, who found this incredible pile — all the stuff came up out of the garbage. And she found this incredible pile of fabric. Unbelievable pile, and that's what all those puppets are made out of. One day, I remember, it was like a gold mine or something. Incredible. She came in with this pile of fabric. It was in the garbage; someone had thrown them away.' — (Ernstthal, interview, '79.)

Schumann (Schumann, interview, '79) remembers it as yellow burlap.

11. '... made in some silver and painted bright blue — bright red lips, and the hands were — two hands — fists that clenched together. From inside. And he wore some kind of silky shiny silvery metally dress we found in the garbage can. Not a dress, but a piece of old curtain.' — (Schumann, interview, '79.)

'I also played the other memorable puppet — was the Judas puppet in the Easter play, which was another character. That was a more — it was a difficult puppet because he had to work two ways. There were two hands mounted on one — like a rod — and the head on the

fixion, the first Easter show: possibly only for the second – another, also oil painted, seems to have been made earlier, but either not used or used only in '69.

The Feeder puppet, a Communion puppet,[12] which I had thought first used in the '67 Judson Memorial Church *Crucifixion* according to a note in the museum ('from Last Supper (1963)') was also built in '63/'64, and used in the '64 *Crucifixion*. Its reddish, well-sculpted hands are chunky. It holds a cup in one hand, a loaf in the other, chunky also, rough shaped, but smoothened. It contributed to the solemnity of the Last Supper scene of the '67 *Crucifixion*.

The Spiessers became the mockers of Jesus.[13] They required two or

---

other. And you had to keep yourself out of it so it always was a question of trying to keep yourself formless so that your head didn't stick out or your knees weren't in the wrong place or something. It was a short puppet, very difficult to manage ... the head is on a rod, the hands are on a rod, and there's a drape over the whole thing, so you're underneath this way. You keep trying to manage to keep your head out of the way and to keep your own body invisible under the drape. But it was very flexible. I climbed a ladder. I got up on a series of boxes. I got my head on Christ's knees. I did all kinds of – you know, like kind of sleazy things that Judas might move to do. But the possibilities of getting this difficult thing to – on one hand keep you invisible and another hand had a character of its own. That was my challenge ... This was in Judson. I played the Judas puppet only one year or two years and that was at Papp's City Theater, the first year. (I: What did Judas do?) Judas betrayed Christ. He met him in the garden in the play, climbed the ladder, delivered a kiss, the identifying kiss, and betrayed Jesus. That was the action. but the activity was to get this puppet into kind of like a sleazy but arrogant walk somehow. And to manage to keep it going through all of these encumbrances, you know. The different levels and the ladder and the whole thing, while still remaining invisible, while still being expressive above it and managing two things on your feet also – different, you see. We have hands on one and the head on the other and the feet are doing something else. I like that whole – (I: Your feet were bare?) No, I had shoes. (I: Any shoes?) Any shoes. The drape is long. You could barely see the feet.' — (Palmer, interview, '79.)

12. '... I had the good fortune to get the part that I loved over all the best that I ever did with Schumann, which was the Feeder at the Last Supper. In a puppet covered up with a hand here and one with a glass in it and one with a loaf of bread and fed all of the puppets. And that to me was the very best thing that I ever – the thing that I loved to do the most of all.' — (Levy, interview, '79.)

13. We see the only two-or three-headed Spiesser puppet in *Elements of World War II* in Moore's photos of a November/December '63 Delancey Street performance. According to Schumann (interview, '82) it was built for this piece.

'There were quite important puppets in (*Crucifixion*), that we don't have any more, that were built *before* we had planned the *Crucifixion*. Like the Spiesser. (Elka: They are in the barn.) Yes, but they are destroyed. Maybe five-headed, four or five heads on one piece of green detached rags – five-headed, fabric, and about six or eight hands, flat hands on sticks. So it needed lots of people. So it was really impractical, it never – we used it a lot, this puppet, but it was never satisfying. (Elka: It was sort of a *crowd*. The heads were all different separate heads. They weren't one lump of many heads.) It's a big puppet. It plays about six feet above the curtain. The heads (were) slightly over-life-size, and the hands very much over-life-size.' — (Schumann, interview, '79.)

'We see the – here apparently only two or three-headed Spiesser puppet in *Elements of World War II* in Moore's photos of a November/December '63 Delancey Street perform-

even three operators. They were played above the curtain: perhaps only. They had no inside operator.

The Pointer

'... was originally used in *Elements*, I think, and then it was used for these different versions of *Crucifixion*. He was the Pointer who pointed at moments of importance. Pointed up — that was his usual position. Then he had a position like this. And then he could sort of do a dance, stepping around, pointing to the — for example, when the miracles were done, at the moment where the lame man threw away the crutch, woop, the finger would be there to point and he acted in many plays like that. But originally in that *Elements* — and then in the *Crucifixion* stories — in all of them. In the meantime, we have two Pointers and they are in various street shows. (I: Isn't there a da Vinci John the Baptist that has a finger like that?) That's right. It didn't have to do with that, but I'm sure I had it in my mind, somehow, to —' (Schumann, interview, December '82.)

The Pointer was a development of the Putney Red Man. Whereas the Red Man linked show and audience as indicator from within the show, as figure in it, the Pointer did it as frame-element, its characters only that function ('Behold!').

The Stovepipe Soldiers,[14] a stick puppet requiring several operators, none of them inside it, played overhead, a grimmer and larger version of the earlier *King Story* Three Soldiers puppet, were dispatched for the Slaughter of the Innocents, and apparently were the focus of the 'experiments' constituting *Elements of World War II*. 'They were sometimes played above the curtain and sometimes in front.' (Schumann, interview,

---

ance. It was built for this piece (Schumann, interview, '82). It had these multiple hands and several heads on separate sticks and needed several people to move them.' (ibid.)

14. '... a big puppet, one of the first built on Suffolk Street, that was a group of soldiers on sticks. Grey faces with bags. Stuffed arms, upright sticks mounted to them. They are still in the (Glover) museum, and with the stovepipes that were carried in the horizontal.' — (Schumann, interview, '79.)

'That was made on Suffolk Street before we had Delancey Street, I think. They were made together with these *Christmas Story* puppets, and also used first in this *Elements of World War II* thing that I don't remember much of. But they were all used in that... the others (the other pole puppets (SSB)) all have disguised operations. The rods are inside the dress of the puppet, right? Like the Jesus puppet, you don't see any rods. They're disguised by the dress. Now, with the soldiers, everything is exposed. You see the rods — you don't know what they are. They are rods that have stuffed arms attached to them. And stovepipes — some rods carry a stovepipe — and some of them carry — so it's sort of noodleish kind or arms and — in a way it's all — there's no disguises built into this puppet. Nothing is disguised, it's just a bunch of sticks, stovepipes, stuffed arms and heads. And a bunch of guns... (their heads (SSB)) are identical. They were built over the same clay mold — the heads — and then, no hands, just stuffed arms and upright sticks and stovepipes. And originally played over the curtain like the rest of the *Crucifixion* puppets, and then, later on, operated by people, also used in peace marches for just pounding the sticks on the ground and marching them on the street and in performances, also.' — (Schumann, interview, December '82.)

December '82.) Ernstthal (interview, '79) remembers it as used at one of the earliest or perhaps the earliest anti-war demonstration they went on, in Times Square – not yet played, they just stood there with it (and with other puppets). This was probably in August of '64. It is in the museum, a superb piece, approaching the thing-power of sculpture. Schumann has mounted with it the (stylistically similar) fanged head of the Beast, a dog of war, but originally the soldiers puppet had only four heads, small, three with their mouths open as though receiving or handing out death, the fourth featureless, its nose and mouth collapsed into a flat grim grimace, all set on goitered necks, connected by stuffed tubes of grey cloth, four or five inches in diameter, an irregular light grey connective tissue between them. At the end of two of these canals – their spider's body – are barrels, smooth like mortar launchers, two-and-a-half feet long or so, darker than the heads, and black, rather than, as they, brown, but part of their body.

The Dancers, development of the Blue Man and His Son, required two inside operators:

'... a very strange puppet that I liked a lot and it's totally smashed by now, that I called The Dancers, I think. It's a white dancing puppet that has an arrangement of – two hands are joined – extending them from each other – away from each other – and the heads are on separate sticks. Can you imagine? You can't see that in the picture. See, there's one hand sculpted as a joined hand. The puppet, then, has stuffed arms, you know, part of him that leads into a head with an upright stick. So the dancers – the people who operate this puppet – have to see to – that the stretch between the puppets stays sort of the same – to not distort the arms. (I: Between the puppets?) Between the two puppets. The puppets are two puppets but are really one, because they're connected by these two hands. So it makes a very peculiar movement. They can only spin or move at the same speed – very limited, but I enjoyed that puppet a lot and it was – I used it in *Crucifixion* stories and in various tryouts, but never got a major job for this puppet. (I: And what would you use it in *Crucifixion* for?) Probably to dance around some important event. Like around the Mary of the Annunciation or something like that. Yes, I think that's very possible.' (Schumann, interview, December '82.)

Schumann may have used it in *Crucifixion*, but if it danced around Mary of the Annunciation, that was in the *Christmas Story*.

The Great Warrior,[5] for one inside operator, not built specifically for

---

15. Cf. part IV.3, section 5 on *King Story*. Also:

'... the Soldiers were replaced by the Great Warrior who was one of the really fine puppets. I used to play it a lot. And the Great Warrior was an interesting example. A very great puppet. Because I used to play it, occasionally, comic. We'd do the *King Story* in a comic vein. And I used to play the Warrior as a sumurai. I was screaming Japanese, sounding things and stomping around, and the Warrior could be – was hilariously funny. And yet, when it was real, it was terrifying. So it could be played either way, but – also we played things so much it became more intimate than any friend or more intimate than any person.' — (Ernstthal, interview, '79.)

'Le Grand Guerrier bleu aux deux épées longues et fines gris acier qu'il tient dans ses mains

King Story – 'I just built it – no puppet hardly ever was built for a show' (Schumann, interview, '79) – was in fact Schumann's answer to the Manteos' Orlando Furioso.

The other puppets for *King Story* at this point apparently were still the Putney built ones; Death, perhaps, had a *Totentanz* mask; I presume the King was done with the Putney rod puppet king.

The Red Devil or Big Fool, originally a rod puppet for being played above a curtain, on sticks and with complicated neck movements (Schumann, interview, December '82), but then deprived of its rods and moved directly by hand, a 'big satanic red figure' (Schumann, interview, '79) was like most of these other first big puppets worked with in *Elements*, and, apparently in some early *Crucifixions*, in scenes of Jesus' being tempted on the mountain. Its appellation of 'Fool' – Schumann in '82 refers to it as a 'laughing puppet' (we see laugher puppets again much later in *The Story of Bread* ('80) and *Woyzeck* ('81): the 'Laughing Guy' puppets, also evil) – was given to him because 'he didn't have a voice. He was a kind of Coney Island laughing character. Somebody who laughed and made fun of things.' (Schumann, interview, December '82.) He was used as evil clown impersonating President Johnson in *Speech*: with an inside operator, and outside ones to move his feet, and without a curtain.

In Moore's picture of it in the November/December '63 *Elements*, head back slightly, one mitten-pawed arm up, and both of its stumpy stuffed legs with their fat paws showing outside the curtain, it looks totally unlike any other puppet of Schumann's because of that malformed body: no upper legs and the head an afterthought, off to one side, cross between a frog and a monkey head, pitifully expressive. In this picture it doesn't as yet have the tongue it got later and still has in the museum. It needed two operators, one for the legs (the operator puts his/her arms in them), one for the head and the – apparently one only – arm, plus, it would seem at least originally, a third person to hold it up, for the distinctive feature of this puppet was that it had neck movements provided by a gooseneck lamp joint, so that, unlike with the other rod puppets, the rod holding it up was not also the rod controlling the head (Schumann, interview, '82).

'... later on was changed into something that two people operated – one for the feet, and one for the head and the arms, and now it's sitting in a wheelchair or something like that, and that used to be a puppet that was quite complicated. Because – we tried – we bought ourselves lamp fixtures. We tried to find a joint that was flexible and could be used for a flexible neck, for movements in the neck

---

énormes et de même couleur: avec sa tête lourde et menaçante, gris acier elle aussi et hérissée de pointes, il évoque la Statue de la Liberté ... Dans *Marriage and Revenge of the Statute of Liberty* (1970), revêtu d'une robe avec de faux seins, il représente la Statue de la Liberté ... Le Grand Guerrier exprime l'idée de la violence, d'une certaine violence. Je dirais volontiers qu'il exprime l'idée d'impérialisme.' — (Kourilsky, '71.)

of the puppet to get away from the stiff-necked puppet, and we spent incredibly many hours figuring this, I remember. All kinds of things like ball joints and we never came to a good solution. The lamp fixtures that we used were all much too weak to hold this kind of weight. It had a loose neck, with a separate operation to move the neck, but it always broke and always had to be rebuilt.'

(Schumann, interview, '79.)

'Then he was demounted. He came off his long sticks — and off the complicated system, and people were put inside him. Sometimes two — sometimes, I think, maybe three — I'm not sure of that. But anyway, he got a complicated system of head movements — hand either mounted or operated by somebody from behind. Arm movements — by somebody who was inside. Leg movements — by somebody who was lying underneath or sitting underneath the person who did the arm movements — that could also be. But there was quite a bunch of different ways of moving that character ... he was used for a Johnson speech — with the legs moving quite a bit and freely, being operated by somebody else — arms moving on their own, and the head moving also, separately. He was used in the *Crucifixion* before he was used in these political rallies because, I think, the first *Crucifixions* that had that scene in (the Red Devil as Satan tempting Jesus on the mountain (SSB)) were played over a curtain, so he must have been on his rods still and I doubt that we'd put him back on the rods after taking him off the rods.'

(Schumann, interview, December '82.)

Both in its mobility and in its appearance it was in the Kasperl tradition — in the hand puppet tradition.

Ernstthal (interview, '79) remembers perhaps mistakenly a puppet used in one of the *Crucifixions*, probably during '64-'66, somewhat like this Red Devil, but with two heads:

'... there was one puppet with two heads and we put in goosenecks — like lamps — lamp goosenecks and there was a rod, a second rod, so you could pull the head — it had a neck movement to it, that one with the two heads. And there was a certain tenderness to it.' (Ernstthal, interview, '79.)

The beast[16] was the Beast of the Apocalypse, used in the *Apocalypse* 'experiments' and we see it as part of *Flower Mountain* in a Peter Moore photo parading around Washington Square Park with a big dollar sign affixed to its pelt on July 20, 1965. It seems to have had a Washington debut in the November 27, '65 March on Washington.

Mary and Joseph in the *Christmas Story* were for a while apparently played by masked children, and he made these masks, it seems celastic

---

16. A 'big, big beast with tusks', its skin an old dilapidated Polish pilot's sheepskin coat of Elka's father's turned inside out, its fleece showing, 'and then we put legs on it, sticks into each of the sleeves and we built two more sleeves on the back of the coat. There are four sticks under this animal and then people walk it in. I think they pounded the sticks on the ground and that's why this thing broke so fast. We (still) have the head of it, not the body. The body was nothing but a piece of grey junk fabric.' — (Schumann, interview, '79.)

'It was very high up, and the operators walked these sticks as feet on the ground and it played in *The Flower Mountain* and such shows.'—(Schumann, interview, December '82.)

face masks, at this time, as also, it seems, new ones for the shepherds. He had used a paper maché Mary mask in combination with a cardboard carton puppet body to advertise the '62 Living Theatre *Christmas Story* on the sidewalks of 14th Street.[17] Whether he continued to use this mask (but not with a carton puppet body) for his Christmas shows is not quite clear, nor whether this paper maché mask or a new celastic one was the one he used in '74 as stilt walking White Lady, Savior Angel and/or Angel of Resurrection, an innocent oval, pretty 'village maiden' face. By '65 or '66, there was a giant Mary done by masked grownups.[18] She was probably not a center pole puppet, but a short stick one (cf. infra.).

There is, in the museum, besides a '67 'Blue Madonna' whose label says she was used in the '67 *Christmas Story*, a very small Mary, five to six feet tall from the hem of her elegantly flower patterned, light yellow gown or shroud up, her hands joined flatly, all fingers parallel, in prayer, with a very tall head in the shape of a bass violin – sleek long hair along its sides, flat, painted eyes, a sharp little nose, and a pursed mouth – her expression very severe. She apparently is also one of the '63/'64 puppets.[19]

The Punch and Judy puppets he made them were used not only in children's shows at the Delancey Street Museum, but also in some of the

---

17. 'I also recall that for the performances of the *Christmas Story* in 1963, I used, I guess, and from then on and after a lot, a cardboard box with a figure painted on it, and holes for the arms, to stick the arms out of and a mask mounted in the place where the face looked out. That was the Mary of the *Christmas Story* and I paraded that Mary in the streets and held a bell, and advertised the show that way. The cardboard box slips over the player and is as big as the player, with only the lower part of the legs sticking out underneath, and the mask is mounted on one side of the cardboard box, right underneath its top (with a hole cut into the cardboard underneath it) so it's in the place where your face is.' (Schumann, interview, '79.) It was the same size as the disciple puppets. (ibid.)

18. '*I* did the Mary puppet, which is very – it's just labor, to lift it, and to keep it angled in the right direction. But it's so *moving* to be encompassed by Mary and to have the labor of carrying her. A tremendous experience for me ... She was Mary, which consisted usually of a giant puppet, consisted of walking it out at the right angle, kneeling, turning in one direction and turning in another direction, standing, leaving. Those simple activities meant a lot to me.' — (Palmer, interview, '79.)

19. 'This is an early Mary. She's just not mounted well, and we redressed her. We – her old dress fell apart. She used to be blue and now she has a brown – brownish beige kind of dress that isn't so good for her and she's also a bit smaller – the sticks are smaller – she used to be quite a bit taller. But that is one of the first Marys. She was built together with all these – Jesus and the disciples (I: And what kind of a puppet was she then?) A two-rod puppet. Two rods – one for the head, one for the folded hands. Quite difficult to play – you have to play her very gentle, slow, like many of these, but she had only a few movements that were good for her. Some – little bit of a turn of her head and some kneeling motion that we rehearsed for ever and ever – whoever played her. It's difficult – very restricted. Originally she was played like all the *Crucifixion* puppets, above the curtain.' — (Schumann, interview, December '82.)

Bread and Puppet Theatre's earlier – 1964? – Latino-directed street shows: Punch and Judy as tenants.[20]

He apparently had several Punches. The one 'used for the New York Punch and Judy landlord, cop-beating shows and stuff like that' (Schumann, interview, December '82), the 'black fellow with big, red cheeks and a red nose' (ibid.), had 'a curtain in front of his teeth – so sometimes the teeth could be curtained off when he was sad and his smile would be disguised' (ibid.).

---

20. 'Punch was black, with a long red head, and as big as the *King Story* puppets – as the King and the Red Man. He had a spoon in one hand instead of a cudgel. He was a two-stick operation. One hand was hanging limp on the dress, so the puppeteer had to operate the head with one stick – that was a broom handle that took care of that one – and the other one was the hand that could hit – and he was very big. The house was a tiny *little* house, just as in the *Christmas Story*. Judy was big. The cop was very big – it was a blue cop, one hand with a gun. The landlord was tiny – was a hand puppet, and the house was a tiny little cutout house on a stick.' — (Schumann, interview, '79.)

4. Puppets, masks, '64-'69.

Stylistically, Schumann's mask and puppet output during the '60s is dominated by the 'sculptural' (rather than by the traditional hand puppet and marionette doll-carving, cute or caricatural style of the initial batch of Christ legend figures, an elevated and severe style, idealising Suffering Man. All his great female figures of the '60s are in this line. A few figures are not.

As regards the puppet-technology:

'Yeah, well, there are various lines of inventions. They are not very logical.'
(Schumann, interview, '82.)

Rather than a single line of development, we have

'the exploration of different possibilities of how to make a sculpture move.'
(Schumann, ibid.)

He wanted to come out from behind the screen, onto the floor, and he wanted more gestural possibilities — not necessarily a prolixity of arm gestures, but more freedom and nuance in the configuration of the whole Gestalt. So that was one line of exploration.

On the other hand, the big center-pole puppets had demonstrated their own virtues in church and on the streets, so he was tempted to push that further. Along this line, he went from big to gigantic center-pole puppets, carried from within, but their arms operated — and sometimes their garments distended — by visible outside operators, part of the show. These giant emblematic effigy or display puppets were not very versatile — if Schumann had hoped putting the arm rods outside the garment would liberate the arms to any significant purpose, his hopes were disappointed — but, though verging on the ridiculous, grotesque rather than stately or awesome, still had the power of the big puppets.[1] The legs of the first one,

---

1. 'In the meantime, until that summer of 1966, it was when we did the Harlem workshop, I had played a lot with these puppets and found their limitations in their uses. When you had the rods inside the puppets, there is a restriction to that — to what that puppet can do. So I was very eager to build even bigger puppets and to liberate them in that the rods would be operated from the outside. I also felt strongly for having the operation exposed, to move the puppet where a bunch of people would be the real performers, with the interest of the show. They would carry these effigies, they would throw them down or behead them or run them or down them or up them, whatever was decided — that population who would do that was part of the idea of these puppets, so I came with that idea into that workshop. I told the kids in the schools the winter before the workshop started that I wanted to build giant puppets like they had never seen. So we were ready for them. But what design we would use and how we would do it and all that, that was all up in the air so we did a helluva lot of fooling around and fumbling around and the first time they tried out, in rehearsal, Mother Earth and Uranus and Chicken Little — Chicken Little was the

Uncle Fatso ('65) were those, visible, of the inside operator, but by and large they looked carried rather than moving on their own. Their crucial theatrical aspect was their relation to their outside operators, dwarfed by them, the community of puppeteers in evidence, demonstrating them.[2] Uncle Fatso had a detachable, separately operable striking arm – which may have led on to the idea of separate, headless hand puppets, all hands, two or more, worked in a crowd with corresponding head puppets (the Grey Ladies of '67 – who themselves, some of them, at least, had more than one head). These puppets of course were very heavy – partly because it took quite an armature to support their giant heads, partly because their shoulder cross-pieces (and these in these giant puppets carry the costume) had to be substantial so that tackle by which the operator can operate the head when resting on the center pole on the ground could pass through them, were heavy. E.g. in the '66 Earth Mother the shoulder piece is a rectangular frame strengthened by cross pieces. The shoulder pieces were hooked onto the center pole passing through them, so that the

---

biggest of them all, they all collapsed as soon as we put the stick on the floor – the weight of the head would jam down so it hit the ground so hard that it broke the frame. We just had overdone it – with chicken wire, with framing inside; much too much lumber and middle pieces that had to be taken out. The fault was that we tried to give them too delicate a movement. Later on we found it wasn't necessary to have built them with moving necks, with necks that allowed for swivel movements, for turns and nods of the head. So that kind of thing was hard to build. (I: So Mother Earth had one of these swivel necks?) Yes. (I: Did she have it when you did the show?) Yes. (I: She doesn't have it now?) No, she doesn't have it – we took it out. It didn't pay to have it. The puppet is too big for that, it doesn't need it. Its body moves stronger.' — (Schumann, interview, '79.)

We notice in this account of the making of the giant *Chicken Little* puppets in '66, that Schumann in fact was not resigned to their statuesque immobility or 'effigy' character, but had wanted them more mobile – with head movement. He achieved this at the same time with other puppets – the other line of development. The giant effigy puppets did not come into their own until the '70s, starting with a 4th of July parade in 1970: in outdoors, circus pageant use. During the '60s, he made only restricted use of them – for special effects, e.g. in *Cry*.

2. 'The very big puppets – when they move, for me the community participation – you know, that's sort of what that is to my mind. When one sees the operators and when the operator becomes a feast of a whole bunch of people participating in it – that kind of pageantry effect of that – of these big effigies, even if the movements in themselves are not delicate or can't be developed much – that's an important line in itself. That's something that has been invented at a certain point and now it exists in different forms. With the Dragon it exists in that only the legs stick out – and everybody is inside it – and other puppets it's all visible – that's not such a big difference to me. (I: What's a big difference to me is whether one of your giant puppets, like Uncle Fatso, walks, or, like in the pageants, is brought in, carried – slides in, like effigy carrying.) Right. They should be lighter. That will be, hopefully, another step to be found. How to build them better. How to do lighter building, because now they're so heavy that only very strong people can do them and then, naturally, they don't get much bounce and rhythm to them. They really slide only and that's a disadvantage. They could also step, and so on.' — (Schumann, interview, '82.)

entire weight of the puppet rested on the carrier of the center pole. These giants were the end of one development from the rod through the center-pole puppets: 'nothing more could be developed out of that rod puppet – just one result of a puppet.' (Schumann, interview, '79.) Schumann during the '70s made them lighter by eliminating the head-operating tackle which made it possible to have slim shoulder cross-pieces, and by making the arms suspended from the shoulder piece lighter. But they were still heavy and e.g. in the giant garbagemen puppets of '80 or '81, the puppet's legs were suspended from the shoulder piece. The costliness of modern light but strong materials was the deterrent to their use – e.g. the aluminum and light silks used by the Theatre du Soleil, or the latexes and styrofoams used for most contemporary giant puppets – precluded recourse to these. Some modern puppets are given facial or gestural versatility by lightweight mechanisms or machinery. Here the deterrent to Schumann was not cost but that he did not care for the versatility.

Schumann gave the flexibility they had not initially had to his big puppets by eliminating the center pole and giving the head some independence from the body – a functional equivalent of a neck.[3] He did this in two ways (both first in *Leaf Feeling the Moonlight*, '65): by mounting the puppet heads on pads mounted on top of the operator's head, by mounting them on short sticks held by the operator, going past his or her face and manipulated just below the chin.[4] The latter type in particular he

---

3. 'Puppen leben. Ihre Beweggründe sind Musik. Auch das Musikalische ist unbeschreibbar. Puppen sind Körper mit Köpfen. Und die Köpfe haben Nacken, die man nicht sieht. Aber unterm Kinn steckt im Hals der Puppe die Seele der Puppe.' — (Schumann, *Puppen und Masken*, '73.)

4. '(I: ... and there were some puppets had a mask on a short stick and there was another where the mask was mounted on the head. And either way the center pole was eliminated. (Was that the point of it?) That was a wonderful discovery but it really was more than this pole-eliminating. It (made it possible) to play the puppet in front of a curtain instead of on top of a curtain. On top of the curtain always required long sticks or, you know, like a marionette is there on the stage that's very tall and you come from the top, hold him up. We never tried that then. But the poles, they just made the movements so extremely characterized by poles, by the stiffness of that. And we tried all these methods I told you about: putting lamp necks into the heads to make that move, all kinds of devices to get more movement into the puppets, like the neck bend or at the wrist of the hand also. And all of that wasn't very good and then the real advantage came when we said, oh forget about the curtain. Let's go inside the puppet and play it in front of the curtain. So this was a person inside it. The Great Warrior was done like that, but with these puppets, that was even better, the little pole inside the puppet. You have an elongated figure there and you have incredible mobility with that pole. You can move the head virtually away from your body and still be part of that body so you can get tremendous distortions. So it gave us great flexibility.' — (Schumann, interview, '83.)

'... there were two perfectly new puppets in this show, that I just found by chance, by experimenting, after having made the faces and finding how to deal with them, and that was the one mounting that I described: the mask is mounted to a hat that fits your head and – so that the mask is elongated by the length of your body – it's taller than you by the

thought of as a 'live' puppet and thinks of as one of the most versatile types of puppet he has devised. As with the big center-pole puppets he comes the closest to puppetry sculpture, so with these puppets he came the closest to puppetry dance. With these two puppet types too a line of development ended.

Apart from these lines of development, two new types of puppet came into use, dummies and small — hand-sized or less — figurines, and there were some anticipations of uses of masks or puppets more important later, but the important development, more important than any of these, was in the use of face masks, that is tied on masks covering the performer's face rather than enveloping his or her head.

Dummies were first used in *Fire* ('66): in fixed bas-relief positions, tied to the wall, the positions altered out of view — a very special use. They were built over thrown out tailor's dummies found in the streets: when the Bread and Puppet Theatre did *Fire* in England they found lighter basketry dummies there, which they then used till they were lost or worn out. From '70 onward, Schumann used homemade dummies, with wooden support structures, stuffed with rags and paper. The only really good dummies he ever had, he says (interview, December '83), were small, two-foot-high or so jointed acrobat-dummies made for his circuses of the late '70s by

---

size of the mask on top of your head; and the other style puppet that was new and was invented for that show was the slightly over-life-size rod puppet, a short rod, a very short stick, that you operate inside that bundle of fabric which constitutes the body of the puppet. So, to describe it in more detail, there's a head — a mask — only two of them were beneath full-size heads — so there's a mask, and a short stick that extends some six inches below the chin of the mask — is mounted to the mask. There's fabric mounted, often in two pieces, one at the back of the mask to disguise the hollow inside of the mask, to hang back as a kerchief would from the back head of a woman, and on the chin of the puppet, the rest of the fabric is attached and hanging as long as your body to disguise the operator's body. And that was a new mask at that time — a new puppet at that time. In other places it was used more widely — likely in the *Grey Lady Cantata*. . . . It wouldn't be fair to call it a rod puppet . . . let's call it a live puppet. Because what you have is a figure that looks like an oversized real figure. The operator — the man or the woman who play this puppet are present there inside the figure and they have a little rod — the rod has to be short.'
— (Schumann, interview, '79.)

'I can describe that to you, what I thought was a great step forward in our puppetry with *Leaf Feeling the Moonlight*. The head mounting wasn't such a great step forward, but the rod really was. It was very different from anything that we had done before. The head mounting puppet achieved an elongated movement which we hadn't had before and that's that the whole head becomes the neck of the puppet. So when you have a puppet mounted here, when you mount it, then these movements become larger than life and the arms are free. So the operator could move the gowns attached to the head and so that was that one type. But the other type was even more — turned out to be the best, I think, invention of a puppet so far. That is, that a person is inside a head, a gown, and has a short stick mounted to the front of the head — in the hollow shape there — going inside the profile line, the nose, forehead line of the face, right there. And with that short rod one could not just do exaggerated neck movements, but distortions that are so beyond what the body can

Catherine Schaub. The use of small figurines, evolved out of the use of toy houses, etc. in *Apocalypse* ('63/'64) and in *War Demonstration* and *Flower Mountain* (both '65), was the technique of *When Johnny Comes Marching Home* ('68): the small paper maché group puppets were placed and displaced on a table, their handling, though obscured by the lighting, part of the show. Dummies, but this time full figure, out in front of the stage, and — to a limited extent — manipulated by strings, were next used in *Difficult Life* ('70), and so were small figurines, some of them, this time, small, string-operated jointed figurines.

Among the isolated germinal anticipations of practices important only later on: hand-held masks, covering the performer (*Murder Mystery*, Bob Nichols' *Everyman*) and stick puppets operated overhead, but without curtain: the 'Shark Plane' used in demonstrations, a development — because it was moved: it would swoop down on other figures — of the use in street demonstrations of the 'Stovepipe Soldiers' puppet; and the 'Smiling Cat' kite puppet that Charlie Adams built the body of:

'he had the idea that it took flight, and it would fly — it was carried horizontally, it chased the mice — it had two hands stuck out and was carried on poles like the airplane: one in the neck and two in the arms, and if it was run fast enough, the fabric body would lift itself up so that it flew.'   (Schumann, interview, '82.)

---

do that it is absolutely amazing. And so, it must be, so that you can tip it right there — so the swivel point is under the chin — this is the imitation of our real neck — what we do when we move our head — and you can make that so big that the head can not just go this far, but can tip all the way over, in any direction, and it still looks like a head on a neck. Plus, you do that with one hand and your other arm is free to shape that gown that surrounds you, in any shape that you want to. That one arm is enough to do that. So you can either use that arm to imitate an arm that sits there, by draping the gown over you, or you can just blouse it or pull it together — it seemed like the biggest thing we ever — the best invention of a puppet that we made at that time. It was like a big step forward, and the Grey Ladies and all those things, to me seemed like the — of all the puppets, the best moving ones . . . you can do much more than the person that has it mounted. With it you can make extreme movements that are very, very strong and that one can't achieve in dance. It seemed to me that this was an idea of a dancing puppet that could do things that no dancer can do.' — (Schumann, interview, '82.)

'And I was a White Woman in *The Dead Man Rises*. And that, to me, was a moveable puppet. It was a mask and a giant costume that hid, more or less, your human body. And it was very subtle. And there was a lot of very difficult movement, like you have to hold a posture for a very long time. You have to be able to handle the thing. And I could project myself into that. I could endure and I could see myself as somehow giving through that. (I: The movements are slow.) They're slow and they have to deal with presenting the sculptural head in different lights . . . projector lights. And it also has to do with a certain kind of dance movement and rhythm that has to be maintained. And I like that. . . . The figure was a white face like the moon. A very simple woman's face. And it was imbedded in the most marvelous costume I've ever seen. It essentially was a net. It was like a presentational piece, for presenting this figure over and over again in different situations.' — (Palmer, interview.)

With the use of face masks (systematically in *Murder Mystery* ('64), *Harvard College Questionnaire* ('65) and *Fire* ('66) — there have been few shows of Schumann's in which no face masks at all were used), Schumann, continuing the practice of *Totentanz*, incorporated the masked performer, puppet-like but distinct from the puppet operated by an inside hidden operator into his medium as its second important element. Unlike his *Totentanz* face masks, these face masks were normally derived from life face casts and therefore fit rather closely and well[5] — which helps to make the performer puppet-like. Unlike most of his initial face-cast-derived face masks, e.g. the 'Mary' and 'Joseph' masks of his first Christmas shows, the face masks made and used subsequently during the '60s tended to be — though in crucial regards they were not — passably naturalistic; the caricatural and idealizing aspects were subdued. They tended to look like face casts taken just after death. There were two basic kinds of these face masks made and looking differently. The one kind, the earlier one (*Murder Mystery*), were worked into a plaster cast made from a clay face mold. He could, while for an optimal fit of the eventual mask retaining the relative placements of eyes, nose and mouth, modify the features of the plaster cast away from those of the clay mold and the face, and apparently typically did, obtaining slightly weird, distorted face masks with exaggerated features.[6] Using this technique later, he often used paper maché rather than celastic. The other type of face mask were molded into the face clay mold directly, and so were closer to the original face and to a human face, but face masks obtained from a given clay mold would vary slightly from one another, and he typically gave them an elevation of expression by

---

5. 'I made face masks of people that came to the studio on Delancey Street, and then I molded this clay over the face masks, on the features, so what I got from that was that after the mask was made it would fit people. I could have the eyes correctly placed, the mouth correctly placed and things like that.' — (Schumann, interview, December '82.)

6. (*Murder Mystery*) was a mask show with masks that I made from friends and people in this way: I cast their faces, then I made a positive from the face, a plaster impression, an exact one, from the face. I modeled this clay over these features, people's faces — and then I made a cast from that, and I worked celastic into this negative cast. So the effect that you get from doing that is that you get something that looks very realistic but it is distorted. (Elka: It's very lifelike — but *not* realistic.) It's very lifelike. (It is) not like a real face because I modeled bigger features into it, bigger cheekbones, bigger eyebrows, bigger foreheads, bigger chins, bigger lips. So the set of masks that was used for *Murder Mystery* was a bunch of such masks — and they were painted with flesh colors with shading to make them even more overdone and something that is *more* than the make-up in an actor.' — (Schumann, interview, '79.)

'We'd take the plaster cast of it and we'd put a little plate here or there and thicken it, just a little. It would be a real-type face, but a little jowlier or a little heavier.'—(Ernstthal, interview.)

'(Masks made by the two methods) look somewhat alike because they resemble faces, but if you look closely, (you see) the exaggerated expressions and features that you get when you really model a face over a face. There's something very different to that than in these real life-like faces.' — (Schumann, interview, '83.)

shadowing the primed mask and washing the shadowing.[7] Both techniques yielded human faces rather than those of demons or beasts and rather than e.g. skull masks – their wearers in a show thus exemplars of people – but while the *Murder Mystery* technique enabled him to show the evil in man (cf. e.g. *Chairs/Speech*), the *Fire* techniques enabled him to show human goodness, the transcendentality of spirit.

Schumann continued to use hand puppets (notably in his Christmas shows), but didn't make many (if any). Similarly for the carton box puppets – in the *Chicken Little* ones, representing houses, he used a device occasionally (e.g. *Monument to Ishi*, '75) used later also: he installed small puppet stages into them. Mary and Joseph's donkey in the early *Christmas Stories* was a cutout; I don't think there were any others during the '60s; cutout puppets became important in his work only '75 ff.

Though Schumann during the '60s and (more frequently) later occasionally, chiefly when he didn't have much money, but had much unskilled labor power, reverted to paper maché, most of his masks have been celastic.[8] From '65 onward, except when many duplicates of the same mask had to be made and the plaster cast was simple enough so it would keep its shape and could be kept intact for making them,[9] he tended to make them directly over the clay, dispensing with a plaster cast. This was quicker and spared the mask makers the acetone fumes they inhaled working inside the casts. But until Schumann, in the early '70s, got some exceptional mask makers, the deviation from the clay originals, not compensated for by work with the celastic, was greater than when working

---

7. 'I just took the negative impression of the face and molded the celastic right into that so it's really a copy of a face.' — (Schumann, interview, '83.)

'You get (some) distortions (to begin with). You also get differences in the painting job. that also changes the expression slightly – white with this little bit of grey shading – because I used a kind of wash. I primed them with white and then I put dark into the deeper parts of the mask and then I washed that off so that's – the control is only vague. It's chancey. So as one does this washing one watches a bit how it washes out. You can manipulate them but you don't really control it. You say, "this is good." It's not like brush work. It's different from when you shade with a brush you really do what you want to do and this washing, smearing-on fashion, you don't. You allow it some chance to take place.' — (Schumann, interview, '83.)

8. 'This year we decided we don't have the money for celastic, so we did paper maché. And we did a lot of paper maché work but we didn't do any finesse work. We didn't do anything good. We didn't do work into molds or wood – we just used it for the rough kick – work that can be done by many people without ever having been very skillful. So the work looks a bit that way, you see? There's no fine stuff.'–(Schumann, interview, '82.)

Hoagland, *Let 'em Have*, '83, speaking of work on the '82 circus speaks of
'molding a whole variety of masks from many layers of shopping-bag paper steeped and stiffened in wallpaper glue, and drying and painting these.'

9. 'The plaster cast we build for two reasons. One is, if we want to duplicate a thing – if we want to have something in many copies. If that thing doesn't have too many indentations, so that it can come out of the mold without ripping the mold apart, then we will still make a plaster mold for such duplications.' — (Schumann, interview, '82.)

from casts. The directly made masks were cruder, flattened,[10] and lacked the surface texturing that plaster casts transfer to the mask.[11] To allow for the coarsening, Schumann took to making the clay originals simpler, e.g. those of the Grey Lady masks, made directly over clay in the winter '66/'67, and for sculptural detail relinquished, substituted painting on the mask.

Schumann made some masks for a play of someone else's in '64, Bob Nichols' street play *Everyman* (June '64), a 'bronze gold' celastic God Face 'with a big mouth':

---

10. 'When you work directly over clay you don't get sharp crevices as sharp as they are because you add a layer of material onto it. That's the flatness of it. Things get a little bit flattened out that way.' — (Schumann, interview, '83.)

11. 'The other reason for the plaster cast is the skin quality that shows from this – of the clay original. Because when you cast a clay original with plaster you make a perfect copy of it – in the negative. And when you work into that negative, then you can get, depending on your workmanship – you can get a truthful cast, as truthful as with a bronze cast. As good as anything that is seen in museums – only it's in paper maché, you know, it's material that's worthless, but as a replica it's as good as any bronze or valuable casting material. (With a) plaster cast one can get that and I still do that, but not frequently, only when I need it.' — (Schumann, interview, '82.)

I have the impression that celastic is less suitable than paper maché for this replication of skin texture.

'All the celastic work that we did that was on these Jesus puppets, disciples, was done *into* plaster casts – into lost plaster casts which is a big job, because you make your clay sculpture, you make a cast, then you strike the clay and you work into the negative of the puppet (of the plaster cast (SSB)) – which made us all sick and dizzy because you stick your head into acetone basically. You really sit inside the mask and work in there. That was the curse of our puppets, but the result is incredibly better than when you work over clay. Because (working directly over) clay you add the thickness of your material to the original. So that's just simply not as good. Until we made *use* of that method and I made my sculptures *simpler* and learned how to do that, how to make use of the softness of the clay underneath, and then you can continue your sculpture there (working with the celastic (SSB)), so that you really create the original with the celastic.' — (Schumann, interview, '82.)

Schumann is here indicating two ways of compensating for the aesthetic losses of working directly over the clay: a sculpturing approach to putting on the celastic and 'simpler' clay sculptures. The former wasn't developed 'till '73 ff., but the latter apparently was a way Schumann already during the '60s adapted to the shift after the first batch of puppets, to sculpturing directly over the clay – together with increased recourse to painting the finished masks:

'But one can also use celastic well over clay without such detail job. One just has to consider this loss of detail that happens when you put on your coat of celastic. So you make a fairly raw original and figure out how much bulk you *want* there. You allow for a lot more roughness and you figure out how much of the detail you can do with the painting job. You know, so instead of, for example, instead of working a hell of a lot on an eye – when you *sculpt* an eye an eye is a big problem, it's a big piece of sculpture in itself. What you indent, what you bring out – every part in it is three-dimensional. The ball of the eye, the lid of the eye, what hangs over from the forehead into the eye – we eliminate all this, for example, and make this one smooth shape and you paint the eye *on*. So this mixture of using painting as some of the detail is a successful way of accelerating.' — Schumann, interview '82.)

'... sort of like a sun with rays on the sides coming out of it and strong features, mounted on a stick. It had no hand. It also had no dress to it. It was just held up. The mouth was like a megaphone and I believe it was used that way – that somebody stood on a chair and said things through that mouth.'

(Schumann, interview, '83.)

as well as 'Creature' masks, an insect one, one 'like a fly in purples and pinks, painted, with wires sticking out' (ibid.), and perhaps two more and a skull mask, and an 'Indian Chief'.

But the first important puppets, after the first set of the fall of '63 and the winter of '63/'64, built by Schumann probably in the summer of '64, those of 'Yama, King of Hell', a stationary seated puppet, and a three-headed 'Demon' puppet for three performers, were designed with a specific show in mind, the *Birdcatcher in Hell* (October '74-January '65). Both, as also the mask (off a life mask taken from Charlie Adams' face) and the clothing of the Birdcatcher, the musician 'puppets' and the (only occasionally used)[12] birds, were all blue.

Yama

'... was a smoke-blowing, balloon-bubbling, three-people-operated monster. It was sitting. The back operator operated the head. I think the back operator needed support for the balloon blowing – that's why I think it was three. But probably in some pictures it was only two. So the back operator was sitting on something elevated, to hold up the head, and to operate the head, to move it, and in front, somebody did the arms, which were sort of sausage-like, irregular – fingers coming out of the wrists. I don't think there were feet. It had no face. It was a big, distorted demon face, with no eyes. (Elka: All sort of blobbish globs.) Just sort of a *mouth*, and a nose.'

(Schumann, interview, '79.)

'He had a bulged-out, big stomach that covered up his operators. Blue balloons were attached to his horns. And the people inside had tubes that blew up the balloons, so that there was a movement in the face, bubbling up balloons.'

(Schumann, interview, December '82.)

'Now, the characters were as follows: There was Yama, the King of Hell – that was two people, one having this incredibly big head – that was almost shapeless, strangely enough – almost shapeless, this kind of strange, demonic head with tubes and horns and trunks coming out ... blue also – the whole thing blue ... almost this shapeless quality to it – almost this shapeless face – with hands – these big hands – with like – just like balls with fingers coming out in every direction – a very shapeless kind of strange, enormous creation. Beany Kunitz, who is a friend of mine, a local hippie, essentially, he's now a carpenter, and Irving Oyle, I believe, were the original players and it had feet – these big feet,

---

12. 'It was in a few performances, but I don't think the birds were used much in that. There were some performances with birds and then others with only other forms of demons, with no birds. It's built – the body has bird legs sort of like a seagull shape – wings. I think a person's arms were meant to be in those wings, the mask worn on the head.' — (Schumann, interview, December '82.)

blue also – blue fabric, blue everything, and there was two guys in it so he could move his feet separately from his head. There were two people in it so it had a lot of movement. There was one guy on his hands and one guy holding the feet – it was a full, you know, four-handed deal.' (Ernstthal, interview, '79.)

'(I: Was this a new kind of puppet – did you think of it that way?) Yeah. Yeah. (I: How would you characterize it?) As a piece of sculpture. It wasn't a face anymore. It was a face only because it had some holes in it and a face only because of – the performers. It was about in the place where a face is, but it doesn't resemble anything like a face. It just has some half elephant trunks sticking out of it and some crevices and elevations. That's about all there is. Yes, that was an interesting thing to me and the same thing with the hands. The hands were just – there was no resemblance to hands. It was just sort of spiking kinds of shapes instead of hands. The distortions were mellowed a bit by – that all of that was in one color without any shading. Everything was just an autumn blue. The cloth a little bit different tone and all the faces in that strong blue and that pulled it all together and made it all so that it didn't jar quite so much.'

(Schumann, interview, '83.)

The three demons, 'faceless blue creatures with celastic faces' (Schumann, ibid.) were

'... three people in a demon suit with three heads – also totally shapeless – almost just like blobs of clay – again blue. And they had these gong rattles – like a big lid of a plastic – you know, a cardboard barrel that has lids that fit over it – those kind of lids – big tin lids like tin with bolts and nuts hung in front of them so it was like a rattle on a stick – and they were demons, and they moved, three of them, together. They were always moving around together.'

(Ernstthal, interview, '79.)

'... a three-headed puppet with wiggling tongues. The tongues were all detached and separate pieces that wiggled around in the mouths of the puppets. It had six arms, or something like that – very close together. It was very hard to wear this thing, I remember.' (Schumann, interview, December '82.)

'Very restricted movement. What it was was three heads and three hands arbitrarily stuck on a piece of fabric and then after that thing was built we had to figure out how three people could possibly be fitted into that. And it was very awkward because they couldn't really fit. They could hardly move anymore. They were in there, the cloth was so – the mounting was so close to each other there was no cloth in between them so they could just about shuffle a little bit and do this much movement with one arm; that was about all. So it wasn't a thing that was invented for some movement. It was more like the thing was made and then somehow we wanted to use it. Very restricted, more than any we used. In that whole play there were pretty crazy useless things used. Some masks just didn't lend themselves to a lot of *movement*. It was sort of helpful in the play but movement-wise they were silly the way they were built.'

(Schumann, interview, '83.)

'(I: Were the demons the musicians too?) No. That was a puppet – a faceless puppet. Just a blue, baggy kind of shape, with blue attached as a shroud and then these people were the musicians. The demons had screams – voices, but no instruments.' (Schumann, interview, '83.)

Murder Mystery, October 3, 1964 ff., for a short while presented along with *Birdcatcher*, was a mask rather than a puppet show. No particular costumes were made to go with the face masks, the play was done in everyday clothes. The masks were the realistic but exaggerated masks made inside plaster casts of life masks but distorted from them, and with one another, central big one, that of the Mountain, 'fluffy, sort of loose, barely recognizable as a face, features that melted into each other—nothing protruded in the face' (Schumann, interview, December '82). 'Painted grey and shaded', and bigger than the others, 'longish', it had sort of a quiet kind of face (Schumann, interview, '79). It looked like the later (1977) *Masaniello* 'people' masks, held in front of their faces by the performers. The performer knelt behind the mask, so it covered him — the Mountain was all face. There was a narrator, unmasked but apparently off-stage; the Mountain; a mute, unmoving chorus of watchers; and the performers of all the characters in the mystery, taking successive masks from a table, replacing one mask by another, as the narrator identified the character and said what he or she did. The *Murder Mystery* masks and others like them were later used in *Speech/Chairs*, often worn on the back of the head.

Harvard College Questionnaire, of the spring of '65, used just two masks: for a performer asking questions, his own face mask, for each of the performers in a chorus of answerers, somebody else's life mask, identical copies of which were used for each of them, the idea being that this use of life masks would yield expressionless or 'petrified' faces.

Among the masks Schumann lent Bob Nichols for his street show *Digging for the Poverty Program* (May '65) was his first witch mask, mophaired, with a corrugated brow, made not too much earlier. It remained in use in his theatre for a decade, was used, e.g. in *Grey Lady Cantata III* and *Emilia* (both '71) — his next witch masks weren't made till the spring of '75.

Yama and the three demons puppet were followed by Uncle Fatso, built that summer ('65), appearing then once, in a show performed by its builders, the children in an East Harlem Negro block, but beginning a long and grand career in the Bread and Puppet Theatre from the *Chicken Little* of the summer of '66 onward, and probably used in demonstrations before then. Just Uncle Fatso to its builders (neither the Landlord, nor President Johnson in effigy, nor Uncle Sam), and really just Uncle Fatso afterward also: the plutocrat of old, Moneybags with a touch of the Boss.[13] Its head was not, like the *Crucifixion* puppets', made by the 'lost

---

13. '... cet 'oncle gros lard' qui deviendra une des figures les plus célèbres du Bread and Puppet Theatre, la tête de turc des manifestations, Sa Majesté Carnaval, en quelque sorte. Il a l'air méchant: une énorme bouche grimaçante, d'épais sourcils noirs, des poches sous les yeux, de grosses bajoues, un nez épaté. Sur la tête, un chapeau haut de forme américain. A la main, un énorme cigare, et de la fumée sort de sa bouche: un acteur habite ce mannequin géant.' — (Kourilsky, '72.)

mold' process or from plaster casts at all, but directly from the clay. From then onward, the '60s masks were as a rule made directly over clay. An inside operator carried him, an outside one his striking arm: which was hooked on, detachable, a puppet in its own right. Schumann can't remember whether gestures of his other arm, the one with the fist holding his cigar, required an outside operator or not: but is sure that in parades, at any rate, he had at most two operators. He was used both one-armed – with his smoking arm only, with his hitting arm only – and two-armed, and in this case either arm could go either side.

Seated now in the museum, he is perhaps ten feet tall from the large, flat and pink feet protruding from his bulky black pants up to his broad-brimmed top hat with its red, white and blue band (a few stars scattered on its crown), itself maybe $2\frac{1}{2}$ ft. tall: the suggestion of a gambler in its brim. He wears a black smock with a flowered elegant tie hanging down over it and over the broad expanse of the dirty white soft collar: a sinister, threatening clown. His face is tough, his mouth twisted in a complex curve as though he were snarling or grunting an order. It is a dark apoplectic night-time brownish purple. He is staring at you meaningfully, his cheeks hang but are not fat. His smock makes him pear-shaped – his smock and his short, stumpy voluminous legs. The way he was made is interesting: by collective, playful labor under restrained, but incisive management.[14]

---

14. 'What we did was we brought a lot of clay up from Delancey Street and they had a little store to operate from, and got the kids working on the clay. I wanted to make a big face, to build a base from bricks and scraps of wood, tied them together with twine and wire, had them throw the clay on – which was fun, to just take a handful of clay and smash it as hard as you can on that base. Then, once we had a big lump of clay sitting there on the table, I had them do a face, I had them do a nose. A bunch of kids worked on the nose, got another bunch of kids to work on the left eye, got a bunch of kids to work on the left ear. As long as they did not disturb each other's traffic, it seemed to be all right. Everyone worked on a different feature in that face and then they messed it up too much, so I walked in, kicked them out and changed it so it wouldn't fall apart and collapse, which is a technical problem with these amounts of clay. And then, out of that whole mess of people, moving that chunk of clay and digging hands into various part of it, we got Uncle Fatso. Then I had older kids help me with the celastic work on it. After the celastic was dried, cut him open, cut into two pieces, bend him, mount it, and put very bad paints on it, that later on turned out not to be waterproof... I don't think I ever had people work on a puppet like that. People jumping around on a piece of clay and I act like a conductor and tell them what to do, where to start, where to add more, things like that. That was new. The final product was probably something I probably controlled – most of it, and made most of the decisions, but it still was a large contribution of little kids' hands in that face... Then we invented the body. The hands were probably made at the same time with the face, but the body became a sewing project more than anything – the suit, the fancy suit, the tie – (I: Is that the one he still has?) I don't think so. Make it all look like a fancy suit, that was the goal. We had a bunch of teenage girls who really enjoyed it. Several of them were just on the tie – I remember that, they were very proud. Uncle Fatso was such a popular enterprise on this block. Everybody knew him by name. The kids called him Uncle Fatso even when he was in clay. (I: Wasn't his face called the Landlord or something?) No, he was just

With him were made a large number of paper maché-headed rats, and little puppet theatre houses that were also puppets.[15]

Uncle Fatso was the first of Schumann's gigantic puppets, so heavy and their poles so long that they 'don't have much movement, really' (Schumann, interview, '82), but because of their size and ponderousness, not only like the '63/'64 tall dowel puppets having an effect of super-human awesomeness, but one of supra-human overweaning dominance by virtue of the fact 'that one sees the operators and that the little operators and the big, godly figure are in the picture together – all that, and that a whole crowd operates one.' (Schumann, interview, '82.) The effect of this to Schumann, however, is not one of dominance and subordination, but of a community effort:

'The very big puppets, when they move – for me the community participation, you know, that's sort of what that is to my mind. When one sees the operators and when the operation becomes a feast of a whole bunch of people participating in it – that kind of pageantry effect of that – of these big effigies – that's something that has been invented at a certain point and now it exists in different forms. With the Dragon it exists, though only the legs stick out and everybody is inside it, and in other puppets it's all visible – that's not such a big difference to me.'
(Schumann, interview, '82.)

He built a few more of these giants in '66: cf. infra.

In the fall of '65, Schumann built puppets of the two new types, constructed to allow the operators inside them new types of movement that I have discussed (IV(1).5) for *Leaf Feeling the Moonlight*. A 'White Lady' puppet and a 'Dead Man' puppet were of the kind in which the head is moved by a short handle inside it, the others of the kind in which the puppet head is mounted on the operator's.

Both of the 'White Lady's' operator's arms were under her gown, 'operating' it, not visible: the puppet was armless. She 'looked very much

---

called Uncle Fatso. That's the name that stuck to him. So the further building was just distributing the leftover jobs: pole mounting, hand mounting, the little tube into the mouth to make him be able to smoke, to puff smoke out of the tube, the ring on the left hand finger, the cigar into the hand and such problems. Distribution of jobs among quite a few kids and teenagers.' — (Schumann, interview, '79.)

15. 'At the same time, while we built Uncle Fatso, we also built a lot of one man puppet stages – on this block, like on any block, (there were lots of) cardboard boxes – so we had a few pieces of string and mounted these cardboard boxes on the kids and then cut holes which made them into walking stages, fringes of fabric, so that the legs of the kids were disguised, and painted the boxes with the kids and had hand puppets with them, and out of that came a whole bunch of little puppet shows.

The third project in the building was to build the rats – a whole bunch of rat masks, with the kids, in paper maché, and those rats were the gang of the landlord, and I think simply shrouded – a flat rat face that was horizontally mounted on top of the head of each kid and have a shroud attached to it that covered up the kids. The holes were cut in the area of the eyes so they could see.' — (Schumann, interview, '79.)

Japanese. Very – like white masks, like white Beauty Ladies in Noh plays. Very gentle dancing puppet, very slow motion' (Schumann, interview, '82). Schumann in '79 remarks especially on these short-stick puppets: they were 'the most versatile, the biggest in scope, in movement scope' of his puppets, the 'danciest' – 'live puppets' (ibid.). It was a 'very challenging puppet to move – very difficult, very versatile, very rewarding as a method. More than any other technique' (ibid.). He used their construction technique frequently thereafter, e.g. for the Grey Ladies of the *Bach Cantatas* ('67, '70-'76). The other construction type – mask mounted on top of the operator's head – was used e.g. for the 'Vietnamese Ladies' with their sculpted hair and long necks (cf. infra). The *Leaf* puppets were used again in the play that grew out of *Leaf, Dead Man Rises* ('67). Schumann does not remember the short-stick ones ever being used in street demonstrations.

Probably also in the course of '65, Schumann built another puppet or perhaps a whole set of stylistically similar puppets, used in street demonstrations (e.g. October 16, '65) and apparently not otherwise, Grey Mothers with babies, technically somewhat distinct, 'more like Uncle Fatso' (Schumann, interview, '83):

'... it was a grey face, it was uniform grey, the whole thing was painted in greys, and it had one stick going – it was a tall one, over twelve feet, I would say, tall puppet, that had a stick to carry the head, *then* it had a second stick that operated *two* hands, that extended from the belly of the woman through some big wire hoop, *away* from the woman, and carried a baby. There were two pieces of sculpture used in this mask, one was the head and the other one was two hands holding a baby child, the two hands holding the baby attached to a wire hoop, and the wrists of the hands were sleeve, carried the sleeves that led around the wire hoop to the body – to the fabric that represented the body of the woman.'

(Schumann, interview, '79.)

'It's one operator who does the whole job. Because of that the head doesn't have much flexibility because he has to have (the stake) in the holster or (there has to be) a long stick. The second stick is a hoop that runs through the sleeves into the dress – and then has a vertical stick which helps too. So the operator holds onto that vertical stick and to the upright of the head, so the movements are restricted to turning (and) a slight up and down movement. That is a great difference from the flexibility you get from having just to care for one rod in the puppet and that (one) a short stick.' (Schumann, interview, '83.)

He much later (1977) used the same construction for a Madonna in his *Masaniello*.

Fire (January-June '66), though he built one or two puppets for the second run of it in '68, the Worm, symbolizing the sickness of fear,[16]

---

16. '... an animal, a worm-like creature with an elongated face, with little teeth on both sides. A blind creature that crawled on the ground. It had a skin of grey fabric behind.' — (Schumann, interview, '79.)

replacing the shark head of the 'Shark Plane' and a red figure that apparently consisted of hands and a costume only,[17] was essentially a face mask (and dummy) show, the third face mask show after *Murder Mystery* and *Harvard College Questionnaire*, all the (five) performers in it (except for two or three maskless and uncostumed, isolated, contrastingly prosaic figures) as well as background live looking dummies wearing slight variants of the same close fitting white face mask, all derived from a few casts[18] made from the face of a Chinese girl, Li Minh,[19] a face mask 'made a day or two before we did a big demonstration in New York' and 'meant specifically for' this demonstration, a demonstration the Schumanns remember as a Memorial Day parade,[20] and in which, as in later parades, it was used as mask of the 'Vietnamese Woman' figures.[21] Unlike the *Murder Mystery* masks, these *Fire* face masks were made inside the original face casts.

The impression given by *Fire* was that the masks moved slightly and wore slightly different expressions in the eight scenes. In part, this may have been due to slight – and probably intended – variations in the masks made from the casts.[22] They are small, and because of their large, lowered

---

17. '... a pair of hands (with) pointed fingers and a red costume, meant for somebody who stood on a box or a chair, so that it was an elongated figure that had no face and had just these two big hands.' — (ibid.)
18. Schumann, in the Christmas season of '65, to earn money was making plaster face casts for people to use as Christmas presents.
19. 'We did the masks of this girl Li Minh, who I heard, by the way, really had a bad time after that. I once heard a rumor – Margo or someone told me – that she went a little bit nuts after that. She was Chinese. And somehow we just met her – it was very brief – it was a brief encounter – made three casts of her face, and all those masks are out of those three casts.' — (Ernstthal, interview, '79.)
20. The Bread and Puppet theatre probably used these masks in the May 30, '66 Memorial Day parade, but that would make their use, if this was the first street one, postdate their use in *Fire*. I have no record of a Bread and Puppet '65 Memorial Day parade, but of course there were other parades in '65. I think the *Fire* or Vietnamese Woman mask was first used in a silent vigil for Norman Morrison and Roger La Porte on the U.N. Plaza on November 26, '65. They were used often in street demonstrations, e.g. November 27, '65 in Washington, D.C., March 26, '66, in the second Fifth Avenue Peace Parade, on a Memorial Day parade, May 30, '66, in Madison Square Garden, December 8, '66.
21. There seems to have been an additional figure in *Fire*, like the masks not made for it, probably one of the background dummies, but not like the others, a tailor's dummy, 'the figure of the woman holding the baby, these big hands with the baby in them.' (Elka, Schumann interview, '79), 'later used in the *Grey Lady Cantata*' (Elka, ibid.). This may have been that red figure. Schumann thinks it was made for an anti-war parade, the one with the Shark Plane. If so, it would have been one of the Vietnamese Ladies, not the red figure without a face.
22. 'I cast her four times at least, if not five times, and made the – she had slightly different expressions on her face every time I made them, so when you now see the masks, they are not just different in that they are painted slightly differently, but they really are slightly different in expression.' — (Schumann, interview, '79.)

lids, quiet, though not saintly. Their wearers look more like abbesses than like nuns: self assured. Dennison's description of their expression (IV(3).12) is correct. For the last scene of *Fire*, for figures coming in to look at the victim, he made some blind Vietnamese Woman masks — without eye slits, so the performers would move and hold their heads like blind people as they looked.[23]

The dummies had been 'built on tailor dummies that we had found on the streets' (Schumann, interview, '79). They were not ideal for touring.[24] When *Fire*, in the spring of '68, was taken on tour to Europe, they took a few of them along (ibid.) and built 'quite a few' (ibid.) over there — took four or five, apparently, built five or six in Europe.

Masked performers and dummies were intermingled as background figures and their stances were changed for different scenes:

'And I do remember — I did remember a couple of weeks ago that I have my *Fire* beads. If you remember — the necklace around the figures. As the cluster of figures is made up of mannequins and human beings and at each of the seven changes, the guy who opens and closes the curtain must go in and assist the people to change the shapes and configurations. And to reset the dummy figures. To know who is what, they wore different colors of necklaces — cheap, discrete kind of necklaces — so, if I were wearing amber, he would know it's George and George is in the next configuration to be doing that — as opposed to what he's going to do in the fourth, which will be bent over. And he always could quickly spot me with the amber beads. (I: Well, wouldn't you know yourself?) No, because the masks, which were those masks of the raped Vietnamese women — there was no way you could move to your new group without being taken there — fitted in there. Because he had to first change the arms on a mannequin figure and then tuck you around it and set your arms. So that he was in complete control. You were all mannequins being moved, some of them more useful than others — human.'

(Ashley, interview, '82.)

Late in '65 or early in '66, perhaps more probably the latter (it was used in a March 26, '66 Fifth Avenue peace demonstration and its fish head was used during the first production of *Fire* (January-June '66), Schumann made his 'Shark Plane', 'the big airplane that Paul Williams helped us build. It was mounted on three sticks and covered with cloth. The head was mounted to it, a celastic head and face, and the rest of it

---

23. 'That's a blind mask, now. Blind masks are made in the same style that I described for the *Fire* show. In the last scene of *Fire* there were several blind people coming in — and I cared for that — they were really blind. (I: You mean the Putney *Fire* show?) No. The Delancey Street *Fire*. So they have no eye slits and people had to wear them and they were really blind. Couldn't see anything. So they were coming in and looking at the lady after she burned and then going out again.' — (Schumann, interview, December '82.)

24. Touring with the big puppets has posed problems generally. E.g. for that '68 European tour the theatre as yet didn't have the boxes they used later on: '... we just used a refrigerator box and cut it in half and ran across the edges with celastic and actually we took it along as private luggage. The whole first tour was done without any freight expenses.' — (Schumann, interview, '79.)

was the airplane.' (Schumann, interview, '79.) It was used in a number of parades, and later on in various productions, e.g. as the Raven in a Grimm fairy tale, *The Three Ravens* ('69) and a crucifix in *The Cry* ('69).

In the Shark Plane parades, held overhead by a number of skull-masked carriers in black, it would dive down on a long line of manacled women in white – the long-necked and long-headed 'Vietnamese Lady' puppets with their large hands that Schumann made for this parade to go with the Shark Plane: a puppet whose head is mounted on top of the operator's. The focal figure in the February '67 *Wounds of Vietnam* was one of them, and so, apparently, was the Woman Taken in Adultery in some of the *Christmas Stories*;[25] and they were later used in the first *Domestic Resurrection Circus* (that of 1970). Two of these ladies are victimized in the spring/summer '67 *Speech* and/or in the spring/summer '68 *Speech/Chairs*. Their enveloping white head masks with their sculpted hair are penis-shaped. They have definitely oriental features, not only the slit, angled, narrow eyes, but the protruding mouths. Their expression is self assured, slightly humorous, their operators looked through holes in their white garments.

'I think that for the first parade with the Shark Plane we also built a group of tall white woman puppets that had Chinese features, and long hands and were tied to the heads of the operators. Baskets were sewn into the bottoms of the heads. The heads had a sculpted *neck*. Mostly, the heads that we had done up to then were heads that reached from the top of the head to the chin and then the neck was where the fabric started. But with these Vietnamese women, for the parade we had made elongated necks that were supported in the back by hair that was also part of the sculpture, and was painted black. The women were painted white with very light grey shading in their faces. They were dressed in white. They had long hands, about a foot and a half long ... (I: The costumes were attached right to the heads and hands?) ... and hands – the operators were inside. There was one operator inside each puppet. (I: Did you use them again?) We used them later in the *Domestic Resurrection Circus* – in the first – on Cate Farm. (Elka: They haven't been used much since.) (I: So they're really parading puppets.)'

(Schumann, interview, '79.)

---

25. 'I did the Lady Who Was Taken in Adultery. That was one of my favorite roles, in the Christmas play. That was a giant-like puppet which is mounted on a basket on the head, so that you have mobility of the head and two hands. That was one of the roles that I remember very much ... like a vignette, sort of ... the vignette was simply the woman being taken out and being stoned and then resurrected. So it was probably three minutes' worth of work, but to me a tour de force, because it's very hard to manage those things and make them beautiful. Mostly the puppets are rod puppets, so you have very limited things you can do with it, like the Twelve Apostles, the disciples. It's just a single rod with a head, you know. You can just move it around, so it's a sculptural display rather than a movement display. The others, the ones that were mounted on the head or had independent hands, were much more moveable and they were expressive in their way and that was what I saw as the beauty of the thing. (I: What did it take?) Very strong body. Good coordination. And the ability to visualize how it looked from the outside while you're managing from the inside. (I: Any kind of attitude?) Oh, a mental attitude? For me, since I was invisible, I just became whatever character I was.' — (Palmer, interview, '79.)

I am not sure when the skull masks used in the parade were made. Schumann thinks (ibid.) that these parade skull masks, made from several different molds (plaster casts), 'in two parts', were used in a peace parade as early as '64, and therefore 'definitely' made in '64 (ibid.). Either these or other skull masks were apparently also used in another parade, a Thanksgiving Day parade, probably of November 24, 1966, in which food is pulled away from 'Vietnamese Women.' (Schumann, interview, '79.)

When Margo Sherman joined the Bread and Puppet Theatre in '66, they were 'building some new demon masks for the *Crucifixion* show' (Sherman, interview, '79). These masks were for a bunch of Negro kids from central Harlem that Catherine Merrill brought down from 134th Street and who were in that Easter show, surrounding the Jesus puppet throughout it: 'Big demon masks. Paper maché masks painted with bright colors and smeared up with shellac to make them shiny. They had all kinds of colorful dresses and ribbons hanging', (Schumann, interview, '79) '. . . wildly colored ponchos and then these demon masks' (Schumann, interview, December '82). Such gay little demons still infiltrate Schumann's show. I saw them, in the *Fight Against the End of the World* in '82, little flame-red demons clearing the stage after the end of the world, removing the litter of possessions of Adam and Eve's cheated progeny, and after the Last Judgment clearing it of their truncated corpses, Satan's turds. They are gay creatures, exotic but thoroughly part of the world, active everywhere, not local phenomena like, for instance, the colorful little fish one sees plentiful around coral reefs. It is interesting that Schumann still likes to have Negro kids do them – something about the syncopated energy of movement of the great race of Afro-Americans. About this time, too, around '66, he replaced, as King Herod's mask in the *Christmas Story*, the *Totentanz* 'Big Mask' by a new one, pink, toothy, the tongue sticking out, with a mop beard (Schumann, interview, December '82). In the '70 circus a line of manacled Vietnamese women were pulled into play by a string passing through his teeth – pulled into his mouth.

In addition to a 200-ft. dragon, whose Canal St. body soon fell apart,[26] and some face masks for children, the Bread and Puppet Theatre, during the summer '66 South Bronx children's workshops produced three giant puppets, Mother Earth, the Professor and Chicken Little,[27] and at a

---

26. But reborn green, this dragon concludes the '67 Newport Folk Festival and in '68 is seen circling Washington Square Park on Halloween and its progeny populates Schumann's circuses '70 following.
27. '. . . pink and had a big belly and it was pink. It was like a childlike, great big pink – it was a chicken, it was a chicken face, he was like a really creamy chickenlike face.' — (Ernstthal, interview, '79.)

Harlem workshop that summer a fourth, the Fox. These puppets, with which, in addition to Uncle and the rats from the preceding summer — supplemented by additional rats — and some older 'small masks and puppets like the Witch mask and things like that' (Schumann, interview, '79), they put on the first (outdoor) showings of *Chicken Little* of May-October '67, were not only considerably bigger than the *Crucifixion* generation of puppets, but required operators outside of them (and therefore visible).[28] Like Fatso's and most of the masks since the summer of

---

28. '... it was a kind of city organization project of which I was the artistic head. (I: So you had a bigger crew working with you?) Yes, I had about ten or so paid puppeteers, among them, Jules, Bob Ernstthal, Arnie, Lydia, various choral — quite a few. (I: How long was this — this was a workshop for the whole summer?) Yes, for the whole summer ... (I: Did the kids in the workshop do most of — did they make the face also on the big puppets — Mother Earth? Like for Uncle Fatso?) Well, it was, as I described, the process of starting the little kids with a bunch of clay and helping them to make something, any kind of similarity to a face or a head or hand or foot, for that matter, feet were made also, and then my getting into it and using it for my purposes, for making the faces, but using a lot of the kids' ideas. I think the kids had more of an outlet in the smaller masks than in these big ones, so in the big ones I ended up doing a lot of work, and on the small ones, the kids ran free much longer — until I stepped in and stopped them and decided that the mask was *finished* or made changes.

I also felt strongly for trying to have the operation exposed, to move the puppet where a bunch of people would be needed to move that puppet, and that bunch of people would be the real performers, with the interest of the show. They would carry these effigies, they would throw them down or behead them or run them or down them or up them, whatever was decided — that population who would do that was part of the idea of these puppets, so I came with that idea into that workshop. I told the kids in the schools the winter before the workshop started that I wanted to build giant puppets like they had never seen. So we were ready for them. But what design we would use and how we would do it and all that, that was all up in the air, so we did a helluva lot of fooling around and fumbling around and the first time they tried out, in rehearsal, Mother Earth and Uranus and Chicken Little — Chicken Little was the biggest of them all — they all collapsed as soon as we put the stick on the floor. The weight of the head would jam down so it hit the ground so hard that it broke the frame. We just had overdone it — with chicken wire, with framing inside, much too much lumber and metal pieces that had to be taken out. The fault was that we tried to give them too delicate a movement. Later on we found it wasn't necessary to have built them with moving necks, with necks that allowed for swivel movements, for turns and nods of the head. So that kind of thing was hard to build. (I: So Mother Earth had one of these swivel necks?) Yes. (I: Did she have it when you did the show?) Yes. (I: She doesn't have it now?) No, she doesn't have it — we took it out. It didn't pay to have it. The puppet is too big for that, it doesn't need it. Its body moves stronger.

Uranus (subsequent name of the Fox (SSB)) had legs that had horizontal sticks coming out of the heel, so two people could hop around and dance, perform acrobatics and do pretty marvelous hops and runs — giant steps, can sit and scratch his nose with his toes if he wants to, so he is very versatile. Then another different mounting was that of Chicken Little. He had a rod in the middle like the others, going up into the head and then the legs larger than — the feet bigger than those of Uranus — had holes in their knees. The legs were

'64, their masks were modelled directly over the clay. Chicken Little wasn't much used subsequently, the Professor was used in a '67 Newport Festival version of *Speech*, together with 'the chorus of rats, that were his clientele, his public' (Schumann, interview, '79). I don't know of other uses. Uranus, who in *Chicken Little* was the Fox, and Mother Earth, were used in a Central Park New Year's show December 31, '68, and then in the '68-'69 *Cry of the People for Meat*. He was occasionally used as King Herod.

At the museum now, Mother Earth's giant grey hands rest on sturdy 8 ft. poles, and she herself measures perhaps 10 ft. from the hem of her lace apron (a perky paper flower on its little white belt) to the top of her grey head: tortured, grotesque muscular grey cheeks above the thick-lipped open mouth, blue eyes, not large, staring upward, a sturdy chest. Her

---

from fabric and there were windows carved in the middle and the kids were put into each leg and the walking around of these kids, at least for the first time we did it, was quite funny. They walked and danced inside these legs and couldn't coordinate their movements. But the try at coordination was funny.

There were different building ideas. Chicken Little was different from Uranus. Mother Earth was different from Chicken Little. She had no feet, she had neck movements. The Professor didn't have a neck movement but he had a string around him to his pipe, so his pipe could wiggle; also he did not have feet but he had a window in the middle of his belly and little puppets were played in his belly because from whatever speech he had he got a bellyache. Also, he had tiny little crippled hands in contrast to the other puppets that had oversized hands which are very expressive and they sort of dwarf the giant to a certain extent, and the Professor's hands were tiny little ones for the intellectual and decadent and sort of pitiful. (I: So, there was a puppet show playing inside the Professor? He had a stage inside of his stomach?) Yes. Don't ask me what performed there, I don't remember what type of bellyaches he had and what the relationship of the belly to his head was. His head often used Johnson's speeches.

The big dragon was also done during that time. And the skin building of the dragon was done by dozens and dozens of kids. Over a long period of time. All kinds of junk that Jules and I collected down on Canal Street, where Jules had access to a basement. Some hardware man had stored up useless parts of all kinds of things and we just picked up all that junk and all of that was used and made a heavy skin for a dragon with that – built with very fllimsy fabric, so it ripped shortly after it was built. It was a big, big dragon and it really was half a block long and fit 100 kids inside it. (I: For the head of the dragon that was made – two separate parts, one for the bottom jaw, one for the top – there was also work done by the kids the same way you were doing the other puppets?) Less than that. I designed it – I made it out and then the work was to make all these many, many, teeth and made out where the neck was and the idea for the jaw being the part that is carried by wheels and the top part being on an axle that is carried above and could move on an axle that was designed for it. It was a big thing, so naturally, many, many hands went into it.

Chicken Little was only a little part of this workshop. The workshop consisted of dance classes and story telling classes and clay building and carpentry, building dozens of little stages and little lean-to sheds, that is, prepared from 1×2 collapsible structures that were done with patchwork fabric and the roof was patchwork fabric. (I: Were those stages like the ones that were used in the workshop the year before?) No, no, these were all built and invented at that time, these little stages that are meant for little plays. The goal was to create a festival that would then travel through the parks. — (Schumann, interview, '79.)

fingernails are dirty. She doesn't look friendly, but neither does she look unfriendly: strained. Uranus is 14 ft. tall, his center pole a tree trunk, 2½ to 3 inches in diameter. Black coat, red bowtie, white shirtfront, stubby reddish hands. His purplish face is warts all over, there are gaps between his teeth, a nigger-mouth is open way across his face, he has a squashed-up, up, broad-nostrilled nose. The index finger of his short right hand is pointing as though he were giving a directive. Black, narrow pants and giant, naked, flecked feet, a red rag head-covering. A terrible sky-principle, he is like Mother Earth (he is a head taller than she), primarily grotesque. Both of them are more terrible than funny, but hardly frightening.

Schumann also made masks for the child performers in the *Chicken Little* show, initially 'true life mask casts' (Schumann, interview, December '82) of the individual casts, then transformed:

'They were used for many purposes. The kids wore them originally — they didn't want to have their own faces, so they wore their own masks. Then, a lot of them were transformed from boys' faces to girls' faces. They found that funny, and hats and wigs were put on them. And they were painted oddly, some of them. Some were painted blue with pink lips — and different colors. Very light faces would be painted very dark and the other way around. That was a trick that the kids went along with — that was funny. So they performed in all these little skits in *Chicken Little*, but also in the little skit that went before that show. And later on they were shepherds in the *Christmas Story* — these masks. There were several *Christmas Stories* where these masks were the shepherds.'

(Schumann, interview, December '82.)

In the summer of '66, Schumann added another face to his repertory of female figures for street demonstrations (Vietnamese women, Vietnamese Ladies, Grey Mothers with babies): he painted masks made from face casts 'black, and sort of painted them charred black — black with grey shades in it' (Schumann, interview, '79). These napalm-charred women appeared in his August 6, '66 Hiroshima Day parade. The masks were later painted over, variously used, e.g. painted over with pretty colors for the pretty partying ladies at the beginning of *Grey Lady Cantata II*, perhaps for the heroine of *Emilia*.

Sometime in '66, probably[29] late in '66, Schumann, at the Astor Library, built the Grey Lady puppets that he then used in the *Bach Cantata #140* of February '67. He built them for an 'outdoor action', or at any rate, during the time of rehearsals of the *Cantata*, first used them in a street demonstration (Schumann, interview, '79): single- and multi-

---

29. But perhaps early in '66: 'a whole big series which we didn't use that much, because that was one of the things that didn't quite fit in. It didn't quite work. Later on it was in the *Bach Cantata* and then in the *Cry of the People for Meat* they were used also. But it seemed like a big production number and we didn't really use it for a while as I remember. We kind of did it all and went through all the production of it and then didn't use them right away.' — (Ernstthal, interview, '79.)

handed, mop-haired, grey-shrouded Ladies of Sorrow[30] whose masks, made over clay, without plaster casts, and operated on short handles hand-held inside them, though different from one another, resembled that of the Grey Mother with baby of '65.[31]

Whereas the Vietnamese women and Ladies, white-faced, did not have much of a career – or any – in Schumann's indoor theatre after '66, these Grey Ladies are key pieces of his indoor theatre '70 ff., starting with *Lamentation* and *Mississippi* (featuring a single Grey Lady with moveable teardrop), then in the series of *Grey Lady Cantatas* ('70-'75).

The '66 *Chicken Little* puppets had been giant machines operated by puppeteers, in the line from the *King Story* through the *Crucifixion* puppets; the gestural line. The Grey Ladies had been more the kind of puppet worn as a garment, its body that of the puppeteer, who in it was less an operator, more a performer, sort of a slow dancer doing something akin to mime; in the dance-line of puppets originating *Leaf*. In this line also, and perhaps the last puppets in it, were the armless, tubular disciple puppets, used for a Last Supper scene in the '67 *Crucifixion*, and made about that time. Schumann wanted a choreographic effect that he felt the arms would have disturbed. A separate Feeder puppet enabled the disciples to eat and drink. In the *Bach Cantata #140* of '67 the Grey Ladies, in the *Crucifixion* of '67, the armless disciples functioned as dance puppets. When they reappeared in the Coney Island Black plays of '70, their use was half-way to the theatrical. The gestural and the dance traditions had merged.

---

30. The use of 'lady' for many of Schumann's female puppets may partly derive from the New York City (Jewish?) indiscriminate use of the term for 'woman'. It may also relate to the traditional Latin use of the term for the mother of god and particularly for the particular local mothers of god by which the Catholic plebes were wont to replace the pagan local deities and protective spirits. Actually, the various lady puppets were not ladylike, i.e. do not evoke the supposedly refined and sensitive women of a nobility. They do in appearance derive from medieval virginal mothers, other-worldly and suffering.

31. 'They were different (from earlier puppets (SSB)) in that they had many, many faces. It was arbitrary. We dyed a lot of fabric scraps and whatever we could and we had somebody donate fabric from scrap fabrics from a store on Broome Street, and we dyed all that grey. Then we made a lot of hands, a lot of heads, and then mounted these heads and hands fairly arbitrarily onto pieces of grey fabric. Big groups of puppets, many, many heads together in one shroud. Many hands together in one shroud. (Elka: But also separate single figures.) Yes. (Elka: You know who might be sort of the mother or the – the first one of the Grey Ladies was really that big woman holding the baby, because she was grey, and her face was very similar to the Grey Ladies that came afterward.) Yes, that's true. (The heads) were all done over clay. They were all different. I made many, many clay pieces. (Elka: I remember there was a great reminding of everybody to keep an eye out for mops, discarded mops in the street, which we used for the hair. And also mop handles for the sticks to be mounted.)' (Schumann, interview, '79.) I.e. the Grey Lady heads and the Grey Lady hands were different puppets.

'Les Dames Grises, avec leur tête craintive aux cheveux de ficelle penchée mollement sur leur corps long et maigre comme un échalas, habillées de grosse toile à sac, expriment l'épuisement mental et physique. En masse elles suggèrent l'idée d'un peuple à bout de forces sous la férule de l'occupant.' — (Kourilsky, '71.)

With the 'Johnny puppets' (and the similar 'Madonnas'), made soon after the troupe got the use of the Old Courthouse, at the beginning of '68, the first more important batch of puppets since the Grey Lady and the armless disciple ones – small, ten to twelve inches high, jointless doll puppets of paper maché – the puppeteer functions somewhat as a child or other person playing with something, dolls or other little play figures; they are lifted up, carried in the hands, put down. When Schumann first fabricated them, he experimented with other ways of using them: on sticks, or put on the heads of puppeteers shrouded in dark fabric like hats or like big masks (Schumann, interview, '79). Finally, i.e. for the *Johnny Comes Marching Home* of March '68, he used them as table puppets:

'I think that the first one was made in the Courthouse, when we moved to the Courthouse. They were used on the second European tour, not the first. With *The Cry*. The Johnny puppets, plus an equally big set of Madonnas with flowers painted on them, I think were all made in a workshop session in the Courthouse, when we invited people to participate in a building workshop. The Madonnas were actually meant for an event that never took place. We wanted – I don't remember with which peace organization – to build altars in the streets of New York and burn these Madonnas made from paper maché. But that never happened. We still have some of them. The Madonnas were made over clay with a few layers of paper maché, newspaper and paper paste on it, and then when that was dry, they were cut up, mounted together, and painted. They were little dolls, about twelve inches or something like that, similar to the Johnny puppets."
(Schumann, interview, '79.)

The Johnny puppets are seated, kneeling or stretched out prone, black and white and dark and light grey, dressed men and women. The prone ones, larger than the others, perhaps 2 ft. long, are sleeping or seem afraid. Some of them are women with babies. The seated figures are partly-hatted burghers, round bodied, 18 inches or so tall, seated as though on chairs, Philistines, partly women with flowers on their black dresses, in black handkerchiefs, white faced (as are all these Johnny puppets), but all in black as though in mourning – with Madonna faces. The kneeling figures seem in sorrow over bereavements – their bodies curved, their hands on, over, by their necks.

The neckless Beast head masks and puppets – half of the body of the operator disappears in the mask (Schumann, interview, '83) – made during the summer of '68 in Maine and used then in one or two local shows entitled *The Bible* and in a show bearing the same title at the summer of '68 Newport Folk Festival, and definitively from March '69 onward in *The Cry of the People for Meat*, were the last important set of puppets of the '60s.[32] Except for two new soldier puppets – 'with breast-

---

32. Among the puppets he lost when during his '69 tour the city repossessed the Courthouse, was a 'super monster' apparently on the lines of King Yama:
'He made one of these huge gents, enormously detailed and baroque, in fact, masks

plates, with heads that were worn on the operator's head and with mailing tubes as guns, celastic fists that held onto these mailing tubes' (Schumann, interview, '79) that Schumann (ibid.) thinks had been used for a *Crucifixion* earlier, *The Bible* and *Cry* had no new puppets other than the Beasts – *Cry* used the Grey Ladies for a bombing scene, the Shark Airplane as crucifix, the Jesus and disciple puppets, the Mary mask from the *Christmas Story*, the Great Warrior as Kronos decapitating his father Uranus.

'(I: What did the Beasts represent to you? I mean, how did they strike you – I mean, they are ugly buggers.) I found them beautiful, in some strange way, when they were all together. They are – they are gargoyles. (I: They don't scare you – they are not just endearing, which you can also think?) Yeah, they are scary. (I: What did you think of that sort of –) My first reaction, when I saw them all white, I thought, well, they are going to get painted. But they didn't, they stayed white. And they – it seemed like marble to me, like marble statues moving, because they were all white and a little bit of color they got from the dirt just gave them highlights that they didn't have before – made them – and the older they got, the more warm they got – the better they got. And I felt that there was something ancient, very ancient about them and I felt that they caught the essence of the Bible ... This is why, because they looked so old, they looked so old and they looked so – and with this sound that he was making, it seemed like a very primitive kind of thing happening. (I: But what is the relation between these dumb Beasts and mostly en masse, on the one hand, and the Bible on the other, specifically?) I think to be honest about it, I was so overwhelmed with the picture of it that I didn't analyze it very strongly. I felt it so much, somehow, I felt this wave, I felt the waves of humanity, or – and then, you see, taking them off, and the people coming up, it was like prehistoric – the prehistoric leading to the birth of man, so to speak. There was something of that for me. The geneologies and then, because the pictures were so strong, they were stronger than any pictures I had ever experienced in my life. Most, stronger than any ritual I had experienced being brought up in a Jewish family. And any of those rituals that I experienced as a child – these, I felt like we were creating rituals that related more to really how I felt than the others they were making me go to as a child.'

Levy, interview, '79.)

'(I: Was there anything technically distinctive about the Beast masks – in the way they were worn or the way they were made?) Not in the making – in the wearing, yes. We tried all kinds of things ... how they would be worn, strapped down or not. They were tied on the backs of people to be played backwards so that you would have your back to the audience. They were tied in front. We ended up having crossed shoulder straps and then those people crawling in them most of the time, sometimes getting up. We hadn't had a mask like that before. Half of the body of the operator disappears in the mask. They were crawling on their knees with their hands – the hands were like the front legs of the Beasts. (I:

(Ashley probably means small faces on the larger face (SSB)), just before leaving to go on the tour out of the Courthouse, when it was lost, and during the transition it disappeared. Later, somebody said it was seen in a commercial movie.'—(Ashley, interview, May '82.)

It went over the shoulders.) And it slipped down on people there, too. Bent forward with it. (They had straps?) Straps that go – the mask is here, sits on you like so, down to the stomach, like this, and then straps over the shoulders crossing over, attaching the mask to your back. (I: In the back it doesn't go down that far, or does it?) On the back there is no mask. There is a sort of a poncho attached to the mask that falls over your back, that disguises your back, so when you're on your knees that poncho becomes the body.' (Schumann, interview, '83.)

They have pointed triangular teeth in gaping mouths, no lips: their upper lips are pronounced nostrils. No eyes. Pointed ears. Bulky, blind – all instinct – they are forward-tending: clumsily. Originally they were all white – unpainted. Some were used as dragon heads in circuses, '70 ff.

5. Schumann's theatre religious: designed to inspire awe.

The Christian specifications apart, Schumann's theatre has a religious air. The size, manner and mien of his puppets, and the slow ceremonious movements of the performers are calculated to inspire awe. This was so especially during the '60s, but was so also in his splendid pantheist pageants from '74 onward, and his use of religious music, increasing from '72 onward, supported this effect. But awe, even awe at human accomplishments, is a religious sentiment, and one relating directly to the most objectionable feature of all religion: the abdication of individual judgment in an overwhelming illusion that one is in the presence of supernatural power. Awed, one is overawed. This emotional tyranny is most noxious when, as is usually the case with religion, a moral claim is presented. It perverts morality, which, if it is anything, is free personal choice, into authority. Nor is the aweing of others improved by sweetness or humility, e.g. the humility of humorous touches, or the sweetness of a mere, modest servant of truth. That doesn't make the one awed less of a slave. It merely saves the awer the onus of imputable tyranny. Schumann's theatre has something oppressive about it.

The form of the theatre in its main aspect of choreographed stately ceremony supports the perception of it as not merely secularly moralistic, but religious; and in its second dominant aspect of childlike simplicity it has a specific Christian resonance, though of course not the Scholastic one. Man's reason is a foolishness before God and one of pride's seductions: the foolishness of faith saves. Schumann's theatre is not only generically religious. It has Christian trappings.[1]

---

[1]. Barry Goldensohn (*Iowa Review*, Spring '77, *Peter Schumann's Bread and Puppet Theatre*.), who sees the 'religious vision' of Schumann's theatre as 'choosing as its main symbols resurrection and redemption (,) ... made impersonal and public, not emblems of personal salvation' mentions as part of its religious aspect the distribution of bread:

'The use of Bread is a part of the public ritual of communion and an integral part of the theater. You are sitting at an Easter Play, you have been a witness to the Passion and the puppets which grew enormous for the great event lie collapsed in a heap before the Cross. The puppeteers have crawled out, shrunken after the event to their normal size. They pass through the audience handing out chunks of bread. It is not the usual mush but a dark, heavy bread, made of hand-ground rye, not flour, and it requires strong teeth. You sit there in a communal ritual tearing at it murderously. Is there only one myth and ritual? The puppeteer who hands me the bread is a friend. I whisper: "Mayra, what is a nice Jewish girl like you doing here?"

"What are *you* doing here?"

From what am I defending myself with bad tasting jokes? This event is quite different from the audience role at Riverside Church, listening to the *B Minor Mass*, or hearing vespers at the Camaldoli Hermitage: we are sharing a chaw of the seasonal god. In this theater the bread is a direct assault on aesthetic distance.

In the setting of the *Easter Play*, bread is offered as an echo of the Eucharist and one is thrust into the role of the surprised communicant, but in other pieces its function is more modest. The bread is an offering, ostentatiously so, and it therefore has an unavoidable ceremonial flavor. Something is shared, and the audience is jarred out of passivity by the act of eating together. Schumann *intends* the bread to be a reminder that you come to the theater not just for entertainment, which is for the skin, but also for vital sustenance, which is for the stomach. That he should assign this meaning reveals the habits of mind of a confirmed allegorist, since it is, after all, gratuitous. Since he leaves out sustenance for the head and heart, it also suggests that he is a primitive and an anti-sentimentalist.'

6. The Christianism of Schumann's theatre.
If mere device a dangerous one.
Probably more than mere device.

Schumann, into the early '70s, regularly celebrated, at Christmas and Easter, the birth, life and death of Our Savior; the figures of the Christ myth are prominent in his theatre; the figure of Mary, during the '60s at least provides the image of all women and that of Christ and his disciples pretty much that of men; he has afforded us glimpses of a supreme (more stern than benign) father deity (*Emilia*, '70; 4th of July parade '70; *Stations*, '72; various 'circuses' during the '70s and early '80s) in a manner contrasting with his comic presentation of the older gods of the Greeks. Guardian, consoling, saving angels appear again and again; and so do the Devil, red, and the Bone- or Skull-man, black and white, of medieval iconography, bearing the wages of sin. Though no longer done only or at all around Christmas and Easter, his formally Christian output continues throughout the '70s, *Stations* (Easter '72 and following), *Bach Cantata #140*, first version (Christmas '74), second version ('76 circus), *Joan of Arc* and *Carmina Burana* ('77), *Ave Maris Stella* ('77 and '78 circus), *Washerwoman Nativity* ('79). Such could be and has been considered the politically convenient and artistically more than legitimate use of an existing iconic vocabulary known to his audience.[1] The story is *the* story to him, and he knows the text – and seems to have done a fair amount of attentive reading in the Old Testament as well.

That those Christian references are not merely political expedients or artistic devices is suggested by the choice of some of them, e.g. an emphasis on the Last Supper in the celebration of Easter, the inclusion of the Annunciations to Mary and to the shepherds in that of Christmas.

But his theatre has had central aspects of content as well, that in the

---

1. 'If there would have been other interesting festivals here in the U.S. (besides Christmas and Easter (SSB)), I would have chosen them, too. For me to use the Christian stories was very rewarding. First of all, I knew them well, I had grown up with them, and they are warm and powerful, and I like them, so I use them for that reason, but I very much wanted to play things that I could do with what I wanted to and that I would know I could rely on people recognizing them – knowing them. And there were many good things about that, also, we had a church. To get into a church seemed to me a great advantage. To be able to play in a church, in contrast to a theatre. That was a good find when we found Spencer Church.' — (Schumann, interview, '82.)

To Christmas and Easter, Schumann added, but later, and less assiduously observed, Thanksgiving ('67, '68, '70) and Independence Day ('68, '70 following). But the manner of his observance of these, points up the sincerity of his observance of Easter and Christmas. His feelings were not engaged. Irony, directed at the warlike, well-appetited Pilgrim Fathers, was the essence of his Thanksgiving shows, and up to '76 or so, of his Independence Day parades as well.

context of those celebrations and iconic references may be and probably legitimately should be considered Christian: a pacifism that despite some allusions seems distinct from the fashionable Hindu one grounded in respect for life, and yet seems not merely moralistic but religious; a nearly total absence not only of the erotic, but of women (or, for that matter, men) under the aspect of actual or potential sexual attractiveness, coupled with a central image of idealized motherhood and a less preponderant but, I think, clearly discernible ideal image of the home as focus of a (monogamous) family; but above all, images of human life and indications as to how it should be lived, conveyed as much by the sculpture of the figures' physiognomies as by their constellations and deportment and by the significance of tableaux and events, that in their central aspects, to my mind are quintessentially Christian: of human existence as characterized by suffering and guilt, and nevertheless also by hope; and of the right life as on the one hand simple to the point of asceticism and free of rage and carnal desire and of action for their satisfaction, and on the other hand devoted to the discharge of duties or the observance of a moral law conflicting with, if not contrary to, human nature – whence the guilt: the suffering being due to deviations (as in war) from those duties or that law, the hope unwarranted but real, and thus suspiciously like the Christian's hope for God's mercy, though the theatre does not tell us its justification, nor even what it is a hope for: it could possibly be hope for a life without suffering. The turn from nature that renders the Gospels so dreary, and the antagonism to human nature that renders Paul's letters so repulsive seem, though this is an observation that needs qualification (cf. infra), basic to his work: as much as the imagery of violence, though not the pariah's revelry in imagined revenge, of John's revelation.

Against its interpretation as Christian there is really only one major argument: there is no suggestion of the divine nature of Christ: the emphasis is on his teachings and works, not on his person, there is no resurrection[2] and there is no redemption by his blood.

---

2. Asked to explain the name of his circuses, '*Our Domestic Resurrection Circus,*' Schumann, regarding 'resurrection,' said:

'... and "resurrection" because one has to steal that term from the religious clubs, or from the religious traditions and can't allow it to belong to that category of mankind. It has to – it's applicable. It's a term that can be profaned – that can be used outside of church and Christianity. It doesn't belong to them, it belongs to all of us. (I: As an event in individual lives and also –) Yeah. As a necessity in communal life as well as a – even if just a provocation – a provocational idea, in an individual life. There's no description of a realistic – a biological resurrection attempted, right, we are not telling a *fairy* tale. We don't have that. But we are calling this – what happens after all the elements that we used in the show *die* that what follows that death – that picks all that up again – we're calling that the resurrection – in imitation of the religious folks who created that.'

'(I: In *Stations of the Cross* there is a suggestion of the resurrection of Christ.) A suggestion? It's really – (I: More than a suggestion?) The last station is Christ, and he's laid down and everyone lies down. Then the people begin to sing *The Lord is Risen*. It's a

I have not mentioned among its Christianoid features what has been his theatre's main feature as regards content: almost without exception, his shows not only are concerned with morals and are moralistic, but show Evil and Goodness – the Good – in opposition to one another, and show them as simple and their distinction as evident and clear-cut. I know of only one show that dealt with moral 'problems,' *Reiteration* ('68), the problem of resistance by violence to violence, and only one admitting of a coincidence of good and evil, *Wolkenstein ('78).*[3] I think he shares this world view and preoccupation with Christianism, but I don't think they in his case derive from it, and the forms he gives the opposition between good and evil seem to me only occasionally and not in their essence Christian.

From at least the mid-'70s onward, Schumann coupled the Christian references and reverberations with theatrical promotions – notably the pageants of his annual circuses – of what has seemed – and seems in his own mind to have been – a more personal religious world view of his, centered, so far as I can make out, on the notions that human lives are part of a human history that is an unending repetition of struggle between good and evil in which the good is forever vanquished but forever reemerges, a cycle of death and resurrection, and where the good is itself the animating or the life principle of the historical and natural or cosmic cycles, and is a feminine principle of fertility and nurture – and of passive acceptance (which qualifies the notion of a 'struggle'), while evil is a male principle of ordering, aggression, and of domination, a death principle or death force. These views, or views of this general sort – we are here dealing with art, not with analytic discourse – have, I would say, been his from the very beginning, and can be glimpsed in his production of the '60s as well: but in his later pageants they became a little more explicit, and their presentation now seemed the very point of the work, the dominant and formative purpose: the pageants (or the circuses of which they were part) have seemed

---

round and we figured a way of singing it so that people would get up as they joined. So I think that's pretty –' — (Elka, interview.)

According to Hoagland, *Let 'em Have*, '83, the Village maskmaker Ralph Lee mentioned as Schumann's primary 'limitation' that 'he is stalled' in 'the one oracular pattern of death and resurrection, an idee fixe which repeats and repeats.'

This is true though snidely put, obsession being the state of everybody big time, but resurrection in Schumann's work is not that of individuals, whether son of god or descendant of Adam, but the regeneration of forms in nature and history. Nevertheless, Schumann shows Jesus, light of the world, metaphorically crucified over and over again, and by this metaphor coyly invites misinterpretation.

3. Hoagland, *Let 'em Have*, '83, reporting on Ralph Lee's views on Schumann's work:

'... that his techniques are better suited to an issue such as the Vietnam War, which can reasonably be portrayed in stark juxtapositions, than to more complicated, "artistic" productions, such as *Wolkenstein*, his tale of a sixteenth-century poet-composer, half of whose soul winds up in Heaven and half in Hell.'

to be and were intended to be religious community festivals, offered as 'modern' replacements of Easter and Christmas. There is no personal deity in this world view, there is nothing to worship, there is no salvation. It is certainly not the Christian world view – in fact, the Church of Rome has recurrently combated and condemned its likes. But Schumann, presenting at these circuses also Christian 'morality plays,' seems to see no conflict. The Christianizing injunction of his morality plays, '74-'79, to do battle against evil, inserts into the moral dichotomy of his pageants the dichotomy of good natural and evil civilized man. His reinterpretation of the theistically divine essence – pure soul – of man as natural life principle, a pantheistic cosmic essence, apparently to him is a negligible detail.

But this cyclical view of Schumann's seems to me a reinterpretation of the Christian finite-curve view. The reason it has seemed this to me is that though it has varied over the years, with fair persistence a sense is conveyed that death is the gateway to life, as Christ's death was for humanity, and as a Christian's death is for him or her personally.

The foregoing concerns story and doctrine. But the puppets – and their movements – are perhaps even more important in giving his theatre – especially of course his Christmas and Easter shows, but the others, too – their Christian resonance. Schumann presumed that his Christ puppet – not labeled 'Christ', but labeled 'Vietnam' or whatever, or not named – would be recognized as such even when not appearing in one of the Christian tales: e.g. in street parades. And similarly for his Mothers of God. And he was right: the feeling was in them. The feeling: museum goers or art students might have made the connection by way of what they knew of renaissance or medieval inconography; but to make it by way of contemporary popular iconography would have often been hard even for practicing Catholics. His Christ looks like God become man or like man partaking of divinity: Schumann caught the central mystery in his sculpture; and by the calm, even cold compassion of his benediction as well as by the reconciled sadness of his resignation is Christ. He cannot be mistaken for mere man – moral exemplar or whatever. E.g. his contrast in this respect to the disciple puppets is definite (and astounding). His large angel puppets similarly unequivocally share the feeling of the annunciatory angels in the Gospels and in Christian iconography: they have their peculiar ethereality, spirituality, purity (and their majesty). Similarly, finally for his death puppets and masks: their fearsomeness is not a churchyard-superstitions one, but an eschatological one, they convey the connotation of punishment. I mention these puppets in particular – and not also e.g. his disciples or Marys – because their mere appearance, independent of story carries religious transcendentalism, and specifically the Christian one, into his shows: not merely a relation to it in terms of a story. Their visual connotations are theological. This is also true of his Godface mask: but in its case the reverberation is not specifically or at least not unequivocally Christian. His great female puppets and masks of the '60s also have aspects of Mary — of divinely chosen vessels: but since (like Mary herself from a Protestant viewpoint) they are not themselves supra-natural, we don't necessarily respond to them in their religious aspect. Those other masks and puppets make the unequivocally Christian, not only generically spiritualist or religious, or moralist, statement he in terms of the overt content of his shows generally avoids.

It is a remarkable fact, that among Schumann's collaborators during the '60s, neither the Jews (e.g. Ernstthal, Sherman, Levy), nor the political radicals (e.g. Ernstthal, Eckhardt) objected to his Christian gesture, nor even thought it weird. They thought it merely use of handy elements of the culture, almost a clever steal, or a focus on essential realities that the Christian mythology gave Schumann a grip on but that so to speak most any other religion might have enabled him to deal with, had he happened to have been raised within it.[4]

---

4. Ernstthal felt the overtly Christian references pertained to the same mid-XXth century apocalyptic realities that the counter-culture mysticisms of the '60s, analogously borrowing from Hinduism and Buddhism, were dealing with, and that they no more committed Schumann or the Bread and Puppet Theatre to any religious dogma than the theatre's leftist political stand committed it to any political dogma:

'I couldn't say I felt any Christian vibration at all. None. As Christianity, as a religion. None. Zero ... what I saw was that his feeling was to make religion real, as in a sense of the true feeling of what religion means, and God. And the search for God and the quality of God and the — we were making the myths real. Like, people say we did the Crucifixion every year, the Christmas story every year, but the point was not religious, the point was to make the mythology of the time real to him and into reality. (I: You speak of God now. In the summer of '63, was that person mentioned between you?) No ... Peter is a very — like I said, anything to do with anything organized; namely, religion, or anything like that, is taboo to discuss, which is really the — because it would have become a Christian theatre or religious theatre, or whatever. It was, if anything, a mythological — it was more mythology than religion. In other words, we were dealing with the Judeo-Christian mythology of — that was current in the world that we were in. But we took that mythology and infused it with a living feeling. That was the point. So in a way, religion — in a way, the word and the ideas of religion never came up..... So in a way, religion — and that's why I really liked — that was my favorite — that was one thing that really held it together. Or held us together, because we — we —. It was infusing mythology of the day with the real, the reality of it. And that, to me, in a way, the Apocalypse and all — and the Revelation — to me that's what was happening. That's what happened in the '60s in New York. It happened. But it happened on the mental plane. Through drugs, and the whole experience was a crashing through into the post-Christian era, which is now. That was the turmoil of the times. So now religion and all that is — I don't follow it, frankly, I don't follow it or care for it. But what we were dealing with was the reality and not the religion. In the same way we were not dealing with politics. We were dealing with the reality. The reality of what we saw. The immediate experience, as opposed to the theory. Even these things you see that he wrote, these little paragraphs and stuff — streets and theatre, you know, the few things — they're all very, very — like woodcuts, almost. They're blocked out. He never dabbled. He never discussed them. And that's why we were so good. That's why he kept going so long, when other people crashed on their ass. Including the Mime Troupe and all those others, because they were constantly dealing with ideology. I never dealt with

A language is charged with the shared values of its speakers. Its use conveys presuppositions of all disagreements possible within it. This goes a fortiori for a language whose terms are the images of a mythology. Thus, for instance, it is impossible to take an anti-Communist stand in the Communist lingo, or to talk in the language of the Christians without promoting their dogma. Joining the ongoing dialogue between the speakers of a language, you enter their special universe of discourse: which is why the special vocabularies of dogmas are precious to their adherents, and why vituperation, cf. Luther up to 1524, is crucial to rebellion. An art of Christian references may be heretic, but it will not be unchristian. A theatre of Mary, Jesus, Gabriel and Peter automatically places the spectator in a world in which God and heaven rather than nature, sin and redemption rather than the joys of living, eternity rather than history and the now, and death rather than life, are the great realities, and in which discontent is a blemish and violence on behalf of survival a discord: regardless of what the author makes Mary, Jesus and the angels and

---

ideology and no one would care about ideology, because it wasn't the *point*. It was how much clay and how much, you know, just work. Just do it. Doesn't matter. Including the Christian stories. We *evoked* the mythology, the reality of the mythology.... Probably *because* I was a Jew I didn't care for how dangerous it was. Like if it was Anna (Bob's wife (SSB)), who had an oppressive history with the Catholics, she probably would be upset about it. But to me it was mythological, and it was a great story – it's the most powerful story. It's also – has to do with that primitive level of theatre which is kind of theatre like *Orlando Furioso* or the Greek tragedies, where *everybody* is in the story. When they came to the theatre they all knew the story already. So it was something very familiar – I like that idea. Plus, it had to do with the spiritual – explorations of what was holy and spiritual and all that, which is essentially what I was thinking about and concerned with. So it had to do with the most elemental concerns – plus it wasn't expressing anything that's holy – and especially if you can get it across and get that feeling – couldn't possibly be oppressive – it could only be inspirational – actually, if you can really carry it off. Like this Christian stuff now and the religious theatre or things that I see now – are just absurd. But the marriage of folk tradition with the mythological tradition of Christianity and reviving it totally is a great experience.' — (Ernstthal, interview.)

A generic non-dogmatic mysticism, related to Schumann's 'work ethic', made the shows good when they were good:

'And at *other* times, we'd have all elaborate shows in churches and this and that and it would be not so great, or medium. So the ethic was, if it's good in a way, it has to do with –I felt, to me–it had to do with the influence, probably to Peter it was more like Christian mysticism. It was the mystic in him. To me, it had to do with the Eastern mysticism which was beginning to flow in the late '50s, early '60s, which I came from – which was that the – every act has a meaning, and there's an inner value to things. Something like that, right? The act itself – like in Catholicism and stuff, it's the Mass. But the act itself has the value.' — (Ernstthal, interview.)

'(I: And what were you doing then? You were propagandizing Christianity?) (Laugh) It's funny, I never thought of it that way. I really fell in love with those stories about Jesus. And the puppets, one fell in love with the puppets. Mary – very beautiful puppet. It was wonderful to act out the story. It was very passionate. It gave meaning to your life....' — (Sherman, interview.)

apostles do or say. Unless, of course, he is simply grossly blasphemous, and even then. (But Schumann's iconography was never blasphemous.) It won't do, therefore, to say that you are merely using convenient symbols. They take over. Insensibly, you find yourself caught. As, I believe, Schumann has: expressing only one half of his own nature. And in any event, the specific Christian references almost force a Christian understanding of his theatre.

Schumann says he 'feels warmly' about the myth – from his childhood days – but anchoring his work in these slimy grounds was not a good idea. My father's choice of Marx – the Saint-Simonian, etc. – utopian vision was better: Marx' conception, 1832-48, of a communist world commonwealth – before he added on the dictatorship of the proletariat bit – has some nobility. Of course, that choice, still reasonable in the 1920s, after all the Russian horrors of the '30s became a little bit difficult. And in this perspective, maybe Schumann picked Jesus-and-Mary instead, because the socialist-anarchist vision of the working class ideologues of the first half of the 19th century could no longer be sustained, picked it, really, because of the idea of a 'hope' that he somehow sniffed in it, just pallid enough, a ghostly wistfulness, that a decent man still *could* sustain. But the images resulting from that choice, though moving on the spot, always leave one a little queasy. Like in all honesty, he was serving his guests spoilt meat.

I could almost be comfortable with its evocations of the Christ myth and of its personages. These are homey familiar images, a story told me over and over again in my childhood, and that, though I am not much interested in, slides off my back. But the dogma, though dead, has been long in decaying, the corpse stinks, and its poisonous miasma is infectious. And whether explicitly or by its use of Christian metaphors, Schumann's theatre, to varying extents, has conveyed the Christian death anxiety, asceticism and cult of guilt, and has grounded them in a distrust of and deep unease about natural man, though notably male man, in fear of if not in enmity toward him, and though not in a dismissal of the natural world, yet in a vitalistically pantheist bonification of it, that seems and to him apparently has seemed at least marginally Christian – Christian in the sense of the mystics, perhaps, if not of the scholastics.

7. Christianity teaches submission to power, guilt, fear of death, the rejection of the world and the taming of the flesh.

The Christian faith is ugly. Its message is aimed at the poor and what it tells them is to accept their lot. It is centered on guilt. And it exploits the fear of death. It is in all three regards a detriment to dignity. Underlying these ugly features is its rejection of the natural: its dismissal of nature and its enmity to natural man.

Nature does not exist in the New Testament, in the Old Testament it is merely something useful to man and demonstration of Jehovah's engineering capacities, in Christian theology it is the place of man's trial. Christian mystics, other than some Germans trespassing into pantheism, don't escape these constraints:

'Praised be my lord god with all his creatures and specially our brother the sun who brings us the day and who brings us the light: fair is he and shines with a very great splendor. O lord, he signifies to us thee.

Praised be my lord for our sister the moon and for the stars the which he has set clear and lovely in the heaven.

Praised be my lord for our brother the wind and for air and cloud, calms and all weather by the which though upholdest life in all creatures.

Praised be my lord for our sister the water who is very serviceable unto us and humble and precious and clean.

Praised be my lord for our brother fire through whom thou givest us light in the darkness and he is bright and pleasant and very mighty and strong.

Praised be my lord for our sister the earth, the which does sustain us and keep us and bringeth forth divers fruits and flowers of many colors and grass.

Praised be my lord for all who pardon one another for his love's sake and who endure weakness and tribulation: blessed are they who peaceably endure: for thou, o, most highest shalt give them a crown.

Praised be my lord for our sister the death of the body from which no man escapeth — woe to him who dieth in mortal sin. Blessed are they who are found walking by thy most holy will for the second death shall have no power to do them harm.

Praise ye and bless the lord and give thanks unto him, and serve him with great humility.'

Francis of Assisi, *Canticle of Created Things*, 1225, translated from the Italian by Matthew Arnold.)

Christianity attempts to bribe us into submission by an appeal to our fear of death. To not want to die is natural, and to know that one will is the spur of all ambition. But to dwell on one's death not only is morbid, shameful and futile, a waste of precious energy, but is a distraction from the fact (obscured by the leap of sexual reproduction) of one's continued existence in one's descendants. Attention to this fact, though also a kind of selfishness, not only is less ignoble than the wish that one oneself might live forever, it is a balance against fear of death and the wellspring of one of men's most admirable features – utopianism.

But the two features of the religion that I find most objectionable are its social pacifism – its instruction to the poor not to fight back – and its theory of sin: that to our guilt feelings there corresponds, as sin in a divine order (the real world behind the appearance of nature), real guilt.

Christian pacifism has consistently accommodated itself to war between nations; some closet casuistry apart, never even concerned itself with it; certainly has no record of opposition to it; but has a record of support covering the era of European expansion. It has instead been channeled toward the poor. The proneness of those disadvantaged by social arrangements to attempt to alter these or to circumvent them by crime or rebellion, even when not wise as – the balance of forces being what it is apt to be, and the obtaining social arrangements often being the best arrangeable – is often the case, is natural and often the only dignified and honorable thing to do. But this does not to the spokesman of Christianity excuse these tentatives. Only exceptionally have the gospels inspired rebellion; they have regularly served to endorse existing social order as god-willed, and the violence of repression has not impeded their use in support of it. The amorphous stance of Christianity against requiting violence by violence, which, in principle, applies as much to the violence that always and everywhere has upheld social order – and so war – in fact has been a stand against the counter-terrorist violence of the poor.

Guilt in its two forms of guilt of non-performance and guilt of transgression as interiorized social regulator, in the contexts of acculturation and sexual restraints peculiar to our species, instituted and set by family power structure, is obviously not a Christian invention. But Christianity (like Judaism) not only reenforces the guilt intrinsic to civilization and guilt's associates, shame and self-doubt, it attaches it to our natural drives and satisfactions (notably, but not only, of course, to sex and violence), enlarges its scope so that it comes to attach to everything naturally desirable, to life itself; and having pampered this hideous vampire, it urges us not just to live with it, but to make it our image and monitor: to reduce life for the sake of reducing guilt, and to direct its energy into repentance: for the sake of a phantasmagorical hope, repulsive in its selfishness, and of a phantasmagorical father.

. The mystery of our redemption by the blood of God's consubstantial son is not fortuitously clad in the metaphor of a son's tortured self-sacrifice to (and sacrifice by) his father, arch metaphor of repression of human nature, the bad habit that sons must overcome to be men, and though it is charmingly a mystery, has for its conceptual essence the affirmations (1) that our guilt is real and that we can never make up for it by ourselves and be quits, but are forever in debt: a vicious lie, if meaningful; but that (2) we should structure our lives into expiations of guilt: evil counsel. Christianity extends and brings to bear on the individual the Jewish burden of the broken covenant, and is, like Judaism, a gospel of guilt,[1] a depressing religion.

Schumann's art seems to me tainted by this pernicious mystery.

The accent on our guilt, the liberal view taken of what we should feel guilty about, the urging to focus on our guilt, the stress on our life's finitude implicit in the suggestion that we had better arrange for a good life later, and the advice to forget about our earthly life's hardships are all given sense by the dismissal of nature — the world — as mere background to our relations with one another and with god, to a moral life conceived as striving to be worthy of god's concern, an artful tapestry hung in the void, and by the identification of our natural self — violent, sexual, voracious — as our enemy. Contempt for the world and hatred of him/herself make the Christian: a dual hatred of nature.

---

1. Ernstthal on the topic of Schumann and free — guiltless — love:

'Like the "sexual revolution", so-called. In a way, sex lost. And probably he tried — but he could never — the thing is, he would never give up his guilt — because he would give up the mainspring of his art. Because our great stuff was all based on guilt: *Fire* was based on guilt, in a certain way. I mean, it was to depress people and to make people feel for the sacrifice of others. And all the stuff that was good was predicated on guilt and anxiety. And morality — and a finger pointing at everybody, saying: "Look at you, you fat pigs — while other people are starving." Best example was the *Eating and Drinking in the Year of Our Lord*, when the Pilgrims are there and we had that big feast at Spencer Church. Food was — just scarfing out like maniacs, right? And then this Vietnamese woman comes. What did she do? She turned the plates over or — you know, this kind of heavy handed trip. So Peter could never — he probably wanted to dabble in it but I think he could never get over his — the guilt.' — (Ernstthal, interview.)

'I think that Peter feels himself to have very, very human traits and part of those ... part of being human is that you will err, you will sin and you will do things that you might regret having done later but the flesh is weaker (Laugh) than the spirit. And I wouldn't exactly ... I mean he might feel ... I can't really say that he feels guilt .... I think he might feel sometimes sorry for pain or bad feelings he has inflicted on other people. I think he might feel very sorry for that but I think he, as far as his own personal guilt, he sort of has this attitude: that there are demons that live in me and live in all of us and they make me do things that sometimes I wish I wouldn't do, but I do them, so I can't help it so I'm not going to be guilty .... Yeah. There are things that make him do things so I don't really think he holds himself guilty but victim of his foibles .... I mean I think in his mind there's the constant fight between the good and the evil .... And I think he believes it exists in each person, that conflict. And so you're constantly fighting in yourself for the good to win.' — (Fernandez, interview.)

8. Nature in Schumann's theatre: Not the real McCoy. Life worshipped, clipped of its exuberance.

The effective stance of Schumann's theatre toward the natural world has varied. During the '60s, a mountain – a large, amorphous, grey mask – is the unregarding, mute witness of a crime (*Murder Mystery*, '64), the free world of the birds, victims of human voracity throws a vestment of blue on men and on men's demon torturers and pursuers (*Birdcatcher*, '65), River and Night – large puppets – appear as stately black agencies of courtship, also a flashlight moonbeam and a paper rose (*Leaf*, '65), and when this ethereal love turns into a farewell (*Dead Man Rises*, '67), a grey landscape (painted panels) is the backdrop. There was nothing particularly Christian about all this. It did not dismiss nature. It psychologized it. When finally (*Cry*, '69) Mother Earth appears (a giant puppet), it is as the mother of war, and life makes its entrance (having heretofore appeared only – *Pied Piper*, '65 – as the urbanite's pal, the rat) in piteous but terrifying form: as crawling toothed beast, incitement to the fatal human passion for domination.[1]

---

1. 'Und eine Sache, die wir, die hat mich immer bitter böse gemacht, das waren diese beasts. Weil ich, ich hab'n andres Natuverständnis, ich bin praktisch jahrelang durch die Gegend gezogen, mal hier, mal da. Ich bin aus ganz bestimmten Gründen, ich hab das aus ganz bestimmten Gründen gemacht. Ich hatte 'n Ziel, selbst, wenn ich ziellos gegangen bin. Ich mir morgens gesagt, so, wo biste denn heute, wa, bei Avignon, naja dann geh'n wir mal eben zu Fuss Richtung Chambery, dat ist ungefähr so 450 Kilometer weiter oder wat oder 'n bisschen weniger, ich weiss so nicht mehr. Und, naja, dann kriegt man Blasen an die Füsse, aber dat spielte alles keine Rolle, dat war äusserlich. Ich wollt, ich wollte Landschaften aufsaugen, Landschaften und Menschen, die wollt ich in mir sammeln, damit ich dann später alles verwenden kann. Und dat, dat is 'ne Arbeit. Ich hab das immer als Arbeit betrachtet und ich hab vor jedem Tag, den ich mit zuen Augen durch die Gegend gegangen bin, manchmal bin ich nämlich krank, ich bin Asthmatiker und wenn ich sowat kriege, dann is zu, dann bin ich zu, dann hab ich, dann kann mich nichts aufnehmen. Da hab ich, ich hab viel bemerkt. Ich hab über, ich hab 'n ganz andres Verständnis bekommen zu dem, wat man hier Natur sagt. Allein schon das Wort Natur stört mich, dat erinnert mich so an, ich weiss nicht an wat, an Doktor Ulrichs Fichtenberge oder irgendsowat. Die Deutschen mit ihrer Natur, ja, Lederhosen-Natur. Natur war für mich immer wat Magisches, wat ich mir nie ganz erklären konnte, und ich immer wusste, dat darin Geheimnisse liegen, die ich gerne wissen möchte, weil die für mich nützlich sind und weil die direkt wat mit'm Menschen zu tun haben. Und ich hab auch gemerkt, dat, dat bestimmte Dinge einen beeinflussen können, die man normalerweise als tote Gegenstände betrachtet. Und darin sind die Christen Meister. Ich hab mir immer, ich hab mir immer, ich hab zum Beispiel immer Tiere gehabt. Ich habe in'ner Eastside hab ich, hab ich Hunde gehabt. Der Peter war manchmal ganz verzweifelt, dann musst er meinen Hund anfassen, der hatte Junge gekriegt und so. Der konnte da nix mit anfangen. Die Elka auch nicht. Die konnten sich mit, die hatten 'n bestimmten Draht nicht. Ich kann, ich fahr 'ne Zeit und dann bin ich mit'm Tier 'n Kumpel, dann kenn ich das Tier ganz genau, das Tier kennt mich und dann sind wir gut in

In 1970, the year Schumann leaves the city for the country, a different perception of nature manifests itself, and nature becomes more important in his theatre. Heaving green hills in one play (*Difficult Life*) endorse the country in juxtaposition to the crowded city and provide a setting for fornication, woods and a wintry landscape in another (Grey *Lady Cantata II*) are a setting for death, and a white exhuberant tree on the light blue sky of a curtain (in *Lamentation, Mississippi*) figures as tree of life. In this year also, a lantern globe, then the sun, later the earth first appears among the theatre's symbols (in *Difficult Life*), as well as (in the summer circus) a large blue and white ship (with the tree of life for its sail), the Ark for All, evoking air and water, clouds and the foam of waves, and this year or next, white flower banners, large red, yellow and blue flowers done in a naive style. In '72, Schumann, for the first time, having never done so in his Easter shows, celebrates spring (*Marriage of the River Winooski*), celebrates the earth in a *Hallelujah* praising its beauty and bounty if properly used and warning against destructive misuse of it, and in a major play (*Simple Light*) commences the history of the world not with creation but with a 'geological' period, done with turbulences of black plastic, presents fighting against the backdrop of a winter tree and a half moon banner, and double-mask lovers in a night of shredded newspaper snowfall, a full moon mask rising. The heroine, representing the simple light that Schumann in this play sets against the darkness of crowds, of fighting and of the actions of leaders and of their followers, enters, accompanied by landscapes, parties with cutout clouds on sticks, survives a tempestuous sea voyage (the storm at sea a black tentacled octopus), a hurricane, metaphor for the destructive forces of commerce and war, and a passage through a dark frightening forest (the trees, masks on poles), inhabited by owls and fanged beasts. The play ends on the vision of a white carousel of noble animals, sheep. Nature as herself, not merely as metaphor or as spiritualized element of the life of the spirit, but as essential relatum of man, real in itself, positive and negative, thus

---

Fahrt, dann kann man 'ne Menge erleben. Dann lässt dat Tier zu, dat man reinstipst, dat man zum Beispiel auch mal 'ne Zeit selber Hund sein, grad 'n Hund sein, irgendwat und, und so entwickelt sich auch 'ne Ehrfurcht und 'ne Achtung. Und, und dat hat mich irgendwie nie gestört, sonst hätte, wenn der Peter so empfunden hätte, wie ich, dann wär er nie auf die Idee gekommen, diese, diese, die Massenproduktion von den Beasts aufzunehmen. Dat war ja 'ne richtige Massenproduktion, konnt er sich richtig dran berauschen, ja .... Die Dinger werden auch wieder 'ne symbolische Bedeutung haben. Da steht irgendwat sündhaftes drin, so schlecht und sündhaft. Ich konnte mit diesen moralischen Begriffen, da konnt ich nicht viel mit anfangen .... Wo ich mich jedes mal drüber geärgert habe, dat war die Beastszene, weil, weil ich 'n anderes Verständnis zur, zur Urmutter hab, zur Erde und zu allem, nicht. Für mich existiert kein Beast in dem Sinne. 'n Beast ist für mich die, die gestaltgewordene Grausamkeit des Menschen, das ist für mich 'n Beast. Sonst gibt es kein Beast – ich wüsste nicht, ich hab noch keins gesehen ....' — (Eckhardt, interview.)

suddenly enters Schumann's theatre during these transitional years 1970-1972. There is, again, nothing particularly Christian about this perception. On the contrary, it relates the 'good' to an existence of man in which he/she relates to nature.

A third approach emerges in 1974. Schumann now is his annual pageants, at least up to that of '78, these pageants being central to his work during this period, presents Nature not only as real relatum of man, but as the whole of reality, of which man is a part, and identifies its Life and Resurrection as the perpetual resurrection of Life from its recurrent conquest by Death. Life is the Good, and right action consists in supporting it, Death is Evil, and wrong action supports Death or kills, Death and Evil always but never finally win out over Life and the Good. These pageants are part of outdoor 'circuses,' the first two of which he presents in '70 and '71, but whereas these first two circuses, like certain other earlier shows (the park shows of '65 and '66, the '71 *Birdcatcher*) merely use the landscape as setting for the show, from '74 onward, with the pageants also only now becoming a distinct, important and separate element, the landscape, in the pageants, becomes part of the show. Typically, in these four circuses ('74-'77), the aforementioned *Hallelujah* is performed, there is a maypole dance around a giant benign female nature deity, the Domestic Resurrection Goddess, decked out in painted and real wild flowers, in grasses and reeds, and there is a profusion of animals (wild and domesticated), fantastic and comic ones in a pastiche of circuses that is part of the 'circus,' mostly white, gentle ones of a lyrically abstractive realist sort in the pageant part, e.g. white horses and white birds in the '74 circus. In the '74 circus these animals are, with giant white Indians, and various white females, the representatives of the forces of Life and Nature and of the Good, in a battle between the White and the Red (the forces of Hell). In the following three circuses, they figure in variants of a story (*The White Horse Butcher*) representing the violation of Nature/Life/ the Good by technological and commercial civilization. This treatment of Nature – during this period concentrated in the circuses and in particular in their pageants, pretty well absent in other shows – is not particularly Christian, it is un-Christian, perhaps even anti-Christian. It presents man as part of Nature, and defines morality in terms of role in natural process. A skit of '78 (*St. Francis Preaches to the Birds*, 'sideshow' in the '78 and '79 'circuses', and in that of '81, dedicated to St. Francis), defining the relation of man to natural creatures as one of siblinghood, is the last appearance of this view.

This explicit and central non-Christian presentation of man in Nature (other than by that evocation of St. Francis in '78) disappears from Schumann's work after '77. He still does the circuses, the white animals walk in his pageants, there is a maypole dance (in '78 and '82 around the female Nature deity, in '79 and '81 around a stern father God), but the landscape once again seems more background and setting than part of the show, and the pageants now deal with the destruction of the human community (given an agricultural and rural cast) by civilization (defined by commerce, technology and war). The productive reproduction, by the use of or out of Nature, of the family and the community, rather than Nature and rather than the relationship to Nature required for that reproduction, is now the focus, and the accent is on the danger to Nature, to that relationship, and to the family and the community, rather than on any of these. This is not a return to a Christian view, for man still appears as part of Nature and as in essence natural, e.g. a weird little ritual under the eye of the '82 Domestic Resurrection deity counterposes innocent play in Nature – or planting as play with Nature! – and harmonious refreshment by her to family and community in what seems a radical rejection of civilization and cultural order, but it is a reversal of the previous relationship between man and Nature: Nature now – for instance in a three-part parade, *Fight Against the End of the World* in '82 – is weak and in need of man's protection against the evil in man.

Nature, thus, after a period of only marginal appearance as negligible concomitant of man's emotional life and moral struggles, source of metaphor, itself metaphor of spirit, emerges in Schumann's work as important element, first as agreeable and appropriate setting and utility, next as reassuring matrix and, again, utility, finally as life-support and utility endangered by man: in a Christian perspective – if we discount the use of its Judaic identification as utility in Christian teleological arguments for God's existence – only in a first phase, and then only negatively, by its neglect; but what at first sight appears a definitely non-Christian or even anti-Christian, namely pantheist perspective in another phase, that of his Nature-celebrating circus pageants.

But this pantheism is itself neo-Christian: an anthropocentric and adynamic, formalist vitalism, not a glorification of Nature as reality independent of, greater then, overarching man, as embodiment of ontologically primary power, drive and force to which man relates only as incidental by-product. If we disentangle his – after initial neglect – persistent utilitarian respect for Nature – in and of itself not particularly Christian, but issuing into a neo-Christian moralist spiritualism: the 'man' its utility for whom makes it worthy of our esteem is not natural man but moral man – from other, less anthropocentric appreciation of it, we find an image of Nature as pacific assembly of graceful forms designed for self-reproduction but devoid of drive. Schumann's world of Nature totally lacks intrinsic dynamism. Life is its essence, but it is life without push. Life without exuberance, wildness or selfishness. The self-reproduction of this Nature is purely a matter of design: of harmony. For this design or harmony no reason appears: no reason in Nature. This is first of all a totally false image of Nature, and one that could only occur to a Christian.

Secondly, it in the Christian manner counterposes man, as by his free will sole source of evil, to intrinsically decent Nature. And thirdly, it does not displace Christian cosmology, but invites complementation by the Christian hypothesis of a benevolently patristic agency setting up Nature for the benefit of man (and for his own glory): as only conceivable explanation for that harmony and design.

The image of Nature in Schumann's pageants '74-'77 seems to substitute for the personal deity of the Christians a life principle. To the Christians, of course, this is a betrayal of Christ, and makes of Schumann a non-Christian. But it is a false image of Nature that could have occurred only to a Christian — to a Christian anxious to preserve his faith in a benign universe, morally legislative, yet charitable: made for man, affording a chance for redemption and actively making up for the ravages of man's free will.

Life is the fortuitous upshot of fact — of a deversification and scattering of matter happening to accord opportunities for its occasional combination into self-reproducing conglomerates. To the cerebrally organized among these conglomerates, this self-reproductive power seems good. But to stand in awe of this seeming goodness is merely to stand foolish conceitedness on its head: a fear-born anxiety reaction dressing conceitedness up in humility. To a non-Christian, a *reassuring* cosmic vitalism — one identifying life as good and as stronger than death, and so able to come up with a morality and some manner of 'hope' — is in essence Christian — and apt to be inspired by Christian faith. Whether Schumann '74-'77 proposed this vitalism in the spirit of a Pascalian gambler, and whether after '77 he lost faith in it is not clear. And in any event, the image of Life in Schumann's theatre is reductive: an appreciation of the stillness of its achieved forms, a fearful appreciation only of its conservative aspect of self-perpetuation, an unwillingness to accept its core: self-seeking antagonistic struggle.

What is missing in Schumann's theatre is the exuberance of Life. It itself is an instance of such exuberance — the many splendid diverse masks, the oppositional political stance, etc. But Schumann seems to deny it to others as though improper: Evil is in his masks the only thing exuberant — prolific, thunderous. With access to color. And he for himself apologetic: justified by moral purpose: if he is going to spread the word, doesn't he need effective puppets? Notice how simple the flowers are on his banners: modest, their color unsophisticated. And apology for his art — his own exuberance — seems essential to it: it presents itself as having high purpose and as being in the service of the public, a moral act, the contribution of a fellow citizen; and as of the simplest sort possible, not the production of a superior intelligence; as shaped only for the most effective presentation of a message that should be delivered; not as representative of him 'as an individual'; and as rough, not finished, imperfect; as well as impermanent, not made to last, of the moment: not for the sake of vanity. Its deliberate imperfections proclaim: I am only doing the minimum necessary to get my point across — proclaim an artist's restraint of his artistry. Just as Schumann's art disclaims its own wild, mad self-extrojecting and self-seeking exuberance, so it disclaims Nature's: reducing it to a paradigm of a Christian life.

9. Schumann on human nature:
Better repress it. Repressed human nature the ideal.

Schumann in his theatre over the last twenty years has with some shifts that may be only shifts of accent defined his position on human nature and on how life had best be lived in terms of three major dichotomies: the Good and the Evil, the People and the Others, Woman and Men. In an overall way, he identified the People and Woman with the Good, the individuals not of the People and Men generally with the Bad. Since the terms of the dichotomies are not congruent, this equation is slightly askew. Schumann's mind is on different tracks when thinking in terms of the People/Others than when thinking in terms of the gender dichotomy, and Good and Bad on the two tracks are not identified in quite the same way. Furthermore, his work deviated a little from the position indicated during a quasi-revolutionary period '69-'72 and perhaps his position wavered during an apocalyptic period starting at the end of the '70s; and a personal elitism, defined on the one hand by contempt for, sometimes, around '72 (*Simple Light*) almost a horror of, sometimes (in the '82 circus), a basic unease with respect to the People, on the other hand by a Romantic elevation of the Artist, qualifies and perhaps contradicts that basic position. But to the extent his work is consistent with the equation, it works out as endorsement of repression — self-repression. In this respect it can be considered neo-Christian.

In Schumann's theatre, '63-'83, there have appeared on the one hand a variety of fantasy figures, legendary, mythological, symbolic — God, Christ and his disciples, Mary, angels, devils, skullmen, demons, dragons — imaginations of womanhood varying the image of Mary, some more oriental, some more Germanic, some more ordinary woman, some more lady — as well as animals, on the other, more or less abstractive and symbolic or more realistic figures representing people or classes or types of types of people. The general development was toward an increased individuation of these during the '80s. His people figures have provided a theatrical anthropology, abstractly foreshadowed by and in terms of social and gender roles specifying a view of the condition of humanity presented by symbolizing fantasy figures. Though all of Schumann's theatre has addressed us in moral terms, its message has been on two levels, a more metaphysical, neither pre- nor pro-scriptive one concerning the Human Condition, conveyed by sculpture and movement abstractly, and a more clearly ethical one, conveyed by roles and story, in more specific terms. It is this latter, Schumann's theatrical anthropology, I am here concerned with. Its significant divisions are by gender and by relation to power.

Setting aside the gender division, humanity in his shows divides into the People (ordinary people, the common man, the mass of humanity),

Rulers, where sometimes a relatively innocuous reigning authority is distinguished from a violent ruling one, rulers' agents – expert advisers, representing the intellect, not unlike the fiscal court Jews of the Middle Ages; salesmen-ideologues, agents of corporate rule; technician-bureaucrats; guardian torturers – and insurgent individuals: Artists and Resistance Fighters, these latter partly identified with youth, Sir Galahads, St. Georges, partly with Woman and the People, Joans of Arc.

The People – a traditional and modern though not contemporary category – first crops up as the white-headed stick puppets hurrahing the Great King's decision to make war in the *Great King Makes War* ('62/'63) and afraid of the Dragon in *King Story I* ('63/'64) and then killed by the Great Warrior, and as the funny little Punch and Judy derived stick and hand puppets that in the *Christmas Stories* of the '60s refuse Mary shelter and save or try to save the Innocents, their children or wards, from slaughter, later (*When Johnny Comes Marching Home*, '68) show up as the equally small paper maché 'Johnny' dolls, individuals or couples, stout and homely, patriotic homebodies and beer guzzlers, in both guises obviously, definitely *manipulated*. In a play of '69, by its title an indictment of them, *The Cry of the People for Meat*, the People, done by unmasked performers, appear only in a brief scene, *The Birth of the People of the World*; as a beast-born mass of zombies in which the women are helped to move by the men: sinful humanity before the flood. This darker, elitist and paranoid view of them is again expressed in '72 (*Simple Light*): the People are represented by dark-hooded crowds and large multiple-face crowd masks. But by '74 they emerge in a new, less morbid, though not too flattering guise, as dour garbagemen, unwilling and dumb workmen, played by masked, workmen-dressed performers, a little later ('77 ff.) complemented by robust, cheery washerwomen, charmless, but nice, also masked, costumed performers, but soon appearing in an idealizing format, as giant puppets. The washerwomen, representing both The People and Woman, even (*Washerwoman Cantata – Ah!*, '78), though only in a humorous and fairy tale way, engage in a little bit of activism – resistance, though at the same time (*Washerwoman Cantata Nativity*, '78) we see them passively submitting to Herod's murder of their children. They are in any event far from having the grandeur of Joyce's washerwomen, as far as from the squalor and toughness of Zola's or Picasso's laundresses.[1] As for

---

1. Schumann intended both his garbagemen and his washerwomen to be positive images! The former were modeled on the Goddard College janitors whom he claimed he liked, the latter – I would say – on his wife, possibly also on some other non-People people, Grace Paley, Mabel Dennison, friends of the family's.
'The garbagemen idea came from these Goddard College garbagemen, from the maintenance crew at Goddard College, and the first one I made was really a portrait of the Goddard College maintenance men. And they were good-natured and we liked them and

popular resistance: the only time the People in Schumann's theatre actively opposed power was in some performances, '69-'71, of *King Story* in which the People rises and kills the Great Warrior: a change of this play quasi-imposed on Schumann by his group and soon abandoned by him.

The People's (and Woman's) terrorization by the violence of aggressive war has been the theatre's main subject throughout its existence in an almost continuous way — fading out a little during the last two years of the U.S. engagement in Vietnam, '72, '73. '63/'64 he experimented with remembrances of World War II and apocalyptic visions (in which Man revenges God on Man); during the '60s and up to the '71 *Birdcatcher*, dedicated to a small-time terrorist (as of this writing most popular of the salesmen in his father-in-law's jewelry store in Columbus, Georgia) in the employ of the U.S. government making war on women and children, his theatre in the streets and indoors focused on the U.S. engagement in Vietnam, portraying it as war on a population and chiefly on women and

---

they were very nice people so we wanted that characteristic in them.' — (Schumann, interview, '82.)

Hoagland, whose perception of them (*Let 'em Have*, '83) derives from the '82 circus, sees the garbagemen as:

'grotesque ... with slackened cheeks like victims of Bell's palsy, who represent the ravages of the Industrial Revolution':

'Schumann's exemplary human beings are his Garbagemen and Washerwomen, who are worn mostly as masks and puffed stomachs by assistants and who look like thirty-year veterans of difficult marriages, of cold northern winters and tedious employment. They move with a joyless slowness, buttoned into bruise-colored faces afflicted with stoicism, with beer bellies of defeat, dull labor, and impoverishment.

"Don't run. Never run! You're Garbagemen!" Schumann shouted in rehearsals. Work as such has no nobility in his cannon, and for ten years or so the Garbagemen have been carrying out a variety of maintenance and cleanup chores (sometimes very grisly cleanups) in his pageants and circuses. The men of affairs — businessmen, newspaper readers in dark suits and ties — who plague and exploit them, brutalizing even their children, do get some pleasure from "working", but it is only an evil delight. The Washerwomen, with their downcast eyes and dented foreheads, their lantern jaws and mannish noses — created as unenviable helpmeets and coequals to the Garbagemen in 1977 at the time of a surge in the women's movement were preceded by many Gray Ladies who ironed or mopped their way through presentations he calls "cantatas."...

Also, he created his first Garbagemen from the model of the college's maintenance crew in their green coveralls and caps, with frigid-seeming Vermont faces and a dairy farmer's matter-of-fact equanimity in the face of pregnancy and birth and death. Handy at any task, these early Garbagemen were rather sinister, compared with the present Glover variety. They never initiated evil doings — evil ideas were the province of the businessmen in suits and ties. But with an insignia on their cap bills that looks like a broken-tailed swastika or two crossed hammers, these country men could be roused from passivity to carry out any ugly job that might be suggested, like throwing babies into wheelbarrows or cleaning out a gas chamber. In the fresh glimpse he had got of his new country setting, he didn't yet see the local people through rose-colored glasses; he could have recognized, for instance, that Vermont country boys would be as likely as any other Americans to perpetrate a My Lai massacre.' — (Hoagland, ibid.)

children, from '74 to '79 his pageants took up the theme in a generalized way, from '80 (*This is*) onward, humanity's impending nuclear mass suicide is a major theme.

Repressive terror, the state's war on the home population, though discernible during the '60s (the Great Warrior's slaying of the People in *King Story*, Herod's baby-extermination project in the *Christmas Story*), after first emerging as central theme in a special context, Black repression '70-'73 (*Mississippi*, '70, the various versions of *Attica*, '71-'73), became a major theme in a somewhat general form only '77-'81: the terror of a revolutionary state in *Masaniello*, '77/'78, and in *Cambodia*, '80, terror per se – though clearly still a state's – not as in Francisco Goya's *Disasters of War*, undistinguishably the terror of an occupying army and the population's insurgent counter-terror – in *Goya*, '81. And, with reference to the treatment of the Indians in the U.S., state terrorism, here indistinguishable from its twin, aggressive war, faintly emerges in the circus pageants, '74-'76 or so.

War, terrorization of another people – or war when it is this: one may read into his *Simple Light* of '72 and '76 circus, his '82 circus pageant a tolerance of the violence of 'old-fashioned' battle-field-fought non-imperialist war between nations of equal strength – has been one of four species of violence Schumann's theatre has dealt with, the other three being terrorization of a people by its own state, the violence of resistance movements (*A Man*, '67, *Reiteration*, '68, *Cry*, '69), and the senseless violence of troubled poor people (*McCloud*, '72, *Woyzeck*, '81, *Diagonal Man*, '82.)

Schumann's stand on violence is defined by his distinction of violence exerted by the state, the holders of authority and power, whether in aggressive wars or against their own populations, from all other violence (resistance against that violence, individual violence), by the overwhelming preponderance in his work of the indictment of that repressive violence exerted by the powerful over positions on the other types of violence, and by his amalgamation of state violence at home and abroad into one type of violence, terrorization of a people and finally, in last place only, by a general abhorrence of violence. E.g., attacked on peace parades, he would not fight back. He would not hit his children: he would shut them up in the toilet for bad language – such as 'fuck you.' (Eckhardt, interview.) His position on resistance by counter-violence has been ambiguous, tending to a forgiving attitude, verging on endorsement. Individual, apolitical violence he has presented as regrettable but incidental, a response to social pressure. Furthermore, his indictment of the state's war on the people has consistently distinguished the proximate perpetrators of this violence – who, after all, are common men, the sons of the people – from the real responsibles, the rulers and their enterprising servants. The former, soldiers, police, prison guards, are not exactly absolved, but they appear as dehumanized tools of war or as bumbling slobs, not as beasts – Herod's soldiers in his *Christmas Stories* being examples of both, the soldiers in his '60s peace parades more of the former. They appear not as evil men, but as men acting under the pressure of circumstance – e.g. the son in *A Man Says*, or Lt. Calley in *Birdcatcher* – essentially themselves victims, like those small-time killers actuated by passion, despair or brutish self interest.

(Alienation, perhaps foreshadowed by *Consumer Cycle* rituals in the '70 and '71 circuses, emerges as a major theme in '81/'82 (the circus pageants of '81 and '82, *Story*, '81). Schumann links it to violence: it is the People's alienation that enables the State to sell it on war. Schumann's preoccupation with violence and the state prevented him from ever dealing with it, in its linkages with consumerism and the division of labor as an independent major theme.)

The evil ones in his theatre have been the People's rulers, of whom Herod is the archetype, other exemplars being Presidents Johnson (Uncle Fatso in the '60s parades, sometimes the Red Devil) and Nixon (the King of Hell in the '71 *Birdcatcher*), and the revolutionary dictator Masaniello in the '77 *Masaniello*. (In his earliest anti-war play, *King Story*, the ruler, the King, is not so much evil as foolish: the Great Warrior whom he calls in is evil, but he represents war itself, not the military.) The image of rulers is that of ruthlessly raging men, angry at heart, passionately selfish, infinitely irritated by opposition, moved by hunger for power, perhaps by fear.

The rulers in his theatre tended to have advisers, bespectacled academi- not unlike Henry Kissinger (*King Story, Christmas Story, Chicken Little*), agents of evil but fearful, mean and foolish rather than evil: perverters of intellect. After a while other types of agents of evil appeared, still related to state power, '75 following the 'Butchers', '81 and following, the 'Salesmen', the former insensitive and dumb looking, the latter foolishly clever, the former brutal despoilers, the latter insidious defrauders, both definitely businessmen, but with a bureaucratic and sometimes even military aura, and not commercial enterprisers, but employees. Both are aggressive – enterprising. The violence of the butchers is primarily technological, they are the engineers of progress, that of the salesmen primarily commercial, they are its salesmen, neither is in the least passionate, in a rage, or even angry. They are not innocents, however, there is malice in them, a hatred of and a contempt for innocence and the natural. Only the salesmen are agents of war, the butchers represent the despoilers of nature in a bureaucratic-commercial-technological civilization.

The People appears as the terrorized and alienated victim of power, power being largely identified with the state. Two other themes, distinctly minor in the theatre, complement this theme: one which all in all we can probably characterize as a theme of escape, that of the Artist, and the theme of resistance, that of the Resistance Fighter.

Johnny puppets, paper mache figures 6–12 inches tall, first used in *When Johnny Comes Marching Home*, 1968.
(Photo: B. Brown)

Johnny puppets, 1968.
(Photo: R. Bellak)

Johnny puppets, 1968.
(Photo: H. Widmer)

The Crucifixion,
Spencer Memorial
Church, 1966.
(Photos:
R. Joyce)

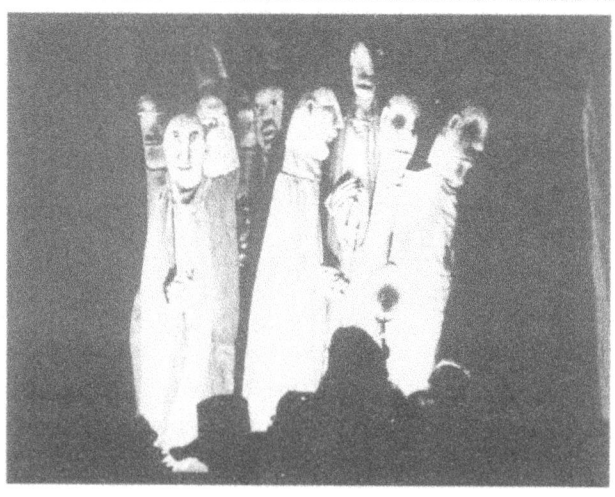

The Crucifixion, 1968.
(Photo: P. Moore)

Rinaldini, The Great Robber, crankie with male and female choruses, December 8, 1967.
(Photo: F. McDarrah)

Anti-Vietnam War Peace March near Washington Square Park, March 6, 1965.
(Photo: F. McDarrah)

Street rallies,
New York City,
1965.
(Photos: R. Joyce)

Street rallies, New York City, 1964–65.
(Photos: R. Joyce)

In support of latino housing agitation, Peter Schumann, Lower East Side, November 30, 1964.
(Photos: R. Joyce)

First of the Fifth Avenue Peace Parades, October 16, 1965.
(Photos: F. McDarrah)

First of the Fifth Avenue Peace
Parades, October 16, 1965.
(Photos: F. McDarrah)

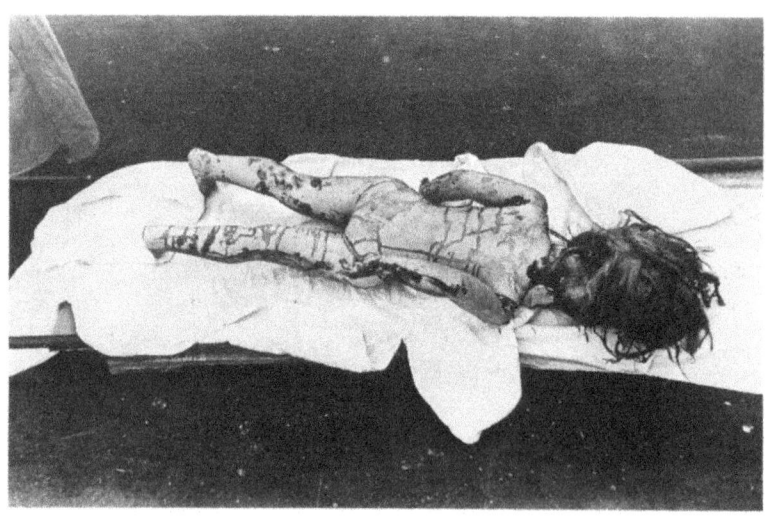

The Resistance Fighter, one might have thought, would be a major figure in Schumann's theatre, and — as in Hölderlin's *Hyperion*, a book focusing on the Resistance Fighter's disappointment in the People — the true incarnation of ideal humanity. This may be Schumann's secret feeling, but the fellow hardly appears in his theatre. The Resistance Fighter was represented by the young, male and female, unmasked operator-performers of *Cry* who constructed the Christ with Gun of that play — a broken gun, apparently — by the prankishly homicidal children of the '75 circus skit, *Uncle Fatso Play*, by the child that overcomes its fears in the '82 *Fear*, perhaps by the '76 Mountain Man of Chile, in the circus sideshow of that name, or by the Salvadorean guerilla fighter in an '81 sideshow called *Goya*. But most importantly the Resistance Fighter has appeared as Woman: the nurse or day care supervisor trying to protect the Innocents from Herod's soldiery in some of the *Christmas Stories*, the woman that perhaps kills the soldier that killed her son in *A Man* ('67) and *Reiteration* ('68), perhaps the heroine of his '77 *Joan of Arc*, the washerwoman of his first *Washerwoman Cantata* ('79), the women in *Seven Obsessions* ('81). These women are the true heroes of Schumann's theatre.

Though for a moment, '68/'69, Schumann's — or perhaps only the Bread and Puppet Theatre's — position is equivocal, neither resisting youth nor the Woman Resistance Fighter employ violence: they put up some other kind of resistance, the nebulousness of which the '82 *Fight Against the End of the World* parade illustrated.

Schumann as the proper form of resistance fighting seems to have in mind propaganda against the evils besetting the People, war and alienation: exemplified by his own activity, but not necessarily in artistic form. Such propaganda, if I read his images aright, is to be coupled with spiritual self-purification and subsistence-activity, both forms of personal resistance to alienation. His portrayal of the People — object of the propaganda — and of the powers of the forces promoting war and alienation make it seem highly doubtful whether this resistance fight could have any impact at all. Resistance therefore effectively seems to come down to that personal resistance: which in and of itself is simply withdrawal.

Schumann's view of the Artist is the Romantic view and is carried, first of all, by the image, from the beginning till now, of himself in his shows as narrator, announcer and fiddler, hirsute, gnomish, charming and in good shape, with no touch of the carney or con man, but a 19th century European cliché of the wandering artist close to a bum; by his portrayals of the poet and musician Wolkenstein, a prototype of this cliché, in the '78 *Wolkenstein*, as a miserable egoist, torn between the good and the bad, but of course as artist presumably one of mankind's benefactors, ray of light in the vale of tears; of the artist Goya in his '81 *Goya* as observant recorder of the horrors mankind inflicts upon itself, profoundly dejected by them; of Josephine in his '84 *Josephine the Singer* as an irritable, self-centered bitch, totally concerned only with being shown the adoration due her gifts, unmindful of the sufferings of humanity; and of Michelangelo in his *Ineffective Man – Dream Woman* ('82) as a depressed and troubled individual, only occasionally erupting into creative work; and his sympathetic portrayal of the misfit (not an artist, though he may have started out Michelangelo) in his '82 *Diagonal Man*, a man so repelled by role-playing, he ends up with the role of the bum, whom Schumann presents as in contra-distinction to the run of humanity at least half alive. That the Diagonal Man to Schumann represents the artistic type is supported by the image of puppeteers as vagrants in certain of his manifestos. These images are all confessions more than exhortations to emulation.

The Artist appears, then, as observer, horrified by the People's suffering, as self-concerned sinner, performer for the great as social misfit, tortured by society's demand for conformity. Art appears as successful refusal to be victimized or alienated. The Artist appears as morally dubious and unhappy individual.

Rather clearly, Schumann does not advise us to try for a withdrawal into art. Rather clearly, also, though on inspection this turns out apt to be another kind of withdrawal, though one graced by a conscience-absolving gesture he advises us to become Resistance Fighters. But the Resistance Fighter is not an opponent of authority per se. He/she is an opponent of power used in violence, specifically: a defender and would-be-savior of the People. The People – the mass of humanity – a bunch of dumb, spineless slobs though they might be – is to be our object of concern – as, incidentally, according to the Rulers and their ideologues, they have always been the Rulers' objects of concern. The People is the Resistance Fighters' raison d'etre.

As I read Schumann's message in re the People, taking into account that he is addressing his theatre to the People, not to what has mostly been his actual audience, it is:

'I, Schumann, through my theatre make jovial fun of you, allow you to see I think I am above you, am quite critical of you in certain respects, on occasion ('69-'73) have even, thinking of you as The Crowd, The Masses, fallen into paranoid fantasies about you, and of late have been telling you outright that I'm not sure any more you are who I thought you were. You may discount some of this as a foolish puppeteer's attempt to entertain you: some of it as the perverse arrogance of an Artist. Some of it is didactic in intent – forgive my presumption! Actually, you, the People, are O.K. More: you live the ideal life – once we discount the distortions wrought by war, terror, commerce and technology, as well as, let's admit it, some not so pretty habits and tendencies, unfortunately, but in the last analysis, let us hope, not disastrously apt to creep into your life, exaggerations of your very virtues. I commend you, the People, for your conscientiousness and your industry, your respect for and many kindnesses to others, your attachment to home, family and community, your peaceableness, your decency and fairness, you care for law and order and of the rights of others, and your solicitous love for the fruit-bearing earth and its animals and seasons, for the natural world in which you live and that sustains you.'

>   Mich aber unsummet
>   Die Bien, und wo der Ackersmann
>   Die Furchen machet, singen gegen
>   Dem Lichte die Vögel. Manche helfen
>   Dem Himmel. Diese siehet
>   Der Dichter. Gut ist es, an andern sich
>   Zu halten. Denn Keiner trägt das Leben allein.
>   (F. Hölderlin, *Die Titanen*.)
>   Nämlich immer jauchzet die Welt
>   Hinweg von dieser Erde, dass sie die
>   Entblösset, wo das Menschliche sie nicht hält.
>   (F. Hölderlin, *Der Einzige*.)

The virtues listed have characterized the People in his theatre. They are of a sort to entail submission to authoritative power, support of its wars and other schemes, seduction by its technology and commercial blandishments. But in and of themselves they define the good life and are paradigmatic for humanity.

Just as in fact he has only occasionally and to a relatively minor extent managed to have the People for this audience – of his '60s street parades for peace, of his Coney Island shows in '70 and '72, of his circuses in northern Vermont, '76 ff. – i.e. has designed his theatre for a desired but largely fictive audience, so the People appearing in it and to which it is addressed is to some extent a non-existing fabricate: an amalgam of long-gone German burghers and U.S. farmers and small town folk, and in any event has excluded large sections of the actual People – the population of the large cities, much of the industrial working class. But fictitious or not, and however exclusive, it has served Schumann to convey his ideal of human existence.

Or part of it: an idealization of Woman complements the theatre's idealization of the People.

Woman first appears in his theatre as the Mary in his '60s *Christmas Stories*, the nurturing mother, persecuted by power, shielding her son. His peace parades of the '60s extended this image to Vietnamese peasant women and mothers, with or without babies, bombed or strafed. She reappears in *Fire* ('66), with the added character of non-violent – self-immolating – Resistance Fighter (no son in evidence) and in the '67 *A Man Says Goodbye to His Mother*, as mother losing her son to war. *Reiteration* ('68) puts the propriety of her resistance in question. The peace parade image of passively suffering women persists with only slight alterations through the early '70s: the mother has become Germanic rather than oriental (Grey Lady puppet rather than Vietnamese Woman), and now appears also as wife doing household chores (*Emilia*, '71 or courageous mainstay of the household (*Simple Light*, '72), as well as dutifully obedient daughter, acquiescing in her father's immolation of her (*Jephtha*, '74). From first signs, '75-'78, that independence from men, even opposition to them, and perhaps objectives other than their nurture might be compatible with proper womanhood (*Grey Lady Cantata #6*, '75, *Dirty Woman's Dream*, '75, *Joan of Arc*, '77, *Wolkenstein*, '78, *Masaniello* in which the mother disavows her killer son, '78), an idealized image of robust, cheery, self-assured, independent and active Woman emerges in '79-'81 (the first *Washerwoman Cantata*, '79, *Story of Bread*, '80, *Woyzeck* and *Seven Obsessions*, '81). This Woman is still child-raiser and homemaker, however, her basic function — in which she is now allowed or even required to exercise independent, energetic initiative — still support of the male. *Diagonal Man* ('82) makes this clear: though man needs Woman to help him, he is the creative one — for good and bad. The circuses of the early '80s make it clear that her role is in the family.

Significantly, I think, the gestures of love — of tenderness or attachment — not only between husband and wife but also between mother and child are missing in this theatre. Woman is source, nurtrice, protectress, but not lover or loving.

Men in relation to Woman appear partly — marginally, but importantly — as the victimizers — soldiers, rulers, butchering technocrats (the variants of *White Horse Butcher*, '75-'78), lecherous and inconstant lovers (cf. infra), partly as dependents — sons — protected by her, nurtured. No ideal figure of Man, corresponding to that of Woman, appears in the theatre. But a type image appears because the Rulers and their servants are men, as is the Artist. This type is predominantly negative. While Woman in this theatre incorporates and is defined by both the basic form of creatively, namely fertility (consider in contrast the pitifully vicious legend of Eve's creation from Adam), and the basic form of aid, namely maternal childnuture, men are primarily characterized as destructive, selfish and competitively antagonistic, and only secondarily or even just incidentally as — culturally — creative: a creativity that Schumann's images of the Artist and of the evils of civilization render suspect, make seem ultimately perhaps destructive. It would not be saying too much that Woman in this theatre appears as representative of basic life force, of the natural good itself — of fertile nurturing Nature, as deification of which the faintly smiling 'Domestic Resurrection Goddess' has presided over some, though not all of the circuses, '75 ff. — while men appear as typifications of a basic death force: the two forces conceived, however, as interdependent and — in a world conceived as process — complementary.

Eroticism, carnal love, sexual drive have been virtually absent from

Schumann's theatre. The chief exception to this cluster '70/'72: as though in a release of the quasi-revolutionary energies gathered '68/'70: a scattering of small paper maché copulations – the image of fornicators on a heaving springtime hill, apt symbolization of sexual passion as prime form of the life force,[2] but very discrete – two or three young women naked on the stage, some sculptures of naked women. He would drily refer to the paper maché copulators as 'copulating couples' – 'wie bei 'ne Bullenzucht." (Eckhardt, interview.) Carlene Fernandez thinks he would have gone further in this direction except for Elka.

There are little comic books by Schumann with copulations in them and his beautiful woodcut print book *White Horse Butcher* of '77 has a sequence of cuts of a female body, young and slender, small-breasted, that express erotic passion with the intensity of 'lyricism': not the mind's fake passion of romantic love, mask of impotence or seduction, nor the comfortable density of feeling between partners in compulation: not attachment, but drive. But the book as a whole seems expression of guilt – expression of an unwillingness to be tied, of resulting feelings of having misused another person. This complex of feelings appears also and more explicitly in the sculptures of the '80/'81 *Chapel of the Condemned* (horny demons and their female victims), but in his theatre only in the costumes of the '71 *Birdcatcher*, i.e., his theatre condemned erotic passion during the same brief period when it faintly commended it by a faint positive expression of it.

What briefly and furtively emerged in those sculptures and prints was an image of man as lecher, and as by his lechery a victimizer of women. Male lechery in the sexual area parallels male violence in the political and male technical and commercial ingenuity in the economic area. That concupiscent love for Schumann ranks with fighting and with commercialized

---

2. '(I: Naked couples in *Uncle Fatso?*) Small ones and big ones, yes ... it was an explosion of, for me, saying, where are all these tits and asses coming from ... he was creating a large number of naked ladies, all very voluptuous and all very much Elka Schumann, I assumed ... it's the first time I remember them. And I remember that they all looked like – at that point, now, I'm saying to myself, he's fucking all these young girls – or some of them – or one of them – or whatever – and yet he is making naked ladies that are all Elka Schumann. Huge bottoms, thighs, breasts – and obviously he had an eye for a nice young maiden. Then, you remember there was the presentation of the Vermont landscapes and he carried a naked lady, Anique Detolle, on his back. I was shocked .... The hill shakes – the earth moves. And then the actual naked woman, which I thought was very shocking. And then I don't remember anything else until I went up (to Cate Farm in '70 (SSB)) and found these very large reliefs that were four feet high of naked women – very – nipples – (in the *Vermont Papermaché Cathedral* (SSB)). I don't remember any eroticism except those – that one moment (when) the earth actually shook when they were fucking – then the one naked woman, which was an erotic kind of thing – she turned – she was a symbol, but it wasn't even a symbol of eroticism, somehow. It wasn't erotic. So, we're back only to this one moment of fucking. And then afterwards, these relief forms. I don't remember any eroticism in any of the shows.' — (Ashley, interview.)

and/or industrialized life as evil, and as evil to which men are powerfully tempted is something he has refrained from putting in his theatre, perhaps because it is the one evil to which he has been powerfully attracted himself: but it is an essential feature of his position.

The frank sex stuff, '70-'72, was exceptional. there was a moment of tenderness between Adam and a very chaste Eve in '69 (*Cry*). Love between the sexes was the theme of the '65 *Leaf Feeling the Moonlight*, but is here a matter of the poetry of adoration and courtship; when in its derivative, *Dead Man Rises* ('67), a man and a woman go to bed together, the cohabitation seems ambiguously a suicide pact or other union in death; the lovers in *Simple Light* ('72) are tragic and as nighttime creatures put in analogy to fighters; carnal desire in the '81 *Woyzeck* is betrayal and a prelude to murder, and its consummation a tragic scene, and in the *Goya* of '81, seduction turns into rape and murder. Except a little, for that brief period, the sex drive has been censored out of Schumann's theatre; when it appears, it is a destructive force. Schumann's repression of the sex drive both in the image of Man offered by his theatre, and in its ideal of Him/Her precisely parallels the absence of drive, power, force in his image of Nature. This shows it's not just due to prudery, let alone Elka's censorship. Rather it's a matter of generalized timidity: for which drive: exercise of power and force – is Bad and the Good is form. Since Schumann is not timid – his drives are strong and he is driven – this is a matter of principle.

The ethical implications of the theatre's image of Man's sexual dichotomy are largely the same as those of its image of Man's social dichotomy (People/Rulers): the good life is lived in performance of duty dictated by man's integration into the life cycle of Nature and requiring self-restraint and self-denial. They go beyond them by a more positive accent on the social nature and unselfishness of this life, its character of giving – Woman is essentially generous, whereas the People is not.

What is absent in this ethics are any roles for passion and play and for their most intense form, the activity of intelligence. On the contrary: it advises us to curb the exuberance of life. E.g.: as violence, whether in resistance of otherwise, and as sexual passion.

Why self-restraint and self-denial? The theatre's answer to this question is given by its anthropological images of the bad, of men, of the possessors of power and authority. They are bad precisely because they reject restraint and wish to deny themselves nothing. For proneness to violence, to lechery, to the prideful play of the intellect in commerce and technology, the passions for domination of others and of nature, for sexual possession, for being better than others are parts of human, though especially male, nature, not the vices of a few. They thus require self-restraint, and, since their restraint does violence to human nature so that their restraint involves loss, self-denial. The good life has to be a stunted life.

The sweetness of a great feeling for ordinary people, for mothering woman and for little children has suffused the productions of the Bread and Puppet Theatre. It has equally been suffused by a great sadness at the hardships and sufferings these same parties have perennially been exposed to, and by a harshly tragic sense of the native power of death over human life, the lives of individuals, of peoples and perhaps of humanity. These are the three dominant strains. In conjunction they have engendered an almost petty stance in favor of self-repression and against exuberance.

The position outlined seems to me close to the Christian one, or at least easily confounded with it, especially when presented in the context of Christian iconography and myth. Close to and easily confounded with not so much gospel morality based on disdain for the world, but its ecclesiastic – medieval – reinterpretation, appreciating the natural man's proclivity to transgressions and perversions of the divine order.

In both cases, in the end, there is an uneasy suspicion of people as they are, a fearful awareness of human nature, a view of man as prone to evildoing and as corruptible; an ideal of a simple human life in which these tendencies are kept in check; and an accent on inhibition and restraint.

In their detail and underpinnings, the two ideologies differ toto coelo. The church supported temporal authority, Schumann opposes it as primary source of evil. The church played with the notions of original sin, salvation, redemption, we don't find any of this in Schumann's theatre. Schumann hides his guilty distrust of human nature in an appreciation of the People and Woman that fictionalizes their repressed condition as the simplicity of an elemental naturalness; the Church tended to see the People and Woman as particularly prone to corruption and most in need of control by itself and by temporal authority. The church saw Natural Man as prone to evil, Schumann by that fiction is able to represent him/her as good.

But in the end the two moralities are very similar: their central injunctions: Beware of your proneness to evil! Restrain yourself! Don't let your passions and appetites, your imagination, your intellect run away with you! Keep things simple and traditional: beware of innovation and daring enterprise!

Both in the end are conservative moralities of guilt and cowardice.

The neo-Christian ethics of Schumann's theatre is animated by (and his theatre conveys) a high respect for life and for human life in particular. But by its cautionary accent it is repressive. Hypocrisy, transgression and guilt would be rampant in any group or society professing it, the only alternatives to depression. His theatre's projection of the natural order that it in preference to the Christian divinely ordained one hypostasizes, unlike the Christian one's, is an incitement to action changing the status quo. But the timidity his ethics counsels weakens the incitement. It makes all action, political or artistic, seem fraught with danger: both to the agent and to others: ethically dubious.

10. The beauty of Schumann's position. A eulogy of saintliness in the historical perspective of the restrained poor and weak and the unrestrained rich and powerful.

Christianity has for nearly 2,000 years pressed the ideals of pacifism and asceticism on the laboring poor; in the context of a religious ideology presenting them as means of salvation, of an improvement of a 'soul' and for this improved 'soul's' eternal blissful life. Not only has this employment of them made them odious, especially when presented in the context of Christian references (as by Schumann), but the abstemious and pacific person idealized in terms of them in this employment, whether oaf or hypocrite, is repulsive: conflicted to the point of hysteria, mean and grim, self-righteous, and simply deprived, a poor kind of human being, stunted and deballed.

On the other hand, human life since it based itself on agriculture has divided into the perforce abstemious and relatively pacific life of the laboring poor and the self-indulgent and violent life of their exploiters, the unhappy constrained restraint of the ones, a brutish, uncivilized state, confronting the grotesque over-indulgences and aggressive brutalities of the others, also a brutish, uncivilized state. Relative to this historical reality, pacifism and asceticism outline policies of restraint, of gentleness and self-denial, for the poor defining the ideal of saintliness, for the privileged that of the gentleman (lady). Gentlemanliness, a privileged condition, is of no concern to Schumann, but his theatre can be viewed as celebration of saintliness.

Saintliness is a consistent rendering of direct services to individuals other than oneself, rendered them for their sake, not one's own, not injurious to third parties, and at a gross real cost to oneself, obvious to oneself, approximating a total sacrifice of oneself, and involving the choice of the advantage of those others in preference to one's own advantage.

It is not something one can in good taste recommend to others. Recommending it to the poor is obscene. Its practice is unavailable to the well-off: living comfortably is by definition incompatible with saintliness: it requires relinquishing the ordinary amenities of life, if necessary even the necessities. But the poor can and not infrequently do act in a saintly manner – to the point of approximating saintliness.

The people canonized by the Roman Catholic Church tend not to be saints at all, but martyrs to the faith and/or deserving servants of the Church. But these ecclesiastic deceptions aside, Christian saintliness differs from genuine saintliness, is a pseudo-saintliness, because the Christian saint's goodness expresses itself in sacrificial services in the salvation of souls, and only incidentally and instrumentally in actually doing something for their supposed possessors, and is in any event nullified either by the pseudo-saint's Christian egoism, viz. concern for his or her own salvation, or by his or her delusive reliance on God's subsequently, in the hereafter, making good his or her losses, or at least on these being there rendered relatively negligible by an eternity of bliss: besides which the Christian saint, disdainful of the satisfactions of natural man, cannot count these losses for much in the first place, and may even consider them improvements in his or her condition. The genuine saint, on the other hand, renders genuine services and makes genuine sacrifices. One may forgive a Christian saint his (her) mischief on the grounds of delusions, but it is not a very admirable person. The genuine saint has no expectations of future rewards, but on the contrary clearly realizes he (she) is genuinely mortal, so that everything given figures as definite loss, something irrevocably foregone: a sacrifice.

To celebrate genuine saintliness — not quite ordinary, yet not altogether extraordinary — within the family, in the place of work, on the battleground, in jails — simple acts of material aid, unostentatious gestures of friendliness or compassion, or perhaps of love, alleviating discomfort, hunger, pain, part of the tissue of ongoing social life — is not necessarily to hold it up as example. It is simply an expression of recognition and admiration. It is not a celebration of the poor: though saintliness is their prerogative, they do not necessarily avail themselves of their opportunity. Much less is it a celebration of the condition of poverty or of the division of humanity mentioned: for if the sacrifices attaching to it are represented as compensated for on the grounds that goodness is its own reward (on which grounds poverty and that division might be justified as preconditions of goodness), it is no longer saintliness that is being celebrated. On the contrary: a celebration of saintliness requires clear exposition of the hard life of the poor. This precludes celebrations of saintliness from being joyous: they are grim and sad. Nor does the celebration of saintliness preclude celebration of crime and rebellion, alternative modes of transcendance of their situation for the poor, if they can muster the strength for them. But the primary condition for decency in these celebrations is that they be clearly not celebrations of choices or life styles presupposing privilege; and that they be not so general as to deprive the poor of the special credit due initiative under difficult conditions.

Schumann's theatre can be viewed as celebration of saintliness (in particular that of the women among the poor, and the mothers more especially) because its Christian aspects, though by their mere presence in the same work inviting interpretation of this saintliness as Christian pseudo-saintliness, in fact are not such as to constrain the spectator to this interpretation. Schumann's plays do not suggest that people have souls independent of their bodies: his masks deny the Christian hypostasis of mind; and there is no perspective in his plays onto a life after this. Goodness appears as hard but real, even ordinary, an admirable fact of life.

> '... denn nie genug
> Hatt er von Güte zu sagen
> Der Worte damals, und zu erheitern, da
> Er's sahe, das Zürnen der Welt.
>
> (F. Hölderlin, *Patmos*, second version.)'

11. How I feel about it. Saintliness is nice but the release of greedy passion is the good.

Personally, I admire individuals strongly affirming themselves, and that do so in an individual and concrete manner by effort and action (or merely by not taking any shit); without the backing of or reliance on the institutionalizations of power, economic, political, ideological or other; and especially when they take serious personal risks in doing so, not playing it safe (in fact, I admire risk-takers of any sort), and when they do it in opposition to those institutionalizations (in fact, I admire rebels of any sort). Schumann himself is a case in point. And I admire equally those that affirm themselves in the flesh, carnally, or in the spirit, mentally, and those also that sacrifice their self-production and expression one way for the sake of their self-affirmation the other, and those that want to have it both ways. On the other hand, I strongly object to hypocrites, bullies and pompous people, and to those who deal as agents of institutionalized power with others even when they are not hypocrites, bullies or pompous, but just impersonal. The vast majority of people are neither of the one kind or the other, and I have nothing to say about them. They are merely nice people. I don't despise them at all. I don't fault them for their lack of self-affirmation: life is tough for most people. I credit them for not having gravitated to the niches of service to power.

My taste thus goes for the energetic and adventurous who go it on their own. Without affirming any ethics or morality in the matter, and certainly not wanting to preach to anybody, or to give advice to the generality, I view their self-production as 'good'. The fact is, that they tend to hurt people (besides often enough getting hurt themselves), and to do so in a blatant way. They tend to hurt people not nearly as much as the 'bad' kind of people I mentioned who are in their various ways mostly all terrorists of (institutionalized) power, and whose hurting of people is therefore so much a part of the way things are that it's sort of invisible; and besides, institutionalized power, even though its particular form is mostly at least partially dysfunctional and perverted, does tend to have a social function and to be in one form or another needed and useful (to all of us), so that the rationales covering up the misdeeds of its agents in fact have some substance. And the nice people at most torture one another quietly. But as regards the hurting of people by the kind of people I like – and I should add that I consider hurting people, especially when they are not themselves of the 'bad' kind, bad – my position is that it can't be helped. I feel it's regrettable but incidental. One should worry about it and try to avoid it, but worrying about it too much will inhibit the elan characterizing the people I said I like, and on the whole I think we should try more to make up for hurting people than try to avoid hurting them – and I incline to think that those people I like in fact do somewhat tend to make up for the damage they – incidentally, by temperament, through the risks they take and simply because they need help they can't requite – do.

I tend to forget the traditional kind of goodness – going out of your way to help others, making sacrifices for the sake of others, care-taking, active concern, generosity, making allowances: the approaches to saintliness. The epitome of it of course is parental and perhaps more particularly maternal concern, especially because children quite naturally tend to be ungrateful – to take it for granted. My feeling here generally is more one of gratitude and appreciation than of admiration or enthusiasm. My neglect is perhaps to some extent excused by the fact that this second class of good people overlaps with my first class, partly because this plain goodness is intrinsically risky and requires an excess of energy (it has nothing to do with the sloppiness of non-calculation), partly because the self-productive adventurers can't be bothered to be pettily selfish and tend to get a kick out of extending a helping hand here and there, helping others along. Also, I tend to be a little suspicious of plain goodness when it goes beyond the family or a love relation. First there is the large class of cases in which it comes down to participation in understood arrangements of mutual help as need or opportunity arise: fine relations as compared to commercial ones, but hardly to the point here. Second, the good person seems often played for a sucker, knowingly exploited, and the relationship seems sick. Thirdly, the exercises of plain goodness sometimes alleviate sufferings the cause of which had better be attacked and effectively substitute for this attack and perpetuate this cause. Finally, the good person often either has traces of nasty malice or else is a meddler who wants to run the lives of others and uses his or her help to them to perpetuate their dependency and/or prove his or her superiority and/or right to righteousness.

But I don't want to deny that plain goodness makes this world a better place to live in.

There is also the great adventure of our species, the creative evolution of culture. Since the days of our unsettled hunting and gathering ancestors and the archaic agricultural villagers, this marvellous enterprise has been carried on primarily – at its creative edge – in the big cities, and among these primarily in the capitals of empires, and it is here, in the big cities and in the empires, that men, especially if socially advantaged, can live most fully under the press of that process (I wouldn't necessarily consider it progress) taking their risks in contributing to it creatively. (It is hard to stand the city if you don't have a place in the country.) The big cities, built and serviced in the service of the rich and powerful by the great masses of the suffering urban poor, consume the produce that in the countryside is produced by the rural poor, and the poor, also in the service of the same exploiters, as their soldiers, conquer and defend the empires, maiming and killing their like. Furthermore, the great majority of those most benefiting from all this suffering, the rich and powerful are pompous and hypocritical bullies, odious parasites in no way contributing to that evolution. I don't know if the adventure has been or is worth its cost. I admire the splendor of the big filthy and insalubrious cities and the self-confidence of culture in the great empires, and the active players in the great power game, the great organizers, oppressors, exploiters and spillers of blood. I see no great evil in them, and more good than evil.

I think very few people – a few pathetic perverts – except momentarily want to hurt anybody. People aim at the good, their own, that of others. Action is by and large positively motivated: the bad things happen incidentally. Evil does not exist as quality of the mind. It *does* exist as quality of social orders. Namely as feature of systems of social roles such that performance in some of them tends to purchase good for some at the relatively big expense of others. About this I think two things: that it does not make such social systems wholly evil, though it might at times make them worse than some then achievable others; and that there have been few if any social systems that did not have evil in them. I suspect that even before agriculture male dominance and the dominance of elders were partly evil in this sense.

Summing up: I think that the idea that human nature should change is ridiculous: it's not only impossible (except by genetic engineering: but the eugenic genetic engineering apt to be undertaken will be contaminated by our present makeup), it's not even called for. And I don't think we should retreat from that great gamble and game of cultural evolution. Communal life is the stilted intercourse of hypocritical morons, deathly afraid to deviate. As for the atom bomb: how, except by its use in the establishment of a worldwide empire to control it, are we going to control it? Nothing interesting can be achieved without hurting people.

I think this pretty much outlines why I don't much care for either the Christian ethics or for the ethics I perceive in Schumann's theatre (though not in his life).

12. The shows of Jesus. The condition of humanity. The persecuted and the poor.

While his Nativity has been on the whole humorous, Schumann's Passion has been tragic, some humor in the demonstration of parables and/or miracles notwithstanding. Both have lacked in anger – there is no anger in any of Schumann's work – their dominant mood perhaps, even in the case of the Nativity, sadness, their feel the sadness of Proverbs rather than the anger of the Prophets (nor, presumably, of Jesus, cleansing the temple of the bankers). Their common theme, as done by Schumann, is the danger to which Jesus, innocent baby or man and teacher of good will, is exposed from other men, and that he should be so ill welcomed and dealt with is the cause of the sadness. But they differ with regard to this theme, for while the child is exposed to the murderous rage of Herod, gross and anxious, the King, the man is judged by the people, the accent of Schumann's Passion, unless I am mistaken, having been on this ('give us Barrabas!') rather than on Pontius Pilate or the High Priests (I don't think the proconsul ever appeared: the priests may have); so that while the *Christmas Story* has tended to carry an anti-authoritarian message – the three kings do homage, but they lack the regal bearing in medieval iconography attesting to their status: they appear mysteriously as sages rather than as rulers, and as foreigners, exotic in the manner of 'natives' perceived by white children – the *Crucifixion* has rather carried the deeper sadness of a warning against the jealous rages of the common man, resenting being told how to live, though it is of course the same common man that in the *Christmas Story* has no room for the refugee family. His Passions have been Crucifixions: the Resurrection that in the myth makes slight of the sufferings of the victims of power is absent from Schumann's rendition: the play is set up to contrast the message to the punishment. His Nativities have been set up to make us feel the marvel that any newborn child is to its parents; and how tough the world is for those not favored by inheritance at birth – a matter that American ideology ignores.

His Nativity generally comprised the annunciation to Mary, the trek to Bethlehem and the rejection there, only beasts (the cows in a stable), but not men willing to put them up, the homage paid by the Wise Men of the East, King Herod's anxiety, consultations, plot, the flight to Egypt: the traditional elements, presented as to children, strung together in a story – Schumann telling, at Christmastime, the story traditionally told at Christmastime, not really vouching for its truth, but neither by the light humor raising any doubts or maintaining any distance: the story is a happy one because Herod's persecutions fail: the miraculous intervention of an

Angel every Christmas saves the Innocents or at least resurrects them[1] – and, of course, Jesus escapes. That this is the savior of mankind, redeeming it from the curse of mortality put on Adam's descendants and subsequently on account of the chosen people's disloyalty aggravated, is not Schumann's point in telling this story – the little fellow is announced as 'king.' The same show done in Germany might almost be kind of shitty, because there it would fit so well in with the confectionary displays, the creches, the petty bourgeois sentimentality orgiastically deployed at the end of December: with what's accepted, done official, right, the main thing. But in the USA where Christianity is a fervently selfish and individualistic striving, a verbal matter of promises and contracts, its festive and neo-communal aspects in the hands of the Jewish and Christian retail trade intent on unloading a maximum of shoddy on the poor – the Puerto Rican parents lugging the huge cartons of plastic priced at $29.95 milling on newspaper-strewn 14th Street just before Christmas – vs. the Nutcracker Suite at Lincoln Center – the show functions as oppositional celebration of the family, of interiority and child's innocence: the little family is poor, poor, poor, and the three wise old men offer homage, not gold. And the little child comes into the world in the shadow of power, the state's repression, murder itself, rampant. The show, as Schumann does it, offers, deliberately, a marginal diversion in a harsh world: what people can at most, and barely, afford by way of taking their eyes away momentarily from their troubles. The centerpiece of the show is the pregnant woman, seated on a funny (as often as not a cutout) donkey, led by a slightly – almost equally – funny man, her husband. There is no emphasis on this image, no attempt to render it grandiose, but there it is: the central piece of human existence, the pregnant woman under the aspect of a need for a home, the poor husband, hard put to provide it.

His Passion, after more restricted versions initially,[2] generally, I think, came to comprise an elucidation of the life – role – of Jesus: to tell us who it is that is found guilty and is killed: his teachings, both the verbal ones – parables and blesses-be's[3] – and those by act, miracles, are evoked by

---

1. Schumann thinks that the babes were slaughtered in the earliest *Christmas Stories* – I suppose the Living Theatre one done in '62. It seems unlikely as regards the children's one in Putney in '62. If so the *Washerwoman Nativity* of '78 is the second one in which the children are slaughtered – otherwise the first.
2. A script in the Bread and Puppet Theatre fiiles that Schumann, because of the presence in it of the 'Spiesser' puppet, inclines to think (Schumann, interview, December '83) is of an early version at the Spencer Memorial Church, is restricted to the preparations for Easter, the betrayal, the last supper, Gethsemane, the trial and the crucifixion and death, its text (narrated by the Rev. Glenesk), with some additions from other gospels, from Luke, xxii, l-xxiii, 46. It ends, in lieu of a resurrection, with a dance – two puppets joined into one by their celastic hands.
3. Sometimes Schumann would bless Blacks among the crippled, the poor in mind, etc.:
'Das war so, so, ja, zum Beispiel das ging los mit "blessed be the lame" oder wat nicht

little skits, and what we see is a good man – someone that was good: the person is not dwelt on, there is no psychology, life story, or adoration – and a teacher, and the thrust of the teaching is that strife is to be avoided and that men should help one another – non-exorbitant demands, in a way, almost what one would naturally want to do anyhow, but in practice, of course, requiring a good deal of self-control, so that when people manage a life along these lines even just approximately – as very many (ordinary) people within the limits of competition and anxiety do – some admiration is due them. If this sounds simple-minded and modest – whether compared to the various popular doctrines of self-realization, the occasional ideals of self-abnegation, or the more lyrical and overreaching doctrines of love of oneness with nature and with others – that is how the evocation of Jesus in these shows affects one. It is precisely by contrast to the modesty of these ambitions, and of the teaching of them, that the power of the counter forces strikes one, and that the eventual success of the attempt to eliminate the messenger and abort the message (Pilate and the priests, but above all, the people's stand, accomplishing what Herod did not) stuns one. Alas! Schumann does not deal with the real killing of the message: the freezing of it into the glittering edifice of a house of power – event repeated (Lenin as Paul) in our century. Gethsemane may appear in an image – the man almost crushed by the burden of his mission – and the Last Supper, image of greatness, this, the still moment before the wave breaks, the instant when a man folds up his life, swallows it, as it were, in a gulp before stepping out of it (Schumann absorbing the 'it is done' on the cross into it), at some point became a part of it – the picture of the giant figures around the table conveying also the grave charge on those – frail men – transmitting the message, and we glimpse the horrible isolation of the traitor – the verdict of guilty is reproduced, a verdict that appears a verdict over those rendering it, and where those rendering it (not that they necessarily appear in the show) appear to be the ordinary people of all ages, meanly resenting the presumption of being told what to do, desperately impatient of being told things they more or less know are true, but – in a tough world – don't quite feel up to acting according to, and the show ends with an evocation of the death of Jesus as a horrible cataclysm, a horrendous event rending the world, mostly an image of a crucifixion, e.g. the puppeteers tying the puppet to a sharkish aeroplane and/or hoisting it aloft as on a gibbet, no longer majestic but piteously limp, i.e. nothing evokes a resurrection,[4] the divinity of the Christ. The show itself certifies the survival of the message.

---

noch alles und "blessed be the black" und dann war'd für mich aus. Nicht, dann hab ich gesagt, du bist bescheuert, dat beweist mir nur, dass du über, 'ne Sache gar nicht nachdenkst. Du, du spielst da 'ne schwarze Figur und lässt die mitten von, von Lahmen und Krüppeln und Armen usw. und Irren reintanzen.' — (Eckhardt, interview.)
4. 'You know, Bob (Ernstthal) and I were after him all the time. When he did his

Easter time is of course a happy time of the year, the poor take repossession of their sidewalk living rooms, the girls emerge from the cocoons of their winter coats, and the Christian message is a springtime one, Christ has arisen! In this springtime ebullience, Schumann's show, a minute speck in the big city panorama, struck a discordant note, happening on it, we looked into it as into an open mass grave framing the victims of a massacre. Its message was not one of hope, but of near despair, more realistic, gave rise to unease. It is all very well to say that Christ has arisen, but what if he died and his death was ours?

The two shows do not teach the lesson of humility. They focus on violence, and identify it as *the* evil — which, from a Christian viewpoint, as, in act, opposite of love, it is. They do not, however, as historically Christianity has, associate — by their choice of images and accent — violence with resistance of the poor and oppressed to poverty and oppression, but with the violence of the powerful and the violence done the poor and oppressed, presenting humanity at large — common men — the mass of the poor and oppressed presumably included, as merely the foolish ancillaries of the powerful. While thus definitely not preaching resistance, they do not preach non-resistance either.

As Schumann has generally included the telling of the generations from Abraham to Jesus in his Christmas story and the beatitudes in his Easter story, his Christmas story has in effect had the aspect of a history of mankind, seen in the aspect of the advent of Jesus;[5] and his Easter story the aspect of a gospel lesson, of instruction in the teachings of Jesus. The Christmas story, at the end of the year, sums up our past: the Easter story, in stirring spring, defines our present. Or any present, any of the presents making up that past, even: defining it as time of struggle of men with themselves and with one another to put in practice and live according to the teachings of Jesus: an almost hopeless struggle.

The two shows have presented a view of the Human Condition more general than that of the theatrical anthropology I discussed. Humanity is shown in a fated division into persecutors and persecuted, and as by and large, overwhelmingly the latter; identified as the mass of laboring, suffer-

---

Crucifixion. I remember what Bob said to him. He said, "Peter, you always do the crucifixion, but you never deal with the resurrection." Peter was downright pessimist ... And that's what he and I used to argue about all the time — that the world isn't like that exclusively, that that's only one face of the world — that if you turn it around it's just as beautiful as it is ugly. And that used to drive him right up the wall. He's get so *furious.* (I: Well, what would be his rejoinder to that?) Well, it's terrible. People are dying.' — (Oyle, interview.)

The first Passion to refer to the resurrection is the '71 *Stations of the Cross*: it concludes with a general singing of *The Lord is Risen.*

5. The aspect of *The Christmas Story* of Universal History is striking in a series of charcoal drawings entitled *Christmas Story* that Schumann presented to the December '68 issue of *Sing Out*, a multiplication of the living, an accumulation of the dead.

ing and oppressed poor, trying to get along, weak, worried and guilt-ridden, but supportive of one another, capable of somber kindness. The Poor rather than the People is the visually operative category.

While *The Christmas Story*, more of a regular story, has been more or less set in its outline and staging since the second ('63) or third ('64) production of it, the *Crucifixion* up to '72, being, as done by him, less of a story — not particularly focusing on the plot against Jesus — more a confrontation of elements, varied greatly from year to year. Seeing a few versions of each, the feeling I got was that while doing the Christmas show was a devotional duty to Schumann, though one it was a pleasure to discharge — fun, in fact — the persentation of the death of Jesus was each time a serious challenge, not just artistically but because its problem, the rejection of the Savior, was so important to Schumann, and so painful.

Christmas when I was a child and even now is above all the tree, the clear light from it, the color of the fruit (my mother hung apples and tangerines from it), the glitter (of colored tin foil wrapped around two or three pieces of candy, more than of the ultra-thin crystal balls); and then — but this more particularly from my childhood — the odor of spice from the cookies that were baked, sometimes long in advance. The day was a warm day in the house, with everything cold outside, and snow-draped. Secondly, the singing, the voices weak, the melody almost foolish it was so familiar, but the fact of singing in the house a glorious outburst. There is no theology in this, religion was carried by the church bells in town, and their point was merely: look, by God, how well off we are, after all, with the days so short, and everything cold, hard and dark around the houses. The birth of the lord was as nothing to me compared with the arrival of the magi, their conical hats glittering in the dark stable. And winter was by no means over: at Christmas time, the worst of it was yet ahead.

Schumann's Nativity on the whole was a fun play — not unlike a Christmas tree. But to me it lacked the magic of the tree. I would have wished for less sense, and for more mystery in the figures.

Easter when I was a child was a matter of egg hunting — green grass, pussy willows, the wild flowers of spring, typically anything but wild, delicate and tender, rather, but spring itself was out in full force, something like wild — the triumphant shouts and august sorrow from the organ loft of some church with an energetic pastor, the pastor's bittersweet evocations (Palm Sunday) of humiliation and death following the triumphant entry into the Temple City, but humiliation and death followed in turn by a greater, an unbelievable triumph. The sense of it was spring in a succession of springs, the coming of summer: a triumph of powerful nature indifferent to us. Indifferent also to our man-imaging story-analogies to its grandiose and colorful course: without these stories, and that of my culture in particular, doing it any harm, on the contrary, being our own modest contribution to that general magnificent insolence of all things in nature

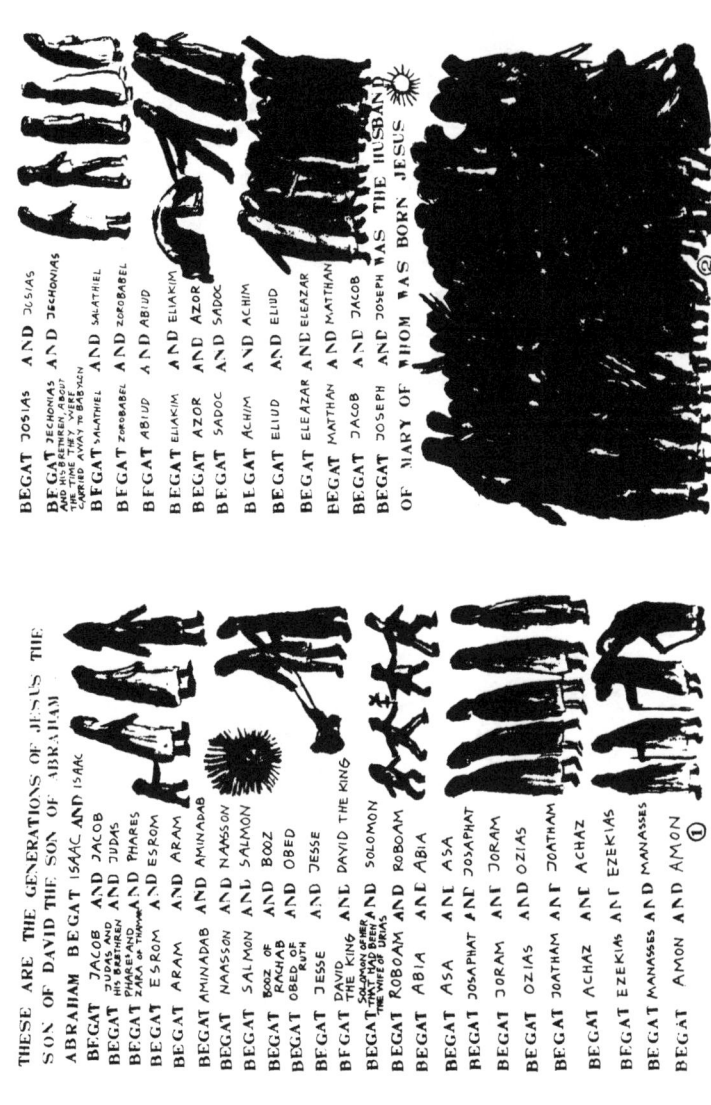

Peter Schumann, *Christmas Story* in Sing Out, December 1968.

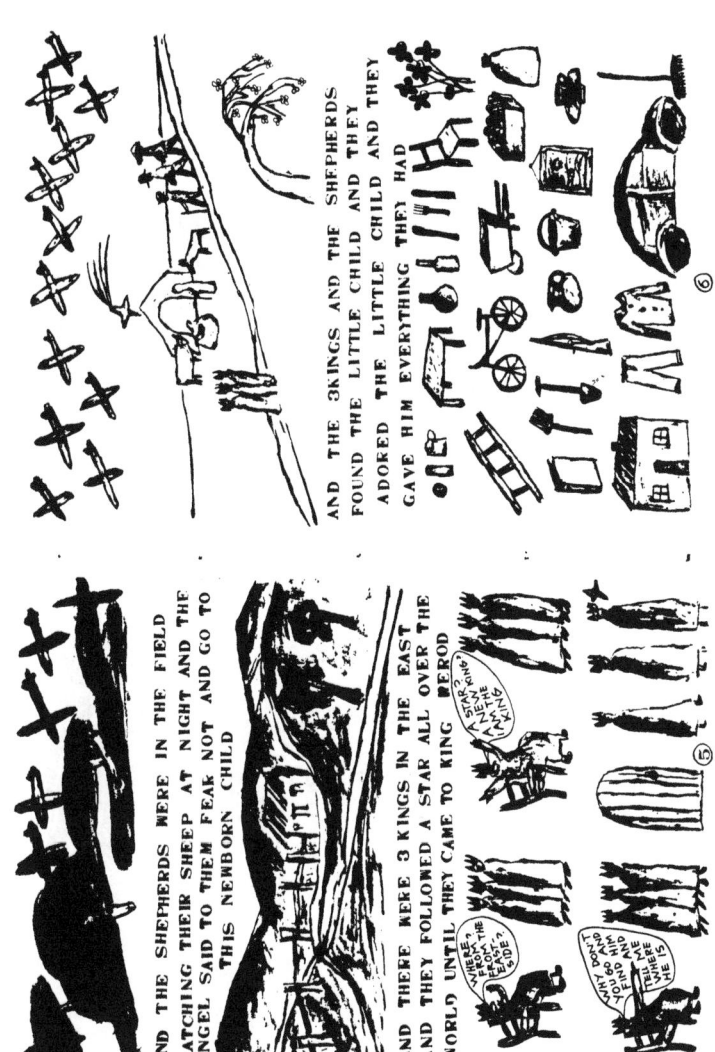

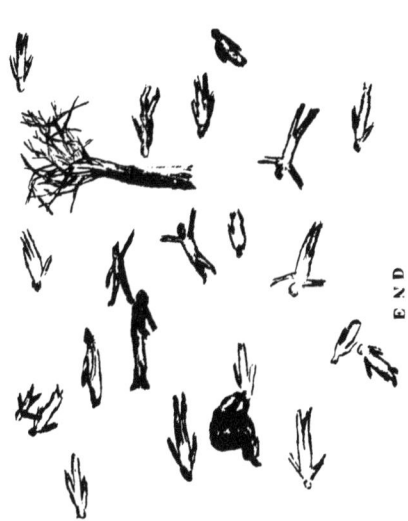

Peter Schumann, *Christmas Story* in *Sing Out*, December 1968.

manifested in spring, something like the violets' wild effort. Bach at the Thomanerkirche and the violets under the hazelnut hedge.

Schumann's passion presented the positive side of human Easter, the by which men add to spring, in the form of the teachings of Jesus (torn by him, as Jesus had torn them, out of the clergy's hands): not in the form of resurrection. What good would life be without the earth? But he heavily played up the myth's tragedy, so alien to spring, and in fact out of all seasons. It was, all in all, a somber play, the way Schumann did it. This recisely is the kind of play to go to, of course, the joyous season of spring: to remind us of our mortality.[6]

---

[6]. 'Easter means the rites of spring achieved through the suffering of prison, torture, and crucifixion. Resurrection is the appearance of young crocus in old snow and the secret power of man to lift his low fate into the light. There is no second fable pushing and directing us so clearly through ourselves. I hope we will always be able to do Easter stories with our puppets.'—(Schumann, Newsletter, '*Bread and Rosebuds*,' November '72.)

13. Observances of Christmas. 1963-69.

Schumann did his first Nativity play in 1962 with Putney grammar school kids, repeating it, but now more definitely as puppetry at the Living Theatre in New York. He did it again, 'The Christmas Story, a happy event,' the next year at the Delancey Street Bread and Puppet Museum (December 20, '63, repeated as The post-Christmas Story, January 4, 11 and 18, '64),[1] having done it, preceded by a parade through the streets, Brooklyn announcing the event, on December 15[2] and 29 at the Reverend William Glenesk's Spencer Memorial Church in Brooklyn (Remsen Street at Boro Hall, Brooklyn Heights), doing it henceforth (until 1972, or perhaps even 1973) regularly each year in somewhat the same form.[3]

---

1. '... a town built to represent Jerusalem, a group of shepherds doing a dance over milk crates, a crankie (for the travelling Joseph and Mary), little hand puppets (for the burghers of Nazareth), a King Herod, a giant angel.' — (Schumann, interview, '79.)
2. There are three Peter Moore photographs of a December 15, '63 (Barbara Moore's data) Spencer Memorial showing.
3. The December 10, 1964 issue of the *Village Voice*, revealing a certain ignorance of the meaning of Christmas, announces that ' "The Nativity" and "The Christmas Story" will be presented during the Christmas season at the Pocket Theatre, 3rd Avenue and 13th Street, performances of the plays which integrate live actors with puppets of various sizes, will be given at 1:30 and 3:00 p.m. on Saturdays and at 1:30 on Sundays. Weekday performances will be given from December 28 through January 1st.' The following issue's Off-Off-Broadway guide tells us that ' "The Christmas Story" and "The Birdcatcher in Hell", (a kiyogen) directed by Peter Schumann are to be presented by the Bread and Puppet Theatre Sunday December 20 at 9 p.m. at Spencer Memorial Church.' An ad by Schumann in the December 24th issue announces performances Saturday, December 24 through Sunday, January 3rd at the Pocket Theatre at 3 p.m., and one in the December 31st issue, 'today through Sunday, January 3rd.'

A Bread and Puppet Theatre booklet of '64, *The Nativity*, presumably informs us of the spirit of this *Nativity*. (cf. Appendix VI.)

In 1965, a large ad by the Bridge Theatre, 4 St. Mark's Place, announces 4 p.m. matinees December 25-28 (adults a dollar, children under 12 50 cents) and evening performances December 24, 27 and 28 (at double matinee prices), *The Christmas Story* in the evening performances – 'featuring: Catherine Merrill, Robert Ernstthal, Peter Schumann and several others' – being presented together with *The Oxfordshire St. George Play*, this latter, 'funny, a real spoof, just a crazy one' (Ernstthal, interview) was done as a 'Christmas play, an original Christmas play with St. George and Father Christmas and Dr. Ball and those traditional mummer's play characters. A lot of balloons and hopping around ... I think we used puppets that we had. Puppets that we found – a Santa Claus mask, sort of disheveled, commercial Santa Claus mask we used. We strung up Christmas lights all over the body of the operator.' — (Schumann, interview, '79.)

Helen Hunter Palmer thought this *Christmas Story* 'a little hearts and flowery' but she 'felt the grace of Peter and the power of possibility of it.... He played a shepherd. He had a staff and his hands were very beautiful. Minimal movement, but very beautifully done.' (Palmer, interview.) Mary was played by a visibly pregnant woman (Helen Rabin).

Fable #10, dated 'Christmas 1965' in some unpublished *Fables* of Schumann's dated

'September 1970' shows how the equation Christ=Vietnam went in Schumann's mind at the time:
'God sends an angel and the angel carries a baby and the angel goes to a woman and says, don't be afraid! But the woman is afraid. And the angel says: this is your son. And then the woman kisses the little baby and gives him apple pie.

Christmas Story

But pretty soon the soldiers come and want to take the baby away from her. She cries and her husband takes a sledge hammer and fights the soldiers. But they kill him. And then the cow and the donkey who are also in the shed with the woman, rise on their hind legs and bite – the soldiers kill them too. And there are three wise men in the east and they follow a star, and when they come to the shed with the poor woman and the poor little baby they argue with the soldiers. But the soldiers won't listen. And the three wise men write letters to the government. But the government won't listen. The three wise men climb on the roof of the shed and burn themselves. And people from all over the world come to help the woman. But the soldiers get more guns and more bombs. And now God has to send an angel again.'

For 1966, an ad of December 22nd in the *Village Voice* reports a shift from Spencer Memorial Church to Greenwich Village: 'Special Christmas Eve Services. Peter Schumann's Bread & Puppet Theatre performing The Nativity Story, Saturday December 24 8 p.m. Judson Memorial Church, 55 Washington Square South. No reservations necessary (an offering will be taken).'

'Judson would be the most exciting show because the audience was always so charged at Judson. I remember we performed on Christmas Eve, late at night, and the funny parts were so funny ... Irving and Bob and Peter were so hilarious that I would almost get sick laughing at the advisory puppets and the hand puppets.' — (Scherman, interview.)

According to George Ashley (interview,) a regular outside participant in Bread and Puppet doings from '66 to '71:

'The State of the Union addresses were used in the *Christmas Story*, in the mouth of King Herod, every year. Herod, normally, was that huge, seated figure of Herod or the Professor or various forms it took, the seated figure, and when you turned it around there was a glove compartment puppet stage in back, where the frock coat was. And it could be turned on wheels, and you open it up – or in various other fashions. But they always used the State of the Union address, every year, for Herod's speech.' — (Ashley, interview.)

Under the title, *The Christmas Story*, the show was repeated at the Reverend Finley Shaef's Washington Square Methodist Church at 33 West 4th Street, and on New Year's Eve at Spencer Memorial Church. He then put it on again, Saturdays and Sundays, January ('67) 7-29, under the title *Nativity*, at the Astor Library Landmark Building for children at 7 p.m. and for grownups, together with the *Oxfordshire St. George Play*, at 8:30 p.m., admission against contributions both times. This was the first piece of Schumann's that Omar Shapli had seen:

'That was when they were at the height of that tradition of doing their Christmas event ... No theatrical equipment or anything, just a big room, and we sat on wooden straightback chairs – there were, I'd say about 150 people there – and watched this event. And I guess to me that was one of the three or four most startling times I've ever spent in a theatrical event. I was quite awed by it. It took me completely by surprise. It was nothing like what I had expected. For one thing, It was just enormously entertaining. The first thing I saw was – I said to myself, how is he going to bring in the Christmas story? Well, he began it with the begats. Immediately I was seeing something that I hadn't prepared myself for. Watching the first three minutes of an event about Christmas which was about so-and-so begat so-and-so, and so-and-so begat so-and-so. With a little march in between as all these various patriarchs at various heights and in various shapes paraded up and bowed to the audience as they went by. From that point on, I was completely entranced. It was obvious what I was going to see was an original and extraordinary experience and it remained that. Everything that happened. It was like miraculous. It was a series of miracles. Things being reinvented at every moment using small or slight physical elements. I was impressed by the extraordinary sophistication of comprehension, of education, of knowledge that must have gone into this, and the ease with which it was thrown away and incorporated. They used everything. I saw what to me appeared to be a very strong Brechtian alienation, and so forth, effect. It seemed to me to be being used for the first time I'd ever seen them being used effectively. (I: Can you give an example?) Sure. Actually, the beginning, to concentrate on that — that whole section of the begats seemed to me in ostensibly focusing on a trivial aspect of an important event, we were somehow illuminated about the core of the event. Now this is hard to justify in a funny way. Except that we were suddenly being told that to talk about the life of Jesus is just as important to talk about who all these various individuals were who were in the line that led to what, by the way? I've never quite understood that in the Bible. We're finding out the generations of Joseph and then we're told that Joseph wasn't the father, anyway. But attention is being paid to details that are not, on the face of it, relevant to what you know the story is going to be about. This makes you think. It makes you curious. It makes you wonder. And not all those questions are answered in the event as they proceed, but it shows you the way you must view what happened after that. That God is in the details. It's like that's where it lies, where it occurs. Of course, the whole mode of work that involves a kind of lightness with material that is not only serious, but is deeply felt by the people who are doing it is a kind of shocking reversal that draws you in. That is, it is clear that we're not seeing a parody of the Christmas story. We're not seeing, even at that time — I guess this is what startled me too — we weren't seeing an atheist portrayal of the Christmas story being used purely for political analogy or whatever, which would have been much more expectable in the '60s. Somehow it was a statement of religious belief as well as a series of very clear political statements within the context of it. All of it thrown away to a degree, in a strange way. All of it kind of lightly allowed to fall. I still remember, in a way — it's the most impressive part of that — Peter's own narrative of the flight through the desert. He stands up there with this unwinding cyclorama, just a simple drawing on a long piece of paper, that gets wound from one end to the other, and he stands up there, then they come to the house and then they walk. I have since found, of course, that Peter is a brilliant story teller and it has to do with just what I was describing. His capacity to throw away in order to emphasize. And somehow the sense that it doesn't matter that much to him, in a way, except, of course, that's because it matters a great deal. That he has no ego stake in what he is doing. It doesn't come out as coy or as insincere. It just seems that the act of doing the event and his part in doing the event isn't particularly important to him. And that the focus is totally on what is happening. I think that, in itself, makes an extraordinary personality in the theatre or in any art form. The ego drive usually manifests itself in other ways. Anyway, that was the first time. (I: What was the political trend or attack?) Herod was very clearly related to either Johnson or whoever the powers that be were at the time. The massacre of the innocents, which doesn't happen in the Schumann play, at least in the versions of it that I've seen, they get away. They don't get massacred because the soldiers are too stupid. They get saved in one way or another. But the massacre of the innocents had very clear reference to the Vietnam war. I think that it was so clear that there was no heaviness about the overtones. It was done, I remember, with little hand puppets. A lot of that . . . . That play had years of life and, of course, every year it bent, I think, to meet the current political scene. But always it ended up with the little German lullaby at the end. I remember at the very end of the piece, a very simple ending, the lullaby to the child. Every time I've seen it, anyway. It was very simple. I mean, it was almost like the traditional end of the Christmas play. The parts that had to do with Herod were the ones that seemed to me to change most year by year. They were the most topical. Other than that, I guess it was very much in keeping with the medieval history of morality plays, where something like that might very well be the part that represents now, always. This represents the present political force of the day and the other aspects of it represent something that to

Peter is timeless and something to fight for and is always in danger, and always in danger of being victimized, overwhelmed, but somehow has a lot of.... I was aware of at least an overtone that I questioned about it, without being particularly hostile with it. I mean, the question had to do with what I felt was a kind of Christian individualism or even anarchic ethic. In other words, a sense that might suggest a kind of permanence to the state of political repression and so forth and a constant duty to resist it. In other words, that there might be some overtone of that and that this you will always have with you and this you must always respond to. A position that I don't really share, that I find essentially very pessimistic on a social level ... part of it had to do with the modern aspects of Herod that we were talking about before. The impliction, even the first time I saw it, was that for thousands of years there'll always be a modern Herod. And the other aspects of it will be more or less always recognizable. You know, the strong, the feminine vulnerability and protectiveness. The motherness of what would you call it? The common people, maybe. But the people. The simple people, maybe, is a better way to express it. You know that there seems to me a question about that – that's all. I mean Peter's work is both very subjective, seeming to come from very strong lines within his own feeling, thought, impulse and instinct and at the same time objectifies itself in such elaborate detail – that's one of the fascinating things about the work, of course ... you're also looking at a very strong statement of a single person in a kind of crisis, perpetual crisis between opposites, that has a pessimistic overtone to it.' — (Shapli, interview.)

Christmas of '67 was celebrated by Saturday evening and Sunday afternoon shows at the Washington Square Methodist Church (contributions) December 9th to January 14th '68 (he was also doing *Fire* there, Monday evenings), except that on Sunday the 17th he gave two performances of something advertised as *The Christmas Story*, 1967, 'a new work commissioned' by the Division of Mass Media of the United Presbyterian Church in the USA,' 'with puppets, carols, master and musicians in the sanctuary' – a different variant of the show? – at Glenesk's Spencer Memorial Church; and on Wednesday, December 20th he did *The Christmas Story* at Public School #122 at 150 First Avenue, in his more immediate neighborhood ('Roast Raffle Tickets 25c, family 50c. Everyone invited.'), apparently under the sponsorship of the Parent Teachers Association. The Christmas Eve celebration was part of a larger celebration at Shaef's church, kicked off by a 'Sun/Son Street Parade' 12:30 to 3:00 p.m. from West 4th Street to nearby Washington Square Park 'with the theme of the birth of the sun as it symbolizes the birth of the spirit of man,' the Bread and Puppet Theatre, the Pageant Players and the Renaissance Chorus of New York participating and (at the church) comprising a performance by Ken Jacobs' Apparition Theatre, dinner, and a Christmas Eve celebration with jazz saxophones, dancing by Jo Leckay and with the Reverend A. Finley Shaef. A. D. Coleman attacked the Brooklyn *Christmas Story 1967* in the December 21 *Village Voice* for being anti-revolutionary: apparently this version of it stops just as Herod's soldiers are about to murder the innocents, Glenesk makes twice repeated appeals for the savior angel to appear, the angel finally appears and saves the children: 'Forget that it is straight out of Peter Pan. That's not what bothers me. I sat there cursing because a supposedly revolutionary theatre had missed a chance to make a powerful revolutionary statement. Surely they know that the angel never comes. Why didn't they say so?' Coleman compares this cop-out unfavorably with the Living Theatre's revolutionary integrity (*The Brig*). I am not aware of Coleman's own contributions to the revolution. Schumann advertised the January 6 and 7 performances with quotes of kid spectators and of the *New York Times* and of Coleman: 'There is no angel. Bad counterrevolutionary theatre.' Criticisms of Schumann's story lines from more genuine revolutionaries within his group were, the next two years, to run along different lines. This performance as well as perhaps one at Bethlehem Lutheran Church may have been a benefit for 'Children of Trinity Lutheran Church.' (Bread and Puppet 'Diary', November '67-March '68). The '67 *Christmas Story* was insufficiently revolutionary for the *Village Voice*, but the *New York Times* dug it as children's theatre: 'A dramatization of the first Christmas that combined reverence and impudence exactly as

The version of the *Christmas Story* described by Nichols in the *Tulane Drama Review* #47 of 1970 is dated by him as of '62, but probably is the December 15 or 29, '63 Spencer Memorial version. The minister with the cymbals is surely Glenesk!

---

they are combined in the medieval mystery plays. The scene is at once the Holy Land and Super America; the time, then and now. Joseph and Mary sleep with the cows because they don't have $26.50 for an oasis-size downstairs double at the Sandy Arms Motel. King Herod prates about the balance-of-payment deficit. The bubble-headed bourgeoisie of Jerusalem dismiss the star in the east as a "publicity stunt for a new picture", The approach may seem campy or sacrilegious. It is neither. The play says that Jesus' world was, in essence, ours; that both need saving. Sensitive older children and their parents will get the message. They will also laugh a lot.' — (Sullivan, *Children's Theaters Bring Some Goodies*, the *New York Times*, December 23, '67 – Schumann's first review in the *New York Times*.)

In 1968, *The Christmas Story* seems to have been first presented on December 7th at the Brooklyn Academy of Music's Poe Forum (*Village Voice* of December 5, '*What's on . . . for children*'), and then also on December 28 at Muse (?), Bedford Avenue and Lincoln Place, Brooklyn (notices ibid., December 19, 26), it was reviewed by Julius Novick in the January 9, '69 *Voice*. It was the first Bread and Puppet production he had seen and except for the 'magnificently sculptured heads' he doesn't like what they are doing — except for occasional satire of the military-industrial complex (King Herod), he finds it lacking in a point of view, religious or other, and without shape, and a failure even as a simple narrative, and the ending leaves the spectator unsatisfied: 'At the moment when the slaughter of the innocents is just about to happen, the company start singing in German, and marches up the aisle and out.' He surmises that the company may perhaps be at a disadvantage indoors, on a stage (a wooden scaffold stage).

I have found no indication of any *Christmas Story* in '69: the presentations of *The Cry of the People for Meat* (which comprised a nativity) at St. Peter's Church in early December, may to some extent have substituted for it, but more importantly, perhaps, Schumann had just returned from a long tour in Europe, had lost his previous base of operations, the Old Courthouse, and had probably in late December either not yet established himself in his temporary substitute for it in Brooklyn or not established himself sufficiently to get up a Christmas show that year.

New York Jewry finally caught up with Schumann's Christian bias that December, however, in Arthur Sainer's hemming/hawing, blathering review of *The Cry of the People* in the *Village Voice* (December 25, '69):

'*The Cry of the People for Meat* has its weaknesses, perhaps the most serious being its failure to deal with the covenants Jehovah made, first with Abraham, then Moses, while devoting an interminable if sometimes charming time to the "begat" sections, that work of some obsessed genealogist. In one sense, the Old Testament can be seen as the struggle of God and the Children of Israel to become worthy of one another. If the Old Testament speaks of anything, it speaks of the pact God makes with his People, promising to be Eternally Present to them. In the context of God's concern for righteousness, the flood makes sense. But in "Cry", the flood is re-enacted as if it were a natural rather than a retributive event, thus trivializing the consequences of one of the great moral catastrophes of the world. If Jesus is to be the culmination of a work that professes to deal with both the Old and the New Testaments, then he must be seen in relation to the God of the Hebrews, and to the success and failure of humanity before his time.'

Sainer subsequently rectified Schumann's error in some miserable dramatic hackwork of his own on Jewish history.

'The masks have a heightened Ubuesque exaggeration, like cartoons. There are three kinds of masks: Herod, the Bugler, and the Soldiers have grotesque masks, as in drawings by Grosz; Joseph and Mary and the three-headed Wise Man recall Picasso's drawings; the three Shepherds are from Brueghel. Confronted with these masks, we see into the souls of the characters, fixed at the moment of the story.

Music, dances, and processions: a bugle, jews'-harp, bongo drums, and recorder (the "people's" concert for Herod), toy horn and tin drum, hand-clapping, and a hymn; the dance of the star (with the drum) leading the Wise Man; the Shepherds' dance; and the final procession up and down the aisle. Music and dance punctuate the action and are the action.

Kinds of speech: exclamations by the crowd, remarks by the gossips, innkeepers, etc. – half-intelligible and handled as pure sound, as part of the music and dance pattern. The "speeches" in the drama are very intermittent. They are burlesque and cartoonlike in the case of Herod and all the puppets. The announcement of the Angel is the poem from the Bible narrative.

The puppets: little four- to six-inch puppets for the householders and populace. Others are all larger. In the Slaughter of the Innocents, there is a Brechtian machine-gun crew with a cardboard machine gun three times as big as the mother's house. The Angel, who rises up from behind the curtain on a pole, stands fifteen feet high. Puppets and the actors converse with each other with no strain on the audience's belief. Their different sizes have the property of emphasis, as in a voice tone.

The staging: a black curtain, suspended from a pipe resting on the church lectern. A pictorial scroll (showing the journey) pulled through a double cylinder by the narrator sitting in the pulpit. The altarpiece is a black and white painting showing the child resting in an arm, and the mask of Mary's face a kind of gray relief-sculpture detached and hung inside the painting. There is one broad spotlight on a movable stand, and a little bull's-eye spot. The light man also plays the recorder.

When the Shepherds and the three-headed Magi with their candles lift up the painting (of the Incarnation) they all sing an old German hymn. "Für Uns Ein Zeit Will Angekommen". At the end, for the procession in which the minister follows them banging a cymbal, they take off their masks, come out from behind the curtain, and we see there are only five people.'

(Robert Nichols, *Christmas Story*, 1962.)

The Reverend Glenesk has described the 'Order (more or less)' of the Christmas services '63 ff. incorporating Schumann's show at his church – following a 'processional' around Brooklyn Heights:

> '*Carol*: "Angels we have
> heard on high".
> The Betrothal of Mary & Joseph.
> The Annunciation
> The Taxation
> The People's Offerings (*parade*)
> Journey to Bethlehem
> Carol: "In Dulci Jubilo" (*the people*)
> Journey of the Kings

Prayers for the Kings
Shepherds in the Fields
The Massacre & King Herod
Petitions to the Angel (*the people*)
The Nativity and the Adoration
Carols: "Old German"
          (*by puppeteers*)
          "Coventry Carol"
          (*the people*)
          "Adeste Fidelis" (*the people*)'

(Glenesk, *Puppets tell the Christmas Story, Face to Face*, December '69.)
The show apparently typically was introduced by the Generations of Jesus:
'The congregation is seated. The sanctuary lights go down. The chancel lights slowly shine on a single chair standing alone up front. There is an almost marching beat heard on a hidden drum. A voice begins a rock-like speech of the generations of Jesus "the song of David, the son of Abraham" when a figure of Abraham appears, climbs up to the lonely chair, sits for a moment, then moves down to the other side and out. The voice of the narrator takes up the genealogy of Jesus "and Abraham begat Isaac, and Isaac begat Jacob" on down the family tree of time to another Jacob who "begat Joseph, and Joseph was the husband of Mary of whom was born Jesus."

Human beings, their faces hidden under masks, in all manner of costume, enter and exist on cue at the narrator's refrain of "begats." The figure of Mary stays. The drum beat stops. Suddenly another voice, this time from high up at the back, through a megaphone, shouts "Fear not, Mary, you shall have a son", and an enormous figure of an angel, ten feet long, seems suspended in the air at the edge of the balcony at the back, bathed in a white light.'   (Glenesk, ibid.)

The show:
'So The Christmas Story by Peter Schumann's Bread and Puppet Theatre begins. We wonder when the little doll-size people we expect at a puppet show are coming on. They do, but only as the little people of Bethlehem where Mary and Joseph found no room in the inn. Peter Schumann puts ten inch puppets and six foot actors together. King Herod stomps on in a mask, ugly, noisy, fat, and smoking a cigar. The three kings are played by one actor, clearly holding on a three-faced mask and speaking for three persons. The star is played by a boy jumping about with a star at the end of a stick, tooting a trumpet, catching the attention of the kings.

The real and fantastic are thrust together, as life-sized Mary and Joseph and donkey (two actors inside the skin) make the rounds of Bethlehem knocking on the doors of houses the size of a large human hand. The little puppets appear on the fingers of the puppeteers behind and below the elevated stage. Peter Schumann himself, when he is not playing the violin or making a sound effect, climbs a small ladder across from the puppet theatre and turns a hand-made scroll, telling the story of the birth of Christ as the actors and puppets act it out. He has put the traditional gospel story simply and into his own plain words, such as "They got up and went home by another way."

The Bread and Puppet Theatre updates the ancient Christmas story by putting Herod's soldiers into modern helmets and uniforms, a scene which sometimes upsets the audience, when the army kills all the children of Bethlehem before their eyes. Like Punch and Judy, this puppet theatre is also violent. But Peter Schumann brings the angel back at the end to kiss the children back to life.'

(Glenesk, ibid.)

The Nativity whose incorporation into *Cry of the People for Meat* (cf. infra) substituted for that year's *Christmas Story*, after, as a political parable, the massacre of the women and children in Ben Suc, Vietnam, doing the massacre of the Innocents, which was in this version for the first time — and for the last, I believe, until the '79 *Washerwoman Nativity* — unintercepted, shows the birth of Jesus — child brought in the teeth of a beast — in the manner of a fairy tale, and immediately follows this fairy tale by a scene, *The Exaltation and Building of Jesus* on the blessings, miracles and sayings of Jesus, heretofore part of the *Crucifixion*, but the Building of Jesus part of which — the blessings — invites interpretation as the true story, not a fairy tale, of who Jesus is and how he comes to be, namely: the Resistance Fighter representing the poor, him/herself arising from among the poor by the decision to resist.

This concludes Schumann's Nativity series of the '60s.

14. Observances of Easter. 1964-1969.

Unlike the Christmas shows, the *Crucifixions* varied a great deal.[1] Schumann started doing them in '64, did five different versions, '64-'68,[2]

---

1. 'But we did *so many* different *Crucifixions* and *Puppet Christs* . . . . Every year different ones. On the Lower East Side, in a church, in Washington Square, what's it called, Judson Church and in Spencer Church – most of them in Spencer Church, I would think, in Brooklyn . . . . Now for me it is impossible to really distinguish between the different Easter plays we did, because we did them quite different from each other every year.' — (Schumann, interview, '79.)

There were some recurrent elements, though:

'There was the trial. Every year Peter would change how he was going to do the trial. And the Last Supper, which was always a very long scene in which we would enter inside of the yellow people and there was a Feeder puppet, that one that has a hand with a cup and another hand with bread . . . . Anyway we used that in one form or another every year in the Crucifixion show – the Last Supper Scene. There's usually a scene with Judas, and the Crucifixion – we'd always use the Airplane, tied up the puppet to the Airplane. And there were very slow scenes always in the *Crucifixion*, very, very slow scenes – the Last Supper.' — (Sherman, interview – she was in these shows '66 ff.)

'The best versions were the earlier versions. It went through a slump when it got into bigger spaces, in my opinion. It went through a certain slump and then got better again. The first versions were in a closed space . . . . We did some at Judson and it got dull. In the middle . . . one of the years . . . it somehow got dull . . . . At one point in the middle it started to be real straight, but then we abstracted it and it got real interesting again . . . . We did it in Judson one year and it was a crowd scene – it was like we had a bigger space to work in. And we did this humming – "hmmmmm" – it got kind of bland. And then I think the next year we decided to go hog wild.' — (Ernstthal, interview.)

2. The Spencer Memorial Church order of service program for Holy Communion on February 4th, '68, which on its cover has a picture of the Bread and Puppet Christ (on the cross), identifies it as a photo of *The Puppet Christ*, 'first produced here for Lent in 1963,' but I think this should have been '1964,' and my record starts with a *Village Voice* notice of March 12th, 1964 repeated on March 19th – Easter Sunday that year was on March 29th – announcing 'Action Bible Readings' 'directed by Peter Schumann and presented by Peter Schumann and company,' Fridays at 9 p.m. at the Bread and Puppet Museum (contributions).

'The loft, which was a – had a defined – a very clearly defined area. These were big, big puppets in a small, small space. And that was quite comical. And they were very – it had a kind of intensity to it, because there were these big puppets in this small space. And it was quite beautiful . . . with the Spiessers, with the whole series of hands, "Kill him, kill him." That was the first *Crucifixion*.' — (Ernstthal, interview.)

My record continues with a large ad of May 21st that same year announcing that 'Peter Schumann's bread & puppet theatre presents *The Puppet Christ* with puppets, masks and music, William Glenesk narrator, saturdays and sundays through June 28, previews May 23 & 24 9 p.m., opening may 30 9 p.m., Spencer Memorial Church.' The Reverend had gotten into the act. the *Off-off Broadway Guide* repeats the information on May 28th as does another ad in the same issue.

'One year, the first year, the puppets played in this manner. There was a big curtain stretched from one pulpit to another in Spencer Church and hung about 6 feet high, all across the altar area. Straight curtain. And above that curtain you saw the play. In front of the curtain, someone to move the lights around and a narrator. So the puppets, elongated –

all the operation was underneath, like *King Story* puppets, and that technique also allowed the use of sticks or signs on sticks where you would only see the sign and not the operator. A lot of chairs, or a table, such devices – can't remember what else besides chairs, sticks, signs.' — (Schumann, interview, '79.)

Schumann having on July 24 and 25 done a 'dance from the *Puppet Christ*' at the Washington Square Gallery (530 Broadway) in a concert comprising work by Rainer, Lucinda Childs, David Gordon and Judith Dunn, the Judson Dance Theatre crowd, and produced by that horrible dyke whose 'personal journalism' at the *Village Voice*, Jill Johnston, was pushing that crowd, then put on *The Puppet Christ*, apparently again *Crucifixion*, at the Judson Memorial Church on August 3 and September 1 and 2, as a benefit for the Mississippi Summer Project, sponsored by the Judson Poets' Theater.

The Spencer *Crucifixion* was the occasion of Schumann's first public programmatic statement, *Bread and Puppets* (cf. Appendix I) – it was in the program: theatre should be an indispensable religious (sacral) activity for both players and audience; his theatre is an extension of sculpture, a cathedral set in motion in its icons.

An ad of March 18th, 1965 repeated April 1st, announces previews of *The Great Passion* for March 21 at 6 and 9 p.m., and performances Sundays at 6 and 9 through April 18th (contributions $1), both at the Spencer Memorial Church. The *Off-off-B'way Guide* gives the same information on April 8th and 15th, and on April 22nd and 29th, and on May 6th and 20th tells of presentations of *The War Against Jesus* Fridays and Saturdays at 8:30 p.m. on the Lower East Side, at Emmanuel Presbyterian Church on East 6th Street, between Avenues C and D: this may have been the same show presented in Brooklyn, or one altered in consonance with the change of title. A note on Elka's copy of Renato Ariza's *La Pasion en marionetas* (*Hablemos*, April 3, 1966, Mexico City, Mexico) says the photos of rehearsals for a Spencer Memorial passion accompanying the article were taken in 1965.

An ad of April 7th, 1966 in the Reverend Glenesk's slightly pompous manner, invites readers 'to celebrate the feast of easter' by attendance at a 'congregation of the arts at the spencer memorial church, brooklyn heights, paul draper, dancer, blanche yurka, actress, james sellars, composer, peter schumann, sculptor, a liturgy of the arts, conducted by william glenesk, chamber ensemble, john sonneborn, organist and choirmaster, sunday april 10 at 11 a.m., with bread & puppet theatre production of the crucifixion, with puppets, masks and music at 9 p.m., repeated sunday april 17.' A separate ad (implemented in the *Off-Off Broadway Guide* of April 21st) announces an April 17th *Crucifixion*, and another performance on the 24th, and another ad announces a May 1st performance, again at Spencer Memorial.

'Then in later productions we changed the puppets, we put a ladder on a dolly – and we put two people on the ladder, one on top and one on the bottom half-way up the ladder – a six-foot step ladder – and these two people that operate the Jesus puppet were wheeled around in that manner.... That was used for another version of the Easter plays to move the puppets – the Jesus puppet and the other puppets – the fabrics got elongated, the sticks got shorter, and the operators got moved inside the puppets and moved the puppets that way. So, there were very different ways of moving these puppets. (I: So they progressed from these giant rod puppets over a curtain to over-life-size puppets moving on a stage.) I don't know if it was '66 or '65 or '64 – I think it was '5 or '6. And one of the players, Catherine, brought a group of children from Harlem on 134th Street and we made masks for them. Big demon masks. Paper maché masks, painted with bright colors and smeared up with shellac to make them shiny. They had all kinds of colorful dresses and ribbons hanging. The whole play was done with this group of demons surrounding the Jesus puppet.' — (Schumann, interview, '79.)

Margo Sherman remembers these dollies of '65 or '66 as being very noisy, a rough, crude effect. I don't know of any other use of dollies in his work.

'Anyway, we went to Glenesk's church and we did one version where there was like revolution. There was explosions – running around hawking the blood of Christ or the water that Pilate washed his hands in. We were selling it in little bottles – it was a very sarcastic version. It was – the parables were done as very loud – there were shots going off and people in the aisles hawking things and selling things – selling remnants of the cross and it was a very loud, mocking, angry type of version.... That was the first one, in Spencer, as I remember, and there were riots breaking out – loud shouts coming from all over and things like that. It was a very loud version. That was a pretty funny version, actually – oh, T-shirts. "Crucifixion '65," I think, it was – I may be wrong, maybe it was '66 – I believe it was '65, though. Selling T-shirts: "I saw the Crucifixion." It was a commercial – a mockery of the commercialism of it. It was an angry version. A funny, silly version.' — (Ernstthal, interview.)

'But I remember one time playing with puppets at Spencer and I believe it was in that version – and I – it was – there were certain scenes that were very poetic – they floated. The puppets floated and they were up above and they had scenes of tremendous tenderness – in some of the scenes. There was one puppet with two heads and we put in goosenecks – like lamps – lamp goosenecks and there was a rod – a second rod so you could pull the head – it was a neck movement to it – that one with the heads. And there was a certain tenderness to it and there was – we did one version there that I remember, that was one of those great moments – that we were completely lifted up into the puppets and it was almost erotic, practically – it was just such a tender, beautiful feeling, we were playing this so for real. It was a great moment. I remember that was one of the moments that was really transcending in the theatre.' — (Ernstthal, interview, '79.)

Margo Sherman, whose first stint with the Bread and Puppet was in the '66 *Crucifixion* – Joseph in a face mask – remembers:

'In those days we used to act out the story of Jesus' life and parables that someone hits you on one cheek, turn the other cheek – if thine eye, I can't remember, arm offend you, cut it off, eye, into the garbage pail – if someone asks you for a coat, give them a cloak, walking a mile – and we had to act these out, with masks on, rapidly. We'd run out from two sides of the stage, and Peter would be sitting over the balcony of the church, playing his fiddle, some very strange sound (sings) like that, with a skull mask on. And he would shout out the parable. We would rush out and do it, run away, and we'd keep it up. And miracles –.... We all played lots and lots of things. That was something very particular about that show, I remember, it was a running show, a sweaty show, because you did a million – you no sooner ran across the stage and did one character or demonstration than you had to run off, change masks, or maybe even get into a puppet, and run on doing something else. And so we were all making a circle constantly between the stage and backstage.... I think it may have been that year that there was a lot of chair banging in the trial scene. We also had a Garden of Gethsemene. And then the children were in those demon masks, that we had made – the new demon masks that were brightly painted. And the children ran out in the end, jumping around the cross – I didn't quite understand that.' — (Sherman, interview.)

In 1967 the theatre had left Delancey Street for the Astor Library Landmark Building and did the *Crucixion* there Friday and Saturday evenings (admission by contribution) starting March 4th, ending with a special Easter Sunday performance in the afternoon – a *Village Voice* notice (March 2, '67) specifying 'the cast consists of 10- to 14-foot rod puppets and choruses of masked performers.'

'The most radical staging we did in the Astor Library was a Passion story which we wanted to do as a fashion show on a walk like one uses in fashion shows. On a very narrow walk where just a person would fit on a walk. I don't know if you recall, but it was – we made one long wall of burlap and played the whole show – the whole Passion story was played in walking, up and down that *bridge*. And they had the podiums.... They're the risers on which people walked.... They were lined up like that, a long wall, and people were sitting like this, so they couldn't see the whole thing at the time – so everything walked and some things were down off that walk, in front of it, like the Pointer and some other things. But that was a monochrome *burlap* color performance with against-the-wall, walking style ... right against the wall.... We had hung burlap there.... And the costumes are burlap. So it was really – it appeared – it hardly stood *out* from the wall. It was a very gentle in tone.' — (Schumann, interview, '82.)

I don't know for sure whether the show was done in a church in '67, but suspect he did it at Judson – the performance(s) that, cf. supra, Ernstthal considered the nadir of their *Crucifixion* series.

An ad in the *Village Voice* of March 28, '68 calls for help with that year's show: 'Many People Needed for Bread & Puppet *Crucifixion Against the War*'–there are to be rehearsals at noon the following Sunday at the Old Courthouse, April 4th at the Judson Memorial Church. Performances that year – April 5-21, at various of the peace-and/or-culture churches – are sponsored by The Angry Arts (become a resistance institution) and advertised as 'for the benefit of the resistance' (the contributions): a 'new production' of *Crucifixion*, and a 'new play' of Bob Nichols', *Peasant Life*, along with it – April 5, 6, 7 and 8, at the Judson Memorial Church, April 12, 13 and 14 at the Washington Square Methodist Church, with two final performances, April 21, by a first ad, being located at the American Place Theatre at St. Clement's Church on West 46th Street, *Crucifixion* in the afternoon, *Peasant Life*, along with *The Pentagon Newsreel* (by the Underground Newsreel) and something called *La Luz* by and with Roberts (Robert?) Blossom.

The Reverend King had gotten his comeuppance on the balcony of his motel April 4th and some or all of the performances April 5 ff. were dedicated to his memory. The program in a preface from Schumann's custom lists the cast of 'puppeteers, musicians, mimes and actors': Charlie Adams, George Ashley, Maurice Blanc, Francesca Borgatta, Joel Cherry, Bob Ernstthal, Mary Kelly, Arnie Lippin, Elizabeth Martinez, Jo-Ellen Sheffield, Peter Schumann, Margo Sherman, Harvey Spevak, Bill Woodkey – and 'many volunteers, including members of the Drew University Seminary.' Michael Smith reviewed the piece for the *Voice* (April 11). He still doesn't dig Schumann's manner:

'... I admire it, without really liking it. Peter Schumann is certainly some kind of genius. The familiar components of *Crucifixion* are abstracted, enlarged, reconstructed as images from a vivid if barely accessible dream (note the hack's use of 'if' (SSB)), and the story is told with a stately solemnity that is too convincing in its pathos to be rightly criticized for its idiosyncratic style.'

Is Smith forgiving Schumann the idiosyncrasy or is he wrongly criticizing him for it?

'J'ai assisté à une autre Passion, dans l'église de Judson Memorial. Du balcon, encombré de bandes magnétiques et de projecteurs, je voyais la scène se remplir de marionnettes gigantesques, représentant le Christ, Marie et les Apôtres. Avec des gestes d'une lenteur terrifiante – chaque mouvement dans l'espace, de la part de ces géants, coupait des blocs de silence que l'on entendair éclater – Marie lavait la face du Christ, avec une éponge au bout d'un long bâton. Judas donnait son baiser. Les apôtres se passaient le pain et le vin. Le choeur de l'église, sur lequel se détachaient ces figures gris craie, bleues, oranges, servait de cadre à cet *acte* religieux, équivalent d'un vitrail de Chartres ou de la sculpture médiévale de Bourgogne. En bas, dans la salle, un conteur commentait chaque tableau en enlevant des feuilles blanches suspendues à une barre transversale fixée sur une petite plateforme. La feuille comportait un dessin, et chaque fois qu'il en changeait, le conteur poussait brusquement sa plateforme vers un groupe de "fidèles" qui peu à peu, à mesure que les gestes du récitant augmentaient en violence, se trouvaient acculés dans un angle de l'église. Le rite, la légende, la foule. On passait de l'art presque immobile à l'art animé du conteur puis au bloc anonyme de la communauté. Trois temps, trois rythmes, trois espaces différents: Peter Schumann, sculpteur et danseur, utilise ces matériaux de l'art moderne pour donner forme à ses mises en scène.' — (Jotterand, *Le nouveau théâtre américain*.)

In the judgment of the group's members, this was their best version of *Crucifixion* and the most daring: Schumann had taken it apart:

'And then I think the next year we decided to go hog wild. It was probably '68 – yeah, right. Easter of '68 – probably – or '67 – that was that version that I mentioned that we shuffled the elements and it was *very* interesting. As I remember, I loved it. I thought it was

and incorporated a sixth one into his '69 *Cry*. This essentially terminated the series. He tapered off by a version in which the parables and beatitudes of Jesus, his message, in a scene entitled *The Building of Jesus* are interpreted as political resistance message, with more than a hint that even violent resistance is called for, and which ends with a Last Supper and a Crucifixion, that no matter how they were finagled with (cf. my account of *Cry* infra) constituted a terrifying and pretty well final finale. – On the Easter Pageants of '70 and '71 and the new Easter play (*Stations of the Cross*) of '72, cf. infra, part V.

---

fabulous – like we took Mary sitting down at a table – eating – and we would talk about the Annunciation. And it was all these elements that were not descriptive of one another, but just put together, flat – just juxtaposed. And they created a real magic, as I remember. That was one of my favorite versions. It was very abstract in a way, and yet it worked also . . . .' — (Ernstthal, interview.)

'In '68 when we did the *Crucifixion*, which was, I thought, for me it was my favorite *Crucifixion* show. The entrance of the yellow people for the Last Supper was excruciatingly slow, and wonderful – I thought it was just – reached a real peak of experience. Everyone felt – I felt – that we had created this landscape of heat, of going, going, going, towards tragedy, and building the tension, never letting it drop for a moment. That *Crucifixion* show we did not perform much. Just a few times at Judson and Washington Square Methodist . . . Mabel was in it. Mabel Dennison. I thought it was – for me it was the most sort of experimental Easter show Peter did. It was the one that was hardest for the audiences to get. It was so abstracted from the story, from the easily caught story, into a relentless – beautiful art, beautiful art – there was a dance. There were two white angel puppets that were connected, and they did a kind of slow spinning dance for the Annunciation. And there was another scene – we performed this in front of an enormous red curtain. Another scene – Bob (Nichols) would read from the Bible. "The one you are looking for, he is not here, he has risen." And Mabel and I, taking turns, we were like two people playing the same character. It was a Mary character, but not in white, and not in blue, but with our hair hanging, and no mask. We'd come out from the red curtain and sit down at a table and drink a glass of water. So, you see what I mean . . . . It was more obscure to an audience, to us it made a lot of sense. And Bob kept reading from the New Testament. And the yellow puppets, the disciples, were kept hidden behind some screens. And their approach to the table for the Last Supper scene was very, very, very slow. And meanwhile there were two people inside of a smaller yellow people puppet, facing each other with a bass drum between them. And they would walk back and forth and stay just like this – beating the drum – but it was much slower. And meanwhile the puppets were just very, very slowly approaching. And the tension was extraordinary.' — (Sherman, interview.)

15. Puppetry for children. 1963-1967.

As I have mentioned, there seems to have been some idea initially that these shows were to be the bread and butter of the Bread and Puppet Theatre. This did not work out. The basic reason seems to have been that Schumann had no interest in and no talent for doing shows for children. The traditions of the country were not available to him: the raw vigor and individualism of the democratic comic strips and cartoon movies of the first third of the century would repulse him no less than the sinister salesman's wit of the TV moppets. He first reached back into his German childhood, then into his memory of silent comedy movies.

The theatre apparently started out with the childish *King Stories*,[1] very soon, keeping these going more or less, enriching the fare with hand puppet versions of German fairy tales, largely gotten up and performed by its two mothers, Eva Eckhardt and Elka:[2] selected for their moral lesson,

---

1. 'In Delancey Street we started kids' shows as soon as we moved in there, in addition to these other projects, but kids' shows were done *all* the time.' (Schumann, interview, '79.) And the first reference I found in the *Village Voice* is in fact in the issue of November 14, '63 in the 'What's On . . . For Children' section: 'Puppet show, Sundays at 4:30 p.m. Bread & Puppet Museum . . . (contribution).' But the next reference in that section is to a show, *Story*, to be presented there March 5, '64 (at the same time): perhaps *King Story II*, which had been showing there evenings together with *King Story I* during February.
2. 'What's On for Children' notices, *Village Voice*, March 12th through April 30th, '64 announce *Fairy Tales* at the Museum, Sundays at 4:40 p.m.

'We (Eva and Elka (SSB)) used puppets that Peter made, little hand puppets, and then we used toys from the children. I remember having the plastic fish for *The Fisherman and His Wife*. Maybe we did that most.' — (Elka, in Schumann, interview, '79.)

'. . . this story of greed. They catch the fish and the fish gives them wishes – the ring – and everything they wish for comes true and she gets more and more stuff and then she wishes it would all go away. That's her last wish and it all goes away and they are happy back where they were. Story of greed. Not like von Stroheim but then, naturally, we took that story because it's about greed and avariciousness.' (Ernstthal, interview, '79.) Ernstthal remembers it as one of the 'attempts that never really came out – the fisherman had a little pole with a little string on it. The wife was shrill like a Punch and Judy. There was also an anti-womanness slant, I would say – women were generally put down – as shrill and silly, like Punch and Judy, or very cultic, like Mary . . . . Anyway, she was shrill. She was constantly kicking him out of the house . . . she would be kicking him out of the house and tell him to go out and he would go and he'd drop a line over the stage and be pulling on something and then this big fish would come up and talk, as a puppet. Then the fish would go down. And then the husband would run back . . . run back to his wife, and the wife, the home, the little cutout house . . . and he'd tell them the story and she would wish for all these things, a mink coat, and this and that, until they had no life left, and she'd wish everything would go away and that was all.' — (Ernstthal, interview.)

They did *The Goose That Lays Golden Eggs*. It carries the same moral. They did *The Emperor's New Clothes*, which they also showed at the Brooklyn Children's Museum, and, at a matinee on the lawn, July 12 '64, at the Ohayo Mountain Hall in Woodstock, New York, where it was advertised as a 'masked play.' The Emperor apparently was decently

and presumably pointed up to drive it home. By early '65 at the latest, probably earlier, they also put on Punch and Judy shows – mixed hand, stick, and rod puppet shows, like the others so far mainly or even exclusively using the older Putney puppets. These were rougher and more fun-oriented, less moralistic: slapstick shows.[3] Schumann was really just feeling his way with these exercises in more or less traditional forms. By the beginning of '66, he was doing his own kind of shows in the tradition of Chaplin, but they now were more for teenagers and grown-ups than for children,[4] and comprised or even mostly consisted of masked mime. Some

---

dressed in toilet paper, a gag that according to an article inspired by Bruno Eckhardt (*Frankfurter Rundschau*, May 25, '68) was soon thereafter stolen for a T.V. show:

'It never really came off, we never liked it. And then we tried and changed this and changed that and worked on it and worked on it, worked on it. Finally we realized this is not working, skip it.' — (Ernstthal, interview.)

When Elka and Eva 'ran out of ideas' (Elka in Schumann, interview, '79), they did Grimm together with children's stories for which Schumann suggested the ideas.

The first review of children's shows, comparing them unfavorable with the Henry Street Settlement House Paper Bag Players' *Fortunately*, 'a thoroughly well-planned afternoon's entertainment for young children,' was probably not too unfair:

'They aren't quite ready to be seen yet. The puppets are marvelous, but the two stories I saw are just terrible.' They are overly moralizing and go on interminably. Once Peter Schumann and his assistants really learn to adjust for working for an audience of young people who are not willing to put up with the drink-your-milk and eat-your-bread stories and get some interesting tales, the shows will probably be great. There is excitement in the puppetry already, but the presentation needs discipline.' — (Peter Share, *Theatre for Children*, *Village Voice*, March 26, '64.)

3. These are the earliest children's shows mentioned in the *Village Voice* since the March '64 fairy tales. The *Voice*'s *Off-Off Broadway Theatre Guide* informs of performances of *Punch and Judy* and of *The Rat Movie*, Saturdays at 9 p.m., January 9, '65 ff.

'They put up a curtain and they come up behind and the baby's crying and he throws the baby out the window and he has to go out and get it and he drives in a car and he cheats the hangman and the police try to arrest him, they arrest him and put him in jail and they're going to hang him and he says I don't know if my head can fit. I don't know how to do this. I've never been hung before. And the hangman says well just do it like this and he puts his head in and he kicks the thing out from under him and the hangman hangs himself and when they all say da da da da da.' — (Ernstthal, interview.)

4. Advertisements in the *Voice* by the Bridge Theatre on St. Mark's Place announce Sunday afternoon performances, February 24 and March 5, 12 and 19, '66:

'Puppets at the Bridge. Peter Schumann's Bread and Puppet Theatre presents *A Winter Story*, the stirring operetta of a *Young Man with a Yellow Hat in the Big City Evicted from Apartment #3*, a musical mask play with violin, v-botts, trumpet, kazoo, hub caps, bells, triangles, piano . . . . Children 50c, adults $1.00.'

A Bridge ad in the June 16 *Voice* advertises a showing of *The Big City Story* – probably the same show – 'an adventure for children' the following Sunday afternoon.

The *Voice*'s 'What's On' column recommended *Winter Story* for children, and the play got them their second review of their children's shows, an enthusiastic one, this time:

'If the doctor advised you to take a daily walk around your mental block, you, as an accompanied or unaccompanied adult, could head in no better direction than the Bridge Theatre on Saturdays at 4, where Peter Schumann's Bread and Puppet Theatre presents a changing program of old and new stories. One speaks sometimes of a show as "moving"

such shows were 'sideshows' at the summer of '66 *Chicken Little* parks project,[5] and then, perhaps with others, and with Punch and Judy and variants of *King Story* showed up again in a 'Slapstick Festival', Sunday

---

and the word has the slight accent of a cliché. There is nothing of the cliché about Schumann's writing or his oversized puppets and masks, and they are moving in precisely the exhilarating way that a trip on the parachute jump at Coney Island or a night-through of excelling talk are moving. You aren't in the same place any more, mentally. My daughter said, looking back on the show, "It left me full of wonders."

After the first astounding seconds of the overture, wherein percussion nearly becomes concussion, child and parent comprehend with delight that they are in for some very powerful theatre, that rare excitement of the unexpectant. As the crowded hour unfolds, no matter what plane is opened to you – humor, irony, satire, tragedy, sentimentality – there is an inevitable and immediate sense of identification: this tale of a near-tragic separation is set in motion because the ethereal heroine keeps a dental appointment; one travels to Mars in a steamer trunk; the nice young man states simply that on his birthday 'everyone gave me nothing.'

There is a remarkable scene in the clubhouse of the rats who live in the hero's apartment house. They have educational T.V. and a rat film is shown. Subtly, relationship to villain-hero tilts and flips; one's loyalty is in abeyance as one sees things from another point of view. The film, a series of drawings rolled from one spool to another, is a play within a play, achieving a high and wildly funny suspense, as Peter Schumann tells the story. A man adopts a rat, who grows into a monster, and attempts to attack the baby. At the last moment, an interfering angel kills the rat. 'What a tragedy!' they all mourn. But, an important but, there is no taint of the "sick" in Schumann's humor.

The abstractions, grotesqueries, exaggerations, and tendresses, the constant root relationship to the 'real' world of city, policy, landlady, apartment number, the alternatively riotous or gentle music, all are extremely vital and comprehensible to children: it is the world of their drawings and imaginations. No less does Schumann's world draw the adult up into it. Here is that rare thing: theatre at its best, at once timeless, undatable, and intricately related to the very day.

On stage are Schumann, Bob Ernstthal, Catherine Merrill, and Charles Adams. I do not have the names of the miracle workers backstage. After the performance, Schumann lets the children examine the delicately wrought masks and puppets – simply perilously one would think yet surviving, he turns the stage over to an avalanche of kids. It is as though the fragility of mask and illusion, by its very tenuousness, is impervious to destruction. There is a beautifully strong security and central calm in Schumann and his work.

Performances are packed. For reservations call the Bridge Theatre 4 St. Marks Place, OR 3-4600. Admission is 50 cents for children under 12, $1 for adults. Every Saturday at 4 p.m. the museum is at 148 Delancey Street, the number YU 2-1535.' — (Victoria Wren, *Village Voice*, March 3, '66.)

'*The Young Man in the Big City.* That was when I was on stage at the Bridge Theatre playing the guitar and singing *Careless Love*. And it was a comedy about – it was kind of like me – or it was kind of like the kid who comes to the city. It was mostly the Candide kind of slapstick, silly narration about a kid who comes to the city. That's one thing I remember. It was again one of these obscure trips that never got to first base. Yeah, I was standing and playing the guitar and it was kind of a spoof. It was a lightweight thing.' — (Ernstthal, interview.)

5. 'Along the way we were making up side shows. And I got to act in sideshows along with the children and the teenagers. And Bob Ernstthal narrated many of them. He made them up and narrated them – they were very funny .... I was doing lots of mime work with face masks on. I was the Hungry Young Man. I was always doing that kind of dancing-mime-acting with a mask on.' — (Sherman, interview.)

'We played *Chicken Little* and then a series of slapsticks. The idea was booth stories, each booth playing a separate story like a carnival thing. And we did *The Hungry Young Man*, which is a very funny slapstick. Again a silent movie type of story, where a guy comes in, I think I did the narration and Margo played the man. And he goes into the restaurant and orders all this food and then can't pay for it. (I: That's Chaplin.) Yeah, and then the boss coming in and throwing him out. It was a real classic slapstick and it was very funny. It was very good. It was one of our most successful ones and we had a whole series of these little slapstick things. There was one in a boat also, where we had waves painted and people moving them so it looked like little waves, and people rowing across the water, sort of like a kind of seaside romance of a fish ... It was very elaborate.'
— (Ernstthal, interview.)

'But at noon Sunday, when the troupe arrived in Tompkins Park in Brooklyn and set up three small stages at home plate on the baseball diamond, they were ready. The children were excited and earnest. "At first we had some trouble with discipline," said Schumann. "Now they discipline themselves."

Nine short skits were presented during the afternoon, narrated by Bread and Puppet member Bob Ernstthal, accompanied on voice and guitar by Cruz Martinez, who came to the summer program from the Lincoln Hospital Neighborhood Service Centers. Occasionally there was also music from a fantastic instrument made of wooden blocks, leftovers from a hardware store, discarded pieces of a fence being torn down by the Parks Department, and unidentifiable objects. "I don't know what you call it – a Steinberg," said Charles Adams, who supervised its creation and played it with 12-year-old Juan Perez.

The children, dancing and miming their parts like small Marcel Marceaus, acted the story of the king who got a cat to chase the rat in his palace. In the end the rat came back, dressed in the king's robes. Or else the king became a rat, that was left for the audience to decide.

They acted out the story of the hungry man who tricked his way into a feast in a restaurant, was ordered by the boss (what an archboss!) to sweep the floor, got into a fight with the waiter, and then, when the stupid-looking cop appeared, told a brilliant sob story.

They also did the story of the princess who never laughed, whose mother was a termagant and father a weakling, and who, in the end, roared with laughter when a clever suitor tricked the father into beating the mother. Oh, they were tuned in all right, those child performers, and their afternoon audience of about 300 children and adults watched, absorbed.

Unfortunately, the group had been unsuccessful in getting bleachers for the spectators and they kept creeping up for a better view. But although some of the smaller spectators found it hard to see at times, most stayed on through the show, from 3:30 to after 5 p.m.'
(Rosa Gustaitis, *The Children Build a Children's Theatre*, *Village Voice*, September 1, '66.)

'De petites marionnettes à gaine qui doivent servir à un spectacle de *Punch and Judy*, sont construites; malheureusement elles seront volées. Les enfants remplaceront alors le spectacle prévu par de courts sketches qu'ils mimeront en mettant différents masques, tandis qu'un marionnettiste accompagné d'un ou plusieurs musiciens racontera l'histoire.

'L'histoire du roi et du rat': un roi à peur d'un rat. Il demande à un chat de chasser le rat et de surveiller son trône. Mais un oiseau arrive et le chat part à sa poursuite. A la fin, le rat revient, revêtu des habits du roi, à moins que ce ne soit le roi qui se soit transformé en rat.

'L'histoire du jeune homme qui a faim': un jeune homme sans le sou a faim dans un grand restaurant. Il commande des dizaines de plats, puis déclare que la nourriture est si mauvaise qu'il ne paiera pas. Cris, bataille avec le serveur. Le patron appelle la police. Le jeune homme pleure: sa mère est à l'hopital, son oncle s'est cassé la jambe la semaine dernière, etc. Tout le monde se met à pleurer avec lui.' — (Kourilsky, '71.)

A list of Elka's (*Tulane Drama Review* #47 (1970)) lists, in addition to *The Hungry Young Man* and *The King and the Rat*, some not mentioned so far: *Rose Robbery, In the*

afternoons, February-September '67 at the Shakespeare Festival Building,[6] the culmination of Bread and Puppet's children shows, and practically also the end of them, insofar, at least, as Schumann had much to do with them. There are no further references in the *Village Voice*, the Bread and Puppet Diary for November '67-March '68 does not record any, the *Blue Raven Beauty* fairy tales of December (?) '67-April '68 (cf. infra) were more for grownups than for children, the summer of '70 and '72 Coney Island shows (cf. infra) were, with the possible exceptions of *Tristan and Isolde* ('70) and *St. George the Dragonkiller* ('72), mainly for grownups, and up in Vermont, after June '70 there were no children's shows I have heard of (other than, initially, some high school *Christmas Stories*) that Schumann had a hand in.

Essentially, I would say, he around '65/'66 slipped out of puppetry for children by way of a half-way house, masked mime derived from the silent

---

Park, The 34-Year-Old Canary, Story of Two Beautiful Ladies Who Went Swimming in the Ocean.

The Man on the Park Bench (Elka's 'In the Park'):

'It was a Chaplin actually, a Chaplinesque story of a man wooing this girl on a park bench, and a bum coming along and kind of horns in on the guy and steals the girl. There's a Chaplin short that is exactly that.' — (Ernstthal, interview.)

6. The *Voice* announces this festival in its 'What's On ... For Children' column on February 23, '67: there will be 'slapstick shows' by the B & P Theatre at the Old Astor Library Sundays at 3 p.m. I think they did children's afternoon shows there every weekend, more or less, till the beginning of November, but the *Voice* record is intermittent: a *Punch and Judy Festival*, July 23 and 30 ('67), a '*Children's Festival*' on August 27 and/or September 3rd, *Punch and Judy* and *The Magic Bag* (?), *The Rat Movie, The Hungry Young Man* ('Puppet shows and slapstick mimes') on September 10th, *Punch and Judy* and *The Magic Bag* again the following Sunday, together with *The Intelligent King Augustus* and *The Great Warrior (King Story II?), Rinaldini, The Great Warrior, El Saco Magico* and *The Hungry Young Man* on October 1st, *The Great Warrior from Japan vs. the Giant Blunderbore from Ohio, The Dead Man Rises, Rinaldini the Great Robber* the following Sunday, and the program of October 1st, with *El Saco Magico* substituted for *Dead Man* and 'an old-time marching band' thrown in, on October 15th. WIN, the resistance magazine, announced slapstick shows for children, Sunday afternoons, March 12th ff., and *Chicken Little* for children, Sunday afternoons in May. *The Militant*, a Trotskyite magazine on October 23rd announced Sunday afternoon 'slapstick mimes and musical puppet shows' running through November 5th.

The *Rinaldini* at Papp's place was a remake of the crankie *Rinaldini* they had done in the summer of '63:

'He goes up on a ladder telling the story. But there was a chorus of people kind of acting it out at the same time and singing the song ... a sing-songy kind of explanation of the story.' — (Ernstthal, interview.)

The Great Warrior from Japan vs. The Giant Blunderbore from Ohio was a version of *King Story*.

'... where instead of the dragon we had Uncle Fatso playing the Giant Blunderbore from Ohio who was the bad guy. And in fact the Warrior took a swipe at him and his pants fell down and then he killed the Red Man and all that. It was a comic demon instead of an evil, scary demon. The demon was a comical one who was Uncle Fatso.' — Ernstthal, interview.)

movies. As far as one can tell from the stories, this genre in his hands was and remained thoroughly derivative, for a moment tempted him — we see it in photos of the '67 *Chicken Little* — but he brutally squashed his temptation by recourse to something along the lines of Brechtian acting and story presentation (Ernstthal, then Levy in *A Man Says Goodbye*): for doing it he was dependent on Margo Sherman's second rate talent for sentimental pathos à la Marcel Marceau and on Ernstthal's inventive wit as story teller and talents as narrative performer, and the appeal to an audience by sentiment and pathos corrupted the coldly moral and tragic address he essentially wanted. The kid stuff — Punch and Judy, fairy tales, silly *King Story* slapstick — he got out of by recourse to it was more in his line, but didn't work. The essential reason it didn't work, I would say, was that he related to the child spectator as puppeteer along the lines of the relation of an old-fashioned European parent to his children: as object to be reared, i.e. tamed; as non-adult to be made over into adult. He therefore, did not show the child-spectator (1) the respect, (2) the affection the modern and especially the American child has come to count as his/her due. These would have hindered rather than promoted the child's transformation into a responsible adult. Refraining from flattery, he made his shows corny rather than cute. American children's art addresses the child in an egalitarian manner: phonily so when with gay frankness pushing on it the liberal ideology of cooperation, genuinely when extending before the child as continuous with its own existence a world of competitively struggling individuals, rabbits or other. Schumann, whether as puppet-sculptor or show-maker made no bones about the status difference between the adult puppeteering educator and the to-be-educated stripling audience member. Right or wrong — I have both approaches — there was no way this could work.

In addition, the couple that children delight in, the small and/or weak, perhaps apparently dumb, good-hearted and/or carefree or silly underdog that ends up on top and the smart aleck or bully lording it over him but in the end getting his comeuppance, the truly dumb one, is lacking in Schumann's repertoire; as also the art of violence with its stop-and-go rhythm, escalations and impossible wish-fulfillment outrange, its employment of all means, its conversion of the world altogether into an ingenious and surprising panoply of instruments of revenge, pursuit, punishment. Schumann doesn't have it in him to expend work, care and fantasy on such: he is against violence. He can no more indulge in a child audience's imaginary destruction of the adult world than he could really let himself go in a glorification of the Vietcong. But brutality is the essence of humor.[7]

---

7. The National Socialists wanted to ennoble fair puppetry by cutting down on its violence: as not in the spirit of the new age. Max Jacob (*Mein Kasperl*, '81) has recorded a practitioner's opposition to this worthy ambition (shared by the 'artistic' puppeteers):

'Meine Herren Kollegen von der künstlerischen Fakultät, davon verstehen Sir nun ganz und gar nichts. Das verhält sich nämlich so: wir Puppenspieler von der Strasse, die wir publik, gegen Tellersammlung, spielen, haben es nicht leicht. Sie wissen es selbst, dass die grossen Menschen wohl sehr gern vor unserer Bühne stehenbleiben und lachen. Wenn aber meine Frau mit dem Teller kommt, dann sind die Zuschauer plötzlich nicht mehr da. Jeder drückt sich, um keinen Groschen geben zu müssen. Da wir einfachen Spieler aber auch Psychologen sind, wissen wir, dass das Publikum immer dann seinen Groschen gibt, wenn es von Herzen lachen kann. Und es lacht immer dann hemmungslos, wenn der Kasper mit der Bratpfanne kommt und den Polizisten oder den Teufel totschlägt. In diesem Moment geht meine Frau schnell mit dem Teller raus und kassiert. Damit sie nun oft Gelegenheit hat, mit dem Teller rauszuhuschen, sind wir genötigt, ebenso oft jemand auf der Bühne totzuschlagen. So ist das, und ich hoffe, dass Sie det verstehen können.'

'Artistic' puppetry worked by no less homicidal irony and satire. Schumann's theatre is occasionally satiric, but never ironic: killing and dying is central to it, but is never humorous: our death, not that of 'the others' is shown.

16. Puppetry with children. 1965, 1966.

In the summers of '65 and '66, under a liberal city administration – Lindsay Mayor, Hoving Parks Commissioner – and with Johnson's Great Society program getting into full swing, Schumann for the only time in his life got involved in work with children, lower class children that had to be seduced into cooperation, Black kids and Puerto Rican kids: a ten-day work project with 50 to 60 kids by him and Bruno Eckhardt, sponsored and paid for by Spanish Catholic Action, on East 100th Street in Harlem in '65,[1] a much larger project in '66, with about 300 kids, with 10 paid volunteers getting $100 a week, lasting two months, sponsored by the New York City Parks Department, centered in St. Mary's Park[2] in a Puerto Rican part of the South Bronx, with a smaller simultaneous operation run from St. Nicholas Park in Harlem.[3]

---

1. 'That was organized by an organization that was called Spanish Catholic Action and that was a summer project that had already started at the time that I got into it on East 100th Street, I believe, between First and Second Avenue. That's supposed to be the most crowded, the most populated block in the whole of New York and it has many problems, but because it is a sort of ill-famed block, a lot of attention is given to this block. At the time I was working there, lots of different social agencies – the Catholic Church, a bunch of nuns going around handing out lollypops to kids. The project that I took over was one that didn't function well. They had spent a lot of money on it. There was an art teacher who got the kids of the block together – grade school kids, got them to paint the walls and sidewalks and everybody got upset in the neighborhood and she had to be fired. She couldn't continue, she wasn't on good terms with the kids, so instead they asked me to do another project, so I went there, with the help of Bruno, something like a week or ten days, a lot of puppets, including Uncle Fatso . . . .' — (Schumann, interview, '79.)
2. 'St. Mary's Park is an oasis of green in a bleak neighborhood inhabited mostly by Puerto Ricans and Negroes. It is a shabby park, though heavily used. "sometimes when it is quiet, we can hear the bottles breaking on the pavement," Schumann said. "Clunk, clunk, in the park." ' (R. Gustaitis, *Bread & Puppet: The Children Build a Children's Theatre, Village Voice*, September 1, '66.)
3. '(I: Was that anything the same as the workshop for the *Pied Piper of Harlem?*) No, it was a known workshop that I had started already in the spring of that year by going to schools in the neighborhood and drumming up interest among kids, in that area of the South Bronx, that is now pretty burned out. It was pretty burned out then actually, and talks with the Council for Parks and Playgrounds who initiated this project, who approached me to do it, and the Parks Department and other people who wanted to contribute to it – that was a much more prepared project, it was not – I knew already that I would do it the winter before it started, so I found the people I wanted to work with during that winter and went into the school and talked with the teachers in the schools and talked with students and described to them what I wanted to do and tried to get the interest for it, sign up sheets and all that kind of work. Found an administrator for it and it was a kind of city organization project of which i was the artistic head.' — (Schumann, interview, '79.)

'There was a lady, I can't remember her name, but she was like a charity lady who wanted us to do workshops for poor kids. This was also the time of the riots, so they were

The official idea was to stimulate talent among the underprivileged,[4] the function to give the neighborhoods a sense of concern, what with their young men, not eligible for college draft deferments, and anyhow satisfied in lieu of employment to serve their country, off to war. The projects gave Schumann a chance to go from big to giant puppets,[5] with work and

---

throwing money at the poor people at that time. And Catherine Merrill was the classic liberal girl and she had some contacts in Harlem and they set us up in the South Bronx in this big parks and recreation center.' — (Ernstthal, interview.)

'Die Park-Behörden in New York mit ganz vernünftigen Leitern haben sich überlegt, dass man in den Slum-Gegenden mehr aus den Parks machen kann als Rasenflächen und Bänke. Sie wollten von uns eine Art Community-Theatre, an dem sich möglichst viele Leute aus der Umgebung beteiligen – gewisse soziale Zentren. Sie stellten uns in Harlem eine Kirche als Arbeitsraum und in der South Bronx, wo hauptsächlich Puertoricaner leben, einen Gärtnerei-Schuppen für die Vorbereitung zur Verfügung. Hier habe ich unentgeltlich für die Kinder der Viertel alle möglichen Werkunterrichte, Schauspielerkurse, Bastelabende gegeben und dabei mit ihnen lauter verschiedene Puppen, Masken und Figurinen zu bauen begonnen. Mit jeder Figur, mit jedem Kostüm entstanden Geschichten, Szenen, Improvisationen. Wir einigten uns dann auf eine Hauptszene: nämlich die alte Kindergeschichte vom 'Chicken Little' mit Riesenpuppen und 13 kleinen Bühnen im Hintergrund, in denen alle Einfälle und Erfindungen der Vorbereitungszeit von Kindern gespielt werden.' — (Schumann, *tendenzen*, November '66-February '67.)

4. 'In a staid-looking building in St. Mary's Park in the Bronx, a hundred-foot dragon arched lazily down a hall. In an adjoining room a boy beat bongo drums. And in still another room a five-foot canary argued with a bearded German sculptor.

The building is St. Mary's Recreation Center, owned by the Department of Parks, which is sponsoring an experimental eight-week program to discover and encourage talent and creativity in chicken from under-privileged neighborhoods.

The sculptor is Peter Schumann, the director of the program, and huge sculpted masks of the dragon and the canary are some of the products of his work with the 150 children in this project and a similar one in St. Nicholas Park in Central Harlem. The children wear costumes with the masks to complete the portrayals.

The project was devised by the Council of Parks and Playgrounds, an advisory committee for the Parks Department.

"We wanted an original creative program to bring in more children and interest them creatively", Mrs. Ann Buttenwieser, president of the council, said recently. "Not necessarily a one-shot deal but to get talent. We went to the Park Commissioner, and he thought it was a great idea."

A $15,000 budget and a staff of 10 have been allocated for the program. The staff includes specialists in music and dance, a seamstress, and Carl Erca, a former professional trumpet player who oversees the program and acts as liaison between the artists and the park officials.

But having fun is the by-product rather than the reason for the program. This is not simply an arts and crafts project to keep children off the streets. It is a serious effort to develop a structure in which vocational skills can be developed and in which artists can make a contribution to society.

"We take this professionally," says Karl Linn, a psychologist and landscape architect and a director of the Council of Parks and Playgrounds. "Our purpose in this program was to develop opportunities for creative artists to be engaged in public service." ' — (*Do-it-yourself Drama is Fostered by City, New York Times*, August 27, 1966.)

5. 'And then the last week before our performances we made up a big show, *Chicken Little*, with big, big puppets. This was the first time Peter had made large, giant puppets.

materials free or paid for, and – the '66 one – to put on his first big show – *Chicken Little* – with a large popular audience. He got these jobs – one or both of the Harlem ones apparently thanks to connections – before he was known otherwise than for his peace parades: his first theatre success, *Fire*, dates from January-June '66, and he got the '66 job during the winter of '65/'66. The establishment was co-opting a gadfly to calm a hornet's nest.[6] The Puerto Rican kids joined in the fun, but the Black kids, especially in '66, refused to cooperate – the Black hustlers involved on the administrative side of the project abandoned with the funds.[7]

And that's what he was so excited about.... So it was all very exciting, because I wasn't really interested in puppet-building. And so I didn't really, really get the thrill of what it meant for someone who had been sculpting things like this to suddenly create eighteen-foot creatures that were operated by three or five people. I liked it, but I wasn't – so attached to it. Anyway, suddenly we had to make up the show, and that's when the kids really came alive.' — (Sherman, interview.)

'And we went to New Jersey, I remember that really well, for empty garbage cans and found this clay pit in a brickyard and we went into this clay pit up to our neck in water and dug out tons and tons of clay. And that's where all these real big puppets come from, from that time, because we came out with just tons of clay ... we made all these great puppets and the dragon, it was on wheels, a great big enormous dragon and all the really big stuff ... the project was very successful. The kids loved it and we loved working with them.' — (Ernstthal, interview.)

6. 'The Bread and Puppet Theatre is composed of painters, poets, musicians, and other artists rather than professional actors. To many New Yorkers it is known mainly by its participation in peace marches, where its grotesque masks and costumes usually attracted some violent attention. Few have seen the troupe's occasional performances in a Lower East Side loft.

When the Council for Parks and Playgrounds suggested to the Parks Department that Peter Schumann run a summer program, however, Commissioner Hoving did not shy away. He was all for trying new things, and was enthusiastic about his concept of the parks as a stage. "They're far out," he commented not long ago, "but so what? Why not?" ' — (R. Gustaitis, *Bread & Puppet, Village Voice*, September 1, '66.)

7. 'The project in Harlem was run by, first of all it was in some kind of a house, like a neighborhood social work house ... (I: It's a rip-off story –) That's right. And the guy ran away with all the money. They were all waiting to get paid and the guy disappeared. Plus I remember it being the scene of the most chaos I'd ever seen in my life. If you can imagine fifteen kids in this house and never being in the same room at the same time but always running in and out of the doors, closing doors, opening doors, knocking on the other side of the doors, coming in, in and out, in and out all the time. It was just frantic. They were mad. I don't know if that's typical or what but these kids were just maniacs. They were just in and out, constantly on the move, running around, running around, never ever doing anything. Never doing anything. And whatever there was to do they would avoid it. They were just wild – I've never seen anything like it. I mean, they were just frantic. They would frantically be running and moving without ever doing anything. And it was total chaos. The one in Harlem was just a fiasco. We saw very soon that we couldn't do anything with them and then the guy ran away with the money and that was the beginning of the end of the Catherine Merrill episode, as I remember it. I may be wrong but I think that after that she was kind of out. Cut out someplace.' — (Ernstthal, interview.)

'The program was organized to run concurrently in St. Mary's Park and Harlem's St.

The guiding idea was to have the shows resulting from the puppet-making to be the kids' — story- and mask- and puppet-wise — but finding them corrupted by television, the Bread and Puppet Theatre took over.[8]

Nobody remembers what the show, for some reason referred to as *The Pied Piper of Harlem*, resulting from the first project was. Schumann remembers it (Schumann, interview, '79) as some kind of interaction between the giant nasty Uncle Fatso puppet built during it who was the Landlord, a large number of rats represented by little kids with rat masks they had made, and who may have been the Landlord's 'gang', and a large number of houses — the houses on that block — represented by little kids with painted cardboard boxes that had holes in them to look like houses, but with curtains inside them so that they were at the same time little puppet stages on which the kids could act out scenes from life with little puppets. Kourilsky ('71) thinks the rats attacked the houses. I.e. the kids would act out their community's life as fight with the Landlord and his rats.

The Black kids were not cooperating, but Schumann in '65 got one of his most powerful puppets out of them, Uncle Fatso, villain in many peace parades. And though he took over from them in the making of the mask mold, it is also one of the few masks with substantial creative contributions by others than himself, these kids. The mask was made directly over the clay. Schumann ordinarily has jealously guarded for himself the prerogative of making the mold. On these projects, the kids got to fool around with the clay and in Uncle Fatso's case, they apparently got quite far.[9]

Nicholas Park, with the performances at the end of the summer bringing the two groups together. But whereas the Southeast Bronx program had seven staff members from the Bread and Puppet Theatre, the one in Harlem had only one and drew more heavily on the community for staff. The lack of expertise and some personality clashes in Harlem proved to be a disappointment. When the show was put on, less than a third of 60 children were from the Harlem group.' — (R. Gustaitis, *Bread & Puppet, Village Voice*, September 1, '66.)

8. 'As the summer wore on, of course, things did not work out exactly as planned. The Punch and Judy shows had to be cancelled because somebody sneaked into the workshop and stole all the small puppets. The plays did not come entirely from the children because, when encouraged to invent plots, they turned to Batman and other things they had seen on T.V. So Schumann and his troupe members sketched out scenes and then had the children improvise within them. The dialogue, the gestures, the complications and refinements in the skits came mostly from the children.' — (R. Gustaitis, *Bread & Puppet, Village Voice*, September 1, '66.)

9. 'What we did was we brought a lot of clay up from Delancey Street and they had a little store to operate from, and got the kids working on the clay. I wanted to make a big face, built a base from brick and scraps of wood, tied them together with twine and wire, had them throw the clay on, which was fun — to just take a handful of clay and smash it as hard as you can on that base. Then once we had a big lump of clay sitting there on the table, I had them do a face, I had them do a nose. A bunch of kids worked on the nose, got another bunch of kids to work on the left eye, got a bunch of kids to work on the left ear. As long as they did not disturb each other's traffic, it seemed to be all right. Everyone

At the conclusion of the project or soon after Uncle Fatso was paraded in the streets locally as Landlord and this way made it into *Newsweek*.

The '66 project was aimed toward shows August 28 to September 4 in four New York City parks in popular – slum – neighborhoods (Americans usually call slums 'ghettoes' in order to obscure their essential character).[10] The Bedford-Stuyvesant one was rained out. The shows were to consist partly of simultaneously repeated daytime skits (originally intended to be Punch and Judy, but the puppets for these got stolen) and a

---

worked on a different feature in that face and then they messed it up too much, so I walked in, kicked them out and changed it so it wouldn't fall apart and collapse, which is a technical problem with these amounts of clay. And then out of that whole mess of people, moving that chunk of clay and digging hands into various parts of it, we got Uncle Fatso. Then I had older kids help me with the celastic work on it. After the celastic had dried, cut him open, cut into two pieces, bend him, mount it, and put very bad paint on it, that later on turned out not to be waterproof. I don't think I ever had people work on a puppet like that. That was new. The final product was probably something I probably controlled most of and made most of the decisions, but it still was a large contribution of little kids' hands in that face. The body became a sewing project more than anything, the suit, the fancy suit, the tie. Make it all. Look like a fancy suit, that was the goal. We had a bunch of teenaged girls who really enjoyed it. Several of them were just on the tie – I remember that, they were very proud. Uncle Fatso was such a popular enterprise on this block. Everybody knew him by name. The kids called him Uncle Fatso even when he was in clay. (I: Did you use the same kids who were working in the workshop for the show?) It wasn't a different group, only many more involved in the show than in the building process. In the building, the problem is always how to deal with the younger kids. I like to do certain primitive kinds of concept like (having them) fool around with a bit of clay and doing the first sketch of the face – the same thing applies to painting, they are able to quickly make a great design and throw it on a piece of cardboard or paper or a mask. But they are unable to use it in consideration of the sculpture or of what it's used for, the mask with its requirements – breathing for noses – so when you work with kids you have to find out what you're going to use them for, what they are good and not good at. So at a certain moment in a workshop like that when the necessity arises, to throw them out or do the work yourself, get some more of the kids to help you with such things and that is the way to work. We did a lot of that in that workshop.' — (Schumann, interview, '79.)

10. A flyer: 'Boys Girls Teenagers Adults Everybody join the GIANT PUPPET CIRCUS for the theater festival in mid-August. Starts July 5.'

'Four "Giant Puppet Festivals" will be presented in four neighborhood parks from August 28 to September 4. Peter Schumann of the Bread & Puppet Theatre will direct the young artists, sculptors, musicians and puppeteers who will participate in the Mobile Theatre Project sponsored by the Council for Parks and Playgrounds in cooperation with the Department of Parks. Each of the four festivals will feature slapstick and puppet shows as well as booths and games throughout the park from 2 to 5:30 p.m. A Dragon Parade through the streets will herald the main show. The festivals will take place in Tompkins Park, at Greene, Marcy and Lafayette Avenues in the Bedford-Stuyvesant section of Brooklyn, on Sunday, August 28; Tompkins Square Park, at East 10th Street between Avenues A and B, on Monday August 29; Saint Nicholas Park, at 135th Street and Saint Nicholas Avenue in Central Harlem, on Saturday, September 3; and Saint Mary's Park, 149th Street and Saint Ann's Avenue in the South Bronx, on Sunday, September 4.' (Notice in the *Village Voice* of August 25, '66, in the *Village Voice* also, on the same date and a week later, in the Off-Off Broadway Guide.)

big nighttime 'puppet festival' — *Chicken Little* — featuring the half-dozen or so giant puppets made, the skits and the festival loosely tied together by the story.[11] *Chicken Little* was given in an enlarged — story-of-the-

---

11. 'Die Hauptszenen spielen wegen der besseren Klarheit nur nachts bei Scheinwerferlicht, die Randbühnen den ganzen Tag über. Hier haben wir unsere grössten Puppen gebaut. Das 'Küken' ganz in rosa Wäschestoff ist fast 5 m hoch und wird von 5 Operateuren bewegt, 2 Kinder rennen mit den Beinen, 3 Erwachsene tragen an Stöcken die Puppe über sich und bewegen — der eine mit einem Seilsystem — Kopf und Flügel. Dann treten eine riesige graue Mama-Henne auf, ein König und sein Marschall, der Fuchs. Die Geschichte ist die, dass das kleine Huhn von Kindern verspottet wird: "Gleich fällt der Himmel runter." Es rennt in seiner Angst zur Mutter, zu anderen Tieren, jeder hat Angst, aber keiner gibt es zu. Das hört die Ratte — natürlich die populärste Figur in diesen Vierteln — sie telephoniert mit einem Riesen-telephon alle Ratten an, die nun durch die ganze Welt rennen, um zu sehen, was die anderen machen. Das sind nun die 13 kleinen Tagesbühnen, auf denen Gott und die Welt fabuliert wird, jedesmal mit dem Schluss, na ja, so ist das Leben, und wenn der Himmel 'runter kommt, was dann? Endlich — das ist wieder Hauptszene nachts — will man den König fragen. Der mit seinen Ratgebern denkt nur ans Fressen und möchte das blöde Huhn als Festmahl haben, Messer und Gabel treten auf als Stockpuppen, aber als der König zulangen möchte, kommt der Himmel wirklich runter mit einer gewaltigen Knall — und Rauchmaschinerie, auf die ich besonders stolz bin. So 20 – 30,000 Leute haben in jedem Park die Szenen gesehen. (Schumann, *tendenzen*, November '66-February '67.)
'Uncle Fatso was hungry. One after another, maidens came before him to recite a menu. He could not be pleased. After each recitation his arm came forward — detached from the body — and socked the maiden. Police then carried her away, sit-in style.
After three maidens had been disposed of, a rat, the Secretary of the Underground, informed His Majesty that the sky was falling and got the same treatment.
"My solution to this grave problem is to have dinner," Uncle Fatso proclaimed and called for Secretary Fox to provide him with some meat.
Just then up came a 12-foot Chicken Little, looking for a place to hide from the falling sky. Fox recommended Uncle Fatso's special atomic shelter and dancing girls showed Chicken the way with signs that spelled "Keep Right". A puff of smoke disposed of the rest of the story. The dancing girls returned with signs spelling: "The End".' — (R. Gustaitis, *Bread & Puppet, Village Voice*, September 1, '66.)
'*Chicken Little*. (Version South Bronx, été 1966.)
Chicken Little joue au ballon avec les "beautiful ladies". Ces belles dames ont des masques aux couleurs brillantes, bleu, rose, vert, etc., et d'extraordinaires perruques de toutes les couleurs, Elles finissent par envoyer le gros ballon sur la tête de Chicken Little. "C'est le ciel qui tombe," lui disent elles, et elles partent en courant. Chicken Little a peur, il appelle Mother Grey Hen pour lui dire que le ciel est en traint de tomber. "C'est impossible — lui répond-elle — il est attaché avec douze épingles dorées," et elle le renvoie jouer. Arrive un petit rat qui, poursuivi par le gros Smiling Cat, se réfugie sous les jupes de Mother Grey Hen. Ce petit rat réapparaîtra constamment dans l'histoire. Il parcourt le monde et assiste à toutes sortes de spectacles étranges. Ici prend place le sketch de "Jeune homme qui a faim." Le rat arrive enfin chez Uncle Fatso qui est dans sa cuisine. L'un après l'autre des serviteurs récitent à Uncle Fatso un menu. Aucun menu ne lui plaît, et à chaque fois son poing se détache et va frapper le serviteur (ce poing mobile est une marionnette à lui tout seul: un acteur le manipule à l'aide d'une tige.) Le rat a beau dire à Uncle Fatso que le viel va tomber: "Ma seule réponse à ce grave problème — retorque-t-il — c'est un bon diner." Il a envie d'un poulet et envoie son premier ministre Fox le chercher. C'est alors que Fox rencontre Chicken Little qui cherche à se protéger du ciel. Il lui recom-

world — format at the Astor Library next spring, and gave Schumann a success at the '67 Newport Folk Festival.

He suffered the little ones to come unto him. Twice a year he rang out the Lord's time of redemption. And then there was the (during the '60s) continuous pressure of an obligation by the challenge of his great puppets to touch up the Peace Movement's onslaught on America's conscience.

---

mande l'abri atomique spécial d'Uncle Fatso. Les voici arrivés devant la cuisine. Danse d'un couteau et d'une fourchette géante (1.50 m), suivie d'une formidable explosion. Est-ce le ciel qui tombe? Est-ce Chicken Little qui est mangé? Un nuage de fumée envahit la scène que les enfants parcourent dans tous les sens en brandissant des pancartes sur lesquelles est inscrit le mot "Fin".' — (Kourilsky, '71.)

Part IV (2).
Street agitation during the '60s.

'Paragraph 240.35. *Loitering.* A person is guilty of loitering when he: ...
4. Being masked or in any manner disguised by unusual or unnatural attire or facial alteration, loiters, remains or congregates in a public place with other persons so masked or disguised, or knowingly permits or aids persons so masked or disguised to congregate in a public place; except that such conduct is not unlawful when it occurs in connection with a masquerade party or like entertainment if, when such entertainment is held in a city which has promulgated regulations in connection with such affairs, permission is first obtained from the police or other appropriate authorities, ...' (New York Consolidated Laws Service. Annotated Statutes with Forms. Penal Law.)

Contents: Part IV (2)

1. The Movement. The three components of the Peace Movement: pacifist, Old Left, New Left. The two intertwining other movements: the Negro and the Youth Movements.
2. Primary form of the Peace Movement: street agitation. Rallies and parades. Spectacle form of verbal communication. 472
3. People telling you in person about the war vs. media coverage. Greater impact of former, but ultimate effect debatable. 476
4. The Bread and Puppet Theatre during the '60s the artistic organ of the Peace Movement in New York City insofar as it was a consensual coalition, though particularly of its pacifist wing. Fade-out of participation with radicalizzation of Movement, '67 ff. A new art form: the puppet parade. 478
5. Richard Tyler marches as *Totentanz* Death in a Living Theatre Strike for Peace. February '62. 490
6. Jesus and his disciples at their business. Fighting the landlord in the Barrio. Winter '63/'64, winter '64/'65. 491
7. August '64 Schumann joins peace agitation under Old Left auspices. 497
8. Or possibly under Liberal Pacifist auspices in March '64. 501
9. April '65. First participation in a large demonstration. Schumann doesn't have his act together yet: reliance on verbal signs. 503
10. October '65. Schumann has mastered the parade art form. A complex two-part parade, its parts meaningful, replacing slogans by images. First parade with puppets other than Jesus and his disciples. 506
11. November '65. Probable first performance of a stationary anti-war street show. 511
12. A street protest of November '65 the origin of Schumann's first theatrical success, *Fire?* 513
13. November '65. Schumann's first grand agitational show. Complex but integral. Large-scale, powerful. Jesus and his disciples gone. 514

14	March '66. Schumann's most famous street show. Simpler than before, but more intense. Beautiful. He is developing the aesthetic dimension of the medium.	519
15	May '66. Theatrical elaboration of stationary street skit.	523
16	May '66. An independent parade of Schumann's, gentle, sorrowful, unaggressive, without reference to aggression.	525
17	August '66. Schumann designs a complex of feeder marches.	530
18	November '66. First hippie-style anti-war demonstration. Schumann tries to adapt.	537
19	November '66. Another street skit added to repertory. More like a play than the preceding one.	541
20	December '66. The anti-war campaign becomes glamorous.	545
21	December '66. Schumann's last demonstration with press coverage.	546
22	April '67. First giant demonstration. Hippie aspects reported on, Schumann's contribution goes unnoticed.	551
23	April-May '67. Hippies vs. hardhats (The People) and the Blacks and Browns.	553
24	Summer '67. Schumann fades out of the picture with a gesture toward the people – militant Latinos.	555
25	August-September '67. The hippie provocateur, the digger, appears on the New York scene.	560
26	October '67. Demonstration as formally insurrectionary, military action swamps gentle Schumann demonstration, his last participation in a big Peace demonstration for $3\frac{1}{2}$ years.	561
27	October '67-August '68. The confrontational style of pacifist non-violent resistance and of the militant hippies (yippies) replaces the Old-Left-Pacifist coalition's genteel style of opinion-voicing.	565
28	Schumann, November '67-March '69. Greenwich Village 'Community' street work. He's essentially out of the larger Peace Movement.	571
29	April-November '69. Harmless anti-war street agitation in Europe.	578

30 November '69. The proper political function of theatre is not to induce action, nor to propose solutions, nor even to define problems, but to induce people to define their problems themselves. 580
31 Summation. Rise and decline of Schumann's anti-war agitation in the '60s. Associated with its liberal phase, he drops out when it becomes radical resistance. 582
32 The sub-text of Schumann's anti-war street imagery during the '60s. The war of power on innocence a marriage of good and evil. 584
33 Communicational form of Schumann's '60s street agitation: spectacle as non-addressive presentation of allegories carrying and pointed up toward strongly addressive moral address. 590

1. The Movement. The three components of the
Peace Movement: Pacifist, Old Left, New Left.
The two interwining other movements: The Negro and
the Youth Movements.

The opposition to the war in Vietnam, i.e. to American intervention and participation during the '60s, the '60s Peace Movement, was a renewed and energized sequel to movements of the '50s opposing the Cold War and its aggravations and/or nuclear armament and the arms race between America and the Soviet Union. Those older and larger objectives were to a large extent lost and forgotten during the '60s. Those of the Peace Movement – opposition to the Vietnam war – replaced them.[1]

The Peace Movement was dual, socialist and pacifist. Some of its leading and most active participants and organizations were partly in one way or another socialist, i.e., basically oriented by a critical attitude toward American social structure ('capitalism') and a hankering for social reform or even revolution. This component of it was itself divided into an Old Left – the communist agents of the Soviet Union, their opponents, the Trotzkyites, etc. – and a New Left, gradually, in the contexts of the Peace Movement and of the Civil Rights Movement, emerging during the '60s, increasingly radicalized, exemplifiable by the Students for a Democratic Society, SDS, younger people, mostly college students.[2] New Left

---

[1]. The sponsors of the New York City 'Peace Walk' on Easter Sunday 1963 in support of the Test Ban Treaty and of the encyclical *Pacem in Terris* did not want opposition to the Vietnam war voiced in signs or speeches. One of them, the Committee for a Sane Nuclear Policy – SANE – told David Dellinger who among others brought up Vietnam, he would not be permitted to speak at any future meetings sponsored by them. These pacifists feared their position would be compromised with those they addressed – 'John F. Kennedy's liberals'. — (Zaroulis and Sullivan, 1984.)

[2]. 'In years to come SDS and the anti-war movement would be thought of as synonymous, but they were never that. SDS had begun as the student branch of the old-time, respected (and respectable) League for Industrial Democracy, which had its roots in the Intercollegiate Socialist Society, founded in 1905 by, among others, the muckraker-novelist Upton Sinclair, Jack London, Clarence Darrow, John Reed, Norman Thomas, Walter Lippmann, and Edna St. Vincent Millay. The ISS viewed itself as an educational – not a revolutionary – organization; it languished during World War I and resurfaced in 1921 as the League for Industrial Democracy, was active for a time in the thirties around the issues of domestic policy and opposition to international entanglements (i.e., war), but it collapsed with the arrival of World War II. In 1945 SLID was revived as the campus arm of LID, which billed itself as a social-democratic group, explicitly anti-Communist.

In early 1960 SLID changed its name to Students for a Democratic Society. Upon receiving a $10,000 grant from the United Automobile Workers SDS was able to name its vice president, Al Haber, a graduate student at the University of Michigan, as its field secretary – that is, paid organizer....

socialism was undogmatic and somewhat inchoate, and at least initially neither Marxist nor revolutionary. It shaded over into the communitarianism and liberal anarchism of the Movement's third major type of supporters – pacifists, mostly older people, many of whom had been active in pre-Vietnam pacifist causes, not infrequently literati, with a bend toward Indian mysticism and doctrines of non-violence, including nonviolent resistance, but also basically oriented by critical attitudes toward modern technology and bureaucratic forms of management – liberals, perhaps rather than radicals, but with communitarian and anarchist ideals.[3] These pacifists were the original instigators and carriers of the

---

In June 1962 some SDS members convened at the FDR camp of the United Automobile Workers in Port Huron, Michigan. After four days and nights of discussion and sometimes argument, they succeeded in revising their constitution so that its explicit anti-Communist language was a little less explicit. This deviation proved to be upsetting to SDS's parent, LID, but after several tumultuous sessions with LID representatives back in New York, and an attempted lockout by LID, SDS remained, for the time being, under LID's wing. During the dispute SDSers had the foresight to remove SDS mailing lists from its office...

The Port Huron Statement's prescription for dealing with these problems, in addition to explicit suggestions, was something called "participatory democracy." This was a method of operation which denigrated strong leadership (which came to be called "elitism") and meant that deciding on a course of action – any course of action – became a nightmare of discussion through which, it was hoped, a consensus would emerge. Often it did not. The authors of *The Port Huron Statement* looked mainly to the universities and to the "New Left" – a term coined by the sociologist C. Wright Mills, who died in the year the statement was born – as agents of change.' — (Zaroulis and Sullivan, 1984.)

3. 'The Women's International League for Peace and Freedom (WILPF), founded in 1915 by, among others, Jane Addams, a pioneer in social work. In 1963 its aims were a complete nuclear test ban treaty; economic planning for disarmament; nonviolent action for human rights; and support of the United Nations.

The War Resisters League (WRL), an outgrowth of the Anti-Enlistment League (1915), founded in 1923 as the American branch of the War Resisters International. WRL offered support to pacifists and conscientious objectors who had no religious ties. It was a "radical pacifist" group, meaning that it followed the Gandhian example of nonviolent direct action/civil disobedience. To protest peacetime conscription after the World War II draft law expired in 1947, WRL sponsored the first draft card burning and turn-in; more than four hundred men participated. In 1948, after the passage of the Selective Service Act, WRL joined other peace groups in founding the Central Committee for Conscientious Objectors. In 1956 WRL started *Liberation* magazine as a forum for social issues – disarmament, civil rights – and the protest tactics of nonviolent direct actions. In the late 1950s and early 1960s WRL members actively protested the civil defense "bomb shelter" programs of the Eisenhower and Kennedy Administrations. WRL Executive Secretary Bayard Rustin organized the massive, landmark March on Washington for Jobs and Freedom in August 1936.

The Committee for Nonviolent Action (CNVA), founded by WRL members in 1957. Its specific purpose was direct-action protest against nuclear weapons. CNVA members sailed into the Pacific Ocean nuclear testing zone in 1958; they entered a nuclear testing base in Nebraska in 1959; they protested at the Polaris (nuclear) submarine base in New London, Connecticut in 1960; they initiated the San Francisco to Moscow Walk for

Peace Movement, and though — under New Left pressure — they accepted the Old Left into a coalition, their stance and ideology at least formally continued to some extent to dominate the Peace Movement in spite of this coalition, and in spite of an increasing role of the New Left, organizationally and numerically and even ideologically. As the Peace Movement expanded, it took in numbers of people to whom all these ideologies were more or less foreign, generic liberals, often academicians or members of the 'professions', ordinary people, neither particularly liberal or radical, but who had taken a dislike to the war, Democratic politicians, Civil Rights and Black Liberation politicians. The leaders and movers of the Movement continued to some extent to be people inspired by one or another of the aforementioned ideologies, and in this sense the Peace Movement can be said to have been Leftist, a movement of the Left. But what defined and gave it what strength it had was its focus on the war. It was an anti-war movement. It entered into coalitions with and was influenced by two other movements, the Negro Movement and the Youth Movement.

The Negro Movement started out — before the Peace Movement — as civil rights movement: carried by a coalition of northern liberals and sympathetic college students with elements in the Negro churches in the South, and focused on restrictions and infractions of the voting rights of southern Negroes, and of a variety of what the Movement claimed to be and established as being their civic rights by segregationist southern practices and statutes. Its protest notably took the forms of freedom marches, sit-ins and court suits. The southern component of this movement soon emerged as a strong and distinct movement in its own right, represented notably by the Reverend King's Southern Christian Leadership Conference and its doctrine of non-violent resistance. During the '60s, it spread to the North, and took on new forms and orientations, notably a focus on the prejudicial economic status of the Negro in the

---

Peace in 1960-61; and they sailed *Everyman I* and *Everyman II* into the Pacific testing zone in 1962.

The Workshop in Nonviolence (WIN), founded in 1965, a New York-based outgrowth of WRL-CNVA whose magazine, *WIN*, had wide readership among activists during the antiwar years....

The National Committee for a Sane Nuclear Policy (SANE), founded in 1959 to work for a nuclear test ban treaty and for disarmament. Its members frowned on the direct-action, non-violent civil disobedience of groups like CNVA, and it refused to allow Communists or socialists in its membership — an "exclusionary" policy.

Women Strike for Peace (WSP), founded in 1961 to work for "general and complete" disarmament and the passage of a nuclear test ban treaty. A self-described "grass-roots" organization, its policy of nonexclusion (membership open to anyone regardless of political affiliation) made it the target of an investigation by the House Un-American Activities Committee in December 1962. Although many WSP members described themselves as middle-class "housewives," they engaged in direct-action tactics — always neatly groomed and dressed. WSP picketed at the UN, the White House, and elsewhere; it was the first group to march on the Pentagon.' — (Zaroulis and Sullivan (1984)).

country as a whole and his de facto segregation in schools and housing in the North. It acquired some younger, non-religious and by no means antiviolence leadership, and in the form of a series of outbursts of anger in northern cities, i.e. in their Negro slums – arson and looting more than attacks on persons – it acquired de facto powerful support from the northern Negro sub-proletariat, unemployed young. This second form of the Negro Movement, a movement for across-the-board national Negro emancipation, partly took the form of a race-oriented Black Liberation Movement.

The Youth or Counter Culture Movement, product of the disintegration (under the impact of economic changes) of intrafamilial authority, with ideological antecedents in beatnik bohemianism, started out in California, notably in San Francisco, and continued to have its base there. It lacked, by its nature recalcitrant to it, the organizational bases of the other two movements, but came to have its own national press and art form, rock,[4] and by these institutions, considerable identity and cohesion as well as a distinct ideology. The rock concert, a party, was its major public form of protest, sartorial and tonsorial displays aside. Antagonistic to institutional restraints and power, notably parental, but also e.g. those of educational institutions, it was largely apolitical, but in the course of the '60s its antiauthoritarianism, its revulsion from the 'middle class' life style, its conflicts with the police (e.g. à propos of drugs), and its adherents' distaste for military service led it into the political arena.

Alliances and influences between these movements and their subcomponents modified the membership, leadership, ideology and forms of action of the Peace Movement in the course of the '60s. The Old Left acquired some – more ideological than organizational – influence on the New Left. There were natural sympathies between the pacifist wing of the Peace Movement and the non-violent resistance wing of the Negro Movement that led to participation by leaders of the latter in the Peace Movement and to a broadening of Peace Movement ideology to take on the cause of civil rights. The Youth Movement, the collegiate New Left and the Peace Movement were natural allies in opposition to the draft. The New Left and the Negro Movement made common cause in the matter of the American Negro's disadvantaged situation in the American economy. From '67 onward some of the Black leadership entered the Peace Movement as auxiliaries, partly seeing the War on Poverty sabotaged by the war in Vietnam, partly on ideological grounds – Black American soldiers fighting colored people. The Youth Movement not only – about the same time – joined with the Peace Movement on the issue of militarism but provided some agitational forms and leadership – hippie, digger, yippie.

---

4. Cf., Appendix XI, R.J. Gleason, *The Greater Sound*. Folk and rock singers were the youth movement's ideologists and representatives.

The three protest movements were symbiotic. Each pointed to its own wrongs or to what it – but once they were pointed to not only it – perceived as such, the Negro Movement not just to a population segment living in virtual misery, but – true evil from the viewpoint of American ideology – virtually excluded from the sphere of competitive self-advancement, the Youth Movement to a family and a school system rendering life miserable and meaningless for adolescents, and beyond this to job opportunities offering no promise of fulfillment, the Peace Movement to a senseless national crime, analogous if not to the horrors of Stalin's advance toward communism, then to those of the German pogrom. As regards this last: even to a citizenry disposed to see things in the perspective of an ongoing historical struggle with world communism, having its nose continually rubbed into napalmed children was not pleasant. The war might be justified, but it was undeniably dirty, and the Peace Movement kept saying, in addition, that even under that perspective, it didn't make sense. Of the three discontent-producing sub-configurations of national life, the war was perhaps not the worst or most evidently evil, but it was one that was actively pursued, an ongoing national enterprise, and the one, therefore, that could if need be be cut down on and eliminated quickly by the authorities. In addition, in spite of the Old Left involvement, the Peace Movement had respectability which the other two movements did not have – it was white, middle-class, academic, and moralistic and law-abiding. The vehemence of the other two movements lent it force, it lent them legitimacy.

The '60s, with '68 the focal year, were a quasi-revolutionary period in the Western world. 1968 parallels 1830, 1848. Why this was so beats me. Things were going well – a bull market, full employment – Schumann's theatre was one of the products of this surge.

Both the mere existence of the two other oppositional movements and their partial confluence with it strengthened the Peace Movement. Oddly, as it became radicalized and more broadly opposed to existing institutions, it also gained wider support in the white middle class, and thence, by '68, gained an echo among its political representatives, notably sectors of or personalities in the Democratic party. At the same time, government opposition to it stiffened and took on repressive and criminal forms: police violence, the subversive activities of the Nixon administration, of the F.B.I., of the C.I.A. The majority of the population and especially the blue collar working class opposed the Peace and the other two movements and supported the war to the end.[5]

---

5. The support given the SDS early on (and given its predecessors) by the socialist Walter Reuther's United Automobile Workers in Michigan was virtually the only link of the Peace Movement to the 'Labor Movement'.

2. Primary form of the Peace Movement: street agitation. rallies and parades. Spectacle-form of verbal communication.

'Congress shall make no law respecting an establishment of religion, or prohibiting the free exercise thereof; or abridging the freedom of speech, or of the press; or of the right of the people peaceably to assemble, and to petition the Government for a redress of grievances.' (Bill of Rights, 1st article.)

Before the politicians – politicians in and out of office – took it up, i.e. for most of the '60s, the Peace Movement did not have the regular political forms, the forms of electoral politics and of intra-government political process, and although it in its entirety could be viewed as petitioning the government, it scarcely, except as occasional propaganda gimmick, took this form – hardly a regular form, anyhow. It took the – more basically democratic and republican – form of expressions of feelings and opinion in communication between citizens. Its basic intent was of course to influence intra-government political process, i.e. government policy (and this rather than, except for its last phase during the '60s the aim of influential electoral politics); but by way of influencing 'public opinion'. Even when staging protests in the capitol, it addressed itself to the citizenry rather than to the governments. During the later '60s, having learned from the rioting northern as well as from the non-violently resisting southern Blacks, it took the secondary form of resistance as distinct from protest, of –though only pro forma–law-breaking sabotage of government activities, notably draft procedures. But its primary form was protest and oppositional agitation, partly in the media – stretching from some, a very small part, of the news coverage on network tv to deploratory and shocked verbiage in liberal or vehemently accusatory verbiage in the Old Left, radical and half-ass Youth Movement 'underground' press – partly 'in the streets': public demonstration/agitation.

Public or street demonstration/agitation not by lone loonies in parks or on street corners (in New York City these ranters are 90% religious nuts), but at and by outdoor meetings – 'rallies' – in squares, parks, malls, on designated street blocks – and by street 'parades' or 'marches', normally not along the sidewalk, but down the middle of the street – both normally in the center of town (in New York City mid-Manhattan) or in the center of some sub-division of it. A march might be preceded by an assembly. It would normally lead to a rally, as way of getting there and as advertisement for it. A rally would normally be preceded by a march. Both in principle required police permits and these were normally requested and almost as normally granted. Both had police protection. Picketing and sit-ins were sub-forms shading off into resistance. Rallies and parades were

advertised in papers read by supporters, in New York City e.g. the *Voice*. Readers of the Old Left, the pacifist and the underground papers were notified by these. Protests were decided on, publicized and organized by committees, unsupported by any clubs, but with some slight support from Old Left party organizations. The committees, local organizing committees, national coordinating and organizing committees, tended to be organized for the purpose of individual protests of campaigns of protest, but some of them stayed in existence for extended periods. Some of them were occupationally or sexually defined – Women's Strike for Peace, Artists and Writers Committee Against the War in Vietnam – some by locality – the Lower East Side Committee for ... – but just about all of them were in name and activity focused on the issue, opposition to the war. Support from unions, union locals, civil rights organizations was relatively slight. Personalities – Dr. Spock, A.J. Muste – were crucial gathering points as speakers at rallies, as figureheads, sometimes as organizers.

Rallies and marches translated the Movement's primary reality, that of verbal communication – conversations, the printing of information, argument and demands and the reading of this writing – into visual form in the public – and civic – space, the appearance in body and person of the writers and readers as marchers and attendants at rallies, as leaders of marches and as speakers. This not only made it a reality inviting notice by the media, but made of it a spectacle[1] (a series of spectacles). It added to

---

[1]. Aryeh Neier, Civil Liberties Union functionary, in his preface to J.B. Fernandez' *In Opposition*, stating his accord with the Founding Fathers' alleged idea that right opinion would prevail given free competition of ideas rationally presented, but taking into account the Maoist Herbert Marcuse's point that the media nowadays are subject to oligopolistic control, in effect argues that in modern society for dissenters to get a hearing, they have to present their ideas *dramatically*: merely rational discourse is 'no longer' enough: the attention of the media (-controllers) has first to be attracted. — (Cf. Appendix XX.)

F. Jotterand traces the form of Peace Movement agitation back to that of Black Civil Liberties agitation, and sees it as form of non-violent resistance:

'Une décision de la Cour suprême, en 1954, déclare la ségrégation des écoles contraire à la Constitution. L'année suivante un pasteur noir de 25 ans, Martin Luther King, est appelé à diriger les mouvements de boycottage contre les transports en commun de Montgomery, ville d'Alabama (un Blanc avait voulu forcer une femme noire à lui céder sa place dans un autobus. La femme avait refusé. La police l'avait arrêtée). C'est le début d'une épopée conduite avec une passion et une science admirables .... La force de King est la non-violence. Par un détour normal à une époque où l'Orient et l'Occident se rapprochent, Luther King emprunte à Gandhi des techniques que celui-ci avait mises au point après avoir lu le livre de Thoreau, l'écrivain du XIXe siècle américain, sur la "désobéissance civile'.

La non-violence n'est pas une résistance passive. Elle est action. King provoque et met en scène ce que les théoriciens du nouvel théâtre appellent des événements (*events*). Cinquante Noirs s'assoient dans un bar aux places réservées normalement aux Blancs. Des enfants et des étudiants se présentent à la porte d'universités ou d'écoles ségréguées. De longues marches s'organisent, défilés interminables d'hommes, de femmes et d'enfants, qui

the opinion-expression and pleading that was the Movement's substance distinct physical activities that its promoters and followers could engage in, and the engagement in which became a pleasant and proud pastime for a significant minority of New Yorkers during the '60s. The addition of the public image – carrying with it, as part of it, some of the verbal communication (speeches at rallies, signs carried by marchers) – added additional communication: to those seeing it or seeing reproductions of or reports on it, and added certain gestures: of physical, personal involvement in the Movement; of a publicizing of this involvement; of an unsolicited address to the public at large; of exercise of a right to the use of public facilities for this expression and address. The Peace Movement as spectacle was the spectacle of masses of people moving or standing united by a common cause: in opposition to the country's (or its elected leadership's) policies, or to the country itself, and, because the spectacle was performed in civic spaces continuous with the city – its typical form, there were of course also rallies in segregated, rented places, indoors – was the spectacle also of invasions of the public space, perturbing public order –

rappellent les pèlerinages du Moyen-Age, quand toute une population accompagnait des reliques d'une église à l'autre. A Einsielden, des images de la vie du saint se dressaient au-dessus de la procession, des hymnes en évoquaient les épisodes, et le théâtre naquit de ces manifestations pour aboutir au "Jeu du Monde" surle parvis de la cathédrale baroque. A Selma, è Birmingham, des pancartes surgissent au-dessus des têtes, les chants se croisent, ponctués de slogans: *"Freedom now!"* Le monde entier, grâce à la télévision, suit de jour en jour la progression de ces "longues marches", drames vivants nourris d'épisodes imprévisibles comme la vie. Leur structure contient des éléments du théâtre: le mouvement dans l'espace; la durée; la représentation, par l'action physique, de sentiments et d'idées; l'attente (le *suspense*); et une ligne générale qui conduit de manière fatale à l'affrontement.

Deux elements nouveaux s'y ajoutent: l'attente est rendue plus dramatique par sa nature aléatoire. Martin Luther King provoque une action qu'il essaie d'infléchir en cours de route avec ses collaborateurs, mais leur pouvoir est limité parl'ignorance de ce que vont faire les autres.... Peu à peu les Blancs, étudiants pluis sympathisants de toute provenance, se joignent aux marches en faveur des *civil rights*, dont l'apogée estla cérémonie du 28 aout 1963 qui réunit 200,000 personnes à Washington. Fête de l'universelle participation. Des troupes de théâtre se produisent en plein air. Il fait une chaleur étouffante. Mahalia Jackson, Joan Baez, Lonnie Sattin chantent. Le *folk-song* américain se mêle aux *blues*. Peu avant le crépuscule, un homme de trente-trois ans donne au spectacle sa signification par un discours que l'on ne peut ré-entendre sur disque sans être ému par son pouvoir d'incantation:

'J'ai fait un rêve
J'ai rêvé qu'un jour sur les collines rouge de Georgie les fils des anciens esclaves et les fils des anciens proprietaires d'esclaves s'assieront ensemble a la table de la fraternite.'

Composé selon une progression qui va vers le chant, avec la reprise des thèmes auxquels la foule répond, le discours est un modèle de poesie dramatique. Il éclate à la fin comme une sonnerie: "Let freedom ring!" Il appelle à la liberation non seulement les Noirs mais les hommes du monde entier qui se donneront la main pour chanter le vieux Negro spiritual: "Free at last!" — (Enfin libres!).

... les marches des civil rights, les nouveaux moyens de communication (la télévision et la radio devenue mobile, personnelle, grâce au transistor ont fait de chaque Americain le spectateur d'événements instantanés...' — Jotterand, *Le nouveau théâtre.*)

and in this respect like picketing, sit-ins, riots — and of the elective confluence of a potentially ever greater proportion of the citizenry (rather than of foregatherings of the predisposed.)

This spectacle was a major feature of the New York public scene of the '60s[2] (and of the Washington and West Coast Bay Area and via tv the national scenes) distinguishing it from that of other decades (except maybe the '30s), exhilarating to some, disquieting to others — especially as it was complemented by the sound of Black militant rhetoric and associated imagery, raised fists, Huey Newton in his African king's cane chair, the sight of looting ghetto crowds and of ghetto conflagrations, the sound of rock, carrying the shouted antagonistic lyrics of its singer, reports of vast crowds of dope-taking, sexually promiscuous youngsters at rock concerts, in toto the spectacle of a disintegration of the social fabric. Actual communists were perceived active behind this scene.

---

2. Cf. Appendix XXIV.

3. People telling you in person about the war vs. media coverage. Greater impact of former, but ultimate effect debatable.

What Schumann and the Peace Movement carried into the streets of New York was the theme of war, and, to some – lesser – extent, its image. The populace was regularly notified by the media there was a war going on: here live performance was added to the airwave representation and the print, i.e. war came up in what were however marginally human confrontations with their attendant peculiar arousals of emotion – human emotions being still geared to direct contact – this being the basic power of impact of street agitation as distinct from media propaganda – and what were also distortions of the familiar landscape of the street, perturbations of the street, and therefore, insofar as this area of modern life, pretty well relegated[1] to dwindling retail commerce and workers' job-home-job transfers (churches still there but inoperative, the bars just off and right on the streets the only significant centers of conviviality), still figures in life, disturbances of the life pattern, welcome or not. People were going out of their way to remind people there was a war going on, taking trouble to do so, trudging up the street, not paid for it, nobody had asked them to, it wasn't any of their BUSINESS, they just barely had a mere right to do it (an afterthought to the Constitution in a revolutionary year): not like turning on the tv, which, like smoking the next cigarette, is your choice, or getting the *Post* or *News*, so you can slip past the front page headlines back to the childhoodlike reassurance of the sports pages, or maybe hear it on the radio, packed in clipped or folksy accents with the weather and the stock market quotations, for absorption as news, news not as this minute's walking-time history of the race, but as part of the constant monitoring of the environment carried on by every animal, to see that everything is alright. A war abroad in the news, as long as the society is still able to handle it alright (and the '60s were prosperous years, bull market years, very much years of progress, not like the 12 years since then – I am writing this in '82), even if your sweetheart or son is out there, when it comes to you as part of the news is ultimately in fact reassuring to hear about, like knowing you are still breathing, the ticking of your heart: no leopard behind the bush. A street parade in this respect is more like the messenger that comes stumbling in out of breath to tell of the approaching

---

1. Except in the slums. The inner city is universally, where not 'cleared', in the U.S. a slum. In the slums, people play, flirt, take dance steps, meet, talk, play dominoes or cards, drink, conduct their dope transactions on the street – overflowing from there into the busiest midtown streets to set up, on two stacked cartons, 3-card monte games, play music for the kitty, sell the mouths of black meat near the tunnels to Jersey or off porno alley, 42nd Street, mug – in the street.

enemy, the battle lost or won: it's upsetting – note how the chorus in Greek drama is upset when the messenger gives them the bad news. If, for instance, there were more or less regular television coverage of hell, on-the-spot reporting from there, with the cameras focusing in on new arrivals, this or that routine of torture, the flames leaping on the screen, shots of Beelzebub back from a conference, speaking a few words into the upheld mike, even the elderly sinner I would say would not be overly disturbed watching from the couch. A news service of course renders services, e.g. the weather news for fishermen or people who have a long walk to the subway or the stock market news for the retired businessman or other smalltime speculator: when a person has set things up so that they can react practically and swiftly to a particular genre of information – not the case for ordinary people and a war.

Whether the Peace Movement had any effect on the war is an open question. The best opinion seems divided.[2]

---

2. The effect would have had to be on the U.S. government, either directly or via public opinion. J.E. Mueller (*War, Presidents and Public Opinion*) concludes it did not sway public opinion: cumulative casualties did. Cf. Appendix XXIII. But:

'Why did President Johnson (in March of 1968 (SSB)) turn from escalation toward disengagement? The book's thesis is that he was forced to do so by political realities within the United States, that the people, ordinary citizens with no authority but the force of their belief and their commitment, simply refused to tolerate the war or the official assumption that there was no alternative to war. The rebellion Johnson faced within his own administration, and the challenge raised by Eugene McCarthy and Robert Kennedy, were the result of a broad-based popular opposition to the war which brought the United States to a point of profound political crisis in late 1967 and early 1968.' — (Mueller, op. cit., pg. xii.)

4. The Bread and Puppet Theatre during the '60s the artistic organ of the Peace Movement in New York City insofar as it was a consensual coalition, though particularly of its pacifist wing. Fade-out of participation with radicalization of Movement, '67 ff. A new art form: the puppet parade.

Schumann was out of touch with and had no interest in the Black Movement, whether the Civil Rights Movement of the early or the Black Liberation Movement of the later '60s. His first real contact took the form of trouble with Black kids and Black administrators (hustlers) during his '66 Harlem workshop work, the next one that of his kids being more or less as a matter of everyday routine beaten up and having their lunch money taken away (end of '60s). Only then, and having gotten his kids out of the city, did the Negro appear in his theatre: during his Coney Island phase in 1970 and 1972 when his audience was Black too. But he never paraded for them.

Hippie culture in the East Village, flower children and all, must have been positively repulsive to him during the '60s: diametrically the opposite of his work cult, sobriety and esteem for sobriety, responsibility and esteem for it, respect for the monogamous family and its life. Conflations of hippie and New Left ideas invaded his group in '69; his work of the period – *Cry of the People for Meat* – shows the influence of this; and some of the attitudes and ideas of the commune movement of the '70s that at least in part grew out of this fusion were congenial to him, show up in his work, ideals of communal living, to some moderate extent,[1] but especially the ecological approach to and ideal of human life – cf. his *Hallelujah* of 1972, and his circus pageants 1974 ff. – and possibly glimpses in his work of something approaching eroticism may be traceable to these sources as well. He has maintained a personal tonsorial and sartorial style close to the hippie style into the '80s, but I would say that older bohemian traditions of self-presentation are in question here. But during the '60s the youth rebellion did nothing for him and he nothing for it.

The Peace Movement, on the other hand, happened to be just his thing, by which I mean that he has been neither an anarchist or pacifist nor either an authoritarian or anti-authoritarian socialist in any strict, dogmatic, sectarian, intellectual or principled sense, whether during the '60s or later, but now is and during the '60s was, more or less all of these in a very general way, as a matter of emotional allegiances, informal concurrences

---

1. Cf. Infra his letter, February 23, '72 to his puppeteers.

and general attitude: so that the *consensus* of the Peace Movement coalition was quite congenial to him, though none of its components pushed in isolation and strictly presented was.[2] The differences, under the circumstances, were not crucial: he is apolitical, i.e. disinclined to push his ideas on others or to commit himself to specific action programs, but this could be dealt with by a metaphorical and non-verbal form of concurrence; expression of his non-sectarian Christian proclivities would not be incongruous, on the contrary, presented shared aspirations within the Peace Movement in a form both anodyne and imposing, as well as appealing to the general public; his Manichean world view, though alien, actually, given the issue of the war, fit in quite well with the opposition between the Movement and the nation; only that world view's pessimist shading was seriously out of kilter, given the Movement's basic general American historical optimism and progressivism and faith in human nature: but this pessimist shading was not sufficiently prominent in Schumann's thinking or work in the '60s to make for incompatibility – though this difference came up in '69.

More important than this concurrence of Schumann's Weltanschauung and the Peace Movement's ideology insofar as it was consensual was the

---

2. I think his more or less perennial political position is probably pretty well expressed by:
'The ways and solutions that have been radically proposed and radically experimented with are inefficient. We can't and we don't want to kill all those bourgeois uncles, small, medium, large-size Nixons, and then start socialism. First of all: they are big and real, we are little and esoteric. Secondly, when studying post-revolutionary societies, we find their achievements not only not exactly befitting the higher aspirations of the masses, but also not fulfilling our own yearning for a free and meaningful life within the regulations of citizenship . . . .' — (Schumann, *Bread & Rosebuds*, November '72.)
'69/'70 he approached what appeared a revolutionary position (*Cry*). But what was in question was not armed struggle for socialism, but the insurrectionary movements of the Third World: with which he sympathized – not being a dogmatic pacifist any more than a dogmatic socialist.
I don't know what Schumann's politics were before he came to America, but since then at any rate his views and sympathies have been on the left. I don't think he cares much for competition, the profit motive, commerce or for what passes for 'material progress', nor thinks the American political system, the universal vote, makes for democracy, i.e. rule of the people. The democratic causes to which he contributed his art before he engaged in the Peace Movement may not have been particularly left, but like the Peace Movement were pretty much sponsored by leftists. I.e. there was a consistency there. He has never with his art come out against communism or the social systems whose ruling bureaucracies claim them to be communist. This makes him look like a fellow traveller. But I suspect his motivation is rather partly 'let everyone sweep before his own door', i.e. try to improve conditions where they live, partly that the big struggle since World War II has not been between the First World and the Second, capitalism and oriental despotism, the USA and Russia, but between the capitalist West, especially the USA, and the Third World: the capitalist countries trying to suppress the Third World peasantries' movements against their exploiters, with the Soviet Union pretty much able to afford being passive, and here Schumann's sympathies were with the Third World. The Vietnam war may have appeared to him part of this struggle.

concurrence of its primary concern, the war in Vietnam, with Schumann's personal and artistic preoccupation with war. The subject matter he was commissioned to deal with was the one he most wanted to deal with and the one that most inspired him.

American involvement in Vietnam, as overt paradigm of the XXth century form of the class struggle, the transnational exploitation/oppression/repression of a proletarian component of humanity by a technologically advanced one, was a godsend to a man of Manichean vision, and, because of its inelegant heavyhandedness, that is, the use of air power in the tradition of the World War II bombardments of civilian Germany, not only of intense personal relevance to him (conditio sine qua non for art) but the perfect foil for a visually oriented moralist responsive to the simply meaningful image.[3]

The war gave Schumann something that he conceived as indispensable, namely an excuse to do art:

'I feel that art in the modern world is generally superfluous. Either we should find a true need for it, or give it up.'
(Schumann interviewed by Brown and Seitz, The Drama Review
(*Tulane Drama Review* #38).

The good cause released his artistic energy and gave it a focus. He had been saddled with a demand, become his own on himself, to render services to humanity. He couldn't just play. On the other hand, neither traditional standards, nor the solution of problems posed by contemporary practice were acceptable to him as justifications. To be a 'good' sculptor or dancer was not necessarily any good at all.

The main point with my feeling about him is that you know he is one of I think the handful of major original theatre artists of the time we live in. And I don't think that is at all understood. (I: That's right . . .) It may be understood more in Europe. I don't know . . . . (It) runs right into the crippled self view of the American theatre at this point. The way the American theatre views itself in its own divisions. The Broadway, Off-off-Broadway, what it views as experimental within the system, you know trhere's something very stark and frightened about it at this point. And Peter's arrogance, I don't know how a humble man can be quite so arrogant, but Peter's arrogant refusal to buy any of that procedure has in a way given the lie to the whole way the American theatre views itself and at the same time it has left him you know permanently on the outskirts in some sort of separate world as far as the American theatre goes . . . . If you were to ask most theatre people . . . where they place the Bread and Puppet Theatre in the American Theatre, I think they would have a hard time answering the question at all. I mean they would say well it's not really theatre, or they would say it's one of the experimental theatres. I don't think there's room for anyone to say it is one of our three or four major theatrical enterprises. Period . . . . You know there is, I think, a cynicism that is partly justified, directed at that 19th century view of the

---

3. Cf. Appendix XXII.

artist as a creator, that is very prevalent among artists. That artists don't like to be viewed as artists in that sense. In a way it's more correct to view yourself as a craftsman or as somebody who knows how to do something and is doing his best at it or is working within the context of historical need or, you know there are all sorts of qualifications, but very few people would want to at least publicly acknowledge that they view themselves as Beethovens, as the kind of brooding creator, you know, the Gordon Craigian view of the theatre ... Peter is of course in an almost literal manifestation of that idea.... (I: But he wouldn't acknowledge that he is.) Oh, I'm sure he wouldn't. (I: In his own view, he's a craftsman, you see...) I understand that that's the way he would view himself. I'm saying that I think that's only half true.... You see, a creator in the Beethoven tradition, certainly he would deny that vehemently and he would mean it. He wouldn't be coy at all ... okay but you've got several you know, the precedence of several thoughts on the subject. I mean particularly with regard to theatre. You have a purely entertainment orientation which seems to me by the way honorable. You know that is I have never thought that the Broadway mentality was dishonorable mentality. It's very straightforward, it says what it says and it does what it does. Sometimes it does it rather well. One may be bored by it. If one is, one doesn't go to it. But it's perfectly straightforward and very few of those people regard themselves as artists or ever have, you know. Some of them do and some of them may even be on a certain level, but it's not part of the root there.

Then you get a political overtone or possibility or potential which is largely Brechtian in its origin, that leads to the fact that one of the points of bankruptcy – I think this is one of the few countries where they've outgrown Brecht without ever having experienced him in a certain way. I mean you think of a lot of people feel oh, we've gone through that kind of Brechtian political thing, now we have to ... What was that? Did that miss me? It seems to have done something bizarre. That means that the interpretation of a man like Brecht, who had kept saying that he's not important as an artist, he's important as a fighter for causes or a political activist, you know, only one drives me to my desk kind of thing, not the voices of the birds in the trees or the political reality around him. You know the legend of a man who gives up being an artist just in order to fight fascism, for his life, and to do all of this has left the kind of mark I think on a kind of socially committed activism in the arts, which is perhaps accepted. Because after all Brecht was an artist, regardless of what he liked to say, who he was or whatever. I mean it was in the context of being an overbearing, overriding and pervasive art.

I think that now when you look at the examples that confront you, you know as an artist in the theatre, now as a worker in the theatre, you have to start from something more basic than any of these forces. It's like what is the need now? You have to begin with maybe it can all go out the window. I think that anyone who really is worth his salt in the theatre has to take the risk of saying I have to examine my position in relation to this, even if the result turns out to be that all of us are in the wrong business, you know. You know it has to examine itself with one of the possibilities that it could self-destruct just like that because there's no place for it to go or nothing for it to do.

I'm saying in a sense, Peter has already done that. In a way, he hasn't depended on any kind of view. He has not depended on even an artistic base. He has created all of that himself. So he is the only working theatrical artist I know who can answer all those questions directly. You know, he is in effect saying, with colossal arrogance perhaps, again for a very humble man, that if this is significant let them come and say so if they want to. And if they don't want to, so what? This is what I do and what I am doing.

Well you can't argue with that. At least I can't, really, as a given point. And it's one of the reasons why I think his theatre is not demoralized and sick in a sense as so much of the rest of it is. In a way it's just like Maurice's challenge to the theologian. It's right in its intellectual aspect, it's wrong in its roots, in its economic and social givens that it accepts in order to do what it's doing. I mean that's a very heavy and complicated condition and it can be very demoralizing if you think very much about it.

If you don't think very much about it it's not demoralizing which is why the Broadway mentality is still a successful mentality ... (I: What you're saying is you have to be a genius today.) ... Would that all of the Lord's people were prophets. Maybe, I don't know that I mean that. You may be right. I mean maybe I'm saying something, maybe taking an absolute disposition that there's no way down from, but I do think that one significance of Peter's work at this point is that it is healthy and thrives. It continues in whatever roots you want to say. Whereas I don't think that in any kind of continuous sense that can be said of any of our other major theatrical forces right now.

I mean I think that certainly the genius, and Peter is unmistakably, again one can say without embarrassment or exaggeration that he's a genius, there are few people you can say that about. I mean that's simply a way of saying that among other things he has the functioning insights to show us something about the conditions we're in. And that's one of the conditions we're in.

You know one of the things, I found myself more and more aware when I go to the theatre of a funny question that I didn't used to ask myself at all, which is what are those people doing there? – meaning the actors. Why are they here? Why do they want me to be here? What's the name of this game anyway? It doesn't seem to be enough anymore to say well this is a theatre and they're actors and they're here to act for me, because I find myself disbelieving more and more in the theatre as the place they should expect me to want to go or I should want to go to. It's kind of a habit that's more and more difficult to understand, you know. Whereas the social aspects of the Bread and Puppet Theatre always answer that question implicitly. Somehow you see that. You're seeing a community of people who seem to share something and for all of their, the autocratic, artistic center of that venture, it is a legitimate functioning community of people who share some sort of – by some sort of free choice – share some sort of esthetic and social way you know. And that is an answer to that question. That's what they're doing here .... Again like Peter, viewing him as an absolute in this set of you know theatrical alternatives, it's very useful to think of that, to consider, all right, this through this absolute method has resolved these problems in this way. Obviously that's not the only way to resolve these problems if they can be resolved. This is difficult times.

You know that business of what business does anybody have doing this sort of thing. I certainly am aware of that. I'm in the very disreputable business of training actors. I'm being a little coy now. Obviously, I'm not so self-denigrating that I think it's a totally disreputable business, but I think you have to be aware of that, that you're in that aspect of it and try to cope with it as you work. It's not like training doctors or butchers or people for whom there is very clear useful things for them to do in society. It has to be reinvented if it's going to be valuable at all.' (Shapli, interview.)

People too shy or modest or perhaps arrogant for naked-faced political agitation – a show of allegiance to a cause that is supposed to impress other people merely because it is one's show, or an addressive voicing of opinion e.g. in the form of a slogan, that is supposed to carry weight – may be willing to engage in masked agitation, being by the mask absolved from direct personal responsibility (as also many actors being not at all nervous about doing weird or outrageous things before a numerous audience in a theatre are in private life unusually reserved).[4] This applies to Schumann himself, I would say.

We may ask: did Schumann hope to change the world? I suspect that though he may have from late '66 or early '67 onward increasingly despaired of his own and the Peace Movement's efficacy (and become increasingly disgusted with the role of agitator and some of the participants in the Movement and the turn they were giving it),[5] virtually abandoning *participation* in it by late '67 or early '68, restricting himself pretty much to making his own statement by showings of *King Story* and *A Man Says Goodbye to His Mother* – he was an agnostic on the question of efficacy from the beginning, doubting, without denying its possibility

---

4. 'One thing I wanted to say about politics is that I remember a conversation with Andy Trompetter in which we both said we wanted to work against the war but we don't like to go to parades, we feel ridiculous, we can't do this, this or that, but the thing we feel comfortable and perfect doing is being in the Bread and Puppet Theatre in a parade. That's the way we feel we can work against the war, with masks.' — (Sherman, interview.)
5. From an interview probably of the summer or early fall of '68:
'Schumann: "I've seen a lot of protests, but few movements. Castro in Cuba: that was a movement. But most of the Vietnam War protests? The hippies? The New Left? and I am disturbed at having the Bread and Puppet called a protest theatre. We are all sick of the Vietnam War. But the theatre must do more than protest . . . ."
TDR: Did ". . . confronting them influence your aesthetics?"
Schumann: "You don't make your point unless a five-year-old girl can understand it. If she gets it, the grownups will too. The show almost has to be stupid. It has to be tremendously concentrated. You need that intensity on the street much more than in a theatre. Indoors you can get by with technique, by sticking to your dialogue, but on the street you come across only if you have your mind on What Has To Be."
TDR: "Does the audience react differently in the street than they do indoors?"
Schumann: "We've had our best – and sometimes our most stupid – performances in the streets. Sometimes you make your point because our point is simply to be there in the street. It stops people in their tracks – to see those large puppets, to see something theatrical outside of a theatre. They can't take the attitude that they've paid money to go into a theatre to 'see something.' Suddenly there is this thing in front of them, confronting them." ' — (Brown and Seitz, *With the Bread and Puppet Theatre, Tulane Drama Review* #38.)

For Schumann's attitude at the end of the '60s, probably at the end of his European tour of '69, cf. part IV(2), section 30, p.580, footnote.

an effect of agitation on public sentiment and alterations of public sentiment on government action, but not letting these doubts prevent him from trying to make his agitation as effective as possible, i.e. holding that if agitation were effective, some forms of it would be more effective than others. More importantly, however, efficacy was for him never the main issue. It was for him rather a matter of absolving a man's, a Christian's and a citizen's or at any rate resident's duty to take a stand against evil and to make his position known to his fellowmen; and to confront the others with what they were doing and not doing. (Thus also Christ's word made sin of much that ignorance would before his advent have excused.)

Schumann has in his art never dealt with National Socialism.[6] (At most one may in the whitefaced moustachio'd military salesmen that in his '81/'82 *Story of One Who Set Out to Study Fear* sell Adam and Eve on civilization see so many Schickelgrubers selling the public rearmament, crusades against the red menace and national greatness.) He was, of course, only 11 when the Third Reich became a memory – could scarcely have made it to HJ Pimpf even. Yet I imagine that one thing that must have bothered him, as it has a generation of younger Germans, was the silence of their fathers and uncles in the face of evil. As one profoundly regrets the occasions on which one failed to take up the challenge to a fight, feeling one's honor irretrievably diminished, so one regrets the times when seeing wrong done one did not at least call it that, and this feeling on behalf of their elders is especially strong among those that were children in the Third Reich. I mention this in partial explanation of Schumann's constant readiness, from '64 or '65 onwards, to protest, given his, I would say, nearly total lack of faith in the effectiveness of protest: it was, at least in part due to a desire not to have spoken up.

The Bread and Puppet Theatre during the '60s became the artistic organ of the pacifist-anarchist-liberal wing of the Peace Movement in New York City. For as long as and to the extent that this wing repre-

---

6. He does take a dim view of it, thinking it killed the German soul, as the Vietnam War did the American:

'Dieser Krieg war nicht so weit weg, wie es erst schien. Menschliche, amerikanische Arroganz, tiefsitzende Gemütlichkeit und Verachtung der Schmerzen, versteckter der zivilisierte Zynismus traten unerwartet zutage. Und ähnlich wie die Offenbarung nationaler Greuel nicht die berühmte deutsche Seele, nicht das deutsche Selbastbewusstsein zerstört hat, so ist auch in USA nichts Grossartiges Nationales geschehen. Kein natürliches Zurückschrecken hat stattgefunden, als Alice Herz, Roger La Porte und Norman Morrison sich selber stifteten, sich öffentlich wie Fackeln anzündeten und verbrannten. Und ähnlich wie Deutschlands unberühmte arme Seele dazumal starb, und die private Geschichte eines Massenmörders der Nation als zukünftige Vorgeschichte seitdem anhaftet, so hat sich auch die amerikanische Seele in diesem kleineren Krieg erschöpft, und der grosse Kriegsheld wird sich von den Todesstössen, die er an andere auszuteilen gedachte, nicht wieder erholen.'

He reverts to the analogy: the speech of the Red Devil as Lyndon Johnson in *Speech* at least on occasion alternated between Texan American and Hitlerian German.

sented the coalitional consensus of the New York City Peace Movement – and it did so decreasingly from '67 onward – the Bread and Puppet Theatre was the organ of the New York City Peace Movement. When from '67 onward the ideas and the protest forms of the Youth and New Left Movements rose to preponderance in the Peace Movement, Schumann faded out of the Movement.[7]

---

7. Ernstthal (interview, '79) distinguishes a non-violent, pacifist Peace Movement dating back to the late '50s from a leftist anti-war (anti-Vietnam-war) movement getting going '62/'63, the two coalescing, e.g. in the 'Fifth Avenue Parades' in '65/'66, and getting big, students and liberals joining, in '67/'68:
'It was the Peace Movement originally. It was the Committee for Non-Violent Action and the War Resisters League and A. J. Muste, David Reynolds, Dave Delinger, a couple, Marge. (?) ... this is going way back, but that was the Peace Movement .... Ban the bomb, the Memphis to New York March, the San Francisco to Moscow March, which Jules Rabin was on ... these were really early, it was against nuclear weapons, nuclear testing, and all that. And that was before Vietnam. That was just nonviolent resistance, Gandhi, Arimsa.
And that had nothing to do with anything left wing. That was Quakers, absolutely, and totally on a pacifist basis. This was like '58, '59, '60.
The first demonstration I was ever at was at General Dynamics in New London, Connecticut in '61 I think. And that was when Ed Sanders swam out to the Nautilus when it was launched. He tried to climb aboard. And that was the CNVA. Committee for Nonviolent Action. Vietnam was not, I don't think it was even happening at that point. It was only disarmament and ban the bomb. So that was the *Peace* Movement.
Then there was the leftists and the anti-war movement group later on in '62 and '63 when Kennedy and Vietnam thing started. And then the Fifth Avenue Day Parades, my remembrance is that was when those things started to come together, when the left wing Communists and the just nonviolent resisters started to find common cause against the war in Vietnam, and came together and also all the students, and people began to be aware of it and it got to be really big, and then the liberals and everybody got on, and it got really, and then it got really big. Then it became, like you got the Fifth Avenue Day Parade.
I mean the original parades, we were picketing the draft board and stuff, 30 people. Or picketing General Dynamics. I was still in college. There were ten people there facing these hordes of workers giving out leaflets that said quit your job .... When the whistle blew you know 10,000 workers come streaming out to go home and there are these little twerps in sandals handing out leaflets saying quit your job, nuclear submarine is dangerous and so forth. They couldn't believe it ....
Anyway, those things came together later and then the Fifth Avenue Parades and they were pretty big scale. But the earlier ones were local, nobody really noticed .... There was one I got knocked over. I was carrying Uncle Fatso and there were right wingers. In '64, '65, '66, there was a lot of counter movement to the Peace Movement, and these marches would have definite hecklers. People would come in and break it up and stuff ... and there was fist fights and stuff like that.' — (Ernstthal, interview.)
The pure anti-war movement, i.e. its heroic phase, ended with '66: opposition to the war became popular:
'Really, within the Movement – and within what was going on – '66 was the cricital year. But it was about three years behind in the public movement. I know it's incredibly fast the way things go in the historical viewpoint – but in the Movement, '66 was the watershed. Because '66 was the year when the –(?) and the feeling of the Movement was pure. '66 was the peak of the – when everything was beautiful. When you could go and meet a girl and kiss her and go make love and then walk away and everybody was happy.

Schumann's art developed as expression of that liberal component of the Peace Movement: not that it wasn't intensely personal, and not that it didn't transcend political issues of the day and political issues altogether,[8] but the Movement provided energy, context and focus.

I mean, it was really the peak. And after that it became — again, the public focus started getting on it. People from all over came into it and it started to decay. In my opinion '66 was the – with the *internal* time – was the climax, was the watershed of it. In the public sphere '68 was the . . . *Fire* was the most – it was the burning – it was dedicated to people who had burned themselves. By '68 people were aware that there was a war in Vietnam. By '68 there was a tremendous Peace Movement. In '66 the Peace Movement was still the Committee for Nonviolent Action, these old-timers: A.J. Muste, Dave McReynolds, you know, the Greenwich Village Peace Center – all of that – were still in the forefront of the Peace Movement. By '68 we would get 500,000 people in the marches, you know. It was a major thing. People like my father and people's parents were beginning to become aware that there was a war in Vietnam. It overthrew Johnson. I mean, the Movement was reaching and doing stuff and had a real effect and everyone was aware of it. *Time* magazine came out against the war in Vietnam – when was that? When was that, in '69 or something? I mean, of all things in the world. And it overthrew the government of Johnson. It was a real force. By '69 it was invaded by the insects in a way – it was just torn apart by the derelicts and the insects. And the mind was – it was overthrown. But before, in '66 it was still bad – it was still a very good chance of getting your head beat in – you know. It was still a good chance that nobody liked you and that they didn't believe there was a war and that there was just a kind of a cleanup thing – there was nothing really happening there. So it was our job – and people burning themselves was the symbol of that – and it was our job to bring that to the attention of the world. When it came to – when it was in the attention of the world there was no longer the job to do because everybody knew it and was talking about it.' — (Ernstthal, interview.)

And Schumann likewise felt that the real anti-war movement for him ended with '66: around the time of a Madison Square pageant of December 8, '66:

'The rally in Madison Square Garden. That was *late*, that was in 1966. (Elka: It was at the very end of the year – December 8.) The end of the war movement – (Elka: It wasn't the end of the war movement.) For us, it seemed like the end of it pretty much. (Elka: It was finally getting popular because big crowds were really . . .)' — (Schumann, interview, '79.)

8. 'In the early sixties, when the Bread and Puppet Theatre's huge puppets and sorrowing masks began appearing in peace parades, it was apparent that they contained a finer knowledge of the heroic nature of the Vietnamese resistance than was yet present in many of the marchers. The pale faces, the gigantic hands in prayer, became emblems for a public morality struggling down Fifth Avenue, the midst of myopic Amerika, to be born. Where had this supraconsciousness come from? What vision had transformed the Amerikan belief in sheer size into a towering witness for humanity? The shock of the puppets – it is always the shock of the Bread and Puppet Theatre – was in the immediacy of their strangeness.' — (K. Taylor, *People's Theater in America*, 1972.)

'(I: I'm not a good interviewer you know, but what does the man stand for and by the man I mean the body of his work as he sort of appears to you at this point. You know there are various dimensions. There is a somehow, well a philosophy of life or a transcendentalism. There is a political sort of stance, and this philosophy of life. I don't know, but there's this whole thing about the family and work and nature. But what is your overall image of his . . .) Well, I guess the nearest I can come to answering that question is that it's the eternal truths, eternal verities. It's the you know the Easter Island, the image of those great figures looming stands for the universal truths. It seemed to me Peter was

The movement in opposition to the war in Vietnam furnished Schumann a raison d'etre and a guide for artistic production that in Germany he had not had; the energy of devoted collaborators to whom he needed

---

quite – this is what he is absorbed in – that whatever his passing interests in politics are, are really passing and that he as much as anybody in the life of the '60s, which is what I'm talking about, the art of the '60s and early '70s, the avant garde in New York, which I was so involved in, he more than any of those people had a way of looking at human beings in their overall view and you know biblical or eternal verities, external truths, I don't know. But virtue is virtue and it existed and sin is sin and it existed and all the nuances and all the subtleties that we're so caught up in – the new freedoms and the nothing's bad . . . . Peter never saw that and I don't think it ever came into his ken . . . . And it gave him an enormous stature and strength.

And I think if he were saying these in any other idiom except the one he was in, we'd have had no time to listen to him. If he had tried to present it in any other art form other than those great puppets, those great majestic puppets coming down Fifth Avenue in a parade against the war in Vietnam, the impact of this wise men of the world and the wise biblical figures out of the past, the great Jews with their eternal truths and they'll go on forever. We shall prevail over everything. It gave – was really breathtaking when you got caught up in something like the war in Vietnam where our stinking government, you know, is blowing the hell out of little people across the Pacific and our outrage was so total that it was such a relief to see they would prevail. And that's what Peter's work always meant. That the human spirit would prevail over the atom bomb, over everything, all the terrible things that were going to happen to us . . . we were going to be wiped off the face of the earth. Somehow, there is Peter's figures, so austere and so without affectation and so paced in their leisurely, you know, hundreds of years to get from one place to another, but one had a view, it was a release that you didn't get from any other art form, particularly the art that I was involved with, the Theatre of the Ridiculous, the Theatre of the Absurd, the Theatre of Cruelty and the whole thing which is really very nerve wracking, very exciting, very nerve wracking.

And then to walk into this eternal calm and truth of Peter's. It's not that the others weren't truthful, they were. But they came from a much smaller dimension; a much more hysterical-dealing, you know, dealing with drugs and the hysteria of angry people, and the war, they didn't understand or – (I: The way you describe it it's a message of hope.) Oh yes, enormous hope. Hope that I actually intellectually don't believe in, since I believe that the world is going to be – that human beings like the dinosaur are on their way out. But something in me, some inhuman and deep response to the fact that that's not true, that there is hope. And that's a wonderful message to get on an emotional level. When you use the images that he used, those great Gothic faces and that great expanse of cloth falling down. That's to my way of looking at things pretty positive. It's not nearly the kind of hope that one can intellectualize. The emotional impact does something to my culture and after all I may be upper middle class from the middle west from middle America from middle you know, from that point of view, nothing European, but the way the European art is translated to us out there in the Midwest, these things were eternal and lasting. These are the people which Schumann spoke to and that's – if I could be religious it would be in the terms of the kind of thing that Peter presented.' — (Bissinger, interview.)

'You know the whole thing though in the '60s, the guerrilla theatres and the whole consortium of sort of leftist and anti-war theatrical groups, in which Bread and Puppet Theatre was grouped. I think the theatre's presence in that always was a kind of uncomfortable association. Because he certainly believed with passionate intensity in the wrongness of the Vietnam war and the importance of stopping it by any means that could be done, I think that there was always a distrust for them by all the other people. Largely

not be grateful, since they, with him, served a higher cause;[9] and an ideal audience, the war-supporting citizenry, who, though they, emphatically did not ask for his art, yet could be seen as in fact objectively in need of it, and whose recalcitrance and indifference absolved him of the sycophancy of bespoke art, as their need for it of the vanity of art for art's sake or for the sake of personal expression.

At the same time, street propaganda and involvement in 'The Move-

---

because he's a Christian you know. Somehow that religious overtone was puzzling to a lot of the bedfellows around that sort of thing and it was something that, yeah he's alright because he's against the war, but that Christian, that mysticism and so forth. Why doesn't he just trim it down to the straight stuff and leave that kind of stuff out? I used to hear that quite a lot.

Again it's one of the interesting things in Peter. It's an extraordinary, whatever else it is, an extraordinary personal integrity to watch in Peter. Because there is I think many times in his life a lot of pressure on him from groups that could not even be considered oppressive or anything like that. From people who admired his work, to emphasize certain directions and he always did it the way he wanted to do it. And it always was a bit disturbing. I mean people were always a little upset because there was always something that they didn't think ought to be there. It was remarkable but why should it do this too? Why is it so slow? Would it be more effective in stirring up the multitudes if it's just a little crisper, you know. This sort of thing. Peter always did it the way he wanted to do it and always expressed what he wanted to express. And that is amazing to me.' — (Shapli, interview.)

9. One gets an impression of the extent to which by '68, the Bread and Puppet Theatre had come to appear a political action group from the reaction to it in Berlin in the summer of '68 of Murray Levy just come from four years with the Free Southern Theatre:

'You see four years in the Black community produces vision that you don't have unless you are there, you see things that you don't see otherwise. And so, over the years there I got my strengths from the Black community, the White community was mostly either indifferent or one would have liked to have killed it. There were a handful of liberals who tried to help us a little bit, you know little crumbs here and there. And then what happened was the change in the Black community was that the Black community didn't want Whites coming in and helping no matter how good willed or what, they wanted to do it themselves, and I was struggling with that new thing, because I didn't see myself as a White. I was having real identity problems. I was going through a lot of changes. And, so when King died it was like God and I packed my bags and I was gone. I was reading in the papers that students were trashing the streets in Berlin, they were breaking it up, they didn't want it to be the way it was. And so I thought well there is the kind of fighting that I want to do, that is what brought me to Germany. That was the first impulse to go to Germany . . . . Well, one of the things that affected me by it too was that, well it was really the first time, that I had seen masks used that way, and it was also the first time that I had seen White actors, I didn't know that that kind of theatre existed in New York. White actors in such a political – who had also political statements to make. 'Cause I had left New York, I had worked on Broadway and had done this whole scene, I had studied here for years and years with Paul Mann, the Group Theatre people and I had left the New York scene and I went down South and then I was in a whole other culture practically, although it wasn't so different, 'cause I grew up in the South Bronx. It seemed to reaffirm my own roots, being in the Black community. I seemed to, at that point, but so that then seeing these White actors and actresses doing things that were as, that were strong, strong for the White community, I thought, wow, you can do that, you can go to the White community too and not cut your balls off first. So to speak.' — (Levy, interview.)

ment' could be seen as still within the realm of popular art, of a kind with the work of medieval stone masons fashioning saints and gargoyles, of the proto-protestant woodcut artists of the 15th century, of the traveling jugglers and puppeteers of fairs, and the market story-tellers, of the lowbrow film-makers of early Hollywood, of the sculptors of burial art in the Roman Republic. Schumann's venue has absolved him of the odium of the artist's privileged existence, by his gifts elevated above the people. It must be added, however, for psychological accuracy, that the work itself, opium of the gifted and energetic, the considerable physical labor of making large puppets: of setting them up and of performing with them, actually for Schumann then was and has continued to be a good in itself and what he really wants, the good cause and the decent populist form merely requirements for allowing him to throw himself into it. He heaps work upon himself. Actually, the man is totally indifferent not only to himself but to his audience, and to his art's political effects on it no less than to its aesthetic effects.

Ernstthal, interview:

'We went to every demonstration and did many of them . . . .'

He invented[10] an art form, the puppet parade, peculiarly adapted to mass parades. Schumann came up with stationary agitational puppet shows that could be done by themselves or at rallies, but his main contribution was the puppet parade. A number of other groups, e.g. the San Francisco Mime Troupe and the Pageant Players, after a while did anti-war skits at rallies or by themselves in parks, but he was pretty much the only one during the '60s to develop this parade art. The fact that his puppets showed up so consistently in New York City peace parades on these occasions meant that they provided them with a consistent image, that, actually, of a mute protest maintained simply as a representation of a de facto state of certain minds irrespective of whether its expression might have any effect on others. The suffering puppets showed up again and again, regardless, so to speak. The consistency of the image reenforced it. In addition, Schumann to some – limited – extent at a certain point seems to have assumed something like design-control over entire marches, though I imagine that in practice it just amounted to being listened to when he suggested adaptations to what he wanted to do with his puppets, plus perhaps an approach to something like a veto power regarding other pageantry than his own. To the extent he achieved this artistic control, it would have added to the efficacy of his imagery: wedding it and each given march more firmly to one another.

---

10. The two most relevant antecedents: Palm Sunday processions with the effigies of Mary or patron saints blessing the houses; July 4th parades with floats.
The great artist of this century in the medium of political propaganda – the parade and the rally as spectacle – was of course A. Hitler. Vide Riefenstahl, *Triumph des Willens*.

5. Richard Tyler marches as *Totentanz* Death in a Living Theatre Strike for Peace. February '62.

Schumann's first contribution to New York City anti-war street agitation was made for him by the Reverend Dickie Tyler leading his Alchemy Players, a 'six piece Alchemy Players unit', the Reverend, finely conscious of the potentially indefinite extent of his organization, says, on the final day of the Living Theatre's World Wide General Strike for Peace, February 4, 1962, on a march from Thompson Street to Times Square, drumming, and wearing the death mask made by Schumann that three months later he wore in Schumann's *Dance of Death* – the little band of weirdos against the atom bomb. That first strike didn't do the job, so Judith and Julian struck again in November, among other things by their sponsorship of the last performance of the *Dance* and of Schumann's mysterious *Burning Towns*. Schumann's career started in that framework.

6. Jesus and his disciples at their business. Fighting the landlord in the Barrio. Winter '63/'64, winter '64/'65.

What inspired him, he says (*tendenzen*, November '66-February '67), by puppet-means to make political statements in the streets, was vox populi. He was in the manner of a medieval parish priest parading his newly made holy effigies around the streets of Brooklyn on December 29, '63,[1] advertising that evening's performance of *The Christmas Story* at the Reverend Glenesk's Spencer Memorial Church and among the comments this inspired in the bystanders some had political allusion. Which gave him the idea.

'Um Publikum zu finden, zogen wir mit den Puppen durch die umliegenden Strassen. Dabei riefen uns die Leute Anspielungen zu – meist aktuelle und politische – und diskutierten mit uns über die Puppen. Nun baue ich meine Figuren und Puppen grundsätzlich mit aus den Meinungen von Laien, Mitarbeitern oder Schauspielern auf – am besten geht das übrigens mit Kindern. Jedenfalls liefen wir bald mit den Puppen durch die Strassen und riefen die Meinungen der Leute aus.' (Schumann, *tendenzen*.)

As the memory of those concerned goes, he got into political street puppetry at the solicitation of a neighborhood – Lower East Side Puerto Rican politico by the name of Bird Aponte connected with the M.P.I., the Movement for Puerto Rican Independence – a leftist outfit, active not only in its nominal cause but also, at any rate during the early '60s, in such causes as improved housing conditions for Puerto Rican immigrants, and possibly also – it would be a little paradoxical – their exercise of voting rights. Rent strike and voter registration agitation, are at any rate what he first got into: I doubt he came out for Puerto Rican independence, too 'political' an issue for him, probably, and, besides, not one where, as with these others, he could view himself as responding simply to neighborhood needs and concerns.

Voter registration, not a particularly leftist cause, was the first cause, it seems – note that Schumann himself never did take out citizenship papers. He just took his new puppets for a walk, Jesus and the disciples. Others provided slogans. If this was his first street demonstration, it would have been in October (when voter registrations drives are mounted) '63: before the Christmas processional in Brooklyn. Elka has a note in her files, 'Nov-

---

1. The Reverend Glenesk (*Face to Face*, December '69) viewed the parade as a processional constituting the first part of the order of that evening's service, gives the itinerary as 'around Brooklyn Heights to the Promenade, the Brooklyn Bridge, downtown to the Supreme Court, Borough Hall', and says it was for a distance of about two miles and took approximately 30 minutes.

'November, 1964/Voter Registration Parade in lower Eastside with big Crucifixion puppets'.

'My feeling is, I'm not sure of this, that the first thing I did with the big puppets was for something called the Voter Registration Drive on the Lower East Side – the Jesus puppets – I believe the voter registration thing was that late fall, with some Puerto Rican and other organizations asking for that kind of thing. (Ephraim: That was just a parade?) Just a parade. We took those parades just like shows. We really composed them – signs and puppets and things – there was a parade that was, I think, organized by Spanish organizations. (Ephraim: And they used the disciple puppets.) Yes, and a big devil puppet – and the big puppets that we called Die Spiesser.' (Schumann, interview, '79.)

'This one is actually the first one – we took the puppets outside. (SSB: For a Lower East Side Voter Registration Parade.) I think that we were on Suffolk Street and we had just made the big *Crucifixion* puppets. That's an obscure moment – I remember that now – and there was a voter registration – really a local kind of thing and there was a Spanish guy who was like a political ward heeler almost in the Lower East Side and he wanted us to go out with him. I think we sort of just walked around with him – something like that – just in the parade and that was the first time. We simply brought them out into the streets and there was no big deal. But they would catch the eye and they would create a little stir and – they were so big – and I think we just walked with them. Maybe there was a landlord/tenant thing – I kind of think we just took them out and walked around on the street. It was a more innocent time – '63 – and all that was more – it was just simple. There was some guy – Hector Gonzalez or something, whom we knew, and he wanted – like big flags or something – and the puppets were part of that. It was something to catch the eye and we just walked around with them one day.' (Ernstthal, interview.)

'(SSB: Lower East Side Voter Registration Parade?) That's the one that we just went out, like I say – I think his name was Gonzalez, or something. He was the local ward guru who got us out to march. That was a proto – in a sense that was one of these first things before we knew what was going on, anything about it at all. We just went out and carried the morale. And I *believe* it was – one of them was labeled "Landlord", the Jesus puppet was a tenant, and there was a bad landlord. Something. But I'm not sure. It may have been also we simply carried them, we simply carried them.' (Ernstthal, interview.)

Ernstthal has a faint idea that the landlord/tenant issue may have been mixed up with the Voter Registration one. It is conceivable though not likely that Ben Reade has it right:

'The troupe's first demonstration came in a parade for voter registration and was simply contrived, consisting of a 14-foot Christ-like puppet labeled "Lower East Side" surrounded by a coterie of figures – "police brutality," "landlord," "Daily News" – cudgeling the Christ with sticks. At the suggestion of the cops, Schumann removed the police figure from the performance.'
(Ben Reade, *The Demonic Protest of the Bread and Puppet Theater, Renewal* (Chicago), April-May '67.)

Kourilsky, '71 (p. 63-64) relates this same Punch and Judy-type parade show to the rent strike context and she is probably right.[2]

His Puerto Rican mentor *may* have gotten him out for Puerto Rican independence as well. In the late-'66 interview in *tendenzen* cited, he says he built, for one of the 'big parades of the Puerto Ricans demonstrating against the brutal exploitation (this sounds like Old Left party lingo! (SSB)) of agricultural laborers and for their national independence ... a wagon with mobile giant puppets: a big boss continuously mistreating the pitiful figure of a campesino.' Maybe. Ernstthal recalls such a flatbed truck show and places it in the incongruous context of a Puerto Rican Day parade with its baseball clubs, bands and pretty 'society' ladies in long dresses: but it is more apt to have been another demonstration on another issue, the California United Farm Workers strike from the fall of '65 onward, which I would for various reasons place in June '67.

Rent strikes[3] and rental agitation on the issues of repairs and heating, rent control,[4] rental rates and changes in rents, and tenants' rights, in the winter of '63/'64 spread from Harlem, where one Jesse Gray was providing leadership, to the Lower East Side, where *The Militant* of January 27 tells us, something calling itself simply the 'Lower Eastside Rentstrike' was coordinating things, specifically, was 'kicking off' the strike by a January 30,'64 rally on Stanton Street, between Chrystie and Forsythe, which *The Militant* of February 10th (locating that Lower East Side Rentstrike outfit at 332 East 4th Street) describes, having mentioned the movement's slogan, 'No Rent for Rats', and that at that time 500 buildings in Harlem, 50 on the Lower East Side, and 45 each in the Bronx and in Bedford-Stuyvesant were on strike:

'Tenants, including many children, marched through the area carrying torches and shouting slogans in Spanish and English to draw a crowd to the meeting which was held in the University Settlement House. The hall, which held some 300 persons, was overflowing.... Someone hung an effigy of a slumlord from a rafter.... Speakers included... Pedro Ortero, vice chairman of the group. Jesse Gray received an ovation....'

The Militant, as apparently the strike movement itself, continues to bear down on rats:

'Five minutes before Brooklyn CORE's rent strike parade started out from the corner of Lexington and Nostrand Avenues on May 2, Police Captain Jenkins of the 79th precinct walked up to Mr. Major Owens, co-ordinator of the parade, and informed him that its main exhibit, a four-foot cage of live rats, caught in Bedford-Stuyvesant tenements would not be permitted, citing an obscure part of

---

2. In one of her photos Ernstthal in some park in front of a partly seated and partly Chinese audience is holding up a door marked 'registration'. She places the show on the Lower East Side in '64. But I suspect it is a performance of the '67 *Chicken Little*, of its third, 'registration' scene – perhaps August 20, '67 in Chinatown?
3. Cf. Appendix XVI.
4. Cf. the *New York Times*, January 8, 9, 24, '64.

New York City's Health Code prohibiting the display of wild animals except in zoos, circuses and laboratories.' (*The Militant*, May 11, '64.)

The paraders complied, displaying signs commending the police department for its concern for the animals, but in subsequent protests to the authorities objected that rats in their parts of the city were domestic. But not domesticated: an article in the July 13th issue of *The Militant* once more told of rats in cribs and of fingers bitten to the bone – on East 6th Street, whither by this time the Schumanns had moved. The *New York Times* on August 30, '64 reports on the Lower East Side rent strikes and says they are organized by a United Tenants Association (president, Roberto Colon) with offices in the house janitored by Richard Tyler, next door to where the Schumanns had lived. At the end of August, August 30 and 31st, the Association is demonstrating in support of a government-funded organization named Mobilization for Youth, in trouble with the city authorities at this time because of press allegations of Communist and/or Trotzkyite infiltration. Mobilization for Youth had been supporting the Association.

'Quand j'habite East 6th Street et qu'il y a une grève, je me sens obligé d'y participer avec ce que je peux faire, c'est à dire avec mes marionettes. Exactement comme Luis Valdez qui vit dans la San Joaquin Valley où il y a une grève des cueilleurs de raisin et qui se joint au mouvement avec le Teatro Campesino. C'est la forme naturelle que prend le théâtre dans ces circonstances. Et le théâtre doit certainement avoir cette immédiateté.' (Schumann, in Kourilsky, '71, p.198.)

Schumann in '64 apparently supports this agitation and these strikes on the streets of the Lower East Side by agitational promenades. Some of these are part of organized parades. One particular Lower East Side organization he remembers cooperating with was called the Independcent Action Committee for Social Progress. Kourilsky ('71, p. 63-4) says it was accused of Communism and dissolved to become Mobilization for Youth. In fact, however, apparently it was formed (according to the *National Guardian* of April 10, '64 sometime before this date, according to a Committee flyer quoted in the F.B.I. files on it on September 20, '64) to pursue Mobilization's goals when Mobilization in '64 fell into temporary disrepute. Another was called something like the Lower East Side Tenants Association.[5] Schumann would take out his big *Crucifixion* puppets, appropriately labeled, e.g. Jesus as 'Tenant,' and perhaps on one occasion on a flatbed truck did the Punch and Judy type show that we

---

5. 'The Lower East Side Tenants Association at the time that we had to do with them was headed by Esther Rand. She was quite a well known Lower East Side Jewish lady who was very active – very radical – very active – very colorful – among all these neighborhood groups. And that was called the Cooper Union or the Cooper Square Tenants Association. Lower East Side Tenants Association, Chapter Cooper Square – something like that. And it was on Second Avenue, their office.' — (Schumann, interview, '82.)

saw Ben Reade placed in a voter registration parade. But he and Ernstthal would also take the Punch and Judy out on their own and do a show on the landlord/tenant theme on a street corner; or they would 'parade' on the burnt-out streets with drum and masks, and stop to do the crankie *Rat Movie*, off a garbage can, with the narrator still masked. The *Rat Movie*

'portrayed a man who finds a stray rat. He takes the rat home, feeds it, watches in horror as it grows finally into a full-blown monster. Afraid that the rat will attack his baby, the man calls the police department. "Sorry, wrong number." The fire department. "Is the rat on fire?" The health department. "Is the rat sick?" Finally, the bureaucracy having failed, an angel swoops down and saves the baby.' (Reade, *Demonic Protest*.)

'Their Punch & Judy show, which played on the street corners and attacked slumlords, was fine with the police so long as the pink-faced puppet portraying the Irish cop did not come to a foul end.' (Reade, ibid.)

'We used Punch and Judy, for landlord, even landlord shows for people who couldn't keep an apartment, the landlord threw them out for various reasons, that was the essence of these Punch and Judy shows. And we did the crankies, we did the *Rat Movie*. That was made during that time. That's a little box. Actually we did it the two of us together, Bob and I. I went around with a dragon mask and a drum and some horns, and we drummed people together and told them we were telling a story. And we put the crankie box on some garbage cans and told the story.... Maybe the narrator wore – had the dragon mask – could be....'
(Schumann, interview, '79.)

The tenant/landlord struggle usually intensifies after Christmas, but reaches a peak in spring just when the worst of winter is over, then dies down. Probably Schumann was active in it from early '64 on: the *National Guardian* shows him still working his crankie at the end of the year.[6] He told Jotterand, the author of *Le Nouveau Theatre Americain*,

---

6. 'These photographs taken on a recent weekend (November 30, '64 (SSB)) demonstrate how the Independent Action Committee for Social Progress on the Lower East Side sought to reach the inhabitants of New York's oldest ghetto with a program calling for better housing, schools, jobs and an end to discrimination. On successive Saturdays this fall (until the weather got too cold), the Committee – with the help of the Bread and Puppet Theatre, which donates its services free – conducted street corner meetings to discuss the miserable conditions under which most of the residents in this area attempt to survive. Speeches in Spanish and English and leaflets about how to impose conditions (form committees, direct action) round out the program. The committee which is in the process of acquiring permanent headquarters holds monthly meetings to which the public is invited.... The Bread and Puppet Theatre is giving daily performances (at 3 p.m.) at the Pocket Theatre, 13th St. and 3rd Ave., until January 3. Performances are also given each Saturday at 8 p.m. at the Bread and Puppet Museum, 148 Delancey St.... It is expected that they'll all return to the street corners as soon as a thaw sets in next spring.' (Unsigned article, *National Guardian*, January 2, '65.) A caption to one of Robert Joyce's photographs reads, 'Crowds at each show usually number 50-100 young and old, black and white' – but the photos show the two showmen alone in the empty streets and their greyness suggests the seasonal cold.

they had

'joué en plein air. Les gens du quartier ou j'habitais refusaient de payer leurs loyers parce que leurs propriétaires laissaient leur apartements s'ecrouler. Nous avons monté un spectacle pour le groupe de la 'Rent Strike' ... et nous l'avons joué devant les résidences des propriétaires, dans les quartiers chics. Ils ont fini par ceder.' (Schumann in Jotterand, op. cit. pg. 147.)

But this is my only source for such excursions.

He found time for at least one more demonstration on the tenant/landlord issues in 1965: sometime after he had built his 'Uncle Fatso' puppet with Negro kids in the summer of 1965, he paraded Uncle Fatso through the streets of Spanish Harlem as Landlord. — (Photo in *Newsweek*, May 23, 1966.)

7. August '64 Schumann joins peace agitation under Old Left auspices.

Elka has a Times Square demonstration of '64 down as the first of the Bread and Puppet peace demonstrations, Schumann conceding that it was an early one. Ernstthal remembers a Times Square demonstration as one of their first peace ones (and thinks of it as one of the earliest anti-war demonstrations in New York City altogether, and as one described in his then friend Ed Sanders' *Tales of Beatnik Glory*).[1] Their descriptions concur

'That very week-end there had been demonstrations in Times Square where club-wielding police on horse had ridden up on the curb into a large crowd packed upon Father Duffy's traffic island – and the blood had dripped from the whacked skulls.' (Sanders, *Tales.*) In the context, this would have been a Friday, March 3rd: which would have placed it in 1964...

Julian Beck's lung was punctured in Times Square by the New York City police on Saturday, March 3rd, 1962 – apparently when his World Wide General Strike for Peace staged a sit-down there. The demonstrators were protesting against President Kennedy's resumption of nuclear testing, 'in the atmosphere.' Joseph Chaikin, founder of the Open Theatre, then in the Living Theatre *Connection*, was arrested. Cf. Michael Smith's *Beck's Condition Okay; McReynolds Blasts Sitters* in the *Village Voice* of March 8, '62 and McReynolds' letter in the March 15 issue. McReynolds spoke for the War Resisters League. This would have been the very early anti-war demonstration Ernstthal remembers. But Schumann hadn't started demonstrating then as yet.

'I think that was probably one (one of the Grey Mother with baby puppets (SSB)), the Fool, and probably the (Stovepipe (SSB)) Soldiers, those are the things that we probably had out there in Times Square – when Beany (Kunitz (SSB)) got arre.... There was a whole bunch of people there, so we went there and the cops knew about it and they came with horses, and I think somebody had pebbles or marbles to throw around to make the horses stumble and fall, and that didn't happen, but the cops were outraged – and they really charged into us.... And – so I tried to organize the gathering up of the puppets and getting the station wagon close that we had there, Bruno's car, I think, to get them in, to get them out of there, and lead them back to safety (laughs), and while we were waiting for the station wagon, Beany sat down on the curb of the sidewalk and then, as we loaded up into the station wagon, the cops arrested him. Just like that. Picked him up, shoved him into their van. And Bruno, who saw that, just in solidarity, for no *particular* reason, hopped on into the van with him (laughs). So I took the puppets home, and they – I think Oyle was there too. (Elka: Obstructing the sidewalk and resisting arrest?) No, not only that, they were accused, later on in the court session, the cops said that Bruno and Beany – no, Beany they let go, for some strange reason. And Bruno there kept and there were two cops testifying, a complete fairy tale, saying that Bruno had put himself flat down into the street in protest and in obstruction of traffic (laughs). So, it was very precarious times because Bruno didn't have a pass. I didn't have a citizenship, I had a green card. But we didn't know how the government would act on those things. We could have lost those green cards.' — (Schumann, interview, '79.)

'(I: Sagen sie, eine Frage, wie war das denn, sie war'n ja kein Amerikaner und der Schumann ist ja auch nie einer geworden. Und, also, sie waren bei diesen Friedensdemonstrationen dabei, wie kommt es, dass man sie nicht einfach herausgeschmissen hat?) Ja, ich weiss dat auch nicht. Wir hatten damals unsere ersten, unsere erste Auseinandersetzung mit der Obrigkeit am Duffy Square. Und am Duffy Square da ging es dann heiss

497

at least as regards an aggression by mounted police.
In fact this appears to have been a demonstration of August 8, '64

zu, und wurde ich auch, ich bin da mit dem Beany, Beany hiess er, (...) also der wurde dann an'n Haaren dann in diese Auto gezerrt und so weiter und bin ich auch mit eingestiegen. Mich hat niemand, mich hat niemand aufgefordert da einzusteigen, ich bin aus freien Stücken da rin. Dann wurde ich auf der Polizeiwache als verhaftet erklärt und grosse Schnauze gehabt, wie üblich, und bin auch nicht, bin nicht geschlagen worden, nix. Und bin aber in Center Street gelandet, zusammen mit den andern. Und da hab ich zum ersten Mal von innen ein amerikanisches Polizeigefängnis gesehen also diese 'Catches' (?) da, nicht. Und da kriecht ich zum ersten Mal so'n Blick hinter die schwierigen Kulissen und da war, da war 'ne Abteilung aus Harlem, die war gerade frisch gekascht worden. Sowat krichten wir nie mit, dat war 'ne andere Welt da oben. Und da hatten 'se einen, einen Bürgerrechtsvertreter, der gehörte sogar, der hatte, der hatte 'ne politische Immunität, dieser Mann. Der stand dort, blutig zusammengeschlagen, mit geplatzter Lippe, mehrere Platzwunden am Kopf, inmitten seiner Getreuen. Und die waren, die waren alle geschlagen worden, konnte man sehen. Die hatten fast alle blutverschmierte Gesichter. Und da hab ich gedacht, (...) wat Du 'n Glück hast. Hättsde so'ne schöne Hautfarbe wie die, dann sähst de jetzt auch anders aus. Ja, und dann, ja, dann wurden wir dann in diesem, dat war so'n Schauprozess, drei Tage ging der. Und da musst ich auch aussagen, so, da hab ich noch den Polizisten da lächerlich gemacht, weil ich, ich weiss nicht, also irgendwie so'n schwerwitzigen Einfall hatte. Ich hab mir unheimlich viele Frechheiten da erlaubt, ja, und man hat mich nicht rausgeschmissen. Dat war wahrscheinlich auch so, dass man (...) ich mein, die Leute wussten, der, der da auf der, da auf der Banke sitzt, der hat so und so viele Genossen noch um sich rum, und wenn wir den aus'm Land rausschmeissen dann gibt es wieder Wirbel und so, dann lassen wir'n lieber in Ruhe. Dat war an sich auch so auch so meine, meine, mein Schutzschild. Wat nicht mein Schutzschild gewesen wäre, waren meine, ich hab ja in New York nie Parktickets bezahlt. Ich hab, ich hab sechs summonses gekriegt, insgesamt, und dann wurde ich gesucht wegen dieses wie nennt sich das nochmal, scofflaw nicht... ja, ja wegen scofflaw und dann, dann kamen die Jungs an. Dat hat aber lang gedauert. Ja, ja der Peter hatte mit sowat keine Schwierigkeiten. Vielleicht, wie ich weg war, ich weiss nicht, aber es war alles ziemlich friedlich um ihn rum. — (Eckhardt, interview.)

Anyway, we brought these puppets up to this demonstration in Duffy Square. The police rode in on horseback, to the demonstration. We grabbed the puppets and took off, because they really started bashing us and stuff. And that was our first demonstration. In fact, that was the first anti-war demonstration of any (?) in New York.... Well, have you ever seen a horse riding down on you? It... they're so big. (I: You got the puppets up there in a car?) Yeah, Charlie Adams, one of Dick Tyler's friends who was like a local guy... he was the one guy who had a car and he had this beat-up Chevy... '53 Chevy station wagon... he had a car, so we used his car constantly. (I: And then you were just standing with the puppets or –?) Just standing with the puppets. There were speeches. This group... I think it was called Youth Against War and Fascism. One of the leaders was a guy named Levi Laub. There was a scandal because one of the guys... one of the other leaders turned out to be an FBI agent later. The whole political thing was really difficult. The demonstrations and all were another thing. But that was the first demonstration we were asked to do and that we in fact did. That was this head-bashing scene.... It was all new. So we just stood there with these horrible looking soldier puppets, protesting the – (I: And one guy was enough to handle these puppets?) No, we had a few. Probably Peter was there and me. As I remember there were six dowels in those puppets. But you could hold, like you could hold two of them. I think two guys were enough for that one. And we didn't do any show or anything.' — (Ernstthal, interview.)

gotten up by an outfit calling itself the May 2nd Committee,[2] though co-sponsored by Youth Against War and Fascism, not only to protest U.S. military aggression in Vietnam but also to assert their right to peaceful assembly in the mid-town area (Sixth to Eighth Avenues, 42nd to 57th Street): there had been a police ban on demonstrations there since the spring of '62:

'A rally in Duffy Square against the military role of the United States in Vietnam was broken up yesterday afternoon by mounted police and patrolmen using nightsticks. A crowd of about 60 had gathered in front of the statue of Father Duffy, between Broadway and 7th Avenue at 47th Street, to hear speeches denouncing the Johnson administration's policies. The police ordered the demonstrators to disperse. They refused. Then, as hundreds of visitors and other bystanders watched, two mounted policemen moved into the crowd.... Phillip A. Luce, a well-tailored young man with a red moustache, was introduced by Levi Laub. Both are under federal indictment for having visited Cuba in violation of a State Department ban.'

(*New York Times*, August 9, '64.)

Robert Joyce caught the 4-Soldiers puppet both still upright in front of Father Duffy's stern face and then lifeless on the ground.

The *Village Voice* did not report these August demonstrations — the issue of November 19 carries a small echo, however, a notice that the May 2nd Committee, a 'radical peace organization', has been picketing the Women's House of Detention in the Village protesting the 'plight of

---

2. The May 2nd Committee 'was under the control of the Progressive Labor Party, a small but militant group founded by former members of the Communist party who sided with Mao Tse Tung in the Moscow-Peking struggle, and it never attracted much of a following.' — (Th. Powers, *The War at Home*, 1973.)

The *New York Times* of May 3rd '64 reports a rally of May 2nd at 110th Street and 8th Avenue i.e. in the Columbia University area, demanding the end of U.S. millitary aid to South Vietnam and the withdrawal of troops, with 400 college students from Columbia, City College, Haverford College participating, organized by the May 2nd Committee, 'an ad hoc student group set up six weeks ago at Yale,' the Socialist Workers Party and the Young Socialist Alliance. The rally was followed by a march to Times Square and the U.N. 'On Broadway there were slight traffic delays as thousands of passersby stopped and stared at the demonstrators. There were no incidents.' (The *New York Times* of August 16th '64 says the May 2nd Committee had their first rally on May 2nd '63.) The May 2nd Committee staged another rally in Duffy Square a week after the first one had been broken up — August 15th '64. This time they were not interfered with, but when they afterward tried to deviate in the direction of downtown from a march eastward to the U.N. that one of the two leaders of the Committee, P.A. Luce (Levy Laub being the other) had negotiated with the police, some of them were arrested, Luce among the first ones. — (*New York Times*, August 16, '64.)

Kennedy had been shot in November '63, and Johnson was president — received the Democratic nomination in August '64. '64 was the year in which he launched the Great Society, the War on Poverty in January, the enactment of Kennedy's civil rights program in July. But August was when he obtained, by way of the Tonkin Gulf incident, congressional authorization for the non-war in Vietnam that was to drag on, wrecking his home reforms, for the next nine years.

Carolyn McFedder, 19, of Portland, Oregon, ... one of the 47 people arrested during a protest against the war in Vietnam last August 15. Her case has not yet come to trial....'

Schumann thus may have entered the Movement under Old Left auspices. But as Ernstthal says, 'the demonstrations were another thing.' He was still, apparently, essentially just standing around with his puppets.

8. Or possibly under liberal pacifist auspices in March '64.

Schumann in '79 inclined to think that their first peace demonstration was, rather, an earlier march that Grace Paley (later the wife of Bob Nichols), one of the chief animators of the Greenwich Village Peace Center, an old-style pacifist organization that became a major link between Schumann and the Movement, invited them on. That would have been in connection with the Peace Center's Easter weekend peace rally in Washington Square Park at the end of March '64 (*Village Voice*, April 2, '64). But their first recorded peace march is the 'Greenwich Village Puppet Parade' (*Village Voice*, March 11, '65) along the south edge of the park, a year later, March 6, '65, sponsored by the Greenwich Village Peace Center:

'Puppet parade for peace . . . to dramatize opposition to the war in Vietnam. The towering characters were created by Peter Schumann for his Lenten season play "*Puppet Christ*." ' (*Village Voice*, March 11, '65.)

'On March 6, 1965, Special Agents of the Federal Bureau of Investigation observed a demonstration which was co-sponsored by the Greenwich Village Peace Center and the Bread and Puppet Theatre. The demonstration consisted of twenty-three persons walking as a group through the Greenwich Village Area of New York City carrying signs protesting the war in Vietnam and America's alleged use of "dirty bombs" therein. Ten of the demonstrators wore Halloween type masks, eight carried poles to which were attached grotesque masks and four carried poles with skeletons atop for the purpose of dramatizing the horrors of war. The demonstration started at 1:00 p.m. and ended at 3:00 p.m. There were no incidents or arrests.' (F.B.I. files: NYfile 62-13318.)

It was a short parade: a skull-masked drummer, his gross head bulldog-like, out front on the sidewalk, 'Bread and Puppet Theater' prominent on his drum, followed by a tall bespectacled lady in blue jeans with a huge sign hung over her, 'We protest bombing of North Vietnam/US support of military dictatorship in South Vietnam', by Christ, arms lifted in what since it can't be benediction is probably exhortation, a sign 'Vietnam' over his chest, his skirt-dress half covering his carrier, Christ in turn backed up by a file of six disciples, with the four-headed soldier puppet as rear guard.

The giant mute puppets make a strong statement, not diminished by the visibility of their carriers, in the nearly empty street. They are above all tall. Schumann has swung into the essential format of his peace agitation. The proximate larger occasion was the beginning of the U.S. bombing of Vietnam in February '65 – 'Operation Rolling Thunder' began February 10th. Johnson had been elected and was pushing through his benign reforms: the new federal voting rights law was passed in August: his speech at Johns Hopkins University in April extended his good will even unto Asia, a billion-dollar program for the Mekong Delta, 'to provide food and water and power on a scale to dwarf even our own TVA' – construction services presumably to be provided by Black & Root. The Black guerilla war of the '60s that had begun with the rioting and looting of Harlem in the summer of '64, continued with the Watts riots (starting four days after the new voting rights law had been passed) of the summer of '65 (Chicago riots, July '66, Detroit riots, and Newark riots, July '67). Large-scale troop commitments in Vietnam, the Americanization of that war, began in late July '65.

It does not seem likely to me that Schumann did not march for peace, having once started, between August '64 and March '65. But I have found no trace of this. And the fact is that street agitation, i.e. agitation protesting against participation in the war in Vietnam, did not in New York City, and probably in the country, really get started until February/March '65, partly because that participation was slight until the February '65 bombings, partly because the civil rights issue (the disarmament and cold war issues having somewhat faded) preoccupied the radical and liberal intelligentsia. So that Schumann's known record is not exceptional. On the other hand, the known mentors of his early peace activities – the May 2nd Committee, the Living Theatre, the Greenwich Village Peace Center – were active before March '65 and it seems reasonable to suppose he marched and/or rallied with or for them.[1]

---

1. Cf. the record of New York City street agitation, Jan. 2, '64-Aug. 3, '68, traceable in the *Village Voice*, Appendix XVIII.

9. April '65. First participation in a large demonstration. Schumann doesn't have his act together yet: reliance on verbal signs.

The two demonstrations we have so far seen Schumann appear in had been sponsored respectively by the conspiratorial Old Left and by the flagrantly respectable pacifist anti-war movement. The next one, a 'March on Washington to End the War in Vietnam' of April 17, '65 – 20,000 demonstrators, an until then unheard-of number – with the February '65 bombings inspiring an until then lacking enthusiasm for it – was initiated, organized and led by the New Left, namely the Students for a Democratic Society, SDS, founded by University of Michigan students in June '62, but the crucial aspect of it, as regards the further history of the Movement was that the insistence of the SDS, and against the opposition of the pacifists, it was ecumenical, the SDS successfully insisting that the Old Left – the Trotzkyite and Communist outfits – not be excluded. This inclusiveness, as an ensuing debate between representatives of the New Left (Staughton Lynd in *Liberation*) and of the Civil Rights Movement (not yet a Black movement) (Bayard Rustin in *Commentary* and *Partisan Review*) brought out, was not just a matter of tactics but expressed an enlargement of the cause: beyond the cause of peace, or even of peace and civil rights, corresponding to the growing radicalism – leftism – of the New Left, its 'rejection of the system': the cause of change in the 'system'. The final paragraph of Lynd's attack (in the June-July issue of *Liberation*) on the limited objectives of the Civil Rights Movement describes the April 17 demonstration as a spectacle generating an inspiring image of revolution:

'At the April 17th march in Washington it was unbearably moving to watch the sea of banners and signs moving out from the Sylvan Theater toward the Capitol as Joan Baez, Judy Collins and others sang 'We Shall Overcome.' Still more poignant was the perception – and I checked my reaction with many others who felt as I did – that as the crowd moved down the mall toward the seat of government, its path delimited on each side by rows of chartered buses so that there was nowhere to go but forward, toward the waiting policemen, it seemed that the great mass of people would simply flow on through and over the marble buildings, that our forward movement was irresistably strong, and that even had some been shot or arrested nothing could have stopped the crowd from taking possession of its government. Perhaps next time we should keep going, occupying for a time the rooms from which orders issue and send to the people of Vietnam and the Dominican Republic the profound apologies which are due; or quietly wait on the Capitol steps until those who make policy for us, and who like ourselves are trapped by fear and pride, consent to enter into dialog with us and mankind.'

Schumann's contribution to this event, to judge by Eli Feiner's photograph in *The Militant* of April 26 ('Star Attraction . . . their dramatic message was much appreciated by other demonstrators.') or by one by Cal Sutliff, printed I don't know where,[1] was still a little ragged, he hadn't quite gotten the hang of it yet – the idea of a unified puppet spectacle, with or without action, as carrier of the message. It was heavily dependent on words, slogans lettered on signs sprinkled throughout it, 'We protest the dirty war/napalm bombing of villages', 'We protest U.S. bombing of North Vietnam/U.S. support of military dictatorship in Southern Vietnam' (the identical sign he'd used in March!), even a sign announcing the show's title 'Gas for Vietnam'; the gas masks on some of the marchers didn't quite go with the face masks on (some of) the sign carriers; and though there was some kind of order in their parade – the skull-masked drummer with the Bread and Puppet drum, the grim-mouthed Great Warrior brandishing his two white wooden swords, big Jesus, his figure a little wormlike, bug-eyed, hands joined as though about to make a pronouncement, presumably followed by the disciples (they are not on these photos) – it's loose and doesn't make a picture.

The time between this march of April 17th '65 and Schumann's next recorded march, on October 16, '65 was an active one for the peaceniks,[2]

---

1. A photo in the *Washington Post* of April 18 shows Jesus outside the Capitol, hands joined in front of his belly, with somebody holding up a toy helicopter next to him, another, ibid., shows him among the 'throng of marchers mov(ing) along the White House sidewalk.' When, at the conclusion of the rally, the 16,000 or so the park police estimated attended it marched 80 abreast (the spectacle that impressed Lynd (SSB)) down the Mall toward the Capitol, chanting 'No more war' and 'We want peace now,' the *Post* reporter among them espied 'six men with a drum, skeleton masks and gas masks, in the middle of their ranks.' This reporter also mentions seven members of the American Nazi party marching in a separate group with signs 'We want dead Reds'. American Nazis in fact showed up at peace rallies consistently – their opportunity as much as the Old Left's.

2. E.g. mentioning only events at which Schumann might have appeared, the May 15 Times Square Old Left rally sponsored by Youth against War and Fascism ('Get the GIs out of the Dominican Republic and Vietnam!'), the June 8 conservative-wing-of-the Movement Emergency Rally on Vietnam in Madison Square Garden sponsored by SANE, featuring speeches by Senator Wayne Morse, Ms. King, Dr. Spock, Norman Thomas and Bayard Rustin, and entertainment by Joan Baez, Irwin Corey, Renee Taylor and the Wilson Dancers and at which cautious Rustin called for 'direct action':

'We know that the Wagner Act which gave labor the right to organize and bargain collectively was empty until workers went into the streets. The civil rights movement has learned this lesson. This is a lesson that must be applied now to the peace movement as well. We must stop meeting indoors and go into the streets.'

There were two small Hiroshima Day observances in New York City, a Hiroshima Day rally at 38th Street and 7th Avenue, addressed by Representative William Fitts Ryan, Democratic candidate for mayor, and a silent march by 400 members of Women's Strike for Peace around the 'Unisphere,' symbol of Robert Moses' unfortunate World's Fair, and a rather bigger one in Washington, D.C., on the first day, August 6, of the 'White House Conference on the Declaration of Conscience,' of an 'Assemby of Unrepresented People,' August 6-9, sponsored by the *Catholic Worker*, the Committee for Non-Violent Action, and I am sure Schumann was in on some of the fun, but I have no record of it. He was doing his children's puppetry workshop in East Harlem that summer (which wouldn't have kept him from doing peace work as well), and on completion of it took the great new puppet the children had built for him – modeled the face of – for a walk through the streets of East Harlem. Ken Wittenberg who had shot him working with the kids took a picture of it that *Newsweek* (issue of May 23, '66, 'Protest Latin style: Spanish Harlem slumlord is caricatured in paper maché.') published. Uncle Fatso henceforth was to represent America in his parades, as Christ so far had represented Vietnam. In the crowded street – with the crowd, given his identification, no doubt responding sympathetically – Uncle Fatso looks like great fun – almost exuberant. But he henceforth for a while lent an aggressive note to some of the Bread and Puppet parades to which patriots responded aggressively.

The Student Peace Union and the War Resisters League, on the last day of which more than 350 people forced the authorities to arrest them. On October 14th, there was a Vietnam rally at West Broadway and Third Street, sponsored by the New York Ad Hoc Committee to Protest the War in Vietnam, at which Conor Cruise O'Brien and David Reynolds spoke, and on October 15th there was a demonstration that in some ways overshadowed the following days:

'David J. Miller, a twenty-two year old pacifist and member of the Catholic Worker Movement, burn(s) his draft card outside the Whitehall Street Army Induction Center in lower Manhattan. His simple act, which was to cost him more than two years in jail, began a movement of personal, almost existential protest against the war which was to spread quickly and evoke an agonized response from students facing the draft across the country ... he climbed to the top of a sound truck, tried to light his card with a match, then hunched over to shield the card with his body and managed to light it with a cigarette lighter which someone handed up to him from the crowd. After a moment he held the burning card up over his head in the dusk. The tiny light, Miller watching it, the silent crowd around him were all picked up by television cameramen and broadcast across the country, a gesture of personal and total opposition.' — (Th. Powers, *The War At Home*.)

10. October '65. Schumann has mastered the parade art form. A complex two-part parade, its parts meaningful, replacing slogans by images. First parade with puppets other than Jesus and his disciples.

Schumann reemerges from the fogs of history walking down Fifth Avenue, holding high the figure of the Christ manacled. This is Saturday, October 16th '65, second day of a weekend of International Days of Protest called by a successor to the Assembly of Unrepresented People, the National Coordinating Committee to End the War in Vietnam, like its predecessor representing a broad coalition of liberal civil rights and pacifist organizations. On the West Coast, i.e. in San Francisco-Berkeley – it's hard to march in Los Angeles – the protests were organized by more or less New Left student groups,[1] comprised police-blocked marches to the Oakland Army Base and led to half-hearted violent conflicts with the Oakland police and Hell's Angels. In New York they were organized by a new coordinating committee, the Fifth Avenue Peace Parade Committee, representing a coalition of traditional pacifist and civil rights groups and consisted, in the main, under the chairmanship of A.J. Muste, though the Socialist Workers and the Progressive Labor Party were represented too, (in spite of an estimated 1,000 hecklers throwing stuff, etc.) in a respectable and peaceful parade, on the whole effectively protected by the police, of about 20,000 people down Fifth Avenue from above the Metropolitan Museum to a rally on 69th Street between Lexington and Park (the Parks Commissioner having refused the use of Central Park). The Fifth Avenue Committee had maintained the inclusionist policy initiated by the SDS in the spring. SANE, not in the Committee, fuddy duddy, as well as the Movement for Puerto Rican Independence (attacked by right-wing Cubans at the beginning of the march, a 'flying wedge of 50 young men bashing through police barricades' according to the *Journal American*'s reporter), the radical Tompkins Square Neighbors for Peace (with an American flag that had skulls and dollar signs for stars), and a group, the Committee to Aid the National Liberation Front, with Vietcong flags and signs equating Vietcong efforts with those of the Watts

---

1. The hippie, then barely emerging from the beatnik, was not yet in evidence politically. The beatniks were at the Berkeley rally represented by the stoned Ken Kesey who, enriching wisdom by art, from time to time interrupted his speech ('There's only one thing's gonna do any good at all ... And that's everybody just look at it, look at the war, and turn your backs and say ... fuck it ...') by playing selections from 'Home on the Range' on his harmonica. But Jerry Rubin was a leader in one of the important student-sponsors of these protests, the Vietnam Day Committee.

rioters, were all in it. And of course just people. The *Times* was favorably impressed.

'Peaceful Protesters Parade Against War. Between 15,000 and 20,000 people marched along Fifth Avenue in a parade protesting America's involvement in Vietnam last Saturday. Though Sunday's press accounts of the march emphasized details of violence and bizarre youthful protest, it was for the most part an orderly affair. Floats and huge signs were displayed only after long intervals of plainly dressed people, many of them adults walking quietly in orderly rows along the street. Many of the spectators who stood behind the police barricades to watch the march remained silent. Of those who openly displayed feelings about one-third cheered. Many opponents of the march held up signs like "traitors should be shot" or "Bomb Hanoi"; others hollered imprecations like "you aren't fit to walk these streets" or "you should be killed." Some marchers retaliated with imprecations of their own, others tried to engage their opponents in conversation, but most remained silent. At a few points along the parade route there was open violence – eggs were hurled, there were fist fights, or attacks with red paint.'

(Paul Cowan, *Village Voice*, October 21, '65.)

Since the spring, Schumann had mastered the parade art form (as with *Leaf* and *Fire* he was that winter to get his indoors art together.) He pulled an image sequence together into an allegory and dispensed with slogans – kept people joining him from bringing them, kept out people that were carrying them. I.e. he had his contingent together as had the Fifth Avenue Committee the march. Just what his show was is not entirely clear. There is a fair agreement that Uncle Fatso, black and corpulent, red-faced, wearing a huge 'All the Way with LBJ' button, was pulling Jesus/-Vietnam and the disciples, gaunt and stately, Buddhistically yellow, in a file as his captives, at some slight distance guarded by a platoon of dog-faced men in black wearing skull masks, marching in step to a drum played by their leader, dressed and masked like them, preceding them, and singing the *Marine Hymn*, the whole followed by four powerful soldier figures, high up in the air, huge expressionless abstract faces, their skulls helmets, with spindly grotesque bodies, and, behind this Four Soldiers puppet used by Schumann in some of his Christmas plays as Herod's death squad, one or more sorrowful Grey Ladies with hempen hair, carrying grey babies in their outstretched arms, a 'band of homebuilt instruments' (Schumann, *Plays and Players*, May '67), a 'bizarre band materializ(ing), clad in grey rags, playing a ghostly cacophony) (*National Guardian*, October 23, '65) bringing up the rear.

This can be pieced together from what different accounts (one by Schumann's intellectual friend, Jules Rabin, in *Liberation* of March '66, one in Kourilsky '71) concur in, and from press photographs. Schumann used the images of the two spring parades I have described, adding the Grey Mothers and substituting Uncle Fatso for the Great Warrior. The two parts of the parade visually conveyed something like the two parts of the verbal slogan carried in the earlier parades, 'We protest U.S. bombing of North Vietnam/U.S. support of military dictatorship in Southern Vietnam.' Some of the photos – they were carried by papers in France and Germany too, one got into *Newsweek* – show the soldiers in front of the marines: the order might have gotten mixed up during the march. Press accounts (the New York *Journal American* and the *New York Times* of October 17th, the *National Guardian* of October 23rd) speak of 'two seven-foot ghosts bearing a badly injured child on a stretcher' (the *Times*), 'two huge ghostly figures, presumably the attendants of the god of war, carry(ing) a stretcher upon which reposed the mangled remains of a life-size doll' (the *Guardian*). Some other group's display? Schumann in the interview in *Plays and Players* quoted claims Uncle Sam Fatso was smoking his cigar. It took a hundred people, he also says in this interview, to put on this show. The left-wing *Guardian* saw his group as the 'outstanding marching contingent', the right-wing *Journal American*, while having to acknowledge his puppets were 'artfully constructed', qualified his 'effigy of President Johnson' as 'vicious', probably as much because Uncle Fatso wore that LBJ button as because he isn't pretty – the Trotzkyite *Militant* later (February 21, '66) took them up on this, captioning their photo of Uncle Fatso '*Unduly Harsh?* Some people though this Bread and Puppet depiction of Vietnam War . . . was a bit strong. Former Master Sergeant's account of what he saw in Vietnam as member of Army Special Forces suggests it may have been an understatement.' The *Militant* had earlier (October 25, '65) acclaimed the show as a 'smash performance' – said it 'stole the show hands down – with savagely satirical attack on U.S. aggression in Vietnam.'

This was one of the few parades they got attacked in, in fact singled out for an attack, and beaten up, the patriots presumably taking their vicious effigy amiss:

'When the marchers came at 68th Street and Park Avenue near the end of the parade route ... about 12 young men lunged into the street and traded blows with the marchers from the Bread and Puppet Theatre, 148 Delancey Street, who carried figures depicting Uncle Sam and a bloodied child on a stretcher. The skirmishers battled for about five minutes before the police could restore order.'
(J. Hanauer, *12,000 March in Viet-Protest, Boos & Foes.*
New York Journal American, October 17, '65.)

'That was in a parade where I was carrying the Jesus puppet, and I think Bruno was carrying Uncle Fatso . . . . We were attacked with cherry bombs, and I got some holes in my . . . . It wasn't all that bad, but people jumped us and cops stepped in and hit us on the head and separated us . . . I carried the Jesus puppet. That was a hard one to carry in the wind. There was a lot of problems because the main pole of the puppets was strapped to your chest in a holster. And your two arms were extended to hold the rods that carried the arms of the puppet, so it was sort of a position that got to be difficult, especially with the wind. So I think Bruno and I only would do that.' (Schumann, interview, '79.)

Apparently Schumann did not believe in fighting back:

'... der grossen Parade (...) gegen den Vietnam-Krieg, die war kilometerlang, die ging ja fast bis Harlem hoch. Und da, ich war der Trommelschläger, nicht, das bin ich da in diesem, in diesem, bei diesen Feierlichkeiten immer gewesen. Ich hatte die dicke Pauke, das war so mein Job, das konnt' ich auch stundenlang machen. Ich hab, ich hab, wenn ich so auf grossen Demonstrationen oder Paraden, da hab ich gut und gerne meine drei bis vier Stunden gekloppt, aber ohne Pause, nicht, (...) Na gut. Da wurden wir angegriffen, und zwar das ging los mit den, mit Übergriffen aus den Zuschauern, die standen da, wir gingen da durch ein Spalier von Leuten, ja, und je weiter dat Richtung down town kam, also ich weiss dat nicht wieso wir da gelandet war'n, da wurden die dann aggressiver.... die Jungs von der American Legion, die wurden dann saufrech. Dat ging los, wie mir einer 'n Trommelstock entreissen wollte und dem hab ich aber, dem hab ich fast die Finger gebrochen, weil der hatte nicht damit gerechnet, dass ich auch was auf'm Kasten hab (...) der wollte mir 'n Trommelstock, weil, ich hab immer gemerkt, auf den Trommler da zog sich immer die Aggression, er macht ja immer den meisten Krach, nicht, und dat war auch was Beängstigendes, dieses, das war 'ne wunderschöne Trommel, die hab ich geliebt, wie sonstwat. Und da war ich, da war ich sauer, dann wurde ich sauer. Und auf einmal hab ich dann vorne, Jesus marschierte vorne, ja dann hab ich gesehen, wie Jesus, machte so'ne Drehung, ja, als wenn er besoffen wäre, und dann klatschte Jesus runter. Und dann hab ich meine Trommel abgeschnallt und bin im Eilstempo an die Spitze gespurtet und dann hab ich Jesus befreit. Dat war, dat war, also irgendwie hat mir meine Wut da Zauberkräfte verliehen, ich kann mir dat nämlich nicht mehr vorstellen. Da war'n fünf sechs Man, die hab'n den Peter, der hat an der einen Seite gezerrt und dann war'n so fünf sechs Slibies(?), die zerrten an'ner andern Seite. Und die hab'n, die hab'n fast alle was von mir sowat furchtbares auf die Schnauze gekriegt. Dat'se, die hab'n losgelassen und ich hab dann nur so'n brennen hinten im Rücken gehabt, da hat mir also so'n Ordnungshüter da mit'm '"Black Jack" ein'n drüber gezogen, damit ich seine Lieblinge in Ruhe und ich hatt zwar selber auch ein'n abgekriegt, aber war nicht so schlimm. Und dann hab ich mich hinterher, hab ich mich über Peter lustig gemacht, nicht, hab ich gesagt, siehste Peterschen, wenn der Ecki da nicht eige... gezischt hätte, da wär dein, na da wär dein schöner Jesus jetzt in Trümmerhaufen. Und Jesus war auch verletzt, der hatte 'ne Beule, die wurde hinterher wieder ausgebessert und dann war er wie neu. Naja, mit dem Ding hab ich ihn manchmal aufgezogen, hat er aber auch seine so, diese, diese prinzipielle Gewaltfreiheit.... Ich hab 'ne ganz bestimmte Einstellung zur Frage der Gewalt und das kann man, wenn man jetzt so auf christlicher Plattform damit, mit diesem Problem rumtanzt, da kann ich mich nur auf Thomas Müntzer beziehen. Und das ist für mich ganz klar und das andere ist für mich so'ne Art Scheinheiligkeit, (...) wenn Gewalt existiert und man muss auch klarstellen, wie Gewalt, wie Gewalt wächst oder so.'

(Eckhardt, interview.)

'There was one I got knocked over. I was carrying Uncle Fatso and there were right-wingers.... these marches would have definite hecklers. People would come in and break it up and stuff... and there was fist fights and stuff like that. I was carrying Uncle Fatso, you know you can't see out.... All of a sudden I hear tick-tick-tick and somebody just jumped on it and the whole thing just toppled over on both of us. Luckily the holder that I was carrying it in ripped or I would have been deballed for sure. Because you know you carry it right there. But anyway it ripped through and it fell down and it shredded . . . .'

(Ernstthal, interview.)

'That outrageous figure . . . Uncle Fatso . . . was, incidentally, assaulted and pulled apart by the parade's end and hasn't reappeared since. The figure of Christ doubling as captive Vietnamese, fourteen feet tall, suffered the loss of an eye and a long gash in his nose in the same trouble.' (Rabin, *Vietnam*.)

'During the Peace March most of the right-wing groups were peaceful. But when they saw Uncle Fatso they jumped at him. They went crazy.'

(Schumann in an interview with Brown and Seitz, *Tulane Drama Review* #38.)

Schumann brought up this beating in various interviews later. He was proud of it.

11. November '65. Probable first performance of a stationary anti-war street show.

Rabin (loc. cit.) says there were half a dozen peace demonstrations by the Bread and Puppet Theatre in '65. Besides the three I have mentioned, there is only one other recorded one I know of, on November 27. That leaves two unaccounted for. Besides the demonstrations before October 16th I have mentioned, at some of which they may have shown up, there were various demonstrations after this date,[1] but two likely occasions for particular shows of theirs presented themselves later that year: a Union Square Rally To Stop the War against Vietnam on Veterans' Day, November 11th, sponsored by Youth Against War and Fascism, an Old Left group, and a silent vigil, sponsored by an 'Artists and Workers Committee' in United Nations Plaza, on November 26th.

J. Edgar Hoover had on November 1st pointed out that war demonstrators in the U.S. 'represented a minority for the most part composed of halfway citizens who are neither morally, mentally nor emotionally mature', adding that this was true 'whether the demonstrator be the college professor or the beatnik', On October 28th, the New York City Council had voted 28 to 2 to make Veterans Day on official Support American Vietnam Effort Day. The Veterans' Day rally is a likely occasion for Schumann's group to have, for the first time perhaps, done a skit they with some variation did again in Washington two weeks later – Ernstthal says they did it on Union Square before they did it at the Washington Monument – and again on May 1st of the following year (again on Union Square): the skit that later became *Speech* or *Chairs*, the first and second time using President Johnson's Johns Hopkins address of April 7, '65, the following May his January 12, '66 State of the Union message.

---

1. For instance, a follow-up on David Miller's gesture of October 15th, sponsored by old-time pacifists, the Committee for Non-Violent Action and the Workshop in Non-Violence, really one and the same group: four pacifists on November 6th burned their draft cards on a public parking lot on 17th Street just east of Broadway as a 'solemn witness against military conscription and war.' By a bill which August 10th of that year had been passed by the House of Representatives sensitive to symbolic actions, 392 to 1 (it was later declared unconstitutional), this rendered them liable to a maximum penalty of $10,000 or a 5-year prison sentence or both. I doubt Schumann would have been there. November 13th there was a Get Out of Vietnam Rally on the 111th Street block between Riverside Drive and Broadway, reserved for it by a street fair permit (*New York Post*, November 14, '65), and sponsored by the May 2nd Movement, SDS and others, at which there was to be a '15 minute dance pageant depicting what was termed "U.S. aggression in Southeast Asia"' (loc. cit.). This was a more likely occasion for Schumann, but not for the two shows I have in mind. Besides which, other entertainment was provided for anyhow (*Village Voice*, November 11, '65): 'Music by (Barbara) Dane and Plastic Arts' was to 'dramatize the program.'

'The first version was in Union Square in New York, '64 maybe. Or '65, say. Say '65. Because in that part we were entertaining at rallies. That was our role, to provide some entertainment. Like you invite folks in to sing. And we were invited to do a skit at a rally. And Union Square indicates that it was still basically a left-wing thing. It was still early. And we did this *Speech*. We had this goofy character reciting a Johnson speech.... Somewhere I have this paper all greasy that I used to read from (it turns out to be the State of the Union Message (SSB).) And that was one version of it. We had people just listening to it. And maybe scratching. We made a comedy of it. I think we used the same speech for this character, you know this ridiculous looking character coming and making this crazy speech and being really goofy. It was just hilarious, totally. Really. We had this Fool, this was called a Fool, and it had that head that fit on the head and hands that were like gloved hands and then feet. It was this fool, and people listening to him and he was saying a Johnson speech. This version was one of the funniest things I have ever seen. The guy was reciting the speech and this crazy puppet was making these gestures, and crossing his legs, and talking and he was the goofiest, it was one of the funniest things we ever did. This was so hilarious, this red guy.... And he had hands. And you know hands with puppets, real hands? Really funny. He would sneeze, and he would cross his legs. And he was giving this very serious speech in a totally ridiculous way.... And we took that speech and made it more serious at the Washington Monument.' (Ernstthal, interview.)

As Ernstthal remembers it, he was inside the Red Devil, a grotesque little bugger, so had had to learn the speech by heart, and was talking through his neck, Schumann working the hands, Dr. Oyle the feet (the three of them changing around, though, on different occasions). There may have been a stage audience of Bread and Puppeteers in addition to them, but if so, it didn't have much of a part. The skit got developed subsequently. (Cf. my accounts infra of *The Press Conference* of May 1st '66; and of the play *Speech/Chairs*.) But if we compared it to Schumann's passive appearance at the August '64 rally, we see that he is by now elaborating and theatricalizing his stationary street shows, just as his parade ones.

Ridiculing the great corrupt populist for selling the poor on murder abroad for welfare at home, Schumann may have in mind that the German people in the '30s bought full employment from Hitler in exchange for their sufferings in the '40s in the war prepared by their labor. The transaction was a special case, and one that didn't work out, of the trade by which the working classes of the advanced nations have in this century generally abandoned the program prepared for them by the socialists of the last century, giving up the aggressive pursuit of class objectives in exchange for a share in the West's Third World loot—cheap raw materials from cheap labor. The reproach to the poor – a moralist approach of immorality – that Schumann arrived at by the end of the '60s (*Johnny, Cry*) is here as yet quite implicit, and probably not as yet in his mind even.

12. A street protest of November '65 the origin of Schumann's first theatrical success, *Fire*?

If we take Rabin's statement about 'half a dozen' Bread and Puppet Theatre demonstrations in '65 seriously, then, even if we pinpoint one of the two 'missing' ones as the November 11 Union Square rally, there is still one missing. Schumann (interview, '79) says that 'the face mask that I cast from the Chinese girl was made into masks that later on served for *Fire*', but that these 'were made just a day or two before we did a big demonstration in New York – I meant them specifically for that.' Rabin (loc. cit.) tells us this Chinese girl, apparently named Li Minh, marched in the October 16th Fifth Avenue parade. As far as my data go, we encounter these Vietnamese Woman masks for the first time in the Washington, D.C. demonstration of Novemberr 27th. Assuming we can rely on both men's memories, they would have been used in some New York demonstration between these two dates. That silent vigil of November 26th, though Schumann does not remember it, and though his attendance at it would have crowded his attendance at a Washington, D.C. demonstration the next day, is the likely occasion. It was in honor of two spectacular war protestors, Norman Morrison and Roger LaPorte. LaPorte, a member of the Catholic Worker organization, had burned himself to death on the U.N. Plaza November 9th, a week after the Quaker Norman Morrison had done so under Defense Secretary McNamara's windows.[1]

The vigil was to be conducted 'in complete silence ... no speeches, slogans or signs' (*Village Voice*, November 25, '65). I suspect members of the Bread and Puppet group attended, wearing the new 'Vietnamese Woman' masks, appropriately garbed. *Fire* was dedicated to those two martyrs (and to Ms. Herz), and was a silent play. Silent participation by these masked figures would in a very Schumannesque fashion have extended its reference to the Buddhist originators of political protest by suicide. But perhaps it would have been considered in bad taste.

---

1. Morrison had been carrying his baby around, barely remembered to put her down before he burned himself up. He left his two-tone Cadillac parked around the corner, key in the ignition. LaPorte, though a devout Catholic, he lived to receive the last rites, assumed the lotus position for his self-immolation, presumably in commemoration of his 1963 Buddhist exemplars in Vietnam. An 82-year-old lady, Ms. Alice Herz, had killed herself by fire in Detroit in March of '65, citing 'the monks in Vietnam.' A Mrs. Jakowski failed November 10th in South Bend – she had forgotten the gasoline, so her neighbor, Henry Wozniak, was able to put out the fire. Mrs. Jakowski had felt that 'the world's problems' were her problems. Her baby had been found smothered in its crib 12 days earlier. Herz, LaPorte and Morrison all used one-gallon gasoline cans. LaPorte and Morrison screamed as they burned. I suppose Ms. Herz did too.

13. November '65. Schumann's first grand agitational show. Complex but integral. Large-scale, powerful. Jesus and his disciples gone.

An ad by the Fifth Avenue Committee in the *Village Voice* of November 11th, '65 announced a November 27 'March on Washington for Peace in Vietnam'[1] on the theme 'Mobilize the Conscience of America'. It offered

---

1. The title of the march differed from that of the April one by substituting 'for peace in' for 'to end the war in', this reflecting the moderation of its organizers, SANE, who were urging not withdrawal but negotiations. But this demonstration also was joined by all factions of the Movement. It was 'decorous' all the same – the *Washington Post* reporters connected the amazing respectability of the demonstrators with the lack thereof of the – scant – hecklers: a few Nazis, Hell's Angels and KKKers congregated into a group. A sharply soaring American casualty rate in November had generated a, for 1965, considerable attendance of about 25,000.

'Even before the International Days of Protest, a third major demonstration had been announced by the Committee for a Sane Nuclear Policy for Saturday, November 27. Convinced that the antiwar movement was antagonizing much of its potential support by its strong language and occasionally belligerent tone, SANE was planning a thoroughly moderate demonstration of concern about, rather than unalterable opposition to, the war. Like the SDS in April, SANE kept tight control over the organization of the march, the list of speakers, and the seventeen approved slogans professionally printed on placards to be carried during the march. Among the slogans: "Stop the bombings," "Respect 1954 Geneva Accords," "War erodes the Great Society" and "Self-determination – Vietnam for the Vietnamese." To avoid criticism that they were being one-sided in their protest, SANE's cochairman Dr. Benjamin Spock, and Harvard Professor H. Stuart Hughes cabled Ho Chi Minh from Washington on October 28:

Our organization helping provide leadership for Nov 27 demonstration in support of ceasefire and negotiated settlement based on 1954 Geneva Accords. Again urge you respond favorably to immediate peace talks. Demonstrations will continue but will not lead to a U.S. pullout.

In Madison, Wisconsin, the National Coordinating Committee to End the War in Vietnam decided to hold its national convention in Washington so the 1,500 delegates and alternates expected to attend could take part in the protest march on Saturday, November 27.

In the aftermath of the International Days of Protest, it first appeared that the energies of the antiwar movement had been temporarily sapped. President Johnson and his administration appeared to be unreachable by those opposed to the war. At best, the President seemed blandly indifferent to the opposition, and at the worst, fully capable of escalating the war to prove his resolve, both to the American people and to the leaders of North Vietnam. In the middle of November, however, the nature of the war was suddenly forced into bold relief by a prolonged battle between American and North Vietnamese troops in the heavily forested Ia Drang Valley. The battle, bloody and inconclusive, brought an end to administration hopes for a quick turn in the tide of the war. American casualties, which had been slowly increasing during the summer as more American troops arrived, suddenly soared. During the week that ended on Monday, November 22, 240

the lure of 'noted entertainers', to perform, before the speakers, at a rally at the Washington Monument following a march around the White House. According to the Washington *Sunday Star* of the 28th ('March Picks Up Steam in Rally, Talks at Monument'), the warmup was provided by a Negro woman folk singer with a tambourine, followed by another singer and by Lew Chandler, one of the Selma-Montgomery marchers of '64, who sang 'Things are in a Jam in Vietnam' to guitar, followed by more singers, followed by 'an anti-war show, complete with false faces, skull masks, a bass drum and loud groans from the actors' given

---

U.S. soldiers were killed in Vietnam, more than three times the highest previous weekly total. The effect on the antiwar movement was electric. When delegates to the NCC convention met in Washington on Wednesday, November 24, they were in an angry, determined mood.

Despite SANE's care to avoid anything like extremism, the divisions in the antiwar movement were immediately apparent. The U.S. Committee to Aid the National Liberation Front of South Vietnam, a tiny group headed by a young man named Walter Teague, began selling NLF flags and buttons and announced it would carry the flags in the march on Saturday. SANE's Sanford Gottlieb, who had gone to great lengths to avoid just such provocations, said the three-hundred monitors of the march would try to discourage the NLF flag carriers, but would not use force. A far deeper source of division was the sharpening, but until then little noticed, contest between the New Left and the Old Left for control of the NCC and the antiwar movement. During the first week in November the New York Committee to End the War in Vietnam, one of the original groups which joined to create the National Coordinating Committee, disbanded as the result of conflict between the Socialist Workers Party, an old-line Trotskyist group, and the SDS over what was called the "single issue" question. The Trotskyists wanted to build a mass movement around the single issue of the war, while the SDS, and the New Left in general, favored an attempt to create a broad radical movement which would emphasize other issues along with the war.

When the NCC held its first plenary session shortly after noon on Thursday, November 25, in Washington's Lincoln Memorial Congregational Temple, it was quickly apparent to those familiar with the techniques of parliamentary maneuver that the Young Socialist Alliance (Trotskyist) was attempting to take over the NCC, initially with the unwitting aid of the Berkeley Vietnam Day Committee. On Friday the YSA tried again with a complicated proposal on credentials intended to leave them with a majority of accredited delegates. When that was voted down they proposed that the NCC adopt three "official" antiwar slogans: "Let's Bring the Troops Home Now," "Self-Determination in Mississippi and Vietnam," and "Freedom Now, Withdrawal Now." A call for immediate withdrawal, the YSA knew, would split the antiwar movement between moderates and radicals; the YSA hoped to dominate the second group, and through them the antiwar movement itself.

The majority of delegates at the convention, young idealists who had little experience with radical politics, which were generally as self-serving as any other kind of politics, were largely bewildered by the YSA's maneuvering. When they finally understood what was going on, they were less angry than disillusioned. They had believed that people in favor of "peace" and "justice" and "civil rights" were afflicted by none of the secrecy and power-hunger of conventional politicians. During the summer the SDS's vice president, a University of Texas dropout names Jeff Shero, had told a magazine writer, "There's practically nobody in the movement that I don't have a great deal of trust in.' At the NCC,

by the Bread and Puppet Theatre. Max Frankel in the *New York Times* of the 28th ('Demonstrators Decorous', one of two articles on the demonstration, the other being headlined 'Asian Communists Sure Public Opinion in US Will Force War's End') describes Schumann's contribution less snidely and with a little more detail:

'At the Sylvan Theater, an outdoor stage beside the Washington Monument, the Bread & Puppet Theatre of Delancey Street in New York produced '*A Pageant of Death Based on President Johnson's Speech at Johns Hopkins.*' The speech, on April 7, was the one in which the president offered unconditional discussions, expressed his opposition to war and weapons, but also voiced the need to employ them in Vietnam. *Doll Bodies Displayed.* A chorus of 30 under the direction of Peter Schumann acted out the deaths of civilians while Mr. Johnson's words were shouted ironically across the great lawn and while a bass drum beat monotonously. The tableau figures wore black drapes and white masks that were replaced by death masks. They ended by carrying out a huge catafalque of doll bodies slain by machine gunners.'

Jules Rabin (loc. cit.) gave a slightly fuller account (reproduced, without

---

the YSA proved there were in fact a great many people in the movement who could not be trusted.

On Saturday, while the majority of the NCC delegates joined SANE's march and rally, the YSA continued to caucus secretly in the basement of the Harrington Hotel in a last-minute attempt to come up with a strategy for capturing the NCC. when one delegate tried to enter, three YSA members guarding the door grabbed him and dragged him away. At the final plenary session held on Sunday, however, the YSA was defeated on the question of how to organize the national committee. The weekend proved a bitter foretaste of the factional fighting that was to plague, and finally cripple, the radical movement in the following years. It is worth emphasizing that there were no villains in this struggle. The Trotskyists were among the most tireless opponents of the war, and groups in the New Left, disillusioned with this or that tactic, would often simply retire from the field. Nevertheless, the Trotskyists were rigid in their politics and were thoroughly out of sympathy with the broader discontent of the student and civil rights movements which, in the beginning, were reluctant to accept socialism as the answer to all problems. The Trotskyists were certain they knew how to organize an end to the war and drove many of their allies half-crazy with takeover attempts. They rarely succeeded but even their failures enjoyed a kind of success. Their ideological rigor set the terms of debate within the movement, and one reason the SDS, for example, eventually declared itself Marxist-Leninist was that old left groups like the Trotskyists and the Progressive Labor Party took a hard revolutionary position. To provide its commitment, the New Left felt itself forced to do the same.

At the demonstration on Saturday, November 27, a cold and windy day, nearly 25,000 people marched around the White House and then gathered at the Washington Monument, as they had in April and August, and would many times again, to listen to speeches on the war. Dr. Spock sternly deplored "the virtual absence of debate in Congress" and proposed that the peace movement support candidates in the 1966 elections "who will refuse to be silenced." Norman Thomas, nearly blind but still a powerful speaker, told the crowd, "I'd rather see America save her soul than her face."

The crowd's strongest response, however, was won by Carl Oglesby, a thirty-year-old former technical writer for a defense contractor in Ann Arbor, Michigan, who had been elected president of SDS in June. Oglesby had once planned to be a novelist but politics

identification of source, by Katzman in his *East Village Other*, May 15-June 1, '66):

'In November, in Washington, the Bread and Puppet Theater presented another pageant on a large scale. The stage was at the foot of the amphitheater behind the Washington Monument. Between the monument and the stage is a broad, shallow bowl of grass where ten or twenty thousand people stood or sat. The performers, numbering about thirty, wore black tunics and alternated between the grey death's-head masks and grey Oriental masks. The Oriental masks, all nearly identical were based on a life mask made of a Chinese girl who had participated in the Fifth Avenue pageant.

A droning voice spoke obligato from off-stage. The voice spoke words about wanting "no wider war," about "the dream of peace and the grievous necessity for bombs and battleships." As the lines were spoken, the chorus wearing Oriental masks went piecemeal before grey executioners (Pilate's Soldiers, now armed with machine guns), were shot and went down on their knees, and stood up again with death's head masks. Following the executions an apocalyptic beast appeared in a setting that was both dirge and pandemonium, and after the beast, a procession of giant mourning mothers, and a mourning population of the dead.'

This in fact seems to have been Schumann's first grand agitational show. He had combined the satire – now given an accent of horror – of his Union Square skit with the elements of his Fifth Avenue parade, magnified for impact on a mass audience, and intensified by choreographed action, not losing but on the contrary strengthening allegorical unity. The integration of the Union Square skit provided the address to government

---

had interrupted his life, as it had the life of his generation. In his speech he expressed the sense of spreading disenchantment that had accompanied each escalation of the war by Johnson. The crowd in Washington had long favored the sort of social measures that Johnson made law in 1965, the year of his legislative triumphs, but the war had canceled out each domestic victory. Vietnam not only absorbed the energies of the administration, but cast doubt on everything else it did. Oglesby focused the confused ambivalence of people who favored Johnson's domestic program and hated his war:

The original commitment in Vietnam was made by President Truman, a mainstream liberal. It was seconded by President Eisenhower, a moderate liberal. It was intensified by the late President Kennedy, a flaming liberal. Think of the men who now engineer that war – those who study the maps, give the commands, push the buttons and tally the dead: Bundy, McNamara, Lodge, Goldberg, the President himself.

> They are not moral monsters.
> They are all honorable men.
> They are all liberals.

We ... are convinced by a few pretty photos in the Sunday supplement that things are getting better, that the world is coming our way, that change from disorder can be orderly, that our benevolence will pacify the distressed, that our might will intimidate the angry....

We have become a nation of young, bright-eyed, hard-hearted, slim-waisted, bullet-headed make-out artists. A nation – may I say it? – of beardless liberals ....' — (Th. Powers, *The War at Home*.)

called for by the locale and address of the demonstration. The photos published by the Washington *Star* and *Post* — and the fact that they were published — attest to his show's raw power: The Grey Mothers with babies, paraded in, weird airborne sculptures of anguish and appeal ('A New York professional group presented life-sized puppets'); a throng of skullmen, not unlike chimpanzees, dressed in black ('Marchers in skull-like masks provide a theatrical touch at Sylvan Theater rally'); stiffly upright as though at an unofficial wake, a large assembly of disparate figures in black blouses, loose over loose dark-grey or black skirts, partly masculine, strong-faced matrons with puffy white faces (the Vietnamese Women's masks), partly Skullmen, each holding a mask of the other kind at their sides ('Dancers in black attire and with skull-like masks provided another theatrical touch'). The sinister and perverse 4-Soldiers puppet appears in *The Militant*, (December 6, '65.)

The women of the Bread and Puppet Theatre had dyed and sewn a great quantity of black garments. Christ and his disciples and their yellow had been replaced by female figures in grey, black and white, the black death reference growing during preceding demonstrations, the Buddhist by Christian invocations of conscience. Though the aggressive (but also jocular) note of Uncle Fatso had been eliminated, relatively gentle plea had been replaced by stark accusation. The women's dance of dying reappears a little over a year later in an indoors anti-war ballet (*Bach Cantata #140*).

14. March '66. Schumann's most famous street show. Simpler than before, but more intense. Beautiful. He is developing the aesthetic dimension of the medium.

The next Bread and Puppet demonstration of record is in the second Fifth Avenue march next spring, March 26, '66, second day of International Days of Protest called by the National Coordinating Committee to end the War in Vietnam. It was the biggest of about half a dozen demonstrations in the U.S. that day, but still of the same order of magnitude as the previous ones, a little over 20,000 demonstrating.

'They poured down Fifth Avenue on Saturday afternoon for hours. The march was dominated by no single group. The politics were from center to left to pacifist to anarchist. What they shared was a hostility to Vietnam. Many, if not most, of the onlookers were friendly. But not all. Some were decked out like Nazis and yelled slogans appropriate to their uniforms, others were ordinary youngsters beaming over their "Bomb Hanoi" placards.' (*Village Voice*, March 31, '66.)

At 86th Street — these young men come from the old, non-Jewish, central European parts of town a few blocks east of there — veterans, having used up their eggs, jumped a group marching under the Vietcong flag. Three of the attackers were arrested.

Schumann had provided what was probably to be his most famous street show, elaborately — for a parade show — choreographed, simpler than his shows of the preceding October and November, but its images more intense, and quite hard to perform in. Also the show was quite beautiful, shockingly so: as ballet. He developed this visual aesthetic dimension of his street agitation starting with the preceding demonstration in Washington. As had since his first Fifth Avenue parade half a year earlier become normal for him, the parade was in two semi-independent sections, i.e. was not a simple statement but a mini-speech, or, more to the point, had a double beat, and each part had its own distinct aesthetic integrity: the first part one of action, drama and black-white contrast, the second one one of simplicity and serenity.

'One contingent of students was led by members of the Bread and Puppet Theater in Greenwich Village. Several members of the theater group wore grotesque two-foot-high papier-mâché headdresses representing Vietnamese women prisoners of war. Others clad in black suits and wearing skull masks, banged on a collection of pipes, oil cans and cymbals. Another group carried a papier-mâché airplane about 10 feet long.'
(*New York Times*, March 27 '66, 'Thousands on 5th Ave. March in Vietnamese Protest.'

'The Bread and Puppet Theatre provided its customary dramatic contingent. Leading were marchers draped in white sheets topped by 2-ft.-high paper maché masks representing Vietnamese women prisoners being kept in line by black-clad men with death-masks playing a weird cacophony on contrived instruments. The men hoisted aloft a 10-ft.-long plane resembling a prehistoric fish. They were followed by a procession of white-draped mourners.'

(*National Guardian*, April 2, '66.)

'Giant puppet heads of Vietnamese women chained together, their stark white faces bound by black blindfolds. A mock wooden airplane, with shark's teeth diving out of the March sky. A band of skullheads, blowing an unearthly tune on horns improvised from washing machine agitators and rattling a dirge on old gasoline cans filled with the nuts and bolts of a mechanized society. The impact was such that the rest of the marchers, all those thousands might just as well have stayed home.'   (Ben Reade, *The Demonic Protest, Renewal*, April-May '67.)

Kourilsky ('71, p. 199) gives a rather complete account:

'De fait, c'est bien sa conception du monde qui peut se lire en filigrane dans les spectacles du Bread and Puppet Theatre, même dans les moins élaborés. A cet égard, la parade du 26 mars 1966 est exemplaire. Le spectacle itinérant se compose de deux parties. Première partie: des hommes en noir aux masques de mort poursuivent avec un avion monstrueux à dents de requin de grandes marionnettes blanches aux masques blêmes, les yeux bandés, et attachées les unes aux autres, comme un troupeau qu'on mènerait à l'abattoir. Accompagnement encore: battements de tambour et bruit de feraille de toutes sortes. Deuxième partie: seule au milieu de la rue, une femme vêtue de blanc, le visage nu; elle joue de la flûte. Elle est suivie d'un long cortège de femmes en blanc qui se déploie sur trois rangs. Toutes les femmes ont le visage recouvert d'un masque de Vietnamienne et chantent une seule note très haute. Celles qui sont en tête du cortège portent en effigie un grand soleil, un croissant de lune et une colombe, les autres tiennent dans leurs bras des brancages.'

The Vietnamese Lady puppets, the puppets' tall heads above their carriers', had to get down on their knees and there bend over, and had to do so in unison and in time with the airplane's descent on them from the rear. And their hands were bound and they were tied to one another!

'I carried one of the white women, again on a basket, mounted. And we were all tied up together, a whole string of us ... maybe there were ten of these large mounted figures, and I remember the exhaustion of the thing. I thought I'd never get through it. Just the physical labor. And in Canada (Hiroshima Day '67 (SSB)) the same thing. I was the white woman, tied up, and the others were like the persecutors. And there was also a wonderful airplane that Peter had developed, that flew. The shark plane. And that was involved too. So the shark would menace the women and the others would torment her and ... sort of the spirit of Vietnam. But the labor of the thing was like pitting myself against ... I never thought I'd live through it, the pressure on my head and the labor of it. And yet I was very attracted to her.'   (Palmer, interview.)

The dove mentioned by Kourilsky was a large painting of a dove, a rather naturalistic study, carried with two hands gripping its upper edge. In a photo in *Liberation*, we see the girl carrying it raising one of her bare hands — strongly contrasting with the intense masked face, shrouded in white, above the painting — to her face, adjusting her mask. Her real hand is monstrously unreal.

Kourilsky saw the show as presentation of a 'conception du monde' — not just a political statement or exhortation, but an allegory — a moralist and historicist one — of the situation of humanity:

'D'un côté, la société mécanisée, la Guerre, la Mort: le Mal. De l'autre, la Vie élémentaire et pure, la Paix: le Bien. Ainsi le Vietnam semble représenter pour Peter Schumann une sorte de paradis perdu, un type de société archaïque où l'on connait encore les valeurs simples, ou les individus ne sont pas dépouillés "des vieux talents humains," où le pain n'est pas "tombé en bouillie." Et la lutte du Peuple vietnamien n'apparaît pas comme une lutte historique, mais comme l'incarnation actuelle d'une lutte éternelle entre le Bien et le Mal.' (ibid.)

I think Kourilsky is exaggerating Schumann's illusions about Vietnamese village life a little (though anarchist communitarian friends of his, e.g. Bob Nichols seem to have had them), and I think that certainly viewers of the parade would not have seen it as idealisation of Vietnamese life, south or north. Its point was not that those people were or their life was good, but that there was a certain innocence about them that made what the U.S. was doing to them bad. But certainly, an ideology idealising peasant life and in particular peasant life of a communal sort, of which life in an 'Oriental village' could be viewed as an approximation, was then developing among the more alienated middle class young in the U.S.A., and from '69 onward for a little while found expression in the commune movement, and Schumann to a certain extent shared these ideals. His show did, in any event, and it was his first street show to do so (*Fire*, then having its first run, had opened in January, and was the first show of his to suggest this view), express a view of the world, and one in terms of approximately the opposition indicated by Kourilsky. The scope of his allegory had expanded. He was using a political demonstration to promote his unpolitical or at any rate not particularly political world view. While this certainly contributed to his show's — and the demonstration's — power, the press reports show that his parade was effective even when its elements were taken in separately and when not all were taken in.

Schumann:

'The parade consisted in part of a repeated action between a group of skull masks led by one skull with a bass drum (Schumann (SSB)), the other skulls carrying, as far as I remember, chimes, improvised chimes from U-bolts and other machine parts. These skulls, these skeleton figures were dressed in black and carried with them the Shark Airplane. During the parade the white women puppets were pulled by a rope that was, I believe, strung to their hands and reached from one to the other — I believe they were all strung in line — or they were bunched up. I am not 100% sure about that. And they were pulled down according to the arrival and the dipping down of the Shark Airplane. And there was a few seconds of stopping the parade and ringing the bell. Then they were pulled up again and marched again and the plane zoomed around and came back to attack them again. That was one section of this parade.' (Schumann, interview, '79.)

'Wir haben ein festes Programm für den ganzen Zug bis zur Farbe und Form der Transparente ausgearbeitet, in deren Mittelpunkt eine agierende Truppe stand. Vorneweg drei Totenmänner mit überlebensgrossen Kopfmasken, die an Stricken elf überlebensgrosse vietnamesische Frauen hinter sich herzogen. Die riesigen Frauen-Puppen wurden von je einer Operateurin auf dem Kopf getragen, die Hände der Frauen waren gefesselt und diese aneinander gebunden. Hinter den Frauen 30 Totenmasken, im Militärschritt, die als Stockpuppe ein Flugzeug mit einem Haifischmaul über sich trugen. Dazu bösartige Zymbeln und Trommeln. Die Frauen wanken durch die Strasse, die Soldaten marschieren immer näher, stossen mit MG-Geknatter das Flugzeug auf sie herunter, die Frauen brechen, nur von den Seilen gehalten, zusammen. Die ganze Gruppe steht bewegungslos. Dann ziehen die drei Totenmänner vorn an den Stricken, zerren die Frauen hoch, die Soldaten fallen zurück, kommen wider näher, stossen auf die Frauen, diese fallen, usw. Am Schluss des Zuges marschieren dann noch 30 Masken von Vietnamesinnen mit Friedensymbolen. Es schmeissen jedesmal einige Leute faule Eier, auch Steine oder provozieren Schlägereien, aber bei dieser Sache sagten viele über uns: "Sie sind zwar alle Feiglinge und Scheisser, aber gut gemacht ist das schon." In eine Art sportlichen Respekts mischt sich dabei echte Empfindung.'

(Schumann in *tendenzen*, November '66-February '67.)

We note here Schumann's claim that the entire parade, not just his part, was designed, and was designed around the Bread and Puppet Theatre and its performance as described. Also the precision required of this performance: hardly sustainable in practice. He had, to an extent, become the Movement's artistic director in New York. It was in keeping with his status, that the *Voice* carried not only a photo of the parade's rear section on its front page ('The Bread and Puppet Women depict the Dead of Vietnam'), but among its photos of celebrities associated with the event – Ginzberg's lover Orlovsky, the sculptor Mark de Suvero, the Reverend Howard Moody of Judson Memorial Church, the venerable socialist-pacifist A.J. Muste – included one of him.

15. May '66. Theatrical elaboration of stationary street skit.

He was back on Union Square on May Day '66, doing a third version of his Johnson-speech skit, now using the president's January 12 State of the Union message, at a demonstration organized by Veterans and Reservists Against the War in Vietnam. Johnson had again promised butter along with the guns.

'Sur une estrade une grosse marionnette buffonne: elle a d'énormes pieds, une énorme tête, mais pratiquement pas de corps. Le Red Man ... est habité par un acteur qui l'anime. Il gesticule dans tous les sens se débattant avec des moustiques. Il est censé tenir un discours que déclame en réalité un acteur devant un micro: c'est le célèbre Message sur l'Etat de l'union .... L'acteur le dit avec un fort accent texan en laissant échapper de temps en temps des bouts de phrase en allemand prononcés a la manière hitlérienne. Un choeur de reporters en noir est aligné à droite de ce gros Lyndon Johnson bouffon. Masqués, l'air abruti, ils l'écoutent délivrer son "message." Pendant le discours ils mettent un autre masque qui leur donne l'air encore plus bête. Enfin, lorsque le President déclare qu'il veut la paix et qu'il donne l'ordre d'ouvrir le feu, ils mettent des masques de mort. Puis l'un d'entre eux prend une bombe insecticide (spray gun (SSB)) pour tuer le moustique avec lequel continue à se débattre le Red Man. Le gros mannequin s'affaise: il est mort.' (Kourilsky, '71.)

How veridical Kourilsky's account of this skit — she entitles this version of it *The Press Conference* — is, I don't know: the journalists' three masks and the mosquito spray (which could have been from *King Story II*) are not mentioned elsewhere and don't sound right. One photo (*tendenzen*, loc. cit.) on which the big-mouth Big Fool puppet that was Johnson is seated on top of some boxes, its tiny hands uplifted weakly, almost seeming to cry, accompanies a text saying the puppet contained a phonograph playing Johnson's speech and identifying the auditors as populace, not journalists. A tape cassette has been mentioned. The scene recorded by B.J. Fernandez (photo #7 in Kourilsky '71) — three white-masked figures lined up next to the Fool in dark pants and blouses, a fourth without a mask but with his face clown-whitened at a stand-up mike — is the one Schumann (interview, '79) remembers. In any event he has clearly since the preceding November developed the skit in a theatrical direction (putting in the 'chorus' of listeners). He did it again, three days later, at a May 4th Vietnam Read-In at Columbia University sponsored by the Columbia Independent Committee on Vietnam. The American Artists Against the War in Vietnam furnished much of the entertainment — Peter Weiss reading excerpts about Auschwitz from his *Marat/Sade*, Brustein, the *New Republic* critic who had made it to head of the Yale Drama Department, reading from *MacBird*, the 'underground play from Berkeley' (*The Militant*, May 16,

'66), a recycled *Macbeth* that accused Ladybird of having put her husband up to Kennedy's murder and that soon was quite a success, Vivecca Lindfors, the leftists' Garbo and a novelist by the name of Truman Nelson reading something else – but I doubt Schumann was a member of it.

'Day before Mother's Day/join the/Women's March/To bring our Men home/ from Vietnam Now!/Saturday May 7 12:30 p.m./beginning at/ U.S. Armory/ 33rd St. and Lexington Ave.... Barbara Dane will sing and the Bread and Puppet Theatre will perform ... Committee for the Women's Peace March/5 Beekman St., 10th Floor.' (*Village Voice*, May 5, '66.)

He did the skit for the ladies – 700 of them according to *The Militant* of March 16th, 'the highlight of the rally ... a short but very funny skit ... satirizing Johnson's pronouncements on the Great Society' (ibid.). The Trotzkyites could dig this – they didn't think the society was going to be so great.

The the skit's further development, cf. my account of *Speech/Chairs* infra.

16. May '66. An independent parade of Schumann's, gentle, sorrowful, unaggressive, without reference to aggression.

On Memorial Day – May 30 – '66, he staged a parade that was quite simple, masks, but no puppets, and relatively unusual in that, though staged jointly with another organization, The Veterans and Reservists to End the War in Vietnam[1] it was in toto a Bread and Puppet parade, not part of a bigger one, but just his own. It apparently was quite effective, impressing bystanders, the establishment press and the Movement representatives, the Left, equally: a single woman leader in white, with a white Vietnamese Woman's mask and a chime, followed by a small group of life figures, but with flowers—daisies or chrysanthemums – which they offered bystanders, and humming on a single note, followed by a small group of men in dark suits and black ties, and carrying a coffin with a sign, 'American dead 4000 – Vietnamese dead 1,300,000.' They walked down from the southwest corner of Central Park along Central Park South, and down Fifth Avenue to Rockefeller Center, where they buried a white doll one of the women had been carrying on the sidewalk (not being allowed into privately owned Rockefeller Plaza) by laying it on the ground and putting flowers around it. Leaflets were passed out during the walk. It took them two hours to walk the half dozen or so blocks. Essentially, Schumann had taken the tail-end of his parade of March 26, its revolving note, and had

---

1. 'Veterans and Reservists to end the War in Viet Nam
Room 1033, 5 Beekman Street
Manhattan 10038
May 26, 1966
For Immediate Release

NEW YORK (May 26) – Members of the Bread and Puppet Theater and Veterans and Reservists to End the War in Viet Nam will move through the streets of midtown Manhattan Memorial Day in memory of the more than four thousand Americans and more than one million Vietnamese killed in Viet Nam since its struggle for independence began two decades ago.

The groups will assemble at Columbus Circle at 1 p.m. Women wearing white costumes (white is the color of mourning throughout Asia) and death masks will begin moving east on Central Park South at 1:30 p.m. They will be followed by veterans and reservists wearing black ties and armbands and carrying a large black casket to symbolize the enormous number of Viet Nam war dead. The walkers will carry hundreds of daisies and offer them to passers-by.

The veterans and reservists will distribute a simple leaflet urging all citizens to commit themselves "to reverence for life and working in every way possible to bring this horrible war to an end."

The walk will end at 50th St. and Fifth Ave. at about 2:30 p.m.
– 0 –
INFORMATION: 661-2567 days, 242-7399 evenings.'

given the girls flowers to carry. Making of the simple cortege a symbolic act, a funeral procession, was a supplemental idea. The action of a man who doesn't like to throw anything away till he has made full use of it. But the end result in terms of effect was new: sorrow conveyed beautifully, an evocation of purity. Aggressiveness had dropped out with Uncle Fatso, now the evocation of aggression was dropped. The address was gentle in tone and content. The two-beat rhythm was retained, however. Schumann paraded as one of the women.

'19 young women draped in white sheets from their heads to their sandals and wearing ashy "death masks" filed slowly along Central Park South and down Fifth Avenue yesterday to protest the war in Vietnam. The specter-like figures who were carrying white, yellow and violet chrysanthemums and humming in a sustained monotone, were followed by ten men who carried a coffin. It bore a sign reading "American Dead 4000 – Vietnamese Dead 1,300,000." About a dozen men and women in dark clothes walked behind the coffin. The cortege was flanked by policemen and by young men, some of them bearded, who passed out leaflets. "Let each of us this Memorial Day commit himself to reverence for life and working in every way possible to bring this horrible war to an end," the handbills said in part. *A Knell is Sounded.* The first of the shrouded women intermittently clanged an iron fork. From afar the sound seemed a knell. Another of the women was carrying a chalkwhite doll in her arms. Many of the passersby appeared embarrassed or awed by the macabre parade. A few small children who were sitting with their mothers on park benches took fright and started crying. A middle-aged man asked loudly: "What sort of a Broadway production is this?" A service man refused the flower that one of the women offered him. A cyclist jeered at the masked figures, "They are afraid to show their faces," he said. The demonstrators who gathered at Columbus Circle at 1 p.m. reached Rockefeller Center at about 3 p.m. and intended to proceed toward Rockefeller Plaza. However, guards barred them, pointing out that the area was private property. The women in white formed a circle on the Fifth Avenue sidewalk in front of Rockefeller Center, placed the doll on the pavement and arranged flowers around it. "The flowers," one member of the group explained, "symbolize our wish for life and peace." The cortege dispersed in a garage on West 49th St. between 5th and 6th Avenues. As the shrouded figures approached the garage, an onlooker said, apparently in earnest: "They're getting gas to burn themselves up," meaning self-immolation, Buddhist style. The protest was organized by the Veterans and Reservists to end the War in Vietnam, an anti-war group, and members of the Bread and Puppet Theater, a Lower East Side unit.'

(Hofman, 'War Foes Stage Macabre Protest, Women lead Mock Funeral Cortege sounding Knell,' *New York Times*, May 31, '66.)

The women's faces were white, not ashy:

'In this Memorial Day parade with just the white – the Vietnamese *Fire*-masks, – the first woman was carrying a chime which she was hitting and everyone was humming one note, and another woman was carrying a doll, that was then put on the ground, and flowers that the older women were carrying were then placed around it.'
(Elka in Schumann, interview, '79.)

Keith Lampe (later a convert to the hippie, then to the yippie style of agitation) cited this march in Dave Dellinger's WIN, the organ of non-violent resistance, as exemplary: by its careful preparation, its aesthetic quality, its seriousness, and because it substituted image for slogan:

'Peter Schumann's Bread and Puppet Theater joined Veterans and Reservists to End the War in Vietnam for a Memorial Day observance — and their efforts brought about the most impressive visual statement yet made by the American Peace movement. Why have we ignored esthetics so long? Nineteen women, carefully coached by Schumann, donned white sheets and masks to lead a mourning procession from Columbus Circle to Rockefeller Plaza via Central Park South. The veterans and reservists, dressed somberly, followed the women and carried a large black coffin in memory of all American and Vietnamese dead since the Vietnamese struggle for independence began twenty years ago. The statistics on the coffin ("American dead 4,000 — Vietnamese dead 1,300,000") were the only verbal element in the procession — though a few veterans walked before and beside the procession and passed out a simple leaflet calling on passers-by to commit themselves to "reverence for life and working in every way possible to bring this horrible war to an end." The event received enormous television coverage in terms generally favorable to the cause of peace. (It is important to note here that the peace movement cannot grow much more unless it scores more points on the television tube; from now on, any action that fails to get broad press coverage must be regarded as merely incestuous.)

It may be that Peter Schumann has more to offer peace groups at this time than anyone else. First, he brings a concern for *movement*: the slow pace and serious posture of the procession was a large part of the power. Second, a concern for *sound*: throughout the ninety-minute procession the women held a single, high, grieved tone that greatly affected passersby; at irregular intervals the lead woman provided a short, sharp, clanging sound to make the whole aural effect strikingly similar to certain Buddhist ceremonies in Japan. Third, of course, *appearance*: Schumann's masks alone make such a strong statement that they should be used at least weekly by small groups of women at various locations in all the five New York boroughs. (Schumann was disappointed that he had time for only one rehearsal — yet if other peace groups would rehearse their actions just once, they would increase their power many times over.)

Schumann rightly criticizes the sloppiness of the March 26th Fifth Avenue Parade. It is time we heeded William Carlos Williams:

"Go with some show of inconvenience."

Too many persons treated the parade as a social event, a Saturday lark, or a shrill form of defiance of the father-generation. I would like to see the Parade Committee hire Schumann for *mise en scene*. He would inconvenience us brilliantly.

There have been too many words, I think. Most of the slogans are exhausted and we must speak with our bodies. The public knows what we want; if we speak nonverbally, they may come to know how much we want it.'

(K. Lampe, *Memorial Day, WIN Magazine*, Volume II, No. 10, June 11, 1966.)

And the Trotzkyites liked it too:

'A unique demonstration against the war in Vietnam, in the form of a funeral procession through the streets of midtown New York, was held on Memorial Day by Veterans and Reservists to End the War in Vietnam and the Bread and Puppet Theatre. About 60 members and supporters of both groups participated...

The demonstration caught most of the holiday strollers and tourists by surprise. The general crowd reaction was one of curiosity, awe and silence, rather than counter-demonstration and jeering. Some spectators joined the procession along the route.'

(R. Wolin, *Bread and Puppet Theatre is Star of N.Y. Antiwar March, The Militant*, June 6, 1966.)

He was on the streets again a week later: June 6, this time in his neighborhood, the Lower East Side, performing for an Old Left-pacifist antiwar rally with ethnic appeal.[1] I don't know what he did:

'Lower East Side Mass Rally/End the War in Vietnam/Bring the Troops Home Now!/Hear/A.J. Muste ... Ted Weiss ... Dixie Bayo, chairman Movement for Puerto Rican Independence .../Entertainment: Peter Schumann's Bread & Puppet/Theatre/Monday, June 6, 7:30 p.m./Central Plaza, 111 Second Ave. at 7th St./Sponsors: Lower East Side Mobilization for Peace Action (LEMPA); Peace Committee District 65, R.W.D.S.U.; Teachers Committee to End the War in Vietnam; East Side Emma Lazarus Club; Veterans for Peace in Vietnam; Youth Against War & Fascism; Lower East Side W.E.B. Dubois Club; Movement for Puerto Rican Independence (M.P.I.); Peace Committee East Side Tenants; Council; New York Workshop in Non-Violence.'

(*Village Voice*, May 26, June 2, '66.)

A propos of the Old Left sponsorship of this rally: he performed *Fire* at the Trotzkyite Militant Labor Forum on June 10th. We may note also that his was no longer the only Movement street theatre group, another, the Pageant Players had emerged.[3]

---

2. 'Youth in our neighborhood are drafted in greater numbers than are young people in other parts of New York City. The poor, especially Negroes and Puerto Ricans, are the first to be sent to Vietnam; sent to slaughter a colored people, also poor, who only want a decent life, free of foreign intervention and with the freedom to decide their own destiny.
— (Flyer, June 6, '66 Lower East Side rally.)

3. 'Under the sponsorship of Tompkins Square Neighbors for Peace, two highly successful performances of an original dance drama protest against the war in Vietnam were presented Friday and Saturday evenings, June 3 and 4, in Lower East Side parks by the Pageant Players. A total of more than 1,500 people attended.

Friday's performance was the first ever given at the Jacob Riis Amphitheatre, the city's newest and best designed park. For once a park for poor people has been built with imagination. It provided a perfect setting for the outdoor drama which told the story of the Vietnamese war in equally human terms. Four of the 10 players represented Vietnamese peasants; four typical New Yorkers; and two, "the rulers of the world, Uncle Sam and his lady." Each group was shown at its daily tasks, with the contrast in style of living vividly depicted. The girding of the Americans for war and their cynical use by the rulers to destroy the people and culture of Vietnam was dramatized in a series of vignettes.

The final scenes showed the resistance of the Vietnamese, their eventual victory and the toppling of "the rulers" by the disgusted people of America.

A second original dance drama called "King Con", a satire based on the monopolistic practices of Consolidated Edison, New York's electric company, was also presented by the talented Pageant Players.

On Saturday night the program was put on in the area in front of the almost completed band shell in Tompkins Square Park. At least half the audience was composed of wide-eyed youngsters who reacted enthusiastically to every move of the dancers.

Also that evening, Jim Morgan, an officer of Tompkins Square Neighbors for Peace, addressed the audience. He told of the group's work to end the war in Vietnam and bring the troops home now and called for the support of all members of the community in building the next Days of Protest, Aug. 6-9, into the most effective demonstration against the war in New York's history.'

(R. Wolin, '*1,500 N.Y. East Siders See Antiwar Pageant*',
(*The Militant*, June 13, '66.)

17. August '66. Schumann designs a complex of feeder marches.

The anniversary of the delivery, by some Americans, of a bomb to the city of Hiroshima on August 6, '45 has been observed by public protests since at least the '50s. As far as I know, Schumann first demonstrated on a Hiroshima Day in '66. The demonstration, sponsored by the Fifth Avenue Peace Parade Committee, partly to increase the area of impact and neighborhood participation,[1] partly to lessen the time required for all the

---

1. Notably a feeder march from Harlem, promoted by SNCC and CORE:
   'The complexion of the peace movement is changing.
   A nearly lily-white crowd of 50,000 anti-war demonstrators paraded down Fifth Avenue last March. By August, a third of the 15,000 protesters who flocked to the midtown Hiroshima Day rally were Negro. Many regulars — students and their families — stayed at Fire Island, but, for once, some residents of the black ghettos came to Times Square. This was something new.
   How widespread Negro opposition to the war in Vietnam is remains debatable. Also obscure is the extent to which advocates of "black power" can cooperate with such unusual coalitions of predominantly white organizations as comprise the Fifth Avenue Vietnam Peace Parade Committee.
   Over ninety groups, compared with thirty last fall, are now loosely affiliated with the Parade Committee: which runs the big anti-war marches. All want to end the war in Vietnam but differ on almost everything else. The pacifists believe in non-violence; the Progressive Labor people preach bloody revolution; SANE thinks the way to peace is through the ballot box. Observers say that the tenuous coalition would collapse if it weren't for the fact that all the members "trust" the Reverend A. J. Muste, chairman of the Parade Committee.
   Indicative of Muste's difficulties was the outburst of New York SNCC director Ivanhoe Donaldson when asked about the "black power" group's role in the anti-war struggle: "We're not inside the peace movement. It's basically all-white. There's no way to relate to that!" Yet, despite his antagonism, Donaldson spoke at the Hiroshima Day demonstration from a platform provided by the Parade Committee.
   A number of SNCC workers were among a group of Negroes arrested last week when they stormed an induction center in Atlanta. The protestors gave out leaflets proclaiming, "We're tired of spilling black man's blood in white man's wars."
   SNCC officially took an anti-war stand in January, 1966. CORE followed at its Baltimore convention with a statement of opposition to the war and a pledge to help men who refused to serve in Vietnam. Brooklyn CORE organized a feeder march for the Hiroshima Day demonstration, as did local Harlem groups such as the Enraged Black Mothers and Afro-Americans to Bring the Troops Home.
   In a speech at the Hiroshima Day rally, Lincoln Lynch, associate director of CORE, castigated the NAACP and the Urban League for treating the war in Vietnam as a "foreign policy matter." He said the more conservative Negro groups fail to recognize that the ordinary Negro sees this war as a white man's war, a war from which the rich get richer and the poor get poorer, a war in which a black man fights and dies, and his buddy comes home and goes on relief, while his white colleague goes on to college."'
   Lynch asked whether democracy in Vietnam was more important than democracy in America. He raged "How can Congress, almost without debate, vote 58 billion dollars to

marchers to arrive at the destination, a Vietnam Day rally, featured feeder marches, to my knowledge the first New York City demonstration to do

---

support ponderous blood-sucking defense machines and haggle like barnyard hens at 2 billion dollars for a poverty program for the poor and the poor black of this nation?"

Negro leaders rarely spoke out in this fashion during either World War I, World War II, or the Korean War, according to Muste – who has been a pacifist since 1915. The 81-year-old Parade Committee chairman said that, in the past,"Except for a few individuals like A. Phillip Randolph, you had no people of prestige in the Negro movement who would link up the cause of war with their economic and social situation." Muste pointed out that Negroes have always benefited economically in previous wars.

Department of Defense figures show that the Army is extremely popular with Negroes. The reenlistment rate for blacks is 45.7 per cent compared with 17.1 per cent for whites. The reason, observers say, is that the American army is more democratic than American society. Not only do Negroes get better education and pay in the services, but they also are treated according to their rank, rather than their skin color. And, of course, they have less to hope for on the outside.

"The biggest obstacle to anti-war feeling in the black ghettos is the high unemployment rate," claims Negro lawyer Conrad Lynn. "The facts of economics are against us. If a boy can't get a job, where else can he go but the Army?" "Negro mothers," Lynn suggested, "would rather see them there than wandering aimlessly around the dope-ridden streets."

Lynn presently handles the cases of 21 Negroes who will not serve in the Army. "They're extremely alienated from American society," Lynn says. "They're very bitter. Every single one of them says he's ready to fight against the U.S."

Lynn recalled that his clients declined to take direct part in a press conference organized by the Parade Committee early this August. They would speak to reporters only after the peace people had had their say. "They're not collaborating with anyone else. This is a fight of the black man against the Army," the lawyer explained.

Muste says there are "as many as 100 men around the country" facing jail sentences because they won't go to Vietnam. Their reasons vary – from the anti-white views of Lynn's clients to a radical pacifism which holds that even accepting classification as a conscientious objector essentially means acquiescing to a special status within the war system.

The Parade Committee has widely publicized the cases of the "Fort Hood Three" – Negro Pvt. James Johnson, Puerto Rican Pvt. Dennis Mora, and Pvt. David Samas. They are currently awaiting court-martial for insubordination because they declined to obey a direct order to go to Vietnam on the grounds that the war is "illegal, immoral, and unjust."

The Fort Hood Three Defense Committee distributes a booklet, containing statements of support from CORE and SNCC, which outlines the experiences and positions of the three men. The strictly factual pamphlet refrains from urging other soldiers to follow the example of the Fort Hood Three. It is given out every Sunday night at the Port Authority Terminal to servicemen returning to Fort Dix. Anti-war leaflets are also distributed regularly by Harlem groups at the 125th Street Army induction center.

"There is also a movement underway to set up an organization of people within the armed services who insist upon their right to criticize the war," according to Muste. "This is stopping short of actually refusing to service." Servicemen signing a public statement of dissent run a "slight calculated risk" of harassment and "even court-martial prosecution" by military authorities, says Keith Lampe of Veterans and Reservists to End the War in Vietnam. The American Civil Liberties Union, he notes, has agreed to defend the soldiers' right to free speech.

The Japan Peace in Vietnam committee announced plans last Friday to set up an American information center in Tokyo. It will provide anti-war literature and advice on

so.[2] He contributed to three of the feeder marches, one from the Lower East Side and the Gramercy-Stuyvesant area, one from Greenwich Village, one from the Upper West Side. This was in fact his last creative *and* large-scale street demonstration until 16 years later. The way the *Voice* (August 4) spoke of the Village feeder march, it sounds as though he were to have the complete design control of it he had had of his small May 30th demonstration: 'designed by Peter Schumann of the Bread and Puppet Theatre, will have as its theme "No More Napalm" ... will be joined by New York University medical students.' My data are equivocal, I am not sure whether it was the East Side or the Greenwich Village march that had the 'No More Napalm' theme – *The Militant* (August 22) says they both did, but whichever did seems to have been dominated by it, and it seems to have been the main of Schumann's three parades: a procession of figures in blackened – male and female – face masks with bloated faces with grim expressions, dressed in and their heads covered by sheets of grey fabric, robed, carrying charred dolls in their arms, most distinctly reproachful victims and sufferers, perhaps humming in a way suggesting a dirge. Somewhere in this march (or in a march, at any rate, involving these same napalm victims) there was a huge faceless beast, dark-grey fabric that covered maybe a dozen people, whose small-looking hands or arms protruded here and there through holes in the fabric, primitive but nasty looking, conveying the idea of people covered by something or buried under something, surmounted by signs on sticks '300,000 dead' 'Nagasaki', 'Hiroshima', 'Vietnam'. The caption to a photo of these women by Fred McDarrah (*Village Voice*, August 11) spoke of 'the victims

---

how to become a conscientious objector to the 50,000 U.S. soldiers stationed in Japan. Liberation editor David Dellinger, who is presently in Japan, said that American peace groups and legal defense committees will supply materials for the Tokyo center.

"The Administration can be made nervous both by G.I. protest and by massive Negro protest. Both things are just beginning to happen now," says Lampe. Observing that he felt "depressed" that day, he added that it would be "utopian" to hope the discontent would become widespread enough to end – or even stop the escalation of – the war. — (Susan Goodman, *Changing the Complexion of the Peace Movement*, Village Voice, Sept. 8, '66, Copyright, Susan Goodman, 1966.)

2. 'Participants gathered in various areas and then marched to Times Square. Those from Brooklyn, Queens and Staten Island marched in their own boroughs and then took subways into Manhattan. In addition to the neighborhood "feeder" marches, a group marched from the UN and a contingent of Veterans and Reservists began their march at Madison Square Park.

As the demonstrators converged on Times Square, they joined in a huge picket line that encircled the triangular area from 42nd to 47th Street. They then marched to Rockefeller Plaza, past the home office of the Dow Chemical Corporation.... Later, A.J. Muste announced a boycott of Saran Wrap, a Dow product.

The rally was held at Park Avenue and 48th Street, with participants filling the long, wide block from Park to Madison Avenues and stretching around Park Ave. to 47th Street.' — (*The Militant*, August 22, '66.)

of Vietnam past and future.' The *New York Times* of August 7 ('Thousands over Nation March to Protest War & Hiroshima'), reporting 800 marchers from Sheridan to Times Square, said, 'leading them were 10 members of the Bread and Puppet Theater wearing grotesque death masks. They carried cow bells that they struck while humming a dirge.' The *Militant* (August 22) spoke of 'ghostlike, grotesquely masked, shrouded figures depicting the attrocities of Hiroshima and Vietnam and the horrors of napalm warfare.'

'Hiroshima Day Parade, we had three groups.... It was one of these theatre parades, with people coming from different parts of Manhattan and converging in one place. And the people from the Puppet Theatre plus all the others ... also divided into three groups. And I think there was one group who were soldiers, they wore T-shirts that were painted to look like soldier jackets. There was another group that was carrying objects that had been burned, I think, household objects, dolls – I can't remember the third group, but it was probably something like skull masks. It might have been something else. It was strenuous. Because, it seemed like all the parades it was either very hot or very cold. And it was so hot that there were some people fainting. And this was not one of those parades where you had to walk for a long time, but you had to wait for a long time, because it was a theatre parade, so you could only go so far and have to wait for another group ... walking and standing, you know, the discipline. You are not standing and conversing with your friend like someone who's not behind a mask, but you are still trying to maintain a form of parade. I was with the group that was carrying the burnt objects. I remember the burned dolls. And we may have also had something like a small chair or a pot – and I remember that Andy – you see my memories are a lot about people, and I was with these people that I knew, and Roger, who's a friend of Andy's and who died two weeks ago, kept trying to get water for the women who were fainting. And Joan, his girlfriend, was there, too. (I: Did you do anything?) No, this was just walking and carrying – (I: Who were the other participants?) It was probably a coalition, mobilization coalition. In this particular parade, we couldn't see the other groups. On Fifth Avenue, it was much more possible to see the people carrying signs saying "Great Neck" or "Trotzkyites" or "Social Workers" or whatever, but in this, we were much more separated. All I remember is the heat, the heat, the heat. I assume that it probably wasn't too friendly, because of the neighborhood. (I: What was the neighborhood?) Around 42nd Street. We were not part of the Greenwich –'—(Sherman, interview.)

'(For) one of the demonstrations, I cast a lot of people's faces, made masks from them and then painted them black and then put them on black costumes and sort of painted them charred black. Black with grey shades in it and then found a lot of dolls in the garbage and I painted those black, charred and burned looking. I remember that as being some special action that was specifically prepared for one of those demonstrations. It was again a large group. Actually, there were quite a few people participating, coming in for rehearsals ... a (parade) that was about the burning of children.... I cast a lot of people who wanted to help with this production, in a studio of the Youth Against War and Fascism – something like that – and I painted them charred and dressed the people in poorly dyed fabrics that it looked also grey and charred. That was another – either Memorial Day parade or some special occasion, where only those things were used. Burnt babies. Dolls that were painted with black paint and those masks and robes.' — (Schumann, interview, '79.)

This parade or these parades carried the idea of a funeral cortege, and focused on the civilian victims, women, mothers, children. The parade from the upper West Side[3] carried the other one of the ideas recurring in

---

3. 'Assembled at the corner of 72nd and Riverside Drive, the feeder march to which I attached myself was ready to go at 11:30 a.m. Led by a group of "Generals" in fancy costumes designed by the Bread and Puppet Theater group, the long column of people – about a thousand of us – wound its way down Broadway in the sun, the marchers vigorous and ready for another of those magnificent happenings which have become the major participatory activities for New York peace people since the first Fifth Avenue parade in October 1965.
Even without crowds lining our Broadway route, with no hecklers, no police harassment, there was exhiliration and joy among the walkers: it was warm and beautiful weather, we talked and joked in our typical white middle-class way, people bumped into old friends, their children were happy, demonstration muscles were loosening up . . . . The virtue of the feeder march idea – showing the various communities within the city that significant numbers of local residents were participants in peace activity, as well as creating the possibility of adding spontaneous walkers to the line – was probably not intended to be proven by us upper west siders: apparently, the feeder march led by Pfc. James Johnson's father, which went through central Harlem on its way to the demonstration, was the most successful of them all. Few people joined the group which left from 72nd Street, and few of us felt there would be any great surprise throughout our westside passage.
Each feeder march faced unique problems. For example, over 50 Staten Islanders walked from Silver Lake Park to the ferry, accompanied by six or eight ex-marines screaming insults; the marines followed them all the way to Times Square. Some demonstrators felt these hecklers increased attention paid to the march and (by contrast) guaranteed it a favorable impression. Edward Weberman walked from South Brooklyn: "At 10:30 the march started down Fulton from Stuyvesant to the Franklin Avenue IND station where about 50 people including two competing peace candidates – Herbert Aptheker and Hal Levin of the 12th CD – took the train. Four of us walked across the Brooklyn Bridge, greeting passersby with "Peace!" or "No More Hiroshimas!" And picking up a drunk along the way. We continued up Broadway until we met the parade at 39th Street."
The main failing of the feeder march idea was shown when we reached Times Square. Until then everything had been easy-going; the mood, the discipline, etc. were loose. We had exchanged some witty repartee with a couple of drunks, we had wound through Columbus Circle in a dignified, impressive manner, and we had presented smiling faces and intelligent leaflets to the denizens of the great automobile showrooms at 57th Street. But once within reach of the major police concentration in Times Square – pre-packaged and malleable as we were after our Broadway jaunt – we were dealt with in such a way as to destroy entirely the whole anticipatory-participatory sense which had been developing. Uninformed of the extent, the direction or the progress of the demonstration, we were shunted into side streets south of Times Square for a half hour, an hour, even more; none of the marshalls could explain what was going to happen next; the afternoon grew hotter, children began to cry, jokes wore thin, apathy set in. We were very well-behaved and most of us stood and waited, unaware of what was happening, trusting in the bureaucratic arrangements which had brought us here and would eventually liberate us from our

Schumann's anti-war parades, that of the march of captive prisoners of war. It was visually less grim, in fact had a humorous touch to it:

'Some 1200 persons marched down Broadway from 72nd Street and Riverside Drive. They were led by a contingent of youths playing funeral dirges on plastic horns and beating a military beat on tin drums. The youths, members of the Bread & Puppet Theater, wore white Tee-shirts with black lines drawn on them to represent military uniforms. They wore paper tricorn hats and epaulettes with general's stars on them. They also carried wooden swords in their belts.... The mock soldiers carried a long banner that said, "Yours is Not to Reason Why, Yours is But to Do or Die." A long rope led from the last soldier in the line to a Youth dressed in green Army fatigues. The rope was tied around his wrist. Following the young man were several dozen women dressed in black. They all carried placards reading, "We regret to inform you..."' — (*New York Times*, August 7, '66.)

'Two dozen members of the Bread & Puppet Theatre played a mock version of "Yankee Doodle Dandy" on toy drums and party noisemakers at Times Square. They were followed by 50 blackclad women, each of whom carried....

Pro-war demonstrators responded by burning a Viet Cong flag, cheering wildly as it burst into flames. "Burn the Reds," they shouted, pointing to the peace demonstration.... On their way from Times Square the peace marchers ran the gauntlet of a dozen members of the Neo-Nazi National Renaissance Party, who stationed themselves at Fifth Avenue and 40th St., to shout, "Democracy stinks.... You'll make a good bar of soap"' — (Carroll, '*Vietniks Mark Hiroshima in Times Square*', *Daily News*, August 7, '66.)

The 'We regret to inform you' led on to Schumann's *A Man Says Goodbye to His Mother*, cf. infra.

Three days later, on August 9th '66, the Dow Chemical Company was picketed, Schumann contributing skull-mask-masked pickets. This was a civil disobedience action, aiming at arrests, but Schumann stayed out of that part of it:

'For Nagasaki Day 1966... representatives from 11 peace organizations demonstrated at the Dow Chemical Company.... The picketing and leafletting began at about 11:30 in front of the statue of Atlas holding up the world across the street from St. Patrick's Cathedral (i.e. in front of Rockefeller Center – Dow

---

standing and waiting here. Some people of course – the less militant, the less committed – began drifting away, confused, slightly chagrined, vaguely unhappy.

Eventually, of course, having arrived at the rally – at 48th Street and Madison Avenue – there was a chance for uplift, there was noise, thousands of people, speeches.... If only we could have heard them. Once again it was clear that the participants, the rank and file, were not the main focus of the demonstration. Obviously there was no guarantee of comfort and dignity to the participants, but without a thorough explication of the day's proceedings in the press or on TV, the kind of experience which most of the marchers had on August 7th 1966 was apt to teach them only the dubious lesson that mass movements rarely function for the benefit of their members.' — (D. Newton, *Direct Action News, Manhattan, Aug. 6, WIN*, August '66.)

The temperature that afternoon was around 90°.

was up on the 29th floor or so (SSB)).... The day was dreary and overcast fitting with the mood of the demonstration. There were about 200 demonstrators and the Bread & Puppet Theater provided a group of death-masked, keening, gong-tapping women. Otherwise the demonstration was absolutely silent. Very few hecklers appeared, most of the spectators being apparently awed at the sombre, silent display. One woman turned to her friend and whispered, "It's scary...". In general there was a basically religious feeling about the demonstration. Before the planned civil disobedience was begun, Peter Boehme of the Fellowship of Reconciliation attempted to talk to the Dow executives. When he was unsuccessful, some 25 others entered the lobby and tried to use the elevators. Denied permission, they sat down in the corridor. In general, the police were considerate, the press was friendly and the action extremely orderly. About 20 minutes later, those who refused to move were arrested very efficiently. Outside, in front of the Atlas statue, the picketing continued for another hour.'

(Anon. *Direct Action News, WIN*, August '66.)

Twenty of them were arrested in the Rockefeller lobby — for disorderly conduct:

'The demonstrators included students, mothers pushing young children in carriages and members of a theatre group dressed in long black robes and skull masks. A spokesman for the Dow company said the company "endorses the right of any citizen to legally and peacefully protest any action with which he disagrees." He also said the company has "a small contract with the Defense Department to supply it with 25 million pounds of napalm a year."'

(*New York Times*, August 10, '66.)

The demonstrators' implicit charge that the Dow Chemical Company was a criminal was given support seventeen years later as regards its sales of 'Agent Orange' to the government for use in the '62-'70 defoliation and crop destruction campaign in Vietnam by company files made public in the course of a veterans' class action suit against the government. They showed Dow knew the Dioxin in the defoliant was toxic because it gave 'chloracne' to the workers that produced the stuff. The suit has been settled and Dow has as far as I know never been indicted (so if by a 'criminal' we mean only someone found guilty of a crime by a court of law, the corporation is not a criminal). Dow, at $7 a gallon, sold a third of the 12.8 million gallons Uncle Sam bought. Whether it compensated its defoliated employees I don't know.[4]

---

4. Cf. R. Blumenthal, *Files Show Dioxin Makers Knew of Hazards*, New York Times, July 6, '83.)

18. November '66. First hippie-style anti-war demonstration. Schumann tries to adapt.

The Fifth Avenue Committee, asking 'Sick of the War?', in the *Village Voice* of November 3, '66 advertises for participants in a November 5 feeder-type march 'to forestall escalation of the war after the November 3 election' (there were by now 400,000 American soldiers in Vietnam, some 215,000 more than a year earlier, some 383,000 more than two years earlier), and for listeners at a 'Mass protest rally', 'just south of Times Square.' Another ad in that issue announces a Guy Fawkes Party for after the demonstration ('Relax after the demonstration with free beer, popcorn and entertainment by the Pageant Players'), admission fee $1, and still another, this one 'aided and abetted by New York Workshop in Non-Violence and Veterans and Reservists to End the War in Vietnam', invites to the march, presenting it as 'a walk for love and peace and freedom with Allen Ginsberg, George Snyder, Paul Krassner, the Fugs, USCO, the Yellow Submarine' and indicating alternative rendezvous at Washington Square or at Tompkins Park in the East Village: 'Bring Mothers, Lovers, Babies, Balloons, Flutes, Flowers, Whistles, Rollerskates and all other beautiful things! – Sign language instead of language in signs! – LOVE STOPS DESTRUCTION!" The gentle hippie is shuffling onto the scene bringing soul.[1] The shift is abrupt from Schumann's stark demon-

---

[1] Keith Lampe welcomes him on behalf of the Movement's pacifist wing in the Workshop in Non-Violence's WIN. Note the 'Learn from the Negro' note:

'The Yellow Submarine Walk October 22 and the Walk *for* Love & Peace & Freedom November 5 mark the tentative beginnings of a community of New Yorkers conscientiously concerned to go beyond rallies, picket lines and parades *against*. For new people drawn to these demonstrations, the question *Are you a pacifist?* is meaningless. After hesitation they'd probably answer it affirmatively. These new people see those demonstrating stridently against the war as belonging to essentially the same society as those conducting the war. Their goal must be to develop their embryonic community into an alternative society.

The consciousness which creates the concern to move beyond *against* is essentially a turned-on one (as in Black Power) and so in most cases cannot be understood by even the very best of the older people. This is why so many former friends of SNCC and CORE do not see that the Black Power concept contains a down-to-the-bones wisdom and is an inevitable evolutionary phase within America. (One straight way to learn this is to spend a lot of time with Haitian or West Indian or African blacks.) This is why most pacifists have such difficulty understanding that the American black, to be whole, cannot return to non-violence till he has won the right to be as violent as everybody else. This is why the new people *for* love can best carry out the SNCC suggestions for white work within white communities.

Because the idea of the Walk for Love & Peace & Freedom is so new, it becomes uniquely unimportant that *New York Times* reporter John P. Callahan found the partici-

strations of August. At the national level, the mood is less gay, but a new coordinating committee is formed.[2]

Schumann, no spoilsport, entered into the spirit of things. He contributed Uncle Fatso to the parade, wearing a crown and a bib identifying him as 'Mr. Peace,' followed by a giant knife and fork ditto. When he started out in the East Village, a balloon was tied to his sleeve. He still looked grim, however. Ginsberg, in a Gandhi-white costume according to the *Voice*, but in a star-spangled one according to the *Daily News*, both agreeing on the Uncle Sam hat — an idea Schumann in the '70s, in a more conciliatory mood, adapted for his circus and July 4th stilt-walks, stole the show from Uncle Fatso.[3]

---

pants "unkempt" and even a little frightening. It is unimportant because not until the general press and public have understood well the necessity for walking *against* the war can they understand the next wisdom of walking *for* peace.

These new people should use their best energies to form and develop their alternative society, but in their spare time they should continue to support demonstrations gently and humanely *against*. — (K. Lampe, '*Black Power and The Yellow Submarine*,' WIN, December 20, '66.)

The *Village Voice* (November 10, '66) carrying front-page photos of Snyder and Ginsberg along with that of the Reverend Muste, on behalf of the liberal establishment, welcomes the Beatifications of the Movement, cf. Don McNeill's report on the parade infra.

2. The National Coordinating Committee to End the War in Vietnam, formed in July '65, active through the spring of '66, had run out of energy (Powers, *The War*). It had not taken part in the Hiroshima Day parade.

'In September, 1966, a new organization called the Mobilization to End the War in Vietnam was formed to sponsor demonstrations between November 5 and 8. On the weekend of November 26, a new meeting in Cleveland was called by the Inter-University Committee to evaluate the November demonstrations and decide what should come next. Noone could argue convincingly that another demonstration would have any more effect than the previous ones, but it was decided to make a major effort anyway. A new group was formed called the Spring Mobilization to End the War in Vietnam under the chairmanship of A.J. Muste. The four vice-chairmen were David Dellinger, editor of Liberation, Ed Keating, publisher of Ramparts; Sidney Peck, a professor at Western Reserve University; and Robert Greenblatt, a professor at Cornell . . . .' — (Powers, ibid.)

3. 'The Yellow Submarine — a 10-foot hero-sandwich-shaped construction of wood, canvas, and a periscope, left over from a peace demonstration of a few weeks ago — was being carried up Third Avenue. The periscope narrowly missed an awning. "DIVE! DIVE!" the bearers shouted.

* * *

An anarchist handbill suggested a mantra:

> Is pollution the solution?
> Will there be a revolution?
> Everything's in dissolution
> No pollution brings solution
> One solution revolution
> One solution revolution
> One solution revolution

* * *

A sound truck followed the feeder march playing not sermons but Supremes. And the Byrds. And the Beatles.

* * *

It was a different sort of peace parade: a pre-election rally that was largely apolitical. The yellow handbills declared that "Love Stops Destruction" and proposed "Sign Language Instead of Language on Signs." A thousand people walked from Tompkins Square to Times Square, joining other thousands to have a good time and stop the war. They had a good time. It was a partial success.

There were traditional elements. Union leaders spoke. A girl sang folk songs and, when saboteurs cut the speaker cable, led peace chants with the enthusiasm of a high school cheerleader. A lady melodiously began her speech "Friends and fellow fighters for peace," and on the edge of the crowd packages of handbills were distributed wholesale to be passed out during the week at churches, induction centers, and schools. But it all seemed a little archaic. Peace play had taken new forms.

The demonstration was organized by the Fifth Avenue Peace Parade Committee in cooperation with the November 8 Mobilization Committee, which had planned a nationwide four-day series of pre-election protest activities. The Mobilization Committee was established at a conference in September to attempt to counteract an anticipated post-election escalation of the war in Vietnam. Specifically, the program was aimed at getting voters to support the peace candidates or, where there are none, to write in the words "Peace" or "U Thant."

Ten feeder marches, from various parts of Manhattan, swelled the crowd at 41st Street and Sixth Avenue to at least 10,000 persons. One of the most colorful marches, a three block long parade of babies, bells, flutes, flowers, and hippies, wound its way from Tompkins Square Park to the Bryant Park site.

The parade from Tompkins Square included a number of props. The Anarchists, who operate out of the Torch Bookstore on East 9th Street, paraded with a "Monster." It was a 10-foot-high assemblage of wheels, chains, wooden shoes, a flag, and a barrel. It was, they said, a "Blood Machine," a "Death Machine." The Bread and Puppet Theatre, led by Peter Schumann, had a large, grotesque papier mache figure labeled "Mr. Peace." A sneering bust of stereotyped Wall Street, pink complexioned and topped with a gold burlap crown, the figure clenched a foot long cigar.

On the way, they walked down 34th Street, filling the block between Fifth and Sixth Avenues. Through the crowds of shoppers in front of Ohrbach's, the people from the Lower East Side went with rollerskates, banners, and bells. Pedestrians seemed amazed, but not hostile. The purpose of the parade was somewhat obscured by the spectacle.

The Tompkins Square contingent merged with a Veterans for Peace march coming up Broadway. Both cheered, and police at the jammed intersection directed foot traffic. Seven blocks later, all converged on Bryant Park.

It was a massive rally, filling all but a lane of Sixth Avenue from 40th to 42nd Streets, and far west on 41st Street. From the steps of Bryant Park, packed like bleachers, one could see a sea of heads, signs, babies on shoulders, and balloons. An occasional balloon would float loose and drift up the side of a glass building. At the intersection, flanked by operating but impotent stoplights, was a large speaker's platform. Over two hours of speeches were delivered. Much of the crowd was oblivious to the formalities. Impossibly jammed but always moving, the crowd was preoccupied with itself. A vacuum would form; a rivulet of bodies would fill it. The mantra singers continued. Peter Orlovsky and friends spread out coats to picnic, and the mass circumnavigated. Conversation dominated. When the sound system was sabotaged, it reigned.

The activities on the speakers' platform seemed to command the attention of those within a radius of a hundred feet or so. There were 13 speakers and a number of additional introductions. Edward Keating, publisher of Ramparts magazine and eloquent like a hometown mayor, called for the impeachment of President Johnson. "When I see the prospect of massive bombing of North Vietnam," Keating said, "I can see no other alternative for massive movement in this country than to call for the impeachment of the President.

This move is necessary to avoid having this country knows as the second Hitler's Germany."

The only visible sign of dissension was a small group of pro-Administration demonstrators beyond the police barricades and the single lane of Sixth Avenue traffic. Late in the afternoon, however, a group of about 10 people filtered into the crowd and began to loudly boo the speakers. Newsmen and police rushed toward the noise. The group included four soldiers in uniform. A short, stocky, middle-aged woman was shouting at a demonstrator.

"We're not on your side, madam, so shut up."

"Go to hell," a soldier shouted.

A news photographer snapped a picture of the woman. "Put that camera down," she yelled. "Get his camera," another person shouted. "Get his film." Jammed together, they lunged toward the man and were suddenly blocked by police. The photographer, trembling, held his camera above the heads of the cops and shot a few more. The police escorted the soldiers away. The woman shoved through the crowd looking for the photographer, who had disappeared. She didn't find him.

It was getting dark, and many of the apolitical Tompkins Square contingent had left. They missed hearing Sue Eanet, the 18-year-old regional coordinator of Students for a Democratic Society. "We have protested," Miss Eanet said. "We have cleansed ourselves by the protests, but we haven't stopped one bomb from falling on the Vietnamese." The people who sang mantras had empathy. But they also had fun. the Rev. A. J. Muste, 81, dean of the New York peace movement, observed that the East Village example was "different from the religious-pacifist orientation, but having a note of delight in it, as well as seriousness, is good."

But the example was catching. Allen Ginsberg, resplendent in white Gandhi pyjamas and an Uncle Sam stars and stripes hat, sang and read last before the crowd of 10,000, "Let Congress execute its own desires," the poet declared. "Let the President execute his own delight," Ginsberg finished triumphantly. "I here alone declare the end of the war." The crowd went wild.' — (Don McNeill, *Village Voice*, November 10, '66. (Copyright Don McNeil, 1966.))

The hippie show of turnedonness in droppedoutness (tunedinness which during the '70s was to show its real virtue as hep consumerism was hard to achieve during a street parade) had been adapted to peace street agitation in the Bay area, California, a year or more earlier. Allen Ginsberg's instructions to Berkeley peace marchers in '65 for turning demonstrations into 'exemplary spectacles ... OUTSIDE the war psychology,' by modifying the Jewish Diasporan response to violence – reasoning, i.e. talking – into the middle class gay's approach to sailors, etc. (loving seduction) provided a suck-arse rationale:

'Masses of flowers – a visual spectacle – especially concentrated in the front lines, can be used to set up barricades, to present to Hell's Angels, police, politicians, and press and spectators whenever needed or at parade's end.... If imaginative, pragmatic, fun, gay, happy, *secure* Propaganda is issued to mass media in advance.... The parade can be made into an exemplary spectacle on how to handle situations of anxiety and fear/threat (such as Spectre of Hells Angels or Spectre of Communism). To manifest by concrete example, namely the parade itself, how to change war psychology and surpass, go over, the habit-image-reaction of fear/violence. That is, the parade can embody an example of peaceable health which is the reverse of fighting back blindly.' — (Ginsberg, *Liberation*, January '66.) (Cf. Appendix XVII.)

The last flower-child hippie type peace demonstration I have noted for New York City took place a year later, November 25, '67. The next West Coast Youth Movement approach to peace demonstration – digger dadaism – had by then already had an impact in New York City. Allen Ginsberg, Phil Ochs and others staged a celebration of the (make-believe) end of the war in Washington Square park: 'A dramatic troupe and a mock-general did droll, deft, anti-draft things in the center of the fountain.' — (Kent, *On a Saturday Afternoon: 'The War is Over!'*, *Village Voice*, November 30, '67.)

19. November '66. Another street skit added to repertory. More like a play than the preceeding one.

An ad in the *Village Voice* of November 10 invites the public to 'join in protest against Pro-Viet Nam War Veterans Day' by coming to a 'Rally and Discharge Paper Burning' on November 11 on the North Plaza of Union Square. It promises that the 'Bread and Puppets will perform', and that A.J. Muste, Joe Mora, Oliver Leeds, Deirdre Griswold, Fred Halstead and Robin Palmer will speak. The rally is sponsored by Veterans and Reservists to End the War in Viet Nam: 'Veterans or reservists who want to burn their papers with us are invited to participate.' I would think that Schumann's contribution was his *A Man Says Goodbye to His Mother* – Kourilsky ('71) had it from him that it was first done this November, and though he says he first did it on order for a Puerto Rican organization,[1] the East Harlem Action Group Against the War in Vietnam (Schumann, interview, '82), this either may not have been so, or he may have given this performance up there, off a flatbed truck, before doing it on Union Square. A year earlier he had done here what later became another little play of his, *Speech* or *Chairs*. *A Man Says* became an important part of his street repertory.[2] It and *King Story* were the lasting pieces

---

1. 'It was in the Shakespeare Company.... It was a request by a Spanish or Puerto Rican neighborhood . . . after they decided to do a rally in which they had a woman whose son was killed in Vietnam speak. So they asked us if we could dramatize this and come to this particular event, and that night we made up this play. Margo (Sherman), Bob (Erntthal), . . . maybe Charlie (Adams) . . . must have been in it. I just wrote down a few lines and then on the basis of that, we made this play. (Elka: . . . you had the text, you had the narration, and how much of that did you make up and how much of it was from this event? This woman who had lost her son –) No. That's it. We learned about that. Yeah. (Elka: Were the scissors, was that something to do –?) No, that was made up. It was not in her story, that her son was killed by a pair of scissors. It just seemed to be the right tool for an American soldier to be killed with.' — (Schumann, interview, '79.)

'. . . our play *Reiteration* was a response to a task; it is based on a play we were asked to do on a street corner in East Harlem. They needed this play within two days. We didn't have anything. We did a rehearsal and there happened to be this little airplane and a baby doll in the studio, and I think that is how the play came together. It was very accidental and it was also because of the task: we were forced to do something in two days that could be done with four players on the street corner and could be carried very easily, and they didn't have money for it either.... We didn't think, "what do we want to achieve in this story?" except at first when we wanted to be on an East Harlem street corner and say to these mothers, some of whom we knew had received that little letter: "Here. Hear this. Here's your letter." That was the reality of this play. The letter is the first sign you get when they kill your son. Our message was to put that letter into a context that was well-known to them, to say it in a way which they probably were not used to themselves.' — (Schumann, The San Francisco Mime Troupe's booklet with a *panel discussion on radical theater.*)

2. '(Elka: Did it change much?) I don't think so. (Elka: I mean, it certainly didn't later,

of his repertory. It introduced something like regular theatre into it: acting, though of a demonstrative rather than representational sort, and a story, a story about individuals, the Son, the Mother, though not about particular individuals. In its street version³ it focused, at least originally,

---

but did you have a very different earlier version of it?) No, no, it stayed pretty much the same. And that we performed a lot then, we went to schools, universities, too, street corners. There was a truck going around New York, it must have been in '66 or '67, with poles against the wall, we then, in that factory truck – we performed in it. It was probably the most used play, the play we did most frequently of any play. (Elka: There was a whole fad then in "Guerilla theatre", and many theatre schools.) That was a bit later, I think. (Elka: and theatre groups – did that come later?) I think so, but then, at that time, I learned to know other groups, like Pageant Players, who also wanted to play in the streets, partially also with masks, and with dragon.' — (Schumann, interview, '79.)

'Some of that stuff came together just easily; some stuff was hard or never worked out and other stuff we did, like *A Man Says Goodbye*, which is, I think, one of the best street shows I've ever seen, it's just so smooth, so perfect in the streets. I remember that we got invited by some group to play on the street corner somewhere and we were working at the Astor Library. That (was) the time we moved there, and I just remember, we went to a side room, right by the front door, with a box of stuff, like props and stuff, and just worked it out. Just an end to the story and it came like in an hour. And it was virtually done and it turned out just so good. I still think it's just a great example of street theatre.' — (Ernstthal, interview.)

'Some of the best shows that I've ever experienced . . . there was one, for instance, that I remember to this day. We were on 14th Street in front of the Con Edison building. You know, 14th Street's a real – East 14th – around Klein's. And we stopped on a flatbed truck. We were sponsored by the Committee Against the War or something. We were giving a version of *A Man* – and these people just walked by and came there and stood. And *every* person out of those 50 or whatever was totally transfixed. In the middle of the city. It was like this zone of total tranquility. Totally quiet. And everyone was totally transfixed. And thoroughly moved. On the street. It was probably one of the best pieces of theatre that's ever been. And it was just *there*. And that happened to be at the *right* moment and the *right* time, and just these people at random. And there it was. And it was just great. It was totally fabulous. — (Ernstthal, interview.)

'A battered truck pulls up and suddenly everything is bustling. It is a late October evening and a small crowd stands around on a corner in the East Village. It is bitterly cold and there is no shelter from the wind. A few moments earlier an archaic old-school leftist railed against the war while three or four persons listened attentively. In everyone's eyes there is apprehension about an antiwar demonstration that is to take place at the Pentagon a few days later. No one speaks of anything else. The members of Peter Schumann's Bread & Puppet Theatre emerge from their truck and begin to arrange props, tune up instruments and slip on their simple costumes. The production is called "A Man Goes To War". Eyes in the audience seem not quite able to comprehend what this story has to say about war. Everyone draws nearer and their foreheads are wrinkled in consternation. Peter stands to one side narrating the pantomime. The acting is slow and deliberate. Their masks are stylized visions of murder and decay. The other members of the cast have formed a semi-circle around the action. They are wearing black ankle-length robes and death masks. When the performance ends the actors silently pack everything into their truck. The night gathers itself together into a bleak chasm and the wind is colder than before.' — (Candy Silberstein, *theater: bread and puppetry, Escapade*, June '68.)

3. I have not been able to get any indications how the pre-'67 version might have differed from the later indoors and street version.

on the mother's bereavement (the theme broached in the '66 Hiroshima Day parade's West Side feeder), in its indoors version later, from the summer of '67 onward, rather on the son's guilt. In September '68, Schumann developed another variant from it, *Reiteration*, which subsequently was the preferred indoors version, at least for a few years – *A Man Says* continued to be done in the street. Cf. infra IV(3) for the indoors *A Man Says*, and for *Reiteration*.[4]

The Bread and Puppet Theatre in a head-on collision of values joined Macy's Department Store in celebrating Thanksgiving (November 24) in public that year:

'The joyful fantasy of Macy's annual Thanksgiving Day parade was followed by a macabre march of anti-war demonstrators dressed in seared, black garments and wearing skull-like masks.... The second parade down Broadway yesterday was made up of 30 men and women opposed to the American involvement in the war in Vietnam. Describing their march as a "Vietnam Thanksgiving," they sought to dramatize the destruction of crops in Vietnam by United States forces. The marchers wore ashen masks and black clothing and carried representations of seared, poisoned crops. The demonstrators who were protected by a cordon of policemen, marched without incident from Columbus Circle to Herald Square.'

(T. Smith, *Contrasts Mark Thanksgiving Day. Festive March is Followed by Antiwar March Here – Many Attend Service, New York Times*, November 25, '66.)

Smith didn't quite get the action of the skit:

'Tout à coup, voici un cortège de femmes en noir, au masque gris foncé comme brûlé, suivies d'hommes avec un masque de mort qui portent une longue table chargée de maïs, table qui, lorsqu'on la regarde bien n'est autre qu'un brancard, arrivé à sa hauteur, elle prend quelque chose dessus, un homme survient, lui retire vivement ce qu'elle a pris, le remet sur la table, et la marche continue, l'action se répétant indéfiniment.' (Kourilsky, '71.)

'... an American pushing Vietnamese women away from a food-laden table, which on second look turned out to be a grim stretcher.' (Reade, *Demonic Protest*.)

The fact that Smith didn't get it is not surprising since American journalists don't look for the plot. How many others among the plebeians along

---

4. '*A Man Says Goodbye* contrasts with a "Black Arts" play staged by LeRoi Jones at an April or May 26, '67 Black Panther rally at the Fillmore auditorium in San Francisco brought up in an article (Steve Pelletiere, *The Panthers, WIN*, Sept. 16, '68) à propos of the trial of Huey Newton July 22, '68 ff.: criticizing the "white community's" inability, because they have never been subjected to the terrorism that the Negro has been subject to, nor the police harassment that the Black Panthers from early '67 onward were subjected to, to appreciate the Black Panther stance and rhetoric of violence – of self-defense: Stokely Carmichael, in a scantily attended, thus little reported, Panther rally at the Fillmore in San Francisco (May 26, 1967) said: "The Black Panthers are doing something that needs to be done." He said that people must be organized, and it must be done on a Carmichael's vision of the genocide-to-come, the only important thing is that the Black community organize to defend itself. This implies that the Panthers are not above

Broadway treating their kids to Macy's contemptuous crap that got a glimpse of Schumann's moving display among the cops at all, took in its brutal accusation? Smith got paid for the tricky little maneuver (made possible by the great paper's style's anodyzing Objectivity) of rejecting responsibility by interposing 'the destruction of crops by United States forces': the poor along that thoroughfare, wont to feast on poisoned food (like Macy's puppets), might simply have been antagonized by the injustice of being told that *they* were taking anybody's food away from them: whereas the truncated sentiment of profound sadness that such a thing should be happening (rather than done by them) filtering through to them through the street's turbulence would be apt to diminish, if only decrementally, their bellicosity. But I don't think this means that Schumann was overreaching in structuring the street skit as action ('I remember that we rehearsed a continued action with food being carried and food being pulled away' (Schumann, interview, '79)) or wrong in letting anger rather than just pity structure it for him: the energy of the emotion probably lent communicative strength to the image, and its action-structure precision. You don't hit a target by aiming at it. The street skit developed into the indoors Thanksgiving shows, *Eating & Drinking . . .*, of '67 and '68.

As far as my information goes, this Thanksgiving parade was his last creative street demonstration, an impressive event designed for the occasion. He from now on tended to rely on standbys adapted in minor ways.

---

terrorizing their own people. Carmichael said as much on February 17: "All of the Uncle Toms, we're gonna sit down and we're gonna talk, and when they flap we're gonna bow . . . and we're gonna try to bring them home, and if they don't come home, we're gonna *off* them."

The Black Panther image is one which a confused, none-too-confident ghetto youth can cherish. By donning the Panther skin, he takes on raw power. This is seductive. Whether the Panther symbol has any meaning to the black working men, the family man, has yet to be proven. The most far-reaching development of the Newton trial and the whole Black Panther movement may be that it sets black son against black parent.

At the same April 26 rally, LeRoi Jones staged a one-act "Black Arts" play in which a black guerilla fighter is pinned down and dying in the rubble of a white American city. His action during the play is to execrate his mother, who, by her endless preaching of Christian love, has cost him his manhood. At his end, the mother comes to comfort her boy, and begins haranguing him for having taken the way of violent Black Nationalism – he shoots her. And the all black, all young crowd at the Fillmore nearly turned themselves inside out applauding.' — (S. Pelletiere, *The Panthers*, WIN, September 16, '68.)

20. December '66. The anti-war campaign becomes glamorous.

'*U.S. Role in Vietnam Assailed at Garden.* United States participation in the Vietnam war was assailed in speeches, songs, plays and poems and with balloons at Madison Square Garden last night. The occasion was a 4½ hour peace rally held by the National Committee for a Sane Nuclear Policy and 36 supporting organizations. A capacity crowd of about 18,000 attended.... Gunnar Myrdal ... Norman Thomas, Floyd McKissick ... I.F. Stone. Entertainment was provided by Peter Seeger, the folksinger; Jules Feiffer, the cartoonist; and a skit satirizing the United States role in the war. At one point hundreds of blue balloons with white peace doves tied to them were released from the ceiling.'
(*New York Times*, December 9, '66.)

Sponsored by moderate SANE (still just demanding negotiations, not immediate withdrawal), it was a leftist class event, televised nationally. Feiffer from the *Voice* was the evening's hit with a Johnson imitation, in Johnson's voice giving Johnson's explanations of past and future escalations. The audience joined Seeger in refrains, e.g. 'Bring them Home! Bring them Home!' There was a theatrical production – readings by Tony Randall, Diana Sands, Shirley Black 'and others'. (*The Militant*, December 19 '66.) To Schumann, who already when he was doing *A Man Says Goodbye to His Mother* on the streets was beginning to feel that the Peace Movement had 'become uninteresting' (Schumann, interview, '79) the end of '66 saw 'the end of the war movement' (ibid.), at least 'for us it seemed like the end of it pretty much', a sentiment his wife relates to the fact that the Movement was 'finally getting popular', attracting 'big crowds.' His participation in Madison Square Garden probably confirmed his feeling – the Movement was taking on a certain gloss.

'(Elka: But that was a pretty elaborately – not elaborately – a pageant we rehearsed several times. The Veterans Against the War rented a hall for you to rehearse somewhere – it was quite far –) It was something with the airplane and the Jesus puppet being crucified on the front of the airplane, and the Vietnamese women – a white Vietnamese woman was used as the figure that got crucified on the airplane, that's how it was – on this grey demon airplane. The rest of the choreography was drums and skeletons marching, and things like that. That's all I recall from that one. But I remember what you said when we rehearsed – several nights, in the hall of some peace movement organization. I guess the War Resisters League. It was hard to find all the people. We needed lots of people.'
(Schumann, interview, '79.)

The crucifixion if properly spotlighted might have been quite effective in the Garden. But I doubt he got the spotlighting. It's out of his Easter shows, and he later occasionally used the airplane, first used in the March 26,'66 Fifth Avenue parade, as crucifix, e.g. in *Cry* ('69).

21. December '66. Schumann's last demonstration with press coverage.

At the end of the year, Schumann organized a demonstration all by himself, and with his own people only, outside of august St. Patrick's. An American cardinal, associated with this church I suppose in his capacity of bishop, Monsignor Spellman, also military vicar for Roman Catholics in the U.S. Army, had for Christmas blessed his sheep in uniform with 'less than victory is inconceivable' and 'total victory means peace,' and speaking at a U.S. naval base in the Philippines had told them, 'you are not only serving your country, but you are serving God, because you are defending the cause of righteousness, the cause of civilization, and God's cause.' His remarks had brushed Schumann the wrong way, and he had decided on a silent vigil in masks and costumes – Mary, Joseph, the shepherds, the three kings – and the Jesus child in Mary's arms, a doll, blood-stained and (according to Joe Flaherty in the *Village Voice* (January 5, '67) grotesque – on the cathedral steps Christmas morning. Police told them they were trespassing on church property, under picketing ordinances had to keep moving – a stationary vigil was out – and – when they had gotten off the steps – that they were obstructing traffic on that sidewalk, had to do it on the sidewalk opposite. At some point, later that morning or the next, the police were better prepared. The demonstrators were informed they could not wear masks, there was a section of the penal code that forbade assemblies of three or more persons with concealed faces except when proceeding to or from a masked ball. The Civil Liberties Union, consulted by Schumann, confirmed this,[1] so Schumann and his people returned with the masks on sticks and signs identifying them – 'I am Mary. My child was napalmed in Vietnam,' etc. This was December 30, and as conclusion they deposited the little Jesus on the cathedral steps as a thoughtful gift to the cardinal:[2]

---

[1] 'The Civil Liberties Union ... sent a telegram to Commissioner Leary asking him not to enforce the statute, which had never been tested in the courts, and saying that the puppeteers were willing to doff their masks or otherwise identify themselves whenever challenged by the police. Nevertheless, the pickets were compelled to unmask.... Calling the police action a "gross misapplication" of the antimask statute adopted in 1888, and an action "specifically designed to thwart the effectiveness of the demonstration," the Civil Liberties Union is seeking a declaratory judgment to enjoin the Police Department from similar use of the statute in the future.' — (*New York Times*, January 9, '67.)
I suppose Schumann was pretty upset, fearing all his street work might be subject to this statute.
[2] '*Vietnam Protesters Picket St. Patrick's.* Wearing black cowls and carrying grotesque masks impaled on poles, eight members of the Bread & Puppet Theater group solemnly picketed St. Patrick's Cathedral yesterday. They were protesting Cardinal Spellman's recent statement calling for an unqualified victory in Vietnam and (presenting) the war as a

'The first time was on Christmas morning, it was cold, and we went with the *Christmas Story* characters to St. Patrick's in honor of Cardinal Spellman, who was one of the bloothhirstiest prowar advocates in America, and we wanted to give him the bloody Jesus doll as a Christmas present. We decided to tell the press about this – Jules (Rabin) felt very strongly that we should have this action recorded by the press (Elka: You didn't know what might happen. You thought you could all be arrested, it was very –) Well, anyway, we went there and we did our first action. There weren't too many people there. It was in the morning. Then cops came and told us that we couldn't do it at that church, we had to move off the sidewalk and we couldn't step up to the church. Anyway, they told us it was illegal to wear masks, so – (Elka: They found an old ordinance dating back to 1890 or something?) That said in New York you can't wear masks unless it's

---

fight for the survival of civilization. For an hour they walked back and forth on the 51st Street side of the cathedral and then circled it twice. A spokesman said they were "mourning for the dead in Vietnam and for the crucifixion of Christ in Southeast Asia." At one point, a marcher placed a doll, splattered with red paint on the sidewalk in front of the cathedral steps at the corner of Fifth Avenue and 51st Street. It was immediately picked up by a detective, one of 25 policemen watching the demonstration. A placard borne by the marcher said "I am Mary. My baby was napalmed in Vietnam." The protest was carried off without incident.' — (*New York Times*, December 21, '66.)

'The demonstration reached its high point when the girl portraying Mary tried to place the blood-stained Jesus doll on the steps of the cathedral. A line of cops blocked her way and told her she couldn't place the doll on the steps. "That's littering," one of Our Finest replied. I looked at heaven hoping that the remark would be forgiven. Since there was no room on the steps for the infant, the girl knelt down and placed the doll on the sidewalk.

Suddenly a guy in a trench coat snatched up the doll and began running down 51st Street. My God, he was abducting Him. What gall! I ran after the guy – this was bigger than the Lindbergh thing. I chased him along 51st Street and he ran into Best and Company. The guy ran into the lost and found department and placed the doll on a desk. "I found this doll on the street, I would like to turn it in to your department". Three city policemen seemed to have set up a sub-precinct in the room. The cop behind the desk placed the doll in a carton and had the kidnaper sign a form.

"May I have this man's name?" the cop behind the desk ordered me out of the room. I protested, "Look, I have the right to know this man's name." The cop behind the desk was losing patience. "Look, you're not getting his name and clear out of here."

The door opened and a police sergeant entered. "What's the commotion in here?" A young, innocent-looking cop answered. "This guy from the press wants to know the name of the guy who brought this doll in here. I don't know what the fuss is about – it was only one of our detectives." The sergeant froze the innocent with his stare. It's going to be a long winter on Staten Island.

The cops unwittingly summed up the protestor's message. As a nation we have lost Jesus.' — (Joe Flaherty, *The Puppets for Peace: Abduction at Cathedral, Village Voice*, January 5, '67.)

'Gee, we did one that we did alone, which was when Cardinal Spellman said that we were doing this to save the people of Vietnam or something and we went with the *Christmas Story* puppets, five of us, on Fifth Avenue, and deposited a burned baby. And there was a lot of attention on that – I remember that because that was one that we did alone and that was really scary – believe me – it was so – it was terrifying. People did *not* like it – *at all*. And there was a lot of press – a lot of press around – and there was only five of us or something.' — (Ernstthal, interview.)

for a carnival dance or something like that. So we just put sticks on the puppets and mounted the fabric from the masks and then left a little hole underneath that exposed our faces, but they knew that we'd be – we had told this cop from this precinct that we would be back. In the meantime, we checked with the Civil Liberties Union, and they also said it would be hard to defeat that thing about the masks. That's why we decided on mounting the masks in this different manner. We had signs, placards, that we carried with us that said things like "I am Mary," ... so that every one of these characters was properly identified, and the donkey signs. The Mary one said I am Mary and my child was napalmed in Vietnam, and she carried a bloody doll.... Anyway, the next day we came back with these masks that weren't masks anymore, that didn't disguise our faces. The cops didn't know what to do. We could be identified so they couldn't move us off the sidewalks. We didn't stand still, we moved like everybody else. A big crowd got together, and by then there was a sensation and there were so many people that you could hardly move. We made several attempts to get up into the church to deposit our doll, which we had told them we wanted to give to Cardinal Spellman. He was the big cardinal in New York, in that church, St. Patrick's.... So anyway we tried to get up there and they blocked our way every time. Finally we just deposited it on the lower step. The doll was immediately snapped up by a plain clothes policeman. he didn't know what to do with it so he brought it to the Lost and Found and some smart *Village Voice* journalist followed him and found the doll.' — (Schumann, interview, '79.)

'A guy in a windbreaker screamed,"When are you going to do this in Hanoi?" A young Marine stood on the cathedral steps, his face devoid of color, biting his lip. "You know what they are – animals, a bunch of animals. I have friends dying over there." The coldness caused the nose of one of the protesters to run. The marine pointed to him "Look at that guy with the snot running down his face – Christ, what a bunch of animals." A young boy asked his father what the group was doing and the man replied, "Oh, they just hate Catholics, son."' — (Flaherty, loc. cit.)

'Ever since Cardinal Spellman's call for "victory" in Vietnam, St. Patrick's Cathedral has been the scene of peace demonstrations. The first was ... by members of the Bread and Puppet Theater.... About a week later 180 people under the sponsorship of the Catholic Peace Fellowship picketed the Cardinal's office around the corner from St. Patrick's.' — (Cakars, *Mass Protest, WIN*, February 10, '67.)

There was a third demonstration, January 22, '67.[3]

---

[3]. 'The mass began at 10:00 as per schedule and proceeded with the usual rites. Elderly ushers led latecomers to their seats in the main body of the cathedral, visitors passed by along side aisles, and the vaulted ceiling echoed the sounds of chanting, of hymns, and of the movements of the reverent. According to instructions in the program provided for the mass, the people rose to stand together after the homily and the priest turned to shut off the pulpit light.

At that moment the demonstrators, who had been sitting near the center aisle towards the front of the cathedral, stepped into the aisle, turned, and began walking back towards the Fifth Avenue exits. Those who were able removed two-by-three-foot reproductions of a weeping Vietnamese child from under their coats and held them at chest level as they walked. Above the child were the words "Thou shalt not kill," and below, "Vietnam."

The St. Patrick's caper was Schumann's last demonstration to get much press notice. This wasn't because there was any radical decrease in the amount of his demonstrating in '67, although there probably was some – I know of a dozen demonstrations of his in '66, only of eight in '67. But on the one hand, Movement agitation, partly due to the increased influence of the campus New Left on its pacifist core, was shifting its accent from legal demonstrations expressing disagreement to illegal protest actions in the nature of non-violent resistance, e.g. resistance to the draft, which besides absorbing some of the energy that might otherwise have gone into legal protest was more newsworthy; on the other hand, legal demonstration to a considerable extent came under the hippie influence that I first noted for the November 5, '66 demonstration, which to some extent may

---

Few of the churchgoers saw the pictures, however, since all but several were immediately taken from the demonstrators by detectives in Sunday attire who had been sitting near them. What those who were close enough to the aisle did see was a group of about fifty people walking determinedly to the rear of the cathedral. The only way to distinguish demonstrator from detective was by watching to see who was holding whom by the arm, shoulder or neck. All walked quickly and silently, and faces looked grimly serious. There was no visible resistance by any of the demonstrators, and no sounds but those of footsteps, of the confiscated pictures rustling and of the whispers and movements among the congregation as they sensed something happening.

The entire demonstration lasted no more than a minute and ended for those within the cathedral as an usher replaced the velvet rope across the aisle after the last of the outsiders had passed by. They could not see the 23 demonstrators in the entrance room within the North-west door, where they were held for some minutes until paddy wagons and police cars were brought to carry them to the stationhouse.

Inside, the Reverend officiating interrupted the mass to calm those present, many of whom were only beginning to understand that something out of the ordinary had occurred. The mass was resumed immediately and completed without further incident.

Reading a prayer during the last parts of the observance, the priest said for his people: "Deliver us, we beg you, O Lord, from every evil, past, present, and to come, and ... in your mercy grant peace in our days, that by your compassionate aid we may be ever free from sin and sheltered from all turmoil."

"Amen," responded the people. – Virginia Moore.

* * *

Obviously the police had been informed in advance despite an effort to keep the demonstration secret. Each arresting officer even had a typed out list of charges to read to those he arrested. The only thing they were not prepared for was the number of demonstrators. Two paddy wagons proved insufficient to contain the 23 and several had to be taken away in squad cars.

Those arrested were made to wait about eleven hours before they were arraigned. Part of the reason for the wait may have been the fact that a liberal Jewish judge was presiding earlier in the day and was replaced in the evening by a Catholic who felt it necessary to accuse the defendants, one of the most "respectable" group of demonstrators ever assembled, of never having heard of the freedom of religion before releasing them on $500 bail apiece.

A group calling itself the Ad Hoc Catholic Committee Against the War in Vietnam has decided to continue confronting St. Patrick's and is planning to picket there every Sunday. – M.C.' — (V. Moore, M. Cakars, *Mass Protest*, WIN, February 10, '67.)

have kept Schumann away, but which in any case tended to attract more attention than Schumann's quieter displays. As long as the Old Left and the pacifists separately and in coalition dominated the New York and Washington Movement street agitation, Schumann stood at the center of it: he naturally represented them. But this from now on was no longer the case. (A.J. Muste, the valuable figurehead of that coalition, died February 11, '67.) He was no longer quite so active; the action no longer was quite of the kind that his contributions would represent; other kinds of action both were more in the spirit of the times and more spectacular and newsworthy. Moreover, the bigger demonstrations in '67 tended to be gigantic, with no longer just tens but hundreds of thousands of participants: on that scale and given the emotional impact of such demonstrations, Schumann's puppets could no longer define or dominate them: they disappeared: the mass of the demonstrators became the overwhelmingly dominant and effective feature – and point – of the demonstrations.

22. April '67. First giant demonstration. Hippie aspects reported on, Schumann's contribution goes unnoticed.

He recalls (interview, '79) parading the 'Grey Lady' puppets he was rehearsing with in January '67 (*Village Voice*, January 19) for a February 2 'Angry Arts' show (his Bach Cantata *#140*) 'in some kind of outside action' during the rehearsals. Some parade in the Washington Square area associated with the program. 'Rev. Schaef & the Bread & Puppet Theatre on Vietnam' given January 8 at the Washington Square Methodist Church (*Village Voice*, January 5)? A parade on the occasion of that Angry Arts Week (January 29-February 2), sponsored by the 'Painters & Writers Protest Organization'?

Hanoi had – for the first time – been bombarded in December '66, the *New York Times* in a noted account reporting on the civilian casualties: the bombardments sabotaged ongoing secret negotiations for a halt in bombardments. The air attacks on North Vietnam were continued and intensified in February '67. March 2, Robert Kennedy; breaking with the administration, in the Senate advocated a halt in the bombings.

The Bread and Puppet Theatre led a 'stop the bombing' march protesting against the 'new escalation' to a ditto rally at St. Marks in the Bouwerie, march and rally under the auspices of the Lower East Side Mobilization for Peace Action (LEMPA), on March 11.

In April, Schumann was gearing up for the New York 'Spring Mobilization' April 15 – advertising (*Village Voice*, April 6, '67) for 'many' volunteers, to be rehearsed the two days before the Sunday demonstration, an assembly in Sheep Meadow, Central Park, at which there was to be a 'Peace Fair', a crosstown march to the U.N., and a rally there, to be addressed by King, Stokely Carmichael and others. This was part of an as it turned out eminently successful national program of the new Mobilization Committee's.[1]

---

1. 'The Easter Sunday be-in in Central Park was incredible; thousands of kids handing you flowers, burning incense, smoking grass, taking acid, passing drugs around right out in the open, taking their clothes off and rolling around on the ground, painting their bodies and faces with Day-Glo, doing Far East-type chants, playing with their toys – balloons and pinwheels and sheriff's badges and Frisbees. They could stand there staring at each other for hours without moving. As I said before, that had always fascinated me the way people could sit by a window or on a porch all day and look out and never be bored, but then if they went to a movie or a play, they suddenly objected to being bored. I always felt that a very slow film could be just as interesting as a porch-sit if you thought about it the same way. And now all these kids on acid were demonstrating the exact same thing.

Suggesting unexpectedly wide Vietnam-weariness, the demonstrations helped stimulate the 'insurgent political campaigns' of '68. (Powers, *The War*.) Sixty-five thousand marched in San Francisco from west of, a quarter to half a million in New York from east of the Mississippi. The scale of the New York demonstration was something new. At Sheep Meadow, draft cards – 175 of them – were burned, overfulfilling a Cornell draft card burning pledge of March 2 – though in other circuits convictions under it had been upheld, the draft card burning law of '65 had the preceding week been held unconstitutional by the U.S. Court of Appeals for the First Circuit. But in an overall way the 'Peace Fair' seems to' have been a hippie event, at least so it seemed to the *New York Times* reporter:

'There were several floats in the parade, including one on which Peter Seeger, the folk singer, rode with a number of children. They sang folk songs like "This Land is Your Land," as they rolled along the line of march.... (A) be-in of several thousand preced(ed) (the) start of (the) parade in the southeast corner of Sheep Meadow: dancing and singing to the music of guitars, flutes and drums. Many of the young people had painted their faces and legs with poster paints. The sweet smell of cooking bananas hung over the group.'

The New York press – *WIN*, the *National Guardian*, *The Militant*, the *New York Post*, the *New York Times*, the *Village Voice*, the *Daily News* – does not report what Schumann did, and he does not remember. I dare say it went unnoticed in a very real sense.

Since the beginning of the year when Thomas Hoving became Parks Commissioner, the kids were using the parks a lot more – and this be-in was the ultimate use so far. In the middle of April, though, Hoving was scheduled to become director of the Metropolitan, and he seemed to be trying to temper his Pop image a little now, going around reassuring people that he wasn't going to turn the Met into a big "happening."

At the end of April there was another be-in – not as big as the Easter one, but big enough so everybody was looking forward to a fantastic summer in the park.' — (Warhol, *POPism*, 1980.)

23. April-May '67. Hippies vs. hardhats (the People) and the Blacks and Browns.

An apercu of New York City street agitation that spring other than the Mobilization suggests he had suddenly become unfashionable. A polarization had occurred, and not only was the People, for a pacific appeal to which his work was designed, on the other side, but the terms of the polarization were such that he could hardly operate within it: his own side was preempted.

A Loyalty Day parade put on by the Veterans of Foreign Wars was on April 29th to show the country that the Spring Mobilization outturn notwithstanding New York City stood behind our boys: the pitiful total of 7,500 paraders — combined totals for Brooklyn and Manhattan — did not disprove this but was embarrassing, so for Patriot's Day, May 13th, a March to Support Our Boys in Vietnam was to furnish the proof. This time, a in 1966 terms decent, 20,000 turned out. A large percentage of them, according to Powers, *The War*, were 'union members, traditionally Democrats and part of the liberal coalition that had dominated American politics since 1932.' There were incidents of violence between the marchers and hippies. (McNeill, 'Armed Forces Parade: Limits of Flower Power,' *Village Voice*, May 25, '67.) March 20th, Armed Forces Day, traditionally the date of military parades, had been declared Flower Power Day[1] by the sponsors of counter-demonstrations that day, the committee for Non-Violent Action (CNVA) and the Workshop in Non-Violence (WIN), representing the pacifist wing of the Movement but anxious 'to bring the hippies into the peace camp' (McNeill, loc. cit.), but when, because of the Patriot's Day troubles, these sponsors, wishing to avoid unpleasantness, withheld their support, Flower Power Day shrunk into a picnic in the park, Lampe's Headfeed,[2] and the unpleasantness was

---

1. 'Now as summer approaches most of the psychedelic community here continues to move from the Hinyana (groove straight forward Nirvana, baby, and skip the planet) to the Mahayana (return to history from those Nirvanic Gates, O Ye Bodhisattvas, and help out) .... Many in the community are expected to attend the Flower Power Day festivities Saturday, May 29 (I guess it should be "May 20" (SSB)), which begin with a Headfeed at 11 a.m. near the Delacorte Theatre off 81st in Central Park – and end with a mammoth Zapping of the Armed Forces Day soldiers as they march down fifth Avenue. Zapping with love: perhaps chicks will spring ecstatically from the crowds and poke flowers into rifle barrels – or men will stretch flower chains across the avenue. Others may have a meditation in Central Park on Buddha's Birthday – May 23.' — (K. Lampe, *East Village Other*, May 15-June 1, '67.)
2. Actually there were some Flower Power demonstrations. The military parade was greeted by chants of 'make love, not war' at 78th Street, and in Central Park members of WIN 'played guitar, preached love and distributed flowers' (*New York Times*, May 21.) Twelve flower people climbed on the Alice in Wonderland statue near 76th Street

delayed until Memorial Day, May 30th, when a gathering of flower people in Tompkins Square Park, singing hare krishna and waiting for the summer's first rock concert to start (*East Village Other*, extra of June 3) was attacked by Captain Fink's 9th Precinct forces, acting on the complaint of residents – according to the *East Village Other* a naturalized person of Slavic descent. Two days later, June 1st, Black and/or Latino kids in that same park threw beer cans at and heckled the Pageant Players, who a year earlier (June 3, 4, '65) had played there to an apparently appreciative audience – the Pageant Players played down the incidents, tracing them to a divergence in musical taste.[3] They performed *King Con, The War Monster, James Bond*.

Essentially, that spring, a hippified Movement confronted not only a hostile, acerbatedly patriotic white working class, but also an antagonistic sub-proletariat of Blacks and Latinos.

Though this doesn't mean there can't have been any, I know of no demonstration of Schumann's (other than in the Mobilization) that spring.

(flower people thought Alice had eaten of the mushroom), one of them getting a summons, eight flower people danced in a witching circle in front of the Metropolitan Museum. (ibid).

3. 'There was a hostile and frantic atmosphere, which may have been due to the fact that we are an all-white group, or to the tensions left over from Tuesday's troubles on the grass. In any case, we are a street theater group, and we are used to heckling, thrown objects, people coming up on the stage, and the like. We know how to handle it peaceably, and we did so that evening. The first two plays were well-received. The third play was not as well-received, though the audience watched throughout. Then, we tried an experiment. We asked for audience participation, in an improvisation about Tuesday's bust-in in the park. It did not play well, and it may have been a mistake to perform it. But it did play without interruption, from beginning to end. As it ended, a knife-fight between two Puerto Ricans broke out in the audience. However, it was quickly stopped, and the crowd waited for the next show. The Pageant Players, having finished their performance, left the park. I returned about 20 minutes later, to discover a white folk-rock group on stage, and an angry crowd of Puerto Ricans demanding Latin music. Some began throwing things, while others set up their own music on Hoving's Hill, with turned-over garbage barrels. The folk-rock group had to finish up behind the lowered, steel, band-shell curtain, amidst great hostility. Meanwhile, a Christine Jorgensen-type woman had lured a huge crowd to her, voluntarily . . .'
— (letter, signature missing, *East Village Other*, June 15-July 1, '67.).

24. Summer '67. Schumann fades out of the picture with a gesture toward the people — militant Latinos.

His activities during the summer suggest that while in the main and on the whole he had given up on New York City, he did make some attempt, opportunity arose, to bridge the gap I have indicated, to work within the polarization on his own terms.[1]

Cesar Chavez' Farm Workers Union had in September of '65 initiated a strike against major grape growers in the San Joaquin Valley, had tried to reenforce it by a national grape boycott, still on in the summer and fall of '67. Schumann remembers doing a Grape Strike parade, and that it was part of a Puerto Rico Day parade:

'That was not an early demonstration, that was one that was quite late – that must have been in the late '60s, that one. I remember that it was during the grape strikes, when the Huelga people had come to New York from the West Coast – the Cesar Chavez people. And they asked us to participate in the Puerto Rican Day thing and they gave us a flatbed truck to perform on and we performed a continuous skit about the grape strike on the back of the truck.'

(Schumann, interview, '82.)

'As far as I can remember we were in every major demonstration and a couple of minor ones like the Puerto Rican Day parade. That I remember really well. We were asked to represent the farm workers ... and we made this flatbed truck little show and that was really funny because it was very lively and it was all Miss Puerto Rico and all these beauty queens and the bands and stuff and then there was us.... Anyway it was the landlord and the poor farmer and the landlord kept beating up the farmer and the farmer would strike back. And it was a fairly simple routine done over and over again. I remember it, I think I was the farmer and it was great because it was really like rabble-rousing, it was a rabble-rousing trip and it wasn't stylized at all. It was really playing to the audience and it was really exciting to do. It was fun to do because right there were just thousands of people and really playing up to the audience. I don't think we even had masks on. It was a very simplistic.... Easily understood by everybody.'

(Ernstthal, interview, '79.)

Luis Miguel Valdez, director of the El Campesino, was in New York City that summer. He is Schumann's likely contact with the La Huelga people,

---

[1]. This was the summer of the Negro riots in Newark across the river (July 9-15) – mainly looting and arson, with more than 20 black people killed, some 1,200 injured, nearly 1,300 arrested (*Village Voice*, July 20, '67.): 3,000 national guardsmen, 375 state troopers.

Out of several thousand words of Johnson's State of the Union report to Congress in the spring of '67 forty-five deal with civil rights. The stress of the speech was on the Safe Streets and Crime Control Act he was going to submit: 'Our country's laws must be respected. Order must be maintained.'

and Schumann probably did his parade that year — June 5th. He wasn't in New York the next two summers. It was an unusual type of show for him to do — like his '64 rent strike Punch and Judys, but also in El Campesino style.

Apparently, he marched for the Chicanos again that fall: the caption under a photo (*WIN*, January 15, '68) of Uncle Fatso in a medium-high black hat on the white band around the top of which is written 'Guimarra' says it's a player of the Bread and Puppet Theatre 'during a demonstration last autumn in support of La Huelga, at the Hudson River pier in Manhattan where the grapes of the struck vineyard were unloaded'.[2]

I am surprised to hear that grapes came by boat to New York in '67, but however they arrived, greeting them by that very specific reference to their painful place of harvest was a moving gesture.

Photographs of Gerhard Gscheidle's, one of which on its back carries the note 'Farmworker Rally/Bread & Puppet Theatre/NYC 1975' show Uncle Fatso, one-armed and threadbare but dapper, his pants striped, a sign across his chest proclaiming him El Patron, loping down the white stripe of a midtown street, on a rope attached to his cigar-carrying right, leading The Farm Worker (a woman without mask, so labelled). A figure with a giant maskhead, the face of a modest functionary, a cop mask, something along the lines of a police cap on his head wearing a uniform coat, in his hand carrying a giant bundle labeled 'lettuce' follows them. Chavez was trying to impose a nationwide boycott of Sacramento Valley lettuce. Schumann's support of La Huelga was the only time he had anything to do with the labor movement, but in fact there hasn't been much labor movement in the U.S. since John L. Lewis' coal strike during World War II.

There was another Hiroshima Day parade in New York City that

---

2. Maury Englander of *WIN* in an accompanying article (*The Third Christmas of La Huelga*) tells his readers of a visit in December '67 to the United Farm Workers headquarters in Delano, California:

'One man in his mid-twenties had been picking fruit since he was twelve. Now with a wife and six children he is a striker. As he talked, he kept glancing at the clock. It was a bit after 9:00 and he was due to begin his shift of picketing at the Guimarra vineyards, some 45 miles away, at ten. At 6:00 the next morning they would be relieved by another crew. For the last 27 months the picketing has continued around the clock, seven days a week. It hasn't been easy. Picketers have frequently been attacked; one was run down by a truck. In the beginning it was necessary to go to court to overrule the county law that required pickets to stand fifty feet apart along the road and forbade the use of bullhorns. Guimarra has been bringing workers in from other parts of the state. Most of them knew nothing of the strike and the bullhorns were the only means of informing them. Whole crews have walked off the job when they found out what was happening. But the job of organizing farm workers has a long hard road ahead.... For more than a thousand men, women and children of Delano, La Huelga has become a daily fact of life. For the past 27 months they have quietly fought their battle for a decent wage and a chance for.... The crisis will come in the spring when the next grape crop will begin.' — (Englander, loc. cit.)

August 6. It was one of the very few Movement stirrings there that summer,[3] and it was of a particularly piteous sort, the commemoration of the attack on Hiroshima being coupled with support of an army physician that had refused service in Vietnam: 'Demand that Dr. Levy be released on bail pending appeal' (from the parade advertisement, *Village Voice*, July 27, '67.). A New York Medical Committee to End the War in Vietnam was among the sponsors. Schumann wasn't there,[4] he was at the 'Youth,

---

3. I know of only two Movement affairs, both at the Village Theatre on Second Avenue (air conditioned, as the ad for the first of them in the *Village Voice*, August 17, points out). The first on August 19 was something chairmanned by Dave Dellinger, sponsored by the National Mobilization and Fifth Avenue Committees, at which H. Rap Brown of SNCC in rather violent terms discussed 'Vietnam and Black America' with the Episcopal Peace Fellowship's Rev. Thomas Lee Hays. There were messages from CORE and from Women Strike for Peace. At the second, on August 24, with the benefits to go, via the Baldwin Benefit Committee, to the 'Harlem Six' and to the 'Black Community of Dorchester County, South Carolina', and with entertainment by Ossie Davis, Dick Davey, the Frank Mitchell Quintet and Bob and Joe, James Baldwin gave 'his first major address in two years.' (*Village Voice*, same issue.) It was called 'No One Heard the Poet. A Comment on Vietnam.'

4. While the Bread and Puppet Theatre was up in Canada, some unpatriotic troublemakers were busy back down in New York:
'It was exactly 12 noon on Sunday, August 6, 1967 – the 22nd anniversary of the A-bombing of Hiroshima. Besides the whoosh of rubber on the West Side Highway, the waterfront was quiet. Two gray destroyers were tied up to the Italian Line's Pier 90 at 50th Street. One was the Italian Nave San Giorgio; the other was the USS Newman K. Perry. Outside on 12th Avenue, police busied themselves with barricades. Detectives milled around – so did reporters. A paddy wagon was parked dockside.

Just north of the pier, a dozen pickets appeared. They wore black armbands and carried signs. The lead picket was a Negro. Her sign said: "DESTROYERS DESTROY PEOPLE."

A little while later, another dozen people approached the pier. They wore black hooded blouses and ashen gray death-head masks on the backs of their heads. They rang tiny bells and clashed hand cymbals.

Both groups, members of the National Mobilization Committee's Direct Action Project, were assigned to the same barricaded area. The masked mourners formed a small circle. Those in mufti marched clockwise around them. The bells tinkled. The signs screamed.
"DANGER, SHIP OF DEATH."
"Tinkle, tinkle, rrring . . .'
"THIS SHIP IS NOT A TOY.'
"Tinke . . .'
"HIROSHIMA – AUGUST 6, 1945/VIETNAM – AUG 6, 1967."
At one o'clock, the general public – mostly families on outings – began lining up to visit the American ship. The police had constructed a maze of wooden barriers and the sheepish visitors began to work their way through it. Behind them came the masked mourners vibrating their bells.

The tingling 12-tone caterpillar inched forward. There was an air of suspense as detectives from the City's "subversive squad" fanned out on the pier. The caterpillar kept moving – until it reached the gangplank of the destroyer.

Commander John A. Smith strode smartly down from his ship to repulse the boarding partly. "I'm going to deny your visit until general visiting is secured," he said. "In view of your aims stated here," Smith waved a yellow flyer, "you appear to be under a mis-

Joy, Peace Day' that Sunday, at Expo '67 in Montreal.[4] On their way to the World's Fair, though, his group participated in a Champlain-to-Montreal Peace Walk:

'Puppets on Peace Walk. The Bread and Puppet Theatre will observe Hiroshima Day by participating in the Champlain-to-Montreal Peace Walk and giving a performance at the arrival rally on Saturday August 5th. New York performances are suspended until August 12. Those wishing to attend the walk or rally may call New York CNVA....' (Notice, *Village Voice*, August 3, '67.)

The 'Peace Pilgrimage' (*WIN*, June 16, '67.) was an afternoon border

---

conception as to the mission and general purpose of a destroyer in the United States Navy, and I will be happy to personally escort you after we permit the large group waiting outside to make their tour."

Rodney Robinson, bearded 23-year old leader of the dirgeful demonstrators, protested that the group wanted "no special privileges."

Commander Smith was adamant. '... WE ARE ONLY CARRYING OUT THE POLICY OF THE UNITED STATES GOVERNMENT.'

Robinson persisted. Smith and his officers were up-tight – so were the police. For awhile, it was a draw. The demonstrators blocked both gangplanks. They were pushed back by a 20-man shoving detail from the destroyer. The public trickled on and off. Officers and enlisted men monitored the scene from the ship. The demonstrators sat down. The police and the navy conferred. The dockmaster arrived, but declined to press charges. The police said they had no case unless someone pressed charges. The pickets sang. the shoving detail shoved some more. It was still a draw.

Then, the demonstrators dropped the papier-mache masks over their faces – violating a section of the Penal Code prohibiting masquerading by three or more persons. The fuzz moved in. One by one, they scooped up the masked figures with stretchers and dumped them head first into the paddy wagon.

The crowd cheered. From inside the wagon came a faint, insistent, dirgeful tingling – and superimposed on this, the sound of singing:
"WE ARE NOT AFRAID..."
"WE SHALL END THIS WAR..."
"WE SHALL BAN THE BOMB SOME DAY..."

The paddy wagon drove off. Pier 90 returned to normal. Burly boilertender David St. Louis clocked the 680th visitor of the day. He was Japanese.' — (L. Kent, '*The Day of Hiroshima: A Visit to a Destroyer*,' *Village Voice*, August 10, '67, Copyright. L. Kent, 1967.)

Robinson's people had been tricked. Robinson, one of Schumann's puppeteers (Schumann, interview, '82) knew the penal code statute, but had relied on the police's earlier disclaimer of jurisdiction on the pier – when they had been asked to protect the demonstrators against molestation from the sailors. The masks were Schumann's.

5. 'The Montreal Expo had opened in May on the banks of the St. Lawrence River with six of my Self-Portraits up there at the U.S. Pavilion, and I flew up to Canada with John de Menil and Fred in Mr. de Menil's jet to see them.

The American pavilion was Buckminster Fuller's big geodesic dome, with its aluminum shades catching the sun, and an Apollo space capsule and a long free-span escalator. Those were things like you'd expect to find at an international exposition. What was unusual was that the rest of the American show was almost completely Pop – it was called Creative America. I remember thinking as I looked around it that there weren't two separate societies in the United States anymore – one official and heavy and "meaningful" and the other frivolous and Pop. People used to pretend that the millions of rock-and-roll 45's the

crossing, bringing money and medical supplies 'for civilian relief in all parts of Vietnam' to the Canadian Quakers. At the Youth, Joy and Peace celebration, they performed *King Story*, and did their parade show with the Shark Plane attacking the Vietnamese Ladies.

---

kids bought every year somehow didn't count, but that what an economist at Harvard or some other place like that said, did. So this U.S. exhibit was like an official acknowledgement that people would rather see media celebrities than anything else.

In the way of art there were works by Rauschenberg and Stella and Poons and Zox and Motherwell and D'Arcangelo and Dine and Rosenquist and Johns and Oldenburg. But a lot of the show was pop culture itself – movies and blow-ups of stars, and props and folk art and American Indian art and Elvis Presley's guitar and Joan Baez's guitar. And these things weren't just *part* of the exhibit; they *were* the exhibit – Pop America *was* America, completely.

The old idea used to be that intellectuals didn't know what was going on in the other society – popular culture. Those scenes in early rock-and-roll movies were so dated now, where the old fogies would hear rock and roll for the first time and start tapping their feet and say, "That's catchy. What did you say you called it? 'Rock and ... *roll*?' " When Thomas Hoving, the director of the Metropolitan, talked about an exhibit there that included three busts of ancient Egyptian princesses, he referred to them offhandedly as "The Supremes." Everybody was part of the same culture now. Pop references let people know that *they* were what was happening, that they didn't have to *read* a book to be part of culture – all they had to do was *buy* it (or a record or a TV set or a movie ticket).'
— (Warhol, *POPism*, 1980.)

25. August-September '67. The hippie provocateur, the digger, appears on the New York scene.

The Haight-Ashbury scene was changing in '67. The flower child's LSD-liberated imagination and pot-calmed feelings were giving way to the nervous energy of speed. This didn't yet make for the violence animating the heroin trade, but it made for a style of confrontation, nervous irony, cunning wit. The point was no longer a gaily playful display of lovingness and of how one was out of it all, paradigmatic theatre, as for instance by a parade celebrating a declaration of the end of the war, but a theatre in which the opponent would participate in the role of fool: making evident to tv watchers the foolishness of violence. This required provocation. The apostles of the new style were the San Francisco diggers. The *Village Voice* salutes their arrival on the local scene in September '67.[1] Their first, and only, big action was the levitation of the Pentagon, October 21st, the only peace demonstration that Schumann participated in that fall, his only one other than the October grape strike one on the piers that I know of.[2]

---

1. Cf. Appendix XVIII.
2. 'During the fall of 1967 the mood of that broad range of activists who referred to themselves as The Movement underwent a sea change. They blamed their failures on themselves, argued that a politics that feared violence was self-defeating, and sought to harden themselves for an escalating struggle.... Those opposed to the war were no longer trying to express a position on the war, to literally *demonstrate* a point of view, but to end it.... Four major demonstrations were held, varying in size from a few hundred to perhaps 75,000, which differed from earlier actions in their militance. Meetings of demonstrators and police had ended in violence before, but now activists expected, planned for, and in a handful of cases even provoked violence. It is important to remember how tentative and symbolic these efforts were; the faintest attempt to push through a police line was sure to result in club-swinging. Occasionally windows were broken, or bottles thrown from the depths of a crowd. In most cases the violence of demonstrators was entirely theatrical, consisting of masses of young men and women pushing, running, waving flags at the end of poles, and shouting slogans.... Middle-class, middle aged, and traditionally liberal elements played almost no part in the four major street actions of the fall of 1967, marking the end of a long transition from liberals to radicals, and from old to young. When the focus of movement activity shifted from civil rights to the war, and from the war as a failure of policy to the war as a symptom of a sick and cruel society, older white and black elements gradually fell to the side.... Opposition to the war in the fall of 1967 was wider than ever, and yet the range of those who took an active part in demonstrations was dramatically narrower than it had been even six months earlier.' — (Th. Power, *The War*.)

26. October '67. Demonstration as formally insurrectionary, military action swamps gentle Schumann demonstration, his last participation in a big peace demonstration for $3\frac{1}{2}$ years.

At the national level, the Mobilization Committee, exhilarated by its April success, i.e. the magnitude of the demonstrations, not any effect of theirs on the war, had since May been planning a repeat on an even bigger scale — there were hopes for a million demonstrators — in Washington, October 21st. Over the summer, more radical elements — the initiatives came from California, but it was a national New Left college campus drive — developed plans for agitation consisting not of shows of opinion in opposition to the war but of actual interference with the war effort, namely a turning in of draft cards and the blocking of access to induction centers: during a Stop the Draft Week, October 16-21. The two projects were coordinated on an organization and on a propaganda level. David Dellinger of the Mobilization Committee asked Jerry Rubin, involved in the anti-draft project:

'to be director for the Washington march, acting as a point of glancing contact between the two. Rubin, with his talent for organizing protests with a certain aesthetic bite, suggested that the October 21 demonstration be held not at the Capitol, but at the Pentagon, the heart and brain of the war machine. The card turn-in on the 16th, the attempts to close down induction centers on following days, and the demonstration at the Pentagon would thus focus on the growing militarization of American society.' (Powers, *The War*.)

'Something that borders on more than symbolic protest' (the terms of a California promoter of the Stop the Draft Week) was to be combined with what the SDS at a June convention had criticized as 'just public expressions of belief.' The SDS and other New Left radicals were urging that action both at induction centers and at the Pentagon step across that border, be a sort actually, if only briefly, 'closing them down.' The Mobilizing Committee

'resolved these strategic disputes by failing to choose among them. The demonstration would begin with a rally at the Lincoln Memorial, would march across the Potomac on the Arlington Memorial Bridge and proceed to the North Parking Lot of the Pentagon where a second rally would be held. At four o'clock, with only an hour or so of daylight remaining, the demonstration would culminate with a nonviolent sit-in where those inclined would be arrested for civil disobedience.' (Th. Powers, *The War*.)

As the Reverend Thomas Hays on behalf of the pacifists and other moderate sponsors put it:

'Individuals will act on their consciences and in their own personal styles. Not all people will take part in the massive sit-in at the Pentagon, and we are not asking people to come to Washington solely on this basis. Those who do not block the Pentagon will surround it in a massive peace-in of picketing, vigiling, music, drama, and rallies.' (Powers, ibid.)

As it turned out, neither the pacifist spectacle of dignified, symbolically significant non-violent acts of civil disobedience, nor the pacifist-Old Left spectacle of the loving spirit (in this case levitating the Pentagon) prevailed: in the media. The turnout was by now-prevailing standards slight (not much above 50,000), the fear or dislike of violence probably keeping away many middle-aged people, and what prevailed, i.e. generated the dominant image that swamped all else was the besieging of the Pentagon:

'There were two main thrusts of activity.... The first was a traditional rally with traditional speeches at the Lincoln Memorial, followed by a mass march across the Arlington Memorial Bridge to the Pentagon in Virginia, where a second rally was held, with more speeches. The speech-making was a good deal more militant than it had been in the past – at the Lincoln Memorial, John Lewis, the first chairman of SNCC, asked for a moment's silence in memory of Che Guevara ... killed ... two weeks earlier; at the Pentagon, Carl Davidson said draft boards would burn—but the rallies themselves were orderly, a "protest" in the familiar mode of "disobedients" expressing an alternate point of view to the public at large and the powers that be. The second main thrust ... was much smaller, involving four to five thousand people at the very most, who attempted to blockade the Pentagon and, briefly, actually invaded its very halls. Just after crossing the bridge ... perhaps a thousand SDS people and New York radicals loosely organized as the Revolutionary Contingent broke from the main body of marchers, moved at a run through the woods between the Potomac and the Pentagon, made a brief feint toward federal troops ..., were turned back ..., felled a fence ... and streamed across the mall to the main steps of the Pentagon. A line of military police was pushed back.... The initial series of rushes ... establish(ed) a beachhead of sorts which was to remain, with some erosion, for the following thirty-two hours.... The rest of the demonstration was a gradual whittling down of these original salients.' (Powers, *The War*.)

A good deal of brutality by soldiers and federal marshals occurred. The demonstrators didn't fight back. But they insisted on staying where they were not supposed to be. The spectacle presented was that of a threat to the federal government and to its military branch in particular, and of a violent elimination of this threat. It was a theatrical spectacle at least inasmuch as the threat was – and was by everyone known to be – illusory. The illusion was created. To create this illusion was the point of the action.[1] 647 people were arrested. The Washington and New York

---

[1] 'OCTOBER 20, 1967: THE PENTAGON BESIEGED. Television transmitted it as an anti-war spectacle (significantly, the networks refused to permit live coverage); it was for those present a high drama of interwoven scenarios. One of every 2,000 Americans – the nation has approximately the same number of millionaires – were gathered at the Lincoln Memorial. They marched across the Potomac and up to the malls of the Pentagon,

papers (other than the radical ones, of course) concurred on two points: the action was deplorable and ugly, the demonstrators were young. The papers ignored the rallies and speeches.

'The throng that assembled here to-day to protest ... was an outpouring of the New Left and a wide array of college students. There was only a sprinkling of

---

where cyclone fences, topped with barbed wire, had been erected. Swiftly the fences went down as "demonstrators" moved to confront, close beneath the building's Mussolinian facade, an involuntary cast placed there by Robert Strange McNamara: several thousand paratroopers, military police, and federal marshalls. The scenario was to disrupt pentagon operations as fully as possible without resort to arms. Defense Secretary McNamara, who was peering from a window, had of course the *force majeure*. But the *force démonstratif* gained the initiative, up to the point where the military used its singular skills. Scaling ropes, flanking maneuvers, inundation by sheer numbers were but part of the repertoire of this humoristic, motley, and audacious legion. The yellow submarine of the hippies, 12 feet long, was passed over heads toward the doors. Smaller contingents of troops were surrounded, talked to, pressed in so tightly they could not use their weapons, allowed to retreat only in disorderly flight, perhaps with helmets swiped or a flower in a rifle barrel. Posters and slogans remembering Che appeared on abutments. Tens of thousands alternated "America the Beautiful" with an ironic "Sieg Heil!" salute chanted to commanding officers on the battlements. Yippies, banners proclaiming solidarity and a victory more than pyrrhic (*We Have One*), moved upon the portals chanting: "Out, Demon, Out!" to a strange music. Before the Pentagon under a golden sun in a crisp breeze, the flag of the Vietnamese National Liberation Front fluttered, blue and red with a gold star. A contingent with flags penetrated through a side door, were beaten at once and expelled. Everywhere there pervaded a spirit of Epic Theatre (so many actions and performers, so much detached awareness of one's deeds even as one acted), even to a Brechtian "narrator" who stood with a bullhorn where he had a commanding view and laconically interpreted events for the majority who could not summon a whole view. The troops tried to seize the narrator; with a little help from his friends he evaded them, not once losing his cool; his ironic commentary set the context for the besiegers. Low overhead the helicopters of the press circled and, visible in their doorways, photographers winding cameras and "shooting" (one constantly recalled the gunship whirlies in 'Nam); the actors in this way too reminded continually of the present moment as history for the making. Sometimes soldiers (their regulation issue: mufti and gasmasks, teargas guns, fixed sheathed bayonets) were brought to admit softly their sympathy for the "protest." And although I did not witness it, this probably happened, as many say it did: A line of troops had been ordered to hold a long incline leading to the Pentagon's doors. Already they'd repulsed several attempts on their line. Now a hippy couple were before them and began to make love. Protestors nearby stood relaxed, and as the boy and girl rubbed each other, kissing deeply, the soldiers grew transfixed, with the couple reaching into shirts and down trousers, loosening clothing, approaching THE ACT. From shock or desire or both, the soldiers were witless when suddenly the demonstrators pierced the military line with a rush, hurling these troops aside to penetrate the doors by the thousands. On the six o'clock news, it perhaps all looked like damnfool spectacle. But not to those there: not to the Pentagon "insiders," and not to that one American in 2,000 who shortly returned to those little Pentagons – the draft boards, the firms profiting from manufacture of terroristic weapons and from exploitation, schools and labs with Defense Department contracts across the land. October 20, 1967 could be said to mark the end of the mass sterile protest parade and the start of an open-ended era of mass, infectious radical dramaturgy.' — (Baxandall, *Spectacles and Scenarios: A Dramaturgy of Radical Activity, Tulane Drama Review* #44, summer 1969. Copyright *The Drama Review* 1969.)

Americans past the age of 30. The predominance of young people was in contrast to the last big peace march here one year ago, when conservatively dressed, middle-aged men and women far outnumbered the young militants. Last year's demonstration was a decorous march around the White House.'

(Herbers, 'Youth Dominates Capital Throng,' *New York Times*, October 22, '67.)

The Bread and Puppet Theatre performed – along with Peter, Paul and Mary, Barbara Dane and Phil Ochs – at the decorous Lincoln Memorial rally. *The Militant*'s was the only notice of it I have found:

'Entertainment before the Lincoln Memorial rally included two performances by the Bread and Puppet Theatre depicting the emergence of militarism and the death of an American pilot. The dramas were conducted in the brutal and moving simplicity of Peter Schumann's presentations, which have come to be a welcome and stimulating part of antiwar demonstrations.'

(*The Militant*, October 30, '67.)

King Story and *A Man Says Goodbye to His Mother*. A warning and a quiet deploration. This was not, from Schumann's viewpoint, the moment for an aggressive show like *Speech*, nor even for a grandiose and proportionately exciting – rather than intimate – evocation of the horrors of war, such as his pageants of victims assailed by planes or even just such as his earlier processions of holy figures made prisoners of war had provided. He was not about to incite to an assault on a government institution; that it was make-believe made it, if anything, worse in his eyes.

This was the last big demonstration he took part in until April '71. But then, as far as I know, it was until then the last big peace demonstration.

27. October '67 - '68. The confrontational style of pacifist non-violent resistance and of the militant hippies (yippies) replaces the Old Left-pacifist coalition's genteel style of opinion-voicing.

Jerry Rubin, now settled in the New York scene, in a critique in the *East Village Other* (December 15-30), of the older-generation style of another Stop the Draft Week at the Whitehall Induction Center, December 5-8, '67, entitled 'Have a Group-In for the Holidays at Whitehall,' gave a political and revolutionary twist to the new theatre introduced by the diggers, calling for guerilla tactics and a guerilla form of organization at demonstrations, based on the presupposition that these would be acts of resistance, but definitely make-believe ones, not designed to attain their stated objective, but to provide an instructive spectacle and the formative experience of acting in it.[1]

---

1. 'Demonstrations are great experiences – where is the person who is not a new and different individual after every action? Our theories meet the test of the cop's club; and the swiftly changing situation frees our thinking. We feel tremendous energy, and the possibilities of our power – the possibilities of mass action to change America.

Action presents everything in intensity and contrast; fellow demonstrators become the closest of comrades; normal things like fire-alarms and garbage cans and street lights become props in a theater of protest. A mass demonstration is a celebration and an affirmation of ourselves and our potential.

The purposes of a mass action are many, but the primary one should be the deepening of a movement of individuals who can change America. And so, the most vital way of seeing an action is how it liberates the individual and enables him to realize himself in new ways.

The stated goals of the demonstration are never the real goals. "Close down the Pentagon." No organizer of that action thought for a moment that we had the power to close down the center of this country's war machine. But that call to action signified an intent; created a good fantasy; told the American people what we thought should happen to the Pentagon.

"Close down Whitehall Induction Center in New York." Same thing. A dramatic way to look at the situation. And the government responds by either calling in the 82nd Airborne, bayonets and all, or mobilizing the entire New York police force, thereby dramatizing for the TV cameras a brilliant theater, in which the nation's military establishments are seen as under seige and in need of the most extreme military protection . . . .

A revolt broke out around 9 A.M. Wednesday. Arguments between demonstrators and monitors grew fierce. A fight broke out over who was to speak at the rally, because the leaders tried to keep control. Finally, people started leaving for expeditions unknown throughout New York.

Joyousness reigned. People jumped on the roofs of cars. Many bystanders waved and showed support for the anti-war insurgency. Drivers beeped hello. Many arguments broke out between pro and con people, and it made beautiful theater. Lindsay's army couldn't clear the streets.

"See!" exclaimed a demonstrator. "It's beautiful! We don't need monitors! We don't need leaders! Every man a leader! We're free!" ' — (J. Rubin, *Have a Group-In, East Village Other*, December 15-30, '67.)

He formally presented some of the theory of it to the New York City Peace Movement in a debate, December 29, '67, at the Trotzkyite Socialist Workers Party's Militant Labor Forum with Fred Halstead, that party's presidential candidate, on the question 'What Policy for the Anti-War Movement?' Rubin proposed substituting a campaign of liberation for the anti-war campaign. The campaign of liberation was to be non-argumentative. It was to consist in theatrical public actings-out of a state of liberation. This would undermine authority and, with luck, might bring down the system of alienation.[2] Halstead, representative of the Old Left — devoted to keeping itself intact as bureaucratic cadre of a sometime-in-the-future revolution — rejected (*The Militant*, January 8, '68.) out of hand his proposal of an anti-authoritarian street theatre for the benefit of the media. David McReynolds, representative of the pacifist wing of the Movement, in an issue of that wing's organ, *WIN* (February 15, '68) in which Rubin's speech was reprinted from *The Militant*, preferring the real-life theatre of non-violent resistance to Rubin's 'antisocial theater' because it was meaningful, also rejected it.[3] But it was clear that because of their

---

2. Cf Appendix XIX.
3. 'Most people like order and stability. It is easy for us to forget that a majority of the voting public is not under 25, that Eisenhower is our most popular national figure, that most Americans aren't black and they aren't poor and they don't smoke pot or drop acid. Haight-Ashbury and the East Village are not America. EVO and the L.A. Free Press and WIN and *all* the underground papers and *all* the little magazines and *all* the radical journals do not, taken together, have a circulation as large as the New York *Daily News*. Most Americans — that vast majority of which you and I are not a part — support their local police, approve the use of tanks and machine guns to put down riots, and think J. Edgar Hoover is a great guy. Baby, that's where it is really at.

This doesn't mean we should speak softly and irritate no one. It does mean the demonstrations we plan should make sense, and not just for ourselves. Demonstrations aren't just for our own "energy release" — they are for changing other people. If I get jailed for blocking an induction center the average guy I meet in a bar will think I'm a godamned-communist but at least I can argue the matter with him, because there was a certain logic to that disruption at that time and place. But how do I explain to sweet old ladies that I urinated on the Pentagon walls because Johnson is emotionally sick? How do I win over neighbors by telling them the trash got thrown in their street because we bombed North Vietnam? Come off it.

Radical actions will create hostility and yet radical actions are necessary and therefore hostility is inevitable — but the job of the radical is not to increase hostility but to make his point while generating as little hostility as possible . . . .

Finally, I want to deal with theater. I have heard about it from Jerry Rubin and I have heard about it from Keith Lampe and I have heard about it from my folk-hero Allen Ginsberg, and I am sick of hearing about it . . . .

One does not have to create artificial drama. If we are not blind we can see that life is filled with it. The drama of birth, the comic ritual of courtship and marriage, the high tragedy of death. Arrest, trial, and prison are genuine theater. There are times when we may create special forms of "living" theater to help people see the drama of life. The Yellow Submarine demonstrations were great, gentle, provocative, and aimed at getting people to see that while we are comic, the Pentagon was, in a sick way, even funnier. But I am against an attempt to turn the peace movement as a whole into artificial theater. I am

shared opposition to authority, the pacifists and the militant hippies weren't that far apart.

During the winter of '67/'68, Rubin formed the Youth International Party (YIP), a political organization for hippies. Schumann's street agitation was as far from the Old Left's verbalism as from the pacifists' civil disobedience activism. But it was even further from the nihilist obstructionism proposed by Rubin, and its dramatic gravity and moral elevation were the opposite of the wild fun Rubin promoted. It is therefore surprising to find the Bread and Puppet Theatre listed as one of the founders of YIP.[4]

---

against the cruelty involved in releasing doves in Grand Central Station in mid-winter, to die by battering against the windows or, if they get out, to die in the frigid air.

I rather approve of Jerry Rubin's blowing everyone's mind at the SWP meeting by having the Lampes come as bodyguards and by playing the Beatles. It was consistent with Jerry's style and helped get across the sense of his poetry. And it is good for serious people to get shaken up. I admit I'm glad I wasn't Fred Halstead, for my vanity would have been wounded, my dignity shaken, and I would have been angry. To be made mock of is very hard to take, but sometimes it can be healthy.

But when so much theater is present at all times I am sorry to see Jerry Rubin or Keith Lampe miss that fact, sorry that they don't realize that by "adding theater to theater" they are behaving as "camp revolutionists." Artificial theater is not the way out – one thinks of Hitler's love of drama – the massive theatricality of the Nazis, with their uniforms and rallies. Theater is not a substitute for the real theater of life. Comedy is fun, but the drama in Vietnam is a long-running tragedy which absorbs or should absorb our attention now.'
— (D. McReynolds, *I am the Eggman!*, WIN, February 15, '68.)

4. '*The Birth of the Yippies*. The Youth International Party (YIP) was founded in New York City on Jan. 16 by some 25 artists, writers, and revolutionaries, including Country Joe and the Fish, the Fugs, the Bread and Puppet Theater, the Pageant Players, Shirley Clarke, Barbara and Marvin Garson, Allen Ginsberg, Arlo Guthrie, Abbie Hoffman, Paul Krassner, Keith Lampe, Phil Ochs, and Jerry Rubin. Here is the new party's very first public word:

"Join us in Chicago in August for an international festival of youth, music and theater. Rise up and abandon the creeping meatball! Come all you rebels, youth spirits, rock minstrels, truth-seekers, peacock freaks, poets, barricade-jumpers, dancers, lovers and artists!

It is summer. It is the last week in August, and the NATIONAL DEATH PARTY meets to bless Lyndon Johnson. We are there! There are 500 of us dancing in the streets, throbbing with amplifiers and harmony. We are making love in the parks. We are reading, laughing, printing newspapers, singing, groping, and making a mock convention, and celebrating the birth of FREE AMERICA in our own time.

A new spirit explodes in the land. Things are bursting in music, poetry, dancing, newspapers, movies, celebration, magic, politics, theater, and life styles. All these new tribes will gather in Chicago. We will be completely open. Everything will be free. Bring blankets, tents, draft cards, body paint, Mr. Leary's Cow, food to share, music, eager skin, and happiness. The threats of LBJ, Mayor Daley, and J. Edgar Freako will not stop us. We are coming! We are coming from all over the world!

The life of the American spirit is being torn asunder by the forces of violence, decay, and the napalm-cancer fiend. We demand the Politics of Ecstasy! We are the delicate spores of the new fierceness that will change America. We will create our own reality, we are Free America! And we will not accept the false theater of the Death Convention.

The first New York City YIP event, March 22, '68, gave a foretaste of the spectacular they got out of the Chicago police five months later.[5]

> We will be in Chicago. Begin preparations now! Chicago is yours! Do it!" ' — (LNS, *The Birth of the Yippies*, WIN, February 15, '68.)
>
> 'In one sense the movement was exhausted at the end of 1967. Militant demonstrations in California, Washington, and New York had resulted in well over a thousand arrests without having any appreciable effect on the government. Other demonstrations not mentioned here, like a huge and bloody anti-draft protest at the University of Wisconsin in November, were turning thousands of students into self-conscious revolutionaries, but nothing had occurred that would have suggested to an objective observer that revolution was any closer. . . .
>
> Jerry Rubin took a different view, arguing that the movement had the capacity to bring down the system by a gadfly warfare which would push the country to the brink of a nervous breakdown:
>
> This system lives by murdering in Vietnam, exploiting the world, and killing black people at home; and we say to hell with middle class "security" and phony status games, we are going to screw up this society. And we can do it too . . . . The goal? A massive white revolutionary youth movement which, working in parallel cooperation with the rebellions in the black communities, could seriously disrupt this country, and thus be an internal catalyst for a breakdown of the American ability and will to fight guerrillas overseas. Thus defeated abroad by peasant revolutionaries, and disrupted within by blacks and whites, the empire of the United States will find itself faced with rebellions from fifteen different directions. (*National Guardian*, November 25, '67.)
>
> Rubin was a little vague about just what blacks and whites were going to *do*, exactly, but this was less significant, for the moment, than the promise of disruption that his appeal embodied. The fact that blacks and young whites could not actually bring down, or take over, the American government was less important than the increasingly real possibility that they might actually try.
>
> This point was not lost on mainstream political figures. In New York City, Joseph L. Raugh, a leader of Americans for Democratic Action and a long-time liberal who had been torn between his support for Johnson's domestic programs and his doubts about the war, told a Democratic group on November 16 that unless a peace candidate ran in 1968, "the rioting at the Pentagon will look like a panty-waist tea party . . . . We've got to turn this horrible frustration from the streets to the ballot box." ' — (Th. Powers, *The War*.)
>
> 5. 'I went to the first Yip-In, midnight March 22 in Grand Central Terminal, fully expecting a hassle with the police. The Yippees had tried to avoid this. They had worded their call deliberately so as not to get the police uptight. But, rather naively, they (or we, I was in on the planning) placed too much faith in our own rhetoric. "It's a spring mating service celebrating the equinox, a back-scratching party, a roller skating rink, a theatre . . . . with you performer and audience. Get acquainted with other Yippees now, for other yiptivities . . . .' None of us considered the cavernous but enclosed terminal a claustrophobic trap. It seemed, instead, a grand place to hold a party. Or so we thought.
>
> The police, however, were uptight. The night before a hippie demonstration at a Lower East Side precinct house had ended up in a battle between egg-throwing hippies and head-cracking tactical patrolmen. The cause of the demonstration was even more ominous. Police on the Lower East Side had been raiding hippie pads, destroying possessions within, busting the inhabitants on drug charges, and subjecting them to indignities. One youth had his hair shorn with the warning that "we're going to get you hippies before this summer."
>
> But within ten minutes after my arrival at Grand Central I knew everything would be all right, like the be-ins of the previous spring. The police made no attempt to keep us out.

And costumes work wonders. People get out of their angry paranoic winter roles into the gentle, playful roles of their fantasies. (The revolution is living the life you dream of living.) I shared popcorn with a crewcutted youth in an ROTC uniform who was overwhelmed by the simple act of sharing, and I overheard two GIs arguing with every well-dressed straight youth, on behalf of the Yippees, telling the straight that these kids with long hair really knew where it was at.

Then, shortly after 1:00 a.m., with no warning and for no apparent reason, about 50 tactical patrolmen charged in from an adjacent waiting room and began cracking skulls. Unable to clear the terminal the first time, they repeated the tactic over and over again. Yippees and commuters alike were bowled over. People were pressed up against the marble walls and beaten. A 60-year-old suburban matron returning from the opera, was threatened with arrest when she tried to stop four police from punching and kicking a youth, under the approving eye of their captain. A number of Yippees were thrown through plate-glass doors. Ron Shea, from Baltimore, had his hands and wrists torn apart as he went through the glass; he won't use them again for six months. Four police seized *Village Voice* reporter Don McNeil, cursed his paper, and sent him flying through glass. WIN photographer Howard Harrison was charged with resisting arrest, for trying to explain that he was on assignment. ACLU lawyer Al Levine described the scene as "the worst example of police brutality I've ever seen outside of Mississippi. Police reacted enthusiastically to the prospect of being unleashed."

The police say we provoked it. Two firecrackers were set off before the initial charge. A dozen or so kids had climbed atop the information booth, pulled hands off the clocks, and defaced them with slogans. A handful of provocateurs from two Lower East Side groups, Black Mask and "Up Against the Wall Motherfucker," were insulting cops, trying to provoke violence as they had succeeded in doing the night before. Violence is their thing; their theory is that kids who are beaten by police become "radical." (Being already "radicalized," they themselves avoid the flailing clubs). But few people joined in their snake dance. The police continued to attack, long after the information booth was cleared and the clock secured.

There is another explanation. Allen Ginsberg refers to the "psycho-political" problem of our time, that is tearing the country apart. Long-haired Yippees represent a new morality. They are free and fearless. Their mere existence is an act of revolution. The police, self-proclaimed paragons of middle-class virtue, straight, uptight, frustrated, beat up the Yippees as parents punish wayward children. "Your sons and your daughters are beyond your command," sings Bob Dylan, but the police demand obedience. America places greater value on a clock face than it does on the living-flesh face of a human being. Police beat Yippees at Grand Central, soldiers napalm Vietnamese at Ben Suc. Each demands obedience of the victim.

The Yippees responded to the attacks with the resiliency that is becoming customary, returning to the terminal floor after each attack. There was some chanting of "fascist cops," which only made the police more frightened and vicious (call a cop a fascist and he usually acts like one), but there was also an awesome and solemn moment when, spontaneously, everyone formed into a slow processional, raised their hands in the "V" Resistance symbol, and hummed the calming Hindu "Om."

Despite the brutality, the arrests, and the poor planning, most participants considered the Yip-in a success. Young, white, middle-class Americans are beginning to get themselves together and YIP has apparently found a key for organizing them. But there is too much organizing to do for us to become side-tracked in hassles with police. We need to liberate people, not places. Confrontations with police seem superfluous. We can organize right under their noses by experiencing community among ourselves and then creating social structures on the basis of the new experience. The Yippee vision of creating an alternative community outside the existing structure is the most revolutionary thing going. But implementing that vision is an awesome, humbling task.' — (M. Jezer, *YIP! WIN*, March 31, '68.)

'The Yip-In was a disaster; not irretrievable perhaps, but certainly unrelieved by success in any respect that I can recognize. If the point was guerrilla theatre, with cops as GIs and Yippees as Vietnamese, who was supposed to draw the lesson? The general public, having seen that defaced clock, would have justified drawing and quartering the lot of us. If the point was *not* to provoke brutality, then I'd say the police did us a grisly favor; without their act, we'd all have died of boredom. There was no way of getting music into that place, and only good acid rock could have thwarted claustrophobia. How long can you bounce a balloon in the air and grin back at the guy who just trod on your toes? And anybody who needs to be "radicalized" with a nightstick is hardly good revolutionary material.

YIP's most planned activity is a Yip-Out in Central Park on Easter Sunday.' — (P. Johnson, *YIP!*, *WIN*, March 31, '68.)

28. Schumann, November '67 - March '69. Greenwich Village 'community' street work. He's essentially out of the larger Peace Movement.

Schumann's street agitation after his Lincoln Memorial appearance in October resumed its small-scale format. It increasingly reverted to its beginnings: rebecame a neighborhood activity.

He made his third annual Union Square Veterans Day appearance on November 11, '67, a rally 'against the war,' as the year before apparently doing *A Man Says Goodbye to His Mother*. The *Voice* ad for the rally (*Village Voice*, November 2) promised 'Two Decorated Veterans of Vietnam (Susskind Show – 10/22).' Barbara Dane, Joe Frazier and Elaine White were the other entertainers.

He provided accompaniment by his troupe for a Neighborhood Peace March, November 25, from the Gramercy Park Friends Meeting House at which a 'peace center' (peace centers gave advice to would-be draft avoiders, evaders, and resisters) had recently been established, to the site, a few blocks east, of a one-hour once-a-week vigil the new center had been running.

He performed *A Man Says Goodbye* – 'A short pantomime about a man being drafted and then killed in war action' (*New York Times*, December 10) – on the steps of St. Peter's Episcopal Church on West 20th, site of another new peace center, as conclusion of a 'Walk of Mourning' ('for the boys who have been killed and those who will be killed' (*Village Voice*, December 7)) by a group – about a hundred of them – of women inblack.

These new peace centers were being established by the original Greenwich Village Peace Center that (or Grace Paley from which) had gotten him out on what he recalls as his earliest peace demonstration – in March '64. Grace Paley was still active there. He had in a sense by the end of '67 come full circle. There were bloody repressions of anti-draft demonstrations – picketing, obstruction – further downtown in Manhattan that December (December 4-8).

Christmas Eve, he did a 'Sun/Son' parade on the theme of 'the birth of the sun as it symbolizes the birth of the spirit of man' in the immediate Washington Square area, sponsored by the Washington Square Methodist Church, the 'Peace Church'. There was a garbage strike on, so February 8 – the Vietcong's Tet offensive had started January 31st – he went on a Village Garbage Parade.[1] Putting on *When Johnny Comes Marching*

---

1. 'GARBAGE PARADE. In the thick of the city's garbage crisis we were asked to provide a parade for a community garbage collection in Greenwich Village. We arrived on the square at eighth street and sixth avenue dressed in top hats and old-fashioned clothing

Home, he performed with Susan Sontag, Eric Bentley, the Open Theatre and Cyrelle Forman at a benefit, March 17, at St. Clement's Church on West 46th, sponsored by the Village Peace Center, for Joan Baez' husband David Mitchell, the Catholic Worker who had been sentenced to two years in the penitentiary for his draftcard burning in October '65, and needed money for appeals – 'Margo (Sherman) hurtled herself against – just slammed herself up against a door and was machine-gunned down. That was moving.' — (Ashley, interview.)

Since his position apparently precluded participation in the more important ongoing street protest, styled as civil disobedience and as police provocation, he began to stress the protest character of his indoors theatre, something he had not been wont to do and ceased to do in the '70s. When he advertised for volunteers, he headed the ad (*Village Voice*, February 1, '68) '*Papier Mache Against the War* ! ! ! !' – a printing and glueing workshop. His performances at St. Peter's in February were advertised (ibid.)

---

where there was a pile of garbage in plastic bags. We greeted the people who were returning from work with music which drew a curious crowd of local store owners and homebound pedestrians. They were informed of the garbage collection and we started to the Gansevoort dump with a trail of followers laden with garbage. Some people we met joined in and the music drew people out of stores and bars along Greenwich Avenue. We continued through the deserted warehouse section until we arrived at the dump. We were greeted with smiles by the skeleton sanitation crew and our paltry load was added to the 50 foot pile of existing garbage. With this as a backdrop we played a movie which consists of a long scroll wound between two spools. Coffee and cookies provided by some friendly citizen were consumed and we returned home.' — (*Bread and Puppet Diary*, November '67-March '68.)

'It was still and dark on Gansevoort Pier. The moon shone down on the black lapping Hudson. A cold wind blew papers against the massive dark buildings lining the long pier. Inside the buildings where garbage is normally dumped and loaded onto barges, it was quiet too. It was Thursday night and the strike was still on.

Faint drums and horns intruded into this Rousseau-like scene. The music came closer, and with it an unlikely parade – surrealistic pilgrims with tall buckled brim hats, long dresses, and bonnets carrying plastic sacks of garbage. They had begun their march at 8th Street and Sixth Avenue. Leaving bundles of garbage behind due to lack of people to carry them, they had walked along Greenwich Avenue losing people all along the way. The 25 frozen people who reached the pier, including some members of the Bread and Puppet Theatre, were there to perform what was obscurely called 'a positive gesture' by organizer, Phyllis Yampolski. She was chicly dressed and accessorized with white Courrege boots and a bag of garbage.

Ceremoniously filing into a long open warehouse containing a mountain of rotting refuse, each member of the procession made his offering to the awesome pile. More music was played, and a story was tod by a barker-like character about a man and woman tricked into leaving their simple country life for a city where they find their simple country things have become garbage. Cheering followed the story. The dumbfounded faces of the policemen and sanitationmen present now showed disgusted amusement. The 'positive gesture' curiously accomplished, very fancy cookies and coffee were passed out. The paper cups were tossed onto the looming garbage heap and the group straggled out. A sense of cold reality returned to Gansevoort Pier leaving the impression that the whole thing never happened. — (*Village Voice*, February 15, '68.)

as 'Theatre of Protest Presentations Directed at Critical Problems of the Day'. His annual Easter play this year was called 'Crucifixion Against the War' and was presented by 'Angry Arts' 'for the benefit of the resistance.' I note, though, that his work at this time was developing an anti-populist tinge – *Johnny*, the *Cry* he started to work on that summer.

He left on his first European tour in April,[2] spent the summer in Maine. While attending Ronnie Davis'[3] Radical Theatre Festival in San Francisco

---

2. While in Europe, he did outdoors political shows, but since they concerned American foreign politics these were only in a very wide sense agitational. E.g. he did *A Man Says Goodbye* at the Hispano-Suiza plant in Bois-Colombes (beginning May '68) and in Nancy, on the Place Stanislas and on the Place de la Carriere (both times in April):

'Les comédiens, à la dernière minute, déposèrent le soldat mort entre les gardes du Palais du Gourverneur en un geste improvisé qu'on jugeait, chez nous, provocateur et qui, accompli par des Américains dans l'esprit du théâtre engagé de New York, était l'exemple d'une rare liberté d'expression et d'un sense sincère de la démocratie.' — (*Le Monde*, April 25, '68.)

The rude guests were forgiven their manners:

'Les soldats ricanant au début, se sont tus en voyant l'homme poignardé par la Vietnamienne.' — (Apocryphal detail reported in *Le Nouvel Observateur*, May 14, '68.)

In England, according to Marowitz, *Village Voice*, May 23, '68, they played in a 'large settlement house auditorium in south London' and gave two street performances, one in Portobello Road and the other at Hyde Park.

Ernstthal (inverview) spoke of performances of *Speech/Chairs* at the Free University of Berlin.

3. Ronald G. Davis started his outdoor performances when Schumann did, in 1962, but seems to have gotten into political shows only in '65, and so far as I know never developed any particular parade theatre.

'1958. R.G. Davis moves to San Francisco following several years of mime study in Paris.

1959. The R.G. Davis Mime Studio and Troupe gives its first performance.

1960. *Eleventh Hour Mime Show* presented weekly under the auspices of the Actors Workshop, then the most progressive and daring of America's residential theatres.

1961. Beckett's *Act Without Words II* performed with the Actors Workshop productions of *Purgatory* and *Krapp's Last Tape*.

First experiments using words with mime technique, a combination well-suited to the commedia dell'arte format.

The Dowry, a commedia adapted from Moliere's *Scapin* and Goldoni's *The Servant of Two Masters*, with additional improvised scenes. This is the Troupe's first commedia dell'arte production, and is performed with masks on a raised portable platform having a simple painted backdrop. The production is viewed as unfavourable competition by the directors of the Actors Workshop, the beginning of a split between them and Davis.

1962. *The Dowry* becomes the first production presented outdoors in the San Francisco city parks during the summer, a practice that continues to the present day. The park performances are free, though donations are solicited.

The Troupe stops performing in the Actors Workshop theatres on a regular basis, though an association remains, and opens its own small studio.

1963. All ties with the Actors Workshop are broken, and as a result Davis loses nearly all of his performers, most being unwilling to give up the possibility of conventional success in the theatre.

The Root, a commedia adapted from Machiavelli's *Mandragola* by Milton Savage, presented at the studio and in the parks.

in September, he put on the only outdoor political performance of his — in the U.S.A. — I have heard of for 1968, a performance of either *A Man Says* or of *King Story* at a rally for Eldridge Cleaver, joint presidential candidate of the Black Panthers and the (white) Freedom (or Peace and Freedom?) Party. (Levy, interview.) During a panel discussion at this festival he said:

'We haven't decided yet, like Ronnie, that we are finished with the demonstrations. I mean it's a constant confusion — for everybody — do you skip a rehearsal and working on what you want to do or do you go and do something for a particular purpose? We do this less than we did a year or two ago. We prefer, more and more, to say no and work on the things we really want to say. But the confusion still exists, because things come up that you feel you can help by being there — by bringing puppets or a little skit. A few years ago we did huge parades down Fifth Avenue. We asked the Parade Committee; we did them. We don't do that anymore. We simply feel New York has seen this and they saw it, and the movement grew. Now something else has to come. But whatever comes, it will be a response to what happens politically in the world. We have not decided what we will do, but it will be in response to politics in our neighborhood, where we live and in response to the larger American scene. One thing that goes on, as Ronnie said, is simply the outgrowth into other groups. What other people take from you, or what you can initiate with other people. Five years ago when we started playing in the street, it was new to New Yorkers. They hadn't

---

Ruzzante's Maneuvers, commedia by Milton Savage, and Jarry's *Ubu Roi*.
1964. *Chorizos*, commedia adapted by Tom Lopez from Saul Landau's scenario, presented for the third summer in the parks, but stopped after eight performances by Davis.
Tartuffe, commedia adapted from Moliere by Richard Sassoon, presented at the San Francisco Mime Troupe theatre at 3450 20th Street.
1965. Tartuffe is staged at the Veterans Memorial Auditorium, marking the acceptance by the Troupe of the need to play in larger spaces, rather than the small studio, in order to attract larger audiences.
Luis Valdez joins the Troupe in May, and leaves in November to found El Teatro Campesino (Farmworkers Theatre), using many of the Davis techniques.
The first production by the Troupe of a play by Brecht, *The Exception and the Rule*. This and later plays encourage the study of Marxism and the political potential of the theatre.
A Minstrel Show, or Civil Rights in a Cracker Barrel, minstrel show by Saul Landau and Davis from traditional and improvised material, based on nineteenth century minstrel productions. The show deals with racial oppression in Watts, the black ghetto area of Los Angeles, shortly before the major riots. It was no longer presented after the riots, in the belief that it has been superceded by rising black consciousness and self expression.
Il Candelaio, commedia adapted from the Giordano Bruno by Peter Berg. Davis is arrested for performing the play in the parks without a permit, which the city had refused to issue because it found "vulgar material" in the script. Davis is found guilty of performing without a permit and sentenced to thirty days (suspended) and one year's probation. On appeal, the permit refusal is ruled unconstitutional.
The Troupe moves to 924 Howard Street.
De Ghelderode's *Chronicles of Hell* premieres at the Commedia Theatre, Palo Alto'. — (R. Toscan and K. Ripley, *The San Francisco Mime Troupe: a Chronology and Bibliography, Theatre Quarterly*, vol. V, 18, '75 ('74?))

had that since the twenties. Now I think there are about five street theatres in New York.'⁴

(Schumann in the San Francisco Mime Troupe's pamphlet
Panel Discussion on Radical Theater, '68.)

This was a good-bye to the Movement, if not necessarily to street agitation.

The fact of the matter seems to be that '68 was not a good year for the Peace Movement. For one thing Johnson's March 31st rejection of military requests for another couple of hundred thousand men and his diplomatic shilly-shallying — partial bombing halt, request for negotiations — but above all, announcement he would not run again (which made people that had been actively opposing the war feel the Movement had gained a victory) sapped the Movement's energy. For another, the rioting at the Chicago Democratic Convention that summer⁵ scared off a good

---

4. A number of politically oriented, leftist or otherwise anti-Establishment theatre groups mainly performing in the streets, in parks and in community centers had, since 1965 when the Pageant Players got together, formed in New York City. Without having researched it, I have the impression that 1967, when Enriquez Vargas abandoned his commedia dell'arte middle class troupe and started his Gut Theatre with local Latino, perhaps mainly Puerto Rican street kids, when the Sixth Street Theatre (masks, mime dance) was formed by people associated with the Angry Arts Committee, some of whom had worked with Schumann, when El Campesino and the San Francisco Mime Troupe both played New York, when Schechner had three different groups doing a play, 'Kill Viet Cong,' in which an audience member is importuned to shoot a supposed Viet Cong, in the streets, was especially a year in which a number of such groups got going. By 1968, Marketta Kimball's and Rick and Levy's City Street Theatre was performing B. Brecht's *Exception and Rule* in Black and Puerto Rican parts of town. By and large these groups disappeared fairly suddenly — often in 1970. The Bread and Puppet influence on them seems to have been considerable and not restricted to the use of masks, but also e.g. to the kinds of stories they acted out, e.g. the Pageant Players' *The War Monster* of '67, and *King Play* and *The Spiritual History of the World ... Or God and Medicaid* of '68 (both in Lesnick, *Guerrilla Street Theater,* '73). The influence seems to have come more from Schumann's *King Story* and *A Man Says Goodbye* than from his parades: these groups were not into parades. The chief differences of these groups from Schumann's theatre was on the one hand their didactic intent, the skits were to educate 'the people' about their true interests and about specific social questions, on the other their folksy, humorous, rough and ready histrionics.
5. At the Convention, a relatively outside candidate with a relatively definite 'peace plank,' McCarthy, was defeated by the candidate of the Democratic party machine and of Johnson, Humphrey: the Chicago city machine, Daley's, and its police aiding. Both the Youth Movement, namely the yippees, and the pacifist wing of the movement, Dave Dellinger and the 'Mobilization', were there, a few thousand of each, say, demonstrating for peace, the yippees doing this by having a party in the park (Lincoln Park) —
'Ginsberg chanted mantras and Abbie Hoffman rapped about revolution for the fun of it, thousands lounged on the grass talking politics or hallucinating on the brownies that Yippie chemists had cooked up.' — (M. Yezer, *The Whole World Was Watching,* WIN, September 16, '68.)
— and by disobeying the curfews and other restrictions imposed by the Chicago police. Some three to four hundred were injured, some four to five hundred arrested, mostly yippie-inspired kids in both categories, though the pacifists did not escape unscathed. The

many earnest people and itself was a sign that people not scared off, people that a couple of years earlier would have put energy into opposing the war, were now looking for more basic social change – whether because resistance had become a habit, or because the government's continuing obscenities in Southeast Asia had spread the idea that policy change required more basic change. Schumann may have kept back from street peace agitation in '68, but there was less of it to engage in in the first place, the withdrawal was general. He seems to have participated in the concurrent radicalization (perhaps especially because he saw May '68 and its immediate radiation in Europe from a first row seat), but the kind of street activity (weathermen, yippie) it went with in the U.S. had nothing to do with puppets, and was alien to his practical turn of mind. Illegal behavior and the confrontations with armed men it led to would to him make sense only if it were a revolutionary commitment to violence with a chance of success – which it could only have as a people's movement, but not as theatre. But for instance the grotesque Martin Luther King Memorial March on April 7, '68 at which Governor Rockefeller marched arm in arm with Harlem Mau Mau chief Charles 37X Kenyatta (who was carrying a sword sheathed in a Bible (*Village Voice*, April 11, '68.)) and Sammy Davis sang 'We Shall Overcome,' the only big New York City demonstration in '68 formally like the ones Schumann had found it possible to lend his services to, was not an occasion for him either.

For '69, there is again only one street appearance of his I know of, on March 18, a show about a stockade murder, done to flip-over narrative, a format he often used later:

'La disproportion des forces en présence m'est apparue le soir du 18 mars 1969 devant les gratte-ciel de *Time and Life*, sur la 6e Avenue où deux petites troupes de théâtre essayaient d'attirer l'attention des foules de Newyorkais qui n'avaient qu'une idée en tête: rentrer chez eux le plus rapidement possible. J'avais assisté, l'après-midi, à une répétition du spectacle à Washington Square, devant une vingtaine de badauds, – mais le *médium* était là: "Je remercie le médium d'être venu, dit le meneur de jeu, et nous espérons qu'il nous suivra à la 51e rue." Le

---

spectacle was on television and in Movement lingo 'brought the war home' to the audience. The violence was the State's: essentially response to the demonstrators' demonstration of disdain for the social order. What was demonstrated was not the evil of the war but (1) that the social order involves a petty control of conduct, (2) beyond consent is based on force. If the demonstrators stated any position on the war or made any points concerning it, this was quite wiped out by the spectacle carrying those two points. In fact, speeches by the demonstrators hardly got into the news media at all. Perhaps the general public got an uneasy sense that the whole unending, bloody, brutal and costly undeclared war in Asia was the same kind of thing: a not really necessary response by force to irritating but essentially unthreatening conduct. The fracas at Chicago – totally negligible when compared to the massacres inflicted on labor from the 1880s to the 1930s and the terrorism that the Negro race was subjected to during approximately the same period – effectively reoriented the Movement from opposition to the war toward opposition to coercion at home.

médium hocha sa tête grisonnante, en épaulant sa caméra. A lui seul, il représentait les cent millions de téléspectateurs qui regarderaient les actualités CBS à 6 heures du soir.

Sur l'esplanade de *Time and Life*, les policiers demandèrent aux acteurs de "circuler", ce qu'ils firent en organisant un mouvement de va-et-vient, brandissant des pancartes, tirant des gosses par la main, menant quelques poussettes – l'attirail habituel. A 5 heures on les autorisa à jouer pendant dix minutes. Grosse caisse, trompettes d'enfants parodiant des marches patriotiques, le *Bread and Puppet* entra immédiatement en action. Grimpé sur une échelle double, un homme raconta l'assassinat de Richard Bunch par une suite de grands dessins qu'il repliait à la façon d'un calendrier. Enfermé dans la prison militaire du Presidio, près de San Francisco, le soldat Bunch avait mis au défi un gardien de le tuer s'il faisait semblant de fuir : "Essaie," avait dit le gardien, qui l'avait abattu. Pour protester contre ce meurtre – Bunch était malade et suicidaire – 27 prisonniers s'étaient assis dans la cour en chantant : "O beautiful America." l'un d'eux présenta une série de griefs à la direction. Trois des soldats furent condamnés à des peines de travaux forcés de quatorze à seize ans, et les autres devaient être jugés le jour même.

Dans le style du *Bread and Puppet*, une immense marionnette symbolisait l'armée, des sacs de papier transformaient en un tour de main les acteurs en prisonniers, on chantait avec accompagnement de kazoos et de trompettes d'enfants : "O beautiful America", mais le fracas de la circulation recouvrait les répliques, et personne ne traversa la rue, depuis le trottoir d'en face. La seconde troupe, les *Pageant Players*, mimèrent ensuite la même histoire, sans l'efficacité visuelle du *Bread and Puppet* "Dans la rue, dit Peter Schumann, il faut donner des images plus grandes que nature."

Deux ou trois cents personnes peut-être, sur les cent mille qui sortaient des bureaux du quartier à ce moment-là, furent atteintes par plusieurs moyens : les pancartes, les images scéniques, les tracts, la musique et le discours, très émouvant, d'un ancien aumônier du Presidio. Combien d'entre elles ont compris de quoi il s'agissait ? Je regardais, en m'éloignant, le groupe dérisoire recommencer son va-et-vient au pied des gratte-ciel. Mais au même instant, dans 109 villes américaines, avaient lieu des manifestations en faveur des soldats du presidio, et j'arrivai à temps à mon hôtel pour voir le reportage télévisé du *médium*. En avril, le procès fut revisé. L'un des condamnés vit sa peine réduite de seize à deux ans de prison.'
(Jotterand, *Le nouveau theatre...*, p.159-61.)

He was protesting, not against the war, but against the repression of protest.

29. April-November '69. Harmless anti-war street agitation in Europe.

This was just before he again left for Europe (mid-April to mid-November '69).[1]

---

1. The group apparently did a great deal of street theatre on this second European tour. They did outdoor shows of *Fire* and *King Story* in Copenhagen, and did *King Story* on the Amsterdam Dam. Schumann says (interview, *l'Art Vivant*, December '69) they did very little street performing in France: probably the events of May '68 were still too much alive there. They had to cancel street appearances in Caen because of ongoing electoral campaigns there. But they did some street performances in the North of France:

'(Elka: there were several times on the tour when the theatre – I remember in France, and in Germany, when we wanted to do street theatre, in France, in a place where there were soldiers stationed, and we ended up doing *King Story* without the puppets, because that had been forbidden. It was in northern France somewhere, and we decided to, despite the prohibition on doing the street theatre, we did do the piece.) The story is a bit more complicated. There were soldiers coming, that we happened to talk to, not in uniform . . . , and so we learned from them that they were forbidden, they were not allowed to come to our performances because we were not the right – (Elka: This was during the Algerian war, wasn't it?) Yes. (Elka: So they were French soldiers?) Yes. So we decided to go there and play in front of the barracks and we went there with some instruments – we wanted to test it out without puppets – and then when we got there, there were plainclothes policemen with clubs and other weapons, and they just beat us up, beat us over the head, beat on the trumpets, beat the women and just got us out of there.' — (Schumann, interview, '79.)

'We would get the band together and we'd go on out and we maybe would do the *King Story*, or maybe we wouldn't, maybe we'd just do parades, inviting people to come to the shows. I remember when we were in Armienne, there were – some soldiers came from the American barracks there and they told us that one of the orders of the day was that no one of those soldiers were to go to the House of Culture in Armienne where we, the Bread and Puppet was performing because there was a Vietcong flag displayed in the show. Have you heard this story? (I: No.) So immediately we said well, we'll have to go and demonstrate it front of the place. So we got our little band together and we made some signs like "Soldiers Should be Allowed to Go to the House of Culture" something like that, we're walking along, playing our instruments and all of a sudden, in front of us there were maybe 40 French policemen and they had hate in their eyes. They charged. They didn't wait for us to approach them. They charged. And they took our instruments and beat them up and they started particularly beating the women in the back, here, the kidney area. Really . . . . So when I saw them kicking Debbie, I remember getting really flipped out – and one of them had torn my sign off of my stick, I had the stick in my hand, and I ran over to one of the cops – there were like this bunch of them kicking her on the ground – everyone is suddenly getting beaten up. I ran over to one of them and I hit him. Gross. I hit him with my stick which had a nail on the end, and I cut his face open – it was as big a shock to me as it was to him, I never expected that to happen, and as soon as his face opened up and his blood started coming out – it was like eh – so the police left her alone and they started to run over to me, and Uwe came and saw this happening and I remember him literally – I don't know how he got through them but he pushed me out between their feet and they beat him up and arrested him. Then we had this big thing, how were we going to get Uwe out of jail. Then we all ran away as fast as we could – that broke up a lot of instruments like horns – I remember my baritone was ruined. They were bad, very bad.

My baritone horn.' — (Leherrissier, interview.)

This fracas almost deprived them of their midsummer place of rest at St. Baume in Provence. The local bishop refused the money for their housing because of it. But then the priest in charge of the shrine of Ste. Magdalene whose skull is kept there allocated money out of this building funds for them to stay at her pilgrims' hospice.

They played outside in Germany quite a bit, though more in the spirit of bringing art to the people than of making politically relevant points. The police were called when they did *King Story* and *A Man* on the Rindermarkt lawn in Munich, but withdrew. In Berlin, in October – it was cold – they did *King Story* and *A Man* in the Märkisches Viertel, a project housing district, in front of a shopping center – being refused service, as hippies, by the local Kneipen, the Forum Theatre, their Berlin sponsor, procured them a bus in which to keep warm on such ventures, – and (televised) in the Wedding, an old-fashioned 19th century working class district, once upon a time stronghold of the communist party – Red Wedding. The Working class population in Germany was uninterested, in Berlin at least actively antagonistic. The kids liked the puppets.

'Nous avons joue *A Man Says Goodbye to His Mother* à Berlin, devant des soldats américains qui devaient peu de temps après partir pour le Vietnam. Les deux côtés étaient très nerveux. C'est une situation que nous aimons bien : pour faire passer l'histoire dans ces conditions, il est important de garder le champ ouvert, il ne faut pas brutaliser les gens ni chercher à leur plaire, mais simplement leur présenter le problème de telle sorte qu'ils le comprennent comme un problème venant d'eux-mêmes.' — (Schumann in Kourilsky '71.)

'I remember at the railroad station at Frankfurt, we had decided to do the *King Story* and *A Man Says Goodbye* right in the railroad station, and that was one of the main places of – where the American army base – and there were very long and very violent discussions after the shows. I remember getting into a terrible argument with a German who was saying America is the greatest, the most wonderful country and all this, and you should be ashamed of doing things against your country – the things we were doing were wrong. So I wasn't always as conservative as I am now (laughs).' — (Elka, in Schumann, interview, '79.)

30. November '69. The proper political function of theatre is not to induce action, nor to propose solutions, nor even to define problems, but to induce people to define their problems themselves.

Schumann in November '69, just before his return to the U.S.A., formulated some notions on the kind of effect on an audience theatre – or his theatre – should aim at. He was summing up his position in opposition to that of the more radical members of his touring group who wanted theatre directly promoting specific political actions on the part of the audience, specifically: revolutionary actions. He held this was not the business of theatre, at any rate not of his theatre, that rather the effect – at two removes from those effects – of stimulating people to work out their problems should be aimed at: at two removes in that it wasn't even theatre's (his theatre's) business to define the problems, let alone the solutions or what was needed to arrive at them.[1]

---

1. 'Certains acteurs me racontent que lorsqu'ils jouent *King Story* dans les usines, ils attachent le drapeau américain à une des pointes de la tête du Grand Guerrier, et ils pensent que de cette façon ils ont politisés la pièce. en realité, que faisons-nous En décorant ainsi les sentiments politiques des gens? Nous les soutenons un peu, nous leur apportons des informations qu'ils possèdent déjà. Mais ce n'est pas là ce que peut faire le théâtre. Nouse devrions agir de façon toute différente: avoir confiance en nos opinions politiques, les faire travailler à l'intérieur de nos pièces et toucher effectivement les gens grâce à elles, à un moment où ils ne s'attendent pas à des arguments politiques. C'est pourquoi les lieux communs, les histoires archi-connues comme la Bible ou les contes de fées, sont si beaux. le public croit qu'il les connaît, mais tout à coup on les éloigne de lui, et il voit comment ça ressort différemment. J'ai l'impression que si on ne déballe pas tout le truc politique, ce pour quoi on est, ce contre quoi on est, si on ne cherche pas à convertir les gens au F.N.L., ou à quoi que ce soit d'autre, il y a une bien meilleure chance de les mettre debout sur leurs jambes et de les amener à agir. Ce que nous voulons, c'est ouvrir quelque chose. Non pas inventer un problème et essayer de le résoudre, mais inventer un problème et le laisser là. Cette ouverture me paraît essentielle. (Kourilsky: Peut-on parler alors d'un théâtre de prise de conscience?) J'ai l'impression que ce que nous faisons se situe avant la prise de conscience. C'est comme si on "chauffait" la pensée de quelqu'un pour la mettre en route. Eveiller la conscience? Oui, peut-être le terme est-il exact en fin de compte. Cependant, dans ce que nous essayons d'atteindre, je crois qu'il y a plus de tripes que de conscience, il s'agit de quelque chose qui se trouve plus bas, qui est plus simple et plus facile d'accès que la conscience. Par exemple, que fait un musicien? Et je me sens musicien moi-même. Il ne réveille pas la conscience grâce à des sons, mais certainement il peut frapper avec des sons, atteindre l'homme quelque part.

Ce que nous faisons n'est pas un travail d'interprètation sur la situation dans laquelle nous vivons ou sur le système que nous subissons, c'est une "sensibilité à" (*what we feel for*) qui vient du coeur tout entier et qui est complètement engagée. Nous n'avons pas de solution pour le théâtre –. Quand j'habite East 6th Street et qu'il y a une grève, je me sens obligé d'y participer avec ce que je peux faire, c'est-à-dire avec mes marionnettes. Exactement comme Luis Valdez qui vit dans la San Joaquin Valley où il y a une grève des cueilleurs de raisin et qui se joint au mouvement avec le Teatro Campesino. C'est la forme naturelle que prend le théâtre dans ces circonstances. Et le théâtre doit certainement avoir cette immédiateté. Mais j'ai l'impression que ce n'est pas toute sa raison d'être. Nous réagissons à ce qui existe, à une situation politique et sociale, mais nous nous efforçons aussi de trouver vraiment notre vie, de trouver ces valeurs qui ne sont pas encore trouvées, et le vrai théâtre essaie de créer cela....' — (Schumann, interview of '68 or '69, in Kourilsky '71.)

Kourilsky concludes:

'Sans doute pense-t-il, comme Brecht, dont il se rapproche précisément par la volonté de ne pas engluer le spectateur dans le spectacle, que le théâtre peut aider l'homme à y voir plus clair et l'amener à prendre conscience de la nécessité de changer le monde dans lequel il vit. Mais il ajoute aussitôt, rejoignant ainsi Artaud, que le but d'un spectacle est de "s'emparer de l'auditeur pour en faire un adepte du nouveau monde", car "le théâtre est une forme de vie et de révolution en soi". En réalité, c'est la vertu rédemptrice de l'art, de l'imagination et du rêve que Peter Schumann croit avant tout.'

31. Summation. Rise and decline of Schumann's anti-war agitation in the '60s. Associated with its liberal phase, he drops out when it becomes radical resistance.

Summing up: starting, probably in October '63, with some Voter Registration Drive parading, and going on to housing problems- and rent-strike-related street activity, extending probably from January '64 into the early months of '65, both in a Leftist, Puerto Rican and neighborhood context, Schumann got into peace agitation possibly as early as March '64 (pacifist-liberal context, Greenwich Village Peace Walk) or else by August of '64 (Times Square rally, Old Left context), doing his first large-scale, formally as yet inept parade in April '65 (March on Washington, Old Left-pacifist liberal coalition context), getting the format of his parade shows together by October '65 (first Fifth Avenue march, same context), that of his stationary shows by November '65 (*Speech* on Union Square, Veterans' Day), doing his first grand – large-scale and formally successful, i.e. beautiful and powerful – demonstration, combining aspects of rally and parade, later that same November (November 27, March on Washington), and his most famous and perhaps most artistic one in March '66 (second Fifth Avenue parade), his last grand one in August '66 (Hiroshima Day), the last creative one in November '66 (Thanksgiving parade), and the last one with media impact in December '66 (St. Patrick's picketing). Up to the summer of '66, the context continues to be that coalitional one. Continuing, but his activity somewhat diminished in scale, scope and frequency, and reverting somewhat to the contexts of '64 and of the first half of '65 – 'social' agitation in a Latino, peace agitation in a Greenwich Village pacifist-liberal context – through '67, his last big demonstration (and the Movement's) is in October '67 (March on Washington), the context now a coalition extended to the New Left and 'underground culture', his contribution swamped. Except for some European street excursions, largely politically irrelevant there, he is virtually absent from the streets in '68 and '69. I.e.: the floruit of his New York City peace demonstrations extends only over the relatively brief period summer of '64 to end of '66, and that only, making liberal allowance for a scarcity of data during the first year or so of this period.

Movement street agitation slackened off considerably after '67, but Schumann's relative fade-out in '67, besides suggesting that his inactivity in '68 and '69 was not just due to this – nor to his European tours those two years – but was due at least in part to whatever caused that '67 fade-out, has to be otherwise accounted for. The obvious proximate cause is the Youth Movement's incursion into the Movement, which from the fall of

'67 onward amounted almost to a take-over. It shifted, whether we have in view non-violent resistance or hippie, then digger and then yippee provocation, the accent of Movement demonstration from voicing of opinion and appealing to conscience into the showing of disaffection, and — once the hippie phase during the second half of '67 had passed — into the suffering of provoked violence.[1] This shift had other causes in turn, but proximately it took away the Movement context of peaceful and at least in its style (whatever the extreme-right reactions at the time) non-provocative voicing of opinion and appeal to conscience into which Schumann's street art had been inserted and for which it had been designed: of which it had been the intensified and non-verbal theatrical form. All witnesses concur that Schumann was never afraid of getting beaten up, and though he may have been a little afraid of being kicked out of the country, fear seems not to the point.

The displacement of focus from the mass parade of dissidents to the shoving or shoved throng of resisters or confrontations between the state and defiers of its order was the context of Schumann's fade-out. He himself had initially effected another change of form: displacing verbal protest, chanted or in repeating signs, mostly both, by the mute progression of images. That reform, only a partial one, of course, had attended a shift in leadership from the Old Left to a coalition dominated by pacifist liberals. The reform that shoved him off the scene then reflected a shift in leadership from this coalition to the New Left and the Counterculture, to the radical young.

---

1. At the beginning of the year you could pick up your phone and Dial-A-Poem, and by June, you'd be able to even Dial-A-Demonstration — you called a number and a recording actually told you where the public protests around town were that day. The star of my movie *Sleep*, John Giorno, the stock-broker-turned-poet, was the Dial-A-Poem organizer, and the Architectural League was the sponsor. John told me that it was the porno poems that got the most calls.

Astrology and other occult things like numerology and phrenology and palmistry were getting more popular all the time — I mean, there were suddenly Zodiac signs everywhere.

The new style was violence — hippie love was already old-fashioned. In '68 Martin Luther King, Jr. and Robert Kennedy both got assassinated, the students at Columbia took over the whole campus and fought with the police, kids jammed Chicago for the Democratic National Convention, and I got shot. Altogether, it was a pretty violent year.' — (Warhol, *POPism*, 1980.)

32. The sub-text of Schumann's anti-war street imagery during the '60s. The war of power on innocence a marriage of good and evil.

Schumann's political street art of the '60s came in two forms, the stationary show, the parade. Of course, if a parade stops recurrently for the performance of some action, the translationally moving puppets becoming mobile in place, you have a combination of the two; you approach a combined form simply if you walk down the street in a strange costume and perhaps a mask, especially if you do it drumming – and the lead drummer was a fixture of Schumann's street shows – and then do your stationary show; and you get a fusion of the two if your performance space is extended and your performance includes a reasonably elaborate entrance of your puppets moving to some spot within it, as was the case with most of his Washington D.C. shows.

His stationary shows at first normally were done as overture to speeches at advertised rallies organized by others; from '67 onward increasingly rather as sole focus of a meeting, and on their own and unsponsored and unadvertised – especially, it seems, during his two European tours. They normally not only had a story and action – an interaction between the figurants – but this defined them, they were a presentation of it. E.g. *Speech* which started out as a puppet's comic non-story illustration of a speech supposedly given by it developed into an interaction between the speaker and listeners.

The parades on the other hand, though they often – and over time increasingly – comprised an action-element – typically an allegory of modern war in the form of some kind of slaughter of innocents – did not rely on this for their impact, but essentially were allegorically meaningful combinations of processionally successive allegorically meaningful elements, e.g.: captor and captives. Such allegories of relationships could be thought of as spatial analogues to actions. His parade shows not infrequently comprised two sections, like two successive sentences, grammatically independent, but clearly coupled by their relating topics, e.g. reenforcing and typically comprised both one-of-a-kind figures and lines or crowds of figures of a kind, e.g. one captor and many captives of a kind. In all respects the line of development of both stationary shows and parades was toward increased complexity, more action, coherence and organization.

As he withdrew from participation, he shifted from parades to more stationary shows: even if part of a rally, they were more self-contained – only rarely apparently, were his parades seen as separate segments of a parade, usually rather as the parade's statement in puppet form, as gathering up into image of the whole parade's meaning: visual climax of a visual show: whereas in a stationary show part of a rally, the speeches claimed more importance and defined the meeting: which did not make the stationary show just a part of that so-defined meeting, but made it show up and stand out as non-integral feature—'entertainment': on its own.

Parades and stationary shows required different techniques.[1] In an unsponsored stationary show the audience has to be pulled in, attracted, held (in a sponsored one they are apt to be captive, there and bound to stay), on a parade they are more or less surprised (though on a well-sponsored one some are apt to have been pre-attracted), the show has come to or upon them. Secondly, assuming an audience, there is less time to make a point on a parade than by a stationary show, you don't have time for a build-up, almost, nor hardly for a story, the image has to strike, and if you are presenting more than an unchanging tableau, you have to repeat your action over and over. Schumann tended to try to get beyond the travelling tableau (monstrous war figure leading oriental captives) into the area of build-up and story, of action (women nobly trudging, plane attacks women, women pitifully – though gracefully – collapse); and even when he didn't show much action, tended to try for a succession of different tableaux, a peppering with images, the images somewhat relating (his *End of the World '82* tri-partite parade the prime example). The idea here was the arrested pedestrian watching at least that whole segment of the parade going by, one to whom a more complex statement could be delivered, but also, the more elaborate the Bread and Puppetry contingent got, the greater the identification of the whole parade with it – and vice versa: its show got to seem *the* statement made by the parade, and it seemed less just another, perhaps independent, co-constitutive element of it, more an integral part, *its* statement.

The formal progression during the '60s was something like from skits and tableaux vivants of a very simple static or repetitive sort in '64, to more complex and large-scale imagery in '65, to allegorical masques with simple action in '66, to simple, narrative, effectively didactic theatre pieces in '67-'69.

In content, the progression was from a presentation of the sufferings of the poor by those of Christ during '64; a presentation ditto of the sufferings of the victims of capitalist/imperialist aggression during '65; a presentation of that same species of sufferings by the image of (male) soldiers killing women and, more particularly, mothers, of the death of

---

1. 'Wir haben zwei Techniken: wir führen auf der Strasse oder auf Lastwagen kurze Scenen auf, die in einigen Gesten und Worten eine ganze Geschichte zusammenfassen, und wir organisieren lange Paraden für die "Friedensmärsche." Während der Märsche fängt die Vorführung immer wieder neu an.' — (Schumann, interview in *Die Weltwoche*, May 17, '68.)

women and children by fire from the air in '66; and an indictment of participation in armed aggression (whether primary or as retribution or in self-defense) by fable on the theme 'who lives by the sword shall die by the sword' in '67 and '68; with perhaps a shift of accent in this theme toward a justification of armed resistance in '69.

Setting aside skullmen, representing war or agents of war or the net import of war, death, and various kinds of soldier figures, the main figures appearing in Schumann's parades were: Christ and his disciples, symbols not only of suffering but also of moral injunction, a variety of female figures, usually coming in groups – his 'Vietnamese Women', 'Vietnamese Ladies', mothers with child – symbols of goodness, patiently-borne suffering, victimhood, and Uncle Fatso, symbol of greed and brutality. The women after a while replaced Christ and his men, Uncle Fatso came and went, lending an accent both jocular and aggressive.

My mental image of a Bread and Puppet Theatre street demonstration is of War, thick-headed, giant, clumsily swaying above the grey messy clump of people bothering to carry him through the streets, his black and white or grey-faced skull above his congruent frock coat which disappears among the shoulders of the demonstrators, the whiteness of his cheeks inimical to the stone of the buildings beyond the sidewalks, other puppets, their character indistinct and confusing, below and around him: War, a familiar and though mysterious yet reassuring, almost comfortingly homey figure, rather than, say, the glaring and dismal black figure of Death: his relatively slow bobbing passage evoking an unease (and not at all antagonism) among the pedestrian crowd akin to the intuition of a disease carried within oneself. The Prophet's wail: but silent.

In fact, however, it was mostly other, at first the suffering of Man of Peace, with a horde of His picayune disciples largely, in a swan-glide, among the horde of automobiles, ascending the avenue like a bunch of sandwichmen, most miserable of salesmen, weird cousins of the Garment Center Jews; later, flocks of Ladies, Women, or Mothers, white, charred or grey, of European cast of face or Oriental mein, human-size and up but asphalt-bound, bending and rising in an orchestrated wave of white, grey, black, gawky, but vaguely evocative of a peace not of these streets, giving momentary rise to a submerged longing for a somehow better life. I.e. not the mute prophet in the strident guise of a caricature, but something meek, male or female.

The dominant and predominant image of the Bread and Puppet anti-war demonstrations was that of women aggressed against; more particularly mothers or mothers with babies; aggressed against by men, formally identified as death-dealers; the aggression in the form of burning by air warfare. A subsidiary image was that of the powerful, evil and ridiculous – male – political figure: as often as not a hypocritical war monger, and one way or another a fomentor of war and a war profiteer. It carried the leftist dimension of the anti-war stance. The female image was provided by the shrouded, flower- or leaf-bearing Vietnamese Women with their small inward faces, or by the manacled and/or blindfolded Vietnamese Ladies with the large prayerful hands and spiritually detached regards, or by the mournful, ghostlike Grey Ladies, sometimes by dead women with charred faces; the male image by demonically skull-masked men in black, henchmen of Death, or by a grey clump of dumb soldiers, or by a gibbering Fool that was equivalently a satanically red devil, or by Uncle Fatso, the obese figure of jovial greed. War appeared as a shark that was also an airplane.[2]

This sexist[3] image complements the identical sexism of Schumann's other art, e.g. the traditional portrayal of Joseph the Cuckold as Mary's weak and foolish partner, of the good mother's son as killer in *A Man Says Goodbye to His Mother*, of the self-immolating victim in a play, *Fire*, dedicated to three self-immolators two of whom were men as a woman; etc. etc. The People thus later appear divided into dumb and lazy garbagemen and strong, capable washerwomen.

This sexist image was in no way, either in the street art or in the other, weakened by the image of Jesus and his disciples, since these in no way appeared as ideal, let alone representative men, but hardly as males at all, but rather as representatives of spirituality, neither sexually male, nor fathers: essentially neuter. This secondary image may in a marginal way also, have been sexist, namely to the extent that this male spirituality is distinguished from that of the female figures by an expressive accent of

---

2. 'Primal struggle between the good guys and the bad guys. There's good guys and there's bad guys. And sometimes the bad guys are fire. Well, his good guys are usually women and his bad guys men. Usually men attacking the women and then you can get very Freudian and make a ... I mean, you could do a Freudian sexual thing out of any one of these plays. That they are all forms of rape. There is the erotic thing in them, but – you'd have to do a little pushing, but it would float.' — (Oyle, interview.)

Dr. Oyle in fact prefers a Jungian interpretation: Schumann's theatre is about the eternal struggle between goodness (the female, light) and evil (the male, darkness), but presents a deficient vision of it, in that Schumann lacks a sense of the complementarity of the two principles, of their unity in a reciprocal dependency. (Oyle, interview.) But Dr. Oyle, who denies the reality of the objective world, lacks even a sense of the struggle, i.e. prefers to deny his awareness of it: a translation of impotence into mendacity characteristic of the Californian-oriental stance. Schumann's deficient presentation of the struggle between male evil and female goodness, on the other hand, seems to me honorably to express male sexual guilt, his expiation being work, the usual, but therefore not necessarily invalid male excuse.

3. 'He made all the decisions, and I kind of fell in with that because of the kind of person I was. The people who had stronger personalities had a harder time with Peter ... someone like Helene (Hunter Palmer), who was a very – she used to argue with Peter. And she kept saying, Peter doesn't like strong women. And then I remember Carol Grossberg used to say the same thing, she would argue with Peter and say, you know, he just hates strong women, he likes women to be meek, victims, etc.' — (Sherman, interview.)

something like worry, a corrosive working of thought, indication in no way that of intellect, let alone superior intellect, but rather of (lifelong) moral struggle: of a war with self that has left no trace in the women's faces, careworn or otherworldly. As I read them, the faces Schumann has given Jesus and his Apostles express male consciousness of male sinfulness and the struggle to overcome it, at most: the unlikely victory in this struggle. As though Schumann's Eve never took a bite from the apple that, blamelessly tricked by the serpent, she got Adam to chew on.

Angels, of course, are really neither male nor female, but, as their rural doubles, creatures of women's tales, the fairies, tend to be female, so angels, the lieutenants of God in myths told by men, tend nevertheless to be males – Gabriel or Michael. Schumann so represents them – they did not appear in the street parades – but as men with a female cast like that of Leonardo's St. John the Baptist, their sternness softened by something like the aged pederast's lifetime gentle adminstration of care to delicate pricks, Walt Whitman's bloodsucking lovingness. Goodness is female.

More abstractly considered, and it was at this level that the puppets and masked figures exerted their power over those that saw them, his street shows over and over again presented the image of an opposition between innocence and evil. They showed it more simply than his indoor pieces and even his Christian observances, and therefore more strongly. Since this is an opposition with which 'common people', and in particular the 'ordinary' American – in Europe the opposition is more apt to be that of decency and evil – habitually operate, the spectators could not help but be touched, in a basic way sharing his standpoint, though disagreeing more or less vehemently as to what it was that was evil and which was the innocent party, the wily oriental or John Wayne. He's wrong, they might think, but he's a moral man. His values are ours.

As his images presented the opposition, it consisted in the active opposition of evil to innocence – innocence was a passive party to it. And evil is not only more powerful than innocence – he always showed evil as the winner, innocence as sufferer or vanquished – never even resisting – it is associated with power: war appeared as metaphor for exercise of power, and evil and power were identical. The sense of this identification, however, its tendency, was not so much that power is bad (though this is a proposition that Schumann would probably agree with without too many qualifications), as that evil consists in the exercise of power, has this as its expression, so to speak, and in particular in the destructive exercise of power over innocence and the innocent. And just as evil appeared as power over innocence, so innocence appeared not just as lack of guilt, let alone as the world's goodness, but as intrinsically exposed to the attack of evil, i.e. as suffering and as suffering the onslaught of evil in particular. Beyond the war indictment, three equations emerged – notably in his more abstract parade shows – one of evil with power, one of goodness with innocence, and one of innocence with suffering, and with them an intrinsic relationship between active power and suffering innocence and thus between evil and goodness: each in its nature the correlate of the other. I.e. the image of a marriage of suffering innocence to victimizing power, of good and evil. Beyond their political content, his puppet parades — showing the reiterated action of evil, the reiterated suffering of innocence, the persistence of the action — dimly — only dimly — evoked this marriage. The concept is sinister. We encounter it in de Sade's *Justine* where that union in action is the source of arousal, and in John's Revelation, where it defines society under the rule of the Beast. In Schumann's parades it carried the suggestion of a fatedness of the very evils protested against. In his thought and work it related backwards to the interdependency of Life and Death in his *Totentanz*, forward to the conception of an interdependency of female creative givingness and male destructiveness in a cosmic cycle of nature presented by his '70s circus pageants.

33. Communicational form of Schumann's '60s street agitation: spectacle as non-addressive presentation of allegories carrying and pointed up toward strongly addressive moral address.

The necessity of getting attention quickly and (briefly) holding it against the street's competition, required a striking image – puppets and action – in the parades, but one very functional in yielding its meaning quickly and completely, and with poignancy, but not competing with that meaning: except for the poignancy, the same as for a tv commercial. Unlike in regular theatres, the audience hadn't paid yet: the show had to suck them in. Discretion was out of place. But on the other hand there was a point to be made. It could be unpleasant: the audience wasn't expected back, it didn't have to be catered to.

Appearances at parades and rallies, as well as independent appearances of the Bread and Puppet Theatre constituted a use of art in protest. The group was perceived as theatre group by the press and almost certainly by people seeing the parade or attending a rally. For one thing, the contingent was quite frequently identified by name on a prominent drum. More importantly, the artistic quality and nature of the puppets was apparent. They had aesthetic appeal.

The war images Schumann disseminated were the World War II dive bomber, prisoners of war, World War I soldiers in units of a machine gun or a mortar crew – killing (the skullmen), bereavement (the mothers) – not fear. He offered them to people who, unlike the males among the students to whom during the beginning '70s he shifted his agitation, were not in any personal danger. His images were in no way up-to-date – more World War I and II and German. (Even his mother image turned out German and pre-dishwasher/laundromat.) Their action, then, was that of art, not of news: an affect-focused symbolization for retention and delayed effects, grabbing people beyond their immediate concerns and the defense mechanisms set up for everyday intercourse in an area of more profound apprehensions.

This artistic incursion involved the addition of visual imagery to verbal statement: written signs, chanted or shouted vocalisms. This was more than the addition of or a changeover to a different medium. Whereas the verbalisms were couched as protests, as demands and/or as indictments (accusations), Schumann's images had the form of statements of fact, albeit in artistic form, i.e. the form of allegorical representations of essential reality or of what the artist conceived to be the essential reality, and albeit, also, that these imaged analogues of statements of fact had moral implications and were obviously designed to have them: the reality the images reported on had moral lineaments, was structured in terms of good and bad, right and wrong. Though effectively appeals for action, their form of address was representational, not oppositional, imperative or accusatory – or even just suggestive or supplicatory. They told the public 'something wrong is being done here', and thus raised for the public the questions of whether this was not perhaps so, and what were they going to do about it – did they not share the responsibility?

To some extent Schumann seems for a spell to have succeeded in substituting his puppets for the usual display of written slogans and the shouting of them, quite standard features of street agitation of a political sort, e.g. the rallies through the years, not just the '60s, of civil servants – cops, firemen, teachers, garbagemen – in Foley Square around City Hall, or the Old Left – Communist, Trotzkyite – rallies and marches from the 1930s onward and even now. The pacifist or pacifist/anarchist core of the Peace Movement would even in this verbal agitation have tended toward a New England gentility and town meeting give-and-take moderation, but the other factions toward the customary stridency ('militancy'), the macho or pseudo-tough-guy (or, from the prophets through Marx, Jewish) style – typically in the form of 'demands' and of declarations of intent to fight, with more or less implicit (phony) threats of violence. You will remember the photos of upraised clenched fists, faces with shouting mouths, an unaesthetic confusion of signs and banners with thick black lettering – 'stop' this or that, 'no more' this or that. The replacement or even just partial mollification of this verbal militancy by Schumann's puppets moved street agitation toward an insinuative approach.

Though not formally – the puppeteers did not attempt audience contact, they were busy with their puppets, related to these, and/or were masked, and in this respect identified with the roles defined by their masks (and costuming), in which roles they had no immediate relation to the spectators – and a picture is less addressive than a verbalism to begin with – these images had a terribly direct address: to the spectators on the street or at a rally, and, I suspect, to a television audience, though not, I would say, to newspaper readers looking at photos because of reportorial alienation: the informational aspect of the photo displaces – at least in a newspaper – the impact the object photographed would have had, viewed directly.

His images addressed who saw them directly by their content, namely by their moral reference. They by this claimed relevance to everybody and intimate, personal relevance at that – e.g.: not to be evaded by a disclaimer of interest in politics. There was of course a political judgment involved (the U.S. is the culprit), and the spectator was apt to contrast or reject its validity, but the image's raising of the moral issue on the one hand exerted a strong direct force on the spectator to do just this and thus to deal with that judgment – rather than just react against its being made on the street, or react against those making it, avoiding dealing with it – on the other hand, the spectator's support of the war was apt to be a support of his country bypassing the moral issue posed, and Schumann's images would tend to stimulate him to consider the matter in this regard, the moral one, and here he might have to admit that the war though in an isolatedly political regard O.K. and to be supported, was morally a little dubious and at the very least regrettable. This was to a certain extent an expectable effect because the values posed by Schumann's imagery were largely shared by the spectators – everybody is sorry for civilians that get hurt, mothers and babies or just defenseless women raise protective feelings in men, comradely feelings in women, and when Schumann's imagery was, as it was initially, more on the Christian side, the Christian spectator – as well as the Jewish one living in a Christian society – would be reminded of the undeniable pacifist bias of his religion (the Jew of that aspect of the culture shared by him/her), and could not reject the 'argument' out of hand. Even the value judgment posed by the figure of Uncle Fatso – the ruthless profiteer – in America has a certain appeal, the more so since the figure, a caricature, has its comic aspects: the appeal of populism: the moneymakers, the greedy rich still have a place in the popular imagination and are regarded with some dislike and suspicion, and the older popular suspicions that they are for something in the commonwealth's larger enterprises though sometimes dormant are not extinct.

That the evident moral tenor of Schumann's images had a religious tinge strengthened his statement in all of these regards: the motives this, to the spectator, would imply to be his, were that much more respectable and to be respected (whereas political motives in America are subject to cynical suspicion); religious appeals (and in America, really just about any religion's) have a right to be heeded, people feel they should take that kind of sentiment into account, and in fact often the more so the weaker their own religiosity (a matter of bad conscience and of a feeling of missing out on something); and, though in a vague way, the spectator would feel he was being addressed within the framework of an at least partial and general concurrence of attitudes.

Schumann at the end of the '60s and during the early '70s was fond of telling interviewers, his theatre did not present solutions to problems, but only the problems. He had consistently presented problems, namely indicated things about society and about American society in particular that he considered wrong, e.g. the war in Vietnam. These were 'problems' in the sense that in principle, in a democracy, his audiences were in a position to do something about them. He has refrained from offering solutions in the sense that his pieces never have said just what to do about these wrong things. E.g. in his street agitation he never called for immediate withdrawal or for negotiations with the Vietcong or for interference with the draft. At the same time it was made eminently clear to spectators that something urgently needed to be done, and that they shared the responsibility for doing something, and that the show was designed to make this point. Though ostensibly factual in form – presentation of problems, if you want – almost all his art during the '60s, street and indoors, by its moralism still also had the form of an appeal for action – with the particular action unspecified in its particulars, but generally specified by the indication of something wrong, and with the appeal emanating from the images, not from the imagers. I.e. he didn't just raise the question of whether such and such was right or wrong. Even though after the '60s he continued to point to things that were in his view bad, this appeal to action disappeared. His theatre lost this form. Those remarks to interviewers in actual fact express this change of attitude and at the same time cover it over by a pretense that nothing has changed. With this change in view, we would have to say that during the '60s his theatre did more than just present problems: it urged that they be solved – by the audience. Its accent was on this appeal: not on the exposition of what was wrong. It was agitation, not just presentation.

The difference between his theatre's moral appeal of the '60s and the moralistic exposition of his subsequent theatre – the difference between saying 'you shouldn't do this' and 'such and such wrong is being done' – expressed itself in a very simple way in the organization of its formal elements: during the '60s they were organized tightly toward maximal understandability – clarity – and moral impact, subsequently toward a maximal faithfulness to what he meant and felt, and toward what he meant meant to him, i.e. toward emotional poignancy, and both at the expense of that clarity and of that exhortation.

What in any event, he believed in, and his practice during the '60s to some extent conformed to this, was that agitation to be effective must not be arrogant or contemptuous (fault and weakness of much left-wing, virtue and strength of right-wing agitation), nor provocative (but his presentation of Uncle Sam and Uncle Fatso surely was provocative), i.e. should avoid rude shocks to sentiment, but that it should rather try to make people think by appealing to what are already their sentiments and to their conscience. I.e. don't affront prejudices head on, mollify people by appeal to an area of concurrence: in a non-antagonistic frame of mind, they will be better able to consider what you are saying. True. But the 'presentation of problems' formula is shitty – the word has been arrogated by psychiatry and social welfare, and of course Schumann never came even near presenting the question of *whether* to pursue the war as a 'problem.' And as for the conciliatory approach: it behooves the weaker party.

His idea, of course, neither in the '60s nor at the end, in '70/'73 (taking in these three years of his Vermont-local and national-campus agitation), was to suck the public's arse, in the process insinuating the appropriate suppository relieving the patriotic congestion. It was, rather, not to affront culture or common man, but to work out of their potentials. Or: not to come on militantly, as faction opposing another faction.

The strangeness of Schumann's puppets may make one think of them as personal expressions and figments of his private imagination, and in the case of some of them as art works in some tradition within some artistic medium — sculpture, puppetry, theatre. But as he used them in his street shows, they were rather apt to be perceived as public types and imagery out of the popular imagination and as standard moral abstractions relating to public popular values, idiosyncratic, to be sure, but still of this sort, in fact deviating from the more ideal types (whether as regards image or as regards value) rather like the considerable proportion of popular imagery throughout the ages marked by artisanal ineptness and by the anti-didactic naivete associated with a lack of formal schooling has differed from the slick stereotypes.[1] This is not to say that in his case ineptness or naivete is really in question: just that popular imagery and values have always had this range, and that his personal genius and background made his products more similar to this portion of it than to the other.

By not relating to the street audience, the Bread and Puppet Theatre related that audience more directly and strongly to what it did, the show. In this regard also, however, it significantly modified the normal patterns of Movement street agitation; it made the show and its performance — the communication as act and as product — as unimportant as themselves, the performers of the show, the communicators: in terms of the self-presentation of the communication, i.e. as far as what manner, form and context of the *show* drew attention to or signified as topic — if not in terms of the response of the audience to the big puppets. The communication presented itself and the communicators as the incidental and negligible, merely instrumental occasioners of the communication. Its communicated focus was on its topic, the moral responsibility or guilt of those addressed: whereas in Peace Movement street agitation independent of it, the focus was not or not only on the topic (the war and its evils), but also or even primarily on the communicators, the marchers or ralliers, and on the communication, the march or rally. That it was the puppeteers who were making an anti-war statement was not relevant to that statement; and neither was the making of it, the puppet show, except by its anti-war

---

1. 'The not achieving seems to my very important for the achieving. That they didn't quite get what they wanted — this trouble that they always had in these folk arts — that probably made for their greatness very often — that they wanted to do probably, sugary, stupid stuff and they didn't get it and on the way to that sugary stuff they made weird things. Like in the paintings and the picture-story stuff they did where they tried very much to imitate professional painters of the period but they didn't succeed but they painted them awkward and this awkwardness is so much better than the professional painters they tried to imitate.' — (Schumann, interview, '82.)

meaning. It invited no attention to its organization or form; its organization or form invited attention to the evils of the war; were designed to attract this attention and to convey this meaning: provided no comment about the show. The actual effect surely was not altogether this. People have pre-established attitudes about shows, and to some extent pay attention to a show and judge it as a show in addition to perhaps being concerned with its meaning: discount the self-abnegation of a performance as formal device. But to a considerable extent I imagine the projected indications that the show was not the point were effective.

The artistic nature and quality of Schumann's contribution not only shifted the mode of address to greater innocuousness and immediacy – both – but had two further effects: to some extent they justified – to the public – his group's making the statement made, the question 'who the fuck do they think they are, shooting off their mouths' did not arise regarding art and especially not as regards this not unappealing, pretty good art; and there was a kind of flattery in being presented with this art: an effort had been gone to, and the ordinary pedestrian could not refuse a certain appreciation.

Schumann's street agitation in all these regards was a 'good faith' operation: even if perhaps in truth not much effect on the public – the street public or the public found through the media – could be expected, and even less further effect on government, yet this artistic allegorical moral appeal, formally hardly even at all addressive, but by its universality and moralism in fact most directly addressive, but above all inoffensive, even: appealing was altogether and seriously – in good faith – designed for effect: if effect were possible, it would have it. It wasn't just a self-satisfying voicing of opinion or a deliberately obnoxious liberation of feelings, the two forms characterizing the Movement's street agitation before and after (and around) Schumann.

Movement street agitation was altogether spectacle, presentation of image, and in these senses theatre: these aspects of it swamping the aspect of it as rational discourse, incepted dialogue, informational enterprise. On the one hand, and especially earlier on, the image of a mass in motion and of sincere people – of a combination of decency, sincerity and concern, no doubt sincere enough, but put forward as itself an argument – on the other hand, and especially later on, images of disaffection from the social routine and from the social system's character or system and images of lively high spirits and of a clash of both this liberated state and this elan with the system, a clash in which the system appeared as brutal and as linked with often petty regulation and with a standardization of conduct imposed on life. Schumann's stuff diverged from both of these forms of spectacle in two ways. First, it was the spectacle of an obviously sincere social gesture, a communication into which work and talent had gone. Secondly, it was formally in the nature of spectacle.

It was not the only kind of Movement spectacle, formally spectacle, though it was pretty much the only kind of formal parade spectacle, occasional inept masks and puppets made by others aside, not only irritating by their ineptness, rather than aesthetically seductive, but inexpressive: not making their point, and in any case rare. Most other Movement street spectacle art was either folksinging or theatre: street or rally skits, occasional plays done in parks, some of the street skits designed for audience involvement, theatre generally of a folksy and humorous sort.

The overall distinguishing feature of Schumann's things relative to this other art — the aesthetic quality of it aside — was its economy. It concentrated on the issue — pretty much the one issue of war, but when the issue was rents, a strike of agricultural laborers or the treatment of prisoners, that issue — it was in all its features shaped to convey what it was about; it concentrated on the general, abstract features of the issue; it represented them directly: the puppets and puppet actions represented moral abstractions, universals, not people; and none of it was spent on providing entertainment, amusement or shocks by which to focus attention. Unlike the folk singers it didn't sell the artist's personality — it had an impersonal form — unlike the other theatre, it did not represent individuals, dispensed with psychology,[2] did not illustrate the issues but allegorically denoted them. It did not divert and did not provide mood, anger or enthusiasm, say.

It thus helped Movement street agitation achieve a concentration of content, not just to a single issue — the war — but to abstract features of this issue. This simplification was eminently appropriate to the Movement when it was coalitional, this calling for an avoidance of stands on issues on which there was divergence within it, and specifically when it was a coalition of liberal pacifists (predominantly concerned with the war, not for instance with civil rights or the evils of the social system) with Old Leftists, coalition within which, in the tradition of the 'popular front', and for strategic reasons, the Old Left played down its dogmatism and revolutionary historical outlook, so that the peace concern of the liberal pacifists outwardly prevailed.

It went beyond the Movement message and added to it in one

---

2. 'Ich glaube nicht, dass die schauspielerische Darstellung eines Problems zu seiner Lösung führen kann, aber sie bringt den Leuten, seien sie nun Hausbesitzer oder Mieter, Pazifisten oder Soldaten, auf der einen oder auf der anderen Seite der Barrikade, die Deutung der Probleme zum Bewusstsein. Man muss das Interesse der Leute wecken, ohne sich in den Details zu verlieren, ohne alle Aspekte der Fragen begreifflich machen zu wollen. Die Passanten auf der Strasse sind nicht empfänglich für realistische Schauspiele. In diesem Bereich bietet ihnen der Film alles, was sie sich nur wünschen können. Man muss deshalb Metaphoren schaffen, überraschende, ungestüme Scenen ohne jede Psychologie, die echt wirken, weil wir an das glauben, was wir spielen. Mit den Masken und den Puppen, von denen gewisse bis zu drei Meter hoch sind, vermögen wir einen Eindruck von "echter als das Leben" zu schaffen.' — (Schumann, interview, *Die Weltwoche*, May 17, '68.)

respect: anchoring its visual condemnation of the war in a view of life, intimated by the appearance of the puppets and by features of the allegories of some of the parade shows. I think, however, that by and large this personal ideology of Schumann's came across to spectators merely as moral tone and religious aura, not as specific ideas nor a personal standpoint. His personal ideology was the more inobtrusive as he did not fashion his street work to express it, but simply used it and could not help doing so – to express opposition to the war.

Schumann's street theatre during the '60s addressed and to some extent reached a popular audience, the public – generally lower middle or working class: on the Lower East Side sub-working class – generally a non-theatre-going public – that might happen to encounter his puppets. This impact was lessened on the one hand by the demonstrations generally taking place on weekends when fewer and fewer working class people would be on the streets, and often on the less 'popular' avenues (Fifth rather than Seventh), on the other by some tendency toward a selection of sympathizers perhaps not qualifying as 'popular' at rallies, but even along parade routes. He addressed this public in an argumentative way: did not merely confront it with factional opinion, numbers or sincerity of belief. He sought, by his popular imagery and that imagery's general moral rather than narrowly political meanings to address them on common ground. A German critic; Dieter Herms, though speaking equally of the San Francisco Mime Troupe and of the Teatro El Campesino, and speaking as regards the Bread and Puppet Theatre not of its agitational work during the '60s, but of work of '70-'71 (*Mississippi, Birdcatcher*) has given a neo-Marxist formulation of this achievement:

'Drei im besten Sinne radikale Theatergruppen, die seit 1959, 1961 baziehungsweise 1965 bestehen, die San Francisco Mimo Troupe, das Bread and Puppet Theatre und El Teatro Campesino, zeigen aufgrund einer kontinuierlichen Produktion und eines stetig wachsenden Publikumzspruches, dass ein politisches Agitationstheater in den USA, insofern als es sich künstlerischer Mittel bedient, die volkstheatermässigen Konventionen entstammen, durchaus nicht vom psychedelischekstatischen Theater abgelöst wird, sich nicht nur neben diesem behauptet, sondern es an Breitenwirkung übertrifft. Das lässt sich zunächst äusserlich am Radius der Aufführungsgeographie darlegen.

Literatur und Theater sind gemeinhin Ware. Verlage und Bühnen beschäftigen Autoren, Regisseure und Darsteller in einem ökonomischen Produktionsvorgang. Der Konsument der Produkte kauft sich als Zuschauer die Aufführung oder als Leser das Buch. Die politischen Theatergruppen stellen sich – schon um der Freiheit der politischen und künstlerischen Aussage willen –, wenn irgend möglich, ausserhalb diese Verwertungsprozesses. Sie gehen als Strassentheater zu einem Publikum, das sonst nie ins Theater gehen würde. Sie sprechen Klassen und Schichten an, die nicht zum etablierte bürgerlichen Bildungspublikum gehören.

Die Werbe- und Vertriebsmechanismen der Kultur- und Bewusstseinindustrie werden bewusst gemieden. Politisches Volkstheater, vor dem Hintergrund von Distributions- und Rezeptionsprozessen definiert, das die Distributions-verhältnisse des herrschenden Kulturapparates gezielt unterläuft, muss leztlich als ein Theater im Rahmen von Gegenöffentlichkeit verstanden werden. Gegenöffentlichkeit – das ist potentiell die Gesamtheit der lohnabhängig Arbeitenden, also die Mehrheit der Bevölkerung, das "Volk". Das politische Theater, das in diesem Rahmen tätig ist, begreift sich daher wesentlich als Instrument, den Erfahrungsbereich seiner spezifischen Öffentlichkeit zu strukturieren Die Texte und Aufführungen geben somit Lernhilfen; sie wollen Lern- und Sozialisationsprozesse in Gang setzen, die die produzierenden Gruppen selbst (in einer tendenziellen Identität von Produzent und Rezipient) und das konsumierende Zielpublikum im Bereich konkret begrenzter Öffentlichkeitsräume (Campus, Farm, community) zur Organisation des eigenen Lebenszusammenhangs befähigen.'

As regards the Bread and Puppet Theatre:

'Das zentrale künstlerische Gestaltungsmittel für die politische Aussage ist die Puppe; als gigantische Siebenmeterpuppe, als normal lebensgrosse und als am Stab vor dem Gesicht getragene "pole puppet". Die Puppe dient jedoch nicht der subtilen Differenzierung im Sinne einer Vielschichtigkeit der Aussage, sondern vereinfacht und reduziert alle Problematik auf ihre grundlegenden Gesetzmässigkeiten. Mit den Puppen wird alle Verschwommenheit – etwa psychologischer Characterdarstellung in Drama – auf typische und alltäglich fassbare Zeichen gebracht.

Es wird damit – im Gegensatz zur gespielten Geistesgestörtheit des strengen Guerillatheaters – ein positiver Weg gefunden, ein durch herrschende Manipulationsmittel vorprogrammiertes und sozialisiertes Publikum mit kritischen Inhalten zu konfrontieren und ihm Verständnis und Einsichten über seine Lage zu vermitteln. Es wird in seiner Abgestumpftheit gleichsam new sensibilisiert. Puppen, Masken, und einfache Schlaginstrumente sind so die strategisch adäquaten Formen, um relevante politische Inhalte einem Zielpublikum nahezubringen, das zur arbeitenden Bevölkerung der unteren und mittleren Klassen gehört.'

(D. Herms, *Mime Troupe, El Teatro, Bread and Puppet – Ansätze zu einem politischen Volkstheater in den USA, Maske and Kothurn*, 1974 or 1975.

Schumann did not, however, address this audience on the nature of the society, nor did he urge it to change that nature, or even intimate that such a change would be desirable. His address was neither reformist nor revolutionary. It was not an attempt to alter consciousness: it was an appeal to conscience. There was, even in his Latino-oriented rent strike and voter registration or grape strike agitation, no social message. In the main he confined himself to the topic of the war, did not suggest any causes of it, opposed it on moral rather than political grounds. I say this not to diminish the achievement of his '60s agitational theatre – to my mind it was grandiose – but merely to define its nature.

Part IV(3).
Indoors theatre during the '60s.

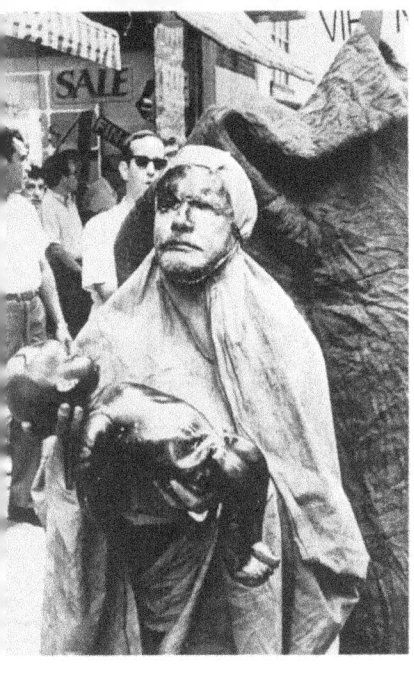

Hiroshima Day Walk, August 6, 1966.
(Photos: F. McDarrah)

Demonstration at St. Patrick's Cathedral, December 1966.
(Photo: Karl Bissinger)

Bread and Puppet Memorial Day Parade, May 30, 1966.
(Photo: Allyn Baum, New York Times Pictures)

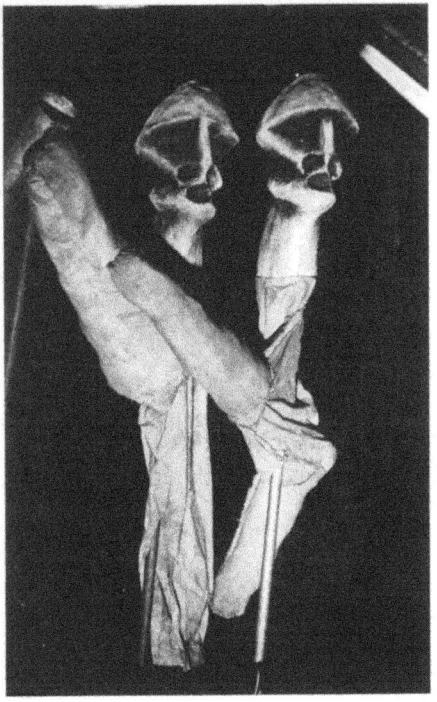

The Elements of World War II,
at 148 Delancey Street, 1963.
(Photos: P. Moore)

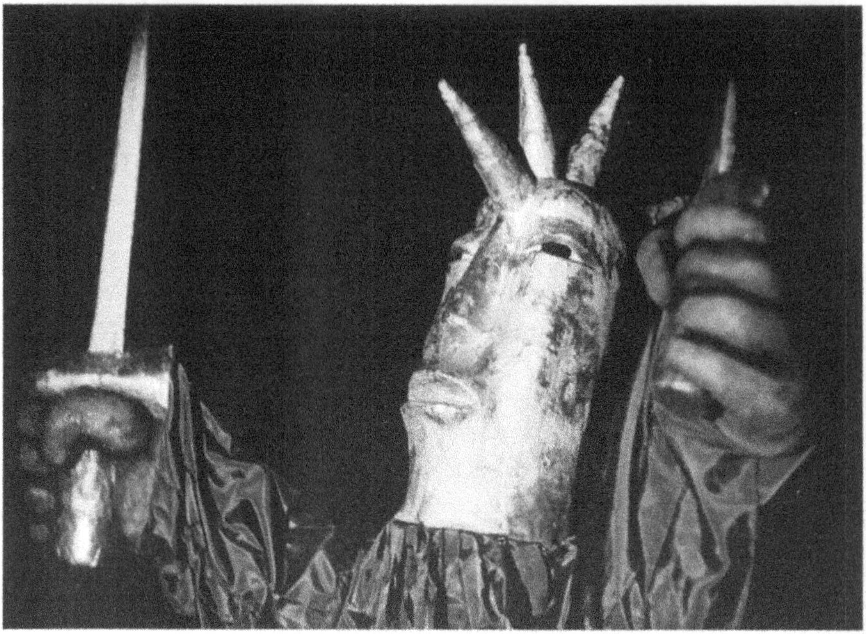

King Story I, 148 Delancey Street, 1964.
(Photos: P. Moore)

King Story, Dolores Park, San Francisco,
California, September 1968.
(Photos: G. Gscheidle)

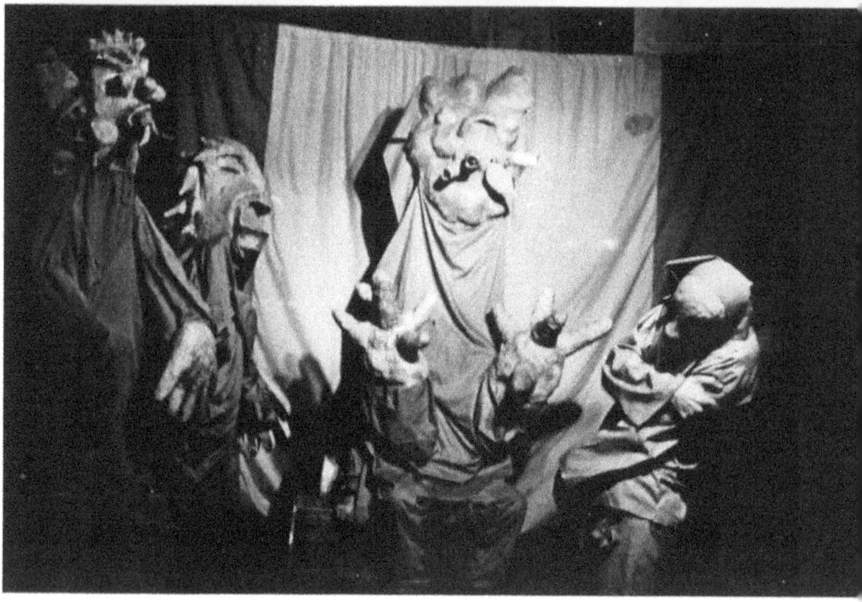

The Birdcatcher in Hell, 148 Delancey Street, 1964.
(Photos: P. Moore)

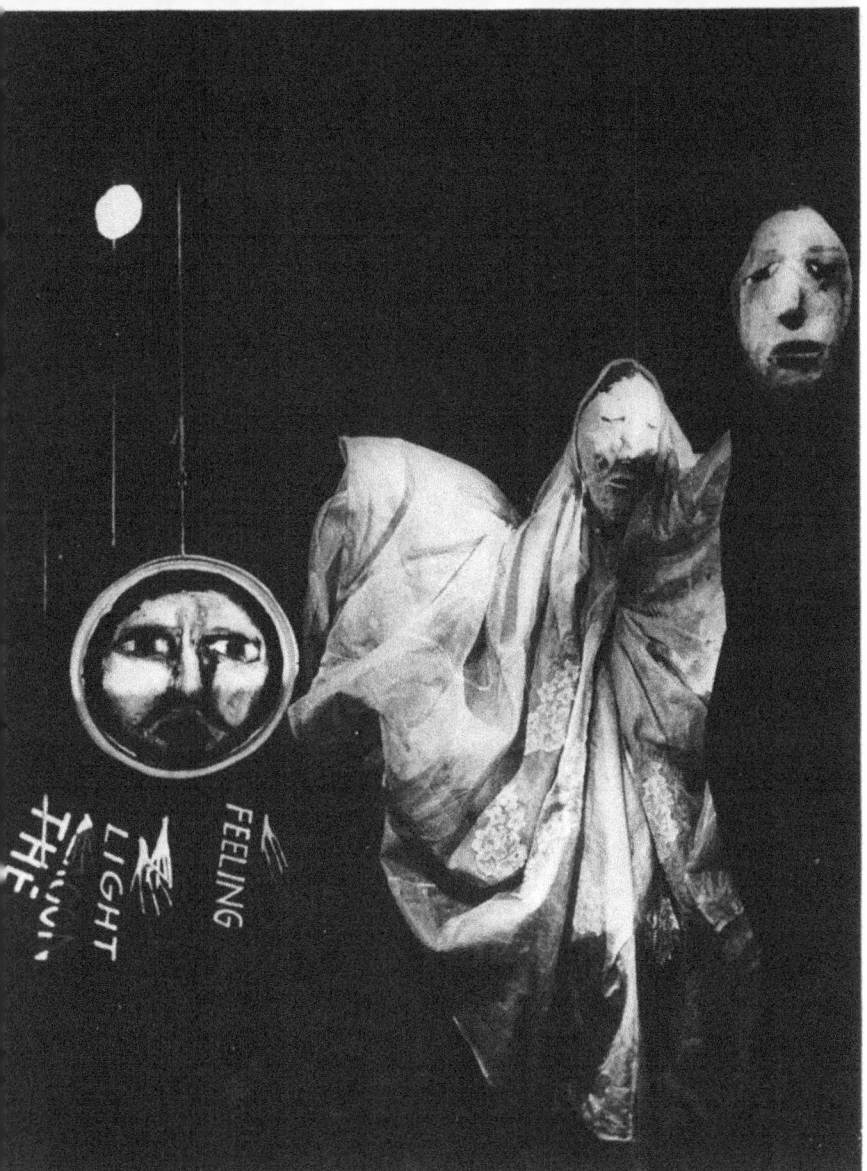

Leaf Feeling the Moonlight, The Bridge Theater,
New York City, November 1965.
(Photo: K. Bissinger)

Fire, New York City, 1966.
(Photos: R. Alazraki)

Dead Man Rises, Astor Memorial Library, New York City,
May – November 1967.

A Man Says . . .,
Panhandle,
San Francisco,
California,
September 1968.
(Photos:
G. Gscheidle)

The Cry of the People for Meat, March–December 1969. (Photo: W. Bredel)

(Photo: P. Moore)

Demonstration for 'The Chicago Seven', Foley Square, February 16, 1970.
(Photo: F. McDarrah)

Peter Schumann in 1968.
(Photo: G. Gscheidle)

Contents: Part IV(3)

1. Yields of his street agitation for his indoor theatre. The unabashed involvement of the spectator in guilt. Space. A broken up show. — 603
2. The New York period: creation, development, extension of his new mask-puppet medium. Initial two year experimental period getting away from a traditionalist conception. Possible subjacent ideal of replacing verbal language by sound and music: scarcely ever attained. Persistent problem of use of verbal language incidentally dealt with. — 614
3. November-December '63. *Elements of World War II.* — 618
4. Winter '63/'64. *Apocalypse.* — 620
5. February-April '64. *King Story.* — 621
6. October '64-November '65: Schumann temporarily gives up on the big puppets, develops his medium along other lines. — 628
7. October '64. *Murder Mystery.* — 629
8. October '64-January '65. *The Birdcatcher in Hell.* — 632
9. January-March '65. *Harvard College Questionnaire.* — 639
10. May-July '65. *Flower Mountain.* — 641
11. November '65. *Leaf Feeling the Moonlight.* Interaction of big puppets. — 642
12. January-June '66. *Fire.* Effective use of masks. — 646
13. February '67. Sufferings of Vietnam, two further pieces: *Wounds of Vietnam, Bach Cantata #140 (Grey Lady Cantata#1).* — 664
14. May-October '67. *Chicken Little, or The Story of the World.* — 672
15. May-August '67, *Speech* and, February '68 ff., *Chairs.* — 678
16. May-November '67, *(The) Dead Man Rises.* — 684
17. July-November '67, *A Man Says Goodbye to his Mother.* — 691
18. November '67, *Eating and Drinking in the Year of Our Lord 1621-1967.* — 696
19. January-March '68. *When Johnny Comes Marching Home.* — 701
20. April-June '68. The first European tour. Fame in France. — 710

21	September '68. *Reiteration*.	716
22	June '68-March '69. The making of *The Cry of the People for Meat*. (*The Bible, Blue Raven Beauty*, The Motherfuckers.) Jehovah as the Satanic essence of man. History: The son's perennial struggle against and defeat by the father.	725
23	March-December '69. *The Cry of the People for Meat*. Pessimistic glorification of resistance, even armed.	743
24	April-November '69. Touring Europe with *Cry*. The Maestro stays atop of chaos (the cunning of the artist).	769
25	December '69, New York City. Flat on his arse.	781

1. Yields of his street agitation for his indoor theatre. The unabashed involvement of the spectator in guilt. Space. A broken up show.

Schumann started building big puppets in his store front living quarters on Suffolk Street in the fall of '63 even before he had a performance space, though his Judson Memorial Church and Living Theatre connections from the previous winter and his encounter with the Rev. Glenesk of Spencer Memorial Church during the summer probably made him think he might get to use them for a Christmas show and/or an Easter one. He got the Delancey Street loft, a space he could perform in, in November or so. He now entered a prolonged period of experimentation with the new puppets working his way around to in front of the curtain and to operational distinctions and correlations between his modes of performance (cf. III.1). He had what he felt were satisfactory results at the end of a year (*Murder Mystery*, the first version of *Birdcatcher*). But the experimentation continued and it wasn't until the end of a second year, with *Leaf* of November '65 and *Fire* of January '66, that he arrived at what we might call an operational method – not a formula or a routine, of course, but a set of solutions and techniques that he could choose between, develop further and add to: a mastery of the medium he had created: that medium itself, we might say. Confidence.

Now this, of course, was also the period during which he got into, developed and, in the same sense, arrived at a method for the street use of his puppets. What at first sight is striking is the total opposition between their crude and free deployment in the great parade shows of October '65-March '66 and their fine and intimate use indoors November '65-January '66. *Leaf* and *Fire* of all his shows of the '60s by their finesse and control were formally – aesthetically – the furthest from not only his parade but also from his rally shows, and not only just because they were done in a small space the smallness – and enclosedness – of which Schumann's staging emphasized (he didn't use large indoor space until *Bach Cantata* of February, *Chicken Little* of May '67): he was doing indoors what he couldn't do outdoors. But – it seems to me – his first street use of his puppets inspired his development of an indoor medium in basic regards. I don't mean it provided him with particular procedures or specific precepts. I mean it guided him in working it out. His theatre puppetry, and that of the '60s in particular, was basically shaped by his agitational street puppetry.

His street agitation first of all I would say gave him for his indoors puppetry of the '60s the courage for its distinctive form: for a directly presented content of moral issues, for directly and focally moralistic core-meanings, directly implicating his audiences. Moral content not as coyly incidental fillip to a tale, nor as authorial viewpoint, but as the content itself, with everything else incidental to it, and in the form of a stark opposition between good and evil.[1] No pretense of entertainment or art being the primary concern. His indoors theatre of the '60s in this regard was an extension of his street theatre.

Secondly, it gave his theatre the stylistic features I have tried to describe (Part III), the features of a naive theatre: strength and simplicity of gesture for clarity of meaning, delineation of essence, roughness and crudity and illusion-breaking alienatory effects to prevent aesthetic absorption distracting from message.[2] These devices are essential on the street to be able to

---

[1] 'Some of our shows are good and some are bad. But all of our shows are for Good and against Evil.' — (Schumann, *Streets and Puppets*, preamble to Schumann, *God Himself* '67.)
[2] Ron Argelander in '76 (*Bread & Puppet's Domestic Resurrection: The War is Over*, *Soho Weekly News*, August 19, '76.) retrospectively characterizes Schumann's theatre style of the '60s:
'stripping away unnecessary information from story line, abstracting movements, and substituting simple symbolic actions for the more complicated ones.'
'They belong in the street. I am not being snide. The genius of Peter Schumann's group is that its extravagant imagery speaks best to crowds out in the open rather than to an "audience" conventionally awaiting a theatrical performance. Schumann insists he has nothing to do with the theatre and he is right. By theatrical standards, the group's work is naive and crude without simplicity and direct impact (the reverse virtues of naivete and crudeness). But as a unique kind of public spectacle, it is incomparable. Like the medieval pageants and pre-Elizabethan touring companies it resembles, the company organizes moving totems to convey disturbing political insights. It is a mistake to write them off as primitives or amateurs. They are both primitive AND amateur; the mistake is in writing them off.
What has fascinated me about the Bread and Puppet Theatre is the way in which it extends theatrical conventions outside of the conventional theatre. It is precisely because the work does not belong in a theatre that it is so theatrically exciting. It poses not so much a development of form as an alternative environment and, in that sense, is in the mainstream of an avant-garde theatre work. It reaffirms the essential theatricality of public rituals.' — (C. Marowitz, *theatre abroad. London: off-off B'way. Village Voice*, September 5, '68.)
'(I: How do street performances influence your aesthetics?) You don't make your point unless a five-year-old girl can understand it. If she gets it, the grown-ups will too. The show almost has to be stupid. It has to be tremendously concentrated. You need that intensity on the street much more than in a theatre. Indoors you can get by with technique, by sticking to your dialogue, but on the street you come across only if you have your mind on What Has To Be Done. Everything should be focused, and everything will become awkward and lame if your guts aren't in what you're saying. Just look at the Peace Marches, hippies happily singing while carrying photos of burnt children. People running around with coffee and sandwiches. But carrying pictures of burnt children is something very hard to do, something very heavy. And unless you know that, you don't get your message across. Most of our street performances taught us how to concentrate, how to get across. We learned how to make large crowds stop drinking cokes and start to listen.' — (Schumann in Brown and Seitz, *With the Bread and Puppet Theatre*, *Tulane Drama Review* #33, Winter '68.)

compete and get across. In a theatre – indoors – they are not at all needed that way, but now are (were for Schumann) needed to prevent the traditional consumerism from taking over, and to keep a leash on the artist's temptation of artistic pride. Where on the street finesse would finesse you right out of the picture, in a theatre it would allow art to absorb your meaning. What in a theatre become alienatory devices to show the work, on the street is unavoidable—some guys, women carrying some homemade puppets.

Thirdly, Schumann developed an art of staging focused on climactic constellations of figures figuring as significancies. His staging over the years can be described as attempting (as the photographs show, successfully) to achieve strong – visually, pictorially, spatially strong – groupings; in undisturbing – in the simplest – ways often with something like a counterposing of individuals and groups, notably of large individual 'puppets' and groups of masks as recurrent, perhaps even as the standard or normal organizing principle; the occurrence and succession of these groupings enlivened, one might say softened, by human movement, whether that of unmasked performers or operators implementatively and presentationally active or that of masked or shrouded mimes; and with an emphatic tolerance of messy and incidental slips of gesture, stance, costume or 'machinery' (props, ropes, wood), most of the time left in as a factual environment or background of the essential pictorial relationships, compelling a more active activity in grasping these, but by way, here, of actually strengthening them.

There are two crucial considerations, it seems to me, behind this kind of staging. On the one hand the mute, non-verbalizing figures that are Schumann's staging elements are not perceived as having egos (such as are represented by actors). Psychological states and processes (attributed to the stage figures by the audience) are not available for defining stage relationships. The stage image must be created without reference to them: on a purely spatial, pictorial level. On the other hand, the gestural and sculptural abstraction of these figures very much facilitates pictorial configurations that are both striking and significant. To signify the (psychological) relationships between the characters represented by actors by pictorial arrangements is much harder.

My description probably exaggerates the static character of Bread and Puppet performances. One does have a sense that the strong groupings, pictorial effects are achieved – come about. But no great shaping effort seems put into the movements creating them. E.g. until the mid-'70s there was virtually no art of entrances and exits – something precluded, really, most of the time, by Schumann's spurning the use of the stage space (as self-contained unit) or of its opening to the audience (as place-where-the-picture-happens) as orienting aid for his groupings. The groupings crucially comprise gesture. But gesture is a motion resolving into pose. Or when they comprise movement other than achievement of gesture it is apt to be a pattern subsisting in a place, notably linear procession, circular tour, sequential iteration of gesture. The impression of movement, grosso modo, attaches to the 'softening' or 'enlivening' movement of operators and/or mimes. And the persistent background of mess from which the relational pictorialities detach themselves also helps to keep the performances non-static.

The groupings achieved by Schumann are very good and good enough to make him a very good theatre director. But I don't think there is much to learn from studying his particular groupings. They are of a traditional modernistic sort and don't indicate any relationships between the figures that are much out of the ordinary in theatrical practice. What is remarkable about them apart from their independence of any restfulness and ordering of stage space and stage frame is their clarity and strength: they have the quality of decisive, convincing statements. This is rarely achieved or even attempted in theatre, in fact is somewhat suspect to contemporary directors – it is more of an opera tradition, though expressionist theatre in Germany and Russia around World War I attempted it also. Schumann arrived at it, I would say, by way of his outdoor demonstrations: where the city was the mess, and the statement the point.

Finally, his street work taught him staging that makes place incidental, defining space by placed objects rather than by a frame, and compositions by the relations between their components rather than in terms of a predefined space (and the performance as a whole by what the spectators can be induced to make of it, rather than by the place where it is offered). In traditional theatre, the viewer relates the actors into a scenic image by their places on the stage, in terms of its limits and in terms of decor and props, and in terms of their roles in the play (plot, character, psychology of the character), and partly focuses on them as self-contained wholes. In Schumann's theatre, perception construes the image starting from individual figures as elements of composition. On the street you are not in a theatre, your puppets damn well have to create their space and – forcibly – their relations. There is no frame. The show is not supposed to be there. As with the musical groups you come across when the weather gets warmer, around Sheridan Square in the Village, outside Penn Station/Madison Square Garden, along 42nd from Fifth to Seventh, this creates an intense rapport between the pedestrian that chooses to stop and watch and the group, though at the same time the pedestrians's freedom any second to drop off or walk on is extraordinary, his/her attention thoroughly his or her choice. The space does not support the show, but it doesn't absorb it either e.g. into the status of a performance at such and such a theatre. The artistic advantage is the spectator's concentration on what is being done, concentration not only of perception but of acute critical judgment. The spectator's attention has not been currupted either by status given the performance by its locale, nor by his/her having gone to the trouble to come and see/hear it, nor by his/her outlay on a ticket that opened a closed door, privilege of admittance. In the case of street agitation (rather than of street artists performing for the take), the performers appear as equally free: they do desire to be heard/seen (or they wouldn't have come): but this has been their sovereign choice: no – e.g. economic – necessity constraining them to their appearance appears. This also promotes a focus on the show, not to be seen as expression of a constraining force, but autonomously itself offered for consideration.

Schumann and not only in the '60s but also later tried in his indoors shows to repress the show's exclusion of the audience and the confrontational aspect of the relation of theatre to audience, and after to reproduce this free situation – encounter in freedom – and this direct relation of spectator to performance. This was consonant with his basic conviction that art ought to spring freely and genuinely from–as appropriate response to–the situation and the artist. But to keep on arranging–or just choosing – performance situations that would both as regards the performance space and the spectator space approximate these conditions was a further matter, a special effort calling for special restraints once he was into doing theatre regularly. It called for avoidance of regular theatres and of admission charges, as far as either was financially feasible, for improvised irregular seating, and most important of all for an inappropriateness of the performance space to theatre, and to the particular show shown – in its demensions, decor and everyday functions so that the show would be seen to make space for itself, and the performers would be seen to have come there for doing a show – momentary campers. Dispensing normally with the elevated stage, the framing proscenium and the front curtain, he shared the performance space with the audience – the opposite of 'environmental theatre's' substitution of performance for spectator space, not that theatre's total extension of performance space, but negation of the difference between it and viewing space, and, in principle at least, ideally, an insinuation of theatre into living space. He recreated the shared space of street agitation.

In all four regards, it wasn't that street agitation put him in mind of general principles, rather it strengthened pre-existing inclinations by affording them a field, or even: required him to follow them and gave him some practice within their scope. These general ideas – hardly that, inclinations – had to be worked out, that is: working back and forth between the street and indoors, he came up with practices roughly delineable as supra. Found it could be done; then worked out how to do it.

The underlying attitude – doing theatre as a useful and basic service to the community – may antedate his street agitation. But there is no evidence for this. It has since the fall of '63 been expressed by the distribution of bread at the end of performances, a gesture suggesting that the performance was intended as a vital aid akin to furnishing the staff of life, that in theatre situation the theatre people functioned as givers, and that the spectators, sharing one loaf, relate to one another as members of a community, with the further connotation that a theatre performance renews the union of the spectators in one God, the performer functioning as priest, a role that in his later circuses Schumann assumed himself, slicing the implausibly many loaves now, a miracle at a wedding, and putting butter or aioli on them, the butter if not the aioli (Schumann thinks of garlic as as vital as bread) adding the suggestion that man does not live from bread alone, an addendum qualifying the original gesture of distributing the broken bare bread by intimating that maybe theatre gives more than just subsistence nourishment. But though the underlying attitude was not developed by his street agitation, his street agitation, I would say, affirmed him in the maintenance of it.

Before Schumann got into street agitation, his audiences were children, occasionally a college audience, splatters of alienated New York art lovers, intelligentsia. His street agitation had 'the people' as audience. It gave him a different concept of audience: as an undifferentiated crowd to which he related only as fellow human beings living in one and the same commonwealth. From sometime in '65 or '66 onward, he constructed his pieces for presentation to the People: as though his audience were some segment of that mass, (1) not the peculiar group of individuals present, (2) not as in any way other than the People. Each of his pieces from *Leaf* ('65) or *Fire* ('66) onward to *Cry* ('69) addressed the People. Neither that, as I have suggested, the People as he thought of it was a fiction, nor that neither this phantasmagoric People, nor any part of it, but mostly a bunch of alienated sophisticates was his actual audience, affected this.

The street audience didn't have to be entertained or pleased or in other ways, e.g. by Art, given value for money it hadn't paid – the street agitator, unlike the showman, is not a debtor – and self expression was out of place and would have been obstructive. The occasion for the address to it justified a severely direct approach, the locale a certain primitiveness. On the other hand, Schumann, assuming them 'ordinary people', could freely share with them basic simple values he could presume them to share, and the putting forward of which was in any event strategically advisable.

The audience that Schumann's indoor theatre got in the USA from about 1966 onward, though starting in 1976 he got a popular audience also up in Vermont, consisted mainly of sympathizers, adherents or fellow travellers of the Peace and other Resistance movements, more or less genteel and often professional people, politically radical or liberal, but more the latter, college students or college educated: people whose views and feelings largely coincided and at any rate did not clash with what they discerned as the views and feelings of his theatre, who watched his shows with a good warm feeling, and did not come to be instructed or altered or brought up short or troubled in their minds in any way, but rather to be confirmed.³

But however his indoors audiences might misinterpret the bread he broke with them, Schumann carried over the attitude and the liberty of his street agitation into his indoors shows (other than his kids' shows and his religious observances – to the kids he owed the amusement grownups owe children, at Christmas and Easter he didn't present shows, he staged celebratory feasts of communion): he owed them only an indication of duty – the most effective and veridic possible. Street agitation gave Schumann the liberty of doing theatre as unapologetically moralist address. When, after the '60s, his communicational mode changed (cf. I.14), this street agitational aspect of it, direct moral address disappeared. But other aspects derived from street agitation remained, and even this aspect was – at least from '75 onward – transmuted rather than simply abandoned.

The figures of his '60s street shows – including the rally figures of Mother, Son, King, Warrior – probably got across to people as moralistically illustrative icons (with religious reverberations) out of a slightly dated popular iconography, not particularly art, and not particularly personal. The same figures augmented by others and as used – their roles conditioning perception of them – in his indoors shows of the same period, though somewhat mysterious – not in any American tradition since the Aztecs – probably, had they taken the trouble, would have been categorized by viewers as an artist's representations of figures of ordinary experience, moralistically abstract and elevated, possibly with mystic reverberations: but again not as art (though surely not as not art either), nor (though surely quite personal) as personal expressions. Playing for these smaller audiences of people that managed to make it there, he still did not allow himself the self-indulgence or the license either of art for art's sake or of a focus on personal experience: the self-indulgence and licence that had, though abortively, guided him during his period of unsettlement up to '63. He merely expanded his participation in a realm of popular emblems (and their coordinate popular values) in an attempt at a public art relating to public experience, a wider and less rigid public domain, still moralistically abstractive, but also reflecting more personal values and perspectives than in his '60s indoors work. I see the shift from a reasonably modernistic style and an orientation toward art and expression during his Munich and Putney periods to an if only incidentally personal manner and an orientation toward moral thrust and an ascetic capture of the generic experiences of ordinary life of his New York period indoors ('theatre') art as the result

---

3. 'TDR: Who are your best audiences?
Schumann: Kids. And the people that are just usually in a place. At Montreal the best audiences were the people who swept up, the cops. The audience which doesn't go to the theatre is always the best audience.' — (Brown and Seitz, *With the Bread and Puppet Theatre*, an interview, *Tulane Drama Review* #38)

of his street work. He did not confine his indoors work to the populism of his street work. But his street work taught him the feasibility and power of an orientation toward the ordinary and toward moralistic definition. An 'orientation toward': his stuff was as weird as always, and as personal.

One thing his street work gave Schumann was a total independence of theatre architecture and engineering, of the dependency on fixed means that in concert with industry generally European theatre art has developed since the 16th century – on the performance art factory, the fixed theatrical capital. To some considerable extent the big puppets obviate a raised stage, their sculpture-power and mask-fascination proscenium encadrement, and their deployment in dance-like mime (together with the use of written signs) accoustic engineering: all advantages – ways of being independent of industrial culture – derived from his '60s focus on showing in the street. He developed a theatre independent of the fixed lighting apparatus on which European directors have depended so heavily for mood and of the separation from the audience on which European actors have depended to a large degree for the illusionist magic of acting styles developed with a view to it, of the fly space making European scene changes bearable, or the hidden-from-sight wing space allowing the naturalistic entrances and exits so important to traditional European acting styles and directing.[4] On the street, the whole operation from setting up to dismantling and throughout is on all sides visible to the public. The show has to create itself in this openness. This effectively meant that conventional theatres were

---

4. 'Die sozialen Ungerechtigkeiten, die hat jeder auch so, von denen, die ich kenne, auf seine eigene Art verdaut. Und Viele oder Einige sind davon irgendwie beeindruckt worden, dat sie ihr Innerstes verändert haben oder sind wacher geworden und so. Und ich hab zum Beispiel nur so 'ne theoretische Kenntnis von, von 'ner Idee gehabt, ja, ich hab da, ich hab, zum ersten Mal (on the Lower East Side (SSB)) so ist mir dat vor'n Kopp geknallt, wohin solch ein System führt, wie und die Auswirkungen und die Weiterentwicklung, die Vergrösserung dieses Problems in eine Katastrophe, wat ja auch wirklich so sein wird, nicht. Also dat glaub ich wohl, weil es gibt ken Weg zurück. Ja, gut, dat war sein Problem genauso wie mein's, damit fertig zu werden. Und dat war eben, wir haben auch viel darüber geredet. Er hat sich meine Bilder angeguckt – er konnt da nicht mit machen. Ich hinterher auch nicht. Ja, wofür is'n Bild gut? Um an'ne Wand zu hängen, nicht, da so'n komischen Klecks. Und ist schön, freust dich, wenn de'n Bild verkauft hast und irgendwie so'n kleiner Kunstliebhaber der hängt sich dat in'ne Bude – und dat ist nicht, wofür du arbeitest, dat ist für mich irgendwat anderes, dat ist dann 'n Fehlschuss, 'n Schuss in die Hose. Naja und da hatte Peter doch wirklich die besseren Mittel. Er hatte einige Mittel nicht, aber dat war irgendwie gut und ist auch immer noch gut, für jeden, der lernen will und machen will. Ich meine gut, ich mach jetzt, ich mach wat anderes, aber für mich ist dat, ist dat dat beste Mittel Dingel zu verdeutlichen, nicht war, so und so verdeutlichen . . . (I: Theater meinen Sie?) Ja, ja, nicht alles Theater. Dieses, dieses Theater: Puppen mit Schauspielern und Tanz mit was, mit allem, was das Theater an den Menschen zu bieten hat. Die, die, auch diese Zersprengung der traditionellen Bühne, dieses komische, diese Punch and Judy – Barock-Szenerien da von Nancy oder so, ja, unabhängig zu sein von Kulissen, unabhängig zu sein von Bühne, nur sich selber zu haben und sein Werkzeug und überall zu spielen, wo man . . . .' — (Eckhardt, interview.)

not only distasteful to Schumann because of their select public and because their special-place aura implied a separation of art from life distasteful to him, but actually constrained the operation of his peculiar theatre art in ways that he had to make special efforts to overcome.

His key device over the years became something quite simple: the curtain placed in space. He has not always used it (especially perhaps not '70-'73), but I suspect that at least during the '60s he used it in most of his shows. On occasion it might be replaced by one or more rigid panels. The curtain often, perhaps mostly, has been visibly hand held on vertical poles at both sides, and has been put up and taken down in view of the audience. 'In space': it does not extend across that stage. The curtain may be simply red or white, or it may have a painting on it. If it has a painting on it, the painting either is not that of a landscape or of a room that the action is taking place in, or if it is, is, for instance as regards perspective, non-'realistic', i.e. the place of action is faked, but is at most indicated in another medium, that of painting. The curtain provides the visual focus. It has been Schumann's standard substitute for a frame, whether that of a theatre's architecture, or one created within that architecture. It tells the audience that the performers are aliens who have penetrated into instituted society and that it is these intruders that are talking to them: not intituted society through representatives. Derived from the front curtain in hand puppet theatre, where it hides manipulation, Schumann used it as focusing device in street rallies. In shows using both hand puppets and big puppets it became the effective backdrop for the big puppets in front of it. Finally it became a generic space-defining device, a formal device for reproducing the street performance situation.

The indications 'up-stage', 'down-stage', 'stage-left', 'stage-right' are not merely conventions and conveniences, but indicate the essence of staging in contained (closed off) space and of perception of its products. Schumann broke with the principles of this staging. He substituted instituted focus for frame: as element defining locus, and, therefore, relation in space. The curtain in space is a device for frameless theatre, but only a device. The instituted focus is moveable, and can break away from such a curtain. E.g. a choral or processional group of performers or a giant puppet exercising some of the space-organizing power of a sculpture – or a narrator with or without a flip-over story book, or a group of singers or musicians – can assume the rule of perceptual center of gravity: for a moment, a scene or the duration of a show. The institution and shifting about of a focus – the organizing and reorganizing of stage space by staging – has been (I would say) the major preoccupation of Schumann as director and has given his shows their essential aesthetic dynamics. This is neither work-wise nor for an audience the same as what a frame-dependent director or actor does in creating or shifting focus of action and attention: the restful reliance on the grid is absent.

When during his second period c. '70-c. '73, he developed an interest in distancing show from audience and, with a view to this, in creating the effect of 'theatre', he therefore, having already developed his special theatre art, did not and could not seek out the traditional theatre-factory, but created special stages that he could put up in any space – like a little home puppet theatre.

Rather than placing his groupings and processes of figures in a pre-arranged and independently defined stage space or frame, Schumann has almost invariably defined an amorphous space or a space defined by functions alien to theatre by the groupings and movements of his figures, or by the focal point of a placed curtain. When he has not done so (notably in the early '70s, but already during the mid and later '60s on isolated occasions), he has arranged a clearly theatrically artifact stage or stage frame as integral part of the performance. Both this absence of a stage representing the world, a universe complete in itself, into which the spectator (outside of it) looks, and the persistent primacy of the figurants in his shows (notably, of course, the large puppets and the masked performers) over their place and over their relations (the absence in his show of a representation of 'objective' society in which the fate of history places men) have rendered appreciation of his stagecraft difficult.

When we look at photos of his earliest puppet shows (his shows of '62/ '63, other than *Totentanz*) we do not yet find that later stagecraft. From some time in the earlier '60s onward (the *Murder Mystery* of '64?), his puppets pull space together into a unity and create an ordered system of relations between them. In those earliest shows no such unity or order is instituted. In fact, Schumann's attempt seems initially to have been more to destroy conventional theatre space by placements above, in front of and away from a curtain, than to create one by the power of his masks and puppets. If what I am saying here about the peculiarity of his stagings is correct – and much of what I am saying here is an inference from photos, and photos tend to misrepresent performances both by their abstraction from the three-dimensional physicality of the performers (and in Schumann's case, puppets) and from the time dimension – it helps to understand the preoccupation of his play-making rehearsals with the gestural potentials of his puppets and masks; his staging depends on these. They ordinate his pictorial compositions and choreography.

The first seven of his twenty-one non-agitational-street, non-church and non-children shows of the '60s were developed as indoors shows for indoor showing (November '63-March '65). Of the other fourteen, seven (May '65-November '67) had agitational antecedents: *Flower Mountain, Fire, Chicken Little, Speech, A Man Says Goodbye, Eating and Drinking, Bach Cantata.*

'Wenn soviel von den Räumen, vom Theaterherkommen die Rede ist, dann deshalb, weil sich der Stil dieser seit 1965 in New York existierenden Truppe am ehesten verstehen lässt, wenn man ihn mit der Strasse in Verbindung bringt. Die übergrossen Puppen, deren verlangsamte Bewegung, die Kraft zur Selbstbesinnung und zur (auch für andere) augenfälligen Versenkung – das alles erklärt sich auch daraus, dass das Bread and Puppet eine neue Einfachheit gesucht und gefunden hat, die sich weder auf literarische Vermittlungen noch auf das simple Anbiedern an die Strassenrealität verlassen möchte. Anders als andere Strassentheater tragen die Leute dieser New Yorker Truppe daher auch keinen zu Schnickschnack vergröberten Realismus unter die Leute, der, wie bei den meisten Strassentheatern, zwischen Holzhammerpointen eines verflachten Kabaretts und dem Handel mit linken Devotionalienkitsch schwankt. Vielmehr hat die Truppe eine Kunstform entwickelt, die spröde nur auf sich verweist, die vergrössernd verfremdet, die Bewegungen verzögert: statt der plappernden Oberflächenkopie eines Alltags, der Leuten stets Entscheidungen nach einem Wortwechsel vorgaukelt, wird die Welt in die Schatten grosser, einfacher Theaterzeichen gebannt.

Zweierlei ist dabei wichtig. Einmal, dass die Truppe in ihren Aufführungen gegen die "Strasse" die schleppend genauen, übergrossen Bewegungen und einfachen Gesten seiner starr ausdrucksvollen Puppen setzt, also Kunstzeichen autonomer Bildlichkeit, die auch keine "rein zufällige" Ähnlichkeit mehr mit "lebenden oder toten Personen" kennen. Zum anderen (und das scheint mir noch wichtiger): die Truppe hat, sicher auch aus ihrer ursprünglichen "provisorischen" Situation eine Tugend machend, mit jenem Hinterherhecheln nach den Rockschössen der Technik aufgehört, mit der das übliche Theater so gerne zeigt, dass es "fast" so perfekt und illusionistisch sein kann wie Film und Fernsehen.

Aus diesem Mittel resultiert der archaisch anmutende Zug der Aufführungen, jenes Bemühen um einen vortechnischen Theaterzauber, der die Fäden nicht nur zeigt, an dem die Puppen tanzen, sondern aus denen Zeigen gerade seinen unverwechselbaren Stil der anti-illusionistischen Illusionen gewinnt.'

(H. Karasek, *Traumatische Genauigkeit*, *Theater Heute*, February 1972.)

2. The New York period: creation, development, extension of his new mask-puppet medium. Initial two year experimental period getting away from a traditionalist conception. Possible subjacent ideal of replacing verbal language by sound and music: scarcely ever attained. Persistent problem of use of verbal language incidentally dealt with.

During these years, then, the '60s, of witness-bearing in the streets of the city, boldly exposing it to the blind gaze of his puppets, and these to its stony glare, years rhythmed by his observances of the Redeemer's troubled birth and promising death, he in a series of largely indoor productions developed his different puppet theatre: essentially tragic (rather than as traditional puppet theatre essentially comic), lyrically poignant (rather than like it, romantically dramatic), and moralistically didactic:[1] presenting human predicament by confrontations between symbolic abstractions rather than in stories of motivated actions and responses); but retaining of traditional European puppetry its naive form.

The difference of this puppetry from most traditional puppetry, though especially hand puppetry and marionettry, arose largely from or was made possible by a few technical or formal choices: (1) the use, though not exclusively, of large and giant puppets, as big as or bigger than human beings (Aristotle's distinction between comedy and tragedy might be relevant here: it is hard, though not impossible, cf. e.g. Robert Anton's puppetry, to achieve either tragedy or lyricism with very small puppets); (2) ways of constructing puppets that unlike what is the case in marionette theatre, and even in Bunraku allow for or even constrain to manipulations subordinating the manipulator to the puppet, and thus generate a dignity for it virtually precluded when we see it as the puppeteer's thing, and that give to the puppet's movements (and to the movements of its garments) a stateliness similar to that of ritual dance (absent in the stiff or – mostly – jerky movements of most traditional puppets); (3) a disinterest in providing the masks with psychologically expressive expressions or the puppets with any great mobility of head, arms or legs, such as would allow gesticulation as distinct from the execution of a few large gestures: an approach to them, effectively, as sculptures, by way of movement capable only of simple, abstractly defined movements; (4) a use of depth

---

1. I would not call his theatre 1970 ff. moralistically didactic. During the early '70s, the subject became suffering rather than the causing of suffering, and the style expository – cryptically expository – with respect to the human condition (one of suffering). During the later '70s, he changed to a style of religious communion.

(not just e.g. of perspective such as traditional puppetry in the Venetian trompe l'oeil tradition sometimes provides by perspectival backdrops, a kind of depth that cannot overcome traditional puppetry's across-the-stage flatness) created by choice of performance space and by placement and paths of displacement in that space, and giving to each puppet a space of its own, defined by it (seeming its emanation), a space like that of monumental sculpture and of sculpture integrated into architecture in a dominant position, but perceived as the puppet's moral reality, and to a set of puppets a derivative space of mutual relevance derived from the interiority created for each puppet by its space; (5) the abandonment of dialogue, of the talking puppet: narration, announcements, separate vocal delivery of dialogue elements, or, occasionally, written signs substituting; this reduction of the verbal going hand in hand with an attempt to provide the visual show with a complement of sound and music instead.

I think Schumann himself to some extent thought of what he was doing in terms of 'puppetry' and in fact in terms of traditional European puppetry: his experience of which was extremely limited. I.e. he was in fact initially liberating himself from restraints of some such parochial conception of puppetry. But he was at the same time developing his new compound medium of puppet operation and masked performance; and was in addition trying to cut down reliance on verbation inappropriate to this medium and to develop a musical complement for it instead.

The majority of the shows during the '60s and later dealt with war, generally as an apocalyptic event, and implicitly pleaded for action to interdict war. But one does not get the impression of a theatre designed to address us on war (or to convey a view of life for which war could be the central illustration, a view of life as structured by an opposition between good and evil), or designed to convey *any* preoccupation of its maker's, but rather that of an artistically experimental theatre, exploring the potentials of a medium its maker has invented. Not, not at all, as though it didn't matter to Schumann what he was dealing with or what he was telling the public, but as though a double reassurance, that he *was* dealing with fundamental matters and *was* telling people the right thing, what they needed to hear, and that he was doing this naturally, being himself directly concerned with these fundamentals, and moved by them in his 'innermost being', had liberated him into a furious preoccupation with his art, with its very terms. He felt at ease turning out the products of this experimentation as though they were almost incidental—happy also, that in thus continuing the productive orgy of his earlier years, he was now, almost as though by fortunate chance, constrained within the limits of a medium he had lucked into the limits – the defined variables of which – mask, puppet – made it possible – in however tentative a way – to gauge success and failure of the experiments as embodied in these products of theirs. He explores this part of the medium, that part.

With *Leaf* and *Fire*, the former a puppet play – large puppets – the latter a mask (and dummy) play, both making a very sparse use of language, the former using written signs, the latter short vocal announcements, he in the winter of '65/'66 attained to a basic security in handling the medium: up to then it had been a matter of getting away from the traditional format of hand puppet over-a-curtain puppetry, inappropriate for large puppets. As regards puppets, this breakthrough coincided with the development of two new types of large puppets; as regards masked performers, with the development of a ceremonial gestique embodying a concept of the masked performer as a pseudo-puppet. Schumann has never verbally made any distinction between masked performance and play with puppets, partly because of the continuity that the live puppet, the puppet with an inside operator, established between what we might otherwise regard as two distinct media, partly because when he got into using masked performers – with *Murder Mystery* in the fall of '64 and with *Harvard Questionnaire* early in '65 – he probably thought of it as an extension of the puppet medium. *Cry*, his first attempt at a long play, concludes the period. I suspect the breakthrough here lay in the use of unmasked operators (clad in formal white) as significant theatrical figures – not just operators but quasi-performers.

His '60s period thus divides into a constitutively experimental part, fall of '63-winter '65/'66, and a developmentally experimental part following it.

The flavor of the first two, preeminently experimental years of this period – roughly coinciding with his work at the Delancey Street Museum (November '63-July '66) – is conveyed by some remarks of his of '82 à propos of *Murder Mystery* (October '64):

'That was one of the more together or successful Delancey Street shows. There were lots of shows done up there – lots and lots of them – every week new shows, but they were lousy, most of them. They were thrown together in an hour or two and then performed. Many, many titles – I don't recall them now, but there were many, many different shows. This was a period when things were pretty wild there, on Delancey Street. Kids' shows were totally improvised, and other shows were ideas, but then they were not rehearsed. The *Murder Mystery* I remember better because it did achieve some form. And others – they were what was the trying of – they were very different staging ideas, I would think – that's all it was. (I: I'd like to know a little bit about what happened to the staging over this period of seven years or so – you know, whether there was any tendency, any line, sort of – and whether, at any time you found a form in any sense – formula or form.) Well, I would say, at that time it would be fair to say that I didn't, because I – for me, the difference of doing a total improvisation and just a fresh idea, and forming something to – repeatable – something like a product that then would exist, and one could really repeat it – was a big struggle. I didn't know which was better – which one should adhere to. We had these different philosophies mixed up. I believed very much in this improvisational effect. I believed in that one doesn't have to give anything to people – that the littlest thing would be the best, and that if one would say one word in an hour, that would be plenty – or if one would show one tableau for half an hour it would be plenty. And I didn't mean to either make it enjoyable for the audience or make it enjoyable for the players. Getting into puppetry was how to combine – how to make a language out of sculpture and music. It was a very difficult enterprise in that it was so open-ended; there was no tradition one could lean on or there was no tradition one could imitate – there was nothing there. It felt so open that I was enjoying the variety more than the search for results, really. The use of objects – of how they get used – the – nothing on stage was very interesting, or appearances of objects above a curtain – that was very interesting – what to do with language – that was a big problem all the time – how to do that – whether one would start, tell a story, or just give a little words and glimpses . . . . It was very inconclusive, all these things, and they were all interrupted by outside demands that came in, like a voter registration parade, I remember, or things that were – (I: See, I was just wondering, you see, whether you arrived during that period at a concentrated, organized, controlled, intensive sort of thing which then, perhaps, you discarded, subsequently.) That's how it was, I think. One would arrive at a result – like the *Murder Mystery* was a result of a bunch of shows that didn't click at all. And so was *Leaf Feeling the Moonlight*. Those were two of the first ones where I really felt, "I've got something there." But there were a dozen shows in between that were – that had titles and had ideas but nothing was achieved – you know, it didn't work, between the narration and what was done there.' (Schumann, interview, '82.)

Schumann here formulates his central problem as that of 'how to make a language out of sculpture and music', and suggests that this problem centrally came down to the problem of the use of language – of word-language: whether to use it, how much and in what form to use it, and what the relation of stage image to verbal language was to be. He wanted sculpture and music – and I assume the term 'music' here is to cover both (non-verbal) sound, e.g. literally music, and movement – to function as in combination a language. But there is no show of his that I know of that is totally without verbal language. He found it indispensable, it would seem. So the problem was on the one hand how to make a language out of puppets and masks, their deployment and movement, and out of music and other non-verbal sound, how, on the other hand to use words without destroying or impairing the integrity and primacy of that language.

3. Schumann's theatre proper during the '60s.
The shows: November-December '63.
Elements of World War II.

Schumann started experimenting with theatre use of his big new 'Jesus puppets' – indoors, for adults, not for religious observances – as soon as he had the work loft on Delancey Street. He is not sure whether he started by trying to adapt the *Apocalypse* he had done during the summer to the new puppets or started with something called *Elements of World War II*, perhaps a development of the War act of his *Story of the World*.[1] There is no record of performances of the former, Peter Moore photographed the latter on various weekends, November 2, '63 to December 7. *Elements* was probably his first show.

He and Elka don't remember it too well. They have a hard time distinguishing it from the later *War Demonstration* (perhaps a reworking of it) and perhaps also confuse it with *Flower Mountain*. Elka seems to relate it to Joos' *Green Table*. It

'was a tryout to use these giant puppets as war puppets, in the manner of the *King Story*. Above a curtain with voices from outside doing the voices for them. I don't ever – I think I never got a performing shape for that. I bet I performed it. But if, then it was just a very loosely knit sequence of these puppets moving and some voices with them and some sticks, and some odd ends. A puppet extravaganza with big puppets. (Elka: In that show and in several other shows from that time I remember a very important element that you experimented with constantly: the idea of building a town, a little city out of blocks on an artificial mountain, on some kind of little hillock, some green fabric over some kind of a bunk that represented a hill, and then building towns, villages out of simple children's blocks, I guess the kind that the kids were using, playing with at that time, our children. And I think – I somehow remember you wanting to show something like World War II or destructioin on that scale.) I remember that. (Elka: On the scale of little children's blocks.) Yes, there were bombing raids performed with little airplanes, just as we used later on for *Man Says Goodbye*, with little figures, and, you were right, cardboard boxes, little houses sitting on them, little trees, little cows hanging from them, with wires hooked into them. If I – I think, that the big puppets were in that – at least the Big Fool, we called him – this big satanic red devil figure and possibly the big Jesus figure and some of the disciple figures. I would think that they were in it. But in a manner where they were used like *King Story* puppets, like rod puppets. With the rods inside these things, the

---

1. 'The first experiments for a play I did with (the Jesus puppets) was called something like *History of World War II*. I think I tried an *Apocalypse* with the big puppets again, after I had the big puppets – I searched around for quite a few things before I performed shows with them. One was about World War II, another one was the *Apocalypse*, I think.'
— (Schumann, interview, '79.)

puppets being held up high by puppeteers who wore holsters and carried these puppets around in their belts and operated the arms above them. (Elka: Wasn't this show like a — the plans for this show — inspired somehow by some cartoon or so in some magazine showing — a political cartoon showing two political leaders sort of playing chess on a table that consisted of a landscape, moving towns around, and moving —) Could be. (Elka: I somehow remember that so clearly as though that's something you were trying to capture or were trying to do a show with this feeling of big figures —) So what you're saying is that probably the puppets weren't operated above the curtain but maybe — (Elka: I don't know. I just remember the landscape part of it and this sort of table top show on a table top with things being manipulated by people right there. It seems to me that it was also one of the shows where the title was almost more important than the show — that the show didn't really jell into anything.) You could say it just as well the other way around, the title was unimportant and the show itself was important but it shouldn't have had such a bombastic title. (Laughter.)'

(Schumann, interview, '79.)

It had the Big Fool and the Stovepipe Soldiers puppet in it, and 'the rest was organization, noises and how the puppets marched' (ibid.). Moore's photos suggest it was done above the curtain, and that Elka's memory is at fault — no toy city on a hill.

4. Winter '63/'64. *Apocalypse*.

Apocalypse, he thinks consisted of 'a lot of acts from the (New Testament) *Apocalypse*,' (ibid.), and though done with 'not much puppets – more objects and some masks' (ibid.),

'was also done with these big puppets, and it was done with garbage that we started collecting. I remember a whole big bag of buttons that looked like gold. They looked like gold coins, and then we had found an old scale and we had a big stick collection from mops – what way they were used there is no way of telling. (Elka: I'm sure you used broomsticks for puppet dowels.) Yes, but we also used sticks for stick dances, for just stick pounding, for sound, but also for stick dances above the curtain. I remember that.' (ibid.)

It featured the big Beast puppet, built for it: not too much like the Beast of *Revelations* xvii, mount of the Babylonian Whore, the Great City, but who will 'hate her and make her solitary and bare, and will eat her flesh and will burn her fire.'

There is no way of knowing how much or what he got out of the theme: the theme of war between the evil ones.

5. February-April '64. *King Story*.

Schumann's next[1] production was a double bill of *King Stories I* and *II*. *King Story II* may have been *The Great King and the Mosquito* more or less unchanged. It became part of the children's repertory. *King Story I*

---

1. The record of Schumann's 'theatre proper' constituted by *Village Voice* ads and notices starts with it. The first Delancey Street shows advertised in the *Voice* had been Sunday afternoon children's shows – probably *King Story II* and other things – November 16, '63 ff. (*Village Voice* 'For Children' column, November 14). Performances of *King Story I*, 'a tragedy with puppets, directed and presented by Peter Schumann', Saturdays at 9 p.m. were announced in the 'Off-Off B'way' column January 30 (performance of February 1), February 6, 13, 27. But starting with the *Voice* of February 6, Schumann in the *Voice* advertised Saturday and then Friday and Saturday evening performances of '2 kingstories/ tragedy and comedy with puppets': apparently presenting both *King Stories* together for adults, a double bill still advertised for March 28, April 4 and April 11. We can thus speak of a first run of *King Story*, February 1 – April 11, '64. He presented the double bill at the Ohayo Mountain Hall in Woodstock, New York on July 11th, but the first performance of it after the April ones mentioned in the *Voice* are those of November 7-22, '65 at the Bridge Theater together with *Leaf* (cf. infra). Since the *Voice* records performances at Delancey Street, October '64 ff., he may in fact not have put it on again till then.

I got most of my dates for Schumann's '60s performances from notices and advertisements in the *Voice*. Schumann believes they present a quite incomplete picture – disliking his work, the *Voice*, he thinks, often did not publish notices even when they had been informed by the theatre. I think Schumann is a little paranoid here. Sometimes, I suspect the theatre may not have gotten notices in on time.

'They know nothing, these people. (I: No, but there are the announcements.) Oh, I see. But even that is unreliable because I remember from then that they were so hostile to us that they very often did not print our announcements. Very often. We had so much trouble with them – they gave us nothing but trouble. They either refused or out of negligence they did not print announcements. (I: Why? Just bitchiness or –) Bitchiness, yes. They disliked us very strongly. I don't know why – I personally disliked the reviewers and I think that was the reason. (I: Yeah, but that was later on.) No. Right in the beginning, I remember. You must have read some of these old reviews, or remember them, about *King Story*: the most ridiculous thing they've ever seen and stuff like that. They hated it and we hated them. But we needed them to advertise the shows. (I: Of course. But, also, do you think that the people in the advertising area there would know anything about what anybody else did, or –) Yeah – you're right – maybe not. Maybe I was a bit hyped up about that. Isn't it the editor that decides all these things – of what is worthwhile being – (I: I don't think they would know about it. Of course, in the early days it was a small paper.) Yeah, it was a small paper – it was maybe all the same people did that – (I: You thought it was a conspiracy.) I thought it was a conspiracy.' — (Schumann, interview, '82.)

On the whole, the *Voice* record for the '60s is probably fairly complete.

King Story, at least from '67 onward became part of the Bread and Puppet repertory, indoors, and as anti-war street show, with *A Man Says Goodbye* his most frequently performed anti-war street show. It was done under the title *The Great Warrior* at the Astor Memorial Library May to September '67, October 21, '67 at the Lincoln Memorial in Washington, D.C., in September '68 at the San Francisco State College Festival of Radical Theatre. The last performance of it as anti-war agitation that I have found mentions of are showings in August '70 at the Puppeteers Festival in Connecticut (in opposition to ROTC), and showings by splinter-groups of the Bread and Puppet Theater, e.g.

gradually developed from scene 6 of *The Story of the World*[2] and from *The Great King Makes War*, and became *King Story* – perhaps only at the Bridge in November '65. It was Schumann's response to the combat-rich Manteo shows.[3] It was still done mostly over the curtain – a red fabric screen, mounted on two wooden poles, held erect by a trumpeter on one side, by the narrator on the other, i.e.: not part of the installation, but element of the play – but the Great Warrior, sometimes with grand entrances through the audience, now encountered the Dragon and Death in front of the curtain, and did his killing in front of it. The '62 combats

---

some by Murray Levy's Stomachache Theatre at the Emmanuel Church in Boston, Massachesetts in February '71. There are isolated showings of it even later, e.g. Sue Bettmann and Sam Kerson, according to a Newsletter of Elka's on February '75, did it in Peru, in South America, in the winter of '74/'75. By this time the Vietnam war had ended and the play had left the category of 'agitation': it was merely instructional. Schumann did it, with his later *Hallelujah*, during a winter-of-'75/'76 European tour, on the street in Switzerland, at the university in Athens, Greece, outdoors in North Africa, and, supported by the local left-wing municipal administrations, in some Tuscan towns, e.g. (Catalogue, *Bread and Puppet/Masaccio* exhibition, Florence) at an occupied factory in Pontadera on February 11, '76, in Pistoia on February 4, '76, and again in Tuscany, on a subsequent visit, in October of '76. It shows up as a 'sideshow' as does *A Man Says Goodbye*, in the August '77 *Circus*, done by some visiting group, and the Bread and Puppet Theatre did it as a street show on two European tours in '78, e.g. in Copenhagen in May '78 and – but this time done only by some Bread and Puppet regulars travelling without Schumann – in Barcelona in October. On these '78 tours it was done as first part of a street trilogy comprising also *Dead Man Rises* ('67), and ending with the later *Hallelujah*: it had now become part of a new anti-war agitation of Schumann's: against nuclear armament.

2. To judge from the one review of this show – a human interest story about these 'three young German artists' – his first in New York City since the one of *Totentanz*, though preceding one of his children's shows by only four days:

'Audiences have been doing a double take. They come prepared to laugh – it's a puppet show, isn't it? But as cymbals clash to open the first story, a spikeheaded monster – the size of a Watusi tribesman – leaps from the curtain, bellows, and brandishes two enormous swords in the face of a gasping front row. There follows music (newest instrument is a jungle jim (sic) of organ pipes and General Motors auto parts), dance, every conceivable size of puppet and two short plays with the simplest story lines.

Too human kings start wars by mistake, soldiers die "slowly, beautifully." The people mourn their dead horses. Kings number one through five are killed. "The rest die at home." The daily newsreel tells about it and justice doesn't triumph in the end. It doesn't take long for the satire to sting the smiles off watching faces.

Silence greeted the play's finish the first night. The performers looked blankly at each other behind the curtain – "We thought everyone had left." When they walked out, the room erupted in applause." — (G. Sheehy, *Giving Them Bread & Puppets*, *New York Herald Tribune*, March 22, '64.)

3. '*King Story* was a reaction to the Sicilian puppets. I remember that very clearly even though I had already rod puppet shows. But to make the *King Story* I didn't succeed to get that until I saw these Sicilian puppets in Hurleyville. They gave me a real kick. How to confront puppets with each other. They didn't have any shape before – before I saw this Hurleyville show. Also it wasn't called the *King Story*.' — (Schumann, interview, '82.)

between carton puppets had become ennobled.[4] Death's victory over the Great Warrior was added to the story.[5]

'Once there was a Good King/ and the King had a Priest/ and the King had a Red Man/ and the King had a Blue Man and His Son/ and the King had Good People./ One day, a Great Warrior/ came into the King's country/ and offered his services/ and he sent him away./ Then a terrible Dragon appeared in the King's country/ and the People were afraid/ and the King was afraid/ and he called for the Great Warrior./ But the Priest implored the King not to ask/ the Great Warrior for help/ and the Blue Man and His Son implored the King/ not to ask the Great Warrior for help./ But the King was afraid/ and the People were afraid/ and the King called for the Great Warrior/ and the Great Warrior fought the Dragon/ and the Great Warrior killed the Dragon/ and then the Great Warrior killed the King/ and then the Great Warrior killed the Priest/ and then the Great Warrior killed the Red Man/ and then the Great Warrior killed the Blue Man and His Son/ and then the Great Warrior killed the People/ and then the Great Warrior was alone/ and Death came/ and Death killed him.'
(Narrative of *King Story*, c. '65, Bread and Puppet Theatre mss.)

Also, Schumann had made an opera out of it:

'The lines of the text are interspersed by melodic singing which is idiosyncratic to the individual puppets and which changes as the puppets express greetings, fear

---

4. 'The Great Warrior came in instead of the soldiers. In the summer we did it with this three-headed soldier puppet. And they were kind of comic looking. It definitely had that red nose foolish soldier's image, like Schwejk or something. They looked – they had that funny red nose, red cheeks, so they were not threatening. And then we made the Great Warrior puppet with these big swords, fitted into the hands, and silver. Just all silver. The mask and the hands were silver – and the swords. It was a silver head and he had this blue, this *blue* metallic covering on, and the head was fitted. It was one of these with the head fitted (so it would fit on your forehead), the head coming up, and then these rubber straps under here. And that was terrific. And it also created a very – it was much heavier – and more dynamic and scarier piece of *theatre* and you also had these huge swords. So they would kill. It became a real dance. It became a very great – we'd stand over there – yayayayaya. It became very powerful because of this warrior. I did it and Bruno did him. I think I did it a lot. Bruno did it some. We traded around. We would trade around, but I did it a lot. Everyone had their own character. Bruno did it very loudly and grotesquely.'
— (Ernstthal, interview.)
5. 'I remember being very happy finding out about this Great Warrior and what I tried – what I remember doing with that puppet was something – was one of these Gautama Buddha stories that he tells his disciples that was about a great demon who fought the Buddha. He uses one arm and hits the Buddha. And that arm breaks as he touches him. In the story prior to this the Buddha tells him "there's no sense in fighting me." And the demon doesn't believe him and then he uses another of his many arms – until he is completely delimbed and then he finally uses his head and he gets stuck on the Buddha with his head. And only then does he give up and get persuaded to better reason. And the Buddha uses this as an illustration of the great strength of this demon, of the great spirit of this great demon. And what the Great Warrior does is as in this story – that he fights with everything he has until he gets killed.' — (Schumann, interview, '82.)

and other emotional responses.'   (Bread and Puppet Theatre *King Story* mss.)[6]

By '67, the show at Papp's place, under the title *The Great Warrior*, looked like this:

'There is a good king in a happy land. The King appears – a graceful orange-red puppet in robes and crown, oriental looking. His hands are like those of a Giacometti sculpture, elongated and delicate. When the King speaks it is a strong, extenuated bit of melody. (Each of the characters has a specific vocal identification, made by the puppeteers. The Narrator "translates" these sounds into the story.) The Priest, a yellow puppet, also slightly oriental looking, enters, hands in a praying attitude. His voice is similar to the King's in intonation but in a different key. The Red Man is introduced in the same way, and then the Blue Man and his Son. Finally, the people appear – strange, hollow-eyes, elongated gray masks. They look flat seen from the front, but take on a variety of expressions in profile or when grouped.

The Narrator announces the mighty Warrior. He has come from a distant land. He is seven feet tall, and enters with slow, heavy tread, dressed in a purple robe with a huge silver head covered with spikes – as if his head and helmet were one. He carries two huge swords. The King asks the Warrior if he can farm, cook, and so on. No, the Warrior is trained only to kill. The King says there is no need for killing in his land. There is no enemy. The Warrior leaves disconsolately.

The drums beat loudly, the cymbals clash, and a terrible, huge Dragon head, like those in children's books, appears. The King and his people are frightened and the King wishes to call the Warrior back. Each of his people appears in turn to implore the King not to send for the Warrior. But the King decides he must, and the trumpet sounds.

The Warrior kills the Dragon, to drums and cymbals. The King appears to thank the Warrior and the Warrior – with ominous, stolid brutality – kills the King. A strange, lonely sound, like the plucking of a low chord, is heard as the King's hand, like a gilded claw, is the last thing to disappear below the red curtain.

Then each of the other characters appears and is killed by the Warrior. Each death is followed by silence and the falling chord. There is no one left in the city.

---

6. 'The *King Story* is like a miniature Wagnerian opera, with the King singing Ah, ah, ah, ah, boom, and then the priestess ah, ah, ah, ah and the Red Man has ah, ahaaahh, . . . and the Blue Man with two voices and one note . . . and they come in harmonies or fifths or whatever they come into . . . .' — (Levy, interview.)

'The narration was too complicated for me to do in a short time 'cause the *King Story* has all to do with drum beats and appearances and coming in and so I did the King, and that is what I stayed with Peter for years and years, I was doing the King. I was like his classical King, he said . . . behind the screen, singing loud.' — (Ernstthal, interview.)

'*King Story* was terrifying. Bruno was the Great Warrior. And when he came stomping in the Great Warrior, I was afraid, a grownup, I was afraid. The voices when they were singing in *King Story* were shrill and harsh and strong and there was nothing pretty about it . . . (Catherine Merrill) was in *King Story* too, because I can remember her high voice – high, high soprano voice.' — (Sherman, interview.)

In the Moore February '64 photo of the show there is still a female puppet. But the female voice was retained in the show even when it definitely no longer had a female role.

The great Warrior is all alone. He turns front and stares at the audience. Then Death appears, a death's head tapping a drum. The Warrior faces him, strikes him, but Death does not die. The Warrior strikes again and again. Death says, "Come with me." The Warrior drops his swords and follows Death.'
(Anonymous description, *Tulane Drama Review* #38, winter of '68.)

September '68, California:

'Yeah, in San Francisco, we did it outside a lot and when we did it then at the festival inside at the big theatre.... We set up the screen outside, the puppets lay back behind the People, behind the screen, come behind the screen, come behind the screen there were three of us, behind the screen there was Peter, and Charlie Adams on either side, and the Great Warrior would go off somewhere and hide. So three, four, five, six, and first appearance of little People puppets, just heads on sticks, that appear. The screen just so, just so that the chin like of the head moves in profile or full face and the sounds of that are just blah, blahs, musical development, talkin' nonsense. And then that builds to a crescendo and there is a drum beat and the People, the People go, the drum beats, and the narrator says "Once there was a good King", the King appears, sings, dances, and bows. "And the King had a Priest", the Priest appears and they bow to each other – dances in the Priest and bow to each other, the Priest dances out, "the King had a Red Man", and the Red Man appears and dances in and bows to the King – it is homage to the King. "The Blue Man and His Son" – he appears to bow to each other, the Blue Man and His Son go out. "And the King had good People", and these little white heads appear, say "Good morning ... Hello, King ... Good Morning, King, ... Nice day, King ... Isn't it a good day, King" ... "One day a Great Warrior came into the King's" ... and the Warrior and the drums and the cymbals, and the Warrior comes through the audience to the screen, and offers his services to the King, but the King refused to accept his services, turns his back on him and sends him away.... He comes from, usually from the distance, from behind the tree and through the audience. That is the revelation.... Sometimes when it is in small places and not enough People, someone else has to come running out from behind the screen and go back, but this is coming from distance, it is very nice. One time at San Jose, we did it in an amphitheatre outdoors and the Great Warrior came from a quarter of a mile away, came slowly up but we had invited the students to put on death masks, and precede him like a little army that time. So that it made it a little grander, the whole piece. And, then, the King sent the Warrior away and then the People are nervous.... Then a terrible Dragon came into the King's ... and that is usually had to come from behind when there were so few People because one of the three operators has to then get into the Dragon, but when there are more People the Dragon comes from another direction. Winds its way to the ... and then the King calls for the Great Warrior and the Great Warrior kills the – fights with the Dragon – kills the Dragon and then the Great Warrior kills the King, and the Priest and the Red Man and the Blue Man and His Son and then the Great Warrior kills the People, which is the ending we had then. And then the Great Warrior was alone and Death came and, then, people would put on death masks and walk up to the Great Warrior and try to hit him ... take the sword and break it. Death would break it.'
(M. Levy, interview.)

During Schumann's revolutionary period, under pressure from his group to infuse a little historical optimism into the play, in 1969, the People gets to kill the Great Warrior.[7] We see this victory in a photo of a street performance's final scene (*Frankfurter Rundschau*, June (?) 7, '69): behind the red cloth, stretched out by two skull-masked attendants, the People's elongated heads on stilts have been joined by a cowled performer in the 'Vietnamese Woman' masks, and a (collectively) raised sword is coming through the cloth toward the Great Warrior, on his knees, collapsing backwards. Another 'revolutionary' ending, presumably of this period, is

---

7. 'It was terrible. Because of the – all the students taking over the universities. The people in the company who were very, very politically involved, more than with theatre actually, insisted that we change the end of the *King Story*, and that the Great Warrior could not kill the People.... They made Peter change it so that the Great Warrior tried to kill the People, and he's there – bang, bang, bang – trying to kill the People, and the People puppets keep bouncing back, bouncing back, and finally the two people holding the red curtain down over the Great Warrior who crumbles under it, and the puppeteers are standing there holding up triumphantly the People puppets. As you can tell from my face, I didn't like it either.... (I: Why do you say "had to.") Nobody made Peter do it. Well, I guess like everybody he is affected by the needs and desires of other people who he is working with. (I: You say it as though it wasn't fair, or terrorism.) I felt, the way I experienced it, was that he was forced into it by Bruno and Carol and people like that – just the constant meetings, talking, arguing – that he had to give in. We used to have a lot of meetings on tour, a lot of political discussions, a lot of anger, people screaming at each other. It was a very violent time.' — (Sherman, interview.)

'But then when we did it in Europe in the '69 tour there were – there was a big faction who felt that there was – that it was too negative – that they wanted the People to win. And so the ending got changed to the People – tried to kill the People and we'd throw him down with the whole red screen just standing there with the puppets, which I went along with – I thought it was okay, but personally speaking I felt that the other ending was harder.... Tougher. I don't think that to be political means to tell people you are going to win. I think to be political sometimes – it is – to be more political is to show it in all of its hideous reality. Bruno and Carol – they didn't want to have this ending of the Death coming and killing the People – but I don't think there was a big fight about it, there was a discussion and Peter agreed to let it end up the other way – with – he tried to kill the People – he starts swinging at the People and the People go back and start saying 'Bah, baa, baa' and louder and louder, until, coming back – the People like a wave coming back – until we charged, and knocked the red screen over, and wrapped him in the red screen, and stood triumphant like this, screaming or something. It seemed to make some people happy, and it didn't upset me. I felt the other ending was better but I went with this one. It didn't rape the piece – it didn't make the piece weaker in any way.' — (M. Levy, interview.)

'Bruno (Eckhardt) was with us at that time and his beef was that it's too abstract – it's too arty for Death to take the Great Warrior because it was a political show about the military and at the end the People should triumph over the Warrior. And a red flag should be waved. And, in fact, we did some things like that – we did some experiments like that. Death kills the People but the People kept coming back, somehow – and the Warrior gets worn out and is in fact defeated.' – (Ernstthal, interview.)

Early on during this '69 tour, as a politically similar, but more or less specifically anti-American and/or anti-capitalist move, Uncle Fatso had been – for a while – substituted for the Great Warrior.' — (Lippen, interview.)

reported in Heilmeyer and Fröhlich's *now/Theater der Erfahrung* ('71): 'Then the people rises: the puppets become ever bigger, and, finally the red cloth buries the Warrior beneath itself.' This was still the ending at a left wing benefit in New York City January 24, '70, but by the spring of that year, out on Coney Island the old ending was, according to Françoise Kourilsky, back. It remained the ending subsequently, though perhaps with minor variations, e.g. Barry Goldensohn (*Peter Schumann's Bread & Puppet Theater, Iowa Review*, spring '77) describes an ending from the early '70s: 'As the Knight stands alone, seemingly triumphant, Death emerges from behind the screen in a mask that is half skull, half helmet, with a body of rags. He wrestles the Knight in a slow dance and finally kills him.' Goldensohn cites this play as prime example of the 'primitivism' of Schumann's theatre and of its 'drastically simple' 'moral and political context.'

6. October '64-November '65: Schumann temporarily gives up on the big puppets, develops his medium along other lines.

Having for half a year struggled to find a way to use his big puppets, Schumann gave up: apparently stymied. I suspect he felt that *King Story* was too much still just one big puppet's, the Great Warrior's, show, not a solution to make them interact, and that while his heavy, stiff center-pole puppets were suitable for the ceremonial of his Christmas and Easter shows, they weren't really for theatre 'proper'. For a year and a half, in five shows, he worked along other lines, didn't use them, and when he finally in November '65 put on another big puppet show (and resumed *King Story*), he used puppets of a new construction.

The first two of these exploratory ventures yielded mask plays, *Murder Mystery*, almost as brief as *King Story*, 15-20 minutes long, done only three times (October 3, 10, 17, '64), as companion piece to the other one, *The Bridcatcher in Hell*, a poetic mime dance piece with stationary puppets, which was done together with a *Birdcatcher* by Bob Nichols, an adaptation of the same Japanese original into a satire on U.S. involvement in Vietnam.[1] He next again took up the theme of *Elements*, but this time without the big puppets, using, rather, small toy props, and little cutouts and pictures: *War Demonstration* (January 23-March 27, '65), an experiment he repeated in *Flower Mountain*, an outdoor show (May 29-July 10, '65), which had one big, unmoving puppet in it, the Beast. *Harvard College Questionnaire*, a choral piece chronologically the fourth (February 20-March 27, '65), was like *Murder Mystery* again a mask play, further exploring the mask medium. All of these shows were out in the open, there was no curtain.

In *Murder Mystery*, the narrator used 'little instruments to punctuate moments of change' (Schumann, interview, '82). In *Birdcatcher* the demons had 'gong rattles – big tin lids with bolts and nuts hung in front of them' (Ernstthal, interview), and for Schumann's dancing there were either flute or string sounds (Schumann, interview, '79). *Harvard College Questionnaire* was an essay at choral chanting. *War Demonstration* had a 'big band' – horns and drums and supporting instruments.

---

[1] 'The most important performer (in Bob's show) was Yama who was painted up, I painted him up, as an Indian chief, crazy, paints all over him, almost in the nude, sitting on the throne, playing like a crazy man. He was this 3/4 crazy, hard-of-hearing and stuttering old man . . . .' — (Schumann, interview, '79.)

7. October '64. *Murder Mystery*.

As Schumann in '79 remembers *Murder Mystery*, it called for more performers than his other shows of the earlier '60s, seven or eight:

'There was a Narrator who told the story and played *some* parts himself, like the Murderer's part, and possibly the Woman's. I think I did that. And then there was a group of masks that stood there in different positions and represented the Neighbors that watched all this and listened to all this. And then there was one big grey mask in it. That was the Mountain. That was just one big grey mask similar to the grey masks we are using now, that were for *Masaniello*, and that we are using now for the *Nativity* – a longish kind of face, I don't have it anymore. It was sort of a quiet kind of face. Painted grey and shaded. That was the face of the Mountain and the Police was the same as all the others, a face mask, and the Judges were also the same: also face masks. (Elka: It was very powerful ... I remember watching it and being very moved by it. It was very mysterious and very – short.) It was a murder mystery that doesn't say anything, who was murdered or why he was murdered, it only stated the mystery.'
(Schumann, interview, '79.)

'And there was a Truck Driver. I think only the Mountain speaks and the Narrator says all the rest of the lines. It starts with a Mountain. That's where the murder happened, and the Mountain says, "I'm so and so old, I'm a mountain" – somebody behind it saying that, and then the murder mystery started.'
(Schumann, interview, '82.)

The masks Schumann had built up to this time generally didn't fit too well. He developed a new mask-building technique for this mask play that resulted in fitting masks but still allowed him some of the sculptural freedom of his earlier masks: he took face casts, built molds over them, and got his celastic masks from these molds.

'It was sort of an exaggerated face that came out of that. They were pretty weird looking. They were painted with skin colors, and they were standing there like this – and it was a chorus job, that whole thing – a chorus of people, the Villagers, in these masks, standing there. The Mountain was a tall mask that somebody held and knelt down with it in the middle of what was the performing space. Then, a group of people, with these strange masks on, were standing on one side. Like observers. And the Narrator was standing on the other side of the Mountain, probably kneeling, not standing, with little instruments to punctuate moments of changes. The Man and the Woman were done by the same performer as the Mountain, taking off the Woman's mask to become the Man and taking off the Man mask to become the Woman. Otherwise there was no movement in the thing, it was a piece of narration with these few things in it. There was no arrangements in the room at all. It was in an open space. The frame was given as in a piece of sculpture. That these people would be standing there and hardly moving. And the murder mystery is really about nothing. One doesn't know whether there is a murder or not.'
(Schumann, interview, '82.)

Ernstthal remembers it ('an experimental piece . . . that never developed . . . it never jelled. It never really came out. We tried it a number of times') as a 'one man show, same as a one man band,' '*one* guy with a whole series of masks who played the whole show,' at first Schumann the narrator, and he the performer, then the other way around; the masks lying on a table:

' "A Man was killed in the woods today" – put on the mask – "I am the Man" – "A Murderer was caught in the woods today" – put on the mask – "I am the Murderer" – "the Police" – puts on another mask – "came to investigate" . . . It was like *Rashomon* almost. You didn't know *what* happened . . . I think, as I remember, it wasn't like he got caught or was punished or anything like that . . . I wasn't clear what happened. Or if he was killed. It had a kind of floating iffy ending to it . . . .' (Ernstthal, interview.)

The program cover suggests that his memory of how it was done may be more accurate – that Schumann is remembering the play as he would have liked it to be:

They are both though probably thereby accurately describing the poetic eeriness of the production, exaggerating the play's openness: the text makes clear that a murder has been committed and that the accused truck driver committed it: suggesting, however, that rather than the execution of an evil intent a murder is an act of desperation, and the staging suggesting that (therefore, one might say) a murderer's guilt is shared by his victim and judges, and that in the time-perspective of enduring nature it is not an important feature of what happened, a view of murder all in all also taken by a later play of Schumann's, *Harvey McCloud:*

'MAN: A man was caught in the woods today. I am the man. I am accused of murder.

WOMAN: A woman was killed in the woods today. I am the woman. The tourists found the dead body when they tried to climb the great mountain. Our mountain which they could not climb.

MAN: The tourists found me in the woods near the corpse. My hands smeared with blood, a rock in my hand smeared with blood.

MOUNTAIN: I am the mountain. I am blind. I am 500,000,000 years old.

POLICE: We are the local police.

MAN: Since I was silent the local police beat me up. Since my hands were smeared with blood they accused me of murder.

JUDGES: We are the judges.

MAN: Since the blood on my hands was the blood of the dead woman they accused me of murder. I am a single man. I ran away from Babylon. The Whores and the Millionaires and the polluted air of Babylon kill thousands of children. The pigeons are killed. Dances in the street are not allowed. Music is not allowed.

I am a truck driver. I am 40 years old. I drove my truck into the woods today. My shirt is torn. My pants are torn. The woman bit into my hands. My hands hurt. My shoes are torn. My feet hurt. It is getting cold. The tourists and the police and the local people they keep me here. They won't let me go.'

8. October '64-January '65.
The Birdcatcher in Hell.

Schumann got the Birdcatcher[1] out of the '57 Grove Press collection of Noh translations by Arthur Waley. Who, between him and Nichols, came up with the idea I don't know. The play is not a Noh play, but a 'kiyogen', one of the farcical interludes with which Noh balanced its high spirituality, this one going with the Noh *Ukai*, story of the redemption of a cormorant fisher, hell-bound for having fished in sacred waters, but absolved for having given refuge to a priest.[2] In the kiyogen, a splendid satire on justice, the hero, guilty, not of the establishment charge of poaching, but of the real though of course unavoidable crime of killing living beings, is accorded a three-year delay in response to his defense that not he, but the falcons fed the cormorants by his noble customers are the guilty ones, the

---

1. After its first three October '64 performances (advertised as of a 'noh play') together with the 'mask play' *Murder Mystery*, admission to both one dollar, Schumann, October 24-December 12, apparently ran it by itself ('traditional Noh play adapted and directed by Peter Schumann'), showing Nochols' 'modern version, written and directed by Robert Nichols,' 8 and 10 P.M. on Saturdays. He did it again, December 20th, together with the *Christmas Story*, at Spencer Memorial Church, January 6th '65 at the Museum, together with *Rat Movie*. This, at least is the *Voice* record.

'It was an inside show, but we *did* perform it once, in Harlem, in a parking lot, because two Frenchmen who had traveled around the globe with some sort of puppet show wanted to make a movie for the UNESCO movie collection had to have a show in Harlem of peaceful undertakings – an absolutely inappropriate (?) show in Harlem, because they thought that was so much the *real thing*.... So they got us a parking lot. They wanted to make a movie of it, and it coincided with some other invitation that we had for that neighborhood, so we played this piece up there.... Out in the street. And unfortunately, at the beginning of the show they had set up a platform, about five feet high, so people could see, a real tall platform, and at the beginning of the show I was sweeping the glass away from the parking lot with a broom. I stood near the platform and jumped down and jumped on my toe and, if you look at my toe now, it was damaged. We did the show but my toe was completely messed up. Bill Baird was there and he wrapped it up. (Laughter.) People came from around there, but it wasn't the show, probably, that we would have chosen to do.' — (Schumann, interview, '79.)

2. Schumann in *Puppen und Masken* (1973) tells the fable of this ghost play, 'Birds of Sorrow,' told him, he says, by a Noh actor (probably much after he first did the kiyogen):

'In olden days there was a kind of bird that hid its young so carefully in the reeds that no hunter could find them, indeed so well were the bird babies hid that even their own parents could not find them again when they returned from gathering food. But then they were made a present of two words, one given to the children so that their parents could recognize them, and one to the parents, learned by the children so they could answer their parents. The secret of the hunters of this kind of bird consisted in learning these two words. But that was not enough. For when a birdcatcher through the deceptive use of the words succeeded in finding a nest with young ones, the parents of the little birds despaired so terribly, they cried tears of blood, and who was struck by such a tear of blood had to die, or had to suffer horrible pains. So the birdcatchers had to carry umbrellas on this hunt.'

THE BIRDCATCHER IN HELL

A KYOGEN

BY THE BREAD AND PUPPET THEATER

 TO THE HUNT
TO THE HUNT

TO THE BIRDHUNT

 AND SUDDENLY FROM THE HILL OF DEATH MANY BIRDS CAME FLYING

THEN SWIFTER THAN SIGHT HIS POLE DARTED AMONG THEM

 HE COOKED THEM AND OFFERED THEM TO THE KING

 LET ME EAT IT
LET ME EAT IT
LET ME EAT IT

 LET US EAT IT
LET US EAT IT
LET US EAT IT

YOU HAVE GIVEN US SUCH A TREAT THAT I WILL SEND YOU BACK TO THE WORLD TO GO ON BIRDCATCHING FOR ANOTHER THREE YEARS YOU SHALL CATCH MANY BIRDS THEY SHALL NOT ELUDE YOU BUT FALL FAST INTO THE FATAL SNARE SO HE REPRIEVED TURNED BACK TO SEE HIM GO BE STOWED A JEWELLED CROWN WHICH KIYOYORI BORE RESPECTFULLY TO THE TERRESTIAL PLANE THERE TO BEGIN HIS SECOND SPAN OF LIFE

 WELL THERE REALLY WASN'T MUCH HARM IN IT

 IT WAS THE FALCONS WHO WERE TO BLAME NOT I

 TAKE YOUR POLE AND HERE AND NOW GIVE US A DEMONSTRATION OF YOUR ART

 NOTHING COULD BE SIMPLER

YAMA THE KING OF HELL STANDS AT THE MEETING OF THE WAYS

HIS MINIONS

YAI
YAI
YAI
YAI
YAI
YAI

KIYOYORI THE BIRDCATCHER

ALL MEN ARE SINNERS WHAT HAVE I TO FEAR MORE THAN THE REST I WAS VERY WELL KNOWN ON EARTH UNTIL I WAS CAUGHT IN THE WIND OF IM PERMANENCE AND HERE I AM MARCHING TO THE SUNLESS LAND WITHOUT A PANG I LEAVE THE WORLD WHERE I WAS WONT TO DWELL HERE I AM ALREADY AT THE MEETING OF THE SIX WAYS OF EXISTENCE I THINK ON THE WHOLE I'LL GO TO HEAVEN

HA HA

THAT SMELLS LIKE A MAN

A SINNER

WE MUST REPORT HIM

COME ON YOU SINNER COME ON

YAI YOU'RE SHOWING A GREAT DEAL MORE SPIRIT THAN MOST SINNERS DO WHAT WAS YOUR JOB ON EARTH?

BIRDCATCHER

BIRDCATCHER? THAT'S BAD I'M AFRAID YOU'LL HAVE TO GO TO HELL

LET'S ASK KING YAMA ABOUT THIS
YAI
YAI
YOU ARE A VERY BAD MAN AND MUST GO TO HELL

BUT THE BIRDS I CAUGT WERE SOLD TO GENTLEMEN TO FEED THEIR FALCONS ON

clemency shown him of course having nothing to do with the dinner of roast fowl he offers his judges. The Noh-consuming aristocracy showed its vigor in partaking also of these hors-d'oevres mocking it.

Except for cutting an introductory scene and making a few other cuts, Schumann pretty much used the kiyogen as he found it, fable and dialogue. There was nothing political about it. Maybe he thought he could leave the political allusions to Bob. If he figures the audience would get a Vietnam analogy, the probably fooled himself.[3] As he staged it, it was an intensely poetic and somewhat mysterious fairy tale, and a dance piece for himself as the Birdcatcher.

'So our play was really just the kiyogen, the take-off – the scene of the ghost play (about) the soul of the Birdcatcher who catches birds all his life and cannot be redeemed. This kiyogen makes fun of it, and then the big King of Hell likes the taste of these little birds so much, when the Birdcatcher is challenged by the demons, by the King of Hell, he gives a demonstration of his art, he catches little birds, he fries them, and presents them to the King of Hell, and the King of Hell loves them and sends him back to earth to catch more. (Schumann laughs.) Anway, we played it as an analogy to the war in Vietnam.) It was extremely appropriate.'
(Schumann, interview, '79.)

'The whole play was in blue. There was no other color. (Elka: Why?) The color of the sky, I think that was my idea – with this color, the play lifted up into the sky – see, you use a color, either traditionally, to speak with tradition, or you make it so that you *hit* people with it and they say "Oh! how comes it *is* blue?" And I guess this was just a little twist like that, to say that it *has* to be blue, but it was great fun. But it is not very comfortable to look at, not a lovely blue, not a peaceful blue, like blue is supposed to be, but it's esoteric, strong.'
(Schumann, interview, '79.)

In the '73 *Puppen & Masken*, he explains the off-blue: 'Das Stück war damals ganz in blau um den amerikanischen Himmel zu denonzieren'. When I interviewed him in '82, he quoted Goethe's 'Blau ist das Leiden des Himmels'.

What he in fact tried to do was turn the kiyogen back into a Noh play:

'The first verion (of *Birdcatcher*) was an idea for creating a show in bright blue. It was all ultramarine blue and it was the idea to do with the kiyogen the opposite of what the Japanese wanted to do with it. In the Noh cycle the kiyogen is a

---

3. Schumann in '79 thinks his feelings at the time were that his own poetic version would suggest the same political analogues as those made explicit by Nichols' adaptation – made too explicit, he thinks. It 'gave it all away, telling the story of the Birdcatcher . . . everybody could figure out themselves what it meant in those days. He just made it from (the old newspaper story of) the helicopter pilot . . . that was shot down. This was the time when America still pretended there was no *war*, that they were only advisors. And there were helicopter pilots shot down – how come a helicopter pilot was shot down, if they're only advisors over there. They were obviously in action, shot down in action, so he used that, and made it into a very clear anti-Vietnam-war statement. A bit too obviously true.'
— (Schumann, interview, '79.)

ridicule of the ghost story. It takes the theme of the ghost story and makes fun of it. And in our version, that fun-making was meant to be subdued and not really be fun-making, but to make again a holy old ghost story out of it. And so the beauty of the blue and the beauty of the performance and the beauty of the sounds, which were metal sounds on sticks of the demons and, I think, some flute sounds – either flute or strings, I'm not so sure now. But the *Birdcatcher* also had some other than just rattling sounds in it.' (Schumann, interview, '82.)

'I played Kiyoyori (the Birdcatcher). (My) mask was made from Charlie Adams' face, but very much changed. (I wore) blue. Blue all over. Blue loose shirt, loose pants, baggy knees. Bob Ernstthal must have done the text. *One* narrator. All (the puppets) were made for the show. (Elka: . . . they had blue lips . . .) There was Yama, there were three demons as the text requires, then there were three musicians that were sort of faceless blue creatures with celastic faces that played strange metal instruments that we built for the show, and there was the Birdcatcher, and there was a narrator. And a little hibachi with fire was used, if I recall that right, for the frying scene. It was a smaller show, much less elaborate and much shorter (than the later *Birdcatcher*).'[4] (Schumann, interview, '79.)

Ernstthal remembers the piece as by its discretion and control a uniquely civilized moment in the theatre's history. Civilization for Schumann as for many of us is oriental.

'It was a prelude to *Fire* because it was using the space in a similar way. And it was a *very* – it was great in many ways. It was different – it was a departure from what we had done before – very much . . . . The first major departure was that it was from a script. That was absolutely unheard of . . . . For another thing it was a very obscure point that was made . . . . I hate to admit it, but it was so obscure that I never really got it . . . . I know the story and I know what the point of the story was. Why he did it or what it had to do with anything I can't really tell you. The Birdcatcher was in hell because he killed birds and the King of Death ate the birds and said they were very good 'and in fact, the birds are so good that you should go back to life for more years.' It was a wry, dry twist that was fairly obscure and always has been, frankly, to me. I mean, it has to do with Peter's wry side or – but it wasn't sarcastic – it was very peculiar – it was a unique thing, actually . . . . It was one of the most interesting shows we ever did . . . . We made a bank of lights that was on the audience side of the skylight . . . . And we built an electric box – a light box, out of cardboard. Now that I think of it it must have been incredibly dangerous – covered on the inside with tin foil with three flood-

---

4. 'Le spectacle du Bread and Puppet Theatre etait tout en bleu. Peter Schumann jouait ou plutot dansait le role de l'oiseleur. Yama etait une immense marionnette actionée par deux acteurs: un pour la tête – une tête monstrueuse d'ou sortaient des ballons de baudruche – l'autre pour les enormes mains aux cinq gros doigts ecartés. Ses demons l'entouraient: trois acteurs enfermés dans un meme sac, et un choeur de musiciens sans visage humain, la tête recouverte d'un masque bleu informe, qui faisaient sortir des sons etranges d'instruments variés, agitant des plaques d'aluminium, tapant avec des batons sur des bidons vides, etc. Du haut d'un echafaudage un narrateur disait le texte qui accompagnait les mouvements des acteurs.' — (Kourilsky, '71.)

lights in it. You know, just a homemade — like a lighting box — like a footlight box or something. And we installed it up on the audience side of the skylight to shine down on the stage. And we covered it with blue gels: so the light was blue. And then in the back of the skylight space — between the end of the skylight and the wall, was only a small space — you know, a few feet, like a crawl space almost, so just ahead of that, so I could get up there behind this big blue drape.... We didn't enclose it, but it was that idea of making a defined space. I don't believe the sides were enclosed — I think it was just in shadow. So anyway, it was all blue. Then there was a throne of blue fabric — covered with blue fabric — made out of milk cartons — and all the puppets and all the characters and everything was in blue — the same color. So it was a totally monochromatic show. And I was above the back curtain on a ladder. I can't remember if my face was blue or if I had a blue shirt and a blue, even, makeup — possibly — well, we never used makeup — I kind of think it was just me. And I had a few instruments and I narrated the text using different voices for the different characters. And like for the demons I had a long cardboard tube from the inside of a bolt of fabric and you'd do different things with my voice — and that was the narrator. And then the puppets with people in them moved to the text — to the sound.... There was Yama, the King of Hell — that was two people, one having this incredibly big head — that was almost shapeless, strangely enough — almost shapeless, this kind of strange, demonic head with tubes and horns and trunks coming out.... Blue also — the whole thing blue. Almost this shapeless quality to it — almost this shapeless face — with hands — these big hands — with like — just like balls with fingers coming out in every direction — a very shapeless kind of strange, enormous creation. Beany Kunitz, who is a friend of mine, a local hippie, essentially, he's now a carpenter, and Irving Oyle, I believe, were the original players and it had feet — these big feet, blue also — blue fabric, blue everything, and there was two guys in it so he could move his feet separately from his head. There were two people in it so it had a lot of movement. There was one guy on his hands and one guy holding the feet, it was a full, you know, four-handed deal. And there were demons — there were three people in a demon suit with three heads — also totally shapeless — almost just like blobs of clay — again blue. And they had these gong rattles — big tin lids like tin with bolts and nuts hung in front of them so it was like a rattle on a stick — and they moved, three of them together. And then there was (Kyoyori?), the Birdcatcher, which was Peter in a lifelike — a man-like mask, also dressed totally in blue. And this is where he started — did dancing. He was in a way a dancer in this one — he became a dancer. It showed us that aspect of him — of being a dancer ... like a bird dancer. He would really dance. He would really make dance movement and be graceful, which was, you know, very stunning. But he was very graceful and it was like a mimed-out dance movements: "Oh please, tell me" — but it was all mimed and I was doing the voices. And there were the demons and the Birdcatcher — and they would move when the voice would come. And it was a real — in a way it was a piece of art. It had art, but like I said, it presaged *Fire* a little because it was a controlled space — it was monochromatic and it told a story. Abstract and strange as it was. It was a real story about the Birdcatcher. And the King says: "Show me an example of your art." And he goes around and does this dance of snaring the birds and roasting them over the fire. There was a signpost: "Heaven-Hell." It starts out with Yama. It starts out: "I

am Yama, King of Death' – and he's instructing the demons, right? "If any sinners come along, fall upon them and send them straight to hell." And then: "We tremble and obey." And they go around and they stand on the side. Then: "Here comes Kiyoyori, the man." He really got the – he was good at this. Peter's a very good dancer. Anyway: "I am Kiyoyori, the Birdcatcher. Here I am at the meeting of the ways." And then the demons set on him and drag him and there's a fight. And I remember another – one moment in it which was that I thought Peter was going to lead me, as the narrator, in one of the performances, and Peter thought – he was waiting for me to lead him – as the narrator, so it was this moment when nobody moved. And I was waiting for him and he was waiting for me – and it lasted a long time. I remember it so well – because it was total – it was one of those moments in theatre when everything kind of drops. And the audience and everybody just froze – ping! And it lasted for – god – it must have been two or three minutes solid. And finally it broke and I said something, I think and it went on. But it was one of those timeless moments – nobody even sneezed – nobody even moved. It was really strange. That, possibly, is where we got the idea for the – *A Man Says Goodbye* – the tableau at the end – being real still – I doubt it, but it's possible, because I remember that moment as being one of those moments that just held – it just held and held and held. It was just there. That was just intense. The original *Birdcatcher* was a controlled play in a defined space.'
(Ernstthal, interview.)

In short, Schumann identified with the Birdcatcher and his beautiful production said, 'Lord knows I'm a miserable sinner, but won't these delicious little puppetry birds I roast redeem me just a little bit?'

The puppets are all out in front of the curtain now, but immobile. The masked dancer gives life to the show.

9. January-March '65. *Harvard College Questionnaire, War Demonstration.*

War Demonstration was shown at the Museum Saturdays January 23-February 6 together with the *Rat Movie* (a crankie) and with a narrated showing of prints of Eckhardt's called *The God Pan, King Scheisskopf and his Clown*, and then, until March 27 together with *Harvard College Questionnaire*.

Harvard College Questionnaire used for text a questionnaire sent Bob Ernstthal when he applied for admission, 'so amazingly inhuman and stupid,' Schumann 'loved it.' It struck Schumann as a ready-made choral work and he tried (he thinks the piece was a disaster) to make something like a cantata from it, a solo voice posing the questions, a group of voices answering, the text the main thing, with no puppets, only a set of masks, all probably, he thinks (interview, '79) taken from Bob's face: 'casting Bob's face and putting it on Bob, so that it would be expressionless – that was the idea for it – and then making a lot of similar kind of petrified faces from one other face and putting them all on a bunch of people – all the same.' (ibid.) Its 'staging idea' as he recalls it in '82 was 'how to do something good in the open without any theatrics':

'That was another of these really stinking, lousy shows – it was nothing – there was very interesting material from Bob Ernstthal applying to Harvard College and getting all these questionnaires – these wonderful ridiculous questionnaires, and we just tried to make a piece of music of that by questioning the questions and by accelerating the questions and re-using questions all the time and then, what was done with it was mask-wearing, position-taking, a few props may have been used and maybe some of the things were written on paper and held up. I don't think a curtain was used at all. Neither for going away nor for coming on. It was all done open.' (Schumann, interview, '82.)[1]

For *War Demonstration*, the group built 'these little landscapes. We built a whole landscape' on the floor of the Delancey Street Museum, 'taking

---

1. Bob thinks the core of the questionnaire was along the lines of 'do you own or have access to.' The show was 'a spoof on questionnaires. It was like a chanted version of this ridiculous army questionnaire to find out how many possessions you had, and what you thought about certain things. Do you have a hat, do you have a cap, do you have a tennis racket, do you have golf clubs, do you have a fishing rod? It was this litany of these objects and success. It was like a spoof on questionnaires and college life. My recollection is that it didn't have masks. That we did it without any masks or any theatrical devices. I think we got the sound part down really well. But as I remember the visual part was undeveloped. It was almost done *a capella*. As I remember it. That was a peculiar experiment also. But it was almost like a chant. It was almost like you were in a choral rendition of this questionnaire. It was like a musical interlude.' — (Ernstthal, interview.)

most of the place, (there was) very little place left for the audience' – which, Schumann remembers with a laugh, thinking of the lack of audience, caused no difficulty – and the spectacle involved

'flying around with an airplane, and changing lights a lot. It was not a show, it was a set of puppets, but with little cutouts, and little paintings.'

(Schumann, interview, '79.)

Much of Schumann's and Elka's description of *Elements* supra apparently applies equally to *War Demonstration*, or may *be* of *War Demonstration*: a war in children's toys, as child's game – toy planes and a toy landscape.

Ernstthal:

'It was a big mountain of a village. A big mountain of landscape with little objects a predecessor of *Johnny Comes Marching Home*. It was in a way like one of those big woodcuts. It was also a predecessor of *A Man Says Goodbye to His Mother* because we used a toy airplane. It was this big village, and it was a big village like a model railroad village set up on this big piece of burlap over I guess a pile of milk cartons or something, so it was like a mountain. And on the mountain were cutouts hung into the burlap, of houses and stuff and then when it was flat little cars, little toy houses. It was like a landscape, a built up landscape on this mountain and then somebody came in with an airplane and then he'd go down on the thing and there would be a loud crash and the houses would blow up or something. It was a slow buildup of the destruction of this landscape in 3-D. It was a lot like a woodcut, like a graphic presentation. With a kind of graphic flat, two-dimensional story telling. Like processing a crankie movie. I think it was black and white. We did it a few times.' (Ernstthal, interview.)

10. May-July '65. *Flower Mountain*.

Schumann's next production, *Flower Mountain* (May-July '65), apparently a further variant on the *Elements/War Demonstration* material, was again, like *Birdcatcher*, produced in tandem with a Bob Nichols play, *Digging for the Poverty Program*, for which Schumann furnished masks.[1] Both were presented as street plays jointly by the Bread and Puppet Theatre and the Greenwich Village Peace Center, and under the aegis of Bob Nichols. Because of its relatively elaborate and miniature set, *Flower Mountain* does not really seem to have had street play character.

'That was like his ant's trip. It was under *great* big canvas and I think it has a whole village set ... and the whole thing took place on this big cloth mountain and there were figures on it or something.' (Ernstthal, interview.)

'A big mountain with houses and flowers and cows and trees hanging from it, and all kind of war machinery that moved. It was done with some – probably some of the equipment from what was formerly called *War Demonstration*, but (had) the big *Beast* in it. I was blowing horns and playing drums and there were several support instruments with the horns and drums, I think.... The whole *Flower Mountain* consisted of people holding up the big big candles and a big piece of burlap. I think there were some little puppets sticking their heads and bodies out of the canvas. Hand puppets. I'm not sure.'(Schumann, interview, '79.)

It was supplemented by a crankie (shown by Helen Rabin) with no story – 'armies and armies and armies marching and guns and guns moving.' (Schumann, interview, '82.) The band music apparently preceded entries – or the entry? – of the Beast.

---

1. 'Street Plays Planned, Participants Sought. The Greenwich Village Peace Center and the Bread & Puppet Museum plan a spring carnival of plays, vaudeville, and juggling acts, to be performed outdoors at Thompson St. & Washington Square South ... The initial program, consisting of six short plays and happenings, will be given on Saturday & Sunday afternoons beginning on May 22. Among the future participants are the Judson Poets Theatre, the Hardware Poets, the N.Y. Poets Theatre, Dick Higgins, Remy Charlip, Aileen Pasloff, and the Fugs. Other groups interested in participating should contact Robert Nichols at ....' (notice, *Village Voice*, April 15, '65.)

'Street Plays. The Village Peace Center and the Bread and Puppet Theatre will present two street plays "Digging for the Poverty Program" and "Mountain Flower" (sic) at 4 p.m. on Saturday & Sunday May 29 & 30, at the Churchyard of St. Marks in the Bouwerie, 2nd Ave. & 10th St.' (*Village Voice* notice, May 27, '65). They were done again on June 5th at Metro-North Community Center, 331 East 100th Street (a foray out of the Village, into, I believe, a Puerto Rican neighborhood), and then were presented at the Bread & Puppet Museum, together with a 'miscellany by the Fugs', by the Greenwich Village Peace Center, June 17 through July 10th. Whether the Fugs, a left wing rock group, played at all of these June-July performances, I do not know.

Bob's interest in street plays lasted beyond '65: the Judson Poets Theatre presented *Scenes from a Street Play* by him at (but inside) the Judson Memorial Church, October 7-24, '66.

11. November '65. *Leaf Feeling the Moonlight*.
Interaction of big puppets.

Leaf Feeling the Moonlight (November '65),[1] is the first of Schumann's plays to be done at something like a regular theatre, and is well-nigh unique in his output both in being a personal statement and in expressing a not only tender but happy mood.

With *Murder Mystery* and *Birdcatcher* it was one of his very very few apolitical shows, and like *The Dead Man Rises* by which two years later he took it back, expression of feeling, a picture of a mood, free of morality (which is to say guilt) and of the obsession to make sure one will have done for others at least as much as a man should do for his fellow men; but very special, apparently, by its lyricism, avowed in its advertisement as 'poem', and expression, I suspect, of joy: if Ernstthal is right, a love poem to the lady that in it did the Lady's part, a love that Ernstthal thinks was (guiltily) consummated, but that, if I read the Schumann of that time right, perhaps wasn't, as then the guilt might have squelched the joy, at least for working purposes, though then again, the incandescence of joy, flesh of Angels, is in men scarcely ever achieved except by the combustion of fear in the carnal consummation of desire, a white play with black in it. That Schumann still feels guilty about this play is shown by the evasiveness of his recollections, he has difficulty recalling the girl's name, he tries to present the play as fortuitous outcome of experimentation with puppets, he says its sections had the words of its title for names, but it had four sections and the third apparently was not 'the', but 'love'.

'It started with building of the puppets and then experimenting with the movements of the puppets, adding sounds and objects, building hands with words that

---

1. 'The Bridge/ Peter Schumann's/ Bread and Puppet Theatre/ *King Story One*/ a tragedy with puppets/ *Leaf Feeling the Moonlight*/ a poem in puppets, in four parts. Note: If your notion of a puppet show is something that's cute, fey, quaint, you're in for something of a shock. Sundays & Mondays, Nov. 7, 8, 14, 15, 22; 8 p.m. 4 St. Marks Place. $2.00 (reservations accepted).' (Rather large ad in the *Village Voice* of November 4, '65.) I have found no further mention of productions of this play until the *Village Voice* of May 18, '67, when the *Off-Off-Broadway Guide* announces it, to be done, together with an 'Untitled New Play', identified by an ad in the same issue as *Speech*, at the Astor Memorial Library Landmark Building the following Saturday, May 20th. An ad of May 25th announces 'one new piece' as companion piece of *Speech* on the 27th probably *Dead Man Rises*, the piece Schumann changed it into. Maybe the May 20th *Leaf* already was *Dead Man Rises*. In the *Off-Off Broadway Guide* of May 25th, the 'new piece' of the 27th is still referred to as *Leaf*. And the May 26, '67 issue of *WIN* alerts us of the presentation, every Saturday, of the 'Bread and Puppet repertory (program II)', consisting of *Leaf* and *Speech*.

ended up with the arbitrary line, *Leaf Feeling the Moonlight* . . . . (It) consisted of meetings of these puppets, solo dances, group dances of them, beginnings and ends of scenes that were indicated by words that were carried by paper maché hands and sounds that separated scenes from each other and sounds like bells and chimes and sounds that accompanied movements. A shakuhachi, another type of a flute as I recall, also some bone rattles, South American bone rattles and I would think some junk instruments, assorted chimes. *Leaf Feeling the Moonlight* had no text other than these words. Leaf, Feeling, (inaudible: Love?), Moonlight. (Elka: That's one of my favorite lost shows . . . . It was one of these shows where each scene as you watched was somehow maybe incomprehensible or hard to fathom and yet the sequence of all these things together made the show. You didn't understand it, it didn't tell a story, but it was like a perfect –) But it felt like a story. (Elka: No, it felt like a poem, it was completely lyrical and captured some essence of what the title says. I mean it didn't have a story – it was some kind of yearning, a red rose, and a struggle and a fight, and problems – all these very romantic elements, but it was done – it was abstract. It was something you had to figure out from watching. It was very beautiful.)'

(Schumann, interview, '79.)

'There is no action. It was a dance piece of these puppets and it was a bit like a marriage or proposal of marriage that happened in it. An older man and a younger man – or were they more like two suitors – (I: You mentioned a father at some point –) A father – I would think so – a father and a suitor and a beautiful lady – the White Lady. And the light in the last scene being the success of the marriage or the dancing of the suitor and the lady. That was the most story line that was in it – no more than that. I performed the man – one of the men. The young man, I think. Yes, I had my mask mounted on my head so that was the young man, and the old man was a stick puppet. A puppet with a short stick. *Leaf Feeling the Moonlight* was just painted words – each one of the words (of the title) became an act. That sounds like a very artificial way of dealing with language, you know, to just do that, but it worked, somehow, with the puppets and the things. There was a frame. (It) had two front curtains, so that hands could come out from the sides and could be played horizontally. So, the title of the show would appear on these white hands that would come in – sculpted hands that would come in and hold that word up. And the puppets also would have entrances and exits that way. (The show) was done with black curtains (and the backdrop) also was black. (The space left for the performance between the side curtains and in front of the back curtain) was very small – very, very small. Maybe six feet wide and the depth probably no more than four feet.' (Schumann, interview, '82.)

The Bridge program describes the contents: 'a lovely lady in the moonlight meets a hand with a rose.'

'*Leaf Feeling the Moonlight* was incredibly romantic and a love story.'

(Sherman, interview.)

'It had to do with a spotlight, there was a spotlight of light and he tried to touch it. It was a love poem to Catherine Merrill, if I may say so. It was the first love story that we attempted.' (Ernstthal, interview.)

643

Schumann did the young man, Merrill the lady. Sherman, Merrill's rival, and Ernstthal, Schumann's, concur it was not only a love poem addressed to her, but had his yen for her for subject matter. (They also concur he had an affair with her, a matter of suspicion.)

Schumann cites as one of the reasons he could not recreate this play later (cf. *Dead Man Rises* infra), that he didn't have a shakuhachi player. Apparently he felt it had been essential to the play.[2]

The play was the first to use two new kinds of puppets with which Schumann feels he achieved a breakthrough as regards mobility: unlike the pole puppets, they were capable of head movements, and in one of them – in which the puppet head is mounted on top of the performer's head – used for the lover and his love – the performer had both hands free, in the other – in which the puppet head is mounted on a short stick – one hand to modify the draping of his or her dress, he can

> 'use his other hand and arm to bulge out the fabric and to give the fabric delicate movement. It's the most versatile puppet that we invented. That style is one – is the danciest of them. The biggest in scope, in movement scope of all the puppets.'
> (Schumann, interview, '79.)

The White Lady's costume, attached to her puppet head

> 'was a bunch of white gauzy kind of fabric that we had found in the garbage can and that was old looking and ripping apart but lovely looking and fluffy, gave a lot of body to this creature.' (Schumann, interview, '79.)

Leaf, then, was a dance mime piece, and the first of Schumann's pieces, really, in which big puppets interacted in space: in a very small, black-limned space. I think that with it, Schumann attained to self assurance in the handling of large sized puppets, as with its sequel, *Fire*, rehearsed as *Leaf* ran, in the handling of masks.

I note that Schumann so far had stayed away from the Vietnam war: his war pieces so far were still digestings of World War II. From *Fire* onward, he was to dwell on Vietnam, he commenced sturdily moral address, engaged theatre. Up to this point there was something quite private about his theatre, in fact verging on the a- if not immoral.

In a quite mellow mood, in a spirit of forgiveness, he dwelt in *Birdcatcher*, himself dancing that clever knave, on the pleasures of the hunt – indeed, pigeons, ortolans and so on and so forth, properly prepared, are

---

2. 'It's a Japanese flute. It's an ancient Japanese instrument. Quite different from our Western flutes in that one uses the breath, not just for sound production, but for amplifying of breath sound. When you breathe into an instrument – on our Western flutes, the idea is always to do voice imitation with flute – that's what the medieval people thought of – and the Japanese flute just – you wander – the breath – you know the way breath sounds into the flute and you use that, and you pitch that, with your *fingers*. So it's like "Whooo" – it's similar to, really breath sounds. There's a much greater variety of sound in it than our flutes ever have.' — (Schumann, interview, '82.)

delicious. The intimate frame there weas blue. He is dancing before Baal Shem. In *Murder Mystery*, a complicitous veil of uncertainty — who can know? who will ever know? — is spread over the rapist's intimate engagement with his victim, his murder of her in the quiet of the woods. Apologies are made for him — look at all the big killers. Such acts, of rage, revenge, out of bitterness, frustration, are self-liberations, akin to the prick's thrust toward the womb. The tourists and the villagers are upset, disapprove — but in the mountain's granite not even a momentary glint reflects the thrusting knife, the throttling hands are undistinguishable from the roots of the bushes and trees underground all around. In *Leaf*, framed narrowly in black, within the poesy, the woman's clothes are removed, her skin is touched, her legs opened, she is invaded, flesh joins flesh, the whole world notwithstanding: the bonds of matrimony burst.[3] In short, Schumann, experimenting with his puppets, here burst forth in passion and sinfulness. A wholly different theatre than in fact he came up with could have emerged at this point: private, poetic, in empathy and sympathy embracing the individual, i.e.: transgression. But Schumann immediately conquered this weakness, disavowed himself by a tragic counterpiece, *Fire*, celebrating ultimate self-denial, suicide under the voluntary duress of morality. And a while later, unable to redo *Leaf*, he reproduces it (*Dead Man Rises*, '67) in renunciatory form, equating unlawful sex — love — with a suicide pact. We encounter this same two-beat operation of guilt again a few years later: the discrete celebration of carnality in *The Difficult Life of Uncle Fatso* of early '70 is countered by a tragic obsequy to death (*Grey Lady Cantata #2*, summer of '70), and is followed and denied by an indictment of ruthless male sexuality (the second *Birdcatcher*, '71).

More directly, he does penance immediately for these personal indulgences and in particular the expression of private delight in *Leaf*, by three pieces on the theme of suffering, on the suffering of others, the suffering of the Vietnamese: *Fire* ('66), and *Wounds of Vietnam* and *Bach's Cantata #140* ('67).

---

3. In an essay, *Unruhen, Gift und Geschrei* (Poland, May '72), written during or at the end of a subsequent phase of passionate self-affirmation, Schumann equates being in love to intoxication by the poison of a love potion and describes the consequences:
'The channels through which (a man's) thought drives toward the marked-out goal are inundated by merry spring rivers.'
The swimmer is threatened but sped on.

12. January-June '66. *Fire*.
Effective use of masks.

Schumann was preparing *Fire* (first run, January-June '66; second: November '67-April '68)[1] when he first put on *Leaf*. Its combination of intensity and intimacy may reflect the same mood. *Fire* was his breakthrough into recognition by the New York artistic community.[2] Its success at the Nancy theatre festival in the spring of '68 procured him the kind and measure of fame he was to attain.

It was his response to the airborne American carnage in peasant Asia in the form of an homage both to its victims and to responses to it on the

---

1. *Fire* apparently was first done at the Museum Saturday evenings (sometimes twice), from January 22, '66 onward. The last presentation in this run I have found a reference for was on June 11th. On June 10th (*The Militant*, June 20, '66), it was done at the Militant Labor Forum. It may not have run quite continuously all Saturdays during this period. Entrance was against 'contributions.' An ad of February 3 carries a dedication: 'IN MEMORIAM Alice Herz, Norman Morrison, Roger Laporte', three people that in protest against the napalm bombing of Vietnam set fire to and so killed themselves. Two special Friday performances on May 20th carried an admission of $1.50 and were for the benefit of the New York Workshop in Nonviolence.

It was then given a second run at the Washington Square Methodist Church, Monday evenings at 8:30 from November 20th '67 to April 1st '68. The Bread and Puppet Theatre had lost its temporary base at the Astor Library Landmark Building at the end of October '67: the Reverend Shaef's Washington Square Methodist 'Peace' church from at least the Angry Arts Week of January 29-February 5, '67 onward the center of the Peace Movement insofar as it was neither Old nor New Left (the Greenwich Village Peace Center moved itself and its 'draft counseling', i.e. help with draft evasion/avoidance there in March '68) became their performance base November '67-February '68. The run of *Fire* here provided a beacon for this pacifist wing of the Peace Movement.

2. '*Fire* was our first step in a certain way into real recognition. I feel that's why Joe Papp invited us in. So that was our entree you know into the more set-up theatrical world. *Fire* was in revival in 1968 when Christian Dupavillon came from the (Nancy) Festival, invited us.... He said will you come to Paris and we'll pay your way. We said oh yeah sure, you know, and then we'll go to Russia you know, okay sure. I remember real disbelief. We didn't even think of it twice. I remember we thought well wouldn't that be fun and then.... That's too much, really, because we still felt obscure, because of Peter's insistence that the world was evil and success wasn't in the vocabulary. To be a success or a modest success, shit on it, was essentially his attitude.' — (Ernstthal, interview.)

The '66 *Fire* was probably the proximate cause of the Obie (*Village Voice* Off-Broadway Award) Schumann received on May 21 that year.

Ernstthal (interview) remembers other performances of the revived *Fire*: perhaps at the Riverside Church, and at a midtown, perhaps Lutheran, church, but thinks that because it required a 'rather elaborate installation', it didn't move around too much. But they took it to Europe that spring of '68, and subsequently played it a great deal, both in Europe and the U.S. The last performances of it I have data on were given in May '70 at the University of Maryland and at Emory University in Atlanta, Georgia; by a sub-group travelling without Schumann at a theatre festival in Shiraz, August/September '70; and at the gymnasium of the Neighborhood House in Madison, Wisconsin, in September '72.

part of certain others than himself, responses that he may have felt more adequate than his own — their self-immolation by fire. Like almost all of Schumann's theatre it represents the incursion of evil, specifically male evil, war, into simple life, specifically into the innocence of female life. But its distinctive feature is that it shows and endorses a response by life to evil by which life does not lose its innocence: its self-termination by what in Schumann's iconography is peculiarly the means of evil against life, fire. The play thus represents the ideology of non-violent resistance, and in fact was that ideology's artistic high point in the U.S. It will be another year before Schumann again (with *A Man Says Goodbye to his Mother*) takes up violent resistance (the theme, really, of *King Story* too, except that here the powerful fight the powerful.) In its form, *Fire* realizes Schumann's '62 program of a sacral theatre in which performers and spectators jointly contemplate the perennial essences of human existence. It seems probably that the masks used in *Fire* were first used at a silent vigil of November 26, '65 on the U.N. Plaza for Norman Morrison and Roger Laporte, having been made for this use, and that *Fire* was suggested to Schumann by this street demonstration, both as regards its subject matter and its form — of a silent vigil.

Fire is the first of his three plays dealing directly with Vietnam (it, *Wounds of Vietnam, Bach Cantata #140*). Up to now he had in his indoors — his 'puppetry as art' — work faced backwards to World War II (*Elements, War Demonstration, Flower Mountain*): January '66-February '67 he deals with the current war, the subject of his politics becomes the subjects of his art-as-art, and he wraps up the subject (*A Man Says Goodbye* of '67 is again more universal). It was the last piece he did at the Delancey Street Museum, and with it he passed from apprenticeship to mastery.

The play has been described in a masterly fashion by George Dennison:[3]

---

3. Copyright George Dennison 1966, 1970.
Robert Nichols wrote the first review of *Fire*, seeing it as Schumann's best work since *Totentanz* and the '63 *Christmas Story*, the work in between having been marred by Schumann's 'deeply-felt social and personal conviction, a commitment to poverty – which can seem like sheer clumsiness' and by Schumann's attempt, as mask-maker and sculptor to 'communicate on the simplest level as if to children. The skill is primitive in the manner of medieval woodcuts and certain religious cartoons; and often appears anti-intellectual or an offense to taste': but in *Fire* the commitment and the primitiveness 'are fused by the material in the way that in Picasso's Guernica passion and ruggedness are fused':

'There are twenty or more white masks, some of which are sewn on dummy figures. They are from the life-mask of an Asian woman, and are identical. The real actors wear the same mask. The face is very beautiful and changes expression throughout the play. The beginning of each of the eight short episodes is signaled by the striking of a gong. The action is simple and grave, and has great suspense. The five real actors wear the same black costume as the dummies; at first it is not possible to tell which is which. The living animate the dead. Both sets of figures move, and are moved, through the sequences of the drama.

'Peter Schumann's *Fire* (which I count among the finest plays I have seen), more than any play I have seen has the quality of prayer.

Prayer (for me) is a childhood memory, but I remember things like these: a peopling of death with human forms; a vague yet affecting sense of the scale of things; a notion of the preciousness of life, and of its vulnerability; a touch of fear, since fate is everywhere and has little to do with one's wishes.

The effect is uncanny, but also direct and compassionate: as when they eat a meal, dance with each other, or untie knots from the rope around each other's hands. The figures are transcendent; their life follows you out of the theatre.' — (Nichols, *Village Voice*, February 17, '66.)

Nichols names as actor-musicians Ernstthal (bass), Charlie Adams (trumpet), and Schumann (violin), and as 'the two other performers', Kathy Solomon and Catherine Merrill.

Bob's review was followed (March 10) by one brilliantly exposing its writer Michael Smith, then baron of the *Voice*'s 'theatre journal' department, as the kind of person that acquires ideological power, a shithead. He reviews it together with five other plays and some Melies movies:

'All day Saturday I accompanied Remy Charlip and a bunch of students (mostly girls) from Sarah Lawrence and Earlham College on a marathon, or merry-go-round, of theatrical events. After a Chinese breakfast.... Next stop (the fourth; after the Japanese dinner (SSB)) was Peter Schumann's Bread and Puppet Museum on Delancey Street. His new work, "Fire", is his strangest yet and an extraordinary experience. I'm not sure whether Schumann's attitude is uncompromising or fanatical. He makes harsh demands on the audience, imposing his own ponderous rhythm, inscrutable and indifferent to "entertainment values." "Fire", dedicated to those who immolated themselves over the Vietnam war, is a formal succession of more or less static images, as self-contained as a poem and nearly perfect. It is hard to distinguish between the masked actors and the dummy figures. Together with the manner of presentation, this suggests an inhumanity and denial of life at odds with Schumann's humanitarian message. Next stop, after a Greek supper, was the Caffee Chino's 1 a.m. show. The group had dwindled to two girls, Remy and me. Michael Benedikt's tiny play, "The Vaseline Photographer" gets a concise straightforward production by ....'

That *Fire* was getting Schumann some attention even uptown is suggested by Jean Hewlett's culinary and personal interest item on Schumann, *Sculptor Finds Art in Baking, Too*, with three (!) photos of him making his bread in the *New York Times* of March 7, '66.

The *New York Times* didn't mention it until January 18, '68 – a 'haunting tableau ... still and chiselled' – and never reviewed it.

Smith's inhouse review was followed in the *Voice* (June 2, '66) by the guest-review ('speak out the arts') of George Dennison's from which he later derived the *Tulane Drama Review* piece. Nichols had suggested that Schumann's work up to *Fire* was clumsy, simpleminded and tasteless, Smith had found inhumanity and denial of life in the harsh, ponderous and inscrutable *Fire*, Dennison, like Nichols warmly appreciative of it ('most moving theatre I have seen this season'), instead of doing it the justice of a full treatment, as he did later, when it was established as a resistance classic, used it as exhibition piece in a disquisition on true and false ritual in the theatre, counterposing the true ritual – giving artistic form to the actual life and feelings of the participants – of Genet's *The Blacks* and Schumann's *Fire* – to the false ritual – artfully created in detachment from life and moving not by its truth but by its art – of Weiss' *Marat/Sade* and of Artaud's prescriptions. This strongly makes the point that *Fire* is not protest, nor moral challenge nor incitement to

I have tended to think of prayer under its aspects of supplication and faith. I am more impressed now by the rationality of prayer. To kneel, to bow one's head, and then to rise is to affirm, in a profoundly rational spirit, one's human place in a world only in small part human. If prayers are addressed to God or to gods they nevertheless signify to other men that we have arrived at some sort of outer limit.

---

action, and is not consciousness-changing, but merely consciousness-raising — and, like prayer, probably pacifying!

'(*Fire*) is concerned with political and moral issues. Yet it is not a protest play; nor does it attempt to convey a message or a point of view, but rather to deepen an awareness that is common to all men and which might be described as the sorrow of the dead. . . . Like Genet, Schumann is uncovering, and deepening, specific emotions which already exist in the experience of the audience. In part these pertain to the war in Vietnam, but more importantly they belong to our feelings about death and the basic human dependencies which the fact of death makes vivid to us. There is little in our culture capable of saving these facts in redemptive public forms. Schumann has accomplished this.'

Schumann shares Dennison's feelings about *Marat/Sade*:

'A pretentious piece of bullshit. When you mix so much money and so much talent and so much fabrication, you lose your humble human persuasion. It was the most tremendous piece of theatrical fabrication I have seen in a long while. I felt sorry for them. And it is an insult to the real suffering of people.' — (Schumann, quoted in Michael Thomas, *Pavement Artists, Plays and Players*, May '67.)

This was during the remaining '60s an important line of division. The seductive power of Artaud/Brook operated in surprising places. E.g. on the Pageant Players:

'We looked around us: Brecht seemed the best of the political playwrights but was so European, intellectual, communist. He saw America as an outsider. We needed to be indigenous in spirit and content. Most other political drama, especially American, seemed hackneyed or heavyhanded, with a few exceptions from the 30s. *Marat/Sade* – the play that turned many of us on to theater! All that music, body movement, choreography, color, energy! Good lessons there. Everyone we knew came out of *Marat/Sade* stoned by the beauty, remembered the story, the history, the image of the asylum and the rich, but none of the arguments or politics stuck in my head or anyone else's I knew.

And both of these still in that "theater." Playing for an elite. Audience glued to their seat. The cost for a show like that staggering. And it was such an exception to the rest of the professional B'way genre of which it was *still* clearly a member, anyway.' — (M. Brown, *Some Dynamics and Aesthetics in Pageant Players Street Theater*, in Lesnick, *Guerrilla Street Theater*, '73.)

The only review of the '66 *Fire* not in the *Voice* I know of was in the Trotzkyite *The Militant* (June 20, '66) – of the performance at the Militant Labor Forum.

Karl Bissinger, the Peace Movement photographer, had seen Schumann's '62 Christmas *Organ* piece:

'Then I remember going through a period where I saw various things of Peter's thinking very much the rhythm of these pieces were so out of touch with my rhythm, my American rhythm, I found it very ponderous and very difficult. And I was always interested . . . . And very often I felt that it was his lacking but in fact I found out it was my lacking and how that came about, there are two sequences about that time. One was in the basement of the Washington Square Church. He did a thing called *Fire*, and somehow or other I was relaxed enough and at ease enough and calmed down from my usual hypertension to fall into a rhythm. It was almost hypnotic. Then I began to get his way. It was like yoga. I began to feel as I gave in to this wonderful piece . . . . It's one of the most wonderful pieces

Fire has many of these aspects of prayer. It speaks from a similar borderline or outer limit of experience. It is not a protest play, and is not propagandistic; rather it *responds* to the horrors of Vietnam, responds modestly and truly, and enables us to respond. To some extent, it is a service for the dead. Beyond this it manifests certain of the deep premises of the human condition: the unquitableness of life, our dependencies on each other, the social nature of the self. Taken together, these are the visceral/spiritual background of all emotion and all feeling, but especially of such emotions as terror, compassion, moral outrage, the sense of justice, sorrow. In some sense Schumann's play is like a dream. The dream does not express emotion, but pulls us deeply into the matrix of emotion. Our landscape now is both logical and pre-logical. To see its shapes is to feel them. They are ambiguous, but not confused. The dream verges on nightmare, recovers itself and deepens. Finally it releases us – and we feel that we have conceived a prayer for the victims of our world.

I have not been speaking fancifully. If one were to watch only the audience, one would come to some such conclusions as these.

I first saw *Fire* four years ago at the tiny Bread and Puppet loft on Delancey Street. The seats were filled and I stood in the back. Two burly young men came in – perhaps not so young, in their late twenties, but wearing jackets like adolescents, minus the skull and bones. They swaggered and bulked their shoulders, smiled guardedly, looked everywhere, and put their heads together. An actress in black robes was distributing programs. She held a loaf of bread under one arm, and broke it and handed out pieces as she went. The two men,

---

I'd ever seen of anybody's. An extraordinary calm. I began to understand his rhythm. What he was asking of me as an audience. And it works.

So that each time from then on I would go in you know an hysterical man, all keyed up and whatnot and then consciously you know begin to work the piece. I mean one does that with any work of art you know. It demands something of you and you respond to it usually unconsciously. This time I very consciously ... I think this is the first time I became aware of a kind of oriental quality, particularly in Peter's work, but in a lot of other works that I'd never – what I'm trying to say is that like so many Americans, particularly, those are the only people I know, Americans have no time for anything. You've got to have immediate satisfaction. Immediate results or you reject it. You simple have nothing more to do with it. I think that's the way we respond to movies. The Keystone comedies we were raised on. Pow pow pow. Great you know. It works. And that kinds of excitement. And it never comes – American jazz. Everything is immediate. A response that you respond to, like this. But the slow ability to take in anything I think is very foreign to American culture.

And what Peter had in a couple of simple lessons, somehow or other, I must have been aware of it or I wouldn't have subjected myself to it over and over ... was that I too, I am responsible as much as the art. You know there's an audience and there's an audience. You've got to work together or it doesn't work. And it has always been my expectation that the artist would work his ass off for me you know and therefore I had to do something, something has to be out here to be receiving. But it was minimum. It really was. Sometimes it was just the price of the ticket. Demand, demand.

But the idea that art can be give and take, you really have to bring a lot to it. I knew this intellectually, but I didn't know it in my bones. I think it's fair to say that this is the first time I ever received this. But I had known this intellectually and I probably even found it a loss in myself. My inability to read the literature of another time. It's very

smiling skeptically now, leaned against the wall and folded their arms, as if they meant to be spectators forever. But now here was the bread lady! And she was breaking off pieces of bread! Their faces changed abruptly into children's faces. They held out their hands, looking first at the girl, then at the pieces of bread lying on their open palms. Furtive glances. Others too were looking around, but all were chewing — and so they popped the bread into their mouths and began to chew. One could see the comment pass across their faces. "Not bad." It was a coarse rye, tangy and substantial. Everyone was chewing, tasting the same taste, settling more comfortably on benches, looking around. In fact, we were eating together, consuming the communal loaf.

Fire is dedicated to Alice Henry, Roger LaPorte, and Norman Morrison, three Americans who killed themselves by fire because of their country's crimes in Vietnam.

The play begins with the stroke of a bell. The small curtain opens on two rows of robed and masked figures sitting in chairs. The masks are the whitened faces of the Vietnamese dead. The hands, too, are masks, with the result that their groping, sensitive gestures are both less than life and larger. A placard on a stand tells the name of the scene, which is *Monday*. The figures murmur and mumble. It is not quite talk, but the "twittering like bats" Odysseus heard in the underground. Hands rise and fall. The faces cannot move; yet something like movement — like awareness, feeling, longing — seems to flit across the eyes and lips and cheeks. The bell sounds again. The talking ceases. The curtain is closed.

---

difficult for me to read anything but contemporary things. And I think that was because of this immediate response . . .

But certainly *Fire* — *Fire was* the first time I remember actually being so elated that I had given a response and changed.' — (Bissinger, interview.)

Catherine Merrill, Bob's femme fatale, was still around:

'She was there and that was kind of the height of it. And I think a lot of the tension — this may be off the wall — but I remember this — and a lot of the pressure — you know how *Fire* was very pressurized? And its extremely intense and very dense quality? That was around the time when she was creating a little bit of waves in the theatre. That kind of feeling — that was her nature. She had a very internal, tense, inward-looking, complicated, neurotic nature and Peter and I were both quite fascinated with it. And I think a lot of that pressure got translated somehow into the show . . . I think I lost out on Catherine — was part of it — and then I bounced out.

Fire came together rather quickly, as I remember . . . It was our best show. It was, in a way, when it all came together in terms of length, breadth, intensity . . . Some of them were constantly changing and like I was saying — about rehearsal and changing the elements and switching it around and on and on and on. But *Fire* wasn't like that, as I remember. *Fire*, as I remember, we practically did it in one week. It was almost like that. I mean, we wanted to do a show in a room — we hung the drapes . . . we hung that black cloth in the space that we had at Delancey Street and . . . we kept that space going . . . the editions of the masks were all there piled up, and we just put 'em around — on the drapes — made the setting — made the — I think there was a question about the front wall at one time — if it was going to be black, or something. You know, very minor things — but then there was that stand with the little signs — the days of the week — and the ball — ding — and with the little clamp light on it and all those things really came together all at once. And the idea of doing it "A week in the life of" — that kind of thing and . . . The really good shows came out very fast.' — (Ernstthal, interview.)

Schumann's masks are extraordinary. In themselves they are works of art. But they were made for theatre, that is, to evoke and suggest many things, and to seem to move. One becomes aware only slowly of their power and beauty. They are touched by the consciousness we imagine hovers anxiously over boundaries of sleep and death. The eyes are closed, yet we sense the power of sight behind the protuberances of the lids. The lips are variously opened, closed, half-closed, fixed in transitional positions between smiling, grimacing, speaking and drinking. The faces seem to have been struck a blow, though there is no evidence of wounds, only awareness recoiling upon itself, recapitulating sight and touch after it has been removed from all intercourse with persons and things. I thought of Rilke's line in "Orpheus, Eurydice, and Hermes", as translated by Lowell:

> Her hands were still ringing and tingling . . .
> And when the god suddenly gripped her
> and said with pain in his voice, "He is looking back at us"
>
> she didn't get through to the words
> and answered vaguely, "Who?"

The bell tolls again. The curtain is drawn aside. The scene is *Tuesday*. A robed figure, awkward, intense, and tender, touches bread and lifts a goblet to the lips of each of the seated figures. Heads lift to receive the food. There is a sensitive confusion of almost-hands, a deep subsiding, hardly visible, of each face after it has been touched by bread. When all have been fed, the bell tolls again. The figures are motionless. The curtain is drawn across.

The bell tolls again. We begin to hear it now also as a tolling for the dead. A haunting, broken music is being made onstage by sticks, rattles, a damaged zither, a fiddle that sounds like the scraping of a shoe. Slowly, with patriarchal dignity, brittle anxiety, and something that is like a solemn agreement that joy must be observed on holy days, the figures dance. It is *Wednesday*. The bell tolls. The figures cease to move. The curtain is drawn across.

The following scene (*Thursday*) is one of uncanny power. The figures are seated facing in a double row from the front of the stage to the back. A newcomer appears among them, bound with a heavy rope. The sensitive, groping hands reach out to him. The attention of the sightless eyes is like wondering. His own hands, too, fall awkwardly against the rope . . . until by failing and failing again, those hands have finally freed him. He stands in the center of the stage and holds out the rope for all to see. We do see it. The rope is uncanny. The bell tolls and the curtain is drawn across.

The *Friday* stage is dark. A figure turns on an overhead light. The one who was freed of the rope lies under covers on a cot. One sits on a chair beside him. Others hover in back. A loud rattling is heard offstage. The seated figure rises and the others come forward. They look long at the one on the cot . . . and then lift the covers and draw them slowly over his face. The bell tolls.

The silence of all these scenes becomes a setting for the horrible noise of the next (*Saturday*), a shrieking, metallic whine and roar like the noise of a siren and the splintering of bone. A light on stage swings wildly in all directions. The effect is like *Guernica*. The figures move, but as if frozen in confusion. A large, demonically ungainly, snuffling creature flops among their feet. The bell tolls in the din. Sound and motion cease. The light is turned out. The curtain is drawn across.

Sunday is played in silence, following the tolling of the bell. The seated and standing figures suggest meditation. One turns his back and lifts his hands in prayer. But his hands have begun to move upward to his face, and continue to move in inexplicable gestures. He turns to us again, and we see that he has covered his face with blood. The bell tolls. The placard is touched by a masked figure, and — like those before it — falls to the floor.

The penultimate scene is called *Fire*. The silence deepens. Two figures slowly swathe the others in dark red bands. The bell tolls.

The last placard names the scene *End*. The robed, masked figures are seated. A Vietnamese woman, whose mask is like the face of death in old age, and whose white robes are like the splendor of a sacred celebration, stands alone just off center of the stage. And now in perfect silence something shocking occurs. Two figures enter, bare-armed and bare-handed, dressed in blue jeans and scivvy shirts, wearing masks of Western faces. They are lugging cinderblocks. Their motions are the motions of workmen at work — and they appear brutal, profoundly alien, almost inhuman in the deeply human setting the others have created. They place the cinderblocks around the white-robed woman, and surround her with a little fence of wire... and then withdraw. There is silence again — but it is a different silence, an acidic, profoundly dislocated, appalling silence. The aged woman holds a roll of bright red tape. With deliberate movements — movements at once practical, prosaic, and ceremonious — she tears long strips of the tape and fastens them to her robe near her feet. The red strips become numerous, and move higher, beginning to entwine her and hamper her movements. One wrist is immobilized against her chest, but the fingers still tear and fasten the strips. The strips cross her mouth now, and her cheeks, and finally lie across her eyes. She folds in upon herself and topples forward, sagging heavily against the fence. There is a long silence. Something has been restored. The bell tolls.

All the theatre now is in darkness. The play is over and everyone knows it, yet no one applauds or moves. The silence is ours as well as theirs. We are unwilling to part with it. Finally the houselights are turned on. Some few clap their hands. Others move shufflingly. We make our way to the door, walking like convalescents.

Since the question of ritual has been so important since Artaud, I would like to say something about it here, though I think not much need be said.

There is ceremoniousness in *Fire*, but no ritualism as such. Schumann, like Genet, knows that rituals cannot be invented on the stage. They exist exclusively in the audience, though in latent forms — and therefore must be uncovered. There can be nothing exotic, nothing merely ritualistic in this process — only penetration of what *is*, in its local and immediate shapes. The powers which accomplish this are familiar powers (and they are powers, not theories): intelligence, insight, imagination, modesty in experience, pride in art, and the poetic gift of inspiration. It was, after all, Artaud's disease which made him imagine (wish desperately) that actors, playwrights, and directors might compete from the stage with social forms many centuries in the making.'

(G. Dennison, *Fire, Tulane Drama Review* #47.)

Kourilsky ('71) has described it more concretely as theatre production, and indicating a structure (life-death-the war). Also she gives details and indicates changes in successive productions. And unlike Dennison, she brings out the play's moral challenge to the audience.

'*Fire* se joue dans un lieu précis qui ne peut recevoir qu'un nombre limité de spectateurs, une cinquantaine, en principe. C'est un lieu clos par de hautes tentures noires sur lesquelles peuvent être accrochées des bannières faites à partir de bois gravés de Peter Schumann qui rappellent certaines gravures sur bois expressionnistes, notamment celles de Frans Masereel: des paysages à différentes heures du jour, survolés par des avions. A une extrémité du rectangle se trouve la scène séparée de la salle par une tenture rouge faiblement éclairée par deux projecteurs latéraux recouverts de papier d'emballage. L'attention des spectateurs confinés dans une chambre noire qui empêche toute dispersion se trouve répercutée sur ce rideau rouge, d'autant plus que de derrière le rideau parvient une musique douce, simple et étrange (bouts de bois frappés l'un contre l'autre, cordes pincées, ongles heurtant une bouteille vide, etc.) qui rend la scène sensible et impose peu le peule silence. Rapprochés physiquement les uns des autres dans cet espace étroit, réunis par l'écoute, les spectateurs forment un groupe dont l'intimité se trouve renforcée par une autre activité commune: ils mangent tous un morceau de pain que leur donne une femme habillée tout en noir, cheminant lentement à travers la salle jusqu'à ce qu'elle atteigne le rideau rouge devant lequel elle dit à voix faible la dédicace: "*Cette pièce est dédiée aux trois Américains, Norman Morrison, Alice Hertz et Roger La Porte qui se sont immolés pour protester contre la guerre au Vietnam*".

Ce prélude prépare les spectateurs et leur apporte déjà un certain nombre d'informations; il expose les thèmes du spectacle et en indique d'emblée le *sens*: c'est une pièce *contre* la guerre au Vietnam que nous allons voir. Dans cette salle tendue de noir, faiblement éclairée, les spectateurs se défendent mal de l'impression d'être réunis pour une veillée mortuaire, d'autant plus que la femme en noir qui distribue le pain ressemble à quelque pleureuse. Cette distribution du pain évoque, en outre, pour le public occidental auquel le Bread and Puppet s'adresse, le rite chrétien eucharistique. Au thème de la mort se relie celui de la violence (le rouge) qui s'oppose directement au thème de la non-violence, de la vie simple et fragile, introduit par la musique. Ces trois thèmes se trouveront développés dans le spectacle à tel point que je distinguerais volontiers trois mouvements.

Premier mouvement: la vie

LUNDI

Lorsque le rideau rouge s'ouvre lentement de gauche à droite, manipulé à l'aide d'une longue perche en bois, le spectateur est frappé par le tableau insolite qui s'offre à lui: c'est un autre monde auquel il se trouve soudain confronté, un monde de morts-vivants où les acteurs dont le corps est dissimulé sous longue robe noire, le visage recouvert d'un masque blanc, les mains gantées de blanc, ou masquées (longues mains décharnées qui rappellent certaines sculptures de Giacometti), se confondent totalement avec des mannequins de taille humaine ou encore avec les masques habillés d'une tunique noire à cagoule qui, accrochés à la tenture côté jardin, paraissent aussi "vivants" que des acteurs.⁴ Dans cette chambre noire qui prolonge la salle et dont le seul élément décoratif est constitué par une toile de fond en noir et blanc qui représente une colline, un village, des arbres,⁵ toute l'attention se porte sur les visages blancs et les mains blanches qui sont les véritables protagonistes du drame. Seules notes de couleurs qu'on oublie vite: les fins colliers de perles vives que portent les Vietnamiennes.⁶ La scène est faiblement éclairée par les deux projecteurs latéraux de la salle et par une lampe obscurcie par un papier d'emballage, installée côté cour. A la tige de fer qui la supporte sont fixés une tablette, une pince à dessin, une clochette (ou une simple plaque de métal) et un bâtonnet. Lorsque la Vietnamienne qui a ouvert le rideau l'a accroché, elle prend un carton blanc sur la tablette, le présente au public – c'est le titre du tableau: "*Lundi*" et le fixe à la pince à dessin, puis elle frappe une fois sur la clochette et sort ou bien va s'asseoir, tout à côté, regardant le tableau qui s'anime.⁷

Groupées en arc de cercle sur deux rangs, les Vietnamiennes sont repliées sur elles-mêmes. La douleur inscrite sur leurs masques crayeux, elles restent immobiles, comme figées dans une attente anxieuse. Du "village" monte un marmonnement confus, une sorte de plainte qui peut évoquer la prière. En fait, les femmes parlent, elles "bavardent" – dit même Schumann qui demande toujours aux acteurs de prononcer à voix basse des phrases "réelles".⁸ Mais de leur dialogue, dont on a

---

4. Lorsque *Fire* a été joué à Paris, salle Wagram, en novembre 1969, les mannequins que le B Puppet Theatre avait laissés à New York ont été remplacés par des acteurs. Mais habituellement la pièce n'est jouée que par cinq acteurs, tous les autres habitants du village sont des mannequins ou des masques. Il y a en général quatre mannequins debout, deux mannequins assis, et environ dix masques accrochés à la tenture.
(Leherrissier on replacing the dummies by live performers: 'It really lost a lot of its charm for me – a lot. It was like it was breathing too much.' — (Leherrissier, interview.))
5. En 1967, lorsque *Fire* a été repris à New York, après une interruption de plus d'un an, Peter Schumann a remplacé la composition plus géométrique qu'il avait utilisée à la création, par un des paysages de *The Dead Man Rises*.
6. 'I did remember a couple of weeks ago that I have my *Fire* beads. If you remember, the necklaces around the figures. Ah – as the cluster of figures is made up of mannequins of human beings and that at each of the seven changes, the guy who opens and closes the curtain must go in and assist the people to change the shapes and configurations. And to reset the dummy figures. To know what is what, they wore different colors of necklaces. Cheap, discrete kind of necklaces. So, if I were wearing amber, he would know it's George and George is in the next configuration to be doing that – as opposed to what he's going to be doing in the fourth, which will be bent over. And he always could quickly spot me with the amber beads. (I: Well, wouldn't you know yourself? Wouldn't the performer know?) No, because in the masks, which were these masks of the raped Vietnamese woman . . . and as you were part of this overall grouping, there was no way you could move to your new group without being taken there – fitted in there. Because he had to first change the arms on the mannequin figure and then tuck you around it and set your arms. So that he was in complete (control) – you were all mannequins being moved – some of them more useful than others, human.' (Ashley, interview.)
7. Tout dépend, en fait, du nombre d'acteurs dont dispose Peter Schumann. S'ils sont trop peu nombreux, le maître de scène – Schumann lui-même le plus souvent – soit sortir pour accomplir certaines tâches, apporter le pain le mardi, etc., ou faire le bruitage nécessaire.
8. Exemples: 'Hier j'ai été à la campagne rendre visite à mes parents. Ma mère est très âgée maintenant', etc. Les acteurs inventent les phrases qu'ils veulent. Il s'agit cependant toujours d'une conversation ayant trait à la famille et rappelant des événements passés.

l'impression que quelque chose l'empêche de s'accomplir pleinement, le public ne perçoit qu'un murmure. Toute communication avec ce monde lui est refusé, le village semble le rejeter comme un intrus et à son tour il se sent pétrifié.

La Vietnamienne qui fait fonction de "maître de scène" s'est levée, elle frappe la clochette et le murmure s'arrête. Elle libère le carton sur lequel est inscrit le jour et ferme le rideau. Les mêmes gestes exécutés sans hâte se répèteront au début et à la fin de chaque tableau.

MARDI

Autour d'une table recouverte d'une nappe blanche et disposée au centre de la scène se trouvent réunies les Vietnamiennes. Elles restent immobiles un moment. Du fond de la scène arrive une Vietnamienne avec une écuelle qu'elle pose sur la table. Les mains au-dessus de la table se mettent alors à bouger, les femmes prennent un morceau de pain, le portent à leur bouche, le tendent à leur voisine, tournant parfois vers elle très légèrement le visage. Bientôt la "servante" revient avec un bol qu'elle pose sur la table, sort, puis revient avec un autre bol. Elle fait chaque Vietnamienne l'une après l'autre, en commençant par les masques qui sont accrochés à la tenture pour finir par le maître de scène, puis elle boit à son tour. La scène se passe dans le plus grand silence, mais c'est un silence familier, modulé par les légers bruits que fait la Vietnamienne en se déplaçant, beaucoup moins pesant que celui de tableau précédent, alourdi par les murmures. Le groupe n'est plus ramassé sur lui-même, il se déplie comme s'il permettait maintenant aux spectateurs de pénétrer dans son intimité. Tout concourt à donner cette impression de début de vie et à amorcer une détente: la couleur blanche, l'extension du volume dans l'espace, l'apparition d'une surface plane où l'oeil peut se reposer et de lignes horizontales qui viennent contrebalancer l'effet dramatisant des verticales, l'amplification des mouvements qui se poursuivra dans le tableau suivant.

MERCREDI

Tout le corps maintenant se met à bouger: trois couples dansent très lentement en se déplaçant à peine, tandis que les autres Vietnamiennes dispersées sur la scène qui est donc maintenant totalement "animé", jouent une musique qui rappelle celle du prélude, à la différence près que le violoniste ne se contente pas de pincer les cordes de son violon, mais tire de son instrument une sorte de mélodie frêle et plaintive.

Ce mouvement d'ouverture à la vie va s'arrêter là. Le village, en effet, va se trouver dérangé par l'apparition d'un élément étranger vers lequel tous les regards désormais convergeront, et qui apporte avec lui la mort.

Deuxième mouvement: la mort

JEUDI

Lorsque le rideau s'ouvre, le spectateur est de nouveau frappé par le spectacle qui s'offre à lui. Il s'était habitué peu à peu au village et commençait même à se "détendre" avec lui. Or, plusieurs éléments créent soudain un déséquilibre plastique et sonore par rapport aux tableaux précédents et réinstallent la tension. Brutalement le son d'une trompe déchire le silence (en coulisse quelqu'un souffle dans un bidon vide) et entre deux rangées de Vietnamiennes aux bras tendus horizontalement, les mains tremblantes, pénètre un homme ligoté, le visage et les mains nues. Au fur et à mesure qu'il avance, les mains des Vietnamiennes s'appliquent, patiemment et fébrilement tout à la fois, à faire tomber la corde. Arrivé sur le devant de la scène, l'homme se penche, ramasse la corde et la tend à bout de bras pour la montrer au public.

Profondeur du champ où l'oeil s'enfonce, lignes brisées, son agressif de la trompe qui à quatre reprises perce le silence, mouvements saccadés des mains qui seules bougent, le reste du corps et les visages mêmes restant immobiles, tout contribue à créer chez le spectateur un malaise accru par l'incertitude dans laquelle il se trouve d'identifier l'étranger: est-ce un prisonnier américain que le village délivre? Est-ce un Vietnamien?

Il faut ici faire une remarque. A l'origine, l'homme portait le masque d'un Noir, peint en blanc, et ses mains étaient gantées de blanc: il faisait donc partie du même monde que les Vietnamiennes, et la scène se chargeait d'un sens politique facilement déchiffrable; elle mettait en lumière la solidarité des Vietnamiens opprimés avec leurs frères noirs. C'est en avril 1968, au moment du Festival de Nancy, que, brusquement, Peter Schumann a décidé que le "rôle" serait tenu désormais par un acteur au visage nu – l'acteur étant du reste choisi en fonction des qualités plastiques de son visage anguleux, fortement charpenté.[9] On imagine aisément ce qui a pu séduire Peter Schumann: le contraste de ce visage nu avec les masques. De fait, l'image gagne en force ce qu'elle perd en lisibilité immédiate: le visage nu et les mains nues de l'homme accentuent son caractère d'"étranger" qui dérange la communauté des Vietnamiennes.

VENDREDI

Pour la première fois depuis le début du spectacle, l'éclairage change: les deux projecteurs latéraux de la salle s'éteignent. Seule reste allumée la faible lampe qui éclaire le titre du tableau: "*Vendredi*". Mais bientôt une source lumineuse unique – une ampoule nue – va violemment éclairer la scène.

L'attention du public se porte sur l'"étranger" qui, allongé sur un banc disposé en biais au milieu de la scène, occupe maintenant une partie importante de l'espace, et vers lequel convergent les regards des Vietnamiennes. Celles-ci se trouvent pour la plupart groupées, immobiles, côté jardin. L'une d'entre elles, cependant, après avoir allumé le lampadaire, s'assied au chevet de l'homme et se met à lire. Une autre, penchée au-dessus de lui, remonte sa couverture, le couvrant jusqu'au cou. Elle se retournera très lentement lorsqu'une Vietnamienne venant du fond de la scène lui aura légèrement touché l'épaule. La Vietnamienne sort. On entend alors un bruit assourdissant en provenance des coulisses (quelqu'un secoue un seau rempli de ferraille), et l'homme laisse tomber sa tête sur le côté. La femme ferme son livre, l'autre se penche pour couvrir le visage du mort, puis elle va s'appuyer sur l'épaule d'une des Vietnamiennes, comme pour pleurer. Toutes les femmes s'inclinent alors très légèrement l'une vers l'autre. La Vietnamienne assise au chevet de l'homme se lève et éteint la lumière.

Avec ce vendredi – jour de la mort du Christ – la référence au mythe chrétien introduite dès le prélude se précise. Le découpage en sept tableaux renvoie-t-il à

---

9. Maurice Blanc et German Mouré ont tenu successivement le rôle. Ce sont deux acteurs que Schumann fait du reste volontiers jouer 'à visage découvert': ils seront respectivement Adam et Joseph dans *The Cry*.

la semaine sainte? Le geste de la Vietnamienne qui vient toucher l'épaule de sa compagne évoque-t-il la trahison de Judas? Mais ne s'agit-il pas tout simplement d'un habitant du village qui vient prévenir les autres d'un danger? Là encore interprétation reste ouverte, et plusieurs lectures sont possibles: elles varient selon les références "culturelles" due spectateur. Quoiqu'il en soit, l'homme est traité scéniquement comme un élément étranger qui bouleverse las vie du village. Le déséquilibre plastique et sonore introduit au tableau précédent se précise, il va s'accentuer dans le tableau suivant, la mort étant le signal du déchaînement de la violence, et le thème de la guerre introduit dès l'arrivée du prisonnier va se développer dans le troisième mouvement.

Troisième mouvement: la guerre

SAMEDI

Les Vietnamiennes sont maintenant groupées côté jardin, immobiles, contre la tenture noire. Elles resteront dans la même position jusqu'à la fin du spectacle. Leur visage est tourné vers le haut et leurs bras sont levés dans un geste de refus et de défense, comme pour se protéger de l'attaque dont elles sont victimes. Dans la salle comme sur la scène les lumières sont éteintes. On entend un sifflement strident, presque insoutenable (produit par l'amplificateur d'un magnétophone). Une Vietnamienne (serviteur de scène "invisible") tient une lampe à la main et dans un vaste mouvement circulaire du bras balaie avec sa lumière blanche aveuglante la scène et la salle, éclairant successivement le groupe des Vietnamiennes et celui des spectateurs (qui souvent se protègent les yeux en mettant leur bras devant le visage, répétant ainsi l'attitude des femmes sur la scène). Aux pieds des Vietnamiennes avance lentement en rampant un horrible animal gris qui peut apparaître comme le "monstre de la guerre", mais qui évoque aussi bien ces hommes atomisés réduits à l'état de larves monstrueuses après le bombardement d'Hiroshima, auquel la lumière et le son peuvent également faire penser: on se rappelle les descriptions des rescapés d'Hiroshima qui disent avoir perçu "d'abord un bruit étrange, puis une lumière à l'éclat intensément clair et tout à fait blanc".

DIMANCHE

L'éclairage revient à "la normale": c'est le même que celui des premiers tableaux. Mais il se passe quelque chose d'insolite. La Vietnamienne qui fait office de maître de scène frappe plusieurs fois la clochette: sonne-t-elle la messe, ou le tocsin?[10] Puis au lieu de s'asseoir (ou de sortir) elle traverse toute la scène pour aller s'agenouiller côté jardin, tout près du rideau noir. Lorsqu'elle se relève, son visage est maculé de sang. Elle a en fait changé de masque: d'où ces gestes qu'on lui a vu faire, comme si elle se lacérait les joues. S'est-elle mutilée dans un geste de refus de la guerre? Toujours est-il que la couleur rouge introduite ici pour la première fois dans le spectacle va désormais envahir la scène, et que l'ordre des jours paraît détraqué: le "feu" va ajouter un huitième jour à la semaine.

---

10. A Paris, à la salle Wagram, en november 1969, cette volée de cloches a été supprimée. La Vietnamienne frappait un seul coup, comme d'habitude, ce qui rendait moins sensible ce bouleversement, de 'rituel' et du temps. En revanche, tout récemment, Peter Schumann a supprimé l'action pour ne garder que le son de la clochette que la Vietnamienne frappe sans discontinuer pendant toute la durée du tableau.

FIRE

Au fond de la scène une immense marionnette rouge indique de ses index géants le travail à accomplir: ses bras qui battent l'air mécaniquement ressemblent aux ailes d'un avion. Un acteur accroupi côté cour et entièrement recouvert d'un tissu rouge, tourne une crécelle, tout à la fois signal d'alarme et bruit du crépitement du feu. Deux autres acteurs jettent sur les femmes du village une pièce d'étoffe rouge sous laquelle elles disparaissent peu à peu, tandis que le maître de scène attise avec une lampe les flammes de tissu qui semblent danser dans la lumière.

Le thème de la guerre a supplanté les deux autres, celui de la vie, comme celui de la mort "humaine", la mort d'un homme entouré d'amis qui le veillent et qui le pleurent. Plus aucune trace d'humanité sur le plateau: plus de visages ni de mains, une masse informe.

Si le spectacle s'arrêtait là, son sens serait essentiellement pessimiste, et le spectateur, terrifié, ne s'en sentirait pas pour autant responsable de ce qui se passe sur scène: la violence de la guerre paraît irrésistible, la progression du feu inéluctable. Le tableau final, qui n'a pas de nom, donne à la pièce sa véritable dimension.

FINALE

Le maître de scène se contente de frapper la clochette et sort. Entre une Vietnamienne entièrement drapée de blanc. Elle regarde les formes brûlées et va se placer au centre de la scène, face au public, immobile. Soudain le silence est troublé. Trois hommes portant des masques d'Occidentaux, les mains nues, pénètrent sur la scène avec des poteaux de bois, des cordes et du treillis et se mettent à dresser un échafaudage autour de la femme. Ils se déplacent lourdement et leurs mouvements disgracieux, le bruit qu'ils font en bougeant, la brutalité de leur apparence, contrastent avec le calme, le silence et la grâce fragile dont le village laisse le souvenir et qu'on retrouve dans cette femme en blanc. Ils sortent. Le silence revient. La Vietnamienne reste immobile un instant encore, puis elle se penche jusqu'à terre et commence à dérouler un rouleau de scotch rouge: sans hâte, méthodiquement, elle déchire des morceaux de ruban qu'elle colle tout le long de sa robe blanche, qu'elle enroule autour de ses poignets, puis de ses bras. Pendant qu'elle se brûle, les trois Occidentaux entrent. Ils ont changé de masque: aveugles, ils tournent en tâtonnant autour d'elle, puis ressortent.[11] Les mouvements de la femme deviennent de plus en plus difficiles, mais elle continue à se détruire, et dans le silence le bruit du scotch déroulé et déchiré évoque le crépitement des flammes et le bruit de la chair qui grésille. Elle colle maintenant les morceaux de ruban rouge sur ses joues, sur sa bouche, sur ses yeux. Puis elle s'écroule en se recroquevillant lentement sur elle-même, s'écrasant contre le treillis, entraînant dans sa chute des bouts de bois qui tombent n'importe où, parfois même dans la salle.[12] Une plainte

---

11. 'Blind masks are made in the same style that I described for the *Fire* show. In the last scene of *Fire* there were several blind people coming in – and I cared for that – they were really blind. So (the masks) have no eye slits and people had to wear them and they were really blind. Couldn't see anything. So they were coming in and looking at the lady after she burned and then going out again.' — (Schumann, interview, December '82.)

12. A l'origine les hommes apportaient non pas du bois, mais des socles d'écran et du treillis. La cage ainsi construite était plus solide et résistait à la chute. L'image proposée différait sensiblement de celle-ci: la Vietnamienne semblait alors enfermée dans une prison.

presque imperceptible – une seule note très haute – qui semble monter du groupe des Vietnamiennes brûlées accompagne sa mort. Un homme entre, regarde le cadavre, va frapper la clochette et mettre le mot *"Fin"*. Rideau. Silence. Personne n'applaudit....

Devant un tel spectacle le public occidental, et plus particulièrement le public américain, ne peut que se sentir mis en accusation. En effet, l'image finale qui lui est proposée n'est pas seulement celle d'un suicide, c'est celle d'un meurtre dont il se rendrait coupable. Bien que la femme occupe sur la scène une place centrale et que sa robe blanche appelle toute une série de significations qui tournent autour de l'idée de martyre, de sacrifice, de rachat, de pureté, elle n'accapare pas toute l'attention du spectateur. Celle-ci se porte aussi sur les hommes qui enferment dans une cage cette femme en blanc – nonne bouddhiste ou davantage encore figure de Paix et d'Amitié – puis sur ceux qui tournent autour d'elles, aveugles. Leurs masques, différents de ceux que nous avons vus jusqu'alors, leurs mains nues, la façon dont ils bougent, le bruit qu'ils font, sont trop choquants pour que nous puissions les oublier. Or, leurs visages sont nos visages à nous Occidentaux, c'est notre propre image qu'ils nous renvoient, nous donnant à voir notre complicité, ou – au mieux – notre aveuglement. "Même les plus sympathisants sont aveugles" – dit Schumann. C'est donc à dessiller les yeux des spectateurs qu'il tente de s'employer tout au long de *Fire*. Il s'agit de montrer aux Américains ce qu'ils font subir au peuple vietnamien, de leur "faire penser" la guerre, de recharger ce mot, qui à force d'être galvaudé, s'est vidé de toute réalité. La guerre, c'est la vie quotidienne bouleversée, l'accomplissement des activités les plus élémentaires entravé, toute communication par la parole ou par le geste rendue impossible, tout mouvement condamné; la guerre menée par les Américains au Vietnam, c'est la destruction méthodique de tout un peuple. Et de ce génocide, les spectateurs ne sont pas tenus quittes. Certes *Fire* n'exprime pas des idées complexes, Peter Schumann ne cherche pas à clarifier la situation, à dévoiler les rouages de la guerre ni à indiquer une solution.' (Kourilsky, '71. (Copyright Françoise Kourilsky 1971.))

Kourilsky, unlike Dennison, who like most Americans that came to see the play came with a clear conscience, saw the play challenge American audiences, and saw it constructed toward this end. The play's effect on Nicole Zand, whose review of it did much to establish Schumann in France, was in this regard closer to that on Dennison than to that on Kourilsky:

'Ce qui fut si remarquable dans ce court spectacle, c'est qu'avec des moyens techniques extrêmement simples – une crécelle, un violon, une ampoule nue, une soupière, quelques masques – Peter Schumann arrive, réellement, et sans mots, sans agression terroriste sur la conscience ou sur les sens, à cerner la guerre et à faire passer de façon éclairante une vision du Vietnam; et soudain, mieux que les plaidoyers idéologiques, les films de bonne volonté, les images d'enfants napalmés, il nous donne la "réalité" même de cette guerre.'

(N. Zand, *Le Monde*, April 26, '68.)

Schumann himself, in a letter of November '69 inviting three North Vietnamese delegates to a Paris production, gives a straightforward account of what happens:

'The play is a mime play without words. It describes seven days in a village in Vietnam. A group of Vietnamese women, chattering, eating, drinking, dancing, liberating an American who comes to them in ropes, who dies amongst them. They are haunted by an air raid. They are burnt by fire. Amidst the dead bodies of the burnt, three Americans set up a cage for a Buddhist nun, they leave her in the cage and she slowly burns herself to death.'

'*Fire* was a great success because of the time it was in. Because it was a time before Vietnam was considered a national issue and a big deal, so it was this incredible elegy, and the feeling was so in step with the time, that it was a tremendous success and a really incredibly powerful piece, and it was right at the right time. It wouldn't have any impact when people aren't feeling a proto guilty feeling, the early stirrings of guiltiness. It wouldn't work so well. But it really worked. I would even go so far as to say that we even recognized it was a masterpiece. I mean we understood that it was, that we had something here that was great.... And it affected audiences always the same way.... We closed the curtain at the end and there would be this silence, as if there was no one there. I mean they could have been standing packed in the back, packed in the entranceway, you know. People stuffed in the theatre. And there was this silence. Dead silence. And maybe after a few minutes you'd hear somebody would clap and then maybe it would just die out and then be quiet and then we'd hear shuffle shuffle. And we'd open the curtain in five minutes, not a soul. Everyone had just walked out. It was so powerful.... There was something there that was really stirring. Because it was heavy.' (Ernstthal, interview.)

Ernstthal in '79 in retrospect saw *Fire* as, inter alia, having self-sacrifice as its subject matter, and thus the self-sacrificing idealism characteristic, as he saw it, of the resistance movement up to but not beyond '66.

According to Schumann's notebooks of October '65 when *Fire* was in rehearsal there were three arrangements of *Fire* before the one shown:

'Fire (1st arrangement)
1) Mon.   singing, standing, solo
2) Tues.   eating
3) Wed.   lightbulb and bed
4) Thurs. dancing
5) Fri.   rope and bugle
6) Sat.   arrival
7) Sun.

Fire (2nd)
1) Mon.   singing, standing
2) Tues.   table, attendant, no sound
3) Wed.   dancing, trumpet, violin, bass
4) Thurs. rope, bugle, speaking hands
5) Fri.   noise, airplane, animal, sun
6) Sat.   lightbulb, bed, blanket, book
7) Sun.   3 X drum

Fire (3rd)
1) Mon.   slow movement
          later, one coming from left, high singing
2) Tues. eating, drinking and attendant (faster)
3) Wed.   dance, trumpet starts faster, bass starts
4) Thurs. rope and horn (not trumpet)
5) Fri.   bed, lamp, book, blanket
6) Sat.   airplane, sun and animal
7) Fire. all fabric
          end-sign in the end.'

(From Sainer, *Radical Theatre Notebook*.)

From the same source: burning pays off:

'The Funny NY Times.
Mr. Baker's Special Fire-Philosophy
1) Draft card does not burn
2) Church burns well
3) Supermarket even better
   Moral: little burning is no good
   Big burning: the government moves in and listens
   Furthermore: in old times people burned people
   Now: nomore
   Better: government burns people (e.g., vicious Vietcong burn sunny American sons)
some governments are not strong enough (or too humane) — they burn effigies instead (as in USA) — sometimes people burn cities — cities are good — Germans, Russians, Americans — then libraries
(Hitler did not like books)
(Negroes don't like books — in Africa they burn real American wisdom libraries, which are there to make people learn something; they just have to wait another few hundred years until they get educated, that's all.)
Now, also: a wife may burn a husband, or rather the soup
                    or a hole with the cigarette
                    or a pot with peas in it
                    or an envious neighbor
                    or nothing
It does not mean anything anyway: burning is good, solid old human hardware, go ahead, young friend, burn draft cards. (comparison of Nazi German and contemporary NY Times style Vietnam reporting)'

Schumann in '72, in conversations reported by Sainer, told him he had conceived of *Fire* as an upbeat celebration of suicide as a life-affirming act:

'I took the title from a poem by Goethe, "Selige Sehnsucht" ("Holy Longing"). Goethe in a collection called West-Östlicher Diwan was writing in the style used by Persian poets from the twelfth through the sixteenth centuries. There was an incredible weltanschaung to that poetry. Some of the lines in the poem are

> Sagt es niemand nur den Weisen
> Weil die Menge gleich verhohnet
> Das Lebend'ge will ich preisen
> Das nach Flammentod sich sehnet...
>
> (Tell nobody, only the wise
> Because the crowds immediately show contempt.
> The living will I praise
> Who longeth for death in the flame...)

I never think of the play as dark. For me the ending is a liberation, not a folding up. It's not a degenerate idea to burn oneself for one's convictions, it's a tremendous statement for life. It's a jubilant statement.

Sometimes the play was performed where the audience simply took it as another example of modern, avant-garde theatre. They were viewing it for its aesthetics rather than its content.

In a way we really did *Fire* for ourselves, it wasn't important whether many or a few saw it. It was something like pure communication, the doing it was the most important element.

Sometimes performers in *Fire* don't get what you get from it. When that happens there's no technique, no teaching that can help. There has to be a full-sized commitment.

The masks are all based on the face of one girl. I cast masks of her five or six times.

The forbear of *Fire* was *Leaf Feeling the Moonlight*. I wanted to see what could be done with great restrictions. I haven't been able to recreate *Leaf Feeling the Moonlight*, however. I never could remember it properly after we did it. But I based *The Dead Man Rises* on it.'

The old fornicator's *Selige Sehnsucht* tells us: when you are fucked out, you better start thinking of higher forms of coitus, the which the Geheimrat does not specify but presents as, like plain fornication, forms of self-destruction:

> Und so lang du das nicht hast,
> Dieses: Stirb und werde!
> Bist du nur ein trüber Gast
> Auf der dunklen Erde.

Such appreciative reference of Schumann's to the subtle old man allows us to appreciate how much we and Schumann have lost by Schumann's wilful decision to be and remain simple-minded in his art: a kind of self-destruction of Schumann's enabling him to be the artist he is – becoming by dying. The lightness of tone of Goethe's poetry is marvelous.

13. February '67. Sufferings of Vietnam, two further pieces: *Wounds of Vietnam, Bach Cantata #140 (Grey Lady Cantata #1)*.

During the summer of '66, Schumann was busy with the *Chicken Little* parks project. He moved his theatre to Papp's place. What else, apart from street agitation — as part of which he may in November have created *A Man Says Goodbye* — he did from September onward I don't know. In February '67, he comes up with two further pieces on the Sufferings of Vietnam, with *Fire* the only ones specifically on this topic, both done within the framework of the Week of the Angry Arts Against the War in Vietnam (January 29-February 5),[1] *Wounds of Vietnam* once on February 4th, at the Washington Square Methodist Church, as part of Robert Nichols' contribution to the week, *Viet Life (An Act of Respect for the Vietnamese People)*,[2] and *Bach Cantata #140*, the 'Wake Up!' cantata as

---

1. The Week was announced as a joint project of the Painters and Writers Protest Organization and of 'Angry Arts Week' at a Peace Readout, January 13. Carol Grosberg — in '69 and perhaps then already an occasional performer with the Bread and Puppet Theatre, one of the feminist editors of the *Rat*, successor, after a feminist take-over, of the *Village Voice*'s East Village radical analogue, the *East Village Other* — was coordinator at the offices in the basement of the Washington Square Methodist Church, of the Greenwich Village Peace Center, the proximate sponsor of the Week. There was another Week of the Angry Arts etc. in Philadelphia, May 7-13, 1968, at the University of Pennsylvania. The Bread and Puppet Theatre performed here on May 9, following a performance of Brecht's 'Three Clowns' by the Theatre of Living Arts.

2. 'Robert Nichols needs people for a project during the Week of the Angry Arts Against the War in Vietnam ... Nichols is organizing a theater program, called "Viet Life", as an act of concern and respect toward the Vietnamese people. It will consist of short segments demonstrating, describing and otherwise expressing various aspects of Vietnamese history, culture and daily life. Participants will include the Bread and Puppet Theatre, the Pageant Players, and a group directed by Saul Gottlieb. Anyone interested in joining the project and preparing a segment should call Nichols ... for details and suggested topics.' (Notice at the end of Michael Smith's weekly Theatre Journal in the January 12 issue of the *Village Voice*.)

Nichols' project, though ostensibly anarchistically permissive, was to present an idealization of the Oriental Village that Marx, though with an accent on its resistance to imperialism, had viewed as basis of Oriental Despotism:

'VIETNAMESE LIFE PROJECT
related events:
"Big-and-medium name" theater, music and dance evenings
Painters/Movie makers college
Small Action Projects on the streets and around town
All-medium Happening
(If you are interested in joining any one of these events contact Carol Grosberg and she will put you in touch with the various producers.)

Schumann refers to it, first of a series of 'Grey Lady' cantatas, done with the Judson Chamber Ensemble and the Judson Choir — the first piece of Schumann's with music by a group of something like professionals — and to be done to pre-existing 'regular' music — twice, on February 2 and 5, at the Village Theatre (admission $1).

Wounds of Vietnam as Schumann remembers it

'was done in the basement of Washington Square Church and we had Irving Oyle read — we used as a text a reading of descriptions of different degrees of burns. (Elka: Clinical descriptions. Out of these medical books, right?) Yes. And as an action we used things that we had read in the papers like that a newspaper was used instead of bandaging material for horrible burn wounds in lack of any other materials. (Elka: Wasn't it one of the white puppets with the very long heads? — and the person that played that was lying down —) Yes. Lying down. (Elka: And the action was just sort of turn and be wrapped up and being unwrapped?) Yes, being wrapped up.' (Schumann, interview, '79.)

"VIETNAMESE LIFE"

The purpose of this is to perform an Act of Respect. Episodes and aspects (1-3 minutes each) will be presented by 20-30 poets and 3 theater groups, with the help of other performers: painters, dancers, musicians and film makers. Material will be selected by each participant, with complete latitude as to artistic means, solo or group performance, descriptive information or abstract, etc. The individual will then be responsible for rehearsals and presentation. There is only one limitation: the pieces must be about the Vietnamese People: to make them present to the audience and to ourselves. The artist is not primarily expressing his own feelings and attitudes towards the war. (This is done in the programs listed above.)

Overall Framework: this will be the responsibility of the general producer, and the visual- and-sound staff. The separate episodes will be put together in two rehearsals during the last week in January. The aesthetic form will be the result of the individual offerings and will not be determined in advance. However we must all see to it in the beginning that the selections chosen will cover a substantial range of Vietnamese life.

A suggested list of episodes is attached. Participants may select one or several, or substitute their own. A possible grouping of episodes (10-20 each) might be:

GROUP 1 Landscape and People
GROUP 2 The Foreigners — through Dien Bien Phu
GROUP 3 The Two Vietnams — through assassination of Diem
GROUP 4 The Big War

Theater Groups: these will be responsible for a specifically dramatic structure, which will occur at intervals during the episodes by individual artists. There are actually in Viet Nam certain events and experiences that recur. For instance the villagers always grow food, and hide it. The hamlets elect their chiefs, and these are replaced by phoney ones, and the real functions in shadow. The villagers are always taken away and put into camps, and then return. The villagers are always raising children, protecting themselves and binding up wounds. These events are continually repeated, with only the cast of characters changing: the Japanese, the French, the Quisling Government, the American Army. Thus the recurring dramatic episodes could be organized around a certain cast of characters: The Villagers/ the Fighters/ the Generals/ the Diplomats/ the Police. The Theater Groups

Marlene Nadle (cf. her criticims of the *Vietnamese Life Project* supra) appreciated *Wounds* for its unaggression:

'The most effective part of it did not even attempt to storm the audience's shock barriers. In Peter Schumann's Bread and Puppet presentation, a physician simply came on the stage and lectured in disapassionate medical language to five students in white masks. As the lecture continued, the manned-puppet began to move slowly, to extend a gigantic hand toward the audience, to try to bind up its wounded fingers with sliding sheets of newspaper, and, in that fumbling awkward gesture, captured all the helplessness of people caught in war.'
(M. Nadle, *The Unsolved Problem, Village Voice*, February 9, '67.)

But she got the show wrong: she read the victim's attempted self-help into it: Schumann was showing passive suffering.

The anonymous 'The Talk of the Town' reviewer of the Angry Arts Week Against the War in Vietnam in the February 11, '67 issue of *The New Yorker*, who apparently shared Nadle's feelings about the program generally, of *Wounds* gives what looks like a precise account:

'The center of the room was cleared and the Bread and Puppet Theatre took over. A doctor (played by a real-life New York physician) read a detailed scientific lecture on the treatment of burns to six "students" wearing expressionless masks. The doctor stressed the life-or-death importance of keeping victims as nearly sterile as possible, to reduce the danger of infection. His lecture was interrupted by a banshee wail from an electronically amplified fiddle, and a girl's voice began to read a dispatch from a *Manchester Guardian* correspondent describing the

---

might make their selections from this cast of characters. Theater scenes should be 5 to 10 minutes each.'

The eventual program was chromatic:

'Vietnamese Life Project. "These are the people we are killing." . . . February 4, continuous, 3 pm-9 pm. Green show 3-5 pm, landscape/faces/ceremonies/wounds. Red show 5-7 pm, houses/rice growing/village life/guerrillas. Blue show 7-9 pm. City life/night transportation/water/hunger. An act of respect for the Vietnamese people by poets, actors and other artists . . .' — (Ad, *Village Voice*, February 2, '67.)

'The success of their seven-hour presentation at the Washington Square Church was equally doubtful.

Even the pre-sold audience that formed the constant and changing line outside the church could not escape the effect of seeing bombs on TV every night over dinner.

Their sensibilities had apparently become almost as calloused as those of other Americans. The first piercing tapes of bombs in the "Viet Life" presentation produced a sense of real shock. Yet, as the dancers and actors continued to portray peasants planting rice and cringing from bombs, peasants carrying supplies and cringing from bombs, building bridges and again cringing from bombs, a kind of immunity set in. The words the poets spoke on the stage became a cerebral accounting of the suffering, and without much visceral impact. Many in the audience became as narcotized as the Vietnamese peasant in Margaret Fuller's mime skit who did not even glance up from her chopsticks when the raids began.

The actors and artists in "Viet Life" were aware of the problem of trying to get through media-dulled sensibilities. It was one of the main reasons for taking a new approach. They tried to portray the Vietnamese people speaking for themselves rather than just delivering

actual conditions in civilian hospitals in South Vietnam, where doctors are often forced to brush flies away from patients' wounds during operations, and old newspapers are used for emergency bandages. On the linoleum floor alongside the students' chairs lay, wrapped in a dirty sheet, a woman wearing outsize hands, made of some shiny plastic, and an outsize plastic head. While the doctor's scientific lecture and the girl's dispassionate voice kept up an antiphonal drone, the figure of the woman writhed in a wordless agony; a long red scarf oozed from underneath her sheet, and mock bandages of shredded newspaper fluttered around her. The banshee wail of the fiddle rose like an air-raid siren and was abruptly cut off, leaving behind it a charged silence.'

Dr. Irving Oyle gave a factual account of the performance in the first edition of his *The Healing Mind, A Physician Looks At the Mysterious Ability of the Mind to Heal the Body*, but in the second and revised edition (Celestial Arts, Millbrae, California, '79) attempted a creative reconstitution of it, based on his Jungian analysis of Schumann's preoccupations with the struggle between good and evil:

'ONE/My Ego, the Doctor. Peter the Puppetmaster — a fascinating fellow. Creator, director, heart and soul of the theater, he is a totally dedicated artist — perhaps a genius. Visions, dreams, and myths constitute the elemental stuff of Peter's artistry. In his mind's eye he encounters vivid visual images, and jots them down in German into his omnipresent brown spiral notebook, capturing them in an intricate intervweaving of *Hochdeutsch* and quick sketches. From there they are transformed into theatrical pieces — "moving sculptures" — whose form and comportment attempt to replicate the original image.

---

peace movement harangues. It was also the reason Saul Gottlieb and the Free Theatre were banned from performing in the church.

Gottlieb's solution to the public's immunity to the shock of war is the "theatre of cruelty." In order to move people to greater commitment, he wanted to make horror real to the point of nausea.

The Reverend A. Finley Schaef wouldn't have it. Not because he wanted a USO version of Vietnam, but because he feels deeply about public resignation to war and the ineffectiveness of the various peace actions. He believes that art must have some element of affirmation or people will be catapulted into complete resignation.

The two argued the aesthetics of the situation while sitting out the show in Mr. Schaef's study. The rest of the Free Theatre was outside the church picketing and trying to persuade the other artists not to perform there.' — (M. Nadle, *The Unsolved Problem. Angry Arts: Aiming Through The Barrier, Village Voice*, February 9, '67.)

'(Bob Nichols) said, all these artists are doing their own, doing their work against the war but it's all about their self-expression. I want to organize a project in which there will be real information about Vietnamese people that will be conveyed, and that's the one rule. So we did a piece that we made up about where there were wounded people but no bandages in the hospital and so the wounds had to be wrapped up in newspaper. Mitch Goodman did a piece using slides, about waterways, I think, rivers. Irene Fornes did a piece demonstrating marriage, a Vietnamese peasant marriage. It was twelve hours long, so every half hour or so somebody else would get up and do their presentation. I think the Pageant Players did a piece about transporting things by bicycle at night.' — (Sherman, interview.)

Visionary psychologist Dr. C. J. Jung saw the same sights. He described them as "Primordial images ... symbols older than historical man ... eternally living, outlasting all generations – the groundwork of the human psyche." A fascinating concept! Archetypal apparitions bubbling up from the bottomless sea of nerve impulses swimming around in our five-million-year-old human brain.

Puppets, their personalities, stage sets and scripts all appear autonomously and fully formed; they rise up from the part of Peter some psychologists call *creative unconscious*. Where do they come from? What is this source of visions which in material form we seen on the stage? Peter experiences a light show in his head, strobe-like flashings of nerve-cell firings – patterned neural discharges in the infinitely intricate circuitry of the ninety percent of his brain which neither knows nor notices the existence of the entity, the other ten percent calling itself "Peter."

Can a doctor give up a thriving suburban general practice and find happiness, professional satisfaction, and an ample income serving the poor of a big-city ghetto? The question is not a come-on for a soap opera. It is a question Dr. Irving Oyle asked himself in real life – and the answer was a firm Yes!

(*Medical World News*, September 1968.)

If that quote were a come-on for a soap opera, the opus in question might be entitled, "My Ego, the Doctor." Allow me to introduce myself. I am the author, the puppetmaster. At that point in my career, professional satisfaction and ample income materialized as a by-product of the activities of my ego, the doctor. An experimental clinic I had set up on New York's lower East Side supplied high-quality health care service in an urban ghetto area. Happiness and personal satisfaction during that period flowed from my involvement with Peter Schumann's Bread and Puppet Theater.

The prime purpose of the Bread and Puppet Theater is the physical manifestation of Peter's mythic visions. For Peter, people and puppets serve as vehicles. He creates the latter out of paper, plastic, wood, wire, and paint, faithfully following the pattern set by the spontaneous firings and flashings of his twenty billion brain cells. The energy emitted by these fantastic creations attracts other people who simply pick them up and animate them – give them life.

In the old days, Peter regarded middle-class American doctors with a contempt bordering on outright hatred. He tolerated my ego, the doctor, the way one would tolerate a wart: as a warp in the character structure of my personality, the puppeteer. I became conscious of these two – my ego, the doctor, and my personality the puppeteer – during a performance.

At the rehearsal earlier, Peter shoved a paper into my hand and growled, "I want you to get out on the stage and play Irving the Doctor. I want you to read the stupid doctor talk on this paper, and then explain it to the audience. Tell it to them in plain talk so they know what it means, and put on that costume you guys usually wear." Having just come from hospital rounds, I was clothed in the correct costume: shined shoes; white shirt with button-down collar and silk tie; expensive, sharply creased one-hundred-percent-wool trousers; topped by a tweedy wool jacket with a stethoscope sticking casually out of one pocket, while a thermometer, a pencil light and a ballpoint pen peeked coyly out of another.

Picking up Peter's paper, putting on my glasses, I stepped onto the stage and acted the role of "Me", the doctor.

The plot concerned the plight of a puppet called the "White Lady." Twelve feet tall, she wore a flowing white robe which trailed ten feet behind her, concealing two human animators. One puppeteer manipulated the massive hands so they covered the distraught White Lady's face while the other allowed her huge head to angle forward as she slowly sank to the floor.

She was "Universal Woman", under attack by an evil-looking black monster which had slithered up from the unfathomable depths of Peter's imagination. Thirteen feet long, with a five-foot wing span, the fanged monster was guided along its malevolent course by a pair of Peter's puppeteers. They were dressed in black, in the style of Japanese *Bunraku* puppetry. Visible to the audience, the trio, one black monster puppet and two black-robed puppeteers, combined to form a single organism, the "War Weapon", an instrument of death which, constructed and controlled by human hands, had just napalmed the White Lady. Prostrate on the ground, the duo within the White Lady executed a series of writhing movements as I read a paper entitled "The Effects of Flaming Napalm on the Human Body." This accomplished, the script called for all action to freeze. Players and puppets fused into a single sculpture. Suspended in space and time, the image filled the consciousness of the onlookers as the players remained motionless for a full fifteen minutes. "That way", said Peter, "they won't forget."

That's when it happened, during the fifteen minutes of immobility and silence: As actors often do, I allowed my mind to wander out into the audience, trying to imagine how I looked to the people out there. My eyelids drooped, and in a flash I saw — in my mind's eye, three-D and living color — an image of myself as I stood on the stage: shined shoes, white shirt with button-down collar . . . only I was a puppet! Behind me, moving my limbs and speaking my lines, was a black-robed figure, the puppeteer, my self. In the audience, enjoying the show immensely, sat a clown. The clown in the audience was me. The shadowy, robed puppeteer kept up a constant patter of critical comments — "You're weaving a bit; watch your breath, slow and regular; that's fine, looks pretty good now" — as he directed the puppet-doctor on the stage. Having left my body (in a sense), I was hallucinating three different versions of my own self.

Fifteen minutes passed. The play ended. I left the stage wondering which was the real me, and pondering the problem of who had had the hallucination. Beneath the wondering and pondering lay a certainty, an intuitive knowing. Peter's vision, (the White Lady, Black War Machine, and hooded puppeteers) and my image of a three-part self, sprang from a single source — our common human brain.'   (I. Oyle, *The Healing Mind*, 2nd edition, Chapter I.)

Bach Cantata #140:

'Battements de grosse caisse prolonges. Une centaine de marionnettes géantes grises s'effondrent lentement, decouvrant peu a peu les musiciens et les chanteurs du Judson Chamber Ensemble qui vont jouer la Cantate #140 de Bach, *Wachet auf, ruft uns die Stimme* . . . . Entre chaque mouvement, les battements de grosse caisse reprennent et les "Dames Grises" sont de nouveau tuées. À la fin de la Cantate, elles se relevent lentement et reviennent à la vie.'

(Kourilsky, '71.)

'The Judson Chamber Ensemble and the Bread and Puppet Theater translate Bach's Cantata 140 into a dialogue of music and movement. In the foreground, a sea of Peter Schumann's immense figures, gray in grayness, move to the beat of

non-Bach drums – stretching high, then falling bit by bit, a quivering, while enormous hands continue to reach up. Then all is still – a death-like mass of crumpled forms.
The gentle notes of Bach: "Sleepers awake, the voices call to us..."
Some stirring of the giant hands, heads with strange immobile faces...
"Stand up and light your lamps!"
Puppets arise to those hypnotic, unrelenting drums, casting shadows from new rays of light (no longer gray but now pale gold like candles or the rising sun). From huddled heads, the hands emerge as though in supplication. And slowly then again, they fall.
"Lo. He comes. Go forth to greet him."
The figures rise again, the drums again – more urgent now.
And cycles continue, expanding in the beauty of the music ... the eloquent, motionless masks, the romanesque long hands, the expressive power of the writhing, reaching forms ... shapes receding into sound and then awakening once more in concentric outward-growing circles.'

(D. Lane, *The Angriest Voice*, WIN, III, No. 5, '67.)

Ernstthal has a vivid but mistaken memory of it – there were no babies:

'a Bach cantata, with this whole landscape, this whole giant stage full, proscenium, full scale, stage *full* of these ladies, with babies.... The babies like this, in the hands, the two hands.... And the Bach cantata *played*, and in between the movements there was this machine gun sound, and they all ... fall down, until at the end they are all dead. Very simple theatrically. I always thought pretty exciting. It was made for a big proscenium stage.' (Ernstthal, interview.)
'So, during that winter, we rehearsed that cantata and that was rehearsed in the Courthouse. We had not moved into the Courthouse yet, but we rehearsed in the cellar of the Courthouse. Actually it was different, because it was difficult to rehearse this piece with a lot of people. There were 100 people when it was finally done, big groups of hands and separate from them, big groups of puppets, Grey Lady puppets. The *Bach Cantata* required a vast stage – it didn't have a very vast – that stage was very shallow that we had to use, but it *wanted* a *gigantic* stage, as we had to fit all these – Judson Choir and Chamber Orchestra plus a big group of kettle drums that we had rented for the occasion, plus all these puppets and I would think some light instruments that were stationed in front.'

(Schumann, interview, '79.)

'The first *Grey Lady Cantata* was done with *big* crowds of grey ladies in contrast to a solo one and in contrast to *hands* – that was all it was.... The hands were separate – were built separately, separate gowns, and operated by separate operators. So there were scenes where only the hands moved and scenes where only the heads moved. And then the solo Grey Lady played her own cantata part. (I: What distinguishes her role?) I don't have that very clear any more. I know that it has to do with the cantata directly and that she was used for the solo parts of either the alto or the soprano in the cantata – so it has to do with the musical structure of the cantata.' (Schumann, interview, '82.)

An undated account of the six *Grey Lady Cantatas* in Elka's files, by its style by Schumann, retrospectively describes this first one as

'variations of the falling and rising of large groups of heads and hands, orchestrated by movements of light.'

The Grey Lady puppets were of one of the two new more flexible types he had developed in '65, their single or multiple heads on short sticks. The concept of the 'Grey Ladies' was

' "anarchist woman" – a woman that suffers history but doesn't organize herself against the effects of history – but simply suffers history and reacts primitively against these effects of the state. Doesn't do anything and these sort of dull women, quite beautiful, to my mind, were the theme (of the succession of *Grey Lady Cantatas* (SSB))'.   (Schumann, interview, '82.)

14. May-October '67. *Chicken Little, or The Story of the World.*

From his images of Vietnam suffering, Schumann in the spring of '67 jumped into satire in the form of puerile but grand, raucous, large-style comedy, his only work of this kind, using not the big images of suffering-bearing womanhood, but giant grotesque puppets and masked and unmasked costume mime: a picaresque reworking of his child-performed parks *Chicken Little* of the summer before, expanded into a history of humanity from creation to destruction (the Christian model that has governed Schumann's thinking) incorporating various of its side-show skits, narrated by Bob Ernstthal, its hero the loony Chicken Little mimed bare-face by Margo Sherman:[1] *Chicken Little, or The Story of the World*. It was his unreviewed chief spring and summer offering at his new base camp in Joseph Papp's emerging theatrical emporium, and in July at the Newport Folk Festival[2] procured him his second breakthrough into public

---

1. 'We redid *Chicken Little* as an enormous show. And I was the star, the lead, Chicken Little. And not only that, I had to take off my mask. I was rehearsing without the mask because it was hot and sweaty in New York, and they said, oh, oh, that's good, you have to leave the mask off. And this was really terrifying, to have my face naked .... Oh how funny Bob was. He narrated the entire show. He would just stand at the mike and he would narrate and do all the voices and we would act everything out in mime. It was very funny and wonderful and exciting and fulfilling. Hardly anthing's been that way since. We performed for thousands of people. It was extraordinary.' — (Sherman, interview.)
2. Performances of *Chicken Little, or The Story of the World*: *Village Voice, Off-Off Broadway Guide*: Astor Library Landmark Building, Friday and Saturday evenings, Sunday afternoon, May 5-7, '67, Friday evening and Sunday afternoon, May 12-14. *Village Voice What's On ... For Children*: Sunday afternoon, May 20. Ads in *Village Voice*: Sunday afternoon, May 21, Friday evening, May 26, Sunday afternoon, May 28, Friday evening, June 2, Sunday afternoon, June 4. *Off-Off Broadway Guide*: Friday and Saturday evenings, June 3 and 4, Sunday afternoon, June 5 (similarly for June 30-July 2, July 7-9).

He advertised for 'puppeteers, mimes, musicians, 1 stage manager' for the Newport performance in the June 15 *Voice*. At the July 10-16 seventh Newport Folk Festival, the first, I believe, to feature theatre – Luis Valdez' Teatro Campesino performed in the July 13 'Hootenanny' program – the Bread and Puppet Theatre performed as part of the July 12 'Children's Program' and for the July 14 'Workshops.' A free outdoor evening show at Gottesman Plaza, West 91st Street and Amsterdam Avenue, on July 31st, sponsored by the Goddard-Riverside Community Center and Goddard Towers (*Village Voice* ad of July 27) may have been *Chicken Little*. Then the *Off-Off Broadway Guide* in the *Village Voice* indicates another Saturday evening performance at the Astor Library on August 19, and finally (August 17) there is a notice, 'Puppets in Chinatown. The Bread and Puppet Theatre will give its last performance of *Chicken Little* ... on Sunday, August 20, at 3 p.m. in Chinatown's Columbus Park (at Mulberry Street). The performance will be sponsored by the Downtown New York Arts Festival.' But apparently it wasn't quite final for an ad (October 19) announces 'On tour this weekend. Bread and Puppet Theatre. Final perfor-

acceptance after gaining recognition by the New York intelligentsia with *Fire*: recognition by the 'kids,' the national youth counter-culture.[3]

'1. Le Début. *"Au début il n'y avait rien"* — hurle dans un mégaphone Bob Ernstthal entrant en scène porté sur les épaules de plusieurs acteurs qui vont le déposer par terre près d'un micro. C'est lui qui racontera l'histoire et parlera à la place des différents personnages. Une grande partie du texte est improvisée.

"Voice Chicken Little" : un jeune garçon assis sur une chaise est déposé au milieu de la scène. Il a l'air totalement ahuri. Margo Sherman qui joue Chicken Little est grimée en Pierrot et habillée en clochard : pantalons en lambeaux, chapeau trop grand, parapluie cassé à la main.

"Et voice Eve" : entre une grande belle femme, outrageusement maquillée, l'air stupide et peu commode. (Les marionnettistes l'appellent entre eux Miss America, car elle a une robe blance avec des bandes rouges.)

Chicken Little et Eve se regardent et tombent dans les bras l'un de l'autre, cependant que l'annonceur continue à crier une quantité d'autres noms, à la manière d'un aboyeur présentant les invités d'un grand bal : le Cardinal et Mrs. Spellman, etc. Les personnages entrent deux par deux, la tête recouverte d'un masque tout en largeur qui paraît deux fois plus grand que leur corps. Musique par l'orchestre du Bread and Puppet Theatre qui se trouve côté jardin. Les musiciens sont tous en

---

mance of *Chicken Little* Saturday October 28 at the Astor Library Landmark Building.' This was their very last performance there for the time being, they had to leave the place, the October 26 *Off-Off Broadway Guide* announcing it as '*Chicken Little (Says Goodbye to Shakespeare.)*' Whether they did it there weekends July 21-22 ff., at least till the Chinatown performance, or even beyond, I do not know.

3. According to the *Christian Science Monitor* (August 18, '67), the Bread and Puppet Theatre 'drew the largest audiences.' To the lady from the *Providence Evening Bulletin* (July 15), the Bread and Puppet puppeteers were hippies: 'Turned-on puppetry is a craft for the hippies — men, women and some smallish children — from New York City.' The *Newport Daily News* (July 15) spoke of the 'German immigrant' and his 'flower power cohorts' and termed their performance 'a kind of theater of the grotesque,' 'filling the stage with movement and pantomimed jibes at the world and its pretenses', and particularly appreciated its 80 ft. green dragon — at the conclusion of the festival 'marched across stage by 20 Newport school children who had been recruited by the puppeteers': it 'breathed smoke and made a fearful noise.'

'The *Chicken Little* that we played at Newport, which was just unbelievable .... That was so successful. It was an outstanding event. 10,000 people on their feet. Screaming and applauding and going nuts. People just like throwing flowers at us. It was great .... We were housed at a college for ladies, a girls school is in Newport for society ladies, a kind of finishing school .... The people there treated us so incredibly well. It just sticks in my mind. People who ran it, Ralph Minsler, and the people who were running it treated us so well. We were like slum people somehow. Rough and ready workers. They considered us as workers, culture workers or whatever you want to call it .... But we were in a scruffy mode. We were not in American successful. We were in the scruffy workers kinds of mode. And they treated us so well. I remember because it was a surprise somehow. We'd never been treated that way it seemed like and it was just elegant. It was just lovely. They fed us well. The rooms were nice. I mean it was definitely not on the tour circuit. We had done a lot of touring to the girls schools .... But Newport was a new dimension. Good treatment.' — (Ernstthal, interview.)

uniforme: blue-jeans et tricot de corps sur lequel sont peintes des médailles et des épaulettes. Valse.

2. *Le Paradis.* Chicken Little fait un somme. Quelqu'un laisse tomber une pomme sur sa tête. Il se réveille persuadé que le ciel tombe. Eve veut manger la pomme, mais Uncle Fatso survient: c'est son jardin, et s'ils mangent cette pomme, il leur enverra son poing dans la figure. Entre le dragon qui les incite à manger la pomme. Pendant tout ce temps Newton muni d'une règle n'arrête pas de mesurer la distance qui sépare la tête de Chicken Little du sol. Finalement Eve croque la pomme et la tend à Chicken Little. Le poing d'Uncle Fatso se détache pour aller les frapper. Tout le monde sort, sauf Chicken Little et Eve qui restent assommés par terre.

3. *Mère Terre.* Mother Earth donne naissance à tous les personnages de la pièce – et à quelques autres – qui sortent masqués de dessous sa jupe grise: le policier, la logeuse acariâtre, l'oiseau, etc. Dès leur naissance, les "enfants" sont "déclarés". Une porte sur laquelle est inscrit le mot *"Registration"* apparaît. Ils frappent à la porte, quelqu'un leur tape sur la tête avec un bâton, ils tombent, se relèvent, "entrent", rejoignent l'orchestre après avoir pris un instrument de musique. Le tout sous un feu roulant de questions tirées de deux formulaires d'inscription, l'un à l'Université Harvard, l'autre à une crèche de Brooklyn, les deux constamment mêlés, ce qui donne lieu aux pires inepties. Quand tous les personnages sont nés, l'orchestre entonne le fameux "Happy Birthday to you" (Bon anniversaire).

4. *Le mariage de Chicken Little.* Les préparatifs d'un grand mariage. Tout le monde s'habille. On arrange des fleurs, on déroule un tapis, on dresse un dais. Le photographe est là. Note discordante: un acteur se débat avec des bidons remplis de pierres et attachés les uns aux autres dont il essaie s'enrouler en faisant un vacarme épouvantable. L'orchestre joue "Here Comes the Bride" (Voici la mariée). Procession, mais rien ne se produit. Nouvelle procession: rien. Au bout de la troisième fois, une actrice surgit déguisée en pasteur, la Bible à la main: *"Blablabla..."* Le pasteur tend à Chicken Little et Eve des bracelets. Ils sont mariés.

5. *Le divorce de Chicken Little.* Dispute entre les deux époux au sujet d'une soupe aux pois (pea-soup). Le ton monte, la soupe devient de plus en plus mauvaise, elle tourne en "sea-poup": ils divorcent.

6. *Appartement no. 4.* Une Maison en bois montée sur une tige. Chicken Little regarde par la fenêtre. La logeuse acariâtre brandissant son balai vocifère contre lui (scène typiquement "Lower East Side"). Elle finit par s'emparer de la maison: il est à la porte.

7. *Le jeune homme qui a faim.* C'est le sketch déjà représenté dans le South Bronx. Le restaurant est "figuré" par une musique typique et par une table. Les plats sont en papier mâché. A la fin de la scène, le jeune homme, le serveur, le patron et le policier pleurent tous ensemble, et s'essuient les yeux avec un rouleau de papier W.C.

8. *Le Roi et le rat.* Chicken Little cherche du travail et un de ses amis lui propose un job dans un nightclub. Il fera partie du Choeur des Anciens: trois hommes habillés de façon extravagante, exécutent, en s'aidant de leur canne, des pas de danse, pour accompagner la chanteuse, Eve Schmaltz Vénus (schmaltz est un mot d'origine judéo-allemande, qui désigne en américain une musique sirupeuse). Eve chante l'histoire du Roi et du rat que miment des acteurs portant des masques. C'est le sketch inventé dans le South Bronx. A la fin de la scène, comme à la fin

des scènes précédentes – mais personne jusqu'ici ne l'avait écouté – Chicken Little dit au Roi que le ciel tombe : le Roi convoque tous les rats du royaume.

9. *Le Cercle des rats* (The Rat Clubhouse). Au son de l'hymne des 'marines' (From the Halls of Montezuma), une bande de rats arrivent en rampant sur la scène. Le Roi s'approche d'eux, les appelle chacun par leur nom (tous les noms des membres du gouvernement des Etats-Unis y passent) : *"Hello Dean, comment ça va ?"* etc., puis leur annonce que le ciel tombe. Que faire ? Les suggestions les plus stupides sont lancées, lorsqu'enfin le plus petit des rats, Lyndon, propose d'appeler le Conseiller. (On se rappelle que l'engagement américain au Vietnam a tout d'abord pris la forme de l'envoi d'*advisers*, de "conseillers".) Entre le Professeur, aux accents de "Hail to the Chief" (Salut au Chef), l'hymne officiel joué lorsque le Président entre dans un lieu public. Le Professeur parle : "I am glad that you asked me to come here today and so happy that I could come. We are the best fed and the best paid and the best educated people in the world and that is something we ought to be proud of. We produce more goods, we transport more goods and we use more goods than anyone in the world. We own almost a third of the world's railroad tracks. We own almost two thirds of the world's automobiles and we don't have to wait 3 years to get a new one either. We own half the trucks in the world. We own almost half of all the radios in the world. We own a third of all the electricity that's produced in the world. We own a fourth of all the steel. Our health conditions rank favorably with those of other countries in the world and although we have only about 6 percent of the population of the world we have half of its wealth. And bear in mind that other 94 percent of the population all would like to trade with us. Maybe a better way of saying it is that they would like to exchange places with us. But don't you help them exchange places with us, because I don't want to be where they are. Ha ha ha ha ha ha ha ha ha ha ha ha ha ha ha ha ha ha ha ha ha ha ha ha ha ha ha ha ha ha ha ha ha ha ha ha ha ha ha ha ha ha ha ha ha ha ha ha ha ha ha ha ha ha ha ha ha ha ha ha ha ha ha ha ha ha ha ha ha." (The Professor's Address to the Rats, from Bread and Puppet Theater *Chicken Little* Festival Program, 1967.) Ce sont les termes mêmes d'un discours du Président Lyndon B. Johnson, prononcé à la Baltimore Junior Chamber of Commerce au printemps 1967. Le Bread and Puppet répétait alors *Chicken Little* et décida d'y inclure ce discours. Pendant tout le temps que le Professeur parle, Chicken Little, impatient, tourne autour de cet énorme mannequin de six mètres de haut, le frappe, essaie de l'interrompre, et finit par obtenir la convocation d'une Conférence.

10. *La Conférence.* Une par une, de gigantesques marionnettes entrent : Mother Earth, Fox, Johnny Appleseed – célèbre héros américain, qui aurait, selon la légende, traversé tous les Etats-Unis à pied, un pot sur la tête, en semant sur son passage de la graine de pomme (*apple-seed*). Les marionnettes s'embrassent, bavardent entre elles, tandis que Chicken Little sur le devant de la scène paint des pancartes "Au secours", "Trop tard", etc., qu'il montre au public.

11. *Chicken Little parcourt le monde en annonçant que le ciel tombe.* Chicken Little est debout sur une chaise au milieu de la scène, tandis que l'orchestre du Bread and Puppet joue un grand morceau de son invention : "la Symphonie du Monde". Il essaie de parler. Tous les membres de l'orchestre parcourent maintenant la scène dans tous les sens avec leurs instruments. Ils finissent par former un cercle autour de Chicken Little qui peut enfin prononcer son discours : "Listen I was lying

under a tree and the westwind blew and it was a beautiful day and I was dreaming of roses that grew around me and of white horses flying through the air when suddenly a piece of sky fell on my head and I woke up and I saw that the sky was falling and so I came here to tell you about it, see, look up, the sky is falling, it's falling on everybody, on you. (Chicken Little's Address to Mankind, from Bread and Puppet Theater *Chicken Little* Festival Program, 1967.) Début de manifestation sur la scène, on brandit des pancartes, on crie des slogans, mais bientôt tout le monde se dispute et se met à déchirer les pancartes. Chicken Little, épuisé, se couche et dort.

12. *La Marche aux enfers*. Chicken Little se met autour du cou un énorme coeur rouge sur lequel est écrit "Go to Hell" (Allez au diable) et prend la tête du défilé: tous les acteurs marchent lentement en soufflant dans leurs instruments. Lorsqu'ils sont arrivés à l'autre extrémité de la scène, une porte sur laquelle est inscrit "Enfer" apparaît. Chicken Little frappe à la porte, elle s'ouvre et tous les acteurs sortent de scène. On entend une grande explosion.

13. *La Fin*. Le dragon apparaît environné de fumée, avec des acteurs tout autour de lui qui jouent de la musique. Grande danse finale.'

(Kourilsky, '71.) (Copyright Françoise Kourilsky 1971.)

'It was a journey story. He was this innocent fool who travelled around having all kinds of things happen to him, getting into fights, his wife divorced him, getting kicked around by the landlord, by the restaurant boss. I think, oh yes, he led some sort of march against the bad guys – Hell, maybe it was Hell or the President, I don't remember, but I do remember this march across the stage, and Peter said, 'Oh, we have to have a symphony', you know, everything was so early instruments, but hardly anyone could, we had only maybe two or three real musicians. So there was a lot of clanging and marching. Oh, there was – the funniest scene. It was a ball, a big dance. And Bob Ernstthal would stand at the mike announcing all the people who had come to the party, like in England, like you would imagine, all the royal people standing at the top of the stairs and being announced, the Duke and Duchess of Windsor, but he made up other names, and he said, Cardinal and Mrs. Spellman – And these were all these heads, enormous heads with little people inside of them, coming out and waltzing. One of the people in the company played the fiddle, and would sit on a chair with his back to the audience, playing a waltz while these puppets, who were just giant heads with little bodies, waltzed around. And I thought that was hysterically funny ... It was very, very long and we had to perform it. And they said, "You can't do an hour and a half show, you only have forty minutes." So we had to run it, absolutely run through the whole show, till it was short enough. That was exciting, very exciting for me.' (Sherman, interview.)

This was the first time Valdez of El Campesino had seen work of Schumann's:

'Bread and Puppet: that, too, is a cultural shock. It works with reality on two levels, neither of which is even vaguely like the "realistic" theater. I first saw them at the Newport Folk Festival. The puppets to begin with: those huge, fantastic

puppets. The production was *Chicken Little*. Peter took theatrical realism and blew it apart and said, people have different visions; people are something else; people can be fifty feet high. There are other forces working in this universe besides this realistic shit. Life goes beyond that, it's much more mystical; it's much more magical; it's more acid-like. And these huge figures come in at the beginning and the Mother Earth figure started creating all these creatures; they come out from under her skirt. She laid an egg and out came a creature with a bill and a funny looking face. All different forms of creation. Beautiful image. Yes, and the kid, six years old I think with a papier-mache head. He was a cop. A cop running with a club hitting everybody. Three feet high, a cop.'
(Valdez, in the San Francisco Mime Troupe's booklet on the September '68 San Francisco Radical Theatre Festival.)

'We sort of succeeded. We did a show that worked on this big stage and for this folksy audience, who wanted to hear beautiful songs.' (Schumann, ibid.)

Beyond the comedy, the play, though like the preceding three Suffering-of-Vietnam plays about the war in Vietnam and propaganda against it, differed from them in being neither about Vietnam nor about suffering, but about the U.S. and action: the war-making of the leaders, the indifference of the population, the disunity of the resistance. Pushing things, we could say it was a plea for unity in resistance. This was consonant with his growing alienation from the Movement (cf. supra, part IV(2).31). He did not in his work repeat this plea nor this address to the resistance. But *Chicken Little* shares with the two propaganda pieces that in '67 entered his indoors repertory, *Speech/Chairs* and *A Man Says Goodbye* the turn from victimized Vietnam to victimizing America.

15. May-August '67, *Speech*, and February '68 ff., *Chairs*.

Schumann, as we have seen (part IV.2) had done outdoor agitational shows utilizing presidential speeches as early as November '65, perhaps on November 11, definitely on November 27th (*A Pageant of Death Based on President Johnson's Speech at Johns Hopkins*). By May '66, the skit included an audience listening to the speech. The skit reappears in *The Rat Clubhouse* in *Chicken Little*, addressed to the chorus of rats that were the Professor-Chief's 'clientele, his public' (Schumann, interview, '79). These were nominally identified as members of government. Under the title of *Speech*, it enters his indoors repertory at the Astor Library May-August '67,[1] and a further variant of it, entitled *Chairs*, is among − or is worked out during − the 'protest presentations' at St. Peter's Church in February '68.[2]

Both *Speech* and *Chairs* take off from that '65 pageant's central idea: the harmless mass of consumers, the general public, turning into ogres when their bellies are threatened. Schumann saw this nexus in the coupling in Johnson's speeches of materialistic identifications of the Great Society and of boasts of American material achievements with threats to foreign nations, and sometimes heard it made directly by Johnson − they are all envious of us, we've got to protect ourselves. The communists impose the image of the war maker on the greedy capitalist: Schumann saw him as the Dr. Jekyll side of Mr. and Mrs. Average Man. This insight went back to − and the staging of part 4 of *Chairs/Speech* indicated this − but went beyond, his discovery in the '50s of the cultured German bourgeoisie's easy complicity in the Nazi regime's Lebensraum-ideology-based regime of terror: went beyond it in extending the indictment to the People, and in focusing it on a charge of base materialism. The insight could be presented by the use of masks: skull masks exchanged for only slightly weird face masks; and of chairs: the masks turned toward the audience to remind it

---

1. The first performance of *Speech* mentioned in the *Village Voice* is that of May 20th, '67 at the Astor Memorial Library Landmark Building. It was done there again the next two Saturdays, but whether it continued to be done or not, the first performances after this we hear of are of July 22nd and 29th. It was probably done at Expo '67 the following weekend, and is listed again for a New York performance of August 19th. It's done July 19 and 20 at the Long Wharf Theatre in New Haven, in November at the Harvard Epworth Methodist Church in Boston.

2. The *Voice* noted performances February 2, 5, 16, 23:

'And we did a series of four Friday nights in which we did the chair piece. That church has since been torn down, and they built in that block-long space the Citicorp building and the church is now a corner of it.' — (Ashley, interview.)

They did it March 30 and 31 at the First Radical American Theatre Festival at the Washington Square Memorial Church, and then took it to Europe.

of *its* complicity; the chairs of the willing listeners to promises of plenty turning into symbols of aggressive weapons – the horde of swine (but quite decent people: note infra in part 2 of *Speech/Chairs* how loving they are) stirred up into a run of wolves. Beyond this indictment looms the Christian view of man: weak flesh ever ready to abandon the path of salvation under the sting of concupiscence, greed.

Speech:

'The starkest episode features a young man reading aloud (with no attempt at mimicry) President Johnson's last State of the Union address, accompanying himself on drum and gong: as he reads, a silent black-clad audience masked in sculpted faces of sepulchral white (each mask a wonder of grief, or pain, or blank indifference beyond the reach of either) acts out its patterned charades of suffering, death, unreachability, horrifyingly underlining the ironies of the rosy materialism and self-congratulation (*our* self-congratulation) that suffuses the speech. These figures sit as an audience, facing the speaker, but then turn their masks to the backs of their heads – masks that stare out at us in pain and silence as the voice drones on. They writhe in anguish on the floor, clattering and clacking away with hand-rattles that sound like the music of dry bones in a high wind; and each is led out in a *marche macabre* by a skeleton of death, voiceless and dignified, who remains until the speaker is finished and follows him offstage. This is didacticism transmuted into art, pain into visual poetry, outrage into communicable sympathy.' (Unsigned review, *Boston*, vol. 59, #12, December '67.)

Speech then, in February '68, was developed into *Chairs* by an elaboration of the audience's interaction with their chairs into a more abstract visual and aural ballet that was then again partly abandoned in favor of a careful articulation of the indictment.

Kourilsky '71 treats the two pieces as identical. I suspect her reconstruction of *Chairs/Speech* is closer to *Chairs*. According to it, the playlet divides visually into four parts, Part 1 to presidential speechifying (done by an unmasked performer in everyday dress in an absolutely neutral tone into a microphone, occasionally punctuated by cymbal beats or drum beats on a big box) about how great America is and how much even better we have got to make it, Part 3 to speechifying ditto about how this war needs to be fought and will be fought, Part 2 between the two parts of the speech, Part 4 after the speech ends. Before the speech begins, the choir – 15 performers in black with white distorted face masks – dragging their chairs enter, leave, reenter, leave, leaving the chairs on the stage: the audience sets the stage: a symbolization of democratic elections.

1 During a pause in the speech ...	Quatre hommes habillés en noir et masques entrent et alignent les chaises devant l'orateur (dos au public). Ils sortent.
	(a sentence of the speech.)
	Battements de grosse caisse.

	Battements de grosse caisse. (No speech.) (No speech.)	Un personnage habillé en noir et masqué, est apporté et posé devant les chaises. Cet homme-marionnette remue les bras avec raideur, en faisant un mouvement à chaque battement de tambour comme s'il prononçait un discours.
	(Speech commences)	Le personnage est emporté hors de scène.
		Les personnages du choeur entrent un par un, très lentement, et s'asseoient face à l'orateur. Chaque personnage tourne son masque pour l'avoir sur sa nuque. Ainsi les masques regardent le public dans les yeux.
		Ils opinent lentement de la tête, de bas en haut, stupidement, tandis que le discours continue.
2		L'orateur frappe la cymbale une fois.
		Les personnages remettent leur masque sur leur visage, se retournent avec leur chaise et s'alignent face au public. Ils tournent maintenant leur tête de gauche à droite, très lentement. Après quelques instants, ils se lèvent, avancent ensemble leur chaises, s'asseoient de nouveau en faisant le même mouvement de tête. Ce jeu se répète une fois. Un homme se lève et s'approche d'une femme assise sur une chaise. Elle se lève, il passe sa main lentement sur la joue de la femme (il continuera le même geste jusqu'à la fin de la scène). Un deuxième homme se lève, s'approche d'une autre femme, fait le même geste, mais cette fois-ci la femme cache son visage dans ses mains. Il arrête son geste. Un troisième homme s'approche d'une autre femme. Lorsqu'il pose la main sur sa joue, elle tombe.
		Le narrateur frappe la cymbale une fois.
		Les personnages du choeur disposent les chaises en cercle, au milieu de la scène, et sortent.
3	Battements de grosse caisse.	Un personnage portant un masque de mort est amené sur la scène et placé au milieu des chaises. Il remue ses bras avec raideur, comme s'il prononçait un discours.
		Le personnage est emporté hors de scène.

Battements de grosse caisse.	Tous les personnages du chœur entrent. Ils portent des masques de mort, ont les bras levés et les bougent avec raideur. Ils avancent jusqu'au milieu des chaises et marchent de long en large, comme s'ils faisaient un discours aux chaises. Ils sortent.
Criquets.	Les personnages du chœur entrent en rampant rapidement, un criquet dans chaque main. Ils se glissent sous les chaises, les renversent lentement et les placent sur leur dos.
L'orateur frappe la cymbale une fois.	Les personnages du chœur s'immobilisent et arrêtent les criquets.
Battements de grosse caisse.	Les personnages du chœur quittent la scène lentement un par un, en laissant les chaises.

(The speech continued for a while.)

4

	Un personnage en blanc apporte un drap blanc qu'il étend par terre à droite de la scène. Il sort et entre de nouveau en compagnie d'une grande marionnette blanche représentant la 'dame vietnamienne' qu'il place sur le drap. Les personnages du chœur entrent. Ils portent des masques de morts. Ils se disposent sur deux rangs, à gauche de la scène, face à la marionnette.
Criquets.	Ils marchent sur la marionnette en levant le genou gauche et le bras gauche et en faisant claquer les criquets qu'ils ont dans la main. Cette marche constitue une étrange parodie d'un défilé nazi.
Noir. (The light has been a uniform white up to this point.)	Les personnages du chœur s'arrêtent.
Appareil à lumière stroboscopique réglé lentement et dirigé sur la 'dame vietnamienne'.	La marionnette oscille lentement et s'incline légèrement en avant. Le personnage en blanc, debout devant la marionnette fait le même mouvement.
Lumière.	Les personnages du chœur regagnent leur place à gauche de la scène et recommencent la marche.
Noir.	Ils s'arrêtent.

Lumière stroboscopique.	La 'dame vietnamienne' et le personnage en blanc tombent.
	Les personnages du chœur ôtent leurs masques, entourent la marionnette, lèvent légèrement le drap blanc pour permettre aux deux manipulateurs de se retirer. La tête et les bras de la 'dame vietnamienne' sont alors portés sur le drap blanc hors de la scène.

'En contrepoint, le jeu scénique n'a apparemment rien à voir avec les propos tenus par l'orateur. Des personnages habillés tout en noir et masqués "jouent" avec des chaises, les apportent en les trainant, s'asseoient dessus, se lèvent, les renversent, etc. Aucune de ces actions n'a une signification évidente, précise; elles finissent cependant par susciter chez le spectateur une anxiété que le discours voudrait précisément assoupir au moyen d'une rhétorique habile, et le malaise créé est d'autant plus vif ce chœur de personnages en noir qui constitue l'auditoire du Président Johnson n'est pa là pour dénoncer ou ridiculiser ses paroles, mais pour renoyer au public l'image de sa propre indifférence et de sa complicité; les acteurs assis face à l'orateur, leur masque sur la nuque, l'air hébété, regardent les spectateurs les regardent et écouter comme eux le discours. Celui-ci s'achève par ces affirmations catégoriques: "Nous faisons ce que le devoir nous commande. Cette tâche doit être la nôtre", et c'est alors seulement que l'"Histoire" se déroule: les personnages du chœur qui portent maintenant des masques de mort marchent à trois reprises – cette marche constitue une étrange parodie d'un défilé nazi – sur une grande marionnette blanche de quatre mètres de haut représentant une Vietnamienne, accompagnée d'un personnage de taille humaine drapé de blanc: les deux personnages s'inclinent à chaque fois un peu plus et finissent par tomber.' (Kourilsky, '71.)

'What makes any theatrical performance memorable is the tanacity of the images it leaves behind. The images of the Bread and Puppet Theatre haunt one for weeks aftwerward. I still find it hard to forget the dead, passive, gaping faces that peered into mine as Lyndon Johnson's words were perfunctorily reproduced in the piece called "Chairs." Here, Schumann counterpoints the hollow political prose of a Presidential address with scarifying entrances and exits by hooded bodies pushing chairs, marching in time, or just sitting with poached-egg eyes watching us watch them. The actions in the piece correspond to the very watching us watch them. The actions in the piece correspond to the very anxieties the words are intended to allay. As we listen to sentiments about peace and sacrifice, we receive stark impressions of the deadly realities the words are trying to divert us from. By the end, we have simultaneously experienced the drone of hollow rehetoric and the terrible sins it commits. It is a piece charged with political contempt but with all its anger mysteriously subdued. It's something like being hit on the head with a hammer wrapped in cottonwool.'
(C. Marowitz, *theatre abroad. London: off-off-B'way. Village Voice*, May 23, '68.)

'Rollerne:

En udraber. Medlemmer af den amerikanske kongres, hoge og duer. Friheds-

gudinden. Kongresmedlemmerne baerer masker. Frihedsgudinden er er stor dukke.

Handlingen: (sat i scene af Bread and Puppet Theatre's leder, Peter Schumann) Scenen er tom. Kongresmedlemmerne begynder at rykke frem pa deres stole. Kongresmedlemmerne forlander scenen. Scenen er fuld af stole. Udraberen begynder til monotont stortrommeakkompagement at udrabe en tale af L.B. Johnson til den amerikanske kongres. Kongresmedlemmer kommer og gar, saetter og rejser sig. Duerne prover at vende ansigtet den anden vej. Det betyder ingenting. Hogene – der er kun hoge tillbage – appellerer til hende med heil-march. Hun svarer ikke. Hogene prover igen. Hun vaerger for sig. Hogene prover igen. Og frihedsgudinden synker sammen i ruinerne af kongressen. Hogene ser pa hende og traekker pa skuldrene. Talen er slut.'

(politisk revy.)

16. May-November '67, *(The) Dead Man Rises.*

In I would say typical fashion creating one of his little mysteries – like not committing himself all his life long on the Divinity of Jesus – Schumann evades questions about the structure and content of *Leaf*, but *Dead Man Rises*, done more or less every Saturday at the Astor Library from early May to November '67,[1] he says, was a revision of it: he found he could not reconstruct it from memory – had lost his notes – had no shakuhachi.[2] I suppose his mood had changed. The question is really how were they the same, did they relate at all. Both were about a relation between a man and a woman (Schumann doing the Lover in *Leaf*, the Dead Man in *Dead Man*) apparently going from an approach/searching/being-drawn through a conjunction to not a separation but a representation of effects, possibly happiness; apparently the same number of the same kind of puppets being used[3] – essentially three puppets, (neither the *Tulane Drama*

---

1. The *New Leader* of May 8, '67 reviews as part of the 'current program' of the Bread and Puppet Theatre at the Astor Library a play entitled 'Leaf Feeling the Moonlight' which as far as one can make out in the review seems to be *Dead Man Rises*: I presume that the *Leaf Feeling the Moonlight* according to the *Village Voice Off-Off-Broadway Guide* of May 18 presented May 20th is also *Dead Man Rises*, and that *Dead Man* is the 'untitled new play' according to the *Village Voice* presented May 27 and June 3rd. The first performances of it under its name listed in the *Village Voice* are on July 21, 22 and 28 and August 19th. The *Village Voice* next, and finally, lists performances of September 16th and October 7th. According to a notice in *The Militant* of October 23rd it's still done Saturday evenings – through November 4th. I suppose, Schumann at first did it under the old title, then untitled, and under the new title only June 10th or soon after. It was frequently performed later in Europe and the USA. The last performance of it that I know of was given by Murray Levy's Stomachache Theatre, a Bread and Puppet splinter group, at the Emmanuel Church in Boston in February '71.
2. '(Elka: *Leaf Feeling the Moonlight*... (laughing) is one of my favorite lost shows.) Yeah, later on when we had this place in the Shakespeare Company, we tried to recapture that, but I had lost my notebook, and there was no way of finding again what was into the show. Also, I had a musician friend there who played beautiful shakuhachi and that was part of the *Leaf Feeling the Moonlight* performances. (Elka: And your attempt to recreate *Leaf Feeling the Moonlight* ended in *Dead Man Rises*.) I sort of got disgusted that we couldn't find it and then I wrote the *Dead Man Rises* story. (Elka: I remember somehow the time when you were working on *Dead Man Rises* and you were – the impression is frustrating rehearsals that just couldn't get it, couldn't get it, and then a real feeling of now I've got it, now I've got it.) It was just the writing of the text that did that. I just wrote the text. (Elka: But the text was *Leaf Feeling the Moonlight*.) No. Not at all. *Leaf Feeling the Moonlight* had no text.' — (Schumann, interview, '79.)
3. '(Ephraim: Were there puppets and masks made for that show?) No, it was the old *Leaf Feeling the Moonlight* that we couldn't get together, and then I wrote this text instead that was used. (Ephraim: So you used the same props that you had for that show.) No we didn't use any more the hands or the signs that I described for *Leaf Feeling the Moonlight*.

Review #38 ('68) synopsis, nor Kourilsky '71 mentions Morning), Man, Woman and a third party, in *Leaf* perhaps an Older Man or the Father, in *Dead Man* the River — the Night and Morning figures in *Dead Man* being incidental, and perhaps one or two similar incidental figures figuring in *Leaf*. Like *Leaf*, *Dead Man* seems to have been a personal statement with no moral, political or social import, pure puppetry also in not involving masked performers but only the big puppets (the Bunraku type "attendant" in *Dead Man* a symbol, since in fact he did not figure as puppet operator), closer to an allegorical dance piece than to mime, and highly and intentionally obscure: done in almost total darkness, even during its 'Morning' section. The 'Plainfield, Vermont, March 1971' version of it published by K. Taylor (Taylor, *People's Theater in America*, '72) is probably a Bread and Puppet Theatre script. I doubt it differs much from the '67 version: the attendant might have been added by '71, the Morning puppet substituted for dressing the risen man in yellow in the morning, and perhaps a dance of the woman and the risen man in the morning as added also.

'THE DEAD MAN RISES[4]

Puppets: The Woman
The River
The Night
The Morning
The Dead Man
(The puppets are all over life-size, white masks and long black robes, except the Woman, who is all in white.)[5]

An Attendant in a black shirt and hood

Props: Bridge (a large wooden block or foot-stool)
One pair white women's shoes
Length of cloth or cord
Pillow
Piece of dark fabric
Silver leaves

They were not in anymore. Instead we used some other props, but no new puppets were built. Now we used the footstool as a bridge, we used the green ribbon to tie the river to the woman — a few small pieces of props — (Ephraim: So the woman and the man, the white and the black puppet, were made — they were made for *Leaf Feeling the Moonlight*?) Yes. Right. But the screens were painted for the river story, for *The Dead Man Rises*. (Ephraim: . . . all the puppets that were in *Dead Man Rises* and the props, they were used before it in the parades?) No. Not at all. The *Dead Man Rises* puppets were not in parades. No.' — (Schumann, interview, '79.)
4. Plainfield, Vermont, March 1971 script.
5. '*Characters*: A woman — a six-foot puppet with flowing white robes and a long, delicate, gentle gray-white face. The Dead Man — six or seven foot tall in gray-black robes. The River — an eight-foot puppet in black robes. The Night — a black puppet, only the head

Backdrop: Three screens showing greyish landscapes, mounted in[6] cinderblocks

Instruments: Bell
Soft horn (length of common garden hose, violin, cello, rattle, ocarina also used)

Other Equipment: Ladder
Three Flashlights
Microphone
Amplifier
Speaker
Floodlight
Dimmer

Darkness. Then a small, dim floodlight gradually illuminates the playing area which is established by three grey-toned paintings on fabric, hung separately from standing poles at right, left and center stage upstage; and by a large circle on the floor, outlined by green branches or sea shells. The Attendant, in black hood and shirt, kneels at SR.

A tall puppet figure all in white, the Woman, appears from behind a screen, pauses, then slowly starts to circle[7] the playing area. As she reaches the center downstage, a whispered, amplified voice is heard:

WHERE ARE YOU GOING? (Bell)
I AM GOING TO THE RIVER. (Bell)
WHY ARE YOU GOING? (Bell)
THE RIVER IS COLD. (Bell)
WHERE IS THE RIVER? (Bell)
THE RIVER IS FAR AWAY.

Breathing sound is heard while Woman completes circle. (Bell)
Silence. Then whispered voice:

HERE IS THE BRIDGE. (Bell)

Attendant steps into the circle and places bridge at the feet of the Woman, then returns to original place. (Bell) River puppet enters and stands center stage.

THIS IS THE RIVER.
ARE YOU THIRSTY?
YES. (Bell)

The Woman kneels and drinks.

---

visible, an ugly Chinese face. All these are body puppets moved by a person inside. The Narrator, downstage right, speaks into a megaphone with a small bell attached to it.' — (Anonymous, *Tulane Drama Review* #38 (**Winter '68**) synopsis.)

6. '*Set*: The same as for *A Man Says Goodbye to His Mother*.' (*Tulane Drama Review* synopsis.)
  'Sur un tapis de sol noir, devant trois toiles peintes sur tissu blanc, représentant des paysages champêtres dans des tonalités grises.' — (Kourilsky, '71.)
7. 'Les acteurs se déplacent en glissant plus qu'en marchant, avec des mouvements extrêment lents qui rappellent les conventions du théâtre de no japonais.' — (Kourilsky, '71.)

THE WATER IS COLD. (Bell)

The Woman stands up.

I WANT TO TAKE MY SHOES OFF AND WADE IN THE RIVER.

The Attendant steps in, removes the Woman's shoes and places them downstage center; then he returns to his original position. The Woman steps behind the River and the two puppets circle the stage together in a gentle, gliding motion. Two handheld flashlights illuminate their faces, following them as they move very slowly. Soft horn wail sounds with this movement. (Bell) They turn. (Bell) The Dead Man puppet enters and lies down. Flashlight shines on his face. He is blindfolded (masking tape over his eyes). (Bell) Then the whispered voice:

THERE IS A DEAD MAN LYING IN THE RIVER.
WHAT WILL YOU DO WITH THE DEAD MAN?
I WILL TIE THE DEAD MAN TO THE BACK OF THE RIVER
AND TAKE HIM TO MY HOUSE. (Soft horn)

With the help of the Attendant, the Woman raises the Dead Man and places him behind the River puppet, supporting him with her body and clasping the River. The Attendant ties the three figures together with a cord or strip of cloth, and returns to original position. The three figures circle the stage together. (Soft horn throughout this movement; then bell) Whisper:

HERE IS THE BRIDGE.

The Attendant brings in the bridge, puts it down: unties the puppets, and returns to original position with the cord. The River exits. Whisper:

FROM HERE I HAVE TO CARRY THE DEAD MAN TO MY HOUSE.

The Woman carries the Dead Man on her back, circling the stage. (Bell; heavy breathing; bell) Whisper:

DID YOU GO THE RIVER?
YES.
WAS THE WATER COLD?
YES. (Bell)
DEAD MAN, I WILL PUT YOU INTO MY BED.

The Woman puts the Dead Man down on the floor. The Attendant enters and places a pillow under his head. The Dead Man lies on his side, facing the audience. (Bell)
The Night puppet enters and stands behind and at the head of the Dead Man. Whisper:

THIS IS THE NIGHT.

The Night covers the Dead Man and the Woman with a dark cloth, then exits. (Bell) There is almost no light on the stage. A flashlight shines on the two puppets. The Morning puppet, which entered during the darkness, rises behind them. Whisper:

THIS IS THE MORNING. (Bell) Full floodlight on.
DEAD MAN, I WILL OPEN YOUR EYES. (Bell)

The Attendant removes the blindfold, takes the pillow, and returns to original position. The Dead Man and the Woman rise. (Bell rings often) Now they dance, face to face, arms outstretched, rocking and circling the stage, and the bell continues to ring.[8] When they reach the back curtain area, silvery leaves flutter down on them from over the top of the back screen. They exit. The River enters and walks slowly downstage center. A flashlight shines on his face. He kneels before the Woman's shoes. The Attendant enters, ties the shoes on the back of the River, and returns to original position. The River rises, turns and exits slowly. A flashlight shines on the shoes. (Soft horn throughout) Whisper:

THE RIVER FINDS THE LADY'S SHOES AND CARRIES THEM ON HIS BACK. (Softhorn)

The flashlight shines on the backdrop, then goes out. The End.'

The piece seems to me to be making the compound statement: love is women's vivification of men; it is their union in death (or: a woman's love for a man is her suicide:), the union in love and death of a man and a woman is the highest form of life.

This dialectic of death and life, though not as applied to sexual love, seems the same as in *Totentanz* according to the explication of *Totentanz* in Schumann's '62 manifesto, and also the underlying Goethean idea of *Fire* (suicide as highest affirmation of life). I doubt, however, that this dialectical message was perceptible to any spectator: or was meant to be.[9] I see

---

8. 'The Dead Man rises and in the morning a yellow robe is put on him and he and the Woman go off.' — (*Tulane Drama Review* synopsis.)

9. 'The first half of Peter Schumann's current offering at his Bread and Puppet Theater, "Leaf Feeling the Moonlight," inches forward lugubriously. So do the puppets themselves, cowled presences eight or nine feet high, like monks and nuns off a canvas by Rouault, their white mouths and eye sockets full of dumb, unchanging anguish, and no backs to their heads.

They advance and recede – Faulkner's favorite adverb, "terrifically," applies here – in front of a shabbily painted landscape. A stagehand sits in the front row and points a wavering flashlight at them, and from the rear of the cavernous room another white beam, slightly rainbowed at its rim, hits the landscape and goes in and out of focus. The puppets incline toward one another, then separate, appear and reappear. They are mesmerized by a plastic pink rose the size of a chrysanthemum which, in this sepulchral context, seems flaming red.

Electronic music growls like a decrepit Wurlitzer being tuned by unpracticed hands, while from time to time a sort of chair up front breathes in a sighing diapason, as if to imitate a man sleeping or dying.

The solemnity is occasionally dispersed by feet that scurry about the edges of the room – somebody is organizing something, preparing something – and once by the crying of a little girl in the audience who is frightened by the spookiness. A French horn suddenly croaks. It drives the figures out of sight. They return. Again the horn wards them off. They keep coming back. Eventually it deflates them with its hoarse shouts. They go down very slowly into darkness.

One could scrabble endlessly for meanings and conclusions in this piece of work. Yet it may be no more than a formal exploration of the medium. A puppet has its own life, and that life is governed by its size in relation to the size of a human being, as well as the

it as the arcane metaphysics underlying Schumann's work, tragic *and* life-affirming, the bit of news censored out of Schumann's plays, imparted by his masks. If he had stayed in Germany, he would have struggled to express it. The imperfect suppression of it made him a great artist.

Schumann disclaims this meaning:

'I don't agree that the second one – (*Dead Man Rises* (SSB)) was an unhappy or tragic play. I think it didn't capture this – the finesse of the first one, of the *Leaf Feeling the Moonlight* because it was more of a story – one can call that a ridiculous story, but it is a story of a dead man coming back to life. And even though the joy isn't played with fanfares or very visibly, that's the theme of it. This finding of a dead man and for no reason and with nothing much to show other than the fact of it that he's put next to the lady and that he comes back to life. The impression that it's dark and tragic is from the darkness of the colors and the slow motion and subduedness of the way it's done, I would think, right, more than from the – (I: A feeling I had was that a possible way of looking at it was that the marriage is that she commits suicide. So that they join one another in death.) Ah-hah. But I meant it as a real crazy resurrection – for no reason – just that with that language one could do that. One could say that somebody would come back to life and one could do it on the stage.' (Schumann, interview, '82.)

In '68 he claimed the show 'clearly' expressed his disgust with city life!

'We don't take a problem-solving attitude. We just try, with each show, to be a little real. We want to evoke a direct emotional response to what is happening – like protesting the war or urban society, or telling kids about violence in our children's plays. We have a show – *The Dead Man Rises* – which doesn't prescribe a thing. It's a clear expression of outrage and disgust with city life. It's an answer to living in the city. It's a celebration of something else, maybe love.'

(Schumann in Brown and Seitz, *With the Bread and Puppet Theatre, Tulane Drama Review* ‡38 (Winter '68).)

Barry Goldensohn thought it a religious play on resurrection and redemption:

'The Bread and Puppet Theater was deeply involved with the civil rights and anti-war protest movements and is marked by their political moralism.

Underlying these moral and political concerns is a religious vision that chooses as its main symbols resurrection and redemption. These are made impersonal and public, not emblems of personal salvation. *The Dead Man Rises* is an early

---

gestural limitations imposed (and for an artist, the opportunities afforded) by its range of activities. Schumann's huge dolls appear to swim through the air; their movement belies their bulk. They do not "walk" like people with their shoulders rising and falling or swaying to compensate for changes of balance, even though there is an actor inside each one. They glide rather as a female character does in the Peking Opera or a Noh performer does as he takes 10 minutes to traverse the few feet of *hashigakura* from the entrance curtain to the stage area.... What Schumann achieves is to match a grisly appearance to graceful actions. This, one feels, is how a tree might travel if it could get off its roots and pace the earth.' — (A. Bermel, *Doll Houses, The New Leader*, May 8, '67.)

example of this theme. In a darkened loft, a small, dim spot of light appears before a gray painted fabric screen. An Attendant, barely visible in black robes, kneels at the side. A tall white puppet, the Woman, slowly circles the stage and enters the light. The Attendant whispers through a megaphone, and rings a bell to distinguish the "speakers."

WHERE ARE YOU GOING? (Bell)
I AM GOING TO THE RIVER. (Bell)
WHY ARE YOU GOING? (Bell)
THE RIVER IS COLD. (Bell)
WHERE IS THE RIVER? (Bell)
THE RIVER IS FAR AWAY.

The Attendant breathes heavily into the megaphone while the Woman walks around the circle of light.

With these few beginning words and actions, stylized and abstracted in manner, we have been carried into a world of profound inwardness. The power and the suddenness of the artifice – disconnected speakers engaging in an interior dialogue, oversized puppets, the absence of color, and the physical helplessness of the puppet figures – place the action in a dream realm that has many features of the inner lives of children.... The primitive morality, the resurrection of the Dead Man as a reward for the devotion of the Woman, is in keeping with the technique. Despite the inwardness, the Woman of this play is not individualized, and the emphasis throughout the work is still on the public nature of the religious issues, the implications for public morality.'

Helen Palmer, who did the Woman in '67 (cf. her description, II.6) and saw the play as a precognition of her separation from the Movement and subsequent discovery of her psychic powers, thought the play was about the Woman's journey, that 'there was great happiness at the end,' and that

'the journey was an inner one, that I went alone, that I found there something that was dead, that resurrected itself. And in the end there was a union of some kind. That may be very mystical, but that's how I saw it....
(Palmer, interview.)

'I will say that the next work (after *Fire* (SSB)) that might be mentioned as being totally overwhelming was *Dead Man Rises*. I have no idea how long *Dead Man Rises* lasts. I don't know – I saw it in a revival at Coney Island, for example, and I thought, well now I'm going to be able to study how it works. But again, the noise of Coney Island all around me disappeared and for – whether it lasts 15 minutes or five minutes or an hour and five minutes, I have no idea, because the power of that piece was such that I always say about it that I stopped breathing. It's a poem – the only poem that I've ever seen on the stage – and one stops breathing throughout the duration of it.'   (Ashley, interview.)

17. July-November '67, *A Man Says Goodbye to his Mother*.

Like Speech, A Man Says Goodbye to his Mother goes back to a street play. It may have been done on the street as early as November '65, but Kourilsky '71 dates its first outdoor showings as of November '66 and is probably right. Its theme had appeared in a Hiroshima Day parade of August 6, '66. In this parade, the soldier that as the Son is the non-hero of the play is presented as manacled victim dragged along by a military leadership. Schumann presented the play indoors at the Astor Library from July to September or November '67.[1] In September '68 it was extended into a version called *Reiteration* (cf. infra, IV.3, 21) which during '69 replaced it for indoor performances, but it stayed in the Bread and Puppet repertory into the late '70s.

I have no doubt that on different occasions it was varied in some details, notably as regards the penultimate scene of the Mother's killing of the Soldier — the Death figure narrator may not always have guided her arm, she may not always have received a skull mask, and perhaps also whether the narrator or the Mother initially gives the Son the bag with his war gear may have varied; and I doubt there always was as much musical accompaniment as Kourilsky's account indicates — but in the main it re-

---

1. The play first is mentioned in the *Village Voice* in its *Off-Off Broadway Guide* of July 20, '67: performances the 21st and 22nd, at the Astor Library. We next hear of performances of it on August 12th, 13th and 19th, and then again on October 16th. It was probably among Schumann's Hiroshima Day offerings, August 5th, 6th and/or 7th at Expo '67 in Montreal, Canada, as well as at the July 10-16 Newport Folk Festival, on the return trip from which it was done, July 19th and 20th, together with *Dead Man* and *Speech* at the Long Wharf Theatre in New Haven, the three playlets being advertised in the New Haven Register of July 16th as 'powerful adult entertainment', presented by this 'wild protest theater straight from New York City and the Newport Folk Festival', 'offering a message of demonic protest, punctuated by fifteen-foot high puppets and apocalyptic visions' and a 'delicious mixture of the marvelous with the macabre.' *The Militant* of October 23 lists it as one of three plays presented at the Astor Library Saturday evenings through November 4th: 'a mime-ballad play for masked players and musicians.'

It was done at the Adams School for the Neurologically Disturbed, 'followed by discussion.' (Bread and Puppet Diary, November 1967-March 1968). It went to Europe in '68 and '69. On the '69 tour it was sometimes billed as *War Theatre*.

2. '(Elka: Just for the record, the last time the *Man Says Goodbye* was done was on this tour to Spain two years ago (October (?) '77 (SSB))? Or was it done in the *Circus* the following year? Maurice (Blanc) did it two circuses ago, didn't he?) Yeah, I think so. Avram Patt did it two circuses ago with Maurice. (Elka: Ephraim and Maurice did it in 1974 on Cate Farm, during the *Circus*, you know?) Yes, and in the meantime it was done in Spain. The puppeteers who did it were very unsatisfied with it, with doing it, complaining about it, with the kind of reactions they collected from it. (Ephraim: But it hasn't really been done since — since then. You did it a lot then. Elka: Well, it *has* —. Ephraim: It *has*, but not much.) Not much at all. No. Very seldom.' — (Schumann, interview, '79.)

mained constant. Lasting about a quarter of an hour, it was a small masterpiece.

A Man Says was done with one or two skull-masked musicians, normally a trumpeter in addition to a drummer, a skull-masked narrator, a performer for the son, unmasked, in army fatigues or work clothes, and a performer for the mother, wearing a silver-grey mask as the son's mother, a Vietnamese mask as the mother of the child he kills.[3]

The narrated text (according to the Bread and Puppet *Reiteration* script) and the action (according to Kourilsky's reconstruction):

A MAN SAYS GOODBYE TO HIS MOTHER: she gives him the bag, they embrace. (Trumpet and drum tune starts and continues during much of the following.) HE GOES TO A COUNTRY FAR AWAY. IT IS A DANGEROUS COUNTRY: THE MAN NEEDS A GUN: the narrator shows the audience the gun and gives it to the man who shoulders it. IT IS A DANGEROUS COUNTRY: THE MAN NEEDS A GAS MASK: the narrator shows the gas mask to the audience, gives it to the man, the man puts it around his neck. IT IS A VERY DANGEROUS COUNTRY: THE MAN NEEDS AN AIRPLANE: the narrator shows the audience the (toy) plane and gives it to the man who puts it into his bag. – WHILE THE MAN IS WALKING (the man marches) (music off, sound of steps) HE IS SHOT IN THE ARM (cymbal clash, the man cries out): the man raises his arm. (Music back on:) the woman puts a bandage around his arm. HE GETS A MEDAL: the narrator shows the audience the medal and goes and puts it around the soldier's neck. – HE COMES TO A VILLAGE. THIS IS THE VILLAGE: the narrator shows the Vietnamese Woman mask to the audience and gives it to the woman who replaces her grey mask by it.

---

3. 'Narrator, standing at stage left, downstage, wears a skull mask and carries a sack. The sack contains props. A Woman, stands center stage in black robes, wearing a silver-grey mask. A Man stands center stage, wearing army fatigues or ordinary work clothes. A Trumpeter and a Bass Drummer stand at stage right, wearing skull masks.' (Bread and Puppet mss. of *Reiteration*.)

'Le narrateur, ... il a avec lui tous les accessoires. Deux musiciens. En principe un trompettiste et une grosse caisse; mais la trompette peut être remplacée par un mirliton. Ils doivent avoir aussi une paire de cymbales et une crécelle ... Une femme .... Elle porte la musette.' — (Kourilsky, '71.)

'Narrator, standing stage right, down front, wears a skull mask and carries a large sack over his shoulder. He looks like a beggar or a character from the *commedia*. His bag is full of props. A trumpeter stands upstage right, also in a skull mask. A woman in black robes with a silver-grey face mask stands center stage with her son, who wears no mask and is in army fatigues.' — (Anonymous synopsis, *Tulane Drama Review* #38, Winter 1968.)

This last source also describes a set:

'Three monochromatic backdrops painted on white sheets – an Asian village below the mountain. One drop is center, the others on either side: a drop and wing effect.'

The Bread and Puppet set indication:

'The street, or anywhere.'

THE WOMEN ARE COOKING SOUP: the narrator gives the soup kettle to the woman who mimes stirring it. THE MAN TAKES HIS AIRPLANE AND LOOKS FOR HIS ENEMY (music off: musicians and/or performers cry aaaaaaaaaaaaaaaaaaaaaaaaaaa):[4] the man takes the plane out of his bag and makes it tour over his head. THE VILLAGE IS AFRAID. – THE PEOPLE GO INTO THE FIELDS TO GATHER THEIR CROPS: the narrator gives the woman a small green branch. THE MAN POISONS THE CROPS: the man puts on his gas mask, the narrator gives him a piece of grey cloth, and the man drops it on the branch. – THE PEOPLE ARE AFRAID. THEY HIDE IN THEIR HOUSES: the narrator gives the woman a paper cutout of a house. She puts it in front of her face. THE MAN LIGHTS A MATCH AND BURNS THE HOUSES: the man lights a match and is about to burn the house, but the narrator stops him: THE NEW YORK CITY FIRE DEPARTMENT DOES NOT ALLOW THE BURNING OF HOUSES. SO THE MAN TEARS THE HOUSES TO PIECES: the man tears up the paper cutout. – THE CHILDREN ARE AFRAID. THEY HIDE WITH THEIR MOTHER: the narrator hands the mother a doll, she cradles it in her arms, rocks it. THE MAN TAKES HIS AIRPLANE AND LOOKS FOR HIS ENEMY. HE BOMBS THE CHILDREN (music off, musicians and/or performers cry aaaaaaaaaaaaaaaaaaaaaa): the man takes the plane out of his bag again, makes it turn over his head, then over the woman. (Cymbal clash.) The man holds his plane over the woman and the child. THE CHILDREN DIE (music back on): the woman slowly puts the doll down. THE WOMAN TAKES HER SCISSORS AND ATTACKS THE MAN (trumpet off, increasingly rapid drum beats): the woman stoops and picks up the scissors, rises and raises her arm to attack the man. The narrator takes her arm and guides it as she stabs the man in the back. AND DEATH LEADS HER HAND AND SHE STABS HIM[5] AND THE MAN DIES: the man falls. (Three drum beats. No more music.) – AND A LETTER IS SENT TO HIS MOTHER: the woman puts her grey mask back on, the narrator gives her a black carton envelope, she opens it and raises it above her head for the audience to read: 'We regret to inform you.' AND HIS BODY IS BROUGHT TO HER: the woman walks over to the dead man. AND SHE TAKES A WHITE SHEET: the narrator gives her a white sheet. AND SHE COVERS HIM: the woman covers him with the sheet.

---

4. *Tulane Drama Review* synopsis: 'all the characters make the buzzing sound of an airplane.'
5. Kourilsky has AND SHE KILLS HIM where the *Reiteration* script has AND DEATH LEADS HER HAND AND SHE STABS HIM: probably the latter text was not in *A Man*, but was introduced into *Reiteration*.

In the *Tulane Drama Review* synopsis the play ends:

'The Woman puts the dead child on the ground, pulls a pair of scissors from her robe and stabs the Son through the heart. The Narrator stands over the dead Son, covers his face with a sheet; there is a long, silent pause. He and the Woman carry the body off. Both the Narrator and the Woman are now wearing skull masks.'

'The story is narrated in presentational style by a symbolic figure (Death) and then translated into a series of symbolic actions performed in a slow and deliberate manner by masked puppet-like figures. There are no wasted movements, no superfluous dialogue, and no extraneous political rhetoric.'
(R. Argelander, *Bread and Puppet's Domestic Resurrection: The War is Over, Soho Weekly News*, August 19, '76.)

'(I: Could you describe the '68 version a little, you know as it was distinct from the '69.) Well, in the '68 version it was the classic . . . death leads her hand and she stabs – the village picks up the scissors and death leads her hand and then he comes over with a death mask and leads her hand until she stabbed him. Which I didn't find that offensive, or anything. I found it theatrical and I didn't feel that it took away from what *she* was doing, I thought that the death was in the *hand*, it wasn't, I didn't find it so mystical the way some people did. Mystical or . . . . it didn't occur to me that anything in it was unclear or not political enough. I just thought it was better than ice cream . . . . when I did it, I fought to have death do that too, I thought it was right. I thought – somehow it felt right. (I: How did some people see it as mystical?) Well, they say, well, death's leading her hand, no she is doing it herself, the Vietcong are strong enough they are doing it themselves without death helping them out. So, that is very crudely put but, but, but I was just, I was breathless when I saw it and I, and it was very strong . . . . I felt it was she. I thought it was the village, I thought it was the Vietnamese striking back. And that death leading her hand, it is death that she is wielding that the village is wielding in return for what they are getting. I didn't think that it was someone putting her up to it. I thought that the hand was then the hand of death, coming down to strike. It has, it goes back to Peter's old, to Peter's good and evil things, but I didn't think that it took away from the strength of the village. (I: But evil in the sense that there is some evil in that act.) Yes. And there *is*, for me . . . . Some evil is unavoidable, I mean, I mean not killing doesn't stop the killing either. I mean killing is going to happen anyway, I think.'

(Levy, interview.)

But to Schumann, as Murray Levy agrees,[6] identifying the Woman with Death in this manner makes her partake of evil. Whether this amounted to a condemnation of resistance, and if it did, should be done, agitated the Bread and Puppet group during their '69 European tour, and the performance probably was varied accordingly sometimes. The issue whether to meet violence with violence or turn the other cheek became focal in *Re-*

---

6. Levy came to the Bread and Puppet in '68 from the Free Southern Theatre and with them had done my father's *The Rifles of Mrs. Carrar*, which, not at all in the spirit of SNCC and Martin Luther King, advocates resistance to violence by violence: the slain son's mother distributes the guns.

iteration. It was really not raised by *A Man*, which presents the circle of violence as such. Like *Speech/Chairs*, however, *A Man* raised the issue of complicity. This issue had been absent in the three earlier *Sufferings of Vietnam* pieces, not even broached in *Fire*, when in productions anterior to the spring of '68, the villagers had given aid to a captured American identified as Negro, or in a metaphor of the U.S. rural pacification program, unmasked Americans imprisoned the self-immolator.

18. November '67, *Eating and Drinking in the Year of Our Lord 1621-1967*.

Development of a November 24, '66 anti-war parade, this show like the Christmas and Easter shows and like the later July 4th parades is integrated into the national calendar of feasts, but negatively, not picking up on the propriety of the Lord's Prayer, but a disgusted comment on the gluttonous essence of Thanksgiving, feast of hogs in a starving world, like *Speech/Chairs* a reproach to an overweight nation.[1] It's the first appearance of the Noble Savage in Schumann's work. He reappears in the circus pageants of the mid-'70s. The playlet's anti-materialism links the '62 *Ceremony of the Things* with the *Consumer Cycle* of the '70 circus. As for how it was done, I don't know: apparently there were no puppets and, except for the Vietnamese Woman mask on one performer, no masks. I presume costuming touches identified the pilgrims. It was billed as a 'new work commissioned by the presbytery of New York.'

'It was a Thanksgiving celebration ... in the sanctuary of the church. Large tables (had been) set up, and the congregation had been eating, and we knew about this, and we were asked to do something, and we asked the Reverend Glenesk and his Elders to leave all the food and all the things there at the end of the Thanksgiving dinner .... The first part of the action (was) the meeting of the Chief Massassoit who was a wild man who came down from the balcony, and was dressed up wildly and painted wildly (Elka: That was Maurice (Blanc). (Then) there was the countdown with the cannon – where the two groups would get into position –) They would *almost* be about to shoot him, and then decided, just at the moment when the gun was to *shoot* – there was a real countdown – they did not shoot, they dropped the gun instead, and *cheered*, and invited the chief to the table, to commemorate that first meeting of the Pilgrims and the friendly Indian chief .... And then we sat down around this table and passed around among

---

1. *Village Voice* ad of November 16, '67: performances at Spencer Memorial Church, Thanksgiving Day, November 23 and the following Sunday, November 26, '67. *Eating and Drinking* etc. (now: '*In the Year of Our Lord 1968*') was done in '68 at Judson Memorial Church, and, under the sponsorship of the Greenwich Village Peace Center, at Washington Square Methodist Church on December 4. Something like it had in between been fifth of the 'experimental plays' (*Bread and Puppet Theatre Diary November '67-March '68*) done at St. Peter's Church January-February '68. The November or December '68 show was repeated more or less identically, except for adaptation to a peculiar space –' something like a pit, the people had to look down to see anything, ... very awkward to perform in' (Schumann, interview, '79) – in the Goddard College Library, the 'D Basement Studio,' on November 21, '70. I am not aware aware of any '69 show.

According to a note by Elka on a script of this performance, it was done again, on Cate Farm, in '71, but no performance of it in '71 is listed in the January '73 Bread and Puppet Theatre history of the Bread and Puppet Theatre.

each other a tin with rouge and people picked up the rouge out of that tin and smeared it broadly over their lips, made huge ugly lips on everybody, and then the eating started. (Elka: No, first was the eating. The rouge came way later at the very end, because it was a very *jolly* scene (at first (SSB)), with everyone sitting there saying "let us give thanks to the Lord." People would pick up the salt shaker and put salt on corn flakes or turkey or whatever – for his glory, forever. And that was when Margo came out dressed as a Vietnamese woman with the baby.) The scene changed, as Ma pointed out, with this smearing of the rouge on the lips, and this starting to eat and the Vietnamese Woman going around and taking the food out of people's mouths. (Elka: Didn't you send somebody to the library to find all these things? Because *you* didn't know anything about Chief Massassoit.) Yes, the *text* was used also . . . we performed the text that was *read*, that described this moment of the meeting. (Elka: Who did the reading?) Charlie (Adams) did.' (Schumann, interview, '79.)

By the summer of '69 at the Royal Court Theatre, London, the piece looked like this:

'Begins with the appearance of the near-naked Indian who slowly crawls forward on a plank into the centre of the auditorium and there sits erect, watching the stage. The lights come up on brightly-coloured, childlike cloths of trees and flowers. "Let the pilgrims appear!" declares a narrator, who then proceeds to read an account of the arrival of the Pilgrim Fathers on 21 November 1620. The pilgrims enter through the auditorium and stand below the stage, laughing and sending up the official record, telling the audience how it really was. "We didn't find any people – only savages!" One of them produces an arrow shot at them by an Indian – "We saved it to show you!"

"Let the wind blow on the 21st November 1620!" says the narrator, and the actors blow through their hands.

"Let the birds sing on the 21st November 1620!" declaims the narrator, and the actors warble and flute and trill.

"Let the leaves fall!" – and from the roof of the theatre descend large green leaves plucked from the plane trees in the square outside.

"Let the first snow-flakes fall!" and pieces of torn white paper flutter down on the audience. "Now let's start the hail storm!" wise-cracks one of the actors.

A table is brought on, plates, mugs, food are distributed and the Red Indian is invited to take the place of honour in the centre where he sits nobly and impassively throughout the following action, totally ignored by the actors. The company begin to say grace and this develops into a syncopated improvisation with the recurring phrase – "For His mercy endureth for ever." At its climax and the clapping and chanting stop abruptly and cease. Schumann's voice is heard saying – "Who does not give food to all people." There is silence. The actors remove their outer clothing, smear red round their lips, and then proceed to eat and drink with a concentrated gluttony. For a long time we hear nothing but the absorbed munch and crackle of food, the dribble of liquid poured into mugs. Then the Vietnamese peasant woman in black, bearing her dead baby, appears. She is a recurring symbol in all Schumann's work and the central character in the playlet, *A Man Says Goodbye to his Mother*.

Now the figure moves slowly from actor to actor in silent rebuke, brushing the food from their hands, turning the plates over and placing the mugs upside down. Gradually all stop eating and stand in silence, stunned, lurid blood-red liquid glistening around their mouths. The woman disappears. Suddenly the Indian sings – "When Jesus wept a falling tear." The play is over. There is silence. The cast slowly pack up. There is no applause. We are stunned. One of the actors calls out – "That's it, folks!" Quietly the audience leaves, though many sit on thoughtfully, or move on to the stage to mingle with and talk to the actors. The entire work has the impact of an early American primitive painting, naive, intensely felt, a simple yet sophisticated folk tale, sacramental in its impact.'

(J. Roose-Evans, *Experimental Theatre*, 1973.)

And by '70/'71:

'SCENE I

Thunderstorm. Lighting. Chief Massasoit paraded in by beasts with torches.

SCENE II

Pastor: Let the sun shine on Chief Massassoit on the 16th day of November, in the Year of Our Lord, 1620.
(All lights turned on. Paper sun held behind Chief Massassoit.)
Let the Pilgrims arrive on the 16th day of November, in the Year of Our Lord, 1620.
(Pilgrim gentlemen in tophats, ladies in shawls enter with instruments, playing and singing:)

"We gather together to ask the Lord's blessing,
He chastens and hastens His will to make known.
The wicked oppressing, now cease them from distressing,
Sing praises to His name, He forgets not His own."

Pastor: Let the wind blow on the 16th day of November, in the Year of Our Lord, 1620. (All blow.)
Let the last leaves fall on the 16th day of November in the Year of Our Lord, 1620.
(Fall leaves are scattered.)
Let the pine woods smell on the 16th day of November in the Year of Our Lord, 1620.
(Aerosol pine smell sprayed around.)
Let the first snowflakes fall on the 16th day of November in the Year of Our Lord, 1620.
(Paper scraps dropped from balcony and flung around.)

Pastor recites text of the hardships of life in the New World:

Let us seriously consider this poor people's present condition, the more to be raised up to admiration of God's goodness towards them in their preservation: For being now passed the vast ocean, and a sea of troubles before in their preparation, they had now no friends to welcome them, no inns to entertain or refresh them, no houses, much less towns, to repair unto to seek help or succor; the Barbarians that Paul the Apostle fell amongst in his shipwreck, at the Isle of Melito, shewed him no small kindness, Acts XXVIII, but these savage Barbarians, when they met with them (as after will appear) were readier to fill their sides full of arrows, than otherwise; and for the season it was winter, and they that know the winters of that country, know them to be sharp and violent, subject to cruel and fierce storms, dangerous to travel to known places, much more to search unknown coasts. Besides, what could they see but a hideous and desolate wilderness full of wild beasts and wild men? And what multitudes of them there were, they then knew not.

Necessity now calling them to look out a place for habitation, and night coming on, they betook themselves to their rendezvous, and set out their sentinels, and rested in quiet that night.

But presently, all on a sudden, about the dawning of the day, they heard a great and strange cry. The cry of the Indians was dreadful, (their note was after this manner, Woach, woach, ha hach, woach) . . .

(All through the text, the Pilgrims participate in a lively and loud manner, commenting on, correcting, interrupting the Pastor's words. Now they fall silent.)

Chief Massassoit:

(Screams, long, weird, amplified, or whistles into cupped hands.)

(Lights out. Only lantern or candles of Pilgrims. Pilgrims get into positions: alarm, chaos, terror, protection, aggression, readying gun, aiming; men around weapon which is made of instruments, tophats, cardboard; women huddling in back. And Chief Massassoit gets into position to throw spear. After each count positions are changed, during speaking positions are frozen.)

Pastor:	Let the Pilgrims and Chief Massassoit meet on the 16th day of
(or man	November in the year of Our Lord, 1620:
shouting	TWO MINUTES LEFT.
through	Let the Pilgrims and Chief . . .
megaphone)	ONE MINUTE THIRTY SECONDS LEFT.
	Let the Pilgrims and Chief . . .
	ONE MINUTE LEFT.
	FIFTY SECONDS LEFT.
	FORTY SECONDS LEFT.
	THIRTY SECONDS LEFT.
	TWENTY SECONDS LEFT.
	TEN SECONDS LEFT.
	9 . . . 8 . . . 7 . . . 6 . . . 5 . . . 4 . . . 3 . . . 2 . . . 1 . . .
	NO TIME LEFT.

(At cymbal clash Pilgrims throw down gun, Chief Massassoit throws down spear, all clap hands and sing fast the hymn: We Gather Together. Pilgrims rush to Massassoit, welcoming him. Men bring in long table, chairs; women spread out dropcloth under table, tablecloth, bring in food. Massassoit is greeted, led to place of honor. All take seats.)

Pastor: O give thanks to the Lord
Who gives food to all flesh
For his mercy endureth forever.

All Pilgrims: O give thanks to the Lord who gives:
         (peanut butter) (sauerkraut) (rice krispies) (beefsteak) (watermelon, etc.)
         To all flesh for His mercy endureth forever.

(All Pilgrims chant in unison, clap hands, bang spoons, in different rhythms, and take turns picking up article of food and calling out its name as substitute for 'food'.)

Pastor: Who does not give food to all people.
(or Pilgrim)

(All fall silent. Pilgrims take off costumes, underneath are ordinary clothes. They smear red (ketchup, stage blood which is on the table) on their mouths and begin a slow-motion real eating and drinking. A woman in black with FIRE mask and baby doll in her arms, enters and walks slowly around the table, taking food, cups from mouths and hands of the eating Pilgrims, until all have ceased eating. Then she leaves. All sit quiet.)

Chief   When Jesus wept, the falling tear
Massassoit: In mercy flowed beyond all bound.
(sings)   When Jesus groaned, a trembling fear
            Seized all the guilty world around.
            (hymn by Josh Billings)'

(Bread and Puppet Theater mss.,
Goddard College, Vermont, November, 1970.)

'Our great stuff was all based on guilt .... Best example was the *Eating and Drinking in the Year of Our Lord* when the Pilgrims are there and we had that big feast at Spencer Church. Food was — just scarfing it out like maniacs, right? And then this Vietnamese woman comes. What did she do? She turned the plates over or — you know — this kind of heavy-handed guilt trip.'   (Ernstthal, interview.)

19. January-March '68. *When Johnny Comes Marching Home.*

During the winter of '67/'68, Schumann was rerunning *Fire* at the Washington Square Methodist Church and, January 26-February 23, Friday evenings did 'protest presentations directed at critical problems of the day' at St. Peter's Church (*Village Voice Off-Off-B'way Guide*, February 1,8,15), in the *Bread and Puppet Diary November '67-March '68*, a report to a fund granter, more civilly referred to as 'experimental plays':

'Rehearsals were held on Tuesday nights and were open to the public. Several of the plays used the materials which had recently been made at our workshop. After all the plays the cast remained for coffee and discussion with the audience, and during one of the plays instruments were handed out to the audience, who joined in the playing. The plays were: January 26: a silent drama, using 1 foot high papier maché figures, manipulated by actors; February 2: a slapstick farce, based on one of our newspapers; two hand-painted movies, with band sound, and audience participation; February 16: a mask drama, based on current events; February 23: a play based on a modern interpretation of the feast of Thanksgiving.' (*Bread and Puppet Diary November 67-March '68.*)

The 'silent drama' was probably the first version of *When Johnny Comes Marching Home*, a play that like *Eating and Drinking* modifies his Vietnam protest by developing his criticism, incipient in *Speech/Chairs*, of the war-supporting U.S. Common Man: an angry switch on *A Man Says Goodbye*. Here the boy comes home and the parents welcome him – the killer. It was his contribution, March 30 and 31 '68, to the First American Radical Theatre Festival[1] at the Washington Square Methodist Church, a festival organized by the Radical Theatre Repertory, a booking agency that Saul Gottlieb had organized early in '68.[2]

---

1. 'First American Radical Theatre Festival. Open Theatre, Pageant Players, Bread & Puppet Theatre, The Performance Group, The Gut Theatre. Sat March 30 & Sun March 31, 8:30 pm. Washington Square Methodist Church, 133 W 4th St. Benefit for *Radical Booking Agency*, nation-wide cooperative including above ensembles plus: San Francisco Mime Troupe, El Teatro Campesino, Minneapolis Fire House Theatre, Boston OM Theatre Workshop, Black Troupe of N.Y. Contribution: $3 & $2.' (*Village Voice* ad of March 21, '68.) An ad of March 28 specifies the performances: the Open Theatre, an improvisation, the Pageant Players, *James Bond*, the Gut Theatre, *City Trips*, the Performance Group, *Ritual* (a birthscene from their *Dionysius in 69* (SSB)), the Bread & Puppet Theatre, *Chairs* & *Johnny Comes Marching Home.*
2. 'Pour établir des liens plus étroits entre ces théâtres radicaux et les aider à organiser leurs tournées, Ronnie Davis avait eu l'idée d'une sorte de coopérative, mais l'association *Radical Theatre Repertory* (R.T.R.) organisée au début de 1968 par un ancien membre du Living Theatre, Saul Gottlieb, et par Oda Jurges, est vite devenue une sorte de vaste potpourri rassemblant des théâtres dont certains n'avaient de radical que le nom qu'ils

Developing the use of small figures and toys of the '65 *War Demonstration*, into an elaborate placing, replacing and removing of small – around 12 inches tall – doll figures and groups of doll figures made of paper maché, *Johnny* constitutes an extension of Schumann's medium. Its technique is that of movie-making: a succession of groupings in front of an imaginary camera. The 'Johnny puppets' hadn't been made for *Johnny*. Schumann tried using them in various other ways – on sticks, mounted on the heads of shrouded performers – before he did this table show with them, 'in which they would be used like little demonstration pieces' (Schumann, interview, '79), but this 'experiment' was

'the one that was most successful.... We put them on the table, and take them off the table whenever they are needed. That was a very flexible show.'
(Schumann, interview, '79.)

One of the earlier experiments was that January 'silent drama':

'We also used them several times in events that were one-time events, where they were used on the floor. I remember one of them in a church in New York somewhere, in midtown Manhattan, where a cello player, Andy Woodner, she was a cellist who was also with us in Maine, and the Johnny puppets to the sound of that cello and percussion sound were moved diagonally across a room. A slow progression of inching them forward and then creating a clash situation, where all the ones that were soldiers in the army met the other ones that were peaceful Johnnies and women Johnny puppets.' (Schumann, interview, '79.)

The inspiration for the play came from the destruction of the Vietnamese

---

s'attribuaient: en 1968, la Daytop Theatre Company (formée d'anciens drogués) jouait *The Concept* off-Broadway dans le circuit commercial normal à cinq dollars la place, tandis que le Performance Group jouait *Dionysos in '69* off-off-Broadway, dans un garage savamment aménagé, pour le même prix, et le même public averti. Le Theatre in the Street dirigé par Patricia Reynolds, théâtre idéalement intégré (trois Noirs, trois Blancs, trois Porto-Ricains) qui grâce à des subventions et à l'aide d'un superbe camion doté des derniers perfectionnements techniques, fait l'aumône d'un répertoire classique (Goldoni, Shakespeare, Tchekov) aux habitants "Déshérités" des quartiers noirs et porto-ricains de New York, voisinait avec le Gut Theatre (le Théâtre de la Tripe) dirigé alors par Enrique Vargas. Dans le quartier porto-ricain de East Harlem, Vargas travaillait avec des bandes d'adolescents auxquels il demandait d'improviser des sketches à partir de leur expérience quotidienne. Les enfants avaient fini par créer leur propre commedia dell'arte dont les principaux types étaient Papo (le Porto-Ricain) et Captain America.

Fin mars 1968, le premier Festival du Théâtre radical américain organise par la R.T.R. a lieu à la Washington Square Methodist Church (y participent l'Open Theatre, le Gut Theatre, les Pageant Players, le Performance Group et le Bread and Puppet Theatre). En 1969, Saul Gottlieb et Oda Jurges consacrent le plus clair de leur activité à organiser la tournée du Living Theatre aux Etats-Unis, d'où le mécontentement de certaines troupes s'estimant négligées et des dettes importantes mettant en danger l'existence de la R.T.R.: celle-ci ne pourrait être "sauvée" que par la Fondation Rockefeller qui offre une subvention, dont les membres "radicaux" ne veulent évidemment pas. Composée comme elle l'était, la R.T.R. ne pouvait qu'éclater.' — (Kourilsky, '71.)

village of Ben Suc, reported in the *New York Times* of January 11, 13 and 16, '68 (and subsequently described by Orville Schell in the *New Yorker*).

The focus now is on war crimes. Schumann's mood has changed from sadness to anger, and the performance-rhythm correspondingly from the elegiac to staccato. The Johnny puppets are what in Schumann's home country are called 'Kleinbürger': effectively the patriotic American white-but-ethnic blue collar class: Schumann is not about to idealize the parents among them:

'Come on mothers throughout the land, pack your boys off to Vietnam. Come father don't hesitate send your son off before it's too late, and you can be the first ones in your block to have your boy come home in a box.'

(Fourth verse of Country Joe and the Fish's '68 *Fixing to Die Rag* – Country Joe in '68 had three LPs among the top ten.)

The Bread and Puppet Theater 1969 script:

'Set: A table, perhaps 15 feet long, covered with a white cloth, is placed at center stage.

The table is illuminated from the front by flood lights mounted at the tops of two long wooden poles stuck into concrete blocks.

The cast, as members of a band, is gathered at stage right.

Props: Small papier-maché (or Celastic) figures of

    Seated Men
    Soldier Johnny
    Seated Johnny
    Mrs. Johnny
    Mrs. Johnny and Child
    Cook
    Women with upraised arms
    Male and female, double figure
    Soldiers, walking, aiming guns, kneeling
    Dead bodies
    Tanks
    Cart
    Automobile
    Mourning women
    Mourning women, painted with flowers, holding babies and –
    Cardboard table with papier-maché cup, plate, and food
    Wooden airplane
    Small cardboard "TV" set
    Large cardboard "TV" set

Other Equipment: Loudspeaker, amplifier, microphone; tape recorder and taped street noises; strobe light; large wooden door, painted white; pink spot light, mounted on long pole.

Costumes: Black cloth skirt and hooded shirt

Waiter costume (red jacket, fantastic mask, napkin on arm)

All other members of cast wear ordinary street clothes, dark in color.

(JOHNNY COMES MARCHING HOME is a table puppet play. The story is told by a series of tableaux displayed on a large table, by puppeteers performing specific tasks around and behind the table, and by music and narration.)

The stage is totally dark.

The band, grouped at stage right, plays "Johnny Comes Marching Home" and repeats the tune playing vigorous rhythmic variations.

In darkness, the Seated Johnny puppet is placed on the table and the narrator says

NUMBER ONE. JOHNNY

Two flood lights, mounted on either side of the table on poles set in concrete blocks, illuminate the tableau.

Light is cut and the band resumes playing "Johnny Comes Marching Home" in new, tight, chopping variations.

In darkness, a prop TV set and the Mrs. Johnny puppet are placed on the table; both Mrs. Johnny and Johnny are arranged facing the TV set. The narrator says

NUMBER TWO. TEE-VEE

The flood lights illuminate the tableau.

Light is cut, and the band plays "The Star Spangled Banner".

In darkness, the Johnny and Mrs. Johnny puppets are removed and replaced with a single puppet of Johnny and Mrs. Johnny embracing.

The narrator makes the noise of a juicy kiss and the lights illuminate the tableau.

Light is cut and the band resumes playing the national anthem while

> the embracing couple puppet is removed and replaced by the Seated Johnny puppet;
>
> an automobile is placed at one end of the table;
>
> a wooden door, painted white, is placed at stage right near the table and held by a puppeteer;
>
> a puppeteer stands near the table amid a group of Seated Men puppets placed on the floor.

NUMBER THREE. ARRIVAL OF FRIENDS

The lights come on as one of the musicians makes the noises of a car's motor, the stopping of the car, the opening and closing of the car door, and puppeteers at either end of the table, using a long rope, pull the papier-maché automobile across the length of the table. When the car reaches the end of the table, and the car stops, a knocking is heard at the door, the puppeteer operating the door shouts

WHO IS IT?

and the puppeteer standing among the Seated Men and holding one before him, shoulder high, replies

IT'S MAURICE!

and the door is pivoted open and the Seated Man Maurice puppet is placed on the table next to Seated Man Johnny as a voice on the microphone, supplemented by puppeteers gathered close to the table roar a welcome

COME IN, MAURICE. HAVE A SEAT. HOW ARE YOU?
LONG TIME NO SEE!

The door closes. The car moves across the table again and the previous action and sounds are repeated until all eight or nine of Johnny's friends have arrived for a visit, and have been seated. Each arrival results in different groupings of Seated Men puppets. The scene ends when the automobile on its last crossing drives off the end of the table crashing to the floor; the band and amplified voice make the sound of a car crash; the light is cut. The entire scene is played with a frenetic exuberance.

In darkness, the narrator announces

NUMBER FOUR. LET'S EAT.

The light comes on. A Waiter, in a fantastic mask, wearing a red coat, with a napkin over his arm and in baggy pants, enters with a table. He puts the table before the Seated Men puppets who are arranged in a semi-circle; the Waiter offers food and drink to the Seated Men, while the band members vocalize a gabble of voices in cut phrases. The light is cut.

In darkness, the narrator announces

NUMBER FIVE. DEAD WOMAN.

The light comes on. A Woman, in black, enters dragging a papier-maché cart with a rope. On the cart lies a papier-maché figure of a Dead Woman. Upon reaching the table, the Woman takes the small table from among the Seated Men and hands it to the Waiter. The Woman then lifts the Dead Woman puppet, gently, and places it where the table had been in the center of the semi-circle of Seated Men; the Woman then exits. The light is cut.

In darkness,   (Tape recorded street noises begin.)

all of the Seated Men are turned facing away from the body, but still in a semi-circle;

the Waiter puts the prop table out of sight under the large table;

Seated Man Johnny is replaced with Marching Soldier Johnny Puppet,

and the narrator announces

NUMBER SIX. JOHNNY.

The light comes on to illuminate the tableau.

The light is cut; the tape recorded street noises are cut. In darkness, the table is cleared of the Seated Men and the Marching Johnny puppets. A Mourning Woman puppet is placed near the Dead Woman puppet. The narrator announces

NUMBER SEVEN. MOURNING

In silence, the light comes on to illuminate the tableau.

The light is cut.

The narrator announces

NUMBER EIGHT. DEAD BODIES

The light comes on and the Woman in black enters, dragging the cart which bears a Dead Body puppet. With the help of the Waiter the Woman lifts the body from the cart and places it on the table. The Woman exits with the cart and returns with another Dead Body, and repeats the previous action, making trip after trip until six or seven bodies are heaped on the table. The woman exits with the cart. The light is cut.

In darkness, very quickly,

> all Dead Body puppets are moved;
>
> some 5 or more Mourning Women are set out covering the table top;
>
> a puppeteer stands at the center behind the table;
>
> a puppeteer, standing at stage left, near the table, holds a small wooden airplane;
>
> a puppeteer stands nearby holding a long pole on which is mounted a pink spot light;
>
> a puppeteer, holding a strobe light, kneels downstage center;
>
> the Woman in black robes is standing facing the door which stands at stage right.

The narrator announces

NUMBER NINE. METAMORPHOSES.

The lights come on to illuminate the tableau.

The light is cut. The pink spot light comes on and, very closely, follows the action of the puppeteer with the airplane. The plane flies in a great sweeping circle and slowly comes down to a stop near the heads of the Mourning Women puppets. Action freezes. The pink spot is turned off; the strobe light comes on and the puppeteer behind the table removes the Mourning Woman who had been bombed, placing her under the table. The strobe is cut and the pink spot comes on, again following the airplane. This action is repeated three more times and after each bombing one or more Mourning Women are removed. This scene ends with the strobe light still flashing.

(The puppeteers make a humming sound for each airplane attack.)

NUMBER TEN. BEN-SUC.

Without stopping, and with the strobe light flashing, several puppeteers enter quickly and place the Mourning Women puppets at one side of the table; puppeteers from the other side have simultaneously set out a group of Soldier puppets at their end of the table, facing/aiming at the Mourning Women. The strobe light is cut.

(During the following scene all of the puppeteers continually yell out the text which is printed at the end of this script, ... Simultaneously, tape recorded street noises are heard.)

The strobe light comes on again and the Soldier and Mourning Women puppets are replaced by a tank aiming at a grouping of three Women puppets which have upraised arms. The strobe light is cut.

The strobe light comes on again, and the Tank and Women are replaced by a single Shooting Soldier aiming at a Single Woman. The strobe is cut. (This action is repeated three more times, ending in darkness and silence.)

The strobe comes on – aimed at the Woman in Black – while machine gun noises are made on the microphone and the Woman, slowly, staggers, sags, and falls to the floor dead. The strobe is turned into the eyes of the audience while the Woman resumes her standing position in front of the door. The strobe turns back to light the machine-gunning and death of the Woman. The action is repeated three more times, ending in darkness.

In darkness, the band plays "Johnny Comes Marching Home" with distortions of tempo and sharp cuts, while the Shooting Soldier and Single Woman puppets are replaced by the Marching Soldier Johnny puppet, and the narrator announces

NUMBER ELEVEN. COMING HOME.

The flood lights come on to illuminate the tableau.

The light is cut, and in darkness the band plays "Johnny Comes Marching Home" in a very fast tempo; the Mrs. Johnny puppet is placed on the table, greeting Johnny, and the narrator announces

NUMBER TWELVE. HOME.

The flood lights come on to illuminate the tableau.

The light is cut, and in silence the Soldier Johnny puppet is replaced by the Seated Johnny puppet. The narrator announces

NUMBER THIRTEEN. HOME.

The flood lights come on to illuminate the tableau.

The lights are cut and in silence a small prop TV set is placed on the table; Seated Johnny and Mrs. Johnny are turned to face the TV. The narrator announces

NUMBER FOURTEEN. HOME.

The flood lights come on to illuminate the tableau.

The lights are cut and in silence the small TV is replaced by a large cardboard TV. In it sits a puppeteer; the strobe light is stuck through a hole in the back of the box. The strobe is turned on, creating the silhouette of a TV newsbroadcaster who gesticulates and mouths (as narrator reads on microphone)

> A HELICOPTER EQUIPPED WITH LOUDSPEAKERS BEGAN BROADCASTING THIS MESSAGE: "ATTENTION PEOPLE OF BEN SUC! YOU ARE SURROUNDED BY REPUBLIC OF SOUTH VIETNAM AND ALLIED FORCES. DO NOT RUN AWAY OR YOU WILL BE SHOT AS V. C. STAY IN YOUR HOMES AND WAIT FOR FURTHER INSTRUCTIONS. YOU WILL NOT BE HURT IF YOU FOLLOW INSTRUCTIONS." THEN CAME A SECOND MESSAGE TELLING MEN, WOMEN AND CHILDREN, "GO IMMEDIATELY TO THE SCHOOLHOUSE. ANYONE WHO DOES NOT GO TO THE SCHOOLHOUSE WILL BE CONSIDERED A VIETCONG AND TREATED ACCORDINGLY." MOST OF THE RESIDENTS, CONSIDERED TO BE PASSIVE VIETCONG, FOLLOWED THE INSTRUCTIONS. FORTY-ONE DID NOT AND DURING THE DAY THEY WERE TRACKED DOWN AND KILLED. ONE HUNDRED MALES, 15 TO 45 YEARS OLD, UNABLE TO PROVE THEIR IDENTITY...[3]

Light and sound cut.'

'Bread & Puppet did a paper-maché parable on war, the reaction and reverberations: Hail Vietnam, alma mater who gave birth to all this theater. Their use of puppets is as sophisticated a technique as the also-used strobe-lights in the performance, and the B & P handles both dramatically. The death-ray feeling grows during the wierd use of a tiny plane whose shadow is thrown in huge magnification around the dark walls as it buzzes its way around the room on the end of a long pole. Somehow the body-snatching of the puppets was better than anything LeRoi ever wrote home about. Every time the plane hovered, a bunch of puppets was whisked off in dead silence.'

(L. Eliscu, *Theatre? East Village Other*, April 5-11, '68.)

The action of the play was so quick and the puppets so small that Eliscu's account pretty much covers what the audience got.

Schechner's Performance Group was doing the Birth Scene from his *Dionysius in '69* at this Festival, and Schechner interrupted the Pageant Players' *James Bond* on May 31st coming running in to announce Johnson's announcement that he wasn't going to send additional troops to Vietnam and was not going to run again: the Resistance Movement's pseudo-victory.

'There was an eclipse of the moon and Johnson announcing that he wouldn't run for president ... and that was an incredible event ... I remember standing on the church (steps) watching the moon get red and eclipsed. The announcement of Johnson came at the same time and it was really ecstatic ... Schechner, those guys were there – *Dionysius in '69*. But as you might have guessed, we were really at

---

3. Text from the *New York Times* of January 11, 13 and 16, 1967.

odds with those kinds of things because they were just the opposite. We were very, very controlled, real strict, and they were exploring the sexual, sweaty scene – muchs more – sweatiness – really a lot. Schechner was also an intellectual – and coming from different aspects of things. But that event was a real highlight in things.' (Ernstthal, interview.)

A reporter for *Die Weltwoche* (May 17, '68), speaking of the Pageant Players' 'sehr bemühende und ungeschickte' performance that evening, claims the audience when informed of Johnson's decision began to dance to rock music, and that the Reverend (Shaef) turned to them, saying 'Let us thank God for this act of liberation, presaging peace. Dance, be joyous, but remember that smoking in the church is prohibited.'

20. April-June '68. The first European tour. Fame in France.

Christian Dupavillon, a cultured Frenchman with some position in French cultural affairs, impressed by *Fire*, had gotten the theatre invited to the April '68 Festival Mondial du Theatre Jeune in Nancy,[1] and April 10 Schumann went, taking Sherman, Ernstthal and Maurice Blanc, his two actors and his narrator. They toured Europe for six weeks – after Nancy a week in Amsterdam, some performances in Utrecht, a week in London,[2] a week in Berlin. The Oyles went with them and the Eckhardts joined them in Europe but apparently didn't perform too much. They did *Fire, Dead Man Rises, A Man, Chairs/Speech, King Story*.

They were a tremendous success in France – in particular because of the inwardness, discretion and elegance of *Fire*[3] – somewhat less of a success

---

1. 'And Christian Dupavillon came to see (*Fire*) in the wintertime. And afterwards this guy came backstage with a ridiculous French accent and said, 'Do you want to come to a theatre festival in France?' And we laughed, because he was funny, had a funny accent, and it's like someone coming up to you and saying, would you like to make a movie in Hollywood. The Puppet Theatre? It wasn't part of our frame of reference. It was a joke. The theatre world, the *Village Voice* despised us, except for Arthur Sainer. We didn't think that people noticed us much.' — (Sherman, interview.)
2. 'Peter Schumann's Bread and Puppet Theatre, after a thumping success at the Nancy Festival, had a pretty hard time in London. As the result of gross mismanagement on the part of the Institute of Contemporary Arts, they were almost prevented from giving their first performance and, after winning that one, were forced to cancel the others. They did, however, play in a large settlement house auditorium in south London and give two street performances, one on Portobello Road and the other at Hyde Park.' — (Marowitz, *theatre abroad, Village Voice*, May 23, '68.)
3. '... la diversité des tendances exprimées invitant à la réflexion.
Par exemple, des boborygmes et des reptations de "Sir and Lady Macbeth" (Leo de Bernadinis et Perla Peragalo, de Rome) revivant, agrippés à un bidet, l'horreur de leur crime, au silence et à la quasi-immobilité des acteurs du "Bread and Puppet Theatre" de New York, nous faisant partager, dans "Fire", sept jours de la vie d'un village vietnamien qui finira par être detruit par le feu, il y a tout un monde: celui qui sépare un théâtre uniquement préoccupé de l'état intérieur de l'individu, tournant sans fin en rond sur lui-même, d'un théâtre ouvert sur le monde qui voudrait être pour les autres – comme le dit Peter Schumann, fondateur et directeur de la troupe new yorkaise depuis 1961 – "un aliment aussi essentiel que le pain". Et, bien que les deux spectacles supposent l'absence de tout texte, l'un, terriblement "bavard", dans une débauche de sons et de lumières, ne dit rien; l'autre dit tout avec les moyens les plus simples ....
A la fin d'un spectacle qui montre d'une façon intense, avec une telle économie de moyens, la réalité même de la guerre, il est évident que les spectateurs n'ont aucune envie d'applaudir et il est impossible d'imaginer une seconde que les cinq acteurs puissent revenir saluer le public. Nous sommes aux antipodes d'un spectacle du "Living Theater" ou même du "US" de Peter Brook, ou les acteurs, immobiles sur la scène, veulent gener le public qui

elsewhere, but all in all this was the first time that critics and audience consecrated Schumann as a Major Artist.[4] Future bookings were assured. They played in regular, even high class theatres for chichi audiences,[5]

---

ne sait s'il doit rester, applaudir ou sortir. Nulle provocation ici, nulle agression, nul exhibitionnisme, nul "artifice". Mais la plus simple beauté et la plus grande efficacité." — (*Théâtre aux quatre coins, le nouvel Observateur*, May 14, '68.)

'Une troupe qui n'était encore jamais venue en Europe, et dont on parle actuellement beaucoup aux Etats-Unis, le Bread and Puppet Theatre, aura créé le premieur grand choc de ce Festival mondial.... A Nancy, elle présente deux fois par jour, jusqu'à la fin du Festival, *Fire*....

Ce qui est si remarquable dans ce court spectacle, c'est qu'avec des moyens techniques extrêmement simples – une crécelle, un violon, une ampoule nue, une soupière, quelques masques, un rouleau de scotch rouge pour figurer les flammes – Peter Schumann arrive, réellement, et sans mots, sans agression terroriste sur la conscience ou sur les sens, à cerner la guerre et à faire passer de façon éclairante une vision du Vietnam; et soudain, mieux que les plaidoyers idéologiques, les films de bonne volonté, les images d'enfants napalmés, il nous donne la "réalité" même de cette guerre.

Le théâtre, même lorsqu'il est "théâtre de protestation", peut-il avoir une action sur le monde? Peter Schumann lui-même avoue n'en rien savoir. "Je ne crois pas que notre métier soit de protester," dit il, "mais de dire ce qu'il faut dire, ce qu'il est bon de dire." Et il est évident qu'il sait le dire admirablement." — (N. Zand, *Revelation du "Bread and Puppet" de New-York au festival de Nancy, Le Monde*, April 25, '68.)

4. 'I went through the first European tour. See, in a way – I was with the theatre until it got really successful – and '68 was the climax of that. We went to the festival at Nancy – theatre festival – and really we were lionized by the public there and that's when we went to Paris – and there was – the riots – they were in 1968 – and it was just this fabulous tour.... We were lionized by the festival and by, in general, the European intelligentsia there. And that was our first really gigantic success.... Everyone wanted us to play at *their* theatre and.... It was a tremendous success, and we went to Amsterdam, Paris, London and Berlin – at the Forum Theater in Berlin – and it was just great – totally great and absolutely fantastic. It was wonderful....

Also Nancy was a time when I got a taste of people trying to interview us. It was really exciting. Peter also got some relieved, although he would never show it. It was exciting. We were in demand. People were coming – please play at our place. Please come to Paris. Please come to London. Because it was our idea, since it was a lengthy trip, we had an original idea to go to Nancy, go to the festival, maybe Peter would go and see his parents, and then we'd go home. And if we could we would travel around according to what happened. But as it turned out all these theatre managers and stuff from Europe would come to this festival and book acts. So Amsterdam was calling us, Berlin, and all this stuff was happening. So we went through this tour from Nancy that was really interesting.' — (Ernstthal, interview.)

5. 'It could be quite yucky. Because we never had a chichi audience in New York, and suddenly we became a theatrical success in Europe, and it was the thing to do to come and see the Bread and Puppet Theatre. And a lot of people didn't like it or didn't understand it. Like in London we played at a chic little museum, the ICA I think it was called, and it was terrible there, it was horrible.... And Amsterdam, we worked at the Mickery, that was also horrible, terrible, at the time, it was way out in the country, a tiny little converted farmhouse, and again it was upper class chichi people who would drive out from Amsterdam to see this *Fire*. And they didn't like it and we didn't like them.' — (Sherman, interview.)

'Because "Fire" demands more than aesthetic appreciation from an audience, sometimes

whose enthusiasm in France was probably more disturbing to Schumann[6] than their antipathy in Berlin,[7] and they did street performances to ab-

---

elegant society crowds were able to view the play only from a limited current vampire-surrealism fad. They would comment on how effectively the white Vietnamese masks "worked" against the black cloth background, or how much they were impressed by our controlled stillness and movements.' — (M. Blanc, *Clowning with the Life Force, Village Voice*, September 5, '68.)

6. 'Travelling through Europe, Peter was suddenly put on the spot in a way he hadn't been in the States; theatre scholars and active craftsmen had read the recent interview in *The Drama Review*. Suddenly he was a world leader. And as we moved through Europe Peter was made to evaluate and reevaluate everything he had formerly designed and believed.' — (Blanc, *Clowning with the Life Force, Village Voice*, September 5, '68.

'And Peter could be very, very moody, more often on tour than at home. And it was so hard on tour, I was so afraid of him on tour, because he would get into such dark moods. Because we were having a lot of bad experiences and very disappointing experiences. That ridiculous place in London, the other stupid place in Amsterdam, were just terribly disappointing. And Peter would be so angry about it, and so he wouldn't be giving a lot of jokes and good nature to us . . . .' — (Sherman, interview.)

7. 'And *Fire* was terribly moving. People in the audience in Berlin – it played at the Forum Theatre and it was a midnight show, and it was the jet set from Berlin was coming and they weren't into it. So they were, they, I mean a lot of them were, and the Americans who came were devastated by it, but the Germans a lot of them, who came, the West Berliners who came, were, some of them made fun while it was going on, the ritualization of it, they weren't into, they wanted more action and less meditative stuff. And it is a meditation. I think that things have changed in Germany now, there is now more place for meditation. I know among the people that I know there is an awful lot of concentration on meditating and finding your center and working from inside out, rather than outside in. And I thought that *Fire* was a play that worked from inside to outside, not from outside to inside.' — (Levy, interview.)

'Then we went to Berlin. And by this time we had been in so many cities and we had such a reputation, that we thought for sure we'd be able to get work here. And Peter begged and pleaded for a place to perform. We got a job performing in the hallway of the Free University. In the hallway, off a staircase. And it was rough . . . students, classes breaking. And then we wanted a theatre where we could do *Fire* and he went four or five times begging to let us perform in his theatre . . . And he finally agreed to it. I don't know why he finally did, but he did . . . But we couldn't even go on at regular theatretime. We had to go on at 11:00 or midnight. There was a Peter Handke play, and after their show was over . . . at 11:00 they would quickly get off the stage, I don't think they had much of a set . . . . And we'd have to race on and quickly set up . . . . To do *Fire* and then be hissed at by the audience who would sit there, I don't understand German but, you know, saying things like . . . .' — (Sherman, interview.)

'The officials were tough on Bruno as we approached Berlin through the East German border where we got a taste of the repressive bureaucracy of East Berlin when we tried to visit the Berliner Ensemble. Peter was denied entrance because he was carrying a can of film (Jules Rabin's footage of the Bread and Puppet Theatre in the summer of '66 in East Harlem and the South Bronx) which we wanted to have Helene Weigel see. I went over myself easily the next two days, but Peter and Bruno still having German citizenship had had enough of grim reminders of the past.

Our initial entry into Berlin by train from Amsterdam was a tremendous shock. We were greeted by 30 chanting students who carried flags and expected us to be their vanguard against their "new Nazi leaders." Some of them were Americans from the exile

solve their consciences.[8] Their protest against American misdeeds in Asia sat only too well with bourgeois audiences disturbed by the revolutionary outbreak of May '68, and only too glad to demonstrate a capacity for moral outrage not focused on them. Still and all, Paris appreciation must have made up for the ignorant carpings and grudging mumblings of the New York critics, and fortified Schumann's artistic resolve — at a time when the ethical impetus on him of opposition to the war was weakening, and he needed it. And for Margo, Bob, and Maurice it was a magnificent

---

group called the U.S. Campaign Against the War. One of the latter was Murray Levy, formerly of the Free Southern Theatre, who acted as our liaison, etc. in Berlin.

That first night in Berlin Peter had long discussion with the militant Marxists who had volunteered to help us find places to perform whether on boards or in town squares. Aggressively they suggested new endings to our plays as they considered them too quietistic, too mystical, too resigned. A friend of Bruno's, Kott, who I believe had once been one of Brecht's aides was a gentle yet persistent gadfly on these matters. He was convinced that most reform is at this time impossible; assisting the death of freedom he said were the supposedly innocent stockholders and people with bank accounts who were in effect also shareholders and murderers of yellow men in Asia.

We performed in the Ford Building the night the Berlin students took over the Free University anticipating that the police would interrupt the speeches before we had a chance to do "Chairs." Untrue to form they did not come. We played on the Ku Damm at the Forum Theatre evenings at 11 to the Berlin jet set who laughed at the death scene and the air raid scene. And during the fire scene I found a new daemonic energy to wrestle in effect with the hardened cynicism and insensitivity out there. I threw the cloth flames over the mangled and twisted mannequins with a new intensity and power. To Peter, who is seldom lacking in courage, those performances are a bad memory, but to me they are reminders of how fear can disappear in the face of bestiality.

On our last day in Berlin Bob, Margo, Peter, Bruno and I were driven to a sidewalk next to the U.S. Army PX where we performed a short anti-war play. Fortunately we were being televised by the Cologne TV. The MP's merely had the German police take our names and passport numbers; otherwise, friends told us, we would have been beaten or arrested. Then, commitments in Denver and Newport brought us home.' — (M. Blanc, *Clowning with the Life Force, Village Voice*, September 5, '68.)

8. ' "Bread and Puppet" auront terminé leur séjour nanceien comme ils l'avaient commencé, au coeur de la ville, dans la rue. Hier matin ils ont debarqué leur grosse caisse et leurs accessoires au milieu de la place de la Carrière. En costumes noirs et avec les masques, tambour en tête et cymbales à l'appui, ils ont marché vers le terre-plein du palais du Gouverneur, suivis par les spectateurs devenus manifestants sans le savoir.

Aux marchés du Palais près des sentinelles, les comédiens jouèrent "A man says good bye to his mother" et cette aventure de guerre et de paix prit un profond relief. Les comédiens, a la dernière minute, deposèrent le soldat mort entre les gardes du Palais en un geste improvisé qu'on jugerait, chez nous, provocateur et qui, accompli par des Américains dans l'esprit du théâtre engagé de new York, était l'exemple d'une rare liberté d'expression et d'un sens sincère de la démocratie.' – (*Le Monde*, April 25 '68.)

The reviewer in the *Nouvel Observateur* (May 14) reports that the soldiers at the Palais du Gouverneur 'ricanant au début, se sont tus en voyant l'homme poignardé par la Vietnamienne dont il vient d'empoisonner la récolte, de détruire la maison et de tuer l'enfant.' What in a society like the U.S. that never had a peasant agriculture seems simplistic in Schumann's work, in one that has had one (and still had one in the mid-20th century) seems essentialist.

pay-off, anonymous though they might be. Not for Bruno, anarchist and revolutionary, who saw his Luther corrupted by the princes, and for whom the big event was not the Bread and Puppet accueil, but the approach, that spring, of revolution in France. His vivid and sympathetic interest in this contrasted with what, as far as I have been able to ascertain, was an attitude of nervous indifference on Schumann's part.[9] (When five years later the working classes stirred in East Germany, though my father eventually sided with the government, his interest was intense and his sympathies were with the insurgents.) The fourth important experience of the tour for Schumann, after the fancy theatres and the bourgeois public, the recognition verging on fame, and the mirage of revolution that did not stir him, was that the group made money. Their playing supported them and they came away with a small profit. He had found a way to support his art.

---

9. Eckhardt in Paris in May '67:
'Und dat war für mich 'ne sehr anstrengende Zeit. Ich hab gewartet bis die Leute eingeschlafen sind. Ich weiss nicht warum ich das gemacht habe, ich hätte ja auch sagen können, ich geh mal eben, aber meistens bin ich, hab ich mich so davon gestohlen und bin dann morgens wieder los und war dann aber immer rechtzeitig wieder da, wenn der Minibus kam um uns, um unsere Truppe abzuholen nach, da wo wir dann spielen wollten, das war'n Vorort, ich weiss jetzt nicht mehr genau. Und ich hab mich die ganze Nacht dann da draussen aufgehalten, um zu gucken, was da los ist. (I: Und was war mit Schumann, seine Reaktion dazu?) Der hat überhaupt keine Durchsicht. Der hat, seine Reaktion dazu die war, die war sehr gemischt, die war nicht eindeutig. Und vor allen Dingen hat er damals schon angefangen so, der fängt an sich zurückzuziehen. Ich hatte damals so meinen grossen Mao-butten da an'ner Jacke und dat war nun, naja, sehr, dat hat ihm alles nicht gefallen.... Aber gut, dat war 'ne Provokation. Dat waren diese dicken Mao-Dinger, da ist ja dat ganze Volk mit rumgelaufen, so diese Klötze. War natürlich 'n Ärgernis, nicht. Ich hab, naja gut, ich hatte für'n Mao-Tse-Tung 'ne ganze Menge übrig, hab ich auch heute noch. Und die Leute die auf'n Barikaden standen, dat waren auch zum grössten Teil Maoisten und da hab ich mich natürlich hingezogen gefühlt, nicht. Ja, bin ich da gewesen. Ich stand nicht hinter der Barikade, ich meine, ich war 'n Schatten. Ich hab alle Leute als Clown benutzt, um da rumzuspringen ohne dass man mich kascht. Ich bin nur einmal in 'ne heikle Situation gekommen, da ham'se mich mit diesen verdammten Pfefferkuchen beschossen. Und ich hatte auch immer so'n Anorak an, so'n Ding und die sind daran abgeprallt, ja, und haben nur so kleine Brandstellen hinterlassen.... Und dann kam 'ne unheimliche Flut von Informationen auf uns zu, die ich verdauen musste und so und das waren alles Sachen, die den Peter einen Scheissdreck interessierten. Ich hab mich damals zum Beispiel interessiert für die, für die Landkommunen in China. Ich find Kommunen gut und die ersten Kommunen, ich weiss nicht, es hat überall Kommunen gegeben. Die amerikanischen Ureinwohner, die haben immer nur so in diesen Kommunen gelebt, deren Kultur besteht ja daraus. Und ich hab irgendwie an so 'ne Wiederkehr von, von, von, dat war natürlich auch 'ne Illusion, ich weiss es nicht, ich hab an irgendwat Neues geglaubt, hat mich berauscht. Und die ersten Gedichte, die von den Bauern selber geschrieben waren, die waren nicht von Parteifunktionären und so weiter geschrieben. Die waren, die waren von den Leuten selber geschrieben, die ja noch gar nicht mal so richtig schreiben konnten. Und dat alles, dat hat mich unheimlich fasziniert. Und dat sollte so auch irgendwie zur Sprache kommen oder sollte sich irgendwie ausdrücken. Ja, nicht, in Paris hat es sich ausgedrückt, gegen dieses ganze, dieser ganze Unwille gegen dieses starre, man kann schon sagen Polizeidik-

tatur da, nicht, in dem man auf die Barikaden ging. Dat war 'ne Euphorie, die war ungeheuer, die Leute haben wirklich wat gezeigt. Und da war 'ne Aufbruchstimmung zu 'ner ganz neuen Sache, irgendwie kriegte man frische Luft in'ne Lunge, die war auch meistens voll Tränengas, ja, aber dat war wat.' — (Eckhardt, interview.)

'There was a strike in a factory – performing there, going inside the factory, being taken to lunch and discovering what a French union was like. And then of course, May of '68 in Paris, there we were, in your apartment, all sleeping on the floor, because we could only ... it was half the apartment? On the red tiles. And all of a sudden something was happening in Paris, in your neighborhood, and we didn't know what it was. And some of us were scared. I was scared. Bruno wasn't scared. He would go out almost every night, very late at night, walking around, observing, watching everything, and he would come back the next morning to report on what had happened. Tearing up the grates in the streets, and students fighting. And then we marched with the people on May Day .... In Paris. (I: How was that?) I think it must have been different for everybody. I felt like, in a daze, I didn't know what was happening. Peter looked the way I felt, but maybe he was a lot more aware than I perceived. Bruno was thrilled .... (I: Schuman looked how?) A little dazed at what's happening, and I'd feel out of my waters and feel somehow I am in support and yet at the same time I don't really feel like this is my world. I felt comfortable with puppets and with theatre. Bruno was thrilled, because he was always very, very political. (I: But Schumann not thrilled ...) I don't know. You see, I never talked to him about things like that. I'm sure that he and Bob talked, and he and Bruno talked .... I think we had to go to, it must have been Berlin .... I think we left the next day. We did that long, hot walk with everybody on May Day. And then it got to the end of the place, prescribed route, and then there was some discussion, what are we gonna do, where are we gonna go, and then a lot of people ran off and occupied buildings, but we didn't go with them. The Sorbonne, the – I forget the name of the theatre, the one where Jean-Louis Barrault ....' — (Sherman, interview.)

21. September '68. *Reiteration*.

Returned from Europe, Schumann in a Maine retreat commenced the work that led to his last play of the '60s, *The Cry of the People for Meat*, but on his return to New York, toward the end of August, he interrupted this work, and put in two weeks at the Old Courthouse expanding *A Man Says Goodbye* to *Reiteration* from about 12 minutes to about an hour and a half – and changing a play addressed to the public and opposing the war to a play addressed, really, to the Resistance Movement itself and debating the proper forms of resistance, i.e. expressing squeamishness about homicide[1] – and then went to San Francisco, hippie heaven, to show it at a Radical Theatre Festival there, the second one after New York's first, symposium and workshop on the theatrical forms of resistance, organized by Ronnie Davis, then still in charge of the San Francisco Mime Troupe. Besides *Reiteration* they did *King Story*, *Dead Man Rises* and the *Rat Movie*, at San Francisco State and various places in the Bay Area. He was showing off his art to the other boys – Davis of the Mime Troupe, Valdez of El Campesino – who, it seemed to him were stuck in worn-out theatrical conventions. The 'kids' – this was the sunset of the flower kids – lapped up his stuff, viz. the mysticism-religiosity that made Valdez and Davis uneasy, and that right along everybody has known Schumann is into without anybody ever being able to lay their hands on evidence that would convict. Because of its repetitions, *Reiteration* had an aspect of ritual and of hypnotism that other groups were grooving with (Performance Group, Living Theatre) and that the 'kids' could dig. Both Valdez and Davis borrowed from him,[2] he didn't from them: in fact, what mime of Davis' he saw may have contributed to his effective decision to cut down on the mime that since '66 the Bread and Puppet had been getting into.

They took *Reiteration* to Europe in '69, not as replacement of *A Man*, but as indoor version of it. Unlike *A Man*, it didn't stay in the repertory.

---

1. '*Reiteration* ... was a second part to *Man Says Goodbye to His Mother*. We tried using that theme and milling it around and demonstrating man's fate a bit more intensely and asking some questions that were pertinent to that scene. Why and how come a man should go and do what this man did, and whether or not he should get punished for this. That was basically the idea of a court martial.' — (Schumann, interview, '79.)
2. E.g. El Campesino made a crankie out of *A Man* and performed it accompanied by mime. — (Levy, interview.)
'He gave it to a Chicano group too, you know he trained them how to do it and gave them the masks and so forth so they could go on doing it in their area. I think he did that on several occasions, where he gave that piece to people to use it.' — (Shapli, interview.)

The last performance of it I know of was in Toronto in August '70.

The original expansion of *A Man* into *Reiteration* consisted in the addition of three parts: a repeat of the play in which the text had been abbreviated but the mime expanded, and which stops just before the Vietnamese mother kills the G.I., the narrator stopping her; a trial of the soldier in which he is questioned by the woman, first as the killed child's mother, then as his mother, then as the Vietnamese mother again – questioned as to the facts, the narrator reporting questions and answers; this trial ending with his mother's preparing him for his execution and handing his gun to some other performer, and with his execution or not, depending on whether a member of the group is willing to execute him;[3] and a trial of the woman by the group for which there was no set text, so that it depended on the questions asked by the questioners whether the Vietnamese woman appeared more guilty or more justified and on their and her actions whether she ended up with only her guilt or as resistance fighter. The first part, the recapitulation, apparently was dropped after the September '68 performances.[4]

The next text (according to the Bread and Puppet *Reiteration* script) and action (according to the reconstruction in Kourilsky '71) before the repetition of the play was dropped went somewhat like this (the lines initially are all the skull-masked narrator's):[5]

'HIS MOTHER IS COOKING SOUP: the woman, wearing the soldier's mother's grey mask, mimes stirring the soup. THE MAN SAYS GOODBYE TO HIS MOTHER: the man and the woman embrace. HE GOES TO A

---

3. At some performances the gun was offered to members of the audience, e.g. in the August '70 Toronto one. (E. Thalenberg, *Not by Bread Alone*, artscanada, December '70.)
4. 'Plus, there was a bunch of mime scenes that were made up in the fall of '68. Which we did only then – which had to do with me as a Vietnamese woman – like running from the man – it was a lot of work on your knees – a lot of mime work on the knees – moving around – planting crops – hiding – falling – we did it just then, at that time, for the Festival, and then when we did the show a year later, that part was cut out and we kept only the trial – the man is brought to trial and the woman is brought to trial.' — (Sherman, interview.)
5. 'The troupe preceded its first play, "Reiteration,". with a hypnotic percussion and wind instrument dirge that lasted at least 20 minutes while everyone was getting settled. This foreshadowed the fact that music is an integral part of the performance, as are other sound effects, and dialogue or narration is quite secondary. "Reiteration" ... is composed of a lengthy series of short vignettes announced by beautifully inscribed banners: "Story," "We," "Territory," "All People," "Poison," and so on .... Grotesque death masks and throbbing, human-like cries from a horn make "Reiteration" exceptionally effective until the reiteration finally becomes tedious." — (J. L. Wasserman, *Bread and Puppet Theater*, San Francisco Chronicle, September 28, '68.)

COUNTRY FAR AWAY: the man marches (sound of steps) continuing during the mime following.) IT IS A DANGEROUS COUNTRY: he marches. THE MAN NEEDS A GUN: he marches, holds out his gun. THE MAN NEEDS A GAS MASK: he marches, holds out his gas mask. THE MAN NEEDS AN AIRPLANE: he marches, holds out his airplane. HE COMES TO A VILLAGE: the woman puts on the Vietnamese Woman mask. THE WOMEN ARE COOKING SOUP: the woman mimes stirring soup. THE CHILDREN ARE AFRAID: she takes the doll in her arms and cradles it. THE MAN TAKES HIS AIRPLANE: he circles the plane over his head. HE BOMBS THE CHILDREN: he stops it over the woman. THE WOMAN TAKES THE SCISSORS: she puts the doll down, and takes up the scissors, and makes as if to attach the man. The narrator stops her.

THE MAN IS BROUGHT TO TRIAL. THIS IS A POT WITH NO SOUP IN IT: the narrator takes the pot and shows it to the audience. THIS IS POISON: the narrator picks up the piece of grey fabric and shows it to the audience. THIS IS A HOUSE WHICH HAS BEEN BURNED: the narrator picks up the pieces of paper into which the cut-out of the house has been torn and shows them to the audience. THESE ARE DEAD CHILDREN: the narrator picks up the doll and shows it to the audience. THIS GUN IS HIS GUN: the narrator walks over to the man and points to the gun or motions to it with his head. (From here on the man and the woman also speak.) (M:) THIS GUN IS MY GUN: the man touches the gun or looks at it. (N:) THIS GAS MASK IS HIS GAS MASK: the narrator shows the gas mask. (M:) THIS IS MY GAS MASK: the man touches the gas mask. (N:) THE MEDAL IS HIS MEDAL: the narrator shows the medal. (M:) THIS IS MY MEDAL: he touches his medal. (N:) THIS AIRPLANE IS HIS AIRPLANE: the narrator shows the plane. (M:) THIS IS MY AIRPLANE: the man touches the plane. (N:) THE WOMAN SAYS THERE IS NO SOUP IN THE POT: the woman takes the pot. (W:) THERE IS NO SOUP IN THE POT: she shows the pot to the man. (N:) THE MAN SAYS, I'M NOT GUILTY. (M:) I AM NOT GUILTY. (N:) THE WOMAN SAYS, MY CROPS ARE POISONED: the woman picks up the piece of gray fabric. (W:) MY CROPS ARE POISONED: she shows the piece of fabric to the man. (N:) THE MAN SAYS, I AM NOT GUILTY. (M:) I AM NOT GUILTY. (N:) THE WOMAN SAYS, MY HOUSE IS BURNED: she shows the pieces of paper to the man. (N:) THE MAN SAYS, I AM NOT GUILTY. (M:) I AM NOT GUILTY. (N:) HIS MOTHER SAYS, IS THIS YOUR GUN? The woman puts on the grey mask. (M:) IS THIS YOUR GUN? (N:) THE MAN SAYS, THIS IS MY GUN. (M:) THIS IS MY GUN. (N:) HIS MOTHER SAYS, IS THIS YOUR GAS MASK? (M:) IS THIS YOUR GAS MASK? (M:) THIS IS MY GAS MASK. (N:) HIS MOTHER SAYS, IS THIS YOUR MEDAL? (M:) IS THIS YOUR MEDAL? (N:) THE MAN SAYS, THIS IS MY MEDAL. (M:) THIS IS MY MEDAL.(N:) HIS MOTHER SAYS, IS THIS YOUR AIRPLANE? (M:) IS THIS YOUR AIRPLANE? (N:) THE MAN SAYS, THIS IS MY AIRPLANE. (M:) THIS IS MY AIRPLANE. The woman takes off the grey mask, puts on the Vietnamese Woman mask. (N:) THE MAN SAYS, YES. (M:) YES. (N:) THE WOMAN SAYS, IS THIS CHILD DEAD? She picks up the doll. (W:) IS MY CHILD DEAD? She shows the doll to the man. (N:) THE MAN SAYS, YES. (M:) YES. (N:) THE WOMAN SAYS, CAN YOU BRING THIS CHILD BACK TO LIFE? (W:) CAN YOU BRING THIS CHILD BACK TO LIFE? (N:) THE MAN SAYS, NO, I CANNOT BRING THIS CHILD BACK TO LIFE. (M:) NO, I CANNOT BRING THIS CHILD BACK TO LIFE. The woman walks over to the man, takes his gun, gas mask, medal, and the bag with the airplane in it, puts them on the floor, undoes the bandage over his arm and puts it over his eyes. The man sings. She takes his gun and offers it to someone in the group, preferably a woman. To rapid strong beats from the bass drum, that someone either shoots the man, the man falling down slowly, or hands the gun on to someone else, who shoots him or in turn hands it on . . . (As Kourilsky describes the action she saw in '69, the man gets shot.) The woman takes the man's boots off him and puts them on and goes to stand stage center facing the audience, sometimes two other performers carrying the man's corpse off, sometimes the corpse remaining there. The performers other than the woman are standing around her, looking at her. What follows is improvised. The performers question the woman, utilizing or not the objects she took from the man. Depending on her answers, they take them off the stage or not. Eventually they have all been taken off and they have all left, and the woman remains alone on the stage. She leaves.'

Kourilsky gives samples of the questions she heard the woman being asked and of her answers:

'ARE YOU GOING TO COOK SOUP IN THIS POT AGAIN? (YES) – IS THIS YOUR CHILD? (YES) – WILL YOU HAVE OTHER CHILDREN (silence or YES) – DO YOU NEED THIS GUN? (YES) – DO YOU WANT THIS GUN? (NO) – ARE THESE YOUR SCISSORS? (YES) – DO YOU KNOW THIS MAN? (NO) – HAS THIS MAN KILLED YOUR CHILD? (YES) – DO YOU WANT TO TAKE THIS GUN? (YES) – DO YOU WANT THIS GAS MASK? (YES) – DO YOU WANT THIS AIRPLANE? (YES or no) – DID YOU KILL THIS MAN? (YES) – WOULD YOU KILL HIM AGAIN?) (YES or silence) – IF YOUR CHILD HAD GROWN UP AND HAD ENLISTED WITH THE ENEMY, WOULD YOU HAVE KILLED HIM? (silence) – WHAT ARE YOU GOING TO DO NOW? (silence).'

The play is doubly open-ended. Conceivably nobody would be found willing to shoot the soldier at the end of his trial;[6] and the interrogation of the

---

6. 'We never came to a real conclusive – how to do this, you know, whether the man ought to be shot or not. I just disliked our pacifist faction in the theatre and I sided more with German (Mouré) who was a Colombian and who very much thought that, *yes*, the gun *should* be used on the man, and his explanations were from his *country*, you know, from – and I remember that very well, that I was much more impressed with his point of view and that I thought let's support *that*. But it was left open, what was done in the end, and that was the difficulty. So people would do very different things at the end and then discuss it.' — (Schumann, interview, '82.)

mother might end up with her with all the soldier's gear, fully armed, a soldier of the Resistance. This last, in fact, seems to have happened repeatedly during the group's '69 European tour: Sherman who did her speaks of being given his gear as 'presents' by the group as though this had been the normal ending.

The group during this tour was torn by political dissent. There were heated off-stage arguments between Ernstthal and Schumann about nonviolence, the Nuremberg trials, etc. The dispute spilled over into performances: In Sweden, as Sherman (interview) remembers it, Ernstthal had come to feel that the woman should be punished – killed – for killing the soldier and Leherrissier agreed with him. After several nights the questioning of the woman had taken the form of an onstage discussion of this, and Leherrissier decided to act out the verdict. She approached Margo Sherman and tried to push her down: to enact the mother's execution. She wasn't strong enough, Margo remained standing. As at this point she was the armed resistance fighter: Leherrissier had unwittingly supplied the audience with the opposite of what she intended: a reaffirmation of violent (armed) Resistance. Ernstthal left the group soon after this incident.

Reiteration is a *Lehrstück sui generis* in that it is designed not to propound or support a thesis, but to ask a question of the audience (and not only of it but of the performers as well), or to induce it (and them) to ask themselves a question, a viz., whether homicide is ever and/or under what circumstances it is justified, in particular retributive or self-defensive homicide.[7] In keeping with the anarchist communitarian spirit of '68, it

---

7. 'Osvaldo Otávio Pires was brought handcuffed into Elio's Bar in the Jardim Guanhambu slum on the outskirts of Sao Paulo at about 8 A.M. on April 2. Over 100 men, women and children had gathered in the small wooden building to await his arrival.

Mr. Pires, 33 years old, was thrust onto a bench facing the crowd and the handcuffs were removed. He was allowed to smoke a cigarette and drink a glass of rough liquor, but no one moved when he asked to see his two small children. Witnesses recalled that his hands were trembling.

Mr. Pires, long feared in Jardim Guanhambu, then heard an array of charges of armed assault brought by people filling the bar. After 20 minutes, participants in the meeting later told reporters, a voice was heard to say, "All those in favor of death raise their hands." Dozens of arms were lifted; apparently no one objected.

Mr. Pires was pushed out of Elio's Bar and the crowd fell on him with sticks, poles and stones. Once he lay dead in the dusty street, the police were called. When they arrived, they took the names and addresses of 43 people who said they had joined in the lynching. No arrests were made.

Last December in São Paulo, a 54-year-old District Attorney, Jéferson Figueira, grabbed a 15-year-old boy who was being chased along a downtown street after stealing a gold necklace from a woman. Witnesses said Mr. Figueira threw the boy to the ground and, with a large crowd watching impassively, jumped on him until he was dead. Once again, no charges were brought.

gave some leeway to the performers (and perhaps even the audience) in framing and in loading the question, i.e. gave improvisation a substantive function. Its repetitions were not pro forma, but served to drive home the gravity of the facts: the moral import of actions. It clearly conveyed the view that guilt attaches to homicide: but left it open whether justification might not balance or even outbalance it. In '69 in Europe ending with the presentation of the woman as resistance fighter it took the form of an implicit endorsement of violent resistance. At the same time, as the Stockholm incident shows, it left room for the advocacy of non-violent resistance, albeit in the paradoxical form of violence used against the resistance fighter. I note also that the play may require the performer favoring armed resistance and/or violent treatment of the agents of oppression to go beyond the verbal into an enactment of execution: a psychological trial of the performer.

Though open, the play of course, posing its question to the Resistance in '68-'70, questioned the use of violence not only by the Vietcong and its

---

In the large slum area of Rio de Janeiro known as the Baixada Fluminense, death squads reportedly comprising off-duty policemen have operated for over 20 years against criminals. According to local politicians, these death squads are generally sponsored by the numbers game bosses, known as bicheiros, who assume responsibility for maintaining order in each community.' — (Alan Riding, *New York Times*, iv/15/'84.)

'In 1939, (Bonhoeffer) traveled to the United States to lecture at the invitation of Reinhold Niebuhr. Many of Pastor Bonhoeffer's colleagues urged him not to return to Germany.

' "He spent less than a month here," Professor Godsey recalled. "He paced the room upstairs here at Union, smoking his cigarettes, fighting his conscience. He finally made his dramatic decision to return."

"I watched him cross the street, board the ship and disappear," Professor Lehmann recalled last week. The two would never meet again. Pastor Bonhoeffer was imprisoned for two years for his part in the plot to kill Hitler and was hanged on April 5, 1945.

"Why did he enter into violence?" Professor Godsey asked. "This is the question Christian people have the most trouble with. The conditions under which Gandhi had to work were so completely different than those faced by Bonhoeffer."

In the end, he said, Pastor Bonhoeffer "felt violence was the only alternative."

"He said that if a madman is driving down the street hitting people, it is the duty of the church not just to bind the wounds of those injured but to stick a spoke into the wheel to stop him," Professor Godsey said.

Professor Bethge told the gathering in James Chapel that Pastor Bonhoeffer had been among the very few church leaders who moved into active resistance in Germany.

"People who never pass the threshold ask how the Pastor Bonhoeffer could justify theologically his identification with the plotters," Professor Bethge said. "The question is obsolete and macabre."

He said the question should actually be worded "the other way around: how can Christian people as accomplices of crimes justify theologically their nonaction?" ' — (K. A. Briggs, *Friends Recall A Theologian Slain by Nazis, New York Times*, April 15, 1984.)

North Vietnamese supporters, but by American (or French) revolutionaries, and in this respect would have to be judged counter-revolutionary. We may also note that though the play questioned violent resistance, its failure to evoke the usual defense of perpetrators of war crimes that they were acting under orders (let alone the one that they were fighting for their country) amounted to a condemnation of violence when not resistance.

The play has similarities to my father's *Die Massnahme* and *the Trial of Lukullus*, but Schumann denies there was any influence.[8]

It puts the group on stage. The group as such is (in the trial of the woman) featured as performer, and in the act of making the play. This was again in the spirit of the times. *Cry*, the following year, in its climactic scene, the arming of Jesus (intensified and abstracted form of the woman's arming in *Reiteration*), repeats this on a grander scale, but Schumann now formalizes it by putting them in uniform, an ironic twist undercutting the anarchism of the gesture – his people were not aware of the irony.

In the first part of *Reiteration* (=*A Man*), narration has the usual function of by telling them what is going on addressing the play to the audience, though not the two other functions narration often has and by which the play is made an object for the audience shared with the narrator: comment on the play, formal address to the audience e.g. by cajoling or insulting. This restricted but still traditional role of narration had been its role in Schumann's work up to this time. In the remainder of *Reiteration* it no longer had this function. It was obviously not needed either in the recapitulation of the play that was dropped (the audience already knew what was going on), nor in the soldier's trial: the characters spoke their own lines. Not supplying any need of its for information, it no longer addressed the play to the audience. It was no longer a link to the audience. Instead it had become a part of the play as non-addressive as the visual part. But resituated within the show, it had two new functions: to

---

8. Eric Berne, who left the Mime Troupe for the Bread and Puppet Theatre not long after seeing them in San Francisco in September '68, quoted in Kourilsky '71:

'A vrai dire, deux raisons m'ont incité à entrer au Bread and Puppet Theatre. Je voulais apprendre l'art des marionnettes, mais surtout ... j'aurais travaillé avec lui parce que *Reiteration* m'avait beaucoup impressioné: les techniques qu'il utilise pour raconter l'histoire de l'homme qui dit au revoir à sa mére, la façon dont il fait jouer le soldat, m'ont immédiatement fait penser à Brecht. Et pour moi qui avais lu certains des *Ecrits sur le théâtre*, qui avais toujours été hanté par Brecht sans jamais l'avoir vu jouer correctement aux Etats-Unis, à tel point que je me disais parfois que c'était peut-être tout simplement une tradition morte, *Reiteration* a été une extraordinaire découverte.'

strengthen the play's contentual moral address to the audience, and to give the makers of the play/(the group) responsibility for this address. The group's collective appearance as makers of the play within the play served the same two functions. Narration was to play the same role in *Cry*.

'The technique of the radical theater is in your commitment and your understanding of the political nature of reality. With Schumann, I see very heavy pacifist, religious-mystical stuff. Some of it I don't agree with. Last night's performance (of *Reiteration*) was not pacifist. It was much stronger, but I don't know if Schumann believes in the Viet Cong defense of their own country as an absolute necessity.... Schumann's beautiful, strong images, his very deep commitment, seems a religious commitment — which is something I don't have and Mime Troupe people do not tangibly know of — or know of but haven't faced. We talk about television, and rock bands and the plastic world, we deal with it. We are middle class people, Mime Troupe middle class people. We have to get it out of our systems, but it's very hard because we've all lived with it. Schumann brings just a whole different beautiful thing. The time is much different. People don't like to go through that time. I'm committed to that time because I know something about (it) and the people. I like that torture, if it's torture. Bread and Puppet time space is very different, it's sculptured time; quite different from commercial theater.... Teatro's time is more like our time and Luis is more theatrical than sculptural.... I don't think you will find the images Peter Schumann brings to the theater any place in the U.S. What he brings is Brechtian, very European, medieval images, very strong, beautiful, sculptured images. Nobody makes masks for the stage as well as he does, very strong, very powerful; he knows what to do with the face. But he's a sculptor, not necessarily a director. After last night's performance, he said it was an anti-show; the Mime Troupe does a show-show. We do trip, trip, trip, and they do an anti-show. In other words, he doesn't perform at all. You can do that if you are Peter Schumann. If you are not Peter Schumann, you have to learn how.'

(R. G. Davis, in the San Francisco Mime Troupe 1968 pamphlet, *Panel Discussion on Radical Theater*.)

'What Ronnie said is true: our play is an anti-play, a performance which is not really a performance. The Mime Troupe and Campesino have a lot of theatricality, and this is their work. In that is their message, and in that is their love. With us it is certainly not so, the play usually grows out of a workshop: after working with people for a time you get to the point where you put it together, and you put it on in front of people.... We don't have this big interest in theater, like Ronnie has and like Luis has. Most of the people in the company are not actors or mimes. Most come for political reasons. We actually have a hard time with actors, when we do get actors into plays.... The Mime Troupe obviously has the stress on the play. It brings the story across by doing a lot of things with it. And we do it the other way around: take everything out and leave just this little bit which is the story.... We are just not enough of the theater to feel we could do more than the story itself and a few lines.... In '*Reiteration*': at first we had other lines in, like we had her spilling the soup, and the airplane bombing the soup, and stuff like that. The play had a little too much sidetrack. And we had to cut it out. It didn't work any more; it was getting phony, it was getting picturesque. All the work was constantly trying to get away from the story. So we threw it all out again and ended with just these particular lines.'

(Schumann, ibid.)

22. June '68-March '69. The making of
The Cry of the People for Meat. Jehovah as the Satanic essence of man. History: The son's perennial struggle against and defeat by the father.

On their return from Europe at the end of May or the beginning of June '68, a by now fairly large Bread and Puppet group settled down for the summer, their first retreat from the big city, way up in central Maine, in the inland township of Strong, for a bit of communal living – 'collective living' – a theatre history of theirs of December '79 calls it: 'a commune, but organized ... it was the women who cooked and the men carried water' (Ashley, interview) – and, Schumann being Schumann, for some serious work. The main group – Andy and Amy Trompetter, Murray Levy, the Schumanns and their five kids, Charlie Adams and Mary Kelly – lived in a small house that Mabel Chrystie Dennison had bought for them for $5,000 and had given to them. A smaller group – Darryl Henriquez, Michael Appleby with Sara Peattie, Murray Levy, Andrea Woodner and Margo Sherman lived nearby in a farmhouse Mary Kelly bought. Ernstthal, who had spent two weeks before they went to Europe fixing up the Dennison-bestowed house had left, Adams was the only old-timer around.[1] Gossip has it that Schumann behaved scandalously this

---

1. 'At present there are some county fairs and Upward Bound shows to do in Maine and a projected San Francisco area tour planned for September and October that Peter is still puzzling over in his mind. In the meantime about 20 people are living at the commune. They cooperate on the chores on two farms which lack electricity, running water, and telephone. They pitch in building outhouses, cutting firewood, getting well water, gardening, cleaning up, cooking. They also create ceramics, short books, "crankie" films, puppets, flower presses, quilts, poems, etc. They swim in the "Sandy River" several miles away, drink home-brew wine and beer, sing rounds, and improvise music in an inimitable style whenever verbal tension erupts.
One thinks of "Communitas" and this quotation from the Goodman brothers' book: Men like to make things, to handle materials and see them take shape and come out as desired, and they are proud of their products. And men like to work and be useful, for work has a rhythm and springs from spontaneous feelings just like play, and to be useful makes people feel right.' — (M. Blanc, *Clowning with the Life Force, Village Voice,* September 5, '68.)
'It was wonderful in Strong, Maine. We would work all day long – we would be bitten to chopped meat by those damn mosquitoes. We tried rehearsals with the headlights of automobiles, we tried it with flashlights, we just, nearly died. I can't remember being more uncomfortable. It was absolutely awful. And in trying to work out – he kept trying so many things – the Bible would be kicked all over the place and dragged – I mean, trying to get ideas out of it. And bruised bodies, I mean, it was a terribly physical period. He must have been having a very difficult time; creative outpouring. Because, otherwise, why

summer, openly courting – unsuccessfully – a lesbian musician in the group. Like the communal living, whatever gave rise to this rumor is a sign of Schumann's infection by the counter-culture.

What the group was doing this summer was they were crawling in the

---

would he have done all of that to us? It was incredibly awful. Trying to get this – what is it – Tower of Babel. I mean, I think we spent three days doing every goddamn possible thing on the Tower of Babel, including, someone had found bases of table lamps and we strung ropes through them and we used them as cymbals. Well, all right, everybody had a pair of them and we were banging them on each others' knuckles. I mean, everyone was a bleeding Tower of Babel with these damn things going. And I – whenever things like that happen, I figure that the person is having a dry spell of creativity and, you know, they keep doing until an idea strikes. And I thought that too, of him. It was not a nice thing to say about Peter, but I thought we – I thought we were abused terribly that summer, because he was having a fallow period ... in the evening we would go swimming in a mountain stream and we would drink homemade wine – peach and pear and other wines – get very drunk, and go swimming in this mountain lake at night – whether there was a moon or not – and people would be throwing themselves into this mountain stream. Sometimes it would be four inches deep and sometimes it would be fifteen feet deep. It's a wonder people didn't die – looking back on it – there was no reason why people simply didn't break their brains out.... It was beautiful. The first thing they did was pollute their well by hanging the milk and things in it, and then Peter – the first time I ever saw him in a rage (I mean, a silly rage) was when he was complaining about the health inspectors condemning his well – saying, the water in New York was bad. The water in New York happens to be very good.' — (Ashley, interview.)

'We started working on *The Cry of the People for Meat*, which became the great love of mine, I mean we did it then for a year after that.... Maine was a lot of people, it was a very very rural farm, it was northern Maine, Strong, middle Maine, near farming people. And it was in the back woods there, and there was well, wood burning fire and there were a lot of people. And I had a little tiny closet room where I slept. There was work, the work with Peter starts in the morning and it goes through, and then, when it was too hot we would take a break and go swimming and work at night, with car lights. Set up the cars and light the area so that we could and I was crazy about him ... and there were people there who were upset that there wasn't more time taken for their personal problems, for their personal needs, they came more for therapy than they did to make theatre and so, I didn't share that, at that point, I didn't anyway. I was too, too full of curiosity and excitement, I wanted to learn, I wanted to do it.... There were nights when we were working with these beasts, when I wasn't in, when I would see it and I couldn't believe it – this bordered on something really medieval or whatever, you know, it just struck me as being one of the strongest visual experiences I had ever had. I didn't know what it meant, but I didn't care, I mean, like the Bob Dylan song. Something is happening here and you don't know what it is, do you Mr. Jones, or Mrs. Jones? But I was carried by the intensity and the effort. I thought – I worked myself to a frazzle, really I just threw myself into it, I, through exhaustion, past exhaustion to another state, it was a really strong work. It wasn't like in, like any other theatre I have ever done, which after a certain number of times people want a break. This was a blitz kind of working, that I felt was cleansing in its, it was cleansing to me, 'cause I needed that at that point.... There were people who were terribly upset from the very beginning, when I got there. When I got there they had been there a week or two and there was a faction that was saying: "Schumann doesn't take any time for our personal problems, nothing, nothing, nothing and it is an emotional desert." And it upset him and hurt him I could see it, I didn't feel and I gave him support.... But that created a lot of conflict there, the people who were feeling that were

mud in beast carapaces. No mime, no acting, no Gallic glamor. The Beast puppets, which they made that summer also, were not just masks, but head – rather than just face – masks extended down the back, confining, heavy and uncomfortable – some had several heads – and totally hiding the performer, who moreover had no opportunity for individual performance: the beasts appeared en masse, and the performer's movements resulted from

---

really putting – stopping the work process to a certain extent. They were creating bad vibes and then one day they left. And it was only then that those of us who wanted to be there consciously decided that that was what we were going to do and weren't. And I think because, because of my loyalty at that point Peter and me got very close.'
(Levy, interview.)

'It was the end of May. And then we went to the country. We had bought a little house in Maine that the Dennisons helped us find. And this was going to be our first experimental collective, living in a house in Maine .... I hated it, and I think other people didn't mind it so much. It was very rough. We had no water. We had to bring it from a stream, we had to lug in water in order to cook and eat. And we had to build fires in the stove to cook and to heat water to wash dishes. And May was very, very muggy and buggy .... For me it was very hard because I was an only child, I was brought up in the city and so very, very rough living, having to cook for a lot of people was all new, and I didn't feel equal to it. (I: How about otherwise? I mean, all these different people ...) Yes, very, very crowded, small house. Charlie and Mary bought their own house and a few people lived with them. But we were very, very overcrowded. (I: Very hard on Elka.) It was very hard on Elka but she was much more equal, she was completely more than equal to the task. I remember her once saying something to me about, well I'll just use my housewife's ingenuity, and create meals out of cans and stuff for people. And since we had never done this before, and since conditions were so primitive, we realized that it took four hours for a meal. That meant preparation and cleaning up. Four hours. And we were rehearsing outdoors .... And we were rehearsing in the grass, and the weather was so atrocious and the bugs were so bad that eventually we had to rehearse before eight in the morning. And it was the only time it was cool enough and bugless. And we were working hard to prepare a show for Newport. Peter seemed to be in a bad mood. I was always tired, what happens to me is that when I'm unhappy I get depressed and physically tired and so it's another effort to drag myself to anything. And so I was very, very conscious of how tired I was, always. And crying, and thinking maybe if I go into the woods and look at the trees I'll get happy, or maybe if I write a poem I'll get happy, and the sense of depression will leave me, but it didn't. And I was very uptight and self-protective. I think Andy and Amy were the only people who kind of enjoyed it. And they kept the house. We never went back there .... (I: But you didn't go back to Maine at all, the group as such? And why, because it had been unpleasant, or just because you hadn't intended to stay longer anyhow?) I, well, the idea, of course, was to have a place in the country where we could work and live in the summer time, but I don't even remember talking about it as much. It was somehow unspokenly understood that we didn't like it, that we didn't enjoy it, except for Andy and Amy, who loved it, immediately got involved in gardening, pressing flowers, looking at birds. They really had a feeling for Maine.' — (Sherman, interview.)

'(I: Was there any reason for rehearsing and doing this show in Maine, or had you just bought the house and there was space? Just to get out of the city.) Yes, we wanted to get away from New York. We wanted to have a place, mainly because of the kids. That house seemed right for our family to be during the summer. There was a farm pretty close by that Charlie Adams had so we also had the use of that farm, they had a big barn.' — (Schumann, interview, '79.)

the costume's constraint and from having to move forward and back in the dense crawling throng. A sadistic scene you might say, but that was hardly the point: Schumann had in mind a play about Humanity. The Bible was to furnish the mythological particulars. In the end, in *Cry*, the Beasts figured in relation to and in contra-distinction from Man. But basically they were in their packed throng and collective movement the Urform of Humanity, their essential characteristics persisting in human conduct, that of The People, or that of the counter-culture, commune-minded youth of the late '60s. I think this was in Schumann's mind. They are dumb piggish beasts. They look stupid – definitely so, unlike actual animals who when they don't as they often do look intelligent look possessed of capacities that make absence of intellect no lack. They also look menacing in a weak way and in such fashion that one is embarrassed by being disquieted by them, one's unease qualified to oneself as prejudice by a simultaneous realisation that they seem perfectly harmless. And they are ugly: and one is ashamed that this should bother one. In all three regards they affect one as The People does the intellectual and the Cultured Man – e.g. Schumann.[2]

---

2. 'We started to work on the Bible – which – we said we were going to do the Bible. And we were trying things out with the beasts first, different formations of the beasts. All the things beasts could do, having three together or one. Carrying or crawling or running or putting them on backwards and having them as wings.' — (Levy, interview.)

'I just remember the heat, making the beasts, rehearsing the beasts in the grass, the sense of struggling very hard, harder than we ever had before to make up a show, making up shows had never been difficult before. And suddenly it was incredibly hard, but it's what happens when Peter is working on something very, very new. He's got some stuff that's new, and he's also trying to exploit old stuff to him, and try to use the old stuff to feed the new stuff, and in the beginning it doesn't quite work, and I would help him, I'd be like the assistant director, that week in Newport. And I would watch things, and I'd say, well, maybe we should try this, try that. Well, you have to fail in order to grow. (I: How did he fail that summer?) It was very, very obscure. This new stuff with the beasts wasn't clear yet what they were to do, what their role would be in the show, and the old stuff was not really alive and vivid, either. So that it was just like a patchwork of old and new. I think we had the yellow people from *The Crucifixion*, old puppets, and the beasts. Eventually, it all got worked out in *The Cry of the People*, that show you know. But it was just fumbling, fumbling, and trying one thing or another. Have you ever watched Peter in rehearsals? . . . Well, you know, it's like moving sculpture around. Let's try this, let's try that. Let's try an arrangement this way, a different speed, a different order. A lot having to do with space, speed, slow, fast, use of sound. And through working with these elements discovering the story. (I: And this was in particular so in thise case . . . like something new, you say?) Yeah, the Beasts, this was another new, new thing. (I: What impression did the beasts make?) Well, they were scary . . . . They were very, very hard to operate. They were exhausting because you had to crawl around in them, and run around in them, and fall. Physically, very, very strenuous and frightening. And it wasn't a spiritual experience. It wasn't uplifting, personal gratifying. It was like being, oh, my goodness. It was like being in a demonstration. I'm glad you're asking these questions, 'cause I'm getting a little insight. It was that sense of being anonymous and frightened by the possibility of physical violence. And not having a personality. It was sort of primeval, violent, very, very violent. The mouths opened, and you had to make them open. Teeth. It felt like it had nothing to do with being a person. I never wanted to be a beast.' — (Sherman, interview.)

'That's right, the *beasts* were started in *Maine*. They had started with the idea of *The Cry* already. I had the idea of doing at least the Old Testament if not the whole Bible, with the help of a big group of beasts. That simply was the idea that started me off on *The Cry*. So the beasts were definitely the main bulk of work there. There may have been individual other puppets. There was a lot of rehearsal in Maine. I don't think there was an equal amount of building, in contrast to some of the workshops here. Really a big part is building, much more than rehearsal, but the rehearsals were difficult because we ended up in a buggy oven — it was difficult to rehearse those people constantly catching mosquitoes. They were very nervous rehearsals, I remember. We finally decided to get up at 3:30 in the morning and do it before the sunrise.' — (Schumann, interview, '79.)

'The gas lantern had run out of fuel so we kept the lights of one of the cars trained on the flat stretch between Charlie Adams' House and the workshop barn. (That July day in Maine was much too hot so we slept and decided to rehearse throughout the night.) There we crawled on the ground within celastic beast heads resembling the faces of wolves and wild boars, our bodies smeared with a strong-smelling insect-repellent and Woodman's Dope and wrapped in — burlap. With George Ashley writing down every movement, Peter Schumann announced tasks and improvisation suggestions from a megaphone as he sat on a log stump in the middle of a moving insect fog. With strange ululations and grotesque instrumental noises we accompanied the slithering and violent motions of the "beasts." Distant farms heard the rites and days later sent puzzled, shy, and envious visitors curious to know about Druid or Dionysian pleasures.

The Bread and Puppet Theatre had been commissioned for a new piece by the Newport Folk Festival and Peter, without a clear end in mind, was having us move and do tasks utilizing the one tangible element he had a certainty about: the "beasts." Peter always works without a script. He moves performers (preferably not actors) around in large puppets, masks or bare-faced; tries sounds, juggles ideas and visual effects over and over until certain patterns are pleasing to the secret voice, which one might call almost-rational-instinct, within him. Much of what we produced that night in the way of fodder for the production seemed, felt inspired, right, vital. But Peter wasn't at all satisfied. The next day we tried wild take-offs on the Jacob Joseph stories of the Old Testament and eventually reached a terrible impasse as the parallel between the famous Biblical dreams and the one of Martin Luther King, Jr., suddenly seemed a meaningful, but with further thought, an awkward, forced theme. The efficacy of theatre at this moment was the oppressive question in Peter's mind. And it rose higher in priority for him than the responsibility of getting a new show ready. And yet that he had to do. Earlier in July in Denver at a workshop conference of the National Churches of Christ that we participated in, he had hinted at, made verbal his fears that theatre clearly wasn't enough, that people were becoming immune to anti-war plays or works that spoke to their conscience.

Clare Clouzot's article "Godard and the U.S.," in the summer issue of *Sight and Sound* perhaps sheds some light on Peter's dilemma as an artist and a man. Miss Clouzot quotes Jean Luc Godard, badgered by militant students to be their vanguard, as "supporting the ones who are taking up the guns," but not wishing to abdicate creation for active revolt. Godard is also quoted as saying, "The Third World's problem is that it is hungry. We on the contrary are overfed culturally and we eat things which are culturally unnecessary, so we must learn again what is our real nourishment." Because this last is Peter's fervent belief also he has started a commune in Maine. With the use of his own and Mary Kelly's land and by the hard work of interested friends and puppeteers, the experiment is in the process. The show given on July 26 in Newport was a product of the commune. Peter's frustration at the early rehearsal mentioned above had continued during the rest of the days in Maine and during those long desperate rehearsals on the stage and lawn at Newport. That the performance itself had a certain raw power and satisfying feeling, despite rough moments, did not neutralize the fact that Peter was still troubled by what his best role is in America at this time.' — (M. Blanc, *Clowning with the Life Force, Village Voice*, September 5, '68.)

According to Kourilsky '71,³ Schumann this summer set out on the assumption that the Judeo-Christian mythology in mystic form furnishes the true history and image of Humanity, but, failing in his attempt to extract this history and image for his theatrical purposes – a piece for the '68 Newport Festival – came to consider that assumption false. Unutilisability demonstrated irrelevance, even untruth. Since this assumption has since Hegel and Schleiermacher been the core of Protestant theology (a salvaging operation), this would have been a crucial loss of faith. We may compare this rejection of the Old Testament with my father's account of how during the '20s he embraced Marxism because it enabled him to be 'productive' in the theatre – to portray social reality.

Apparently, the Judaic heritage – which had not featured in his Christmas and Easter plays – the avenging and embracing Deity – stuck in his craw: he could not square it with the human situation as he saw it. His loss of faith amounted to a denial of God: leading over into his shift from a presumptive de- or theism into pantheism in the '70s. *Cry* (cf. infra) enregisters his revolt against God the Father.

The summer's work was a failure, but under the title *The Bible*, they did bits and pieces of what they came up with at one or two local churches, at a Christian drama workshop in Colorado,⁴ and at a Religious Arts

---

3. 'Peter Schumann a construit une série de masques de bêtes et il travaille sur la Bible. "Aussi longtemps que la Bible reste une préoccupation religieuse – dit il – c'est un domaine lourdement chargé de mysticisme, horrible, complètement clos, dont on ne peut rien tirer. Mais quand on arrive à s'emparer d'un "cliché" se usé, à en extraire la fable, la vraie légende, tout à coup on a une vision entièrement neuve; c'est une histoire extraordinaire dont on va faire profiter les gens. L'histoire archi-connue a tant de chances d'être aussi la plus neuve qui soit. C'est comme les contes de fées qui existent partout dans le monde: la-dessous il y a une histoire fascinante, colossale, qui durera toujours." Mais Peter Schumann n'arrivera pas à raconter la Bible: "Dieu allant et venant, tuant tout le monde, embrassant tout le monde." ' — (Kourilsky, '71.)

4. The 20th Annual Drama Workshop: The Contribution of the Arts, specially the Dramatic Arts, to the Person in the Age of Automation, sponsored by the Department of Educational Development, and the National Council of the Churches of Christ, in cooperation with the Christian Society for Drama, at Temple Buell College, Denver, Colorado, July 6-13.

'I got an invitation to go to something, a conference for the National Council of Churches in Denver, Colorado that summer and it had to do with theatre.... I was asked to go up there to run some games workshops, theatre games workshops. And I didn't know that Peter was going to be there. But he was one of the others of those who were hired to conduct sessions for the National Council of Churches.... It was very exciting for me because it was my opportunity to meet and to get to know Peter. He was only up there with Margo and with Maurice Blanc.... It was the first time I'd seen *A Man Says Goodbye to His Mother* in its simple street theatre version.... He did it in several places up there.... (I: Did they do anything else up there?) They were working on a piece about the Bible. It had to do with the Bible. It didn't happen. I think aspects of the work probably ended up *Cry of the People* later on, but it was interesting. They'd take sections of the Bible and simply try them out. Peter would incorporate the Christians into the large set

Festival in Kennebunk, Maine, and, July 26, at the Newport Folk Festival, a show adjudged a failure by Schumann and by most of the people in the group I have talked to.[5] Otherwise, that summer, they participated in parades in Farmington and Phillips, Maine, one of them a 4th of July parade, and laid on some kind of festivity for the locals,[6] two

---

pieces and try to give them each a line to say and things like that. I don't remember really all the details, but I remember I was quite fascinated by it because I know how difficult that sort of thing is. If you were simply doing it off the seat of your pants and why don't we try, you do this, you do this, you stand over there and do that. Somehow he had a very sure feel of it. There's no question.' — (Shapli, interview.)

5. 'What we did was really a rough draft . . . . And it was a very, very rough show. It was not a success.' — (Sherman, interview.)

'The Newport show was, well we in the Puppet Theatre when you are doing, when you are going even to a festival or whatever you are so busy rehearsing and doing that you don't got a helluva lot of chance to see anybody else or to interact. And we were all nervous, it was my first real show, and I was, I think in that show I was the Great Warrior. The angel with the sword and I came to strike Mary, to give her, to impregnate her, I think that that is what I did, one of the things that I did. And I was nervous, would I do it right, and I was practicing all of the time. Newport, I had been to Newport before to see the festival, the Folk Festival and that, the summer that we played there, we were on the same bill with Janice Joplin, I don't know if she came before or after. And then we had a party together and it was nice.' — (Levy, interview.)

'La piece presentée a Newport n'a pas vraiment "d'histoire," les masques sont impressionants, certains mouvements de groupe opposant les hommes et les bêtes sont trés beaux, mais Schumann le reconnaît lui-même: trop hermetique, le spectacle n'a pas touché vraiment le public.' — (Kourilsky, '71.)

'What was done in Maine didn't end up with *The Cry*, it ended up with something that we called *The Bible*, and we performed it in that state of Maine, somewhere in a church on a couple of occasions, and at least a little part of it at the Newport Festival. This was our second time going to the Newport Festival and this production consisted of elements that were then in *The Cry*. I remember one scene where after some action of these grey soldiers that I described earlier, a group of people with*out* masks did a blowing sound and motion, blowing over these soldier puppets, and I also remember that we used a chain saw as the main musical instrument in that production. And also in the church. And later on, when we rehearsed *The Cry*, we tried that again and again, to use the chain saw. We finally ended up not using it, because we didn't have one.' — (Schumann, interview, '79.)

'I find this problem of losing contact with people very real. Like Luis said, it's an artistic problem. You can separate yourself from people by doing something too much inside itself and then it doesn't talk to anybody. At the Newport Folk Festival last year, when Luis was there, we sort of succeeded. We did a show that worked on this big stage and for this folk audience, who wanted to hear beautiful songs. But this year we got completely stuck. We wanted to play the Bible in twenty minutes and we ended up playing nothing but the murder of Cain and Abel in something like ten minutes with these big puppets. It was a show that had nothing to give. It just was in itself. It didn't say anything. It was not even a good show.

At the same time, we felt that for this audience who came there to listen to all the schmaltzy, nice, beautiful singing that went on, it was just the right kind of cold water. It was nice for them to get that and they really thoroughly didn't like it. We felt that was almost an achievement.' — (Schumann, in *Radical Theater Festival San Francisco State College September 1968*/Publication of the San Francisco Mime Troupe.)

6. 'In addition to preparations for *The Cry*, we also prepared a little festival that we invited

undertakings foreshadowing Bread and Puppet activities in Vermont later.

Having returned from San Francisco to New York in late September or early October, Schumann continued working with the Beasts, though apparently initially abandoning the project of a biblical world history, toying with the idea of using them in a play based on Aesop's *Fables* instead,[7] but soon returning to his original project, though now, if we can trust the hint he gives Kourilsky,[8] in an atheist frame and focused on the problem of what future humanity can make for itself without God; and making use of the group-presentation mode of performance adumbrated in

---

the community. In that festival we played a pageant and small puppet shows and decorated and made a museum, using old parts of tools and a few dummies and masks. It was a jolly afternoon. Lots of people came.' — (Schumann, interview, '79.)

'Peter held an open house (fore-runner of the Circuses) at Charlie's place, with exhibits, performances, etc. A lot of (not a *lot*) townsfolk, rather neighbours (*not* from the nearby town, but *lumpen* rural) came to it and the old folk (farmers in their childhood) and the children liked it, and the people from 14 to 50 were non-plussed, disliked it, etc.' (Dennison, private communication, May '82.)

7. 'We were reading *Aesop's Fables*. We were trying to do them and we got into a lot of choral speaking stuff which is something that – there was another theatre – the one – who's the woman who's in the Theatre for the New City? Crystal. I think it's the theatre that she was in. They came over and used the space and they were doing choral speaking. You know where one person would say one word and another person would say another and it would line up to be a sentence. So we were doing *Aesop's Fables* with that kind of stuff and there was something about a lamb? I can't even remember. I remember a phrase "I wasn't even born yet", you know. It was something about I wasn't guilty because I wasn't even born yet. It must have been a sheep and wolf story. I can't remember . . . . (I: Were there masks?) No, I think it was mainly speaking. There were no masks that went with it and I don't even remember action with it. Oh no, wait a minute. There were groups of people, ah, there were groups of people in one place and then we would all have to run and fall in another place. And it was that kind of massing movement and massing together, the sounds of it too. (I: That sounds like the beasts.) Yeah. I think the beast masks were made before the *Fable* work started, so probably the *Fable* work was an attempt to find some character for the beasts which didn't really work out because Aesop's *Fables* are very intellectual and verbal. I don't know, it didn't ever fit very well. But I guess the movement . . . .' — (Lippen, interview.)

One of the Bread and Puppet little illustrated booklets – comic books – 'Workshops 1968-69/New York City' – suggests what a Bread and Puppet Aesop's *Fables* would have been about:

'Right now we need a big set of animals to play Aesop's *Fables*/To show why the wolf dresses in sheep's clothes/Or to demonstrate how the little sheep pollutes the water that the wolf wants to drink/Or instructions on how to learn the language of the wolf.'

8. 'De retour à New York, dans la Old Courthouse, Peter Schumann se sert des masques de bêtes pour raconter des fables d'Esope, montrer "comment le petit mouton salit l'eau que le loup veut boire," etc. Mais ce ne sont pour lui que des "broderies" et il reviendra bientôt à la Bible. "Le système dans lequel nous vivons est encore fondé sur ce livre – dit-il. La façon nous avons de comprendre le monde, les formes mêmes de notre culture s'y trouvent.' Il voudrait donc "fouiller le passé de cet Occident civilisé qui, au seuil de l'avenir, sur le point de créer une nouvelle vie, tend a rejeter son propre mythe, sa propre histoire." ' — (Kourilsky,'71.)

Reiteration. His aim now is a play he can tour in Europe, a big play.[9] Its title, *The Cry of the People for Meat*, discretely — since the dechristianized public wouldn't recognize the reference — states its subject matter to be the problem of how a godless humanity is going to make it to the Promised Land:[10] humanity is belly-run, murderous, and shrinks from the hardships. It is ready by March '69. There are open rehearsals at the Courthouse in March, and showings at some New York colleges — Columbia University, Ithaca — and, April 2 in a Boston discotheque.[11] But in the main — there

---

9. 'I think that very soon after that (returning to New York (SSB)) we definitely planned a big tour to Europe in the spring of '69, with a lot of people, and with a big show.... And so we started at the beginning, spent weeks and weeks and weeks working with the beasts.... It was a very exciting time because it was very organized. The other days were terribly exciting and not organized. And this was just exciting in the sense of every day rehearsing from 10 to 1, a lunch break, and rehearsing again from 2 to 6. That can be very thrilling too, that routine. And you know that the whole thing is going towards building a great big show and taking it on a big tour of Europe. So there was quite a good spirit in the group.' — (Sherman, interview.)

10. 'Fünf Akte mit je fünf bis siebzejn Bildern von der Erschaffung der Welt bis zur Kreuzignung Christi zeigen in seiner Vielfalt von wechselnden Masken immer denselben Grundtrieb des Menschen, sein Verlangen nach Fleisch, nach Opfer, seine Unfähigkeit anderes Leben zu respektieren.' — (D. Herms, *Mime Troupe, El Teatro, Bread and Puppet*, Maske und Kethurn '73-'74).

11. 'Yeah, so it was only performed *in* the Courthouse before we left, so it didn't have any real — well, maybe one performance at Columbia, or several, and another one in Boston in the Paradise or some strange place. Not much anyway. That is, maybe more than I think now ... because I know we'd been to some colleges also, upstate New York, Ithaca. So we did a few performances, but it was a constantly changing show. It was hardly ever fixed into any particular shape.' — (Schumann, interview, '79.)

'On April 2, in the vast, open space of a part-time discotheque called the Ark, near Kenmore Sq., the Bread and Puppet Theater gave a single performance of a play called "The Cry of the People for Meat." It received practically no publicity; it was not very well attended; it drew three reviews in the Boston press. But to my mind, without reservation, "The Cry of the People for Meat" is the most exciting and adventurous piece of new theater we've had all season. As I've indicated, in sleep or awake, the evening is unforgettable.

The play virtually is a vaudeville Happening, a free-ranging experiment spiralling as far from traditional concepts of drama as possible. It spirals right into the collective unconscious, spinning violent dramatic images against our own grim, unknown fears and thereby creating a nightmare that sorrows on and on, rather like the restless Ghost of Hamlet's father and just as demanding. The play begins like a game.

Before it begins the members of the company roam through the Ark, now and then stopping to talk among themselves or to someone in the audience, now and then giving out chunks of bread torn from what appear to be home-made loaves. The open floor is littered with equipment, props, light fixtures, electrical cord, electronic devices, musical instruments and a collection of puppets, three of them 25-30 feet high. Off to one side there's a puppet tableaux, a dozen or more puppets dressed in what looks like grey dust, with faces so eroded by sorrow that their features slip into each other. They lean together in terror on a platform that seems to be an island in placeless time.

Eventually, an announcer signals the beginning of the play. The audience stands or sits where it can. There are no seats, only thin sheets of foam rubber scattered on the floor. There is a drumming sound that's vaguely musical and, at that moment, with the company

were a few subsequent showings in December '69 at St. Peter's Church in New York — the play was made for and shown to just European audiences: during the theatre's second European tour, April to November '69.

Schumann during the winter of '68/'69 was preoccupied by *Cry*, but there was a college tour with something (to Hobart, Williams, Bennington, Goddard) and he did put out one new show, *Blue Raven Beauty*,[12]

---

adjusting costumes, lining up, getting into place and surrounded by all the disarray of equipment it looked like the commedia dell'arte in a junkyard.

This evening's play, the announcer says like a lecturer, is taken from the Old and New Testaments. Selected episodes will be dramatized. And then, without so much as the blinking of an eye, a modern myth begins to assume shape. In the corner stands a mammoth puppet, a huge body topped with a face that might have been chiseled for Mount Rushmore except that the face is sour, lascivious, evil. The teeth would be at home in the mouth of a shark. Red ribboned lips form a highway into a grin. The puppet has derrick-sized hands and wears street clothes. He is God. He moves out like a faintly civilized King Kong and, in a moment, he's in a thick embrace with another mammoth puppet, Mother Earth, grey of face and body. They kiss and copulate, they circle each other in an elephantine waltz. They're watched by a third mammoth puppet, Uncle Fatso. Shortly after the cranking waltz has ended, the announcer drones through the endless recitation of who begat whom from the Bible.

The circus-like atmosphere that, at first, seemed awkwardly beguiling, now changes to a suffocating mood of violence and destruction. Between Christian myth and contemporary symbol, the world turns on insanity. The advance of civilization is counterpointed by a scene of beasts being led into a corral of slaughter. And the beasts, by the way, are absolutely horrifying: Hydrocephalic monsters, greyish white, gorgoneion, with tunnel nostrils that also serve as hollow eyes, with sharply tipped ears, heads without bodies. In one of the most appalling scenes in the play, they slither across the floor in the semi-dark, a horde of heads moaning and moving to a pitiless destruction, and I can't tell you how many times this image has kept me from sleeping.

The meaningless massacre of monsters is followed soon after by the massacre of innocent people. There is violence, destruction and death in every corner of existence. There's a sonic roar of aggression as man's word richochetes inside its own willed torment and God watches, above it all, His towering presence concerned with other matters. Between the struggle for a visionless need for power and conquest, there's the story of Jesus Christ. And there is the serene image of the Virgin Mary who is destroyed by a fish-shaped war plane. Voices murmur for help that will never come and there is the endless cry of the people for meat.

The Bread and Puppet Theater shows everything being made on the spot. The mechanism for the usual theatrical magic is shown for what it is: Mechanism. The result is that the force of illusion is somehow forceful beyond easy belief. The images take over, nightmares inhabit your system, like a virus slipping in under your fingernail and traveling up to the mind where it infects your thought. The company is without equal in the originality of its interest, in the scope of its awareness. This review is written in the hope that they can be brought back to the Ark for a prolonged engagement.' — (K. Kelly, 'A New Theater That Excites and Haunts,' *Boston Globe*, April 13, '69.)

This was Kelly's second review of the play. It is one of the few American reviews of Schumann doing full justice to his work.

12. Done at Open House nights, Fridays, at the Old Courthouse in January and/or February '69, late March or early April at La Mama on East 4th, and on the '69 European tour.

consisting of slightly abstractive adaptations of three Grimm fairy tales, *Sleeping Beauty, The Raven, The Blue Light*, presupposing the audience's knowledge of the stories. As he refers to them on the title page of the mss. – 'in which a child is born ... in which a terrible curse is cast upon the child ... in which everything is solved and the king renders his kingdom to the people' – they seem to have formed some kind of a whole in his mind. This in fact is not so in the mss. text, nor was it the case in the production. He called them 'fables' rather than 'fairy tales': as though to suggest archtypal content or other inner meaning, but this is not evident either. There are glimmers of political significance. They were, I would say, a hasty, unconsidered job. Levy (interview) suggests that they were intended to broaden their repertory beyond the political for the European tour. Though designed for adults, they were on occasion during the '69 tour performed for children.[13] Their form was loose.[14] As in *Reiteration* and *The Cry*, the group figured as collective performer.

I remember one scene. When Sleeping Beauty falls asleep for her

---

13. 'But we did perform them for children. We took them to Europe. And one performance I do remember is in the backyard of the Munich Children's Museum – for many, many children. And it was actually fun to do, even though we realized: Well, this is a real mistake, playing these shows for kids, because they don't really tell the story. One has to guess the story in 'em. So, I think we added a, I did a translation, I did a kind of narrative alongside explaining it as it happened, and that helped. But I remember that one as a good performance. Then we also did that in fancy theatres in France, and so on and that was very boring – to do it to big crowds of people who wanted to see political shows from us – eh – (I: But they were somewhat political –) Yeah, very –.' — (Schumann, interview, August '82.)

14. '*The Blue Light* – it's the Brothers Grimm story, but it was very distorted. It was done with very few masks, I think. It had no stage arrangement at all. It was done in the open.... And they were done – a crowd of people, and single characters simply stepping out of the crowd because the main characters in the play.... There was very little in the way of masks and puppets in (*The Blue Light*), and they were all used openly. A person would put them on himself or herself and would come out.' (Schumann, interview, August '82).

Their setting according to the mss.:

'A painted flower backdrop. Two large, celastic flower-painted lady puppets with babies in their arms are set before the backdrop. A light bulb is hanging from the ceiling with a long cord attached to it.'

According to Jotterand, *Le Nouveau Theatre Americain*, The Raven, a giant grey bird, hanging at one side of the stage, served for entrances and exits throughout the show – but Jotterand is unreliable:

'*Blue Raven Beauty (La beaute et le corbeau blue)*: la fable est tirée de trois contes de Grimm. La representation d'avril 1969, à la Mama a New York, etait une succession d'apparitions de tableaux de rêve, traversées par le passage des petits Bavarois blonds chaussés de bottes (les fils de Schumann). Un mariage, le trone du roi, la sorcière, les trois voleurs, – les images théatrales se succedaient comme un livre dont on tournait les pages en revenant en arrière, en sautant des épisodes. Le corbeau formait le decor à lui tout seul, grand bec gris au milieu de tentures grises qui s'ouvraient pour laisser entrer les acteurs ou les engloutir.'

hundred years sleep, everyone else does too, in turn telling what they were doing when they fell asleep, the Queen first. After the Queen tells it, she starts counting slowly to a hundred:

'After all stories have been told, one by one, in turn, the men players pick up the bass drum and beat it as they cross the stage to the sleeping Princess. There is a player standing there and he slowly strangles each man as he arrives and places the bodies in a great heap. The Queen continues counting through this action until she reaches and ends with ONE HUNDRED YEARS OF SLEEP. An overlifesize puppet, the Great Warrior, with two swords enters, crosses the stage to the strangler and strikes him dead. All the players rise, pick up instruments and . . .' (Mss., *Blue Raven Beauty*.)

October 22nd ('68) Schumann performed *King Story* at the Fillmore East on lower Second Avenue, rock palladium of Bill Graham, Berlin-born rock-impressario who got his start when he left the San Francisco Mime Troupe to manage the Jefferson Airplane. The occasion was a benefit for the Columbia Legal Defense Fund, a fund to aid the 'insurgent' students at Columbia University. Saul Gottlieb, manager of the Radical Theatre Repertory, and at this time of the hugely successful U.S. tour of the Living Theatre returned from Europe and bent on bringing the Paris May to the U.S., had with the aid of Richard Schechner, director of the Performance Group set up the benefit. Illustrating the mood at the time of the 'radical theater' of which Schumann's was a part, and the 'revolutionary' exuberance of it that he resisted but that also was infecting his group and influencing his work of '68-69, the event is of significance for his history. The playwright and poet Jackson MacLow described it soberly in the non-violent resistance magazine *WIN*; the journalist Richard Goldstein peddled its hype in the *Voice*.

'Talking tuf is in; talking luf is out whatever else happened Tuesday night (10/22/68) at the Fillmore East – & plenty else did – these depressing facts were inescapable.

The Open Theatre began the program, a benefit for the Columbia Legal Defense Fund & Ben Morea, who's facing felony charges for defending himself with a knife against thugs in Boston with a short, precisely executed piece in which time was made to go back & forth many times, to the beat of a drum. A small group of kneeling couples in the front alternated between poses of indifference (waving to audiences, etc.) & dying & attempted escape when a couple of other people in front of them shot at them. Another figure (a candidate?) went forward with a hand-shaking gesture & then back. A larger group was at first back of the couples, first warning them when the "riflemen" took aim, later moving around in a precise drill to the left of the kneelers, who faced the right where the riflemen & candidates were placed. This "chorus" recited several speeches in an automaton-like staccato, one syllable per drum beat. Tho they first seemed to be concerned with the victims, their later speeches (I was unable to catch much of what they said) seemed to be stressing their lack of involvement, being good citizens, etc. The alternation of a small number of poses became quite intricate in the small group while the chorus configurations changed. I kept thinking of the scene in Cocteau's "Blood of a Poet" where the hero, peeping thru a keyhole in the "Hotel of Dramatic Follies" sees a Mexican being executed by firing squad, getting up again, being executed by firing squad, getting up again, being executed again, etc., ad infinitum. But the piece didn't have much effect on me perhaps because so many words escaped me despite its being performed well.

After that the tuf talk began. I don't remember the exact order, but Juan Gonzalez, after assuring us that things were still hot at Columbia, read a poem from Berkeley against "the grey-bearded pacifist poets" who supposedly led the young astray into nonviolence, love, mysticism, & dope. Later Ray Brown warned that the black group at Columbia won't be the tail of white radical groups, & Bob Collier (who's served time for allegedly plotting to blow up the Statue of Liberty egged on by my erstwhile fellow-member of Bronx CORE, Detective Ray Wood, alias Ray Woodall, our ultra-militant chant leader at demonstrations) warned that the next election would be the last, that all hell was going to break out after it & that we'd better make sure & be on his side or we'd get ours along with the other pigs. With Collier was a bodyguard who kept one hand in a pocket & edged forward menacingly when anyone objected to what his boss was saying. But why? What did Collier – a man of superb presence & seemingly great intelligence think he was accomplishing by threatening that theatreful of heads, politicals, and political heads? Do people who are really plotting violent revolution go around boasting about it in public & threatening potential allies? The whole bit goes right past me & I don't think it's just because I oppose violent means as leading to violent ends.

Well, somewhere in here the Soul & Latin Theatre, a high school group, began a very long play about life in a typical NYC classroom. The students were all Puerto Rican – 3 girls & 1 boy while the teacher, a very large woman, & toward the end, a dapper male principal or dean, were both played by blacks. The teacher spent most of her time telling the students to 'SHUT UP!' & otherwise insulting them, while the latter talked back to her more & more strongly until she fainted. Then one of the girls had to slap her to bring her to, the principal appeared, more hassles, on & on & on. It obviously might have gone on forever, & of course it really does, but the audience after loyally cheering the students & booking the authorities over & over got tired of it & said so. It still kept on, however, & I didn't find it the least bit boring. It wasn't entertaining & wasn't meant to be, but it all rang so true that I was fascinated all the way through.

Then (I think it was then), as if to make up for the previous death of jollity, Abbie Hoffman came on & proved he is one of America's greatest stand-up comedians. I'd never seen the man live before & I hadn't much liked what I'd seen or heard of him before then, but his account of his Chicago adventures during the convention & afterwards when he went back to stand trial was insanely funny. Yet that was itself troubling. His whole thing was so unrelentingly nutty that I began to wonder whether he was able to act any other way. From the beginning, when he threw off his hat & coat & kicked them off the stage, all through his zig-zag story proving the insanity of police, FBI, & other facets of government he kept up an absent-minded jerky half-dance as if he really had to go pee in the worst way. But his comments were so sharp, his transitions so swift & devastating, that I couldn't help loving him & laughing uncontrollably.

During the intermission I understand that the 6th Street Theatre did an election satire in which a candidate was pumped up until he burst, but my wife & I didn't feel like boring our way thru the crush, so we missed it.

Right after the intermission The Living Theatre began an abbreviated version of *Paradise Now*. Actors moved all over the theatre, in & out over the rows, hoarsely shouting "I don't know how to stop the war!" I don't know what other complaints intervened, but after a while they were saying "I'm not allowed to smoke marihuana!" But this wasn't the Brooklyn Academy of Music & undaunted East Side heads were soon passing joints all over the place, as if to say, "Well you damn well can HERE!" However, much to my surprise, when the actors got to "I'm not allowed to take my clothes off in public!" only 3 people really stripped, & 2 of them were LT actors. Otherwise, bathing suits, loincloths, bras & panties, & skivvies were the rule. Why were all those so willing to risk smoking pot in public so shy about disrobing to the public?

On stage, the more & less unclad ones (almost all LT actors) sat in a circle & passed around joints & a pipe for a while. Then the actors grouped into half-standing ass-fucking teams of 4 or 5 each & then climbed onto each others' back & became totem poles with their tongues thrust out & hands & forearms held out stiffly from elbows with fingers spread wide. Applause & well deserved: it was a startling tableau.

But then the big hassle began, & I'm damned if I can remember how it started. Before the show, an LT actor had told us that they & the eastside anarchist group "Up Against The Wall/Motherfuckers" were going to take over the theatre & force the owner, a certain Bill Graham, to let the East Side community have the theatre free one night a week for whatever they wanted to have happen in it: free rock concerts, town meetings, plays, etc. The story was that UATW/M had approached Graham about this & that he'd said they could have it for $450 or some such sum. Agitation for a free night at the Fillmore has been going on for several weeks, but nothing else had come of it. Now there was Ben Morea & Tom Newman of UATW/M at the microphone stage right, with innumerable people around them, pressing these demands, & after a while calling for Graham to come up on stage.

When he did he kept rehashing past conversations, "& then what did I say? & then what did *you* say?" ad nauseam. There were hundreds milling around on stage by then, it seemed, & somebody brought on a mimeograph & started running off leaflets then & there while somebody else was silk-screening blue-or-red-on-orange posters that said something about "revolution" (a term so run into the ground these days that my only reponse can be "Anarchist Revolutionism Forever!") The hassle went on literally for hours. I can't begin to do a blow-by-blow, but I couldn't help admiring Graham's guts as he stood up to a few thousand angry heads, saying that if they tried to *force* him to do anything, they'd only get the theatre over his dead body.

After a while he was saying that they could have the theatre one night a week if they let him know what they'd do with it & he approved. But Julian & Ben & a few other objected to this, saying that "no one man should have the right to decide such a thing" & all thru this was the continuing threat that "the community" was going to occupy the theatre from then on (as the mimeo'd leaflets were recommending) until it got what it wanted. Then an agreement seemed to be reached that he'd allow a town meeting the following week on Wednesday in which the community might decide what to do with the theatre on the free days, if any. But still no one got off the stage. The Bread & Puppet Players wanted to put on their "King Play," but couldn't for a very long time. Then they did.

Their precise and formal puppet, mask, drum & trumpet piece was performed before & above a bright red cloth. (Earlier, this or a similar cloth had been wound & rewound among the crowd on stage, & still earlier, someone had put a red cloth on the right-hand loudspeaker assemblage, which caused someone else to put a *black* cloth or coat on the left-hand one, but whether this meant that communism & anarchy were working hand-in-hand or at loggerheads was quite unclear.) This story was as simple as possible. A Great Warrior offered his services to a Good King. The latter refused at first, but later, when threatened by someone else, engaged the GW, who then killed the GK, the Head Priest, & all the People. Then Death came. GW tried to kill him, failed, and then fell before him. Then Death (dear Charley Adams in a scary mask & an old brown hat) went away beating his drum. The End.

It was pushing 2 AM by then, so after a short conversation with Judith & Julian, we went home & never did find out how the show ended. The Fillmore East is still there & Graham still owns it.'

(J. Mac Low, *Up Against the Wall Theatre,*
or Where Have All The Flowers Gone, Motherfucker?,
WIN, November 15, '68.) (Copyright Jackson MacLow 1968.)

'Antonin Artaud played the Fillmore East on October 22 — electric shock and all. The occasion was a benefit for the Columbia students' legal defense fund. The program included the cream of New York's radical theatre crop (Living Theatre; Performance Group; Pageant Players; Bread and Puppet Theatre; Open Theatre), two local street troupes (6th Street Theatre and New York Free Theatre) and a taste of the high school underground (Soul and Latin Theatre). Also present was a stellar corps of hip brothers in the struggle (Juan Gonzalez, Ray Brown, Ben Morea, Bob Collier), assorted veterans of the Lincoln Park Brigade (Abbie Hoffman, Paul Krassner, Bob Fass), and a cast of thousands who had never been immortalized in any Norman Mailer epic of the revolution, and who were therefore (notwithstanding a visceral need for publicity) groovy and pure.

There were speed freak saints doing a jig of liberation in the balcony, and West Side liberalatti crouching in the pews below. There were Black Panthers stalking Village highrisers in the aisles, their every step an indelible mince of cool. There were earth mothers holding moon children in their arms. There were media men (that dwindling core of reporters who work the radical beat) with a gleam of their pens and a glaze in their eyes. And there was the pride of the math commune, lavaliered with slogans, lips pursed, brow furrowed, his entire face transformed into a pink fist . . . .

The evening had been organized to benefit two causes: it might yield an abundant breadcrop for the student coffers, and it might engender a sense of solidarity among New York's most unorthodox theatre community. For there is something about the street theatre experience which defies standardization. This could be because (unlike rock) it remains structurally undefined, depending for its vitality only on the expectations of its audience. In the context of latent range, it is possible to be deeply aroused by the kind of stark pageantry they used to throw at renegade serfs. Great street theatre functions as a stained glass window to the soul, and the lesson it flashes through those vibrantly tinted panes is the liberation of emotion, in the absence of consequence.

No wonder the Living Theatre stunned Europe (and, pinched America) as the quintessential street theatre, ready to do battle not with dogma, but with restraint. And no wonder Eric Bentley refused to appear on the same stage with Julian Beck. He foresaw the resurrection of Artaud last Tuesday night, when he predicted that the Living Theatre would disrupt the proceedings. To disrupt (in ecstatic-anarchist slang) is to render spontaneous, and therefore, free.

The evening began, sedately enough, with a word-ballet by the Open Theatre. It was a pleasant exercise in desperation, with the cast feigning assassination one moment, and socialization the next ("I am a small man . . . I mind my own affairs . . . I stay alive.") But it became apparent that this audience was after more than closet revolt. It wanted to participate in a bloodletting, with the victim in absentia. A long selection from the Hard Core, a Columbia SDS newsletter, drew audience-fire with its tirade against the hip-rock-flower crusade ("Your disciples are dying in the streets, gurus/You have been among the philistines too long . . . . Is it not time to admit that hate as well as love redeems the world?") And an interminable skit called "Classroom" ended with the audience screaming "Strike, strike" at the young actors who were rebelling against their teacher. But this was no tribute to the gilded memory of Clifford Odets. In the youth-Marxism of this movement, it is now against then, and image against authority. "Make class war," a voice from the rafters rang out, and the pun went uncontested.

How appropriate that the Living Theatre should choose that moment to begin its performance of "Paradise Now." The actors emerged mysteriously from the depths of their own audience, like a demon whale leaping out of water. In that moment when you can't tell for the spray and power what is fish and what is sea, the actors sprang from their places, and it was impossible to separate act from experience. The audience simply disappeared under the weight of its own emotions.

"Oh wow," a kid behind me said. "Some chick back there is tripping out, screaming that she can't travel without a passport." A tall cat with lean blond hair occupied the center aisle like an indignant stag, shouting "I don't know how to stop the war." A lady shrank from his spittle. Another smiled the vacant grin of indigestion. But then he was surrounded by kids, who danced around him screaming "I DO know how to stop the war," and this litany continued for five minutes, like a furious Hail Mary.

Onstage, 100 people were dancing, chanting, or stomping away. Many who knew the scenario by heart were stripping in anticipation. A couple started shagging stage center, surrounded by cheering admirers. A skinny kid ripped off his shirt and peeled away his jeans. He stood in the velour-blue spotlight, in a beard and jockey shorts, as his friends shouted "C'mon, Mark, take it all off."

The actors too, had bared their bodies; they slipped onstage, formed an even circle, and passed the pipe around. Neighborhood kids moved among the actors, whistling and shouting "Naked City." A pale woman stood backstage in a simple pair of underpants. "I feel like I've done something," she whispered, slipping her bra in place. "You know . . . I can't stand the war . . . they're killing babies over there."

The performance "ended" in a huge swirling dance of OM. From the audience, it looked like a transplanted chunk of Central Park on some mythical Easter Sunday. To watch that orchestrated tumult from beyond the footlights was to understand why young radicals are fascinated by the erasure of barriers between life and theatre, and why liberals are terrified to see those boundaries disappear. Because, in truth, that audience was watching itself. The theatre had vanished; instead, the Becks had turned the Fillmore East into a street.

At that moment – as though timing were all that was involved – Ben Morea grabbed the microphone and announced on behalf of the Motherfuckers that the Fillmore East had been liberated. He proceeded to demand that Bill Graham turn the house over to "the community" once a week, gratis. Graham's eyes did a soft roll in their sockets as he walked into the spotlight to make the confrontation complete.

The "liberation" had been planned. Morea proceeded to tell his audience that Graham had refused repeated requests to use the hall. Graham denied the charge, and Morea announced that the Fillmore would be free or the community would burn it down. "If you want the theatre to be free," Graham replied, "then buy it." The confrontation turned into a debate about the future of radical theatre in a fascist state. Graham, faced with all the standard charges (exploitation of the hip masses, authoritarianism, and just plain straightness), responded with a lame smile. But there was rage in his face. Mark Kaminsky, an organizer of the benefit, began to fear for the other acts. He offered to have the stage cleared, but Graham refused. "The thing is like a big balloon," he said. "You just have to let it run out of air."

But the uprising refused to deflate. Julian Beck stepped in to negotiate, and as is his talent, he succeeded in exacerbating Graham's anger. The audience insisted on capitulation, and someone shouted, "If we don't get the hall, you don't either." Graham stepped to the microphone. "Okay, we can talk about using the place," he said. "But if you try to take it by force, you're gonna have to kill me first."

In a temporary settlement, Graham agreed to open his theatre on Wednesday, October 30, for a "town meeting" at which the Motherfuckers and their allies would attempt to organize a Free Theatre for the Lower East Side. A mimeograph machine was hauled onstage, and leaflets announcing the agreements were run off on the spot. "The community needs a space," the release declared, needs it to survive, grow freaky, breathe, expand, love, struggle, and on. Bill Graham, hippie entrepreneur . . . may tonite have been a little liberated, or he may not. Next Wednesday will tell." On the bottom, in threatening letters, the flyer said: "One Nite a Week or Sky's the Limit."

It was another victory for hippie power. The audience – or that segment of it which had not been exasperated beyond endurance – cheered wildly. "Today the Fillmore," I heard someone mutter, "tomorrow the White House."

The Bread and Puppet Theatre (the only troupe which had not called the scene a bummer and split) set up it instruments and its masks. Director Peter Schumann pleaded with the Motherfuckers to clear the stage (at one point he asked for just five minutes to perform) but the harranguing went on. Two members of the Living Theatre began to shout "You're fired" at the sound crew. Graham was still surrounded by accusers. And Julian Beck held forth backstage on art and revolution. He called the evening "The most exciting production I've seen in the New York theatre." I asked whether he didn't feel uncomfortable in alliance with a movement which counseled violence when necessary to achieve its ends. "This isn't violence," he answered. "It's passion. It's a bourgeois myth to confuse the two."

Julian Beck was right, of course. We had all been victim-heroes of a passion play called "New York City, October 22, 1968." The Living Theatre, delving into the psyche of its audience, had liberated rage. If the communards and the Motherfuckers chose to channel that emotion into revolution, they were not alone in their rationale. They could have played the teacher's strike at the Fillmore that night (Yeshiva gentility turns into righteousness – the Jewish equivalent of anger). They could have turned the whole thing into a Wallace rally, or a rape. They could have played cops, raising their fists into the air, at the red television eye, and shouting "Lindsay/Graham must go." Raising their fists like the kids at Columbia, in a peace-queer salute. Raising their fists to let the whole city know that like everyone else in this place – like every mother's shortbread wonder – they too were pissed.'

(R. Goldstein, *Fillmore Liberation/The Theatre of Cruelty Comes to Second Avenue, Village Voice*, October 31, '68.) (Copyright *The Village Voice*, 1968.)

Schumann got to perform, Schechner didn't. The Motherfuckers, 'self-acclaimed vanguard of the hip-militant coalition' then according to Steve Lerner (*The Lower Eastside: Radicalization of Hip, Village Voice*, November 28, '68) in process of formation, a bunch of decent drug-taking rowdies, New York analogue of the San Francisco Diggers, with touches of the Hell's Angels, weren't only trying to take over the Fillmore but Schumann's Courthouse as well,[15] and while Schumann was gone in Europe in '69 succeeded.

---

15. 'Well, they wanted to get in, they wanted to get in, and we – and I said, look – I used to see them all the time the leaders and so I used to say – look, we are using it ourselves. We are using it every minute too, we are not fucking around here. And they respected that. They said, well, can we have a little piece, can we have a little piece, I said not now. I mean I wasn't afraid of them, I wasn't intimidated by them, at all, in fact, I called one of them a punk and he got real angry, but we didn't get to fighting over it. I didn't feel anybody – I mean I had been through some things, I didn't think that anybody could tell me they were more radical than I was or ready to change more than I was. I mean, I felt that, at that time . . . . (Schumann) knew everybody, to a certain extent, he knew we were also in a situation on the Lower East Side where there were incredible currents pushing, tugging, screaming, the currents of the streets – what was happening on the Lower East Side were the Motherfuckers, the street people, the Vietnam war, the demonstrations – and then to boot, a lot of the people in the group were in accord with all that, if not everybody, and some of the people had very intimate contact – I had intimate contact with the Motherfuckers too – and I counted them among friends – we'd argue. I wasn't afraid at all, but they were pushing. They were saying, get off your arse and you couldn't not hear it.' — (Levy, interview.)

23. March-December '69. *The Cry of the People for Meat.* Pessimistic glorification of resistance, even armed.

Though I had attended some of the Old Courthouse rehearsals in the spring of '69, I saw *The Cry* only in its three showings for the benefit of military base coffee houses and G.I. newspapers at St. Peter's Church on West 20th Street in New York City, December 5, 6, and 7, '69. My account of the play, writen '69/70 (published in *Tulane Drama Review* #47 (1970), follows:

'In terms of content, *Cry* divided into:

I. PROLOGUE IN GREECE

II. THE OLD TESTAMENT AND THE NATIVITY
1. The Beasts of the Earth (before Man) (Gen. 3:8, 28)
2. Breathing Life into Man's Nostrils (and eating from the tree) (Gen. 1:27 and 3:6-7)
3. Attention! Angel! (The expulsion) (Gen. 3:8, 28)
4. Cain's birth (Gen. 4:1-16)
5. Noah's Second Message ("every living thing that moves shall be meat for you") (Gen. 9:3)
6. The Beasts of the Earth (Abel's murder and Cain's nomination) (Gen. 4:7-8)
7. Birth of the People of the World (the children of God and the daughters of men) (Gen. 4:1-4)
8. Noah's Nomination and First Message ("I see that every imagination of the thoughts of your heart is only evil continually") (Gen. 6:5-8)
9. The Flood (Gen 7:17-23)
10. The Herding of the Beasts (Gen. 8:19-21 and/or 9:2)
11. Joseph's Genealogy (the old history) (Matt. 1:1-16)
12. Joseph is Clothed (not in the Bible)
13. Joseph's Dream (Matt. 1:20-21)
14. The Creation of Mary (Luke 1:28-37)
15. The Nativity (cf. Luke 2:7 and 35-37 and Matt. 1:8-21)
16. The Procession to Bethlehem (Luke 2:4)
17. The Arrival of the Three Kings (Matt. 2:1-2, 7-11)

III. HEROD'S WRATH
1. The Message of the Three Kings (Matt. 2:2)
2. Herold's Wrath (Matt. 2:3 and 16-18)
3. The Three Kings' Dream (Matt. 3:12)
4. Joseph's Dream (Matt. 2:13)
5. The Flight to Egypt (Matt. 2:14)
6. Jerusalem's Wrath (not in the Bible)

IV. THE GREY LADIES AND THE WOMAN OF BEN SUC (cf. Matt. 2:16-18)
  1. One Soldier Marching
  2. The Grey Ladies of Bethlehem
  3. Arrival of a Woman with a Baby
  4. The Soldier Fighting the Door
  5. The Air Raid
V. THE CRUCIFIXION
  1. The Exaltation and Building of Jesus (a feast and the Beatitudes) (Luke 6:20 and Matt. 5:4-10) and the Parables
  2. The Three Miracles
  3. The Last Supper
  4. The Crucifixion
  5. An Ascension?[1]

In terms of dramatic movement — strange continuities between scenes, major breaks, alternations of mood and content — the structure seemed to me to be:

I. PROLOGUE IN HEAVEN. PATRICIDE, OR THE PRINCIPLE OF LIFE, VS. RESISTANCE (I supra)
II. HUMANITY BEFORE CHRIST: GOD AGAINST LIFE AND LIFE UNDER GOD (II supra)
  1. Life and Love: The Animal Kingdom and Adam and Eve (II.1-2 supra)
  2. Divine Wrath: the Expulsion (II.3) supra
  2. Be Fruitful and Multiply (II.4)
  4. Divine Reaction and Revenge: Life Set Against Life, or Fratricidal Strife (II.5-6)
  5. Love and Aid between Men and Women (II.7)

---

[1]. The Prologue in Greece derived from the Newport *Chicken Little* by way of a New Year's Eve Party, December 31, '68 in Central Park:

'Bethesda Party. A New Year's Eve Party open to all will be held in Central Park at the Bethesda Foundation (72nd St.) from 11 pm to 1 am. The Bread & Puppet Theatre will present a special New Year's pageant featuring 20-ft. puppets. The terrace will be illuminated with moving lights by Martin Fronstein and decorated with plastic, air-supported structures by Kip Coburn. Tony Lawrence, director of the Harlem Cultural Festival, will m.c. A rock and roll band will play starting at 11 pm. Shortly before midnight, 2 giant piñatas designed by Adolfo Castro will be broken, distributing noise-makers. Clara Walker and the Gospel Redeemers will sing at midnight and 12 giant helium-filled balloons will be released as a symbol of peace for the new year. Ray Baretto and his Latin Soul Brothers will play until the end. Hot drinks and bratwurst and marshmallows will be sold.' — (Notice, *Village Voice*, January 2, '69.)

II. 1-10 was a development of the Newport '68 *The Bible*; II. 11-17, III & IV were in effect a new version of the *Christmas Story*, where IV was inspired by Jonathan Schell's *The Village of Ben Suc* (*The New Yorker*, April '67) and developed themes of the street parades (cf. *Johnny Comes Marching Home*, and of the *Bach Cantata#140*), V was a new version of *The Crucifixion*.

6. Divine Wrath and Punishment, the Perversion of Life: Man the Proprietor (II.8-10)
7. The Old History: Perverted Life or Death in Life (II.11)
8. Hope in Life: the Coming of Jesus (II.12-17)
III. ANTI-LIFE AGAINST LIFE: HEROD'S WRATH, OR BETHLEHEM & VIETNAM (III & IV supra)
IV. LIFE IN HOPE: RESISTANCE (V.1-2 supra)
V. ANTI-LIFE AGAINST LIFE (V.3-4 supra)
VI. HOPE? (V.5 supra)

The performance:

There is no stage, only a floor space & some partitions at the back for costume changes & props. We are at the other end, on tiered benches & on the floor, in a broad half circle. Most of the time, most of the group is out on the floor ("stage left"), often as a band, in a circle, or facing the action. Performers rise from this pool, rejoin it. They are somewhat uniformly dressed in vaguely Buddhist-looking white gym suits.[2] The important piece of stage machinery is a red cloth about ten feet high & twelve feet wide, between two poles. Stretched between them by two pole bearers, its nether edge flush with the ground, it serves as a screen – in this play (originally it was marked "heaven") it marks off the world of God from the mortal world of men & beasts. It is mobile, serves other purposes, & is easily put away when the action does not call for it. As division, background, goal of advance or point of departure, it defines the performing space wherever it is put (generally, "stage right"). The action, in proportion to its power of concentrating attention, makes this definition real. "Onstage" is where the action is.

Maurice Blanc, Schumann's chief actor (Sensitive Hero), in top hat & frock coat, tells us over the P.A. system – Schumann banging on the side of his big drum – that the play consists of the *entire* Bible. He announces the evening's program as a barker at a fair, vaunting the fantastic richness of the offerings inside, the management's grandiose, unstinting ambition. (It is evidently going to be cheap art.) He reads the list of biblical events represented from a scroll, each heading, in circus-act fashion, accompanied by drum rolls & trumpet flourishes. "And now we begin with a prologue which takes place in Greece in which you will see the marriage of the God of Heaven, Uranos, & Mother Earth, the birth of Chronos, & the slaying of Uranos by Chronos."

Prologue in Greece
'Ladies & Gentlemen, the Lord of Heaven, Uranos!' A fifteen-foot colossus, Uncle Fatso,[3] arch-capitalist (a cigar between the knuckles of his fat hand), a

---

2. Paris, Salle Wagram, November '68:
'Pleins feux scène et salle. Les spectateurs entrent, s'asseoient, parlent. De leur côté, les acteurs (une vingtaine) se préparent, aménagent l'espace dans lequel ils vont jouer. Ils sont tous vêtus de blanc, en blue-jeans, avec une chemise, un pull over ou un polo. Autour de leurs genoux et de leurs coudes ils attachent des bandages destinés à amortir les chocs. Sur la nuque, ils portent un masque. Ils prennent chacun un ou plusieurs instruments de musique, grosse caisse, cymbales, cors, petites trompettes d'enfants en plastique, criquets, sifflets, mirlitons, couvercles de casserole, etc., et vont s'installer côté jardin en formant un large cercle. Séance de musique improvisée.' — (Kourilsky, '71.)
3. According to Kourilsky, '71, the 'Fox' from *Chicken Little*.

bloody tyrant when in motion, a man-eating Moloch when standing straight, sways away from the wall he's been leaning against, moving his arms in the awkward gestures of demagogic politicians. He is promenaded about by five performers, allowed to introduce himself to the audience, shown off, retired toward the wall.

'You all know her, you all love her – Mother Earth!' – Her fifteen-foot-high body has been leaning in the other corner, a grotesque mother-figure out of the German petty-bourgeoisie, her face inexpressive but acid – or, on the contrary, depending on mood & lighting, staring, with her mouth pulled open & out, as though fascinated, frozen in eternal terror at a horrible event. She gives a wiggle as she comes out. They meet, embrace, kiss with a loud smack, waltz to the music of the band, grandly part like a parting of the waves.

'And now, Mother Earth gives birth to her last child, Chronos...' The screen flutters violently as she decently gives birth behind it – the boy, a mere nine-footer, agile (there is a performer inside), a great intrepid spiked head, the fixed gaze of combat above truculently set Negro lips – emerging from a heaving hillock of a hundred pounds of newspaper strips on the floor. He is born with his two swords in hand, jagged raw wood splinters, two or three feet in length. He rises, immediately starts to fight his father who is too august really to fight back. Two performers sportscast the fight, passing the mike back & forth while others mount a stepladder behind Uranos, remove his head, toss it into the screen spread out as a trampoline by still others who bounce the head into the rear storage area. Chronos has won.

All this has been done very quickly, at a run, with all the lights on, with the air of enacting something known, for the sake of providing the enjoyment of the act, the "how we do it" in the forefront. One watches the giants in unbelief – they are incredible – & excitedly admires the acrobatics. The killing of one's father is the gayest thing in life, archetype of victory, appropriately done showing off, to hurdy-gurdy music.[4]

The Old Testament & The Nativity
The Beasts of the Earth (before man)

The red screen advances, its carriers wearing the masks of beasts. The lights go out, a hand projector in the litter left on the floor from Chronos' birth is trained on the screen,[5] the screen falls to a cymbal clash, revealing – to a discordant noise on the P.A.[6] – a tight mass or mountain of beasts in a stretched-out, heaving, forward-moving blob on the floor.[7] These beasts, seemingly all gray-white head – the performers' bodies & limbs perfunctorily covered by the burlap-like material attached to the heads – are a picture of horror out of an imaginary low state of

---

4. 'Le Dieu du Ciel décapité est emporté et adossé au fond de la scène, côté jardin. De l'autre côté, on place Mère Terre: c'est en leur présence que se déroulera la suite de l'histoire.' — (Kourilsky, '71.)
5. '... le meneur de jeu (Peter Schumann) se débarrasse de sa grosse caisse pour prendre une lampe, une simple ampoule protégée par un abat-jour en métal cabossé.' — (Kourilsky, '71.)
6. 'Dans un bruit infernal de voitures, de pneus qui crissent, de klaxons, de sifflets de police, de hurlements de sirènes (le bruit de la circulation sur la 2ᵉ Avenue à New York enregistrée sur bande magnétique...' — (Kourilsky, '71.)
7. In Paris, Chronos herded in the beasts — (Kourilsky, '71.)

evolution, but neither savage nor cruel. Their sharp-pointed teeth look brittle, their jaws weak; they have dumb-looking, mostly piggish snouts – creeping things.

Each of the performers straps on at least two beast-heads, some strap on three: one on the head, the others on the arms, with the arm inside. Much rehearsal time was spent on mass movement. Schumann kept telling the performers to bunch together, crawl over one another, speed up, keep down: he got the effect of the primeval horror of scarcely individuated life out of the simple physical difficulty of crawling in a tight mass with those eyeless heads on, & did not call for any manner or style of body movement – a puppeteering, not acting, feat. The effect is a limbless reptilian advance, but heavy & awkward, instinctive rather than purposive.

In their first appearance in the play, the beasts image the pre-human earth, a setting for achievement, but also the panic side of nature. Starting the play with this scene rather than with Adam & Eve makes it a play about "every living thing that moves" rather than about man.

Breathing Life into Man's Nostrils

More or less unnoticeably, among the herd, two human figures, man & woman: transparent cocoons of plastic over their dress, have entered the acting space & now come out from among them & lie down still, in front of the screen. Schumann, wearing no particular costume, comes over with a floodlight, kneels, breathes life into Adam's nostrils, shining the light on this action, slaps him very hard on the back or arse, and Adam rises slowly as though unconscious. Schumann drags the woman upright before Adam. Still in her cocoon up to her neck, she starts slowly to divest him of his with her teeth (& neck & shoulders, rubbing), while Schumann stands there, painting this arduous awakening with white light – the sheen of the plastic, its folds, the pensive Maurice inside. The scene is slow, the silence complete – there is tension of being present at a crucially important step. Eve then shrugs herself out of her own cocoon.

Schumann's role is that of God, but he does not in any way act of God: God is not there. Schumann acts as operator of the theatre – as puppeteer – with "unacted," natural, efficient movements, contributing technological beauty. Adam & Eve are grave & deliberate. Their poetry contrasts with the horror-vision of the creeping things & the comedy of the gods. Except for the operator, they are the first persons – neither puppets nor masked – we have seen. The scene implies natural evolution. The fall from grace – they end up "nude" – is an awakening: in the spiritual though not necessarily the moralistic sense of Gen. 3:5-7. There is no serpent, only the woman. She is the awakener, man is the son of woman – in the spirit of the Jesus-story but not of Genesis where she is first only in sin. They are without sin in this scene, inconcupiscent. Schumann sees the scene as a sensual love story. The ripping off of the cocoon, analogous to a cow's licking her newborn calf clean, is love-making: Eve uses her mouth.

The Expulsion

A sudden cry: "Attention! Angel!"[8] With a horrible noise (the taped sound of

---

8. Schumann's awkward English for 'Obacht! Der Engel!' which combines 'Watch out! Here comes the Lord's servant!' and the military command to come to attention – Jehovah as dreaded martinet.

traffic on Second Ave, at 2:00 P.M., cymbal clashes, "ahs" from the group), the Deity declares Himself: His Angel – the same Great Warrior that was Chronos, horned, blue, a crazy angel – comes out from behind the screen, striking at Adam & Eve. They fall. "So he drove out the man; and he placed at the east of the garden of Eden Cherubims, and a flaming sword which turned every way, to keep the way of the tree of LIFE" (Gen. 3:24). The Angel is Time. Life in moving time is removal from Life.

Cain's Birth

Somehow the expulsion scene changes into another in which Adam seems to be delivering Eve of an attacker with a beast's head, pulling him off her & out of his beast-mask, he clinging to her or she to him. The Angel with very slow, large gestures proceeds to strike the attacker elaborately. He is on the ground, his arms & legs keep sticking up (an ancient gag from burlesque & puppet theatre – but frightful here), the Angel keeps striking them down, he will not die . . . he is down flat, slain. But he comes alive again immediately! – he rises.[9]

This whole scene, though evidently a reference to Cain, is very confused, a mixture of rape, birth, homicide, rescue – images of Divine wrath, procreation, strife & survival. According to Schumann: Eve gives birth, a beast crawls up, she grabs his head, the man Adam pulls Cain out. He is born but is not yet alive. The Angel strikes him alive. It is Cain.

Noah's Second Message

Immediately, Schumann brutally ties a cardboard sign over Cain's eye which says: "Every living thing that moves shall be meat for you." He stands facing the audience, blinded. Cain has – momentarily – become Noah. God's assignment to Noah: "Every moving thing that livest shall be meat for you" (Gen. 9:3) has been inverted in order to eliminate its ritualism (cf. e.g., Deut. 14:21) & to stress its evils: life is to be meat for life. It is a preamble to His basic contract with all living things, His rainbow covenant with the Jews, & is motivated by the savor of burnt meat offerings & by the resigned consideration that "the imagination of man's heart is evil from his youth" (Gen. 8:21). It is severely qualified: He will lay off the floods, let man & animals live, but He reserves the right to all life (Gen. 9:4-6).

The Beasts of the Earth (Abel's murder & Cain's Nomination)

Schumann separates out one of the beasts, carries it before the blinded man, lays it down at his feet. Cain begins to tame it, with slow brutal grace, again & again picking it up & throwing it down. Finally subjugated, the beast stays down, then

---

9. 'Les bêtes s'écartent et le rideau rouge est étendu au milieu d'elles: c'est sur ce tapis de sol que vont se dérouler les actions suivantes. Le Grand Guerrier se tient debout, derrière, présidant la scène. Une bête vient toucher doucement Eve. Adam et Eve se placent de part et d'autre de la bête et tirent sur le masque, découvrant un homme qui reste étendu à plat ventre sur le tapis rouge. Le Grand Guerrier le frappe successivement sur lese poignets, les talons, la tête, et lentement, à chaque coup d'épée souligné par un éclat de cymbales, il lève un bras, une jambe, redresse le buste, frémissant comme un oiseau qui chercherait à s'envoler, puis, d'un brusque mouvement, il se met debout. Derrière lui, le Grand Guerrier tient ses deux épées dressées en l'air." — (Kourilsky, '71.)

crawls over & licks his master's feet. The scene — pivotal, in view of the play's title — is charged with horror: an indictment of blind brutality. It is, also, the play's only sexually charged scene. The cowed beast gropes its way up along its standing master's body, its beast-mask has disappeared, a white human mask appearing underneath. Another performer removes its master's blinder. The beast has become man, has risen; the seeing master now fights him in another long, terrifyingly methodical patient fight — the subjugate's body thumping on the floor. The master of beasts master him. Throughout, the Angel stands watching with his swords up.[10]

The lust for meat — the failure to respect life in all that lives — is why man is wolf unto man, the root of men's mistreatment of one another. The master-servant relationship generalizes brutality. But Schumann here intends not brutality but murder — imperialist war:

Cursed be Canaan; a servant of servants shall he be unto his brethren.

(Gen. 9:25)

For thou art an holy people unto the Lord they God, and the Lord hath chosen thee to be a peculiar people unto himself, above all the nations that are upon the earth.

(Deut. 14:2)

The cry for meat is answered by the sanctification of imperialism (Deut. 12:1-19). Schumann: "Killing the beast gives him all that power to kill his brother." To Schumann's lowing, mooing horn — horns & percussions, no strings, no light instruments, the beat from a gasoline power saw — the beasts advance, then retreat again — as though rejected by God. They carry the body of the victim with them.

Birth of the People of the World

Slowly, with steady pauses, in his strong German voice, to the metronomic clicking of a cricket-instrument, Schumann proceeds to read the genealogy of the patriarchs from Adam to Noah (Gen. 5). As he reads, men & women rise out of the mass of beasts, getting rid of their beast-masks — they are wearing white & dark human masks underneath — & begin a slow, blind, excruciating, zombielike advance toward the screen, the harsh floodlight (actually only 150 watts) shaping the group into plastic, raw sculpture, the more starkly the closer they get. The women are not walking themselves, the men are teaching & helping them by sculpting their arm-, leg- or body-motions into forward poses which they then hold until moved again. The busy arranging by the men contrasts with the slow motion of the women & of the group. The group reaches the screen, crowds against it, some listening to sounds from behind it — but there is not much acting. The evocation of great time is effective, the posing & poses evoke the labor of history. The nonmotion of the moved suggests that the time of man is not yet in motion.

---

10. According to Schumann the full scene is actually: the cowed beast crawls up to Adam & Eve, is born as Cain was before, they pull his mask off, Adam pulls him — Eve's second born, Abel — over to Cain, he writes 'Cain' in red on Cain's forehead. Then, with the mark of Cain on him, Cain proceeds to *kill Abel*. But what I saw renders the essence, which shows that the symbolic efficacy of the staging is independent of its parabolic clarity.

The active role of the men is exceptional in Schumann's theatre. The scene is inspired by the strange passage (Gen. 6:1-4) which tells how the Children of God irritated Him when they began fornication with the Daughters of Men, begetting giants & famous men. Schumann converts the concupiscence displeasing to God (Gen. 6:11) into compassionate aid. The scene is counterpoint to the human aggression in the preceding scenes.

Noah's Nomination & First Message

The reading has reached the name of Noah. Noah climbs on the others' backs, and bends his ear to the upper edge of the screen. Two spindly white hands appear above it, hand Noah a pole, and disappear. Noah speaks to the people, apparently transmitting a message (Gen. 6:5), which only he has heard; the people repeat it in a cry: "I see that every imagination of the thoughts of your heart is only evil continually."

The Flood

Everybody except Noah collapses to the floor, the breath of life has left them (Schumann called for an "explosion"), they have become the flood covering the earth. Noah in a walking motion, pole upheld as a mast, his legs on the backs of two crawling performers, moves through the crowd toward a briefly held up picture of wheat, labeled "Earth."

Nothing in the preceding scene's painful but lovely image of the Birth of the People of the World justifies Divine zoocide. God comes across as petty & mean, an enemy of humanity.[11]

The Herding of the Beasts

The performers have gotten back into the beast-masks. They advance again. Hands drop ropes over the screen. Schumann & a performer (Cain/Noah) brutally round up the beasts, treating them as objects, nervously tying them into a single clump, pulling the rope through nostrils, around horns, etc. The physicality of the action, similar to that of heavy puppeteering, is emphasized, its technical difficulties rather than any acting producing the effect. There are thunderous growling sounds – Second Avenue again – from the amplifiers. A harsh floodlight illuminates the action from above. The mass of beasts is dragged to the screen (the burnt offering of Gen. 8:20-21).[12] This repeats the theme of the preceding scene of dompting, & its brutality relates to the human warmth of the Birth of the

---

11. In the earlier versions, the Flood is more dramatic. The crowd runs back from the screen. They don the beast-masks & approach again, as beasts. Schumann, behind the Angel on whose swords the projector hangs, manipulates him like a human puppet, wrestling him backward & forward by his shoulders so that the projector lights the advancing tangle of beasts. Thunderous sounds, growls. Schumann draws the Angel before them, lifts him up high, illuminating the floor messy with newspaper strips. The beasts collapse on the floor, white masks, giant heads all over. A field of wreckage. God the killer.

12. 'The stage is littered with shredded paper, torn polyethylene, lengths of cable, and Schumann scrambling for his hand-mike, his portable light and script. Yet through the untidiness, the mess, the often blurred effects, he carves his blazing vision of man's ultimate destiny, so that the very mess becomes part of the image of Chaos out of which God created order. It is at this moment that Schumann creates one of his most memorable

People of the World scene as the dompting scene related to the Adam & Eve scene, it generates a musical pattern also found in Genesis: the interaction between men's relation to other living things that move and their own relations to one another.

The beasts are far from pretty. They represent brute life, life in the raw, a potential that can be realized only in & by human solidarity. If Schumann made them pretty like Disney, he would just be back in the property bag — aesthetic property. But Schumann finds them beautiful. They have no eyes, he says, so they are innocent. They are not harmless, but threatening only in a mass.

The biblical reference of the scene is to the disembarcation & offering after the Flood (Gen. 8:19-20). It re-evokes the covenant: the corrupt foundation of pre-Christian history which the following scene of Joseph's genealogy presents.[13]

In truth, the history of the Jews as they told it in the Old Testament is a miserably petty orgy of meanly selfish violence & deceit, serving sexual & economic greed, from the son-cursing Noah & the drunken Lot who devirginized his daughters (having failed to purchase his safety by offering the Sodomites first crack), through the treacherous pimp Abraham trading in his half-sister & wife Sarah, down to the murderous procurer Mordecai & his prostitute niece Esther. It is a classic account of the desperate horror of normal, i.e. selfish, unidealistic, & therefore ahistorical life, torn between death & law & life & lust. Only when we come to the Teachings (Job, the Psalms, Solomon's three books) is there a glimpse of what is called humanity (modesty, justice, wisdom, unselfish piety, *joie de vivre*, love) & in the Prophets some awareness of the misery of the acquisitive condition, in which the fear of death (Luke 1:79) is the driving force that swells the prick & claws the hand.

Joseph's Genealogy

The December version of Joseph's genealogy rather reflects — turning its resignation to humor — the comment of Ecclesiastes:

Vanity of vanities, said the Preacher, vanity of vanities: all is vanity.

---

effects. With the announcement of the Flood, Schumann lifts high his portable light to reveal a moving wave of grotesqe pigs' heads, the Gadarene swine, mankind at its most bestial. Like drovers at a market or shepherds in shearing time, Schumann, assisted by another actor, moves in among them, roughly binding them with ropes as they pile on top of one another, slithering and sliding forward towards the edge of the stage, an avalanche of monstrous heads, manhandling the actors, sweat streaming down his face, he moves in like one possessed against a background of twentieth-century traffic noise on tape, the full-throated roar of modern man. At this moment Schumann carves a theatre image that has all the intensity of Blake. At such moments you cannot but feel he is a "sent" man, a prophet new inspired. It is as though we were present with the artist at the very instant of creating a work of art.' — (Roose-Evans, *Experimental Theatre*.)

13. In the spring version, this scene was a horrible & tragic spectacle. Schumann, with the cricket-instrument, read the begats in darkness, with two slowly flashing strobe-lights illuminating the advance of the groups amidst the eery litter of paper debris & thrown-off beast-masks, a couple acting out each begat: rising together, struggling, falling again: cohabitation, procreation, death in a desperate fusion of orgasm & agony in which death not only wins out over sex, but inhabits it, corroding life, a turgid struggle forever lost.

> What profit hath man of all his labour which he taketh under the sun?
> One generation passeth away, and another cometh:
> but the earth abideth forever.
>
> The thing that hath been, it is that which shall be;
> and that which is done is that which shall be done:
> and there is no new thing under the sun.
>
> (Eccles. 1:2-4, 9)

It begins with a series of tiny comic hand puppets, gradually growing bigger and bigger, quickly appearing high above the screen as though seen from far away. One of the pole-holders chants the name of each patriarch as he appears, after being announced by Schumann. They are followed by masked performers, heinous & hilarious, life-size but fantastic creatures in crudely improvised children's-show garb suggesting royalty & prophets. They each in turn come out from behind the screen, parade across it, disappear. Both sets of personages, though quickly individualizing themselves by some little act or trick of timing[14] & though proud of their sonorous Hebrew names & imbued with their unique importances, are arbitrary creatures of a benignly grotesque phantasy – puppets & masks created for other occasions, for other purposes, & for none. It doesn't matter who these men were. But they become progressively more vivid & monstrous, their masks more hideous, their gestures madder.

The last performer to come out (Maurice) remains, stands very still, easily solemn, a female performer (Margo) behind him. Another performer, kneeling before him, takes a succession of small thin face masks out of a bundle left by the preceding impostor, putting each in turn before Maurice's immobile face, where Margo holds it briefly, to the reading of a name, & then drops it. The three shadows move on the screen like living clock work. The succession is now grave but quick as though the generations had sped up, in anticipation.

Joseph is Clothed

We reach the name of Joseph. Margo proceeds to dress Maurice (out of that same bundle) in an extremely slow, silent ceremony of investiture. The fatal rush of time has ended. The scene takes a good five minutes. It is a silent scene except for some weird violin noise (the plastic electric toy violin?) over the P.A. The gestures are everyday, but the duration invites respect for the occasion. The scene is interesting for the time & care devoted by one person to another & to an ordinary task. It is a puppeteering variant of the basic theatrical gesture of self-disguise: a costume is put on another. The color of the items of desert clothing are in no way beautiful, they are crude – colorful. (Schumann has an exquisite sense of color but a horror

---

14. The back of the head appears first, then the face – he was looking the wrong way. One sniffs a little. One waves his hand hello. One leaves suddenly as though called away. One comes in very very slowly, but disappears immediately when he sees the audience. David & Solomon: David's face, very big, rises, Solomon, smaller, steps out in front of it. Abraham & Isaac: two white faces, the one growing out of the other, rising behind it. A king rides out in front of the screen on a beast, then the beast comes out, riding on the king. A blue lady pushes a little miserable old man puppet on a chair. A small man, naked on top, with enormous feet, he is all feet, comes out, takes a bow for his feet. A little hand puppet cop comes out, then a much bigger cop, about two feet tall.

of aestheticism, & besides likes to take a chance on others' choices, on what's around, on what has been discarded & found on the street – within limits. Spring prop-list: Pair of white strips for sheathing ankles, yellow wrap for body, red belt, orange cloth for arms, green drape, parachute, neckrag, green cloth for cape, yellow cloth for hood.) The scene has a comic twist. After he's dressed up, Joseph is completely covered over with a burnoose, a funny-scary clown's mask, & a tall black hat, smartly slapped into shape by his spouse. Schumann puts the ridicule of the cuckold on him – ending up, after an appearance to the contrary, by bringing out that post-Judaic Negligibility of the Father. It affirms the importance of the Mother & the protective role of the wife. Margo Sherman's pose of softly dreamy sensitivity does not diminish the scene's power as a metaphor of care for another – key to the New Age.

Joseph's Dream

The woman prepares a pallet on the floor, beds down Joseph in it, he sleeps. Schumann walks over, hands her a pair of large cymbals, she kneels down on one knee, and with a wide ecstatic gesture, looking down at him, clashes the cymbals in his ear. Schumann's walking over is "unnecessary," a theatrical effect – except that it suggests that a transcendental agency is involved in the action, Margo here representing the Angel of the Lord in Joseph's dream (Matt. 1:20-23). The action now takes on the precision of pre-destination. Joseph rises, advances to the screen, and, reaching under it with drumsticks (handed to him by Schumann), drums sharply on a bass drum behind it. There is the cry "Attention! Angel!", the screen falls, there is nothing, i.e., no God, behind it, but the Angel (still the Great Warrior, Chronos) strides out and strikes the woman down.

The Creation of Mary

The Mother of God, a large pole puppet, tall, blue, her great hands joined in prayer, is brought out, and advances. The stricken Mary rises from the floor & gets into the puppet, becoming the Blessed Virgin (cf. the Annunciation, Luke 1:26-37). The lights go out.

The Nativity. The Procession to Bethlehem. The Arrival of the Three Kings.

Small red and green lights flicker on and off, a breathtaking Christmas tree, and a toothy, bloody-red-mawed monsterheaded dragon that has been dangling high up from the center rafters slips down with a small baby doll, painted white, between its teeth. Joseph, now a tiny figure of fun between the Angel and Mary, takes it and presents it to Mary – and *all* the lights in the house go on bright, and a chant-

---

15. In the earlier versions, Joseph's dressing did not end up funny. Furthermore, it was rendered awful by a screaming – a wailing, howling – at first rebellious, challenging, then more plaintive, which was kept up continuously by an uncostumed girl off to one side under a sign, 'Earth.' This voice of the Earth gave the ceremony a transcendental dimension. The girl (Leherissier) left the company & nobody else could do it, but, in any event, now Earth no longer calls for or takes notice of the Change of the Times. When Joseph drummed, the screen dropped, the Lord – actually Uranos – was revealed. Joseph shielded his eyes, the Blue Mary came forward, enormous in the light, her right arm in a splendidly angular gesture.

ing procession arrives with the Three Kings – a small performer with three crowned puppet heads, riding on a beast.[16]

Biblical reference, e.g., Revelation 12, will hardly clarify why the child Jesus should be brought in the mouth of a dragon. Graphically, the image (first in *Sleeping Beauty*, '68) evokes the ideas that innocence and life have to be snatched out of the dangerous muzzle of the world but also that innocence gives power over evil. Then, the image of the child in danger is in fact Schumann's emblem of the Christian era. Then again, presumably Schumann is spoofing the miracle of the Virgin Birth and the Fathership of the Holy Ghost by bringing in a fairy tale motif. One reference may be to the Chinese New Year's dragon. There is a faint echo of Jesus in the manger: in Schumann's *Christmas Story*, the ox is the only one in Bethlehem willing to put up Joseph & his family & Joseph shakes its hoof in thanks. And finally, that the Redeemer should be brought to us by a beast, & a particularly terrible but also a nasty, low sort of beast, not unlike a *serpent*, signals the end of the covenant against life – assigns to the serpent in the new life an opposite role than which the Jews assigned it in the old. There is no evil.

Herod's Wrath

The following scene emerges rapidly out of the preceding one. (In fact, Herod is supposed to arrive with the Three Kings.) King Herod is carried in on a chair; he sits, a lone figure, the light on him, a golden paper crown on his head, drumming like mad on a drum between his legs. A Soldier's streamlined bulb of a head-mask with attached angularly hunch-backed tunic & a fat bland staff of a musket, all uniform in dead-gray, are brought out; the Angel-Chronos is undressed, & dressed in them. We are shown how soldiers are made by kings (Matt. 2:3), but the public assumption of this role also ambivalently points to the responsibility of choice & to the common humanity of all carriers of all roles, evil or good. Dressed up, the man is an alien monster & a tool for murder, his skull a helmet, his hump a cache. He stands, bayonet off guard.

---

16. The spring action-outline is different, from Mary's getting into the pole puppet onward:

The people get back into the beast heads and, simultaneously, colored blankets are placed on two of the beasts; the narrator sweeps a path through the shredded paper; a length of green fabric is unrolled along the cleared path; Mary and Joseph mount the beasts; the people who assist Mary and Joseph put on colorful robes, string bells around the necks of some of the beasts and walk along as Shepherds beside and behind Mary and Joseph, in a procession that slowly crosses the stage to the far side, along a green path, to where a woman who has been shrieking awaits them.

Suddenly a musical chanting is heard from the other side of the stage, the Three Kings appear, riding a beast and traveling the same path the procession had followed. Mary and Joseph and the Shepherds join the Three Kings in the chant.

The light is cut; a red and green flicker light comes on, aimed at the far side of the stage. From under the red screen crawls a fantastic dragon bearing a white-painted baby in its mouth. The dragon crawls very closely across the stage to Mary's feet. Throughout this scene can be heard the gentle noises of woodland creatures, birds, crickets, & frogs. The woman who has been howling steps forward & takes the baby from the mouth of the dragon. The light is cut.

The Message of the Three Kings. Herod's Wrath. The Three Kings' Dream. The Flight to Egypt. Jerusalem's Wrath.

Mary leaves, the Three Kings approach Herod, mark his face with red grease paint. He gets up, wrestles them down, sits, his face a grimace-mask of fright.[17] The Three Kings get up, start to ride off, stop, say (Schumann holding the microphone as if for press conference statements), "We return to our own country, but by a different way" (Matt. 2:12), change course, ride off again — their departure is jocular in effect. The Soldier is still standing. Schumann whispers into the microphone, to Joseph, "Take the child and flee," and suddenly the tableau resolves into a wild scrimmage, the whole cast pursuing Joseph, who is running with the baby in his arms as if it were a football. After a moment of madness they return. With their fingers they contort their faces into hideous grimaces. Herod is hunched over his drum, his face a mask of idiot pain & evil, sharply turned over his shoulder, rigidly held toward the audience (good acting, puppet-style). The screen is spread over all of them, like a sheet over a corpse, & they are taken out. Only the Soldier is onstage. He marches up & down in guardstep, his boots stomping, a gray distorted figure, powerful, mechanical. Schumann starts to beat on his big drum. This moment lasts. Its image of bestially dumb, great power is frightening.

The Grey Ladies & The Woman of Ben Suc

One Soldier Marching

A white door with a sign saying "Bethlehem" on it advances toward the Soldier & the audience, carried by a performer in a white gym suit. Behind it advances a group of woman-figures, the Grey Ladies, tenebrous mothers of sights & tears, their faces corroded by suffering and inured to suffering, accusing. They are grey puppets, perhaps seven feet tall, but seem taller, their sad-colored winding-sheets attached to their mop-wigged sculptured heads. As the Soldier patrols & the group advances in a processional ooze, Schumann, in a regular cadence & matter-of-fact voice, counts off the time of day, hour by hour up to 5:30, mentioning breakfast at 8 & lunch between 12 & 1. This is humorous but also contrasts unsuspecting civilian life with its impending doom, & beyond this makes us mindful of the contrast between the routine of the unconcerned and its secular background of horrors. Behind the advancing city, the shark-nosed plane which Schumann uses to crucify Jesus is lined up by performers & also advances, its wings protruding slightly. The scene builds up tension, a fear that something terrible is going to happen. The drumming stops.[18]

---

17. 'Pour lui faire part de la naissance du Christ, les Rois Mages se contentent de caresser le visage d'Hérode. Au départ, la scène comportait un dialogue entre Hérode et un messager: "Ce sont les trois Mages? – Oui. – Ils viennent de l'Est? – Oui. – Suivant une étoile? – Un nouveau roi est né? – Oui". Mais il a très vite été inutile. En guise de réponse, Hérode renverse les Rois Mages et fait une épouvantable grimace: il est en colère. Dans la dernière version de *The Cry*, l'expression était encore plus resserrée. Les Mages ne caressaient plus le visage du roi, mais le maquillaient avec un crayon gras bleu; sa grimace en était encore plus terrible: ce qu'ils disaient le mettait en colère; les deux actions étaient liées.' — (Kourilsky, '71.)

18. 'Cette extrême concentration peut conduire Schumann à un style elliptique qui n'est pas

That the city *advances* to its doom, Schumann says, is "just a visual effect." It clashes with the meaning of Schumann's reading of the times of day. But the greatness of Schumann's theatre is that his stage-effects, though not designed by him *for* this, carry large ideas.

The Grey Ladies of Bethlehem

The masks of the Grey Ladies are abstracts of the faces of Silesian/Thuringian poor peasant women of Wendic or other Slavic blood. Their crudity & passivity give the scene a dimension *independent* of its horror & pity & of the multiple evo-

---

sans nuire parfois à la clarté du récit, à cette lisibilité immédiate qu'il recherche pourtant avant tout. Mais elle aboutit le plus souvent à une extraordinaire intensité d'expression. A cet égard la scène de l'attaque de Bethléem dans *The Cry* paraît exemplaire. Elle est toute entière construite sur l'interaction de deux plans: l'armée, le village. Interaction plastique: le soldat gris marche sur le devant de la scène de long en large, la porte blanche derrière laquelle se trouvent massées les Dames Grises avance du fond de la scène selon une ligne oblique qui finira par rejoindre la transversale. Interaction sonore: aux coups frappés sur la grosse caisse en alternance avec les pas du soldat répond la rengaine frêle et plaintive du violon électrique, puis l'énumération des heures et des activités de la journée. Schumann n'est pas parvenu d'emblée à cette rigueur de composition et à cette intensité d'expression. Cette "Scène des Dames Grises" est une de celles qui ont été le plus travaillées. Sans entrer ici dans le détail des répétitions, je voudrais relever les changements les plus remarquables qui se sont effectués peu à peu. La concentration des deux plans dans un même espace-temps en est sans doute le plus important. Au départ, en effet, le montage était différent: les deux "thèmes",l'armée et le village, donnaient lieu à des scènes séparées qui se succédaient. On voyait d'abord le soldat marcher devant un paysage gris; parfois même plusieurs bannières étaient tendues successivement derrière lui: une forêt, une forêt qui brûle,une ville, une ville qui brûle, un désert, la montagne, et on entendait les coups frappés sur la grosse caisse. Puis, noir: la bannière placée au centre de la scène était ôtée: lumière: on découvrait alors les Dames Grises assises en demi-cercle autour d'une table, et on entendait le son plaintif du violon. A un stade plus primitif des répétitions (en janvier 1969), la scène comportait même certains éléments de dialogue. Un choeur dirigé par Peter Schumann formulait des courtes questions: "Tuer les enfants? Au-dessous de deux ans? Est-ce vrai? Tous au-dessous de deux ans? Mon enfant?' Sur chaque "oui" tombait un coup de tambour. Lorsque le soldat arrivait, il demandait: "Y a-t-il quelqu'un à la maison?"; une des femmes disait: "Jai peur", etc. Peu à peu le texte sera supprimé. Seule subsistera la citation extraite du *New York Times*: "La semaine dernière les avions en forme de poisson ont survolé nos champs etc.", dite par une actrice tout en gris, assise, repliée sur elle-même, au milieu des grandes marionnettes. Encore Peter Schumann trouvant que la citation, telle qu'elle était dite, apportait une information déjà donnée par l'image, et qu'elle ajoutait même une note sentimentale, parlait-il constamment de la supprimer. Il ne sera satisfait que lorsqu'il l'aura véritablement mise de côté: l'actrice récitera le texte, assise côté jardin, tout en regardant, en spectatrice, l'action qui se déroule. De la même façon les éléments "décoratifs" seront supprimés : plus de bannières, le violon suffira à "peindre" le paysage tout comme il peint *aussi* le village (on songe à l'emploi du *shamisen* dans le théâtre japonais). Plus de tables ni de chaises, la porte suffira à représenter la maison et pourra même au-delà de cette fonction représentative revêtir un caractère magique, devenant objet rituel. Sans doute n'est-il pas inutile de noter que c'est en plein air, au cours des répétitions de l'été 1969 à la Sainte-Baume que la scène s'est transformée de façon décisive: sur le grand pré où *The Cry* était désormais joué, tout devait être plus concentré qu'à l'intérieur, et le moindre détail pittoresque ou simplement "réaliste" sonnait faux.' — (Kourilsky, '71.)

cations of Schumann's reading. Later, when the plane squashes them, we notice that their masks are unprotesting, even unsurprised.

Arrival of a Woman with a Baby

The group of grey women is now out front; the performer carrying the door turns it, it is open. A tall female puppet (masked & shrouded performer), also in grey, but not one of the Ladies, younger, advances carrying a small naked child-doll with its arms out as though playing. Her beautiful, sensitive, emaciated face & elongated figure, its wrinkled (tinted & bleach-burned) drapery in the receding-small-wave curves of sculptured stone, are off the Naumburg dome. She continues advancing through the audience, as a woman's taped voice reads over the P.A. system in a struck monotone:

> I wanted to stay. Last week the fish-shaped planes flew over our fields. My husband didn't know what they were. He stood up & they shot him down & killed him. I wish I had stayed & got killed too, but I was afraid I would only be wounded & that there would be no one to take care of me.

The understatement (according to the spring action-outline by "the Woman of Ben Suc," from *The New York Times*, January 16, 1967) carries.

The Soldier Fighting the Door

The drumming & marching resume. As the lights go out, the Soldier approaches the door (closed again); in strobe lighting, he commences to batter down the door with the butt-end of his gun, the group behind it swaying as he hammers. In a protracted, magnificently physical scene of violence & destruction, the door slowly, inexorably goes down as the fish-plane rises behind the women in the flickering light.

The Air Raid

The door is down. The women are exposed. The marching Soldier advances through the audiences, a threatening presence, as the drumming resumes & as the fish-nosed plane, looming above the women, grey as they, slowly smashes them to the ground, silent in the noise of drums & boots. Large grey-white celastic hands from the groups of victims are still up in the air. Drums. They are now just a mess on the floor, the fish-plane on top of them. End of drumming.

A feeling of terror, pity, & regret – drainage of emotions.

The Crucifixion

The Exaltation & Building of Jesus

An indeterminate, pretty intermission follows. The white litter, all over the floor, is swept & kicked into a corner by the white performers, like a group of angels in their random motion. Bird twitters from small bird-shaped noise-makers mix with the papery noise of the sweeping and low small-talk among the audience. The headless Uranos in his black suit, white cuffs, white shirt-front, is standing up flatly against the side brick-wall, his hands happening to point pistol-like at the audience.

The cast comes out gradually, with various gear, mostly their instruments, the beast-masks tied to their backs. They assemble in a group on the floor, a bottle is passed around, a ring has formed, music, light dance-music with a Near Eastern flavor, begins sporadically, a feast emerges from the intermission. The audience joins in, clapping.

The feast sets the tone of the merry life of Jesus, bringer of the still serviceable word of life:

> Sing aloud unto God our strength:
> make a joyful noise unto the God of Jacob.
>
> Take a psalm, and bring hither the timbrel,
> the pleasant harp with the psaltery.
>
> Blow up the trumpet in the new moon,
> in the time appointed, on our solemn feast day.
>
> (Ps. 81:1-3)

The Beatitudes

The next two scenes gaily present this word (eight of the nine beatitudes in Matthew 5 & nine parables) as a message of resistance for which the play is a frame: "Think not that I am come to send peace on earth: I came not to send peace, but a sword" (Matt. 10:34).[19]

Cardboards with the individual Blessed-ares are successively held up. Schumann reads each beatitude in a slightly muffled, strong voice over the rhythmic music dominated by the beat of the drums, as if giving directions to a large crowd at a public event, repeating them like current political slogans, known verities professed, as though exhorting a rally of sympathizers to affirmative repetition. There is a note of friendly satire in this.

Blessed are the poor . . .

A member of the group breaks away from the concert, tossing the beast-mask off his back into a corner as he runs, gets the screen, brings it out, the two poles joined, waves it as the Red Flag. Jubilation from the group. He assumes a central position as standard-bearer.

For each of the following slogans performers on the run suspend a symbolic ornament from the revolutionary representative of the poor.[20]

Blessed are the meek . . .

A white doll is tied to his arm.

---

19. In the early versions of the play, the beatitudes were introduced by a light-feast. The performers assembled stage-center wearing the beast-masks. The amplifier mooed, lowed, the sound gradually growing into a wordless chant. It was dark but Schumann could be seen among his beasts, gesturing. A candle projected a shadow of his arm across half the ceiling. Gradually, more & more candles were lit, finally there were hundreds. Then all the houselights went on.
20. Schumann has preferred Luke's 'blessed are the poor' to Matthew's 'blessed are the poor in spirt.' Though the Sermon on the Mount is more 'social' throughout in Luke 6:20-21, Schumann quotes Matthew 5:3-10, for the other beatitudes.

Blessed are those who mourn . . .

He is draped in white, his face covered with one of the small white Oriental woman masks from *Fire*, smiling, with the certainty of victory – or of righteousness making success irrelevant.

Blessed are those who hunger and thirst after righteousness . . .

Bags of fruit, beads, cooking pots, flowers are hung on him – the music becomes louder & more strident, it has the force of scandal, the feast is turning into a rebellion.

Blessed are the merciful . . .

A black hand-puppet is brought to him, kisses him, is tied to him.

Blessed are the pure in heart . . .

A large red heart is hung low around his neck, a crown of bells put around his head, & small tools are suspended from his shoulders. The cumulative emotional impact of this ritual, resuscitating Christianity, is considerable – the pride of resistance & the joy of liberation.

Blessed are the peacemakers . . .

A Viet Cong flag is put in his left hand, a toy rifle strapped around his neck.[21]

---

21. Martin Gottlieb – whose mind *Cry* blew – 'one of the most remarkable theatre pieces I have ever seen – such theatre, so extravagantly original and so intense in its convictions simply has no comparison in our commercial theatre' (*Women's Wear Daily*, December 12, '69) – parenthetically mentions that the rifle was broken. I didn't notice and nobody else in the audience did.
  'Well, I think most of the contributions came when we were building the Christ figure. The group's . . . Building the scene. It started with a circle making music and that was a free flow of music, the group together, and then one person running in the middle, jumping in the middle and then out of the music came giving that person things. (I: The Christ figure.) The person – he came first, received first the Vietnamese mask and then started to receive things, dressed in robes and things, like the dressing of Joseph. And then at one point somebody gave him a gun and that was shocking to Peter at that point. (I: That was somebody's own idea.) Right. (I: And when did that happen, in New York still? At the Courthouse?) Yes. And that stayed in. (I: And why do you think it was shocking to him?) Shocking not, but I think he was surprised. (I: Why do you think so?) I don't know, because the gun – because later on he broke the gun in half, he didn't want the gun. (I: Who did?) Peter. (I: Didn't want the gun in the play?) Yeah. Not that he didn't want the gun, but he – (I: When did he break it in half?) I don't remember, I just remember him breaking the gun. (I: During the tour?) During the tour. (I: In Europe?) Yes. It was like he was having conflcts about the gun . . . . (I: You don't remember who proposed the gun or who brought it in.) It was the gun and the red flag both were the controversial – (I: In New York.) Things were discussed, I remember, it wasn't just told to us to do, it was something that came out of the impulse the people had. And then we talked about it afterwards. I don't think there were fights about it – (: No, but did he express surprise or shock or doubt before you went to Europe, in New York?) I don't remember.'
— (Levy, interview.)

Blessed are the persecuted . . .

To the sound of wild triumph from the trumpets, a "Free Bobby & Huey" sign is hung on the heroic figure. The ten-foot stepladder & a large Jesus-puppet are brought out. The puppet is put over him. He carefully climbs the ladder to the top, sits, the puppet's sackcloth robe covering his body & the ladder. Jesus appears to stand, towers nearly three times life-size, his large hands (the left dark, the right light) in an open gesture of blessing or perhaps prayer, a red streamer on his right wrist. The mask's expression is utter detachment; he is completely removed from the scene, but still its center & symbol. The horns are blaring, the noise — in the rhythm of the beatitudes — is terrific. The audience claps. Complete silence.[22]

'Blessed are ye, when men shall revile you and persecute you . . . for my sake" is left out.

With some clanging, the instruments are cleared away.

The Parables

Schumann announces the Parables of Jesus. The first three parables are done with the small, white, foot-high, totally inexpressive papier-mache puppets from *Johnny Comes Marching Home*: two seated men with hats & one standing with a gun. Throughout this scene a seven-foot-high masked figure with an enormous hand stands pointing his finger as each parable is done (there is an effect of a V-sign). He points to Jesus &/or to Schumann reading &/or to the action, or lifts his finger-hand in gestures of "Verily, I say unto you" or "Note." As each parable is read, performers jump forward & do a quick burlesque skit.

"A sower sows good seed. At night his enemy sows bad seed among the good. When the fall comes, the bad seeds strangle the good." (Matt. 13:24-30). The little seated man is rushed out, followed by the little gun-man, who shoots him. Schumann: "What do the people say?" The group: "Oioioi."

"Here we have the mustard seed which is indeed the least of all seeds, but, when it grows up . . . look: it is the mightiest of all herbs" (Matt. 13-31-32). The little seated man is held out; a performer runs forward, shows a sign reading "Cuba," another a sign with a list of South American countries. "A sower plants three seeds. The first seed falls by the wayside and the birds carry it away. The second seed falls on rocky soil and is scorched by the sun. But the third seed falls on good soil" (Matt. 13:3-9). A female performer comes in with the little man with the gun, and a sign, "Pentagon," is shown; the figure is put on the floor, is snatched away to the sound of twitterings from the bird-whistles. A seated man is brought in with a sign, "Business," put on the floor; the woman hits it with a

---

22. The reference to the Black Panthers was added in New York, and a performer with a skull-mask seated on the ladder and then covered by Jesus' robe was eliminated.

'Une échelle de 3,50m. de haut est apportée et au son de plus en plus triomphant des trompettes, le vietnamien s'assoit sur la dernière marche, tandis qu'à mi-hauteur prend place une actrice portant un masque de mort. Ils sont revêtus de la marionnette qui représente Jésus . . . . A côté du résistant vietnamien, se glisse un masque de mort: c'est la seule note discordante de cette manifestation, joueuse où le groupe affirme ses convictions politiques, projetant sur scène ses rêves et ses espoirs.' — (Kourilsky, '71.)

little tin disk (the sun) it topples, and is taken out. Another seated figure is brought in with a sign, "Resistance." The woman picks it up & kisses it.

The transparent simple-mindedness of these acts makes them artistic comments on the guilelessness of Jesus. They are not witty: they are done with the humor of gleeful children. The anodyne figures are anybodies. "And if someone asks for your coat, give him your hat also" (Matt. 5:40). Two performers come out, one robs the other of his coat, he gets angry, is about to hit the first, instead graciously gives him his hat.

"And if your eye offend thee, pluck it out and cast it from thee. And if your hand offend thee, cut it off and cast it from thee. For it is better that one member perish rather than your whole body be cast in hell's fire" (Matt. 5:29-30). They come in with a garbage can with a $-sign on it, a cardboard eye, a hand, a red cloth. The eye and the hand are thrown into the can. The cloth is shaken. In Matthew this parable recommends castrating oneself. Here it warns against letting making a living interfere with true purpose.

"And if someone hits you on one cheek, don't run away, but turn the other cheek' (Matt. 5:39). A performer (Arnie) & the Great Warrior enter. Arnie greets him with the peace gesture. The Great Warrior hits his hand & it turns into a fist. Arnie repeats the gesture with the other hand, the same happens. Arnie proceeds to cut the Warrior down with a karate chop, which involves turning his backside to him.

"You can not serve two masters" (Mat. 6:24). Uncle Fatso & a pretty Vietnamese Girl join the Great Warrior. He prepares to strike her. The group shouts, "No! no! no!" He turns on Uncle Fatso. They shout "Yes!" He strikes him. Uncle Fatso bawls. The group wipes his tears with an American flag.

"Let him who is without sin cast the first stone" (John 8:7). The little puppet with the gun is brought out and aimed at the pretty Vietnamese Girl. She pulls a gun out of her sleeve, aims at him. Schumann says: "Jesus says, 'Ready, aim, fire.'" She shoots the little man. Another performer runs along the front row with a mirror for the spectators to look at themselves in.

"Knock and it shall be opened" (Matt: 7:8, Luke 9:9). The white door is brought in, the pretty Vietnamese Girl knocks with nice timidity, the door opens, she is welcomed. Uncle Fatso waddles up, an American flag behind his ear, knocks loud as hell.

GIRL: Who are you?
UNCLE F: Uncle Fatso.
GIRL: What do you want?
UNCLE F: Forward motion is the primary ingredient we are trying to bring to a series of excellent recommendations.
GIRL: It is easier for a camel to go through through the eye of a needle, than for a rich man to get to heaven (Matt. 19:24).
UNCLE F: Bangs on the door, swears.
GIRL: Go to hell.[23]

---

23. A conclusion to this scene and three additional sayings of Jesus interpreted in a Resistance sense were cut in New York:
'Quelqu'un s'approche alors d'Uncle Fatso avec tout un lot de coeurs rouges sur lesquels

The Three Miracles

Schumann's evangely concludes with the Miracles, Jesus' propagandistic paradigms of aid, typically in violation of the Law, here in the Maoist spirit of Che. One performer ties the red streamer hanging from Christ's wrist over his own eyes, one ties the ankle of his awkwardly lifted leg to his thigh, one, wearing a skull-mask, lies down in front of Jesus.

"And now we show you how the blind are made to see." The blind man, to a cymbal clash, removes the ribbon.

"And now we show you how the lame are made to walk." The lame man, to a cymbal clash, removes the ribbon, puts his foot down, does a jig.

"And now we show you how the dead are brought to life." The prone man, to a cymbal clash, rises, takes off his mask. All this is done very quickly, like a magician's act or rather like a parody of a magician's act:

> For the Jews require a sign, and the Greeks seek after wisdom: but we preach Christ crucified,
> unto the Jews a stumbling-block, and unto the Greeks foolishness;
> but unto them which are called, both Jews and Greeks,
> Christ: the power of God and the wisdom of God.
>
> Because the foolishness of God is wiser then men;
> and the weakness of God is stronger than men.
>
> For ye see your calling, brethren,
> how that not many wise men after the flesh,
> not many mighty, not many noble are called:
> but God hath chosen the foolish things of the world
> to confound the wise;
> and God hath chosen the weak things of the world
> to confound the things which are mighty.
>
> (I Cor. 1:22-27)

---

est écrit en plusieurs langues: "Va en enfer". "Eh! j'ai un télégramme pour toi. Va au diable!". Il lui jette les coeurs à la figure et tous les acteurs font tourner Uncle Fatso sur lui-même en le poussant dehors.

"Méfiez-vous des faux prophètes".

Une bête arrive, tenue en laisse par un acteur. Elle représente un peuple opprimé. Il est arrivé que le marionnettiste, au lieu de revêtir un masque de bête, mette le masque d'un Noir. Uncle Fatso entre de nouveau, suivi d'un acteur en jaquette et chapeau haut de forme qui brandit une pancarte sur laquelle est inscrit "Paix" et ouvre la bouche comme s'il faisait un discours, tandis qu'à côté de lui une actrice joue de la flûte. Soudain le poing d'Uncle Fatso se détache, porté par un acteur, et va assomer la bête à qui il parle de paix.

"Mais les premiers seront les derniers et les premiers les derniers".

La Vietnamienne et les acteurs brandissant le drapeau du F.N.L. poursuivent Uncle Fatso et le font sortir de scène.

Jésus dit aussi: "Vous êtes la lumière du monde. Ne la cachez pas. Laissez-la briller".

Un acteur craque une allumette et met le feu à un écriteau: "Livret militaire".' — (Kourilsky, '71.)

St. Paul speaking the mind of Peter Schumann.

The Last Supper

Lights on, three tables are put together in front of Jesus to form one very long table, a white cloth is placed over it; Schumann's homemade rye bread (1 Cor. 10:16-18) is laid out. Performers pick up the loaves, distribute chunks among the audience.[24] At the same time, a female performer brings out a water kettle and anoints Jesus' hands very slowly (she later moistens his face).

Twelve performers now advance, inside the Disciple puppets, intoning an angelic om, in a very slow procession from behind the audience to & around the table, and sit down facing us, on both sides of Jesus. They are tall, tubular, armless, sack-cloth figures of many unreal races, with the misshapen heads of larvae & the serious up-tight expressions of businessmen, administrators, emperors, the middle-aged faces of men carrying grave public responsibilities — faces perhaps crippled by life — careworn, awe-inspiring, but certainly not appealing, not beatific. Eight of the robes are mustard-colored, the upper part of one of these, extending over the Disciple's mouth, is black; three are in different reds. The twelfth Disciple comes in holding a clump of yellow bread & a roughhewn blue mug, & very very slowly gives them to each in turn to eat & drink, each leaning forward slightly when his turn comes (this leaves the after-image of a wave-motion). Jesus is immobile during this. It is a gigantic spectacle of great tension, a moment approaching what the sacred would be if there were any: "For as often as ye eat this bread and drink this cup, ye do shew the lord's death TILL HE COME" (1 Cor. 11:26).

The Crucifixion

The chant rises in intensity as the last few Disciples are given bread & wine — the fanged beast's head still hanging from the rafters, a red rag like a sliver of raw meat dangling from one of its fangs. Jesus is given to eat & drink; the chant now grows very loud. There is a sudden terrific screaming. The tall figures of the Disciples topple & crush over the table, the table crashes to the floor. The fish-headed plane rises behind Jesus. The lights go out.[25]

---

24. In Paris, in November:
'Une énorme marionnette bouffonne — l'Homme Rouge — apparaît en haut du balcon, côté cour. L'acteur qui l'habite chante un air d'opéra, puis demande: "Peux-tu changer ces pierres en pains?" En bas, le meneur de jeu ou un autre membre de la troupe, répond: "L'homme ne vit pas seulement de pain". Du haut du balcon, les miches sont alors descendues dans un panier. Les acteurs les mettent sur la table. Ils rompent le pain, en mangent, et vont le distribuer dans la salle.' — (Kourilsky, '71.)

25. In Paris in November:
'Sa tâche accomplie, il (the Feeder (SSB)) va s'agenouiller devant Jésus, les mains posées sur la table. Explosion brutale, gigantesque. Les murmures se changent en cris, en hurlements. Les bruits de voiture retentissent de nouveau, les disciples se débarrassent violemment de leur marionnette et renversent la table qui se fracasse par terre, puis ils courent prendre l'avion-requin qu'ils font avancer à toute vitesse horizontalement à travers la scène pour le dresser soudain, comme une croix, derrière le Christ dont le corps disparaît sous les draperies grises: seul son long visage à l'expression absente, résignée, reste visible, dominé

An Ascension?

Jesus is taken down (off his cross), lit by two flashlights. He is laid out on the floor, the flashlights on him, performers busily crowding around him in the dark. There is the sound of rope being pulled. The lights go on, the monster is on the floor, the Jesus-puppet in its mouth (Rev. 12:4). The overhead lights go off, the flashlights are still on, & the dragon, with Jesus' head in its mouth & Jesus' hands tied up over its dragon-head in prayer, is hauled up to the rafters. It may be an ascension. It looks like a hanging. It is the recurrent disappearance of a permanent vision. The performers all lie prone on the floor.[26]

> And now remaineth faith, hope, charity, these three:
> but the greatest of these is charity.
>
> (1 Cor. 13:13)'

Apparently Schumann had in the winter of '68/'69 come to see a way of using the Jewish God myth — the image of a murderous and repressive

---

par la tête monstrueuse de l'avion-croix. Silence. Pleins feux scène et salle. C'est en général ici que se termine le spectacle.' — (Kourilsky, '71.)

'Devenus soudains des "marines", les acteurs vont chercher l'avion et y crucifient le "Sauveur" et avec lui l'image de la nouvelle vie rêvée où la guerre et la faim auraient été abolies. Fin abrupte, qui coupe brutalement le contact qui avait été établi avec la salle, et qui laisse le spectateur dans un curieux état d'insatisfaction et d'attente. Le spectacle se termine par des points de suspension. Bien souvent du reste les membres de la troupe sont amenés à dire au public: "C'est tout".' — (Kourilsky, '71.)

26. A Berlin paper in an article '*Puppen auf dem Hinterhof* from Schumann's introductory remarks in German before a street performance of *Cry* in the working class district the Wedding in October quotes 'We play the whole Bible, the Old and the New Testament — all in two hours. But we only go as far as the Crucifixion. For the Resurrection must now be done on earth itself.'

'Parfois, cependant, il y a une suite: une courte Résurrection. Celle-ci a été ajoutée tardivement, à la demande du groupe qui pensait que la fin de *The Cry* était trop pessimiste. Elle n'a jamais été vraiment "trouvée", sans doute parce que pour Schumann la vraie fin est la Crucifixion.

Noir. Seul le faisceau d'une lampe de poche se promène lentement sur le Christ, éclairant tel détail de son visage ou de ses mains. On entend des bruits de cordes tirées. Le remue-ménage dure assez longtemps. Puis les lumières s'allument sur la scène et dans la salle: le Christ "vidé" du Vietnamien est ficelé à l'avion. Tous les acteurs sont allongés par terre. Soudain, ils se relèvent, ils ont de petits sifflets-oiseaux et commencent à "gazouiller" gaiement.

Autre fin (jouée lors des toutes dernières représentations de *The Cry* à Paris, et reprise à New York): quand les lumières s'allument, le Christ "vidé" se trouve dans la gueule du dragon qui remonte lentement vers les cintres, tandis que les acteurs restent allongés par terre.

On le voit: les images proposées n'ont pas été "contrôlées". Ces deux versions de la Résurrection sont contradictoires. Dans la première, on pourrait voir le triomphe des hommes sur les dieux, le monde occidental se libérant du mythe chrétien, tandis que la seconde suggère l'idée de l'Ascension. Mais on peut dire aussi tout simplement que le dragon remporte la promesse de vie nouvelle apportée avec l'enfant. C'est sans doute cette interprétation plus littérale, plus "païenne", que préfèrerait Peter Schumann.' — (Kourilsky, '71.)

reigning Deity. He interpreted it as image of the domination of human history by violence and oppression, and counterposed to it an image, in the forms of rebellion and hope likewise perennial in human history, of a reign of peace on earth – derived from a reinterpretation (in the sense of the Resistance Movement) of the New Testament, as that other image was derived from the Old Testament. The Jewish god in *Cry* figures as Satan, and Satan as symbol of the evil in men.[27] The power of *Cry* is this clash of black and white. Becoming infected, September-December '68 with the euphoria of Resistance – the blind elan of the counter-culture youth movement just before its collapse – he momentarily possessed the inner wherewithal theatrically to express an utterly black vision of mankind's modus operandi throughout its history, the rampaging violence of power jealously asserting its authority.[28]

The Living Theatre (*Paradise Now, Frankenstein*) and the Performance Group (*Dionysius in '69*) simultaneously staged similar oppositions, but white/future/youth/hope in their case was not Resistance in its simple real meaning of political, armed resistance, but loving community, i.e. fucking around – and specifically abstention from politics and above all from counter-violence.

---

27. The New York reviewer of *Cry*, preoccupied by recovering his Jewish identity saw Schumann's rejection of Jehovah as weakness of the play:
' " The Cry of the People for Meat" has its weakness, perhaps the most serious being its failure to deal with the covenants Jehovah made, first with Abraham, then Moses, while devoting an interminable if sometimes charming time to the "begat" sections, that work of some obsessed genealogist. In one sense, the Old Testament can be seen as the struggle of God and the Children of Israel to become worthy of one another. If the Old Testament speaks of anything, it speaks of the pact God makes with his People, promising to be Eternally Present to them. In the context of God's concern for righteousness, the flood makes sense. But in "Cry," the flood is reenacted as if it were a natural rather than a retributive event, thus trivializing the consequences of one of the great moral catastrophes of the world. If Jesus is to be the culmination of a work that professes to deal with both the Old and the New Testaments, then he must be seen in relation to the God of the Hebrews, and to the success and failure of humanity before his time.
But the force of the work overcomes its inability to make a coherent moral development of the Bible.' — (A. Sainer, *Theatre: The Cry of the People for Meat. Village Voice*, December 25, '69.)

28. 'I loved doing the show. I think a lot of people in the company didn't. We were always working on it. It was changing all the time. It had occurred to me soon after we arrived that it was a tragedy, that it had formed like a Greek tragedy . . . and that a lot of the people in the company didn't realize that . . . obviously, it wasn't like a Greek tragedy, it had a lot more characters. But I guess it must have felt that way in that it was trying to deal on a very basic level with strong forces than run through mankind. Things that are bigger than individuals, and the violence. Most of Peter's shows had a lot of violence in them in those days, and that was quite evident to us. And I felt, I don't know, it just hit me one day, maybe I was wrong, but this was a tragedy, this a real honest-to-goodness tragedy, it's one that's being created in our time by the person I thought was the greatest theatre maker in the world. (I: A tragedy is something that ends badly. Why did this end badly?) It ended with the Crucifixion.' — (M. Sherman, interview.)

Cry is unique among Schumann's works both by its radically negative image of God and for being an almost unequivocal endorsement of armed resistance.

It is also the last of his plays in which the group figures within the play as makers of the play. This role of the group's in its fifth act – blessings and sayings of Jesus – tends to put the onus of (or the credit for) the play's radicalism on them. It also reflects the anarchist and communal mood of the group at this time. He made them wear uniforms – flower children white – for this collective performance role.

He ditched authorial group presence immediately after *Cry*: but the uniformly white crew reappeared as carriers and worshippers of nature goddesses and as celebrators of ever reborn nature in his circuses. In *Cry*, the white suggested the pure aspirations of the Resistance and Youth Movements, in the Hallelujahs and Pageants of his circuses subsequently rather the purity of spirit of acolytes at (pantheist and humanitarian) services.[29] Theatrically, this uniform identifies the members of his group as such – as performers: whereas if they appeared in the performances doing the same

---

29. The authorial performing group in *Cry*:

'The actors look at us thoughtfully, gently, still rapt in the mysteries they have enacted. Without manifestoes, without dogmatic utterances, without aggression, this company presents a truly poor theatre, a holy theatre. Their very materials (apart from the superbly-made masks) are the creased and old clothes, lengths of material, curtains, found in any jumble sale. They dress up in whatever they can find, adapting with the complete conviction of a child. They make do, pretend. One could not call them professionals in the accepted sense. They bring no conventional set of skills, sophistication or polish to their performance. The plays are presented with a simplicity that radiates from the inner certainty of Schumann and his followers. One feels that the first Franciscans must have been like this: it is impossible to separate the quality of their life from their work.' — (Roose-Evans, *Experimental Theatre*.)

'From the instant that the troupe begins to warm up for its performance, with a percussive force that's even more moral than musical, with an urgent and childishly joyous blast of trumpets, you know there's serious work afoot. It's almost uncanny how the company, barely conscious of it, conveys a sense of having collided with some abiding experience that flickers about its self, a contemplative almost peace that modifies, challenges, and at times almost oddly obliterates what we believe to be the work at hand.

It's not only that life is making art, but that life has been backed into a corner and forced to remake its art before our eyes, that it is coaxing, goading, comforting, and pounding at its creation so that the work seems continuously in the process of being born. The work seems inevitably to be affected by what's transpired on the street an hour before the performance. Public events are embraced as if they were private triumphs and transgressions. The dirty war, in particular, has intensified the radicalization of this theatre, has given new life to the politics of aesthetics.' (A. Sainer, *Village Voice*, December 25, 1969.)

In the later circuses:

'These volunteers wear white clothing in performance. White dress lends his troupe a pacifist or innocent air, as if they were a clean slate to write on. But the white pants, white sheeting, places them at one remove from the rest of humanity too – "like a butcher," said a slightly unsettled psychiatrist sitting on the hillside during a rehearsal, or like members of some vaguely unnerving cult.' — (Hoagland, '83.)

things, but wearing everyday clothes, they would be identified as individuals – private parties – active in the theatre. In *Cry*, this theatrical sense of the whites in fact conflicted with their performance in it as collective makers of the play: reduced it from a strong communitarian statement to a mere tautology. But this was hardly noticeable at the time. Schumann, an ironical man, may have thought of it, though. Within the limits of uniform and of a play to perform, the group came on to the audience as themselves, present in the performance – including Schumann – as makers and presenters of the play: a more restrained form of what the Living Theatre and the Performance Group were doing and having their huge successes with at the time, more restrained in that they gave the audience bread (and in *Cry* occasionally wine) but otherwise didn't involve it, i.e. there was no audience-participation, and in that there was no aggression toward the audience, as in both of those cases there was (loving aggression).

Schumann had been present within the show 'doing the lights' and narrating and metaphorically directing (moving the people learning to walk, taming the animals). Formally this was in line with the group's on-stage residence, actions and celebrations in *Cry*, with the on-stage donning and removal of masks in the spring '69 *Blue Raven Beauty* and with the group's collective on-stage shaping of the ending of *Reiteration* in the fall of '68 and the modified function of narration in *Reiteration*. Schumann in the winter of '69/'70 came to feel, and may already have come to feel in Europe, that this was a weakness of the play's: the finger pointing to the play was missing.[30] But narration had never yet so far served him as finger pointing to the play. What really bothered him, I would say, was that with *Cry* by integrating the making of the show into the show (of which the 'inside' narrator was only one aspect) he had reached the extreme of his theatrical form of the '60s, viz. direct address to the audience by (moral) content, without formal address to it, and he now no longer felt up to this moral commitment – and specifically because it had landed him in almost unequivocal endorsement of armed resistance, i.e. murder – and wanted to do shows not only without such strengthened moral address, but without moral address altogether. This required a 'finger pointing to the show' – not necessarily any kind of narration, but a frame.

Cry, the crucifixion of Jesus as Resistance Fighter notwithstanding came across as endorsement of armed resistance. This was not quite unequivocal,

---

30. (Elka: In *The Cry* . . . you were right *in* the show – you were the light man –) And the narrator, and the operator of things, I would move people around – when they learned how to walk, I would pull the beasts on the rope, and things like that – (Elka: Yes, but you were *inside* the piece . . .) But it was an *inside* job. And the whole piece suffered from this whole thing's being muddled up and no clear taking a stand, and showing people what we were doing – that pointed finger and stick that somebody who addresses the public needs was missing. *The Grey Lady Cantata* had that. For the first time.' — (Schumann, interview, '79.)

however. First there were Schumann's two little jokes: the death figure hidden under the cloak of that militant Jesus and his inobviously broken gun. And Kourilsky '71 points out that it's his disciples that crucify the *Cry* Jesus. More importantly, there was the crucifixion itself. Some members of the Bread and Puppet group during the European tour felt the ending the play with the Crucifixion amounted to a definitive declaration of lack of faith in the Resistance struggle. Others, who agreed with the otiosity of counter-violence, felt that ending betokened lack of faith in personal salvation. Whence, by democratic process or moral blackmail, and/or because Schumann himself thought even hopeless resistance (including armed resistance), or at least the vivifying hope for a better future, morally appropriate and a spiritual sine qua non of human existence, one or the other of two endings were occasionally tacked on to the Crucifixion: the one in New York, Jesus up in the sky, ready for rebirth, or the one I have quoted Kourilsky on, the resurrection of the performers, tooting on bird whistles.

Some Schumann fans feel that *Cry* was his artistic high point:

'Why has he changed? Are his interests changed? Are the ideas he has reduced, somehow? I mean, the elegance – the form – the intricacy of the work that was done on *The Cry* for instance – which was so structured, so elegant, so powerful as a dance piece – just as dance – and pageant – he's never done anything quite like that since and I'm wondering if it's because he has different people to work with .... None of the people that are with him now are crazy.'

(Ashley, interview.)

24. April-November '69. Touring Europe with *Cry*.
The Maestro stays atop of chaos (the cunning of the artist).

> 'Leicht fanget aber sich
> In der Kette, die
> Es abgerissen, das Kälblein.'
> (F. Hölderlin, *Auf falbem Laube ruhet...*)

Cry had been planned for Europe, and its size — it was both by far the longest play Schumann had so far done, lasting from an hour and a half to two hours plus, in fact it was the first long play of his, and the one with — by far — the most characters in it and requiring the most performers and the most puppet gear — in '68 they had been able to take all the theatre gear as personal luggage — is an indication of the confidence in his European market and of the booking contacts '68 had given him. It was a totally new level of operation for him and one that with ups and downs he maintained henceforth. The tour started out with around 20 people, and Schumann took his family for the first half of the tour. Moving around in Europe, it grew to 25-30. During their mid-tour communal rest period by Mary Magdalene's grave in Ste. Baume in the south of France in August there were 70-80 people in and around the group.[1] The tour covered most of Europe[2] and lasted more than seven months (April 10 to the second half of November). He brought along the stuff for and he performed six to eight other plays besides *Cry*[3]. He played not only in regular theatres,[4] but

---

1. 'And it was also more open as far as letting people — as we traveled, people entered the theatre, entered the group and played in the shows. A few of them, I guess, stayed almost the whole tour, but I remember after Ste. Baume there were several new faces that stayed on for a couple of months more. I think on other tours it's been a much more closed group.' — (Schumann, interview, '79.)
  'And a lot of people on tour, not only the original 19 or 20 or more, plus children, but we would pick up people in every city. It was that time, I think all the companies did that. The Open Theater probably did that too. You meet people in each city and they join you and travel with you for a while.' — (Sherman, interview.)
2. Nancy again, the Premio Roma Festival, Milan, Turin, Grenoble, the Experimental Festival in Frankfurt, Munich, Paris, Le Havre, Caen, Amiens, Bordeaux, London, the Bitef Festival in Belgrade, Copenhagen, Stockholm, Berlin, Poznan, Wroclaw, Amsterdam, Brussels, Liege, Namour — and finally again Paris.
3. *King Story, Reiteration, A Man, The Christmas Story, Johnny, Dead Man, Blue Raven Beauty*. At the Comedie de Caen, May 20, they did a *Litany of Breath*, based on a poem of my father's. They did *Fire* in Paris.
4. 'The show was big, and it didn't adapt easily to places, so often the theatres were way too small. We had to invent all kinds of tricks on how to cope with that, and entrances and

did street performances and played in factories.⁵ The tour was supposed to be managed by an outfit called Productions d'Aujourd'hui Berger, but

---

exits, in this show, were – even though they were flexible, there were requirements for running off and hopping on and for moving a lot of equipment around that were never fulfilled in the same way. No two places were alike, it seemed, on this tour.' — (Schumann, interview, '79.)

5. 'In der Dämmerung spielten sie in Berlin, ganz bewusst die Stunde wählend, in der sich Realität und Traum vermengen, vor ebenso bewusst gewählter Kulisse: Im Märkischen Viertel, einer freudlosen Ansammlung von Wohnsilos, gegen den Menschen gebaut. Hier, weitab von jeder urbanen Vergnügung, wollen sie Spielfreude begreiflich machen, bringen sie Fabeln und Märchen für die Armen – unkompliziert, in scheinbar kindlicher Vereinfachung. Ein andermal spielen sie ihr umfangreichstes Stück in Wedding auf einem der vielen Altberliner Hinterhöfe, die vom Vorderhaus her mit jedem neuen Hof dunkler, trostloser und dreckiger werden, abgebröckelte Fassaden, blinde Fenster und stinkende Mülltonnen stecken den Raum ab für die grotesken, überdimensionalen Figuren aus Pappmaché. Stets hängen aus den Fenstern der deprimierenden Mietskasernen geringschätzig lächelnde, deren Neugier überhand nimmt, wenn . . . .' (R. Lorenzen, *Theater auf der Strasse. Die 'Bread and Puppet'-Bühne*. In the Krefelder edition of some (?) German newspaper, December 31, '69.)

The German press reports concur in noting the lack of interest of the proletarian adults, the children's vivid appreciation. The working class audience was as antagonistic, in fact, as the toughs that heckled Schumann's parades in New York City in the mid-'60s.

'Bread and Puppet Theater
Strassentheater, New York:
3.10
um 17 Uhr in Kreuzberg, Hohenstaufenplatz:
    falls es regnet: in der Turnhalle der Robert-Koch-Oberschule, Böckhstrasse 5-6
4.10
um 17 Uhr Britz-Süd, Einkaufzentrum an der Oufschmidtstrasse:
    falls es regnet: under der Aula der 1. Grundschule in der Wutzkyallee 68
5.10
um 16 Uhr in Wilmersdorf, Olivaer Platz;
falls es regnet: in der alten Mensa der Technischen Universität, Hardenbergstrasse
um 21 Uhr in der alten Mensa der Technischen Universität, Hardenbergstrasse
    'The Cry of the People for Meat'
7.10
um 17 Uhr im grossen Saal der Gauss-Akademie, Liltticher Strasse 20
9.10
um 17 Uhr in Dahlem, Henry-Ford-Bau, Garystrasse Stoltzmannstrasse:
    falls es regnet: in der Halle des Henry-Ford-Bau vor dem auditorium maximum
Eintritt frei

'Berliner Festwochen 1969 in Verbindung mit dem forum theater.'

'Un groupe de jeunes beatniks, une dizaine environ de garçons et de filles, se sont produits dans notre ville, après avoir parcouru plusieurs localités de la région.

Ils ont parcouru la ville pour annoncer le spectacle qu'ils ont ensuite donné devant l'Ecole de filles: un bien curieux spectacle où le récitant de la tragédie antique, les Marionnetes et les acteurs à masques jouaient chacun leur rôle, sur un fond de melopée que scandaient tambour et pipeau.

they felt they were being misbooked by these people,[6] so dropped them and Pascal Ortega whom the Productions d'Aujourd'hui Berger had sent them as road manager (to replace their initial road manager Michael Appleby) planned the second half of their tour.[7] According to Ernstthal, Schumann had reinvited him into the company, asking him to take over from him and be in charge for the tour's autumn part, but this – Ernstthal feels because he had been too critical of *Cry*, in front of everybody criticizing it for being too downbeat in its second half[8] – didn't work out, and Ernstthal in fact quit the company before the tour was over.

Mais ce "Chicken little theatre" a le mérite d'exprimer sous cette forme, une condamnation sans équivoque de la guerre, qui se fait toujours contre la volonté des peuples
"Le peuple implora le roi: je n'ai pas demandé l'aide du grand guerrier..."
On peut certes sourire devant ce "comant qui nous est si peu familier". Mais le rire s'arrête et fait place au respect quand qu'elle qu'en soit la forme, se révèle l'amour de la paix chez les générations montantes.
Ce groupe sera à Digne lundi soir où il donnera un spectacle au Lido.' — (En Plein Air Samedi/ Théâtre beatnik dans notre ville, *La Marseillaise*, Marseille, October 20, '69.)
6. 'Okay, so then after Rome – I don't remember what the order was, but we went back across the Alps about eight times in that spring part of that tour, because the scheduling was so screwed up. We were traveling to Italy doing a one-night stand and going back to France and doing a two-day stand and coming back. What's that university town in France by the mountains? Grenoble.' — (Leherrissier, interview.)
7. 'Productions d'Aujourd'hui Berger and Collette, I forget her last name, the man and woman who ran a booking agency in France, and they were supposedly booking our whole tour. We went over with the thought, that okay, we'll let them book the first part of the tour, the first three months, and maybe we'll stay in Europe more after that. And we didn't like what they were doing, and they sent somebody to travel around with us, Pascal Ortega. And, of course, we were suspicious of him because he came from management, but what happened was he became one of us, and not one of them, and after three months, and feeling not good about the way they were handling us, we decided not to work with them any more, and to extend the tour for another three or four months, and let Pascal do all the booking. We had a vacation, and then we had a summer residency, and Pascal did the bookings for the fall.... And so we were able to have a much better time in the fall tour, better arrangements, better housing, earn money, not feel that we were being cheated by producers.' — (Sherman, interview.)
8. 'In January Peter called me and said: "We're getting together this great, big European tour for '69" – twenty-five people, big show, and it was going to be for six months – and going to Poland and, I mean, *all over the place*. And he said: "Really, I don't want to take it for six months, I don't want to be away from my family for that long. So why don't I take it for half the time and then you take it for half the time?" And there I was like Cincinnatus at the plow – right? – and I thought: "Oh no, what should I do?" And on one hand I was thinking it would be really fun, because touring is a grind in a way, but it's fun and it's a way to get around. Anyway, I thought about it and I decided no, I don't really want to. And I think I actually changed my mind a couple of times – back and forth – but my last answer was no. I didn't really want to do it again ... what happened was we left New Mexico and became total hippies and wound up through various things – on the beach in Hawaii on our way to India.... My wife and I and another couple – wound up on the beach in Hawaii – penniless, without any papers, without virtually any clothes – and totally at our wits' end. Because when you become a real hippie – if you want to really do it – what that thing was – you wind up – the idea is spiritual poverty – and going

They were by and large[9] a huge success, both with the regular bourgeois theatre audience and the pimps of the dailies bringing in these Johns,

along on the natural energy and all that – I don't want to really go into all of it – but what I found was that what happens is that you become at the mercy of any schlemiel in a car. The person who's walking is at the mercy of any schmuck in a car. So, I realized that something was upside down and this was the wrong tactic and I should really do what I know and etcetera. So I decided to go to Europe – meet the theatre – they were in London at the time – I think they had just gotten there – and go with the theatre and do that. Because I really knew it – I was good at it and I liked it – it was fun. So, anyways, I flew to Europe with my wife – I saw the show – it was *The Cry of the People For Meat*, and then afterwards they saw me and everybody was real happy because, I think Peter is a hard case to deal with and people were really happy that I was there and felt it was really good and everything. And then they all gathered around – and I remember this really well – afterwards – and Peter asked me in front of everyone what I thought of the show. Unfortunately, I was stupid enough to – I told them what I really thought of it .... Peter, I would say, by the success – Peter was forced into a position of taking it all on himself, due to mistrust. Paranoia was rampant also, at those times – really rampant – and when I criticized the show, I think, that created a wedge between us, you see, because he had developed the show when I wasn't there, and it created – that was a wedge, you see. So he tried to do everything. If I had been an administrator and had gone through the development and everything, it would have – everything – I don't want to be self-serving, but I do feel everything would have been a little easier, because we would have had things worked out beforehand. But to come upon the show – and everybody gather round and say: "What do you think?" – and then you tell them. They've been working on this for months.' — (Ernstthal, interview.)

9. 'In Paris recently the bourgeois critics either disliked or ignored it, and from their own point of view they were right to do so, for it has no G-strings, no nakedness, no eroticism, and nothing to titillate or horrify or disgust the senses. The avant-garde critics have been brought up on Brecht, Ionesco, and Beckett equally could make nothing of it. They were gloomily estranged by its having no author, practically no text, no actors who can speak clearly, and apparently no knowledge of the rules of preparation, climax, and catastrophe. They resented the stage being a confusion of plastic bags, heaps of newspaper cuttings, and gigantic dolls; and they could see no point in what they heard – the beating of drums, the shrill blowing of whistles – being a dissonance and a discord .... In view of the attitude of the audience at the Royal Court, and of the fact that in Paris only the extreme Left and the students of the Sorbonne recognised it for what it is – a tender and unforgettable contemporary humanitarian statement in revolutionary theatrical terms.' — (Hobson, *Carnival Heartcry, London Sunday Times*, June 24, '69.)

'And so we arrived in Nancy, and we were probably the most important performers at the festival, and we were performing in this little house of culture which was part of this Louis XIV art Rococo wedding cake theatre, and also we were performing in a tent outside the town. I found out only later that Nancy is like this super ultraconservative place. I didn't know. We were in this tent outside the town for 500, and the first night we performed, there were 3,000 people inside the tent. It was so packed that the people were coming onto the stage, and I really got scared, it was like this huge number of people, and they were worried because there were these heaters – people were like spilling onto the stage, and I was just – it was like unbelievable for me because in America, we'd go to a college, and they'd like us and afterwards we'd have a little party and everyone would say "very good" if they really liked you – "well, thank you." But this was completely different, these people were absolutely enamored of the Bread and Puppet. And the show was good, it was really working. So everything felt very positive, and that was like a

and with the large public of counter-culture 'kids,',[10] i.e. the privileged beneficiaries of higher education, the former won over by Christian accents and good-natured humor, the latter by the group's hippie image (cleaner and less cum-encrusted than that of the Living Theatre, but still . . .) and by the theatre's balance of mystic reverberation and tone of intransigent (yet unaggressive) radicalism. Least of all perhaps in Germany: Schumann didn't really make it there till his next tour, with work of his next period.

Though on stage they looked like one big happy group of young idealists, the group was rent by dissension. In Europe, this was the year after the revolution didn't happen, and the radical young, though unwilling to acknowledge that the moment had passed,[12] were (as essentially had been Schumann since '67) turning away from the one worthwhile though rarely, except for fascists and others on the Right, reasonable project of mobilizing The People and turning to other avenues of escape from salaried servitude to the system: which affected the group as exterior climate and because of the European recruits. The weakening of the unifying force of opposition to the war in Vietnam and the system's evident stability in America – Johnson was out, but Nixon was in – had the same effect in America[12] and on Americans in the group. The two avenues of

---

terrific start for that tour, we really went off after that – we just took off. They would accost us on the street and say to us, "Oh, you're Bread and Puppet," and then they would want to talk to us all about it, like what it is to work with the great Bread and Puppet and yak yak yak. It was pretty flattering basically. I remember going into bars and having people come over and buying us drinks and all this stuff. It was nice. Then we went to Rome . . . . They were very bad – they cheated us and they didn't want to pay us all the money and it was ugly. Plus the Italians weren't all as enthusiastic as the French. They were quite a bit more reserved . . . . I don't think they really liked the show that much, although they did give us the first prize at that festival.' — (Leherrissier, interview.)
10. 'That was the first big tour, that was the tour where the theatre really took off as a major – had major publicity there. In the newspapers. It was a really big surprise, we were being greeted – wild. And our public was to a major extent – the freaks were coming – the politicals and freaks and being very enthusiastic.' — (Levy, interview.)
11. 'I do remember France and the people screaming the call from '68 which was "Ce n'est pas le bout, continuez le combat" the end of the chant. (I: What is the change again?) "It's only the beginning, let's continue the struggle." and in Germany too, and all over. It was startling to me.' — (Levy, interview.)
12. 'The sexual freedom and the dope freedom movement was in full swing. The Living Theatre – I think at that time – was doing *Paradise Now* – and they were in Algeria, or something, sucking up all the hashish in town and there was Peter. This old-fashioned, moralistic, beer-drinking – really straight, in a way – person, caught in these currents – right – and Bruno also – like that it was okay to get drunk and get stoned and this and that and it's not really for everyone. In other words, in general, like you say, '68 was the climax, but '69 on Haight Street it was boarded up from one end to the other because the predators were coming in on the "do your own thing" movement and the sociopaths and the people who said do your own thing – "That's for me, man – I feel like cuttin' your head off. I feel like punching you know a knife into your stomach to see it bleed."

the escape beckoning were opposite: violent opposition, verbal and if possible not only verbal to the system in isolation from and effectively in opposition to The People vs. withdrawal into personal redemption by private cultivation of the spirit.[13] Schumann[14] and many in the group, while taking the position of neither faction, 'politicals' or 'hippies,' but rather groping their way toward the radical accommodation of the '70s – ecology, return to the land, genteel and, in principle, practical communes, continued dialogue with The People in the form of gentle, reasonable, pacifist and environmentalist agitation – were unable to make prevail or even just to offer any rigid opposition to the demands of either faction, who didn't fight with one another very much, but in shifting alliances, structured by personal relationships, fought Schumann and tried to influence him and the group's work. Schumann shared the hippies' distaste for violence, the politicals' idealism and concern for how people lived. There were endless arguments, personal attacks, affronts, antagonisms, crises. The issues were group democracy[15] – how were decisions to be

---

Manson – all the stuff – was happening. So it just peaked out, and so ripened out and rotted – all at the same time. When I saw Manson, by the way, I was in Denmark – when I read about it – it took me months to get over it because I knew – I'd been so close to the total hippie freedom experiment – that I saw that just on the other side of it was murder. You know what I mean – like LSD makes you feel out of your body and stuff and it's really spiritual. But you get a guy who's been in jail all his life taking it – or lots of people – taking it and it will either completely fuck their mind up or, say well, it's just body – it's just somebody's body – let's watch it bleed – like the Rolling Stones, right -- let it bleed. So, all of '69 was this real chaos and to me it was like the Apocalypse. It was the beasts just rising out of the people – because freedom was given to them – total freedom was given to them and nobody's ready for it – nobody's ready for it.' — (Ernstthal, interview.)
13. 'And then we went on a wonderful vacation to all these great places – to Germany, to see his parents and southern France, and then we started to play the show again – rehearse it again, and play it and what happened was, again, a reflection of the times – very much – was that there were two sort of factions in the theatre. Like I said, we got our people because of political beliefs. But on one hand they were the mystics, who believed in good triumphing, and on the other side were the political people with the hard-core Communists essentially, who believed that society was fucked and things were bad. That was the essential split. It went, you know, through San Francisco, through the whole world at that time – this split between those factions.' — (Ernstthal, interview.)
14. Schumann's position of '68/'70 is expressed in his answer of October '69 to a three-part questionnaire submitted to him and to other participants in the Second International Festival of Students Theatre (University of Wroclaw (Breslau), October 18-26), by the revue *Polska*, an answer, *The World has to be Demonstrated Anew*, published in *WIN*, July '70 — (cf. Appendix IV).
15. 'Bruno would talk about "the people" – "the people's decision" – a lot of political cant and rhetoric, as I remember, dealing with maybe how decisions should be made . . . within the group – what we should vote on – or "It's the people's theatre" – something like that – I think on those lines – you know what I mean? – that we do the work in the theatre, therefore we should have the say in what goes on – which I don't believe, either. I mean, I didn't believe that . . .'. — (Ernstthal, interview.)

'(Elka: Wasn't there a vote taken at the end where the money should go, whether it

arrived at, what areas should the group will extend to – where – for whom – to perform[16] – on the streets, in factories at universities,[17] in

---

should go to the people or to the theatre, and everyone decided . . .) The people decided to give it to people. So the theatre ended up with nothing. (Elka: Well, we had some.)' — (Schumann, interview, '79.)

16. 'On one hand there were those who wanted to go to the people – that they felt there was a political . . . . Like I say, it was definitely the time – it was the strain of that time that caused this. It was happening everywhere. And I'll try to remember – the issue had to do with – theatres. Playing in theatres for money . . . . Bruno thought we should go to the factories – right? We should go to the streets – we should play for free – we should get our message to the people. We should condemn the theatre owners – condemn the theatrical promoters. And essentially condemn and deny the actual people who had put this stuff together for us – because obviously there was a guy – there were some people – who were interested in putting the tour on. But they felt we should bolt from them and condemn them as capitalists – and we should go to the factories . . . . and Peter felt that he had to honor his commitments – that it didn't matter who you – Peter had the attitude: I shit on the audience – what do I care where I do it? You know what I mean? Peter is – what I loved about him too was that he was so incredibly apolitical in a certain way. For all his political theatre he was not staunch enough. What I'm saying is: for all his politics he was a very undogmatic person. And he didn't give a shit who the audience was – really. Plus, there was the feeling that: why should you play to the workers? And then not play to the capitalists? You see, we were popular – see, here comes – you know what I'm saying? The pitfalls of popularity. Because people would flock to the theatres to see – at the same time in Europe the Black Panthers were being lionized – in French intellectual circles. Eldridge Cleaver was considered – really, you know, a tremendous ideologue and really smart and all that. So the Bread and Puppet Theatre was considered really hot stuff. So the liberals flocked to it and when we'd play a show we were jammed constantly. But then there were those who felt that this was a cop-out. It happened to Bob Dylan – it happened all up and down the line. It was: You're copping out; you're being a capitalist; you're making money; you're doing this or that and the other thing. The first thing that Peter told me when he called me in New Mexico was that everybody would be paid – Look, taking thirty-five people and plane loads of equipment to Europe is no small matter. And then there was a certain amount of logistics and a certain amount of money that was involved. And some of the places we played were fairly well-paying – obviously – and the crowds flocked to see us and naturally there was – I'm not aware of it – but there was obviously a money – there was money – thousands of dollars – being passed around . . . so at certain places we would get paid, and other places we wouldn't get paid and then there were the political people who came on the tour to make a political message. They were communists and they wanted to provoke the bourgeois – épater the bourgeois – right? – and stick it to 'em and the reason they were there was for that. And then there were the old-timers, more; Margot and myself and Maurice Blanc and a few other people who felt that it was an artistic and humanistic message that we were bringing – see? And it was for the show itself and who cares what the politics were behind it. But, it got bunched up. There were a lot of political hassles which Peter, frankly, was not adept at – nor does he care.' — (Ernstthal, interview.)

17. 'And the political stuff, fighting and stuff began when we went to Europe . . . . Because '68 was, moved onto '69, and there were student uprisings wherever we went. People taking over the universities, and asking us to perform, and we having to perform in theatres for money, and sometimes liking it and sometimes hating it. And then going to the schools and performing for free for the students. Once we actually left a place, I think it's the only time we've done that. It was in, must have been the Piccolo Teatro, Milano.' — (Sherman, interview.)

theatres, in certain theatres judged particularly bourgeois – whether admissions should be charged, and the plays themselves, notably *King Story, A Man, Reiteration* and *Cry*, but in particular their endings, were an issue. Schumann felt the plays were his. But not only was he dependent on the group, he was himself at this time to some extent caught up in communitarian ideology, and living with the group could not as he could earlier in New York simply as equal but as author and director and puppet maker insist on having his way; being now clearly the leader such insistence would now blatantly conflict with the anti-authoritarianism of his work. He maneuvered, compromised, tried to keep the tour going and his plays intact ideologically and artistically.[18] At that, though, though he and his family and the Eckhardts had just spent a relatively harmonious two weeks' holiday together in Germany, he had Eckhardt courtmartialed out of the group,[19] substantially for insubordination, in Ste. Baume, and

---

18. 'And Peter was trying to ride herd on all of this and it was like thirty people by that time in the cast and Bruno, his old friend, was really a hard-core political guy by then. Very adamant and stuff and Peter essentially mocked Bruno and also used the technique in the group – which was that he would accuse someone of something – of *doing* something – and make him – and *really* condemn him for it – and then forgive him. Thereby gaining an incredible power over everyone. It's as if I said to you: "Cigars are just the worst habit and I think they're disgusting . . . but it's okay, because it's you." See what I mean? – what kind of position it puts you in? And he did this to Bruno – dealing with politics and stuff . . . . But he was trying to hold it – he was straddling because he was trying to hold it together. He was trying to hold the tour together as best he could. But that's his *worst* position in the world. He is *not* a manipulator – no, that's wrong – he *is* a manipulator of people, but he's not an administrator. He has no talent for it.' — (Ernstthal, interview.)

Note that the break between Davis and the Mime Troupe about this time also involves the self-assertion of his group. 'Production problems on Brecht's *Congress of the Whitewashers* contribute to the erosion of Davis' authority' in '68, according to Toscan and Ripley, *The San Francisco Mime Troupe, a Chronology, Theatre Quarterly*, vol. V, #18; and in 1970 Davis 'leaves the Troupe and collective creation becomes the dominant approach.' — (ibid.)

19. '(Elka: I don't know if you want to go into that. It seems as though, the '69 tour, you didn't talk about that. In my mind, it seemed almost like a watershed, a landmark . . .) Not in my mind. (Elka: Maybe because it came so close to our moving out of New York, but it seemed to embody, the tour and the people on the tour, seemed to embody the essence of that whole decade of the sixties, of the political turmoil and the extreme – the freedom that people took to express themselves or to do what they wanted on the tour. On that tour and with that piece there was more flexibility and people were allowed or you allowed them or whatever to do more in determining how the piece was done . . . of a violence within the group and people arguing and fighting on stage in sort of undisciplined (laughs) — that never happened again.) It was quite jolly. (Elka: So you just dismiss it. I just watched, I didn't take part.) Yeah, that's true. It was very – a lot of fights. (Elka: A lot of disagreements among the people. In a way, the fact that a group of people who disagreed so much were able to stay together and work on one piece for nine months – I think that's a pretty amazing thing.) We had to throw out only one person. (Elka: Who was that?) Uwe Krieger – and everything else – with these minor disagreements in this group we . . . stayed together to the end. (Elka: Another thing that made this time so unusual was that maybe until now, you had been the – maybe this is a wrong interpretation, but I think of you as

similarly got rid of Leherrissier's lover, the other extremist in the group, the Berlinese Uwe Krieger, before they went to Poland, Leherrissier (more one of the 'hippies') leaving with him; and Ernstthal, another im-

---

being the pushing force of a group of people, the one who would *dare* to do something and be like in the forefront of what action was taken politically and organizing parades and taking part in things, and on this tour there were quite a number of people who were way, way more radical or extreme than you were. Maybe they were pretty unbalanced too. I think you started, you found yourself more and more in the role of the person sort of holding back and pulling people back from experimenting or being too far out. Also politically, I remember at some point, terrible arguments with Bruno – he was the radical, sort of the super-Marxist – very violent, and also I guess very egotistical kind of radicalism, and – not just me, but several of us women had found his position at one point so hard to take, because he was scorning the group of middle-aged people who had come to the hostel, on a sort of a weekend retreat and he was looking at them and sort of scorning them as these fat Spiesser – that complacent middle class, and I don't know how violently he expressed his scorn but it was very strong, and then we found that these were the remnants of the resistance in France, they were people who had fought against the Nazis, and now they were 40 years old or 50 years old, but they were also religious people.) They had their meetings there. They were all active members of the Resistance. They used to have meetings there, and they had come there for their annual meeting. Bruno didn't know this. We all didn't know this. (Elka: But even before we found out, I know that a group of us just found Bruno's radicalism so hollow and so empty, it didn't make sense anymore. It was too opposed to everything that was traditional. Without thinking whether it was good or bad. It seemed mindless.) Several people in the group took their radicalism to a practical – to places where we in practice had to deal with people, which was in theatres, and so they were very radical with stage hands and stage people and didn't allow them to do what they wanted to do and thought that it was too bourgeois, too this and that to have the curtain go up or the fire curtain come down. They made a helluva lot of trouble out of these simple arrangements that exist in the traditional theatre, so a lot of hostility and poor performing came from the very bad relationships with French and Italian and German stagehands – so I think that's what more or less means my conservatism and Bruno's radicalism. Those were the big moments of radicalism. To try to get into a fistfight with stagehands. — (Schumann, interview, '79.)

20. 'Ja, dat war, der dicke Knaller, also wo ich, wo ich wirklich gesagt hab, jetzt ist Schluss, dat war in dem Kloster am, ich weiss nicht, St. Baume. Da hatte der Peter 'ne Generalsitzung einberufen, dat war wie 'ne Gerichtsverhandlung. Das war so, wir hatten 'ne Gruppenzeitung gemacht, wo jeder seine Meinung äussern konnte, und da hab ich meine natürlich auch dazu gegeben. Und die war dann so, dass der Peter das als 'ne ungeheure Provokation ansah und verlangte, dass ich (...), er wollte mich rausschmeissen.

Dat ging um diesen, dat warn, dat warn, politische, für mich war dat'ne politische Auseinandersetzung. Dat ging los mit dem Streit um die Posters. Wir hatten uns Siebdruckmaterial besorgt und haben dann Posters gemacht über die Show. Und ich hab Posters gemacht über "Das Salz der Erde". Dat waren vietnamesische Freiheitskämpfer, die hab ich, dat waren immer so zwei Reihen von Guerilleros, die, die, so in voller Montur und unten drunter hab ich 'n Spruch geschrieben. Ich weiss jetzt nicht mehr, welcher Spruch dat war, aber der Spruch, der stammte nicht von mir. Der war, irgendwie kam der aus der Quelle die dem Peter auch vertraut sein müsste. Und da gab es den ersten Ärger. Und da hab ich 'n zweites Blatt grad gemacht und zwar das kannt ich nicht aus'm Kopf, das hab ich, das hab ich abgezeichnet, von Photo. Ich hab das nur 'n bisschen verändert. Dat waren drei Guerilla-Kämpfer, die auf'm zerschossenen Hubschrauber stehen. Und war an sich 'n sehr bekanntes Photo (...). Und die Plakate waren sehr schön, dat ist nicht jetzt

portant 'hippie' left in Scandinavia.[21] And Eckhardt, the revolutionary, and Ernstthal, the hippie, of course, were his two oldest associates.

I have mentioned the issues concerning the plays' endings. In *A Man*, apparently Death's leading the arm of the Vietnamese woman when she kills the soldier was at least for a time eliminated. In *King Story*, instead of the Great Warrior's killing the People, and then Death him, the People were made to rise and vanquish him, smothering him under the red puppet

---

so, weil ich dat, weil ich sagen will, wie schön, ich dat gemacht hab, die waren einfach schön geworden und die wurden auch am schnellsten verkauft. Dat Geld kam in die Theaterkasse, für unsere weitere Existenz und so. Und dat hatte, dat hatte den Peter gewurmt, dat war, und dann hatt er so und dann hat er angefangen seine Autorität auszuspielen gegen die ich auch irgendwie so machtlos war und (...) Rollen, die ich früher gemacht habe, anderen zuzuteilen, nicht. Und dat war auch sowat, naja, da war dat Ding gelaufen, dat wusst ich ganz genau. Wir haben uns dann in Berlin nochmal ernsthaft unterhalten, ich hab gesagt, Peter, ich hau jetzt nicht ab, ich geh erst, wenn du gehst. Aber ich geh jetzt nicht. Vor allen Dingen, wat sollt ich denn machen? Wo soll ich denn hingehen, soll ich im Strassengraben schlafen? Ich hatte, ich hatte kein zu Hause mehr. Ich war von meiner Familie weg, ich hatte mich vom Peter getrennt und meine Zukunft war ungewiss. Und wie ich dann vom Theatre weggegangen bin, da kriegt ich 700 Mark ausgezahlt, dat war mein Anteil. Ich war ziemlich sauer, er hatte 'ne ganze Menge, also für Theater, er wollte sich-'n Zirkuszelt kaufen und so weiter. Und der hat natürlich da wat auf die hohe Kante gelegt. Ich bin dann mit den 700 Mark nach Berlin, ich bin zwischendurch krank geworden, wie die abgefahren sind, dann hab ich wegen der Delly, an der ich sehr gehangen hab (...) aber ich wollte nicht wegen der rüberfahren. Da hab ich, da hab ich in, in, da hab ich in Paris in so 'ne Art Nervenzusammenbruch gekriegt mit 'nem sehr starken Asthmaanfall. Und die Leute, bei denen ich da einquartiert war, dat warn, dat warn französische Spiessbürger. Die haben sich nicht viel um mich gekümmert, die kriegten da hinterher Angst, dat mir nicht doch irgendwat zustösst und dann haben die doch 'n Artzt geholt. Dat haben die bezahlt auch. Und da hatte ich, ich hatte überhaupt keine Medikamente und dann hab ich Medikamente gehabt und dann hab ich mich eines Morgens, ich hab da acht Tage im Bette gelegen, in so'ner kleinen Kammer, ich hab auch in der ganzen Zeit so gut wie nix gegessen. Dann hab ich mich voll mit Medikamente gestopft und bin morgens um vier oder um fünf, praktisch mitten in der Nacht, bin ich zum Gare d'Lyon (?) oder wie dat heisst gefahren und hab mich in 'n Zug gesetzt Richtung Germany. Und da, da hat so mein neues Leben angefangen, eines von meinen einigen, wieder angefangen, ja.' — (Eckhardt, interview.)

21. 'We went to Denmark and in Stockholm we were staying at the KFUM – it was the YMCA, and it was getting worse and worse and Peter was finally saying: "If you don't like, it leave." But, of course, nobody had any money. People were fighting all the time and it was getting – people were not liking each other – it was degenerating. I mean, that's okay. That happens – and it was degenerating and getting scrappy. People were fighting and not liking each other. There was no more common purpose – it was getting – poor – it was getting difficult. Finally, Peter was saying "If you don't like it, leave" – which was *another* idle threat. Because how would they leave? Nobody had any money – or – plus, they would face – like exile and be really stupid – and look stupid, and it would hurt the theatre and would do this and do that.... I think it was late August – early September.... So I think it may have been like September 3rd – something like that. Anyway, so I said: "Well, fuck you. I'm leaving. If that's the way you're going to treat people and that's what it's going to be like – I'm leaving" – which I did.' — (Ernstthal, interview.)

curtain. In *Reiteration*, the interrogation of the mother settled down to her being progressively armed and ending up as justified Resistance Fighter, instead of, as seems previously to have been the case, refusing the arms and ending up unarmed but with the guilt of her killing the soldier attaching to her; though on the other hand on one memorable occasion in Sweden, there was an attempt to wrestle her down in symbolization not only of that guilt, but of her liability to punishment for it. Both the hippies and the politicals objected to *Cry* ending with the Crucifixion.[22] At first, according

---

22. 'Which was, that I felt that it was a tremendous beginning – a wonderfully promising, dynamic, poetic beginning – the beginning sequences – but then the ending was shitty, it just ended with the Crucifixion – everybody yelling and screaming and tying up Jesus – and it just ended flat because – if it's the story of the world, the story of Jesus is the story of the Resurrection – that's how it ends – he's resurrected from the dead and it's – life goes on. In other words, it's a life-affirming message, in my opinion – that's the end of the story. It's that man triumphs over death, etcetera, etcetera. You know what I mean? The end of the story is a life-affirming, ongoing, godly-feeling, positive message – but they just had this tremendous buildup – right through Noah and these wonderful scenes with the beasts and up and up and up and then, bang! He just cut it and that was the end. And it just left you like: "Well, so what? Why did I go all the way up this wonderful"... to me, it was like switching gears, and it's a real cop-out to call Jesus a Vietnamese, just because they happen to be having a war right now... why the fuck should it end with some Vietnamese liberation fighter? That's stupid. Because look what they did in – look what's going on now.... (I: But what about the perennial struggle for liberty as being the idea there, maybe – something like that? Which doesn't have much hope, but –) That's what I'm saying, the show had nothing to do with that.... The show didn't have to do with it. The show was supposed – to be, it was the story – it was the biblical mythology of the evolution of the world, and it had a spiritual basis. And switching it to political at the end, it's a cop-out. And this is – like I said before, I think this is where Peter and I were really sympathetic together and everything was on this spiritual – that's my bent – that's my particular bent in life – is toward the spiritual. Not towards religion or anything, but towards the spiritual. I mean, I wound up in India where I saw history and I saw spirituality from a different angle... I also felt that Peter... was actually in a conflict between the life-affirming values and the life-defeating values. And I felt like at this time his crucifixion – ending it with the crucifixion – was, in a way, he didn't want to seem soft. He didn't want to seem like a hippie. He didn't want to seem like a mushy-headed liberal. He wanted to maintain this tough stance of: that the world is fucked and the world is in a crucified state and not that it's coming out into a more beautiful or evolving state. This is where hippies and Peter were always at odds and I think that Peter opted for that old line at this point and made a statement *against* the movement towards freedom and evolution and peace and all that. And I think that's where it started to go awry – for me, in my opinion, because I was – I was definitely on the mystic side of things and my feeling was that the show should resolve and leave people with the feeling; "I can do it," See.... (I: Wouldn't that also have been Bruno Eckhardt's – I mean that faction's general...) Now wait – now that you mention it, probably that was true. That was true. Right. So in that sense we were around together again – because probably Bruno wanted to – on the other – no – I felt slightly different but in a way the same, you're right. I felt like it should have been that life triumphs. That the spirit triumphs over the flesh and that the spirit is resurrected and heaven is coming, or – you know, that kind of message of: "God wills it, let the..." – in the Apocalypse it says: "Let those who are stupid be stupid still – let those who are mean still – but God triumphs and life goes on." – that kind of feeling – and I had

to Kourilsky, only sometimes and late in the tour, a slight resurrection of the performers was added, the lights go on and they get up and blow gaily on bird whistles – the hippie emmendation; for the last performances in Paris and for the New York ones the ending I described was added: an ascension which to the politicals signaled the continuing necessity cum possibility of a revolutionary transformation, and to Schumann probably justified hopeful non-violent resistance in spite of its perpetual re-defeat. At some point, earlier in the tour, Uwe Krieger as Christ apparently simply refused to come down off the ladder after he was crucified, Schumann had to drag him down. At another point, apparently, Schumann broke Christ's gun. My father in response to government criticism changed his condemnation of war in *The Trial of Lukullus* to one of wars other than wars of national defense. I like the revision process in the Bread and Puppet Theatre in the summer of '69 better.

---

no political ax to grind. Bruno, I think, wanted to incite people. That's the difference. I think he thought that it should have incited people to go and blow up the Bank of America or go and overthrow the government. He felt it should be a political move – to incite people. To be more of a didactic and well, you know, to incite people to go up against the government – to go out on the street – to go out and fight. Fight, fight, fight.' — (Ernstthal, interview.)

'All the people in the company were always asking for a resurrection. And the last week in Paris, after eight months of touring, he finally added a resurrection.' — (Sherman, interview.)

25. December '69, New York City.
Flat on his arse.

As I have previously told, Schumann on his return to New York City found he had lost his base of operations, the old Jefferson Courthouse. The Pageant Players, a leftist group he had let use it had let the Motherfuckers use it, and the City not liking their use of it, had reappropriated it. The extremism that had given him such trouble on the tour had done him in.[1] The loss very probably contributed to his decision soon after to leave the city.

From the tour's profits he had managed to wrest[2] around $2500 for himself — capital for the theatre and living expenses. It seemed a lot but it didn't go far.

He had come to dislike *Cry*. The reason he gives is that it involved too much 'acting,' depending on it, and (thus) really hadn't been puppet theatre any more at all:[3] by 'acting' meaning performance by unmasked

---

1. 'The Courthouse was gone. Murray Levy had given the key to the Motherfuckers and they had wrecked it or something.' — (Leherrissier, interview.)
'When we came back to New York the cops had taken away from us the old Jefferson Courthouse on Second Avenue workshop home theater. The city had removed the Pageant Players and rerented the place to an opera and film enterprise. Dozens of puppets, masks – including the largest supermonster ever – musical instruments and tools were missing.' — (Schumann, Newsletter, '*Bread and Rosebuds*,' April 25, '70.)
2. I suspect the '69 tour had been one of the tours George Ashley talked to me about that created nasty arguments about money:
'I heard (from Tanith Noble in Paris (SSB)) all the stories about the bad times on the tours and the meanness amongst people about money.... They were always fighting about money – coming back on the bus, people were saying: I want my share of the money. I remember people being very cranky about money. (I: The European tour?) Their European tours – coming back and being very angry with Peter about they needed money and they didn't have any. And Peter saying, fuck off, I'm going to take the money for the circus whether you like it or not. Maybe he didn't on one occasion, but I know they were very angry and there were hard feelings. Seemed like every tour they came back – whether – even in the States they sometimes had quarrels about money.... They should have known they were on the search for the Holy Grail, or something, and they couldn't expect to come away rich from a European tour. Peter did say to me one time – very early on – that he felt guilty about using celastic at a hundred dollars a roll when he didn't have money to give to his puppeteers. When it would be much cheaper to use paper maché. Except that paper maché was too heavy and it wasn't flexible and it didn't travel as well. So, that he felt guilty but he had no other recourse. He had to use celastic.' — (Ashley, interview.)
3. 'Well, the end of the '69 tour was like a splitting, saying, "this is enough of this kind of theatre," "let's do something else." (I: Why did you decide that this is the end of this kind of theatre?) Because it was acting. There was a lot of performing in it that was performing. And on account of that I don't like acting. I find bad acting better than good acting. I just

individuals, effective because of their use of their looks and their projection of their (strong) personalities. He denies that what bothered him was its use (as in *Reiteration* and *Blue Raven Beauty*) of the appearance within the play of the group as makers of the play – the distinguishing peculiarity of it and of those other plays, and the one-time formal appearance in his work of the anti-authoritarian communal ideal that emerged into prominence in avant garde theatre and the youth movement at that time. But I suspect that this was what above all bothered him after the '69 tour.

His situation at this time may be summarized as follows. Having invented a new kind of theatre, he was now a master in its art. He had attained to recognition as a major artist in the Old World, and had achieved critical success in the New (Konnoff, interview, '83, describes the mood of the group in December '69: 'Everybody was used to being sort of famous and performing a lot'). Though he had never been in vogue in New York City, he was now definitely out of vogue. During the '60s, Off-off-Broadway theatre had established itself. It was in a mode of sex, violence and ego totally alien to his. This mode was in vogue. Though he was not quite broke, he was poor as always. But his fame might now suffice to support this theatre by means of college and European tours. He was fed up with his crew, partly because they had the hutzpe to expect rewarding parts, partly because they viewed his theatre, the Bread and Puppet Theatre as theirs or at least as of a sort entitling them to exert political (radical) pressure on him, and as intrinsically a (radical) political theatre. He had himself in his work assumed a decidedly revolutionary political

---

don't appreciate when the show depends on that. The real interest, the movement of puppets and the painted things and all the sounds and all that got sort of swallowed up by people's personal performing with these things. I didn't care for it all any more when we played it in New York. I wanted to change the theatre – so – it was good – it was a good time to say bye-bye, and to go different ways and that's what most people did .... (I: So, in the beginning of the tour, the show, because of the people who were in it, it changed that way? They moved the show away from what you wanted it to be and you decided that there had to be a big change.) I'm talking about the end of the tour, not the beginning of the tour. (I: But it changed from the beginning. In the beginning it wasn't that way.) Well, maybe in the beginning I wasn't aware of how the show depended on performances and on expositions of that sort, of how a person would perform something. (Elka: But the actors you had who were important in it like Margo and Maurice and Irene and Bill – they were kind of the prominent people in it, were very strong. You weren't dissatisfied with *them*, were you? Or where you simply dissatisfied with people being more important than the puppets and masks?) What kind of question is this? (Elka laughs).' — (Schumann, interview, '79.)

'I hated *The Cry of the People for Meat* by the time we came back from the European tour – I remember that – and during the performance in New York, where we did our last performance of it, I felt: What am I doing here working with actors. I have no interest in this – with all this performing. Do you remember that? (Elka: Yeah, I remember that.) That's not what I want to do. I want to work with puppets – with things that move – (Elka: And have no personality clashes or –.)' — (Schumann, interview, '82.)

stance, but was repulsed by the political dogmatism it seemed to imply, as well as by its apparent ethical implications (endorsement of violent resistance). The form of the Peace Movement in which he had flourished as artist, namely a quasi-continuous street agitation, had virtually disappeared, and in any event public protest as such was no longer its key form: the peculiar deployment of his new kind of theatre had become otiose. In truth, I would say, the environment of hippies and radicals he had worked himself into had become hateful to him, its fervors and sincerities, no less than its arrogantly naive shallowness suffocated him. *Cry* had, in content and form, summed up an epoch of his creativity for him, and had wound it up: an epoch in which his theatre, in content and form, was an extension of the Peace Movement. He wanted to strike out in a new direction, 'develop'. Unbeknownst (or almost) to his associates and audience, he had over a period of two years or more changed focus. It was now at least as much on the meanness of the masses of the People as on the obsessive greed of the High and Mighty. Also, legitimate theatres seemed more inappropriate than ever to him for his kind of theatre, his distaste for them (and perhaps their audiences) was stronger than ever. He conceived the idea that his theatre should have the form of a travelling circus reaching the traditional circus audiences (children as well as adults, the working and lower middle classes, rural and small town people as well as or perhaps even rather than urban audiences): i.e. those masses of the people whose basic attitudes needed to be changed.

www.ingramcontent.com/pod-product-compliance
Ingram Content Group UK Ltd.
Pitfield, Milton Keynes, MK11 3LW, UK
UKHW022209230426
12048UKWH00016BA/745

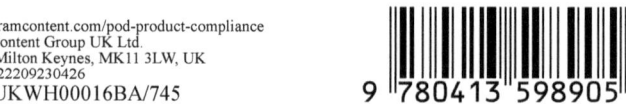